A

GRAMMAR

OF THE

GREEK LANGUAGE

BY

ALPHEUS CROSBY,

PROFESSOR OF THE GREEK LANGUAGE AND LITERATURE IN DARTMOUTH COLLEGE.

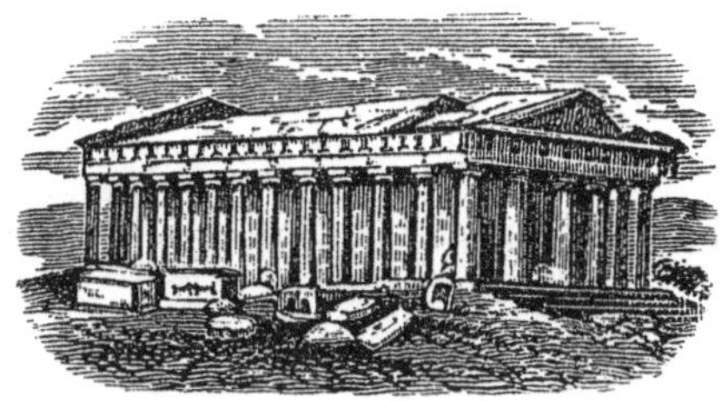

Μέμνησθ' Ἀθηνῶν Ἑλλάδος τε.

ÆSCHYLUS.

TWENTY-NINTH EDITION.

BOSTON:

CROSBY, NICHOLS, LEE, & CO.,

117 WASHINGTON STREET.

1860.

"The LANGUAGE OF THE GREEKS was truly like themselves, it was conformable to their transcendent and universal Genius. * * * * THE GREEK TONGUE, *from its propriety and universality, is made for all that is great, and all that is beautiful, in every Subject, and under every Form of writing.*" — Harris's *Hermes*, Bk. III. Ch. 5.

"Greek, — the shrine of the genius of the old world; as universal as our race, as individual as ourselves; of infinite flexibility, of indefatigable strength, with the complication and the distinctness of nature herself; to which nothing was vulgar, from which nothing was excluded; speaking to the ear like Italian, speaking to the mind like English; with words like pictures, with words like the gossamer film of the summer; at once the variety and picturesqueness of Homer, the gloom and the intensity of Æschylus; not compressed to the closest by Thucydides, not fathomed to the bottom by Plato, not sounding with all its thunders, nor lit up with all its ardors even under the Promethean touch of Demosthenes!" — Coleridge's *Study of the Greek Classic Poets*, Gen. Introd.

CAMBRIDGE:
UNIVERSITY PRESS.

PREFACE TO THE SECOND EDITION.

THE following pages are the result of an attempt to supply what was believed to be a desideratum in the list of Greek text-books; viz. a grammar which should be portable and simple enough to be put into the hands of the beginner, and which should yet be sufficiently scientific and complete to accompany him through his whole course. The volume from which the elements of a language are first learned becomes to the student a species of mnemonic tables, and cannot be changed in the course of his study without a material derangement of those associations upon which memory essentially depends. The familiar remark, "It must be remembered that, if the grammar be the first book put into the learner's hands, it should also be the last to leave them," though applying most happily to grammatical study in general, was made by its accomplished author with particular reference to the manual used by the student.

In the preparation of this work, the routine of daily life has obliged me to keep constantly in view the wants of more advanced students; and, for their sake, an attempt has been made to investigate the principles of the language more deeply, and illustrate its use more fully, than has been usual in grammatical treatises, even of far greater size. At the same time, no pains have been spared to meet the wants of the beginner, by a studious simplicity of method and expression, and by the reduction of the most important principles to the form of concise rules, easy of retention and convenient for citation. Many valuable works in philology fail of attaining the highest point of utility, through a cumbrousness of form, burdensome alike to the understanding and the memory of the learner. They have been the armor of Saul to the youthful David. I have not, however, believed that I should consult the advantage even of the beginner by a false representation of the language, or by any departure from philosophical accuracy of statement or propriety of arrangement. Truth is always better than falsehood, and science than empiricism.

To secure, so far as might be, the double object of the work, it has been constructed upon the following plan.

First, to *state* the usage of the language in comprehensive rules and condensed tables, to be imprinted upon the memory of the student. For convenient examples of the care with which brevity and simplicity have been here studied, the reader will permit me to refer him to the rules of syntax, as presented to the eye at a single view in ¶ 64, and to the elementary tables of inflection and formation.

Secondly, to *explain* the usage of the language, and *trace its historical development*, as fully as the limits allowed to the work, and the present state of philological science, would permit. The student who thinks wishes to know, not only *what is true*, but *why it is true;* and to the philosophical mind, a single principle addressed to the reason is often like the silver cord of Æolus, confining a vast number of facts, which otherwise, like the enfranchised winds, are scattered far and wide beyond the power of control.

Thirdly, to *illustrate* the use of the language by great fulness of remark and exemplification. In these remarks and examples, as well as in the more general rules and statements, I have designed to keep myself carefully within the limits of Attic usage, as exhibiting the language in its standard form, except when some intimation is given to the contrary; believing that the grammarian has no more right than the author to use indiscriminately, and without notice, the vocabulary, forms, and idioms of different ages and communities, —

"A party-color'd dress
Of patch'd and pye-ball'd languages."

The examples of syntax, in order that the student may be assured in regard to their genuineness and sources, and be able to examine them in their connection, have been all cited from classic authors in the precise words in which they occur, and with references to the places where they may be found. In accordance with the general plan of the work, these examples have been mostly taken from the purest Attic writers, beginning with Æschylus, and ending with Æschines. It was also thought, that the practical value of such examples might be greatly enhanced to the student by selecting a single author, whose works, as those of a model-writer, should be most frequently resorted to; and especially, by selecting for constant citation a single work of this author, which could be in the hands of every student as a companion to his grammar, in which he might consult the passages referred to, and which might be to him, at the same time, a text-book in reading, and a model in writing, Greek. In making the choice, I could not hesitate in selecting, among authors, Xenophon, and among his writings, the Anabasis. References also abound in the Etymology, but chiefly in respect to peculiar and dialectic forms.

The subject of euphonic laws and changes has received a larger share of attention than is usual in works of this kind, but not larger than I felt compelled to bestow, in treating of a language,

> "Whose law was heavenly beauty, and whose breath
> Enrapturing music."

The student will allow me to commend to his special notice two principles of extensive use in the explanation of Greek forms; viz. the precession of vowels (i. e. the tendency of vowels, in the progress of language, to pass from a more open to a closer sound; see §§ 28, 29, 44, 86, 93, 118, 123, 259, &c.), and the correspondence between the consonants ν and σ, and the vowels α and ε (§§ 34, 46. β, 50, 56–58, 60, 63. R., 84, 100. 2, 105, 109, 132, 179, 181, 200, 201, 213, 248. *f*, 300, &c.).

In treating of Greek etymology, I have wished to avoid every thing like arbitrary formation; and, instead of deducing one form from another by empirical processes, which might often be quite as well reversed, I have endeavoured, by rigid analysis, to resolve all the forms into their elements. The old method of forming the tenses of the Greek verb one from another (compared by an excellent grammarian to "The House that Jack built"), is liable to objection, not only on account of its complexity and multiplication of arbitrary rules, but yet more on account of the great number of imaginary forms which it requires the student to suppose, and which often occupy a place in his memory, to the exclusion of the real forms of the language. To cite but a single case, the second aorist passive, according to this method, is formed from the second aorist active, although it is a general rule of the language, that verbs which have the one tense want the other (§ 255. β). Nor is the method which makes the theme the foundation of all the other forms free from objection, either in declension or in conjugation. This method not only requires the assistance of many imaginary nominatives and presents, but it often inverts the order of nature, by deriving the simpler form from the more complicated, and commits a species of grammatical anachronism, by making the later form the origin of the earlier. See §§ 84, 100, 256. V., 265. In the following grammar, all the forms are immediately referred to the root, and the analysis of the actual, as obtained from classic usage, takes the place both of the metempsychosis of the obsolete, and of the metamorphosis of the ideal.

Those parts of Greek Grammar of which I at first proposed to form a separate volume, the Dialects, the History of Greek Inflection, the Formation of Words, and Versification, I have concluded, with the advice of highly esteemed friends, to incorporate in this; so that a single volume should constitute a complete manual of Greek Grammar. To accomplish this object within moderate limits of size and expense, a very condensed mode of printing has been adopted, giving to the volume an unusual amount of matter in proportion to its size. I thank my printers, that, through their skill and care, they have shown this to be consistent with so much typographical clearness and beauty. It has also been found necessary to reserve for a separate treatise those parts of the first edition which were devoted to General Grammar, and which it was at first proposed to include in the present edition as an appendix. I submit to this necessity with the less reluctance, because a systematic attention to the principles of General Grammar ought not to be deferred till the study of the Greek, unless, in accordance with the judicious advice of some distinguished scholars, this should be the first language learned after our own; and because the wish has been expressed, that these parts might be published separately for the use of those who were not engaged in a course of classical study.

I cannot conclude this preface without the expression of my most sincere thanks to those personal friends and friends of learning who have so kindly encouraged and aided me in my work. Among those to whom I am especially indebted for valuable suggestions, or for the loan of books, are President Woolsey, whose elevation, while I am writing, to a post which he will so much adorn, will not, I trust, withdraw him from that department of study and authorship in which he has won for himself so enviable a distinction; Professors Felton of Cambridge, Gibbs of New Haven, Hackett of Newton, Sanborn, my highly esteemed associate in classical instruction, Stuart of Andover, and Tyler of Amherst; and Messrs. Richards of Meriden, Sophocles of Hartford, and Taylor of Andover. Nor can I conclude without the acknowledgment of my deep obligations to previous laborers in the same field, to the GREAT LIVING, and to the GREAT DEAD — *Requiescant in pace!* It is almost superfluous that I should mention, as among those to whom I am most greatly indebted, the honored names of Ahrens, Bernhardy, Bopp, Buttmann, Carmichael, Fischer, Hartung, Hermann, Hoogeveen, Kühner, Lobeck, Maittaire, Matthiæ, Passow, Rost, Thiersch, and Viger.

A. C.

HANOVER, Oct. 13, 1846

PREFACE TO THE TABLES.

THE following tables have been prepared as part of a Greek Grammar. They are likewise published separately, for the greater convenience and economy in their use. The advantages of a tabular arrangement are too obvious to require remark; nor is it less obvious, that tables are consulted and compared with greater ease when printed together, than when scattered throughout a volume.

The principles upon which the Tables of Paradigms have been constructed, are the following: —

I. *To avoid needless repetition.* There is a certain ellipsis in grammatical tables, as well as in discourse, which relieves not only the material instruments of the mind, but the mind itself, and which assists alike the understanding and the memory. When the student has learned that, in the neuter gender, the nominative, accusative, and vocative are *always* the same, why, in each neuter paradigm that he studies, must his eye and mind be taxed with the examination of nine forms instead of three? why, in his daily exercises in declension, must his tongue triple its labor, and more than triple the weariness of the teacher's ear? With the ellipses in the following tables, the paradigms of neuter nouns contain only *eight* forms, instead of the *twelve* which are usually, and the *fifteen* which are sometimes, given; and the paradigms of participles and of adjectives similarly declined contain only *twenty-two* forms, instead of the usual *thirty-six* or *forty-five.* See ¶ 4.

II. *To give the forms just as they appear upon the Greek page,* that is, *without abbreviation and without hyphens.* A dissected and abbreviated mode of printing the paradigms exposes the young student to mistake, and familiarizes the eye, and of course the mind, with fragments, instead of complete forms. If these fragments were separated upon analytical principles, the evil would be less; but they are usually cut off just where convenience in printing may direct, so that they contain, sometimes a part of the affix, sometimes the whole affix, and sometimes the affix with a part of the root. Hyphens are useful in the analysis of forms, but a table of paradigms seems not to be the most appropriate place for them. In the following tables, the affixes are given by themselves, and the paradigms are so arranged in columns, that the eye of the student will usually separate, at a glance, the root from the affix.

III. *To represent the language according to its actual use, and not according to the theories or fancies of the Alexandrine and Byzantine grammarians.* Hence, for example,

1. The *first perfect active imperative*, which has no existence in pure writers, has been discarded.

2. For the imaginary *imperative* forms ἵσταθι, τίθετι, δίδοθι δείκνυθι, have been substituted the actual forms ἵστη, τίθει, δίδου, δείκνυ.

3. Together with analogical but rare forms, have been given the usual forms, which in many grammars are noticed only as exceptions or dialectic peculiarities. Thus, βουλευέτωσαν and βουλευόντων, βουλεύσαις and βουλεύσειας, ἐβεβουλεύκεισαν and ἐβεβουλεύκεσαν (¶ 34) ; βουλευέσθωσαν and βουλευέσθων, βουλευθείησαν and βουλευθεῖεν (¶ 35) ; ἐτίθην and ἐτίθουν (¶ 50) ; ἦς and ἦσθα, ἔσεται and ἔσται (¶ 55).

4. The *second future active* and *middle*, which, except as a euphonic form of the first future, is purely imaginary, has been wholly rejected.

IV. *To distinguish between regular and irregular usage.* What student, from the common paradigms, does not receive the impression, sometimes never corrected, that the *second perfect* and *pluperfect*, the *second aorist* and *future*, and the *third future* belong as regularly to the Greek verb, as the first tenses bearing the same name ; when, in point of fact, the Attic dialect, even including poetic usage, presents only about fifty verbs which have the second perfect and pluperfect, eighty-five, which have the second aorist active ; fifty, which have the second aorist and future passive ; and forty, which have the second aorist middle ? The gleanings of all the other dialects will not double these numbers. Carmichael, who has given us most fully the statistics of the Greek verb, and whose labors deserve all praise, has gathered, from all the dialects, a list of only eighty-eight verbs which have the second perfect, one hundred and forty-five which have the second aorist active, eighty-four which have the second aorist passive, and fifty-eight which have the second aorist middle. And, of his catalogue of nearly eight hundred verbs, embracing the most common verbs of the language, only fifty-five have the third future, and, in the Attic dialect, only twenty-eight.

To some there may appear to be an impiety in attacking the venerable shade of *τύπτω*, but alas! it is little more than a shade, and, with all my early and long cherished attachment to it, I am forced, after examination, to exclaim, in the language of Electra,

> Ἀντὶ φιλτάτης
> Μορφῆς, σποδόν τε καὶ σκιὰν ἀνωφελῆ,

and to ask why, in an age which professes such devotion to truth, a false representation of an irregular verb should be still set forth as the paradigm of regular conjugation, and made the Procrustes' bed to which all other verbs must be stretched or pruned. The actual future of *τύπτω* is not *τύψω*, but *τυπτήσω*, the perfect passive is both *τέτυμμαι* and *τετύπτημαι*, the aorists are in part dialectic or poetic, the first and second perfect and pluperfect active are not found in classic Greek, if, indeed, found at all, and the second future active and middle are the mere figments of grammatical fancy. And yet all the regular verbs in the language must be gravely pronounced defective, because they do not conform to this imaginary model.

In the following tables, the example of Kühner has been followed, in selecting *βουλεύω* as the paradigm of regular conjugation. This verb is strictly regular, it glides smoothly over the tongue, is not liable to be mispronounced, and presents, to the eye, the prefixes, root, and affixes, with entire distinctness throughout. This is followed by shorter paradigms, in part merely synoptical, which exhibit the different classes of verbs, with their varieties of formation.

From the common paradigms, what student would hesitate, in writing Greek, to employ the form in *-μεθον*, little suspecting that it is only a variety of the first person dual, so exceedingly rare, that the learned Elmsley (perhaps too hastily) pronounced it a mere invention of the Alexandrine grammarians? The teacher who meets with it in his recitation-room may almost call his class, as the crier called the Roman people upon the celebration of the secular games, "to gaze upon that which they had never seen before, and would never see again." In the secondary tenses of the indicative, and in the optative, this form does not occur at all; and, in the remaining tenses, there have been found only five examples, two of which are quoted by Athenæus from a *word-hunter* (*ὀνοματοθήρας*), whose affectation he is ridiculing, while the three classical examples are all poetic, occurring, one in Homer (Il. Ψ. 485), and the other two in Sophocles (El. 950 and Phil. 1079). And yet, in the single paradigm of τύπτω, as I learned it in my boyhood, this "needless *Alexandrine*,"

"Which, like a wounded snake, drags its slow length along,"

occurs no fewer than twenty-six times, that is, almost nine times as often as in the whole range of the Greek classics.

With respect to the manner in which these tables should be used so much depends upon the age and attainments of the student, that no directions could be given which might not require to be greatly modified in particular cases. I would, however, recommend,

1. That the paradigms should not be learned *en masse*, but gradually, in connection with the study of the principles and rules of the grammar, and with other exercises.

2. That some of the paradigms should rather be used for reference, than formally committed to memory. It will be seen at once, that some of them have been inserted merely for the sake of exhibiting differences of accent, or individual peculiarities.

3. That, in learning and consulting the paradigms, the student should constantly compare them with each other, with the tables of terminations, and with the rules of the grammar.

4. That the humble volume should not be dismissed from service, till the paradigms are impressed upon the tablets of the memory as legibly as upon the printed page, — till they have become so familiar to the student, that whenever he has occasion to repeat them, "the words," in the expressive language of Milton, "like so many nimble and airy servitors, shall trip about him at command, and in well-ordered files, as he would wish, fall aptly into their own places."

In the present edition, the Tables of Inflection have been enlarged by the addition of the Dialectic Forms, the Analysis of the Affixes, the Changes in the Root of the Verb, &c. Tables of Ligatures, of Derivation, of Pronominal Correlatives, of the Rules of Syntax, and of Forms of Analysis and Parsing, have also been added. Some references have been made to sections in the Grammar.

A. C.

HANOVER, Sept. 1, 1846.

⁂ The volume of Tables contains pp i, ii, vii - xii, 9 - 84.

CONTENTS.

TABLES.

I. Tables of Orthography and Orthoëpy.

II. Tables of Etymology.

1*

BOOK IV. PROSODY.

¶ 3. C. Vocal Elements.

I. Vowels, Simple and Compound.

[§§ 24-26.]

	Orders.		Class I. A Sounds.	II. O Sounds.	III. E Sounds.	IV. U Sounds.	V. I Sounds.
Simple Vowels.	Short,	1.	ᾰ	ο	ε	ῠ	ῐ
	Long,	2.	ᾱ	ω	η	ῡ	ῑ
Diphthongs in ι.	Proper,	3.	ᾰι	οι	ει	ῠι	
	Improper,	4.	ᾳ	ῳ	ῃ	ῡι	
Diphthongs in υ.	Proper,	5.	ᾰυ	ου	ευ		
	Improper,	6.	ᾱυ	ωυ	ηυ		

II. Consonants.

[§§ 49-51.]

A. Consonants associated in Classes and Orders.

Orders.	Class I. Labials.	Class II. Palatals.	Class III. Linguals.
1. Smooth Mutes,	π	κ	τ
2. Middle Mutes,	β	γ	δ
3. Rough Mutes,	φ	χ	θ
4. Nasals,	μ	γ	ν
5. Double Consonants,	ψ	ξ	ζ

B. Additional Semivowels.

λ ϱ σ

Consonants (Second Arrangement).

Single Consonants,
- Mutes,
  - Smooth, π, κ, τ.
  - Middle, β, γ, δ.
  - Rough, φ, χ, ϑ.
- Semivowels,
  - Liquids, λ, μ, ν, ϱ, γ nasal
  - Sibilant, σ.

Double Consonants, ψ, ξ, ζ.

III. Breathings.

[§ 13.]

Rough Breathing, or Aspirate (῾).

Smooth or Soft Breathing (᾿).

II. ETYMOLOGY.

¶ 4. REMARKS. I. To avoid needless repetition, alike burdensome to teacher and pupil, and to accustom the student early to the application of rule, the tables of paradigms have been constructed with the following *ellipses*, which will be at once supplied from general rules.

1. In the paradigms of DECLENSION, the *Voc. sing.* is omitted whenever it has the same form with the Nom., and the following cases are omitted throughout (see § 80);

α.) The *Voc. plur.*, because it is always the same with the Nom.

β.) The *Dat. dual*, because it is always the same with the Gen.

γ.) The *Acc.* and *Voc. dual*, because they are always the same with the Nom.

δ.) The *Acc* and *Voc. neut.*, in all the numbers, because they are always the same with the Nom.

2. In the paradigms of ADJECTIVES, and of words similarly inflected, the *Neuter* is omitted in the *Gen.* and *Dat.* of all the numbers, and in the *Nom. dual;* because in these cases it never differs from the Masculine (§ 130. ϵ).

3. In the paradigms of CONJUGATION, the *1st Pers. dual* is omitted throughout, as having the same form with the 1st Pers. plur., and the *3d Pers. dual* is omitted whenever it has the same form with the 2d Pers. dual, that is, in the primary tenses of the Indicative, and in the Subjunctive (§ 212. 2). For the form in -μεθον, whose empty shade has been so multiplied by grammarians, and forced to stand, for idle show, in the rank and file of numbers and persons, see § 212. N.

4. The compound forms of the PERFECT PASSIVE SUBJUNCTIVE and OPTATIVE are omitted, as belonging rather to Syntax than to inflection § 234, 637).

II. The regular formation of the tenses is exhibited in the table (¶ 28), which may be thus read; "The —— tense is formed from the root by affixing ——," or, "by prefixing —— and affixing —— (or, in the nude form, [illegible] application of this table, the forms of the root [illegible], if it has more than a single form (§ 254).

[illegible] of translation (¶ 33), the form of the verb must, of [illegible] to the number and person of the pronoun; thus, *I am planning, thou art planning, he is planning*, &c. For the MIDDLE VOICE, change the forms of "*plan*" into the corresponding forms of "*deliberate*"; and, for the PASSIVE VOICE, into the corresponding forms of "*be planned.*"

IV. The Dialectic Forms, for the sake of distinction, are uniformly printed in smaller type. In connection with these forms, the abbreviations Æol. and Æ. denote Æolic; Alex., Alexandrine; Att., Attic; Bœot. and B., Bœotic; Comm., Common; Dor. and D., Doric; Ep. and E, Epic; Hel., Hellenistic; Ion. and I., Ionic; Iter. and It., Iterative; O., Old; Poet. and P., Poetic.

V. A star (*) in the tables denotes that an affix or a form is wanting. Parentheses are sometimes used to inclose unusual, doubtful, peculiar, or supplementary forms. In ¶¶ 29, 30, the ϰ and ϑ of the tense-signs, as dropped in the *second tenses* (§ 199. II.), are separated by a hyphen from the rest of the affix.

¶ 6. II. Analysis of the Affixes.

[The figures in the last column denote the declensions.]

	Connecting Vowels.			Flexible Endings
	Dec. I.	Dec. II.	Dec. III.	
Sing. Nom.	α (η)	ο	*	ς. Fem. 1, *. Neut. 2, ν, ι, *
Gen.	α (η)	ο	*	(οθ) ος. 2 and Masc. 1, ο.
Dat.	α (η)	ο	*	ῐ.
Acc.	α (η)	ο	*	ν, ᾰ. Neut. 3, *.
Voc.	α (η)	ο (ε)	*	*
Plur. Nom.	α	ο	*	ες. 1 and 2, ι Neut. ᾰ.
Gen.	α	ο	*	ων.
Dat.	α	ο	*	(εσι). 3, σῐ. 1 and 2, ις.
Acc.	α	ο	*	(νς) ᾰς. Neut. ᾰ.
Dual Nom.	α	ο	*	ε.
Gen.	α	ο	*	ιν. 3, οιν.

	D.	σκιαῖς	θύραις	γλώσσαις	τιμαῖς	μνάαις, μναῖς
	A.	σκιᾶς	θύρᾱς	γλώσσᾱς	τιμᾱ́ς	μνάᾱς, μνᾶς
D.	N.	σκιᾱ́	θύρᾱ	γλώσσᾱ	τιμᾱ́	μνάᾱ, μνᾶ
	G.	σκιαῖν	θύραιν	γλώσσαιν	τιμαῖν	μνάαιν, μναῖν

¶ 8. Dialectic Forms.

S. N. ᾱς, Ion. ης · ταμίης, βορῆς.
ης, Dor. ᾱς · ναύτᾱς, Ἀτρείδᾱς.
Old, ᾰ · ἱππότᾰ, μητίετᾰ.
ᾱ, Ion. η · σκιή, θύρη.
ᾰ, Ion. η · Ep. ἀληθείη, κνίσση.
η, Dor. ᾱ · τιμᾱ́, ψυχᾱ́, γᾶ.
G. ου, Old, ᾱο · Ἀτρείδᾱο, Βορέᾱο.
Ion. εω, ω · Ἀτρείδεω, Βορέω.
Dor. ᾱ · Ἀτρείδᾱ, Ἑρμᾶ.
ᾱς {Ion. ης · σκιῆς, θύρης.
ης {Dor. ᾱς · τιμᾶς, γλώσσᾱς.
Ep. ηθε(ν) · Αἰσύμηθεν.
D. ᾳ {Ion. ῃ · ταμίῃ, θύρῃ.
ῃ {Dor. ᾳ · ναύτᾳ, τιμᾷ.
Ep. ηφι(ν) · θύρηφι(ν).

A. αν {Ion. ην, εᾰ (masc.); ταμίην, Ἀρισταγόρην, -εᾰ.
ην {Dor. ᾱν · ναύτᾱν, τιμᾱ́ν.
V. ᾱ, Ion. η · ταμίη.
ᾰ, Poet. η · Αἰήτη Ap. Rh.
η, Dor. ᾱ · Ἀτρείδᾱ, Μενάλκᾱ.
Old, ᾰ · νύμφᾰ, Δίκᾰ.
P. G. ῶν, Old, ᾱ́ων · Ἀτρειδᾱ́ων.
Ion. έων · Ἀτρειδέων, θυρέων.
Dor. ᾶν · Ἀτρειδᾶν, θυρᾶν.
D. αις, Old, αισι · ναύταισι, θύραισι.
Ion. ῃσι, ῃς · θύρῃσι, πέτρῃς
A. ᾱς, Ion. εᾰς (masc.); δεσπότεᾰς
Dor. ᾰς · Μοίρᾰς, νύμφᾰς.
Æol. αις · ταὶς τιμαίς.

¶ 9. IV. Nouns of the Second Declension

A. Masculine and Feminine.

		ὁ, *word.*	ὁ, *people.*	ἡ, *way.*	ὁ, *mind.*	ὁ, *temple.*
S.	N.	λόγος	δῆμος	ὁδός	νόος, νοῦς	νᾱός, νεώς
	G.	λόγου	δήμου	ὁδοῦ	νόου, νοῦ	νᾱοῦ, νεώ
	D.	λόγῳ	δήμῳ	ὁδῷ	νόῳ, νῷ	νᾱῷ, νεῴ
	A.	λόγον	δῆμον	ὁδόν	νόον, νοῦν	νᾱόν, νεών, νεω
	V.	λόγε	δῆμε	ὁδέ	νόε, νοῦ	
P.	N.	λόγοι	δῆμοι	ὁδοί	νόοι, νοῖ	νᾱοί, νεῴ
	G.	λόγων	δήμων	ὁδῶν	νόων, νῶν	νᾱῶν, νεῶν
	D.	λόγοις	δήμοις	ὁδοῖς	νόοις, νοῖς	νᾱοῖς, νεῷς
	A.	λόγους	δήμους	ὁδούς	νόους, νοῦς	νᾱούς, νεώς
D.	N.	λόγω	δήμω	ὁδώ	νόω, νώ	νᾱώ, νεώ
	G.	λόγοιν	δήμοιν	ὁδοῖν	νόοιν, νοῖν	νᾱοῖν, νεῷν

B. Neuter.

		τὸ, *fig.*	τὸ, *wing.*	τὸ, *part.*	τὸ, *bone.*	τὸ, *chamber.*
S.	N.	σῦκον	πτερόν	μόριον	ὀστέον, ὀστοῦν	ἀνώγεων
	G.	σύκου	πτεροῦ	μορίου	ὀστέου, ὀστοῦ	ἀνώγεω
	D.	σύκῳ	πτερῷ	μορίῳ	ὀστέῳ, ὀστῷ	ἀνώγεῳ
P.	N.	σῦκᾰ	πτερᾰ́	μόριᾰ	ὀστέᾰ, ὀστᾶ	ἀνώγεω
	G.	σύκων	πτερῶν	μορίων	ὀστέων, ὀστῶν	ἀνώγεων
	D.	σύκοις	πτεροῖς	μορίοις	ὀστέοις, ὀστοῖς	ἀνώγεῳς
D.	N.	σύκω	πτερώ	μορίω	ὀστέω, ὀστώ	ἀνώγεω
	G.	σύκοιν	πτεροῖν	μορίοιν	ὀστέοιν, ὀστοῖν	ἀνώγεῳν

¶ 10. Dialectic Forms.

S. N. ος, Laconic, ορ · παλεόρ, § 70.4.
G. ου, Ep. οιο · τοῖο λόγοιο.
Dor. ω · τῶ λόγω.
(Ion. εω · Βάττεω, Κροίσεω.)
Ep. οθε(ν) · οὐράνοθεν.
ω (contracted from αου), Ep. ωο · Πετεῶο.
D. ῳ, Old, οι · Ἰσθμοῖ, τοῖ δάμοι.
Ep. οφι(ν) · αὐτόφι, ζυγόφιν.
Ep. οθι · οὐρανόθι, Ἰλιόθι.

S. D ῳ, Bœot. ῡ · αὐτῦ, τῦ δάμῡ.
P. N. οι, Bœot. ῡ · καλῦ, Ὅμηρῡ.
(G. ων, Ion. έων · πετσέων, πυρέων.)
D. οις, Old, οισι · τοῖσι λόγοισι.
Bœot. ῡς · τῦς ἄλλῡς προξένῡς
A. ους, Dor. ως, ος · τὼς λόγως, τὼς λύκος, παρθένος.
Æol. οις · ἀνδρείοις πέπλοις, τοὶς νόμοις.
D. G. οιν, Ep. οιϊν · ἵπποιϊν, ὤμοιϊν.

¶ 11. V. Nouns of the Third Declension.

A. Mute.

1. Labial. / **2. Palatal.**

		ὁ, *vulture.*	ἡ, *vein.*	ὁ, *raven.*	ὁ, ἡ, *goat.*	ἡ, *phalanx.*	ἡ, *hair*
S.	N.	γύψ	φλέψ	κόραξ	αἴξ	φᾰ́λαγξ	θρίξ
	G.	γῡπός	φλεβός	κόρᾰκος	αἰγός	φάλαγγος	τρῐχός
	D.	γῡπί	φλεβί	κόρακι	αἰγί	φάλαγγι	τριχί
	A.	γῦπα	φλέβα	κόρακα	αἶγα	φάλαγγα	τρίχα
P.	N.	γῦπες	φλέβες	κόρακες	αἶγες	φάλαγγες	τρίχες
	G.	γῡπῶν	φλεβῶν	κοράκων	αἰγῶν	φαλάγγων	τριχῶν
	D.	γυψί	φλεψί	κόραξι	αἰξί	φάλαγξι	θριξί
	A.	γῦπας	φλέβας	κόρακας	αἶγας	φάλαγγας	τρίχας
D.	N.	γῦπε	φλέβε	κόρακε	αἶγε	φάλαγγε	τρίχε
	G.	γῡποῖν	φλεβοῖν	κοράκοιν	αἰγοῖν	φαλάγγοιν	τριχοῖν

3. Lingual.

α. Masculine and Feminine.

		ὁ, ἡ, *child.*	ὁ, *foot.*	ὁ, *sovereign.*	ἡ, *grace.*	ἡ, *key.*
S.	N.	παῖς	πούς	ἄναξ	χᾰ́ρῐς	κλείς
	G.	παιδός	ποδός	ἄνακτος	χάρῐτος	κλειδός
	D.	παιδί	ποδί	ἄνακτι	χάριτι	κλειδί
	A.	παῖδα	πόδα	ἄνακτα	χάριτα, χάρῐν	κλεῖδα, κλεῖν
	V.	παῖ		ἄνᾰ		
P.	N.	παῖδες	πόδες	ἄνακτες	χάριτες	κλεῖδες, κλεῖς
	G.	παίδων	ποδῶν	ἀνάκτων	χαρίτων	κλειδῶν
	D.	παισί	ποσί	ἄναξι	χάρισι	κλεισί
	A.	παῖδας	πόδας	ἄνακτας	χάριτας	κλεῖδας, κλεῖς
D.	N.	παῖδε	πόδε	ἄνακτε	χάριτε	κλεῖδε
	G.	παίδοιν	ποδοῖν	ἀνάκτοιν	χαρίτοιν	κλειδοῖν

β. Neuter.

		τὸ, *body.*	τὸ, *light.*	τὸ, *liver.*	τὸ, *horn.*			τὸ, *ear*
S.	N.	σῶμᾰ	φῶς	ἧπᾰρ	κέρᾰς			οὖς
	G.	σώμᾰτος	φωτός	ἥπᾰτος	κέρᾱτος,	κέραος,	κέρως	ὠτός
	D.	σώματι	φωτί	ἥπατι	κέρᾱτι,	κέραϊ,	κέρᾳ	ὠτί
P.	N.	σώματα	φῶτα	ἥπατα	κέρᾱτα,	κέραα,	κέρᾱ	ὦτα
	G.	σωμάτων	φώτων	ἡπάτων	κερᾱ́των	κεράων,	κερῶν	ὤτων
	D.	σώμασι	φωσί	ἥπασι	κέρᾱσι			ὠσί
D.	N.	σώματε	φῶτε	ἥπατε	κέρᾱτε,	κέραε,	κέρᾱ	ὦτε
	G.	σωμάτοιν	φώτοιν	ἡπάτοιν	κερᾱ́τοιν,	κεράοιν,	κερῷν	ὤτοιν

¶ 12. B. Liquid.

	ὁ, *harbour.*	ὁ, *deity.*	ἡ, *nose.*	ὁ, *beast.*	ὁ, *orator.*	ἡ, *hand*
S. N.	λιμήν	δαίμων	ῥίς	θήρ	ῥήτωρ	χείρ
G.	λιμένος	δαίμονος	ῥινός	θηρός	ῥήτορος	χειρός
D.	λιμένι	δαίμονι	ῥινί	θηρί	ῥήτορι	χειρί
A.	λιμένα	δαίμονα	ῥῖνα	θῆρα	ῥήτορα	χεῖρα
V.		δαῖμον	ῥίν		ῥῆτορ	
P. N.	λιμένες	δαίμονες	ῥῖνες	θῆρες	ῥήτορες	χεῖρες
G.	λιμένων	δαιμόνων	ῥινῶν	θηρῶν	ῥητόρων	χειρῶν
D.	λιμέσι	δαίμοσι	ῥισί	θηρσί	ῥήτορσι	χερσί
A.	λιμένας	δαίμονας	ῥῖνας	θῆρας	ῥήτορας	χεῖρας
D. N.	λιμένε	δαίμονε	ῥῖνε	θῆρε	ῥήτορε	χεῖρε
G.	λιμένοιν	δαιμόνοιν	ῥινοῖν	θηροῖν	ῥητόροιν	χεροῖν

Syncopated.

	ὁ, *father.*	ὁ, *man.*	ἡ, *mother.*	ὁ, ἡ, *dog.*	ὁ, ἡ, *lamb.*
S. N.	πᾰτήρ	ἀνήρ	μήτηρ	κύων	(ἀμνός)
G.	πατέρος, πατρός	ἀνέρος, ἀνδρός	μητρός	κυνός	ἀρνός
D.	πατέρι, πατρί	ἀνέρι, ἀνδρί	μητρί	κυνί	ἀρνί
A.	πατέρα	ἀνέρα, ἄνδρα	μητέρα	κύνα	ἄρνα
V.	πάτερ	ἄνερ	μῆτερ	κύον	
P. N.	πατέρες	ἀνέρες, ἄνδρες	μητέρες	κύνες	ἄρνες
G.	πατέρων	ἀνέρων, ἀνδρῶν	μητέρων	κυνῶν	ἀρνῶν
D.	πατράσι	ἀνδράσι	μητράσι	κυσί	ἀρνάσι
A.	πατέρας	ἀνέρας, ἄνδρας	μητέρας	κύνας	ἄρνας
D. N.	πατέρε	ἀνέρε, ἄνδρε	μητέρε	κύνε	ἄρνε
G.	πατέροιν	ἀνέροιν, ἀνδροῖν	μητέροιν	κυνοῖν	ἀρνοῖν

¶ 13. C. Liquid-Mute.

	ὁ, *lion.*	ὁ, *tooth.*	ὁ, *giant.*	ἡ, *wife.*	ὁ, *Xenophon.*
S. N.	λέων	ὀδούς	γίγᾱς	δάμαρ	Ξενοφῶν
G.	λέοντος	ὀδόντος	γίγαντος	δάμαρτος	Ξενοφῶντος
D.	λέοντι	ὀδόντι	γίγαντι	δάμαρτι	Ξενοφῶντι
A.	λέοντα	ὀδόντα	γίγαντα	δάμαρτα	Ξενοφῶντα
V.	λέον		γίγᾰν		
P. N.	λέοντες	ὀδόντες	γίγαντες	δάμαρτες	
G.	λεόντων	ὀδόντων	γιγάντων	δαμάρτων	
D.	λέουσι	ὀδοῦσι	γίγᾱσι	δάμαρσι	
A.	λέοντας	ὀδόντας	γίγαντας	δάμαρτας	
D. N.	λέοντε	ὀδόντε	γίγαντε	δάμαρτε	
G.	λεόντοιν	ὀδόντοιν	γιγάντοιν	δαμάρτοιν	

	ἡ, *Opus.*
S. N.	Ὀποῦς
G.	Ὀποῦντος
D.	Ὀποῦντι
A.	Ὀποῦντα

¶ 14. D. Pure.

α. Masculine and Feminine.

	ὁ, *jackal.*	ὁ, *hero.*	ὁ, *weevil.*	ὁ, ἡ, *sheep.*	ὁ, *fish.*
S. N.	θώς	ἥρως	κίς	οἶς	ἰχθύς
G.	θωός	ἥρωος	κῐός	οἰός	ἰχθῠ́ος
D.	θωΐ	ἥρωϊ (ἥρῳ)	κῐΐ	οἰΐ	ἰχθῠ́ϊ
A.	θῶα	ἥρωα, ἥρω	κίν	οἶν	ἰχθύν
V.					ἰχθῠ́
P. N.	θῶες	ἥρωες	κῐ́ες	οἶες, οἶς	ἰχθῠ́ες, ἰχθῦς
G.	θώων	ἡρώων	κῐῶν	οἰῶν	ἰχθῠ́ων
D.	θωσί	ἥρωσι	κῐσί	οἰσί	ἰχθῠ́σι
A.	θῶας	ἥρωας, ἥρως	κῐ́ας	οἶας, οἶς	ἰχθῠ́ας, ἰχθῦς
D. N.	θῶε	ἥρωε	κῐ́ε	οἶε	ἰχθῠ́ε, ἰχθῦ
G.	θώοιν	ἡρώοιν	κῐοῖν	οἰοῖν	ἰχθῠ́οιν

	ὁ, *knight.*	ὁ, ἡ, *ox.*	ἡ, *old woman.*	ἡ, *ship.*
S. N.	ἱππεύς	βοῦς	γραῦς	ναῦς
G.	ἱππέως	βοός	γρᾱός	νεώς
D.	ἱππέϊ, ἱππεῖ	βοΐ	γρᾱΐ	νηΐ
A.	ἱππέᾱ	βοῦν	γραῦν	ναῦν
V.	ἱππεῦ	βοῦ	γραῦ	
P. N.	ἱππέες, ἱππεῖς	βόες	γρᾶες	νῆες
G.	ἱππέων	βοῶν	γρᾱῶν	νεῶν
D.	ἱππεῦσι	βουσί	γραυσί	ναυσί
A.	ἱππέᾱς, ἱππεῖς	βόας, βοῦς	γρᾶας, γραῦς	ναῦς
D. N.	ἱππέε	βόε	γρᾶε	νῆε
G.	ἱππέοιν	βοοῖν	γρᾱοῖν	νεοῖν

	ὁ, *cubit.*	ἡ, *city.*	ἡ, *trireme.*
S. N.	πῆχῠς	πόλῐς	τριήρης
G.	πήχεως	πόλεως	τριήρεος, τριήρους
D.	πήχεϊ, πήχει	πόλεϊ, πόλει	τριήρεϊ, τριήρει
A.	πῆχυν	πόλιν	τριήρεα, τριήρη
V.	πῆχυ	πόλι	τριῆρες
P. N.	πήχεες, πήχεις	πόλεες, πόλεις	τριήρεες, τριήρεις
G.	πήχεων (πηχῶν)	πόλεων	τριηρέων, τριήρων
D.	πήχεσι	πόλεσι	τριήρεσι
A.	πήχεας, πήχεις	πόλεας, πόλεις	τριήρεας, τριήρεις
D. N.	πήχεε	πόλεε, πόλη	τριήρεε, τριήρη
G.	πηχέοιν	πολέοιν	τριηρέοιν, τριηροῖν

	ἡ, *echo.*	ἡ, *shame.*	ὁ, *Socrates.*
S. N.	ἠχώ	αἰδώς	Σωκράτης
G.	ἠχόος, ἠχοῦς	αἰδόος, αἰδοῦς	Σωκράτεος, Σωκράτους
D.	ἠχόϊ, ἠχοῖ	αἰδόϊ, αἰδοῖ	Σωκράτεϊ, Σωκράτει
A.	ἠχόα, ἠχώ	αἰδόα, αἰδῶ	Σωκράτεα, Σωκράτη, Σωκράτην
V.	ἠχοῖ	αἰδοῖ	Σώκρατες

	ὁ, *Piræus.*	ὁ, *Hercules.*
S. N.	Πειραιεύς	Ἡρακλέης, Ἡρακλῆς
G.	Πειραιέως, Πειραιῶς	Ἡρακλέεος, Ἡρακλέους
D.	Πειραιέϊ, Πειραιεῖ	Ἡρακλέεϊ, Ἡρακλέει, Ἡρακλεῖ
A.	Πειραιέᾱ, Πειραιᾶ	Ἡρακλέεα, Ἡρακλέᾱ, Ἡρακλῆ
V.	Πειραιεῦ	Ἡράκλεες, Ἡράκλεις (Ἥρακλες)

β. Neuter.

	τὸ, *wall.*	τὸ, *town.*	τὸ, *honor.*
S. N.	τεῖχος	ἄστῠ	γέρᾰς
G.	τείχεος, τείχους	ἄστεος, ἄστεως	γέρᾰος, γέρως
D.	τείχεϊ, τείχει	ἄστεϊ, ἄστει	γέραϊ, γέρᾳ
P. N.	τείχεα, τείχη	ἄστεα, ἄστη	γέραα, γέρᾱ
G.	τειχέων, τειχῶν	ἀστέων	γεράων, γερῶν
D.	τείχεσι	ἄστεσι	γέρασι
D. N.	τείχεε, τείχη	ἄστεε	γέραε, γέρᾱ
G.	τειχέοιν, τειχοῖν	ἀστέοιν	γεράοιν, γερῷν

¶ 15. Dialectic Forms.

S. G. ατος, Ion. εος · κέρεος, τέρεος.
εος, Ion. ευς · Θέρευς, Θάμβευς.
έως, Ep. ῆος · βασιλῆος.
Ion. and Dor. έος · βασιλέος.
εως, Ion. and Dor. ιος · πόλιος.
ιδος, Ion. and Dor. ιος · Κύπριος.
Dor. ιτος · Θέμιτος.
οῦς, Dor. and Æol. ῶς, οῖς · ἀχῶς, [ἀοῖς.
D. εῖ, Ep. ῆϊ · βασιλῆϊ.
Ion. εϊ · βασιλέϊ.
ει, Ion. ῑ · πόλῑ, δυνάμῑ.
ιδι, Ion. ῑ · Θέτῑ, ἀπόλῑ.
A. ν, Poet. α · εὐρέα, ἰχθύα.
όα, Ion. οῦν · Ἰοῦν, Λητοῦν.
Dor. ων · Ἧρων, Λατών.
έᾰ, Ep. ῆᾰ · βασιλῆᾰ.
Ion. έᾰ · βασιλέᾰ.
Dor. ῆ · βασιλῆ.
V. ες, Æol. ε · Σώκρατε.

P. N. εῖς, Old Att. ῆς · βασιλῆς.
Ep. ῆες · βασιλῆες.
Ion. έες · βασιλέες.
εις, Ion. and Dor. ιες · πόλιες.
αα, Poet. ᾰ · γέρᾰ, κρέᾰ.
Ion. εα · γέρεα, τέρεα.
G. ων, Ion. έων · χηνέων, ἀνδρέων.
έων, Ep. ήων · βασιλήων.
εων, Ion. and Dor. ίων · πολίων.
D. σι(ν), Old, εσι(ν) · χείρεσι.
Poet. σσι(ν) · ἔπεσσι.
εσσι(ν) · πόδεσσιν.
εσι(ν), Ep. εσφι(ν) · ὄχεσφιν.
Ion. ισι(ν) · πόλισι.
A. έᾱς, Ep. ῆᾰς · βασιλῆᾰς.
Ion. έᾰς · βασιλέᾰς.
Comm. εῖς · βασιλεῖς.
εις, Ion. and Dor. ιας · πόλιας.
D. G. οιν, Ep. οιϊν · ποδοῖϊν, Σειρήνοιϊν.

¶ 16. VI. Irregular and Dialectic Declension.

		ὁ, *Jupiter.*			ὁ, *Œdipus.*			ὁ, *Glus.*
S.	N.	Ζεύς,		Ζᾶν (Dor.)	Οἰδίπους			Γλοῦς
	G.	Διός,	Ζηνός,	Ζᾶνός	Οἰδίποδος,	Οἰδίπου	Οἰδιπόδᾱο, -ᾱ, -εω,	Γλοῦ
	D.	Διί,	Ζηνί,	Ζᾶνί	Οἰδίποδι,	[(poet.),	[D. -ῃ, -ᾳ, A. -ην,	Γλοῦ
	A.	Δία,	Ζῆνα,	Ζᾶνα	Οἰδίποδα,	Οἰδίπουν	[-ᾱν, V. -η, -ᾱ	Γλοῦν
	V.	Ζεῦ			Οἰδίπου		[(Ep. and Lyr.)	Γλοῦ

		Attic.	ὁ, *son*	Homeric.				Doric.	ἡ, *ship.* Ionic.
S.	N.	υἱός		υἱός				ναῦς (νᾶς)	νηῦς (νῆϋς)
	G.	υἱοῦ,	υἱέος	υἱοῦ,	υἷος,	υἱέος		νᾶός	νηός, νεός
	D.	υἱῷ,	υἱεῖ		υἷι,	υἱέϊ,	υἱεῖ	νᾶΐ	νηΐ
	A.	υἱόν		υἱόν,	υἷα,	υἱέᾰ		ναῦν (νᾶν)	νῆα, νέα, νηῦν
	V.	υἱέ							
P.	N.	υἱοί,	υἱεῖς		υἷες,	υἱέες,	υἱεῖς	νᾶες	νῆες, νέες
	G.	υἱῶν,	υἱέων	υἱῶν,		υἱέων		νᾶῶν	νηῶν, νεῶν
	D.	υἱοῖς,	υἱέσι	υἱοῖσι,	υἱάσι,			ναυσί, νάεσσι	νηῦσι, νήεσσι, νέεσσι,
	A.	υἱούς,	υἱεῖς	υἱούς,	υἷας,	υἱέας		νᾶας	νῆας, νέας [ναῦφι

		Attic.	τὸ, *spear.*	Homeric.		Homeric.	τὸ, *cave.*
S.	N.	δόρυ		δόρυ		σπέος,	σπεῖος
	G.	δόρατος,	δορός (poet.)	δούρατος,	δουρός	σπείους	
	D.	δόρατι,	δορί, δόρει (poet.)	δούρατι,	δουρί	σπῆϊ	
P.	N.	δόρατα,	δόρη (poet.)	δούρατα,	δοῦρα		
	G.	δοράτων			δούρων	σπείων	
	D.	δόρασι		δούρασι,	δούρεσσι	σπέσσι,	σπήεσσι

Homeric Paradigms.

		ὁ, *knight.*	ἡ, *city.*		
S.	N.	ἱππεύς	πόλις		
	G.	ἱππῆος	πόλιος,	πτόλιος, πόλεος (πόλευς Theog.),	πόληος
	D.	ἱππῆϊ	(πόλῑ Hdt.),	πτόλεϊ, πόλει,	πόληϊ
	A.	ἱππῆα	πόλιν,	πτόλιν	(πόληα Hes.)
	V.	ἱππεῦ			
P.	N.	ἱππῆες, ἱππεῖς	πόλιες (πόλῖς Hdt.),		πόληες
	G.	ἱππήων	πολίων		
	D.	ἱππεῦσι	πολίεσσι (πολίεσι Pind., πόλισι Hdt.)		
	A.	ἱππῆας	πόλιας (πόλῖς Hdt.), πόλεις,		πόληας

		ὁ, *Ulysses.*				ὁ, *Patroclus.*		
S.	N.	Ὀδυσσεύς,		Ὀδυσεύς		Πάτροκλος		
	G.	Ὀδυσσῆος,	Ὀδυσσέος,	Ὀδυσῆος,	Ὀδυσεῦς	Πατρόκλου,	-οιο,	Πατροκλῆος
	D.			Ὀδυσῆϊ,	Ὀδυσεῖ	Πατρόκλῳ		
	A.	Ὀδυσσῆα,	Ὀδυσσέα,	Ὀδυσῆα,	Ὀδυσῆ	Πάτροκλον,		Πατροκλῆα
	V.	Ὀδυσσεῦ,		Ὀδυσεῦ		Πάτροκλε,		Πατρόκλεις

¶ 17. VII. Adjectives of Two Terminations.

A. Of the Second Declension.

	ὁ, ἡ (*unjust*)	τὸ	ὁ, ἡ (*unfading*)	τὸ
S. N.	ἄδῐκος	ἄδικον	ἀγήρᾰος, ἀγήρως	ἀγήραον, ἀγήρων
G.	ἀδίκου		ἀγηράου, ἀγήρω	
D.	ἀδίκῳ		ἀγηράῳ, ἀγήρῳ	
A.	ἄδικον		ἀγήραον, ἀγήρων, ἀγήρω	
V.	ἄδικε			
P. N.	ἄδικοι	ἄδικα	ἀγήραοι, ἀγήρῳ	ἀγήραα, ἀγήρω
G.	ἀδίκων		ἀγηράων, ἀγήρων	
D.	ἀδίκοις		ἀγηράοις, ἀγήρῳς	
A.	ἀδίκους		ἀγηράους, ἀγήρως	
D. N.	ἀδίκω		ἀγηράω, ἀγήρω	
G.	ἀδίκοιν		ἀγηράοιν, ἀγήρῳν	

B. Of the Third Declension.

	ὁ, ἡ (*male*)	τὸ	ὁ, ἡ (*pleasing*)	τὸ	ὁ, ἡ (*two-footed*)	τὸ
S. N.	ἄῤῥην	ἄῤῥεν	εὔχᾰρις	εὔχαρι	δίπους	δίπουν
G.	ἄῤῥενος		εὐχάρῐτος		δίποδος	
D.	ἄῤῥενι		εὐχάριτι		δίποδι	
A.	ἄῤῥενα		εὐχάριτα, εὔχαριν		δίποδα, δίπουν	
V.	ἄῤῥεν		εὔχαρι		δίπου	
P. N.	ἄῤῥενες	ἄῤῥενα	εὐχάριτες	εὐχάριτα	δίποδες	δίποδα
G.	ἀῤῥένων		εὐχαρίτων		διπόδων	
D.	ἄῤῥεσι		εὐχάρισι		δίποσι	
A.	ἄῤῥενας		εὐχάριτας		δίποδας	
D. N.	ἄῤῥενε		εὐχάριτε		δίποδε	
G.	ἀῤῥένοιν		εὐχαρίτοιν		διπόδοιν	

	ὁ, ἡ (*evident*)	τὸ	ὁ, ἡ (*greater*)	τὸ
S. N.	σαφής	σαφές	μείζων	μεῖζον
G.	σαφέος, σαφοῦς		μείζονος	
D.	σαφέϊ, σαφεῖ		μείζονι	
A.	σαφέα, σαφῆ		μείζονα, μείζω	
V.	σαφές		μεῖζον	
P. N.	σαφέες, σαφεῖς	σαφέα, σαφῆ	μείζονες, μείζους	μείζονα, μείζω
G.	σαφέων, σαφῶν		μειζόνων	
D.	σαφέσι		μείζοσι	
A.	σαφέας, σαφεῖς		μείζονας, μείζους	
D. N.	σαφέε, σαφῆ		μείζονε	
G.	σαφέοιν, σαφοῖν		μειζόνοιν	

¶ 18. VIII. Adjectives of Three Terminations.

A. Of the Second and First Declensions.

	ὁ (*friendly*)	ἡ	τὸ	ὁ (*wise*)	ἡ	τὸ
S. N.	φίλιος	φιλίᾱ	φίλιον	σοφός	σοφή	σοφόν
G.	φιλίου	φιλίᾱς		σοφοῦ	σοφῆς	
D.	φιλίῳ	φιλίᾳ		σοφῷ	σοφῇ	
A.	φίλιον	φιλίᾱν		σοφόν	σοφήν	
V.	φίλιε			σοφέ		
P. N.	φίλιοι	φίλιαι	φίλιᾰ	σοφοί	σοφαί	σοφᾰ́
G.	φιλίων	φιλίων		σοφῶν	σοφῶν	
D.	φιλίοις	φιλίαις		σοφοῖς	σοφαῖς	
A.	φιλίους	φιλίᾱς		σοφούς	σοφᾱ́ς	
D. N.	φιλίω	φιλίᾱ		σοφώ	σοφᾱ́	
G.	φιλίοιν	φιλίαιν		σοφοῖν	σοφαῖν	

Contracted.

	ὁ (*golden*)	ἡ	τὸ
S. N.	χρύσεος, χρῡσοῦς	χρυσέᾱ, χρυσῆ	χρύσεον, χρυσοῦν
G.	χρυσέου, χρυσοῦ	χρυσέᾱς, χρυσῆς	
D.	χρυσέῳ, χρυσῷ	χρυσέᾳ, χρυσῇ	
A.	χρύσεον, χρυσοῦν	χρυσέᾱν, χρυσῆν	
P. N.	χρύσεοι, χρυσοῖ	χρύσεαι, χρυσαῖ	χρύσεᾰ, χρυσᾶ
G.	χρυσέων, χρυσῶν	χρυσέων, χρυσῶν	
D.	χρυσέοις, χρυσοῖς	χρυσέαις, χρυσαῖς	
A.	χρυσέους, χρυσοῦς	χρυσέᾱς, χρυσᾶς	
D. N.	χρυσέω, χρυσώ	χρυσέᾱ, χρυσᾶ	
G.	χρυσέοιν, χρυσοῖν	χρυσέαιν, χρυσαῖν	

	ὁ (*double*)	ἡ	τὸ
S. N.	διπλόος, διπλοῦς	διπλόη, διπλῆ	διπλόον, διπλοῦν
G.	διπλόου, διπλοῦ	διπλόης, διπλῆς	
D	διπλόῳ, διπλῷ	διπλόῃ, διπλῇ	
A	διπλόον, διπλοῦν	διπλόην, διπλῆν	
P. N	διπλόοι, διπλοῖ	διπλόαι, διπλαῖ	διπλόᾰ, διπλᾶ
G.	διπλόων, διπλῶν	διπλόων, διπλῶν	
D.	διπλόοις, διπλοῖς	διπλόαις, διπλαῖς	
A.	διπλόους, διπλοῦς	διπλόᾱς, διπλᾶς	
D. N.	διπλόω, διπλώ	διπλόᾱ, διπλᾶ	
G.	διπλόοιν, διπλοῖν	διπλόαιν, διπλαῖν	

¶ 19. B. Of the Third and First Declensions.

	ὁ (*black*)	ἡ	τὸ	ὁ (*all*)	ἡ	τὸ
S. N.	μέλᾱς	μέλαινᾰ	μέλᾰν	πᾶς	πᾶσᾰ	πᾶν
G.	μέλᾰνος	μελαίνης		παντός	πάσης	
D.	μέλανι	μελαίνῃ		παντί	πάσῃ	
A.	μέλανα	μέλαινᾰν		πάντα	πᾶσᾰν	
P. N.	μέλανες	μέλαιναι	μέλανα	πάντες	πᾶσαι	πάντα
G.	μελάνων	μελαινῶν		πάντων	πασῶν	
D.	μέλασι	μελαίναις		πᾶσι	πάσαις	
A.	μέλανας	μελαίνᾱς		πάντας	πάσᾱς	
D. N.	μέλανε	μελαίνᾱ		πάντε	πάσᾱ	
G.	μελάνοιν	μελαίναιν		πάντοιν	πάσαιν	

	ὁ (*agreeable*)	ἡ	τὸ	ὁ (*sweet*)	ἡ	τὸ
S. N.	χαρίεις	χαρίεσσᾰ	χαρίεν	ἡδύς	ἡδεῖᾰ	ἡδύ
G.	χαρίεντος	χαριέσσης		ἡδέος	ἡδείᾱς	
D.	χαρίεντι	χαριέσσῃ		ἡδέϊ, ἡδεῖ	ἡδείᾳ	
A.	χαρίεντα	χαρίεσσᾰν		ἡδύν	ἡδεῖᾰν	
V.	χαρίεν			ἡδύ		
P. N.	χαρίεντες	χαρίεσσαι	χαρίεντα	ἡδέες, ἡδεῖς	ἡδεῖαι	ἡδέα
G.	χαριέντων	χαριεσσῶν		ἡδέων	ἡδειῶν	
D.	χαρίεσι	χαριέσσαις		ἡδέσι	ἡδείαις	
A.	χαρίεντας	χαριέσσᾱς		ἡδέας, ἡδεῖς	ἡδείᾱς	
D. N.	χαρίεντε	χαριέσσᾱ		ἡδέε	ἡδείᾱ	
G.	χαριέντοιν	χαριέσσαιν		ἡδέοιν	ἡδείαιν	

¶ 20. C. Of the Three Declensions.

	ὁ (*great*)	ἡ	τὸ	ὁ (*much*)	ἡ	τὸ
S. N.	μέγᾰς	μεγάλη	μέγα	πολύς	πολλή	πολύ
G.	μεγάλου	μεγάλης		πολλοῦ	πολλῆς	
D	μεγάλῳ	μεγάλῃ		πολλῷ	πολλῇ	
A	μέγαν	μεγάλην		πολύν	πολλήν	
V.	μεγάλε			(*many*)		
P. N.	μεγάλοι	μεγάλαι	μεγάλᾰ	πολλοί	πολλαί	πολλά
G.	μεγάλων	μεγάλων		πολλῶν	πολλῶν	
D.	μεγάλοις	μεγάλαις		πολλοῖς	πολλαῖς	
A.	μεγάλους	μεγάλᾱς		πολλούς	πολλάς	
D. N.	μεγάλω	μεγάλᾱ				
G.	μεγάλοιν	μεγάλαιν				

Homeric Forms of πολύς.

	ὁ		ἡ	τὸ
S. N.	πολύς, πουλύς	πολλός	πολλή	πολύ, πουλύ, πολλόν
G.	πολέος		πολλῆς	
D.	(πολεῖ Æsch.)	πολλῷ	πολλῇ	
A.	πολύν, πουλύν	πολλόν	πολλήν, πουλύν	
P. N.	πολέες, πολεῖς	πολλοί	πολλαί	(πολέα Æsch.) πολλά
G.	πολέων	πολλῶν	πολλάων, πολλέων	
D.	πολέσι, -έσσι, -έεσσι	πολλοῖσι, -οῖς	πολλῇσι	
A.	πολέας, πολεῖς	πολλούς	πολλάς	

S.	ὁ (*mild*)	ἡ	τὸ	P. οἱ		αἱ	τὰ
N.	πρᾶος	πραεῖᾰ	πρᾶον	πρᾶοι,	πραεῖς	πραεῖαι	πραέα
G.	πράου	πραείᾱς			πραέων	πραειῶν	
D.	πράῳ	πραείᾳ		πράοις,	πραέσι	πραείαις	πραέσι
A.	πρᾶον	πραεῖᾰν		πράους,	πραεῖς	πραείᾱς	

¶ 21. IX. Numerals.

	M. (*one*)	F.	N.	M. (*no one*)	F.	N.	M., *none*.
S. N.	εἷς	μίᾰ	ἕν	οὐδείς	οὐδεμία	οὐδέν	P. οὐδένες
G.	ἑνός	μιᾶς		οὐδενός	οὐδεμιᾶς		οὐδένων
D.	ἑνί	μιᾷ		οὐδενί	οὐδεμιᾷ		οὐδέσι
A.	ἕνα	μίᾰν		οὐδένα	οὐδεμίαν		οὐδένας
	Ep. Dor.	Ion. Ep.		Late.	Ion.	Late.	Ion.
N.	ἔεις, ἧς	μίη, ἴᾰ		οὐθείς	οὐδεμίη	οὐθέν	οὐδαμοί, N. -ά
G.		μιῆς, ἰῆς		οὐθενός	οὐδεμιῆς		οὐδαμῶν
D.	ἰῷ	μιῇ, ἰῇ		οὐθενί	οὐδεμιῇ		οὐδαμοῖς
A.		μίην, ἴᾰν		οὐθένα	οὐδεμίην		οὐδαμούς, F. -έας

	M. F. N., *two*.		M. F. N., *both*.
D. N. A.	δύο, δύω		ἄμφω
G. D.	δυοῖν, δυεῖν (Att.)	P. D. δυσί (rare)	ἀμφοῖν

	Ep.	Ep.	Ion.
N.	δοιώ	δοιοί, -αί, -ά	
G.			δυῶν
D.		δοιοῖς, -οῖσι,	δυοῖσι
A.		δοιούς, -άς	

	M. F. (*three*)	N.	M. F. (*four*)	N.
P. N.	τρεῖς	τρία	τέσσᾰρες, τέτταρες	τέσσαρα, τέτταρα
G.	τριῶν		τεσσάρων, τεττάρων	
D.	τρισί		τέσσαρσι, τέτταρσι	
A.	τρεῖς		τέσσαρας, τέτταρας	
	Poet.			
D.	τριοῖσι			

Ion. τέσσερες, Dor. τέτορες and τέττορες, Æol. and Ep. πίσυρες, &c.; Dat., Ep. and in late prose, τέτρᾰσι.

¶ 22. x. Participles.

1. Present Active.

	ὁ (*advising*)	ἡ	τὸ
S. N.	βουλεύων	βουλεύουσᾰ	βουλεῦον
G.	βουλεύοντος	βουλευούσης	
D.	βουλεύοντι	βουλευούσῃ	
A.	βουλεύοντα	βουλεύουσᾰν	
P. N.	βουλεύοντες	βουλεύουσαι	βουλεύοντα
G.	βουλευόντων	βουλευουσῶν	
D.	βουλεύουσι	βουλευούσαις	
A.	βουλεύοντας	βουλευούσᾱς	
D. N.	βουλεύοντε	βουλευούσᾱ	
G.	βουλευόντοιν	βουλευούσαιν	

2. Present Active Contracted.

	ὁ (*honoring*)		ἡ		τὸ	
S. N.	τῑμάων,	τιμῶν	τιμάουσᾰ,	τιμῶσᾰ	τιμάον,	τιμῶν
G.	τιμάοντος,	τιμῶντος	τιμαούσης,	τιμώσης		
D.	τιμάοντι,	τιμῶντι	τιμαούσῃ,	τιμώσῃ		
A.	τιμάοντα,	τιμῶντα	τιμάουσᾰν,	τιμῶσᾰν		
P. N.	τιμάοντες,	τιμῶντες	τιμάουσαι,	τιμῶσαι	τιμάοντα,	τιμῶντα
G.	τιμαόντων,	τιμώντων	τιμαουσῶν,	τιμωσῶν		
D.	τιμάουσι,	τιμῶσι	τιμαούσαις,	τιμώσαις		
A.	τιμάοντας,	τιμῶντας	τιμαούσᾱς,	τιμώσᾱς		
D. N.	τιμάοντε,	τιμῶντε	τιμαούσᾱ,	τιμώσᾱ		
G.	τιμαόντοιν,	τιμώντοιν	τιμαούσαιν,	τιμώσαιν		

3. Liquid Future Active. 4. Aorist II. Active

	ὁ (*about to show*)	ἡ	τὸ	ὁ (*having left*)	ἡ	τὸ
S. N.	φανῶν	φανοῦσᾰ	φανοῦν	λιπών	λιποῦσᾰ	λιπόν
G.	φανοῦντος	φανούσης		λιπόντος	λιπούσης	
D.	φανοῦντι	φανούσῃ		λιπόντι	λιπούσῃ	
A.	φανοῦντα	φανοῦσᾰν		λιπόντα	λιποῦσᾰν	
P. N.	φανοῦντες	φανοῦσαι	φανοῦντα	λιπόντες	λιποῦσαι	λιπόντα
G.	φανούντων	φανουσῶν		λιπόντων	λιπουσῶν	
D.	φανοῦσι	φανούσαις		λιποῦσι	λιπούσαις	
A.	φανοῦντας	φανούσᾱς		λιπόντας	λιπούσᾱς	
D. N.	φανοῦντε	φανούσᾱ		λιπόντε	λιπούσᾱ	
G.	φανούντοιν	φανούσαιν		λιπόντοιν	λιπούσαιν	

5. Aorist 1. Active. | 6. Aorist Passive.

	ὁ (*having raised*)	ἡ	τὸ	ὁ (*having appeared*)	ἡ	τὸ
S. N.	ἄρᾱς	ἄρᾱσᾰ	ἆρᾰν	φανείς	φανεῖσᾰ	φανέν
G.	ἄραντος	ἀράσης		φανέντος	φανείσης	
D.	ἄραντι	ἀράσῃ		φανέντι	φανείσῃ	
A.	ἄραντα	ἄρᾱσᾰν		φανέντα	φανεῖσᾰν	
P. N.	ἄραντες	ἄρᾱσαι	ἄραντα	φανέντες	φανεῖσαι	φανέντα
G.	ἀράντων	ἀρᾱσῶν		φανέντων	φανεισῶν	
D.	ἄρᾱσι	ἀράσαις		φανεῖσι	φανείσαις	
A.	ἄραντας	ἀράσᾱς		φανέντας	φανείσᾱς	
D. N.	ἄραντε	ἀράσᾱ		φανέντε	φανείσᾱ	
G.	ἀράντοιν	ἀράσαιν		φανέντοιν	φανείσαιν	

7. Perfect Active. | 8. Perfect Active Contracted.

	ὁ (*knowing*)	ἡ	τὸ	ὁ (*standing*)	ἡ	τὸ
S. N.	εἰδώς	εἰδυῖᾰ	εἰδός	ἑστώς	ἑστῶσᾰ	ἑστώς, ἑστός
G.	εἰδότος	εἰδυίᾱς		ἑστῶτος	ἑστώσης	
D.	εἰδότι	εἰδυίᾳ		ἑστῶτι	ἑστώσῃ	
A.	εἰδότα	εἰδυῖᾰν		ἑστῶτα	ἑστῶσᾰν	
P. N.	εἰδότες	εἰδυῖαι	εἰδότα	ἑστῶτες	ἑστῶσαι	ἑστῶτα
G.	εἰδότων	εἰδυιῶν		ἑστώτων	ἑστωσῶν	
D.	εἰδόσι	εἰδυίαις		ἑστῶσι	ἑστώσαις	
A.	εἰδότας	εἰδυίᾱς		ἑστῶτας	ἑστώσᾱς	
D. N.	εἰδότε	εἰδυίᾱ		ἑστῶτε	ἑστώσᾱ	
G.	εἰδότοιν	εἰδυίαιν		ἑστώτοιν	ἑστώσαιν	

9. From Verbs in -μι.

	ὁ (*having given*)	ἡ	τὸ	ὁ (*having entered*)	ἡ	τὸ
S. N.	δούς	δοῦσᾰ	δόν	δύς	δῦσᾰ	δῦν
G.	δόντος	δούσης		δύντος	δύσης	
D.	δόντι	δούσῃ		δύντι	δύσῃ	
A.	δόντα	δοῦσᾰν		δύντα	δῦσᾰν	
P. N.	δόντες	δοῦσαι	δόντα	δύντες	δῦσαι	δύντα
G.	δόντων	δουσῶν		δύντων	δυσῶν	
D.	δοῦσι	δούσαις		δῦσι	δύσαις	
A.	δόντας	δούσᾱς		δύντας	δύσᾱς	
D. N.	δόντε	δούσᾱ		δύντε	δύσᾱ	
G.	δόντοιν	δούσαιν		δύντοιν	δύσαιν	

¶ 23. XI. Substantive Pronouns.

[To those forms which are used as enclitic, the sign † is affixed. The initials affixed to dialectic forms denote, Æ. Æolic, B. Bœotic, D. Doric, E. Epic, I. Ionic, O. Old, P. Poetic.]

A. Personal.

	1st P. *I.*	2d P. *thou.*	3d P. *his, her.*
S. N.	ἐγώ	σύ	*
G.	ἐμοῦ, μοῦ†	σοῦ†	οὗ†
D.	ἐμοί, μοί†	σοί†	οἷ†
A.	ἐμέ, μέ†	σέ†	ἕ†
P. N.	ἡμεῖς	ὑμεῖς	σφεῖς
G.	ἡμῶν	ὑμῶν	σφῶν
D.	ἡμῖν	ὑμῖν	σφίσι(ν)†
A.	ἡμᾶς	ὑμᾶς	σφᾶς
D. N.	νώ	σφώ	
G.	νῷν	σφῷν	σφωΐν†

Homeric Forms.

S. N.	ἐγών, ἐγώ	σύ, τύνη	
G.	ἐμέο, ἐμεῖο, ἐμεῦ, μεῦ†, ἐμέθεν	σέο†, σεῖο, σεῦ†, σέθεν, τεοῖο	ἕο†, εἷο, εὗ†, ἕθεν†
D.	ἐμοί, μοί†	σοί, τοί†, τεΐν	ἑοῖ, οἷ†
A.	ἐμέ, μέ†	σέ†	ἕ†, ἑέ, μίν†
P. N.	ἡμεῖς, ἄμμες	ὑμεῖς, ὔμμες	
G.	ἡμέων, ἡμείων	ὑμέων, ὑμείων	σφέων†, σφείων, σφῶν
D.	ἡμῖν, ἥμιν, ἧμιν, ἄμμι(ν)	ὑμῖν, ὔμμι(ν), ὔμμ'	σφίσι(ν)†, σφί(ν)†, σφ'
A.	ἡμέας, -έας, ἧμας, ἄμμε	ὑμέας, -έας, ὔμμε	σφέας†, -έας†, σφεῖας, σφᾶς†, σφέ†
D. N.	νῶϊ (νῶϊν?)	σφῶϊ (σφῶϊν?), σφώ	
G.	νῶϊν	σφῶϊν	
D.	νῶϊν	σφῶϊν, σφῷν	σφωΐν†
A.	νῶϊ, νώ	σφῶϊ, σφώ	σφωέ†, σφώ† or σφω'

Additional Forms.

S. N.	ἰών, ἰώ B.	τύ D., τού B.	
G.	ἐμέος, ἐμεῦς, ἐμοῦς D.	τεῦ†, τέος, τεῦς, τεοῦς, τεοῦ D.	Ϝέθεν Æ., ἑοῦς D., ἑεῖο E.
D.	ἐμίν D.	τίν D.	Ϝοῖ† Æ., ἵν or ἵν D.
A.		τέ, τύ† D.	Ϝέ† Æ., νίν† D. P.
P. N.	ἡμέες I., ἁμές D.	ὑμέες I., ὑμές D.	Neut. σφέα† I.
G.	ἁμῶν D., ἀμμέων Æ.	ὑμμέων Æ.	
D.	ἁμίν D., ἄμμεσι(ν) Æ.		φίν†, ψίν† D., ἄσφι Æ.
A.	ἁμέ D.	ὑμέ, ὔμμε D.	ψέ† D., ἄσφε Æ.
D. N.	νῶε B.		

B. Reflexive.

	1st P. M. (*of myself*)	F.	2d P. M. (*of thyself*)	F.
S. G.	ἐμαυτοῦ	ἐμαυτῆς	σεαυτοῦ, σαυτοῦ	σεαυτῆς, σαυτῆς
D.	ἐμαυτῷ	ἐμαυτῇ	σεαυτῷ, σαυτῷ	σεαυτῇ, σαυτῇ
A.	ἐμαυτόν	ἐμαυτήν	σεαυτόν, σαυτόν	σεαυτήν, σαυτήν
P. G.	ἡμῶν αὐτῶν	ἡμῶν αὐτῶν	ὑμῶν αὐτῶν	ὑμῶν αὐτῶν
D.	ἡμῖν αὐτοῖς	ἡμῖν αὐταῖς	ὑμῖν αὐτοῖς	ὑμῖν αὐταῖς
A.	ἡμᾶς αὐτούς	ἡμᾶς αὐτάς	ὑμᾶς αὐτούς	ὑμᾶς αὐτάς

	3d P. M., *of himself.*	F., *of herself.*	N., *of itself.*
S. G.	ἑαυτοῦ, αὑτοῦ	ἑαυτῆς, αὑτῆς	
D.	ἑαυτῷ, αὑτῷ	ἑαυτῇ, αὑτῇ	
A.	ἑαυτόν, αὑτόν	ἑαυτήν, αὑτήν	ἑαυτό, αὑτό
P. G.	ἑαυτῶν, αὑτῶν	ἑαυτῶν, αὑτῶν	
D.	ἑαυτοῖς, αὑτοῖς	ἑαυταῖς, αὑταῖς	
A.	ἑαυτούς, αὑτούς	ἑαυτάς, αὑτάς	ἑαυτᾰ́, αὑτᾰ́

New Ionic.

S. G.	ἐμεωυτοῦ	ἐμεωυτῆς	σεωυτοῦ	σεωυτῆς
D.	ἐμεωυτῷ	ἐμεωυτῇ	σεωυτῷ	σεωυτῇ
A.	ἐμεωυτόν	ἐμεωυτήν	σεωυτόν	σεωυτήν

S. G.	ἑωυτοῦ	ἑωυτῆς		P.	ἑωυτῶν	ἑωυτῶν	
D.	ἑωυτῷ	ἑωυτῇ			ἑωυτοῖσι	ἑωυταῖσι	
A.	ἑωυτόν	ἑωυτήν	ἑωυτό		ἑωυτούς	ἑωυτάς	ἑωυτᾰ́

3d P. S. G. αὐταύτω, -ᾶς, D. -ῳ, -ᾳ, A. -ον, -ᾶν, -ο·
P. G. αὐταύτων, D. -οις, -αις, A. -ως, -ᾶς, -ᾰ, Dor.

C. Reciprocal.

	M. (*of one another*)	F.	N.		M. N.	F.
P. G.	ἀλλήλων	ἀλλήλων		D. A.	ἀλλήλω	ἀλλήλᾱ
D.	ἀλλήλοις	ἀλλήλαις		G.	ἀλλήλοιν	ἀλλήλαιν
A.	ἀλλήλους	ἀλλήλᾱς	ἄλληλᾰ			

P. G.	ἀλλάλων Dor.	ἀλλάλων Dor.		D. G.	ἀλλήλοιϊν Ep.
D.	ἀλλάλοισι, -οις	ἀλλάλαισι, -αις			
A.	ἀλλάλους	ἀλλάλᾱς	ἄλλαλᾰ Dor.		

D. Indefinite.

	M. F. N., *such a one.*		M.
S. N.	ὁ, ἡ, τὸ δεῖνα	P.	οἱ δεῖνες
G.	τοῦ, τῆς δεῖνος		τῶν δείνων
D.	τῷ, τῇ δεῖνι		*
A.	τόν, τήν, τὸ δεῖνα		τοὺς δεῖνας

¶ 24. XII. Adjective Pronouns.

A. Definite.

	Article.			Iterative.		
	M. (*the*)	F.	N.	M. (*very, same, self*)	F.	N.
S. N.	ὁ	ἡ	τό	αὐτός	αὐτή	αὐτό
G.	τοῦ	τῆς		αὐτοῦ	αὐτῆς	
D.	τῷ	τῇ		αὐτῷ	αὐτῇ	
A.	τόν	τήν		αὐτόν	αὐτήν	
P. N.	οἱ	αἱ	τά	αὐτοί	αὐταί	αὐτά
G.	τῶν	τῶν		αὐτῶν	αὐτῶν	
D.	τοῖς	ταῖς		αὐτοῖς	αὐταῖς	
A.	τούς	τάς		αὐτούς	αὐτάς	
D. N.	τώ	τά		αὐτώ	αὐτά	
G.	τοῖν	ταῖν		αὐτοῖν	αὐταῖν	
S. N.		ἅ D.			αὐτά D., -έη I.	
G.	τοῖο E., τῶ D.	τᾶς D.		αὐτοῖο E., -έου I.	αὐτᾶς D., -έης I.	
D.		τᾷ D.		αὐτέῳ I.	αὐτᾷ D., -έῃ I.	
A.		τάν D.			αὐτάν D., -έην I.	
P. N.	τοί E. D.	ταί E. D.				
G.		τάων O., τᾶν D.		αὐτέων I.	αὐτάων O., -ᾶν D., -έων I.	
D.	τοῖσι O.	ταῖσι O., τῇσι, [τῇς I.		αὐτοῖσι O., -έοισι I.	αὐτῇσι, -ῇς, -έῃσι I.	
A.	τώς, τός D.			αὐτέους I.	αὐτέας I.	

	Relative.			Demonstrative.		
	M. (*who*)	F.	N.	M. (*this*)	F.	N.
S. N.	ὅς	ἥ	ὅ	ὅδε	ἥδε	τόδε
G.	οὗ	ἧς		τοῦδε	τῆσδε	
D.	ᾧ	ᾗ		τῷδε	τῇδε	
A.	ὅν	ἥν		τόνδε	τήνδε	
P. N.	οἵ	αἵ	ἅ	οἵδε	αἵδε	τάδε
G.	ὧν	ὧν		τῶνδε	τῶνδε	
D.	οἷς	αἷς		τοῖσδε	ταῖσδε	
A.	οὕς	ἅς		τούσδε	τάσδε	
D. N.	ὥ	ἅ		τώδε	τάδε	
G.	οἷν	αἷν		τοῖνδε	ταῖνδε	

Possessive.

1 P. S. ἐμός
P. ἡμέτερος
D. νωΐτερος Ep.

2 P. S. σός
P. ὑμέτερος
D. σφωΐτερος Ep.

3 P. S. ὅς Poet.
P. σφέτερος

Dialectic and Paragogic Forms.

S. N.	ὅ O.	ἅ D.	ὁδί	ἡδί	τοδί
G.	οἷο, ὅου E.	ἕης E., ἅς D.	τουδί	τησδί	
D.		ᾇ D.		&c.	
A.		ἅν D.			
P. D.		ἧσι, ἧς E.	τοισίδε O., τοῖσδεσι, τοῖσδεσσι E.		

1 P. P. ἁμός, ἀμός O., ἁμέτερος D., ἄμμος, ἀμμέτερος Æ.
2 P. S. τεός D. E.
P. ὑμός O., ὔμμος Æ
3 P. S. ἑός E. D.
P. σφός O.

Demonstrative.

	M. (*this*)	F.	N.	M. (*so much*)	F.	N.
S. N.	οὗτος	αὕτη	τοῦτο	τοσοῦτος	τοσαύτη	τοσοῦτο, τοσοῦτον
G.	τούτου	ταύτης		τοσούτου	τοσαύτης	
D.	τούτῳ	ταύτῃ		τοσούτῳ	τοσαύτῃ	
A.	τοῦτον	ταύτην		τοσοῦτον	τοσαύτην	
P. N.	οὗτοι	αὗται	ταῦτᾰ	τοσοῦτοι	τοσαῦται	τοσαῦτᾰ
G.	τούτων	τούτων		τοσούτων	τοσούτων	
D.	τούτοις	ταύταις		τοσούτοις	τοσαύταις	
A.	τούτους	ταύτᾱς		τοσούτους	τοσαύτᾱς	
D. N.	τούτω	ταύτᾱ		τοσούτω	τοσαύτᾱ	
G.	τούτοιν	ταύταιν		τοσούτοιν	τοσαύταιν	

Paragogic Declension.				Mixed Paragogic Forms.
S. N.	οὑτοσί	αὑτηΐ	τουτί	τοσουτοσί, ἐκεινοσί, ὁδεδί, τουτογί, τουτοδί.
G.	τουτουΐ	ταυτησί		τυννουτουΐ, κεινουΐ, τηλικαυτησί.
D.	τουτῳΐ	ταυτῃΐ		τυννουτῳΐ. Adv. οὑτωσί, ἐνθαδί, νυνί, δευρί.
A.	τουτονί	ταυτηνί		τοσουτονί, τοσονδί, τοιουτονί, ἐκεινονί, τηνδεδί.
P. N.	οὑτοιΐ	αὑταιΐ	ταυτί	τοιουτοιΐ, τοιαυταιΐ, τοιαυτί, ταυταγί.
G.	τουτωνί, &c.			τοσουτωνί, ἐκεινωνί, &c.

B. Indefinite.

	Simple Indefinite.		Interrogative.		Relative Indefinite.		
	M. F. (*any, some*)	N.	M. F. (*who?*)	N.	M. (*whoever*)	F.	N.
S. N.	τὶς	τὶ	τίς	τί	ὅστις	ἥτις	ὅ τι
G.	τινός, τοῦ		τίνος, τοῦ		οὗτινος, ὅτου	ἧστινος	
D.	τινί, τῷ		τίνι, τῷ		ᾧτινι, ὅτῳ	ᾗτινι	
A.	τινά		τίνα		ὅντινα	ἥντινα	
P. N.	τινές	τινά,	τίνες	τίνα	οἵτινες	αἵτινες	ἅτινα, ἅττα
G.	τινῶν	[ἅττα	τίνων		ὧντινων, ὅτων	ὧντινων	
D.	τισί		τίσι		οἷστισι, ὅτοισι	αἷστισι	
A.	τινάς		τίνας		οὕστινας	ἅστινας	
D. N.	τινέ		τίνε		ὥτινε	ἅτινε	
G.	τινοῖν		τίνοιν		οἷντινοιν	αἷντινοιν	

Homeric Declension of τὶς, τίς, and ὅτις = ὅστις.

S. N.	τὶς	τὶ	τίς	τί	ὅτις	ὅ τι, ὅ ττι
G.	τέο, τεῦ		τέο, τεῦ		ὅτευ, ὅττεο, ὅττευ	
D.	τέῳ, τῷ				ὅτεῳ, ὅτεῴ	
A.	τινά		τίνα		ὅτινα	
P. N.	τινές	ἄσσα	τίνες			ὅτινα
G.			τέων		ὅτεων	
D.					ὁτέοισι	
A.	τινάς				ὅτινας	ἄσσα
D. N.	τινέ					

¶ 25. B. Table of Numerals.

I. Adjectives.

		1. Cardinal.	2. Ordinal.
Interrog.		πόσοι ; *how many?*	πόστος ; *which in order?* οι, *one of how many?*
Indef.		ποσοί, *a certain number.*	
Rel. Ind.		ὁπόσοι, *how many soever.*	ὁπόστος, *whichsoever in order.*
Dimin.		ὀλίγοι, *few.*	ὀλιγοστός, *one of few.*
Augment.		πολλοί, *many.*	πολλοστός, *one of many,* οι, *one following many.*
Demonst.		τόσοι, *so many.*	
Relat.		ὅσοι, *as many.*	
1	α′	εἷς, μία, ἕν, *one.*	πρῶτος,-η,-ον, *first.*
2	β′	δύο, δύω, *two.*	δεύτερος,-ᾱ,-ον, *second.*
3	γ′	τρεῖς, τρία, *three.*	τρίτος,-η,-ον, *third.*
4	δ′	τέσσαρες, τέσσαρα, *four.*	τέταρτος, *fourth.*
5	ε′	πέντε, *five.*	πέμπτος, *fifth.*
6	ϛ′	ἕξ, *six.*	ἕκτος, *sixth.*
7	ζ′	ἑπτά, *seven.*	ἕβδομος, *seventh.*
8	η′	ὀκτώ, *eight.*	ὄγδοος, *eighth.*
9	ϑ′	ἐννέα, *nine.*	ἔνατος, ἔννατος, *ninth.*
10	ι′	δέκα, *ten.*	δέκατος, *tenth.*
11	ια′	ἕνδεκα, *eleven.*	ἑνδέκατος, *eleventh.*
12	ιβ′	δώδεκα, *twelve.*	δωδέκατος, *twelfth.*
13	ιγ′	τρισκαίδεκα, δεκατρεῖς	τρισκαιδέκατος
14	ιδ′	τεσσαρεσκαίδεκα	τεσσαρακαιδέκατος
15	ιε′	πεντεκαίδεκα	πεντεκαιδέκατος
16	ιϛ′	ἑκκαίδεκα	ἑκκαιδέκατος
17	ιζ′	ἑπτακαίδεκα	ἑπτακαιδέκατος
18	ιη′	οκτωκαίδεκα	ὀκτωκαιδέκατος
19	ιϑ′	ἐννεακαίδεκα	ἐννεακαιδέκατος
20	κ′	εἴκοσι(ν)	εἰκοστός
21	κα′	εἴκοσιν εἷς, εἷς καὶ εἴκοσι	εἰκοστὸς πρῶτος
30	λ′	τριᾱκοντα	τριᾱκοστός
40	μ′	τεσσαράκοντα	τεσσαρακοστός
50	ν′	πεντήκοντα	πεντηκοστός
60	ξ′	ἑξήκοντα	ἑξηκοστός
70	ο′	ἑβδομήκοντα	ἑβδομηκοστός
80	π′	ὀγδοήκοντα	ὀγδοηκοστός
90	ϙ	ἐνενήκοντα	ἐνενηκοστός
100	ρ′	ἑκατόν	ἑκατοστός
200	σ′	διᾱκόσιοι,-αι,-α	διᾱκοσιοστός
300	τ′	τριᾱκόσιοι	τριᾱκοσιοστός

400	υ'	τετρακόσιοι	τετρακοσιοστός
500	φ'	πεντακόσιοι	πεντακοσιοστός
600	χ'	ἑξακόσιοι	ἑξακοσιοστός
700	ψ'	ἑπτακόσιοι	ἑπτακοσιοστός
800	ω'	ὀκτακόσιοι	ὀκτακοσιοστός
900	ϡ	ἐνακόσιοι	ἐνακοσιοστός
1,000	͵α	χίλιοι,-αι,-α	χιλιοστός
2,000	͵β	δισχίλιοι	δισχιλιοστός
10,000	͵ι	μύριοι,-αι,-α	μυριοστός
20,000	͵κ	δισμύριοι	δισμυριοστός
100,000	͵ρ	δεκακισμύριοι	δεκακισμυριοστός

	3. Temporal.	4. Multiple.
Inter.	ποσταῖος ; *on what day?*	
1.	(αὐθήμερος, *on the same day.*)	ἁπλόος, ἁπλοῦς, *simple, single*
2.	δευτεραῖος, *on the second day.*	διπλοῦς, *double.*
3.	τριταῖος, *on the third day.*	τριπλοῦς, *triple.*
4.	τεταρταῖος, *on the fourth day.*	τετραπλοῦς, *quadruple.*
5.	πεμπταῖος, *on the fifth day.*	πενταπλοῦς, *quintuple.*
6.	ἑκταῖος, *on the sixth day.*	ἑξαπλοῦς, *sextuple.*
7.	ἑβδομαῖος, *on the seventh day.*	ἑπταπλοῦς, *septuple.*
8.	ὀγδοαῖος, *on the eighth day.*	ὀκταπλοῦς, *octuple.*

	5. Proportional.	II. Adverbs.	III. Substantives.
Inter.	ποσαπλάσιος ; *how many fold?*	ποσάκις ; *how many times?*	ποσότης, *quantity, number.*
Dim.		ὀλιγάκις, *few times.*	ὀλιγότης, *fewness.*
Augm.	πολλαπλάσιος, *many fold.*	πολλάκις, *many times.*	
1.	(ἴσος, *equal.*)	ἅπαξ, *once.*	μονάς, *monad.*
2.	διπλάσιος, *twofold.*	δίς, *twice.*	δυάς, *duad.*
3.	τριπλάσιος, *threefold.*	τρίς, *thrice.*	τριάς, *triad.*
4.	τετραπλάσιος	τετράκις, *four times.*	τετράς, τετρακτύς
5.	πενταπλάσιος	πεντάκις	πεντάς
6.	ἑξαπλάσιος	ἑξάκις	ἑξάς
7.	ἑπταπλάσιος	ἑπτάκις	ἑβδομάς
8.	ὀκταπλάσιος	ὀκτάκις	ὀγδοάς
9.	ἐννεαπλάσιος	ἐννεάκις, ἐνάκις	ἐννεάς
10.	δεκαπλάσιος	δεκάκις	δεκάς
20.	εἰκοσαπλάσιος	εἰκοσάκις	εἰκάς
100.	ἑκατονταπλάσιος	ἑκατοντάκις	ἑκατοντάς
1,000.	χιλιοπλάσιος	χιλιάκις	χιλιάς
10,000.	μυριοπλάσιος	μυριάκις	μυριάς

C. Tables of Conjugation

¶ 26. I. The Tenses classified.

Relations.	Time.	I. Primary. 1. Present.	2. Future.	II. Secondary. 3. Past.
1. Definite.		PRESENT. γράφω, *I am writing.*	* *I shall be writing.*	IMPERFECT. ἔγραφον, *I was writing.*
2. Indefinite.		* *I write.*	FUTURE. γράψω, *I shall write.*	AORIST. ἔγραψα, *I wrote.*
3. Complete.		PERFECT. γέγραφα, *I have written.*	* *I shall have written.*	PLUPERFECT. ἐγεγράφειν, *I had written.*

¶ 27. II. The Modes classified.

I. DISTINCT.

A. Intellective.

1. Actual.	2. Contingent. α. Present.	β. Past.
INDICATIVE.	SUBJUNCTIVE.	OPTATIVE.
γράφω, *I am writing.*	γράφω, *I may write.*	γράφοιμι, *I might write*

B. Volitive.

IMPERATIVE.

γράφε,
Write.

II. INCORPORATED.

A. Substantive.	B. Adjective.
INFINITIVE.	PARTICIPLE.
γράφειν, *To write.*	γράφων, *Writing.*

¶ 28. III. Formation of the Tenses.

Prefixes.	Tenses.	Affixes. Active.	Middle.	Passive.
	PRESENT,	ω, μι	ομαι, μαι	
Augm.	IMPERFECT,	ον, ν	όμην, μην	
	FUTURE,	σω	σομαι	θήσομαι
	FUT. II.,			ήσομαι
Augm.	AORIST,	σα	σάμην	θην
Augm.	AOR. II.,	ον, ν	όμην, μην	ην
Redpl.	PERFECT,	κα	μαι	
Redpl.	PERF. II.,	α		
Augm. Redpl.	PLUPERFECT,	κειν	μην	
Augm. Redpl.	PLUPERF. II.,	ειν		
Redpl.	FUT. PERF.		σομαι	

¶ 29. IV. AFFIXES OF THE

			Present.		Imperfect.	
			Nude.	Euphonic.	Nude.	Euphonic
Ind.	S.	1	μι	ω	ν	ον
		2	ς	εις	ς	ες
		3	σι(ν)	ει	*	ε(ν)
	P	1	μεν	ομεν	μεν	ομεν
		2	τε	ετε	τε	ετε
		3	νσι(ν), ᾶσι(ν)	ουσι(ν)	σαν	ον
	D.	1	μεν	ομεν	μεν	ομεν
		2	τον	ετον	τον	ετον
		3	τον	ετον	την	ετην
Subj.	S.	1		ω		
		2		ῃς		
		3		ῃ		
	P.	1		ωμεν		
		2		ητε		
		3		ωσι(ν)		
	D.	1		ωμεν		
		2		ητον		
		3		ητον		
Opt.	S.	1	ίην	οιμι		
		2	ίης	οις		
		3	ίη	οι		
	P.	1	ίημεν, ῖμεν	οιμεν		
		2	ίητε, ῖτε	οιτε		
		3	ίησαν, ῖεν	οιεν		
	D.	1	ίημεν, ῖμεν	οιμεν		
		2	ίητον, ῖτον	οιτον		
		3	ιήτην, ίτην	οίτην		
Imp.	S.	2	θι, ς, ε	ε		
		3	τω	έτω		
	P.	2	τε	ετε		
		3	τωσαν, ντων	έτωσαν, όντων		
	D.	2	τον	ετον		
		3	των	έτων		
Inf.			ναι	ειν		
Part.		N.	ντς, ντσᾰ, ν	ων, ουσᾰ, ον		
		G.	ντος, ντσης	οντος, ούσης		

ACTIVE VOICE.

			Future.	Aorist.	Perfect.	Pluperfect.
Ind.	S.	1	σω	σᾰ	κ-ᾰ	κ-ειν, κ-η
		2	σεις	σᾰς	κ-ᾰς	κ-εις
		3	σει	σε(ν)	κ-ε(ν)	κ-ει
	P.	1	σομεν	σᾰμεν	κ-ᾰμεν	κ-ειμεν
		2	σετε	σᾰτε	κ-ᾰτε	κ-ειτε
		3	σουσι(ν)	σᾰν	κ-ᾱσι(ν)	κ-εισαν, κ-εσαν
	D.	1	σομεν	σᾰμεν	κ-ᾰμεν	κ-ειμεν
		2	σετον	σᾰτον	κ-ᾰτον	κ-ειτον
		3	σετον	σᾰτην	κ-ᾰτον	κ-είτην
Subj.	S.	1		σω	(κ-ω)	
		2		σῃς	(κ-ῃς)	
		3		σῃ	(κ-ῃ)	
	P.	1		σωμεν	(κ-ωμεν)	
		2		σητε	(κ-ητε)	
		3		σωσι(ν)	(κ-ωσι-ν)	
	D.	1		σωμεν	(κ-ωμεν)	
		2		σητον	(κ-ητον)	
		3		σητον	(κ-ητον)	
Opt.	S.	1	σοιμι	σαιμι	(κ-οιμι)	
		2	σοις	σαις, σειᾰς	(κ-οις)	
		3	σοι	σαι, σειε(ν)	(κ-οι)	
	P.	1	σοιμεν	σαιμεν	(κ-οιμεν)	
		2	σοιτε	σαιτε	(κ-οιτε)	
		3	σοιεν	σαιεν, σειᾰν	(κ-οιεν)	
	D.	1	σοιμεν	σαιμεν	(κ-οιμεν)	
		2	σοιτον	σαιτον	(κ-οιτον)	
		3	σοίτην	σαίτην	(κ-οίτην)	
Imp.	S.	2		σον	(κ-ε)	
		3		σᾰτω	(κ-έτω)	
	P.	2		σᾰτε [των	(κ-ετε)	
		3		σᾰτωσαν, σάν-	(κ-έτωσαν, κ-όντων)	
	D.	2		σᾰτον	(κ-ετον)	
		3		σᾰτων	(κ-έτων)	
Inf.			σειν	σαι	κ-έναι	
Part.	N.		σων, &c.	σᾱς, σᾱσᾰ, σᾰν	κ-ώς, κ-υῖᾰ, κ-ός	
	G.		σοντος	σαντος, σᾱσης	κ-ότος, κ-υίᾱς	

¶ 30. V. Affixes of the

		Pres.		Imperf.		Perf.	Plup.
		Nude.	Euph.	Nude.	Euph		
Ind.	S. 1	μαι	ομαι	μην	όμην	μαι	μην
	2	σαι, αι	ῃ, ει	σο, ο	ου	σαι	σο
	3	ται	εται	το	ετο	ται	το
	P. 1	μεθα	όμεθα	μεθα	όμεθα	μεθα	μεθα
	2	σθε	εσθε	σθε	εσθε	σθε	σθε
	3	νται	ονται	ντο	οντο	νται	ντο
	D. 1	μεθα	όμεθα	μεθα	όμεθα	μεθα	μεθα
	2	σθον	εσθον	σθον	εσθον	σθον	σθον
	3	σθον	εσθον	σθην	έσθην	σθον	σθην
Subj.	S. 1		ωμαι			(μένος ὦ)	
	2		ῃ			(μένος ᾖς)	
	3		ηται			(μένος ᾖ)	
	P. 1		ώμεθα			(μένοι ὦμεν)	
	2		ησθε			(μένοι ἦτε)	
	3		ωνται			(μένοι ὦσι-ν)	
	D. 1		ώμεθα			(μένω ὦμεν)	
	2		ησθον			(μένω ἦτον)	
	3		ησθον			(μένω ἦτον)	
Opt.	S. 1	ίμην	οίμην			(μένος εἴην)	
	2	ιο	οιο			(μένος εἴης)	
	3	ιτο	οιτο			(μένος εἴη)	
	P. 1	ίμεθα	οίμεθα			(μένοι εἴημεν)	
	2	ισθε	οισθε			(μένοι εἴητε)	
	3	ιντο	οιντο			(μένοι εἴησαν)	
	D. 1	ίμεθα	οίμεθα			(μένω εἴημεν)	
	2	ισθον	οισθον			(μένω εἴητον)	
	3	ίσθην	οίσθην			(μένω εἰήτην)	
Imp.	S. 2	σο, ο	ου			σο	
	3	σθω	έσθω			σθω	
	P. 2	σθε	εσθε			σθε	
	3	σθωσαν, σθων	έσθωσαν, έσθων			σθωσαν, σθων	
	D. 2	σθον	εσθον			σθον	
	3	σθων	έσθων			σθων	
Inf.		σθαι	εσθαι			σθαι	
Part.	N.	μενος, -η, -ον	όμενος, -η, -ον			μένος, -η, -ον	
	G.	μένου, -ης	ομένου, -ης			μένου, -ης	

Middle and Passive Voices.

	Fut. Mid.	Aor. Mid.	Aor. Pass.	Fut. Pass.
Ind. S. 1	σομαι	σάμην	ϑ-ην	ϑ-ήσομαι
2	σῃ, σει	σω	ϑ-ης	ϑ-ήσῃ, ϑ-ήσει
3	σεται	σατο	ϑ-η	ϑ-ήσεται
P. 1	σόμεϑα	σάμεϑα	ϑ-ημεν	ϑ-ησόμεϑα
2	σεσϑε	σασϑε	ϑ-ητε	ϑ-ήσεσϑε
3	σονται	σαντο	ϑ-ησαν	ϑ-ήσονται
D. 1	σόμεϑα	σάμεϑα	ϑ-ημεν	ϑ-ησόμεϑα
2	σεσϑον	σασϑον	ϑ-ητον	ϑ-ήσεσϑον
3	σεσϑον	σάσϑην	ϑ-ήτην	ϑ-ήσεσϑον
Subj. S. 1		σωμαι	ϑ-ῶ	
2		σῃ	ϑ-ῇς	
3		σηται	ϑ-ῇ	
P. 1		σώμεϑα	ϑ-ῶμεν	
2		σησϑε	ϑ-ῆτε	
3		σωνται	ϑ-ῶσι(ν)	
D. 1		σώμεϑα	ϑ-ῶμεν	
2		σησϑον	ϑ-ῆτον	
3		σησϑον	ϑ-ῆτον	
Opt. S. 1	σοίμην	σαίμην	ϑ-είην	ϑ-ησοίμην
2	σοιο	σαιο	ϑ-είης	ϑ-ήσοιο
3	σοιτο	σαιτο	ϑ-είη	ϑ-ήσοιτο
P. 1	σοίμεϑα	σαίμεϑα	ϑ-είημεν, ϑ-εῖμεν	ϑ-ησοίμεϑα
2	σοισϑε	σαισϑε	ϑ-είητε, ϑ-εῖτε	ϑ-ήσοισϑε
3	σοιντο	σαιντο	ϑ-είησαν, ϑ-εῖεν	ϑ-ήσοιντο
D. 1	σοίμεϑα	σαίμεϑα	ϑ-είημεν, ϑ-εῖμεν	ϑ-ησοίμεϑα
2	σοισϑον	σαισϑον	ϑ-είητον	ϑ-ήσοισϑον
3	σοίσϑην	σαίσϑην	ϑ-ειήτην	ϑ-ησοίσϑην
Imp. S. 2		σαι	ϑ-ητι	
3		σάσϑω	ϑ-ήτω	
P. 2		σασϑε	ϑ-ητε	
3		σάσϑωσαν, σάσϑων	ϑ-ήτωσαν, ϑ-έντων	
D. 2		σασϑον	ϑ-ητον	
3		σάσϑων	ϑ-ήτων	
Inf.	σεσϑαι	σασϑαι	ϑ-ῆναι	ϑ-ήσεσϑαι
Part. N.	σόμενος	σάμενος	ϑ-είς, ϑ-εῖσᾰ, ϑ-έν	ϑ-ησόμενος
G.	σομένου	σαμένου	ϑ-έντος, ϑ-είσης	ϑ-ησομένου

¶ 31. VI. Analysis of the Affixes of Conjugation.

	Tense-Signs.					Connecting Vowels.												Flexible Endings.					
						Indicative.				Subjunctive.	Optative.				Imperative. Infinitive. Participle.			Subjective.			Objective.		
	Future and Aorist, Active and Middle. Future Perfect.	Perfect and Pluperfect Active.	Aorist Passive.	Future Passive.	Present and Imperfect. Perfect and Pluperfect Passive.	Present, Imperfect, and Future.	Aorist Active and Middle. Perfect Active.	Pluperfect Active.	Aor., Perf., and Pluperf., Passive. Pres. and Imperf. of Verbs in -μι.		Middle of Verbs in -μι.	Active of Verbs in -μι. Aorist Passive.	Present and Future.	Aorist Active and Middle.	Present and Future. Perfect Active.	Aorist Active and Middle.	Aorist and Perfect Passive. Present of Verbs in -μι.	Primary.	Secondary.	Imperative. Infinitive. Participle.	Primary.	Secondary.	Imperative. Infinitive. Participle.
S. 1	σ	κ-	θ-ε	θ-ησ	*	ο	ᾰ	ει	*	ω	ι	ιη	οι	αι				μ (μῐ, *)	μ (ν, μῐ, *)		μαι	μην	
2	σ	κ-	θ-ε	θ-ησ	*	ε	ᾰ	ει	*	η	ι	ιη	οι	αι	ε	ᾰ (ο)	*	ς (σθᾰ)	ς (σθᾰ)	θ (θῐ, ς, ε, *)	σ-αι	σ-ο	σ-ο
3	σ	κ-	θ-ε	θ-ησ	*	ε	ᾰ (ε)	ει	*	η	ι	ιη	οι	αι	ε	ᾰ	*	τ (σῐ, *)	τ (*)	τω	ται	το	σθω
P. 1	σ	κ-	θ-ε	θ-ησ	*	ο	ᾰ	ει	*	ω	ι	ιη	οι	αι				μεν	μεν		μεθᾰ	μεθᾰ	
2	σ	κ-	θ-ε	θ-ησ	*	ε	ᾰ	ει	*	η	ι	ιη	οι	αι	ε	ᾰ	*	τε	τε	τε	σθε	σθε	σθε
3	σ	κ-	θ-ε	θ-ησ	*	ο	ᾰ	ει (ε)	*	ω	ι	ιη	οι	αι	ε (ο)	ᾰ	*	ντ (νσῐ)	ντ (ν, εν), σᾰν	τωσᾰν, ντων	νται	ντο	σθωσᾰν, σθων
D. 1	σ	κ-	θ-ε	θ-ησ	*	ο	ᾰ	ει	*	ω	ι	ιη	οι	αι				μεν	μεν		μεθᾰ	μεθᾰ	
2	σ	κ-	θ-ε	θ-ησ	*	ε	ᾰ	ει	*	η	ι	ιη	οι	αι	ε	ᾰ	*	τον	τον	τον	σθον	σθον	σθον
3	σ	κ-	θ-ε	θ-ησ	*	ε	ᾰ	ει	*	η	ι	ιη	οι	αι	ε	ᾰ	*	τον	την	των	σθον	σθην	σθων
Inf.	σ	κ-	θ-ε	θ-ησ	*										ε (ει)	ᾰ	*			ν, ναι, ι			σθαι
Part.	σ	κ-	θ-ε	θ-ησ	*										ο	ᾰ	*			ντ-ς (τ-ς)			μεν-ος

¶ 32. VII. Dialectic Forms (see §§ 241–253).

Subjective.

Singular.

1 *Ind.* Pr. ω, Old μι· ὄρημι, κάλημι.
άω, ῶ, Ion. έω· ὁρέω, φοιτέω.
Ep. όω, ώω· ὁρόω, μενοινώω.
έω, ῶ, Ep. είω· νεικείω, πνείω.
Fut. ω, Dor. ῶ· ᾀσῶ, πεμψῶ.
σω, Dor. ξῶ· δικαξῶ, κομιξῶ.
ῶ, Ion. έω· ἀγγελέω, φανέω.
Impf. ν, Iter. σκον· ἔχεσκον, φέρεσκον.
Ion. α· ἐτίθεα, ἦα, ἔα.
αον, ων, Ion. εον, Ion. and Dor. ευν· ἠγάπευν.
Aor. σα, Dor. ξα· ἐκόμιξα, ἔφθαξα.
Iter. σασκον· στρέψασκον, ὤσασκον.
Plup. ειν, Ion. εα· ᾔδεα, ἐτεθήπεα.
Old Att. η· ᾔδη, ἐπεπόνθη.
Subj. ω, Ep. ωμι· ἴδωμι, ἵκωμι.
ῶ, Ep. είω, ώω, &c.; δαμείω, θείω, γνώω.
2 ς, Old σθα· εἴπησθα, βάλοισθα.
εις, Dor. ες· ἀμέλγες, συρίσδες.
άεις, ᾷς, Dor. ῇς· ὁρῇς, τολμῇς, λῇς.
Ep. άᾳς· ὁράᾳς, ἐάᾳς.
3 σι, Dor. τι· τίθητι, φατί.
Subj. ῃ, Ep. ῃσι· ἄγῃσι, θέῃσιν.

Plural.

1 μεν, Dor. μες· εὕρομες, δεδοίκαμες.
Subj. ωμεν, Ep. ομεν· ἀγείρομεν, ἴομεν.
2 *Subj.* ητε, Ep. ετε· εἴδετε.
3 νσι, Dor. ντι· φαντί, ἔχοντι.
ουσι, Æol. οισι· κρύπτοισιν, στάξοισιν.
άουσι, ῶσι, Ep. όωσι, ώωσι· βοόωσιν, δρώωσι.
Dor. ᾶντι· πεινᾶντι.
έουσι, οῦσι, Ion. εῦσι· ποιεῦσι.
Dor. εῦντι· φιλεῦντι, μενεῦντι.
ᾶσι, Ion. έᾱσι· ἱστέᾱσι, ἑστέᾱσι.
ᾱσι, Æol. αισι· φαισί.
ᾱσι, ον, Alex. αν, οσαν· εἴρηκαν, ἤλθοσαν.
σαν, Old ν· ἔσταν, ἤγερθεν.

Inf. ναι, Æol. ν· μεθύσθην, ἄντλην.
Dor. and Ep. μεν· κριθῆμεν, φάμεν.
Ep. and Æol. μεναι· μιχθήμεναι, θέμε-
ειν, Dor. εν· συρίσδεν, βόσκεν. [ναι.
Dor. and Æol. ην· εὑρῆν, ἄγην.
Poet. έμεν, έμεναι· ἀξέμεν, ἀξέμεναι.
εῖν, Ion. έειν· ἰδέειν, παθέειν.
άειν, ᾷν, Ep. άᾳν· ὁράᾳν, ἐλάᾳν.
Dor. ῆν· ὁρῆν, σιγῆν.
όειν, Dor. ῶν· ὑπνῶν, ῥιγῶν. [κην.
έναι, Dor. and Æol. ειν, ην· δεδύκειν, τεθνά-
Ep. έμεν· πεπληγέμεν.

Pt. ῶν, Ion. έων· ἀγγελέων, ἐρέων.
άων, ῶν, Ep. όων, ώων· ὁρόων.
ᾱς, ᾶσα, Æol. αις, αισα· ῥίψαις, -αισα.
ουσα, Æol. οισα· ἔχοισα, φέροισα.
άουσα, ῶσα, Ep. όωσα, ώωσα, άωσα· ὁρόωσα.
G. όντος, Ep. ῶτος· βεβαῶτος, κεκμηῶτος.

Objective.

Singular.

1 έομαι, οῦμαι, Ion. and Dor. εῦμαι· φοβεῦμαι.
σομαι, Dor. σοῦμαι, σεῦμαι· ἑξοῦμαι, ᾀσεῦμαι.
οῦμαι, Ion. έομαι· φανέομαι, ὀλέομαι.
μην, Dor. μᾱν· δυνάμᾱν, ἱκόμᾱν.
Iter. σκόμην· πελεσκόμην, μνησασκόμην.
2 ῃ, Ion. εαι, *Subj.* ηαι· ἔσεαι, πίθηαι.
Hel. εσαι· πίεσαι, καυχᾶσαι.
ου, Ion. εο· ἔπλεο, φράζεο.
Ion. and Dor. ευ· ἔπλευ, φράζευ.
Ep. ειο· ἔρειο, σπεῖο.
ω, Ion. αο· ἐδέξαο, ἐπίσταο.
Dor. ᾱ; ἐπάξᾱ, ἤρᾱ.
σαι, σο, Ep. αι, ο· βέβληαι, ἔσσυο.
έεαι, έεο, Ion. έαι, έο· φοβέαι, φοβέο.

Plural.

1 μεθα, Poet. μεσθα· ἀγόμεσθα, ἐσόμεσθα.
3 νται, ντο, Ion. αται, ατο. κέαται, ἕατο.
ανται, αντο, Ion. έαται, έατο· δυνέαται.
οντο, Ion. έατο· ἐβουλέατο, ἱκέατο.
άονται, ῶνται, Ep. όωνται, ώονται· αἰτιόωνται.
άοντο, ῶντο, Ep. όωντο, ώοντο· ἐμνώοντο.
Du. 3 σθην, Dor. σθᾱν· κτησάσθᾱν, ἱκέσθᾱν.
Inf. άεσθαι, ᾶσθαι, Ion. έεσθαι· χρέεσθαι.
Ep. άασθαι· ὁράασθαι.
Dor. ῆσθαι· πειρῆσθαι.
εῖσθαι, Ion. έεσθαι· φανέεσθαι, ὀλέεσθαι.

¶ 33. VIII. The Active Voice of the

			Present.	Imperfect.
Ind.	S.	1 *I* 2 *Thou, You* 3 *He, She, It*		
	P.	1 *We* 2 *Ye, You* 3 *They*	*am planning,* or *plan.*	*was planning* or *planned.*
	D.	1 *We two* 2 *You two* 3 *They two*		
Subj.	S.	1 *I* 2 *Thou, You* 3 *He, She, It*		
	P.	1 *We* 2 *Ye, You* 3 *They*	*may plan,* *can plan,* or *plan.*	
	D.	1 *We two* 2 *You two* 3 *They two*		
Opt.	S.	1 *I* 2 *Thou, You* 3 *He, She, It*		
	P.	1 *We* 2 *Ye, You* 3 *They*	*might plan,* *should plan,* *would plan,* *could plan,* or *planned.*	
	D.	1 *We two* 2 *You two* 3 *They two*		
Imp.	S.	2 *Do thou* 3 *Let him*		
	P.	2 *Do you* 3 *Let them*	*be planning,* or *plan.*	
	D.	2 *Do you two* 3 *Let them two*		
Infinitive,			*To be planning,* or *To plan.*	
Participle,			*Planning.*	

VERB βουλεύω (¶ 34) TRANSLATED.

Future.	Aorist.	Perfect.	Pluperfect.
shall plan, or *will plan.*	*planned,* *have planned,* *had planned,* or *plan.*	*have planned.*	*had planned*
	may plan, *may have planned,* *can plan,* *can have planned,* *plan,* or *have planned.*		
should plan, or *would plan.*	*might plan,* *might have planned,* *should plan,* *should have planned,* *would plan,* *would have planned,* *could plan,* *could have planned,* *plan,* or *have planned,*		
	plan, or *have planned.*		
To be about to plan.	*To plan,* or *To have planned.*	*To have planned.*	
About to plan.	*Having planned,* or *Planning.*	*Having planned.*	

¶ 34. IX. ACTIVE VOICE OF THE

		Present.	Imperfect.	Future.
Ind. S.	1	βουλεύω	ἐβούλευον	βουλεύσω
	2	βουλεύεις	ἐβούλευες	βουλεύσεις
	3	βουλεύει	ἐβούλευε	βουλεύσει
P.	1	βουλεύομεν	ἐβουλεύομεν	βουλεύσομεν
	2	βουλεύετε	ἐβουλεύετε	βουλεύσετε
	3	βουλεύουσι	ἐβούλευον	βουλεύσουσι
D.	2	βουλεύετον	ἐβουλεύετον	βουλεύσετον
	3		ἐβουλευέτην	
Subj. S.	1	βουλεύω		
	2	βουλεύῃς		
	3	βουλεύῃ		
P.	1	βουλεύωμεν		
	2	βουλεύητε		
	3	βουλεύωσι		
D.	2	βουλεύητον		
Opt. S.	1	βουλεύοιμι		βουλεύσοιμι
	2	βουλεύοις		βουλεύσοις
	3	βουλεύοι		βουλεύσοι
P.	1	βουλεύοιμεν		βουλεύσοιμεν
	2	βουλεύοιτε		βουλεύσοιτε
	3	βουλεύοιεν		βουλεύσοιεν
D.	2	βουλεύοιτον		βουλεύσοιτον
	3	βουλευοίτην		βουλευσοίτην
Imp. S.	2	βούλευε		
	3	βουλευέτω		
P.	2	βουλεύετε		
	3	βουλευέτωσαν βουλευόντων		
D.	2	βουλεύετον		
	3	βουλευέτων		
Infin.		βουλεύειν		βουλεύσειν
Part.		βουλεύων		βουλεύσων

Regular Verb *βουλεύω, to plan, to counsel.*

Aorist.	Perfect.	Pluperfect.
ἐβούλευσα	βεβούλευκα	ἐβεβουλεύκειν
ἐβούλευσας	βεβούλευκας	ἐβεβουλεύκεις
ἐβούλευσε	βεβούλευκε	ἐβεβουλεύκει
ἐβουλεύσαμεν	βεβουλεύκαμεν	ἐβεβουλεύκειμεν
ἐβουλεύσατε	βεβουλεύκατε	ἐβεβουλεύκειτε
ἐβούλευσαν	βεβουλεύκᾱσι	ἐβεβουλεύκεισαν, ἐβεβουλεύκεσαν
ἐβουλεύσατον	βεβουλεύκατον	ἐβεβουλεύκειτον
ἐβουλευσάτην		ἐβεβουλευκείτην
βουλεύσω		
βουλεύσῃς		
βουλεύσῃ		
βουλεύσωμεν		
βουλεύσητε		
βουλεύσωσι		
βουλεύσητον		
βουλεύσαιμι		
βουλεύσαις, βουλεύσειας		
βουλεύσαι, βουλεύσειε		
βουλεύσαιμεν		
βουλεύσαιτε		
βουλεύσαιεν, βουλεύσειαν		
βουλεύσαιτον		
βουλευσαίτην		
βούλευσον		
βουλευσάτω		
βουλεύσατε		
βουλευσάτωσαν, βουλευσάντων		
βουλεύσατον		
βουλευσάτων		
βουλεῦσαι	βεβουλευκέναι	
βουλεύσᾱς	βεβουλευκώς	

¶ 35. X. Middle and Passive Voices of

(In the Middle Voice

		Present.	Imperfect.	Future Mid.
Ind S.	1	βουλεύομαι	ἐβουλευόμην	βουλεύσομαι
	2	βουλεύῃ, βουλεύει	ἐβουλεύου	βουλεύσῃ, βουλεύσει
	3	βουλεύεται	ἐβουλεύετο	βουλεύσεται
P.	1	βουλευόμεθα	ἐβουλευόμεθα	βουλευσόμεθα
	2	βουλεύεσθε	ἐβουλεύεσθε	βουλεύσεσθε
	3	βουλεύονται	ἐβουλεύοντο	βουλεύσονται
D.	2	βουλεύεσθον	ἐβουλεύεσθον	βουλεύσεσθον
	3		ἐβουλευέσθην	
Subj. S.	1	βουλεύωμαι		
	2	βουλεύῃ		
	3	βουλεύηται		
P.	1	βουλευώμεθα		
	2	βουλεύησθε		
	3	βουλεύωνται		
D.	2	βουλεύησθον		
Opt. S.	1	βουλευοίμην		βουλευσοίμην
	2	βουλεύοιο		βουλεύσοιο
	3	βουλεύοιτο		βουλεύσοιτο
P.	1	βουλευοίμεθα		βουλευσοίμεθα
	2	βουλεύοισθε		βουλεύσοισθε
	3	βουλεύοιντο		βουλεύσοιντο
D.	2	βουλεύοισθον		βουλεύσοισθον
	3	βουλευοίσθην		βουλευσοίσθην
Imp. S.	2	βουλεύου		
	3	βουλευέσθω		
P.	2	βουλεύεσθε		
	3	βουλευέσθωσαν, βουλευέσθων		
D.	2	βουλεύεσθον		
	3	βουλευέσθων		
Infin.		βουλεύεσθαι		βουλεύσεσθαι
Part.		βουλευόμενος		βουλευσόμενος

THE REGULAR VERB *βουλεύω, to plan, to counsel.*

to deliberate, to resolve.)

Aorist Mid.	Perfect.	Pluperfect.
ἐβουλευσάμην	βεβούλευμαι	ἐβεβουλεύμην
ἐβουλεύσω	βεβούλευσαι	ἐβεβούλευσο
ἐβουλεύσατο	βεβούλευται	ἐβεβούλευτο
ἐβουλευσάμεθα	βεβουλεύμεθα	ἐβεβουλεύμεθα
ἐβουλεύσασθε	βεβούλευσθε	ἐβεβούλευσθε
ἐβουλεύσαντο	βεβούλευνται	ἐβεβούλευντο
ἐβουλεύσασθον	βεβούλευσθον	ἐβεβούλευσθον
ἐβουλευσάσθην		ἐβεβουλεύσθην
βουλεύσωμαι		
βουλεύσῃ		
βουλεύσηται		
βουλευσώμεθα		
βουλεύσησθε		
βουλεύσωνται		
βουλεύσησθον		
βουλευσαίμην		
βουλεύσαιο		
βουλεύσαιτο		
βουλευσαίμεθα		
βουλεύσαισθε		
βουλεύσαιντο		
βουλεύσαισθον		
βουλευσαίσθην		
βούλευσαι	βεβούλευσο	
βουλευσάσθω	βεβουλεύσθω	
βουλεύσασθε	βεβούλευσθε	
βουλευσάσθωσαν, βουλευσάσθων	βεβουλεύσθωσαν, βεβουλεύσθων	
βουλεύσασθον	βεβούλευσθον	
βουλευσάσθων	βεβουλεύσθων	
βουλεύσασθαι	βεβουλεῦσθαι	
βουλευσάμενος	βεβουλευμένος	

Table X. completed.

		Aorist Pass.		Future Pass.
Ind. S.	1	ἐβουλεύθην		βουλευθήσομαι
	2	ἐβουλεύθης		βουλευθήσῃ, βουλευθήσει
	3	ἐβουλεύθη		βουλευθήσεται
P.	1	ἐβουλεύθημεν		βουλευθησόμεθα
	2	ἐβουλεύθητε		βουλευθήσεσθε
	3	ἐβουλεύθησαν		βουλευθήσονται
D.	2	ἐβουλεύθητον		βουλευθήσεσθον
	3	ἐβουλευθήτην		
Subj. S.	1	βουλευθῶ		
	2	βουλευθῇς		
	3	βουλευθῇ		
P.	1	βουλευθῶμεν		
	2	βουλευθῆτε		
	3	βουλευθῶσι		
D	2	βουλευθῆτον		
Opt. S.	1	βουλευθείην		βουλευθησοίμην
	2	βουλευθείης		βουλευθήσοιο
	3	βουλευθείη		βουλευθήσοιτο
P.	1	βουλευθείημεν,	βουλευθεῖμεν	βουλευθησοίμεθα
	2	βουλευθείητε,	βουλευθεῖτε	βουλευθήσοισθε
	3	βουλευθείησαν,	βουλευθεῖεν	βουλευθήσοιντο
D.	2	βουλευθείητον		βουλευθήσοισθον
	3	βουλευθειήτην		βουλευθησοίσθην
Imp. S.	2	βουλεύθητι		
	3	βουλευθήτω		
P.	2	βουλεύθητε		
	3	βουλευθήτωσαν,	βουλευθέντων	
D.	2	βουλεύθητον		
	3	βουλευθήτων		
Infin.		βουλευθῆναι		βουλευθήσεσθαι
Part.		βουλευθείς		βουλευθησόμενος

¶ 36. XI. (A.) MUTE VERBS. i. LABIAL.

1. *Γράφω, to write.*

ACTIVE VOICE.

	Present.	Future.	Aorist.	Perfect.
Ind.	γράφω	γράψω	ἔγραψα	γέγραφα
Subj.	γράφω		γράψω	
Opt.	γράφοιμι	γράψοιμι	γράψαιμι	
Imp.	γράφε		γράψον	
Inf.	γράφειν	γράψειν	γράψαι	γεγραφέναι
Part.	γράφων	γράψων	γράψας	γεγραφώς
	Imperfect.			Pluperfect.
Ind.	ἔγραφον			ἐγεγράφειν

MIDDLE AND PASSIVE VOICES.

	Present.	Future Mid.	Aorist Mid.	3 Future.
Ind.	γράφομαι	γράψομαι	ἐγραψάμην	γεγράψομαι
Subj.	γράφωμαι		γράψωμαι	
Opt.	γραφοίμην	γραψοίμην	γραψαίμην	γεγραψοίμην
Imp.	γράφου		γράψαι	
Inf.	γράφεσθαι	γράψεσθαι	γράψασθαι	γεγράψεσθαι
Part.	γραφόμενος	γραψόμενος	γραψάμενος	γεγραψόμενος
	Imperfect.	2 Aor. Pass.		2 Fut. Pass.
Ind.	ἐγραφόμην	ἐγράφην		γραφήσομαι
Subj.		γραφῶ		
Opt.		γραφείην		γραφησοίμην
Imp.		γράφηθι		
Inf.		γραφῆναι		γραφήσεσθαι
Part.		γραφείς		γραφησόμενος

PERFECT, Ind.		Imp.	Inf.	PLUPERFECT.
S. 1	γέγραμμαι		γεγράφθαι	ἐγεγράμμην
2	γέγραψαι	γέγραψο		ἐγέγραψο
3	γέγραπται	γεγράφθω	Part.	ἐγέγραπτο
P. 1	γεγράμμεθα		γεγραμμένος	ἐγεγράμμεθα
2	γέγραφθε	γέγραφθε		ἐγέγραφθε
3	γεγραμμένοι [εἰσί	γεγράφθωσαν, γεγράφθων		γεγραμμένοι [ἦσαν
D. 2	γέγραφθον	γέγραφθον		ἐγέγραφθον
3		γεγράφθων		ἐγεγράφθην

¶ 37. Labial. 2. Λείπω, *to leave*.

Active Voice.

	Present.	Imperfect.	Future.	2 Perfect.	2 Pluperfect.
Ind.	λείπω	ἔλειπον	λείψω	λέλοιπα	ἐλελοίπειν
Subj.	λείπω				
Opt.	λείποιμι		λείψοιμι		
Imp.	λεῖπε				
Inf.	λείπειν		λείψειν	λελοιπέναι	
Part.	λείπων		λείψων	λελοιπώς	

Aorist II.

	Ind.	Subj.	Opt.	Imp.	Inf.
S. 1	ἔλιπον	λίπω	λίποιμι		λιπεῖν
2	ἔλιπες	λίπῃς	λίποις	λίπε	
3	ἔλιπε	λίπῃ	λίποι	λιπέτω	Part.
P. 1	ἐλίπομεν	λίπωμεν	λίποιμεν		λιπών
2	ἐλίπετε	λίπητε	λίποιτε	λίπετε	λιποῦσα
3	ἔλιπον	λίπωσι	λίποιεν	λιπέτωσαν, λιπόντων	λιπόν
D. 2	ἐλίπετον	λίπητον	λίποιτον	λίπετον	λιπόντος
3	ἐλιπέτην		λιποίτην	λιπέτων	λιπούσης

Middle and Passive Voices.

	Present.	Future Mid.	Perfect.	Aorist Pass.
Ind.	λείπομαι	λείψομαι	λέλειμμαι	ἐλείφθην
Subj.	λείπωμαι			λειφθῶ
Opt.	λειποίμην	λειψοίμην		λειφθείην
Imp.	λείπου		λέλειψο	λείφθητι
Inf.	λείπεσθαι	λείψεσθαι	λελεῖφθαι	λειφθῆναι
Part.	λειπόμενος	λειψόμενος	λελειμμένος	λειφθείς
	Imperfect.	3 Future.	Pluperfect.	Future Pass.
Ind.	ἐλειπόμην	λελείψομαι	ἐλελείμμην	λειφθήσομαι

Aorist II. Middle.

	Ind.	Subj.	Opt.	Imp.	Inf.
S. 1	ἐλιπόμην	λίπωμαι	λιποίμην		λιπέσθαι
2	ἐλίπου	λίπῃ	λίποιο	λιποῦ	
3	ἐλίπετο	λίπηται	λίποιτο	λιπέσθω	Part.
P. 1	ἐλιπόμεθα	λιπώμεθα	λιποίμεθα		λιπόμενος
2	ἐλίπεσθε	λίπησθε	λίποισθε	λίπεσθε	
3	ἐλίποντο	λίπωνται	λίποιντο	λιπέσθωσαν, λιπέσθων	
D. 2	ἐλίπεσθον	λίπησθον	λίποισθον	λίπεσθον	
3	ἐλιπέσθην		λιποίσθην	λιπέσθων	

¶ 38. ii. Palatal. *Πράσσω* or *πράττω*, *to do.*

Active Voice.

	Present.	Future.	Aorist.	1 Perfect.	2 Perfect.
Ind.	πράσσω, πράττω	πράξω	ἔπραξα	πέπρᾱχα	πέπρᾱγα
Subj.	πράσσω, πράττω		πράξω		
Opt.	πράσσοιμι, πράττοιμι	πράξοιμι	πράξαιμι		
Imp.	πρᾶσσε, πρᾶττε		πρᾶξον	[ναι	[ναι
Inf.	πράσσειν, πράττειν	πράξειν	πρᾶξαι	πεπραχέ-	πεπραγέ-
Part.	πράσσων, πράττων	πράξων	πράξας	πεπραχώς	πεπραγώς

Imperfect.	1 Pluperfect.	2 Pluperfect.
ἔπρασσον, ἔπραττον	ἐπεπράχειν	ἐπεπράγειν

Middle and Passive Voices.

	Present.	Imperfect.	Future Mid.
Ind.	πράσσομαι, πράττομαι	ἐπρασσόμην, ἐπραττόμην	πράξομαι
Subj.	πράσσωμαι, πράττωμαι		
Opt.	πρασσοίμην, πραττοίμην		πραξοίμην
Imp.	πράσσου, πράττου		
Inf.	πράσσεσθαι, πράττεσθαι		πράξεσθαι
Part.	πρασσόμενος, πραττόμενος		πραξόμενος

	Aorist Mid.	Aorist Pass.	Future Pass.	3 Future.
Ind.	ἐπραξάμην	ἐπράχθην	πραχθήσομαι	πεπράξομαι
Subj.	πράξωμαι	πραχθῶ		
Opt.	πραξαίμην	πραχθείην	πραχθησοίμην	πεπραξοίμην
Imp.	πρᾶξαι	πράχθητι		
Inf.	πράξασθαι	πραχθῆναι	πραχθήσεσθαι	πεπράξεσθαι
Part.	πραξάμενος	πραχθείς	πραχθησόμενος	πεπραξόμενος

		Perfect. Ind.	Imp.	Inf.	Pluperfect.
S.	1	πέπραγμαι		πεπρᾶχθαι	ἐπεπράγμην
	2	πέπραξαι	πέπραξο		ἐπέπραξο
	3	πέπρακται	πεπράχθω	Part.	ἐπέπρακτο
P.	1	πεπράγμεθα		πεπραγμένος	ἐπεπράγμεθα
	2	πέπραχθε	πέπραχθε		ἐπέπραχθε
	3	πεπραγμένοι [εἰσί	πεπράχθωσαν, πεπράχθων		πεπραγμένοι [ἦσαν
D	2	πέπραχθον	πέπραχθον		ἐπέπραχθον
	3		πεπράχθων		ἐπεπράχθην

¶ 39. iii. Lingual. 1. *Πείθω, to persuade.*

(2 Perfect, *to trust;* Middle and Passive, *to believe, to obey.*)

Active Voice.

	Present.	Future.	1 Aorist.	2 Aorist.	1 Perfect.	2 Perfect.
Ind.	πείθω	πείσω	ἔπεισα	ἔπιθον	πέπεικα	πέποιθα
Subj.	πείθω		πείσω	πίθω		πεποίθω
Opt.	πείθοιμι	πείσοιμι	πείσαιμι	πίθοιμι		πεποιθοίην
Imp.	πεῖθε		πεῖσον	πίθε		πέπεισθι
Inf.	πείθειν	πείσειν	πεῖσαι	πιθεῖν	πεπεικέναι	πεποιθέναι
Part.	πείθων	πείσων	πείσας	πιθών	πεπεικώς	πεποιθώς

	Imperfect.				1 Pluperfect.	2 Pluperfect.
	ἔπειθον				ἐπεπείκειν	ἐπεποίθειν

Middle and Passive Voices.

	Present.	Future Mid.	2 Aor. Mid.	Aorist Pass.	Future Pass.
Ind.	πείθομαι	πείσομαι	ἐπιθόμην	ἐπείσθην	πεισθήσομαι
Subj.	πείθωμαι		πίθωμαι	πεισθῶ	
Opt.	πειθοίμην	πεισοίμην	πιθοίμην	πεισθείην	πεισθησοίμην
Imp.	πείθου		πιθοῦ	πείσθητι	
Inf.	πείθεσθαι	πείσεσθαι	πιθέσθαι	πεισθῆναι	πεισθήσεσθαι
Part.	πειθόμενος	πεισόμενος	πιθόμενος	πεισθείς	πεισθησόμενος

	Imperfect.
	ἐπειθόμην

		Perfect.			Pluperfect.
		Ind.	Imp.	Inf.	
S.	1	πέπεισμαι		πεπεῖσθαι	ἐπεπείσμην
	2	πέπεισαι	πέπεισο		ἐπέπεισο
	3	πέπεισται	πεπείσθω	Part.	ἐπέπειστο
P.	1	πεπείσμεθα		πεπεισμένος	ἐπεπείσμεθα
	2	πέπεισθε	πέπεισθε		ἐπέπεισθε
	3	πεπεισμένοι [εἰσί	πεπείσθωσαν, πεπείσθων		πεπεισμένοι [ἦσαν
D.	2	πέπεισθον	πέπεισθον		ἐπέπεισθον
	3		πεπείσθων		ἐπεπείσθην

¶ 40. 2. *Κομίζω, to bring.*

(Middle, *to receive.*)

Active Voice.

	Present.	Future.	Aorist.	Perfect.
Ind.	κομίζω	κομίσω	ἐκόμισα	κεκόμικα
Subj.	κομίζω		κομίσω	
Opt.	κομίζοιμι	κομίσοιμι	κομίσαιμι	
Imp.	κόμιζε		κόμισον	
Inf.	κομίζειν	κομίσειν	κομίσαι	κεκομικέναι
Part.	κομίζων	κομίσων	κομίσας	κεκομικώς
	Imperfect.			Pluperfect.
	ἐκόμιζον			ἐκεκομίκειν

Middle and Passive Voices.

	Present.	Future Mid.	Aorist Mid.	Aorist Pass.
Ind.	κομίζομαι	κομίσομαι	ἐκομισάμην	ἐκομίσθην
Subj.	κομίζωμαι		κομίσωμαι	κομισθῶ
Opt.	κομιζοίμην	κομισοίμην	κομισαίμην	κομισθείην
Imp.	κομίζου		κόμισαι	κομίσθητι
Inf.	κομίζεσθαι	κομίσεσθαι	κομίσασθαι	κομισθῆναι
Part.	κομιζόμενος	κομισόμενος	κομισάμενος	κομισθείς

	Imperfect.	Perfect.	Pluperfect.	Future Pass.
Ind	ἐκομιζόμην	κεκόμισμαι	ἐκεκομίσμην	κομισθήσομαι
Opt.				κομισθησοίμην
Imp.		κεκόμισο		
Inf.		κεκομίσθαι		κομισθήσεσθαι
Part.		κεκομισμένος		κομισθησόμενος

Attic Future.

	Active.		Middle.	
	Ind.	Inf.	Ind.	Inf.
S. 1	κομιῶ	κομιεῖν	κομιοῦμαι	κομιεῖσθαι
2	κομιεῖς		κομιεῖ	
3	κομιεῖ	Part.	κομιεῖται	Part.
P. 1	κομιοῦμεν	κομιῶν	κομιούμεθα	κομιούμενος
2	κομιεῖτε	κομιοῦσα	κομιεῖσθε	
3	κομιοῦσι	κομιοῦν	κομιοῦνται	
D. 2	κομιεῖτον	κομιοῦντος	κομιεῖσθον	

¶ 41. XII. (B.) Liquid Verbs.

1. Ἀγγέλλω, *to announce.*

Active Voice.

	Present.	Imperfect.	2 Aorist.	Perfect.	Pluperfect.
Ind.	ἀγγέλλω	ἤγγελλον	ἤγγελον	ἤγγελκα	ἠγγέλκειν.
Subj.	ἀγγέλλω		ἀγγέλω		
Opt.	ἀγγέλλοιμι		ἀγγέλοιμι		
Imp.	ἄγγελλε		ἄγγελε		
Inf.	ἀγγέλλειν		ἀγγελεῖν	ἠγγελκέναι	
Part.	ἀγγέλλων		ἀγγελών	ἠγγελκώς	

Future.

		Ind.	Opt.	Inf.	Part.
S.	1	ἀγγελῶ	ἀγγελοῖμι, ἀγγελοίην	ἀγγελεῖν	ἀγγελῶν
	2	ἀγγελεῖς	ἀγγελοῖς, ἀγγελοίης		ἀγγελοῦσα
	3	ἀγγελεῖ	ἀγγελοῖ, ἀγγελοίη		ἀγγελοῦν
P.	1	ἀγγελοῦμεν	ἀγγελοῖμεν, ἀγγελοίημεν		ἀγγελοῦντος
	2	ἀγγελεῖτε	ἀγγελοῖτε, ἀγγελοίητε		ἀγγελούσης
	3	ἀγγελοῦσι	ἀγγελοῖεν		
D.	2	ἀγγελεῖτον	ἀγγελοῖτον, ἀγγελοίητον		
	3		ἀγγελοίτην, ἀγγελοιήτην		

Aorist I.

		Ind.	Subj.	Opt.	Imp.
S.	1	ἤγγειλα	ἀγγείλω	ἀγγείλαιμι	
	2	ἤγγειλας	ἀγγείλῃς	ἀγγείλαις, ἀγγείλειας	ἄγγειλον
	3	ἤγγειλε	ἀγγείλῃ	ἀγγείλαι, ἀγγείλειε	ἀγγειλάτω
P.	1	ἠγγείλαμεν	ἀγγείλωμεν	ἀγγείλαιμεν	
	2	ἠγγείλατε	ἀγγείλητε	ἀγγείλαιτε	ἀγγείλατε
	3	ἤγγειλαν	ἀγγείλωσι	ἀγγείλαιεν, ἀγγείλειαν	ἀγγειλάτωσαν, ἀγγειλάντων
D.	2	ἠγγείλατον	ἀγγείλητον	ἀγγείλαιτον	ἀγγείλατον
	3	ἠγγειλάτην		ἀγγειλαίτην	ἀγγειλάτων

Inf. ἀγγεῖλαι. Part. ἀγγείλας,-ᾱσα,-αν · G.-αντος,-άσης.

Middle and Passive Voices.

	Present.	2 Aor. Mid.	1 Aor. Pass.	2 Aor. Pass.
Ind.	ἀγγέλλομαι	ἠγγελόμην	ἠγγέλθην	ἠγγέλην
Subj.	ἀγγέλλωμαι	ἀγγέλωμαι	ἀγγελθῶ	ἀγγελῶ
Opt.	ἀγγελλοίμην	ἀγγελοίμην	ἀγγελθείην	ἀγγελείην
Imp.	ἀγγέλλου	ἀγγελοῦ	ἀγγέλθητι	ἀγγέληθι
Inf.	ἀγγέλλεσθαι	ἀγγελέσθαι	ἀγγελθῆναι	ἀγγελῆναι
Part.	ἀγγελλόμενος	ἀγγελόμενος	ἀγγελθείς	ἀγγελείς

	Imperfect.	1 Future.	2 Future.
Ind.	ἠγγελλόμην	ἀγγελθήσομαι	ἀγγελήσομαι
Opt.		ἀγγελθησοίμην	ἀγγελησοίμην
Inf.		ἀγγελθήσεσθαι	ἀγγελήσεσθαι
Part.		ἀγγελθησόμενος	ἀγγελησόμενος

FUTURE MIDDLE.

	Ind.	Opt.	Inf.	Part.
S. 1	ἀγγελοῦμαι	ἀγγελοίμην	ἀγγελεῖσθαι	ἀγγελούμενος
2	ἀγγελῇ, ἀγγελεῖ	ἀγγελοῖο		ἀγγελουμένη
3	ἀγγελεῖται	ἀγγελοῖτο		ἀγγελούμενον
P. 1	ἀγγελούμεθα	ἀγγελοίμεθα		ἀγγελουμένου
2	ἀγγελεῖσθε	ἀγγελοῖσθε		ἀγγελουμένης
3	ἀγγελοῦνται	ἀγγελοῖντο		
D. 2	ἀγγελεῖσθον	ἀγγελοῖσθον		
3		ἀγγελοίσθην		

AORIST I. MIDDLE.

	Ind.	Subj.	Opt.	Imp.
S. 1	ἠγγειλάμην	ἀγγείλωμαι	ἀγγειλαίμην	
2	ἠγγείλω	ἀγγείλῃ	ἀγγείλαιο	ἄγγειλαι
3	ἠγγείλατο	ἀγγείληται	ἀγγείλαιτο	ἀγγειλάσθω
P. 1	ἠγγειλάμεθα	ἀγγειλώμεθα	ἀγγειλαίμεθα	
2	ἠγγείλασθε	ἀγγείλησθε	ἀγγείλαισθε	ἀγγείλασθε
3	ἠγγείλαντο	ἀγγείλωνται	ἀγγείλαιντο	ἀγγειλάσθωσαν, ἀγγειλάσθων
D. 2	ἠγγείλασθον	ἀγγείλησθον	ἀγγείλαισθον	ἀγγείλασθον
3	ἠγγειλάσθην		ἀγγειλαίσθην	ἀγγειλάσθων

Inf. ἀγγείλασθαι. Part. ἀγγειλάμενος.

	PERFECT. Ind.	Imp.	Inf.	PLUPERFECT.
S. 1	ἤγγελμαι		ἠγγέλθαι	ἠγγέλμην
2	ἤγγελσαι	ἤγγελσο		ἤγγελσο
3	ἤγγελται	ἠγγέλθω	Part.	ἤγγελτο
P. 1	ἠγγέλμεθα		ἠγγελμένος	ἠγγέλμεθα
2	ἤγγελθε	ἤγγελθε		ἤγγελθε
3	ἠγγελμένοι εἰσί	ἠγγέλθωσαν, ἠγγέλθων		ἠγγελμένοι ἦσαν
D. 2	ἤγγελθον	ἤγγελθον		ἤγγελθον
3		ἠγγέλθων		ἠγγέλθην

¶ 42. Liquid. 2. *Φαίνω, to show.*

(2 Perf. and Middle, *to appear.*)

Active Voice.

	Present.	Future.	Aorist.	1 Perfect.	2 Perfect.
Ind.	φαίνω	φανῶ	ἔφηνα	πέφαγκα	πέφηνα
Subj.	φαίνω		φήνω		
Opt.	φαίνοιμι	φανοῖμι, φανοίην	φήναιμι		
Imp.	φαῖνε		φῆνον		
Inf.	φαίνειν	φανεῖν	φῆναι		πεφηνέναι
Part.	φαίνων	φανῶν	φήνας		πεφηνώς
	Imperfect.				2 Pluperfect.
	ἔφαινον				ἐπεφήνειν

Middle and Passive Voices.

	Present.	Imperfect.	Future Mid.	Aorist Mid.
Ind.	φαίνομαι	ἐφαινόμην	φανοῦμαι	ἐφηνάμην
Subj.	φαίνωμαι			φήνωμαι
Opt.	φαινοίμην		φανοίμην	φηναίμην
Imp.	φαίνου			φῆναι
Inf.	φαίνεσθαι		φανεῖσθαι	φήνασθαι
Part.	φαινόμενος		φανούμενος	φηνάμενος

	1 Aor. Pass.	2 Aor. Pass.	1 Fut. Pass.	2 Fut. Pass.
Ind.	ἐφάνθην	ἐφάνην	φανθήσομαι	φανήσομαι
Subj.	φανθῶ	φανῶ		
Opt.	φανθείην	φανείην	φανθησοίμην	φανησοίμην
Imp.	φάνθητι	φάνηθι		
Inf.	φανθῆναι	φανῆναι	φανθήσεσθαι	φανήσεσθαι
Part.	φανθείς	φανείς	φανθησόμενος	φανησόμενος

	Perfect. Ind.	Perfect. Imp.	Perfect. Inf.	Pluperfect.
S. 1	πέφασμαι		πεφάνθαι	ἐπεφάσμην
2	πέφανσαι	πέφανσο		ἐπέφανσο
3	πέφανται	πεφάνθω	Part.	ἐπέφαντο
P. 1	πεφάσμεθα		πεφασμένος	ἐπεφάσμεθα
2	πέφανθε	πέφανθε		ἐπέφανθε
3	πεφασμένοι εἰσί	πεφάνθωσαν, πεφάνθων		πεφασμένοι ἦσαν
D. 2	πέφανθον	πέφανθον		ἐπέφανθον
3		πεφάνθων		ἐπεφάνθην

¶ 43. XIII. (C.) Double Consonant Verbs.

1. *Αὔξω* or *αὐξάνω*, *to increase.*

Active Voice.

	Present.		Future.	Aorist.	Perfect.
Ind.	αὔξω,	αὐξάνω	αὐξήσω	ηὔξησα	ηὔξηκα
Subj.	αὔξω,	αὐξάνω		αὐξήσω	
Opt.	αὔξοιμι,	αὐξάνοιμι	αὐξήσοιμι	αὐξήσαιμι	
Imp.	αὖξε,	αὔξανε		αὔξησον	
Inf.	αὔξειν,	αὐξάνειν	αὐξήσειν	αὐξῆσαι	ηὐξηκέναι
Part.	αὔξων,	αὐξάνων	αὐξήσων	αὐξήσας	ηὐξηκώς
	Imperfect.				Pluperfect
	ηὖξον,	ηὔξανον			ηὐξήκειν

Middle and Passive Voices.

	Present.		Future Mid.	Aorist Mid.
Ind.	αὔξομαι,	αὐξάνομαι	αὐξήσομαι	ηὐξησάμην
Subj.	αὔξωμαι,	αὐξάνωμαι		αὐξήσωμαι
Opt.	αὐξοίμην,	αὐξανοίμην	αὐξησοίμην	αὐξησαίμην
Imp.	αὔξου,	αὐξάνου		αὔξησαι
Inf.	αὔξεσθαι,	αὐξάνεσθαι	αὐξήσεσθαι	αὐξήσασθαι
Part.	αὐξόμενος,	αὐξανόμενος	αὐξησόμενος	αὐξησάμενος
	Imperfect.			
	ηὐξόμην,	ηὐξανόμην		

	Perfect.	Pluperfect.	Aorist Pass.	Future Pass.
Ind.	ηὔξημαι	ηὐξήμην	ηὐξήθην	αὐξηθήσομαι
Subj.			αὐξηθῶ	
Opt.			αὐξηθείην	αὐξηθησοίμην
Imp.	ηὔξησο		αὐξήθητι	
Inf.	ηὐξῆσθαι		αὐξηθῆναι	αὐξηθήσεσθαι
Part.	ηὐξημένος		αὐξηθείς	αὐξηθησόμενος

¶ 44. 2. Perfect Passive of *κάμπτω*, *to bend*, and *ἐλέγχω*, *to convict.*

		Indicative.		Imperative.	
S.	1	κέκαμμαι	ἐλήλεγμαι		
	2	κέκαμψαι	ἐλήλεγξαι	κέκαμψο	ἐλήλεγξο
	3	κέκαμπται	ἐλήλεγκται	κεκάμφθω, &c.	ἐληλέγχθω, &c.
P.	1	κεκάμμεθα	ἐληλέγμεθα	Infinitive.	
	2	κέκαμφθε	ἐλήλεγχθε	κεκάμφθαι	ἐληλέγχθαι
	3	κεκαμμένοι [εἰσί	ἐληλεγμένοι [εἰσί	Participle.	
D.	2	κέκαμφθον	ἐλήλεγχθον	κεκαμμένος	ἐληλεγμένος

¶ 45. XIV. (D.) Pure Verbs. i. Contract

1. *Τῑμάω, to honor.*

Active Voice.

		Present Ind.		Present Subj.	
S.	1	τῑμάω,	τιμῶ	τιμάω,	τιμῶ
	2	τιμάεις,	τιμᾷς	τιμάῃς,	τιμᾷς
	3	τιμάει,	τιμᾷ	τιμάῃ,	τιμᾷ
P.	1	τιμάομεν,	τιμῶμεν	τιμάωμεν,	τιμῶμεν
	2	τιμάετε,	τιμᾶτε	τιμάητε,	τιμᾶτε
	3	τιμάουσι,	τιμῶσι	τιμάωσι,	τιμῶσι
D.	2	τιμάετον,	τιμᾶτον	τιμάητον,	τιμᾶτον

		Imperfect.		Present Opt.		
S.	1	ἐτίμαον,	ἐτίμων	τιμάοιμι,	τιμῷμι,	τιμῴην
	2	ἐτίμαες,	ἐτίμας	τιμάοις,	τιμῷς,	τιμῴης
	3	ἐτίμαε,	ἐτίμα	τιμάοι,	τιμῷ,	τιμῴη
P.	1	ἐτιμάομεν,	ἐτιμῶμεν	τιμάοιμεν,	τιμῷμεν,	τιμῴημεν
	2	ἐτιμάετε,	ἐτιμᾶτε	τιμάοιτε,	τιμῷτε,	τιμῴητε
	3	ἐτίμαον,	ἐτίμων	τιμάοιεν,	τιμῷεν	
D.	2	ἐτιμάετον,	ἐτιμᾶτον	τιμάοιτον,	τιμῷτον,	τιμῴητον
	3	ἐτιμαέτην,	ἐτιμάτην	τιμαοίτην,	τιμῴτην,	τιμῳήτην

		Present Imp.		Present Inf.	
S.	2	τίμαε,	τίμα	τιμάειν,	τιμᾶν
	3	τιμαέτω,	τιμάτω	**Present Part.**	
P.	2	τιμάετε,	τιμᾶτε	τιμάων,	τιμῶν
	3	τιμαέτωσαν,	τιμάτωσαν,	τιμάουσα,	τιμῶσα
		τιμαόντων,	τιμώντων	τιμάον,	τιμῶν
D.	2	τιμάετον,	τιμᾶτον	G. τιμάοντος,	τιμῶντος
	3	τιμαέτων,	τιμάτων	τιμαούσης,	τιμώσης

	Future.	Aorist.	Perfect.	Pluperfect.
Ind.	τιμήσω	ἐτίμησα	τετίμηκα	ἐτετιμήκειν
Subj.		τιμήσω		
Opt.	τιμήσοιμι	τιμήσαιμι		
Imp.		τίμησον		
Inf.	τιμήσειν	τιμῆσαι	τετιμηκέναι	
Part	τιμήσων	τιμήσας	τετιμηκώς	

Middle and Passive Voices.

	Present Ind.		Present Subj.	
S. 1	τῑμάομαι,	τιμῶμαι	τιμάωμαι,	τιμῶμαι
2	τιμάῃ,	τιμᾷ	τιμάῃ,	τιμᾷ
3	τιμάεται,	τιμᾶται	τιμάηται,	τιμᾶται
P. 1	τιμαόμεθα,	τιμώμεθα	τιμαώμεθα,	τιμώμεθα
2	τιμάεσθε,	τιμᾶσθε	τιμάησθε,	τιμᾶσθε
3	τιμάονται,	τιμῶνται	τιμάωνται,	τιμῶνται
D. 2	τιμάεσθον,	τιμᾶσθον	τιμάησθον,	τιμᾶσθον

	Imperfect.		Present Opt.	
S. 1	ἐτιμαόμην,	ἐτιμώμην	τιμαοίμην,	τιμῴμην
2	ἐτιμάου,	ἐτῑμῶ	τιμάοιο,	τιμῷο
3	ἐτιμάετο,	ἐτιμᾶτο	τιμάοιτο,	τιμῷτο
P. 1	ἐτιμαόμεθα,	ἐτιμώμεθα	τιμαοίμεθα,	τιμῴμεθα
2	ἐτιμάεσθε,	ἐτιμᾶσθε	τιμάοισθε,	τιμῷσθε
3	ἐτιμάοντο,	ἐτιμῶντο	τιμάοιντο,	τιμῷντο
D. 2	ἐτιμάεσθον,	ἐτιμᾶσθον	τιμάοισθον,	τιμῷσθον
3	ἐτιμαέσθην,	ἐτιμάσθην	τιμαοίσθην,	τιμῴσθην

	Present Imp.		Present Inf.	
S. 2	τιμάου,	τιμῶ	τιμάεσθαι,	τιμᾶσθαι
3	τιμαέσθω,	τιμάσθω		
P. 2	τιμάεσθε,	τιμᾶσθε		
3	τιμαέσθωσαν,	τιμάσθωσαν,	**Present Part.**	
	τιμαέσθων,	τιμάσθων	τιμαόμενος,	τιμώμενος
D. 2	τιμάεσθον,	τιμᾶσθον	τιμαομένη,	τιμωμένη
3	τιμαέσθων,	τιμάσθων	τιμαόμενον,	τιμώμενον

	Future Mid.	Aorist Mid.	Perfect.	Aorist Pass.
Ind.	τιμήσομαι	ἐτιμησάμην	τετίμημαι	ἐτιμήθην
Subj.		τιμήσωμαι		τιμηθῶ
Opt.	τιμησοίμην	τιμησαίμην		τιμηθείην
Imp.		τίμησαι	τετίμησο	τιμήθητι
Inf.	τιμήσεσθαι	τιμήσασθαι	τετιμῆσθαι	τιμηθῆναι
Part.	τιμησόμενος	τιμησάμενος	τετιμημένος	τιμηθείς

	3 Future.	Pluperfect.	Future Pass.
Ind.	τετιμήσομαι	ἐτετιμήμην	τιμηθήσομαι
Opt.	τετιμησοίμην		τιμηθησοίμην
Inf.	τετιμήσεσθαι		τιμηθήσεσθαι
Part.	τετιμησόμενος		τιμηθησόμενος

¶ 46. Contract. 2. *Φιλέω, to love.*

Active Voice.

	Present Ind.		Present Subj.	
S. 1	φιλέω,	φιλῶ	φιλέω,	φιλῶ
2	φιλέεις,	φιλεῖς	φιλέῃς,	φιλῇς
3	φιλέει,	φιλεῖ	φιλέῃ,	φιλῇ
P. 1	φιλέομεν,	φιλοῦμεν	φιλέωμεν,	φιλῶμεν
2	φιλέετε,	φιλεῖτε	φιλέητε,	φιλῆτε
3	φιλέουσι,	φιλοῦσι	φιλέωσι,	φιλῶσι
D. 2	φιλέετον,	φιλεῖτον	φιλέητον,	φιλῆτον

	Imperfect.		Present Opt.		
S. 1	ἐφίλεον,	ἐφίλουν	φιλέοιμι,	φιλοῖμι,	φιλοίην
2	ἐφίλεες,	ἐφίλεις	φιλέοις,	φιλοῖς,	φιλοίης
3	ἐφίλεε,	ἐφίλει	φιλέοι,	φιλοῖ,	φιλοίη
P. 1	ἐφιλέομεν,	ἐφιλοῦμεν	φιλέοιμεν,	φιλοῖμεν,	φιλοίημεν
2	ἐφιλέετε,	ἐφιλεῖτε	φιλέοιτε,	φιλοῖτε,	φιλοίητε
3	ἐφίλεον,	ἐφίλουν	φιλέοιεν,	φιλοῖεν	
D. 2	ἐφιλέετον,	ἐφιλεῖτον	φιλέοιτον,	φιλοῖτον,	φιλοίητον
3	ἐφιλεέτην,	ἐφιλείτην	φιλεοίτην,	φιλοίτην,	φιλοιήτην

	Present Imp.		Present Inf.	
S. 2	φίλεε,	φίλει	φιλέειν,	φιλεῖν
3	φιλεέτω,	φιλείτω	**Present Part.**	
P. 2	φιλέετε,	φιλεῖτε	φιλέων,	φιλῶν
3	φιλεέτωσαν,	φιλείτωσαν,	φιλέουσα,	φιλοῦσα
	φιλεόντων,	φιλούντων	φιλέον,	φιλοῦν
D. 2	φιλέετον,	φιλεῖτον	G. φιλέοντος,	φιλοῦντος
3	φιλεέτων,	φιλείτων	φιλεούσης,	φιλούσης

	Future.	Aorist.	Perfect.	Pluperfect.
Ind.	φιλήσω	ἐφίλησα	πεφίληκα	ἐπεφιλήκειν
Subj.		φιλήσω		
Opt.	φιλήσοιμι	φιλήσαιμι		
Imp.		φίλησον		
Inf.	φιλήσειν	φιλῆσαι	πεφιληκέναι	
Part.	φιλήσων	φιλήσας	πεφιληκώς	

Middle and Passive Voices.

	Present Ind.		Present Subj.	
S. 1	φιλέομαι,	φιλοῦμαι	φιλέωμαι,	φιλῶμαι
2	φιλέῃ, φιλέει,	φιλῇ, φιλεῖ	φιλέῃ,	φιλῇ
3	φιλέεται,	φιλεῖται	φιλέηται,	φιλῆται
P. 1	φιλεόμεθα,	φιλούμεθα	φιλεώμεθα,	φιλώμεθα
2	φιλέεσθε,	φιλεῖσθε	φιλέησθε,	φιλῆσθε
3	φιλέονται,	φιλοῦνται	φιλέωνται,	φιλῶνται
D. 2	φιλέεσθον,	φιλεῖσθον	φιλέησθον,	φιλῆσθον

	Imperfect.		Present Opt.	
S. 1	ἐφιλεόμην,	ἐφιλούμην	φιλεοίμην,	φιλοίμην
2	ἐφιλέου,	ἐφιλοῦ	φιλέοιο,	φιλοῖο
3	ἐφιλέετο,	ἐφιλεῖτο	φιλέοιτο,	φιλοῖτο
P. 1	ἐφιλεόμεθα,	ἐφιλούμεθα	φιλεοίμεθα,	φιλοίμεθα
2	ἐφιλέεσθε,	ἐφιλεῖσθε	φιλέοισθε,	φιλοῖσθε
3	ἐφιλέοντο,	ἐφιλοῦντο	φιλέοιντο,	φιλοῖντο
D. 2	ἐφιλέεσθον,	ἐφιλεῖσθον	φιλέοισθον,	φιλοῖσθον
3	ἐφιλεέσθην,	ἐφιλείσθην	φιλεοίσθην,	φιλοίσθην

	Present Imp.		Present Inf.	
S. 2	φιλέου,	φιλοῦ	φιλέεσθαι,	φιλεῖσθαι
3	φιλεέσθω,	φιλείσθω		
P. 2	φιλέεσθε,	φιλεῖσθε		
3	φιλεέσθωσαν,	φιλείσθωσαν,	**Present Part.**	
	φιλεέσθων,	φιλείσθων	φιλεόμενος,	φιλούμενος
D. 2	φιλέεσθον,	φιλεῖσθον	φιλεομένη,	φιλουμένη
3	φιλεέσθων,	φιλείσθων	φιλεόμενον,	φιλούμενον

	Future Mid.	Aorist Mid.	Perfect.	Aorist Pass.
Ind.	φιλήσομαι	ἐφιλησάμην	πεφίλημαι	ἐφιλήθην
Subj.		φιλήσωμαι		φιληθῶ
Opt.	φιλησοίμην	φιλησαίμην		φιληθείην
Imp.		φίλησαι	πεφίλησο	φιλήθητι
Inf.	φιλήσεσθαι	φιλήσασθαι	πεφιλῆσθαι	φιληθῆναι
Part.	φιλησόμενος	φιλησάμενος	πεφιλημένος	φιληθείς

	3 Future.		Pluperfect.	Future Pass.
Ind.	πεφιλήσομαι		ἐπεφιλήμην	φιληθήσομαι
Opt.	πεφιλησοίμην			φιληθησοίμην
Inf.	πεφιλήσεσθαι			φιληθήσεσθαι
Part.	πεφιλησόμενος			φιληθησόμενος

¶ 47. Contract. 3. Δηλόω, *to manifest.*

Active Voice.

	Present Ind.		Present Subj.	
S. 1	δηλόω,	δηλῶ	δηλόω,	δηλῶ
2	δηλόεις,	δηλοῖς	δηλόῃς,	δηλοῖς
3	δηλόει,	δηλοῖ	δηλόῃ,	δηλοῖ
P. 1	δηλόομεν,	δηλοῦμεν	δηλόωμεν,	δηλῶμεν
2	δηλόετε,	δηλοῦτε	δηλόητε,	δηλῶτε
3	δηλόουσι,	δηλοῦσι	δηλόωσι,	δηλῶσι
D. 2	δηλόετον,	δηλοῦτον	δηλόητον,	δηλῶτον

	Imperfect.		Present Opt.		
S. 1	ἐδήλοον,	ἐδήλουν	δηλόοιμι,	δηλοῖμι,	δηλοίην
2	ἐδήλοες,	ἐδήλους	δηλόοις,	δηλοῖς,	δηλοίης
3	ἐδήλοε,	ἐδήλου	δηλόοι,	δηλοῖ,	δηλοίη
P. 1	ἐδηλόομεν,	ἐδηλοῦμεν	δηλόοιμεν,	δηλοῖμεν,	δηλοίημεν
2	ἐδηλόετε,	ἐδηλοῦτε	δηλόοιτε,	δηλοῖτε,	δηλοίητε
3	ἐδήλοον,	ἐδήλουν	δηλόοιεν,	δηλοῖεν	
D. 2	ἐδηλόετον,	ἐδηλοῦτον	δηλόοιτον,	δηλοῖτον,	δηλοίητον
3	ἐδηλοέτην,	ἐδηλούτην	δηλοοίτην,	δηλοίτην,	δηλοιήτην

	Present Imp.			Present Inf.	
S. 2	δήλοε,	δήλου		δηλόειν,	δηλοῦν
3	δηλοέτω,	δηλούτω		**Present Part.**	
P. 2	δηλόετε,	δηλοῦτε		δηλόων,	δηλῶν
3	δηλοέτωσαν,	δηλούτωσαν,		δηλόουσα,	δηλοῦσα
	δηλοόντων,	δηλούντων		δηλόον,	δηλοῦν
D. 2	δηλόετον,	δηλοῦτον	G.	δηλόοντος,	δηλοῦντος
3	δηλοέτων,	δηλούτων		δηλοούσης,	δηλούσης

	Future.	Aorist.	Perfect.	Pluperfect.
Ind.	δηλώσω	ἐδήλωσα	δεδήλωκα	ἐδεδηλώκειν
Subj.		δηλώσω		
Opt.	δηλώσοιμι	δηλώσαιμι		
Imp.		δήλωσον		
Inf.	δηλώσειν	δηλῶσαι	δεδηλωκέναι	
Part.	δηλώσων	δηλώσας	δεδηλωκώς	

Middle and Passive Voices.

	Present Ind.		Present Subj.	
S. 1	δηλόομαι,	δηλοῦμαι	δηλόωμαι,	δηλῶμαι
2	δηλόῃ,	δηλοῖ	δηλόῃ,	δηλοῖ
3	δηλόεται,	δηλοῦται	δηλόηται,	δηλῶται
P. 1	δηλοόμεθα,	δηλούμεθα	δηλοώμεθα,	δηλώμεθα
2	δηλόεσθε,	δηλοῦσθε	δηλόησθε,	δηλῶσθε
3	δηλόονται,	δηλοῦνται	δηλόωνται,	δηλῶνται
D. 2	δηλόεσθον,	δηλοῦσθον	δηλόησθον,	δηλῶσθον

	Imperfect.		Present Opt.	
S. 1	ἐδηλοόμην,	ἐδηλούμην	δηλοοίμην,	δηλοίμην
2	ἐδηλόου,	ἐδηλοῦ	δηλόοιο,	δηλοῖο
3	ἐδηλόετο,	ἐδηλοῦτο	δηλόοιτο,	δηλοῖτο
P. 1	ἐδηλοόμεθα,	ἐδηλούμεθα	δηλοοίμεθα,	δηλοίμεθα
2	ἐδηλόεσθε,	ἐδηλοῦσθε	δηλόοισθε,	δηλοῖσθε
3	ἐδηλόοντο,	ἐδηλοῦντο	δηλόοιντο,	δηλοῖντο
D. 2	ἐδηλόεσθον,	ἐδηλοῦσθον	δηλόοισθον,	δηλοῖσθον
3	ἐδηλοέσθην,	ἐδηλούσθην	δηλοοίσθην,	δηλοίσθην

	Present Imp.		Present Inf.	
S. 2	δηλόου,	δηλοῦ	δηλόεσθαι,	δηλοῦσθαι
3	δηλοέσθω,	δηλούσθω		
P. 2	δηλόεσθε,	δηλοῦσθε		
3	δηλοέσθωσαν,	δηλούσθωσαν,	**Present Part.**	
	δηλοέσθων,	δηλούσθων	δηλοόμενος,	δηλούμενος
D. 2	δηλόεσθον,	δηλοῦσθον	δηλοομένη,	δηλουμένη
3	δηλοέσθων,	δηλούσθων	δηλοόμενον,	δηλούμενον

	Future Mid.	Aorist Mid.	Perfect.	Aorist Pass.
Ind.	δηλώσομαι	ἐδηλωσάμην	δεδήλωμαι	ἐδηλώθην
Subj.		δηλώσωμαι		δηλωθῶ
Opt.	δηλωσοίμην	δηλωσαίμην		δηλωθείην
Imp.		δήλωσαι	δεδήλωσο	δηλώθητι
Inf.	δηλώσεσθαι	δηλώσασθαι	δεδηλῶσθαι	δηλωθῆναι
Part.	δηλωσόμενος	δηλωσάμενος	δεδηλωμένος	δηλωθείς

	3 Future.		Pluperfect.	Future Pass.
Ind.	δεδηλώσομαι		ἐδεδηλώμην	δηλωθήσομαι
Opt.	δεδηλωσοίμην			δηλωθησοίμην
Inf.	δεδηλώσεσθαι			δηλωθήσεσθαι
Part.	δεδηλωσόμενος			δηλωθησόμενος

¶ 48. Pure Verbs. ii. Verbs in -μι.

1. Ἵστημι, *to place, to station.*

(2 Aor., Perf., Plup., and 3 Fut., *to stand.*)

ACTIVE VOICE.

Present.

		Ind.	Subj.	Opt.		Imp.
S.	1	ἵστημι	ἱστῶ	ἱσταίην		
	2	ἵστης	ἱστῇς	ἱσταίης		ἵστη
	3	ἵστησι	ἱστῇ	ἱσταίη		ἱστάτω
P.	1	ἵσταμεν	ἱστῶμεν	ἱσταίημεν,	ἱσταῖμεν	
	2	ἵστατε	ἱστῆτε	ἱσταίητε,	ἱσταῖτε	ἵστατε
	3	ἱστᾶσι	ἱστῶσι	ἱσταίησαν,	ἱσταῖεν	ἱστάτωσαν, ἱστάντων
D.	2	ἵστατον	ἱστῆτον	ἱσταίητον,	ἱσταῖτον	ἵστατον
	3			ἱσταιήτην,	ἱσταίτην	ἱστάτων

Inf. ἱστάναι. Part. ἱστάς,-ᾶσα,-άν· G.-άντος,-άσης.

Imperfect.

S.	1 ἵστην	P.	ἵσταμεν	D.	
	2 ἵστης		ἵστατε		ἵστατον
	3 ἵστη		ἵστασαν		ἱστάτην

Aorist II.

		Ind.	Subj.	Opt.		Imp.	Inf.
S	1	ἔστην	στῶ	σταίην			στῆναι
	2	ἔστης	στῇς	σταίης		στῆθι (στᾱ)	
	3	ἔστη	στῇ	σταίη		στήτω	Part.
P.	1	ἔστημεν	στῶμεν	σταίημεν,	σταῖμεν		στάς
	2	ἔστητε	στῆτε	σταίητε,	σταῖτε	στῆτε	
	3	ἔστησαν	στῶσι	σταίησαν,	σταῖεν	στήτωσαν, στάντων	
D.	2	ἔστητον	στῆτον	σταίητον,	σταῖτον	στῆτον	
	3	ἐστήτην		σταιήτην,	σταίτην	στήτων	

	Future.	1 Aorist.	Perfect.	Pluperfect.	3 Future.
Ind.	στήσω	ἔστησα	ἕστηκα	ἑστήκειν, εἱστήκειν	ἑστήξω
Subj.		στήσω	ἑστήκω		
Opt.	στήσοιμι	στήσαιμι			ἑστήξοιμι
Imp.		στῆσον			
Inf.	στήσειν	στῆσαι	*		ἑστήξειν
Part.	στήσων	στήσας	ἑστηκώς		ἑστήξων

	Perfect II.					Pluperf. II.
	Ind.	Subj.	Opt.	Imp.	Inf.	
S. 1	*	ἑστῶ	ἑσταίην		ἑστάναι	*
2	*	*	ἑσταίης	ἕσταθι		*
3	*	*	ἑσταίη	ἑστάτω	Part.	*
P. 1	ἕσταμεν	ἑστῶμεν	&c.		ἑστώς	ἕσταμεν
2	ἕστατε	*		ἕστατε	ἑστῶσα	ἕστατε
3	ἑστᾶσι	ἑστῶσι		&c.	ἑστώς, ἑστός	ἕστασαν
D. 2	ἕστατον	*			ἑστῶτος	ἕστατον
3					ἑστώσης	ἑστάτην

MIDDLE AND PASSIVE VOICES.

Present.

	Ind.	Subj.	Opt.	Imp.	Inf.
S. 1	ἵσταμαι	ἱστῶμαι	ἱσταίμην		ἵστασθαι
2	ἵστασαι	ἱστῇ	ἵσταιο	ἵστασο, ἵστω	
3	ἵσταται	ἱστῆται	ἵσταιτο	ἱστάσθω	Part.
P. 1	ἱστάμεθα	ἱστώμεθα	ἱσταίμεθα		ἱστάμενος
2	ἵστασθε	ἱστῆσθε	ἵσταισθε	ἵστασθε	
3	ἵστανται	ἱστῶνται	ἵσταιντο	ἱστάσθωσαν, ἱστάσθων	
D. 2	ἵστασθον	ἱστῆσθον	ἵσταισθον	ἵστασθον	
3			ἱσταίσθην	ἱστάσθων	

Imperfect.

S. 1	ἱστάμην	P.	ἱστάμεθα	D.	
2	ἵστασο, ἵστω		ἵστασθε		ἵστασθον
3	ἵστατο		ἵσταντο		ἱστάσθην

Fut. Mid. στήσομαι. Aor. Mid. ἐστησάμην. Perf. ἕσταμαι. Pluperf. ἑστάμην. 3 Fut. Mid. ἑστήξομαι. Aor. Pass. ἐστάθην. Fut. Pass. σταθήσομαι.

¶ 49. 2. The Second Aorist πρίασθαι, *to buy*.

	Ind.	Subj.	Opt.	Imp.	Inf.
S. 1	ἐπριάμην	πρίωμαι	πριαίμην		πρίασθαι
2	ἐπρίω	πρίῃ	πρίαιο	πρίασο, πρίω	
3	ἐπρίατο	πρίηται	πρίαιτο	πριάσθω	Part.
P. 1	ἐπριάμεθα	πριώμεθα	πριαίμεθα		πριάμενος
2	ἐπρίασθε	πρίησθε	πρίαισθε	πρίασθε	
3	ἐπρίαντο	πρίωνται	πρίαιντο	πριάσθωσαν, πριάσθων	
D. 2	ἐπρίασθον	πρίησθον	πρίαισθον	πρίασθον	
3	ἐπριάσθην		πριαίσθην	πριάσθων	

¶ 50. Verbs in -μι. 3. Τίθημι, *to put.*

ACTIVE VOICE.

Present.

	Ind.	Subj.	Opt.	Imp.
S. 1	τίθημι	τιθῶ	τιθείην	
2	τίθης	τιθῇς	τιθείης	τίθει
3	τίθησι	τιθῇ	τιθείη	τιθέτω
P. 1	τίθεμεν	τιθῶμεν	τιθείημεν, τιθεῖμεν	
2	τίθετε	τιθῆτε	τιθείητε, τιθεῖτε	τίθετε
3	τιθέᾱσι, τιθεῖσι	τιθῶσι	τιθείησαν, τιθεῖεν	τιθέτωσαν, τιθέντων
D. 2	τίθετον	τιθῆτον	τιθείητον, τιθεῖτον	τίθετον
3			τιθειήτην, τιθείτην	τιθέτων

Inf. τιθέναι. Part. τιθείς,-εῖσα,-έν· G.-έντος,-είσης.

Imperfect.

		P.	D.
S. 1	ἐτίθην, ἐτίθουν	ἐτίθεμεν	
2	ἐτίθης, ἐτίθεις	ἐτίθετε	ἐτίθετον
3	ἐτίθη, ἐτίθει	ἐτίθεσαν	ἐτιθέτην

Aorist I. Aorist II.

	Aorist I. Ind.	Aorist II. Ind.	Subj.	Opt.	Imp.
S. 1	ἔθηκα	*	θῶ	θείην	
2	ἔθηκας	*	θῇς	θείης	θές
3	ἔθηκε	*	θῇ	θείη	θέτω
P. 1	ἐθήκαμεν	ἔθεμεν	θῶμεν	θείημεν, θεῖμεν	
2	ἐθήκατε	ἔθετε	θῆτε	θείητε, θεῖτε	θέτε
3	ἔθηκαν	ἔθεσαν	θῶσι	θείησαν, θεῖεν	θέτωσαν, θέντων
D. 2		ἔθετον	θῆτον	θείητον, θεῖτον	θέτον
3		ἐθέτην		θειήτην, θείτην	θέτων

Aor. II. Inf. θεῖναι. Part. θείς, θεῖσα, θέν· G. θέντος, θείσης

	Future.	Perfect.	Pluperfect.
Ind.	θήσω	τέθεικα	ἐτεθείκειν
Opt.	θήσοιμι		
Inf.	θήσειν	τεθεικέναι	
Part.	θήσων	τεθεικώς	

MIDDLE AND PASSIVE VOICES.

Present.

	Ind.	Subj.	Opt.	
S. 1	τίθεμαι	τιθῶμαι	τιθείμην,	τιθοίμην
2	τίθεσαι, τίθῃ	τιθῇ	τίθειο,	τίθοιο
3	τίθεται	τιθῆται	τίθειτο,	τίθοιτο
P. 1	τιθέμεθα	τιθώμεθα	τιθείμεθα,	τιθοίμεθα
2	τίθεσθε	τιθῆσθε	τίθεισθε,	τίθοισθε
3	τίθενται	τιθῶνται	τίθειντο,	τίθοιντο
D. 2	τίθεσθον	τιθῆσθον	τίθεισθον,	τίθοισθον
3			τιθείσθην,	τιθοίσθην

	Imp.	Inf.	Imperfect.
S. 1		τίθεσθαι	ἐτιθέμην
2	τίθεσο, τίθου		ἐτίθεσο, ἐτίθου
3	τιθέσθω	Part.	ἐτίθετο
P. 1		τιθέμενος	ἐτιθέμεθα
2	τίθεσθε		ἐτίθεσθε
3	τιθέσθωσαν, τιθέσθων		ἐτίθεντο
D. 2	τίθεσθον		ἐτίθεσθον
3	τιθέσθων		ἐτιθέσθην

Aorist II. Middle.

	Ind.	Subj.	Opt.	Imp.	Inf.
S. 1	ἐθέμην	θῶμαι	θείμην (θοίμην)		θέσθαι
2	ἔθου	θῇ	θεῖο	θοῦ	
3	ἔθετο	θῆται	θεῖτο	θέσθω	Part.
P. 1	ἐθέμεθα	θώμεθα	θείμεθα		θέμενος
2	ἔθεσθε	θῆσθε	θεῖσθε	θέσθε	
3	ἔθεντο	θῶνται	θεῖντο	θέσθωσαν, θέσθων	
D. 2	ἔθεσθον	θῆσθον	θεῖσθον	θέσθον	
3	ἐθέσθην		θείσθην	θέσθων	

	Fut. Mid.	Aor. Pass.	Fut. Pass.	Perfect.	Pluperfect.
Ind.	θήσομαι	ἐτέθην	τεθήσομαι	τέθειμαι	ἐτεθείμην
Subj.		τεθῶ			
Opt.	θησοίμην	τεθείην	τεθησοίμην		
Imp.		τέθητι		τέθεισο	
Inf.	θήσεσθαι	τεθῆναι	τεθήσεσθαι	τεθεῖσθαι	
Part.	θησόμενος	τεθείς	τεθησόμενος	τεθειμένος	

¶ 51. Verbs in -μι. 4. *Δίδωμι, to give.*

ACTIVE VOICE.

Present.

	Ind.	Subj.	Opt.	Imp.
S. 1	δίδωμι	διδῶ	διδοίην (διδῴην)	
2	δίδως	διδῷς	διδοίης	δίδου
3	δίδωσι	διδῷ	διδοίη	διδότω
P. 1	δίδομεν	διδῶμεν	διδοίημεν, διδοῖμεν	
2	δίδοτε	διδῶτε	διδοίητε, διδοῖτε	δίδοτε
3	διδόασι, διδοῦσι	διδῶσι	διδοίησαν, διδοῖεν	διδότωσαν, διδόντων
D. 2	δίδοτον	διδῶτον	διδοίητον, διδοῖτον	δίδοτον
3			διδοιήτην, διδοίτην	διδότων

Inf. διδόναι. Part. διδούς,-οῦσα,-όν· G.-όντος,-ούσης.

Imperfect.

S. 1	ἐδίδων, ἐδίδουν	P.	ἐδίδομεν	D.	
2	ἐδίδως, ἐδίδους		ἐδίδοτε		ἐδίδοτον
3	ἐδίδω, ἐδίδου		ἐδίδοσαν		ἐδιδότην

Aorist I. Aorist II.

	Aor. I. Ind.	Aor. II. Ind.	Subj.	Opt.	Imp.
S. 1	ἔδωκα	*	δῶ	δοίην (δῴην)	
2	ἔδωκας	*	δῷς	δοίης	δός
3	ἔδωκε	*	δῷ	δοίη	δότω
P. 1	ἐδώκαμεν	ἔδομεν	δῶμεν	δοίημεν, δοῖμεν	
2	ἐδώκατε	ἔδοτε	δῶτε	δοίητε, δοῖτε	δότε
3	ἔδωκαν	ἔδοσαν	δῶσι	δοίησαν, δοῖεν	δότωσαν, δόντων
D 2		ἔδοτον	δῶτον	δοίητον, δοῖτον	δότον
3		ἐδότην		δοιήτην, δοίτην	δότων

Aor. II. Inf. δοῦναι. Part. δούς, δοῦσα, δόν· G. δόντος, δούσης.

	Future.	Perfect.	Pluperfect.
Ind.	δώσω	δέδωκα	ἐδεδώκειν
Opt.	δώσοιμι		
Inf.	δώσειν	δεδωκέναι	
Part.	δώσων	δεδωκώς	

MIDDLE AND PASSIVE VOICES.

Present.

	Ind.	Subj.	Opt.	Imp.
S. 1	δίδομαι	διδῶμαι	διδοίμην	
2	δίδοσαι	διδῷ	δίδοιο	δίδοσο, δίδου
3	δίδοται	διδῶται	δίδοιτο	διδόσθω
P. 1	διδόμεθα	διδώμεθα	διδοίμεθα	
2	δίδοσθε	διδῶσθε	δίδοισθε	διδόσθε
3	δίδονται	διδῶνται	δίδοιντο	διδόσθωσαν διδόσθων
D. 2	δίδοσθον	διδῶσθον	δίδοισθον	δίδοσθον
3			διδοίσθην	διδόσθων

Inf. δίδοσθαι. Part. διδόμενος.

Imperfect.

S.		P.	D.
1	ἐδιδόμην	ἐδιδόμεθα	
2	ἐδίδοσο, ἐδίδου	ἐδίδοσθε	ἐδίδοσθον
3	ἐδίδοτο	ἐδίδοντο	ἐδιδόσθην

Aorist II. Middle.

	Ind.	Subj.	Opt.	Imp.	Inf.
S. 1	ἐδόμην	δῶμαι	δοίμην		δόσθαι
2	ἔδου	δῷ	δοῖο	δοῦ	
3	ἔδοτο	δῶται	δοῖτο	δόσθω	Part.
P. 1	ἐδόμεθα	δώμεθα	δοίμεθα		δόμενος
2	ἔδοσθε	δῶσθε	δοῖσθε	δόσθε	
3	ἔδοντο	δῶνται	δοῖντο	δόσθωσαν, δόσθων	
D. 2	ἔδοσθον	δῶσθον	δοῖσθον	δόσθον	
3	ἐδόσθην		δοίσθην	δόσθων	

	Fut. Mid.	Aor. Pass.	Fut. Pass.	Perfect.	Pluperfect.
Ind.	δώσομαι	ἐδόθην	δοθήσομαι	δέδομαι	ἐδεδόμην
Subj.		δοθῶ			
Opt.	δωσοίμην	δοθείην	δοθησοίμην		
Imp.		δόθητι		δέδοσο	
Inf.	δώσεσθαι	δοθῆναι	δοθήσεσθαι	δεδόσθαι	
Part.	δωσόμενος	δοθείς	δοθησόμενος	δεδομένος	

¶ 52. Verbs in -μι. 5. Δείκνῡμι, to show.

ACTIVE VOICE.

Present.

	Ind.	Subj.	Opt.	Imp.
S. 1	δείκνῡμι	δεικνύω	δεικνύοιμι	
2	δείκνῡς	δεικνύῃς	δεικνύοις	δείκνῡ
3	δείκνῡσι	δεικνύῃ	δεικνύοι	δεικνύτω
P. 1	δείκνῠμεν	δεικνύωμεν	δεικνύοιμεν	
2	δείκνυτε	δεικνύητε	δεικνύοιτε	δείκνῠτε
3	δεικνύᾱσι, δεικνῦσι	δεικνύωσι	δεικνύοιεν	δεικνύτωσαν, δεικνύντων
D. 2	δείκνῠτον	δεικνύητον	δεικνύοιτον	δείκνῠτον
3			δεικνυοίτην	δεικνύτων

Inf. δεικνύναι. Part. δεικνύς,-ῦσα,-ύν· G.-ύντος,-ύσης.

Imperfect.

S. 1	ἐδείκνῡν, ἐδείκνῠον	P. ἐδείκνῠμεν	D.	
2	ἐδείκνῡς, ἐδείκνῠες	ἐδείκνυτε		ἐδείκνῠτον
3	ἐδείκνῡ, ἐδείκνῠε	ἐδείκνυσαν		ἐδεικνύτην

Future δείξω. Aorist ἔδειξα.

MIDDLE AND PASSIVE VOICES.

Present.

	Ind.	Subj.	Opt.	Imp.
S. 1	δείκνῠμαι	δεικνύωμαι	δεικνυοίμην	
2	δείκνυσαι	δεικνύῃ	δεικνύοιο	δείκνυσο
3	δείκνυται	δεικνύηται	δεικνύοιτο	δεικνύσθω
P. 1	δεικνύμεθα	δεικνυώμεθα	δεικνυοίμεθα	
2	δείκνυσθε	δεικνύησθε	δεικνύοισθε	δείκνυσθε
3	δείκνυνται	δεικνύωνται	δεικνύοιντο	δεικνύσθωσαν, δεικνύσθων
D. 2	δείκνυσθον	δεικνύησθον	δεικνύοισθον	δείκνυσθον
3			δεικνυοίσθην	δεικνύσθων

Inf. δείκνυσθαι. Part. δεικνύμενος.

Imperfect.

S 1	ἐδεικνύμην	P. ἐδεικνύμεθα	D.	
2	ἐδείκνυσο	ἐδείκνυσθε		ἐδείκνυσθον
3	ἐδείκνυτο	ἐδείκνυντο		ἐδεικνύσθην

Fut. Mid. δείξομαι. Aor. Mid. ἐδειξάμην. Perf. δέδειγμαι. Pluperf. ἐδεδείγμην. Aor. Pass. ἐδείχθην. Fut. Pass. δειχθήσομαι.

¶ 53. 6. *Φημί, to say.*

Present.

	Ind.	Subj.	Opt.	Imp.	Inf.
S. 1	φημί, ἡμί	φῶ	φαίην		φάναι
2	φής, φῄς	φῇς	φαίης	φάθι	
3	φησί	φῇ	φαίη	φάτω	Part.
P. 1	φἄμέν	φῶμεν	φαίημεν, φαῖμεν		φάς
2	φἄτέ	φῆτε	φαίητε, φαῖτε	φάτε	
3	φᾶσί	φῶσι	φαίησαν, φαῖεν	φάτωσαν, φάντων	
D. 2	φἄτόν	φῆτον	φαίητον, φαῖτον	φάτον	
3			φαιήτην, φαίτην	φάτων	

Imperfect.

			P.	D.
S 1	ἔφην,	ἦν	ἔφαμεν	
2	ἔφης,	ἔφησθα	ἔφατε	ἔφατον
3	ἔφη,	ἦ	ἔφασαν	ἐφάτην

Synopsis of Associated Forms.

Active Voice.

	Present.		Imperfect.	Future.	
Ind.	φημί,	φάσκω	ἔφην, ἔφασκον	φήσω,	ἐρῶ
Subj.	φῶ,	φάσκω			
Opt.	φαίην,	φάσκοιμι		*	ἐροῖμι, ἐροίην
Imp.	φάθι,	φάσκε			
Inf.	φάναι,	φάσκειν		φήσειν,	ἐρεῖν
Part.	φάς,	φάσκων		φήσων,	ἐρῶν

	1 Aorist.		2 Aorist.	Perfect.	Pluperfect.
Ind.	ἔφησα,	εἶπα	εἶπον	εἴρηκα	εἰρήκειν
Subj.	φήσω,	εἴπω	εἴπω		
Opt.	φήσαιμι,	εἴπαιμι	εἴποιμι		
Imp.	*	εἶπον	εἰπέ		
Inf.	φῆσαι,	εἶπαι	εἰπεῖν	εἰρηκέναι	
Part.	φήσας,	εἴπας	εἰπών	εἰρηκώς	

Middle and Passive Voices.

Pres. Inf. φάσθαι, Part. φάμενος· Perf. Imp. S. 3 πεφάσθω· Imperf. ἐφασκόμην· Perf. εἴρημαι, Plup. εἰρήμην, 3 Fut. εἰρήσομαι, Aor. Pass. ἐῤῥήθην, ἐῤῥέθην, Fut. Pass. ῥηθήσομαι.

¶ 54. Verbs in -μι. 7. Ἵημι, *to send.*

ACTIVE VOICE.

Present.

		Ind.	Subj.	Opt.	Imp.	Inf.
S	1	ἵημι	ἱῶ	ἱείην		ἱέναι
	2	ἵης	ἱῇς	ἱείης	ἵει	
	3	ἵησι	ἱῇ	ἱείη	ἱέτω	Part.
P	1	ἵεμεν	ἱῶμεν	ἱείημεν, ἱεῖμεν		ἱείς
	2	ἵετε	ἱῆτε	ἱείητε, ἱεῖτε	ἵετε	
	3	ἱᾶσι, ἱεῖσι	ἱῶσι	ἱείησαν, ἱεῖεν	ἱέτωσαν, ἱέντων	
D	2	ἵετον	ἱῆτον	ἱείητον, ἱεῖτον	ἵετον	
	3			ἱειήτην, ἱείτην	ἱέτων	

		Imperfect.	Aorist I.	Aorist II.				
			Ind.	Ind.	Subj.	Opt.	Imp.	Inf.
S	1	ἵην, ἵουν (ἵειν)	ἧκα	*	ὧ	εἵην		εἶναι
	2	ἵης, ἵεις	ἧκας	*	ᾗς	εἵης	ἕς	
	3	ἵη, ἵει	ἧκε	*	ᾗ	εἵη, &c.	ἕτω	Part
P.	1	ἵεμεν	ἥκαμεν	εἶμεν	ὧμεν			εἵς
	2	ἵετε	ἥκατε	εἶτε	ἧτε		ἕτε	
	3	ἵεσαν	ἧκαν	εἶσαν	ὧσι		ἕτωσαν, ἕντων	
D	2	ἵετον		εἶτον	ἧτον		ἕτον	
	3	ἱέτην		εἵτην			ἕτων	

Future, ἥσω. Perfect, εἶκα. Pluperfect, εἵκειν.

MIDDLE AND PASSIVE VOICES.

Present.

		Ind.	Subj.	Opt.	Imp.	Inf.
S	1	ἵεμαι	ἱῶμαι	ἱείμην, ἱοίμην		ἵεσθαι
	2	ἵεσαι, ἵῃ	ἱῇ	ἵειο, ἵοιο	ἵεσο, ἵου	
	3	ἵεται	ἱῆται	ἵειτο, ἵοιτο	ἱέσθω	Part.
		&c.	&c.	&c. &c.	&c.	ἱέμενος

		Imperfect.	Aorist II. Middle.				
			Ind.	Subj.	Opt.	Imp.	Inf.
S.	1	ἱέμην	εἵμην	ὧμαι	οἵμην		ἕσθαι
	2	ἵεσο, ἵου	εἶσο	ᾗ	οἷο	οὗ	
	3	ἵετο	εἶτο	ἧται	οἷτο	ἕσθω	Part.
		&c.	&c.	&c.	&c.	&c.	ἕμενος

Fut. Mid. ἥσομαι. 1 Aor. Mid. ἡκάμην. Perf. εἶμαι. Plup εἵμην. Aor. Pass. εἵθην. Fut. Pass. ἑθήσομαι.

¶ 55. 8. Εἰμί, *to be.*

PRESENT.

	Ind.	Subj.	Opt.	Imp.	Inf.
S. 1	εἰμί	ὦ	εἴην		εἶναι
2	εἶς, εἶ	ᾖς	εἴης	ἴσθι	
3	ἐστί	ᾖ	εἴη	ἔστω (ἤτω)	
P. 1	ἐσμέν	ὦμεν	εἴημεν, εἶμεν		Part.
2	ἐστέ	ἦτε	εἴητε, εἶτε	ἔστε	ὤν
3	εἰσί	ὦσι	εἴησαν, εἶεν	ἔστωσαν,	οὖσα
				ἔστων, ὄντων	ὄν
D. 2	ἐστόν	ἦτον	εἴητον, εἶτον	ἔστον	ὄντος
3			εἰήτην, εἴτην	ἔστων	οὔσης

	IMPERFECT.	FUTURE. Ind.	Opt.	Inf.
S. 1	ἦν, ἦ, ἤμην	ἔσομαι	ἐσοίμην	ἔσεσθαι
2	ἦς, ἦσθα	ἔσῃ, ἔσει	ἔσοιο	
3	ἦν	ἔσεται, ἔσται	ἔσοιτο	Part.
P. 1	ἦμεν	ἐσόμεθα	ἐσοίμεθα	ἐσόμενος
2	ἦτε, ἦστε	ἔσεσθε	ἔσοισθε	ἐσομένη
3	ἦσαν	ἔσονται	ἔσοιντο	ἐσόμενον
D. 2	ἦτον, ἦστον	ἔσεσθον	ἔσοισθον	
3	ἤτην, ἤστην		ἐσοίσθην	

DIALECTIC FORMS.

PRESENT.

Ind.	Subj.	Imp.	Part.
S. 1 ἐμμί D.	S. 1 ἔω I.	S. 2 ἔσο, ἔσσο P.	M. ἐών I.
2 εἶς I.	εἴω E.	Inf.	F. ἐοῦσα I.
ἐσσί P.	3 ᾖσι E.	ἔμεν E.	ἐοῖσα D.
3 ἐντί D.	ἔῃσι E.	ἔμεναι E.	εὖσα D.
P. 1 εἰμέν I.	P. 1 ὦμες D.	ἔμμεν P.	ἔᾶσα D.
εἰμές D.	3 ἔωσι I.	ἔμμεναι E. Æ.	N. ἐόν I.
ἐμέν P.	Opt.	ἦμεν D.	Gen.
3 ἐντί D.	S. 2 εἴησθα P.	εἶμεν D.	ἐόντος I.
ἔᾶσι E.	ἔοις, 3 ἔοι I.	εἶμεναι D.	εὖντος D.

IMPERFECT.

S. 1 ἔην E.	S. 2 ἔης P.	S. 3 ἔην I.	P. 3 ἔσαν I. P.
ἔον E.	ἔησθα E.	ἦς D.	ἔσσαν P.
ἔσκον It.	ἔας I.	ἔσκε It.	ἔσκον It.
ἔα I.	3 ἤην E.	P. 1 ἦμες D.	ἔασαν I.
ἦα I.	ἦε(ν) I.	2 ἔατε I.	εἴατο E.

Dialectic Forms of εἰμί, *to be*.

Future Ind.

S. 1	ἔσσομαι E.		S. 3	ἔσεται E.		P. 1	ἐσόμεσθα P.
2	ἔσεαι I.			ἔσσεται E.			ἐσσόμεθα E.
	ἔσσεαι E.			ἐσεῖται D.		2	ἔσσεσθε E.
	ἔσσῃ P.			ἐσσεῖται D.		3	ἔσσονται E.
	ἐσσῇ D.						ἐσοῦνται D

¶ 56. 9. *Εἶμι, to go.*

Present.

	Ind.	Subj.	Opt.	Imp.	Inf.	Part
S. 1	εἶμι	ἴω	ἴοιμι, ἰοίην		ἰέναι	ἰών
2	εἶς, εἶ	ἴῃς	ἴοις	ἴθι (εἶ)		ἰοῦσα
3	εἶσι	ἴῃ	ἴοι	ἴτω		ἰόν
P. 1	ἴμεν	ἴωμεν	ἴοιμεν			
2	ἴτε	ἴητε	ἴοιτε	ἴτε		
3	ἴᾱσι	ἴωσι	ἴοιεν	ἴτωσαν, ἰόντων, ἴτων		
D. 2	ἴτον	ἴητον	ἴοιτον	ἴτον		
3			ἰοίτην	ἴτων		

Pluperfect II., or Imperfect.

	S.	P.	D.
1	ᾔειν, ᾖα (ἤϊα)	ᾔειμεν, ᾖμεν	
2	ᾔεις, ᾔεισθα	ᾔειτε, ᾖτε	ᾔειτον, ᾖτον
3	ᾔει(ν)	ᾔεσαν	ᾐείτην, ᾔτην

Middle (*to hasten*). Present, ἵεμαι. Imperfect, ἱέμην.

Dialectic Forms.

Present.

Ind.		Subj.		Opt.		Inf.
S. 2	εἶς I.	S. 1	εἴω P.	S. 3	εἴη E.	ἴμεν E. D.
	εἶσθα E.	2	ἴῃσθα E.		ἰείη E.	ἴμεναι E.
		3	ἴῃσι E.			ἴμμεναι E.
P. 3	εἶσι P.	P. 1	ἴομεν E.			ἴναι P.

Imperfect.

S. 1	ἤϊα I.	P. 1	ἤομεν E.	D. 3	ἴτην E.
3	ἤϊε I.	3	ἴσαν E.		
	ᾖε E.		ἤϊσαν I.		
	ἴε E.		ἤϊον E.		

Mid. Fut. εἴσομαι, Aor. εἰσάμην, Ep. (§ 252).

¶ 57. Pure Verbs. iii. Second Aorists.

1. Aorist II. of *βαίνω*, *to go*.

	Ind.	Subj.	Opt.	Imp.	Inf.
S. 1	ἔβην	βῶ	βαίην		βῆναι
2	ἔβης	βῇς	βαίης	βῆθι (βᾶ)	
3	ἔβη	βῇ	βαίη	βήτω	Part.
P. 1	ἔβημεν	βῶμεν	βαίημεν, βαῖμεν		βάς
2	ἔβητε	βῆτε	βαίητε, βαῖτε	βῆτε	
3	ἔβησαν	βῶσι	βαίησαν, βαῖεν	βήτωσαν, βάντων	
D 2	ἔβητον	βῆτον	βαίητον, βαῖτον	βῆτον	
3	ἐβήτην		βαιήτην, βαίτην	βήτων	

2. Aorist II. of *ἀποδιδράσκω*, *to run away*.

	Ind.	Subj.	Opt.	Inf.
S. 1	ἀπέδρᾱν	ἀποδρῶ	ἀποδραίην	ἀποδρᾶναι
2	ἀπέδρᾱς	ἀποδρᾷς	ἀποδραίης	
3	ἀπέδρᾱ	ἀποδρᾷ	ἀποδραίη	Part.
P. 1	ἀπέδρᾱμεν	ἀποδρῶμεν	&c.	ἀποδράς
2	ἀπέδρᾱτε	ἀποδρᾶτε		
3	ἀπέδρᾱσαν	ἀποδρῶσι		
D. 2	ἀπέδρᾱτον	ἀποδρᾶτον		
3	ἀπεδράτην			

3. Aorist II. of *γιγνώσκω*, *to know*.

	Ind.	Subj.	Opt.	Imp.	Inf.
S. 1	ἔγνων	γνῶ	γνοίην (γνῴην)		γνῶναι
2	ἔγνως	γνῷς	γνοίης	γνῶθι	
3	ἔγνω	γνῷ	γνοίη	γνώτω	Part.
P. 1	ἔγνωμεν	γνῶμεν	γνοίημεν, γνοῖμεν		γνούς
2	ἔγνωτε	γνῶτε	γνοίητε, γνοῖτε	γνῶτε	
3	ἔγνωσαν	γνῶσι	γνοίησαν, γνοῖεν	γνώτωσαν, γνόντων	
D. 2	ἔγνωτον	γνῶτον	γνοίητον, γνοῖτον	γνῶτον	
3	ἐγνώτην		γνοιήτην, γνοίτην	γνώτων	

4. Aorist II. of *δύνω*, *to enter*, *to put on*.

	Ind.	Subj.	Opt.	Imp.	Inf.
S. 1	ἔδῡν	δύω	δύοιμι		δῦναι
2	ἔδῡς	δύῃς	δύοις	δῦθι	
3	ἔδῡ	δύῃ	δύοι	δύτω	Part.
P 1	ἔδῡμεν	δύωμεν	δύοιμεν		δύς
2	ἔδῡτε	δύητε	δύοιτε	δῦτε	
3	ἔδῡσαν	δύωσι	δύοιεν	δύτωσαν, δύντων	
D. 2	ἔδῡτον	δύητον	δύοιτον	δῦτον	
3	ἐδύτην		δυοίτην	δύτων	

7

¶ 58. XV. (E.) Preteritive Verbs.

1. Οἶδα, *to know.*

Perfect II.

		Ind.		Subj.	Opt.	Imp.	Inf.
S	1	οἶδα		εἰδῶ	εἰδείην		εἰδέναι
	2	οἶδας,	οἶσθα	εἰδῇς	εἰδείης	ἴσθι	
	3	οἶδε		εἰδῇ	εἰδείη	ἴστω	Part.
P.	1	οἴδαμεν,	ἴσμεν	εἰδῶμεν	&c.		εἰδώς
	2	οἴδατε,	ἴστε	εἰδῆτε		ἴστε	
	3	οἴδᾱσι,	ἴσᾱσι	εἰδῶσι		ἴστωσαν	
D.	2	οἴδατον,	ἴστον	εἰδῆτον		ἴστον 3 ἴστων	

Pluperfect II.

S.	1	ᾔδειν,	ᾔδη	P. ᾔδειμεν,	ᾖσμεν	D.	
	2	ᾔδεις,	ᾔδης,	ᾔδειτε,	ᾖστε	ᾔδειτον,	ᾖστον
		ᾔδεισθα,	ᾔδησθα				
	3	ᾔδει(ν),	ᾔδη	ᾔδεσαν,	ᾖσαν	ᾐδείτην,	ᾔστην

Future, εἴσομαι, εἰδήσω. Aorist, εἴδησα.

2. Δέδοικα or δέδια, *to be afraid.*

		Perfect II.				Pluperf. II.
		Ind.	Subj.	Imp.	Inf.	
S.	1	δέδια	δεδίω		δεδιέναι	ἐδεδίειν
	2	δέδιας	δεδίῃς	δέδιθι		ἐδεδίεις
	3	δέδιε	δεδίῃ	δεδίτω	Part.	ἐδεδίει
P.	1	δέδιμεν	δεδίωμεν		δεδιώς	ἐδέδιμεν
	2	δέδιτε	δεδίητε	δέδιτε		ἐδέδιτε
	3	δεδίᾱσι	δεδίωσι	δεδίτωσαν		ἐδέδισαν
D.	2	δέδιτον	δεδίητον	δέδιτον		ἐδέδιτον
	3			δεδίτων		ἐδεδίτην

1 Perf. δέδοικα. 1 Pluperf. ἐδεδοίκειν. Fut. δείσομαι. Aor. ἔδεισα.

¶ 59. 3. Ἧμαι, *to sit.*

		Perfect.				Pluperfect.
		Ind.	Imp.	Inf.	Part.	
S.	1	ἧμαι		ἧσθαι	ἥμενος	ἥμην
	2	ἧσαι	ἧσο			ἧσο
	3	ἧσται	ἥσθω			ἧστο
P.	1	ἥμεθα				ἥμεθα
	2	ἧσθε	ἧσθε			ἧσθε
	3	ἧνται	ἥσθωσαν, ἥσθων			ἧντο
D.	2	ἧσθον	ἧσθον 3 ἥσθων			ἧσθον 3 ἥσθην

INTRODUCTION.

§ 1. The Ancient Greeks were divided into three principal races; the Ionic, of which the Attic was a branch, the Doric, and the Æolic. These races spoke the same general language, but with many dialectic peculiarities.

The Ancient Greek Language (commonly called simply *the Greek*) has been accordingly divided by grammarians into four principal Dialects, the Attic, the Ionic, the Doric, and the Æolic. Of these the Attic and Ionic were far the most refined, and had far the greatest unity within themselves. The Doric and Æolic were not only much ruder, but, as the dialects of races widely extended, and united by no common bond of literature, abounded in local diversities. Some of the varieties of the Doric or Æolic were separated from each other by differences scarcely less marked than those which distinguished them in common from the other dialects. Of the Æolic, the principal varieties were the Lesbian, the Bœotian, and the Thessalian. The Doric, according as it was more or less removed from the Attic and Ionic, was characterized as the *stricter* or the *milder* Doric; the former prevailing in the Laconic, Tarentine, Cretan, Cyrenian, and some other varieties; the latter in the Corinthian, Syracusan, Megarian, Delphian, Rhodian, and some others.

§ 2. The Greek colonies upon the coast of Asia Minor and the adjacent islands, from various causes, took the lead of the mother country in refinement; and the first development of Greek literature which secured permanence for its productions, was among the Asiatic Ionians. This development was Epic Poetry, and we have, doubtless, its choicest strains remaining to us in the still unsurpassed Homeric poems. The language of these poems, often called *Epic* and *Homeric*, is the old Ionic, with those modifications and additions which a wandering bard would insensibly gather up, as he sang from city to city, and those poetic licenses which are always allowed to early minstrelsy, when as yet the language is unfixed, and critics are unknown. Epic poetry was followed in Ionia by the Elegiac, of which Callinus of Ephesus and Mimnermus of Colophon were two great masters; and this again by Ionic Prose, in which the two principal names are Herodotus and Hippocrates, who chose this refined dialect, although themselves of Doric descent. In distinction from the Old Ionic of the Epic poets the language of the Elegiac poets may be termed the Middle Ionic, and that of the prose-writers, the New Ionic.

§ **3.** The next dialect which attained distinction in literature was the Æolic of Lesbos, in which the lyric strains of Alcæus and Sappho were sung. But its distinction was short-lived, and we have scarce any thing remaining of the dialect except some brief fragments. There arose later among the Æolians of Bœotia another school of Lyric Poetry, of which Pindar was the most illustrious ornament. As writing, however for the public festivals of Greece, he rejected the peculiarities of his rude native tongue, and wrote in a dialect of which the basis consisted of words and forms common to the Doric and Æolic, but which was greatly enriched from the now universally familiar Epic. He is commonly said, but loosely, to have written in the Doric.

§ **4.** Meanwhile, the Athenians, a branch of the Ionian race, were gradually rising to such political and commercial importance, and to such intellectual preëminence among the states of Greece, that their dialect, adorned by such dramatists as Æschylus, Sophocles, Euripides, Aristophanes, and Menander, by such historians as Thucydides and Xenophon, by such philosophers as Plato and Aristotle, and by such orators as Lysias Æschines, and Demosthenes, became at length the standard language of the Greeks, and, as such, was adopted by the educated classes in all the states. It became the general medium of intercourse, and, with a few exceptions, which will be hereafter noticed, the universal language of composition. This diffusion of the Attic dialect was especially promoted by the conquests of the Macedonians, who adopted it as their court language. As its use extended, it naturally lost some of its peculiarities, and received many additions; and thus diffused and modified, it ceased to be regarded as the language of a particular state, and received the appellation of the COMMON DIALECT OF LANGUAGE.

The Attic and Common dialects, therefore, do not differ in

any essential feature, and may properly be regarded, the one as the earlier and pure, the other as the later and impure, form of the same dialect. In this dialect, either in its earlier or later form, we find written nearly the whole that remains to us of ancient Greek literature. It may claim therefore to be regarded, notwithstanding a few splendid compositions in the other dialects, as the national language of Greece; and its acquisition should form the commencement and the basis of Greek study.

The pure Attic has been divided into three periods; the *Old*, used by Thucydides, the Tragedians, and Aristophanes; the *Middle*, used by Xenophon and Plato; and the *New*, used by the Orators and the later Comedians. The period of the Common dialect may be regarded as commencing with the subjection of Athens to the Macedonians.

§ **5.** Of the Doric dialect, in proportion to its wide extent, we have very scanty remains; and of most of its varieties our knowledge is derived from passages in Attic writers, from monuments, and from the works of grammarians. In Greece itself, it seems scarcely to have been applied to any other branch of literature than Lyric Poetry. In the more refined Dorian colonies of Italy and Sicily, it was employed in Philosophy by the Pythagoreans (Archytas, Timæus, &c.), in Mathematics by the great Archimedes, in Comedy by Epicharmus and his successors, and in Pastoral Poetry by Theocritus, Bion, and Moschus.

§ **6.** To the universality acquired by the Attic dialect, an exception must be made in poetry. Here the later writers felt constrained to imitate the language of the great early models. The Epic poet never felt at liberty to depart from the dialect of Homer. Indeed, the old Epic language was regarded by subsequent poets in all departments as a sacred tongue, *the language of the gods*, from which they might enrich their several compositions. The Æolic and Doric held such a place in Lyric Poetry, that even upon the Attic stage an Æolo-Doric hue was given to the lyric portions by the use of the long α, which formed so marked a characteristic of those dialects, and which, by its openness of sound, was so favorable to musical effect. Pastoral Poetry was confined to the Doric. The Dramatic was the only department of poetry in which the Attic was the standard dialect.

§ **7.** Grammar flourished only in the decline of the Greek language, and the Greek grammarians usually treated the dialects with little precision. Whatever they found in the old Ionic of Homer that seemed to them more akin to the later cultivated Æolic, Doric, or even Attic, than to the new Ionic they did not hesitate to ascribe to those dialects. Even in the common language, whatever appeared to them irregular or peculiar, they usually referred to one of the old dialects, terming the regular form *κοινόν*, *common*, though perhaps this form was either wholly unused, or was found only as a dialectic variety On the other hand, some critics used the appellation *κοινός* as a term of reproach, designating by it that which was not pure Attic. In the following Grammar, an attempt will be made to exhibit first and distinctly, under each head, the Greek in its standard form, that is, the Attic and the purer Common usage; and afterwards to specify the important dialectic peculiarities. It will not, however, be understood that every thing which is ascribed to one of the dialects prevails in that dialect throughout, or is found in no other. This applies especially to the Doric and Æolic, which, with great variety within themselves (§ 1), are closely akin to each other; so that some (as Maittaire) have treated of both under the general head of Doric; and in the following Grammar some forms will be simply mentioned as Doric, that also occur in the Æolic. By the term Æolic, as employed by grammarians, is commonly denoted the cultivated Æolic of Lesbos; as the term Ionic is usually confined to the language spoken (though, according to Herodotus, with four varieties) by the Ionians of Asia Minor and the adjacent islands.

§ **8.** It remains to notice the modifications of the later Greek. The Macedonians, who had previously spoken a rude and semi-barbarous dialect of the Greek, retained and diffused some of the peculiarities of their native tongue. These are termed *Macedonic*, or, sometimes, from Alexandria, the principal seat of Macedonian, and indeed of later Greek culture, *Alexandrine*.

The Greek, as the common language of the civilized world, was employed in the translation of the Jewish Scriptures, and the composition of the Christian. When so employed by native Jews, it naturally received a strong Hebrew coloring; and, as a Jew speaking Greek was called *Ἑλληνιστής* (from *ἑλληνίζω*, *to speak Greek*), this form of the language has been termed the *Hellenistic* (or by some the *Ecclesiastical*) dialect. Its peculiarities naturally passed more or less into the writings of the fathers, and through the diffusion of Christianity exerted a great general influence.

Another influence modifying the Greek came from the language of the Roman conquerors of the world. Of necessity, the Greek, notwithstanding the careful compositions of such scholars as Arrian, Lucian, and Ælian, and the precepts of a class of critics, called Atticists, was continually becoming more and more impure. The language of the Byzantine period was especially degenerate. Since the destruction of the Eastern Empire by the Turks, the fusion of the Byzantine and Ecclesiastical Greek with the popular dialects of the different districts and islands of Greece has produced the MODERN GREEK, or, as it is often called, by a name derived from the Roman Empire in the East, ROMAÏC. This language has been especially cultivated and refined within the present century, and has now a large body of original and translated literature.

§ **9.** The Greek, therefore, in its various forms, has never ceased to be a living language; and it offers to the student a series of compositions, not only including many of the highest productions of genius, but extending through a period of nearly three thousand years.

BOOK I.

ORTHOGRAPHY AND ORTHOËPY.

Γραμμάτων τε συνθέσεις
Ἐξεῦρον αὐτοῖς.

Æschylus, Prom. Vinct.

CHAPTER I.

CHARACTERS.

[¶¶ 1, 2.]

§ **10.** The Greek language is written with *twenty-four letters*, *two breathings*, *three accents*, *four marks of punctuation*, and a few other characters.

1. For the Letters, see Table, ¶ 1.

Remarks. 1. Double Forms. Sigma *final* is written ς; *not final*, σ; as, στάσις. In compound words, some editors, without authority from manuscripts, use ς at the end of each component word; thus, προςεισφέρεις. The other double forms are used indifferently; as, βοῦς or ϐοῦς

2. Ligatures. Two or more letters are often united, except in recent editions, into one character, called a *ligature* (ligatūra, *tie*); as, ϗ for καὶ, ȣ for ου, σθ for σθ, ϛ (named στὶ or στίγμα) for στ. For a list of the principal ligatures, see Table, ¶ 2.

§ **11.** 3. Numeral Power. To denote numbers under a thousand, the Greeks employed the letters of the alphabet, as exhibited in the table, with the mark (ʹ) over them; as, αʹ 1, ιʹ 10, ιβʹ 12, ρκγʹ 123. The first eight letters, with Vau, represented the nine units; the next eight, with Koppa, the nine tens; and the last eight, with Sampi, the nine hundreds. The thousands were denoted by the same letters with the mark *beneath* · as, εʹ 5, ͵ε 5,000, κγʹ 23, ͵κ͵γ or κ͵γ 23,000, ͵αωμά 1841.

NOTES. *α*. Vau, in its usual small form (ϛ), resembles the ligature for στ (§ 10). Hence some editors confound them, and employ ΣΤ, as the large form of Vau, to denote 6.

β. Sometimes the Greek letters, like our own, denote ordinal numbers, according to their own order in the alphabet. In this way the books of Homer are marked; as, Ἰλιάδος, Α, Ζ, Ω, *The Iliad, Books I., VI., XXIV.*

γ. Another method of writing numerals occurs in old inscriptions, by which Ι denotes *one*, Π (for Πέντε) *five*, Δ (for Δέκα) *ten*, Η (for Ηεκατόν, § 22. α) *a hundred*, Χ (for Χίλιοι) *a thousand*, Μ (for Μύριοι) *ten thousand*. Π drawn around another numeral multiplies it by five. Thus, ΜΧΧ[Π with Η]ΗΗ[Π with Δ]ΔΔΙΙΙ = 12,676.

§ 12. 4. ROMAN LETTERS. By the side of the Greek letters in the table (¶ 1), are placed the Roman letters which take their place when Greek words are transferred into Latin or English; as, *Κύκλωψ*, *Cyclops*.

NOTES. *α*. The letter *γ* becomes *n*, when followed by another palatal; but, otherwise, *g*; as, ἄγγελος, Lat. *angelus*, Eng. *angel*; συγκοπή, *syncope*; λάρυγξ, *larynx*; Αἴγῑνα, *Ægīna*.

β. The *diphthong* αι becomes in Latin *æ*; οι, *œ*; ει, ῑ or ē (before a consonant almost always ῑ); ου, ū; and υι, *yi*; as, Φαῖδρος, *Phædrus*; Βοιωτία, *Bœotia*; Νεῖλος, *Nīlus*; Δαρεῖος, *Darīus*; Μήδεια, *Medēa*; Μοῦσα, *Mūsa*, Εἰλείθυια, *Ilithyia*.

A few words ending in αια and οια are excepted; as, Μαῖα, *Maia*, Τροία, *Troia* or *Troja*; so also Αἴας, *Ajax*.

γ. The improper diphthongs ᾳ, ῃ, ῳ, are written in Latin simply *a, e, o*; as, Θρᾴκη, *Thrācē*, ᾍδης, *Hādēs*, Θρῇσσα, *Thressa*, ᾠδή, *ōdē*. But in a few compounds of ᾠδή, ῳ becomes *œ*; as, τραγῳδία, *tragœdia*, Eng. *tragedy*.

δ. The *rough breathing* becomes, in Latin and English, *h*, while the *smooth* is not written; as, Ἕκτωρ, *Hector*, Ἔρυξ, *Eryx*, Ῥέα, *Rhea* (the *h* being placed after the *r* by the same inaccuracy as after the *w* in our *while*, pronounced *hoo-ile*; since in both cases the breathing introduces the word).

§ 13. II. The BREATHINGS are the SMOOTH or SOFT (᾿), and the ROUGH (῾), also called the ASPIRATE (aspīro, *to breathe*). The first denotes a gentle emission of the breath, such as must precede every initial vowel; the second, a strong emission, such as in English is represented by *h*. One of these is placed over every *initial vowel*, and over every *initial* or *doubled* ρ.

NOTES. 1. An *initial* υ has always the rough breathing to assist in its utterance (as in English an initial long *u* is always preceded by the sound of *y*; thus, ὗς, ὑμεῖς, as, in English, *use*, pronounced *yuse*, *union*); except in the Æolic dialect, and in the Epic forms ὔμμες, ὔμμι or ὔμμιν, ὔμμε.

2. An *initial* ϱ requires, for its proper vibration or rolling, a strong aspiration, and is therefore always marked with the rough breathing; as, ῥέω. When ϱ is *doubled*, the first ϱ has the smooth breathing, and the second the rough; as, Πύῤῥος. See § 62. β.

3. In diphthongs (except ᾳ, ῃ, and ῳ), the breathing is placed over the second vowel; as, αὐτός, οὗτος. See § 26.

4. In place of the rough breathing, the Æolic seems commonly, and the Epic often, to have used the digamma (§ 22. δ), or the smooth breathing. In Homer we find the smooth for the rough particularly in words which are strengthened in some other way; as, εὔκηλος, οὖλος, οὖρος, ἠέλιος, ὔμμες, for ἕκηλος, ὅλος, ὅρος, ἥλιος, ὑμεῖς.

§ 14. III. The ACCENTS are the ACUTE (′), the GRAVE (\`), and the CIRCUMFLEX (˜ or ˆ). For their use, see Prosody.

§ 15. IV. The MARKS OF PUNCTUATION are the COMMA (,), the COLON (·), the PERIOD (.), and the NOTE OF INTERROGATION (;), which has the form of ours (?) inverted.

To these, some editors have judiciously added the NOTE OF EXCLAMATION (!).

§ 16. V. OTHER CHARACTERS.

1. CORONIS and APOSTROPHE. The mark (᾿), which at the *beginning* of a word is the *smooth breathing*, over the *middle* is the CORONIS (κορωνίς, *crooked mark*), or *mark of crasis*, and at the *end*, the APOSTROPHE (§ 30); as, ταὐτά for τὰ αὐτά, ἀλλ᾿ ἐγώ for ἀλλὰ ἐγώ.

2. The HYPODIASTOLE (ὑποδιαστολή, *separation beneath*), or DIASTOLE (διαστολή, *separation*), is a mark like a comma, placed, for distinction's sake, after some forms of the article and relative pronoun, when followed by the enclitics τέ and τὶ; as, ὅ,τε, τό,τε, ὅ,τι, to distinguish them from the particles ὅτε, τότε, ὅτι. Some editors more wisely omit it, and merely separate the enclitic by a space.

3. The HYPHEN, DIÆRESIS, DASH, and MARKS OF PARENTHESIS and QUOTATION are used in Greek as in English.

4. Among the other signs used by critics and editors, are BRACKETS [ ], to inclose words of doubtful authenticity; the OBELISK († or —), to mark verses or words as faulty; the ASTERISK (*), to denote that something is wanting in the text; and MARKS OF QUANTITY, viz. (¯), to mark a vowel or syllable as *long*; (˘), as *short*; (⏔ or ⏕), as *either long or short.*

PRONUNCIATION.

§ 17. There are three methods of pronouncing Greek which deserve notice; the ENGLISH, the MODERN GREEK, and the ERASMIAN.

The pronunciation of every language, from the very laws of language, is in a continual process of change, more or less rapid. And in respect to the Greek, there is full internal evidence, both that its pronunciation had materially changed before its orthography became fixed, and that it has materially changed since. Therefore, as there is no art of embalming sounds, the ancient pronunciation of the Greek can now only be inferred, and, in part, with great uncertainty. Modern scholars have commonly pronounced it according to the analogy of their respective languages. The English method, which has prevailed in the schools of England and this country, conforms, in general, to the analogy of our own tongue, and to our method of pronouncing the Latin. The Modern Greek method (also called the Reuchlinian, from its distinguished advocate, the learned Reuchlin) is that which now prevails in Greece itself. It is given below, as exhibited in the Grammar of Sophocles. The Erasmian method (so named from the celebrated Erasmus) is that which is most extensively followed in the schools upon the continent of Europe, and which conforms most nearly to the prevailing analogy of the continental tongues.

NOTE. To avoid confusion, the terms *protracted* and *abrupt* are employed below to denote what, in English orthoëpy, we commonly call *long* and *short* sounds; and the term *ictus* (*stroke*, *beat*), to denote that stress of the voice which in English we commonly call *accent*. For the proper use of the terms *long* and *short*, and *accent*, in Greek grammar, see Prosody.

A. ENGLISH METHOD.

§ 18. 1. SIMPLE VOWELS. η, υ, and ω have always the protracted sounds of *e* in *mete*, *u* in *tube*, and *o* in *note*; as, θηρσί, τύπτω, σφῶν.

ε and ο have the abrupt sounds of *e* in *let*, and *o* in *dot*; except before another vowel, and at the end of a word, where they are protracted, like *e* in *real*, and *o* in *go*; as, λέγω, λόγος· θεός, νόος· δέ, τό.

α and ι are, in general, sounded like *a* and *i* in English; when protracted, like *a* in *hate*, and *i* in *pine*; when abrupt, like *a* in *hat*, and *i* in *pin*. At the end of a word, ι always maintains its protracted sound; but α, except in monosyllables, takes the indistinct sound of *a* in *Columbia*; as, θηρί, λέοντι· πρᾶγμα, φιλία· τά.

NOTE. If α or ι receives the *ictus*, whether primary or secondary, and is followed by a single consonant or ζ, it is protracted in the penult, but abrupt in any preceding syllable; as, ἄγω, ἐλπίζω· γράφετε, φιλέω, Ἀθηναῖος. From this rule is excepted α in any syllable preceding the penult, when the vowel of the next syllable is ε or ι before another vowel (both without the ictus), in which case α is protracted; as, πατέω, νεανίας, γαλεομυομαχία.

2. Diphthongs. The diphthongs are, for the most part, pronounced according to the prevailing sound of the same combinations in our own language; ει like *ei* in *height*, οι like *oi* in *boil*, υι like *ui* in *quiet*, αυ like *au* in *aught*, ευ and ηυ like *eu* in *Europe*, *neuter*, ου and ωυ like *ou* in *thou*; αι is sounded like the affirmative *ay* (*ah-ee*, the two sounds uttered with a single impulse of the voice), and υἱ like *whi* in *while*. Thus, εἰδυῖα αὐτοί, πλευσοῦμαι, ηὖξον, θωῦμα, υἱός.

3. Consonants. The consonants are pronounced like the corresponding letters in our own alphabet, with the following special remarks.

γ, κ, and χ are always hard in sound: γ being pronounced like *g* in *go* (except before a palatal, where it has the sound of *ng* in *long*, § 49); κ and χ like *c* in *cap*, and *ch* in *chaos*, i. e. like *k*; as, γένος, ἄγγος (pron. *ang-gos*), κῆρυξ, χέω.

θ has the sharp sound of *th* in *thin*; as, θεός.

σ has the sharp sound of *s* in *say*; except in the middle of a word before μ, and at the end of a word after η and ω, where it sounds like *z*; as, σβέσαι· κόσμος, τῆς, ὡς.

σ and τ never have the sound of *sh*; thus Ἀσία is pronounced *A'-si-a*, not *A'-shi-a*; Κριτίας, *Krit'-i-as*, not *Krish'-i-as*.

At the beginning of a word, ξ sounds like *z*, and ψ like *s*; and, of two consonants which cannot both be pronounced with ease, the first is silent; as, Ξενοφῶν, ψηφίζω, Πτολεμαῖος, βδέλλιον. So, in English, *xebec*, *psalm*, &c.

4. Breathings. The *rough* has the sound of *h*; the *smooth* has no sound; as, ὅρος, ὄρος. See § 13.

5. Ictus. The primary ictus is placed according to the following

Rule. In *dissyllables*, the *penult* takes the ictus. In *polysyllables*, the penult, if *long*, takes the ictus; but, if *short*, throws it upon the antepenult. Thus, πατήρ, pron. *pa'-tēr*, γράφητε, *gra-phē'-te*, γράφετε, *graph'-e-te*.

Note. If two or more syllables precede the primary ictus, one of these, receives a secondary ictus, in placing which the ear and formation of the word will decide.

B. Modern Greek Method.

§ 19. "α and ᾳ are pronounced like *a* in *father*; after the sound I (ι, η, ει, οι, υ, υι) it is pronounced like *a* in *peculiarity*. αι like ε. αυ, ευ, ηυ, ωυ, before a vowel, a liquid, or a middle mute (β, γ, δ) are pronounced like *av*, *ev*, *eev*, *ov*, respectively; in all other cases, like *af*, *ef*, *eef*, *off*. β like *v*. γ before the sounds E and I is pronounced nearly like *y* in *yes*, *York*; in all other cases it is guttural, like the German *g* in *Tag*. γγ and γκ like *ng* in *strongest*. γξ like *nx*. γχ like *ng-h*, nearly. δ like *th* in *that*. ε like *e* in *fellow*, nearly. ει like ι. ευ, see αυ. ζ like *z*. η and ῃ like ι. ηυ, see αυ. θ like *th* in *thin*. ι like *i* in *machine*. κ like *k*. λ like *l*; before the sound I, like *ll* in *William*. μ like *m*. μπ like *mb*, as, ἔμπροσθεν pronounced *émbrosthen.* μψ (μπσ) like *mbs.* ν like *n*; before the sound I, like *n* in *oNion.* The words τὸν, τὴν, ἐν, σὺν, before a word beginning with κ or ξ, are pronounced like τὸγ, τὴγ, ἐγ, σὺγ before κ or ξ (see γκ, γξ); e. g. τὸν καιρόν, ἐν ξυλόχῳ, pronounced τὸγκαιρόν, ἐγξυλόχῳ; before π or ψ they are pronounced τὸμ, τὴμ, ἐμ, σὺμ; e. g. τὸν πονηρόν, σὺν ψυχῇ, pronounced τὸμπονηρόν, σὺμψυχῇ. ντ like *nd*, as, ἔντιμος pronounced *éndimos.* ξ like *x* or *ks.* ο like *o* in *porter.* οι like ι. ου like *oo* in *moon.* π, ρ, like *p*, *r*. σ like *s* in *soft*; before β, γ, δ, μ, ρ, it is sounded like ζ; e. g. κόσμος, σβέσαι, Σμύρνη, pronounced κόζμος, ζβέσαι, Ζμύρνη; so also at the end of a word, τοὺς βασιλεῖς τῆς γῆς, pronounced τοὺζβασιλεῖς τῆζγῆς. τ like *t* in *tell.* υ like ι. υι like ι. φ like *ph* or *f.* χ like German *ch* or Spanish *j.* ψ like *ps.* ω and ῳ like *o.* ωυ, see αυ.

"The *rough breathing* is silent in Modern Greek. So far as *quantity* is concerned, all the short vowels are equivalent to the long ones. The written *accent* guides the stress of the voice. The accent of the *enclitic*, however, is disregarded in pronunciation. But when the attracting word has the accent on the antepenult, its last syllable takes the secondary accent; e. g. δεῖξόν μοι, pronounced δείξονμοι, but λέλεκταί μοι has the primary accent on the first syllable λε, and the secondary on κται."— *Soph. Gr. Gr.*, pp. 21, 22.

C. ERASMIAN METHOD.

§ **20.** The Erasmian method differs from the English chiefly in sounding α protracted like *a* in *father*, ι protracted like *i* in *machine*, η like *ey* in *they*, αυ like *ou* in *our*, ου like *ou* in *ragout*, υι like our pronoun *we*, and ζ like a soft *dz.*

HISTORY OF GREEK ORTHOGRAPHY.

§ **21.** That the Greek alphabet was borrowed from the Phœnician is abundantly established both by historical and by internal evidence.

According to common tradition, letters were first brought into Greece by Cadmus, a Phœnician, who founded Thebes. In illustration, we give the common Hebrew alphabet, which is substantially the same with the old Phœnician, placing the corresponding Greek letters by the side. It should be remarked, however, that the forms of the letters in both alphabets have undergone much change. It will be noticed that most of the Oriental names of the letters, when transferred to the Greek, require modification in accordance with the law respecting final letters (§ 63), and that this is commonly effected by adding α.

	Hebrew.			Greek.		Hebrew.			Greek.
א	Aleph	Α	α	Alpha	ל	Lamed	Λ	λ	Lambda
ב	Beth	Β	ϐ	Beta	מ	Mem	Μ	μ	Mu
ג	Gimel	Γ	γ	Gamma	נ	Nun	Ν	ν	Nu
ד	Daleth	Δ	δ	Delta	ס	Samech	Σ	σ	Sigma
ה	He	Ε	ε	E (psīlon)	ע	Ayin	Ο	ο	O (mīcron)
ו	Vau	Ϝ	F	Vau	פ	Pe	Π	π	Pi
ז	Zayin	Ζ	ζ	Zeta	צ	Tsade	Ξ	ξ	Xi
ח	Hheth	Η	η	Eta	ק	Koph	Ϙ		Koppa
ט	Teth	Θ	ϑ	Theta	ר	Resh	Ρ	ρ	Rho
י	Iod	Ι	ι	Iota	ש	Shin	ϡ		San or Sampi
כ	Kaph	Κ	κ	Kappa	ת	Tau	Τ	τ	Tau

§ **22.** This borrowed alphabet received in the course of time important modifications.

α. The original Phœnician alphabet had no proper vowels. The Greeks, therefore, employed as such those letters which were nearest akin to vowels, viz. A, E, F, H, I, and O. In the transition of these letters into vowels there appears to have been nothing arbitrary. A, as the soft or entirely open breathing, naturally passed into the most open and deepest of the vowels. E and H, as weaker and stronger forms of the palatal breathing, naturally became signs of the shorter and longer sounds of the palatal vowel *e*; in like manner, the lingual breathing I passed into the lingual vowel *i*, and the labial breathing F into the labial vowel *u* (compare *i* and *y*, or in some languages *j*, and also *u* and *v* or *w*); O appears to have been originally a nasal breathing, and was hence employed to represent the vowel most akin to a nasal, *o*. The aspirate use of E and F still continued for a period, and hence these letters when employed as vowels were distinguished by the addition of ψῖλόν, *smooth*; thus "Ε ψῖλόν, Ὗ ψῖλόν. It will be observed that the last of these letters, when used as a vowel, was somewhat changed in form, and was put at the end of the old alphabet. The aspirate use of H prevailed still later, even to the period of the highest Greek refinement, and when at length it had yielded to the vowel use, the grammarian Aristophanes of Byzantium, who flourished at the court of Alexandria, about 200 years B. C., is said to have divided the old character into the two marks, ⊢ for the rough, and ⊣ for the smooth breathing. These marks were abbreviated to ˪ ˩ or ˥ ˥, and were afterwards rounded to their present forms, ʽ ʼ. To the same Aristophanes has been ascribed the first use of marks of accent and punctuation.

β. The sibilants Σ, Ξ, and Ϡ exchanged places in the alphabet; so that Ξ came after N, Ϡ after Π (hence called Σαμπῖ, *the S which stood next to Pi*), and Σ after P.

γ. To the Phœnician alphabet, the Greeks added the aspirates Φ and X, the double consonant Ψ, and the sign for long *o*, Ω. These new letters they placed at the end. In distinction the short *o* was now termed "Ο μῖκρόν, *small O*; and the long *o*, Ὦ μέγα, *great O*. The names of the other new letters were formed by simply adding a vowel to aid in sounding them; thus, Φῖ, Χῖ, as, in English, *be*, *ce*.

δ. In the softening of the language, the labial breathing F, and also Ϙ and Ϡ, which were only rougher forms of K and Σ, fell into disuse, and these letters were retained only as numeral characters; F and Ϙ in their proper places in the alphabet, but Ϡ at the end. Thus employed, they were termed *Episēma* (ἐπίσημον, *sign, mark*). See ¶ 1, § 11.

F was also named from its form the *Digamma*, i. e. the double gamma; and from its being longest retained among the Æolians, the *Æolic Digamma*. It is still found upon some inscriptions and coins. In Latin it commonly appears as *v*; thus, Fιδεῖν, video, *to see*, Fοῖνος, vinum, *wine*. Its restoration by Bentley to the poems of Homer has removed so many apparent hiatuses and irregularities of metre, that we cannot doubt its existence in the time of Homer, though apparently even then beginning to lose its power. The general law in respect to the disappearance of F, appears to be the following: *Before a vowel or an initial ρ, it is usually dropped, or becomes one of the common breathings; but otherwise, it usually passes into the cognate vowel υ*; thus, βοFός, βοFί, βόFες (Lat. *bovis*, *bovi*, *boves*) become βοός, βοΐ, βόες; but βόFς, βόFν, βόF, βοFσί become βοῦς, βοῦν, βοῦ, βουσί (¶ 14).

§ 23. The alphabet in its present complete form was first adopted by the Ionians (cf. § 2), and hence termed Ἰωνικὰ γράμματα. In Attic inscriptions it was first used in the archonship of Euclīdes, B. C. 403.

The Greeks first wrote, like the Phœnicians, from right to left; and then alternately from left to right and right to left (as it was termed, βουστροφηδόν, i.e. *as the ox turns with the plough*). In this mode the laws of Solon were written. Herodotus, however (II. 36), speaks of the method of writing from left to right as the established custom of the Greeks in his time. Till a very late period the Greeks wrote entirely in capitals, and without marking the division of words. The small cursive character first appears in manuscripts in the eighth century, though there is evidence of its having been used earlier in the transactions of common life.

That there should be great variety in the orthography of the dialects results of necessity from the fact, that in each dialect words were written as they were pronounced. The Greeks had no standard of orthography until the prevalence of the Common dialect (§ 4).

CHAPTER II.

VOWELS.

[¶ 3.]

§ 24. The Greek has *five simple vowels*, and *seven diphthongs*. Each of the simple vowels may be either long or short, and each of the diphthongs may have either a long or short prepositive, or first vowel.

REMARKS. 1. Of three vowels, the long and short sounds are represented by the same letters (ᾰ, ᾱ; ῐ, ῑ; ῠ, ῡ); but of the other two, by different letters (ε̆, η̄; ŏ, ω̄).

NOTES. *α*. The long sounds of these two vowels occur far more frequently than those of the other three, and are hence distinguished by separate characters.

β. When speaking of letters, and not of sounds, we say that the Greek has seven vowels; and call ε and ο the *short vowels*, because they always represent short sounds, η and ω the *long vowels*, because they always represent long sounds, and α, ι, and υ, the *doubtful vowels*, because their form leaves it doubtful whether the sound is long or short.

γ. There is strong evidence, that, in general, these vowels were pronounced in the same manner as the corresponding vowels are now pronounced upon the continent of Europe; i. e. α, like *a* in *father*, *wall*, *fan* (not as in *hate*); η, ε, like *e* in *they*, *then* (not as in *mete*); ι like *i* in *machine*, *pin* (not as in *pine*); ω, ο, like *o* in *note*, *not*; υ like *u* in *tube*, *bull*. They will hence be thus placed upon the *scale of precession* or *attenuation*.

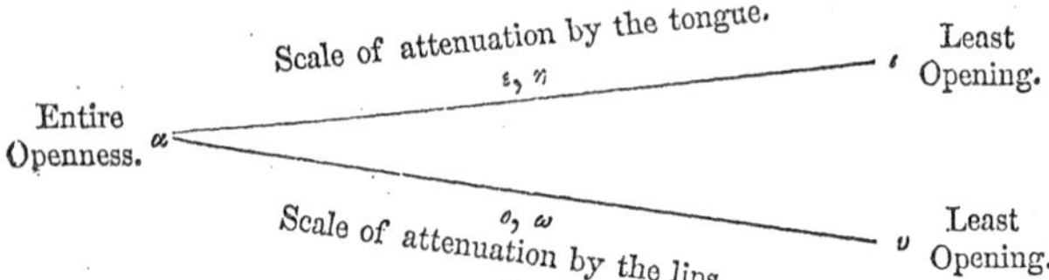

In general, α, ε, and ο are termed the *open*, and υ and ι the *close* vowels; but α is more open than ε and ο, and ι is somewhat closer than υ.

§ **25.** 2. In the Greek diphthongs, the voice always passes from a *more open* to a *closer* sound; and the subjunctive, or last vowel is always ι or υ. Hence the combinations possible are only *seven*, or, counting separately the proper and improper diphthongs, *fourteen*. Of these, ωυ scarcely occurs, except in the Ionic dialect.

A *short* prepositive left time for the full utterance of the subjunctive vowel, and the diphthong was then termed *proper*, as really combining two sounds; but a *long* prepositive nearly or quite crowded out the sound of the subjunctive, and the diphthong was then termed *improper*, as though diphthongal only in appearance.

3. After α long, η, and ω, the subjunctive ι so lost its sound, that it was at last merely written beneath the prepositive, if this was a small letter, and was then termed *iota subscript* (subscriptus, *written beneath*). With capitals, it still remains in the line, but is not sounded. Thus, ᾞΑιδης or ᾅδης, pron. *Hādēs*, Ἤιδη or ᾔδη, *ēdē*; Ὠιδή or ᾠδή, *ōdē*.

NOTES. α. The ι subscript is often written where it does not belong, from false views of etymology; as in the Epic dative θύρῃφι, for θύρηφι (¶ 8); and in the aorist of liquid verbs, which have αι in the penult of the theme; thus, from φαίνω, αἴρω (roots φαν-, ἀρ-), ἔφῃνα, ᾖρα, ᾄρω, for ἔφηνα, ἦρα, ἄρω · so Perf. II. πέφῃνα, for πέφηνα.

β. In some cases the best critics differ; thus, in the infinitive of verbs in -άω, some write τιμᾷν, as contracted from τιμάειν, and others τιμᾶν, as contracted from an older form τιμάεν. So in the adverbial forms πῇ, ὅπῃ, or πῆ, ὅπη, and the like.

§ **26.** 4. In diphthongs, except the three just mentioned (ᾳ, ῃ, and ῳ), the breathings and accents are written over the second vowel, and thus often mark the union of the two vowels · as, αὐτή, *herself*, but ἀϋτή, *cry*; ηὖδα, but ἤϋσε · αἵρεσις (ᾰ) but Ἅιδης (ᾱ).

If two vowels which might form a diphthong are pronounced separately the second is marked with a diæresis (§ 16. 3); as, ἀϋτή, ἤϋσε.

☞ For a full exhibition of the Greek vowels, simple and

compound, see the Table (¶ 3). They are there divided into *classes*, according to the simple sound which is their sole or leading element, as *A sounds*, &c.; and into *orders*, according to the length of this sound, or its combination with other sounds, as *short vowels*, &c. The classes are arranged according to the openness of the vowel from which they are named. Vowels belonging to the same class are termed *cognate*.

§ 27. The Greek vowels are subject to a great number of EUPHONIC CHANGES, which may be referred, for the most part, to two great heads, the PRECESSION OF VOWELS, and the UNION OF SYLLABLES.

These changes diminish the effort in speaking, by reducing the volume of sound employed, or by preventing hiatus, and lessening the number of syllables.

I. PRECESSION OF VOWELS.

§ 28. The great tendency in Greek to the precession or attenuation of vowel sounds shows itself,

1.) In the change of simple vowels.

Precession especially affects α, as the most open of the vowels, changing it, when short, to ε and ο, and, when long, to η, and sometimes to ω.

Hence these three vowels may be regarded as *kindred*, and are often interchanged in the formation and inflection of words. Thus, in the verbs τρέπω, στρέφω, we find the root in three forms, τραπ-, τρεπ-, and τροπ-, στραφ-, στρεφ-, and στροφ-; and in ῥήγνῡμι, we find the forms ῥαγ-, ῥηγ-, and ῥωγ-. This interchange is also illustrated by the connecting vowels inserted, for the sake of euphony, in the inflection of words. Thus, in the first declension, the connecting vowel is α, but in the second, ο, for which in one case ε appears. In the indicative active, the connecting vowel in the aorist and perfect is α (passing, however, into ε in the 3d pers. sing.; compare the imperative βούλευσον), while in the present, imperfect, and future, it is ο before a liquid, but otherwise ε.

§ 29. 2.) In the lengthening of the short vowels, and in the general laws of contraction. Thus,

α. The long vowel is regarded as the short vowel doubled that is, ᾱ = ᾰᾰ, η = εε, ω = οο, ῡ = ῠῠ, and ῑ = ῐῐ. Whenever, therefore, in the formation of words, a short vowel is lengthened, or two short vowels of the same class are united in sound, the corresponding long vowel ought to result. But through precession, which especially affects the long open vowels, ᾰ, unless it follows ε, ι, ρ, or ρο, is usually lengthened, not to ᾱ, but to the closer η, and εε and οο commonly form, not η and ω, but the closer diphthongs ει and ου, which are hence termed the *corresponding diphthongs* of ε and ο.

β. Contraction more frequently exhibits some attenuation of vowel sound. See §§ 31 – 37. This naturally appears less in the earlier than in the later contractions. Compare βασιλῆς with βασιλεῖς (§ 37. 2).

NOTE. A similar tendency to pass from a more open to a closer sound appears in the general law for the formation of diphthongs (§ 25. 2).

II. UNION OF SYLLABLES.

§ **30.** The most important changes belonging to this head are, A. CONTRACTION, which unites two successive vowels in the same word; B. CRASIS (*κρᾶσις, mingling*), which unites the *final* and *initial* vowels of successive words; and C. APOSTROPHE or ELISION, which simply *drops* a final vowel before a word beginning with a vowel.

In poetry, two vowels are often united in pronunciation, which are written separately. This union is termed *synizēsis* (*συνίζησις, placing together*), or *synecphonēsis* (*συνεκφώνησις, pronouncing together*).

A. CONTRACTION.

§ **31.** Contraction takes place in three ways; by *simple union*, by *absorption*, and by *union with precession*. From the law of diphthongs (§ 25. 2), two vowels can unite without change only when the latter is ι or υ, and the former a more open vowel. In other cases, therefore, either one of the vowels is *absorbed*, i. e. simply lost in the other, which, if before short, now of course becomes long; or else *precession* takes place, changing one of the vowels to ι or υ, which then forms a diphthong with the other vowel. The following are the general rules of contraction, with the principal cases belonging to each, and the prominent exceptions.

NOTE. An ι, when absorbed in α, η, or ω, is written beneath it. The laws of contraction take effect, without regard to an ι subscript, or the subjunctive ι of the diphthong ει; as, αη ᾳ, αει ᾳ (§ 33).

§ 32. I. Two vowels, which can form a diphthong, unite without further change. Thus,

	become	as			become	as	
ᾱϊ	ᾳ,	ῥᾱΐστος	ῥᾷστος.	οϊ	οι,	ἠχόϊ	ἠχοῖ.
εϊ	ει,	τείχεϊ	τείχει.	ωϊ	ῳ,	λώϊστος	λῷστος.
ηϊ	ῃ,	Θρήϊσσα	Θρῇσσα.	υϊ	υι,	νέκυϊ	νέκυι (Ep.).

EXCEPTION. ᾰϊ, like ᾱϊ, becomes ᾳ; as, γήρᾰϊ, γήρᾳ· unless, with Thiersch, we prefer to write γήραι.

§ 33. II. α, (1.) before an *E* sound (¶ 3), absorbs it; but (2.) before another *A* sound, is itself absorbed. (3.) α, or (4.) η, with an *O* sound, forms ω. Thus,

		become	as				become	as	
(1.)	αε	ᾱ,	τίμαε	τίμᾱ.		οα	ω,	ἠχόα	ἠχώ.
	αει	ᾳ,	τιμάεις	τιμᾷς.		αω	ω,	τιμάω	τιμῶ.
	αη	ᾱ,	τιμάητε	τιμᾶτε.		ωα	ω,	ἥρωας	ἥρως.
	αῃ	ᾳ,	τιμάῃ	τιμᾷ.		αοι	ῳ,	τιμάοιμι	τιμῷμι.
(2.)	αα	ᾱ,	γέραα	γέρᾱ.		αου	ω,	τιμάουσι	τιμῶσι.
	αᾳ	ᾳ,	μνάᾳ	μνᾷ.		ουα	ω,	οὔατος	ὠτός.
	ααι	αι,	μνάαι	μναῖ.	(4.)	οη	ω,	δηλόητε	δηλῶτε.
(3.)	αο	ω,	τιμάομεν	τιμῶμεν.		οῃ	ῳ,	διδόῃς	διδῷς.

EXCEPTIONS. α. The closer η takes the place of ᾱ in the contract forms of four *every-day* verbs; viz. πεινάω, *to hunger*, διψάω, *to thirst*, χράομαι, *to use*, and ζάω, *to live*; as, πεινάειν πεινῆν, χράεσθαι χρῆσθαι. Add the verbs κνάω, σμάω, and ψάω· the Subjunctive of verbs in -μι, as, ἱστάῃ (from ἵστημι) ἱστῇ· and the liquid Aorist (see § 56).

β. In *adjectives*, ο before α and η is absorbed; as, διπλόα διπλᾶ, διπλόαι διπλαῖ, ἁπλόη ἁπλῆ.

γ. In οὖας, *ear*, the Nominative singular becomes οὖς by an absorption of the α, but the other forms are contracted according to the rule; as, ὠτός, ὦτα.

δ. For the change of οῃ into οι, in verbs in -οω, see § 37. 3.

§ 34. REMARKS. 1. α, taking the place of ν before ο (§ 50) is contracted like ε; thus, in the Acc. plur., (λόγονς, λόγοας) λόγους, (γλῶσσανς, γλώσσαας) γλώσσᾱς, (οἶνς) οἶας οἶς, ἰχθύας ἰχθῦς, πόλεας πόλεις, βόας βοῦς, μείζονας (μείζοας) μείζους· in themes of Dec. III., (ἕνς, ἑας) εἷς, (φανέντς, φανεας) φανείς, (ὀδόντς, ὄδοας) ὀδούς, (ῥίνς, ῥιας) ῥίς· in feminine adjectives and participles, (φανέντσα, φανεασα) φανεῖσα, (ἄγοντσα, ἀγοασα) ἄγουσα· in the 3d pers. plur. of verbs, (βουλεύονσι, βουλευοασι) βουλεύουσι, (τίθενσι) τιθέᾱσι τιθεῖσι, (δίδονσι) διδόᾱσι διδοῦσι, (δείκνυνσι) δεικνύᾱσι δεικνῦσι.

NOTES. α. By a similar contraction with βόας βοῦς, we find also νᾶας ναῦς and γρᾶας γραῦς (¶ 14). In like manner ναῦς occurs in the Nom. plur. by contraction from νᾶες, but only in late writers.

9*

β. For χοέας χοᾶς, see § 116. ϵ. For Κλήμης, Οὐάλης, see § 109. β.

§ **35.** 2. When α long is contracted with an *O* sound, there is usually inserted before the ω an ε, which, however, is not regarded in the accentuation as a distinct syllable; as, νᾱός (νως) νεώς (¶ 9), Μενέλᾱος Μενέλεως, Ἀτρείδᾱο Ἀτρείδεω (¶ 8).

So sometimes, chiefly in the Ion. (§§ 48. 1, 242. a), when α is short.

§ **36.** III. (1.) εα becomes η, and (2.) εε, ει. (3.) ε and ο, with ο, form ου; but (4.) with other *O* sounds are absorbed. (5.) In other combinations not already given (§ 32, 33), ε is absorbed. Thus,

		become	as				become	as	
(1.)	εα	η,	τείχεα	τείχη.		οιε	οι,	οἶες	οἶς.
	εᾳ	ῃ,	χρυσέᾳ	χρυσῇ.		εου	ου,	φιλέουσι	φιλοῦσι.
(2.)	εε	ει,	πόλεες	πόλεις.		οω	ω,	δηλόω	δηλῶ.
	εει	ει,	φιλέειν	φιλεῖν.		οῳ	ῳ,	νόῳ	νῷ.
	ειε	ει,	κλεῖες	κλεῖς.		οοι	οι,	νόοι	νοῖ.
(3.)	εο	ου,	ἐφίλεον	ἐφίλουν.		οου	ου,	δηλόου	δηλοῦ.
	οε	ου,	δηλόετε	δηλοῦτε.	(5.)	εαι	αι,	χρύσεαι	χρυσαῖ.
	οει	ου,	μελιτόεις	μελιτοῦς.		εη	η,	φιλέητε	φιλῆτε.
	οο	ου,	νόος	νοῦς.		εῃ	ῃ,	φιλέῃ	φιλῇ.
(4.)	εω	ω,	φιλέω	φιλῶ.		ηε	η,	τιμήεντος	τιμῆντος.
	εῳ	ῳ,	ὀστέῳ	ὀστῷ.		ηει	ῃ,	τιμήεις	τιμῇς.
	εοι	οι,	φιλέοιτε	φιλοῖτε.		υε	ῡ,	ἰχθύες	ἰχθῦς.

§ **37.** Exceptions. 1. εα preceded by ε, ι, ρ, or ρο (§ 29), or in the *plural* or *dual* of the *first* or *second declension*, becomes ᾱ; as, ὑγιέα ὑγιᾶ, ἀργυρέας ἀργυρᾶς, ἀργυρέᾳ ἀργυρᾷ, συκέας συκᾶς, συκέᾱ συκᾶ, ὀστέα ὀστᾶ. Yet φρέαρ, Gen. φρέατος φρητός (§ 104).

2. In the *dual* of the *third declension*, εε becomes η; as, τείχεε τείχη. In the older Attic writers, we find the same contraction in the Nom. plur. of nouns in -ευς; as, βασιλέες βασιλῆς (incorrectly written -ῇς), instead of the common βασιλεῖς.

3. In verbs in -οω, the syllables οῃ and οει, except in the Infinitive, become οι (i. e. the ο and ι unite, absorbing the η and ε); as, δηλόῃ δηλοῖ, δηλόεις δηλοῖς. But δηλόειν (Infin.) δηλοῦν, διδόῃς (from δίδωμι) διδῷς (§ 33).

4. In the termination of the second person singular passive, εαι is contracted into ῃ or ει, and ηαι into ῃ; as, βουλεύεαι βουλεύῃ or βουλεύει, βουλεύηαι ουλεύῃ.

5. For special contractions of ε in the augment, see §§ 188, 189.

Remark. Contraction is omitted in many words in which it might take place according to the preceding rules; particularly in nouns of the third declension, and in dissyllabic verbs in -εω.

B. Crasis.

§ **38.** Crasis (1.), for the most part, follows the

laws of contraction, disregarding, however, an ι final, which, according to the best usage, is not even subscribed. But often (2.), without respect to these laws, a final, or (3.) an initial vowel is entirely absorbed.

Crasis occurs mostly in poetry. It is commonly indicated by the coronis (̓) (§ 16), except when this mark is excluded by the rough breathing; as, τἀμά, οὑμοί. When an initial vowel has been absorbed without any further change, the words are more frequently separated in writing; as, οἱ 'μοί. The same is sometimes done when a final vowel has been absorbed. And, hence, cases are often referred to *aphæresis* and *apostrophe* which properly belong to crasis. For the change of a smooth mute to its cognate rough, when the second word is aspirated, see § 65. For the accent, see Prosody.

§ **39.** The principal words in which the final vowel is subject to crasis are the following:

α. The *article;* thus, for

(1.)	ὁ ἐκ, ὁ ἐπί,	οὑκ, οὑπί.	For	ἡ ἀρετή,	ἁρετή.
	οἱ ἐμοί,	οὑμοί.		αἱ ἀγαθαί,	ἁγαθαί.
	ὁ ὄρνις,	οὕρνις.		τοῦ αὐτοῦ,	ταὐτοῦ.
	τῷ ἐμῷ, τῇ ἐμῇ,	τὠμῷ, τἠμῇ.		τοῦ ἡμετέρου,	θἡμετέρου.
(2.)	ὁ ἀνήρ,	ἁνήρ, or, less Attic, ὡνήρ.	(3.)	ὁ οἶνος,	ᾦνος.
				οἱ ἐμοί,	οἱ 'μοί.
	τῷ ἀνδρί,	τἀνδρί.		τοῦ ὕδατος,	θοὔδατος.

NOTES. 1. The *neuter forms* τό and τά are especially subject to crasis thus, for

(1.)	τὸ ἐναντίον,	τοὐναντίον.	For	τὰ ὅπλα,	θὦπλα.
	τὸ ὄνομα,	τοὔνομα.	(2.)	τὸ ἀληθές,	τἀληθές.
	τὸ ἱμάτιον,	θοἰμάτιον.	(3.)	τὰ αἰσχρά,	τᾀσχρά.

2. In crasis, ἕτερος, *other*, retains the old form ἅτερος · thus, for

(2.)	ὁ ἕτερος,	ἅτερος.	For	τοῦ ἑτέρου,	θἀτέρου.
	τὸ ἕτερον,	θἅτερον.		τῷ ἑτέρῳ,	θἀτέρῳ.

§ **40.** β. The *conjunction* καί, *and;* thus, for

(1.)	καὶ ἄν, καὶ ἐάν,	κἄν.	For	καὶ ὁ, καὶ οἱ,	χὠ, χοἰ.
	καὶ ἐν, καὶ ἐκ,	κἀν, κἀκ.	(2.)	καὶ εἰ, καὶ οὐ,	κεἰ, κοὐ.
	καὶ ἕτερος,	χἄτερος.		καὶ ὑπό,	χὐπό.
	καὶ εἶτα,	κᾆτα.	(2, 3.)	καὶ ἡ ἄγχουσα,	χἤγχουσα,

γ. A few other *particles;* thus, for

	ἤτοι ἄρα,	ἠτᾶρα.	For	μηδέπω ἐν,	μηδέπω 'ν.
	μέντοι ἄν,	μεντἄν.		ποῦ ἐστιν,	ποῦ 'στιν.
	οὔτοι ἄρα,	οὐτᾶρα.		πρὸ ἔργου,	προὔργου.
	ει μη ἔχοιμι,	εἰ μὴ 'χοιμι.		ὦ ἀγαθέ,	ὦ 'γαθέ.
	μὴ εὕρω,	μὴ 'ὕρω.		ὦ ἄνθρωπε,	ὦ 'νθρωπε.

δ. Some forms of the *pronouns*; thus, for

ἐγὼ οἶδα,	ἐγᾦδα.	For ὃ ἐφέρει,	οὑφόρει.
ἐγὼ οἶμαι,	ἐγᾦμαι.	οὗ ἕνεκα,	οὕνεκα.
μοὶ ἐδόκει,	μοὐδόκει.	ὅτου ἕνεκα,	ὁθοὕνεκα.
σοί ἐστιν,	σοὖστιν.	ἃ ἄν, ἃ ἐμέ,	ἄν, ἀμέ.

The few cases which remain are best learned from observation.

C. Apostrophe, or Elision.

§ 41. Apostrophe affects only the short vowels ᾰ, ε, ῐ, and ο, and sometimes, in poetry, the passive terminations in αι (and perhaps οι in the enclitics μοί, σοί, τοί). In monosyllables (except the Ep. ῥά, and a few rare or doubtful cases), ε only is elided.

For the mark of apostrophe, see § 16. For the accentuation, see Prosody.

Elision is most common,

1.) In the prepositions, and other particles of constant use; as, ἀφ' ἑαυτοῦ (for ἀπὸ ἑαυτοῦ, § 65), ἐπ' ἐκεῖνον, κατ' ἐμέ, and, in composition (where the sign ' is omitted), ἀνέρχομαι, διελαύνω, πάρειμι· ἀλλ' ἐγώ, ἄρ' οὖν, γ' οὐδέν, μάλ' ἄν, ὅθ' ὁ (ὅτε ὁ), τάχ' ἄν.

2.) In a few pronouns, and in some phrases of frequent occurrence; as, τοῦτ' ἄλλο, ταῦτ' ἤδη· γένοιτ' ἄν, ἔσθ' ὅπου (ἔστι ὅπου), λέγοιμ' ἄν, οἶδ' ὅτι, φήμ' ἐγώ.

§ 42. Remarks. α. Elision is less frequent in ι, than in the other short vowels above mentioned. Particularly, it is never elided by the Attics in περί or ὅτι (which might then be confounded with ὅτε); and never in the Epic ἐσσί (2d person singular of εἰμί). It is never in prose, and very rarely in Attic poetry, elided in the Dative singular, which might then be confounded with the Accusative. The forms which take ν *paragogic* (§ 66) are not elided in prose, except ἐστί.

β. Elision is least frequent in Ionic prose. In Attic prose, it is found chiefly in a few words, but these often recurring. In poetry, where hiatus is more carefully avoided, its use is far more extended. In respect to its use or omission in prose, much seems to depend upon the rhythm of the sentence, the emphasis, the pauses, and the taste of the writer. There is, also, in this respect, a great difference among manuscripts.

DIALECTIC VARIATIONS.

§ 43. The dialectic variations in the vowels may be mostly referred to the heads of Precession, Union or Resolution, Quantity, and Insertion or Omission.

§ 44. I. Precession prevailed most in the soft Ionic, and

least in the rough Doric and Æolic; while the Attic, which blended strength and refinement, held a middle place. E. g.

1. Long α, for the most part, is retained in the Doric and Æolic, but in the Ionic passes into η; while in the Attic it is retained after ε, ι, ρ, and ρο, but otherwise passes into η (§ 29). Thus, Dor. ἁμέρᾱ, Att. ἡμέρᾱ, Ion. ἡμέρη · Dor. δᾶμος, πᾱγά, ὠκύτᾱς, Att. and Ion. δῆμος, πηγή, ὠκύτης · Dor. and Att. σοφίᾱ, πρᾶγμα, Ion. σοφίη, πρῆγμα. So, even in diphthongs, Ion. νηῦς, γρηῦς, for ναῦς, γραῦς, and in Dat. pl. of Dec. I., -ῃσι, -ῃς, for -αισι, -αις.

Note. The use of this long α produced, in great measure, the Doric feature called πλατειασμός, *broad pronunciation*, which was imitated by the Attics in the lyric parts of their drama (§ 6).

2. Short α is retained by the Doric in some words, where, in the Attic, it passes into ε; and in some (particularly verbs in -αω) by the Attic, where it becomes ε in the Ionic. Thus, Dor. τράφω, Ἄρτᾰμις, ὅκᾰ, φρᾰσί, Att. τρέφω, Ἄρτεμις, ὅτε, φρεσί · Att. ὁράω, φοιτάω, τέσσαρες, ἄρσην, Ion. ὁρέω, φοιτέω, τέσσερες, ἔρσην.

3. In nouns in -ις, -εως, the characteristic ε commonly passes, in the Ionic, into ι throughout; as, πόλις, ιος, ιι (contracted into ῑ according to § 29. α), ιν, ιες, ίων, ισι, ιας (contr. ῑς).

4. As the long of ε and ο, or the contraction of εε and οο or οε, the stricter Doric prefers the long vowels η and ω to the closer diphthongs ει and ου; while, on the other hand, the Ionic is particularly fond of protracting ε and ο to ει and ου or οι. Thus, Dor. χήρ, δῶλος · Gen. of Dec. II., τῶ ὠρανῶ · Infin. εὑρῆν, χαίρην, ὑπνῶν · for χείρ, δοῦλος, τοῦ οὐρανοῦ, εὑρεῖν, χαίρειν, ὑπνοῦν. Ion. ξεῖνος, μοῦνος, ποίη, for ξένος, μόνος, πόα. Att. κόρος, ὄνομα, ὄρος · Ion. κοῦρος, οὔνομα, οὖρος · Dor. κῶρος, ὤνομα, ὦρος. Both the Doric and Ionic have ὦν for οὖν, *therefore*, contracted from ἐόν.

5. Other examples of precession or the interchange of kindred vowels (§ 28) are the following; in some of which, contrary to the general law of the dialects, the Ionic has a more open sound than the Attic, or the Attic than the Doric or Æolic; Att. ᾱ̓εί, ᾱ̓ετός, Ion. αἰεί, αἰετός · Att. κάω, κλάω, Ion. and Com. καίω, κλαίω · Att. θᾶκος, Ion. θῶκος · Ion. τράπω, τάμνω, μέγαθος, Att. τρέπω, τέμνω, μέγεθος · Ion. ἀῤῥωδέω, Att. ὀῤῥωδέω · Ion. μεσαμβρία, Att. μεσημβρία · Dor. and Ep. αἰ, Att. εἰ · Dor. θνᾱ́σκω, Ion. and Att. θνήσκω, Æol. θναίσκω · Att. στρατός, βραχέως, πάρδαλις, Æol. στροτός, βροχέως, πόρδαλις · Att. ὄνομα, Æol. ὄνυμα · Att. ἑρπετόν, Æol. ὄρπετον.

§ 45. II. Union or Resolution. A. The Contraction of vowels prevailed most in the vivacious Attic, and least in the luxurious Ionic. By the poets, it is often employed or omitted according to the demands of the metre. There are also dialectic differences in the mode of contraction, which, for the most part, may be explained by precession. E. g.

1 In contracting α with an *O* sound, the Doric often prefers ᾱ to the closer ω; in the first declension, regularly. Thus, Dor. Ἀτρείδᾱ, τᾶν θυρᾶν (¶ 8), Ποσειδᾶν, -ᾶνος, πεινᾶντι, διαπεινᾶμες, πρᾶτος, for Ἀτρείδου (uncontracted -ᾱο), τῶν θυρῶν (-άων), Ποσειδῶν, -ῶνος (-άων, -άονος), πεινῶντι (-άοντι), διαπεινῶμεν (-άομεν), πρῶτος (-όατος). A like contraction appears in proper names in -λᾱος; as, Dor. Μενέλᾱς, for Μενέλᾱος.

2 For the contraction of εε and οο or οε, see § 44. 4.

3. With the Ionics and some of the Dorics, the favorite contraction of εο and εου is into ευ, instead of ου. This use of ευ for ου sometimes extends to cases where this diphthong results from a different contraction. Thus, φιλεῦμεν, φιλεῦ, ἐμεῦ, θέρευς, for φιλοῦμεν (-έομεν), φιλοῦ (-έου), ἐμοῦ (-έο), θέρους (-εος)· ἐδικαίευ, ἐδικαίευν, δικαιεῦσι, in Herodotus for ἐδικαίου (-οε), ἐδικαίου (-οον), δικαιοῦσι (-όουσι)· λωτεῦντα Μ. 283, for λωτοῦντα (-όεντα).

4. The Dorics (but not Pindar), contrary to the general law of the dialect, commonly contract α with an *E* sound following, into η; as, ἐρώτη, σιγῆν, λῆς, from ἐρώτας, σιγάειν, λάῃς. Cf. § 33. α.

5. In the contractions which follow the change of ν before σ (§ 58), the Æolic often employs αι and οι, for ᾱ and ου; as, Acc. pl. ταὶς τιμαίς, τοὶς νόμοις, for τὰς τιμάς, τοὺς νόμους · Nom. sing. of adj. and partic. μέλαις, τύψαις, τύψαισα, ἔχοισα, for μέλᾱς, τύψᾱς, τύψᾱσα, ἔχουσα · 3d pers. pl. of verbs, φαισί, κρύπτοισι, for φᾶσί, κρύπτουσι. The Doric has here great variety, both employing the simple long vowels, the short vowels (as though ν were simply dropped before σ), the common diphthongs of contraction (§ 34), and the Æolic diphthongs; thus, Acc. pl. τέχνᾱς and τέχνᾰς (Theoc. 21. 1); τοὺς λύκους and τὼς λύκος (Theoc. 4. 11); εἷς and ἦς, *one*; Μοῦσα, Μῶσα (Theoc.), Μοῖσα (Pind.), and Laconic Μῶα· Nom. sing. of partic. φράσαις (Pind. Ol. 2. 108), ἰδοῖσα (Ib. 73). So, likewise, οι for ου before σ in ἀκοίσω, Theoc. 11. 78.

6. The Ionic use of ωυ for αυ in a few words, appears, at least in some of them, to have arisen from a union of ο and α to form ω; thus, for ταὐτό, ἐμαυτοῦ, σεαυτοῦ, ἑαυτοῦ, Ion. τωὐτό, ἐμεωυτοῦ, σεωυτοῦ, ἑωυτοῦ, from τὸ αὐτό, ἐμέο αὐτοῦ, σέο αὐτοῦ, ἕο αὐτοῦ. In the reciprocal pronouns, the ωυ passed into the other cases. We find also Ion. θωῦμα, τρωῦμα (yet better τρῶμα), for θαῦμα, τραῦμα. In all these words, ωυ is written by some with a diæresis; as, θώϋμα.

§ 46. B. Vowels which appear only as diphthongs in the Attic are often RESOLVED in the other dialects, especially the Ionic and Æolic, into separate sounds. In the Ionic, the resolution of ει, with ε prolonged, into ηϊ, is especially common; as βασιληΐη, κληΐς, for βασιλεία, κλείς.

NOTES. α. On the other hand, the Ionic in a few cases employs contraction where the Attic omits it, particularly of οη into ω; as, ἱρός, ἔβωσα, ἔνωσα, βωθέω, ὀγδώκοντα, for ἱερός, ἐβόησα, ἐνόησα, βοηθέω, ὀγδοήκοντα.

β. The fondness of the Ionic for a concurrence of vowels leads it, in some cases, to change ν to α (§ 50) after a vowel (which, if before α, now becomes ε); as, Ἀρισταγόρεα, ἐδυνέατο, for Ἀρισταγόραν, ἐδύναντο.

C. In CRASIS, the Doric and Ionic often differ from the Attic by uniting the ο of the article with α and αι initial, to form ω and ῳ; as, τὸ ἀληθές, τὠληθές· οἱ ἄνδρες, ὦνδρες· οἱ αἰπόλοι ᾡπόλοι.

In the following crases, which are found in Herodotus, and the two first also in Homer, the smooth breathing has taken the place of the rough; ὁ ἄριστος, ὤριστος· ὁ αὐτός, ὡὐτός· οἱ ἄλλοι, ὦλλοι. Other dialectic crases are, Dor. ὁ ἔλαφος, ὤλαφος· ὁ ἐξ, ὤξ· καὶ ἐκ, κὴκ· καὶ εἶπε, κῆπε· Ion. ὁ ἕτερος, οὕτερος.

§ 47. III. Quantity. For a short vowel in the Attic, the other dialects often employ a long vowel or diphthong, and the converse. Thus,

Ion. διπλήσιος for διπλάσιος· Ion. ἐπιτήδεος, εὑρέη, ἀπόδεξις, μέζων, κρέσσων, for ἐπιτήδειος, εὑρεῖα, ἀπόδειξις, μείζων, κρείσσων· Dor. and Ep. ἕταρος for ἑταῖρος· Æol. Ἀλκᾶος, ἀρχᾶος, for Ἀλκαῖος, ἀρχαῖος. See §§ 44. 4; 45. 5.

Note. The poets, especially the Epic, often lengthen or shorten a vowel according to the metre. A short vowel when lengthened in Epic verse usually passes into a cognate dipthong; as, εἰλήλουθας for ἐλήλυθας, A. 202.

§ 48. IV. Insertion or Omission. Vowels are often inserted in one dialect which are omitted in another; and here, as elsewhere, a peculiar freedom belongs to the poets, especially the Epic. These often double a vowel, or insert the half of it (i. e. the *short* for the *long*), for the sake of the metre, particularly in *contract verbs*; as, κρήηνον ἐέλδωρ, for κρῆνον ἔλδωρ, A. 41, φάανθεν, ἡβώωσα, ὁρόω, ὁράας, γελώοντες, φόως, γαλόως, ἐείκοσι, for φάνθεν, ἡβῶσα, ὁρῶ, ὁρᾷς, γελῶντες, φῶς, γάλως, εἴκοσι.

Remarks. 1. The Ionic is especially fond of the insertion of ε; as, Gen. pl. ἀνδρέων, χηνέων, αὐτέων, for ἀνδρῶν, &c.; 2 Aor. infin. εὑρέειν, λιπέειν, for εὑρεῖν, λιπεῖν.

2. In the Doric and Epic, the particles ἄρα, ἀνά, κατά, παρά, ἀπό, ὑπό, and ποτί (Dor. for πρός), often omit the final vowel before a consonant, with such assimilation of the preceding consonant as euphony may require; as, ἄρ σφως, ἂμ βωμοῖσι, ἄγκρισις, ἀνστάς (§ 68. 3), κὰδ δύναμιν, κὰπ φάλαρα (§ 62. β), κὰκ κεφαλῆς, κὰγ γόνυ, καχχεῦαι, κὰρ ῥόον, κάλλιπον, καμμίξας, πὰρ Ζηνί, ἀππέμψει, ὑββάλλειν, πὸτ τόν. When three consonants are thus brought together, the first is sometimes rejected; as, κάκτανε, ἀμνάσει, for κάκκτανε, ἀμμνάσει. So, sometimes in the Doric, even before a single consonant; as, καβαίνων.

Notes. α. From the close connection of the preposition with the following word, these cases are not regarded as making any exception to the rule in § 63. Compare § 68. β. The two words are often written together, even when there is no composition; as, καδδύναμιν, ποττόν.

β. In these words, the final vowel was probably a euphonic addition to the original form. Compare ἀπό and ὑπό with the Latin *ab* and *sub*. The old form πρότ, in accordance with the rule (§ 63), became πρός and προτί, whence ποτί.

γ. Some of these forms even passed into the Attic, and into Ionic prose; as, κατθανεῖν (poet.), ἀμβάτης (Xen.), ἀμπαύομαι (Herod.).

δ. Ἄρα has also, by aphæresis, the Epic form ῥά, which is enclitic.

CHAPTER III.

CONSONANTS.

[¶ 3.]

§ 49. The Greek has eighteen CONSONANTS, represented by seventeen letters.

They are exhibited in the Table (¶ 3) according to two methods of division, employed by orthoëpists. Consonants of the same class, according to the first method, are termed *cognate;* of the same order, *coördinate.*

REMARKS. 1. The letter γ performs a double office. When followed by another palatal, it is a *nasal;* otherwise a *middle mute.* As a nasal, it has *n* for its corresponding Roman letter; as a middle mute, *g* (§ 12). For its pronunciation, see § 18. 3.

2. From the representation of the Latin *v* by β (*Virgilius*, Βιργίλιος), it is probable that in the ancient, as in the modern Greek (§ 19), the middle mutes approached nearer to the aspirates than in our own language, and that, in forming them, the organs were not wholly closed.

§ 50. 3. The semivowels ν and σ have corresponding vowels in α and ε; that is, α may take the place of ν, and ε of σ, when euphony forbids the use of these consonants; as, ἐφθάραται for ἔφθαρνται, σπερέω (contracted σπερῶ) for σπέρσω See §§ 34, 46. β, 56 – 58, 60, 63. R., &c.

NOTE. In like manner, υ is the corresponding vowel of the old consonant F. See § 22. δ.

§ 51. The following laws, mostly euphonic, are observed in the formation and connection of words

A. IN THE FORMATION OF WORDS.

I. A *labial mute* before σ forms with it ψ; and a *palatal*, ξ; thus,

	become	as			become	as	
πσ	ψ,	λείπσω	λείψω.	κσ	ξ,	κόρακς	κόραξ.
βσ	ψ,	Ἄραβς	Ἄραψ.	γσ	ξ,	λέγσω	λέξω.
φσ	ψ,	γράφσω	γράψω.	χσ	ξ,	θρίχς	θρίξ.

NOTE. In like manner, ζ is the union of a lingual with a sibilant sound, and in many words has taken the place of σδ; e. g. adverbs of place in -ζε, as, for Ἀθήνασδε, Ἀθήναζε, for Θήβασδε, Θήβαζε· and many verbs in -ζω; as, for μελίσδω, μελίζω, for φράσδω, φράζω. In these verbs, the old forms remain in the Æolic and Doric (§ 70. V.). For a lingual *before* σ, see § 55.

§ 52. II. Before a *lingual mute*, a (1.) *labial* or (2.) *palatal mute* becomes *coördinate* (§ 49, ¶ 3), and (3.) a *lingual mute*, σ; thus,

		become		as			become		as
(1.)	βτ	πτ,	τέτριβται	τέτριπται.		χδ	γδ,	βρύχδην	βρύγδην.
	φτ	πτ,	γέγραφται	γέγραπται.		κθ	χθ,	ἐπλέκθην	ἐπλέχθην.
	πδ	βδ,	ἕπδομος	ἕβδομος.		γθ	χθ,	ἐπράγθην	ἐπράχθην.
	φδ	βδ,	γράφδην	γράβδην.	(3.)	ττ	στ,	ὠνόματται	ὠνόμασται.
	πθ	φθ,	ἐλείπθην	ἐλείφθην.		δτ	στ,	ψεύδτης	ψεύστης.
	βθ	φθ,	ἐτρίβθην	ἐτρίφθην.		θτ	στ,	πέπειθται	πέπεισται.
(2.)	γτ	κτ,	λέλεγται	λέλεκται.		τθ	σθ,	ὠνομάτθην	ὠνομάσθην.
	χτ	κτ,	τέτυχται	τέτυκται.		δθ	σθ,	ἐφράδθην	ἐφράσθην.
	κδ	γδ,	πλέκδην	πλέγδην.		θθ	σθ,	ἐπείθθην	ἐπείσθην.

EXCEPTION. Two lingual mutes may remain together, if both are radical; as, πράττω, 'Ατθίς.

§ 53. III. Before μ, a *labial mute* becomes μ, a *palatal*, γ, and a *lingual*, σ; thus,

	become		as		become		as
πμ	μμ,	λέλειπμαι	λέλειμμαι.	χμ	γμ,	τέτυχμαι	τέτυγμαι.
βμ	μμ,	τρίβμα	τρίμμα.	τμ	σμ,	ὠνόματμαι	ὠνόμασμαι.
φμ	μμ,	γράφμα	γράμμα.	δμ	σμ,	ᾆδμα	ᾆσμα.
κμ	γμ,	πέπλεκμαι	πέπλεγμαι.	θμ	σμ,	πέπειθμαι	πέπεισμαι.

Except in a few such words as ἀκμή, κευθμών, νεοχμός, πότμος· and some others from the dialects; as, in Homer, ὀδμή, ἴδμεν, ἐπέπιθμεν, κεκορυθμένος, ἀκαχμένος.

§ 54. IV. ν before a (1.) *labial* or (2.) *palatal*, is changed into the *cognate* nasal (§ 49, ¶ 3); and (3.) before a *liquid*, into that liquid; thus,

		become		as			become		as
(1.)	νπ	μπ,	συνπάσχω	συμπάσχω.		νγ	γγ,	συνγενής	συγγενής.
	νβ	μβ,	ἐνβάλλω	ἐμβάλλω.		νχ	γχ,	συνχαίρω	συγχαίρω.
	νφ	μφ,	συνφέρω	συμφέρω.		νξ	γξ,	ἐνξέω	ἐγξέω.
	νμ	μμ,	ἐνμένω	ἐμμένω.	(3.)	νλ	λλ,	ἔνλογος	ἔλλογος.
	νψ	μψ,	ἔνψῦχος	ἔμψῦχος.		νρ	ῤῥ,	συνράπτω	συῤῥάπτω.
(2.)	νκ	γκ,	ἐνκαλέω	ἐγκαλέω.					

NOTES. *α*. Enclitics are here regarded as distinct words; thus, ὅνπερ, τόνγε. We find, however, final ν changed in like manner upon old inscriptions; as, ΜΕΜΦΣΥΧΑΣ, for μὲν ψυχάς (Insc. Potid.); so, ΑΓΚΑΙ, ΤΟΛΛΟΓΟΝ, and even ΕΣΣΑΜΟΙ (cf. §§ 57. 5, 68. 3), for ἂν καί, τὸν λόγον, ἐν Σάμῳ.

β. Before μ in the Perfect passive, ν sometimes becomes σ and is sometimes dropped; as, for πέφανμαι, πέφασμαι· for κέκλινμαι, κέκλιμαι.

γ. Before κ in the Perfect active, ν was commonly dropped, or the form avoided, except by later writers; as, for κέκρινκα, κέκρικα.

§ **55.** V. A *lingual* or *liquid* should not precede σ. This is prevented in various ways.

1. A *lingual mute* is simply dropped before σ; thus, σώματσι παῖδς, πείθσω become σώμασι, παῖς, πείσω.

§ **56.** 2. In *liquid verbs*, the σ formative of the Future and Aorist is changed into ε (§ 50), which (1.) in the *Future* is contracted with the *affix*, but (2.) in the *Aorist* is transposed and contracted with the vowel of the *penult*.

Thus, in the Fut. and Aor. of the liquid verbs, *ἀγγέλλω, to announce, νέμω, to distribute, κρίνω, to judge, πλύνω, to wash*, and *δέρω, to flay*, for

(1.)	ἀγγέλσω,	(ἀγγελέω)	ἀγγελῶ·	(2.) ἤγγελσα,	(ἠγγεελα)	ἤγγειλα.
	νέμσω,	(νεμέω)	νεμῶ·	ἔνεμσα,	(ἐνεεμα)	ἔνειμα.
	κρίνσω,	(κρινέω)	κρινῶ·	ἔκρινσα,	(ἐκριενα)	ἔκρῖνα.
	πλύνσω,	(πλυνέω)	πλυνῶ·	ἔπλυνσα,	(ἐπλυενα)	ἔπλῦνα.
	δέρσω,	(δερέω)	δερῶ·	ἔδερσα,	(ἐδεερα)	ἔδειρα.

NOTES. α. Here αε commonly passes into η, unless ι or ρ precedes; thus, *σφάλλω, to cause to slip, φαίνω, to show* (roots σφαλ-, φαν-), have in the Aor. (ἔσφαλσα, ἐσφαελα) ἔσφηλα, ἔφηνα· while *πιαίνω, to fatten, περαίνω, to complete* (roots πιαν-, περαν-), have ἐπίᾶνα, ἐπέρᾶνα. But *ἰσχναίνω, to make lean, κερδαίνω, to gain, κοιλαίνω, to hollow out, λευκαίνω, to whiten, ὀργαίνω, to enrage, πεπαίνω, to ripen*, have ᾱ in the penult of the Aor.; *τετραίνω, to bore*, η; and *σημαίνω, to give a signal, μιαίνω, to stain*, both η and ᾱ. *Αἴρω, to raise*, and *ἅλλομαι, to leap*, have ᾱ, which in the Indicative is changed by the augment into η; thus, ἦρα, ἄρω, ἄραιμι.

β. A few poetic verbs retain the old forms with σ; as, *κέλλω, to land*, κέλσω, ἔκελσα· *κύρω, to meet with, to chance*, κύρσω, ἔκυρσα· ὄρνῡμι (r. ὀρ-), *to rouse*, ὄρσω, ὦρσα· *φύρω, to knead*, ἔφυρσα. Add these forms, mostly from Homer, ἦρσα, ἔλσα, ἔρσα, θέρσομαι, κέρσω, ἔκερσα, διαφθέρσω, ἤερσα.

§ **57.** 3. In the *Nominative*, the formative σ (1.) after ρ, and sometimes (2.) after ν, becomes ε, which is then transposed, and *absorbed* (§ 31) by the preceding vowel; as, for

(1.)	ψάρς,	(ψαερ)	ψάρ.	(2.) παιάνς,	(παιαεν)	παιάν.
	πατέρς,	(πατεερ)	πατήρ.	λιμένς,	(λιμεεν)	λιμήν.
	ῥήτορς,	(ῥητοερ)	ῥήτωρ.	δαίμονς,	(δαιμοεν)	δαίμων.

Except in δάμᾰρ (§ 109).

4. In the *Dative plural* of the third declension, ν preceding σ *without* an intervening τ, is *dropped;* as, for

μέλανσι,	μέλασι.	For δαίμονσι,	δαίμοσι.
λιμένσι,	λιμέσι.	ῥινσί,	ῥισί.

So also *with* τ, in the Dat. pl. of *adjectives in* -εις; as, for χαρίεντσι, χαρίεσι.

5. In the *feminine* of *adjectives in* -εις, ν before σ becomes σ; as, for χαρίεντσα, (χαρίενσα) χαρίεσσα.

§ **58.** 6. Otherwise, ν before σ is changed into α, which is then *contracted* with the preceding vowel (§§ 34, 50); as, for

	Nom. Masc.			Nom. Fem.	
μέλανς,	(μελαας)	μέλᾱς.	For πάντσα,	(πάασα)	πᾶσα.
φανέντς,	(φανεας)	φανείς.	φανέντσα,	(φανέασα)	φανεῖσα
δόντς,	(δοας)	δούς.	δόντσα,	(δόασα)	δοῦσα.
δύντς,	(δυας)	δύς.	δύντσα,	(δύασα)	δῦσα.
ῥίνς,	(ῥιας)	ῥίς.		Dat. Plur.	
Verbs in 3d Pers. Plur.			πάντσι,	(πάασι)	πᾶσι.
ἵστανσι,	(ἱστάασι)	ἱστᾶσι.	φανέντσι,	(φανέασι)	φανεῖσι.
τίθενσι,	τιθέᾱσι,	τιθεῖσι.	δόντσι,	(δόασι)	δοῦσι.
δίδονσι,	διδόᾱσι,	διδοῦσι.	δύντσι,	(δύασι)	δῦσι.
δείκνυνσι,	δεικνύᾱσι,	δεικνῦσι.		Future.	
ἵνσι,	ἵᾱσι.		πένθσομαι,	(πεασομαι)	πείσομαι.
			σπένδσω,	(σπεασω)	σπείσω.

NOTES. α. The forms τιθέᾱσι, διδόᾱσι, and δεικνύᾱσι were used by the Attics, for the most part, without contraction; ἵᾱσι received no contraction.

β. In nouns, if νθ precede σ, the ν is retained; as, for ἕλμινθς, ἕλμινς, for ἕλμινθσι, ἕλμινσι (yet others, ἕλμῖσι). It is also retained in some forms in σαι and derivatives in -σις, from verbs in -αίνω, as πέφανσαι from φαίνω, πέπανσις from πεπαίνω· and sometimes in the adverb πάλιν, and the adjective πᾶν, in composition. Add the Homeric κένσαι, Ψ. 337. For ἐν, σύν, and ἀν, see § 68. 3. In the rough Argive and Cretan, ν seems to have been extensively retained before σ; thus, ἐνς, τιθένς, for εἰς, τιθείς.

§ **59.** 7. In the Dative plural of *syncopated liquids*, and of ἀστήρ, *star*, the combination -ερσ-, by metathesis and the change of ε to α, became -ρασ-; as, for πατέρσι, πατράσι· for ἀστέρσι, ἀστράσι.

8. Elsewhere the combinations λσ and ρσ were permitted to stand, except as σ *radical* after ρ was softened in the new Attic to ρ (§ 70); as, ἄῤῥην, *male*, θάῤῥος, *courage*, κόῤῥη, *temple*, *cheek*, for the older ἄρσην, θάρσος, κόρση. The combination μσ is unknown in classic Greek.

§ **60.** VI. Between two consonants, σ *formative* is dropped, and ν is changed to α (§ 50); as, for

γεγράφσθαι, γεγράφθαι· for λέλεγσθε, λέλεχθε· for ἔφθαρνται, ἐφθάραται.

NOTE. So the compound προσσχών is written by some προσχών.

§ **61.** VII. Before κ *formative*, a *labial* or *palatal mute* unites with it in the cognate *rough*, and a *lingual mute* is dropped; thus,

	become	as			become	as	
πκ	φ,	κέκλοπκα	κέκλοφα.	χκ	χ,	δεδίδαχκα	δεδίδαχα.
βκ	φ,	εἴληβκα	εἴληφα.	τκ	κ,	ὠνόματκα	ὠνόμακα.
φκ	φ,	γέγραφκα	γέγραφα.	δκ	κ,	πέφραδκα	πέφρακα.
κκ	χ,	δέδεικκα	δέδειχα.	θκ	κ,	πέπειθκα	πέπεικα.
γκ	χ,	πέπραγκα	πέπρᾱχα.				

§ **62.** VIII. If *rough mutes* begin two successive syllables, the *first* is often changed into its cognate *smooth*, especially (1.) in *reduplications*, or (2.) when both letters are *radical*; but (3.) in the *second person singular* of the *Aorist imperative passive*, the *second* rough mute is changed; thus, for

(1.)	φεφίληκα,	πεφίληκα.	(2.) θριχός,	τριχός.
	χέχρημαι,	κέχρημαι.	θαχύς,	ταχύς.
	θέθυκα,	τέθυκα.	θρέχω,	τρέχω.
	θίθημι,	τίθημι.	(3.) βουλεύθηθι,	βουλεύθητι.

NOTES. α. Upon the same principle, ἕχω becomes ἔχω· and whenever ῥ is reduplicated, the first ῥ becomes *smooth*, and, as it then cannot stand at the beginning of a word (§ 13. 2), is transposed; as, for ῥέῤῖφα, ἔῤῥῖφα. Yet we find, by a softening of the second ρ, ῥερυπωμένα ζ. 59, ῥεραπισμένα Anacr. Fr. 105, ῥερῖφθαι Pind. Fr. 281.

β. So, to avoid excessive aspiration, a rough mute is never preceded by the same rough mute, but, instead of it, by the cognate smooth; as, the Epic κὰπ φάλαρα, for κὰφ φάλαρα (§ 48. 2); so, Σαπφώ, Βάκχος, Ἀτθίς· and, upon the same principle, Πύῤῥος (§ 13. 2).

§ **63.** IX. The semivowels ν, ρ, and ς, are the only consonants that may end a word. Any other consonant, therefore, falling at the end of a word, is either (1.) *dropped*, or (2.) *changed* into one of these, or (3.) *assumes a vowel*; thus, for

(1.)	σῶματ,	σῶμα.	For κέρατ,	κέρας.
	μέλιτ,	μέλι.	εἰδότ,	εἰδός.
	ἄγοντ,	ἄγον.	ἧπατ,	ἧπαρ.
	ἐβούλευοντ,	ἐβούλευον.	ἐβούλευομ,	ἐβούλευον.
	παῖδ,	παῖ.	ἵστημ,	ἵστην.
	γύναικ,	γύναι.	ἐτίθημ,	ἐτίθην.
	ἄνακτ,	ἄνα.	(3.) βουλεύοιμ,	βουλεύοιμι.
	γάλακτ,	γάλα.	τίθημ,	τίθημι,
(2.)	φῶτ,	φῶς.	στῆθ,	στῆθι.

REMARK. A word can end with two consonants, only when the last is σ; as, ἅλς, γύψ (γύπς), νύξ (νύκς), κόραξ. Hence the *formative* ν of the Accusative is changed into α (§ 50) after a consonant, except in a few cases, in which a lingual mute preceding ν is dropped; thus, for

γύπν,	γῦπα.	For κλεῖδν,	κλεῖδα and κλεῖν.
κόρακν,	κόρακα.	ὄρνιθν,	ὄρνῖθα and ὄρνιν.
παῖδν,	παῖδα.	γέλωτν,	γέλωτα and γέλων.

§ **64.** X. A consonant is sometimes *inserted* or *transposed*, to soften the sound. Thus,

1. When a *simple vowel* is brought by inflection or composition before an *initial* ῥ, a smooth ρ is inserted; as, ἔῤῥωσα, ἄῤῥωστος, ἐπιῤῥώννῡμι, from ῥώννῡμι (ἐ-, ἀ-, and ἐπί prefixed) but εὔρωστος (the *diphthong* εὖ prefixed).

2. When, by syncope or metathesis, a nasal is brought before λ or ρ, the cognate middle mute is inserted; as, from ἀνέρος, (ἀνρός) ἀνδρός, from μεσημερία, μεσημβρία.

Note. If the nasal is initial, it is then dropped from the difficulty of sounding it; e. g., the roots of βλίττω and βλώσκω are thus changed; μελιτ-, μλιτ-, μβλιτ-, βλιτ-; μολ-, μλο-, μβλο-, βλο-; so βροτός, *mortal*, derived from μόρος, Lat. *mors*.

3. Transposition especially affects a liquid coming before another consonant; as, for θόρσκω, θρώσκω, for βέβαλκα, βέβληκα.

§ **65.** B. In the Connection of Words.

I. When a *smooth mute* is brought by (1.) *crasis* or (2.) *elision* before the *rough breathing*, it is changed into its cognate *rough*; as, for

(1.) καὶ ὁ, καὶ οἱ,	χὠ, χοἰ.	For νύκτα ὅλην,	νύχθ' ὅλην.
τὸ ἱμάτιον,	θοἰμάτιον.	And in composition, from	
τοῦ ἑτέρου,	θἀτέρου.	ἀπό and ἵημι,	ἀφίημι.
ὅτου ἕνεκα,	ὁθοὔνεκα.	δέκα and ἡμέρα,	δεχήμερος.
(2.) ἀπὸ οὗ,	ἀφ' οὗ.	ἑπτά and ἡμέρα,	ἑφθήμερος.

Note. In some compounds, this change takes place with an intervening ρ; and in some words, it appears simply to have arisen from the tendency of ρ to aspiration (cf. § 13. 2); as, φροῦδος (from πρό and ὁδός), φρουρός (πρό ὁράω), τέθριππον (τέτταρες, ἵππος); φροίμιον (πρό, οἶμος), θράσσω from ταράσσω.

§ **66.** II. Some words and forms end either *with* or *without* a *final consonant* according to euphony, emphasis, or rhythm.

In most of these cases, the consonant appears not to belong to the original form, but to have been assumed. In some cases, however, the reverse appears to be true; and some cases are doubtful.

1. *Datives plural in* ι, and *verbs of the third person in* ε and ι, assume ν at the end of a sentence, or when the next word begins with a vowel; as,

Πᾶσι γὰρ εἶπε τοῦτο· but, Εἶπεν αὐτὸ πᾶσιν.
Πᾶσι λέγουσι τοῦτο· but, Πᾶσιν αὐτὸ λέγουσιν.

10*

NOTES. *α*. So, likewise, *adverbs of place in* -σι (properly datives plural the adverb πέρυσι, *last year*, the numeral εἴκοσι (commonly), the demonstrative -ι preceded by σ (sometimes), the Epic case-ending -φι, and the Epic particles κέ, νύ, and νόσφι · as, ἡ Πλαταιᾶσιν ἡγεμονία· εἴκοσιν ἔτη. See § 211. N.

β. The ν thus assumed is called ν *paragogic*. It is sometimes employed by the poets before a consonant to make a syllable long by position; and in most kinds of verse, some of the best editors write it uniformly at the end of a line. In Ionic prose it is generally neglected, but in Attic prose it is sometimes found even before a consonant in the middle of a sentence. In grammars and lexicons, a paragogic letter is commonly marked thus: εἴκοσι(ν).

§ **67.** 2. The adverb οὕτως, *thus*, commonly loses σ before a consonant; and ἄχρι and μέχρι, *until*, often assume it before a vowel; as, οὕτω φησί· μέχρις οὗ.

3. Some other words have poetic or dialectic forms, in which a final ν or ς is dropped or assumed; as, local adverbs in -θεν (poet., chiefly Ep., -θε), numeral adverbs in -κις (Ion. -κι), ἄντικρυς, ἀτρέμας, ἔμπας, πάλιν, εὐθύ(ς), ἰθύ(ς).

§ 68. C. Special Rules.

1. The preposition ἐξ, *out of*, becomes ἐκ before a consonant, and admits no further change; as ἐκ κακῶν, ἐκσεύω, ἐκγελάω, ἔκθετος, ἐκμάσσω.

2. The adverb οὐ, *not*, before a vowel, assumes κ, which becomes χ before the rough breathing; as οὔ φησι, οὐκ ἔνεστιν, οὐχ ὕει, οὐκέτι.

NOTES. *α*. The adverb μηκέτι, from μή and ἔτι, follows the analogy of οὐκέτι.

β. In these words, ἐκ and οὐκ may perhaps be regarded as the original forms. That in certain situations these forms are retained is owing to their close connection as proclitics, or in composition, with the following word, and therefore forms no real exception to the rule in § 63. When orthotone, they conform to the rule, the one by assuming ς, and the other by dropping κ.

3. In composition, the preposition ἐν, *in*, retains its ν before ρ and σ; while σύν, *with*, drops its ν before σ followed by another consonant, and before ζ; but before σ followed by a vowel, changes ν to σ; as, ἐνράπτω, ἐνσείω (yet ἔρρυθμος oftener than ἔνρυθμος); σύστημα (for σύνστημα), συζυγία· συσσεύω (for συνσεύω), συσσιτία.

NOTE. The Epic ἀν for ἀνά (§ 48. 2) here imitates ἐν · as, ἀνστάς, ἄνσχετος.

DIALECTIC VARIATIONS.

§ **69.** A. The dialects often *interchange* consonants; most frequently,

I. COGNATE MUTES (§ 49); as, Ion. αὖτις, δέκομαι, for αὖθις, δέχομαι· Æol. ἀμπί for ἀμφί.

NOTES. *α*. The soft Ionic was less inclined than the Attic to the rough mutes; hence, in the Ionic, the smooth mute remains before the rough breathing (§ § 65, 68. 2); as, ἀπ' οὗ, δεκήμερος, οὐκ ὕει. In some compounds, this passed into the Attic; as, ἀπηλιώτης, from ἀπό and ἥλιος.

β. Aspiration is sometimes *transposed;* as, Ion. κιθών, ἐνθαῦτα, ἐνθεῦτεν, Καλχηδών, for χιτών, ἐνταῦθα, ἐντεῦθεν, Χαλκηδών.

II. COÖRDINATE MUTES (§ 49); as, Ion. and Æol., κ for π in *interrogative* and *indefinite pronouns* and *adverbs;* thus, κοῖος, κοῦ, κοτέ, for ποῖος, ποῦ, ποτέ· Dor., κ for τ in πόκα, ὅκα, τόκα, for πότε, ὅτε, τότε, and in similar *adverbs of time;* Æol. πέμπε for πέντε, φήρ for θήρ· Æol. and Dor. γλέφαρον for βλέφαρον, δᾶ for γῆ· Dor. ὀδελός for ὀβελός, ὄρνιχος for ὄρνιθος.

III. LIQUIDS; as, Dor. ἦνθον, βέντιστος, for ἦλθον, βέλτιστος· Ion. πλεύμων for πνεύμων.

§ 70. IV. σ with other letters; e. g.

1. The Ionic and Old Attic σσ and ρσ pass, for the most part, in the later Attic, into ττ and ῤῥ; as, τάσσω τάττω, γλῶσσα γλῶττα, ἄρσην ἄῤῥην. See § 59. 8.

2. Dor. τ for σ; as, Ποτειδάν, ἔπετον, εἴκατι, for Ποσειδῶν, ἔπεσον, εἴκοσι. This appears especially in the 2d personal pronoun, and in the 3d pers. of verbs; as, τύ, τέ, for σύ, σέ (Lat. *tu, te*); φατί, φαντί, λέγοντι, for φησί, φασί, λέγουσι (Lat. *legunt*).

3. Dor. σ for ν in the verb-ending of 1st pers. pl. μες for μεν (Lat. *mus*); as, λέγομες for λέγομεν (Lat. *legimus*).

4. The Laconic often changes θ to σ, and final ς to ρ; as, παλεόρ Ar. Lys. 988, σιόρ, σέλω, for παλαιός, θεός, θέλω· ποῖρ for παῖς (Lat. *puer*, compare *Marcipor*).

V. The DOUBLE CONSONANTS with other letters; as, old ξύν, later and common σύν (in the Lat. *cum* the σ has been dropped, instead of the κ); Æol. Ψαπφώ for Σαπφώ· Æol. σκένος, σκίφος, for ξένος, ξίφος· Dor. ψέ, ψίν, for σφέ, σφίν· Ion. διξός, τριξός, for δισσός, τρισσός.

For ζ, we find, in the Æolic and Doric, σδ, δδ, and δ; as, ὕσδος, μελίσδω (§ 51. N.), παίδδω, μάδδα, Δεύς, for ὄζος, μελίζω, παίζω, μάζα, Ζεύς.

§ 71. B. Consonants are often *doubled*, *inserted*, *omitted*, and *transposed* by the poets, especially the Epic, for the sake of the metre; as, ἔλλαβον, φράσσομαι, νέκυσσι, ὅσσος, ὅππως, ἔδδεισε, for ἔλαβον, &c.; πτόλεμος, πτόλις, διχθά, νώνυμνος, ἀπάλαμνος, for πόλεμος, πόλις, δίχα, νώνυμος, ἀπάλαμος· ἔρεζον, Ὀδυσεύς, Ἀχιλεύς, φάρυγος, for ἔῤῥεζον, Ὀδυσσεύς, Ἀχιλλεύς, φάρυγγος· κραδίη, κάρτερος, βάρδιστος, for καρδία, κράτερος, βράδιστος.

BOOK II.

ETYMOLOGY.

Ἔπεα πτερόεντα.
Homer.

§ 72. Etymology treats of the INFLECTION and of the FORMATION OF WORDS; the former including DECLENSION, COMPARISON, and CONJUGATION, and the latter, DERIVATION and COMPOSITION.

For the distinction between the *radical* and the *formative* part of words, and the use of the terms *root*, *prefix*, *affix*, *open* and *close* or *vowel* and *consonant* affixes, *characteristic*, *pure* and *impure* words, *mute*, *liquid*, *liquid-mute*, *labial*, *palatal*, and *lingual* words, *theme*, *paradigm*, &c., see General Grammar.

CHAPTER I.

PRINCIPLES OF DECLENSION.

§ 73. The two classes of SUBSTANTIVES (including Nouns and Substantive Pronouns) and ADJECTIVES (including the Article, Adjectives commonly so called, Adjective Pronouns, and Participles) are declined to mark three distinctions, GENDER, NUMBER, and CASE.

NOTE. Adjectives receive these distinctions merely for the sake of conforming to the substantives to which they belong.

A. GENDER.

§ 74. The Greek has three genders; the MASCULINE, the FEMININE, and the NEUTER.

NOTES. α. Nouns which are both masculine and feminine, are said to be of the *common* gender.

β. To mark the genders of Greek nouns, we employ the different forms of the article, in the singular, for the masculine, ὁ; for the feminine, ἡ; for the common, ὁ, ἡ; and for the neuter, τό: in the plural, for the masculine, οἱ; for the feminine, αἱ; for the common, οἱ, αἱ; and, for the neuter, τά: as, ὁ ταμίας, *steward*, ὁ, ἡ τροφός, *nurse*, τὸ σῦκον, *fig*.

In like manner, the different cases and numbers, according to their gender, are marked by different forms of the article; as the Gen. sing. masc. by τοῦ, &c.

γ. In the case of most animals it is seldom important to distinguish the gender. Hence in Greek, for the most part, the names of animals, instead of being common, have but a single gender, which is used indifferently for both sexes. Such nouns are termed *epicene* (ἐπίκοινος, *promiscuous*). Thus, ὁ λύκος, *wolf*, ἡ ἀλώπηξ, *fox*, whether the male or the female is spoken of.

δ. Words which change their forms to denote change of gender are termed *movable;* and this change is termed *motion;* as, ὁ βασιλεύς, *king*, ἡ βασίλεια, *queen;* ὁ σοφός, *wise*, ἡ σοφή, τὸ σοφόν.

ε. In words in which the feminine may either have a *common* form with the masculine or a *distinct* form, the *Attic* sometimes prefers the common form, where the *Ionic* and *Common* dialects prefer the distinct form; as, ὁ, ἡ θεός, *god*, *goddess*, and ἡ θεά or θέαινα, *goddess*. So, likewise, in adjectives.

§ **75.** The masculine gender belongs properly to words denoting *males;* the feminine, to words denoting *females;* and the neuter to words denoting *neither* males nor females. In Greek, however, the names of most things without life are masculine or feminine, either from the real or fancied possession of masculine or feminine qualities, or from a similarity in their formation to other nouns of these genders.

Thus, for the most part, the names of *winds* and *rivers* (from their power and violence), and also of the *months*, are *masculine;* and the names of *trees*, *plants*, *countries*, *islands*, and *cities* (regarded as mothers of their products or inhabitants) are *feminine;* while nouns denoting mere *products*, or implying *inferiority* (even though names of persons), especially *diminutives*, are *neuter;* as, ὁ ἄνεμος, *wind*, ὁ Βοῤῥᾶς, *Boreas*, ὁ ποταμός, *river*, ὁ Νεῖλος, *the Nile*, ὁ μήν, *month*, ὁ Ἑκατομβαιών, *June–July*, ἡ συκῆ, *fig-tree*, ἡ μηλέα, *apple-tree*, ἡ ἄπιος, *pear-tree*, ἡ ἄμπελος, *vine*, ἡ βύβλος, *papyrus*, ἡ χώρα, *country*, ἡ Αἴγυπτος, *Egypt*, ἡ νῆσος, *island*, ἡ Σάμος, *Samos*, ἡ πόλις, *city*, ἡ Λακεδαίμων, *Lacedæmon;* τὸ σῦκον, *fig*, τὸ μῆλον, *apple*, τὸ τέκνον, *child*, τὸ ἀνδράποδον, *slave*, τὸ γύναιον, dim. of γυνή, *woman*, τὸ παιδίον, *little boy* or *girl*.

§ **76.** The gender of nouns, when not determined by the signification, may be, for the most part, inferred from the form of the theme or root, according to the following rules.

I. In the FIRST DECLENSION (¶ 7), all words in -ας and -ης

are *masculine;* all in -α and -η, *feminine;* as, ὁ ταμίας, ὁ ναύτης· ἡ οἰκία, ἡ τιμή.

II. In the SECOND DECLENSION (¶ 9), most words in -ος and -ως are *masculine*, but some are *feminine* or *common;* words in -ον and -ων are *neuter;* as, ὁ λόγος, ὁ νεώς· ἡ ὁδός, ἡ ἕως, *dawn;* ὁ, ἡ θεός, *god*, ὁ, ἡ ἄρκτος, *bear;* τὸ σῦκον, τὸ ἀνώγεων.

Except when the diminutive form in -ον is given to feminine proper names; as, ἡ Λεόντιον, ἡ Γλυκέριον.

III. In the THIRD DECLENSION (¶¶ 11–14),

a. All words in -ευς are *masculine;* all in -ω and -αυς, *feminine;* and all in -α, -ι, -υ, and -ος, *neuter;* as, ὁ ἱππεύς, ὁ ἀμφορεύς, *amphora;* ἡ ἠχώ, ἡ ναῦς· τὸ σῶμα, τὸ μέλι, *honey*, τὸ ἄστυ, τὸ τεῖχος.

b. All *abstracts* in -της and -ις, and most other words in -ις are *feminine;* as, ἡ γλυκύτης, *sweetness;* ἡ δύναμις, *power*, ἡ ποίησις, *poesy;* ἡ ῥίς, ἡ πόλις.

c. All *labials* and *palatals*, all *liquids* (except a few in which ρ is the characteristic), and all *liquid-mutes* are either *masculine* or *feminine.*

d. Nouns in which the root ends in,

1.) -ωτ-, -εν-, or -ντ-, are *masculine;* as, ὁ γέλως, -ωτος, *laughter;* ὁ λιμήν, -ένος· ὁ λέων, -οντος, ὁ ὀδούς, ὁ γίγας, ὁ ἱμάς, -άντος, *thong.*

Except τὸ οὖς, ὠτός, *ear*, τὸ φῶς, φωτός, *light* (both contracts), ἡ φρήν, φρενός, *mind*, and a few names of cities (§ 75); as, ἡ Ῥαμνοῦς, -οῦντος, *Rhamnus.*

2.) -δ-, or -θ-, are *feminine;* as, ἡ λαμπάς, -άδος, *torch*, ἡ ἔρις, -ιδος, *strife*, ἡ χλαμύς, -ύδος, *cloak;* ἡ κόρυς, -υθος, *helmet.*

Except ὁ, ἡ παῖς, παιδός, *child*, ὁ πούς, ποδός, *foot*, ὁ, ἡ ὄρνις, -ῑθος, *bird.*

3.) -ατ-, or -ᾰ-, are *neuter;* as, τὸ ἧπαρ, -ατος, τὸ κέρας, -ᾱτος, τὸ γέρας, -ᾰος.

B. NUMBER.

§ 77. The Greek has three numbers; the SINGULAR, denoting *one;* the PLURAL, denoting *more than one;* and the DUAL (duālis, from duo, *two*), a variety of the plural, which may be employed when only *two* are spoken of.

Thus, the singular ἄνθρωπος signifies *man*, the plural ἄνθρωποι, *men* (whether two or more), and the dual ἀνθρώπω, *two men.*

REMARK. The dual is most used in the Attic Greek. In the Æolic dialect (as in the Latin, which it approaches the most nearly of the Greek dialects) and in the Hellenistic Greek, the dual does not occur, except in δύο, *two*, and ἄμφω, *both* (Lat. *duo*, *ambo*).

C. Case.

§ 78. The Greek has five cases;

1. The Nominative, expressing the subject of a sentence.
2. " Genitive, " the point of departure, or cause.
3. " Dative, " the indirect object, or accompaniment.
4. " Accusative, " direct limit.
5. " Vocative, " address.

Notes. α. From the general character of the relations which they denote, the Nominative, Accusative, and Vocative are termed the *direct*, and the Genitive and Dative, the *indirect* cases.

β. The Nominative and Vocative are also termed *casus recti*, *the right cases* and the other three, *casus obliqui*, *the oblique cases*.

γ. For a fuller statement of the use of the cases, see Syntax.

D. Methods of Declension.

§ 79. Words are declined, in Greek, by annexing to the root certain AFFIXES, which mark the distinctions of gender, number, and case. There are three sets of these affixes; and hence arise three distinct methods of declining words, called the FIRST, SECOND, and THIRD DECLENSIONS.

The first of these methods applies only to words of the masculine and feminine genders; the second and third apply to words of all the genders. In some of the cases, however, the affixes vary, in the same declension, according to the gender; so that, to know how a word is declined, it is necessary to ascertain three things; 1. its *root*, 2. the *declension* to which it belongs, and 3. its *gender*.

The mode in which the gender is marked has been already stated (§ 74, β). From the theme (i. e. the Nom. sing.) and the gender, we can often determine at once the root and the declension. If it is necessary to mark these explicitly, it is commonly done by giving, with the theme, the Genitive singular, or its ending. *If the Genitive singular ends in* -ας *or* -ης, *or in* -ου *from a theme in* -ας *or* -ης, *the word is of the first declension; if it ends in* -ου *from a theme in* -ος *or* -ον, *the word is of the second declension; if it ends in* -ος, *the word is of the third declension. The root is obtained by throwing off the affix of the Genitive;* or it may be obtained by throwing off any affix beginning with a vowel.

Thus the nouns, ὁ ταμίας, *steward*, ἡ οἰκία, *house*, ἡ γλῶσσα, *tongue*, ὁ δῆμος, *people*, and ὁ Ἄραψ, *Arab*, make in the Genitive, ταμίου, οἰκίας, γλώσσης, δήμου, and Ἄραβος. From these genitives, we ascertain that ταμίας, οἰκία, and γλῶσσα belong to the first declension, δῆμος to the second, and Ἄραψ to the third. By throwing off the affixes -ου, -ας, -ης, and -ος, we obtain the roots ταμι-, οἰκι-, γλωσσ-, δημ-, and Ἀραβ-. The words are then declined by annexing to these roots the affixes in the table (¶ 5).

§ 80. In the declension of words, the following GENERAL RULES are observed.

I. The masculine and feminine affixes are the same, except in the *Nominative* and *Genitive singular* of the *first* declension. The neuter affixes are the same with the masculine and feminine, except in the *direct* cases, *singular* and *plural*.

II. In *neuters*, the three *direct* cases have the same affix, and in the plural this affix is always ᾰ.

III. The dual has but two forms; one for the *direct*, and the other for the *indirect* cases.

IV. In the *feminine singular* of the *first* declension, and in the *plural* of all words, the *Vocative* is the same with the Nominative.

§ 81. REMARKS. 1. The use of the Voc. as a distinct form is still further limited. Few substantives or adjectives, except proper names and personal appellatives and epithets, are sufficiently employed in address to require a separate form for this purpose. Hence the *participle*, *pronoun*, *article*, and *numeral* have no distinct Voc.; and in respect to other words which are declined, the following observations may be made.

α. *Masculines* of Dec. I. are commonly names or epithets of persons, and therefore form the Voc. sing.

β. In Dec. II., the distinct form of the Voc. is commonly used, except for euphony or rhythm; as, Ὦ φίλος, ὦ φίλος, *my friend! my friend!* Ar. Nub. 1167. Φίλος ὦ Μενέλαε Δ. 189. Ἠέλιός τε Γ. 277. To avoid the double ε, θεός, *god* (like *deus* in Latin), has, in classic writers, no distinct Voc.; yet Θεέ St. Matth. 27. 46.

γ. In Dec. III., few words, except proper names and personal appellatives and epithets, have a distinct Voc.; and even in those which have, the Nom. is sometimes employed in its stead, especially by Attic writers; thus, Ὦ πᾶσα πόλι Ar. Ach. 971; but Ὦ πόλις Soph. Phil. 1213. Αἶαν Soph. Aj. 89; but Ὦ φίλ' Αἴας Ib. 529. In many words of this declension, the Voc. cannot be formed without such a mutilation of the root as scarcely to leave it intelligible (§§ 63, 101).

§ **82.** 2. An inspection of the table (¶ 5) will likewise show, that, in regular declension,

α.) The Nom. sing. masc. and (except in Dec. I.) fem. always ends in ς.

β.) The Dat. sing. always ends in ι, either written in the line or subscribed.

γ.) The Acc. sing. (except in neuters of Dec. III.) always ends in ν, or its corresponding vowel α (§ 50); and the Acc. plur. masc. and fem. is always formed by adding ς to the Acc. sing. (§§ 34, 58).

δ.) The Gen. plur. always ends in ων.

ε.) In Dec. I. and II., the affixes are all *open* (i. e. begin with a *vowel*), and all constitute a distinct syllable. In Dec. III., three of the affixes, σ, ν, and σι, are *close* (i. e. begin with a *consonant*), and of these the two first, having no vowel, must unite with the last syllable of the root.

ζ.) In the singular of Dec. III., the direct cases neut., and the Voc. masc. and fem., have no affixes.

Note. It follows, from nos. ε and ζ, that words of Dec. I. and II. are *parisyllabic* (par, *equal*), that is, have the same number of syllables in all their cases; but words of Dec. III. are *imparisyllabic*, that is, have more syllables in some of their cases than in others.

3. The Table (¶ 6) exhibits the affixes as resolved into their two classes of Elements; I. Flexible Endings, which are *significant* additions, marking distinctions of number, case, and gender; and II. Connecting Vowels, which are *euphonic* in their origin, and serve to unite the flexible endings with the root. For farther illustration, see the following sections upon the history of Greek declension.

E. History of Greek Declension.

§ **83.** The early history of Greek declension is beyond the period not merely of written records, but even of tradition. It can be traced, therefore, only by the way-marks which have been left upon the language itself, and by the aid of comparative philology. The following view of the subject has much evidence in its support, and serves to explain the general phenomena of Greek declension, and of the use of the numbers and cases.

Greek declension was progressive. At first, the simple root was used, as in some languages even at the present day, without any change to denote number or case; thus, ἰχθύ, *fish*, γύπ, *vulture*, whether one or more were spoken of. Then the *plural* number was marked, by affixing to the root ε, the simple root, of course, now becoming *singular*, as each new formation limits the use of prior forms; thus,

Singular,	ἰχθύ, *fish*,	Plural,	ἰχθύε, *fishes*.
	γύπ, *vulture*,		γῦπε, *vultures*.

The next step was to make a separate form, to express the *indirect*, as distinguished from the *direct* relations. This was done by annexing ι to the root, and this form became plural by adding one of the common signs of the plural, ν. We have now the distinction of case; thus,

	Singular.	Plural.
Direct Case,	ἰχθύ	ἰχθύε
	γύπ	γῦπε
Indirect Case,	ἰχθύϊ	ἰχθύϊν
	γυπί	γυπίν

§ 84. Each of these cases was afterwards subdivided. (A.) From the Direct Case were separated, in the *masculine* and *feminine* genders, two new cases, the one to express the *subject*, and the other the *direct object*, of an action, i. e. the *Nominative*, and *Accusative cases*.

The *Nominative* was formed by adding ς, as the sign of the *subject*, to the old Direct forms; thus, Sing. ἰχθύς, γύπς, Plur. ἰχθύες, γῦπες.

The *Accusative* was formed by adding to the root, as the sign of the *direct object*, ν, which in the plural took one of the common signs of the plural, ς; thus, Sing. ἰχθύν, γύπν, Plur. ἰχθύνς, γύπνς, or, by the euphonic change of ν into its corresponding vowel (§§ 58, 63, R.), Sing. γῦπα, Plur. ἰχθύας, γῦπας.

(B.) From the Indirect Case was separated a new case to express the *subjective*, as distinguished from the *objective* relations, i. e. the *Genitive*. This was formed by affixing θ, or commonly, with a euphonic vowel, οθ. In the plural, this took the plural affix ν; thus, οθν. But by the laws of euphony, which afterwards prevailed, neither θ, nor θν could end a word (§ 63). Therefore, θ either was changed to ς, or was dropped, or assumed the vowel ε (commonly written with ν paragogic εν, § 67. 3); and οθν became ων by the absorption of the θ (θ, perhaps, first passing into σ, as in the singular, then σ being changed into its corresponding vowel ε, and this absorbed). Thus οθ became ος, ο, or οθεν; and οθν, ων.

The old Indirect Case remained as a *Dative*, without change, except that a new plural was formed by annexing the dative sign ι (§ 83) to the Nominative plural.

§ 85. The plural had now throughout a new form, but the old form had so attached itself to various names of incessant use, that in most of the dialects it was still preserved. But these household plurals, which could not be shaken off, would be principally such as referred to objects double by nature or custom, as the eyes, hands, feet, shoes, wings, &c. Hence this form came at length to be appropriated to a *dual* sense, though in the time of Homer this restriction of its use seems not as yet to have been fully made. The simple form of the root was likewise retained in the singular as a case of address (*Vocative*), in words in which there was occasion for such a form, and the laws of euphony allowed it. In the plural the Vocative had never any form distinct from the Nominative. We have now the three numbers, and the five cases, which, with the euphonic changes already mentioned, appear thus.

Sing.	Nom.	-ς	ἰχθύς	γύπς (γύψ)
	Gen.	-ος	ἰχθύος	γυπός
	Dat.	-ι	ἰχθύϊ	γυπί
	Acc.	-ν, -α	ἰχθύν	γῦπα
	Voc.	*	ἰχθύ	
Plur.	N. V.	-ες	ἰχθύες	γῦπες
	Gen.	-ων	ἰχθύων	γυπῶν
	Dat.	-εσι	ἰχθύεσι (ἰχθύσι)	γύπεσι (γυψί)
	Acc.	-ας	ἰχθύας	γῦπας

Dual Dir.	-ε	ἰχθύε	γῦπε
Indir.	-ιν	ἰχθύϊν (ἰχθύοιν)	γυπίν (γυποῖν).

For the sake of completeness, we have added in the table above two later modifications; viz., the common shorter Dat. plur., formed by dropping ε (unless one chooses to form it from the Dat. sing. by inserting the plural sign σ); and the Indirect Case dual prolonged by inserting ο, after the analogy of the Gen. sing. and plur.

§ 86. We have exhibited above the primitive nude declension, now called the *third*. But subsequently two other modes of declension sprang up, having connecting vowels, which united the flexible endings to the root; the one having ο, now called the *second* declension; and the other, α, now called the *first*. These declensions chose rather to drop than to change the final ϑ of the Gen. sing., apparently to avoid confusion with the Nom.; and likewise to retain the old Direct Case as a Nom. plur., which became afterwards distinguished from the dual by a different mode of contraction, its more frequent use leading to precession. In all the affixes of these declensions in which two vowels came together, contraction naturally took place in one or another of its forms; and in the Dat. plur. a shorter form became the more common one, made either by dropping ι from the longer form, or by adding the plural sign ς to the Dat. sing. For ε in the Voc., instead of ο, see § 28. We give as an example of Dec. II., *ὁ λόγος, word*, and of Dec. I., *ὁ ταμίας, steward.*

Sing. Nom.	λόγ-ο-ς,	λόγος	ταμί-α-ς,	ταμίας
Gen.	λόγ-ο-ο,	λόγου	ταμί-α-ο,	ταμίου
Dat.	λόγ-ο-ι,	λόγῳ	ταμί-α-ι,	ταμίᾳ
Acc.	λόγ-ο-ν,	λόγον	ταμί-α-ν,	ταμίαν
Voc.	λόγ-ο,	λόγε	ταμί-α,	ταμία
Plur. N. V.	λόγ-ο-ε,	λόγοι	ταμί-α-ε,	ταμίαι
Gen.	λογ-ό-ων,	λόγων	ταμι-ά-ων,	ταμιῶν
Dat.	λογ-ό-εσι,	λόγοισι, -οις	ταμι-ά-εσι,	ταμίαισι, -αις
Acc.	λόγ-ο-ας,	λόγους	ταμί-α-ας,	ταμίας
Dual N. A. V.	λόγ-ο-ε,	λόγω	ταμί-α-ε,	ταμία
G. D.	λόγ-ο-ιν,	λόγοιν	ταμί-α-ιν,	ταμίαιν

In the Nom. and Acc. sing. of these declensions, the primitive direct form, without ς or ν appended, was sometimes retained; as, Nom. Θυέστᾰ, ἱππότᾰ (§ 95. 2; compare the Latin *nauta, poēta*), ὁ· Acc. νεώ, ἕω, Ἄθω (§ 97). So the neuters τό, ἄλλο, αὐτό, ἐκεῖνο, ὅ (§ 97).

§ 87. We have thus far treated only of the *masculine* gender. In the *neuter* (which occurs only in the second and third declensions), since things without life have no voluntary action, the distinction of subject and object is obviously of far less consequence, and therefore in this gender the separation of the Nom., Acc., and Voc. was never made. The place of these three cases continued to be supplied by a single Direct Case, which in the singular of Dec. III. was the simple root, and in the singular of Dec. II. ended in ον (the ν being either euphonic, or more probably having the same force as in the Acc., and marking the *objective* character of the gender). The plural has the same form in both declensions, simply appending, instead of the old ε, ᾰ (which, as the corresponding vowel of ν (§ 50), is more *objective* in its character), and without a connecting vowel. We give, as examples, *τὸ δάκρυ* (poetic), *tear*, of Dec. III., and *τὸ σῦκον, fig*, of Dec. II.

Sing.	N. A. V.	δάκρυ	σῦκ-ον
	Gen.	δάκρυ-ος	σύκ-ου
	Dat.	δάκρυ-ι	σύκ-ῳ
Plur.	N. A. V.	δάκρυ-α	σῦκ-α
	Gen.	δακρύ-ων	σύκ-ων
	Dat.	δάκρυ-σι	σύκ-οις
Dual	N. A. V.	δάκρυ-ε	σύκ-ω
	G. D.	δακρύ-οιν	σύκ-οιν

§ 88. The distinction of subject and object is less striking in the *feminine* than in the masculine ; and hence, in the *first* declension, where there are no neuters with which a distinction must be maintained, the feminine is distinguished from the masculine by not appending the *subjective* ς in the Nom. sing. (§ 84), and by retaining the form ος in the Gen. sing., as the reason for preferring the shorter form does not now exist (§ 86). The ο of this ending is absorbed in the preceding α, unless one chooses to consider the ς as here appended without the euphonic vowel (§ 84. B). In all the other cases, the feminine has precisely the same form as the masculine. Thus, ἡ σκιά, *shadow*,

Sing.	Nom. σκι-ά,	σκιά	Plur.	Nom.	σκιαί
	Gen. σκι-ά-ος,	σκιᾶς		Gen.	σκιῶν
	Dat. σκι-ά-ϊ,	σκιᾷ		Dat.	σκιαῖς
	Acc. σκι-ά-ν,	σκιάν		Acc.	σκιάς

For the precession which has taken place so extensively in the singular of Dec. I., see § 93.

§ 89. In the earlier Greek, the prevalent mode of avoiding hiatus was not, as afterwards, by contraction, but by the insertion of a strong breathing or aspirate consonant (cf. § 117). Of these the most prominent appears to have been the digamma (§ 22. δ). And, although this has disappeared from the language, yet it has left other consonants which have either taken its place, or which were used in like manner with it. The insertion of these consonants, together with different modes of contraction, has given an especial variety of form, in the *first* and *second declensions*, to the *Dative singular*, which, as the primitive indirect case (§ 83), originally performed the offices of both the Genitive and the Dative. Thus, we find,

1.) The ι appended with the insertion of φ, the natural successor of the digamma. This form is Epic, and from its being used as both Gen. and Dat., and sometimes even supplying the place of these cases in the plural, is evidently of great antiquity. E. g.

Gen. Sing. Dec. I. ἐξ εὐνῆφι Ο. 580, β. 2 ; ἀπὸ νευρῆφιν Θ. 300 : Dec. II. ἀπὸ πασσαλόφι Ω. 268 ; ἐκ ποντόφιν ω. 83 ; ἀπὸ πλατέος πτυόφιν Ν. 588 ; Ἰλιόφι κλυτὰ τείχεα Φ. 295 ; ἀπ' αὐτόφιν Λ. 44.

Dat. Sing. Dec. I. ἦφι βίηφι πιθήσας Χ. 107 ; ἅμ' ἠοῖ φαινομένηφιν δ. 407, Ι. 618 ; ἑτέρηφι Π. 734 ; θύρηφιν ι. 238 : Dec. II. παρ' αὐτόφι Μ. 302 ; ἐπὶ δεξιόφιν Ν. 308 ; θεόφιν Η. 366.

Gen. and Dat. Plur. Dec. II. ὄσσε δακρυόφι πλῆσθεν Ρ. 696, Ψ. 397, δ. 705 ; ἀπ' ὀστεόφιν ξ. 134 ; ἀμφ' ὀστεόφιν π. 145 ; ἰκριόφιν μ. 414.

NOTES. α. The φ likewise appears in the *Dative plural* of a few words of the *third declension*, where it seems to have been inserted for the sake of lengthening the preceding syllable; as, ὄχεσφι for ὄχεσι. These forms were also used as both Gen. and Dat.; thus, Gen. κατ' ὄρεσφι Δ. 452; πρόσθ'... ὄχεσφιν Ε. 107; ἀπὸ στήθεσφιν Ξ. 214; διὰ δὲ στήθεσφιν Ε. 41: Dat. σὺν ὄχεσφι Π. 811; ὄρεσφι Λ. 474 (cf. 479), Χ. 139.

β. The following forms in -φι(ν) require special notice; (*a*) ἐσχαρόφιν ε. 59, and κοτυληδονόφιν ε. 433, which are formed as from nouns of Dec. II., while the themes in use are ἐσχάρη of Dec. I., and κοτυληδών of Dec. III.; (*b*) κράτεσφι Κ. 156, and Ἐρέβεσφιν (probably the correct form for Ἐρέβευσφιν Ι. 572, Hom. Cer. 350, Hes. Th. 669), which appear to have plural forms, though singular in their use; (*c*) ναῦφιν, an irregular plural form for ναῦσι, Ν. 700; also used as Gen. Π. 246, &c.; (*d*) the Epic adverb ἶφι, *with might*, Α. 38, which appears to be an old Dat. sing. from ἴς.

γ. Compare with these forms in -φι, the Latin Datives *tibi, sibi, nobis, vobis, deabus, sermonibus, rebus*, and the Latin adverbs of place in *-bi;* as, *ibi, alibi, utribi*, from *is, alius, uter*. The forms in -ηφι when used as Datives are often written incorrectly with an ι subscript (-ῃφι, § 25. α), as though φι had been added to the complete Dat. form. For the ν paragogic, see § 66. α.

§ **90.** 2.) The ι appended with the insertion of θ. This form became adverbial (chiefly poetic), denoting the *place where;* as, οἴκοθι, *at home*, ἄλλοθι, *elsewhere*, αὐτόθι, ὅθι, Κορινθόθι. It was mostly confined to the *second declension*, and, in the few instances in which it was made from nouns of other declensions, it still imitated the forms of this. Traces of its old use as the Indirect Case still remain in Homer; thus, Gen. οὐρανόθι πρό, = πρὸ οὐράνου, Γ. 3, Ἰλιόθι πρό Θ. 561, ἠῶθι πρό ζ. 36; Dat. κηρόθι Ι. 300, ο. 370.

3.) The ι appended with the insertion of χ. This form appears only in the Epic ἧχι (improperly written by some ᾗχι, cf. 89. γ), for the adverbial Dative ᾗ, *where*, Α. 607.

4.) The ι contracted with the preceding ο in the second declension into οι (§ 32). This simpler mode of contraction now scarcely appears except in adverbial Datives; as, οἴκοι, *at home* (but οἴκῳ, *to a house;* cf. in Latin, *domi* and *domus*), πέδοι, Ἰσθμοῖ, οἷ, ὅποι. Yet ἐν Ἰσθμοῖ Simon. Fr. 209; ἐν Πριανσιοῖ Inscr. Cret.; τοῖ δάμοι Inscr. Bœot.

5.) The common form, in which the ι is absorbed by the preceding vowel; as, α-ι ᾳ, ο-ι ῳ; thus, θύρᾳ, οἴκῳ, Ἰσθμῷ.

§ **91.** The forms of the Genitive in -οθεν or -θεν (§ 84. B) remained in the common language only as adverbs, denoting the *place whence;* as, οἴκοθεν, *from home*, ἄλλοθεν, αὐτόθεν, Ἀθήνηθεν. As examples of their use as decided Genitives, may be cited ἐξ Αἰσύμηθεν Θ. 304, ἐξ οὐρανόθεν Θ. 19, ἀπ' οὐρανόθεν λ. 18; and the pronominal forms ἐμέθεν, σέθεν, ἕθεν, which even occur in Attic poets.

CHAPTER II.

DECLENSION OF NOUNS.

I. The First Declension.

[For the affixes and paradigms, see ¶¶ 5-8.]

§ **92.** For the original affixes of Dec. I., which all had α as a connecting vowel, see §§ 86, 88. In most of these affixes, α either became part of a diphthong, or else, either through contraction or the force of analogy, became long. Short α however remained in the *singular*,

1.) In the *direct cases* of *feminines*, whose characteristic was σ, a double consonant, or λλ; as, γλῶσσᾰ, γλῶσσᾰν (¶ 7), δίψᾰ, *thirst*, δόξᾰ, *opinion*, ῥίζᾰ, *root*, ἅμιλλᾰ, *contest*.

Notes. α. Add a few feminines in -λα, and some in -να, particularly *female appellatives;* as, παῦλᾰ and ἀνάπαυλᾰ, *rest*, ἔχιδνᾰ, *viper*, μέριμνᾰ, *care*, δέσποινᾰ, *mistress*, λέαινᾰ, *lioness;* likewise ἄκανθᾰ, *thorn*.

β. Add, also, many feminines in -α pure and -ρα. These have mostly a diphthong in the penult, and may all be recognized by the accent, except the proper names Κίῤῥᾰ, Πύῤῥᾰ, and the numeral μίᾰ, *one*. The principal classes are, (*a*) Polysyllables in -εια and -οια, except abstracts in -εια from verbs in -ευω; as, ἀλήθειᾰ, *truth*, εὔνοιᾰ, *good-will*, βασίλειᾰ, *queen*, but βασιλείᾱ, *reign*, from βασιλεύω· (*b*) Female designations in -τρια; as, ψάλτριᾰ, *female musician:* (*c*) Dissyllables and some polysyllabic names of places in -αια; as, μαῖᾰ, *good mother*, Ἱστίαιᾰ· (*d*) Words in -υια; as, μυῖᾰ, *fly:* (*e*) Most words in -ρα, whose penult is lengthened by a diphthong (except αυ), by ῡ, or by ῤῥ; as, μάχαιρᾰ, *sword*, γέφῡρᾰ, *bridge*, Πύῤῥᾰ.

γ. The accent commonly shows the quantity of final α in the theme. Thus, in all *proparoxytones* and *properispomena*, it must be *short* by the general laws of accent; while, by a special law of the declension, it is *long* in all *oxytones*, and in all *paroxytones* in -α, Gen. -ας, except the three mentioned in Note β.

2.) In the *Vocative* of nouns in -της, and of *gentiles* and *compound verbals* in -ης; as ναύτης (¶ 7), Σκύθης, *Scythian*, Πέρσης, *Persian*, γεωμέτρης (γῆ, *earth*, μετρέω, *to measure*), *geometer*, μυροπώλης (μύρον, *perfume*, πωλέω, *to sell*), *perfumer*, Voc. ναῦτᾰ, Σκύθᾰ, Πέρσᾰ (but Πέρσης, *Perses*, a man's name, Voc. Πέρση), γεωμέτρᾰ, μυροπῶλᾰ.

§ **93.** In the singular, long α passed, by precession, into η, unless preceded by ε, ι, ρ, or ρο (§ 29); as, ναύτης, ναύτη, Ἀτρείδης, Ἀτρείδην, Ἀτρείδη, γλώσσης, γλώσσῃ, τιμή, τιμῆς, τιμήν·

but ταμίᾱς, ταμίᾳ, σκιᾱ́, σκιᾶς, θύρᾱ, θύρᾱν (¶ 7), ἰδέᾱ, *idea* χρείᾱ, *need*, χρόᾱ, *color.*

NOTE. Long α likewise remains in the pures, πόᾱ, *grass*, στοᾱ́, *porch*, γύᾱ, *field*, σικύᾱ, *gourd*, καρύᾱ, *walnut-tree*, ἐλάᾱ, *olive-tree*, Ναυσικάᾱ, *Nausicaa*; in the words, ἀλαλᾱ́, *war-cry*, ἐπίβδᾱ, *day after a feast*, σκανδάλᾱ, *trap-spring*, γεννάδᾱς, *noble*; and in some proper names, particularly those which are Doric or foreign; as, Ἀνδρομέδᾱ, Λήδᾱ, Φιλομήλᾱ, Λεωνίδᾱς, Ὕλᾱς, Σύλλᾱς· and it became η after ρ or ρο in the words δέρη, *neck*, κόρη, *maiden*, κόρρη, *cheek*, ἀθάρη, *pap*, ῥοή, *stream*; in some proper names, as Τήρης· and in compounds of μετρέω, *to measure*, as γεωμέτρης (§ 92. 2). In some words, usage fluctuates between long or short α and η; as, Ἀράσπᾱς Cyr. vi. 1. 31, Ἀράσπης Ib. v. 1. 4, πεῖνᾰ and πείνη, πρύμνᾰ and πρύμνη.

§ **94.** CONTRACTS. A few nouns, in which the characteristic is α or ε, and feminine adjectives in -εα and -οη, are contracted; as, μνάᾱ μνᾶ, Ἑρμέᾱς Ἑρμῆς, βορέᾱς βοῤῥᾶς (ρ being here doubled after contraction), συκέα συκῆ, *fig-tree*, χρυσέα χρυσῆ, διπλόη διπλῆ. For the rules, see §§ 33, 36, 37; for the paradigms, ¶¶ 7, 18.

DIALECTIC FORMS.

§ **95.** 1. In the affixes of this declension, the *Doric* dialect retains throughout the original α; while in the singular, the *Ionic* has η in most of those words in which the *Attic* and *Common* dialects have long α, and even in some in which they have short α, particularly derivatives in -εια and -οια (§ 44); thus, Dor. τιμᾱ́, τιμᾶς, τιμᾷ, τιμᾱ́ν· Ion. σκιή, σκιῆς, σκιῇ, σκιήν· Ep. ἀληθείη, εὐπλοίη, New Ion. ἀληθηΐη, μίη, for ἀλήθειᾰ, εὔπλοιᾰ, μίᾰ.

2. In words in -ης, the *primitive Direct Case* in -ᾰ is sometimes retained by Homer and some of the other poets as Nom. (§ 86), for the sake of the metre or euphony; as, ὁ αὖτε Θυέστᾰ B. 107; ἱππότᾰ Νέστωρ B. 336; μητίετα Ζεύς A. 175; βαθυμῆτα Χείρων Pind. N. 3. 92; ἱυκτᾰ Μενάλκας Theoc. 8. 30. So in feminines in -η, the poets sometimes retain the old short α in the Voc.; as, νύμφᾰ φίλη Γ. 130; Ὦ Δίκᾰ, Sapph. 66 (44). On the other hand, Αἰήτη Ap. Rh. 3. 386, for Αἰῆτᾰ, Voc. of Αἰήτης.

3. The old *genitive* affixes, ᾱο and ᾱων, which often occur in the Epic writers, were contracted as follows:

α.) In the *Ionic* dialect, they were regularly contracted into ω and ων, with the insertion of ε after a consonant (§ 35); as, Ἀτρείδαο (Ἀτρείδω) Ἀτρείδεω, Ἀτρειδάων (Ἀτρειδῶν) Ἀτρειδέων· Βορέᾱο Βορέω, Ἑρμείω O. 214, ἐϋμμελίω Δ. 165, Ἀσίω B. 461.

β.) In the *Doric*, ᾱ absorbed the following vowel, and the affixes became ᾱ and ᾶν (§ 45. 1); as, Ἀτρείδαο Ἀτρείδᾱ, Ἀτρειδάων Ἀτρειδᾶν.

γ.) In the *Attic*, ᾱο and ᾱων were contracted into ου (by precession from ω, §§ 28, 29) and ῶν; as, Ἀτρείδαο (Ἀτρείδω) Ἀτρείδου, Ἀτρειδάων Ἀτρειδῶν.

§ **96.** 4. In the *Accusative of masculines*, the Ionic often changes ν to ᾰ, the old connecting vowel α now becoming ε (§ 46. β); as, δεσπότεᾰ Hdt. i. 11, pl. δεσπότεᾰς Ib. 111, for δεσπότην, δεσπότᾱς.

5. The dative plural in Homer commonly ends in -ησι, or -ῃς before a

vowel (which may be referred to apostrophe). There are, however, a few instances of -ῃς before a consonant (σῇς καί A. 179, πέτρῃς πρός η. 279, &c.) and two, where we even find -αις, which ought, perhaps, to be changed to -ῃς (ἀκταῖς M. 284, θεαῖς ε. 119). An old contraction into -ᾶσι, instead of -αισι, remained in the common language in adverbs of place; as, Πλαταιᾶσι, *at Platææ*, θύρᾶσι.

6. For the Epic Gen. in -θεν, see § 91. For the Epic Datives in -φι, -θι, and -χι, see §§ 89, 90. For the Doric and Æolic forms of the Acc. plur., see § 45. 5.

7. Antique, Ionic, and Doric forms are sometimes found in Attic writers; particularly,

α.) The Dor. Gen. in -ᾱ, from some nouns in -ας, mostly proper names; as, ὀρνιθοθήρας, *fowler*, Γωβρύας, Καλλίας· Gen. ὀρνιθοθήρα, Γωβρύα, Καλλία. So all contracts in -ᾶς; as, βοῤῥᾶς, G. βοῤῥᾶ (¶ 7).

β.) The Ion. Gen. in -εω, from a few proper names in -ης; as, Θαλῆς, Τήρης· Gen. Θάλεω, Τήρεω.

γ.) The old Dat. plur. in -αισι, which is frequent in the poets. So, in Plato, τέχναισι Leg. 920 e, ἡμέραισι Phædr. 276 b.

II. The Second Declension.

[For the affixes and paradigms, see §§ 86, 87; ¶¶ 5, 6, 9, 10.]

§ **97.** The flexible endings of the Nominative and Accusative singular are wanting (§ 86),

1.) In the *theme* of the *article;* thus, ὁ for ὅς.

2.) In the *neuter* of the *article* and of the *pronouns* ἄλλος, αὐτός, ἐκεῖνος, and ὅς· thus, τό, ἄλλο, αὐτό, ἐκεῖνο, ὅ, for τόν, ἄλλον, &c.

Note. In crasis with the article (§ 39), and in composition with the pronouns τοῖος and τόσος, the neuter αὐτό more frequently becomes αὐτόν· thus, ταὐτόν and ταὐτό, for τὸ αὐτό· τοιοῦτον and τοιοῦτο, τοσοῦτον and τοσοῦτο.

3.) Frequently in the *Accusative* of the *Attic declension* (§ 98), particularly in ἡ ἕως, *dawn*, ἡ ἅλως, *threshing-floor*, ἡ Κέως, ἡ Κῶς, ἡ Τέως, ὁ Ἄθως· thus, Acc. νεών and νεώ (¶ 9), ἕω, Ἄθω. So, in the adjectives ἀγήρως (¶ 17), ἀνάπλεως, *full*, ἀξιόχρεως, *competent*.

§ **98.** Contracts. If the characteristic is α, ε, or ο, it may be contracted with the affix according to the rules (§§ 33–37). See ἀγήραος (¶ 17), ὀστέον, νόος (¶ 9). The contract declension in -ως and -ων, from -αος and -αον, is termed by grammarians the *Attic Declension* from its prevalence among Attic writers, although it is far from being peculiar to them (§ 7).

Notes. α. The number of words belonging to the Attic declension is small. In some of them, the uncontracted form does not occur, or occurs only with some change. Thus, for ἀνώγαον, εὔγαος (which are compounds of γάα, the original form of γῆ, *earth*, and from which come by contraction ἀνώγεων, εὔγεως) we find the extended forms ἀνώγαιον v. 4. 29, εὔγαιος or εὔγειος. Some of them are variously declined. See §§ 123. γ, 124. γ.

β. If the characteristic is long α, ε is inserted after the contraction (§ 35) thus, ναός (νώς) νεώς (¶ 9), ναοῦ (νῶ) νεώ, ναῷ (νῷ) νεῷ, ναόν (νών) νεών· Plur. ναοί (νῷ) νεῴ, &c.

γ. In the Attic declension, the Nom. plur. neut. is contracted, like the other cases, into ω; thus, ἀγήρω (¶ 17), as if from ἀγηρά-ο-α, a form with the connecting vowel. See § 87.

DIALECTIC FORMS.

§ **99.** 1. The affix of the Gen. sing. ο-ο (§ 86), which was commonly contracted to ου, or, in the Æolic and stricter Doric, to ω (§ 44. 4), was often prolonged by the poets, especially the Epic (sometimes even by the Tragic in lyric portions), to οιο; thus, πόντου Ἰκαρίοιο B. 145; δόμου ὑψηλοῖο α. 126; οἷο δόμοιο α. 330; θεοῦ Pind. O. 2. 37; θεοῖο Ib. 6. 60; μεγάλω Δίος Alc. 1 (20); ἐρχομένοιο Id. 37; ποταμοῖο...Ἀνάπω Theoc. 1. 68; μαλακῶ χόρτοιο Id. 4. 18. The Epic genitives Πετεῶο (Δ. 327, &c.) and Πηνελεῶο (Ξ. 489) are made by a single contraction, with the usual insertion of ε (§ 98. β), from the original forms Πετάοο, Πηνελάοο. The Epic *dual* forms in οιϊν, which alone are used by Homer, arise from a mere poetic doubling of ι (§ 48).

2. Some proper names in -ος have the Gen. sing. in Herodotus, after the analogy of Dec. I.; as, Κροῖσος, Κροίσεω viii. 122, but Κροίσου i. 6; Βάττεω iv. 160; Κλεομβρότεω v. 32. The Gen. plur. forms πεσσέων (Hdt. i. 94) and πυρέων (Id. ii. 36), if genuine, may be referred to the Ionic insertion of ε (§ 48. 1).

3. The old Dat. plur. in -οισι is common in the poets of all classes, and in Ionic prose. So, even in Plato, θεοῖσι Leg. 955 e.

4. For the Epic Gen. in -οθεν, see § 91. For the Epic Datives in -οφι and οθι, and the old Dat. in -οι, see §§ 89, 90. For the Doric and Æolic forms of the Acc. plur., see § 45. 5.

5. Contracts in -ους from -οος occur in Homer, though rarely; as, νοῦς κ. 240 (elsewhere νόος). In words in -εος, -εον, he sometimes protracts the ε to ει (§ 47. N.), and sometimes employs synizesis (§ 30).

III. THE THIRD DECLENSION.

[For the affixes and paradigms, see §§ 85, 87; ¶¶ 5, 6, 11-16.]

§ **100.** In this declension, the Nominative, though regarded as the theme of the word, seldom exhibits the root in its simple, distinct form. This form must therefore be obtained from the Genitive, or from some case which has an open affix (§§ 79, 82. ε).

REMARKS. 1. Special attention must be given to the euphonic changes which occur in those cases which have either *close* affixes, or *no* affixes; that is in the Nominative and Vocative singular, the Dative plural, and the Accusative singular in -ν. For these changes, see in general §§ 51, 55, 57–59, 63.

2. The flexible ending of the Acc. sing. in this, as in the other two declensions, seems to have been originally ν. But the ν was so extensively changed into α in accordance with § 63. R., that the α became the prevailing affix, and was often used even after a vowel. It will therefore be understood that the affix is α, if no statement is made to the contrary. When the affix is ν, the root receives the same changes as in the theme (§ 110).

Words of the third declension are divided according to the characteristic, into Mutes, Liquids, Liquid-Mutes, and Pures.

A. Mutes.

[¶ 11.]

§ 101. Labials and Palatals. These are all either masculine or feminine, and in none is the Voc. formed except γυνή (N. γ).

Notes. α. For the ψ and ξ in the theme and Dat. pl., see § 51.

β. In θρίξ, the root is θριχ-. In those cases in which χ remains, θ becomes τ, according to § 62. In ἡ ἀλώπηξ, -εκος, *fox*, the last vowel of the root is lengthened in the theme. Compare § 112. α.

γ. Γυνή, *woman*, *wife*, which is irregular in having its theme after the form of Dec. I., and also in its accentuation, is thus declined: S. N. γυνή, G. γυναικός, D. γυναικί, A. γυναῖκα, V. γύναι· P. N. γυναῖκες, G. γυναικῶν, D. γυναιξί, A. γυναῖκας· D. N. γυναῖκε, G. γυναικοῖν. The old grammarians have also cited from Comic writers the forms, A. γυνήν, P. N. γυναί, A. γυνάς, according to Dec. I.

§ 102. Masculine and Feminine Linguals. These lose their characteristic in the theme and Dat. pl. (§ 55), in the Acc. sing., when formed in ν (§§ 63. R., 100. 2), and in the Voc. (§ 63).

Notes. α. If a palatal is thus brought before σ, it unites with it in ξ (§ 51), as (ἄνακτς, ἄνακς) ἄναξ (¶ 11), ἡ (νύκτς) νύξ, *night*; if to the end of a word, it is dropped (§ 63), as (ἄνακτ, ἄνακ) ἄνα. This distinct Voc., however, is used only in addressing a god; otherwise, ὦ ἄναξ (or, by frequent crasis, ὦναξ).

β. For the change of ο when brought before the affixes ς and ν, or to the end of a word, see §§ 112. α, 113. 3.

γ. Barytones in -ις and -υς form the Acc. sing. in both α and ν, the latter being the more common affix; as, χάρις (¶ 11), ἡ ἔρις, *strife*, ὁ, ἡ ὄρνις, *bird*; Acc. χάριτα and χάριν (as the name of a goddess, the form in -α is always used, and sometimes, also, in poetry; but, otherwise, the form in -ν, yet see H. Gr. iii. 5. 16), ἔριν and poet. ἔριδα, ὄρνιν and poet. ὄρνιθα. So also, κλείς (¶ 11), ὁ γέλως, *laughter*, and the compounds of πούς, *foot*; thus, Acc. κλεῖδα and κλεῖν, γέλωτα and γέλων, Οἰδίποδα and Οἰδίπουν (¶ 16), δίποδα and δίπουν (¶ 17). Add ὁ ἔρως, *love*, Acc. ἔρωτα and rare poetic form ἔρων. So παῖς, when resolved by the poets into πάϊς, may have Acc. πάϊν, Ap. Rh.

4. 697. In oxytones, the accent served to prevent the lingual from falling away.

§ **103.** Neuter Linguals. In these, the characteristic is always τ, which, in the theme, is commonly dropped after μα, but otherwise becomes ς or ϱ (§ 63); as, σῶμα, φῶς, κέρας, ἧπαϱ (¶ 11), εἶδός (¶ 22), from the roots σωματ-, φωτ-, κερατ-, ἡπατ-, εἰδοτ-.

Note. The τ is also dropped in μέλι, μέλιτος, *honey;* in γάλα, γάλακτος, *milk*, which also drops κ; and in γόνυ, γόνατος, *knee*, and δόϱυ, δόϱατος, *spear*, which then change α to υ (compare § 113). In the poetic ἦμαϱ, ἤματος, *day*, τ is changed into ϱ after μα; and in ὕδωϱ, ὕδατος, *water*, and σκῶϱ, σκατός, *filth*, τ is changed into ϱ, and α into ω. See § 123. γ.

§ **104.** Contract Linguals. A few linguals drop the characteristic before some or all of the open affixes, and are then contracted; thus, κλεῖδες (κλεῖες) κλεῖς, κλεῖδας (κλεῖας) κλεῖς· κέϱᾰτος κέϱαος κέϱως, κέϱᾰτα κέϱαα κέϱᾱ (¶ 11); τὸ τέϱας, *prodigy*, P. N. τέϱᾰτα τέϱᾱ, G. τεϱάτων τεϱῶν· ὁ χρώς, *skin*, S. D. χρωτί (χρωΐ) χρῷ (in the phrase ἐν χρῷ). So, in Homer, from ὁ ἱδρώς, *sweat*, ὁ γέλως, *laughter*, ὁ ἔρως, *love*, S. D. ἱδρῷ, γέλῳ, ἔρῳ, for ἱδρῶτι, &c.; A. ἱδρῶ, γέλω, for ἱδρῶτα (ἱδρῶα), γέλωτα. Compare §§ 107, 119, 123. α.

Note. In the following words, the contraction is confined to the root

τὸ οὖς, ὠτός, *ear* (¶ 11), contracted from the old οὖας, οὔατος (§ 33. γ).

τὸ δέλεαϱ, *bait*, Gen. δελέατος, δέλητος.

τὸ στέαϱ, contr. στῆϱ, *tallow*, Gen. στέᾱτος, στητός.

τὸ φϱέαϱ, *well*, Gen. φϱέατος (ᾱ or ᾰ), φϱητός (§ 37. 1).

Remark. Those linguals in which a liquid precedes the lingual will be treated as a distinct class (§ 109).

B. Liquids.

[¶ 12.]

§ **105.** Masculine and Feminine Liquids. In these, except ἅλς, *salt*, *sea* (in the singular, only Ionic and poetic), the characteristic is always ν or ϱ. For the changes in the theme and Dat. pl., see §§ 57 – 59. When the characteristic is ν, it depends upon the preceding vowel whether the ν or the ς is changed in the theme; as follows.

1.) If an *E* or *O* vowel precede, the ς is changed; as in λιμήν, -ένος, δαίμων, -ονος (¶ 12); ὁ μήν, μηνός, *month*, ὁ χειμών, -ῶνος, *storm*, *winter*.

Except ὁ κτείς, κτενός, *comb*, the numeral εἷς, ἑνός, *one* (¶ 21), and the Ionic ὁ μείς (as from root μεν-, yet Gen. μηνός) for μήν, *month* (Hdt. ii. 82).

2.) If α precede, in *nouns* the ς is changed, but in *adjectives* the ν; thus, ὁ Πάν, Πανός, *Pan*, ὁ παιάν, -ᾶνος, *pæan*; but μέλᾱς, -ανος (¶ 19), τάλᾱς, -ανος, *wretched*.

3.) If ι or υ precede, the ν is changed; as in ῥίς, ῥινός (¶ 12), ὁ δελφίς, -ῖνος, *dolphin*, ὁ Φόρκυς, -ῡνος, *Phorcys*.

NOTES. α. The ν remains in μόσυν, -ῡνος, *wooden tower*; and most words in -ις and -υς have a second, but less classic form, in -ιν and -υν; as, ῥίς and ῥίν, δελφίς and δελφίν, Φόρκυς and Φόρκυν.

β. In the pronoun τίς, (¶ 24), the ν of the root τιν- is simply dropped in the theme. Yet see § 152. β.

REMARK. VOCATIVE. In the Voc. of Ἀπόλλων, -ωνος, *Apollo*, Ποσειδῶν, -ῶνος, *Neptune*, and ὁ σωτήρ, -ῆρος, *saviour*, the natural tone of address has led to the throwing back of the accent, and the shortening of the last syllable; thus, Ἄπολλον, Πόσειδον, σῶτερ.

§ **106.** SYNCOPATED LIQUIDS. I. In a few liquids of familiar use, a *short vowel* preceding the characteristic is syncopated in some or most of the cases; as follows.

1.) In these three, the syncope takes place before *all* the *open* terminations:

ἀνήρ, *man* (¶ 12). For the insertion of the δ, see § 64. 2.

κύων, *dog* (¶ 12), which has, for its root, κυον-, by syncope, κυν-. In this word, the syncope extends to the Dat. plur.

ἀρνός, *lamb's* (¶ 12), which has, for its root, ἀρεν-, by syncope, ἀρν-. The Nom. sing. is not used, and its place is supplied by ἀμνός.

2.) These five are syncopated in the *genitive* and *dative singular*:

πατήρ, *father*, and μήτηρ, *mother* (¶ 12).

ἡ θυγάτηρ, *daughter*, G. θυγατέρος θυγατρός, D. θυγατέρι θυγατρί.

ἡ γαστήρ, *stomach*, G. γαστέρος γαστρός, D. γαστέρι γαστρί.

ἡ Δημήτηρ, *Ceres*, G. Δημήτερος Δήμητρος, D. Δημήτερι Δήμητρι· also, A. Δημήτερα Δήμητρα.

NOTES. α. In these words, the poets sometimes neglect the syncope, and sometimes employ it in other cases than those which are specified.

β. For the Dat. pl., see § 59. Γαστήρ has not only γαστράσι (Dio Cass. 54. 22), but also in Hipp. γαστῆρσι.

§ **107.** II. In *comparatives* in -ων, the ν is more frequently syncopated before α and ε, after which contraction takes place; as, μείζονα (μείζοα) μείζω, μείζονες (μείζοες) μείζους, μείζονας (μείζοας) μείζους (¶ 17). Compare §§ 104, 119, 123. α.

NOTE. A similar contraction is common in the Acc. of Ἀπόλλων, *Apollo*, and Ποσειδῶν, *Neptune*; thus, Ἀπόλλωνα, (Ἀπόλλωα) Ἀπόλλω (iii. 1. 6); Ποσειδῶνα, Ποσειδῶ. See, for both the uncontracted and the contracted forms, Pl. Crat. 402 d, e, 404 d, 405 d. So, likewise, ὁ κυκεών, -ῶνος, *mixed drink*; Acc. κυκεῶνα, and, rather poetic, κυκεῶ (κ. 316; κυκειῶ Λ. 624); ἡ γλήχων, -ωνος, *pennyroyal*; Acc. γλήχωνα, γλήχω (Ar. Ach. 874); and by a like syncope of ρ, ὁ ἰχώρ, *ichor*; Acc. ἰχῶρα and (only E. 416) ἰχῶ.

§ **108.** NEUTER LIQUIDS. A few nouns, in which ρ is

the characteristic, are neuter. They are, for the most part, confined to the singular, and require, in their declension, no euphonic changes of letters.

NOTE. In ἔαρ, *spring*, and the poetic κέαρ, *heart*, contraction takes place in the root; thus, N. ἔαρ, poetic ἦρ, G. ἔαρος, commonly ἦρος, D. ἔαρι, commonly ἦρι· N. κέαρ, in Homer always κῆρ, D. κῆρι.

C. LIQUID-MUTES.

[¶ 13.]

§ **109.** All nouns of this class are either masculine o feminine. The characteristic of the class is ντ, except in the feminines δάμαρ, -αρτος, *wife*, ἕλμινς, -ινθος, *worm*, πείρινς, -ινθος, *carriage-basket*, and Τίρυνς, -υνθος, *Tiryns*. The τ or θ is affected as in simple linguals (§ 102). When, by the dropping of τ, ν is brought before ς in the theme, it depends upon the preceding vowel whether the ν or the ς is changed (§§ 57, 58), according to the following rule: *If an O vowel precede, the ς is changed; otherwise, the ν.*

Thus, λέων, -οντος, Ξενοφῶν, -ῶντος (¶ 13), ὁ δράκων, -οντος, *dragon*; but γίγᾱς, -αντος (¶ 13), ὁ ἱμάς, -άντος, *thong*, ὁ Σιμόεις, -εντος, *the Simoïs*, δεικνύς, -ύντος, *showing*.

NOTES. α. Except ὀδούς, -όντος, *tooth* (¶ 13; yet Ion. ὀδών Hdt. vi. 107), and participles from verbs in -ωμι; as, δούς, δόντος (¶ 22), from δίδωμι, *to give*.

β. Some Latin names received into the Greek have -ης in the theme, instead of -εις; as, Κλήμης, -εντος, *Clemens*, Οὐάλης, -εντος, *Valens*.

γ. If the characteristic is -νθ-, the ν remains before ς (§ 58. β). In δάμαρ (¶ 13), the ς is simply dropped in the theme.

REMARKS. 1. A few proper names in -ᾱς, -αντος, form the Voc. after the analogy of the theme; that is, ν becomes α, and is then contracted; thus, Ἄτλᾱς, -αντος, V. (Ἄτλαντ, Ἄτλαν, Ἄτλαα) Ἄτλᾱ· Πολυδάμᾱς, V. Πολυδάμᾱ.

2. Nouns and adjectives in -εις, -εντος, preceded by ο or η, are usually contracted; as, ὁ πλακόεις πλακοῦς, *cake*, G. πλακόεντος πλακοῦντος· τιμήεις τιμῆς, *honored*, F. τιμήεσσα τιμῆσσα, N. τιμῆεν τιμῆν, G. τιμήεντος τιμῆντος, &c.

D. PURES.

[¶ 14.]

§ **110.** The euphonic changes in the declension of pures may be mostly referred, (I.) to a special law of Greek declension, and (II.) to contraction.

I. SPECIAL LAW OF GREEK DECLENSION. *The short vowels, ε and ο, can never remain in the root, either before the affixes ς and ν* (¶ 5), *or at the end of a word.* Hence,

§ **111.** (A.) Before the affixes ς and ν, ε becomes η, ι, υ, or ευ; and ο becomes ω or ου; as follows.

1.) In *masculine nouns*, ε becomes ευ in *simple*, and η in *compound* words; as, *simple*, ὁ ἱππεύς, -έως (¶ 14; root ἱππε-), ὁ βασιλεύς, -έως, *king*, ὁ ἱερεύς, -έως, *priest*, ὁ Θησεύς, -έως, *Theseus*, ὁ Μεγαρεύς, -έως, *Megarian; compound*, ὁ Σωκράτης, -εος (¶ 14; from σῶς, *entire*, and κράτος, *strength*), ὁ Ἀριστοτέλης, -εος, *Aristotle*, ὁ Δημοσθένης, -εος.

Except the simples ὁ Ἄρης, -εος, *Mars*, ὁ σής, σεός, *moth;* and the following, in which ε becomes υ or ι, ὁ πῆχυς, -εως, Acc. πῆχυν (¶ 14), ὁ πέλεκυς, -εως, *axe*, ὁ πρέσβυς, -εως, *elder* (properly an adj.); ὁ ἔχις, -εως, *viper*, ὁ ὄφις, -εως, *serpent*, ὁ πρύτανις, -εως, *president*, and also κόρις, κύρβις, μάρις, and ὄρχις.

2.) In *feminine* and *common nouns*, ε becomes ι; as, ἡ πόλις -εως, Acc. πόλιν (¶ 14), ἡ δύναμις, -εως, *power;* ὁ, ἡ μάντις, -εως, *prophet*, *prophetess*.

§ **112.** 3.) In *adjectives*, ε becomes υ in *simple*, and η in *compound* words; as, *simple*, ἡδύς, -έος, Acc. ἡδύν (¶ 19), γλυκύς, -έος, *sweet*, ὀξύς, -έος, *sharp; compound*, ἀληθής, -έος, *true*, εὐτελής, -έος, *cheap*, σφηκώδης, -εος, *wasp-like*, τριήρης, -εος, *having three banks of oars*, or, as a substantive (ναῦς, *vessel*, being understood), *trireme* (¶ 14).

Except a few simple adjectives, in which ε becomes η; as, σαφής, -έος (¶ 17), πλήρης, -εος, *full*, ψευδής, -έος, *false*.

4.) In *monosyllables*, ο becomes ου; otherwise, ω; as, βοῦς, βοός, Acc. βοῦν (¶ 14), ὁ, ἡ ῥοῦς, ῥοός, *sumach*, ὁ χοῦς, χοός, *heap of earth;* but αἰδώς, -όος (¶ 14).

Notes. α. This rule applies also to *linguals* in which ο precedes the characteristic; thus, πούς, ποδός (¶ 11), and its compounds, Οἰδίπους, -οδος (¶ 16), δίπους, -οδος (¶ 17); but εἰδώς, -ότος (¶ 22).

β. In feminines of more than one syllable, in which the characteristic is ο, the affix ς is changed to ε, and is then absorbed. Thus from the root ἠχο- is formed the theme (ἠχος, ἠχοε) ἠχώ (¶ 14). So ἡ πειθώ, -όος, *persuasion*, ἡ Λητώ, -όος, *Latona*, &c. Except, as above, αἰδώς, and the Ionic ἡ ἠώς, *dawn*. These feminines in -ω and -ως have no plural or dual, except by metaplasm (§ 122); unless, perhaps, εἰκούς (§ 123. α) is to be regarded as simply contracted from εἰκόας.

§ **113.** (B.) In cases which have *no affix*, ε *characteristic* becomes ι, υ, or ευ, or else assumes a euphonic ς; and ο *characteristic* becomes οι or ου; as follows.

1.) If the theme ends in -ης, ε becomes ες; but, otherwise

is changed as in the theme; thus, Nom. neut. σαφές (¶ 17), ἡδύ (¶ 19); Voc. τρίηρες, Σώκρατες, πόλι, πῆχυ, ἱππεῦ (¶ 14), ἡδύ (¶ 19).

2.) In the theme of *neuter nouns*, ε assumes ς, becoming itself ο (§ 28); as, τὸ τεῖχος, -εος (¶ 14), τὸ ἔθνος, -εος, *nation*, τὸ ὄρος, -εος, *mountain*.

Except τὸ ἄστυ, -εος, *town* (¶ 14), the Epic τὸ πῶϋ, -εος, *flock*, and a few foreign names of natural productions in -ι, as τὸ πέπερι, -εως, *pepper*.

3.) In the *Vocative*, ο becomes οῖ, if the theme ends in -ώ or -ώς; but ου, if it ends in -ους; as, ἠχοῖ, αἰδοῖ, βοῦ (¶ 14); and in like manner (cf. 112. α), Οἰδίπου (¶ 16).

§ **114.** REMARKS. 1. After the analogy of ε and ο, α *characteristic* becomes αυ in γραῦς and ναῦς (¶ 14), and assumes ς in the theme of *neuters;* as, τὸ γέρας, -αος (¶ 14), τὸ γῆρας, -αος, *old age*.

2. In the *Accusative singular* of pures, the formative ν becomes α (§ 100. 2) except when the theme ends in -ας, -ις, -υς, -αυς, or -ους; thus, θώς, ἥρως, ἱππεύς, τριήρης, αἰδώς, ἠχώ (¶ 14), σαφής (¶ 17); Acc. θῶα, ἥρωα, ἱππέα, τριήρεα, αἰδόα, ἠχόα, σαφέα; but ὁ λᾶς, *stone*, κίς, οἶς (contracted from ὄϊς), πόλις, ἰχθύς, πῆχυς, γραῦς, ναῦς, βοῦς (¶ 14), ἡδύς (¶ 19); Acc λᾶν, κίν, οἶν, πόλιν, ἰχθύν, πῆχυν, γραῦν, ναῦν, βοῦν, ἡδύν.

NOTE. Proper names in -ης, -εος, for the most part, admit both forms of the Acc.; as, Σωκράτης (¶ 14), A. Σωκράτη (Plat.), Σωκράτην (Xen.); ὁ Ἄρης, *Mars*, A. Ἄρη and Ἄρην.

3. When the characteristic is changed to a *diphthong* before σ in the theme, the same change is made before σι in the *Dative plural;* as, ἱππεῦσι, βουσί, γραυσί, ναυσί (¶ 14).

§ **115.** II. CONTRACTION. For the general laws, see §§ 31–37. The following remarks may be added.

1. Pures in -ης, -ος, -ώ, and -ώς, -όος, are contracted in *all* the cases which have *open* terminations. See τριήρης, Σωκράτης, Ἡρακλέης, τεῖχος, ἠχώ, αἰδώς (¶ 14), σαφής (¶ 17). Add a few neuters in -ας; as, τὸ γέρας (¶ 14), τὸ κρέας, *meat*.

NOTES. α. Of nouns in -ώ and -ώς, -όος, the uncontracted form scarcely occurs, even in the poets and dialects.

β. In proper names in -κλέης, contracted -κλῆς (from κλέος, *renown*), the Dat. and sometimes the Acc. sing. are *doubly* contracted. See Ἡρακλέης (¶ 14). For the later Voc. Ἥρακλες, compare § 105. R. The Nom. pl Ἡρακλέες, in the Ion. form (§ 121. 4), occurs, with Θησέες, Pl. Theæt 169 b.

2. In other pures, contraction is, for the most part, con fined to three cases; the Nom. and Acc. plur., and the Dat sing.

The contractions which are usual or frequent in these words are exhibited in the tables. Contraction sometimes occurs in cases in which it is not given in the tables, and is sometimes omitted in cases in which it is given. These deviations from common usage are chiefly found in the poets.

§ 116. 3. In the Attic and Common dialects, the endings -εος, -εα, and -εας, instead of the common contraction, receive in certain words a peculiar change, which lengthens the last vowel. This change takes place,

a.) In the Gen. sing. of nouns in -ις, -υς, and -ευς, and sometimes of nouns in -ι and -υ; as, πόλις, Gen. πόλεος πόλεως, πῆχυς, -εως, ἱππεύς, -έως, ἄστυ, -εος and -εως (¶ 14), πέπερι, -εως (§ 113. 2). Also ὁ Ἄρης, *Mars*, G. Ἄρεος and sometimes Ἄρεως (as if from a second theme Ἄρευς, cited by grammarians from Alcæus).

b.) In the Acc. sing. and plur. of nouns in -ευς; as, ἱππεύς, Acc. sing. ἱππέᾰ ἱππέᾱ, pl. ἱππέᾰς ἱππέᾱς.

NOTES. α. This change appears to be simply an early and less perfect mode of contraction. From the accentuation of such words as πόλεως, it is evident that the ε (as in Ἀτρείδεω, Μενέλεως, § 35) has not the full force of a distinct syllable; while it is equally evident from the use of the poets, that it has not wholly lost its syllabic power. It seems, therefore, to have united as a species of semivowel (of the same class with our *y* and *w*) with the following vowel, which consequently, as in other cases of contraction, became long. An especial reason for regarding this method of contraction as early, consists in the fact that it is confined to those classes of words which have dropped F or Δ from the root (§§ 117, 118). The poets sometimes complete the contraction by synizesis; as, βασιλέως Eur. Alc. 240, Ἐρεχθέως Id. Hipp. 1095, Ἀχιλλέα Id. Iph. A. 1341. Sometimes, also, the unchanged Gen. in -εος, and rarely the Acc. in -εᾰ and -εᾰς occur in the Attic poets; as, Νηρέος Eur. Ion, 1082, πόλεος Id. Hec. 866, φονέᾰ Ib. 882. The poets likewise employ in the Acc. sing. the regular contraction into ῆ; as, ξυγγραφῆ Ar. Ach. 1150, Ὀδυσσῆ Eur. Rh. 708, and even ἱερῆ Id. Alc. 25. The regularly contracted Acc. pl. in -εις, instead of -εᾱς, became in the later Greek the common form, and although regarded as less Attic, yet is not unfrequent in the manuscripts and editions of genuine Attic writers, particularly of Xenophon; as, βασιλεῖς Mem. iii. 9. 10.

β. If another vowel precedes, the ε is commonly absorbed by the ως, ᾱ, and ᾱς; thus, Πειραιέως Πειραιῶς, Πειραιέα Πειραιᾶ (¶ 14); χοῶς, χοᾶ, χοᾶς (§ 123).

γ. For the earlier contraction of the Nom. pl. of nouns in -ευς into ῆς, see § 37. 2. The uncontracted Θησέες occurs Pl. Theæt. 169 b.

δ. The form of the Gen. in -εως is termed by grammarians the *Attic Genitive.* For its accentuation, see Prosody. The Gen. pl. in -εων accented upon the antepenult is also termed Attic; as, πόλεων. The regularly contracted πηχῶν occurs iv. 7. 16.

ε. The Gen. in -εως is also found in a few adjectives in -ις (as, καλλίπολις, -εως), in ἥμισυς, *half* (Gen. commonly -εως, but also -εος and -ους), and, in later writers, in other adjectives in -υς (thus, βραχέως Plut.).

§ 117. Remarks on the Declension of Pures. The various and peculiar changes in the declension of pures appear to have chiefly arisen from the successive methods which were employed to avoid the hiatus produced by appending the open affixes to the characteristic vowel. Of these methods, the earlier consisted mainly in the *insertion of a strong breathing or aspirate consonant* (cf. § 89); and the later, in contraction. The inserted aspirate became so intimately associated with the root, that its use extended even to the cases which had not an open affix; and although it fell away in the refining of the language (cf. § 22. δ), yet it left distinct memorials of itself, either in a kindred vowel or consonant, or in a prolonged syllable. The aspirates chiefly inserted appear to have been the labial F, and a dental breathing, which was most akin to σ (in Latin it passed extensively into *r*; for distinction's sake, we here represent it by a capital Σ). From the classes of words in which these aspirates were respectively inserted, the former appears to have prevailed in an earlier period of the language, than the latter. In the modifications which subsequently took place, the following law prevailed: *When* (1.) *followed by a vowel, both the aspirates were simply dropped. When not followed by a vowel, the labial breathing united* (2.) *with* α, ε, *and* ο *preceding to form* αυ, ευ, *and* ου, *and* (3.) *with* ῐ *and* ῠ (*except in the Dat. plur.*), *to form* ῑ *and* ῡ; *while the dental breathing* (4.) *at the end of a word became* ς, *and* (5.) *before the affix* ς *lengthened a preceding short vowel.* Thus,

(1.) βοFός βοός, γρᾱFός γρᾱός, κῐFός κῐός, ἰχθῠFος ἰχθῠος, ἱππέFες ἱππέες· αἰδόΣος αἰδόος, τείχεΣος τείχεος, γέραΣος γέραος (¶ 14), σαφέΣος σαφέος (¶ 17).

(2.) γράFς γραῦς, νάFς ναῦς (Lat. *navis*), ναFσί ναυσί, ἱππέFς ἱππεύς, ἱππέF ἱππεῦ, βόFς βοῦς, βόFν βοῦν, βόF βοῦ (¶ 14).

(3.) κῐFς κῑς, κῐFν κῑν, ἰχθῠFς ἰχθῡς, ἰχθῠF ἰχθῡ (¶ 14); but Dat. pl. κῐσί, ἰχθῠσι.

(4.) Nom. neut. σαφέΣ σαφές (¶ 17), τεῖχεΣ τεῖχος (ε passing into its kindred vowel, § 28), γέραΣ γέρας (¶ 14); Voc. ΣώκρατεΣ Σώκρατες, τριήρεΣ τριήρες (¶ 14). The peculiar form of the Voc. of ἠχώ and αἰδώς has arisen from the change of ς to its corresponding vowel (§ 50) and then contraction with precession (§ 29); thus, ἠχόΣ ἠχόι ἠχοῖ (cf. §§ 45. 5, 86, 112. β).

(5.) σαφέΣς σαφής (¶ 17), ΣωκράτεΣς Σωκράτης, αἰδόΣς αἰδώς (¶ 14). For ἠχώ, see § 112. β, and compare ἠχοῖ above (4.). In the Dat. pl. the short vowel remains unchanged; as, σαφέσι.

Note. In adjectives, and in a few masculine and neuter nouns, the diphthong ευ appears to have been reduced to a simple short υ; as, ἡδέFς ἡδῠς, ἡδέF ἡδῠ (¶ 19); πῆχεFς πῆχῠς, πῆχεFν πῆχῠν, πῆχεF πῆχῠ, ἄστεF ἄστῠ (¶ 14).

§ 118. In *feminines*, it was natural that the inserted breathing or consonant should commonly assume a softer form. In this form, it appears to have been most nearly akin to the lingual middle mute δ (cf. § 49. 2); and in a great number of feminines, it acquired a permanent place in the language as this letter. In its previous, and as yet unfixed state, we represent it, for distinction's sake, by a capital Δ. Before this inserted lingual, α could remain, but there was a uniform tendency in ε to pass by precession into ι. It is a remarkable illustration of this, that in the whole declension, there is not a single instance of ε before a characteristic lingual mute. In the progress of the language, feminines in -ε-, or with the inserted lingual -εΔ-, assumed three forms:

1.) The Δ fell away, leaving the vowel of precession ι in the Nom., Acc., and Voc. sing., but the original ε in the other cases; thus, πόλις, πόλεως, πόλει, πόλιν, πόλι· πόλεις, πόλεων, πόλεσι, πόλεις (¶ 14). This became the usual form of feminine pures in -ις, in the Attic and Common dialects.

2.) The Δ fell away, and precession took place throughout. This became the regular form of feminine pures in -ις in the Ionic dialect (§ 44. 3); thus, Ion. N. -ῐς, G. -ῐος, D. -ῐι, always contracted into -ῑ, A. -ῐν, V. -ῐ; Pl. N. -ῐες, sometimes contr. into -ῑς, G. -ῐων, D. -ῐσι, A. -ῐας, commonly contr. into -ῑς; as, πόλις, πόλιος, πόλῑ, πόλιν· πόλιες, -ίων, πόλισι, πόλιας, -ῑς. The ι was also the prevalent vowel in the Doric; thus, Dor. πόλις, πόλιος, πόλῑ and πόλει, πόλιν· πόλιες, πολίων, πολίεσσι and πόλεσι, πόλιας.

3.) The Δ became fixed in the root, and the word passed into the class of linguals. Thus, the root Μεγαρε-, *Megarian*, had two forms, ΜεγαρεϜ- masc., and with precession ΜεγαριΔ- fem.; from the former we have Μεγαρεύς, -έως, *Megarian man*, and from the latter, Μεγαρίς, -ίδος, *Megarian woman*. This became the prevalent mode of declining feminines in -ις, if we except the large class of abstract nouns in -σις. Especially many feminine adjectives, or words which are properly such, are thus declined.

NOTE. We find, also, the same forms in a few masculine or common nouns and adjectives (§§ 111, 119. 2), and even, in a few words, a corresponding neuter formation in -ι (§ 113. 2).

§ **119.** As might have been expected, these three forms are far from being kept entirely separate. Thus,

1.) Some words exhibit both the lingual and the pure inflection, the latter especially in the Ionic and Doric dialects, which were less averse than the Attic to hiatus (§§ 45, 46); as, ἡ μῆνις, *wrath*, G. μήνιδος and μήνιος· ἡ τρόπις, *keel*, G. τρόπιδος, τρόπιος, and τρόπεως· particularly proper names, as, Κύπρις, G. -ιδος, and -ιος· Ἶσις, G. -ιδος and -ιος· Θέτις, G. Θέτιδος Θ. 370, D. Θέτῑ Σ. 407. For similar cases of the use and omission of a lingual characteristic, see § 104; of a liquid characteristic, §§ 107, 123. α.

2.) In some pures in -ις, the Attic adopts, in whole or in part (particularly in the Gen. sing.), the Ionic forms; as, ἡ τύρσις, *tower*, G. τύρσιος vii. 8. 12, but Pl. N. τύρσεις iv. 4. 2, τύρσεων H. Gr. iv. 7. 6, τύρσεσι Cyr. vii. 5. 10; ὁ πόσις, *spouse*, G. -ιος, D. -ει· ἡ μάγαδις, -ιος, *a kind of harp*, D. μαγάδῑ vii. 3. 32; ὁ, ἡ τίγρις, *tiger*, G. τίγριος, and in later writers τίγριδος, Pl. N. τίγρεις, G. τίγρεων· some proper names, as, ὁ Συέννεσις, G. -ιος, i. 2. 12, ὁ Ἶρις, G. -ιος vi. 2. 1: and the adjectives ἴδρις, *intelligent*, νῆστις, *abstemious*. In like manner, ὁ, ἡ ἔγχελυς (§ 117. N.), *eel*, G. ἐγχέλυος, Pl. N. ἐγχέλεις G. ἐγχέλεων· τὸ πέπερι (§ 118. N.), *pepper*, G. -εως and -ιος.

DIALECTIC FORMS.

§ 120. (A.) Dialectic changes affecting the AFFIX.

1. In the poets, especially the Epic, the Acc. sing. sometimes ends in -α, in words in which it has commonly -ν; as, εὐρέα Z. 291, νῆα or νέα, πόληα, for εὐρύν, ναῦν, πόλιν· ἰχθύα Theoc. 21. 45. On the other hand, the New Ionic often forms the Acc. of nouns in -ώ or -ώς, -όος, in -οῦν; as, Ἰώ, *Io*, Λητώ, *Latona*, ἠώς, *dawn*, Acc. Ἰοῦν Hdt. i. 1, Λητοῦν, ἠοῦν. The Æolic and stricter Doric have here -ων for -οῦν (§ 44. 4); as, Ἥρων Sapph. 75 (91), Λατῶν Inscr. Cret.

2. In the Gen. plur., the Ionic sometimes inserts ε (cf. §§ 48. 1, 99. 2); as, χηνέων Hdt. ii. 45, μυριαδέων, ἀνδρέων, for χηνῶν, μυριάδων, ἀνδρῶν.

3. In the Dat. plur., for the common affix -σι(ν), the poets often employ the old or prolonged forms -εσι(ν), -εσσι(ν), and -σσι(ν). See §§ 71, 84, 85. Homer uses the four forms, though -εσι(ν) rarely. The forms -εσσι(ν) and -εσι(ν) are also common in Doric and Æolic prose; and -εσι(ν) is used in Ionic prose after the characteristic ν. Thus, χερσίν A. 14, χείρεσσι Γ. 271, χείρεσι Υ. 468; ποσί E. 745, ποσσί B. 44, πόδεσσιν Γ. 407; ἔπεσιν B. 73, ἔπεσσι δ. 597, ἐπέεσσιν B. 75; δαιτυμόνεσι Hdt. vi. 57. So, Ϝ not passing into υ before a vowel (§ 117), βόεσσι B. 481, νάεσσι Pind. P. 4. 98, ἀριστήεσσι A. 227.

4. In the Dual, the Epic prolongs -οιν (as in Dec. II., § 99. 1) to -οιїν; thus, ποδοιїν Ξ. 228, Σειρήνοιїν μ. 52.

§ 121. (B.) Dialectic changes affecting the ROOT, either simply or in connection with the affix.

1. Many changes result from dialectic preferences of vowels; as, Ion. θώρηξ, νηῦς, γρηῦς, for θώραξ, &c.; Dor. ποιμάν, ὠκύτᾶς, τιμάεις, contr. τιμᾶς, for ποιμήν, &c.; χήρ for χείρ, ὦς for οὖς, βῶς, βῶν, for βοῦς, βοῦν (the Acc. βῶν in the sense of *a shield covered with ox-hide* occurs also H. 738), ἀχῶς for ἠχοῦς, &c. See §§ 44, 45.

2. The dialects and poets vary greatly in the extent to which they employ contraction, and in the mode of contraction. The Epic has here especial license. In the poets, contractions are often made by synizesis (§ 30), which are not written. In respect to the usage of Homer, we remark as follows: (*a*) In the Gen. sing., contraction is commonly omitted, except in nouns in -ώ and -ώς, G. -όος. In a few words, the contraction of -εος into -ευς occurs (§ 45. 3), and there are a few instances of synizesis (which we mark thus, ε͡α); e. g. Ἐρέβευς Θ. 368, θάμβευς ω. 394, θέρευς η. 118; Πηλέ͡ος A. 489, Μηκιστέ͡ος B. 566, πόλι͡ος B. 811. (*b*) In the Dat. sing., both the contracted and uncontracted forms are used in most words with equal freedom; as, γήραϊ and γήρᾳ, θέρεϊ and θέρει, τείχεϊ and τείχει, Πηλέϊ and Πηλεῖ, πόληϊ, πτόλεϊ, and πόλει, ἥρωϊ and ἥρῳ H. 453. The endings -ιι, -υι, and -οι (except in χροΐ) are always contracted (§§ 118. 2, 115. *a*); as, κνήστῖ Λ. 640, νέκυι Π. 526 (this contraction of -υϊ into -υι is Epic), ἠοῖ I. 618. (*c*) The endings -εα, -εων, and -εας are commonly uncontracted, except by synizesis; as, θεοειδέ͡α Γ. 27, ὑψερεφέ͡α δ. 757, ἄλγε͡α Ω. 7, βέλε͡α O. 444, νέ͡α ι. 283; στηθέ͡ων K. 95; πολέ͡ας A. 559, πελέκε͡ας Ψ. 114. So πόλιας Θ. 560. (*d*) The ending -εες is used both with and without contraction; as, πρωτοπαγεῖς νεοτευχέες E. 194. (*e*) The neut. plur. ending -αα is always contracted, or drops one

α (cf. 4. below); as, κέρα, δέπα, γέρᾰ B. 237. The form with the single short α sometimes occurs in the Attic poets; as, κρέᾰ Ar. Pax. 192. (*f.*) Of ὄϊς, *sheep*, οὖς, *ear*, and γραῦς, *old woman*, the following forms occur in Homer; N. ὄϊς, G. ὄϊος, οἰός, A. ὄϊν· P. N. ὄϊες, G. ὀΐων, οἰῶν, D. ὀΐεσσι, οἴεσι, ὄεσσι (cf. § 119. 2), A. ὄϊς. N. οὖς, G. οὔατος· P. N. οὔατα, D. οὔασι, ὠσί (§ 33. γ). N. γρηῦς, γρηῦς, D. γρηΐ, V. γρηῦ, γρηῦ· the Gen. and Acc. are supplied by γραίης and γραῖαν of Dec. I.

3. In *common nouns in* -εύς, the characteristic εϝ before a vowel regularly becomes η, in the Epic; as, ἱππῆος, ἱππῆϊ, ἱππῆᾰ, ἱππῆες (once in Hom. ἱππεῖς A. 151, also βασιλεῖς Hes. Op. 246), ἱππήων (¶ 16), ἀριστήεσσι A. 227 (so, by imitation, βασιλῆας Eur. Phœn. 829). This change also extends to proper names in -εύς (in which the Epic has great freedom in using the long or short vowel according to the metre), to Ἄρης, *Mars* (§ 116. a), and to πόλις. See Homeric Paradigms, ¶ 16. In common nouns in -εύς, this change occurs also in Herodotus, although questioned by critics; as, βασιλῆος, βασιλῆα, vii. 137, βασιλῆϊ iii. 137, βασιλήων vi. 58. The regular inflection of nouns in -ευς, in Ionic prose, and also in the Doric, is in -εος, &c. The Acc. in -ηα or -εα is sometimes contracted by the poets into -ῆ; as, Ὀδυσῆ τ. 136, Τυδῆ Δ. 384, βασιλῆ Hdt. vii. 220 (Oracle). We find βασιλῆες with synizesis Hes. Op. 261.

4. In words whose root ends in εε-, the Epic often unites εε into η (as regularly in proper names in -κλέης), or into ει; but sometimes in the Epic and other poets, and in dialectic prose, one ε is dropped. Still further variety of form is sometimes given by the Epic protraction of ε to ει or η, or by the Ionic or poetic neglect of contraction. Thus, Ἡρακλέης Hes. Th. 318, Hdt. ii. 43, Pind. O. 6. 115; G. Ἡρακλῆος Ξ. 266, Ἡρακλέος Hdt. ii. 43, Pind. O. 3. 20; D. Ἡρακλῆϊ Θ. 224, Pind. I. 5. 47, Ἡρακλέϊ Hdt. ii. 145, Ἡρακλεῖ Pind. P. 9. 151; A. Ἡρακλῆα Ξ. 324, Ἡρακλέᾰ Hdt. ii. 43, Pind. O. 10. 20, Ἡρακλέην Theoc. 13. 73 (for the Attic forms of Ἡρακλῆς, see ¶ 14 and Mem. ii. 1. 21–26); ἀγακλῆος Π. 738: ἐϋκλείας (Acc. pl. of εὐκλεής) K. 281, εὐκλέᾰς Pind. O. 2. 163; ἐϋῤῥεῖος (Gen. of εὐρεής) Z. 508; κλεῖᾰ (pl. of κλέος) Hes. Th. 100: δυσκλέᾰ B. 115, ὑπερδέᾰ P. 330: ἀκληεῖς (Nom. pl. of ἀκλεής) M. 318. For the Homeric forms of σπέος, and for those of Πάτροκλος, which, like some other compounds of κλέος, has forms both of Dec. II. and of Dec. III., see ¶ 16.

5. For the Ionic and Doric declension of words in -ις, -εως, and for the omission of δ in words in -ις, -ιδος, see §§ 118, 119. The Ionic likewise omits the τ in κέρας and τέρας· and then in these, as in other neuters in -ας, -αος, the later Ionic often changes α into ε (§ 44. 2.), except in the theme; as, κέρεος, κέρεϊ, κέρεα, κερέων, τέρεος, γέρεα, Hdt.

6. In ναῦς, the Doric retains throughout the original α, and is here sometimes imitated by the Attic poets. In the Ionic, the α passes throughout by precession either into η, or with short quantity, especially in the later Ionic, into ε. The Attic retains the α in the diphthong αυ, but has otherwise η or ε (the latter having, perhaps, been inserted in the Gen. sing. and pl. after the contraction of ᾱο and ᾱω, according to § 35, and the Gen. dual having followed the analogy of the other numbers). For the Ionic and Doric forms, see ¶ 16; for the Attic, ¶ 14.

IV. IRREGULAR NOUNS.

§ **122.** Irregularities in the declension of nouns, which

have not been already noticed, may be chiefly referred to two heads; *variety of declension*, and *defect of declension.*

A. Variety of Declension.

A noun may vary, (1.) in its *root;* (2.) in its *method* of declension; and (3.) in its *gender* (§ 79). In the first case, it is termed a *metaplast* (μεταπλαστός, *transformed*); in the second, a *heteroclite* (ἑτερόκλιτος, *of different declensions*); in the third, *heterogeneous* (ἑτερογενής, *of different genders*).

Words which have distinct double forms, either throughout or in part, are termed *redundant.* Those, on the other hand, that want some of the usual forms, are termed *defective.*

The lists which follow are designed both to exemplify the different kinds of anomaly, and likewise to present, in a classified arrangement, the principal anomalous nouns. It will be observed, that some of the words might have been arranged with equal propriety under other heads, from their exhibiting more than one species of anomaly.

§ 123. 1. Metaplasts.

Metaplasm has mostly arisen from a change of the root, in the progress of the language, for the sake of euphony or emphasis, chiefly by the precession of an open vowel, or the addition of a consonant to prevent hiatus; while, at the same time, forms have remained from the old root, especially in the poets and in the dialects.

α. With a Double Root, in ον- and in ο-.

ἡ ἀηδών, *nightingale,* G. ἀηδόνος, &c.; from the root ἀηδο-, G. ἀηδοῦς Soph. Aj. 628, D. ἀηδοῖ Ar. Av. 679.

ἡ Γοργώ, -οῦς, and Γοργών, -όνος, *Gorgon.*

ἡ εἰκών, *image,* G. εἰκόνος, &c.; from r. εἰκο-, G. εἰκοῦς Eur. Hel. 77, A εἰκώ Hdt. vii. 69; from r. εἰκ-, by the second declension, Pl. A. εἰκούς Eur. Tro. 1178, Ar. Nub. 559. Yet see § 112. β.

ἡ χελῑδών, *swallow,* G. χελῑδόνος, &c.; from r. χελιδο-, V. χελῑδοῖ Ar. Av. 1411 from Simon.

Compare §§ 104, 107, 119.

β. With a Double Root, in α- and in ε-.

τὸ βρέτας, *wooden image,* poetic, G. βρέτεος, D. βρέτει· Pl. N. βρέτη, G. βρετέων.

τὸ κνέφας, *darkness,* G. Epic κνέφαος, Attic κνέφους Ar. Eccl. 291, later κνέφατος Polyb., D. κνέφαϊ κνέφᾳ Cyr. iv. 2. 15.

τὸ κῶας, *fleece,* poetic, π. 47; Pl. N. κώεα υ. 3, D. κώεσι γ. 38.

τὸ οὖδας, *floor,* poetic, G. οὔδεος, D. οὔδεϊ οὔδει (all in Hom.).

γ. Miscellaneous Examples.

τὸ γόνυ, *knee,* and τὸ δόρυ, *spear,* G. γόνατος, δόρατος, &c. (§ 103. N.). For the various forms of δόρυ (of which in the theme there is even the late form δοῦρας Antiphil. 9), see ¶ 16. Those which occur of γόνυ correspond; thus, Ion. and poet. γούνατος, γούνατα, γούνασι and γούνασσι (I. 488, P. 451, for which some write γούνεσσι); also poet. γουνός, γουνί, γοῦνα, γούνων, and γόνων Sapph. 14 (25), γούνεσσι.

ἡ ἕως, *dawn* (r. ἑα-, Attic Dec. II.), G. ἕω, D. ἕῳ, A. ἕω and ἕων (§ 97. 3) Dor. ἀώς (r. ἀο-), G. ἀόος ἀοῦς · Ion. ἠώς, G. ἠοῦς, D. ἠοῖ, A. ἠῶ and ἠοῦ (§ 120. 1).

ἡ Θέμις, *Themis*, as a common noun, *right, law*, G. Θέμιδος, Epic Θέμιστος β. 68, Ionic Θέμιος Hdt. ii. 50, Doric Θέμιτος Pind. O. 13. 11, also Pl. Rep. 380 a. In the Attic, θέμις occurs mostly in certain forms of expression, where it is used without declension, as an adjective or neuter noun; thus, θέμις ἐστί, *it is lawful; φασὶ ... θέμις εἶναι, they say that it is lawful*, Pl. Gorg. 505 d; τὸ μὴ θέμις, *that which is not lawful*, Æsch. Sup. 335.

ὁ θεράπων, *attendant*, G. θεράποντος, &c.; poet. A. θέραπα, Pl. N. θέραπες Eur. Ion, 94.

ὁ κάλως, *cable* (r. καλα-, Att. Dec. II.), G. κάλω, &c.; Ion. κάλος, -ου, &c., ε. 260 and Hdt.; in the later Epic, Pl. κάλωες, &c., Ap. Rh. 2. 725.

ὁ λαγώς, *hare* (r. λαγα-, Att. Dec. II.), G. λαγώ, A. λαγών, λαγώ, &c.; Ion. λαγός, -οῦ, &c., Hdt., also Pl. N. λαγοί Soph. Fr. 113, A. Dor. (§ 45. 5) λαγός Hes. Sc. 302; Epic λαγωός, -οῦ, Hom.

ὁ, ἡ μάρτυς (in late writers μάρτυρ), *witness*, G. μάρτυρος, D. μάρτυρι, A. μάρτυρα, rarer μάρτυν · D. pl. μάρτυσι · Epic ὁ μάρτυρος, -ου, π. 423.

ὁ, ἡ ὄρνις, *bird*, G. ὄρνιθος (Dor. ὄρνιχος, § 69. II.), D. ὄρνιθι, A. ὄρνιθα and ὄρνιν · Pl. ὄρνιθες, &c.; from r. ὀρνε-, Sing. N. ὄρνις, A. ὄρνιν, Pl. N. ὄρνεις, G. ὀρνέων, A. ὄρνεις and ὄρνις (§ 119). Another form is τὸ ὄρνεον, -ου.

ὁ ὀρφώς and ὀρφός, a sea-fish, G. ὀρφώ and ὀρφοῦ. Compare κάλως, λαγώς.

ἡ πνύξ, *pnyx*, G. πυκνός, D. πυκνί, A. πύκνα · later G. πνυκός, D. πνυκί, A. πνύκα. The proper root is πυκν- (compare the adj. πυκνός); but from the difficulty of appending ς in the theme, transposition took place (§ 64. 3), which afterwards extended, through the influence of analogy, to the oblique cases.

ὁ σής, *moth*, G. σεός, and in later writers σητός.

ἡ σμῶδιξ, *weal*, B. 267, G. σμώδιγγος, &c.; N. pl. σμώδιγγες Ψ. 716.

ὁ φθόϊς, contr. φθοῖς, *cake*, G. φθοιός · N. pl. φθοῖς and φθόεις · also ἡ φθοΐς -ΐδος · N. pl. φθοΐδες. See § 119.

ἡ χείρ, *hand*, G. χειρός and χερός, &c. For the common forms, see ¶ 12. The other forms are also found in the poets and in Ionic prose.

ὁ χοῦς, the name of a measure, G. χοός, &c., like βοῦς (¶ 14); from r. χοε-, the better Attic G. χοέως, χοῶς, A. χοέα χοᾶ, Pl. A. χοέας χοᾶς (§ 116. β); also Dat. Ion. χοέϊ Hipp.

τὸ χρέος (Ep. χρεῖος, § 47), *debt*, G. χρέους · Pl. N. χρέα (§ 37. 1); from r. χραε-, N. (χράος, χρῶς) χρέως, G. (χράεος, χράους, χρῶς) χρέως (§§ 33, 35).

ὁ χρώς, *skin, surface*, G. χρωτός, D. χρωτί (χρῷ, § 104) A. χρῶτα · Ion. and poet. G. χροός, D. χροΐ, A. χρόα.

For Ζεύς, Οἰδίπους, Πάτροκλος, and υἱός, see ¶ 16.

NOTE. Add the poetic Nom. ἡ δώς Hes. Op. 354, = δόσις, *gift*; Acc. λίβα Æsch. Fr. 49, 65, = λιβάδα from ἡ λιβάς, *libation*; Nom. ὁ λῖς Ο. 275, Acc. λῖν Λ. 480, = λέων Γ. 23, λέοντα Σ. 161, *lion* (in the later Epic, Pl. λίες, λίεσσι); Dat. μάστι Ψ. 500, Acc. μάστιν ο. 182, = μάστιγι Ε. 748, μάστιγα Ε. 226, from ἡ μάστιξ, *scourge*; ὁ Σαρπηδών, G. Σαρπηδόνος and Σαρπήδοντος, V. Σαρπῆδον · Nom. pl. στάγες Ap. Rh. 4. 626, = σταγόνες from ἡ σταγών, *drop*; Dat. ὕδει Hes. Op. 61, Theog. 955, = ὕδατι from τὸ ὕδωρ, *water* (so Nom. ὕδος Call. Fr. 466).

§ 124. 2. Heteroclites.

α. Of the First and Third Declensions.

ὁ Ἅιδης, poetic Ἀΐδης, *Hades*, G. ου, &c.; Dec. III. Epic G. Ἄϊδος, D. Ἄϊδι. Another poetic form is Ἀϊδωνεύς, G. -έως, Ion. -ῆος.

ὁ Θαλῆς, *Thales*, G. Θάλεω (§ 96. 7) and Θάλητος.

ὁ λᾶας, contracted λᾶς, *stone*, G. λᾶος, and λάου Soph. Œd. C. 196, D. λᾶϊ, A. λᾶαν, λᾶν, and λᾶα Call. Fr. 104, Pl. N. λᾶες, &c.

ὁ μύκης, *mushroom*, G. μύκου and μύκητος.

ἡ πτυχή, -ῆς, and mostly Ep. πτύξ, G. πτυχός, *fold*.

ἡ φρίκη, -ης, poetic φρίξ, G. φρῑκός, *shudder*, *ripple*.

Notes. a. Add some proper names in -ης, of which a part admit a double formation throughout, as Χάρης· but others only in particular cases; thus Στρεψιάδης, -ου, has (Ar. Nub. 1206) Voc. Στρεψίαδες. Some refer to this head the double Acc. in § 114. N. For γυνή, see § 101. γ.

b. Add, also, the Epic Dat. ἀλκί (always in the phrase ἀλκὶ πεποιθώς E. 299), = ἀλκῇ (ω. 509) from ἀλκή, *might*; Nom. ἡ ἅρπαξ Hes. Op. 354, = ἁρπαγή, *robbery*; Acc. ἴωκα Λ. 601, = ἰωκήν from ἰωκή (E. 740), *battle-din* Acc. κρόκα Hes. Op. 536, = κρόκην from κρόκη, *woof* (also Pl. N. κρόκες Antip. Th. 10. 5); Dat. pl. ῥοδέεσσιν Ap. Rh. 3. 1020, = ῥόδοις from ῥόδον, *rose*; Dat. ὑσμῖνι B. 863, Θ. 56, = ὑσμίνῃ (Υ. 245) from ὑσμίνη, *battle*; Acc. φύγα (only in φύγαδε, *to flight*, Θ. 157, &c.), = φυγήν from φυγή, *flight*; and the Doric Gen. fem. αἰγᾶν Theoc. 5. 148, 8. 49, for αἰγῶν from αἴξ, *goat* (so Gen. νησάων Call. Del. 66, 275, for νήσων from ἡ νῆσος of Dec. II.).

β. Of the Second and Third Declensions.

τὸ δάκρυον and poet. δάκρυ, *tear*, G. δακρύου, D. δακρύῳ· Pl. N. δάκρυα, G. δακρύων, D. δακρύοις and δάκρυσι Th. vii. 75.

τὸ δένδρον and Ion. δένδρεον, *tree*, G. δένδρου, &c.; Dec. III. D. δένδρει, A. δένδρος Hdt. vi. 79, Pl. N. δένδρη, D. δένδρεσι (the more common form of the Dat. pl. even in Attic prose; e. g. Th. ii. 75).

ὁ ἴκτῖνος, *hawk*, G. ἰκτίνου, &c.; Dec. III. rarer A. ἴκτῖνα Ar. Fr. 525, Pl. N. ἴκτῖνες Pausan. 5. 14.

ὁ κλάδος, *twig*, G. κλάδου, &c.; Dec. III. poet. D. κλαδί, A. κλάδα, Pl. D. κλάδεσι Ar. Av. 239, κλαδέεσσι, A. κλάδας.

ὁ κοινωνός, *sharer*, G. κοινωνοῦ, &c.; Dec. III. Pl. N. κοινῶνες Cyr. viii. 1. 25, A. κοινῶνας Ib. 16.

τὸ κρίνον, *lily*, G. κρίνου, &c.; Dec. III. Pl. N. κρίνεα Hdt. ii. 92, D. κρίνεσι Ar. Nub. 911.

τὸ ὄνειρον and ὁ ὄνειρος, *dream*, G. ὀνείρου and ὀνείρατος· Pl. ὄνειρα, and more frequently ὀνείρατα. Derived from ὄναρ (§ 127).

ἡ πρόχοος, contr. πρόχους, *ewer*, G. πρόχου, &c.; Dec. III. Pl. D. πρόχουσι Ar. Nub. 272.

τὸ πῦρ, *fire*, G. πυρός, D. πυρί Dec. II. Pl. N. πυρά, *watch-fires*, D. πυροῖς.

ὁ στίχος, *row*, G. στίχου, &c.; Dec. III. poet. fem. G. στιχός Π. 173, Pl. N. στίχες Pind. P. 4. 373, A. στίχας Ar. Eq. 163.

NOTE. Add the poet. Dat. pl. ἀνδραπόδεσσι Η. 475, = ἀνδραπόδοις from ἀνδράποδον, *slave;* Nom. ἔρος Ξ. 315, Acc. ἔρον Ι. 92, = ὁ ἔρως Γ. 442, *love,* A. ἔρωτα Hom. Merc. 449; Gen. pl. μηλάτων Lyc. 106, = μήλων from μῆλον, *sheep;* Acc. οἶκα (only in οἴκαδε, *homeward,* often in Hom. and even used in Attic prose, vii. 7. 57), = οἶκον from οἶκος, *house;* Pl. N. προσώπατα σ. 192, D. προσώπασι Η. 212, = πρόσωπα, προσώποις, from πρόσωπον, *face.* For Οἰδίπους, Πάτροκλος, and υἱός, see ¶ 16.

γ. Of the Attic Second and Third Declensions.

ἡ ἅλως, *threshing-floor,* G. ἅλω, ἅλωνος, and poet. ἅλωος.

ὁ μήτρως, *maternal uncle,* G. μήτρω and μήτρωος· Pl. μήτρωες.

ὁ Μίνως, *Minos,* G. Μίνω and Μίνωος.

ὁ πάτρως, *paternal uncle,* G. πάτρω and πάτρωος· Pl. πάτρωες.

ὁ ταὼς and ταών, *peacock,* G. ταῶ and ταῶνος· Pl. N. ταῴ, ταοί, and ταῶνες

ὁ τυφώς, *whirlwind,* G. τυφῶ and τυφῶνος.

§ 125. 3. HETEROGENEOUS NOUNS.

α. Of the Second Declension.

ὁ δεσμός, *band,* Pl. τὰ δεσμά and οἱ δεσμοί.

τὸ ζυγόν and ὁ ζυγός, *yoke,* Pl. τὰ ζυγά.

ὁ θεσμός (Dor. τεθμός), *institute,* Pl. οἱ θεσμοί and τὰ θεσμά.

ὁ λύχνος, *lamp,* Pl. τὰ λύχνα and οἱ λύχνοι.

τὸ νῶτον and ὁ νῶτος, *back,* Pl. τὰ νῶτα.

ὁ σῖτος, *corn,* Pl. τὰ σῖτα.

ὁ σταθμός, *station, balance,* Pl. οἱ σταθμοί and τὰ σταθμά, *stations,* τὰ σταθμά, *balances.*

ὁ Τάρταρος (ἡ Pind. P. 1. 29), *Tartarus,* Pl. τὰ Τάρταρα.

β. Of the Third Declension.

τὸ κάρᾱ and (Soph. Ph. 1457) κρᾶτα, *head,* poetic, G. κρᾱτός (τῆς, Eur. El. 140), D. κρᾱτί and κάρᾳ Soph. Ant. 1272, A. τὸ κάρᾱ, τὸν and τὸ κρᾶτα Eur. El. 148 (cf. 150), Fr. Arch. 16, Soph. Œd. T. 263; Pl. A. τοὺς κρᾶτας Eur. Phœn. 1149. The following forms are found in Homer:

S. N.	κάρη					
G.	κάρητος	καρήᾰτος	κρᾱτός	κράᾰτος	κρῆθεν λ. 588	κᾰρήνου
D.	κάρητι	καρήᾰτι	κρᾱτί	κράᾰτι		
A.	κάρη, κάρ Π. 392		κρᾶτα θ. 92			
P. N.	κάρᾱ Cer. 12	καρήᾰτα		κράᾰτα		κάρηνα
G.			κράτων			καρήνων
D.			κρᾱσί, κράτεσφι, Κ. 152, 156			

Other poets (not Attic) have also forms of κάρη as a fem. of Dec. I.; thus, G. κάρης Call. Fr. 125, Mosch. 4. 74, κάρῃ Theog. 1018.

γ. Of Different Declensions.

Dec. I. and II. ἡ πλευρά and τὸ πλευρόν, *rib;* ὁ φθογγός and ἡ φθογγή, *voice*; ἡ χώρα and ὁ χῶρος, *space*: Dec. I. and III. ἡ δίψα, -ης, and τὸ δίψος -εος, *thirst*; ἡ νάπη and τὸ νάπος, *dell*; ἡ βλάβη and τὸ βλάβος, *injury*; ἡ γνώμη and Ion. and poet. τὸ γνῶμα, -ατος, *opinion*; τὸ πάθος and ἡ πάθη, *suffering*: Dec. II. and III. ὁ ὄχος (Dor. ὄκχος), -ου, and τὸ ὄχος, -εος, and also τὸ ὄχημα, -ατος, *carriage*; ὁ and τὸ σκότος (and also ἡ σκοτία), *darkness*; ὁ and τὸ σκύφος, *cup*; &c.

B. Defect of Declension.

§ **126.** 1. Some words receive *no declension*, as the names of the letters, some foreign proper names, and a few other foreign words. Thus, τὸ, τοῦ, τῷ ἄλφα· ὁ, τοῦ, τῷ, τὸν Ἀβραάμ· τὸ, τοῦ, τῷ πάσχα, *passover*.

Note. A word of this kind is termed *indeclinable*, or an *aptote* (ἄπτωτος, *without cases*).

2. A few diminutives and foreign proper names, whose root ends with a vowel, receive ς in the Nom., ν in the Acc., and, if the vowel admits it, an iota subscript in the Dat., but have no further declension; as

ὁ Διονῦς (dim. from Διόνυσος, *Bacchus*), G. Διονῦ, D. Διονῦ, A. Διονῦν, V. Διονῦ.

ὁ Μηνᾶς (dim. from Μηνόδωρος), G. Μηνᾶ, D. Μηνᾷ, A. Μηνᾶν, V. Μηνᾶ.

ὁ Μασκᾶς, G. Μασκᾶ, D. Μασκᾷ, A. Μασκᾶν, V. Μασκᾶ.

ὁ Ἰαννῆς, G. Ἰαννῆ, D. Ἰαννῇ, A. Ἰαννῆν, V. Ἰαννῆ.

ὁ Ἰησοῦς, *Jesus*, G. Ἰησοῦ, D. Ἰησοῦ, A. Ἰησοῦν, V. Ἰησοῦ.

ὁ Γλοῦς. See ¶ 16.

3. Many nouns are defective in *number*. Thus,

α. Many nouns, from their signification, want the plural; as, ὁ, ἡ ἀήρ, *the air*, ὁ χαλκός, *copper*, τὸ ἔλαιον, *oil*, ἡ ταχυτής, *swiftness*. Proper and abstract nouns are seldom found in the plural, except when employed as common nouns.

β. The names of festivals, some names of cities, and a few other words, want the singular; as, τὰ Διονύσια, *the feast of Bacchus*, αἱ Ἀθῆναι, *Athens*, οἱ ἐτησίαι, *the trade-winds*.

§ **127.** 4. Some nouns are employed only in particular *cases*, and these, it may be, occurring only in certain forms of expression. Of this kind are,

δέμας, *body*, *form*, Nom. and Acc. neut.

ἐπίκλην, *surname*, Acc. fem. (= ἐπίκλησιν), commonly used adverbially.

λίπα, *with oil*, Dat. neut., perhaps shortened from λίπαϊ. Some regard it as Acc.

μάλης, *arm-pit*, Gen. fem., only in the phrase ὑπὸ μάλης, *under the arm*, *secretly*; also, in late writers, ὑπὸ μάλην. Otherwise the longer form, ἡ μασχάλη, is employed.

μέλε, Voc. masc. and fem., used only in familiar address; ὦ μέλε, *my good friend*.

ὄναρ, sleep, dream, and *ὕπαρ, waking, reality,* N. and A. neut. See ὄνειρον (§ 124. β).

ὄσσε, eyes, Du. N. and A. neut.; Pl. G. ὄσσων, D. ὄσσοις.

ὄφελος, advantage, and ἧδος (Ep.), *pleasure,* N. neut.

τάν or τᾶν, only Attic and in the phrase ὦ τάν, *good sir, sirrah.*

Notes. α. Add the poet. Nom. and Acc. neut. δῶ (root δωμ-, § 63) A 426, = δῶμα, *house,* κρῖ (r. κριθ-) Θ. 564, = ἡ κριθή, *barley,* ἄλφι (r. ἀλφιτ-) Hom. Cer. 208, = ἄλφιτον, *barley-meal,* γλάφυ, *hollow,* Hes. Op. 531, ἔρι Philet. ap. Strab. 364, = ἔριον, *wool* (compare, with these neuters, βρῖ and ῥά, § 136. β); Dat. fem. δαΐ (ῐ), *battle,* N. 286 (akin to this, Acc. δάϊν Call. Fr. 243); Dat. λιτί Σ. 352, Acc. sing. masc. or pl. neut. λῖτα α. 130, = Dat. and Acc. of τὸ λίνον, *linen;* Acc. fem. νίφα, *snow,* Hes. Op. 533 (from which ἡ νιφάς, -άδος, *snow-flake*); Voc. ἠλὲ O. 128, = ἠλεὲ β. 243, from ἠλεός, *crazed.*

β. A word which is only employed in a *single* case, is termed a *monoptote* (μόνος, *single,* πτῶσις, *case*); in *two* cases, a *diptote;* in *three,* a *triptote;* in *four,* a *tetraptote.*

CHAPTER III.

DECLENSION OF ADJECTIVES AND PARTICIPLES.

[¶¶ 17-20, 22.]

§ 128. Adjectives are declined like substantives, except so far as they vary their form to denote variation of gender (§ 74. δ). In this respect, they are divided into three classes, *adjectives of one, of two,* and *of three terminations.*

Note. In adjectives of more than one termination, the *masculine* is regarded as the primary gender, and the root, theme, and declension of the masculine, as the general root, theme, and declension of the word. The mode of declining an adjective is commonly marked by subjoining to the theme the other forms of the Nom. sing., or their endings; and, if necessary, the form of the Gen. sing. Thus, ἄδικος, -ον · σαφής, -ές · φίλιος, -ᾱ, -ον · ὁ, ἡ δίπους, -οδος, τὸ δίπουν.

§ 129. I. Adjectives of One Termination are declined precisely like nouns, and therefore require no separate rules or paradigms. They are confined, in the language of prose, to the masculine and feminine genders, and some of them are employed in a single gender only. E. g.

1. Masculine. Dec. I. ὁ γεννάδας, -ου, *noble,* ὁ μονίας, -ου, *solitary,* ὁ ἐθελοντής, -οῦ, *voluntary;* Dec. III. ὁ γέρων, -οντος, *old,* ὁ πένης, -ητος, *poor* (yet Hesych. gives ἡ πένησσα).

2. Feminine. Dec. III. ἡ μαινάς, -άδος, *frantic*, ἡ πατρίς, -ίδος, *native*, ἡ Τρωάς, -άδος, *Trojan*, ἡ Δωρίς, -ίδος, *Dorian*.

3. Masculine and Feminine. Dec. III. ὁ, ἡ ἀγνώς, -ῶτος, *unknown*, ὁ, ἡ ἄπαις, -αιδος, *childless*, ὁ, ἡ ἧλιξ, -ικος, *of the same age*, ὁ, ἡ ἡμιθνής, -ῆτος, *half-dead*, ὁ, ἡ φυγάς, άδος, *fugitive*.

NOTE. The indirect cases of adjectives of one termination and of Dec. III., are sometimes employed by the poets as neuter; as, γνώμην τε μεγάλην ἐν πένητι σώματι Eur. El. 372, μανιάσιν λυσσήμασιν Id. Or. 270, δρομάσι δινεύων βλεφάροις Ib. 837.

§ 130. II. ADJECTIVES OF TWO TERMINATIONS have the *same* form for the *feminine* as for the *masculine*, but have a *distinct* form for the *neuter* in the direct cases singular and plural.

REMARKS. α. Adjectives which form the neuter must be either of Dec. II. or III. (§ 79), and, if of Dec. III., cannot have either a labial or a palatal characteristic (§ 101). To adjectives which cannot form the neuter, this gender is sometimes supplied from a kindred or derived root; as, ὁ, ἡ ἅρπαξ, -αγος, *rapacious*, τὸ ἁρπακτικόν.

β. The neuter must have two distinct forms, and can have only two, one for the direct cases singular, and the other for the direct cases plural (§ 80). Hence, every complete adjective must have two terminations. A neuter plural is sometimes given, though rarely, to adjectives which do not form the neuter singular; as, τέκεα πατρὸς ἀπάτορα Eur. Herc. 114, ἔθνεα ... ἐπήλυδα Hdt. viii. 73.

γ. In δίπους (¶ 17), and in similar compounds of πούς, *foot*, the Neuter sing., on account of the difficulty of forming it from the root, is formed from the theme, after the analogy of contracts of Dec. II. (¶ 18); thus, ὁ, ἡ δίπους, τὸ δίπουν· ὁ, ἡ τρίπους, -οδος, *three-footed*, τὸ τρίπουν. Cf. § 136. 2.

§ 131. III. ADJECTIVES OF THREE TERMINATIONS differ from those of two in having a distinct form for the *feminine*.

It is only in the first declension that the feminine has a distinct form from the masculine. These adjectives, therefore, must be of two declensions, uniting the *feminine* forms of the *first* with the *masculine* and *neuter* of the *second* or *third*. The feminine is formed according to the following rules.

RULE I. If the theme belongs to the *second declension*, the feminine affixes of the first are annexed to the *simple root*.

If the root ends in ε, ι, ρ, or ρο, the feminine is declined like σκιᾱ· otherwise, like τιμή (¶ 7, § 93).

Thus, φιλίᾱ, φιλίᾱς· σοφή, σοφῆς· χρυσέᾱ, διπλόη (¶ 18); μακρός, -ᾱ, -όν, *long*, ἀθρόος, -ᾱ, -ον, *dense*; καλός, -ή, -όν, *beautiful*, μέσος, -η, -ον, *middle*, γεγραμμένος, -η, -ον, *written*.

§ 132. RULE II. If the theme belongs to the *third declension*, the feminine affixes of the first are annexed to the *root increased by* σ (i. e. to the theme before euphonic changes).

Thus, from the roots παντ-, χαριεντ- (¶ 19), βουλευοντ-, ἀραντ-, φανεντ (¶ 22), are formed the feminines (πάντσα, πάνσα) πᾶσᾰ, (χαρίεντσα, χαρίενσα) χαρίεσσᾰ, (βουλεύοντσα) βουλεύουσᾰ, (ἄραντσα) ἄρᾱσᾰ, (φανέντσα) φανεῖσᾰ (§§ 55, 57, 58).

The following SPECIAL RULES are observed in the formation of the feminine, when the theme belongs to Dec. III.

1. After ε or ο, the σ which is added to the root becomes ε (§ 50), which is then contracted, with ε into ει, and with ο into υι. Thus, from the roots ἡδε- (¶ 19), and εἰδοτ- (¶ 22), are formed the feminines (ἡδέσα, ἡδέεα) ἡδεῖᾰ, (εἰδότσα, εἰδόσα, εἰδόεα) εἰδυῖᾰ.

NOTES. α. The diphthong ου never stands before the affixes of Dec. I. The concurrence of open vowels which would be thus produced seems to have displeased the Greek ear. Hence the contraction, in this case, of οι into the closer diphthong υι.

β. In the *contracted perfect participles*, which have a long vowel in the last syllable of the root, the σ remains. Thus, from r. ἑστωτ- (contr. from ἑσταοτ-, from the verb ἵστημι, *to stand*) is formed the feminine (ἑστῶτσα) ἑστῶσᾰ (¶ 22).

γ. The fem. termination -εῖᾰ is commonly shortened in Ionic prose, and sometimes in Epic and other poetry, to έᾰ (sometimes Ion. έη, especially in Hipp.); as, βαθέα, εὐρέα Hdt. i. 178, βαθέην Ib. 75, βαθέης E. 147 (but βαθείης B. 92), ὠκέα B. 786, ἁδέα Theoc. 3. 20, ταχεῶν Theog. 715. So, even in Attic prose, Buttmann edits from the best Mss. ἡμισέας Pl. Meno, 83 c. On the other hand, the poets, in a few instances, prolong -έα of the Neut. pl. to -εῖα for the sake of the metre (§ 47. N.); as, ὀξεῖα Hes. Sc. 348, ἁδεῖα Soph. Tr. 122 (so σκιόειν for σκιόεν, Ap. Rh. 2. 404, δακρυόειν Id. 4. 1291).

2. After a liquid, the σ which is added becomes ε, which is then transposed, and contracted with the preceding vowel into a diphthong. Thus, from the roots μελαν- (¶ 19), τερεν- (r. of τέρην, *tender*), πιερ-, are formed the feminines (μέλανσα, μέλανεα) μέλαινᾰ, (τέρενσα, τερεενα) τέρεινᾰ, πίειρᾰ (§ 134. δ) Compare §§ 56, 57.

3. If the root, after the addition of σ, and the consequent changes, ends in ι or ρ, the feminine is declined like σκιά· but if it ends in σ or ν, like γλῶσσα (¶ 7, §§ 92, 93); as, ἡδεῖᾰ, ἡδείᾱς· πᾶσᾰ, πάσης· μέλαινᾰ, μελαίνης (¶ 19); πίειρᾰ, πιείρᾱς. Observe that the α in the direct cases is always short. See § 92.

§ **133.** Of those words which belong to the general class of ADJECTIVES (§ 73), the following have three terminations:—

1. All participles; as, *βουλεύων*, *ἄρας*, *εἰδώς* (¶ 22).

NOTE. In *participles*, which partake of the *verb* and the *adjective*, a distinction must be made between the *root*, *affix*, *connecting vowel*, and *flexible ending* of *conjugation*, and those of *declension*; thus, in the genitive *βουλεύοντος*, the root of conjugation is *βουλευ-*, and the affix *-οντος* · while the root of declension is *βουλευοντ-*, and the affix *-ος*.

2. All comparatives and superlatives in *-ος*; as, *σοφώτερος*, *-ᾱ*, *-ον*, *wiser*; *σοφώτατος*, *-η*, *-ον*, *wisest*.

3. All numerals, except cardinals from 2 to 100 inclusive; as, *διακόσιοι*, *-αι*, *-α*, *two hundred*, *τρίτος*, *-η*, *-ον*, *third*.

4. The article and adjective pronouns, except *τίς* (*τὶς*). See ¶ 24.

5. Simple adjectives in *-ος*, *-εις*, and *-υς*, with a few other adjectives; as, *φίλιος*, *σοφός*, *χρύσεος* (¶ 18); *χαρίεις*, *ἡδύς* · *πᾶς*, *μέλας* (¶ 19); *ἑκών*, *-οῦσα*, *-όν*, G. *-όντος*, *willing*; *τάλας*, *-αινα*, *-αν*, G. *-ανος*, *wretched*; *τέρην*, *-εινα*, *-εν*, G. *-ενος*, *tender*.

NOTES. *α*. For the number of terminations in adjectives in *-ος*, only general rules can be given. For the most part, simples have three terminations, and compounds, but two. Yet some compounds have three, and many simples, particularly derivatives in *-ειος*, *-ιος*, and *-ιμος*, have but two. Derivatives from compound verbs, as being themselves uncompounded, especially those in *-κος*, *-τος*, and *-τέος*, have more commonly three terminations. In many words, usage is variable. See *γ*.

β. Adjectives in *-ως*, of the Attic Dec. II., have but two terminations; as, *ἀγήρως* (¶ 17), *ὁ*, *ἡ* *εὔγεως*, *τὸ* *εὔγεων*, *fertile*. For *πλέως*, see § 135.

γ. In (a.) words in which the Fem. has commonly a distinct form, the form of the Masc. is sometimes employed in its stead. And (b.), on the other hand, a distinct form is sometimes given to the Fem. in words in which it is commonly the same with the Masc. Thus, we find as feminine,

(a.) Adjectives in *-ος* (particularly in Attic writers, § 74. ε), *δῆλος* Eur. Med. 1197, *φαῦλος* Id. Hipp. 435, Th. vi. 21, *ἀναγκαίου* Th. i. 2, *κλυτός* B. 742; Adjectives in *-υς* (particularly in Epic and Doric poetry), *ἡδύς* *μ*. 369, *ἁδέα* Theoc. 20. 8, *θηλύς* T. 97, *πουλύν* K. 27; Comparatives, Superlatives, Participles, and Pronouns (all rarely, except in the dual, see δ.), *ἀπορώτερος* Th. v. 110, *δυσεμβολώτατος* Id. iii. 101, *ὀλοώτατος* δ. 442; *τιθέντες* Æsch. Ag. 560; *τηλικοῦτος* Soph. El. 613, Œd. C. 751.

(b.) *ἀθανάτη* K. 404, *θηροφόνη* Theog. 11, *πολυξένᾱν* Pind. N. 3. 3, *πολυτιμήτη* Ar. Pax, 978, for the common *ἡ ἀθάνατος*, &c. This use is especially epic and lyric.

δ. This use of the masc. form for the fem. is particularly frequent in the *dual*, in which, from its limited use, the distinction of gender is least important; as, *τὼ χεῖρε* vi. 1. 8 (the fem. form *τά* scarcely belongs to classic Greek); *τούτω τὼ ἡμέρα* Cyr. i. 2. 11; *τούτοιν δὴ τοῖν κινησέοιν* Pl. Leg.

898 a.; *δύο τινέ ἐστον ἰδέα ἄρχοντε καὶ ἄγοντε, οἷν ἑπόμεθα·... τούτω* Pl. Phædr. 237 d.; *ἰδόντε καὶ παθοῦσα* Soph. Œd. C. 1676; *πληγέντε* Θ. 455.

§ **134.** To some adjectives, feminine forms are supplied from a kindred or derived root. These forms may be either required to complete the adjective, or they may be only special feminines, used (particularly in poetry and the dialects) by the side of forms of the common gender (cf. § 74. ε). The feminines thus supplied most frequently end in -ις, G. -ιδος, but also in -ας, G. -αδος, in -εια, -ειρα, &c. (for the use of δ as a feminine formative, see § 118). Thus,

α. Masculines in -ης of Dec. I., and in -εύς of Dec. III., have often corresponding feminines in -ις, -ιδος. These words are chiefly patrials and gentiles, or other personal designations, and are commonly used as substantives. Thus, ὁ πολίτης, -ου, *belonging to a city* (θεοὶ πολῖται Æsch. Th. 253), *citizen*, ἡ πολῖτις, -ιδος· ὁ ἱκέτης, ἡ ἱκέτις, *suppliant*; ὁ Σκύθης, ἡ Σκύθις, *Scythian*; ὁ Μεγαρεύς, -έως, ἡ Μεγαρίς, *Megarian*.

β. The compounds of ἔτος, *year* (in -ης, -ες of Dec. III., but sometimes in ης, G. -ου of Dec. I.), have often a special fem. in -ις, -ιδος; as, ὁ, ἡ ἑπτέτης, τὸ ἑπτέτες, *seven years old*, and ἡ ἑπτέτις, -ιδος· τὸν ἑξέτη καὶ τὴν ἑξέτιν Pl. Leg. 794 c.; τὰς τριακοντούτεις σπονδάς Th. i. 23, but τριακοντουτίδων σπονδῶν Ib. 87.

γ. Some compounds in -ης, -ες have a poetic (particularly Epic) fem. in εια; as, ἠριγενής, -ές, ἡ ἠριγένειᾰ A. 477. So μουνογένειᾰ, ἡδυέπειᾰ, θεσπιέπειᾰ Soph. Œd. T. 463.

δ. Add ὁ, ἡ πίων, and ἡ πίειρᾰ, τὸ πῖον, *fat*; ὁ πρέσβυς, *old*, *venerable*, Fem., chiefly poet., πρέσβᾰ, πρέσβη, πρέσβειρᾰ, πρεσβηΐς, πρέσβις· ὁ, ἡ μάκαρ, and ἡ μάκαιρᾰ, *blessed*, poetic; ὁ, ἡ πρόφρων, and Ep. ἡ πρόφρασσᾰ K. 290, *kind*.

§ **135.** Irregular Adjectives. Among the adjectives which deserve special notice are the following.

μέγας, *great*, and πολύς, *much* (¶ 20). In these adjectives, the Nom. and Acc. sing. masc. and neut. are formed from the roots μεγα- and πολε-, according to Dec. III. The other cases are formed from the roots μεγαλ- and πολλ-, according to Dec. I. and II. The Voc. μεγάλε occurs only Æsch. Th. 822. From its signification, πολύς has no dual. For the Homeric inflection of πολύς, see ¶ 20. In Herodotus, the forms from πολλός prevail throughout, yet not to the entire exclusion of the other forms. The Epic forms sometimes occur in the Attic poets.

ὁ πλέως, ἡ πλέᾱ, τὸ πλέων, *full*. The Masc. and Neut. are formed from r. πλα-, according to the Attic Dec. II. (§ 98); the Fem. is formed from r. πλε-. Ion. πλέος, Ep. πλεῖος, -η, -ον. So, likewise, in Att. writers, the plural compounds ἔμπλεοι, ἔκπλεα Cyr. vi. 2. 7, περίπλεα Ib. 33. In like manner ἵλεα Pl. Phædo, 95 a, N. pl. from ἵλεως, -ων, contr. from ἵλαος, -ον.

ὁ πρᾶος (by some written πρᾷος), ἡ πραεῖα, τὸ πρᾶον (πρᾷον), *mild*. In this adj., forms from r. πρα-, of Dec. II., and from r. πραε-, of Dec. III., are blended (see ¶ 20). Ion. πρηΰς.

ὁ, ἡ σῶς, τὸ σῶν, *safe*. In this adj., contract forms from r. σα- are blended with forms from r. σω- (contr. from σαο-), belonging partly to Dec. II. and partly to Dec. III. Thus,

	ὁ, ἡ		τὸ
S. N.	(σάος) σῶς	σῶος iii. 1. 32	(σάον) σῶν
A.	(σάον) σῶν		
P. N.		σῶοι, (σῶες) σῶς	(σάα) σᾶ, σῶα
A.		σώους, (σῶας) σῶς	

There is also an Epic form σόος. With the above may be compared the Homeric ζώς E. 87, Acc. ζών Π. 445, contr. from ζαός, ζαόν, = the common ζωός, ζωόν, *living.*

§ 136. REMARKS. 1. Some compounds of γέλως, *laughter*, and κέρας, *horn*, may receive either the Attic second, or the third declension; as, φιλόγελως, -ων, G. -ω and -ωτος, *laughter-loving*, χρυσόκερως, -ων, G. -ω and -ωτος, *golden-horned*. Shorter forms also occur, according to the common Dec. II.; as, δίκερον, νήκεροι, ἄκερα.

2. Some compounds of πούς, *foot*, have secondary forms according to Dec. II.; as, πολύπους (poet. πουλύπους), *many-footed*, G. πολύποδος and πολύπου· τρίπους, -οδος, and Ep. τρίπος, -ου, X. 164, *three-footed*; Ἶρις ἀελλόπος Θ. 409; ἵπποισιν ἀελλοπόδεσσιν Hom. Ven. 218. See Οἰδίπου (¶ 16), and compare § 130. γ.

3. Among other examples of varied formation, we notice the Homeric ὁ ἐΰς B. 819, and ἠΰς Π. 464, *good, brave*, τὸ ἐΰ Γ. 235, εὖ E. 650 (both adverbial), and ἠΰ P. 456, Gen. ἐῆος A. 393 (cf. § 121. 3), Acc. ἐΰν Θ. 303, and ἠΰν E. 628; Gen. pl. neut. ἐάων Ω. 528; ὁ ἐρίηρος Δ. 266, *trusty*, Pl. ἐρίηρες, ἐρίηρας, Γ. 47, 378; ὁ πολύῤῥηνος λ. 257, *rich in sheep*, Pl. πολύῤῥηνες I. 154 (see also πολύαρνι below, 4. δ); αἰπύς ὄλεθρος N. 773, Ἴλιον αἰπύ O. 71, Ἴλιος αἰπεινή N. 773, πόλιν αἰπήν N. 625, αἰπὰ ῥέεθρα Θ. 369, Πήδασον αἰπήεσσαν Φ. 87; ἀργῆτι Γ. 419, ἀργῆτα Θ. 133, ἀργέτι Λ. 818, ἀργέτα Φ. 127; ἀργύφεον Σ. 50, ἄργυφον Ω. 621; πόλιν ... εὐτείχεον A. 129, πόλιν εὐτείχεα Π. 57; Τροίην ἐριβώλακα Γ. 74, Τροίην ἐρίβωλον I. 329; πολύτλας ε. 171, πολυτλήμων σ. 319, πολύτλητοι λ. 38; &c. Examples of adjectives of double formation, or of synonymous adjectives with different forms, might be greatly multiplied.

4. Among defective adjectives, we notice,

α.) The following, chiefly poetic: ὁ, ἡ ἄδακρυς, τὸ ἄδακρυ, *tearless*, Acc. ἄδακρυν (the other cases supplied by ἀδάκρυτος, -ον); πολύδακρυς, *tearful* (supplied in like manner by πολυδάκρυτος); ὁ πρέσβυς (for fem. see § 134. δ), *old*, as subst. *elder*, *ambassador* (in the last sense G. πρέσβεως Ar. Ach. 93), A. πρέσβυν, V. πρέσβυ· Pl. πρέσβεις, πρεσβῆες Hes. Sc. 245, *elders*, *ambassadors*, G. πρέσβεων, D. πρέσβεσι, πρεσβεῦσιν Lyc. 1056, A. πρέσβεις, Du. πρέσβη Ar. Fr. 495 (the plur. in the sense of *ambassadors* was in common use; otherwise, the word was almost exclusively poetic, and its place supplied by ὁ πρεσβύτης, *old man*, and ὁ πρεσβευτής, *ambassador*); φροῦδος, -η, -ον, *gone*, which, with the Nom. throughout, has only the Gen. φρούδου Soph. Aj. 264.

β.) Poetic feminines and neuters, which have no corresponding masc.; as, ἡ πότνιἄ (and sometimes πότνᾶ), *revered*, τὴν πότνιἄν, αἱ πότνιαι· ἡ θάλειἄ, τὰ θάλεα, *blooming*, *rich* (Hom.), ἡ λῖς and λισσή (always with πέτρη), μ. 64, 79, γ. 293, ε. 412, = λεία, fem. of λεῖος, *smooth*; τὸ βρῖ (r. βριθ-) Hes. ap. Strab. 364, = neut. of βριθύς, *heavy*; τὸ ῥᾳ (r. ῥαδ-) Soph. Fr. 932, = neut. of ῥάδιος, *easy* (compare with βρῖ and ῥᾳ, the neuters δῶ, κρῖ, &c., § 127. α); τὰ ἦρα and ἐπίηρα, *pleasing* (Hom.).

γ.) Poetic plurals which have no corresponding sing.; as οἱ θαμέες K. 264, and ταρφέες Λ. 387 (yet ταρφύς Æsch. Th. 535), *thick, frequent*, αἱ θαμειαί A. 52, and ταρφειαί T. 357 (accented as if from θαμειός and ταρφειός), τὰ ταρφέα Λ. 69, ἐρυσάρματες...ἵπποι Π. 370; οἱ πλέες Λ. 395, τοὺς πλέας B. 129 = πλέονες, πλέονας, *more*.

δ.) Poetic oblique cases which have no corresponding Nom.; as, τοῦ δυσδάμαρτος, *unhappily wedded*, Æsch. Ag. 1319; καλλιγύναικος, *having beautiful women*, Sapph. (135), καλλιγύναικι Pind. P. 9. 131, Ἑλλάδα καλλιγύναικα B. 683; πολύαρνι Θυέστῃ B. 106; πολυπάταγα θυμέλαν Pratin. ap. Ath. 617 c; ὑψικέρᾱτα πέτραν Ar. Nub. 597; χέρηος, χέρηϊ, χέρηα, also Pl. χέρηες, χέρηα (of which χέρεια σ. 229, υ. 310, is a doubtful variation), A. 80, Δ. 400, &c. = χείρονος, &c., *worse*.

CHAPTER IV.

NUMERALS.

[¶¶ 21, 25.]

§ 137. I. NUMERAL ADJECTIVES. Of numeral adjectives, the principal are, (1.) the CARDINAL, answering the question πόσοι; *how many?* (2.) the ORDINAL, answering the question, πόστος; *which in order?* or, *one of how many?* (3.) the TEMPORAL, answering the question, ποσταῖος; *on what day?* or, *in how many days?* (4.) the MULTIPLE (multiplex, *having many folds*), showing to what extent any thing is *complicated*; and the PROPORTIONAL, showing the *proportion* which one thing bears to another.

1. CARDINAL. For the declension of the first four cardinals, see ¶ 21. The cardinals from 5 to 100, inclusive, are indeclinable; as, οἱ, αἱ, τά, τῶν, τοῖς, ταῖς, τούς, τάς, πέντε, *five*. Those above 100 are declined like the plural of φίλιος (¶ 18).

NOTES. *a.* Εἷς, from its signification, is used only in the singular; δύω, only in the dual and plural; and the other cardinals only in the plural (except with collective nouns, in such expressions as ἀσπὶς μυρία καὶ τετρακοσία, 10,400 *infantry*, i. 7. 10, ἵππον ὀκτακισχιλίην, 8,000 *horse*, Hdt. vii. 85). For the dialectic as well as common declens. of the first four cardinals, see ¶ 21. We add references to authors for some of the less frequent forms: ἕεις Hes. Th. 145, ἧς Theoc. 11. 33 (in some Mss.), Inscr. Heracl., ἰῷ Z. 422, οὐδαμέας (by some written οὐδαμάς) Hdt. iv. 114, δοιώ Γ. 236, δυῶν Hdt. i. 94, δυοῖσι Ib. 32, τριοῖσι Hippon. Fr. 8, τέτορες Hdt. vii. 228 (Inscr. Lac.), τέτορα Hes. Op. 696, τετόρων Theoc. 14. 16, πίσυρες ε. 70, πίσυρας Ο. 680, τέτρασι Hes. Fr. 47. 5, Pind. O. 10. 83. Dialectic forms of some of the higher numbers are, 5 πέμπε Æol., 12 δυώδεκα and δυοκαίδεκα Ion. and Poet., 20 ἐείκοσι Ep., εἴκατι Dor., 30 τριήκοντα Ion. (we even find Gen. τριηκόντων

Hes. Op. 694, Dat τριηκόντεσσιν Anthol.), 40 τεσσεράκοντα and τεσσερήκοντα Ion., πετρώκοντα Dor., 80 ὀγδώκοντα (§ 46. α) Ion., 90 ἐννήκοντα τ. 174, 200 διηκόσιοι Ion., 9,000 ἐννεάχῑλοι Ξ. 148, 10,000 δεκάχῑλοι Ib.

β. Εἷς has two roots, ἐν- and μι-. Its compounds οὐδείς and μηδείς (which, for the sake of emphasis, are also written separately, οὐδὲ εἷς, μηδὲ εἷς) have the masc. plur.

γ. The common form of the second cardinal is δύο, shortened from the regular δύω, which is by some excluded entirely from the Attic and from Herodotus. The second form of the Gen. δυεῖν is only Attic, and is even excluded from some of the best editions of good Att. writers. The Dat. pl. δυσί occurs Th. viii. 101. Both δύο (δύω) and ἄμφω, *both* (which is placed in ¶ 21, as partaking of the nature of a *numeral*, with that of an emphatic pronoun), are sometimes indeclinable (in Hom. never otherwise); as, δύο μηνῶν vii. 6. 1, δύο μοιράων K. 253, δύω κανόνεσσι N. 407, χερσὶν ἅμ' ἄμφω Hom. Cer. 15.

δ. For the double forms of τέσσαρες, see § 70. 1. In the compounds δεκατρεῖς, τεσσαρεσκαίδεκα, and its equivalent δεκατέσσαρες, the components τρεῖς and τέσσαρες are declined; thus, δεκατρεῖς, δεκατρία, δεκατριῶν· τοῖς τεσσαρσικαίδεκα. Yet we sometimes find τεσσαρεσκαίδεκα (Ion. τεσσερεσκαίδεκα), and even τεσσαρακαίδεκα used as indeclinable. See Hdt. i. 86, Mem. ii. 7. 2, and Lob. ad Phryn. p. 409. The compounds from 13 to 19 are also written separately: τέσσαρες καὶ δέκα. So τρεῖς γε καὶ δέκα Pind. O. 1. 127, τρία καὶ δέκα Hdt. i. 119.

ε. The cardinals become *collective* or *distributive* by composition with σύν· as, σύνδυο, *two together*, or *two at a time*, vi. 3. 2, σύντρεις ι. 429, συνδώδεκα Eur. Tro. 1076. The distributive sense is also expressed by means of the prepositions ἀνά, κατά, and, in some connections, εἰς and ἐπί· as, ἓξ λόχους ἀνὰ ἑκατὸν ἄνδρας, *six companies, each a hundred men*, iii. 4. 21; κατὰ τετρακισχιλίους, 4,000 *at a time*, iii. 5. 8; εἰς ἑκατόν, 100 *deep*, Cyr. vi. 3. 23; ἐπὶ τεττάρων, *four deep*, i. 2. 15.

ζ. The numeral μύριοι, 10,000, is distinguished from μυρίοι, plur. of μυρίος, *vast, countless*, with which it was originally one, by the accent.

§ **138.** 2. Ordinal. The ordinal numbers are all derived from the cardinal, except πρῶτος, and are all declined with three terminations. They all end in -τος, except δεύτερος, ἕβδομος, and ὄγδοος. Those from 20, upwards, all end in -οστός.

Notes. α. Dialectic forms are, 1 πρᾶτος Dor., 3 τρίτατος Ep., 4 τέτρατος Ep., 7 ἑβδόματος Ep., 8 ὀγδόατος Ep., 9 εἴνατος Ep., 12 δυωδέκατος Ion., 14 τεσσερεσκαιδέκατος Ion., 30 τριηκοστός Ion., &c.

β. Instead of the compound numbers from 13 to 19 in the table (¶ 25), we also find the combinations τρίτος καὶ δέκατος, Th. v. 56; τέταρτος καὶ δέκατος, Ib. 81; πέμπτος καὶ δέκατος, Ib. 83; &c. Also, εἷς καὶ εἰκοστός, Th. viii. 109. See § 140. 1.

3. Temporal. The temporal numbers are formed from the ordinals, by changing the final -ος into -αῖος, -ᾱ, -ον; thus, δεύτερος, δευτεραῖος, -ᾱ, -ον. From πρῶτος, no temporal number is formed. Its place is supplied by αὐθήμερος, -ον.

4. MULTIPLE. The multiple numbers end in -πλόος, contracted -πλοῦς, and are declined like διπλόος, διπλοῦς (¶ 18).

Other forms are those in -φάσιος, chiefly Ion., as, διφάσιος, τριφάσιος · also, δισσός, τρισσός, Ion. διξός, τριξός (§ 70. V.), &c.

5. PROPORTIONAL. The proportional numbers have double forms, in -πλάσιος, -ᾱ, -ον, and, more rarely, -πλασίων, -ον, G. -ονος. Thus the ratio of 2 to 1 is expressed by διπλάσιος -α, -ον, or διπλασίων, -ον, G. -ονος · and that of 10 to 1, by δεκαπλάσιος or δεκαπλασίων. The ratio of 1 to 1, or of equality, is expressed by ἴσος (Ep. ῑσος), -η, -ον.

§ 139. II. NUMERAL ADVERBS. 1. The numeral adverbs which reply to the interrogative ποσάκις; *how many times?* all end in -άκις, except the three first; thus, δεκάκις, *ten times*, ἐννεακαιεικοσικαιεπτακοσιοπλασιάκις, 729 *times*, Pl. Rep. 587 e.

These adverbs are employed in the formation of the higher cardinal and ordinal numbers; thus, δισχίλιοι, *two thousand*, πεντακισχιλιοστός, *five thousandth*.

2. Other numeral adverbs relate to *division*, *order*, *place*, *manner*, &c.; as, δίχα, *in two divisions*, τρίχα, *in three divisions*; δεύτερον, *secondly*, τρίτον, *thirdly*; τριχοῦ, *in three places*, πενταχοῦ, *in five places*; πενταχῶς, *in five ways*, ἑξαχῶς, *in six ways*.

III. NUMERAL SUBSTANTIVES. The numeral substantives, for the most part, end in -άς, -άδος, and are employed both as abstract and as collective nouns. Thus, ἡ μυριάς may signify, either the number 10,000, considered abstractly, or a collection of 10,000. These numerals often take the place of the cardinals, particularly in the expression of the higher numbers; as, δέκα μυριάδες, *ten myriads* = 100,000; ἑκατὸν μυριάδες, *a million*.

§ 140. REMARKS. 1. When numerals are combined, the less commonly precedes with καί · but often the greater without καί, and sometimes also with it.

Thus, πέντε καὶ εἴκοσιν, *five and twenty*, i. 4. 2; τετταράκοντα πέντε, *forty-five*, v. 5. 5; τριάκοντα καὶ πέντε, *thirty and five*, i. 4. 2; σταθμοὶ τρεῖς καὶ ἐνενήκοντα, παρασάγγαι πέντε καὶ τριάκοντα καὶ πεντακόσιοι, στάδιοι πεντήκοντα καὶ ἑξακισχίλιοι καὶ μύριοι, ii. 2. 6; σταθμοὶ διακόσιοι δεκαπέντε, παρασάγγαι χίλιοι ἑκατὸν πεντήκοντα πέντε, στάδια τρισμύρια τετρακισχίλια ἑξακόσια πεντήκοντα, vii. 8. 26. See v. 5. 4, and § 138. β.

NOTES. α. From the division of the Greek month into *decades*, the days were often designated as follows; *μηνὸς βοηδρομιῶνος ἕκτη ἐπὶ δέκα*, *upon the*

[6th after 10] *16th of the month Boëdromion*, Dem. 261. 12; *ἀνθεστηριῶνος ἕκτη ἐπὶ δεκάτῃ*, Id. 279. 17; *βοηδρομιῶνος ἕκτῃ μετ' εἰκάδα*, 'the 26th,' Id 265. 5. In like manner, *τρίτος γε γένναν πρὸς δέκ' ἄλλαισιν γοναῖς*, Æsch Prom. 773.

β. Instead of adding eight or nine, *subtraction* is often employed; as, *νῆες ...μιᾶς δέουσαι τεσσαράκοντα*, *forty ships wanting one* [40 — 1 = 39], Th. viii. 7; *ναυσὶ δυοῖν δεούσαις πεντήκοντα* [50 — 2 = 48], Ib. 25; *δυοῖν δεούσαις εἴκοσι ναυσί*, H. Gr. i. 1. 5; *πεντήκοντα δυοῖν δέοντα ἔτη*, Th. ii. 2; *ἑνὸς δέον εἰκοστὸν ἔτος*, Id. viii. 6 (cf. *ὄγδοον καὶ δέκατον ἔτος*, Id. vii. 18); *ἑνὸς δέοντος τριακοστῷ ἔτει*, *in the thirtieth year, one wanting*, Id. iv. 102. In like manner, *τριακοσίων ἀποδέοντα μύρια*, Id. ii. 13. It will be observed, that the participle may either agree with the greater number, or, by a rarer construction, be put absolute with the less. See Syntax.

γ. The combinations of *fractions* with whole numbers are variously expressed; thus, (a) *τρία ἡμιδαρεικά*, *three half-darics*, i. e. $1\frac{1}{2}$ *darics*, i. 3. 21 (b) Particularly in Herodotus, *τρίτον ἡμιτάλαντον*, *the third talent a half one* i. e. $2\frac{1}{2}$ *talents*, Hdt. i. 50; *ἕβδομον ἡμιτάλαντον* + *τέταρτον ἡμιτάλαντον* = *τάλαντα δέκα*, $6\frac{1}{2} + 3\frac{1}{2} = 10$, Ib. (compare in Lat. *sestertius*, shortened from *semistertius*): (c) Less classic, *δύο καὶ ἡμίσειαν μνᾶν*, *δύω καὶ ἥμισυ δραχμαί*, Poll. ix. 56, 62: (d) *ἐπίτριτον*, *a third in addition*, i. e. $1\frac{1}{3}$, Vect. 3. 9; *ἐπίπεμπτον*, $1\frac{1}{5}$, Ib.: (e) *ἡμιόλιον*, *half as much again*, i. e. $1\frac{1}{2}$, i. 3. 21.

2. The Table (¶ 25) exhibits the most common numerals with some of the interrogatives, indefinites, diminutives, &c. which correspond with them.

CHAPTER V.

PRONOUNS.

I. Substantive.

[¶ 23.]

§ 141. Personal, *ἐγώ*, *σύ*, *οὗ*. The declension of these pronouns is peculiar.

The numbers are distinguished not less by difference of *root*, than of *affix*. Thus, the 1st Person has the *roots*, Sing. *μ*-, or, as a more emphatic form, *ἐμ*-, Pl. *ἡμ*-, Du. *ν*-; the 2d Pers., Sing. *σ*-, Pl. *ὑμ*-, Du. *σφ*-; the 3d Pers., Sing. the rough breathing, Pl. and Du. *σφ*-. Most of the forms have a *connecting vowel*, which in the Sing. and Pl. is -*ε*- (in the Dat. sing. passing into the kindred -*ο*-, § 28), but in the Du., -*ω*-. The *flexible endings* are Sing. Gen. -*ο*, Dat. -ῐ, Acc. none (the primitive Direct Case remained as Acc., while the Nom., in the 1st and 2d Persons, had the peculiar forms *ἐγώ* and *σύ*, and in the 3d, from its reflexive use, early disappeared; compare the Lat. *me*, *te*, *se*; *ego*, *tu*, Nom. of 3d Pers. wanting); Pl. Nom. -*ες*, Gen. -*ων*, Dat. -ῐν (the flexible ending of the old Indirect Case, § 83), Acc. -ᾰς; Du. Nom. -*ε* (in the prolonged forms *νῶϊ*, *σφῶϊ*, the -*ι* appears to have come from an imitation of the Gen.), Gen. -ῐν. In all the forms in common use, the connecting vowel and flexible ending are contracted; thus, ἐμ-έ-ο ἐμοῦ, σ-έ-ο σοῦ, ῾-έ-ο οὗ· (ἐμ-έ-ι, ἐμ-ό-ι) ἐμοί, (σ-έ-ι) σοί, (῾-έ-ι) οἷ· ἡμ-έ-ες ἡμεῖς, ὑμ-έ-ες ὑμεῖς, (σφ-έ-ες) σφεῖς· ἡμ-έ-ων ἡμῶν, ὑμ-έ-ων ὑμῶν, σφ-έ-ων σφῶν· (ἡμ-έ-ῖν) ἡμῖν, (ὑμ-έ-ῖν) ὑμῖν (σφίσι exhibits a different formation without a connecting vowel); ἡμ-έ-ᾰς ἡμᾶς, ὑμ-έ-ᾰς ὑμᾶς, σφ-έ-ᾰς σφᾶς· ν-ῶ-ε νώ, σφ-ῶ-ε σφώ (νώ and σφώ are sometimes written incorrectly νῴ and σφῴ, as if contracted from νῶϊ, σφῶϊ, § 25. α); ν-ῶ-ϊν νῷν, σφ-ῶ-ϊν σφῷν (σφωΐν, from its limited use, remained uncontracted)

§ 142. REMARKS. 1. The Table (¶ 23) exhibits, 1st, the common forms of the personal pronouns; 2d, the forms which occur in Homer, whether common or dialectic; 3d, the principal other forms which occur. The forms to which the sign † is affixed are enclitic when used without emphasis (see Prosody). When the oblique cases Sing. of ἐγώ are not enclitic, the longer forms ἐμοῦ, ἐμοί, ἐμέ are employed.

2. The pronoun οὗ is used, both as a simple personal pronoun, and as a reflexive. In the Attic and Common dialects, however, it is not greatly used in either sense, its place being commonly supplied by other pronouns. The plur. forms σφεῖς and σφέα first occur in Hdt. (vii. 168, i. 46). For the limitations and peculiarities in the use of this pronoun, see Syntax.

3. Besides the forms which are common in prose, the Attic poets also employ, (*a*) the Epic Genitives ἐμέθεν, σέθεν, ἕθεν· (*b*) the Accusatives νίν and σφέ, without distinction of number or gender; (*c*) the Dat. pl. σφίν, which even occurs, though rarely, both in Attic and in other poetry, as sing.; (*d*) the Dat. pl. of ἐγώ and σύ with the ultima short (especially Sophocles); thus, ἡμῐ́ν, ὑμῐ́ν, or ἧμῐν, ὗμῐν. See 5. below.

4. The DIALECTIC FORMS arise chiefly, (*a*) from want of contraction, as, ἐμέο, &c.; (*b*) from protraction, as, ἐμεῖο, σεῖο, εἷο, ἡμείων, ὑμείων, σφείων (§ 47. N.); (*c*) from peculiar contraction, as, ἐμεῦ, σεῦ, εὗ (§ 45. 3); (*d*) from the use of different affixes, as Gen. Ep. -θεν (ἐμέθεν, σέθεν, ἕθεν, § 84), Dor. -ος (ἐμέος, contr. ἐμοῦς, ἐμεῦς, τέος, contr. τεῦς, with ε doubled τεοῦς, and, similarly formed, ἑοῦς); Dat. sing. Dor. -ιν (ἐμίν, τεΐν, τίν, ἵν); (*e*) from the retention of primitive forms without the flexible ending, as ῾ᾱμέ, ἄμμε, ὑμέ, ὔμμε, σφέ (compare the sing. ἐμέ, σέ, ἕ, and see §§ 83, 86); (*f*) from variation of root; as, Dor. τ- for σ- (τύ, τεῦ, τοί, τέ, Lat. *tu*, *tui*, *tibi*, *te*, § 70. 2); Æol. Ϝ- for the rough breathing (Ϝέθεν, Ϝοῖ, Ϝέ· Lat. *s-*: *sui*, *sibi*, *se*); Dor. ῾ᾱμ-, Æol. and Ep. ἀμμ-, for ἡμ- (῾ᾱμές, ἄμμες, &c.); Æol. and Ep. ὐμμ- for ῾ῡμ- (ὔμμες, &c.); Dor. ψ- and φ-, Æol. ἀσφ-, for σφ- (ψίν, ψέ, φίν, ἄσφι, ἄσφε). See Table, and 5. below.

5. We add a few references to authors for the dialectic and poetic forms: ἐγών Α. 76 (used by Hom. only before vowels), Ar. Ach. 748 (Meg.), Ar. Lys. 983 (Lac.), Theoc. 1. 14, Æsch. Pers. 931, ἰώνγα (= ἔγωγε) Cor. 12, ἰώγα Ar. Ach. 898; ἐμέο Κ. 124, Hdt. i. 126, ἐμεῖο Α. 174, ἐμεῦ Α. 88, Hdt. vii. 158, μευ Α. 37, Hdt. vii. 209, ἐμέθεν Α. 525, Eur. Or. 986, ἔμεθεν Sapph. 89; ἐμίν Theoc. 2. 144, Ar. Av. 930; ἡμέες Hdt. ii. 6, ῾ᾱμές Ar. Lys. 168, ἄμμες Φ. 432, Theoc. 5. 67; ἡμέων Γ. 101, ἡμείων Ε. 258, ῾ᾱμῶν Theoc. 2. 158, ἀμμέων Alc. 77; ἧμιν Α. 147, ἧμῐν or ἡμῐ́ν, λ. 344, Soph. Œd. T. 39, 42, 103, Ar. Av. 386, ῾ᾱμῖν Theoc. 5. 106, ἄμμι Α. 384, Theoc. 1. 102, ἄμμιν Ν. 379, Alc. 86 (15), ἄμμεσιν Alc. 91 (78); ἡμέας Θ. 211, Hdt. i. 30, ἧμᾰς π. 372, ῾ᾱμέ Ar. Lys. 95, ἄμμε Α. 59, Sapph. 93 (13), Theoc. 8. 25; νῶε Cor. 16, νῶϊ Δ. 418, Π. 99 (νῶϊν?), νώ Ε. 219,

νῶϊν Χ. 88 : τύ Ar. Lys. 1188, Sapph. 1. 13, τύνη Ε. 485, τού Cor. 2 ; σέο Α. 396, Hdt. i. 8, σεῖο Γ. 137, σεῦ Γ. 206, Hdt. i. 9, σέθεν Α. 180, Eur Alc. 51, τεοῖο Θ. 37, 468, τεῦς Theoc. 2. 126, τεοῦς Theoc. 11. 25 ; τοι Α. 28, Hdt. i. 9, τεΐν δ. 619 (not in Il.), Hdt. v. 60 (Inscr.), Ar. Av. 930, τίν Theoc. 2. 11, Pind. O. 10. 113 ; τέ Theoc. 1. 5, τυ Theoc. 1. 56, Ar. Eq. 1225 ; ὑμέες Hdt. vi. 11, ὑμές Ar. Ach. 760, ὔμμες Α. 274, Sapph. 95 (17), Theoc. 5. 111 ; ὑμέων Η. 159, Hdt. iii. 50, ὑμείων Δ. 348, ὐμμέων Alc. 77 ; ὑμῖν or ὗμιν, Soph. Ant. 308, ὔμμιν Δ. 249, Theoc. 1. 116, ὔμμι Ζ. 77, ὔμμ' Κ. 551 ; ὑμέας β. 75, Hdt. i. 53, ὑμέ, Ar. Lys. 87, ὔμμε Ib. 1076, ὔμμε Ψ. 412, Pind. O. 8. 19, Theoc. 5. 145, Soph. Ant. 846 ; σφῶϊ Α. 336, σφώ Α. 574 ; σφῶϊν Α. 257, ψ. 52 (here considered Nom. by some), σφῷν δ. 62 : ἕο Β. 239, εἷο Δ. 400, ἑεῖο Ap. Rh. 1. 1032, εὗ Υ. 464, εὑ Hdt. iii. 135, ἕθεν Α. 114, Æsch. Sup. 66, Ϝέθεν Alc. 6 (71) ; ἑοῖ Ν. 495, ἵν (or ἶν) Hes. Fr. 66, Ϝοῖ Sapph. 2. 1 ; Ϝε Alc. 56 (84), ἑέ Υ. 171, μιν Α. 29, Hdt. i. 9, νιν Pind. O. 1. 40, Theoc. 1. 150, Æsch. Prom. 55 ; σφεα Hdt. i. 46 ; σφεων Σ. 311, Hdt. i. 31, σφείων Δ. 535 ; σφιν Α. 73, Æsch. Prom. 252, as sing. Hom. H. 19. 19, Æsch. Pers. 759, σφι Β. 614, Hdt. i. 1, σφ' Γ. 300, ψιν Sophr. 83 (87), φιν Call. Di. 125, ἄσφι Sapph. 98 (40) ; σφεας Β. 96, σφέας Hdt. i. 4, σφεῖας ν. 213, σφᾶς Ε. 567, σφε Λ. 111, Theoc. 15. 80, Soph. Ant. 44, ψε Theoc. 4. 3, ἄσφε Alc. 92 (80) ; σφωε Α. 8, σφω or σφω' Ρ. 531 ; σφωϊν Α. 338 : ἐμέος, ἐμοῦς, ἐμεῦς, μεθέν, τέος, τέο, ἑοῦς, &c., cited by Apollonius in his treatise on the Greek Pronoun.

§ 143. 6. History. *α.* The distinction of *person*, like those of *case* and *number* (§ 83), appears to have been at first only twofold, merely separating the person speaking from all other persons, whether spoken to or spoken of. We find traces of this early use not only in the roots common to the 2d and 3d persons, but also in the common forms of these persons in the dual of verbs. The most natural way of designating one's self by gesture is to bring home the hand ; of designating another, to stretch it out towards him. The voice here follows the analogy of the hand. To denote ourselves, we naturally keep the voice at home as much as is consistent with enunciation ; while we denote another by a forcible emission of it, a pointing, as it were, of the voice towards the person. The former of these is accomplished by closing the lips and murmuring within, that is, by uttering *m*, which hence became the great root of the 1st personal pronouns. The latter is accomplished by sending the voice out forcibly through a narrow aperture. This, according to the place of the aperture, and the mode of emission, may produce either a sibilant, a lingual, or a strong breathing. Hence we find all these as roots of the 2d and 3d personal pronouns. In the progress of language, these two persons were separated, and their forms became, for the most part, distinct, although founded, in general, upon common roots.

β. The μ- of the 1st Pers. passed in the old Plur. (which afterwards became the Dual, § 85) into the kindred ν- (compare Lat. *nos*) ; and in the Sing., when pronounced with emphasis, assumed an initial ᾰ (compare the Æol. ἄσφι, ἄσφε), which passed by precession into ε. In the new Plur., the idea of plurality was conveyed by doubling the μ (ἀμμ-, in the Ep. and Æol. ἄμμες, ἀμμέων, ἄμμιν, ἄμμεσι, ἄμμε) ; or more commonly by doubling the ᾰ to η (§ 29), pronounced with the rough breathing (ἡμ-, in ἡμεῖς, &c.), or, in the Dor., to ᾱ (ʽᾱμ-, in ʽᾱμές, ʽᾱμῶν, ʽᾱμῖν, ʽᾱμέ). From this the new Plur. of the 2d Pers. appears to have been formed, by changing, for propriety of expression, α, the deepest of the vowels, into υ, the most protrusive (ὐμμ-, in the Ep. and Æol. ὔμμες, ὐμμέων, ὔμμιν, ὔμμε · and ʽῡμ-, in ὑμεῖς, &c.) With the exception of this imitative plural, the Plur. and Du. of the 2d and 3d persons have the same root, in which plurality is expressed by joining two of the signs of these persons (σφ- = σ + F). In the separation of the two persons, the sign σ- became appropriated to the 2d Pers. (but in the Dor., τ-, as in the Lat., and also in the verb-endings -τε, -τον, -*tis*); and the rough breathing to the 3d Pers. (in an early state of the language, this was F-; in Lat. it became *s*-; while in the article we find both the rough breathing and τ-, and in verb-endings of the 3d Pers. both σ, and more frequently τ).

γ. In the Nom. sing., the subjective force appears to have been expressed by peculiar modes of strengthening; in the 1st Pers. by a double prefix to the μ, thus, ἐ-γ-ό-μ (the γ being inserted simply to prevent hiatus), or, as μ cannot end a word, ἐγόν, which passed, by a change of ν to its corresponding vowel (§ 50) and contraction, into (ἐγοα) ἐγώ (compare the Sanscrit *aham*, the Zend *azem*, the Bœotic ἰώ, the Latin *ego*, and the verb-ending of the 1st Pers. ω in Greek, and *o* in Lat.); in the 2d Pers. by affixing F, which with the preceding ε passed into ῠ in the common Greek (cf. § 117. N.), but in the Bœot. into ου (compare the Lat. *tū*, § 12. β); in the 3d Pers. by affixing Δ (perhaps chosen rather than F, on account of the initial F), before which precession took place (§ 118), so that the form became FίΔ, and from this, ἵΔ or ἴΔ, and, by dropping the Δ, ἵ or ἴ (this obsolete form is cited by Apollonius; compare the Lat. *is*, *ea*, *id*). With this Nom. there appears to have been associated an Acc. ἵν or ἴν, of which μίν and νίν are strengthened forms.

§ 144. B. Reflexive, ἐμαυτοῦ, σεαυτοῦ, ἑαυτοῦ. These pronouns, from their nature, want the Nom., and the two first also the neuter. They are formed by uniting the personal pronouns with αὐτός.

In the Plur. of the 1st and 2d Persons, and sometimes of the 3d, the two elements remain distinct; ἡμῶν αὐτῶν, ὑμῶν αὐτῶν, σφῶν αὐτῶν = ἑαυτῶν. In Homer, they are distinct in both Sing. and Plur.; thus, ἔμ' αὐτόν A. 271, ἐμέθεν περιδώσομαι αὐτῆς ψ. 78, αὐτόν μιν δ. 244. In the common compound forms, the personal pronouns omit the flexible ending, in uniting with αὐτός, and in the 1st Pers., and often in the other two, contraction takes place: ἐμε-αυτοῦ ἐμαυτοῦ, σε-αυτοῦ σαυτοῦ, ἑ-αυτοῦ αὑτοῦ. In the New Ionic, on the other hand, the flexible ending of the Gen. is retained, and is contracted with αυ into ωυ (§ 45. 6): ἐμεο-αὐτοῦ ἐμεωυτοῦ. The other cases imitate the form of the Gen.: ἐμεωυτῷ, -όν. The Doric forms αὐταύτω, αὕταυτον, αὐταύτων, αὕταυτα, &c., which occur chiefly in Pythagorean fragments, are formed by doubling αὐτός. Apollonius cites the comic Nom. ἐμαυτός from the Metœci of the comedian Plato.

§ 145. C. Reciprocal, ἀλλήλων. This pronoun is formed by doubling ἄλλος, *other*. From its nature, it wants the Nom. and the Sing., and is not common in the Dual.

Note. For ἀλλάλων (Theoc. 14. 46), see § 44. 1. For ἀλλήλοιϊν (K. 65), see § 99. 1.

§ 146. D. Indefinite, ὁ δεῖνα. This pronoun may be termed, with almost equal propriety, *definite* and *indefinite*. It is used to designate a particular person or thing, which the speaker either cannot, or does not care to name; or, in the language of Matthiæ, it "indefinitely expresses a definite person or thing"; as, Τὸν δεῖνα γιγνώσκεις; *Do you know Mr. So and So?* Ar. Thesm. 620. Ὁ δεῖνα τοῦ δεῖνος τὸν δεῖνα εἰσαγγέλλει, *A. B., the son of C. D., impeaches E. F.*, Dem. 167. 24. In the Sing. this pronoun is of the three genders; in the Plur. it is masc. only, and wants the Dat. It is sometimes indeclinable; as, τοῦ δεῖνα Ar. Thesm. 622.

NOTE. The article is an essential part of this pronoun; and it were better written as a single word, ὁδεῖνα. It appears to be simply an extension of the demonstrative ὅδε, by adding -ιν- or -ινα, which gives to it an indefinite force (cf. § 152. 1), making it a *demonstrative indefinite.* When -ιν- was appended, it received a double declension; when -ινα, it had only the declension of the article. It belongs properly to the colloquial Attic, and first appears in Aristophanes.

II. ADJECTIVE.

[¶ 24.]

§ 147. All the pronouns which are declined in ¶ 24 may be traced back to a common foundation in an old DEFINITIVE, which had two roots, the *rough breathing* and τ- (cf. § 143. α, β), and which performed the offices both of an *article* and of a *demonstrative*, *personal*, and *relative pronoun.*

REMARKS. α. To this definitive the Greeks gave the name ἄρθρον, *joint,* from its giving connection to discourse, by marking the person or thing spoken of as one which had been spoken of before, or which was about to be spoken of further, or which was familiar to the mind. The Greek name ἄρθρον became, in Latin, *articulus* (*small joint,* from artus, *joint,* a word of the same origin with ἄρθρον), from which has come the English name, *article.* This definitive, when used as a demonstrative, or simply as the definite article, naturally *precedes* the name of the person or thing spoken of; but when used as a relative, usually *follows* it; as, οὗτός ἐστιν ὁ ἀνὴρ ὃν εἶδες, *this is* THE *man* WHOM *you saw;* τὸ ῥόδον ὃ ἀνθεῖ, THE *rose* WHICH *blooms.* Hence, in the former use, it was termed the *prepositive,* and, in the latter, the *postpositive article.* When prepositive, it was so closely connected with the following word that its aspirated forms became proclitic.

β. In the progress of the language, the forms of this old DEFINITIVE became specially appropriated, and other pronouns arose from it by derivation and composition (see the following sections). The forms τός and τή of the Nom. sing. became obsolete.

A. DEFINITE.

§ 148. 1. ARTICLE, ὁ, ἡ, τό. The *prepositive article*, or, as it is commonly termed, simply the *article*, unites the *proclitic aspirated forms* of the old definitive, ὁ, ἡ, οἱ, αἱ, with the τ- *forms* of the *neuter*, the *oblique cases*, and the *dual.*

NOTE. The forms τοί and ταί are also used, for the sake of metre, euphony, or emphasis, in the Ionic (chiefly the Epic), and in the Doric; e. g. τοί A. 147, Hdt. viii. 68. 1 (where it is strongly demonstrative), Theoc. 1. 80; ταί Γ. 5, Theoc. 1. 9. So, even in the Attic poets, τοὶ δέ Æsch. Pers. 423, Soph. Aj. 1404; ταί Ar. Eq. 1329. For the other dialectic forms, see §§ 95, 96 99. For the forms ὁ and τό, see § 97.

2. Relative, ὅς, ἥ, ὅ. The *postpositive article*, or as it is now commonly termed, the *relative pronoun*, has the *orthotone aspirated forms* of the old definitive.

Note. For the old Masc. ὅ (Π. 835, β. 262), as well as for the Neut. ὅ, see § 97. For the reduplicated ὅου (B. 325) and ἕης (Π. 208), see § 48.

§ 149. 3. Iterative, αὐτός, -ή, -ό (§ 97). This pronoun appears to be compounded of the particle αὖ, *again*, *back*, and the *old definitive* τός (§ 147. β). It is hence a pronoun of return (or, as it may be termed, an *iterative* pronoun), marking the return of the mind to the same person or thing.

Notes. α. The New Ionic often inserts ε in αὐτός and its compounds, before a long vowel in the affix (see § 48. 1, ¶ 24). This belongs especially to Hippocrates and his imitator Aretæus; in Hdt., it is chiefly confined to the forms in -ῳ and -ων of αὐτός and οὗτος· e. g. αὐτέῳ, αὐτέων and αὐτῶν, Hdt. i. 133, αὐτέων τουτέων Ib. ii. 3. For the other dialectic forms of αὐτός, see §§ 95, 96, 99.

β. The article and αὐτός are often united by crasis (§ 39); as, αὑτός, ταὐτόν (§ 97. N.) or ταὐτό (Ion. τωὐτό Hdt. i. 53, § 45. 6), ταὐτοῦ, ταὐτά, for ὁ αὐτός, τὸ αὐτό, τοῦ αὐτοῦ, τὰ αὐτά.

§ 150. 4. Demonstrative. The primary demonstratives are οὗτος, *this*, compounded of the article and αὐτός· ὅδε, *this*, compounded of the article and δε (an inseparable particle marking *direction towards*), and declined precisely like the article, with this addition; and ἐκεῖνος, *that*, derived from ἐκεῖ, *there*.

Note. Of ἐκεῖνος (which, with ἄλλος, *other*, is declined like αὐτός, § 97) there are also the forms, Ion. κεῖνος, which is also common in the Att. poets, Æol. κῆνος Sapph. 2. 1, Dor. τῆνος Theoc. 1. 4. In the Epic forms of ὅδε, τοῖσδεσι φ. 93, τοῖσδεσσι K. 462, τοῖσδεσσιν β. 47, there is a species of double declension.

Remarks. α. The definitives τοῖος, *such*, τόσος, *so great*, τηλίκος, *so old*, and τύννος, *so little*, are strengthened, in the same manner as the article, by composition with αὐτός and δε· thus, τοιοῦτος and τοιόσδε, *just such*, τοσοῦτος and τοσόσδε, *just so much*, τηλικοῦτος and τηλικόσδε, τυννοῦτος. These compound pronouns are commonly employed, instead of the simple, even when there is no special emphasis.

β. In declining the compounds of αὐτός with the article and adjective pronouns, the following rule is observed: — *If the termination of the article or adjective pronoun has an O vowel, it unites with the first syllable of αὐτός, to form ου; but is otherwise absorbed.*

Thus, (ὁ αὐτός) οὗτος, (ἡ αὐτή) αὕτη, (τὸ αὐτό) τοῦτο· G. (τοῦ αὐτοῦ) τούτου, (τῆς αὐτῆς) ταύτης· Pl. (οἱ αὐτοί) οὗτοι, (αἱ αὐταί) αὗται, (τὰ αὐτά) ταῦτα· G. (τῶν αὐτῶν) τούτων (¶ 24)· (τόσος αὐτός) τοσοῦτος, (τόση αὐτή) τοσαύτη, (τόσον αὐτό) τοσοῦτο and τοσοῦτον (§ 97. N.)

γ. To demonstratives, for the sake of stronger expression, an ι is affixed, which is always long and acute, and before which a short vowel is dropped, and a long vowel or diphthong regarded as short; thus, οὑτοσί, αὑτηΐ, τουτί, *this here;* Pl. οὑτοιΐ, αὑταιΐ, ταυτί· ἐκεινοσί, *that there;* ὁδί, τοσουτοσί.

Note. This ι *paragogic* is Attic, and belongs especially to the style of conversation and popular discourse. It was also affixed to adverbs; as, οὑτωσί, ὡδί, νυνί, ἐνταυθί, ἐντευθενί. So, in comic language, even with an inserted particle, νυνμενί Ar. Av. 448, ἐνγεταυθί Id. Thesm. 646, ἐνμεντευθενί Ath. 269 f.

§ 151. 5. Possessive. The possessive pronouns are derived from the personal, and are regularly declined as adjectives of three terminations.

We add references for the less common possessives: νωΐτερος, O. 39; σφωΐτερος, A. 216, in Ap. Rh. = σφέτερος, 1. 643, 2. 544; ὅς, Γ. 333, Hdt. i. 205, Soph. Aj. 442; ἁμός or ἀμός, Z. 414, Pind. O. 10. 10, Theoc. 5. 108, Æsch. Cho. 428 (used particularly in the Att. poets as sing.); ἁμέτερος, Theoc. 2. 31; ἄμμος, Alc. 103; ἀμμέτερος, Alc. 104; τέος, γ. 122, Æsch. Prom. 162; ὑμός, α. 375, Pind. P. 7. 15; ἑός, α. 409, Theoc. 17. 50; σφός, A. 534; Ϝός (= ὅς), ὕμμος, cited by Apollonius. For the use of the possessives, particularly ὅς, ἑός, σφέτερος, σφός, and σφωΐτερος, see Syntax.

B. Indefinite.

§ 152. 1. The simple indefinite is τὶς, which has two roots, τιν- and τε-, both appearing to be formed from τ-, the root of the article, by adding -ιν- and -ε- to give an indefinite force (cf. § 146. N.).

Remarks. α. The later root τιν- is declined throughout after Dec. III., but the earlier τε- only in the Gen. and Dat., after Dec. II. (except in the Gen. Sing., which imitates the personal pronouns) with contraction; thus, τῐς, τῐ, τῐνός, τῐσί, &c. (§ 105. β); G. τέο τοῦ, D. τέῳ τῷ, and, in the compound, Pl. G. ὅτεων ὅτων, D. ὁτέοισι ὅτοισι (also Ion. τέων, τέοισι, § 153. γ). For the accentuation, and the forms ἄττα, ἄσσα, see 2. below, and § 153. α.

β. The short ι of τῐς, τῐσί, and the omission of ν in τῐ, suggest an intermediate root τι-, formed from τε- by precession, and afterwards increased by ν (cf. § 119, and ὄρνις, § 123. γ). To this intermediate root may be referred, according to Dec. II., the Æol. τίῳ; Sapph. 55 (34), τίοισιν Id. 109 (113).

2. The interrogatives in Greek are simply the *indefinites with a change of accent* (see Syntax).

Thus, the forms of the indefinite τὶς (except the peculiar ἄττα, which is rarely used except in connection with an adjective, and which is never used interrogatively) are *enclitic;* while those of the interrogative τίς are *orthotone*, and never take the grave accent. In lexicons and grammars, for the sake of distinction, the forms of the indefinite, τὶς and τὶ, are written with the *grave* accent, or *without* an accent.

§ 153. 3. The composition of ὅς with τὶς forms the RELATIVE INDEFINITE ὅστις, *whoever*, of which both parts are declined in those forms which have the root τιν-, but the latter only in those which have the root τε-; thus, οὗτινος, but ὅτεο ὅτου. The longer forms of the Gen. and Dat. are very rare in the Attic poets.

NOTES. α. The forms ἄσσα, Att. ἄττα (§ 70. 1), appear to be shorter forms of ἅτινα, and are said by Eustathius to be compounded of ἅ and the Doric σά = τινά. In certain connections, they passed into simple indefinites, and then, by a softer pronunciation, became ἄσσα, ἄττα.

β. The forms which occur in Homer of τὶς, τίς, and ὅτις, which is the same with ὅστις, except that it has no double declension, are exhibited in ¶ 24. Homer has also the regular forms of ὅστις. The doubling of τ in some of the forms is simply poetic, for the sake of the metre.

γ. References are added for many of the forms of τὶς, τίς, and ὅστις: ὅτις Γ. 279 (ὅστις 167), ὅ ττι Θ. 408; του Cyr. viii. 5. 7, τοῦ; Soph. Œd T. 1435, ὅτου i. 9. 21, τεο π. 305, Hdt. i. 58, τέο; B. 225, ὅττεο α. 124, τευ (§ 45. 3) B. 388, Hdt. i. 19, τεῦ Σ. 192, Hdt. v. 106, ὅτευ ρ. 422, Hdt. i. 119, ὅττευ ρ. 121; τῳ A. 299, i. 9. 7, τῷ; Soph. El. 679, ὅτῳ ii. 6. 23, τεῳ Hdt. ii. 48, τέῳ; Hdt. i. 117, ὅτεῳ β. 114, Hdt. i. 95, ὅτεῷ M. 428; ὅτινα Θ. 204 (ὅντινα B. 188); οἰκτρὰ ἄττα Cyr. ii. 2. 13, ὁπποῖ' ἄσσα τ. 218, ἄττα Rep. Ath. 2. 17, ἄσσα A. 554, Hdt. i. 138, ὅτινα X. 450 (ἅτινα A. 289); τεων Hdt. v. 57, τέων; Ω. 387, τέῶν; ν. 200, ὁτέων κ. 39, Hdt. viii. 65, ὅτων vii. 6. 24; τέοισι Hdt. ix. 27, ὁτέοισιν O. 491, ὁτέοισι Hdt. ii. 82, ὅτοισι Soph. Ant. 1335; ὅτινας O. 492 (οὕστινας Δ. 240).

§ 154. REMARKS. 1. Adjective Pronouns which have not been specially mentioned are regularly declined as adjectives of three terminations (§ 133. 4). For the Correlative Pronouns, and for the Particles which are affixed to pronouns, see ¶ 63, §§ 317, 328.

2. Special care is required in distinguishing the forms of ὁ, ὅς, οὗ, τίς, and τὶς. Forms which have the same letters may be often distinguished by the accentuation; as, οἱ, οἷ, οἵ. Special care is also required in distinguishing the forms of οὗτος, those of αὐτός, the combined forms of ὁ αὐτός, *the same*, and the contracted forms of ἑαυτοῦ.

CHAPTER VI.

COMPARISON.

§ **155.** ADJECTIVES and ADVERBS have, in Greek, three degrees of comparison, the POSITIVE, the COMPARATIVE, and the SUPERLATIVE.

I. COMPARISON OF ADJECTIVES.

In adjectives, the *comparative* is usually formed in -τερος, -ᾰ, -ον, and the *superlative* in -τατος, -η, -ον; but sometimes the *comparative* is formed in -ίων, -ῑον, Gen. -ῑονος, and the *superlative*, in -ιστος, -η, -ον.

A. COMPARISON IN -τερος, -τατος.

§ **156.** In receiving the affixes -τερος and -τατος, the endings of the theme are changed as follows;

1.) -ος, preceded by a long syllable, becomes -ο-; by a short syllable, -ω-; as,

κοῦφος, *light*,	κουφότερος,	κουφότατος.
σοφός, *wise*,	σοφώτερος,	σοφώτατος.

REMARKS. α. This change to -ω- takes place to avoid the succession of too many short syllables. Three successive short syllables are inadmissible in hexameter verse. We also find, for the sake of the metre, κακοξεινώτερος υ. 376, λᾱρώτατος β. 350, ὀϊζῡρώτερον P. 446, ὀϊζῡρώτατον ε. 105. In respect to κενός, *empty*, and στενός, *narrow*, authorities vary.

β. A mute and liquid preceding -ος have commonly the same effect as a long syllable; as, σφοδρός, *vehement*, σφοδρότερος, σφοδρότατος. Yet here, also, the Attic poets sometimes employ -ω- for the sake of the metre; as, δυσποτμώτερα Eur. Ph. 1348, βαρυποτμωτάτας Ib. 1345, εὐτεκνώτατε Id. Hec. 620.

γ. In a few words, -ος is dropped; and, in a few, it becomes -αι-, -εσ-, or -ισ-; as,

παλαιός, *ancient*,	παλαίτερος,	παλαίτατος.
φίλος, *dear*,	φίλτερος,	φίλτατος.
friendly,	φιλαίτερος,	φιλαίτατος.
ἥσυχος, *quiet*,	ἡσυχαίτερος.	ἡσυχαίτατος.
ἐῤῥωμένος, *strong*,	ἐῤῥωμενέστερος,	ἐῤῥωμενέστατος.
λάλος, *talkative*,	λαλίστερος,	λαλίστατος.

NOTES. (a.) Yet also παλαιότερος, Pind. N. 6. 91, φιλώτερος, Mem. iii. 11. 18, φιλΐων (§ 159) ω. 268, φίλιστος, Soph. Aj. 842, ἡσυχώτερος, Id. Ant. 1089.

(b.) The change of -ος into -εσ- belongs particularly to contracts in -οος These contracts, and those in -εος, are likewise contracted in the Comp. and Sup. ; as,

ἁπλόος, *simple*,	ἁπλοέστερος,	ἁπλοέστατος,
ἁπλοῦς,	ἁπλούστερος,	ἁπλούστατος
πορφύρεος, *purple*,	πορφυρεώτερος,	πορφυρεώτατος,
πορφυροῦς,	πορφυρώτερος,	πορφυρώτατος.

But ἀπλοώτερος, *less fit for sea*, Th. vii. 60, εὐχροώτερος, Œc. 10. 11, εὐπνοώτερος, Eq. 1. 10, &c.

(c.) Other examples of -ος dropped in comparison are γεραιός, *old*, σχολαῖος, *at leisure*; of -ος changed to -αι-, εὔδιος, *clear*, ἴδιος, *private*, ἴσος, *equal*, μέσος, *middle* (see δ. below), ὄρθριος, *at dawn*, ὄψιος, *late*, πρώϊος, *early*; of -ος changed to -εσ-, αἰδοῖος, *august*, ἄκρατος, *unmixed*, ἄσμενος, *glad*, ἄφθονος, *bountiful*, ἐπίπεδος, *level*, εὔζωρος, *pure*, ἥδυμος, *sweet* (poet.); of -ος changed to -ισ-, μονοφάγος, *eating alone*, ὀψοφάγος, *dainty*, πτωχός, *poor*.

δ. Μέσος and νέος have old superlatives of limited and chiefly poetic use in -ατος; thus, μέσατος, *midmost*, Ar. Vesp. 1502, Ep. μέσσατος, Θ. 223, νέατος, *last, lowest*, Λ. 712, Soph. Ant. 627, Ep. νείατος, Β. 824. Compare ἔσχατος, (πρόατος) πρῶτος, and ὕπατος (§ 161. 2).

§ 157. 2.) -εις and -ης become -εσ-; as,

χαρίεις, *agreeable*,	χαριέστερος,	χαριέστατος.
σαφής, *evident*,	σαφέστερος,	σαφέστατος.
πένης, *poor*,	πενέστερος,	πενέστατος.

REMARK. In adjectives of the first declension, and in ψευδής, -ης becomes -ισ-; as, πλεονέκτης, -ου, *covetous*, πλεονεκτίστατος· ψευδής, -έος, *false*, ψευδίστατος. Except, for the sake of euphony, ὑβριστής, -οῦ, *insolent*, ὑβριστότερος v. 8. 3, ὑβριστότατος, Ib. 22 (referred by some to ὕβριστος).

3.) -υς becomes -υ-; as,

πρέσβυς, *old*,	πρεσβύτερος,	πρεσβύτατος.

For the sake of the metre, ἰθύντατα Σ. 508.

§ 158. 4.) In adjectives of other endings, -τερος and -τατος are either added to the simple root, or to the root increased by -εσ-, -ισ-, or -ω-; as,

τάλας, -ανος, *wretched*,	ταλάντερος,	ταλάντατος.
σώφρων, -ονος, *discreet*,	σωφρονέστερος,	σωφρονέστατος.
ἅρπαξ, -αγος, *rapacious*,		ἁρπαγίστατος.
ἐπίχαρις, -ιτος, *pleasing*,	ἐπιχαριτώτερος,	ἐπιχαριτώτατος.

NOTES. α. Other examples are μάκαρ, *blessed*, μακάρτατος λ. 483; μέλας

-ανος, *black*, μελάντερος, Δ. 277, and μελανώτερος, Strab.; ἀφῆλιξ, -ικος, *elderly*, ἀφηλικέστερος· βλάξ, -ᾶκός, *stupid*, βλακώτερος, -ώτατος, Mem. iii. 13. 4, iv. 2. 40, for which some read βλακότερος, and βλακότατος or βλακίστατος. From ἄχαρις, *disagreeable*, we find the shorter form ἀχαρίστερος, υ. 392.

β. The insertion of -εσ- is particularly made in adjectives in -ων. Yet some of these employ shorter forms; as, πέπων, *ripe*, πεπαίτερος Æsch. Fr. 244; πίων, *fat*, πιότερος, Hom. Ap. 48, πιότατος, Ι. 577 (as from the rare πῖος, Orph. Arg. 508); ἐπιλήσμων, *forgetful*, ἐπιλησμότατος, Ar. Nub. 790 (ἐπιλησμονέστερος, Apol. 6).

B. Comparison in -ίων, -ιστος.

§ 159. A few adjectives are compared by changing -υς, -ας, -ος, and even -ρος, final, into -ίων and -ιστος. In some of these, -ίων with the preceding consonant passes into -σσων (-ττων, § 70. 1) or -ζων. Thus,

ἡδύς, *pleasant*,	ἡδίων,	ἥδιστος.
ταχύς, *swift*,	θάσσων, θάττων,	τάχιστος.
πολύς, *much*,	πλείων, πλέων,	πλεῖστος.
μέγας, *great*,	μείζων,	μέγιστος.
καλός, *beautiful*,	καλλίων,	κάλλιστος.
αἰσχρός, *base*,	αἰσχίων,	αἴσχιστος.
ἐχθρός, *hostile*,	ἐχθίων,	ἔχθιστος.

Remarks. α. For the declension of comparatives in -ων, see ¶ 17 and § 107. The ι in the affix -ίων is long in the Attic poets, but short in the Epic, and variable in the later.

β. The forms in -σσων and -ζων observe this distinction: -σσων can arise only when the consonant preceding -ίων is κ, χ, τ, δ, or θ; -ζων, only when this consonant is γ. The vowel preceding becomes long by nature, perhaps from a transposition, and absorption or contraction, of the ι. Thus, τᾰχύς (originally θᾰχύς, § 62), θαχίων θᾶσσων, Neut. θᾶσσον (the regular ταχίων is also common in late prose); ἐλᾰχύς (Epic; ἐλάχεια Hom. Ap. 197), *small*, ἐλάσσων· πᾰχύς, *thick*, παχίων (Arat.) πάσσων, ζ. 230; from r. ἡκ-, Comp. ἥσσων, *inferior* (Ion. ἕσσων, Hdt. v. 86); γλῠκύς, *sweet*, γλυκίων (Σ. 109) γλύσσων, Xenophan.; μακρός, *long*, μάσσων poet., θ. 203, Æsch. Ag. 598; κρᾰτύς (Epic, Π. 181), *strong*, κρείσσων (Ion. κρέσσων, Hdt. i. 66); βρᾰδύς, *slow*, βραδίων (Hes. Op. 526) βράσσων Κ. 226; βᾰθύς, *deep*, βαθίων (Tyrt. 3. 6) βάσσων, Epicharm.; μέγας (the only adj. in -ας compared in -ίων, -ιστος), μεγίων μείζων (Ion. μέζων Hdt. i. 202); ὀλῐγος, ὀλίζων, Call. Jov. 72 (ὑπολίζονες Σ. 519). It will be observed that many of these comparatives are merely poetic. Compare the formation of verbs in -σσω and -ζω.

γ. The root of πολύς is πολε-, by syncope πλε-. From this short root are formed the comparative and superlative. Πλέων is a yet shorter form for πλείων. The longer form is more common in the contracted cases and plural, but the neut. πλέον is more used than πλεῖον, especially as an adverb. The neut. πλεῖον sometimes becomes πλεῖν, but only in such phrases as πλεῖν ἢ μύριοι, *more than ten thousand*. The Ionic contracts -εο- into -ευ- (§ 45. 3); as, πλεῦν, πλεῦνος, πλεῦνες, &c. Hdt. ii. 19, i. 97, 199, &c. The Ep. πλέες Λ. 395, and πλέας Β. 129, are comparative in sense, though positive in form.

δ. In the Comp. and Sup. of καλός, λ is doubled, as in the noun τὸ κάλλος -εος, *beauty*. In the adjectives in -ρος which are compared in -ίων and -ιστος, the Comp. and Sup. appear to have come either from a simpler form of the positive, or from a corresponding noun. See § 161. R.

ε. Most adjectives which are compared as above have also forms in -τερος and -τατος; thus, βραδύς, *slow*, βραδύτερος, βραδίων, and βράσσων, βραδύτατος, βράδιστος, and by poetic metath. (§ 71), βάρδιστος, Ψ. 310; μακρός, *long*, μακρότερος and μάσσων, μακρότατος and (ᾱ becoming by precession η, as in the noun τὸ μῆκος, -εος, *length*) μήκιστος, Cyr. iv. 5. 28, Dor. μάκιστος, Soph. Œd. T. 1301. Other examples of double formation are αἰσχρός, ἐχθρός, κυδρός (poet.), *renowned*, οἰκτρός, *pitiable*, βαθύς, βραχύς, *short*, γλυκύς, παχύς, πρεσβύς, ταχύς, ὠκύς, *swift*, κακός (§ 160), φίλος (§ 156. a), &c.

C. Irregular Comparison.

§ 160. Some adjectives in the comparative and superlative degrees are formed from positives which are not in use, from words which are themselves comparatives or superlatives, or from other parts of speech. Some of these are usually referred to positives in use, which have a similar signification and some of which are also regularly compared; thus,

ἀγαθός, *good*,	ἀμείνων,	ἄριστος.
	βελτίων,	βέλτιστος.
	κρείσσων, κρείττων,	κράτιστος.
	λῴων,	λῷστος.

Poet. ἀμεινότερος Mimn. 11. 9; ἀρείων Æsch. Ag. 81, ἀρειότερος, Theog. 548; βέλτερος, Æsch. Th. 337, βέλτατος, Id. Eum. 487; φέρτερος, Id. Pr. 768, φέρτατος H. 289, φέριστος, Soph. Œd. T. 1159, and even Pl. Phædr. 238 d, φέρτιστος, Pind. Fr. 92; λωΐων, β. 169, λωΐτερος, α. 376 (the pos. form λώϊα occurs Theoc. 26. 32); κάρτιστος, A. 266 (§ 71; so always in Hom.). Dor. βέντιστος, Theoc. 5. 76, κάῤῥων, Tim. ap. Pl. 102 d; Ion. κρέσσων (§ 159. β). Late ἀγαθώτατος, Diod. 16. 85.

ἀλγεινός, *painful*,	ἀλγίων,	ἄλγιστος.
	ἀλγεινότερος,	ἀλγεινότατος.
κακός, *bad*,	κακίων,	κάκιστος.
	χείρων,	χείριστος.
	ἥσσων, ἥττων.	

Poet. κακώτερος, ο. 343; χειρότερος, O. 513, χερείων A. 114, χερειότερος] 248 (for the Epic χέρηος, &c., which, though positive in form, are compa-tive in sense, see § 136. δ); ἥκιστος or ἥκιστος Ψ. 531 (ἥκιστα as an adverb was common in Attic prose; Ælian uses ἥκιστος as an adj.), Ion. ἕσσων (§ 159. β).

μικρός, *small*, ὀλίγος, *little*, *few*,	μικρότερος	μικρότατος.
	ἐλάσσων, ἐλάττων,	ἐλάχιστος.
	μείων,	ὀλίγιστος.

Poet. ἐλαχύς, ὀλίζων (§ 159. β); μειότερος Ap. Rh. 2. 368, μεῖστος, Bion, 5. 10 (yet common reading μήονα).

ῥᾴδιος, *easy*, ῥᾴων, ῥᾷστος.

Poet. ῥηΐδιος, λ. 146, ῥήδιος, Theog. 574, ῥηΐτερος, Σ. 258, ῥᾴτερος Pind. O. 8. 78, ῥήϊστος, δ. 565, ῥάϊστος, Theoc. 11. 7, ῥηΐτατος, τ. 577. The common foundation of the forms of this word appears to have been ῥᾱϊΔ- (see §§ 118, 119).

§ 161. 1. Examples of double comparison.

ἔσχατος, *last, extreme*, ἐσχατώτερος (Οὔτε γὰρ τοῦ ἐσχάτου ἐσχατώτερον εἴη ἄν τι. Aristl. Metaph. 10. 4), ἐσχατώτατος, H. Gr. ii. 3. 49.

πρότερος, *before*, comic προτεραίτερος Ar. Eq. 1164;

ΚΛ. Ὁρᾷς; ἐγώ σοι πρότερος ἐκφέρω δίφρον.
ΑΛ. Ἀλλ' οὐ τράπεζαν, ἀλλ' ἐγὼ προτεραίτερος.

πρῶτος, *first*, πρώτιστος, *first of all*, B. 228.

ἐλάχιστος, *least*, ἐλαχιστότερος, *less than the least*, Ep. Ephes. 3. 8.

NOTE. See also examples of a poetic double formation of the Comp. (ἀμεινότερος, ἀρειότερος, &c.) in § 160. For καλλιώτερον Th. iv. 118, is now read κάλλιον.

2. Examples of adjectives in the comparative and superlative degrees, formed from other parts of speech.

βασιλεύς, *king*, βασιλεύτερος, *more kingly, a greater king*, I. 160, βασιλεύτατος, *the greatest king*, I. 69.

ἑταῖρος, *friend*, ἑταιρότατος, *best friend*, Pl. Gorg. 487 d.

κλέπτης, *thief*, κλεπτίστατος, *most adroit thief*, Ar. Plut. 27.

κύων, *dog*, κύντερος, *more dog-like, more impudent*, Θ. 483, κύντατος, K. 503.

κέρδος, -εος, *gain*, κερδίων, *more gainful*, Γ. 41, κέρδιστος, Æsch. Pr. 385.

αὐτός, *himself*, αὐτότερος Epich. 2 (1), αὐτότατος (*ipsissumus* Plaut. Trinum. IV. 2), *his very self*, Ar. Plut. 83.

ἄγχι or ἄγχου, *near*, ἀγχότερος, *nearer*, Hdt. vii. 175, ἀγχότατος, Eur. Pel. 2, oftener ἄγχιστος Soph. Œd. T. 919.

ἄνω, *up*, ἀνώτερος, *upper*, ἀνώτατος, *uppermost*, Hdt. ii. 125.

ἠρέμα, *quietly*, ἠρεμέστερος, *more quiet*, Cyr. vii. 5. 63.

πλησίον, *near* (πλησίος poet. and Ion.), πλησιαίτερος i. 10. 5, πλησιαίτατος, vii. 3. 29, also πλησιέστερος, -έστατος.

προὔργου, *of importance*, προὐργιαίτερος, *more important*, Pl. Gorg. 458 c, προὐργιαίτατος.

ἐξ, *out of*, ἔσχατος, *extreme*.

πρό, *before*, πρότερος, *former*, πρῶτος (§ 156. δ), *first* (Dor. πρᾶτος Theoc. 8. 5, § 45. 1).

ὑπέρ, *above*, ὑπέρτερος, *superior*, ὑπέρτατος and ὕπατος, *supreme* (ὑπερώτατος, Pind. N. 8. 73).

ὑπό (?), ὕστερος, *later*, ὕστατος, *last*.

REMARKS. We find an explanation of these formations in the use of prepositions as adverbs, and of adverbs as adjectives; in the fact that many nouns are originally adjectives; and in the still more important fact, that in the earliest period of language there is as yet no grammatical distinction of the different parts of speech. For other examples of comparatives and superlatives which appear to be formed from nouns, see, in § 160, ἀλγίων, -ιστος (from ἄλγος, -εος, *pain*), and ἄριστος (like ἀρετή, from Ἄρης or a common root, and signifying originally *best in war*), and also § 159. δ, ε. Add the poetic κήδιστος, I. 642, ῥιγίων, -ιστος, A. 325, E. 873, μύχατος, Ap. Rh. 1. 170, μυχοίτατος φ. 146, ὁπλότερος, -τατος, B. 707, Hes. Th. 137, &c.; and, from adverbs, ὀπίστερος, -τατος, Θ. 342, παροίτερος, -τατος, Ψ. 459, Ap. Rh. 2. 29, ὑψίτερος, Theoc. 8. 46, ὑψίων, Pind. Fr. 232, ὕψιστος, Æsch. Pr. 720, &c.

II. Comparison of Adverbs.

§ 162. I. Adverbs derived from adjectives are commonly compared by taking the *neuter singular comparative*, and the *neuter plural superlative* of these adjectives; as,

σοφῶς (from σοφός, § 156), *wisely*,	σοφώτερον, *more wisely*,	σοφώτατα, *most wisely*.
σαφῶς (from σαφής, § 157), *clearly*,	σαφέστερον, *more clearly*,	σαφέστατα, *most clearly*.
ταχέως (from ταχύς, § 159),	θᾶσσον, θᾶττον,	τάχιστα.
αἰσχρῶς (from αἰσχρός, § 159),	αἶσχῖον,	αἴσχιστα.

Note. The adverbial termination -ως is sometimes given to the Comp. as, χαλεπωτέρως, *more severely*, ἐχθιόνως, *in a more hostile manner*. So Sup. ξυντομωτάτως, *most concisely*, Soph. Œd. C. 1579.

§ 163. II. Adverbs not derived from adjectives are, for the most part, compared in -τέρω and -τάτω; as,

ἄνω, *up*,	ἀνωτέρω,	ἀνωτάτω.
ἑκάς, *afar*,	ἑκαστέρω,	ἑκαστάτω.

Remarks. α. The following are compared after the analogy of adverbs derived from adjectives:

ἄγχι or ἀγχοῦ, *near*,	ἆσσον,	ἄγχιστα.
μάλα, *very*,	μᾶλλον,	μάλιστα.

So πρωΐ, *early*, and ὀψέ, *late*, employ forms of the adjectives πρώϊος, ὄψιος (§ 156. c), derived from them. In ἀσσοτέρω ρ. 572, we have a poetic double form (§ 161. N.).

β. Some adverbs vary in their comparison; as,

ἐγγύς, *near*,	ἐγγυτέρω,	ἐγγυτάτω.
	ἐγγύτερον,	ἐγγύτατα.
(Not Att.)	ἔγγιον,	ἔγγιστα.

CHAPTER VII.

GENERAL PRINCIPLES OF CONJUGATION.

§ **164.** Verbs are conjugated, in Greek, to mark five distinctions, VOICE, TENSE, MODE, NUMBER, and PERSON. Of these distinctions, the first shows how the *action* of a verb is related to its *subject;* the second, how it is related to *time;* and the third, how it is related to the *mind of the speaker*, or to *some other action.* The two remaining distinctions merely show the number and person of the subject.

Greek verbs are conjugated both by PREFIXES and by AFFIXES. For the prefixes, see Ch. VIII.; for the affixes, see ¶¶ 28–31, and Ch. IX.; for the modifications which the root itself receives, see Ch. X.

A. VOICE.

§ **165.** The Greek has three voices, the ACTIVE, the MIDDLE, and the PASSIVE.

The ACTIVE represents the subject of the verb as the *doer* of the action, or its *agent;* as, λούω τινά, *I wash some one.*

The PASSIVE represents the subject of the verb as the *receiver* of the action, or its *object;* as, λοῦμαι ὑπό τινος, *I am washed by some one.*

The MIDDLE is *intermediate* in sense between the Active and the Passive, and commonly represents the subject of the verb as, either more or less directly, both the *agent* and the *object* of the action; as, ἐλουσάμην, *I washed myself, I bathed.*

§ **166.** REMARKS. 1. The *middle* and *passive* voices have a common form, except in the *Future* and *Aorist.* In Etymology, this form is usually spoken of as *passive.* And even in the Future and Aorist, the distinction in sense between the two voices is not always preserved.

2. The reflexive sense of the *middle* voice often becomes so indistinct, that this voice does not differ from the *active* in its use. Hence, in many verbs, either wholly or in part, the middle voice takes the place of the active. This is particu-

larly frequent in the *Future*. When it occurs in the *theme* (§ 170. *α*), the verb is termed *deponent* (depōnens, *laying aside* sc. the peculiar signification of the middle form). E. g.

(*α*.) Verbs, in which the *theme* has the *active*, and the *Future* has the *middle* form: ἀκούω, *to hear*, ἀκούσομαι· βαίνω, *to go*, βήσομαι· γιγνώσκω, *to know*, γνώσομαι· εἰμί, *to be*, ἔσομαι· μανθάνω, *to learn*, μαθήσομαι.

(*β*.) Deponent Verbs: αἰσθάνομαι, *to perceive*, γίγνομαι, *to become*, δέχομαι, *to receive*, δύναμαι, *to be able*, ἥδομαι, *to rejoice*.

Note. A Deponent Verb is termed *deponent middle*, or *deponent passive*, according as its Aorist has the middle or the passive form.

B. Tense.

§ **167.** The Greek has six tenses; the Present, the Imperfect, the Future, the Aorist, the Perfect, and the Pluperfect.

1. The Present represents an action as *doing* at the *present time*; as, γράφω, *I am writing*, *I write*.

2. The Imperfect represents an action as *doing* at some *past time*; as, ἔγραφον, *I was writing*.

3. The Future represents an action as one that *will be done* at some *future time*; as, γράψω, *I shall write*.

4. The Aorist (ἀόριστος, *indefinite*) represents an action simply as *done*; as, ἔγραψα, *I wrote*, *I have written*, *I had written*.

5. The Perfect represents an action as *complete* at the *present time*; as, γέγραφα, *I have written*.

6. The Pluperect represents an action as *complete* at some *past time*; as, ἐγεγράφειν, *I had written*.

§ **168.** Tenses may be classified in two ways; I. with respect to the *time* which is spoken of; II. with respect to the *relation* which the action bears to this time.

I. The time which is spoken of is either, 1. *present*, 2. *future*, or 3. *past*.

The reference to time is most distinct in the Indicative. In this mode, those tenses which refer to present or future time are termed *primary* or *chief* tenses, and those which refer to past time *secondary* or *historical* tenses.

II. The action is related to the time, either, 1. as *doing at* the time, 2. as *done in* the time, or 3. as *complete at* the time.

The tenses which denote the first of these relations may be termed *definite*; the second, *indefinite*; and the third, *complete*. For a classified table of the Greek tenses, see ¶ 26.

NOTES. *α*. Some verbs have a *complete future* tense, called the *Future Perfect*, or the *Third Future* (§ 239); but, otherwise, the three tenses which are wanting in the table (¶ 26), viz. the *indefinite present*, the *definite future*, and the *complete future*, are supplied by forms belonging to other tenses, or by participles combined with auxiliary verbs.

β. For the general formation of the Greek tenses, see ¶ 28.

C. MODE.

§ 169. The Greek has six modes; the INDICATIVE, the SUBJUNCTIVE, the OPTATIVE, the IMPERATIVE, the INFINITIVE, and the PARTICIPLE.

1. The INDICATIVE expresses *direct assertion* or *inquiry;* as γράφω, *I am writing;* γράφω; *am I writing?*

2. The SUBJUNCTIVE expresses *present contingence;* as, οὐκ οἶδα, ὅποι τράπωμαι, *I know not, whither I can turn.*

3. The OPTATIVE (opto, *to wish*, because often used in the expression of a wish) expresses *past contingence;* as, οὐκ ᾔδειν, ὅποι τραποίμην, *I knew not, whither I could turn.*

4. The IMPERATIVE expresses *direct command*, or *entreaty*, as, γράφε, *write;* τυπτέσθω, *let him be beaten;* δός μοι, *give me.*

5. The INFINITIVE partakes of the nature of an *abstract noun;* as, γράφειν, *to write.*

6. The PARTICIPLE partakes of the nature of an *adjective*, as, γράφων, *writing.*

NOTES. *α*. For a table of the Greek modes classified according to the character of the sentences which they form, see ¶ 27.

β. In the regular inflection of the Greek verb, the Present and Aorist have all the modes; but the Future wants the Subjunctive and Imperative; and the Perfect, for the most part, wants the Subjunctive and Optative, and likewise, in the active voice, the Imperative. The Imperfect has the same form with the Present, and the Pluperfect the same form with the Perfect, except in the Indicative.

γ. The tenses of the Subjunctive and Optative are related to each other as *present* and *past*, or as *primary* and *secondary*, tenses (§ 168. I.); and some have therefore chosen to consider them as only different tenses of a general conjunctive or contingent mode. With this change, the number and offices of the Greek modes are the same with those of the Latin, and the correspondence between the Greek conjunctive and the English potential modes becomes more obvious.

D. NUMBER AND PERSON.

§ 170. The numbers and persons of verbs correspond to those of nouns and pronouns (§ 164).

NOTE. The Imperative, from its signification, wants the *first person*; the Infinitive, from its abstract nature, wants the distinctions of number and person altogether; and the Participle, as partaking of the nature of an Adjective, has the distinctions of *gender* and *case*, instead of person.

REMARKS. *α.* The *first person singular* of the *Present indicative active*, or in deponent verbs (§ 166. 2), *middle*, is regarded as the THEME of the verb. The ROOT is obtained by throwing off the affix of the theme, or it may be obtained from any form of the verb, by throwing off the prefix and affix, and allowing for euphonic changes. A verb is conjugated by adding to the root the prefixes and affixes in ¶¶ 28 – 30.

β. Verbs are divided, according to the *characteristic*, into MUTE, LIQUID DOUBLE CONSONANT, and PURE VERBS; and according to the *affix in the theme*, into VERBS IN -ω, and VERBS IN -μι (§ 208. 2). For a paradigm of *regular conjugation without euphonic changes*, see ¶¶ 34, 35; for shorter paradigms of the *several classes of verbs*, see ¶¶ 36 – 60.

γ. For a fuller view of the use of the Greek verb in its several forms, see Syntax.

E. HISTORY OF GREEK CONJUGATION.

§ 171. The early history of Greek conjugation can be traced only in the same way with that of declension (§ 83). The following view is offered as one which has much in its support, and which serves to explain the general phenomena of the Greek verb.

Greek conjugation, like declension (§§ 83, 143), was progressive. At first, the root was used, as in nouns, without inflection. The first distinction appears to have been that of *person*, which was, at first, only twofold, affixing μ to express the first person, and a lingual or sibilant to express the other two. Of this second pronominal affix, the simplest and most demonstrative form appears to have been -τ (cf. §§ 143, 148). By uniting these affixes with the root φα-, *to say*, we have the forms,

φάμ, *I* or *we say*, φάτ, *you*, *he*, or *they say*.

§ 172. A *plural* was then formed by affixing the plural sign ν (§ 83), with the insertion of ε to assist in the utterance. Thus,

	1 Person.	2 and 3 Persons.
Sing.	φάμ	φάτ
Plur.	φάμεν	φάτεν

Upon the separation of the 2d and 3d Persons (§ 143. β), the 2d, as being less demonstrative, took in the Sing. the softer form ς (in some cases, σθ or θ, in both which forms the θ would, by the subsequent laws of euphony, pass into ς, unless dropped or sustained by an assumed vowel, § 63); while in the Plur. there was a new formation (cf. §§ 84, 85), in which plurality was marked, in the 2d Pers. by affixing ε (cf. § 83), and in the 3d Pers. by inserting ν (cf. -σ-ι, § 85). The old Plur. now became, as in nouns (§ 85), a Dual, and the system of numbers and persons was complete. Thus,

	1 Pers.	2 Pers.	3 Pers.
Sing.	φάμ	φάς	φάτ
Plur.	φάμεν	φάτε	φάντ
Dual	φάμεν	φάτεν	φάτεν

§ 173. The distinction of *tense*, like those of number, case, and person (§§ 83, 143), was at first only twofold, simply distinguishing a *past* action from a *present* or *future* one. This was naturally done by prefixing ε- (in Sanscrit, ă-), to express, as it were, the *throwing back* of the action into past time (§ 187). This expression, it will be observed, is aided by the throwing back of the accent. With the prefix of ε-, a distinction was also made between the 2d and 3d Persons dual (perhaps because, the more remote the action, the more important becomes the specific designation of the subject). In the 3d Pers. the inserted ε (§ 172) was lengthened to η, while in the 2d Pers., as in both the 2d and 3d Persons of the unaugmented tense, it passed into the kindred ο (§ 28). We have now two tenses, the unaugmented *Primary Tense*, which supplied the place of both the Present and the Future, and the augmented *Secondary Tense*, which expressed past action both definitely and indefinitely, and supplied the place of all the past tenses (§ 168). Thus,

	Primary Tense.			Secondary Tense.		
	1 P.	2 P.	3 P.	1 P.	2 P.	3 P.
S.	φάμ	φάς	φάτ	ἔφαμ	ἔφας	ἔφατ
P.	φάμεν	φάτε	φάντ	ἔφαμεν	ἔφατε	ἔφαντ
D.	φάμεν	φάτον	φάτον	ἔφαμεν	ἔφατον	ἐφάτην

§ 174. At first, there was no distinction of *voice*. The affix merely showed the connection of the person with the action, but did not distinguish his relation to it as *agent* or *object*. This distinction seems to have arisen as follows. A transitive action passes immediately from the agent, but its effect often continues long upon the object. This continuance would naturally be denoted by prolonging the affix. Thus, if I may be pardoned such an illustration, while *the striker* simply says with vivacity τύπτομ, *I strike*, *the one struck* rubs his head and cries τύπτομαι, tŭptom-ah-ee, *I am struck*. Hence the *objective* form was distinguished from the *subjective* (§ 195), simply by the prolongation of the affix. This took place in various ways, but all affecting the *personal* and not the *numeral* element of the affix. If the affix ended with the *sign of person*, it was prolonged by annexing, in the Primary Tense, αι; but in the Secondary Tense (on account of the augment, which had a natural tendency to shorten the affix), the shorter ο, except in the 1st Pers., where a species of *reduplication* seems to have taken place (-μημ, passing of course into -μην, § 63). Thus -μ became -μαι and -μην; -ς, -σαι and -σο; -τ, -ται and -το; -ντ, -νται and -ντο. If the affix ended with the *sign of number*, the preceding *sign of person* took a longer form. In the 2d and 3d Persons, this was σθ (which might be considered as arising from the τ by the addition of θ, since τθ must pass into σθ, § 52). The 1st Pers., in imitation of the others, inserted θ (or, if a long syllable was wanted by the poets, σθ), after which either ο was inserted, to aid in the utterance, or, what became the common form, the final ν passed into its corresponding vowel α (§ 50). Thus -τε, -τον, -την became -σθε, -σθον, -σθην; and -μεν became -μεθον (-μεσθον), or commonly -μεθα (-μεσθα). In respect to the form -μεθον, see § 212. 1. We place the subjective and objective inflections side by side for comparison.

	Subjective.			Objective.		
	1 P.	2 P.	3 P.	1 P.	2 P.	3 P.
Prim. S.	φά-μ	φά-ς	φά-τ	φά-μαι	φά-σαι	φά-ται
P.	φά-μεν	φά-τε	φά-ντ	φά-μεθα	φά-σθε	φά-νται
D.	φά-μεν	φά-τον	φά-τον	φά-μεθα	φά-σθον	φά-σθον

		SUBJECTIVE.			OBJECTIVE.		
		1 P.	2 P.	3 P.	1 P.	2 P.	3 P.
Sec.	S.	ἔφα-μ	ἔφα-ς	ἔφα-τ	ἐφά-μην	ἔφα-σο	ἔφα-το
	P.	ἔφα-μεν	ἔφα-τε	ἔφα-ντ	ἐφά-μεθα	ἔφα-σθε	ἔφα-ντο
	D.	ἔφα-μεν	ἔφα-τον	ἐφά-την	ἐφά-μεθα	ἔφα-σθον	ἐφά-σθη

§ **175.** It will be observed, that all the affixes above begin with a consonant. While, therefore, they could be readily attached to roots ending with a vowel, euphony required that, in their attachment to the far greater number of roots ending with a consonant, a *connecting vowel* should be inserted. This vowel, which was purely euphonic in its origin, was, doubtless also from euphonic preference, -ο- before a liquid, but otherwise -ε- (the formation of the Opt. and the analogy of Dec. II. lead us rather to consider the -ε- as a euphonic substitute for the -ο- than the reverse, §§ 28, 86, 177). As an example of *euphonic inflection* (in distinction from which the inflection without connecting vowels is termed *nude*), we select the root γραφ-, *to write* (¶ 36).

		SUBJECTIVE.			OBJECTIVE.		
		1 P.	2 P.	3 P.	1 P.	2 P.	3 P.
Prim.	S.	γράφ-ομ	-ες	-ετ	γράφ-ομαι	-εσαι	-εται
	P.	γράφ-ομεν	-ετε	-οντ	γραφ-όμεθα	-εσθε	-ονται
	D.	γράφ-ομεν	-ετον	-ετον	γραφ-όμεθα	-εσθον	-εσθον
Sec.	S.	ἔγραφ-ομ	-ες	-ετ	ἐγραφ-όμην	-εσο	-ετο
	P.	ἐγράφ-ομεν	-ετε	-οντ	ἐγραφ-όμεθα	-εσθε	-οντο
	D.	ἐγράφ-ομεν	-ετον	-έτην	ἐγραφ-όμεθα	-εσθον	-έσθην

§ **176.** The distinction of *mode* in the inflection of verbs commences with that of person. For the very attachment of personal affixes makes a distinction between a *personal mode* (i. e. the verb used as finite) and a *non-personal mode* (i. e. the verb used as an infinitive or participle). The latter had doubtless, at first, no affix. But the Infinitive is in its use a *substantive*, commonly sustaining the office, either of a *direct*, or yet more frequently *indirect object* of another word. Hence it naturally took the objective endings of nouns. Of these the simplest and the earliest in its objective force appears to have been ν (§§ 84, 87), which was, accordingly, affixed to the Inf., to express in general the objective character of this mode. To *pure* roots this affix was attached *directly;* but to *impure* roots *with the insertion of* ε to assist the utterance. Thus the Inf. of φα- was φάν ; and of γραφ-, γράφεν. Subsequently, to mark more specifically the prevalent relation of the Inf., that of *indirect object*, the dative affix of Dec. I. (§ 86) was added to these forms; thus, φάναι, γράφεναι. Voice appears to have been distinguished by the insertion, in these forms, of σθ (before which the ν fell away, cf. §§ 55, 57), after the analogy of § 174; thus, Act. (or Subject.) Form, φάναι, γράφεναι · Mid. and Pass. (or Obj.) Form, (φάν-σθ-αι) φάσθαι, (γράφεν-σθ-αι) γράφεσθαι. But the verb is also used as an *adjective*, and, as such, receives declension. The root of this declension, in the Act. (or Subject.) Form, may be derived from the original form of the non-personal mode in -ν, by adding τ, which is used so extensively in the formation of verbal substantives and adjectives; thus, φάν φαντ-, or, with the affix of declension (¶ 5), φάντ-ς, γράφεν γράφοντ-ς (the kindred ο was here preferred as a connecting vowel to ε, cf. § 175). The Mid. and Pass. (or Obj.) form of the Participle may be derived from the same, by a reduplication analogous to that in § 174 (since the Acc. affix, § 84, is strictly a nasal, which could be either *μ* or *ν*, according to euphonic preference; as, βοςέαν, but Lat. *boream*); thus, φάν φάμεν-ος, γράφεν γραφόμεν-ος We have now the single non-personal mode developed into a system of Infinitives and Participles; thus,

	SUBJECTIVE.	OBJECTIVE.
Inf.	φάναι, γράφεναι	φάσθαι, γράφεσθαι
Part.	φάντς, γράφοντς	φάμενος, γραφόμενος

§ 177. In the *personal mode*, a threefold distinction arose. Doubt leads to hesitation in closing a word or sentence; and hence the idea of *contingence* was naturally expressed by dwelling upon the connecting vowel (or upon the final vowel of the root), as if it were a matter of question whether the verb ought to be united with its subject. The strongest expression of contingence, that of *past contingence*, protracted the connecting vowel, or final vowel of the root, to the cognate diphthong in *ι* (¶ 3), and thus formed what is termed the *Optative* mode, which, as denoting past time, takes the secondary affixes; thus, ἔφαμ φαῖμ, ἐφάμην φαίμην, ἔγραφομ γράφοιμ, ἐγραφόμην γραφοίμην. The weaker expression of contingence, that of *present contingence*, as less needed, seems to have arisen later, after the conjugation with the connecting vowels -ο- and -ε- had become established as the prevailing analogy of the language; and to have consisted simply in prolonging these vowels to -ω- and -η-, attaching the same affixes to all verbs. This weaker form, termed the *Subjunctive* mode (yet see § 169. γ), as denoting present time, takes the primary affixes. Thus, γράφομ γράφωμ, γράφομαι γράφωμαι, φάμ φάωμ, φάμαι φάωμαι. The original mode now became an *Indicative*, expressing the *actual*, in distinction from the *contingent*.

A third mode arose for the expression of *command*. This obviously required no 1st Pers.; and in the 2d, it required no essential change, as the tone of voice would sufficiently indicate the intent of the speaker. There would, however, be a preference of short forms, as the language of direct command is laconic; hence, we find in the objective inflection -σο rather than -σαι, and in the subjective, a tendency to drop the affix of the 2d Pers. sing. The 3d Pers., on the other hand, has throughout a peculiar form, in which the affix is emphatically prolonged. This is done in the Sing. subjective by adding ω; thus, -τω. In the objective inflection, -τω, of course, becomes -σθω (§ 174). The old Plur., afterwards the Du., was formed by adding the plural sign ν (§ 172); thus, -των, -σθων. The new Plur. was still further strengthened by prefixing ν (which in the obj. form would make no change, cf. § 176), or by adding the later plur. ending σαν (§ 181. γ) instead of ν; thus, -ντων or -τωσαν, (-νσθων) -σθων or -σθωσαν. In the 2d Pers., it is convenient to regard -θ as the proper flexible ending (§ 172). The system of personal modes is now complete; thus,

SUBJECTIVE INFLECTION.

		INDICATIVE.			CONJUNCTIVE.		
		1 P.	2 P.	3 P.	1 P.	2 P.	3 P.
Prim.	S.	γράφ-ομ	-ες	-ετ	γράφ-ωμ	-ης	-ητ
	P.	γράφ-ομεν	-ετε	-οντ	γράφ-ωμεν	-ητε	-ωντ
	D.	γράφ-ομεν	-ετον	-ετον	γράφ-ωμεν	-ητον	-ητον
Sec.	S.	ἔγραφ-ομ	-ες	-ετ	γράφ-οιμ	-οις	-οιτ
	P.	ἐγράφ-ομεν	-ετε	-οντ	γράφ-οιμεν	-οιτε	-οιντ
	D.	ἐγράφ-ομεν	-ετον	-έτην	γράφ-οιμεν	-οιτον	-οίτην

Imperative.

	2 P.	3 P.	2 P.	3 P.
S.	φά-θ	φά-τω	γράφ-εθ	-έτω
P.	φά-τε	φά-ντων, φά-τωσαν	γράφ-ετε	-όντων, -έτωσαν
D.	φά-τον	φά-των	γράφ-ετον	-έτων

Objective Inflection.

		Indicative.			Conjunctive.		
		1 P.	2 P.	3 P.	1 P.	2 P.	3 P.
Prim.	S.	γράφ-ομαι	-εσαι	-εται	γράφ-ωμαι	-ησαι	-ηται
	P.	γραφ-όμεθα	-εσθε	-ονται	γραφ-ώμεθα	-ησθε	-ωνται
	D.	γραφ-όμεθα	-εσθον	-εσθον	γραφ-ώμεθα	-ησθον	-ησθον
Sec.	S.	ἐγραφ-όμην	-εσο	-ετο	γραφ-οίμην	-οισο	-οιτο
	P.	ἐγραφ-όμεθα	-εσθε	-οντο	γραφ-οίμεθα	-οισθε	-οιντο
	D.	ἐγραφ-όμεθα	-εσθον	-έσθην	γραφ-οίμεθα	-οισθον	-οίσθην

Imperative.

	2 P.	3 P.	2 P.	3 P.
S.	φά-σο	φά-σθω	γράφ-εσο	-έσθω
P.	φά-σθε	φά-σθων, φά-σθωσαν	γράφ-εσθε	-έσθων, -έσθωσαν
D.	φά-σθον	φά-σθων	γράφ-εσθον	-έσθων

§ 178. We have, as yet, but two tenses, the Primary, denoting *present* and *future* time, and the Secondary, denoting *past* time, both *definitely* and *indefinitely*. In a few verbs, mostly poetic, the formation appears never to have proceeded farther. In other verbs, more specific tenses were developed from these, as follows.

1. In most verbs, the Future was distinguished from the Present, and the Aorist (the *indefinite past*) from the Imperfect (the *definite past*) by new forms, in which the greater energy of the Fut. and Aor. was expressed by a σ added to the root (cf. § 84); and consequently, if the old Primary and Secondary Tenses remained, they remained as Present and Imperfect. The Fut. followed throughout the inflection of the Pres., except that it wanted the Subjunctive and Imperative, which were not needed in this tense. The Aor. had all the modes, following in general the inflection of the Pres. and Impf., except that it preferred -α- as a connecting vowel, and simply appended the later affix -ι in the Inf. act. (§ 176); thus,

Subjective Inflection.

	Indicative.			Subjunctive.		
S.	ἔγραφ-σαμ	-σας	-σατ	γράφ-σω	-σης	-σητ
P.	ἐγράφ-σαμεν	-σατε	-σαντ	γράφ-σωμεν	-σητε	-σωντ
D.	ἐγράφ-σαμεν	-σατον	-σάτην	γράφ-σωμεν	-σητον	-σητον

	Optative.			Imperative.	
S.	γράφ-σαιμ	-σαις	-σαιτ	γράφ-σαθ	-σάτω
P.	γράφ-σαιμεν	-σαιτε	-σαιντ	γράφ-σατε	-σάντων, -σάτωσαν
D.	γράφ-σαιμεν	-σαιτον	-σαίτην	γράφ-σατον	-σάτων

Infinitive, γράφ-σαι   Participle, γράφ-σαντ-ς

Objective Inflection.

	Indicative.			Subjunctive.		
S.	ἐγραφ-σάμην	-σασο	-σατο	γράφ-σωμαι	-σησαι	-σηται
P.	ἐγραφ-σάμεθα	-σασθε	-σαντο	γραφ-σώμεθα	-σησθε	-σωνται
D.	ἐγραφ-σάμεθα	-σασθον	-σάσθην	γραφ-σώμεθα	-σησθον	-σησθον

	Optative.			Imperative.	
S.	γραφ-σαίμην	-σαισο	-σαιτο	γράφ-σασο	-σάσθω
P.	γραφ-σαίμεθα	-σαισθε	-σαιντο	γράφ-σασθε	-σάσθων, -σάσθωσαν
D.	γραφ-σαίμεθα	-σαισθον	-σαίσθην	γράφ-σασθον	-σάσθων

Infinitive, γράφ-σασθαι Participle, γραφ-σάμεν-ος

2. In many verbs, by a change of root, a new Pres. and Impf. were formed, which expressed more specifically the action as *doing;* and in some of these verbs, the old Secondary Tense remained as an Aorist (called, for distinction's sake, the *Second Aorist,* § 199. α); and in a few, the old Primary, as a Future (§ 200. b).

§ 179. The *complete tenses* were, probably, still later in their formation. These tenses, in their precise import, represent *the state consequent upon the completion of an action* (τὴν ἐπιστολὴν γέγραφα, *I have the letter written*), or in other words they represent the action as done, but its effect remaining. This idea was naturally expressed by an initial reduplication (§ 190). These tenses admit a threefold distinction of time, and may express either *present, past,* or *future* completeness. The present complete tense (the Perfect) naturally took the primary endings; the past complete tense (the Pluperfect), the augment and the secondary endings; and the future complete tense (the Future Perfect, or Third Future), the common future affixes. In the Perf. and Plup., the *objective* endings were affixed without a connecting vowel; and, of course, with many euphonic changes. See the inflection of (γέγραφ-μαι) γέγραμμαι (¶ 36), πέπραγ-μαι (¶ 38), (πέπειθ-μαι) πέπεισμαι (¶ 39), &c. The *subjective* endings appear to have been at first appended in the same way; thus, Perf. Ind. γέγραφ-μ, Inf. γεγράφ-ναι, Part. γεγράφ-ντς. But all these forms were forbidden by euphony. Hence in the Ind. -μ became -α (which, since μ final passes into ν, may be considered the corresponding vowel of μ as well as of ν, § 50); thus, γέγραφμ γέγραφα· and after this change the inflection proceeded according to the analogy of the Aor., except so far as the primary form differs from the secondary. The α in this way became simply a connecting vowel; thus, γέγραφα (or, if the analogy of the Aor. be followed here also, γέγραφ-α-μ), γέγραφ-α-ς, -α-τ, -α-μεν, -α-τε, -α-ντ, -α-τον. In the Part., ν also became α, which by precession passed into ο (§ 28). Indeed, in Dec. III. no masculine or feminine has a root ending in -ατ- (§ 76. d. 3). *Thus, γεγραφ-ότς. The ν in the Inf., instead of a similar change (as it was followed by α), took -ε- before it; thus, γεγραφ-έναι. In the Plup. act., there* was a kind of double augment, prefixing ε, both to the reduplication, and also to the connecting vowel of the Perf., making the connective of the Plup. -εα-; thus, ἐ-γεγράφ-εα-μ. This εα remained in the Ionic, but in the old Attic was contracted into η, which afterwards passed by precession into ει.

§ 180. The *middle* and *passive* voices were at first undistinguished. The form simply showed that the subject was affected by the action, but did not determine whether the action were his own or that of another. In the *definite* and *complete* tenses, the action is so represented, that this would be commonly understood without special designation. But in the *indefinite* tenses, there would be greater need of marking the distinction. Hence, a special Aor and Fut. *passive* were formed by employing the verb εἰμί, *to be*, as an *auxiliary*, and compounding its past and future tenses with the root of the verb (the augment being prefixed in the Aor., as in other past tenses, and the ε being lengthened in some of the forms from the influence of analogy or for euphony), thus, Aor. ἐ-γράφ-ην, Fut. γραφ-ήσομαι. The old Aor. and Fut. now became *middle*, and the two voices were so far distinct. They had still, however, so much in common, that it is not wonderful that this distinction was not always observed (§ 166. 1). The Aor. and Fut. pass. were afterwards strengthened by the insertion of θ, which came, perhaps, from employing in the composition the passive verbal in -τος, instead of the simple root of the verb; thus, πρακτ-ός ἦν ἐπράχθην. From the prevalence of the θ, the tenses formed with it were denominated *first*, and those formed without it, *second* tenses (§ 199. II.).

§ 181. The system of Greek conjugation was now complete, having *three persons*, *three numbers*, *three voices*, *six modes*, if the Subj. and Opt. are separated, and no fewer than *eleven tenses*, if the *first* and *second* are counted separately. Some remarks remain to be added, chiefly upon *euphonic changes*.

I. By a law which became so established in the language as to allow no exception (§ 63), final μ, τ, and θ could not remain. They were, therefore, either *dropped*, *changed*, *prolonged*, or *both changed and prolonged*; as follows.

1. Final μ, after -α- *connective*, was dropped; after -ο- or -ω- *connective*,* was changed to -α and then contracted with the preceding vowel; after -οι- and -αι- *connective*, and in the primary nude form (§ 173), was prolonged to -μι; and, in all other cases, became -ν. Thus, ἔγραψαμ, γέγραφαμ, ἐγεγράφεαμ became ἔγραψα, γέγραφα, ἐγεγράφεα· γράφομ and γράφωμ became (γράφοα, γράφωα) γράφω, and γράψομ and γράψωμ became γράψω· γράφοιμ, γράψοιμ, γράψαιμ, φάμ became γράφοιμι, γράψοιμι, γράψαιμι, φάμι· ἔγραφομ, ἐγεγράφειμ, ἔφαμ became ἔγραφον, ἐγεγράφειν, ἔφαν.

2. Final τ, in the secondary forms throughout, and in the Perf. sing., was dropped; but, in other cases, was changed into -ς, which after -ε- or -η- *connective* passed into -ι and was then contracted, but otherwise was prolonged to -σι. When, by the dropping of -τ, -α- *connective* became final, it passed into -ε (§ 28). Thus, ἔφατ ἔφα, ἔγραφετ ἔγραφε, ἔγραφοντ ἔγραφον, ἔγραψατ ἔγραψε, ἔγραψαντ ἔγραψαν, γράφοιτ γράφοι, γράψαιτ γράψαι, γέγραφατ γέγραφε· γράφ-ε-τ (γράφες, γράφει) γράφει, γράψ-ε-τ γράψει, γράφ-η-τ γράφῃ (written with the ι subsc. in imitation of the Ind.), γράψ-η-τ γράψῃ· φάτ φάσι, φάντ (φάνσι, § 58) φᾶσι, γράφοντ (γράφονσι) γράφουσι, γράψοντ γράψουσι, γέγραφαντ (γεγράφανσι) γεγράφᾱσι, γράφωντ (γράφωνσι) γράφωσι.

Notes. α. In the prolonged forms of the endings -τ and -ντ, the Doric retained the τ (§ 70. 2); as, φατί Theoc. 1. 51, τίθητι 3. 48, φαντί 2. 45, φιλέοντι 16. 101, ᾠδήκαντι 1. 43, λέγοντι Pind. O. 2. 51, ἐπιτρέψοντι 6. 36.

β. Epic forms of the Subjunctive, with -μ and -τ prolonged to -μι and -σι, are not unfrequent; as, ἐθέλωμι A. 549, τύχωμι E. 279, ἵκωμι I. 414, ἴδωμι X. 450, ἐθέλῃσιν (§ 66) A. 408, παύσῃσι δ. 191, θέῃσιν Σ. 601; so Dor. ἐθέλῃτι (N. α) Theoc. 16. 28. A similar form of the Opt., though not free from doubt, occurs in παραφθαίησι K. 346.

γ. A new form of the 3 Pers. pl. secondary was formed by changing -τ of the Sing. into -σαν (i. e. by *affixing* ν instead of prefixing it, with a change of τ into σ, as above, and the necessary insertion of a union-vowel, which

* in primary forms (§ 209).

here, as after *σ* in the Aor., was *-α-*, § 185). This form, in the Attic, is not used in those tenses which have as a connecting vowel *-ο-* or *-α-*, and scarcely in those which have *-οι-* or *-αι-*; but in most other tenses is either the common form, or may be freely used; thus, for *ἔφαντ, ἐγεγράφειντ, ἐπρᾶχθεντ, ἔφασαν, ἐγεγράφεισαν, ἐπράχθησαν* (§ 183).

3. Final *θ* was dropped after *-ε- connective;* after a short vowel in the root, it became in the 2 Aor. *-ς*, and in the Pres. (except *φημί* and *εἰμί*) *-ε*, which was then contracted with the preceding vowel (*αε* becoming *η*); in other cases (except the irregular substitution of *-ον* for *-αθ* in the Aor.) it was prolonged to *-θι*. Thus, *γράφεθ γράφε, δόθ δός, δίδοθ* (*δίδοε*) *δίδου, φάθ φάθι, γράφηθ γράφηθι*.

§ 182. II. A stronger form of the 2 Pers. sing. subjective was in *-σθ* (compare the Eng. and German *-st*), which, according to § 63, must either drop *θ* and thus become the same with the common form, or assume a vowel. In the latter case, it assumed *α*, becoming *-σθα* (compare the affix *-sti* of the Lat. Perf.). This remained the common form in *ἔφησθα* (¶ 53), *ἦσθα* (¶ 55), *ᾔεισθα* (¶ 56), *οἶσθα, ᾔδεισθα,* and *ᾔδησθα* (¶ 58). Other examples are furnished by the poets (particularly in the Subjunctive, by Homer); as, *τίθησθα* ι. 404, *δίδοισθα* Τ. 270, *ἐθέλῃσθα* Α. 554, *βουλεύῃσθα* Ι. 99, *εἴπῃσθα* Υ. 250, *βάλοισθα* Ο. 571, *κλαίοισθα* Ω. 619, *ἔχεισθα, φίλεισθα* Sapph. 89, *ἐθέλησθα* Theoc. 29. 4, *χρῆσθα* Ar. Ach. 778. This form, like many others belonging to the old language, is termed by grammarians *Æolic*.

III. The objective endings of the 2 Pers. sing., *-σαι* and *-σο*, commonly dropped *σ* in those tenses in which a vowel uniformly preceded (cf. §§ 117, 200. 2, 201. 2), and were then contracted with this vowel except in the Opt.; thus, *γράφεσαι γράφεαι γράφῃ* or *γράφει* (§ 37. 4), *γράψεσαι γράψῃ* or *-ει, γράφησαι γράφῃ, ἐγράφεσο ἐγράφεο ἐγράφου, γράφεσο γράφου, ἐγράψασο ἐγράψαο ἐγράψω, γράψασο γράψαο γράψαι* (the contraction is here irregular), *γράφοισο γράφοιο, γράψαισο γράψαιο*.

§ 183. IV. In the Greek verb, there is a great tendency to lengthen a short vowel before an affix beginning with a consonant. This will be observed in pure verbs before the tense-signs (§ 218); in the tense-signs of the Aor. and Fut. pass. (§ 180); in the *-ε-* often inserted in the Opt. (§ 184); in *verbs in -μι* before the *subjective endings*, especially in the Ind. sing. (§ 224); in the euphonic affixes *-ες* and *-εν* of the Pres. and Fut. act. (§§ 203. *α*, 206. *β*); &c. This tendency does not appear before endings beginning with *ντ*, since here the syllable is already long by position. Of other endings, it appears chiefly before the shorter; hence, before the *subjective* far more than the *objective*, and in the *Sing.* more than the *Plur.* or *Dual.* We give here examples of the two last only of the cases that have been mentioned above: *φᾱμι φημί* (we now change the regular accentuation of the word to that which is usually given to it as an enclitic), *φάς φής, φάσι φησί*, but Pl. *φᾰμέν* · *ἔφᾰν ἔφην, ἔφας ἔφης, ἔφα ἔφη*, but Pl. *ἔφᾰμεν* (¶ 53); 2 Pers. *γράφες γράφεις* (so some form *γράφω* and *γράφει* by lengthening the connecting vowel and dropping the flexible ending), *γράψες γράψεις* · *γράφεν* (the old form of the Inf., § 176) *γράφειν* (this became the common form of the Pres. and Fut. inf. act.), *γράψεν γράψειν*.

NOTE. The old short forms of the 2d Pers. and Inf. in *-ες* and *-εν* remain in some varieties of the Doric; as, *συρίσδες* Theoc. 1. 3, *ἀμέλγες* 4. 3, *συρίσδεν* 1. 14, *βόσκεν* 4. 2, *γαρύεν* Pind. O. 1. 5, *τράφεν* Ar. Ach. 788.

§ **184.** V. The Opt. subjective was often rendered still more expressive, by adding to its connective ε, which was lengthened to η except before ντ (§ 183). This addition was most common before the endings which have no vowel, -μ, -ς, -τ, -ντ. In the 3d Pers. pl. this addition was always made; but, except here, it was never made to -αι- *connective*, and rarely to οι- *connective* except in contract forms. Thus, (γράφ-οι-ντ) γράφοιεν, (γράψ-αι-ντ) γράψαιεν, (φα-ῖ-μ) φαίην, (φα-ῖ-ς) φαίης, (φα-ῖ-τ) φαίη, φαῖμεν φαίημεν, φαῖτε φαίητε, (φα-ῖ-ντ) φαῖεν and φαίησαν, ἀγγελοίην (¶ 41), τιμῴην (¶ 45), φιλοίην (¶ 46).

NOTES. α. In the Aor. opt. act., a special prolonged form arose, in which the connective was that of the Ind. with ει prefixed. This form occurs only in the 2d and 3d Persons sing. and the 3d Pers. pl.; but in these persons was far more common than the other form. Thus, γράψ-ει-α-ς, (γράψ-ει-α-τ, § 181. 2) γράψειε, γράψειαν. This form, like many other remains of old usage, was termed by grammarians *Æolic.* It was especially employed by the Attics; yet was not confined to them, nor employed by them to the exclusion of the other forms; thus, τίσειαν Α. 42, μείνειας Γ. 52, ψαύσειε Pind. P. 9. 213, ἀγγείλειεν Theoc. 12. 19, διαρρήξειας Hdt. iii. 12; ἀλγύναις Soph. Œd. T. 446, δικάσαις Ar. Vesp. 726, φήσαις Pl. Gorg. 477 b, ἁρπαλίσαι Æsch. Eum. 983, φθάσαιεν Th. iii. 49.

β. In analyzing Opt. forms of the 3d Pers. pl., it is often convenient to join the inserted ε with the flexible ending, although in strict propriety it is an extension of the connecting vowel. See ¶ 31.

§ **185.** VI. One important analogy we ought not to pass unnoticed. The oldest inflection both of verbs and of nouns, that of the nude Pres. and Impf., and of Dec. III., had no connecting vowels. The next inflection in order of time, that of the euphonic Pres. and Impf., of the Fut., and of Dec. II., took the connecting vowels -ο- and -ε-; while the latest inflection, that of the Aor., of the Perf. Act., and of Dec. I., took the connecting vowel -α- (cf. § 176). But the analogy does not stop here. As some nouns fluctuated between the different declensions (§§ 124, 125), so some forms of verbs fluctuated between the different methods of inflection. Thus we find,

α.) Verbs in both -μι and -ω, particularly the large class in -ῡμι and -ῠω, as, δείκνῡμι and δεικνῠω, *to show.*

β.) That verbs in -μι whose roots end in ε, ο, or υ, have, in the Impf. act. sing., a second and more common form in -ον; as, ἐτίθην and (ἐτίθε-ον) ἐτίθουν (¶ 50), ἐδίδων and ἐδίδουν (¶ 51), ἐδείκνῡν and ἐδείκνῠον (¶ 52).

γ.) That verbs in -ω have the 2 Aor. *nude,* if the root ends in a vowel, except ι; as, (¶ 57) ἔβην (r. βα-), ἔγνων (r. γνο-), ἔδῡν (r. δυ-); but ἔπιον (r. πι-), 2 Aor. of πίνω, *to drink.*

δ.) Poetic (chiefly Epic) 2 Aorists middle which want the connecting vowel even after a consonant; as, ἆλτο Α. 532; ἄρμενον (Part.) Σ. 600; γέντο (= εἷλετο) Θ. 43; γέντο (= ἐγένετο) Hes. Th. 199, ἔγεντο Theoc. 1. 88; ἐδέγμην ι. 513, δέκτο Ο. 88 (so even Pres. 3 Pers. pl., δέχαται Μ. 147, for δέχνται, § 60), Imp. δέξο Τ. 10, δέχθε Ap. Rh. 4. 1554, Inf. δέχθαι Α. 23, Part. δέγμενος Β. 794; ἐλέλικτο Α. 39; ἵκτο Hes. Th. 481; ἐλέγμην ι. 335, λέκτο δ. 451, λέξο Ω. 650; μιάνθην (3 Pers. du. for ἐμιάνσθην, § 60)*; ἔμικτο α. 433, μίκτο Λ. 354; ὦρτο Ε. 590, Æsch. Ag. 987, ὄρσο Δ. 204, ὄρθαι Θ. 474, ὄρμενος, Λ. 572, Soph. Œd. T. 177; πάλτο Ο. 645; πέρθαι (for πέρθσθαι, §§ 55, 60) π. 708.

* Δ. 146.

β. In the 3d Pers. sing. of the Aor. and Perf. act., -ε- takes the place of -α- ; as, (ἐϐούλευσ-α-τ) ἐϐούλευσε, βεϐούλευκε. See § 181. 2.

γ. In the 3d Pers. pl. of the Plup., -ε- commonly takes the place of -ει-

NOTE. The original connective of the Plup. was -εα-, which remained in the Ion. (§ 179); as, ᾔδεα Ξ. 71, Hdt. ii. 150, ἐτεθήπεα ζ. 166, ἐτεθήπεας ω. 90, ᾔδεε Β. 832, ᾔδεεν Σ. 404, ἐγεγόνεε Hdt. i. 11, συνῄδεατε Id. ix. 58. The earlier contraction into -η- is especially old Attic, but also occurs in the Ep. and Dor. ; as, 1 Pers. ᾔδη Soph. Ant. 18, ἐπεπόνθη Ar. Eccl. 650, κεχήνη Id. Ach. 10 ; 2 Pers. ᾔδης Soph. Ant. 447, ᾔδησθα τ. 93, ἐλελήθης Ar. Eq. 822 ; 3 Pers. ᾔδη A. 70, Soph. Œd. T. 1525, ἐλελήθη Theoc. 10. 38. By precession (§ 29), -η- passed into -ει-, which became the common connective, and in the 3 Pers. sing. is already found in Hom. (arising from -εε); as, ἑστήκει Σ. 557 ; so λελοίπει Theoc. 1. 139. In the 3 Pers. pl., -εα- became -ε-, by the omission of the α, which was only euphonic in its origin (§ 179). So, in the 2 Pers. pl., ᾔδετε for ᾔδειτε, Eur. Bac. 1345.

§ **204.** II. The SUBJUNCTIVE takes the connecting vowels of the Pres. ind., lengthening -ε- to -η- and -ο- to -ω- (§ 177).

Thus, Ind. βουλεύ-ω, Subj. βουλεύ-ω, βουλεύσ-ω· βουλεύ-ει-ς, βουλεύ-η-ς, βουλεύσ-η-ς· βουλεύ-ει, βουλεύ-ῃ, βουλεύσ-ῃ· βουλεύ-ο-μεν, βουλεύ-ω-μεν· βουλεύ-ε-τε, βουλεύ-η-τε· (βουλεύ-ο-νσι, βουλεύ-ω-νσι, § 58) βουλεύουσι, βουλεύωσι· βουλεύ-ο-μαι, βουλεύ-ω-μαι, βουλεύσ-ω-μαι· βουλεύ-ε-ται, βουλεύ-η-ται, βουλεύσ-η-ται.

§ **205.** III. The OPTATIVE has, for its connective, ι, either alone or with other vowels (§§ 177, 184).

RULE. If the Ind. has no connecting vowel, and the base ends in α, ε, or ο, then the ι is *followed* by η in the *subjective* forms, but receives *no addition* in the *objective*. In other cases, the ι takes *before it* α in the Aor., and ο in the other tenses. The connective ι always forms a *diphthong* with the preceding vowel.

Thus, ἱστα-ίη-ν, ἱστα-ί-μην (¶ 48), τιθε-ίη-ν, τιθε-ί-μην (¶ 50), βουλευθε-ίη-ν (¶ 35), διδο-ίη-ν, διδο-ί-μην (¶ 51) ; βουλεύσ-αι-μι, βουλευσ-αί-μην· βουλεύ-οι-μι, βουλευ-οί-μην, βουλεύσ-οι-μι, βουλευσ-οί-μην, βουλευθησ-οί-μην· ἴ-οι-μι (¶ 56), δεικνύ-οι-μι, δεικνυ-οί-μην (¶ 52).

REMARKS. 1. In Optatives in -ίην, the η is often omitted in the Plur., especially in the 3d Pers., and also in the Dual ; as, ἱσταῖμεν, ἱσταῖτε, ἱσταῖεν ἱσταῖτον (¶ 48), βουλευθεῖεν (¶ 35). In the 3d Pers. pl. of the Aor. pass. the longer form is rare in classic Greek (ἐκπεμφθείησαν Th. i. 38).

2. In *contract subjective forms*, whether Pres. or Fut., the connective οι often assumes η ; as, φιλέ-οι-μι, contr. φιλοῖ-μι or φιλοίη-ν (¶ 46) ; ἀγγελοίη-ν (¶ 41, § 56).

NOTES. *α*. The form of the Opt. in -οίην, for -οιμι, is called the *Attic Optative*, though not confined to Attic writers ; as, ἐνωρῴη Hdt. i. 89, οἰκοίητε Theoc. 12. 28. This form is most employed in the Sing., where it is the common form in contracts in -έω and -όω, and almost the exclusive form in contracts in -άω. In the 3d Pers. pl., it scarcely occurs (δοκοίησαν Æschin. 41.

29). It is likewise found in the Perf., as πεποιθοίη (¶ 39) Ar. Ach. 940, ἐκπεφευγοίην Soph. Œd. T. 840, προεληλυθοίης Cyr. ii. 4. 17; and in the 2 Aor. of ἔχω, *to have*, which has, for its Opt., σχοίην in the simple verb (Cyr. vii. 1. 36), but σχοιμι in compounds (κατάσχοις Mem. iii. 11. 11). So ἰοίην (¶ 56) Symp. 4. 16.

β. See, in respect to the insertion of η (ε) in the Opt., § 184.

3. The Aor. opt. act. has a second form, termed *Æolic*, in which the connective is that of the Ind. with ει prefixed; as, βουλεύσ-εια-ς. See § 184. α

§ **206.** IV. In the IMPERATIVE and INFINITIVE, the connecting vowel is -α- in the Aorist, and -ε- in the other tenses.

Thus, βουλεύσ-α-τε, βουλεύσ-α-σθε, βουλεῦσ-α-ι, βουλεύσ-α-σθαι· βουλεύ-ε-τε, βουλεύ-ε-σθε, βουλεύ-ε-σθαι, βεβουλευκ-έ-ναι, βουλεύσ-ε-σθαι, βουλευθήσ-ε-σθαι.

REMARKS. α. Before ν in the *Imperative*, -ο- takes the place of -ε-, and, in the 2*d Pers. sing.*, of -α-; as, βουλευ-ό-ντων, βούλευσ-ο-ν (§ 210. 2).

β. In the *Infinitive* of the Pres. and Fut. act., -ε- is lengthened to -ει (§ 183); as, βουλεύ-ει-ν, βουλεύσ-ει-ν.

§ **207.** V. In the PARTICIPLE, the connecting vowel is -α- in the Aorist, and -ο- in the other tenses.

Thus, (βουλεῦσ-α-ντς, § 109) βουλεύσας, βουλευσ-ά-μενος· (βουλεῦ-ο-ντς, § 109) βουλεύων, (βουλεύ-ο-ντσα, § 132) βουλεύουσα, (βουλεῦ-ο-ντ, § 63) βουλεῦον· βουλευόντων· (βεβουλευκ-ό-τς, §§ 112. α, 179) βεβουλευκώς, (βεβουλευκ-ό-τσα, § 132. 1) βεβουλευκυῖα, (βεβουλευκ-ό-τ, § 103) βεβουλευκός· βουλευ-ό-μενος, βουλευσ-ό-μενος, βουλευθησ-ό-μενος.

§ **208.** The INDICATIVE, IMPERATIVE, INFINITIVE, and PARTICIPLE are *nude* (nudus, *naked*), i. e. have no connecting vowel (§ 175),

1.) In the *Aor.*, *Perf.*, and *Plup.*, *passive*, of *all verbs*.

In the Aor. pass., the flexible endings are affixed, in these modes, to the *tense-sign* (§ 198); in the Perf. and Plup. pass., they are affixed to the *root*; as, ἐβουλεύ-θη-ν (§ 199); βεβούλευ-μαι, ἐβεβουλεύ-μην.

2.) In the *Pres.* and *Impf.* of *some verbs in which the characteristic is a short vowel.* These verbs are termed, from the ending of the theme, VERBS IN -μι, and, in distinction from them, other verbs are termed VERBS IN -ω (§ 209).

The flexible endings are here affixed to the *root*; thus, ἵστα-μεν, ἵστα-σαν· ἵστα-μαι, ἱστά-μην (¶ 48). In the Inf. and Part., the connecting vowels -ε- and -ο- are inserted after ι; thus, ἰ-έ-ναι, (ἰ-ό-ντς) ἰών (¶ 56). So, in the Imperative, ἰόντων. Cf. §§ 185. γ, 205.

3.) In a few *Second Perf.* and *Plup.* forms (§ 186).

The flexible endings are here affixed to the *root*; thus, ἕστα-μεν, ἕστα-θι, ἑστά-ναι (¶ 48). In the Part., the connecting vowel is inserted; as, δεδιώς (¶ 58). So, in the *Inf.*, δεδιέναι, with which compare ἰέναι, above.

C. Flexible Endings.

§ **209.** The *flexible endings* (flexibilis, *change able*) are the chief instruments of conjugation, marking by their *changes* the distinctions of *voice*, *number*, *person*, and, in part, of *tense* and *mode*. They are exhibited in ¶ 31, according to the classification (§§ 195, 196).

Special Rules and Remarks.

First Pers. Sing. The ending -μ, after -α- *connective*, and, in *primary* forms (§ 196. 1), after -ο- and -ω- *connective*, is dropped or absorbed; after -οι- and -αι-, and in the *nude Present* (§ 208. 2), it becomes -μι; in other cases, it becomes -ν; as, (Ind. βούλευ-ο-μ, Subj. βουλεύ-ω-μ) βουλεύ-ω, βεβούλευκ-α, ἐβούλευσ-α (so after -εα-, contr. -η-, § 203. N.); βουλεύσ-αι-μι, βουλεύ-οι-μι, βουλεύσ-οι-μι, ἵστη-μι (¶ 48); ἐβούλευ-ο-ν, ἐβεβουλεύκ-ει-ν, ἐβουλεύθη-ν, βουλευθείη-ν · φιλοίη-ν, ἀγγελοίη-ν (§ 205. 2); ἵστη-ν, ἱσταίη-ν (¶ 48). See § 181. 1.

Note. Τρέφοιν, for τρέφοιμι, occurs for the sake of the metre Eur. Fr. Inc. 152.

§ **210.** Second Pers. Sing. 1. For the form -σθα, see § 182.

2. The ending -θ is dropped after -ε- *connective;* after -α- *connective*, it becomes -ν, with a change of -α- to -ο- (§ 206. α); after a *short vowel in the root*, it becomes in the 2d Aor. σ, and in the Pres. ε, which is then contracted with the preceding vowel (αε becoming η); in other cases, it becomes -θι (see § 181. 3). Thus, βούλευ-ε · βούλευσ-ο-ν · θέ-ς, δό-ς, ἕ-ς (¶¶ 50, 51, 54); (ἵστᾰ-ε) ἵστη, (τίθε-ε) τίθει, (δί-δο-ε) δίδου, (δείκνῠ-ε) δείκνῡ (¶¶ 48-52); φάνηθι (¶ 42), βουλεύθητι (§ 62), ἕστᾰθι (¶ 48), ἴσθι, δέδῐθι (¶ 58), and, in like manner, φᾰθι, ἴθι (¶¶ 53, 56, § 181. 3), and the poet. ἵλᾰθι Theoc. 15. 143, ἐπόμνῠθι Theog. 1195.

Note. In composition, στῆθι, βῆθι, and ἴθι (¶¶ 48, 56, 57) are often shortened to στᾶ, βᾶ, and εἰ · as, παράστᾶ for παράστηθι, κατάβᾶ for κατάβηθι, πρόσει for πρόσιθι.

3. The endings -σαι and -σο drop the σ, except in the Perf. and Plup. pass., and sometimes in the *nude* Pres. and Impf. (§ 208. 2); as, (βουλεύ-ε-αι, § 37. 4) βουλεύῃ or βουλεύει, (βουλεύ-ε-ο) βουλεύου, (ἐβουλεύ-ε-ο) ἐβουλεύου, (ἐβουλεύσ-α-ο) ἐβουλεύσω · βουλεύ-οι-ο, βουλεύσ-αι-ο · βεβούλευ-σαι, βεβούλευ-σο, ἐβεβούλευ-σο · ἵστα-σαι, ἵστα-σο and (ἵστα-ο) ἵστω (¶ 48); τίθε-σαι

and (τίθε-αι) τίθῃ, (ἔθε-ο) ἔθου (¶ 50); δίδο-σο and (δίδο ο) δίδου, (δόο) δοῦ (¶ 51). See § 182. III.

REMARKS. (*a*) The Aor. imperat. is irregularly contracted; thus, (βουλεύσ-α-ο) βούλευσαι. (*b*) The contraction of -εαι into -ει (§ 37. 4) is a special Attic form, which was extensively used by pure writers; and which, after yielding in other words to the common contraction into -ῃ, remained in βούλει, οἴει, and ὄψει. (*c*) In *verbs in -μι*, -σαι remained more frequently than -σο, and was the common form if α or ο preceded. Yet poet. ἐπίστᾳ Æsch. Eum. 86, δύνᾳ or δύνῃ (§ 29) Soph. Ph. 798. Further particulars respecting the use or omission of the -σ- in *verbs in -μι* are best learned from the tables and from observation.

§ **211.** THIRD PERS. SING. The ending -τ becomes -σι in the *nude Pres.*, but in other cases is dropped, or lost in a diphthong; as, (ἵστη-τ) ἵστησι, ἵστη (¶ 48); ἐβούλευε, βεβούλευκε, (βούλευ-ε-τ, βουλεύ-ε-ε) βουλεύει. See § 181. 2.

NOTE. The *paragogic* ν (§ 66), which is regularly affixed only to ε and simple ι, is, in a few instances, found after -ει in the Plup., and follows ῄ in the Impf. of εἰμί, even before a consonant; thus, 3 Pers. ᾔδειν ὡς (¶ 58) Ar. Vesp. 635, ᾔειν οὐδέπω (¶ 56) Id. Plut. 696, ἐπεποίθειν οὐκ Id. Nub. 1347, ἑστήκειν αὐτοῦ Ψ. 691, βεβλήκειν αἰχμή E. 661, ἦν δε i. 2. 3. In all these cases, the ν appears to have been retained from an uncontracted form in -ε(ν). See § 203. N., 230. γ. So Impf. ᾔσκειν εἶρια Γ. 388.

§ **212.** FIRST AND SECOND PERSONS PL., WITH THE DUAL. **1.** The 1st Pers. is the same in the Plur. and Du., having, for its *subjective* ending, -μεν, and for its *objective*, -μεθα, or sometimes in the poets, -μεσθα· thus, βουλεύο-μεν, βουλευό-μεθα, and poet. βουλευό-μεσθα.

NOTE. Of the form in -μεθον (§ 174), there have been found only three classical examples, all in the *dual primary*, and all occurring in poetry before a vowel: περιδώμεθον Ψ. 485, λελείμμεθον Soph. El. 950, ὁρμώμεθον Id. Ph. 1079. Two examples more are quoted by Athenæus (98 a) from a *word-hunter* (ὀνοματοθήρας), whose affectation he is ridiculing.

2. The 2d Pers. pl. always ends in -ε. The 2d Pers. du. is obtained by changing this vowel into -ον; and the 3d Pers. du., by changing it into -ον in the *primary* inflection, into -ην in the *secondary*, and into -ων in the *imperative*. Thus, Pl. 2, βουλεύετε, ἐβουλεύετε· Du. 2, βουλεύετον, ἐβουλεύετον· Du. 3, βουλεύετον, ἐβουλευέτην, βουλευέτων.

REMARK. In the *secondary dual*, the 3d Pers. seems originally to have had the same form with the 2d; and we find in Hom. such cases as 3d Pers. διώκετον K. 364, τετεύχετον N. 346, λαφύσσετον Σ. 583, θωρήσσεσθον N. 301. On the other hand, the lengthening to -ην (with which compare the lengthening of the Plup. affix, § 179) was sometimes extended by the Attics even to the 2d Pers.; as, 2d Pers. εἰχέτην Soph. Œd. T. 1511, ἠλλαξάτην Eur. Alc. 661, εὑρέτην, ἐπεδημείτην Pl. Euthyd. 273 e.

§ **213.** THIRD PERS. PL. 1. The ending -ντ, in the *pri*

mary tenses, becomes *-νσι*. In the *secondary*, after *-ο-* or *-α-* *connective*, it becomes *-ν*; after a diphthong in the Opt., *-εν*; but, otherwise, *-σαν*. Thus, (*βουλεύονσι*, § 58) *βουλεύουσι*, *βουλεύσουσι*, *βεβουλεύκᾱσι*, *βουλεύωσι*· *ἱστᾶσι*, *ἑστᾶσι* (¶ 48); *ἐβούλευ-ο-ν*, *ἐβούλευσ-α-ν*· *βουλεύοι-εν*, *βουλεύσαι-εν*, *βουλευθεῖ-εν*· *ἐβεβουλεύκε-σαν*, *ἐβουλεύθη-σαν*, *βουλευθείη-σαν*· *ἵστα-σαν*, *ἔστη-σαν*, *ἱσταίη-σαν* (¶ 48). See §§ **181, 184.** *β*.

2. In the Perf. and Plup. pass. of *impure verbs*, the 3d Pers. pl. is either formed in *-αται* and *-ατο* (§ 60), or, more commonly, supplied by the Part. with *εἰσί* and *ἦσαν* (¶ 55); as, *ἐφθάρ-αται* Th. iii. **13**, from *φθείρω* (r. *φθαρ-*), *to waste*, *γεγραμμένοι εἰσί*, *γεγραμμένοι ἦσαν* (¶ 36).

Remark. The forms in *-αται* and *-ατο* are termed *Ionic*. Before these endings, a labial or palatal mute must be *rough* (*φ*, *χ*), and a lingual, *middle* (*δ*); as, from *τρέπω* (r. *τραπ-*), *to turn*, (*τέτραπ-νται*) *τετράφαται* Pl. Rep. 533 b; from *τάσσω* (r. *ταγ-*), *to arrange*, (*τέταγ-νται*) *τετάχαται* iv. 8. 5, *ἐτετάχατο* Th. vii. 4.

3. In the *Imperative*, the shorter forms in *-ντων* and *-σθων* (§ 177), which are termed *Attic* (§ 7), are the more common. In Homer, they are the sole forms.

Note. In *ἔστων* and *ἴτων* (¶¶ 55, 56), the old plur. form has remained without change.

§ 214. 1. Infinitive. The *subjective* ending, after *-ει-* connective (§ 206. *β*), has the form *-ν*; after *-α-* connective, *-ι* forming a diphthong with *-α-*; but, in other cases, *-ναι*; as, *βουλεύ-ει-ν*, *βουλεύσ-ει-ν*· *βουλεῦσ-α-ι*· *βεβουλευκ-έ-ναι*, *βουλευθῆ-ναι*· *ἱστά-ναι*, *στῆ-ναι*, *ἑστά-ναι* (¶ 48). See §§ 176, 183.

2. Participle. For the change of *ν* to a connecting vowel in the Perf. act., see § 179. For the *declension* of the Part., see Ch. III., and the paradigms (¶ 22).

§ 215. Remarks. 1. For the regular affixes of the verb, which are those of the *euphonic* Pres. and Impf., and of the regularly formed Fut., Aor., Perf., and Plup., see ¶¶ 29, 30. These affixes are *open* in the Pres. and Impf., and *close* in the other tenses. For the affixes of the Pres. and Impf. of verbs in *-μι* (§ 208. 2), see ¶¶ 29, 30. The affixes of the 2d Aor. act. and mid. are the same with those of the Impf. (§ 199. *α*), or, except in the Ind., the same with those of the Pres. (§ 169. *β*). The affixes of the other tenses denominated *second* (except the *nude* 2d Perf. and Plup., § 186) differ from the regular affixes only in the *tense-sign* (§ 199. II.). The Fut. Perf. or 3d Fut. has the same affixes with the common Fut. act. and mid. (§ 179).

2. Special care is required in distinguishing forms which have the same letters. In *βουλεύω* (¶¶ 34, 35), we remark (besides the forms which are the same in the Plur. and Du., § 212) the following: Ind. and Subj. *βουλεύω*· Fut. Ind. and Aor. Subj. *βουλεύσω*· Ind. and Imp. *βουλεύετε*, *βουλεύεσθε*· Ind.

Pl. 3, and Part. Pl. Dat. βουλεύουσι, βουλεύσουσι · Imp. Pl. 3, and Part. Pl. Gen. βουλευόντων, βουλευσάντων, βουλευθέντων · Act. S. 3, and Mid. S. 2, βουλεύει, βουλεύσει · Subj. Act. S. 3, and Ind. and Subj. Mid. S. 2, βουλεύῃ · Fut. Ind. Mid. S. 2, and Aor. Subj. Act. S. 3, and Mid. S. 2, βουλεύσῃ · Aor. Imp. βούλευσον, Fut. Part. βουλεῦσον · Opt. Act. S. 3, βουλεύσαι, Inf. Act. βουλεῦσαι, Imp. Mid. S. 2, βούλευσαι.

3. With respect to the changes which take place in the root, or in the union of the affixes with the root, the tenses are thus associated: 1. the Pres. and Impf. act. and pass.; 2. the Fut. act. and Mid.; 3. the Aor. act. and mid.; 4. the Perf. and Plup. act.; 5. the Perf. and Plup. pass.; 6. the Aor. and Fut. pass. It will be understood, that whatever change of the kind mentioned above takes place in one of the tenses, belongs likewise to the associated tenses, if nothing appears to the contrary. For the Fut. Perf., see § 239.

II. Union of the Affixes with the Root

A. Regular Open Affixes.

§ 216. When the regular open affixes (§ 215. 1) are annexed to *roots ending in α, ε,* or *ο*, CONTRACTION takes place, according to the rules (§§ 31 – 37). See the paradigms (¶¶ 45 – 47).

NOTES. *α.* Verbs in which this contraction takes place are termed CONTRACT VERBS, or, from the accent of the theme, *Perispomena*. In distinction from them, other verbs are termed *Barytone Verbs*. See Prosody.

β. The verbs καω, *to burn*, and κλαω, *to weep*, which have likewise the forms καίω and κλαίω, are not contracted. Dissyllabic Verbs in -έω admit only the contractions into ει; thus, πλέω, *to sail*, πλέεις πλεῖς, πλέει πλεῖ, πλέομεν, πλέετε πλεῖτε, πλέουσι. Except δέω, *to bind;* as, τὸ δοῦν, τῷ δοῦντι Pl. Crat. 419 a, b.

γ. The contract Ind. and Subj. of *verbs in -αω* are throughout the same. See ¶ 45. The contract Inf. in -ᾶν is likewise written without the ι subsc.; thus, τιμᾶν, as contr. from the old τιμάεν (§§ 25. β, 176, 183). So φιλεῖν, δηλοῦν may be formed from the old φιλέεν, δηλόεν.

B. Regular Close Affixes.

§ 217. I. When the close affixes are annexed to a consonant, changes are often required by the general laws of orthography and euphony; as,

γράφω (¶ 36, root γραφ-); γράψω, ἔγραψα, γέγραψαι (§ 51); γέγραφα, ἐγεγράφειν (§ 61); γέγραμμαι, γεγραμμένος (§ 53); γέγραπται (§ 52); γέγραφθε, γεγράφθω (§ 60).

λείπω (¶ 37, r. λιπ-, λειπ-); ἐλείφθην, λειφθήσομαι (§ 52).

πράσσω (¶ 38, r. πρᾶγ-); πράξω, πράξομαι, ἐπραξάμην, πέπραξο (§ 51) πέπρᾶχα (§ 61): πέπρακται, ἐπράχθην, ἐπέπραχθε, πεπρᾶχθαι (§§ 52, 60).

πείθω (¶ 39, r. *πιθ-*, *πειθ-*); *πείσω*, *ἐπέπεισο*, *ἐπέπεισθε*, *πεπεῖσθαι* (§ 55) *πέπεικα* (§ 61); *πέπεισμαι*, *ἐπεπείσμην* (§ 53); *πέπεισται*, *ἐπείσθην* (§ 52).

ἀγγέλλω (¶ 41, r. *ἀγγελ-*); *ἀγγελῶ*, *ἀγγελοῦμαι*, *ἤγγειλα*, *ἠγγειλάμην* (§ 56); *ἤγγελθε* (§ 60).

Remarks. *α.* In the *liquid verbs* *κλίνω*, *to bend*, *κρίνω*, *to judge*, *κτείνω*, *to slay*, *τείνω*, *to stretch*, and *πλύνω*, *to wash*, *ν* is dropped before the affixes which *remain close* (§ 56), except sometimes in the Aor. pass. (chiefly in poetry for the sake of the metre); as, *κέκλιμαι*, *ἐκλίθην* and *ἐκλίνθην*, Γ. 360, H. Gr. iv. 1. 30; *κέκρικα*, *κέκριμαι*, *ἐκρίθην* and Ep. *ἐκρίνθην*, N. 129.

β. In other verbs, *ν characteristic*, before *μ*, more frequently becomes *σ*, but sometimes becomes *μ* or is dropped (§ 54); as, *πέφασμαι*, *πεφασμένος* (¶ 42); *παροξῦνω*, *to exasperate*, Pf. P. Part. *παρωξυμμένος* or *παρωξῡμένος*.

γ. Before *μ* in the affix, neither *μ* nor *γ* can be doubled; hence, *κέκαμμαι*, *ἐλήλεγμαι* (¶ 44), for *κέκαμμμαι*, *ἐλήλεγγμαι*.

§ 218. II. Before the *regular close affixes*, a *short* vowel is commonly *lengthened*; and here *ᾰ* becomes *η*, unless preceded by *ε*, *ι*, *ρ*, or *ρο* (§ 29); as,

τιμάω (¶ 45), *τιμήσω*, *ἐτίμησα*, *τετίμηκα*, *τετίμημαι*, *ἐτιμήθην*.

φιλέω (¶ 46), *φιλήσω*, *φιλήσομαι*, *πεφίλημαι*, *πεφιλήσομαι*.

δηλόω (¶ 47), *δηλώσω*, *ἐδηλωσάμην*, *ἐδεδηλώμην*, *δηλωθήσομαι*.

τῐ́ω, *to honor*, poet., F. *τῑ́σω*, A. *ἔτῑσα*, Pf. P. *τέτῑμαι*.

φῠ́ω, *to produce*, F. *φῡ́σω*, A. *ἔφῡσα*, Pf. *πέφῡκα*.

ἐᾰ́ω, *to permit*, F. *ἐᾱ́σω*, A. *εἴᾱσα* (§ 189. 3), Pf. *εἴᾱκα*.

θηρᾰ́ω, *to hunt*, F. *θηρᾱ́σω*, A. *ἐθήρᾱσα*, Pf. *τεθήρᾱκα* (§ 62).

Notes. *α.* *Χράω*, *to utter an oracle*, *χράομαι*, *to use*, and *τετραίνω* (r. *τρα-*), *to bore*, lengthen *ᾰ* to *η*; as, F. *χρήσω*, *χρήσομαι*, *τρήσω*. *Ἀλοάω*, *to thresh*, with the common F. *ἀλοήσω*, has also the Old-Att. *ἀλοᾱ́σω*.

β. In the Perf. of *verbs in -μι*, *ε* is lengthened to *ει*, instead of *η* (§ 29); as, *τέθεικα*, *τέθειμαι* (¶ 50); *εἷκα*, *εἷμαι* (¶ 54).

§ 219. Remarks. 1. Some verbs *retain the short vowel*, and others are *variable*; as,

σπᾰ́ω, *to draw*, F. *σπᾰ́σω*, A. *ἔσπᾰσα*, Pf. *ἔσπᾰκα*, Pf. P. *ἔσπασμαι* (§ 221), A. P. *ἐσπάσθην*.

τελέω, *to finish*, F. *τελέσω*, *τελῶ* (§ 200. 2), A. *ἐτέλεσα*, Pf. *τετέλεκα*, Pf. P. *τετέλεσμαι*, A. P. *ἐτελέσθην*.

ἀρόω, *to plough*, F. *ἀρόσω*, A. *ἤροσα*, A. P. *ἠρόθην* (Ion. Pf. P. Part. *ἀρηρομένος*, Σ. 548, Hdt. iv. 97, § 191. 2).

δέω, *to bind*, F. *δήσω*, A. *ἔδησα*, 3 F. *δεδήσομαι*· Pf. *δέδεκα*, Pf. P. *δέδεμαι* (*δέδεσμαι* Hipp.), A. P. *ἐδέθην*.

θύω (¯ῠ), *to sacrifice*, F. *θῡ́σω*, A. *ἔθῡσα*, A. M. *ἐθῡσάμην*· Pf. *τέθῠκα*, Pf. P. *τέθῠμαι*, A. P. *ἐτῠ́θην* (§ 62).

Notes. *α.* Verbs in *-αννῡμι* and *-εννῡμι*, and those in which the root ends in λᾰ-, for the most part retain the short vowel; as, γελάω, *to laugh*, F. γελᾰσομαι, A. ἐγέλᾰσα, A. P. ἐγελάσθην.

β. The short vowel remains most frequently before θ, and least frequently before σ. In the PERFECT and PLUPERFECT, it remains more frequently in the *passive*, than in the *active* voice.

§ **220.** 2. In *seven familiar dissyllables*, mostly implying *motion*, ϝ appears to have been once attached to the root (see §§ 22. δ, 117):

θέω, *to run* (r. θεϝ-), F. (θέϝσομαι) θεύσομαι (θεύσω only Lyc. 1119). See § 166. α.

νέω, *to swim*, F. νεύσομαι, -οῦμαι (§ 200. 3), iv. 3. 12, A. ἔνευσα, Pf. νένευκα.

πλέω, *to sail*, F. πλεύσω, commonly πλεύσομαι, v. 6. 12, or πλευσοῦμαι, v. 1. 10, A. ἔπλευσα, Pf. πέπλευκα, Pf. P. πέπλευσμαι (§ 221).

πνέω, *to breathe*, F. πνεύσω, Dem. 284. 17, commonly πνεύσομαι Eur. Andr. 555, or πνευσοῦμαι, Ar. Ran. 1221, A. ἔπνευσα, Pf. πέπνευκα.

Add ῥέω, *to flow*, καίω, *to burn*, and κλαίω, *to weep*.

221. III. After a *short vowel* or a *diphthong*, σ is usually *inserted* before the *regular affixes* of the *Passive* beginning with θ, μ, or τ; as,

σπᾰω, *to draw* (§ 219), Pass. Pf. ἔσπα-σ-μαι, ἔσπασαι, ἔσπα-σ-ται, ἐσπά-σμεθα· ἐσπα-σ-μένος· A. ἐσπά-σ-θην· F. σπα-σ-θήσομαι.

τελέω, *to finish* (§ 219), Pass. Pf. τετέλεσμαι, τετελεσμένος· Plup. ἐτετελέσμην, ἐτετέλεσο, ἐτετέλεστο· A. ἐτελέσθην· F. τελεσθήσομαι.

κελεύω, *to command*, Pass. Pf. κεκέλευσμαι, κεκέλευσται, κεκελευσμένος· Plup. ἐκεκελεύσμην· A. ἐκελεύσθην· F. κελευσθήσομαι.

REMARKS. α. In some verbs, σ is *omitted* after a *short vowel* or *diphthong* in some it is *inserted* after a *simple long vowel*; and some are *variable*; thus, ἠρόθην, δέδεμαι, ἐδέθην, τέθυμαι, ἐτύθην (§ 219); βεβούλευμαι, ἐβουλεύθην (¶ 35)· χόω, *to heap up*, κέχωσμαι, ἐχώσθην· χράομαι, *to use*, κέχρημαι, ἐχρήσθην· μέμνημαι, *to remember*, ἐμνήσθην· παύω, *to stop*, πέπαυμαι, ἐπαύσθην and ἐπαύθην· ῥώννυμι (r. ῥο-), *to strengthen*, ἔρρωμαι, ἐρρώσθην· δράω, *to do*, δέδραμαι and δέδρασμαι, ἐδράσθην· θραύω, *to dash*, τέθραυσμαι and τέθραυμαι, ἐθραύσθην. It will be observed that the σ is attracted most strongly by the affixes beginning with θ.

β. When σ is inserted in the Perf. and Plup., the 3d Pers. pl. wants the simple form; as, Pl. 3, ἐσπασμένοι εἰσί, κεκελευσμένοι ἦσαν. See § 213. 2.

§ **222.** IV. The *regular close affixes* are annexed with the *insertion of* η,

1.) To *double consonant* roots, except those which end in a *labial* or *palatal mute not preceded by* σ, and those which end in a *lingual mute preceded by* ν; as,

αὔξ-ω (r. αὐξ-, ¶ 43), αὐξ-ή-σω, ηὔξ-η-σα, ηὔξ-η-κα, ηὔξ-η-μαι, ηὐξ-ή-θην αὐξ-η-θήσομαι.

ἕψω, to boil, F. ἑψήσω, A. ἥψησα. *ὄζω, to smell,* F. ὀζήσω, A. ὤζησα.

μέλλω, to be about to, to purpose, to delay, F. μελλήσω, A. ἐμέλλησα and ἠμέλλησα (§ 189. 1).

ἔῤῥω, to go away, F. ἐῤῥήσω, A. ἤῤῥησα, Pf. ἤῤῥηκα.

βόσκω, to pasture, to feed, F. βοσκήσω.

But λάμπω, *to shine,* F. λάμψω, A. ἔλαμψα, 2 Pf. λέλαμπα· ἄρχω, *to lead, to rule,* F. ἄρξω, A. ἦρξα, Pf. P. ἦργμαι, A. P. ἤρχθην· σπένδω, *to make a libation,* F. (σπένδ-σω, §§ 55, 58) σπείσω, A. ἔσπεισα, Pf. P. (ἔσπενδ-μαι, ἔσπενσμαι, § 53) ἔσπεισμαι, A. P. ἐσπείσθην, late Pf. A. ἔσπεικα.

2.) To *liquid* roots in which the characteristic is preceded by a *diphthong*, and to a few in which it is preceded by ε; as,

βούλομαι, to will, F. βουλήσομαι, Pf. βεβούλημαι (Ep. 2 Pf. βέβουλα A. 113), A. ἐβουλήθην and ἠβουλήθην (§ 189. 1).

ἐθέλω, and shortened θέλω, *to wish,* F. ἐθελήσω and θελήσω, A. ἠθέλησα and ἐθέλησα, Pf. ἠθέληκα, and late τεθέληκα.

μέλω, to concern, F. μελήσω, A. ἐμέλησα, Pf. μεμέληκα (Ep. 2 Pf. as Pres. μέμηλα, B. 25), A. P. ἐμελήθην. This verb is commonly used impersonally: μέλει, *it concerns,* μελήσει, &c.

μένω, to remain, F. μενῶ, A. ἔμεινα, 1 Pf. μεμένηκα (cf. 54. γ), 2 Pf. μέμονα.

νέμω, to distribute, F. νεμῶ, and later νεμήσω, A. ἔνειμα, Pf. νενέμηκα, Pf. P. νενέμημαι, A. P. ἐνεμήθην and ἐνεμέθην (R. α).

3.) To a few other roots; as,

δέω, to need, F. δεήσω, A. ἐδέησα (δῆσεν Σ. 100), Pf. δεδέηκα· Mid. δέομαι, *to need, to beg,* F. δεήσομαι, Pf. δεδέημαι, A. P. ἐδεήθην. The Act. is most common as impersonal: δεῖ, *there is need,* δεήσει, ἐδέησε, &c. See R. γ.

εὕδω, to sleep, Impf. εὗδον and ηὗδον (§ 188. N.), F. εὑδήσω.

οἴομαι, to think, F. οἰήσομαι, A. P. ᾠήθην. When used parenthetically, the 1st Pers. sing. of the Pres. and Impf. has the nude forms οἶμαι, ᾤμην. In Hom. we find the forms ὀΐομαι, ὀΐω, οἴω (Dor. οἰῶ Ar. Lys. 156), ὠϊσάμην, ὠΐσθην, with ι commonly long. See R. γ.

οἴχομαι, to depart, to be gone (the Pres. having commonly the force of the Perf.), F. οἰχήσομαι, Pf. ᾤχημαι, and poet. οἴχωκα or ᾤχωκα (R. β) Soph. Aj. 896 (ᾤχηκεν K. 252).

παίω, to strike, F. παίσω, in Att. poetry παιήσω, Ar. Nub. 1125, A. ἔπαισα, Pf. πέπαικα, A. P. ἐπαίσθην.

REMARKS. α. In a few verbs, ε is inserted instead of η (cf. 219); as,

ἄχθομαι, to be vexed, F. ἀχθέσομαι, A. P. ἠχθέσθην.

μάχομαι, to fight, F. μαχέσομαι, μαχοῦμαι (§ 200. 2), A. ἐμαχεσάμην, Pf. μεμάχημαι (Ion. μαχέομαι, Hdt. vii. 104, F. μαχήσομαι A. 298).

β. In a very few verbs, we find the insertion of ο or ω. See οἴχομαι (3. above), ὄμνυμι, ἐσθίω, ἄγω, εἴωθα (in the two last the inserted vowel even precedes the characteristic).

γ. In most of these cases, the vowel is obviously inserted for the sake of *euphony*. That the vowel should be commonly η, rather than ε, results from

§ 218. In δέω, *to need*, and οἴομαι, *to think*, there appears to have been once a digamma, of which we find traces in the Homeric (δέϜομαι) δεύομαι, δευήσομαι, ἐδεύησα, and in the long ι of ὀΐομαι.

§ **223.** V. In a few *liquid roots*, METATHESIS takes place before the terminations that *remain close* (§ 56), to avoid the concurrence of consonants (§ 64. 3); as,

βάλλω (r. βαλ-, transp. βλα-), *to throw*, F. βαλῶ, and in Att. poetry βαλλήσω (§ 222), Ar. Vesp. 222, 2 A. ἔβαλον, Pf. βέβληκα (§ 218), Pf. P. βέβλημαι, 3 F. βεβλήσομαι, A. P. ἐβλήθην.

κάμνω (r. καμ-, transp. κμα-), *to labor, to be weary*, F. καμοῦμαι, 2 A. ἔκαμον, Pf. κέκμηκα.

C. VERBS IN -μι.

[For the paradigms, see ¶¶ 48-57.]

§ **224.** I. Before the *nude affixes*, the CHARACTERISTIC SHORT VOWEL (§§ 183, 208. 2) is *lengthened* (ᾰ becoming η, unless preceded by ρ, § 29; and ι, ει),

1.) In the *Indicative singular* of the PRESENT and IMPERFECT ACTIVE.

Thus, ἵστημι (¶ 48; r. στᾰ-), ἵστην· τίθημι (¶ 50; r. θε-), ἐτίθην· δίδωμι (¶ 51; r. δο-), ἐδίδων· δείκνῡμι (¶ 52; r. δεικ-, δεικνῠ-), ἐδείκνῡν· εἶμι (¶ 56; r. ἰ-), εἶ, εἶσι.

2.) In the SECOND AORIST ACTIVE throughout, except before ντ (§ 183).

Thus, ἔστην, ἔστημεν, στῆθι, στήτωσαν, στῆναι· στάντων, (στά-ντς) στάς· ἀπέδρᾱν (¶ 57; r. δρᾰ-), ἀποδρᾶναι· ἔγνων (¶ 57; r. γνο-), ἔγνωμεν, ἔγνωτον, γνῶθι, γνῶναι· γνόντων, (γνόντς) γνούς.

EXCEPTION. The short vowel *remains*, in the 2 Aor. of τίθημι, δίδωμι, and ἵημι, except in the Inf., where it is changed into its corresponding diphthong (§ 29); thus, ἔθεμεν, θές, θεῖναι, (θέ-ντς) θείς· ἔδομεν, δός, δοῦναι, (δό-ντς) δούς· εἷμεν (¶ 54; r. ἑ-; for the augment, see § 189. 3), ἕς, εἷναι, (ἕ-ντς) εἵς (for the Sing. of these Aorists, see § 201. 3). Except, also, the poet. ἔκτᾰν and οὖτᾰν.

3.) In a few MIDDLE forms, mostly *poetic*.

Thus, δίζημαι (r. διζε-), *to seek*; ὀνίνημι, *to profit*, 2 A. M. ὠνήμην, and later ὠνάμην· πίμπλημι, *to fill*, 2 A. M. poet ἐπλήμην.

§ **225.** II. If the characteristic is ε, ο, or υ, the *singular* of the IMPERFECT ACTIVE is commonly formed with the *connecting vowel* (§ 185. β); thus, ἐτίθεον, contr. ἐτίθουν, ἐτίθεες ἐτίθεις, ἐτίθεε ἐτίθει · ἐδίδοον ἐδίδουν · ἐδείκνυον (¶¶ 50–52).

REMARK. In like manner, the *regular* affixes sometimes take the place of the *nude*, in other forms, particularly in *verbs in -υμι*, which may be regarded as having a second but less Attic theme in -ύω (§ 185. α); thus, δείκνῡμι and δεικνύω, δείκνῡσι and δεικνύει, ἐδείκνυσαν and ἐδείκνυον, δεικνύς and δεικνύων.

§ **226.** III. SUBJUNCTIVE AND OPTATIVE. 1. In the Subj., verbs in -μι differ from other verbs only in the mode of contracting -αη and -οη (§§ 33, 37. 3); thus, ἱστά-ω ἱστῶ, ἱστά-ῃς ἱστῇς · ἱστά-ωμαι ἱστῶμαι, ἱστά-ῃ ἱστῇ · τιθέ-ω τιθῶ, τιθέ-ῃς τιθῇς · τιθέ-ωμαι τιθῶμαι, τιθέ-ῃ τιθῇ · διδό-ω διδῶ, διδό-ῃς διδῷς · διδό-ωμαι διδῶμαι, διδό-ῃ διδῷ · δεικνύ-ω, δεικνύ-ωμαι · ἴ-ω (¶ 56). If, however, ρ precede -αη, the contraction is into α; as, ἀποδρᾷς (¶ 57).

2. VERBS IN -ωμι have a second form of the Opt. act. in -ῴην, which is most frequent in late writers, but is not confined to them; as, ἁλῴη ξ. 183 (ἁλοίην X. 253), βιῴην Ar. Ran. 177 (the other form is not used in this word, perhaps to avoid confusion with the Att. Pres. opt., § 205. 2), βιῴη Pl. Gorg. 512 e.

3. In the Opt. mid., ει, if not in the *initial syllable*, is often changed before the flexible ending into οι, in imitation of *verbs in -ω*; thus, τιθοίμην, ἱοίμην (¶¶ 50, 54), and the compound forms, ἐπιθοίμην, συνθοίμην, i. 9. 7, προοίμην, Ib. 10. So even κρέμοισθε for κρέμαισθε, Ar. Vesp. 298; μαρνοίμεθα for μαρναίμεθα, λ. 513; and ἀφίοιτε for ἀφίειτε, Pl. Apol. 29 d.

4. In a few instances, verbs in -υμι, instead of inserting a connecting vowel in the Subj. and Opt., simply lengthen the υ (cf. § 177); as, διασκεδάννῡσι, διασκεδάννῡται for διασκεδαννύῃ, διασκεδαννύηται, Pl. Phædo, 77 b, d; πήγνῡτο for πηγνύοιτο, Ib. 118 a. Add the poet. ἐκδῦμεν Π. 99, φῦῃ Theoc. 15. 94, δαίνῡτο Ω. 665, δαινῦατο (for -ῡντο) σ. 248; and the similarly formed φθίμην κ. 51, φθῖτο λ. 330.

§ **227.** IV. SECOND AORIST. The 2 Aor. from a *pure root* retains the *primitive nude form*, whatever may be the form of the theme (§ 185. γ); as, ἔβην, ἀπέδρᾱν, ἔγνων, ἔδῡν (¶ 57).

NOTES. α. Except ἔπιον (cf. §§ 205, 208. 2, 3), which yet has the Imp. πῖθι.

β. A few roots are transposed, in order to admit the nude form; thus, σκέλλομαι, *to dry up*, 2 A. (r. σκαλ-, σκλα-) ἔσκλην, *Opt.* σκλαίην, *Inf.* σκλῆναι Ar. Vesp. 160.

γ. We add a list of nude 2 Aorists, which may not be hereafter mentioned: κλάω, *to break*, 2 A. Part. κλάς Anacr. Fr. 16; κλύω, *to hear*, poet., 2 A.

Imp. κλῦθι A. 37, Eur. Hipp. 872, κλῦτε B. 56, Æsch. Cho. 399, redupl. κέκλῦθι K. 284, κέκλυτε Γ. 86; λύω, *to loose*, 2 A. M. λύμην Φ. 80, λύτο 114, λύντο H. 16; φύω, *to produce*, 2 A. ἔφῦν, Cyr. ii. 1. 15, *Subj.* φύω, *Opt.* φύην (§ 226. 4), *Inf.* φῦναι, *Part.* φύς.

Remarks upon Particular Verbs.

Φημί, to say.

[¶ 53.]

§ **228.** (*a*) In certain connections, φημί, ἔφην, and ἔφη are shortened, for the sake of *vivacity*, to ἠμί, ἦν, and ἦ· thus, ἦν δ' ἐγώ, *said I*, Ar. Eq. 634; ἦ δ' ὅς, *said he*, Pl. Rep. 327 b, c; ἦ, *he spake*, A. 219; παῖ, ἠμί, παῖ, παῖ, *boy! I say, boy! boy!* Ar. Nub. 1145. (*b*) The 2 Pers. sing. of the Pres. ind. is commonly written φῄς, as if contracted from φαείς. For ἔφησθα, in the Imp., see § 182. (*c*) To the forms in the table, may be added the Ep. Pres. M. Pl. 2 φάσθε κ. 562, *Imp.* φάο π. 168, φάσθω υ. 100, φάσθε I. 422 (*Inf.* φάσθαι A. 187, Æsch. Pers. 700); Pf. P. S. 3 πέφαται Ap. Rh. 1. 988, *Part.* πεφασμένος, Ξ. 127.

Ἵημι, to send.

[¶ 54.]

§ **229.** (*a*) Many of the forms of this verb occur only in composition. (*b*) Of the contract forms ἱᾶσι and ἱεῖσι (for ἵε-νσι, ἱέασι, § 58), the former is preferred in the Attic, and the latter in the Ionic. (*c*) The Impf. form ἵειν, which occurs only in composition (προΐειν ι. 88, ἠφίειν Pl. Euthyd. 293 a), seems either to have come from ἵην (which is of doubtful occurrence) by *precession*, or to have been formed after the analogy of ἵεις, ἵει, or of the Plup. (*d*) For the Opt. forms ἱοίμην and οἵμην, the latter of which can be employed only in composition, see § 226. 3. (*e*) In the dialects, we find forms from the simpler themes ἵω and ἕω· thus, Impf. ξύνιον A. 273, Imp. ξύνιε Theog. 1240, Pf. P. Part. μεμετιμένος Hdt. v. 108 (§§ 69. α, 192. 3; cf. μεμέθεικα, Anacr. Fr. 78); Pr. ἀνίονται Hdt. ii. 165. In the S. S. we find ἤφιε Mk. 1. 34, ἀφεῖς Rev. 2. 20, Pf. P. ἀφέωνται Mt. 9. 2, 5.

Εἰμί, to be.

[¶ 55.]

§ **230.** In the Present and Imperfect of this verb, the radical syllable ἐ-,

1.) Before a *vowel*, unites with it; thus, (ἐ-νσι, ἐ-ᾶσι, § 58) εἰσί· (ἔ-ω) ὦ, (ἔ-ῃς) ᾖς· (ἐ-ίην) εἴην.

2.) Before ντ, becomes ο (cf. §§ 203, 206); thus, (ἔ-ντς, ὄ-ντς, § 109) ὤν, Imp. (ἔ-ντων) ὄντων (less used than the other forms, Pl. Leg. 879 b).

3.) In other cases, is *lengthened*, as follows.

α.) It becomes εἰ in the forms εἰμί, εἶς, εἶ, εἶναι (cf. §§ 218. β, 224. E). The form εἶ, both here and in ¶ 56, is either shortened from εἶς (which is not used by the Attics), or is a middle form employed in its stead.

β.) In the remaining forms of the Pres., it assumes σ (compare § 221);

thus, ἔ-σ-μέν, ἐ-σ-τέ, ἐ-σ-τόν, ἔ-σ-τω, ἔ-σ-τωσαν, ἔ-σ-των (§ 213. N.). After the σ, the τ in the 3d Pers. sing. is retained; thus, ἐ-σ-τί. Before the σ, ε in the 2d Pers. sing. of the Imperative becomes ἴ by precession (cf. § 118); thus, ἴ-σ-θι.

γ.) In the Impf. it becomes η, and may likewise assume σ before τ; thus, ἦν, ἦτε or rather ἦ-σ-τε. The *Old-Att. form* of the 1st Pers. ἦ (Ar. Av. 1363), and the 3d Pers. ἦν, appear to have been contracted from ἦα and ἦεν (cf. § 179, 201. N., 211. N.). For ἦσθα, see § 182. The *middle form* ἤμην is little used by the more classic writers (Cyr. vi. 1. 9). The Imp. ἤτω, which follows the analogy of the Impf., occurs but once in the classic writers (Pl. Rep. 361 c.), and is there doubtful.

Remarks. a. In the Fut., instead of ἔσεται, the Attics always use the *nude form* ἔσται.

b. Some regard the root of this verb as being ἐσ-, and adduce in support of this view, the Lat. *(esum) sum, es, est, (e)sumus, estis, (e)sunt,* and the Sanscrit *asmi, asi, asti,* &c.

Εἶμι, *to go.*

[¶ 56.]

§ **231.** (*a*) The Pres. of εἶμι has commonly in the Ind., and sometimes in the other modes, the sense of the Fut. (§ 200. b); thus, εἶμι, (*I am going*) *I will go.* (*b*) For ᾔειν, in the Plup., the common Attic form was ᾖα, which appears to be a remnant of the old formation noticed in § 203. N. A Perf. εἶα, corresponding to this Plup., nowhere appears, and some regard ᾔειν (omitting the ι subsc.) as an Impf. doubly augmented (§ 189). For the use of this tense, see § 233. (*c*) For ἴοιμι and ἰοίην, see § 205; for ἴτων, § 213. N.; for ἰέναι, ἰών, and ἰόντων, § 208. 2; for ᾔεισθα, § 182; for ᾔειν in the 3d Pers., § 211. N.; for ᾖμεν, ᾖτε, &c., § 237. (*d*) The *middle forms* ἴεμαι, ἰέμην are regarded by some of the best critics as incorrectly written for ἵεμαι, ἱέμην, from ἵημι (¶ 54).

Κεῖμαι, *to lie down.*

[¶ 60.]

§ **232.** (*a*) This verb appears to be contracted from κέεμαι, a deponent inflected like τίθεμαι (¶ 50); thus, κέεμαι κεῖμαι, κέενται κεῖνται, κέεσο κεῖσο, κέεσθαι κεῖσθαι, κεέμενος κείμενος · ἐκεέμην ἐκείμην · κεέσομαι κείσομαι. In the Subj. and Opt. the contraction is commonly omitted; thus, κέωμαι, Œc. 8. 19, κεοίμην, iv. 1. 16, like τιθῶμαι (also accented τίθωμαι) and τιθοίμην · yet κῆται (also written κεῖται), for κέηται, T. 32, β. 102. (*b*) The Subj. sometimes retains the form of the Ind. (§ 177); as, Subj. διάκειμαι Pl. Phædo, 84 e. (*c*) We find the following forms in the dialects, some of which have the shorter root κε-: Pres. S. 2 κεῖαι Hom. Merc. 254, S. 3 κέεται Hdt. vi. 139, Pl. 3 κέονται X. 510, κείαται Ω. 527, κέαται Λ. 659, Hdt. i. 14; Impf. Pl. 3 ἐκείατο Ap. Rh. 4. 1295, κείατο φ. 418, ἐκέατο Hdt. i. 167, κέατο N. 763; Fut. κεισεῦμαι Theoc. 3. 53 (§ 200. 3); old Pres. as Fut. (§ 200. b) κέω, η. 342, κείω τ. 340. (*d*) Some of the best grammarians regard κεῖμαι as a Perf. having the sense of the Pres. (§ 233).

D. Complete Tenses.

§ **233.** I. In some verbs, the sense of the complete

tenses, by a natural transition (see Syntax), passes into that of other tenses; and the PERFECT becomes, in signification, a *Present;* the PLUPERFECT, an *Imperfect*, or *Aorist;* and the FUTURE PERFECT, a common *Future.* Thus, ἵστημι (¶ 48), *to station*, Pf. ἕστηκα, (*I have stationed myself*) *I stand*, Plup. ἑστήκειν, *I stood*, F. Pf. ἑστήξω, *I shall stand;* μιμνήσκω, *to remind*, Pf. P. μέμνημαι, (*I have been reminded*) *I remember*, Plup. ἐμεμνήμην, *I remembered*, F. Pf. μεμνήσομαι, *I shall remember;* Plup. ᾔειν (¶ 56), *I went.*

REMARK. In a few of these verbs, the Pres. is not used, and the PERF. is regarded as the *theme.* Such verbs, as having a preterite tense for the theme, are termed PRETERITIVE. See ¶¶ *58, 59.*

§ **234.** II. MODES. 1. The PERFECT SUBJUNCTIVE and OPTATIVE are commonly *supplied* by the *Participle* with the *auxiliary verb* εἰμί (¶ 55, § 169. β); thus, Pf. Act. *Subj.* βεβουλευκώς ὦ, *Opt.* βεβουλευκώς εἴην· Pf. P. *Subj.* βεβουλευμένος ὦ, *Opt.* βεβουλευμένος εἴην.

REMARKS. α. Sometimes, however, the Perf. *forms* these modes according to the general rules (§ § 204, 205, &c.), chiefly when it is employed as a *Pres.;* as, ἑστήκω, vi. 5, 10, ἑστῶ, Pl. Gorg. 468 b, ἑσταίην, Ψ. 101 (¶ 48), πεποιθοίην (§ 205. α), δεδίω (¶ 58), Rep. Ath. 1. 11; εἰλήφωσιν Pl. Pol. 269 c, πεπτώκοι v. 7. 26, βεβλήκοιεν Th. ii. 48, πεποιήκοι Id. viii. 108.

β. In the *Perf. pass.*, these modes are formed in only a *few pure verbs*, and in these without a fixed analogy; thus,

καλέω, *to call;* Pf. P. κέκλημαι, *I have been called, I am named, Opt.* (κεκλη-ί-μην) κεκλῄμην, κέκλῃο Soph. Ph. 119, κέκλῃτο, &c.

κτάομαι, *to acquire;* Pf. κέκτημαι, *I have acquired, I possess, Subj.* (κεκτά-ω-μαι) κεκτῶμαι, κεκτῇ, κεκτῆται Symp. 1. 8; *Opt.* (κεκτη-ί-μην) κεκτῄμην, κέκτῃο, κέκτῃτο Pl. Leg. 731 c, or (κεκτα-οί-μην) κεκτῴμην, κεκτῷο, κεκτῷτο Ages. 9. 7.

μέμνημαι (§ 233), *Subj.* μεμνῶμαι, Pl. Phil. 31 a, *Opt.* μεμνῄμην Ω. 745, μεμνῆτο Ar. Plut. 991, or μεμνῴμην, μεμνῷο (or μέμνοιο) i. 7. 5, μεμνῷτο Cyr. i. 6. 3.

For κάθημαι, see ¶ 59. Add *Subj.* βεβλῆσθε Andoc. 22. 41, τετμῆσθον Pl. Rep. 564 c; *Opt.* λελῦτο σ. 238 (cf. § 226. 4).

§ **235.** 2. The Perfect, in its *proper sense*, may have the IMPERATIVE in the *3d Pers. pass.;* but, otherwise, this mode belongs only to those Perfects which have the *sense of the Pres.;* and, even in these, the *Imperative active* is scarcely found except in the *nude form* of the *2d Perf.* (§§ 237, 238); yet ἄνωγε, κεκράγετε (§ 238. β), γέγωνε Eur. Or. 1220, βεβηκέτω Luc. de Hist. Scrib. 45, ἐοικέτω Ib. 49.

§ **236.** III. VOWEL CHANGES. The affixes in -α, -ειν of

the SECOND PERFECT and PLUPERFECT are annexed with the following changes in the preceding syllable.

1.) ε becomes ο, and ει becomes οι; as, *μένω*, *to remain*, 2 Pf. *μέμονα*· *δέρκομαι*, *to see*, poet., *δέδορκα*· *λείπω*, *λέλοιπα* (¶ 37); *πείθω*, *πέποιθα* (¶ 39).

NOTES. (*a*) The same changes take place in the 1st Perf. and Plup. of a few verbs; as, *κλέπτω*, *to steal*, *κέκλοφα*· *τρέπω*, *to turn*, *τέτροφα*· *πέμπω*, *to send*, *πέπομφα*· *δέδοικα* (¶ 58). (*b*) Analogous to the change of ε into ο, is that of η into ω in *ῥήγνῡμι*, *to break*, 2 Pf. *ἔῤῥωγα*. (c) In the following Perfects, there appears to be an insertion of ο or ω (§ 222. β): *ἄγω*, *to lead*, *ἀγήοχα* (§ 191. 2), Dem. 239. 1, *ἐσθίω*, *to eat*, *ἐδήδοκα*, iv. 8. 20 (Ep. Pf. P. *ἐδήδομαι*, *χ*. 56), *εἴωθα* (r. *ἐθ*-), *to be wont*, preteritive, *οἴχωκα* (§ 221. 3). (*d*) In the following dialectic forms, the change or insertion of vowels has extended to the *passive*: *ἀφέωνται* (§ 229. *e*); *ἄωρτο* *γ*. 272, Theoc. 24. 43, for *ἤερτο* or *ἦρτο*, Plup. S. 3 of *ἀείρω* or *αἴρω*, *to raise*; *ἐπώχατο* M. 340, Plup. Pl. 3 of *ἐπέχω*· *ἐδήδομαι* (N. *c*).

2.) Short α, ι, or υ, before a *single consonant*, is *lengthened* (α, not preceded by ε or ρ, § 29, becoming η); as, *φαίνω*, *πέφηνα* (¶ 42; r. *φᾰν*-); *θάλλω*, *to bloom*, *τέθηλα*· *ἄγνῡμι* (r. *ἀγ*-), *to break*, *ἔᾱγα*· *κράζω*, *κέκρᾱγα* (§ 238. β); *κέκρῑγα* (r. *κρῐγ*-), *to creak*, pret.; *μῡκάομαι* (r. *μῠκ*-), *to bellow*, *μέμῡκα*.

EXCEPTIONS. After the Attic reduplication, the short vowel remains; as, *ἐλήλυθα* (§ 191. 2). In *λάσκω* (r. *λᾰκ*-), *to sound*, α is not changed into η in the Att.; thus, 2 Pf. *λέλᾱκα*, Ar. Ach. 410 (*λέληκα*, X. 141).

§ **237.** IV. NUDE FORMS. In the SECOND PERFECT and PLUPERFECT, the connecting vowel is sometimes omitted in the *Indicative plural* and *dual* (§ 186). When this omission takes place, (*a*) the Ind. sing. is commonly *supplied* by forms from a *longer base* (cf. § 201. N.); which forms likewise occur in the *plural* and *dual*, but less frequently; (*b*) the Subj., Opt., Imp., and Inf. are formed after the analogy of *verbs in -μι*; (*c*) the Part. is *contracted*, if the characteristic is α or ο. Thus,

Pf. Ind. *Sing.* *ἕστηκα* (¶ 48; r. *στα*-, base *ἑστα*-, prolonged to *ἑστηκ*-, § 186), *ἕστηκας*, *ἕστηκε*, *Pl.* *ἕστᾰ-μεν* Pl. Gorg. 468 b, and rarely *ἑστήκαμεν*, *ἕστᾰ-τε*, (*ἕστα-ντι*, *ἑστά-ασι*, § 58) *ἑστᾶσι* (*ἑστήκασι* Δ. 434); Subj. (*ἑστά-ω*) *ἑστῶ* and *ἑστήκω*· Opt. *ἑσταίην* (poet.); Imp. *ἕστᾰ-θι* (poet.) Ar. Av. 206; Inf. *ἑστάναι* iv. 7. 9; Part. Ep. *ἑστᾰ-ώς*, *-ότος* T. 79 (also *ἑστηώς* Hes. Th. 519), commonly contr. *ἑστώς* (¶ 22. 8) i. 3. 2, (*ἑστα-ό-τσα*) *ἑστῶσα*, (*ἑστα-ό-ς*) *ἑστώς* and sometimes, by syncope, *ἑστός* Pl. Parm. 146 a, Ion. *ἑστεώς* (§ 48. 1), *-ῶτος* Hdt. ii. 38; also *ἑστηκώς* Pl. Meno, 93 d. Plup. *Sing.* *ἑστήκειν* or *εἱστήκειν*, *-εις*, *-ει*, *Pl.* *ἕστᾰ-μεν*, *ἕστᾰ-τε*, *ἕστᾰ-σαν* i. 5. 13 (*ἑστήκεσαν* Cyr. viii. 3. 9).

Θνήσκω, *to die* (r. *θαν*-, *θνα*-, § 64), Pf. Ind. *Sing.* *τέθνηκα* (base *τεθνα*-, *τεθνηκ*-), *-ας*, *-ε*, *Pl.* *τέθναμεν* Pl. Gorg. 492 e, *τέθνατε*, *τεθνᾶσι* iv. 2. 17, *Du.* *τέθνατον* iv. 1. 19; Subj. *τεθνήκω*, Th. viii. 74; Opt. *τεθναίην*, Cyr. iv. 2. 3;

Imp. τέθναθι X. 365, τεθνάτω Pl. Leg. 933 e, &c.; Inf. τεθνᾰ́ναι Mem. i. 2. 16, τεθνηκέναι Soph. Aj. 474, and Poet. (τεθνα-έ-ναι) τεθνᾶναι Æsch. Ag. 539, Part. τεθνηκώς (fem. δ. 734), τεθνᾰ-ώς, Pind. Nem. 10. 139, commonly contr., with ε inserted (cf. §§ 35, 48. 1), τεθνεώς, -ῶσα, -ώς or -ός, vii. 4. 19, τ. 331, Ep. τεθνηώς or τεθνειώς, -ότος or -ῶτος, α. 289, P. 435. Plup. *Sing.* ἐτεθνήκειν, -εις, -ει, *Pl.* ἐτέθναμεν, -τε, -σαν H. Gr. vi. 4. 16.

Pf. Ind. *Sing.* δέδοικα Cyr. i. 4. 12, and δέδια Soph. Œd. C. 1469 (¶ 58, base δεδι-, δεδοικ-), δέδοικας and δέδιας, δέδοικε and δέδιε· *Pl.* δέδιμεν Th. iii. 53, δέδιτε, (δέδινσι, § 58) δεδίᾱσι Pl. Apol. 29 a; Subj. δεδίω· Imp. δέδιθι Ar. Vesp. 373; Inf. δεδιέναι (§ 208. 3) Rep. Ath. 1. 11, and δεδοικέναι Eur. Sup. 548; Part. δεδιώς Pl. Prot. 320 a (contr. or sync. δειδυῖαν Ap. Rh. 3. 753), and δεδοικώς Eur. Ion, 624. Plup. *Sing.* ἐδεδοίκειν Pl. Charm. 175 a, and ἐδεδίειν, -εις, -ει· *Pl.* ἐδέδιμεν, ἐδέδιτε, ἐδέδισαν Pl. Leg. 685 c (ἐδεδοίκεσαν iii. 5. 18).

Pf. Ind. *Sing.* οἶδα (¶ 58; base ἰδ-, οἰδ-), οἶσθα (for οἶδ-σθα, § 182; οἶδας scarce occurs in the Att., yet Eur. Alc. 780; the Att. poets, by a mingling of forms, sometimes use οἶσθας Eur. Ion, 999), οἶδε· *Pl.* (ἴδ-μεν, § 53) ἴσμεν ii. 4. 6, (ἴδ-τε, § 52) ἴστε, (ἴδ-νσι, the δ becoming σ in imitation of the other persons) ἴσᾱσι, and rarely οἴδαμεν Pl. Alc. 141 e, οἴδατε, οἴδᾱσι· Imp. (ἴδ-θι) ἴσθι ii. 1. 13. Plup. *Sing.* ᾔδειν, *Pl.* ᾔδειμεν, &c., and poet. (ᾖδ-μεν) ᾖσμεν Eur. Hec. 1112, (ᾖδ-τε) ᾖστε, (ᾖδ-σαν) ᾖσαν Æsch. Prom. 451.

Plup. *Sing.* ᾔειν (¶ 56), ᾔεις, ᾔει, *Pl.* ᾔειμεν, -τε, commonly ᾖμεν Pl. Rep. 328 b, ᾖτε vii. 7. 6, ᾔεσαν Cyr. iv. 5. 55, sometimes Ion. ᾖσαν τ. 445, Hdt. ii. 163.

§ 238. In the following examples, the nude forms are chiefly poetic, and, in part, Epic only.

α. PURE. *ἀριστάω, to dine;* Pf. *Pl.* 1 ἠρίστᾰμεν Ar. Fr. 428, Inf. ἠριστᾰ́ναι Ath. 423 a. In imitation of these comic forms, we find also, from δειπνέω, *to sup*, δεδείπνᾰμεν and δεδειπνᾰ́ναι Ath. 422 e, Ar. Fr. 243.

βαίνω, to go; Pf. βέβηκα (r. βα-), 2 Pf. *Pl.* poet. βέβαμεν, βέβατε, βεβάᾱσι B. 134, βεβᾶσιν Soph. El. 1386; Subj. *Pl.* 3 βεβῶσι Pl. Phædr. 252 e; Inf. βεβάναι Eur. Heracl. 610, Hdt. iii. 146, Part. Ep. βεβαώς, -υῖα, -ῶτος, E. 199, Ω. 81, Att. contr. βεβώς, -ῶσα, -ῶτος, Soph. Ant. 67, 996, Œd. C. 314, H. Gr. vii. 2. 3, Pl. Phædr. 254 b. 2 Plup. *Pl.* ἐβέβαμεν, -ατε, -ασαν B. 720.

βιβρώσκω, to eat; 1 Pf. βέβρωκα (r. βρο-), 2 Pf. Part. (βεβρο-ώς) βεβρώς, -ῶτος, Soph. Ant. 1022.

γίγνομαι (r. *γα-, γεν-, γιγν-*), *to become;* 2 Pf. γέγονα, poet. *Pl.* 2 γεγάᾱτε (Ep. for γέγᾰτε) Hom. Batr. 143, 3 γεγᾰ́ᾱσιν Δ. 41; Inf. γεγάμεν (Ep. for γεγάναι) E. 248; Part. Ep. γεγαώς, -υῖα, -ῶτος, Γ. 199, I. 456, Att. contr. γεγώς, -ῶσα, -ῶτος, Eur. Alc. 532, 677. Plup. *Du.* 3 γεγάτην κ. 138

μέμονα (r. *μα-, μεν-*, § 236. 1), *to be eager*, pret., E. 482, μέμονας Æsch. Sept. 686, μέμονε Soph. Tr. 982, *Pl.* μέμαμεν I. 641, μέματε H. 160, μεμάᾱσι K. 208, *Du.* μέματον Θ. 413; Imp. S. 3 μεμάτω Δ. 304; Part. μεμᾰώς, -υῖα, -ῶτος, Δ. 40, 440, Θ. 118, and μεμᾱώς, -ότος, Π. 754, B. 818. Plup. *Pl.* 3 μέμασαν B. 863.

πίπτω, to fall; 1 Pf. πέπτωκα (r. πτε-, πτο-); 2 Pf. Part. Ep. πεπτεώς, -ῶτος, Φ. 503, and πεπτηώς, -υῖα, -ότος and -ῶτος, ν. 98, Ap. Rh. 2. 832, Att. contr. πεπτώς, -ῶτος, Soph. Ant. 697, 1018.

τέτληκα (r. *τλα-*), *to bear*, pret., *Pl.* τέτλαμεν υ. 311; Imp. τέτλαθι A.

586 ; Inf. *τετλάμεν* (Ep. for *τετλάναι*) *γ*. 209; Part. *τετληώς*, *-υῖα*, *-ότος*, *υ*. 23, E. 873.

β. IMPURE. In the nude forms of the first four verbs mentioned below, *τ* passes into *ϑ*, after the analogy either of the 2d Pers. sing., or of the *objective* inflection.

ἄνωγα, *to command*, poet. preteritive, *Pl.* *ἄνωγμεν* Hom. Ap. 528 ; Imp. *ἄνωγε* Eur. Or. 119, and *ἄνωχθι* Id. Alc. 1044, *ἀνωγέτω* *β*. 195, and (*ἀνώγτω*) *ἀνώχθω* Λ. 189, *Pl.* *ἀνώγετε* *ψ*. 132, *ἄνωχθε* Eur. Herc. 241.

κράζω, commonly 2 Pf. *κέκρᾱγα*, *to cry*; Imp. *κέκραχθι* Ar. Vesp. 198, *Pl.* *κεκράγετε* Ib. 415, and *κέκραχθε* Ar. Ach. 335.

ἐγείρω, *to rouse*; 2 Pf. *ἐγρήγορα* · Imp. *Pl.* 2 *ἐγρήγορθε* Σ. 299 ; Inf. *ἐγρηγόρθαι* (as if from *ἐγρήγορμαι*) K. 67.

πάσχω, *to suffer*; 2 Pf. *πέπονθα*, *Pl.* 2 (*πέπονθτε*, *πέπονστε*, § 52, *πέποσστε*, § 55) *πέποσθε* Γ. 99, *κ*. 465.

ἔοικα, *to be like*, pret. (base *εἰκ-*, *ἐοικ-*, §§ 191. 3, 236. 1), *Pl.* trag. *ἔοιγμεν* Soph. Aj. 1239, *Du.* Ep. *ἔϊκτον* *δ*. 27, Plup. *ἐΐκτην* A. 104.

ἔρχομαι, *to come*; 2 Pf. *ἐλήλυθα*, Ep. *Pl.* 1 *εἰλήλουθμεν* (§ 47. N.) *γ*. 81.

πέποιθα, *to trust* (¶ 39 ; base *πεπιθ-*, *πεπειθ-*, *πεποιθ-*, § 236. 1); Imp. trag. *πέπεισθι* Æsch. Eum. 599 ; Plup. Ep. *Pl.* 1 *ἐπέπιθμεν* B. 341.

§ **239.** V. FUTURE PERFECT, OR THIRD FUTURE. The Fut. Perf. unites the *base* of the Perf. with the *affixes* of the Fut. act. and mid. ; as, (ἑστήκ-σω, ¶ 48) ἑστήξω, (γεγράφ-σομαι, ¶ 36) γεγράψομαι.

REMARKS. 1. The Fut. Perf. is scarcely found in *liquid* verbs, or in verbs *beginning with a vowel* (*πεφύρσεσθαι* Pind. Nem. 1. 104, *εἰρήσομαι*, ¶ 53, Cyr. vii. 1. 9), and is frequent in those verbs only in which it has the *sense* of the common *future* (§ 233).

2. (*a*) Of the Fut. Perf. act., the only examples in Attic prose are *ἑστήξω* and *τεθνήξω*, both formed from Perfects having the sense of the Pres., *ἕστηκα* and *τέθνηκα* (§§ 233, 237), and both giving rise to *middle* forms of the same signification (§ 166. 2), *ἑστήξομαι* and *τεθνήξομαι*. (*b*) Other examples of a reduplicated Fut. in the active voice are *τετορήσω* Ar. Pax, 381, and the Ep. *ἀκαχήσω*, Hom. Merc. 286, *κεκαδήσω*, *φ*. 153, *πεπιθήσω* X. 223, *κεχαρήσω*, O. 98 (also *κεχαρήσομαι*, *ψ*. 266), all from verbs which have reduplicated 2 Aorists (§ 194. 3). (*c*) Other examples of the Fut. Perf. *mid.* with the Perf. *act.*, are *κέκλαγγα*, *κεκλάγξομαι* Ar. Vesp. 930, *κέκρᾱγα*, *κεκράξομαι* Ar. Ran. 265, *κέκηδα*, *κεκαδήσομαι*, Θ. 353. (*d*) An example of a reduplicated Fut. mid. with a reduplicated 2 Aor. is *πεφιδήσομαι*, O. 215.

§ **240.** VI. The student will observe, in respect to the complete tenses, the following particulars, which are far more striking in the Act. than in the Pass. voice (§ 256) ; 1. their *defective formation ;* 2. the *entire want of these tenses* in many verbs ; 3. the *comparative infrequency* of their use ; and 4. their more frequent occurrence in the *later* than in the *earlier* writers.

DIALECTIC FORMS.

A. CONTRACTION.

§ **241.** Forms which are *contracted* in the Att. (and which are also commonly contracted in the Dor., but often with a different vowel of contraction) more frequently remain *uncontracted* in Ion. prose, while the Ep. has great freedom in the employment of either *uncontracted, contracted,* or *variously protracted* forms. Here belong, Contract Verbs in -άω, -έω, and -όω (§ 216), the Liquid, Att., and Dor. Fut. (§ 200), the Aor. Pass. Subj. (§ 199), the Subj. of Verbs in -μι (§ 226), and the 2d Pers. Sing. in -αι and -ο (§ 210 3). In these forms, the first vowel is either (I.) α, (II.) ε or η, or (III.) ο. Of these, ε or η is far the most frequently uncontracted.

§ **242.** I. *The first vowel* α. (a.) In the Ion., the α is commonly contracted or changed into ε (§ 44. 2); and when α with an *O* vowel is contracted into ω, ε is often inserted (§ 48. 1, cf. § 35). Thus we find, as various readings, ὁρῶντες, ὁρέοντες, and ὁρέωντες, Hdt. i. 82, 99. So ἐωρῶμεν i. 120, ὡρέομεν ii. 131, χρᾶσθαι vii. 141, χρῆσθαι (§ 33. α) i. 47, χρέεσθαι 157, ἐχρέωντο 53, χρέω (for χράου) 155, ἐμηχανέατο (for ἐμηχανάοντο, one ε dropped; see §§ 243. 2, 248, *f*) v. 63; Subj. of Verbs in -μι, δυνεώμεθα iv. 97, 2 Aor. κτέομεν or κτέωμεν χ. 216, for κτάωμεν, contr. κτῶμεν (see also b. below).

NOTE. In the 2 Pers., the termination -αο commonly remains; as, ἐχρήσαο Hdt. i. 117, ἐπίσταο vii. 209.

(b.) In the Ep., protracted forms are made by doubling the vowel of contraction, either in whole, or in part (i. e. by inserting one of its elements, or its corresponding short vowel, commonly ο with ω, and ᾰ with ᾱ, § 48); and sometimes by prolonging a short vowel, particularly ε used for α to ει; as, ὁράω, contr. ὁρῶ Γ. 234, protracted ὁρόω Ε. 244, ὁράεις ὁρᾷς Λ. 202, ὁράᾳς Η. 448, ὁράων ὁρῶν Ε. 872, ὁρόων Α. 350, ὁρόωσαι Δ. 9, ὁρᾶσθαι λ. 156, ὁράασθαι π. 107, ὁρόωτε Δ. 347, ἀντιόωσαν Α. 31, ἀσχαλάᾳ Β. 293, ἀσχαλάᾳν 297, ἐμνώοντο 686, γελόωντες σ. 40, γελώοντες 111, ἀλόω (Imp. for ἀλάου, -ω) ε. 377; μνάασθαι α. 39, μενοινώω Ν. 79 (μενοίνεον Μ. 59), δρώωσι ο. 324; δρώοιμι 317, ἡβώοιμι Η. 157 (ἡβῷμι 133), (μνάεο, μνάου, μνῶ) μνώεο Ap. Rh. 1. 896, ναιεταώσῃ Γ. 387; μενοινήῃσι Ο. 82, for μενοινάῃ, κέραιε Ι. 203, for κέραε· Att. Fut. ἐλόωσι Ν. 315, η. 319, ἐλάᾳν ε. 290 (see § 200. 2); κρεμόω Η. 83: 2 Aor. Subj. of Verbs in -μι, στήῃς Ρ. 30, στήῃ Ε. 598, στείομεν Ο. 297 (στέωμεν Λ. 348), στήωσι Ρ. 95, στήετον σ. 183; βείω Ζ. 113, for βῶ (¶ 57), βήῃ Ι. 501, βείομεν Κ. 97 (βέωμεν Hdt. vii. 50. 2).

NOTES. 1. α is not prefixed, when the flexible ending begins with τ; as in ὁρᾶ-τε, ὁρᾶ-ται. Yet ἄᾰται Hes. Sc. 101, for ᾶται (ᾱ being resolved into ᾰᾰ, § 29).

2. We also find in Ion. prose, in imitation of the Ep., κομόωσι Hdt. iv. 191, ἠγορόωντο vi. 11. So Dor. κομόωντι Theoc. 4. 57.

(c.) The Dor. sometimes contracts α with an *O* sound following into ᾱ; and commonly α with an *E* sound following into η (§ 45. 1, 4); as, πεινᾶντι Theoc. 15, 148, διαπεινᾶμες Ar. Ach. 751; 1 Aor. *Sing.* 2 ἐπάξᾱ Theoc. 4. 28, for ἐπήξαο, -ω, ἧρᾱ Ar. Ach. 913; τολμῆς Theoc. 5. 35, λῆς 64, ὁρῆτε 110, σιγῆν Ar. Ach. 778, ἐρώτη 800. The latter contraction appears in some Ion. prose-writers (as Hipp.; so θυμιῆται Hdt. iv. 75); and in the Ep. ὁρῆαι ξ.

343 (written by some ὄρηαι, as if from ὄρημι), and in the Du. forms, προσαυδήτην Λ. 136, συλήτην Ν. 202, συναντήτην π. 333, φοιτήτην Μ. 266.

§ **243.** II. *The first vowel* ε *or* η. (a.) In Ion. prose, contraction is commonly omitted, except as εο and εου often become ευ; as, ποιέω Hdt. i. 38, ποιέεις 39, ἐποίεε 22, ποιεόμενος 73, ποιεύμενος 68, ποιεῦσι 131, ποιεῦμαι, ἀξιεύμενος ix. 11; Fut. σημανέω Ib. i. 75, κερδανέεις 35, ἐρέων 5; Aor. Subj ἀπαιρεθέω Ib. iii. 65, φανέωσι i. 41, θέωσι iv. 71 (see § 226. 1); 2 Pers. βούλεαι, τεύξεαι Ib. i. 90, ἐγένεο 35, ἔθευ vii. 209.

NOTES. 1. In like manner, εο, used for αο (§ 242. a), may become υ; as, εἰρώτευν Hdt. iii. 140, εἰρωτεῦντας 62 (εἰρωτέωντος v. 13). So in the Dor., ἠρώτευν Theoc. i. 81, γελεῦντι 90, for γελάουσι, &c.

2. If εε is followed by another distinct vowel, one ε is often dropped; as, φοβέαι, φοβέο Hdt. vii. 52 (φοβεῦ i. 9), for φοβέεαι, φοβέεο. So Ep. ἐκλέο Ω. 202, πωλέο or πωλέαι δ. 811. A similar omission of ο appears in ἀνακοινέο Theog. 73.

3. After the analogy of the contract Pres., the Ion. extends the 2 Aor. Inf. in -εῖν, as if formed by contraction, to -έειν; as, ἰδέειν, παθέειν Hdt. i. 32, φυγέειν I, B. 393 (φυγεῖν 401), πιέειν Δ. 363.

4. The Ion. often renders impure verbs pure, by the insertion of its favorite ε (§ 48. 1); as, συμβαλλεόμενος (cf. συνεβάλλετο) Hdt. i. 68, ἐνειχεε 118, ἀγεόμενον iii. 14, ἐνδυνέουσι 98.

(b.) The Ep. commonly omits contraction if the last vowel is ω, ῳ, οι, or ου (except in the Aor. pass. subj., and in the Perf. subj. εἰδῶ); but otherwise employs or omits it according to the metre (εο, when contracted, becoming ευ; yet ἐπόρθουν Δ. 308, ἀνεῤῥίπτουν ν. 78). Synizesis is frequent when ε precedes a long O vowel, and sometimes occurs in εον, and even in εαι. The Ep., also, often protracts ε to ει, and sometimes doubles the vowel of contraction η. Thus, φιλέοι ο. 305 (yet φιλοίη δ. 692, and φορoίη ι. 320), φιλέωμεν θ. 42, οἰκέοιτο Δ. 18, πειρηθῶμεν Χ. 381, εἰδῶ Α. 515, εἰδέω π. 236; φιλεῖ Β. 197, φιλέει Ι. 342, ἔῤῥει Ρ. 86, ἔῤῥεε Ν. 539, ἔσῃ τ. 254, ἔσεαι Α. 563, ἔσσεαι Σ. 95, ἔσσεαι ζ. 33, γνώσεαι Β. 367, γνώσῃ 365; μυθεῖαι θ. 180 (μυθέαι or μυθέῃ β. 202, § 243. a. 2), νεῖαι λ. 114, for μυθέεαι, νέεαι· ἔπλεο Χ. 281, ἔπλευ Ψ. 69, φράζεο Ε. 440, φράζευ δ. 395, κάλεον Δ. 477, κάλεον θ. 550, καλεῦντο Β. 684; νεικείω Δ. 359, ἐτελείετο Α. 5, ἐρείομεν 62, ἔρειο Λ. 611, σπεῖο Κ. 285; Aor. Pass. Subj. δαμείω σ. 54, δαμείῃς Γ. 436, δαμήῃ Χ. 246, δαμείετε Π. 72; 2 Aor. Subj. of Verbs in -μι, θείω Π. 83 (θέω Hdt. i. 108), θείῃς κ. 341, θείῃ 301, ἀνήῃ Β. 34, θέωμεν ω. 485, θείομεν Α. 143, θείομαι Σ. 409.

(c.) For the Dor. contraction of εο and εου into ευ, and, in the stricter Dor., of εε into η, see §§ 45. 3, 44. 4; e. g. ἐλέγευ Theoc. 1. 86, μάχευ 113, ὡμάρτευν 2. 73, εὖσα 76; ποίη Ar. Lys. 1318. So, in Hom., ὁμαρτήτην Ν. 584, ἀπειλήτην λ. 313.

REMARKS. α. Some varieties of the Dor. change εο into ιο or ιω, and εω into ιω; as, μογίομες Ar. Lys. 1002, ὁμιώμεθα 183, ἐπαινίω 198, for μογέομεν, -οῦμεν, ὁμούμεθα, ἐπαινῶ.

β. The later Dor., from the influence of analogy (§§ 44. 1, 248. d), has sometimes α for η, in verbs in -έω; as, φιλᾶσῶ Theoc. 3. 19, δᾶσας 5. 118 So. Aor. Pass. ἐτύπᾶν Id. 4. 53.

§ **244.** III. *The first vowel ο.* (a.) Here the Ion. and Dor. usually employ contraction, following the common rules, except that the Ion. sometimes uses ευ for ου, and the Dor. ω and ῳ for ου and οι (§§ 44. 4, 45. 3); as, δικαιεῦσι Hdt. i. 133, ἐδικαίευν vi. 15, οἰκειεῦνται i. 4, στεφανεῦνται viii. 59; ὑπνῶν Ar. Lys. 143, μαστιγῶν Epich. 19 (1). The Dor. ω is likewise used by other dialects in ῥιγόω, *to be cold*, and in the Ion. ἱδρόω, *to sweat*; as, ῥιγῶν Ar. Vesp. 446 (ῥιγοῦν Cyr. v. 1. 11), ῥιγῷ Pl. Gorg. 517 d; ἱδρῶσαι Λ. 598.

(b.) The Ep. sometimes protracts the ο to ω, and sometimes employs the combination οω after the analogy of verbs in -άω; as, ἱδρώοντα Σ. 372, ἱδρώουσα Λ. 119, ὑπνώοντας ε. 48; ἀρόωσιν ι. 108, δηϊόωντο Ν. 675, δηϊόῳεν δ. 226; 2 Aor. Subj. of Verbs in -μι, γνώω ξ. 118, ἁλώω Λ. 405, δώῃ μ. 216, δώῃσιν Α. 324 (δῷσι 129), δώομεν Η. 299 (δῶμεν Ψ. 537), δώωσιν Α. 137.

B. Tense-Signs.

§ **245.** 1. In verbs in -ζω, the Dor. commonly employs ξ for σ, in the Fut. and Aor.; as, καθίξας Theoc. 1. 12, for καθίσας from καθίζω, χαρίξῃ 5. 71, ἐκόμιξαν Pind. N. 2. 31. This change appears also in a few other verbs in which short α precedes; as, γελάξας Theoc. 7. 42, ἔφθαξα 2. 115, from γελάω (§ 219. α), φθάνω (§ 278). Similar forms sometimes occur in other poets besides the Dor., for the sake of the metre; as, σφετεριξάμενον Æsch. Sup. 39, ἡλιάξει Ar. Lys. 380, ἐκφλύξαι (φλύω) Ap. Rh. 1. 275.

2. In the Fut. act. and mid., the Dor. commonly adds to the tense-sign ε, which is then contracted with the connecting vowel; as, (ᾀσέω) ᾀσῶ Theoc. 1. 145, (ᾀσέομαι, § 45. 3) ᾀσεῦμαι 3. 38, ποησεῖς 3. 9, ἀξῇ 1. 11, πεμψεῖ 6. 31, δεξεῖται Call. Lav. 116, γρυλλιξεῖτε Ar. Ach. 746, πειρασεῖσθε 743, for ᾄσω, ᾄσομαι, &c. See § 200. 3.

3. The Ep. employs the Att. Fut. (§ 200. 2), both *uncontracted*, *contracted*, and *protracted;* and has also other examples of the Fut. with σ dropped (or of the Pres. used as Fut.); as, ἀνύω Λ. 365, ἐρύουσι 454, χεύω β. 222. So ἐκγεγάονται (from Pf. base γεγα-, see §§ 238. α, 239. c) Hom. Ven. 198.

4. The formation of the 1 Aor. without σ is extended, (*a*) in the Ion. and poet. language, to a very few liquids, in which the characteristic is preceded by a diphthong (cf. § 222. 2), or by another consonant; thus, ἀπούρας Α. 356, ἀπηύρω Æsch. Prom. 28, ἐπαυράμην Hipp., εὔρατο Ap. Rh. 4. 1133, ὄσφραντο Hipp. i. 80: (*b*) in the Alex. and Hellenist. dialects, to a number of verbs which in the classic Greek employ the 2 Aor.; as, ἤλθατε Mt. 25. 36, ἀνείλατο Acts 7. 21.

5. For the doubling of σ by the poets, especially the Ep., to make a short vowel long by position (καλέσσετο Α. 54, ὄμοσσον 76, ἱλάσσεαι 147), see § 71. For Ep. examples of σ retained in liquid verbs, see § 56. β. In ὀφέλλειεν Π 651, β. 334, the λ is doubled to compensate for the loss of the σ.

C. Connecting Vowels.

§ **246.** 1. For -ει- *connective*, the Dor. and Æol. sometimes employ η- (§ 44. 4); as, ἐθέλησθα Theoc. 29. 4, for ἐθέλεις, εὑρῆν 11. 4, for εὑρεῖν, ἄγην Sapph. 1. 19. For the Dor. forms in -ες and -εν, see § 183. N.

2. The Dor. and Æol. sometimes give to the Perf. the connecting vowel of the Pres. (§ 185), especially in the Inf.; as, δεδοίκω Theoc. 15. 58, for δέδοικα, πεπόνθης 10. 1 (see 1. above), ὀπώπη 5. 7, πεποίθει 5. 28; Inf. δεδύκειν

1. 102, γεγάκειν Pind. O. 6. 83, τεθνάκην Sapph. 2. 15; Part. κεχλάδοντας Pind. P. 4. 318, πεφρίκοντας 325. Instances likewise occur in the Ep. of the Perf. passing over into the form of the Pres., and of the Plup. into that of the Impf.; as, κεκλήγοντας M. 125, ἐρρίγοντι Hes. Sc. 228; ἐμέμηκον ι. 439, ἐπέφυκον Hes. Th. 152.

NOTE. In this way new verbs arose, not confined to the Ep.; as, from ἄνωγα, ἀνώγω, *to order*, O. 43, Δ. 287, Hdt. vii. 104, Impf. ἤνωγον I. 578 (ἠνώγειν H. 394), F. ἀνώξω π. 404, A. ἤνωξα, Hes. Sc. 479; from ὤλεκα, ὀλέκω, *to destroy*, Σ. 172, A. 10, Soph. Ant. 1286; from γέγωνα, γεγωνέω and γεγωνίσκω, *to cry aloud*.

3. In the Subjunctive, the Ep. often retains the old short connective (§ 177), for the sake of the metre; as, ἀγείρομεν A. 142, ἴομεν, ἐγείρομεν B. 440, φθιόμεσθα Ξ. 87, φθίεται Υ. 173, εἴδομεν A. 363, εἴδετε Θ. 18.

4. In the following poet. chiefly Ep. forms, the connecting vowel is omitted:

α.) Of Pure Verbs. ἀνύω, *to accomplish;* Impf. ἤνῠτο ε. 243, "ἄνῠτο Theoc. 2. 92, "ἄνῠμες 7. 10.

ἐρύω, Ion. and Poet. εἰρύω, *to draw*, Mid. *to draw to one's self, to protect;* Act. Inf. εἰρῠμεναι Hes. Op. 816; Mid. ἔρῡται Ap. Rh. 1208, εἰρύαται A. 239, ἔρῡσο X. 507, ἔρῡτο Δ. 138, εἴρῡτο Π. 542, ἔρυντο Theoc. 25. 76, εἴρυντο M. 454, ἔρυσθαι ε. 484, εἴρυσθαι ψ. 82; Pass. ἔρῡτο Hes. Th. 301; from the shorter ῥύομαι, ἐῤῥῡτο Soph. Œd. T. 1352, ῥύατο Σ. 515, ῥῦσθαι O. 141; Iter. ῥύσκευ Ω. 730.

σεύω, *to shake*, σεῦται Soph. Tr. 645.

στεῦται, *he takes his stand, purposes*, Γ. 83, στεῦνται Æsch. Pers. 49, στεῦτο B. 597, λ. 583.

τανύω, *to stretch;* τάνῠται P. 393.

β.) Of Impure Verbs. ἔδω, comm. ἐσθίω, *to eat;* Inf. ἔδμεναι Δ. 345.

λείπω, *to leave;* Impf. ἔλειπτο Ap. Rh. 1. 45.

πέρθω, *to lay waste*, Inf. Pass. (πέρθ-σθαι, § 60) πέρθαι Π. 708.

φέρω, *to bear;* Imp. φέρτε I. 171.

φυλάσσω, *to watch* (r. φυλακ-); Imp. προ-φύλαχθε (cf. § 238. β) Hom. Ap. 538.

D. FLEXIBLE ENDINGS.

§ 247. a. 2*d Pers. Sing.* (*a*) For the form -σθα, see § 182. II. (*b*) For uncontracted, variously contracted, and protracted objective forms, see § 243. (*c*) The Ep. sometimes drops σ in the Perf. and Plup. pass.; as, μέμνηαι Φ. 442, contr. μέμνῃ O. 18, Theoc. 21. 41, βέβληαι E. 284, ἔσσυο Π. 585. (*d*) On the other hand, in the S. S., we find σ retained in some contract forms, and in the Presents having the sense of the Fut. πίομαι, φάγομαι · thus, (καυχάεσαι) καυχᾶσαι Rom. 2. 17, ὀδυνᾶσαι Lk. 16. 25, πίεσαι, φάγεσαι Id. 17. 8.

b. 1*st Pers. Pl. and Du.* The Dor. uses -μες for -μεν (§ 70. 3); as, δεδοίκαμες Theoc. 1. 16, εἴδομες 2. 25. For the endings -μεσθα and -μεθον, see § 212.

§ 248. c. 3*d Pers. Pl.* (*a*) For the Dor. -ντι, see § 181. α. (*b*) The Æol. uses -οισι for -ουσι, and -αισι for -ᾱσι (§ 45. 5); as, κρύπτοισι

Alc. 7 (1), στάζοισι Pind. P. 9. 110, φαισί Sapph. 35 (88). (c) In the Alexandrine Greek we find -αν for -ᾱσι of the Perf., and -οσαν for -ον of the Impf.; as, πέφρῖκαν Lyc. 252, ἔγνωκαν St. Jn. 17. 7 (so ἔοργαν Hom. Batr. 179); ἐσχάζοσαν Lyc. 21, ἤλθοσαν LXX. Ps. 79. 1, ἐδολιοῦσαν Rom. 3. 13. So, in the Opt., εἴποισαν Ps. 35. 25, ποιήσαισαν Deut. 1. 44, for εἴποιεν, ποιήσαιεν (d) Rare instances occur in the poets of -ᾰσι in the Perf. with a short penult (cf. § 45. 5); thus the old reading λελόγχᾰσιν λ. 304, νενεύκᾰσιν Antim

(e) In the nude Impf. and 2 Aor., and in the Aor. pass., the Ep. and Dor. often retain the older ending -ν (§ 181. γ); as, ἔστᾰν A. 535, Pind. P. 4. 240 (ἔστησαν N. 488), ἴεν M. 33, Pind. I. 1. 34, τίθεν Id. P. 3. 114, ἔδιδον Hom. Cer. 437, ἔγνον Pind. P. 4. 214, and ἔγνων Ib. 9. 137, ἔφῠν ε. 481, Pind. P. 1. 82, ἤγερθεν A. 57, τράφεν 251, φάανθεν 200, Mosch. 2. 33, ἐφίλᾱθεν Theoc. 7. 60, φάνεν Pind. O. 10. 101. So, in imitation of the Ep., ἐκόρεσθεν Ar. Pax, 1283, ἔκρυφθεν Eur. Hipp. 1247. We even find, as 3 Pers. pl., ᾐείδειν Ap. Rh. 4. 1700, ᾔδειν 2. 65.

(*f*) In the Ion., the endings -ᾰται and -ᾰτο, for -νται and -ντο (§ 213. 2), are the common forms in the Perf. and Plup., are very frequent in the Opt., and are also employed in the Impf., 2 Aor., and nude Pres. ind. Before these endings, a short vowel in the root is not lengthened (§ 218), except in the poets for the sake of the metre, the connective -ε- is used instead of -ο- (§ 203), α and sometimes ει become ε, and consonants are changed according to § 213. R. Thus, οἰκέαται Hdt. i. 142, for ᾤκηνται, ἕαται Γ. 134, Hdt. ii. 86, εἵαται (§ 47. N.) B. 137, ἕατο H. 414, εἵατο Γ. 149, for ἧνται, ἧντο, πεφοβήατο Φ. 206; ἐβουλέατο Hdt. i. 4, for ἐβούλοντο, ἀπικέατο 152; δυνέαται Id. ii. 142, ἐδυνέατο iv. 114, ἀναπεπτέαται ix. 9, for δύνανται, &c.; κέαται Λ. 659, Hdt. i. 14, κείαται Ω. 527, ἐκέατο Hdt. i. 167, κείατο φ. 418, ἀποκεκλέατο Hdt. ix. 50, for κεῖνται, &c. (so, with an intervening consonant, ἐρηρέδαται Ψ. 284, ἐρηρέδατο η. 95, from ἐρείδω); τετρίφαται (r. τριβ-) Id. ii. 93, δεδέχαται (r. δεικ-, Ion. δεκ-) 65 (yet ἀπίκαται vii. 209, cf. § 69. α), κεχωρίδαται i. 140, ἐσκευάδατο vii. 67 (so, as if from verbs in -ζω, ἐληλάδατο η. 86, ἀκηχέδαται P. 637, ἐρράδαται υ. 354, -το M. 431, ἐσταλάδατο Hdt. vii. 89); βουλοίατο Hdt. i. 3, πειρῴατο iv. 139, γευσαίατο ii. 47. The Opt forms in -ατο are likewise used by the Att. poets; as, δεξαίατο Soph. Œd. C 44, πεμψαίατο 602, πυθοίατο 921.

(*g*) In the Imperative, a third form is found in Dor. inscriptions, made by prefixing ν to the flex. ending of the Sing. (cf. § 172); as, ποιούντω (compare Lat. *faciunto*), (διδόνσθω, cf. § 177) διδόσθω Inscr. Corcyr.

d. For the Subj. forms in -μι and -σι, see § 181. β. For the Dor. Sing. 3 in -τι, see § 181. α. For the Dor. Sing. 1 in -μᾱν, and Du. 3 in -τᾱν, -σθᾱν (for -μην, -την, -σθην), cf. §§ 44. 1, 243. c. β.

§ **249.** e. *Iterative Form.* The Ion., especially the Ep., to express with more emphasis the idea of *repeated* or *continued action*, often prolongs the flex. endings of the Impf. and Aor., in the sing. and the 3d Pers. pl., to -σκον, -σκες, -σκε(ν), -σκον in the *subjective inflection*, and to -σκόμην, -σκεο (-ευ, -ου), -σκετο, -σκοντο in the *objective*. This form, which is called the *iterative* (itero, *to repeat*) is likewise used by the Dor. poets, and sometimes in lyric portions by the tragic. It sometimes appears to be used for metrical effect, rather than for special emphasis. It commonly wants the augment. Thus, Impf. ἔχεσκον, *I was in the habit of carrying*, N. 257, ἔχεσκες E. 472, ἔχεσκε 126, Hdt. vi. 12, *Pl.* 3 ἔχεσκον δ. 627, for εἶχον, -ες, -ε, -ον, ὑφαίνεσκεν, *she kept weaving*, β. 104, ἀλλύεσκεν 105, πέμπεσκε, ἐπέμπεσκον Hdt. i. 100, φέρεσκε Theoc. 25. 138, παύεσκε Soph. Ant. 963, μαχέσκετο H. 140, πελέσκεο X. 433, ἐμισγέσκοντο υ. 7, ζωννύσκετο E. 857; 2 Aor. ἴδεσκε Γ. 217, λάβεσκε Hdt. iv. 78, ἐλάβεσκον 130, δύσκεν Θ. 271, γενέσκετο λ. 208, ὀλέσκετο 586, 1 Aor. (only poet.), στρέψασκον Σ. 546, ὤσασκε λ. 599, μνησάσκετο Λ. 566

NOTES. (*a*) That the connecting vowel before -σκ- is ε rather than ο, follows from § 203. (*b*) Before -σκ-, a short vowel remains, and ε takes the place of ει; as, στάσκεν Γ. 217, for ἔστη (r. στα-), δόσκον I. 331, ἀνίεσκε Hes. Th. 157, for ἀνίη, φάνεσκεν Λ. 64, for ἐφάνη (§ 199), ἔσκον H. 153, for ἦν, κάλεσκε Ap. Rh. 4. 1514, for ἐκάλει (καλέεσκε ζ. 402, for ἐκάλεε), καλέσκετο O. 338, for ἐκαλεῖτο, κέσκετο φ. 41, for ἔκειτο. (*c*) Verbs in -άω have commonly the iterative Impf. in -ασκον, sometimes doubling the α for the sake of the metre (cf. 242. b); as, ἔασκες T. 295, for εἴας, ναιετάασκον B. 539; so *Pl.* 1 νικάσκομεν λ. 512, for ἐνικῶμεν. (*d*) There appears to be a blending of Impf. and Aor. forms (or formation as if from a theme in -άω), in κρύπτασκε Θ. 272, ῥίπτασκον O. 23, ῥοίζασκε Hes. Th. 835, ἀνασσείασκε Hom. Ap. 403, from κρύπτω, ῥίπτω, ῥοιζέω, and ἀνασείω.

§ **250.** f. *Infinitive.* In the Inf., instead of -ναι, the Dor. and Æol. commonly retain the old ending -ν (§ 176), or, with the Ep., reduplicate this ending to -μεν (cf. §§ 174, 176), which may be still farther prolonged (chiefly by the poets) to -μεναι. (*a*) Thus the Æol. forms the Aor. pass. inf. in -ην, the Dor. in -ῆμεν, and the Ep. (which also employs the common form) in -ήμεναι; as, μεθύσθην Alc. 28(29), ὀμνάσθην (for ἀναμνησθῆναι) Theoc. 29. 26; διακριθῆμεν Th. v. 79; ὁμοιωθήμεναι A. 187. (*b*) In other tenses, the *nude* Inf. has commonly in the Dor. the form -μεν, in the Æol. -ν and -μεναι, and in the Ep. -ναι, -μεν, and -μεναι; as, θέμεν Theoc. 5. 21, Pind. P. 4. 492, λ. 315, θέμεναι Inscr. Cum., B. 285, Pind. O. 14. 15, θεῖναι Δ. 26 (cf. 57), φάμεν Pind. O. 1. 55, δόμεν Th. v. 77, Δ. 379, δόμεναι A. 98, 116, α. 317, δοῦναι 316, γνώμεναι α. 411; νίκᾶν (§ 251. 2) Alc. 86(15), ἄντλην 11(3); τεθνάμεν O. 497, τεθνάμεναι Ω. 225, ἴδμεν Λ. 719, ἴδμεναι N. 273. So ἱστάμεναι Hdt. i. 17. Before -μεν and -μεναι, a short vowel in the 2 Aor. does not pass into a diphthong (§ 224. E.). (*c*) In like manner the non-Attic poets employ, for -ειν (originally -εν, § 176), the prolonged -έμεν and -έμεναι; as, (ἀκοῦ-εν) ἀκουέμεν A. 547, Pind. O. 3. 44, Theoc. 8. 83, ἀκουέμεναι λ. 380, ἀξέμεν Ψ. 111, ἀξέμεναι 50, χολωσέμεν A. 78, ἐλθέμεναι 151. (*d*) So, in the Perf., πεπληγέμεν Π. 728. For the Perf. inf. in -ειν or -ην, see § 246. 2. The common form in -έναι first occurs in Hdt. (*e*) Verbs in -άω and -έω have a contract form in -ήμεναι; as, (γοά-εν) γοήμεναι Ξ. 502, πεινήμεναι υ. 137, καλήμεναι K. 125, πενθήμεναι σ. 174, from γοάω, πεινάω, καλέω, πενθέω. Yet (ἀέμεναι) ἄμεναι Φ. 70. In ἀγινέμεναι υ. 213, from ἀγινέω, and ἀρόμμεναι Hes. Op. 22, from ἀρόω, the connecting vowel is omitted.

g. *Participle.* For the Æol. contraction into αι and οι in the Part., see § 45. 5; thus, κίρναις Alc. 27, ῥίψαις Pind. P. 1. 86, θρέψαισα 8. 37, ζεύξαισα Sapph. 1. 9, ἔχοισα 77(76), Pind. P. 8. 4, Theoc. 1. 96. For the Fem. -ουσα, the Laconic uses -ωα; as, ἐκλιπῶα, κλεῶα, θυρσαδδωᾶν (§ 70. V.), for ἐκλιποῦσα, κλέουσα, θυρσαζουσῶν, Ar. Lys. 1297, 1299, 1313. So Μῶα 1293 (§ 45. 5).

E. VERBS IN -μι.

§ **251.** 1. The Ion. and Dor. employ more freely than the Att. the forms with a connecting vowel (§ 225), especially in the Pres. sing. of verbs whose characteristic is ε or ο; as, τιθεῖς Pind. P. 8. 14, τιθεῖ α. 192, Hdt. i.

133, διδοῖς I. 164, διδοῖ 519, Hdt. i. 107 ; ἱστᾷ Ib. iv. 103, Imp. καθίστα I. 202 ; προθέουσι (unredupl., for προτιθέᾱσι) A. 291 ; 2 Aor. Opt. προσθέοιτο Hdt. i. 53 ; Inf. συνιεῖν Theog. 565, διδῶν (§ 244. a) Theoc. 29. 9.

2. On the other hand, the Æol., Dor., and Ep. retain the form in -μι in some verbs, which in the Att. and in Ion. prose have only the form in -ω ; as, κάλημι Sapph. 1. 16, ὄρημι 2. 11, φίλημι 79(23), αἴνημι Hes. Op. 681, νίκημι Theoc. 7. 40, for καλέω, ὁράω, &c. ; ἀνέχησι, φέρησι, βρίθησι τ. 111, 112, for ἀνέχει, &c. (unless rather Subj. ἀνέχησι, &c.) ; φορῆναι B. 107.

3. The Ion. changes α *characteristic* before another α to ε (cf. 242. a), and sometimes inserts ε before α (§ 48. 1) ; as, (ἱστάᾱσι, § 58) ἱστέᾱσι Hdt. v. 71, δυνέαται (§ 248. *f*), ἱστέαιτο Hdt. iv. 166. So, in the nude Perf., ἑστέᾱσι Hdt. i. 200, ἑστέατε v. 49.

4. The Ep. sometimes differs from the common language in the length of the characteristic vowel (§ 224) ; as, Inf. τιθήμεναι Ψ. 247, διδοῦναι Ω. 425, ζευγνῦμεν Π. 145, for τιθέναι, &c. ; Part. τιθήμενον K. 34 ; Imp. ἵληθι, δίδωθι γ. 380 (so nude Perf. ἕστητε Δ. 243, 246, for ἕστατε) : 2 Aor. βᾰσαν M. 469, βάτην A. 327, for ἔβησαν, &c.

5. For the Impf. ἐτίθην and ἦν, the Ion. has ἐτίθεα Hdt. iii. 155, and ἦα β. 313, unaugmented ἔα Δ. 321, Hdt. ii. 19. So ἔας Hdt. i. 187, ἦεν A. 381, ἔατε Hdt. iv. 119, ἔασαν ix. 31. Cf. §§ 179, 201. N, 252. b.

§ **252.** 6. *Dialectic forms of εἰμί, to be* (¶ 55). (*a*) Those which arise from different modes of lengthening the radical syllable (§ 230. 3) : ἐμμί Theoc. 20. 32, Sapph. 2. 15, ἐσσί (ι assumed after the analogy of the other persons) A. 176, Theoc. 5. 75, *S.* 3 ἐντί (ν inserted instead of σ) Id. 1. 17, εἰμέν E. 873, Hdt. i. 97 ; Inf. ἦμεν (for which some give the form ἦμες, cf. § 70. 3) Theoc. 2. 41. (*b*) Uncontracted forms, and forms like those of verbs in -ω : ἔᾱσιν B. 125, ἔω A. 119, Hdt. iv. 98, ἔῃσι B. 366, ἔωσι I. 140, Hdt. i. 155, ἔοις I. 284, ἔοι 142, Hdt. vii. 6, ἐών B. 27, Hdt. i. 86, ἐοῦσα Γ. 159, ἐοῖσα Pind. P. 4. 471, Theoc. 2. 64, εὖσα 76, (ἔ-ντσα, § 58) ἔᾱσα or ἔασσα Tim. Locr. 96 a, ἔον A. 762, εὖντα Theoc. 2. 3. (*c*) Variously protracted forms : ἔην (1 P.) Λ. 762, (3 P.) B. 642, Hdt. vii. 143, ἔης Theoc. 19. 8, ἔησθα X. 435, ἤην Λ. 808, εἴω Ψ. 47 ; Impf. iter. (§ 249. *b*), ἔσκον (1 P.) H. 153, (3 P.) Hdt. I. 196, ἔσκε Ib., E. 536, Æsch. Pers. 656. (*d*) Middle forms : ἔσο, commonly ἔσσο α. 302, Sapph. 1. 28, εἴατο υ. 106 (for ἦντο, cf. *S.* 1 ἤμην · others read εἵατο, Ep. for ἧντο from ἧμαι). (*e*) Old short and unaugmented forms : ἐμέν Call. Fr. 294, ἔσαν A. 267, Pind. P. 4. 371, ἔσσαν Id. O. 9. 79. (*f*) For εἶς Π. 515, Hdt. vii. 9, see § 230. α ; for *P.* 3 ἐντί Pind. O. 9. 158, Th. v. 77, Theoc. 5. 109, § 181. α ; for ἔα, ἦα, ἔας, ἦε(ν), ἔατε, ἔασαν, § 251. 5 ; for ἦσι T. 202, and ἔῃσι, § 181. β ; for εἴησθα Theog. 715, ἔησθα, § 182 ; for εἶμες, ὦμες Theoc. 15. 9, ἦμες 14. 29, § 247. b ; for Impf. *S.* 3 (ἦστ) ἦς Theoc. 2. 90, § 230. γ ; for Inf. ἔμεν Δ. 299, ἔμεναι Γ. 40, ἔμμεν Pind. O. 5. 38, Theoc. 7. 28, Soph. Ant. 623, ἔμμεναι A. 117, Sapph. 2. 2, ἦμεν Theoc. 2. 41, εἶμεν (for which some write εἶμες, cf. *a* above) Th. v. 79, Tim. Locr. 93 a, εἴμεναι or ἤμεναι Ar. Ach. 775, § 250. *b* ; for ἔσσομαι Δ. 267, ἔσσεται Δ. 164, Æsch. Pers. 121 (ἔσεται A. 211), § 71 ; for ἔσεαι A. 563, ἔσσεαι Σ. 95, § 243 ; for ἐσσῇ Theoc. 10. 5, ἐσεῖται Eur. Iph. A. 782, ἐσσεῖται B. 393, Theoc. 7. 67, ἐσοῦνται Th. v. 77, § 245. 2.

7. *Dialectic Forms of εἶμι, to go* (¶ 56). (a) The protraction of ῐ to ει (§ 224) likewise appears in *P.* 3 εἶσι (or ἴσι, or perhaps εἰσί from εἰμί, *to be*)

Hes. Sc. 113, Theog. 116, *εἴω* only Sophr. 2 (23), *εἴη* (by some ascribed to *εἰμί, to be*) ξ. 496, Ω. 139, *εἴσομαι* Ξ. 8, *εἴσατο* Δ. 138, *ἐείσατο* O. 415, *ἐεισάσθην* 544. (b) In the Impf., we find both nude forms and forms with a connecting vowel, from the root *ἰ-*, both unaugmented, doubly augmented (§ 189), and doubly augmented with contraction; thus, (*ἦιν*, cf. 251. 5) *ἤϊα* (from which may be formed by contr. the Att. *ᾖα*, § 231. *b*) δ. 427, Hdt. i. 42, *ἤϊε* A. 47, Hdt. i. 65, *ᾖε* M. 371, *ἴε* B. 872, *ᾔομεν* κ. 251, *ἴσαν* A. 494, *ἤϊσαν* K. 197, Hdt. i. 62, *ἤϊον* ψ. 370, *ἴτην* A. 347. (c) The Opt. *ἰείη* (only T. 209) is formed, as if from the root *ἰε-* (cf. § 231. *d*). (d) The Inf. *ἴναι* Ath. 580 c, is the regular nude form. (e) For *εἶς* see § 230. *α*; for *εἶσθα* K. 450, *ᾔησθα* K. 67, § 182; for *ἴῃσι* I. 701, § 181. *β*; for *ἴομεν* B. 440, § 246. 3; for *ἴμεν* A. 170, Pind. O. 6. 108, *ἴμεναι* Υ. 32, *ἴμμεναι* 365, § 250. *b*.

F. Perfect Participle.

§ **253.** 1. In Perf. Participles ending in *-ώς* pure, the Ep. more frequently lengthens the preceding vowel; and the Part. is then declined in *-ότος* or *-ῶτος*, according to the metre. If the preceding vowel remains short, the form in *-ῶτος* is commonly required by the metre. Thus, *βεβαρηότες* γ. 139, *κεκμηότας* Λ. 801, *κεκμηῶτα* κ. 31. See, also, §§ 237, 238.

2. In some fem. forms, the antepenult is shortened on account of the verse, as, *λελᾰκυῖα* μ. 85 (*λεληκώς* X. 141), *μεμᾰκυῖαι* Δ. 435 (*μεμηκώς* K. 362), *ἀρᾰρυίας* Γ. 331, *τεθᾰλυῖαν* I. 208.

CHAPTER X.

ROOT OF THE VERB.

§ **254.** The root of the Greek verb, although not properly varied by inflection, yet *received many changes* in the progress of the language. These changes affected the different tenses unequally, so that there are but few *primitive* verbs in which the root appears in only a single form.

Note. The earlier, intermediate, and later forms of the root may be termed, for the sake of brevity, *old*, *middle*, and *new* roots. The final syllable of the earliest form of the root is commonly short; and the oldest roots of the language are monosyllabic.

§ **255.** The tenses may be arranged, with respect to the degree in which they exhibit the *departure of the root from its original form*, in the following order.

I. The Second Aorist and Second Future.

Remarks. *α.* The 2d Aor. *act.* and *mid.* is simply the *Impf. of an old root*

(§ 178. 2); thus ἔλιπον and ἐλιπόμην (¶ 37) are formed from the old root λιπ- in precisely the same way as ἔλειπον and ἐλειπόμην from the new root λειπ-.

β. The 2d Aor. and Fut. *pass.* are chiefly found in *impure* verbs which *want* the 2d Aor. *act.* and *mid.* They affix -ην and -ησομαι (§ 180) to the simplest form of the root.

γ. These tenses (except the nude 2 Aor. act., § 224. 2) have commonly a short syllable before the affix (§ 254. N.).

δ. In a few verbs, the original root appears to have received some change even in the 2 Aor.; chiefly, in accordance with the prevailing analogy of the tense, to render the root *monosyllabic*, or its *last syllable short* (§ 254. N.), or to enable it to receive the *nude form* (§ 227. β).

§ **256.** II. THE PERFECT AND PLUPERFECT PASSIVE. These tenses have not only a more complete, uniform, and simple formation than the Perf. and Plup. *act.* (§§ 179, 186, 235), but are likewise more common, and are formed in some verbs (see τρέφω, § 263, φθείρω, § 268, &c.) from an earlier root.

III. THE PERFECT AND PLUPERFECT ACTIVE. For the various formations of these tenses, see §§ 179, 186, 234–238.

IV. THE FIRST AORIST AND FUTURE.

V. THE PRESENT AND IMPERFECT. These tenses, with very few exceptions, exhibit the root in its latest and most protracted form.

§ **257.** REMARKS. 1. The 2 Aor. and 2 Fut. are widely distinguished from the other tenses by their *attachment to the original form* of the root; while the Pres. and Impf. are distinguished no less widely by their *inclination to depart* from this form. The other tenses differ comparatively but little from each other in the form of the root. If the verb has *three* roots, they are commonly formed from the *middle* root. See, for example, λαμβάνω (§ 290).

2. Many verbs are DEFECTIVE, either from the *want of a complete formation*, or from the *disuse of some of their forms*. In both cases, the defect is often supplied by other verbs having the same signification (§ 301). In the poets, especially the older, we find many fragments of verbs belonging to the earlier language. These occur often in but a single tense, and sometimes in only a single form of that tense; as, 2 A. *S.* 3 ἔβραχε, *rang*, Δ. 420, δέατο (r. δεα-), *appeared*, ζ. 242, 1 A. ἐκάπυσσεν, *breathed*, X. 467, λίγξε, *twanged*, Δ. 125, Pf. *Pt.* κεκαφηότα, *gasping*, E. 698.

3. On the other hand, many verbs are REDUNDANT, either through a *double formation* from the same root, or the use of forms from *different roots*. It should be observed, however, that two or more forms of the same tense, with few exceptions, either,

(α.) Belong to *different periods, dialects*, or *styles of composition;* thus, κτείνω, and later κτίννῡμι (§ 295); τάσσω (§ 274. γ), A. P. ἐτάχθην, and later ἐτάγην· καίω (§ 267. 3), A. P. ἐκαύθην, and Ion. ἐκάην· πυνθάνομαι and poet. πεύθομαι (§ 290); πείθω (¶ 39), A. ἔπεισα, and poet. ἔπιθον.

Or, (β.) *Differ* in their *use*; thus, 1 Pf. πέπεικα, transitive, *I have persuaded*, 2 Pf. πέποιθα, intransitive, *I trust* (¶ 39); 1 A. ἔστησα, trans. *I placed*, 2 A. ἔστην, intrans. *I stood* (¶ 48). The *second tenses* are more inclined than the *first* to an intransitive use. From the prevalence of this use in the 2d Perf. and Plup., these tenses were formerly called the *Perf.* and *Plup. middle.*

Or, (γ.) Are *supplementary* to each other. See §§ 201. N., 237. *a.*

NOTE. From the various changes which take place in the root, many verbs, together with their common themes, have others, either derived or collateral. In regard to some forms, it seems doubtful whether they should be rather viewed as redundant forms of the same verb, or as the forms of distinct but kindred verbs.

§ 258. The changes in the root of the Greek verb are of three kinds; EUPHONIC, EMPHATIC, and ANOMALOUS.

NOTE. The lists which follow are designed both to exemplify the various changes of the root, and likewise to present, in a classified arrangement, all those verbs upon whose inflection farther remark seemed to be required. It will be observed, that some of the words might have been arranged with equal propriety under other heads, from their exhibiting more than one species of change in the root.

A. EUPHONIC CHANGES.

§ 259. 1. Radical vowels are sometimes changed by PRECESSION (§ 28), α becoming ε, and ε and ο becoming ι.

a. *Change of* α *to* ε.

NOTE. If the α is preceded or followed by a *liquid*, it is sometimes retained in the *Perfect*, particularly the *Perfect passive.*

δέρκομαι (r. δαρκ-, δερκ-), and 2 Pf. δέδορκα, *to see*, poet., Γ. 342, Soph. Œd. T. 389, 2 A. ἔδρακον (§ 262) Eur. Or. 1456, 1 A. P. ἐδέρχθην, Æsch. Pr. 53, 2 A. P. ἐδράκην, Pind. N. 7. 4.

δέρω (r. δαρ-), *to flay*, F. δερῶ, A. ἔδειρα, Pf. P. δέδαρμαι, 2 A. P. ἐδάρην, iii. 5. 9. Poet. and Ion. δαίρω, Ar. Nub. 442, δείρω, Hdt. ii. 39.

δρέπω, *to pluck*, poet. δρέπτω (§ 272), Mosch. 2. 69, F. δρέψω, A. ἔδρεψα. 2 A. ἔδραπον, Pind. P. 4. 231.

πλέκω, *to wreath*, F. πλέξω, A. ἔπλεξα, Pf. P. πέπλεγμαι, 1 A. P. ἐπλέχθην, 2 A. P. ἐπλάκην, A. M. ἐπλεξάμην. In Hipp., Pf. ἐμ-πέπλεχα, δια πέπλοχα.

στρέφω, *to twist*, F. στρέψω, A. ἔστρεψα, Pf. P. ἔστραμμαι, 1. A. P. ἐστρέφθην, 2 A. P. ἐστράφην. Pf. ἀν-έστροφα, Ath. 104 c. 1 A. P. Ion. and Dor. ἐστράφθην, Hdt. i. 130, Theoc. 7. 132. Extended forms, chiefly poet., στρωφάω, ζ. 53, στρωφάομαι, Eur. Alc. 1052, Hdt. ii. 85, F. στρωφήσομαι Theog. 837; στροφέω, Ar. Pax, 175.

τρέπω (Ion. τράπω Hdt. ii. 92), *to turn*, F. τρέψω, A. ἔτρεψα, Pf. τέτροφα (§ 236. *a*) and τέτραφα, Pf. P. τέτραμμαι, 1 A. P. ἐτρέφθην, 2 A. P. ἐτράπην, 1 A. M. commonly trans. ἐτρεψάμην, 2 A. M. intrans. ἐτραπόμην. 2 A. Ep. ἔτραπον, E. 187, F. Pf. τετράψομαι Hesych.

b. *Change of* ε *and* ο *to* ι.

The change of ε and ο to ι is almost wholly confined to syllables which become long in the Pres. and Impf., by the *addition of one or more consonants* as, τίκτω (§ 272. β), κίρνημι (§ 278. δ), ἀμβλίσκω (§ 280).

§ **260.** 2. Some roots are CONTRACTED; as,

ᾄδω, *to sing*, F. ᾄσομαι, A. ᾖσα, Pf. P. ᾖσμαι, A. P. ᾔσθην· contr. from ἀείδω, A. 1, ἀείσομαι, χ. 352 (ἀείσω Theoc. 22. 26, Eur. Herc. 681), &c. For ἀείσεο, see § 185. ε.

ᾄσσω or ᾄττω (§ 70. 1), *to rush*, F. ᾄξω, A. ᾖξα· contr. from ἀΐσσω, Θ. 88, &c. A. P. ἠΐχθην, Γ. 368.

λούω, *to wash*, F. λούσω, A. ἔλουσα, Pf. P. λέλουμαι, A. P. ἐλούθην· contr. from Ep. λοέω, δ. 252, F. λοέσω, &c. From the old r. λο-, we have the Ep. Impf. or 2 A. λόε κ. 361, λόον Hom. Ap. 120, Mid. *Inf.* λόεσθαι or λοέσθαι Hes. Op. 747; and from the same root, or from λου- with the omission of the connecting vowels, are the common shorter forms of the Impf. act. and Pres. and Impf. mid.; as, (for ἐλόομεν or ἐλούομεν) ἐλοῦμεν Ar. Pl. 657, λοῦμαι, λοῦται Cyr. i. 3. 11, λοῦσθαι ζ. 216.

§ **261.** 3. Some roots are SYNCOPATED in the *theme*, chiefly in cases of *reduplication;* as, (r. γιγεν-, γιγν-) γίγνομαι, πίπτω, μίμνω (§ 286): others in the 2*d Aor.* (§ 255. δ); as, (r. ἐγερ-, ἐγρ-) ἠγρόμην (§ 268), ἦλθον (§ 301. 3), Ep. defect. (r. τεμ-) ἔτετμον (§ 194. 3), *found:* others in *other tenses;* as,

καλέω, *to call*, F. καλέσω, καλῶ (§ 200. 2), A. ἐκάλεσα, Pf. (r. καλε-, κλε-) κέκληκα, Pf. P. κέκλημαι, F. Pf. κεκλήσομαι, Ar. Av. 184, A. P. ἐκλήθην (ἐκαλέσθην, Hipp.). Poet., κικλήσκω Æsch. Sup. 217, προ-καλίζομαι, Γ. 19.

μέλω, *to concern* (§ 222. 2); Ep. Pf. P. μέμβλεται, -εσθε, Τ. 343, Plup. μέμβλετο Φ. 516. See §§ 64. 2, 222. α.

NOTE. In regard to some forms, it seems doubtful whether they are best referred to syncope, or to metathesis with, in some cases, contraction; thus, (r. καλε-, κλαε-, κλη-) κέκληκα.

§ **262.** 4. In some roots, METATHESIS takes place, chiefly by changing the place of a *liquid.* This occurs, (*a*) in the *theme;* as, βλώσκω, θνήσκω, θρώσκω (§ 281): (*b*) in the 2*d Aor.* (§ 255. δ); as, ἔσκλην (§ 227. β), ἔτλην (§ 301. 2), ἔδρακον (§ 259. a), ἔπραθον (§ 288): (*c*) in *other tenses;* as, βέβληκα, ἐβλήθην, κέκμηκα (§ 223).

§ **263.** 5. A few roots are changed to avoid a DOUBLE ASPIRATION (§ 62); as,

τρέφω (r. θραφ-, θρεφ- § 259, τραφ-, τρεφ-), *to nourish* (Old τράφω, Pind. P. 4. 205), F. θρέψω, A. ἔθρεψα, Pf. τέτροφα, Pf. P. τέθραμμαι, 1 A. P ἐθρέφθην, commonly 2 A. P. ἐτράφην. Ep. 2 Aor. intrans. or pass. ἔτραφον Ε. 555, Pf. συν-έτροφε Hipp.

NOTE. See, also, ἔχω (§ 300), θάπτω, θρύπτω (§ 272), θύω (§ 219), τρέχω (§ 301), τύφω (§ 270). A few other roots have both aspirated and unaspirated forms; as, τυχ- and τυκ- (§§ 270. 9, 285, 290), χαδ- and καδ- (§ 275. ζ), ψύχω, *to cool*, F. ψύξω, &c., 2 A. P. ἐψύγην, Ar. Nub. 151, and ἐψύχην, Æsch. Fr. 95.

6. In a few cases, a consonant is DROPPED or ADDED for the sake of euphony or the metre; as, λείβω, *to pour out*, Ep. εἴβω, *Π*. 11; δουπέω, *to sound*, A. ἐδούπησα, i. 8. 18, *Δ*. 504, and ἐγδούπησα, *Λ*. 45; λείχω, *to lick*, Pf. P. λελειχμώς Hes. Th. 826. So, in reduplicated forms, πίμπλημι, πίμπρημι (§ 284), and in the Att. Redupl., ἐγρήγορα (§ 268), ἠμύω, *to bow down*, ἐμνήμῡκε *Χ*. 491 (for ἐμήμῡκε, ἐμ- being prefixed according to analogy, § 191. 2, although the η is radical). With χολόομαι, -ώσομαι, *to be angry*, we have also the Ep. (χοόομαι, § 29. α) χώομαι, χώσομαι, *Α*. 80 (see *Γ*. 413, 414).

§ **264.** 7. In some verbs, the omission of the DIGAMMA (§ 22. δ) has given rise to different forms of the root; as,

ἀλεύω (r. ἀλεϜ-, ἀλε-, ἀλευ-), *to avert*, poet. Æsch. Prom. 568, F. ἀλεύσω Soph. Fr. 825, A. ἤλευσα, Æsch. Sept. 87; Mid. ἀλέομαι and ἀλεύομαι, *to avoid*, Σ. 586, ω. 29, A. ἠλεάμην and ἠλευάμην (§ 201. 2). Deriv., ἀλεείνω, Α. 794, ἀλύσκω (§ 273. α).

ἀνα-πνέω, Ep. ἀμ-πνύω (§ 48. 2; r. πνεϜ-, πνε-, πνευ-, πνυ-, πνυν- § 277), *to recover breath*, Χ. 222, A. P. ἀμπνύνθην, Ε. 697, nude 2 A. M. ἄμπνῡτο Λ. 359. From the root πνυ- are formed the extended πινύσκω and πινύσσω, *to make wise*, Æsch. Pers. 830, Ξ. 249, and the Pf. P. πέπνῡμαι, *to be wise*, Ω. 377, referred by some to πνέω, by others to πινύσκω.

ῥέω (r. ῥεϜ-, ῥυ-), *to flow*, F. ῥεύσομαι (§ 220), A. ἔῤῥευσα, and better Att. F. M. (or 2 F. P.) ῥυήσομαι, 2 A. P. (or 2 A. Act. r. ῥυε-) ἐῤῥύην, Pf. ἐῤῥύηκα. Ion. Pres. *Pt*. ῥεούμενοι Hdt. vii. 140. Late F. ῥεύσω.

σεύομαι and σόομαι (r. σεϜ-, σευ-, συ-, σε-, whence σο- § 28), *to rush*, poet. Soph. Tr. 645 (§ 246. α), Æsch. Pers. 25, A. σευάμην (§ 201. 2) Η. 208, Pf., as Pres., ἔσσῠμαι, Ζ. 361, A. P. ἐσύθην or ἐσσύθην, Eur. Hel. 1302, Soph. Aj. 294, 2 A. M. ἐσύμην or ἐσσύμην, Eur. Hel. 1162, Ξ. 519. Ep. A. Act. ἔσσευα Ε. 208. Lacon. 2 A. P. ἀπ-εσσούα Η. Gr. i. 1. 23, for ἀπεσσύη. Observe the augm. and redupl.

χέω (r. χεϜ-, χυ-), *to pour*, F. χέω (§ 200. 2), A. ἔχεα (§ 201. 2), rare and doubtful ἔχῠσα, Pf. P. κέχῠμαι, A. P. ἐχύθην. Ep. F. χεύσω, χεύω β. 222, A. ἔχευσα, ἔχευα, Δ. 269, 2 A. M. ἐχύμην, Δ. 526, Æsch. Cho. 401. Late Pf. κέχῠκα, Anth. Late form, χύνω.

NOTE. See, also, θέω, νέω, πλέω (§ 220), δαίω, καίω, κλαίω (§ 267. 3). An Ep. and Ion. form of πλέω is πλώω, -ώσω, &c., ε. 240, Hdt. vi. 97, 2 A. ἔπλων, γ. 15; extended, πλωΐζω, Th. i. 13.

B. EMPHATIC CHANGES.

§ **265.** Most *impure* roots and many *pure* roots are PROTRACTED in the *Present* and *Imper-*

fect, to express with more emphasis the idea of *continued action*. This protraction takes place,

§ **266.** I. By LENGTHENING A SHORT VOWEL as follows.

In *mute* verbs, ᾰ becomes η; in *liquid* verbs, and in some *mute* verbs, ῐ and ῠ are *simply lengthened*; in other cases, the short vowel is usually changed to a *diphthong*.

In *mute* verbs, the change commonly extends to all the *regular tenses* (§ 215. 1).

1. Change of ᾰ to η.

σήπω (r. *σαπ-*, *σηπ-*), *to rot*, trans., F. *σήψω*, 2 Pf. intrans. (§ 257. β) *σέσηπα*, iv. 5. 12, 2 A. P. *ἐσάπην*.

τήκω, *to melt* (Dor. *τάκω* Theoc. 2. 28), F. *τήξω*, A. *ἔτηξα*, 2 Pf. intrans. *τέτηκα*, iv. 5. 15, 1 A. P. *ἐτήχθην*, commonly 2 A. P. *ἐτάκην*. Pf. P. *τέτηγμαι* Anth.

§ **267.** 2. Change of ᾰ to αι.

δαίομαι (r. *δα-*, *δαι-*), *to divide*, chiefly poet. ο. 140, F. *δάσομαι*, A. *ἐδάσάμην*, Œc. 7. 24, *δέδασμαι*, A. 125, *δέδαιμαι*, α. 23. Kindred, *δαΐζω*, *-ίζω*, *to rend*, Æsch. Ag. 207, *δατέομαι*, *to divide*, Σ. 264, Hdt. i. 216, A. *δατέασθαι* (§ 201. 2).

καθαίρω (r. *καθαρ-*), *to purify*, F. *καθαρῶ*, A. *ἐκάθηρα* (sometimes written *ἐκάθᾱρα*, cf. § 56. α), Pf. P. *κεκάθαρμαι*, A. P. *ἐκαθάρθην*.

καίνω, *to kill*, chiefly poet., F. *κανῶ*, 2 A. *ἔκανον*.

ναίω (r. *να-*), *to dwell*, poet., Soph. Tr. 40, F. *νάσσομαι* (§ 71) Ap. Rh. 2. 747, A. *ἔνασσα*, *built*, δ. 174, Pf. P. *νένασμαι*, Herod. Att., A. P. *ἐνάσθην* Eur. Med. 166. Ep. deriv. *ναιετάω*, Δ. 45.

ὑφαίνω, *to weave*, F. *ὑφανῶ*, A. *ὕφηνα*, Pf. P. *ὕφασμαι* (§ 217. β), A. P. *ὑφάνθην*. From the pure root *ὑφα-*, Ep. *ὑφόωσι* (§ 242. b) η. 105.

φαίνω (¶ 42), *to show*, F. *φανῶ*, &c. The Pf. *πέφαγκα* is late, first occurring in Dinarch., who employs it in composition with *ἀπό*. Kindred poet. verbs, *φαείνω*, *to shine*, μ. 383; from r. *φα-*, Impf. *φάε* ξ. 502, F. *πεφήσεται* P. 155; from r. *φαεθ-*, *Pt.* *φαέθων* Λ. 735, Soph. El. 824.

χαίρω (r. *χαρ-*, *χαιρ-*), *to rejoice*, F. *χαιρήσω* (§ 222. 2), Pf. *κεχάρηκα*, Pf. P. *κεχάρημαι* and *κέχαρμαι*, 2 A. P. *ἐχάρην*. Ep., redupl. F. *κεχαρήσω*, *κεχαρήσομαι* (§ 239. *b*), 2 A. M. *κεχαρόμην* (§ 194. 3), 1 A. M. *ἐχηράμην*, Ξ. 270, 2 Pf. *Pt.* *κεχαρηώς* (§ 253. 1), H. 312. Late, 1 Aor. *ἐχαίρησα*, 2 F. P. *χαρήσομαι*.

3. Various Changes of α.

δαίω (r. *δαϜ-*, *δα-*, *δαι-*), *to burn*, poet. Æsch. Ag. 496, 2 Pf. as Pres. intrans., *δέδηα*, Υ. 18, 2 A. M. *ἐδαόμην*, Υ. 316, Pf. P. *δέδαυμαι*, Call. Ep. 52.

καίω and *κάω* (r. *κᾰϜ-*, *καυ-*, *κε-* § 259, *και-*, *κᾱ-*), *to burn*, F. *καύσω* and *καύσομαι*, A. *ἔκαυσα* and poet. *ἔκεα* (§ 201. 2), Æsch. Ag. 849 (Ep. *ἔκηα* A. 40, *ἔκεια*, φ. 176), Pf. *κέκαυκα*, Pf. P. *κέκαυμαι*, A. P. *ἐκαύθην*. Ion. 2 A. P *ἐκάην*, Hdt. ii. 180.

κλαίω and *κλάω*, *to weep*, F. *κλαύσομαι* or *κλαυσοῦμαι* (§ 200. 3), and *κλαιήσω* or *κλᾱήσω* (§ 222), A. *ἔκλαυσα*, Pf. P. *κέκλαυμαι*, 3 F. *κεκλαύσομαι*, Ar. Nub. 1436. F. *κλαύσω*, Theoc. 23. 34. Late, A. P. *ἐκλαύσθην*, Pf. P *κέκλαυσμαι*, Anth.

NOTE. Κάω and *κλάω* are Att. forms, and are not contracted (§ 216. β). For *καύσω*, *κλαύσομαι*, *δέδαυμαι*, from *κάϜσω*, *κλάϜσομαι*, *δέδαϜμαι*, &c., see § 220.

τρώγω (r. *τραγ-*, *τρωγ-* § 28. 1), *to eat*, F. *τρώξομαι*, 2 A. *ἔτραγον*, Pf P *τέτρωγμαι*. Ion. 1 A. *ἔτρωξα* Hom. Batr. 126.

§ 268. 4. Change of ε to ει.

ἀγείρω (r. *ἀγερ-*, *ἀγειρ-*), *to collect*, F. *ἀγερῶ*, A. *ἤγειρα*, A. P. *ἠγέρθην*. Ep., Pf. P. *ἀγήγερμαι*, Δ. 211, 2 A. M. *ἠγερόμην*, B. 94, *Pt.* sync. *ἀγρόμενος*, H. 134. Ep. forms, *ἠγερέθομαι*, Γ. 231, *ἠγερέομαι*, K. 127; later Ep. *ἀγέρομαι* Ap. Rh. 3. 895.

ἀείρω (r. *ἀερ-*, *ἀειρ-*), *to raise*, poet. and Ion., F. *ἀερῶ*, contr. *ᾱρῶ*, Æsch. Pers. 795, A. *ἤειρα*, Pf. P. *ἤερμαι* (for *ἄωρτο*, see § 236. *d*), A. P. *ἠέρθην*· commonly *αἴρω* (r. *ἀρ-*, sync. from *ἀερ-* § 261, *αἰρ-* § 267), F. *ἀρῶ*, A. *ἦρα*, *Subj.* *ᾄρω* (§ 56. α), Pf. *ἦρκα*, Pf. P. *ἦρμαι*, A. P. *ἤρθην*, 1 A. M. *ἠράμην*, *ᾄρωμαι*, *ᾀραίμην*, Eur. Or. 3, 2 A. M. poet. *ἠρόμην*, *ἄρωμαι*, *ἀροίμην* Soph. El. 34. Æol. *ἀέρρω*, Sapph. 44(73). Poet. deriv., *ἠερέθομαι*, Γ. 108, *ἀερτάζω*, Ap. Rh. 1. 738, *ἄρνῠμαι* Soph. Ant. 903, *αἴνῠμαι* (§ 293. 3), ξ. 144.

ἐγείρω (r. *ἐγερ-*, *ἐγρ-* § 261, *ἐγειρ-*), *to rouse*, F. *ἐγερῶ*, 2 Pf., as Pres. intrans., (the sync. root prefixed, by a peculiar Att. redupl., § 263. 6) *ἐγρήγορα*, Pf. P. *ἐγήγερμαι*, A. P. *ἠγέρθην*, 2 A. M. *ἠγρόμην*. For *ἐγρήγορθε*, *ἐγρηγόρθαι*, see § 238. β. 2 Pf. *Pl.* 3 *ἐγρηγόρθᾱσι* (as from r. *ἐγερθ-*) K. 419. Hipp. has *ἐξ-ήγερτο* and *ἐγείρατο*. Deriv., Ep. *ἐγρηγοράω*, υ. 6, *ἐγρήσσω* υ. 33; late *γρηγορέω*.

εἴλω (r. *ἀλ-*, *ἐλ-* § 259), *to roll up*, *press hard*, Ep. E. 203, A. *ἔλσα* (§ 56. β) A. 409, Pf. P. *ἔελμαι*, Ω. 662, 2 A. P. *ἐάλην*, N. 408. Att. forms, *εἴλλω* or *εἵλλω*, Ar. Nub. 761, Th. ii. 76, and *ἴλλω* Soph. Ant. 340. Deriv. *εἰλέω* or *εἱλέω*, *-ήσω*, *εἰλύω*, *-ύσω* (Ep., A. P. *ἐλύσθην*, Ψ. 393; Deriv. *εἰλῠφάω*, Λ. 156, *εἰλῡφάζω*, Υ. 492), *ἑλίσσω*, *-ίξω* (poet. and Ion. *εἱλίσσω* or *εἰλίσσω*, Æsch. Pr. 1085, Hdt. ii. 38), *ἑλελίζω*, *-ίξω*, Ep. A. 530.

θείνω, *to smite*, poet., F. *θενῶ*, 2 A. *ἔθενον*, Ar. Av. 54, 1 A. *ἔθεινα*, Υ. 481.

κείρω (r. *καρ-*, *κερ-* § 259), *to shear*, F. *κερῶ*, A. *ἔκειρα*, Pf. P. *κέκαρμαι*. F. *κέρσω*, Mosch. 2. 32, A. *ἔκερσα*, κ. 456, *ἐκερσάμην*, Æsch. Pers. 952 (§ 56. β), 1 A. P. *ἐκέρθην*, Pind. P. 4. 146, 2 A. P. *ἐκάρην*, Anth.

μείρομαι (r. *μαρ-*), *to obtain*, chiefly poet., I. 616, 2 Pf *ἔμμορα*, A. 278, Pf. P. *εἵμαρται* (§ 191. 1), *it has been fated*, Pl. Rep. 566 a, *Pt.* *εἱμαρμένος*, later Ep. *μεμόρηται* Ap. Rh. 1. 646, Dor. *μεμόρακται* Tim. Locr. 95 a.

ὀφείλω, *to owe*, *ought* (Ep. *ὀφέλλω* Θ. 462), F. *ὀφειλήσω* (§ 222. 2), 1 A. *ὠφείλησα*, 2. A., used only in the expression of a wish, *ὤφελον*, Pf. *ὠφείληκα*. Kindred verbs, *ὀφέλλω*, *to assist*, poet. (for *ὀφέλλειε*, see § 245. 5), *ὀφλισκάνω*, *to incur* (§ 289), *ὠφελέω*, *to assist*.

πείρω (r. *παρ-*), *to pierce*, F. *περῶ*, Pf. P. *πέπαρμαι*. A. *ἔπειρα*, A. 465, 2 A. P. *ἐπάρην*, Hdt. 4. 94, Ath. 349 c.

σπείρω, *to sow*, F. *σπερῶ*, A. *ἔσπειρα*, Pf. P. *ἔσπαρμαι*, 2 A. P. *ἐσπάρην*.

τείνω (r. *ταν-*), *to stretch*, F. *τενῶ*, A. *ἔτεινα*, Pf. *τέτᾰκα* (§ 217. α), Pf. P *τέτᾰμαι*, A. P. *ἐτᾰθην*. Kindred Ep. forms, *τιταίνω*, B. 390, A. *Pt.* *τιτήνας*

19 *

N. 534; τανύω P. 390, F. τανύσω, &c.; *Imp.* τῆ (contr. from τάς, r. τα-; Ξ. 219; 2 Aor. *Pt.* τεταγών (§ 194. 3; r. ταγ-) A. 591.

φθείρω, *to destroy*, F. φθερῶ, A. ἔφθειρα, 1 Pf. ἔφθαρκα, 2 Pf. ἔφθορα, Pf. P ἔφθαρμαι, 2 A. P. ἐφθάρην. F. φθέρσω, N. 625, F. M. φθαρέομαι Hdt. viii. 108, φθερέομαι ix. 42, 2 A. M. ἐφθαρέατο (§ 248. *f*) Id. viii. 90.

§ 269. 5. Change of ῐ to ῑ.

κλίνω, *to bend*, F. κλῐνῶ, A. ἔκλῑνα (§ 56), Pf. P. κέκλῐμαι (§ 217. *a*), 1 A. P. ἐκλῐθην and ἐκλίνθην, 2 A. P. ἐκλῐνην.

τρίβω, *to rub, to wear*, F. τρίψω, A. ἔτριψα, Pf. τέτρῐφα, Pf. P. τέτριμμαι, 1 A. P. ἐτρίφθην, commonly 2 A. P. ἐτρῐβην.

6. Change of ῐ into ει.

ἀλείφω (r. ἀλιφ-, ἀλειφ-), *to anoint*, F. ἀλείψω, A. ἤλειψα, Pf. ἀλήλῐφα (§ 191. 2) and ἤλειφα, Pf. P. ἀλήλιμμαι and ἤλειμμαι, 1 A. P. ἠλείφθην, 2 A. P. ἠλίφην.

ἐρείκω, *to break*, F. ἐρείξω, 1 A. ἤρειξα, Ar. Vesp. 649, and ἤριξα, Hipp., 2 A. ἤρικον, P. 295, Pf. P. ἐρήριγμαι, Hipp. Collat., Ep. ἐρέχθω, ε. 83.

ἐρείπω, *to cast down*, F. ἐρείψω, A. ἤρειψα, A. P. ἠρείφθην. 2 A., comm. intrans., ἤριπον, E. 47, Plup. P. ἐρέριπτο Ξ. 15, late Pf. P. ἐρήρειμμαι.

See, also, λείπω (¶ 37) and πείθω (¶ 39).

7. Change of ο into ου.

ἀκούω (r. ἀκο-, ἀκου-), *to hear*, F. ἀκούσομαι, A. ἤκουσα, 2 Pf. ἀκήκοα, 2 Plup. ἠκηκόειν (§ 191. 2), A. P. ἠκούσθην. Late, F. ἀκούσω, Pf. P. ἤκουσμαι. Ep. ἀκουάζω, Hom. Merc. 423.

§ 270. 8. Change of ῠ into ῡ.

ἀλγύνω, *to afflict*, F. ἀλγῠνῶ, A. ἤλγῡνα, A. P. ἠλγύνθην.

ὀδύρομαι and δύρομαι, *to lament*, F. ὀδῠροῦμαι, A. ὠδυράμην.

πλύνω, *to wash*, F. πλῠνῶ, A. ἔπλῡνα, Pf. P. πέπλῠμαι (§ 217. *a*), A. P ἐπλῠθην.

τύφω (r. θῠφ-, τυφ- § 263), *to fumigate, to burn*, F. θύψω, Pf. P. τέθυμμαι, 2 A. P. ἐτῠφην.

9. Change of ῠ into ευ.

κεύθω (r. κυθ-, κευθ-), *to hide*, poet. Æsch. Pr. 571, F. κεύσω, 1 A. ἔκευσα, ο. 263, 2 A. ἔκυθον, γ. 16 (κέκυθον, § 194. 3), 2 Pf. κέκευθα, Soph. El. 1120. Ep. κευθάνω, Γ. 453.

τεύχω, *to prepare*, poet., F. τεύξω, A. ἔτευξα, Pf. P. τέτυγμαι, A. P. ἐτύχθην. Pf. *Pt.* intrans. τετευχώς μ. 423, Pf. P. τετεύχαται (§ 248. *f*) β. 63, Plup. ἐτετεύχατο Λ. 808, Pf. P. *Inf.* τετευχῆσθαι χ. 104, F. Pf. τετεύξομαι, M. 345, A. P. ἐτεύχθην, Hipp. Kindred verbs, τυγχάνω (§ 290), τιτύσκομαι (§ 285).

φεύγω, and sometimes φυγγάνω (§ 290), *to flee*, F. φεύξομαι and φευξοῦμαι (§ 200. 3), 1 A. ἔφευξα, commonly 2 A. ἔφυγον, 2 Pf. πέφευγα. Ep. Pf. *Pt.* πεφυζότες (cf. 274. δ) Φ. 6, πεφυγμένος α. 18.

10. Change of ε, in the diphthong ει, to η.

κλείω and *κλῄω*, *to shut*, F. *κλείσω* and *κλῄσω*, A. *ἔκλεισα* and *ἔκλῃσα*, Pf. P. *κέκλεισμαι*, *κέκλειμαι*, and *κέκλῃμαι*, F. Pf. *κεκλείσομαι*, Ar. Lys. 1072, A. P. *ἐκλείσθην*. Ion. *κληΐω*, *-ίσω*, Hdt. iii. 117; Dor. F. *κλαξῶ* or *κλᾳξῶ* Theoc. 6. 32, A. *ἔκλαξα*, &c., as from *κλάζω* or *κλᾴζω* (§ 245. 1).

§ 271. II. By the ADDITION OF CONSONANTS, usually either τ, σ, ν, σκ, or ζ.

Of these consonants, τ is chiefly added to *labial* roots; σ, to *palatal* and *lingual* roots; ν (without further addition, § 289. 2), to *liquid* and *pure* roots; σκ, ζ, &c., to *pure* roots. In a few instances, the *close terminations* are affixed to the protracted root.

§ 272. 1. ADDITION OF τ (see § 52).

α. To Labial Roots.

ἅπτω (r. *ἁφ-*, *ἁπτ-*), *to fasten to, to set on fire*, F. *ἅψω*, A. *ἧψα*, Pf. P. *ἧμμαι*, A. P. *ἥφθην* (*ἅφθην*, Hdt. i. 19, *ἐάφθην*, ν. 543). Kindred, *ἀφάω*, *to handle*, Ion. *ἀφάσσω*, A. *ἤφασα*, Hdt. iii. 69, *ἀπαφίσκω* (§ 296).

βάπτω (r. *βαφ-*, *βαπτ-*), *to dip*, F. *βάψω*, A. *ἔβαψα*, Pf. P. *βέβαμμαι*, 1 A. P. *ἐβάφθην*, commonly 2 A. P. *ἐβάφην*.

βλάπτω (r. *βλαβ-*), *to hurt*, F. *βλάψω*, A. *ἔβλαψα*, Pf. *βέβλαφα*, Pf. P. *βέβλαμμαι*, 1 A. P. *ἐβλάφθην*, 2 A. P. *ἐβλάβην*. F. Pf. *βεβλάψομαι*, Hipp. Ep. *βλάβομαι*, T. 82.

δρύπτω (r. *δρυφ-*), *to tear the flesh*, poet. Eur. El. 150, F. *δρύψω*, 1 A. *ἔδρυψα*, Π. 324, 2 A. *Opt.* *ἀποδρύφοι* Ψ. 187, A. P. *ἐδρύφθην*, ε. 435.

θάπτω (r. *θαφ-*), *to bury*, F. *θάψω*, A. *ἔθαψα*, Pf. P. *τέθαμμαι*, 3 F. *τεθάψομαι*, Soph. Aj. 577, 2 A. P. *ἐτάφην* (§ 263). 1 A. P. *ἐθάφθην*, Hdt. ii. 81. From the r. *θαφ-* in another sense, come the Ep. and Ion. 2 Pf., as Pres., *τέθηπα*, *to be amazed*, Δ. 243, Hdt. ii. 156, 2 A. *ἔταφον*, I. 193; and the late 1 Pf. trans. *τέθαφα*, Ath. 258 c.

θρύπτω (r. *θρυφ-*), *to break in pieces*, F. *θρύψω*, Pf. P. *τέθρυμμαι*. A. *ἔθρυψα*, Hipp., 1 A. P. *ἐθρύφθην*, Anth., 2 A. P. *ἐτρύφην* (§ 263), Γ. 363.

κάμπτω (r. *καμπ-*), *to bend*, F. *κάμψω*, A. *ἔκαμψα*, Pf. P. *κέκαμμαι* (§ 217. γ), A. P. *ἐκάμφθην*. Kindred, *γνάμπτω*.

κλέπτω (r. *κλαπ-*, *κλεπ-* § 259), *to steal*, F. *κλέψω*, A. *ἔκλεψα*, Pf. *κέκλοφα* (§ 236. *a*), Pf. P. *κέκλεμμαι*, 1 A. P. *ἐκλέφθην*, commonly 2 A. P. *ἐκλάπην*. Late 2 A. *ἔκλαπον*.

κόπτω (r. *κοπ-*), *to cut, to strike*, F. *κόψω*, A. *ἔκοψα*, Pf. *κέκοφα*, Pf. P. *κέκομμαι*, 3 F. *κεκόψομαι*, Ar. Ran. 1223, 2 A. P. *ἐκόπην*. 2 Pf. *Pt.* *κεκοπώς* N. 60.

κρύπτω (r. *κρυβ-*), *to hide*, F. *κρύψω*, A. *ἔκρυψα*, Pf. P. *κέκρυμμαι*, 1 A. P *ἐκρύφθην*, sometimes 2 A. P. *ἐκρύβην*. In Hipp., Pf. *κέκρυφα*, F. Pf. *κεκρύψομαι*. For *κρύπτασκε*, see § 249. *d*.

ῥάπτω (r. *ῥαφ-*), *to stitch*, F. *ῥάψω*, A. *ἔῤῥαψα*, Pf. P. *ἔῤῥαμμαι*, 2 A. P *ἐῤῥάφην*.

μάρπτω (r. *μαρπ-*), *to seize*, poet., F. *μάρψω*, O. 137, 1 A. *ἔμαρψα*, Ar. Eq

197, Ep 2 A. μέμαρπον, shortened μίμαπον (§§ 194. 3, 255. δ, 263. 6), and ἔμαπον, Hes. Sc. 231, 2 Pf. μέμαρπα, Id. Op. 202.

τύπτω (r. τυπ-, τυπτ-), F. τυπτήσω (§ 222. 1), 2 A. ἔτυπον, Pf. P. τετύπτημαι and τέτυμμαι, 2 A. P. ἐτύπην. Ion. 1 A. ἔτυψα, Δ. 531, ἐτυψάμην Hdt. ii. 40. For τετυπόντες, see § 194. 3.

β. To Other Roots.

ἀνύω, ἀνύτω (r. ἀνυ-, ἀνυτ-), *to accomplish*, F. ἀνύσω, A. ἤνυσα, Pf. ἤνυκα, Pf. P. ἤνυσμαι. A. P. ἠνύσθην, Hes. Sc. 311. The simpler form ἄνω likewise occurs in the Pres. and Impf. For ἤνυτο, &c., see § 246. α

τίκτω (r. τεκ-, τικτ- § 259), *to beget, to bring forth*, F. τέξω, commonly τέξομαι, 1 A. ἔτεξα, commonly 2 A. ἔτεκον, 2 Pf. τέτοκα, A. P. ἐτέχθην. Late Pf. P. τέτεγμαι. For τεκεῖσθαι, see § 200. γ.

§ 273. 2. ADDITION OF σ.

This letter is sometimes *simply prefixed* or *affixed* to the characteristic, but commonly *unites* with it, if a *palatal*, to form σσ (ττ, § 70. 1), or less frequently ζ, and, if a *lingual*, to form ζ (§ 51. N.), or less frequently σσ (ττ).

NOTES. (1.) Palatals in -ζω are mostly onomatopes. (2.) Linguals in -ζω are mostly derivatives, wanting the second tenses, and, by reason of euphonic changes, nowhere exhibiting the root in its simple form. The characteristic may, however, be often determined from another word. It is most frequently δ, and may be assumed to be this letter, if not known to be another. (3.) In a few instances, σ unites with γγ to form ζ, and even with a labial to form ζ or σσ.

α. Prefixed.

ἀλύσκω (r. ἀλυκ-, ἀλυσκ-), *to avoid*, poet., F. ἀλύξω, A. ἤλυξα. Extended Ep. forms, ἀλυσκάζω Z. 443, ἀλύσκανε χ. 330.

ἐΐσκω (r. ἐϊκ-, εἰκ- § 260, ἐϊσκ-), *to liken*, Ep. Γ. 197 (also ἴσκω δ. 279), Pf. P., as Pres., ἤϊγμαι, *to be like*, Eur. Alc. 1063, Plup. P. ἠΐγμην, δ. 796. The common trans. form is εἰκάζω, -άσω, &c., and the common intrans., the pret. ἔοικα (§ 238. β), for which are also used the simpler εἶκα (having in the 3d Pers. pl. the irregular form εἴξᾱσι Ar. Av. 96; cf. ἴσᾱσι, § 237. οἶδα), and Ion. οἶκα, Hdt. i. 155; Plup., as Impf., ἐῴκειν (§ 189. 5), F. εἴξω, Ar. Nub. 1001. Ep. Impf. intrans. (or Pf.) εἶκε Σ. 520.

ἐνέπω and ἐννέπω (r. ἐνεπ-, ἐνισπ- § 259, ἐνισπ-), *to speak, tell*, poet. Λ. 643, Β. 761, Soph. Œd. T. 350, F. ἐνίψω, Η. 447, and ἐνισπήσω (§ 222) ε. 98 2 A. ἔνισπον, Eur. Sup. 435. Kindred, ἐνίπτω and ἐνίσσω (§ 276. θ), *to reproach*, Ep. Γ. 438, Ο. 198, 2 A. ἠνίπαπον and ἐνένιπον (§ 194. 3). Related to εἶπον (§ 301. 7).

λάσκω (r. λακ-), *to sound, to utter*, poet., F. λακήσομαι (§ 222), A. ἐλάκησα, commonly 2 A. ἔλακον, 2 Pf. λέλᾱκα (§ 236. E.). 2 A. M. λελάκοντο (§ 194. 3). For λελᾱκυῖα, see § 253. 2. Deriv. forms, Ep. ληκέω, θ. 379, Dor. λᾱκέω, Theoc. 2. 24, Att. λακάζω, Æsch. Sup. 872.

β. Affixed.

ἀλέξω (r. ἀλεκ-, ἀλεξ-), *to ward off*, poet. in the Act., F. ἀλεξήσω, Z. 109, 1 A. ἠλέξησα, γ. 346, and ἤλεξα, Æsch. Sup. 1052, 2 A. ἄλαλκον (§§ 194. 3,

261), ἤλκαθον (§ 299) Æsch. Fr. 417; Mid. *to repel*, F. ἀλεξήσομαι, vii. 7. 3 A. ἠλεξάμην, i. 3. 6.

ὀδάξομαι, *to bite*, Ion. and Poet., F. ὀδαξήσομαι, Hipp., A. ὠδαξάμην, Anth., Pf. P. ὤδαγμαι. Act. ὀδάξω, *to smart from a bite*, Symp. 4. 27.

§ 274. γ. Uniting with a Palatal to form σσ (ττ).

ἀλλάσσω or ἀλλάττω (r. ἀλλαγ-), *to change*, F. ἀλλάξω, A. ἤλλαξα, Pf. ἤλλαχα, Pf. P. ἤλλαγμαι, 1 A. P. ἠλλάχθην, 2 A. P. ἠλλάγην.

πλήσσω (r. πληγ-), *to strike*, in composition with ἐκ or κατά, *to strike with terror*, F. πλήξω, A. ἔπληξα, 2 Pf. πέπληγα, Pf. P. πέπληγμαι, 3 F. πεπλήξομαι, Ar. Eq. 272, 1 A. P. ἐπλήχθην, commonly 2 A. P. ἐπλήγην, but ἐξεπλᾰγην, κατεπλᾰγην (-ήγην, Γ. 31, Σ. 225). For πέπληγον, &c., see § 194. 3. The form πλήγνῦμαι (§ 293) occurs Th. iv. 125. In the simple sense *to strike*, the Att. writers associate the Act. of πατάσσω with the Pass. of πλήσσω (§ 301).

πτήσσω (r. πτακ-, πτηκ- § 266), *to crouch from fear*, F. πτήξω, 1 A. ἔπτηξα, poet. 2 A. ἔπτακον, Æsch. Eum. 252, Pf. ἔπτηχα. Ep., from r. πτα-, 2 A. *D.* 3 πτήτην H. 136, Pf. *Pt.* πεπτηώς (§ 253. 1), B. 312 (cf. § 238. α). Kindred, πτώσσω, Δ. 371, πτωσκάζω, Δ. 372.

ταράσσω (r. ταραχ-), *to disturb*, F. ταράξω, A. ἐτάραξα, Pf. P. τετάραγμαι, A. P. ἐταράχθην. From ταράσσω is formed, by metathesis, contraction, and the aspiration of τ before ρ (§ 65. N.), θράσσω (ταρασσ-, τρaασσ-, θρᾱσσ-), F. θράξω, A. ἔθραξα, A. P. ἐθράχθην. Ep. Pf., as Pr. intrans., τέτρηχα (§ 62), H. 346.

τάσσω (r. ταγ-), *to arrange*, F. τάξω, A. ἔταξα, Pf. τέταχα, Pf. P. τέταγμαι, F. Pf. τετάξομαι, Th. v. 71, 1 A. P. ἐτάχθην, rare 2 A. P. ἐτάγην.

φρίσσω (r. φρικ-), *to shudder*, F. φρίξω, A. ἔφριξα, 2 Pf. πέφρῑκα. For πεφρῑκοντας, see § 246. 2.

δ. Uniting with a Palatal to form ζ.

κράζω and 2 Pf. κέκρᾱγα (§ 238. β), *to cry*, F. Pf. κεκράξομαι (§ 239. *c*), 2 A. ἔκραγον. Kindred, κλάζω (§ 277. α), κρώζω, -ωξω, κλώζω.

οἰμώζω (r. οἰμωγ-), *to bewail*, F. οἰμώξομαι, A. ᾤμωξα, Pf. P. οἴμωγμαι (§ 189. 4). A. P. *Pt.* οἰμωχθείς Theog. 1204, late F. οἰμώξω, Anth.

ὀλολύζω (r. ὀλολυγ-), *to shout, to shriek*, F. ὀλολύξομαι, A. ὠλόλυξα.

στενάζω, and poet. στενάχω, *to groan*, F. στενάξω, A. ἐστέναξα. Poet. forms, στοναχέω, Soph. El. 133, στοναχίζω or στεναχίζω, B. 781, A. ἐστονάχησα, Σ. 124.

σφάζω and σφάττω (r. σφαγ-), *to slay*, F. σφάξω, A. ἔσφαξα, 1 A. P. ἐσφάχθην, commonly 2 A. P. ἐσφάγην. Pf. P. ἔσφαγμαι, κ. 532. The shorter root φα- appears in the Ep. Pf. P. πέφᾰμαι, E. 531, F. Pf. πεφήσομαι, N. 829. Hence (r. φα-, φεν- §§ 259, 277), the poet. 2 A. ἔπεφνον (§§ 194. 3, 261).

ε. Uniting with γγ to form ζ.

πλάζω (r. πλαγγ-), *to cause to wander*, poet. (= πλανάω), B. 132, A. ἔπλαγξα, ω. 307; Mid. πλάζομαι, *to wander*, Soph. Aj. 886, F. πλάγξομαι ο. 312, A. P. ἐπλάγχθην Eur. Hipp. 240.

σαλπίζω (r. σαλπιγγ-), *to sound a trumpet*, F. σαλπίγξω, A. ἐσάλπιγξα. Late F. σαλπίσω, &c.

See, also, κλάζω (§ 277. α).

§ **275.** ζ. Uniting with a Lingual to form ζ.

καθίζω (r. ἑ-, ἑδ- § 282, ἑζ-, ἱζ- § 259), *to seat, to place*, F. *καθίσω*, *καθιῶ* (§ 200. β), A. *ἐκάθῖσα* and *καθῖσα* (§ 192. 3), Ar. Ran. 911. Mid. *καθίζομαι*, and rarely *καθέζομαι*, Pl. Ax. 371 c, *to sit*, F. *καθιζήσομαι* (§ 222), Pl. Phædr. 229 a, and *καθεδοῦμαι* (§ 200. γ), Pl. Theæt. 146 a, 1 A. commonly trans. *ἐκαθισάμην*, Dem. 897. 3, and *καθεισάμην* (§ 189. 3), Eur. Hipp. 31 2 A. intrans. *ἐκαθεζόμην*, i. 5. 9. Late, A. P. *ἐκαθέσθην*, Anth., F. M. *καθεδήσομαι*, Diog. Laert. ii. 72. The simple forms are chiefly poet. and dialectic *ἵζω*, *to seat, sit*, B. 53, Æsch. Eum. 18 (extended *ἱζάνω*, Th. ii. 76), A. *εἷσα*, B. 549, *Pt.* *ἕσας*, κ. 361 (Ion. *ὑπ-είσας* Hdt. iii. 126); Mid. *ἵζομαι*, Γ. 162, and rarely *ἕζομαι*, Soph. Œd. T. 32, F. *ἐφ-έσσεσθαι* I. 455, later *εἴσομαι* Ap. Rh. 2. 807, 1 A. *εἱσάμην*, Theog. 12, *ἑσσάμην*, Pind. P. 4. 363, *ἐεσσάμην*, ξ. 295, 2 A. *ἑζόμην*, Æsch. Eum. 3; Pf. P. *ἧμαι*, *to sit* (¶ 59), A. 134, Eur. Alc. 604, of which the comp. *κάθημαι* is also common in Att. prose. Deriv. *ἱδρύω*, -*ύσω*, &c., A. P. *ἱδρύθην* and *ἱδρύνθην* (§ 278. γ).

ὀνομάζω (r. *ὀνοματ-*), *to name*, F. *ὀνομάσω*, A. *ὠνόμασα*, Pf. *ὠνόμακα*, Pf. P. *ὠνόμασμαι*, A. P. *ὠνομάσθην*. Ion. *οὐνομάζω* (§ 44. 4), Hdt. iv. 6, Æol. *ὀνυμάζω* (§ 44. 5), Pind. P. 2. 82, chiefly Ep. *ὀνομαίνω*, B. 488.

φράζω (r. *φραδ-*), *to tell*, F. *φράσω*, A. *ἔφρασα*, Pf. *πέφρακα*, Pf. P. *πέφρασμαι*, A. P. *ἐφράσθην*. Pf. P. *Pt.* *πρo-πεφραδμένος*, Hes. Op. 653. For *πέφραδον*, &c., see § 194. 3. Extended, 1 A. *φράδασσε* Pind. Nem. 3. 45.

χάζω (r. *χαδ-*, *καδ-* § 263. N.), *to drive back, retire* (*ἀνα-χάζω* iv. 1. 16), more frequently, but chiefly Ep., Mid. *χάζομαι*, *to retire*, F. *χάσομαι*, 1 A. *ἐχασσάμην*, Δ. 535. Ep. 2 A. *Pt.* *κεκαδών*, 2 A. M. *κεκάδοντο* (§ 194. 3), F. *κεκαδήσω* (§ 239. *b*).

η. Uniting with a Lingual to form σσ (ττ).

ἀηθέσσω, *to be unused*, Ep. K. 493, A. *ἀήθεσα*, Ap. Rh. 1. 1171.

ἁρμόζω, and Att. *ἁρμόττω* (r. *ἁρμοδ-*), F. *ἁρμόσω*, *ἥρμοσμαι*, Dor. A. P. *ἁρμόχθην*, Diog. Laert. viii. 85.

βλίσσω or *βλίττω* (r. *μελιτ-*, *μλιτ-* § 261, *βλιτ-* § 64. N.), *to take honey from the hive*, F. *βλίσω*, A. *ἔβλισα*.

κορύσσω (r. *κορυθ-*), *to arm*, poet., Pf. P. *Pt.* *κεκορυθμένος* (§ 53), Γ. 18 Eur. Andr. 279. A. M. *Pt.* *κορυσσάμενος* (§ 71) T. 397, Dor. A. *ἐκόρυξα* (§ 245. 1), Theoc. 3. 5.

πάσσω, *to sprinkle*, F. *πάσω*, A. *ἔπασα*, A. P. *ἐπάσθην*.

πλάσσω, *to fashion*, F. *πλάσω*, A. *ἔπλασα*, Pf. P. *πέπλασμαι*, A. P. *ἐπλάσθην*.

θ. Uniting with a Labial to form ζ or σσ.

νίζω (r. *νιφ-*), *to wash*, F. *νίψω*, A. *ἔνιψα*, Pf. P. *νένιμμαι*, A. P. *ἐνίφθην*, Hipp. Late *νίπτω*, Plut., but *ἀπο-νίπτεσθαι* σ. 178.

πέσσω or *πέττω* (r. *πεπ-*), *to cook*, F. *πέψω*, A. *ἔπεψα*, Pf. P. *πέπεμμαι*, A. P. *ἐπέφθην*. Late *πέπτω*.

See, also, *ἐνίσσω* (§ 273. α), *λάζομαι* (§ 290).

§ **276.** Remark. As verbs in -*ζω* and -*σσω* are formed from both palatal and lingual roots, and as pure verbs often pass into verbs in -*ζω*, it is not strange that in some verbs there should be an intermingling of forms. Thus, ἁρπάζω, *to snatch*, F. ἁρπάσω, A. ἥρπασα, Pf. ἥρπακα, Pf. P. ἥρπασμαι, A. P. ἡρπάσθην. Non-Att. F. ἁρπάξω, X. 310, A. P. ἡρπάχθην, Hdt. ii. 90, &c. Late 2 A. M. *Pt.* (r. ἁρπα-, § 227) ἁρπάμενος, Anth.

ἐναρίζω, *to slay, strip*, poet., F. ἐναρίξω, A. 191, A. ἐνάριξα P. 187, and ἠνάρισα, Anacr., Pf. P. ἠνάρισμαι, Soph. Aj. 26, ἠναρίσθην, Æsch. Cho. 347. Primitive, ἐναίρω Θ. 296, 2 A. ἤναρον, Soph. Ant. 871, 1 A. M. ἐνηράμην, E. 43.

ἔρδω (or ἕρδω) and ῥέζω (r. ἐργ-, ῥεγ- § 262, ἐρδ-), *to do*, poet. and Ion. Æsch. Sept. 231, Φ. 214, F. ἔρξω ε. 360, and ῥέξω, Eur. Alc. 262, A. ἔρξα, Æsch. Sept. 924, and ἔῤῥεξα or ἔρεξα, I. 536, Soph. Œd. C. 539 (observe the augment), 2 Pf. ἔοργα, B. 272, 2 Plup. ἐώργειν (§ 189. 5), δ. 693, ἐόργεα, Hdt. i. 127, A. P. *Pt.* ῥεχθείς, I. 250.

μερμηρίζω, *to ponder*, poet., F. μερμηρίξω π. 261, A. ἐμερμήριξα, A. 189, and ἐμερμήρισα, Ar. Vesp. 5.

παίζω, *to play*, F. παίξομαι, παιξοῦμαι (§ 200. 3), A. ἔπαισα, Pf. πέπαικα, Pf. P. πεπαίσμαι. Later, παίξω, ἔπαιξα, πέπαιχα, πέπαιγμαι, ἐπαίχθην.

NOTE. See § 245. 1. The Dorics sometimes extend the palatal forms to other tenses, besides the Fut. and Aor. act. and mid.; as, ἐλυγίχθης (for -ίσθης) Theoc. 1. 98, τέθλαγμαι (θλάω) Id. 22. 45, ἁρμόχθην (§ 275. η).

§ 277. 3. ADDITION OF ν.

In *impure* roots, ν is commonly *prefixed* to the characteristic, but in *pure* roots, *affixed*.

NOTE. In a few poetic forms, ν is prefixed to α characteristic. For the changes of ν before a consonant, see § 54. A short vowel is sometimes lengthened before ν.

α. Prefixed to a Consonant.

ἅλλομαι (r. ἁλ-, ἀνλ-, ἀλλ-), *to leap*, F. ἁλοῦμαι, A. ἡλάμην, *Subj.* ἅλω μαι (§ 56. α), &c., 2 A. ἡλόμην, *Subj.* ἅλωμαι, &c. Ep. nude 2 A. *S.* 2 ἆλσο π. 754, 3 ἆλτο 755, *Pt.* ἅλμενος Α. 421 (§§ 13. 4, 185. δ).

βάλλω (r. βαλ-, βλα- § 262, βολε- §§ 28, 288), F. βαλῶ, &c., see § 223. Ep., F. βλήσομαι, Υ. 335, 2 A. ἔβλην (§ 227. β), φ. 15, ἐβλήμην, Ξ. 39, commonly pass. Λ. 675, *Opt. S.* 2 βλῇο or (r. βλε- § 259, cf. χρείη, πλείμην, § 284) βλεῖο N. 288, *Inf.* βλῆσθαι Δ. 115, &c.; Pf. P. βεβόλημαι, I. 9.

κλάζω (r. κλαγ-, κλαγγ-, κλαζ- § 274. ε), *to clang, to scream*, F. κλάγξω, 1 A. ἔκλαγξα, 2 A. ἔκλαγον, Pf., as Pres., κέκλαγγα or κέκλαγχα, Ar. Vesp. 929 (κέκληγα, B. 222, see § 246. 2), F. Pf. κεκλάγξομαι (§ 239. c). Extended forms, κλαγγέω, Theoc. Ep. 6. 5, κλαγγαίνω, Æsch. Eum. 131, κλαγγάνω Soph. Fr. 782.

σφάλλω (r. σφαλ-), *to deceive*, F. σφαλῶ, A. ἔσφηλα, Pf. P. ἔσφαλμαι, 2 A. P. ἐσφάλην.

στέλλω (r. σταλ-, στελ- § 259), *to send*, F. στελῶ, A. ἔστειλα, Pf. ἔσταλκα, Pf. P. ἔσταλμαι, 2 A. P. ἐστάλην, rarely 1 A. P. ἐστάλθην. For ἐσταλάδατο, see § 248. *f*.

β. Affixed to a Consonant.

δάκνω (r. δακ-, δηκ- § 266), *to bite*, F. δήξομαι, 2 A. ἔδακον, Pf. P. δέδη γμαι, A. P. ἐδήχθην. Poet. Mid. δακνάζομαι, Æsch. Pers. 571.

τέμνω (r. ταμ-, τεμ- § 259), *to cut*, F. τεμῶ, 2 A. ἔταμον and ἔτεμον, Pf τέτμηκα (§ 261), Pf. P. τέτμημαι, 3 F. τετμήσομαι, A. P. ἐτμήθην. Ion. τάμνω, Γ. 105. For τετμῆσθον, see § 234. β. Kindred Ep. τμήγω, Π. 390 (τμήσσω, Mosch. 2. 81), F. τμήξω, 1 A. ἔτμηξα, 2 A. ἔτμαγον, 2 A. P. ἐτμάγην, later ἐτμήγην. Some read τέμει, as Pres., N. 707.

See, also, κάμνω (§ 223).

§ 278. γ. Affixed to a Vowel.

βαίνω, and poet. βάσκω (§ 279 ; r. βα-), *to go*, F. βήσομαι, 2 A. ἔβη (¶ 57 ; see § 227, 242. b, 251. 4), Pf. βέβηκα (see § 238. α). Poet. and Ion., F. βήσω, *I will cause to go*, Eur. Iph. T. 742, 1 A. ἔβησα, Hdt. i. 46. In composition, Pf. P. βέβαμαι and βέβασμαι (§ 221. α), A. P. ἐβάθην. For βήσεο, &c., see § 185. ε. Kindred forms, βάω in Dor. ἐκβῶντας Th. v. 77 ; Ep. βιβάω, Γ. 22, βίβημι, H. 213, βιβάσθω N. 809; Ion. βιβάσκω, Hipp.; the common causative βιβάζω; and apparently the Ep. Pres. used as Fut. (§ 200. b) βέομαι, *I shall walk, live*, O. 194, X. 431, *Pl.* βεόμεσθα (or βιόμεσθα) Hom. Ap. 528.

δύνω (r. δυ-), *to enter*, F. δύσομαι, 2 A. ἔδυν (¶ 57 ; see §§ 227, 226. 4), Pf. δέδυκα. For δυνέουσι, see § 243. 4. The primitive δύω is commonly causative, *to make to enter* (yet = δύνω, ε. 272), F. δύσω, A. ἔδυσα, Pf. ἀποδέδυκα v. 8. 23, Pf. P. δέδυμαι, A. P. ἐδύθην. Chiefly Ep. and Ion., Pres. M. δύομαι, E. 140, A. M. ἐδυσάμην, B. 578, 2 A. P. ἐδύην, Hipp. For δύσετο, &c., see § 185. ε. Later Ep. form, δύπτω, Ap. Rh. 1. 1008, A. *Pt.* δύψας 1326.

ἐλάω, commonly ἐλαύνω, *to drive*, F. ἐλάσω, ἐλῶ (§ 200. 2), A. ἤλασα, Pf. ἐλήλακα (§ 191), Pf. P. ἐλήλαμαι, A. P. ἠλάθην. Ion., Pf. P. ἐλήλασμαι Hipp., A. P. ἠλάσθην, Hdt. iii. 54. For ἐληλάδατο, see § 248. *f*. Ion. and Poet. ἐλαστρέω, Σ. 543.

μάομαι and μαίομαι (r. μα-, μαι- § 267, μεν- § 259), *to seek after*, poet. Soph. Œd. C. 836, ν. 367, Ep. F. μάσσομαι (§ 71) Δ. 190, A. ἐμασσάμην, ν. 429, 2 Pf. μέμονα (§ 238. α). Pres. *Imp.* μῶεο (§ 242. b) Mem. ii. 1. 20 (Epich.), *Inf.* (as from r. μαο-) μῶσθαι Theog. 769. Extended, μαιμάω, -ήσω, Soph. Aj. 50.

πίνω (r. πο-, πι- § 259), *to drink*, F. πίομαι (§ 200. b), later πιοῦμαι (§ 200. 3), 2 A. ἔπιον (§ 227. α), *Imp.* πίε, commonly πῖθι, Pf. πέπωκα, Pf. P. πέπομαι, A. P. ἐπόθην.

τίνω (r. τι-), *to pay, to expiate*, F. τίσω, A. ἔτισα, Pf. τέτικα, Pf. P. τέτισμαι, A. P. ἐτίσθην. Mid. τίνομαι, and τίνυμαι or τίννυμαι (§ 293), *to avenge, to punish*, chiefly poet. Γ. 279, 366, Eur. Or. 323, 1172, Hdt. v. 77. Poet. τίω, *to pay honor to*, F. τίσω I. 142, ἔτισα, Soph. Ant. 22, Pf. P. *Pt.* τετιμένος, Υ. 426.

φθάνω (r. φθα-), *to anticipate*, F. φθάσω, commonly φθήσομαι (§ 219), 1 A. ἔφθασα, 2 A. ἔφθην (§ 227), Pf. ἔφθακα. Ep. 2 A. M. *Pt.* φθάμενος E. 119.

φθίνω (r. φθι-), *to perish, to destroy*, F. trans. φθίσω, φθιῶ, Soph. Aj. 1027, intrans. φθίσομαι, A. trans. ἔφθισα, Pf. P. ἔφθιμαι, Plup. P. and 2 A. M. (§§ 227, 226. 4) ἐφθίμην. Ep., φθίω, Σ. 446, β. 368, A. P. ἐφθίθην, ψ. 331, 2 A. Act. ἔφθιθον (cf. § 299) E. 110. Extended poet. form, φθινύθω, A. 491, α. 250.

δ. Prefixed to α.

See δάμναμαι (§ 298), κίρνημι, κρήμναμαι, πίτνημι, σκίδνημι (§ 293), πέρνημι (§ 285), πιλνάω, πίλναμαι (§ 282).

§ 279. 4. ADDITION OF σκ.

The addition of these letters is commonly attended with the *precession* or *protraction* of the preceding vowel, with *metathesis*, or with the *loss of a consonant*.

α. Without further Change.

ἀρέσκω (r. *ἀρε-*), *to please*, F. *ἀρέσω*, A. *ἤρεσα*, A. P. *ἠρέσθην*. See *ἀραρίσκω* (§ 285).

γηράω and *γηράσκω*, *to grow old*, F. *γηράσω* and *γηράσομαι*, 1 A. *ἐγήρᾱσα*, 2 A. *ἐγήρᾱν* (§ 227), Pf. *γεγήρακα*.

ἱλάσκομαι (r. *ἱλα-*), *to propitiate*, F. *ἱλᾰ́σομαι*, A. *ἱλᾰσάμην*, A. P. *ἱλάσθην*. Kindred Att. forms, *ἱλέομαι* Æsch. Sup. 117, *ἱλεόομαι*, Pl. Leg. 804 b. Ep., *ἱλάομαι*, B. 550, Pf. *Subj.* *ἱλήκω*, φ. 365, *Opt.* *ἱλήκοιμι*, Hom. Ap. 165; forms as from *ἵλημι*, Imp. *ἵλᾱθι* Ap. Rh. 4. 1014, *ἵληθι* (§ 251. 4), Mid. *ἵλᾰμαι* Hom. Hym. 20. 5; later Ep., F. *ἱλάξομαι* Ap. Rh. 2. 808, A. *ἱλαξάμην*, 1. 1093.

μεθύσκω (r. *μεθυ-*), *to intoxicate*, F. *μεθῠ́σω*, A. *ἐμέθῠσα*, A. P. *ἐμεθύσθην*. The intrans. *μεθύω*, *to be drunk*, occurs in the Pres. and Impf.

§ 280. β. Vowel changed by Precession.

ἀμβλόω, commonly *ἀμβλίσκω* (r. *ἀμβλο-*, *ἀμβλισκ-* § 259), *to miscarry*, F. *ἀμβλώσω*, A. *ἤμβλωσα*, Pf. *ἤμβλωκα*, Pf. P. *ἤμβλωμαι*. 2 A. *ἤμβλων* in Suid. Ion. *ἐξ-αμβλέεται* Hipp.

ἀνᾱλόω, commonly *ἀνᾱλίσκω* (r. *ἀλο-*, *ἀλισκ-*), *to expend*, F. *ἀνᾱλώσω*, A. *ἀνήλωσα*, Pf. *ἀνήλωκα*, Pf. P. *ἀνήλωμαι*, A. P. *ἀνηλώθην*. This verb often retains α in the augment (§ 189. 4), especially in the older Att.; and sometimes, in double composition, augments the second preposition (§ 192. 3); thus, A. *ἀνᾱ́λωσα*, Soph. Aj. 1049, *κατηνάλωσα*, Isoc. 201 b.

γ. Vowel Lengthened.

βιώσκομαι (r. *βιο-*, *βιωσκ-*), chiefly in the comp. *ἀνα-βιώσκομαι*, *to revive*, both trans. and intrans., F. *βιώσομαι*, 1 A. trans. *ἐβιωσάμην*, 2 A. intrans. *ἐβίων* (§ 227), *βιῶ*, *βιῴην* (§ 226. 2), *βίωθι*, *βιῶναι*, *βιούς*. Primitive, *βιόω*, *to live*, Fut. *βιώσω*, commonly *βιώσομαι*, 1 A. *ἐβίωσα*, commonly 2 A. *ἐβίων*, Pf. *βεβίωκα*, Pf. P. *βεβίωμαι*. Shorter Ep. forms, *βιόμεσθα* (*βεόμεσθα* Wolf., § 278) Hom. Ap. 528, F. *βώσεσθε* Ap. Rh. 1. 685. For *βιόω*, we commonly find, in the Pres. and Impf., *ζάω*, which again in the other tenses (F. *ζήσω* or *ζήσομαι*, A. *ἔζησα*, &c.) is rare or late. For the contraction of *ζάω*, see § 33. α. From the contr. forms of the Impf. (*ἔζαες*) *ἔζης*, *ἔζη*, appears to have arisen a 1st Pers. *ἔζην* Eur. Alc. 295, and a late *Imp.* *ζῆθι* Anth. The prolonged *ζώω* and *ζόω* (§ 242. b) have given rise to A. *ἐπ-έζωσε* Hdt. i. 120, *Inf.* *ζόειν* Simon. Fr. 231. 17.

§ 281. δ. Metathesis.

βλώσκω (r. *μολ-*, *μλο-*, *βλο-* § 64. N.), *to go, to come* (in the Pres., Ep. and found only in composition, π. 466), F. *μολοῦμαι*, 2 A. *ἔμολον*, Pf. *μέμβλωκα* (§ 223).

θνήσκω (r. *θαν-*, *θνα-*), *to die*, F. *θανοῦμαι*, 2 A. *ἔθανον*, Pf. *τέθνηκα* (§ 237), F. Pf. *τεθνήξω* and *τεθνήξομαι* (§ 239. a). See *κτείνω* (§ 295).

θρώσκω (r. θορ-, θρο-), *to leap*, F. θοροῦμαι, 2 A. ἔθορον. Collat. θόρνυμαι, Hdt. iii. 109.

ε. Consonant Dropped.

χάσκω (r. χαν-, § 55), *to gape*, F. χανοῦμαι, 2 A. ἔχανον, 2 Pf. κέχηνα. Late χαίνω. Extended χασκάζω, Ar. Vesp. 695.

πάσχω (r. παθ-, πενθ- §§ 259, 277, παθσκ-, πασχ-, the aspiration of the θ, which is dropped before σ, being transferred to the κ, which thus becomes χ), *to suffer*, F. πείσομαι (§ 58), 2 A. ἔπαθον, 2 Pf. πέπονθα. Poet. 1 A. *Pt.* πήσας (but πταίσας Dind.) Æsch. Ag. 1624, Ep. Pf. *Pt.* πεπᾰθυίῃ (§ 253. 2) ρ. 555, Dor. Pf. πέποσχα, Epich. 7(2). For πέποσθε, see § 238. β.

§ 282. 5. Addition of δ, ζ, θ, and χ.

ἀμείρω and ἀμέρδω (r. ἀμερ-), *to deprive*, poet. Pind. P. 6. 27, τ. 18, F. ἀμέρσω, A. ἤμερσα, θ. 64, A. P. ἠμέρθην, X. 58.

δίω and δείδω (r. δι-, δειδ- § 269. 6) both Ep. I. 433, Λ. 470, commonly δέδια or δέδοικα (¶ 58, § 237), *to fear*, F. Ep. δείσομαι, O. 299, A. ἔδεισα, Cyr. i. 4. 22; Mid. δίομαι, *to frighten*, poet. E. 763, Æsch. Eum. 357. Deriv. δεδίσκομαι or δεδίττομαι, *to frighten*, διώκω (§ 299), and Ep. δίημι, *to chase*.

νήθω (r. νε-, νηθ- § 266), *to spin*, F. νήσω, A. P. ἐνήθην. Ep. νέω, Hes. Op. 775, A. ἔνησα, Υ. 128, ἐνησάμην, η. 198. Late Pf. P. νένησμαι.

οὐτάζω (r. οὐτα-), *to wound*, F. οὐτάσω, &c. Ep. οὐτάω, χ. 356, F. οὐτήσω, 1 A. οὔτησα, 2 A. *S.* 3 οὖτᾰ (§ 224. E.), *Inf.* οὐτάμεν, -άμεναι, E. 132, 2 A. M. *Pt.*, as Pass., οὐτάμενος, Λ. 659.

πελάζω, and poet. πελᾰθω, Eur. Rh. 555, or πλᾱθω, Soph. El. 220 (r. πελα-, πελαζ-, πελᾰθ-, πλεᾰθ-, πλᾱθ-, §§ 260, 262), *to approach*, F. πελᾰσω, πελῶ (§ 200. 2), A. ἐπέλᾰσα, A. P. ἐπελάσθην and poet. ἐπλᾱθην (§ 261. N.), Æsch. Pr. 896. Ep., πελάω, Hom. Bac. 44, Pf. P. πέπλημαι μ. 108, 2 A. M. ἐπλήμην, Δ. 449; πιλνάω, *to bring near*, Hes. Op. 508, πίλναμαι, *to approach*, T. 93.

πρίω and πρίζω, *to saw*, F. πρίσω, A. ἔπρισα, Pf. P. πέπρισμαι, A. P. ἐπρίσθην.

σώζω (r. σαο-, σω- § 261), *to save*, F. σώσω, A. ἔσωσα, Pf. σέσωκα, Pf. P. σέσωμαι and σέσωσμαι, A. P. ἐσώθην. Ep., σαόω, Call. Del. 22, σαώσω, A. 83, &c.; Pres. *Imp.* (σάοε, σάου, σῶ, § 242. b) σάω ν. 230, Impf. *S.* 3 (ἐσάοε) ἐσάω or σάω Π. 363, Φ. 238; contr. σώω, Ap. Rh. 4. 197; σόω, in the Subj. σόῃς I. 681, σόῃ 424.

τρύω, *to afflict*, F. τρύσω, Pf. P. τέτρυμαι· and τρύχω (r. τρυ-, τρυχ-, τρυχο- § 298), F. τρύξω, Pf. P. τετρύχωμαι, Th. iv. 60. So νέω (§ 220), *to swim*, poet. νήχω, ε. 375; ψάω and ψήχω, *to rub*.

§ 283. III. By increasing the number of syllables, either, 1. by *reduplication*, or 2. by *syllabic affixes*, or 3. by *exchange of letters*.

1. Reduplication.

Reduplication in the root is most frequent in *verbs in -μι* and *-σκω*. It is of three kinds:

a. *Proper*, which belongs to roots beginning with a *single consonant*, with a *mute and liquid*, or with μν, and which prefixes the *initial consonant* with ι, or rarely with ε. See δίδωμι, κίχρημι (§ 284); βιβρώσκω, μιμνήσκω (§ 285).

b. *Attic*, which belongs to roots beginning with a *short vowel followed by a single consonant*, and which prefixes the *two first letters*. See ἀραρίσκω (§ 285).

Instead of repeating the initial vowel, ι is sometimes inserted, in imitation of the proper reduplication. See ὀνίνημι (§ 284).

c. *Improper*, which belongs to roots not included above, and which simply prefixes ι with the *rough breathing*.

Compare §§ 190, 191. 2. 4.

§ 284. α. Verbs in -μι.

δέω, *to bind*, rarely δίδημι (r. δε-, διδε-), v. 8. 24 (Impf. δίδη Λ. 105), F. δήσω. See §§ 219, 216. β.

δίδωμι (r. δο-, διδο-), *to give*, F. δώσω, Ep. διδώσω, ν. 358. See ¶ 51.

ἵημι (r. ἑ-, ἱε-), *to send*, F. ἥσω. See ¶ 54, § 229.

ἵστημι (r. στα-, ἱστα-), *to place*, F. στήσω. See ¶ 48. Poet. 1 A. ἕστᾰσα, M. 56. Late Pf. trans. ἕστᾰκα Anth., Dor. 1 A. P. ἐστάθην Call. Lav. 83. Kindred forms, ἱστάνω in composition only, Dem. 807. 6; rare ἑστήκω (§ 246. N.) Ath. 412 e; late στήκω, Rom. 14. 4; στεῦμαι (§ 246. α).

κίχρημι (r. χρα-, κιχρα- § 62), *to lend*, F. χρήσω, A. ἔχρησα, Pf. P. κέχρημαι. Mid. κίχρᾰμαι, *to borrow*. The primitive sense of the root χρα- appears to be *to supply need*. Hence we have,

1. κίχρημι, *to supply the need of another, by lending him what he requires*. Mid. κίχραμαι, *to supply one's own need by borrowing*.

2. χράω (§ 218. α), *to supply the need of one who consults an oracle, by answering his inquiries*, F. χρήσω, A. ἔχρησα, Pf. P. κέχρημαι and κέχρησμαι, A. P. ἐχρήσθην. Mid. χράομαι, *to consult an oracle*. Poet. χρήζω or χρῄζω, Eur. Hel. 516.

3. χράομαι, *to supply one's own need by making use of a thing*, F. χρήσομαι, Pf. κέχρημαι, A. P. ἐχρήσθην, A. M. ἐχρησάμην. In the Att. contract forms of χράω and χράομαι, η takes the place of α (§ 23. α), which, on the other hand, is commonly retained by the Ion.; as χρᾷ Hdt. i. 55.

4. χρή (3 Pers. sing., for χράει or χρῆσι), *it supplies need*, i. e. *it is useful* or *necessary*, *it must* or *ought to be*, impers.; *Subj.* χρῇ, *Opt.* (χρα-, χρε- § 259) χρείη, *Inf.* χρῆναι, and poet. (χράειν) χρῆν, *Part. Neut.* (χράον, ε inserted after contraction, § 35) χρεών· Impf. ἐχρῆν (with ν paragogic, for ἔχραε, or ἔχρη, cf. § 211. N.) or unaugm. (§ 194. 1) χρῆν· Fut. χρήσει. The participle χρεών is sometimes used as an indeclinable noun; thus, τοῦ χρεών. Personally, S. 2 χρῆσθα (§ 182), *you must*, Ar. Ach. 778 (Meg.); Pf. P., as Pres., κέχρημαι, *to need*, *want*, Eur. Iph. A. 382, α. 13, F. Pf. κεχρήσομαι, Theoc. 16. 73. Kindred, χρῄζω, *to want*, *desire*, Ion. χρηΐζω Hdt. i. 41, Dor. χρῄσδω Theoc. 8. 12, and χρῄδδω, Ar. Ach. 734 (§ 70. V.); Ion. depon. χρηΐσκομαι, Hdt. iii. 117.

5. *ἀπό-χρη, it fully supplies need,* i. e. *it suffices, it is enough; Inf.* ἀποχρῆν· Impf. ἀπέχρη, F. ἀποχρήσει, A. ἀπέχρησε. Ion. ἀποχρᾷ, -χρᾶν, &c. (see 3 above), Hdt. ix. 79. So ἀπεχρέετο (§ 242. a) Id. viii. 14, κατα-χρᾷ i. 164, ἐκ-χρήσει iii. 137. These verbs are also used personally.

ὀνίνημι (r. ὀνα-, ὀνινα-), *to benefit,* F. ὀνήσω, A. ὤνησα, A. P. ὠνήθην, 2 A. M ὠνήμην and ὠνᾰ́μην (§ 224. 3), *Opt.* ὀναίμην, *Inf.* ὄνασθαι, Ep. and Ion. *Imp* ὄνησο τ. 68, *Inf.* ὀνῆσθαι Hipp., *Pt.* ὀνήμενος β. 33. Doubtful 2 A. Act *Inf.* ὀνῆναι Pl. Rep. 600 d; late 1 A. M. ὠνᾰσάμην, Anth.

πίμπλημι (r. πλα-, πι-μ-πλα- § 263. 6), *to fill,* F. πλήσω, A. ἔπλησα, Pf. πέπληκα, Pf. P. πέπλησμαι (Plup. ἐν-επέπληντο Lys. 180. 4), A. P. ἐπλήσθην, 2 A. M. ἐπλήμην (§ 224. 3), *Opt.* (πλη-ί-μην) πλήμην or (πλα-, πλε- § 259) πλείμην (cf. χρείη, 4 above, βλεῖο, § 277. α), *Imp.* πλῆσο, *Part.* πλήμενος. *Imp.* ἐμ-πίπληθι (§ 251. 4) Φ. 311, *Pt.* (r. πλε-) ἐμπιπλείς, Hipp. Collat. Ion. forms, πιμπλάω, -έω, Hes. Th. 880, πίπλω, Hes. Sc. 291 Gaisf., πιμπλάνομαι I. 679. Kindred, πληρόω, and the intrans. πλήθω (2 Pf. πέπληθα, Theoc. 22. 38), whence πληθύω and πληθῦνω.

πίμπρημι (r. πρα-, πιμπρα-), *to burn,* F. πρήσω, A. ἔπρησα, Pf. P. πέπρημαι or πέπρησμαι, A. P. ἐπρήσθην. Pf. ὑπο-πέπρηκα, Hipp., F. Pf. πεπρήσομαι, Hdt. vi. 9, A. ἔπρεσε Hes. Th. 856, Ep. *Subj.* (as from πίμπρω) πίμπρῃσι (§ 181. β) Ar. Lys. 248. Rare Ep. form, πρήθω, I. 589.

NOTE. The epenthetic μ of πίμπλημι and πίμπρημι is commonly omitted, when these verbs, in composition, are preceded by μ; thus, ἐμπίπλημι, but ἐνεπίμπλην.

τίθημι (r. θε-, τιθε-, § 62), *to put,* F. θήσω. See ¶ 50.

REMARK. Φημί (¶ 53) is the only verb in -μι having a monosyllabic root, and beginning with a consonant, which is not reduplicated.

§ 285. β. Verbs in -σκω.

ἀραρίσκω (r. ἀρ-, ἀρε-, ἀραρισκ- § 296), *to fit,* Ep. ξ. 23, 1 A. ἦρσα, Ξ. 167, α. 280, 2 A. ἤραρον Δ. 110, Soph. El. 147 (§ 194. 3), 2 Pf. intrans., as Pres., ἄρηρα, N. 800, also Att. ἄρᾱρα, Æsch. Prom. 60, H. Gr. iv. 7. 6, A. P. ἤρθην Π. 211. Pf. P. ἀρήρεμαι, Hes. Op. 429, Ap. Rh. 1. 787. For ἀρᾱρυῖα, see § 253. 2. Deriv., ἀρέσκω (§ 279), ἀρτύω and ἀρτῦνω, &c.

βιβρώσκω (r. βρο-, βιβρωσκ-, § 280. γ), *to eat* (the Pres. rare), Pf. βέβρωκα (see § 238. α), Pf. P. βέβρωμαι. Ep., 2 A. ἔβρων, Hom. Ap. 127, 2 Pf. *Opt.* (r. βρωθ-; or from new Pres. βεβρώθω) βεβρώθοις Δ. 35, F. Pf. βεβρώσομαι, β. 203; Ion. A. P. ἐβρώθην Hdt. iii. 16; late Ep. 1 A. ἔβρωξα, Ap. Rh. 2. 271; late F. βρώξομαι. The deficiencies of this verb are supplied by ἐσθίω (§ 298) and τρώγω (§ 267. 3).

γιγνώσκω (r. γνο-), *to know,* F. γνώσομαι, 2 A. ἔγνων (¶ 57), Pf. ἔγνωκα, Pf. P. ἔγνωσμαι, A. P. ἐγνώσθην. 2 A. M. *Opt.* συγ-γνοῖτο Æsch. Sup. 216, Ion. 1 A. ἀν-έγνωσα, *persuaded,* Hdt. i. 68.

NOTE. The Ion. (not Hom.) and the later Greek softened γ γνώσκω and γίγνομαι (§ 286) to γῑνώσκω and γῑ́νομαι.

διδάσκω (r. δα-, διδαχ-, διδασκ-), *to teach,* F. διδάξω, A. ἐδίδαξα, Pf. δεδίδαχα, Pf. P. δεδίδαγμαι, A. P. ἐδιδάχθην. Ep., 1 A. ἐδιδάσκησα, Hom. Cer. 144, 2 A. ἔδαον, Ap. Rh. 3. 529, δέδαον (§ 194. 3). From the r. δα- are also formed, with the sense *to learn,* the poet. F. δαήσομαι (§ 222), γ. 187, Pf. δεδάηκα, β. 61, δεδάημαι, Theoc. 8. 4, δέδαα, ρ. 519 (hence δεδάασθαι π. 316.

§ 246. 2), 2 A. P. ἐδάην, Soph. El. 169. Hence, likewise, the Ep. F. contr. (δαέσω, δαέω, § 200. 2) δήω, I. 418.

διδράσκω (r. δρα-), *to run*, used only in composition with ἀπό, διά, or ἐξ, F. δρᾱσομαι, 1 A. ἔδρᾱσα, 2 A. ἔδρᾱν (¶ 57), Pf. δέδρᾱκα. Kindred, δρασκάζω, Lys. 117. 35, δρηστεύω, Hdt. iv. 79.

μιμνήσκω (r. μνα-), *to remind*, F. μνήσω, A. ἔμνησα, Pf. P. μέμνημαι (see § 234. β), 3 F. μεμνήσομαι, Cyr. iii. 1. 27, A. P. ἐμνήσθην. As from μέμνομαι and μέμναμαι, *Imp.* μέμνεο Hdt. v. 105, *Pt.* μεμνόμενος Archil. Fr. 1, *Opt.* Pl. 3 μεμναίατο Pind. Fr. 277. Prim. Mid. μνάομαι, *to remember* (Ep. δ. 106), *to woo*, vii. 3. 18. Collat. forms, μνήσκω, Orph. Hym. 77. 6, μνήσκομαι, Anacr. Fr. 69.

πιπράσκω, and poet. πέρνημι (r. περα-, πρᾱ- § 261, περνα- § 278. δ), *to sell*, Pf. πέπρᾱκα, Pf. P. πέπρᾱμαι, 3 F. πεπρᾱσομαι, vii. 1. 36, commonly used for the rare πραθήσομαι (Ath. 160 f), A. P. ἐπρᾱθην. Ep., Fut. *Inf.* (περάσειν) περάᾳν (§ 245. 3) Φ. 454, A. ἐπέρᾰσα Ο. 428, Pf. P. *Pt.* πεπερημένος Φ. 58. The Fut. and Aor. of this verb are supplied by ἀποδώσομαι and ἀπεδόμην, mid. tenses of ἀποδίδωμι.

τιτρώσκω (r. τρο-), *to wound*, F. τρώσω, A. ἔτρωσα, Pf. P. τέτρωμαι, A. P. ἐτρώθην. Kindred, τρώω, Ep. φ. 293, τορέω, *to pierce*, Ep. Hom. Merc. 283, F. τορήσω, Ib. 178, 1 A. ἐτόρησα, E. 337, 2 A. ἔτορον, Λ. 236 (for τέτορον and τετορήσω, see §§ 194. 3, 239. *b*), τορεύω, Ar. Thesm. 986, τετραίνω (§ 286).

τιτύσκομαι (r. τυκ-, §§ 263. N., 273. α), *to prepare*, Ep. Φ. 342, 2 A. τετυκεῖν (§ 194. 3) ο. 77, τετυκόμην, A. 467.

§ 286. γ. Other Verbs.

ἀκαχίζω (r. ἀχ-, ἀκαχ-, ἀκαχιζ- § 297), *to afflict*, Ep. π. 432, F. ἀκαχήσω, 1 A. ἀκάχησα, commonly 2 A. ἤκαχον, Pf. P. ἀκάχημαι and ἀκήχεμαι (P. 3 ἀκηχέδαται § 248. *f*). Collat., ἄχομαι τ. 129, and ἄχνῠμαι, Soph. Ant. 627, *to sorrow*; Pres. *Pt.* ἀχέων B. 694, ἀχεύων E. 869.

γίγνομαι (r. γα-, γεν- §§ 259, 277, γιγεν-, γιγν- § 261), *to become*, F. γενήσομαι (§ 222), 2 A. ἐγενόμην, Pf. γεγένημαι, 2 Pf. γέγονα (see § 238. α), F. P. γενηθήσομαι, 1 A. trans. ἐγεινάμην, *I begat* or *bore*. Ion. and late A. P. ἐγενήθην, Hipp. For γέντο, see § 185. δ; for 1 Pf. Dor. γεγάκειν, § 246. 2; for ἐκγεγάονται, § 245. 3; for γίνομαι, § 285. N. Kindred, γείνομαι, Ep. X. 477, γεννάω, -ήσω, *to beget.*

λιλαίομαι (r. λα-, λιλα-, § 267), *to desire earnestly*, Ep. N. 253, Pf. P. (one λ dropped, § 263. 6) λελίημαι, Δ. 465. The prim. λάω is used by the Dorics; Theoc. 1. 12.

μένω, and poet. μίμνω, Æsch. Ag. 74, F. μενῶ. See § 222. 2. Ep. deriv. μιμνάζω, B. 392.

πίπτω (r πετ-, πεσ- § 273. β, πιπτ-), *to fall*, F. πεσοῦμαι (§ 200. 3), 1 A. ἔπεσα, commonly 2 A. ἔπεσον, Pf. (πετ-, πτε- § 262, πτο- § 236. *a*) πέπτωκα (see § 238. α). Dor. 2 A. ἔπετον, Pind. O. 7. 126; late Pf. πέπτηκα, Anth. Poet. forms, πίτνω, Soph. Œd. C. 1754, and perhaps πιτνέω (Eur. Ph. 293) and πιτνάω (Pind. I. 2. 39), with which some connect ἔπιτνον as 2 Aor.

τετραίνω (r. τρα-, τετραιν- § 277), *to bore*, F. τρήσω, A. ἔτρησα, Pf. P. τέτρημαι, A. P. ἐτρήθην, A. M. ἐτετρηνάμην. F. τετρανέω, Hdt. iii. 12, A. ἐτέτρηνα ε. 247, A. P. ἐτετράνθην, Anth. Late or doubtful, τιτράω, τιτραίνω, τετρήνω.

2. Syllabic Affixes.

§ **287.** The syllables which are most frequently affixed to protract the root are α, ε, ᾰν, νε, νυ, ισκ, and ιζ.

a. Addition of α and ε.

Remarks. (1.) When α is affixed, ε in the preceding syllable usually becomes ω; but, when ε is affixed, ο. See στρωφάω and στροφέω (§ 259. a). (2.) The vowel which is added is more frequently retained before the close terminations.

α. Addition of α.

βρῡχάομαι (r. βρυχ-), *to roar*, F. βρυχήσομαι, A. ἐβρυχησάμην, A. P. ἐβρυχήθην, 2 Pf., as Pres., βέβρῡχα. Kindred, βρύκω, later βρῡ́χω (Hipp.), *to gnash the teeth*. Similar onomatopes are βληχάομαι and μηκάομαι, *to bleat*, and μυκάομαι, *to low*, F. -ήσομαι, Ep. 2 Pf. μέμηκα, K. 362, μέμῡκα, Σ. 580, 2 A. ἔμακον, Π. 469, ἔμῡκον, E. 749.

γοάω (r. γο-), *to bewail*, Ep. Ω. 664, F. γοήσομαι, 2 A. ἔγοον, Z. 500. Mid. γοάομαι also Att., Soph. Œd. T. 1249.

νωμάω, F. νωμήσω, poet. for νέμω (§ 222. 2), *to distribute*. Also Ep. Impf. νεμέθοντο A. 635.

πέτομαι, poet. πέτᾰμαι, Pind. P. 8. 128, and ποτάομαι, B. 462, Æsch. Sept. 84, later ἵπτᾰμαι, Eur. Iph. A. 1608 (r. πετ-, πετα-, ποτα-, πτα- § 261, ἱπτα- § 283. c), *to fly*, F. πετήσομαι, commonly πτήσομαι, 2 A. ἔπτην, 2 A. M. ἐπτάμην, commonly ἐπτόμην (§ 261), Pf. P. πεπότημαι, A. P. ἐποτήθην. F. ποτήσομαι, Mosch. 2. 141. Other collat. forms, ποτέομαι, T. 357, πωτάομαι, M. 287, πετάομαι, Hdt. iii. 111.

§ **288.** β. Addition of ε.

αἴδεομαι, and poet. αἴδομαι, Æsch. Eum. 549 (r. αἰδ-, αἰδε-), *to respect*, F. αἰδέσομαι, A. M. ᾐδεσάμην, Pf. ᾔδεσμαι (P. 3 προ-ηδέατο, § 248. *f*, Hdt. i. 61), A. P. ᾐδέσθην.

ἄω, ε. 478, and ἄημι, I. 5 (r. ἀ-, ἀε-), *to breathe, blow*, Ep.; *Imp.* ἀήτω, *Inf.* ἀῆναι, *Pt.* ἀείς· Pass. ἄημαι, ζ. 131. Deriv., ἀΐω, O. 252, and ἀΐσθω, Π. 468, *to breathe out, expire*. Kindred, A. ἄεσα, *to breathe in sleep, to sleep*, γ. 151, contr. ἆσα, π. 367.

γαμέω (r. γαμ-), *to marry*, said of the man, F. γαμῶ, A. ἔγημα, Pf. γεγάμηκα, Pf. P. γεγάμημαι. Mid. γαμέομαι, *to marry*, said of the woman, F. γαμοῦμαι, A. ἐγημάμην. Late F. γαμήσω, A. ἐγάμησα, A. P. ἐγαμήθην (γαμεθεῖσα Theoc. 8. 91). Ep. F. M. γαμέσσομαι, *will provide a wife for*, I. 394.

δίζω, *to doubt, consider*, poet. and Ion. Π. 713, Mid. δίζομαι, commonly δίζημαι (§ 224. 3; r. διζ-, διζε-), *to seek*, Theoc. 25. 37, λ. 100, Hdt. i. 95, F. διζήσομαι, A. ἐδιζησάμην.

δοκέω (r. δοκ-), *to seem, to think*, F. δόξω, A. ἔδοξα, Pf. P. δέδογμαι, A. P. ἐδόχθην. Poet. and Ion., F. δοκήσω, A. ἐδόκησα, Pf. δεδόκηκα, Pf. P. δεδόκημαι, A. P. ἐδοκήθην. Impers. δοκεῖ, *it seems*, F. δόξει, &c.

ἐπιμέλομαι and ἐπιμελέομαι (r. μελ-, μελε-), *to take care of*, F. ἐπιμελήσομαι, Pf. P. ἐπιμεμέλημαι, A. P. ἐπεμελήθην.

κτυπέω, to sound, to crash, poet., F. *κτυπήσω*, 1 A. *ἐκτύπησα*, 2 A. *ἔκτυπον*.

κυλίνδω and *κυλινδέω, to roll*, F. (*κυλίνδ-σω*, § 58) *κυλίσω*, A. *ἐκύλῖσα* Pf. P. *κεκύλισμαι*, A. P. *ἐκυλίσθην*. Late F. *κυλινδήσω*. Rare Pres. *κυλίω*, Ar. Vesp. 202. Kindred, *καλινδέομαι, to be busied in*, Cyr. i. 4. 5, *ἀλινδέω* or *ἀλίνδω*, A. *ἤλισα*, Ar. Nub. 32, Pf. *ἤλικα*, Ib. 33.

κύρω and *κυρέω, to meet with, to chance*, chiefly poet. and Ion. Eur. Hipp. 746, Med. 23, F. *κύρσω* (§ 56. *β*), Soph. Œd. C. 225, and *κυρήσω*, Eur. Heracl. 252, A. *ἔκυρσα*, Γ. 23, and *ἐκύρησα*, Hdt. i. 31, Pf. *κεκύρηκα*, Pf. P. *κεκύρημαι*.

πατέομαι (r. *πατ-*), *to taste*, Ion. and Poet. Hdt. ii. 37, F. *πάσομαι*, A. *ἐπάσάμην*, A. 464, Soph. Ant. 202, Plup. *πεπάσμην* Ω. 642.

πορθέω (r. *παρθ-*, *περθ-* § 259, *πορθε-*), *to lay waste*, F. *πορθήσω*, Pf. *πεπόρθηκα*, &c. Poet. *πέρθω*, F. *πέρσω*, Soph. Ph. 114, 1 A. *ἔπερσα*, *α*. 2, Ep. 2 A. *ἔπραθον* (§ 262), A. 367. For *πέρθαι*, see § 246. *β*.

ῥίπτω and *ῥιπτέω* (r. *ῥιφ-*, *ῥιπτ-* § 272), *to throw*, F. *ῥίψω*, A. *ἔρριψα*, Pf. *ἔρρῖφα*, Pf. P. *ἔρριμμαι*, 1 A. P. *ἐρρίφθην*, 2 A. P. *ἐρρῖφην*. For *ῥίπτασκον*, see § 249. *d*. Deriv. *ῥιπτάζω*.

σκέπτομαι, commonly *σκοπέω* or *σκοπέομαι* (r. *σκεπ-*), F. *σκέψομαι*, A. *ἐσκεψάμην*, Pf. *ἔσκεμμαι*, F. Pf. *ἐσκέψομαι*, Pl. Rep. 392 c.

ὠθέω (r. *ὠθ-*), *to push*, F. *ὤσω*, and poet. *ὠθήσω*, A. *ἔωσα* (§ 189. 2), Pf. P. *ἔωσμαι*, A. P. *ἐώσθην*. Late Pf. *ἔωκα*, Plut.; Ep. and Ion., A. *ὦσα*, A. 220 (*πρώσας*, for *προ-ώσας*, Anth.), Pf. P. *ὦσμαι*, Hdt. v. 69; *ἀπ-εώθην* Hipp. Deriv. *ὠστίζομαι, to justle*, Ar. Ach. 42.

§ 289. b. Addition of ἄν.

Remarks. (1.) Roots which receive *ἄν* without further change are mostly *double consonant*. (2.) *Mute roots receiving ἄν commonly insert ν before the characteristic.* (3.) Roots which do not insert *ν* sometimes prolong *ἄν* to *αιν* or *ᾱν*.

α. Without further Change.

αἰσθάνομαι, and rarely *αἴσθομαι* (r. *αἰσθ-*, *αἰσθαν-*), *to perceive*, F. *αἰσθήσομαι* (§ 222. 1), 2 A. *ᾐσθόμην*, Pf. P. *ᾔσθημαι*.

ἀλφάνω (r. *ἀλφ-*), *to find*, poet. Eur. Med. 298, 2 A. *ἦλφον* Φ. 79.

ἁμαρτάνω (r. *ἁμαρτ-*), *to err, to miss*, F. *ἁμαρτήσομαι*, 2 A. *ἥμαρτον*, Pf. *ἡμάρτηκα*, Pf. P. *ἡμάρτημαι*, A. P. *ἡμαρτήθην*. F. *ἁμαρτήσω*, Hipp., 1 A. *ἡμάρτησα*, Orph. Arg. 646, Ep. 2 A. (*ἁμαρτ-*, *ἁμρατ-* § 262, *ἀμβροτ-*, §§ 13. 4, 28, 64. 2) *ἤμβροτον*, E. 287 (*ἅμαρθ'* Δ. 491). Hence (*μ* dropped, cf. *ἀπλακών*, § 296) *ἀβροτάζω*, only in A. *Subj.* *ἀβροτάξομεν* K. 65.

ἀπεχθάνομαι, and sometimes *ἀπέχθομαι* (r. *ἐχθ-*), *to be hated*, F. *ἀπεχθήσομαι*, 2 A. *ἀπηχθόμην*, Pf. *ἀπήχθημαι*.

αὔξω and *αὐξάνω*, poet. and Ion. *ἀέξω* (r. *ἀϜεγ-*, *αὐγ-*, *ἀεγ-*, § 22. *δ*, *αὐξ-*, *ἀεξ-*, § 273), Z. 261, *to increase*, F. *αὐξήσω*, &c. See ¶ 43, and cf. Lat. *augeo*.

βλαστάνω, and poet. *βλαστέω* (r. *βλαστ-*), *to sprout, to bud*, F. *βλαστήσω*, 2 A. *ἔβλαστον*, Pf. *ἐβλάστηκα* (§ 190; Plup. *ἐβεβλαστήκει* Th. iii. 26). 1 A. *ἐβλάστησα*, Ap. Rh. 1. 1131.

δαρθάνω (r. δαρθ-), *to sleep*, usually in composition with κατά, 2 A. ἔδαρθον, Pf. δεδάρθηκα, 2 A. P. poet. ἐδάρθην. Ep. 2 A. ἔδραθον Θ. 296, 2 A. P. ἐδράθην, ε. 471 (§ 262).

ὀφλισκάνω (r. ὀφλ-, ὀφλισκ- § 296), *to incur*, F. ὀφλήσω, 1 A. ὤφλησα commonly 2 A. ὦφλον, Pf. ὤφληκα. Ion. Impf. or 2 A. ὤφλεε (§ 243. 4) Hdt. viii. 26. See ὀφείλω (§ 268).

§ 290. β. With the Insertion of ν (see § 54).

ἁνδάνω (r. ἁδ, ἁ-ν-δαν-), *to please*, poet. and Ion. B. 114, Soph. Ant. 504 F. ἁδήσω, Hdt. v. 39, 2 A. ἕαδον, Id. i. 151, *Subj.* ἅδω, &c., 2 Pf. ἕαδα, I. 173 (ἕαδα, Theoc. 27. 22; 1 Pf. ἅδηκα, Hippon.). For the augm., see § 189. 2. Kindred, ἥδω, *to please*, commonly ἥδομαι, *to be pleased*, F. ἡσθήσομαι, A. ἥσθην (A. M. ἥσατο ι. 353).

ἐρυγγάνω (r. ἐρυγ-), *to disgorge*, 2 A. ἤρυγον. Ion. ἐρεύγομαι, O. 621, F. ἐρεύξομαι, Pf. ἔρευγμαι, Hipp.

θιγγάνω (r. θιγ-), *to touch*, F. θίξομαι, 2 A. ἔθιγον. Lat. *tango*.

κῑχᾰνω or κιγχᾰνω (r. κιχ-), *to find*, poet. Eur. Alc. 477, F. κῑχήσομαι, Soph. Œd. C. 1487, 2 A. ἔκῐχον, Eur. Alc. 22. Ep. κῐχάνω, P. 672, and κιχέω ω. 284 (Mid. *Pt.* κιχήμενος, E. 187), F. κιχήσω, Ap. Rh. 4. 1482, 2 A. (from r. κιχε-, or Pass. with sense of Act.) ἐκῐχην, π. 379, *Subj.* (κιχῶ) κιχείω (§ 243. b), A. 26, &c. 1 A. M. ἐκιχησάμην, Δ. 385.

λαγχάνω (r. λαχ-, ληχ- § 266, λεγχ- §§ 259, 277, λαγχαν-), *to obtain by lot*, F. λήξομαι, 2 A. ἔλαχον, Pf. εἴληχα (§ 191. 1) and λέλογχα, Pf. P. εἴληγμαι, A. P. ἐλήχθην. Ion. F. λάξομαι, Hdt. vii. 144. For 2 Aor. *Subj.* λελάχω, causative, see § 194. 3.

λαμβάνω (r. λαβ-, ληβ-, λαμβ-), *to take*, F. λήψομαι, 2 A. ἔλαβον, Pf. εἴληφα (§ 191. 1), Pf. P. εἴλημμαι, and poet. λέλημμαι, Eur. Iph. A. 363, A. P. ἐλήφθην. Ion., F. λάμψομαι, Hdt. i. 199, Pf. P. λέλαμμαι, iii. 117, A. P. ἐλάμφθην, ii. 89, Pf. A. λελάβηκα (§ 222), iv. 79. For λελαβέσθαι, see § 194. 3. Poet. forms, λάζομαι and λάζυμαι, Δ. 357, Ar. Lys. 209.

λανθάνω, and sometimes λήθω (r. λαθ-, ληθ-), *to lie hid, to escape notice*, F. λήσω, 1 A. ἔλησα, commonly 2 A. ἔλαθον, 2 Pf. λέληθα. Mid. λανθάνομαι and λήθομαι, *to forget*, F. λήσομαι, 2 A. ἐλαθόμην, Pf. λέλησμαι, F. Pf. λελήσομαι, Eur. Alc. 198. Ep. Pf. P. λέλασμαι, E. 834, late 1 A. M. ἐλησάμην, Quint. 3. 99, Dor. A. P. ἐλάσθην, Theoc. 2. 46. For λέλαθον, &c., see § 194. 3 Collat. ἐκ-ληθάνω, η. 221.

λείπω (r. λιπ-, λειπ-), *to leave*, and sometimes in composition λιμπάνω, Th viii. 17, F. λείψω, &c. (¶ 37). Late 1 A. ἔλειψα.

μανθάνω (r. μαθ-), *to learn*, F. μαθήσομαι (§ 222), 2 A. ἔμαθον, Pf. μεμάθηκα. For μαθεῦμαι, see § 200. γ.

πυνθάνομαι, and poet. πεύθομαι Æsch. Ag. 988 (r. πυθ-, πευθ- § 270), *to inquire*, F. πεύσομαι (πευσεῖσθαι Æsch. Pr. 988, § 200. 3), 2 A. ἐπυθόμην, Pf. πέπυσμαι. Ep. 2 A. *Opt.* πεπύθοιτο (§ 194. 3), Z. 50.

τυγχάνω (r. τυχ-, τευχ-), *to happen, to obtain, to hit*, F. τεύξομαι, 2 A. ἔτυχον, Pf. τετύχηκα (§ 222), rarely τέτευχα, Ath. 581 e. Ep. 1 A. ἐτύχησα, Δ. 106. See τεύχω (§ 270).

χανδάνω (r. χαδ-, χανδ-, χενδ- § 259), *to contain*, poet. Ar. Ran. 260, F. (χένδσομαι, § 58) χείσομαι, σ. 17, 2 A. ἔχαδον, Δ. 24, 2 Pf. κέχανδα, Ψ. 268.

§ 291. γ. With αν prolonged.

ἀλδαίνω (r. ἀλδ-), *to nourish*, poet. Æsch. Pr. 540, 2 A. ἤλδανον, σ. 70. Also ἀλδήσκω, *to nourish, to grow*, Ψ. 599, late A. iter. ἀλδήσασκεν Orph. Lith. 364.

ἀλιταίνω or ἀλιτραίνω (r. ἀλιτ-), *to sin*, poet., Hes. Op. 239, 328, 1 A. ἤλιτησα, Orph. Arg. 647, 2 A. ἤλιτον, I. 375, Pf. P. *Pt.* ἀλιτήμενος δ. 807.

οἰδέω and οἰδαίνω (r. οἰδ-, οἰδε- § 288), *to swell*, F. οἰδήσω, A. ᾤδησα, Pf. ᾤδηκα. Also οἰδάνω, trans., I. 554.

ὀλισθάνω and ὀλισθαίνω (r. ὀλισθ-), *to slide, to slip*, F. ὀλισθήσω, 2 A. ὤλισθον. 1 A. ὠλίσθησα and Pf. ὠλίσθηκα, Hipp. Also ὀλισθάζω, Ath. 236 a.

ὀσφραίνομαι, rarely ὀσφράομαι, Ath. 299 e (r. ὀσφρ-, ὀσφρα- § 287), *to smell*, F. ὀσφρήσομαι, 2 A. ὠσφρόμην, A. P. ὠσφράνθην. Ion. 2 A. ὠσφράμην, Hdt. i. 80, late 1 A. ὠσφρησάμην.

See, also, ἱκάνω (§ 292), κιχάνω (§ 290).

§ 292. c. Addition of νε.

βυνέω (or βύω), *to stop up* (r. βυ-), F. βύσω, A. ἔβυσα, Pf. P. βέβυσμαι. Also Pass. βύνομαι, Hdt. ii. 96.

ἱκνέομαι, and poet. ἱκάνω (r. ἱκ-, ἱκαν- § 291), *to come*, F. ἵξομαι, 2 A. ἱκόμην, Pf. ἷγμαι. Ep. ἵκω, K. 142. For ἷκτο and ἷξον, see § 185. δ, ε.

κυνέω (r. κυ-), *to kiss*, F. κυνήσομαι, A. ἔκυσα. The comp. προσκυνέω, *to worship*, is regular: F. προσκυνήσω, A. προσεκύνησα, and poet. προσέκυσα, Ar. Eq. 156.

ὑπισχνέομαι (r. σχ-, ἰσχ-), *to promise*, F. ὑποσχήσομαι (§ 222), 2 A. ὑπεσχόμην, Pf. ὑπέσχημαι, rare A. P. ὑπεσχέθην, Pl. Phædr. 235 d. Poet. and Ion. ὑπίσχομαι Æsch. Eum. 804, Hdt. vii. 104. See ἔχω (§ 300).

§ 293. d. Addition of νυ.

(1.) If α, ε, or ο precede, the ν is doubled, ο becoming ω. (2.) If λ precede, the ν becomes λ. (3.) A *lingual* or *liquid* preceded by a *diphthong* is dropped before νυ.

α. To Pure Roots.

ἕννυμι (r. Ϝε-, ἑ- § 22. δ), *to clothe*, poet., chiefly Ep., F. ἕσσω (§ 71), ο. 337, A. ἕσσα, E. 905, Pf. P. εἷμαι and ἕσμαι, τ. 72, Hdt. i. 47. Prose form, ἀμφιέννυμι, F. ἀμφιέσω, ἀμφιῶ (§ 200. 2), ἠμφίεσα (§ 192. 3), Pf. P. ἠμφίεσμαι. Ion., κατα-είνυον Ψ. 135, ἐπ-είνυσθαι Hdt. iv. 64.

ζώννυμι (r. ζο-), *to gird*, F. ζώσω, A. ἔζωσα, Pf. P. ἔζωσμαι. Late Pf. ἔζωκα, Anth.

κεράννυμι (r. κερα-, κρα- § 261, κιρνα- §§ 259, 278. δ), *to mix*, F. κεράσω, κερῶ, A. ἐκέρασα (κρῆσαι η. 164), Pf. P. κεκέρασμαι, Ath. 576 a, commonly κέκραμαι, A. P. ἐκεράσθην and ἐκράθην. Ep. κεράω, Ω. 363 (κέραις, § 242. b), *Subj.* κέρωνται Δ. 260, as from κέραμαι. Poet. and Ion., κίρνημι, Ar. Eccl. 841, and κιρνάω, Hdt. iv. 52.

κορέννυμι (r. κορε-), *to satiate*, F. κορέσω, A. ἐκόρεσα, Pf. P. κεκόρεσμαι, A. P. ἐκορέσθην. Ep., F. κορέω (§ 245. 3), Θ. 379, 2 Pf. intrans. κεκορηώς (§ 253. 1), σ. 372; Ion. Pf. P. κεκόρημαι Σ. 287. The verb κορέω, *to sweep*, is regular.

κρεμάννυμι (r. κρεμα-), *to suspend*, F. κρεμάσω, κρεμῶ (§ 200. 2), A. ἐκρέμᾰσα, A. P. ἐκρεμάσθην, Mid. κρέμᾰμαι (Act. *Pt.* κρεμάντες Ath. 25 d), and poet. κρήμνᾰμαι (§ 278, δ), Ar. Nub. 377, *to hang*, F. κρεμήσομαι. Also κρημνάομαι, Hom. Bac. 39, *Pt.* κρημνάς, Pind. P. 4. 43, late κρεμάω.

πετάννῡμι (r. πετα-), *to spread, to expand*, F. πετᾰσω, πετῶ, A. ἐπέτᾰσα Pf. P. πέπτᾰμαι (§ 261), A. P. ἐπετάσθην. Ion. Pf. P. πεπέτασμαι, Hdt. i. 62. Ep., πίτνημι, λ. 392, πίτνω, Hes. Sc. 291 Göttl.; late πετάω.

ῥώννῡμι (r. ῥο-), *to strengthen*, F. ῥώσω, A. ἔῤῥωσα, Pf. P. ἔῤῥωμαι, A. P. ἐῤῥώσθην (§ 221. α).

σβέννῡμι (r. σβε-), *to extinguish*, F. σβέσω, 1 A. ἔσβεσα, A. P. ἐσβέσθην. Mid. σβέννῡμαι, *to be extinguished, to go out*, F. σβήσομαι, 2 A. Act. ἔσβην (§ 227), Pf. Act. ἔσβηκα.

σκεδάννῡμι (r. σκεδα-), *to scatter*, F. σκεδᾰσω, σκεδῶ, A. ἐσκέδᾰσα, Pf. P. ἐσκέδασμαι, A. P. ἐσκεδάσθην. Collat. forms, chiefly poet., κεδάω, Ap. Rh. 4. 500, κεδαίομαι, Id. 2. 626, κεδάννῡμι, Anth., A. ἐκέδασσα, E. 88; σκίδνημι (§§ 259, 278. δ), Hes. Th. 875, Th. vi. 98, κίδνημι, Hdt. vii. 140, Eur. Hec. 916.

§ 294. β. To Palatal Roots.

ἄγνῡμι (r. Ϝαγ-), *to break*, F. ἄξω, A. ἔαξα (§ 189. 2), 2 Pf. intrans. ἔᾱγα, *to be broken*, 2 A. P. ἐάγην (Att. ᾱ, Ep. comm. ᾰ). Ion., A. ἦξα, Ψ. 392, 2 Pf. ἔηγα, Hdt. vii. 224, ἦγα, Hipp.; Ep. A. *Opt.* (κατα-Ϝάξαις, καϜ-Ϝάξαις, §§ 22. δ, 48. 2) καυάξαις Hes. Op. 664. In the comp. κατάγνῡμι, the ε of the augm. is sometimes found out of the Ind.; as, A. *Part.* κατεάξας, Lys. 100. 5.

ἀνοίγω and ἀνοίγνῡμι (r. οἰγ-), *to open*, Impf. ἀνέῳγον (§ 189. 2), Π. 221, v. 5. 20, and later ἤνοιγον, H. Gr. i. 1. 2 (Ion. ἀνῷγον, Ξ. 168), F. ἀνοίξω, A. ἀνέῳξα, and later ἤνοιξα, Pf. ἀνέῳχα, Pf. P. ἀνέῳγμαι, A. P. ἀνεῴχθην, and later ἠνοίχθην, Acts, 12. 10. 2 Pf. ἀνέῳγα, *to stand open*, Hipp. The simple οἴγω and οἴγνῡμι are poet., Æsch. Pr. 611, F. οἴξω, A. ᾦξα Ω. 457, ὤϊξα, Ω. 446.

δείκνῡμι (r. δεικ-), *to show*, F. δείξω. See ¶ 52. Ion. (r. δεκ-) δέξω, ἔδεξα, &c., Hdt. iii. 122. Mid. δείκνῡμαι, Ep. *to greet*, I. 196, Pf. δείδεγμαι (§ 47. N.), η. 72. The primary sense of δείκνῡμι is *to stretch out the hand*, and kindred verbs are δέχομαι (Ion. δέκομαι, Hdt. vii. 177, § 69. I.), *to receive* F. δέξομαι, A. ἐδεξάμην, Pf. δέδεγμαι, F. Pf. δεδέξομαι (for ἐδέγμην, &c., see § 185. δ), and the poet. δειδίσκομαι, δειδίσκομαι, δεικανάω, δέχνῡμαι.

εἴργνῡμι (r. ἐργ-, εἰργ- § 268), *to shut in, to confine*, F. εἴρξω and ἕρξω, A. εἶρξα, *Part.* εἴρξας and ἕρξας, Pf. P. εἶργμαι, A. P. εἴρχθην. This verb appears to have been originally the same with εἴργω, *to shut out*, and the distinction which afterwards arose, and which was marked by the difference of breathing, appears not to have been always observed. Ion., in both senses, ἔργω, -ξω, Hdt. iii. 48, Θ. 325 (Ep. ἐέργω, B. 617), and ἔργνῡμι or εἴργνῡμι, Hdt. ii. 86, iv. 69.

ζεύγνῡμι (r. ζυγ-, ζευγ- § 270), *to yoke*, F. ζεύξω, A. ἔζευξα, Pf. P. ἔζευγμαι, 1 A. P. ἐζεύχθην, 2 A. P. ἐζύγην.

μίγνῡμι (r. μιγ-), *to mingle, to mix*, F. μίξω, A. ἔμιξα, Pf. P. μέμιγμαι, 3 F. μεμίξομαι, Æsch. Pers. 1052, 1 A. P. ἐμίχθην, 2 A. P. ἐμίγην. The older form μίσγω (§ 273) is always used in the Pres. and Impf. by Hom. and Hdt. For ἔμικτο, &c., see § 185. δ.

πήγνῡμι (r. παγ-, πηγ- § 266), *to fasten, to fix*, F. πήξω, A. ἔπηξα, 2 Pf.

intrans., as Pres., πέπηγα, 1 A. P. ἐπήχθην, commonly 2 A. P. ἐπάγην. Ep. 2 A. M. *S.* 3 ἔπηκτο (§ 185. δ) Λ. 378. For πήγνῦτο, see § 226. 4. Late πήσσω, Pf. P. πέπηγμαι.

ῥήγνῦμι (r. ῥαγ-, ῥηγ-), *to break*, F. ῥήξω, A. ἔῤῥηξα, 2 Pf. intrans. ἔῤῥωγα (§ 236. *b*), 2 A. P. ἐῤῥάγην. Ep., ῥήσσω, Σ. 571, Pf. P. ἔῤῥηγμαι, Θ. 137; Ion. 1 A. P. ἐῤῥήχθην, Hipp. Kindred, ῥάσσω and ἀράσσω, -ξω, *to smite*.

φράσσω, and rarely φράγνῦμι, Th. vii. 74 (r. φραγ-, φρασσ- § 274), *to fence*, F. φράξω, A. ἔφραξα, Pf. P. πέφραγμαι, A. P. ἐφράχθην. Late 2 A. P. ἐφράγην.

§ 295. γ. To Lingual and Liquid Roots.

δαίνῦμι (r. δαιτ-, δαινυ-), *to entertain, to feast*, poet. Ψ. 29, F. δαίσω, Æsch. Eum. 305, A. ἔδαισα, A. P. ἐδαίσθην. For Opt. δαίνῦτο, see § 226. 4.

καίνυμαι (r. καδ-, καιδ- § 267), *to excel*, poet. γ. 282, Pf. κέκασμαι, Eur. El. 616, *Pt.* κεκασμένος Δ. 339, and κεκαδμένος, Pind. O. 1. 42.

κτείνω, and later κτίννῦμι or κτείνῦμι (r. κτα-, κταν- § 278, κτεν- § 259, κτειν- § 268, κτιννυ- § 259. b, κτεινυ-), *to slay*, usually in composition with ἀπό or κατά, F. κτενῶ, 1 A. ἔκτεινα, poet. 2 A. ἔκτανον Soph. Ant. 1340 (also in Xen., who was partial to poet. forms, iv. 8, 25), and poet. ἔκτᾱν (§ 224. E.), Soph. Tr. 38, 2 Pf. ἔκτονα, 1 Pf., less classic, ἔκτακα (or ἔκταγκα) and ἐκτόνηκα, 2 A. M. poet. ἐκτάμην, Æsch. Pers. 923. Ep., F. κτανέω, Z. 409, 1 A. P. ἐκτάθην, δ. 537; late ἐκτάνθην, Anth. For the passive of κτείνω, the Attic writers employ θνήσκω (§ 281).

ὄλλῦμι (r. ὀλ-, ὀλ-νυ-), *to destroy*, F. ὀλέσω (§ 222. α), commonly ὀλῶ, A. ὤλεσα, 1 Pf. ὀλώλεκα, 2 Pf. intrans. ὄλωλα, 2 A. M. ὠλόμην. Poet. ὀλέκω, A. 10, Soph. Ant. 1286; Impf. iter. ὀλέκεσκεν (or ὀλέεσκεν, as from ὀλέω) T. 135.

ὄμνῦμι (r. ὀμ-), *to swear*, F. ὀμοῦμαι, A. ὤμοσα (§ 222. β), Pf. ὀμώμοκα (§ 191. 2), Pf. P. ὀμώμοσμαι and ὀμώμομαι (§ 221. α), A. P. ὠμόσθην and ὠμόθην. Pres. *Pt.* ὀμοῦντες Hdt. i. 153; late F. ὀμόσω, Anth.

ὀμόργνῦμι (ὀμοργ-), *to wipe off*, poet. E. 416, F. ὀμόρξω, A. ὤμορξα, Eur. Or. 219, A. P. ὠμόρχθην, Ar. Vesp. 560, A. M. ὠμορξάμην, Σ. 124. Collat. ὀμοργάζω, Hom. Merc. 361, late μόργνῦμι.

ὀρέγω, *to stretch out*, and Ep. ὀρέγνῦμι, A. 351, F. ὀρέξω, A. ὤρεξα, A. P. ὠρέχθην, Pf. P. ὤρεγμαι, Hipp., ὀρώρεγμαι, Π. 834.

ὄρνῦμι (r. ὀρ-), *to rouse*, F. ὄρσω (§ 56. β), A. ὦρσα, 2 Pf. intrans., as Pres., ὄρωρα. Ep., F. M. ὀροῦμαι, Υ. 140, 2 A. ὤρορον (§ 194. 3), 2 A. M. ὠρόμην, M. 279 (see § 185. δ, ε); from r. ὀρε-, Impf. ὀρέμην, B. 398, Pf. P. ὀρώρεμαι (§ 191. 2), τ. 377, *Subj.* ὀρώρηται M. 271. Kindred, chiefly poet., ὄρομαι, ὀρίνω, ὀροθύνω, ὀρούω· Lat. *orior*.

πτάρνυμαι (r. πταρ-), *to sneeze*, 2 A. ἔπταρον. 2 A. P. *Pt.* πταρείς, Hipp.

στόρνῦμι, στορέννῦμι, and στρώννῦμι (r. στορ-, στορε- § 288, στρο- § 262), *to strew*, F. στορῶ and στρώσω, A. ἐστόρεσα and ἔστρωσα, Pf. P. ἔστρωμαι, A. P. ἐστρώθην (ἐστορέσθην, Hipp.).

§ 296. e. Addition of ισκ.

ἀμπλακίσκω (r. ἀμπλακ-), *to err*, poet. 2 A. ἤμπλακον Soph. Ant. 910 *Pt.* ἀμπλακών and, to shorten the initial α (§ 263. 6), ἀπλακών Eur. Alc 241.

ἀπαφίσκω (r. ἀφ-, ἀπαφ-), *to deceive*, Ep. λ. 217, F. ἀπαφήσω, A. ἀπάφησα, Hom. Ap. 376, commonly 2 A. ἤπαφον, ξ. 379.

γεγωνέω and γεγωνίσκω (r. γων-, γεγων- § 283, γεγωνε- § 288, γεγωνισκ-) *to call aloud*, F. γεγωνήσω, A. ἐγεγώνησα, 2 Pf., as Pres., γέγωνα, *Subj.* γεγώνω, *Imp.* γέγωνε (§ 235), &c. Ep. Imp. or 2 A. ἐγέγωνεν (or Pf. γέγωνεν) Ξ. 469. See § 246. N.

ἐπαυρίσκομαι (r. αὐρ-, *to get*), *to get at, to reach, to enjoy*, poet. and Ion. N. 733, F. ἐπαυρήσομαι, 2 A. ἐπηῦρον, Λ. 572, 2 A. M. ἐπηυρόμην Eur. Hel. 469, 1 A. M. ἐπαυράμην, Hipp. Also ἐπαυρίσκω, Theog. 111, and ἐπαυρέω, Hes. Op. 417. From the same root, ἀπαυράω (§ 287. α), *to get from, to take away*, poet. A. 430, 1 A. M. ἀπηυράμην, Æsch. Pr. 28; and from the kindred οὐρ- (§ 28), Ep. Aor. *Pt.* ἀπούρας A. 356, ἀπουράμενος, Hes. Sc. 173.

εὑρίσκω (r. εὑρ-), *to find*, F. εὑρήσω (§ 222. 2), 2 A. εὗρον or ηὗρον (§ 188. N.), Pf. εὕρηκα, Pf. P. εὕρημαι, A. P. εὑρέθην (§ 219), 2 A. M. εὑρόμην, and less Att. 1 A. M. εὑράμην.

στερέω and στερίσκω (r. στερ-), *to deprive*, F. στερήσω, A. ἐστέρησα, Pf. ἐστέρηκα, Pf. P. ἐστέρημαι, 1 A. P. ἐστερήθην, poet. 2 A. P. *Pt.* στερείς Eur. Hel. 95. Mid. στέρομαι, *to want*, F., often as Pass., στερήσομαι (ἀπο-στερεῖσθε Andoc. 19. 25). Ep. 1 A. ἐστέρεσα, ν. 262.

§ 297. f. ADDITION OF ιζ.

ἐθίζω (r. ἐθ-), *to accustom*, F. ἐθίσω, -ιῶ (§ 200. β), Pf. εἴθικα (§ 189. 3) &c.; 2 Pf., as Pres. intrans., εἴωθα (§ 236. c). Ep. Pres. *Pt.* intrans. ἔθων I. 540.

ἐλπίζω (r. Ϝελπ-), *to hope*, F. ἐλπίσω, -ιῶ, &c.; Ep. ἔλπω, *to give hope*, β. 91, ἔλπομαι or ἐέλπομαι, and 2 Pf. ἔολπα (§ 191. 3), *to hope*, H. 199, K. 105, Υ. 186, 2 Plup. ἐώλπειν (§ 189. 5), T. 328.

κοναβίζω (r. κοναβ-), *to ring*, Ep. B. 466, A. ἐκονάβησα, B. 334.

πορίζω (r. πορ-), *to furnish*, F. πορίσω, -ιῶ, Pf. πεπόρικα, &c. Poet., 2 A. ἔπορον, Soph. Œd. T. 921 (see § 194. 3), Pf. P. πέπρωται (§ 223), *it is fated*, Σ. 329, *Pt.* πεπρωμένος, Soph. Ant. 1337, Mem. ii. 1. 33.

§ 298. g. ADDITION OF OTHER SYLLABLES.

ἄω (r. ἀ-, ἀδε-), *to be sated, to satiate*, Ep., F. ἄσω, Λ. 818, A. ἆσα, E. 289, and ἄδησα (*Opt.* ἀδδήσειεν or ἀδήσειεν α. 134), Pf. *Pt.* ἀδδηκώς, K. 98, F. M. ἄσομαι, Ω. 717, A. M. ἄσασθαι T. 307. The F. ἄσω and commonly the A. ἆσα are trans., the other forms intrans. For Pres. *Subj.* (ἄωμεν, ὦμεν) ἕωμεν (also written ἑῶμεν, as if from ἑάω) T. 402, see § 242. a; for *Inf.* ἄμεναι, see § 250. e; for Pres. Mid. ἄαται, see § 242. 1. Deriv. ἀσάομαι, Theoc. 25. 240, A. P. ἠσήθην Hdt. iii. 41.

δαμάζω (r. δαμ-), *to subdue*, F. δαμάσω, A. ἐδάμασα, 1 A. P. ἐδαμάσθην, and poet. ἐδμήθην (§ 223), Δ. 99, Eur. Alc. 127, 2 A. P. poet. ἐδάμην, Eur. Med. 647. Ep. Pres. and perhaps Fut. (§ 200. a) δαμάω, A. 61, Z. 368, Pf. P. δέδμημαι, E. 878, F. Pf. δεδμήσομαι Hom. Ap. 543. Collat. poet. forms, δαμνάω, λ. 221, δάμνημι E. 893, Æsch. Pr. 164, δαμαλίζω, Pind. P. 5. 163. Lat. *domo*.

ἕλκω (r. ἑλκ-, ἑλκυ-), *to draw*, F. ἕλξω (ἑλκύσω, Hipp.), A. εἵλκυσα (§ 189. 3; εἷλξα, Orph. Arg. 260), Pf. εἵλκυκα, Pf. P. εἵλκυσμαι, A. P. εἱλκύσθην. Ep. ἑλκέω, P. 395, ἑλκήσω, ἥλκησα, λ. 580.

ἐρωτάω (r. ἐρ-), *to ask*, F. ἐρωτήσω and ἐρήσομαι (§ 222), A. ἠρώτησα,

Pf. ἠρώτηκα, Pf. P. ἠρώτημαι, A. P. ἠρωτήθην, 2 A. M. ἠρόμην. Ep. and Ion., εἴρομαι A. 553, Hdt. iii. 64 (εἰρεόμενος Ib., § 243. 4), F. εἰρήσομαι δ. 61; εἰρωτάω, -έω, δ. 347, Hdt. iv. 145; ἐρέω, H. 128; ἐρεείνω Z. 145.

ἐσθίω, and poet. ἔσθω, Ω. 415, Æsch. Ag. 1597, or ἔδω, ε. 341, Eur. Cycl. 245 (r. ἐδ-, ἐσθ- §§ 282, 52, ἐσθι-), *to eat*, F. ἔδομαι (§ 200. b), Pf. ἐδήδοκα (§ 236. c), Pf. P. ἐδήδεσμαι (§ 222. α), Pl. Phædo, 110 e, A. P. ἠδέσθην· 2 A. ἔφαγον (r. φαγ-, § 301). Late F. φάγομαι (§ 247. d). Ep. 2 Pf. ἔδηδα, P. 542, Pf. P. ἐδήδομαι (§ 236. c).

ἔχθω, Soph. Aj. 459, ἐχθαίρω Eur. Alc. 179, and ἐχθραίνω, Ages. 11. 5 (r. ἐχθ-), *to hate*, chiefly poet., F. ἐχθαρῶ, A. ἤχθηρα.

ὄνομαι (ὀν-, ὀνο-), *to scorn*, Ion. and poet., ὄνοσαι, &c. (see ¶ 51), ρ. 378 F. ὀνόσομαι, A. ὠνοσάμην P. 173, and ὠνάμην, P. 25, A. P. ὠνόσθην, Hdt. ii 136. Deriv., ὀνειδίζω, and poet. ὀνοτάζω, Æsch. Sup. 11.

πεκτέω, Ep. πείκω (r. πεκ-), *to comb, shear*, poet., Ar. Av. 714, σ. 316, F. πεξῶ (§ 245. 2) Theoc. 5. 98, A. ἔπεξα, ἐπεξάμην, Ξ. 176, A. P. ἐπέχθην, Ar. Nub. 1356.

φλέγω, and poet. φλεγέθω, Soph. Tr. 99, *to burn*, F. φλέξω, A. ἔφλεξα, A. P. ἐφλέχθην. Late 2 A. P. ἐφλέγην, Anth.

§ **299.** Remark. A few verbs obtain a 2 Aor. with a short penult (§ 255. δ), through an extension of the root; as, διώκω, *to pursue*, ἐδιώκᾰθον, Ar. Vesp. 1203, Pl. Gorg. 483 a; εἴκω, *to yield*, εἰκᾰθον, Soph. Œd. T. 651; εἴργω, *to exclude*, εἴργᾰθον, Soph. Œd. C. 862 (ἔργᾰθον, Λ. 437, ἐέργᾰθον, E. 147), εἰργᾰθόμην, Æsch. Eum. 566; ἀμῡνω, *to ward off*, ἠμῡνᾰθον, Ar. Nub. 1323, ἠμῡνᾰθόμην, Æsch. Eum. 438; κίω, *to go*, μετ-εκίᾰθον Λ. 52; ἤλκᾰθον (§ 273. β), ἔσχεθον (§ 300). Cf. ἔφθιθον (§ 278). These extended Aorists, which are chiefly poet., are regarded by some as Imperfects, and are commonly so accented.

§ 300. 3. Exchange of Letters.

In the two following verbs, σ passes into ε aspirated (§ 50).

ἕπω (r. σπ-, ἑπ-), *to be occupied with*, Impf. εἶπον (§ 189. 3), F. ἕψω, 2 A. ἔσπον, *Subj.* σπῶ, &c. Mid. ἕπομαι, *to follow*, Impf. εἱπόμην, F. ἕψομαι, 2 A. ἑσπόμην, *Subj.* σπῶμαι, &c. Poet. ἕσπομαι, δ. 826, Impf. (considered by some 2 A.) ἑσπόμην, Γ. 239. A. P. περι-έφθην, Hdt. vi. 15. The act. ἕπω scarcely occurs except in composition.

ἔχω and ἴσχω (r. σχ-, ἐχ-, ἑχ- § 263, ἰσχ- §§ 283. c, 263), *to have, to hold* (in the sense *to have*, the forms ἔχω and ἕξω are preferred; in the sense *to hold*, ἴσχω and σχήσω), Impf. εἶχον and ἴσχον, F. ἕξω and σχήσω (§ 222); 2 A. ἔσχον, *Subj.* σχῶ (comp. διάσχω or διασχῶ, r. σχ- or σχε-), *Opt.* σχοίην (§ 205. α), *Imp.* σχές (σχε- § 288; compare θές, ἕς, § 210. 2), and rarely, in composition, σχέ, *Inf.* σχεῖν, *Pt.* σχών· 2 A. poet. ἔσχεθον (§ 299), Æsch. Pr. 16; Pf. ἔσχηκα, Pf. P. ἔσχημαι, A. P. ἐσχέθην, 2 A. M. ἐσχόμην. Ep. Pf. *Pt.* συν-οχωκότε (§§ 236. 1, 191. 2, 62) B. 218. For ἐπ-ώχατο, see § 236. d; for ἐν-είχεε, see § 243. 4. Ep. deriv. forms, ἰσχάνω, Ξ. 387, ἰσχανάω, E. 89. For the compound ὑπισχνέομαι, see § 292, for ἀνέχομαι, § 301. 2. For the π in ἀμπέχω (ἀμφί, ἔχω), see § 62; and for the various forms of the augm. (Impf. ἠμπ-ειχόμην, 2 A. ἠμπι-σχόμην, ἠμπ-εσχόμην, &c.), § 192. 3.

C. Anomalous Changes.

§ **301.** Forms are sometimes associated, which must be

referred to roots *originally distinct*, or *widely removed* from each other (§ 257. 2); as,

1. αἱρέω (r. αἱρε-), *to take*, F. αἱρήσω, Pf. ᾕρηκα, Pf. P. ᾕρημαι, A. P. ᾑρέθην (§ 219); 2 A. εἷλον (r. ἑλ-, § 189. 3), 2 A. M. εἱλόμην. Poet. 1 A. M. ἐξ-ηρήσατο Ar. Thesm. 761. Doubtful or late F. ἑλῶ, ἑλοῦμαι· Ion. Pf. ἀραίρηκα, Hdt. v. 102, ἀραίρημαι, iv. 66; Ep. 2 A. M. *S.* 3 γέντο for Fέλτο (§§ 69. III., 185. δ) Θ. 43. In the sense *to capture*, the Pass. is commonly supplied by ἁλίσκομαι (r. ἁλ-, whence ἑλ- § 259, ἁλο-, ἁλισκ- § 280), Impf. ἡλισκόμην, F. ἁλώσομαι, 2 A. ἑάλων (§ 189. 2) and ἥλων, *Subj.* ἁλῶ, &c., Pf. ἑάλωκα and ἥλωκα.

2. ἀνέχομαι, *to endure*, a compound of ἔχω (§ 300), F. ἀνέξομαι and ἀνασχήσομαι, 2 A. ἠνεσχόμην (§ 192. 3); F. τλήσομαι (r. ταλα-, τλα- § 261), 2 A. ἔτλην (§ 227), Pf. τέτληκα (see § 238. α). Ep. 1 A. ἐτάλασσα, P. 166. Later Ep., ὀτλέω, Ap. Rh. 3. 769, ὀτλεύω, 2. 1008.

3. ἔρχομαι (r. ἐρχ-), *to go, to come*, Imp. ἠρχόμην· F. ἐλεύσομαι (r. ἐλυθ-, ἐλευθ- § 270), 2 A. ἤλυθον, commonly ἦλθον (§ 261), 2 Pf. ἐλήλυθα (§ 191. 2). Ep. 2 Pf. ἤλυθα, Hes. Th. 660, εἰλήλουθα (§ 47. N.), Dor. 2 A. ἦνθον (§ 69. III.), Theoc. 1. 77, Lacon. ἦλσον (§ 70. 4), Ar. Lys. 105. The Pres. (except in the Ind.), the Impf., and the Fut. are commonly supplied in the Att. by the verb εἶμι (§ 231).

4. ὁράω (r. ὁρα-), *to see*, Impf. ἑώρων (§ 189. 2), Pf. ἑώρᾱκα (ἑόρᾱκα Ar. Pl. 98), Pf. P. ἑώρᾱμαι· F. ὄψομαι (r. ὀπ-), Pf. P. ὦμμαι, A. P. ὤφθην (ὁραθῆναι Pl. Def. 411 a), 2 Pf. poet. and Ion. ὄπωπα Soph. Ant. 6, Hdt. iii. 63; 2 A. εἶδον (r. ἰδ-, the augm. uniting with the ι to form ει), *Subj.* ἴδω, &c., 2 A. M. εἰδόμην, *Subj.* ἴδωμαι, &c.; 2 Pf. οἶδα, (*I have seen*) *I know* (§ 233); Mid., poet., εἴδομαι (r. εἰδ- § 268), *to seem, to resemble*, Æsch. Cho. 178, 1 A. εἰσάμην, β. 791.

Note. In the *preteritive* οἶδα (¶ 58, § 237), the root has four forms, (1.) ἰδ-; ἴσμεν (Ion. ἴδμεν A. 124), ἴστε, ἴσθι, ἴστω (Bœot. ἴττω Ar. Ach. 911), &c.; and Ep., *Inf.* ἴδμεν Α. 719, ἴδμεναι Ν. 273, *Pt.* ἰδυῖα, Α. 608, Plup. *Pl.* 3 (ἴδ-σαν) ἴσαν Σ. 405: (2.) εἰδ-; εἰδέναι, εἰδώς, ᾔδειν, εἴσομαι· and the Ep. *Subj.* εἴδομεν, εἴδετε (§ 246. 3): (3.) οἰδ- (§ 236. 1); οἶδα, οἶσθα, &c.: (4.) εἰδε- (§ 288); (εἰδέω) εἰδῶ, εἰδείην, εἰδήσω (rare, A. 546, Isoc. 5 b), εἴδησα (late). The Plup. is sometimes doubly augmented (§ 189); thus, Ep. ἠείδεις or ἠείδης Χ. 280, ἠείδει or ἠείδη ι. 206, Ion. ἠείδε Hdt. i. 45 (for ἠείδεε, one ε dropped, cf. § 243. 2). In the Dor., we find the verb ἴσᾱμι, perhaps suggested by ἴσᾱσι (§ 237, οἶδα), Pind. P. 4. 441, ἴσης Theoc. 13. 34, ἴσᾱτι 15. 146, ἴσαμεν Pind. N. 7. 21, *Pt.* ἴσας, Pind. P. 3. 52. The deficiencies of οἶδα are supplied by γιγνώσκω (§ 285).

5. τρέχω (r. θρεχ-, τρεχ- § 263), *to run*, F. θρέξομαι, commonly δραμοῦμαι (r. δραμ-), 1 A. ἔθρεξα, commonly 2 A. ἔδραμον, Pf. δεδράμηκα (§ 222), Pf. P. δεδράμημαι. Ep. 2 Pf. δέδρομα, ε. 412. Late and rare F. δραμῶ Ath. 416 f, δράμομαι (§ 200. b), Anth. Deriv., τροχάζω, vii. 3. 46, Ep. τροχάω, ο. 451, τρωχάω, Χ. 163, δρομάω, Hes. Fr. 2. 2.

6. φέρω (r. φερ-), *to bear*, F. οἴσω (r. οἰ-), F. M. οἴσομαι, F. P. οἰσθήσομαι· 1 A. ἤνεγκα (r. ἐνεκ-, ἐνεγκ- § 277), 2 A. ἤνεγκον, A. M. ἠνεγκάμην, Pf. ἐνήνοχα (§§ 191. 2, 236. α), Pf. P. ἐνήνεγμαι, A. P. ἠνέχθην, F. P. ἐνεχθήσομαι. Ion. (r. ἐνεικ- § 268; συν-ενείκεται Hes. Sc. 440) 1 A. ἤνεικα, E. 885 Hdt. iii. 30, 2 A. *Opt.* ἐνείκοι Σ. 147, *Inf.* ἐνεικέμεν Τ. 194, Pf. P. ἐνήνειγμαι, Hdt. ii. 12, A. P. ἠνείχθην, i. 66; 1 A. *Inf.* (ἀνα-οῖσαι) ἀνῷσαι Ib. 157 Late Pf. P. προ-οῖσται Luc. Paras. 2. For οἶσε, &c., see § 185. ε; for φέρτε

§ 246. β; for φέρησι, § 251. 2. Deriv., φορέω, *to carry*, -ήσω, &c. (φορῆναι § 251. 2), δια-, εἰσ-, ἐκ-φρέω (φρείω, Ar. Vesp. 125), *to let pass*, -φρήσω, -έφρησα, -εφρήσθην. Lat. *fero.* — The Aorists ἤνεγκα and ἤνεγκον are both common in the 1*st Pers. sing.* of the *Ind.*, and in the *Opt.*; but in the 2*d Pers. sing.* of the *Imp.*, in the *Inf.*, and in the *Part.*, the forms of ἤνεγκον are preferred; and, elsewhere, those of ἤνεγκα.

7. φημί and φάσκω (¶ 53, § 228; r. φα-, φασκ- § 279), *to say, to affirm*, F. ἐρῶ (r. ἐρ-, ῥε- § 262), Pf. εἴρηκα (§ 191. 1), Pf. P. εἴρημαι, F. Pf. εἰρήσομαι, Cyr. vii. 1. 9, A. P. ἐῤῥήθην or ἐῤῥέθην (Ion. εἰρέθην or εἰρήθην, Hdt. iv. 77); 1 A. εἶπα (r. ἐπ-, εἰπ- § 268), 2 A. εἶπον. Non-Att., Pres. εἴρω β. 162, εἰρέω, Hes. Th. 38; Ion. 1 A. M. ἀπ-ειπάμην, *refused*, Hdt. i. 205; Poet. 1 Aor. (ἔϝειπα) ἔειπα Pind. N. 9. 78, 2 A. ἔειπον K. 445; Ep. 2 A. (r. ἐπ-, ἐσπ- § 273, cf. ἐνέπω) ἔσπον, B. 484. Redupl. forms, πιφαύσκω Æsch. Eum. 620, πιφάσκω, Hes. Th. 655. — The forms of φάσκω, with the F. φήσω, the A. ἔφησα, and the Mid. voice, have commonly the strengthened sense, *to affirm* The 1st Aor. inf. εἶπαι and part. εἴπας are not used by the Attics.

8. ὠνέομαι (r. ὠνε-), *to buy*, Impf. ἐωνούμην (§ 189. 2), F. ὠνήσομαι, Pf. ἐώνημαι, A. P. ἐωνήθην· 2 A. M. ἐπριάμην (¶ 49; r. πρια-). Ion. and late 1 A. M. ἐωνησάμην, Hipp.

CHAPTER XI.

FORMATION OF WORDS.

§ **302.** The Greek, like all other original languages, is the development, according to certain natural laws, of a *small number of germs*, or *primary roots.* These primary roots (which may be termed *radicals*, to distinguish them from the mere roots of inflection) have a significance which is not arbitrary, but founded upon instinctive principles of the human constitution.

NOTE. The much agitated question, whether the radicals of language are *nouns* or *verbs*, has no propriety, inasmuch as the origin of these radicals was prior to grammatical distinctions, and the same radical was used as *noun, adjective, verb*, &c., as the case might require.

§ **303.** Those words in which the radicals appear in their simplest forms are termed *primitive;* and all others are termed *derivative;* while, at the same time, a distinction must be made between simple derivatives, and those words which are formed by the union of other words, and which are termed *compound.*

NOTES. *a.* Of those words which are commonly distinguished as *primitive* and *derivative*, some are directly related to each other as parent and child, while others are merely formations from the same radical, which, however, commonly appears in a simpler form in the one than in the other. It is important to observe this distinction, though the same language is commonly, for the sake of convenience, employed in both cases.

β. In tracing derivations, it is sometimes convenient to assume a theme, either as a primitive, or as a link of connection. We must, however, be cautious in pronouncing that to have been essential in the actual formation of the language, which we find convenient in explaining that formation.

I. Formation of Simple Words.

§ **304.** Simple Words are divided in respect to their formation into three classes.

(I.) Those which consist of the mere radical, without change, except for euphony or emphasis.

(II.) Those which have, in addition, merely the affixes of inflection.

(III.) Those which receive farther modifications.

The Rules and Remarks which follow have respect chiefly to the third class.

A. Nouns.

§ **305.** I. From Verbs. Nouns formed from verbs (or from common radicals, § 303. *α*) denote,

1.) The action of the verb. These are formed by adding to the root of the verb,

a. *-σις* (Gen. *-σεως*, fem.), or *-σίᾱ* (G. *-σίᾱς*, f.); as, *μιμέ-ομαι*, *to imitate*, *μίμη-σις*, *imitation*; *πράσσω* (r. *πρᾱγ-*), *to act*, (*πρᾶγ-σις*) *πρᾶξις*, *action*; *θύω*, *to sacrifice*, *θυσία*, *sacrifice*; *δοκιμάζω*, *to try*, *δοκιμασία*, *trial*.

b. *-η*, *-α* (G. *-ης*, *-ᾱς*, f.); as, *φεύγω* (r. *φυγ-*), *to flee*, *φυγ-ή*, *flight*; *τρέφω*, *to nourish*, *τροφή*, *nourishment*; *χαίρω* (r. *χαρ-*), *to rejoice*, *χαρ-ά*, *joy*; *φθείρω*, *to corrupt*, *φθορά*, *corruption*. Some verbs in *-εύω* have abstracts in *-είᾱ* (§ 92. *β*. *a*); as, *παιδεύω*, *to instruct*, *παιδείᾱ*, *instruction*.

c. *-ος* (G. *-ου*, m.); as, *λέγ-ω*, *to speak*, *λόγ-ος*, *speech*; *σπείρω*, *to sow*, *σπόρος*, *sowing*.

d. *-τος* (G. *-του*, m.); as, *κωκύ-ω*, *to wail*, *κωκῡ-τός*, *wailing*.

e. *-ος* (G. *-εος*, n.); as, *κήδ-ομαι*, *to care*, *κῆδ-ος*, *care*.

f. *-μός* (G. *-μοῦ*, m.), or *-μη* (G. *-μης*, f.); as, *ὀδύρ-ομαι*, *to lament*, *ὀδυρ-μός*, *lamentation*; *μέ-μνη-μαι*, *to remember*, *μνή-μη*, *remembrance*.

Remark. From the tendency of *abstracts* to pass into *concretes*, verbals of Class 1 often express not so much the *action* itself, as the *effect* or *object* of the action, and thus blend with Class 2; as, *γραμμή*, *line*.

§ **306.** 2.) The effect, or object of the action. These are formed by adding to the root of the verb,

-μα (G. *-ματος*, n.); as, *ποιέ-ω*, *to make*, *compose*, *ποίη-μα*, *thing made*,

poem; σπείρω, *to sow,* σπέρμα, *thing sown, seed;* γράφω, *to write,* (γράφ-μα) γράμμα, *letter.* See also § 305. R.

3.) The DOER. These are formed by adding to the root of the verb,

a. -της (G. -του, m.); as, θεά-ομαι, *to behold,* θεᾱ-τής, *beholder;* ποιέω, *to compose,* ποιητής, *poet;* κτίζω, *to found,* κτίστης, *founder.*

b. -τηρ (G. -τηρος, m.), or -τωρ (G. -τορος, m.); as, δίδωμι (r. δο-), *to give,* δο-τήρ, *giver;* σώζω, *to save,* σωτήρ, *saviour;* r. ῥε-, *to speak,* ῥή-τωρ, *speaker orator.*

NOTE. The feminines corresponding to the above (a. and b.) end in -τριᾰ or -τειρᾰ (proparoxytone, G. -ᾱς), or in -τρις or -τις (G. -ιδος); as, ποιήτρια, *poetess,* σώτειρα, *female deliverer;* αὐλητής and -τήρ, *flute-player,* αὐλητρίς and -τρια, *flute-girl;* προφήτης, *prophet,* προφῆτις, *prophetess.*

c. -εύς (G. -έως, m.); as, γράφ-ω, *to paint,* γραφ-εύς, *painter;* φθείρω, *to corrupt,* φθορεύς, *corrupter;* κείρω, *to shave,* κουρεύς, *barber.*

d. -ος (G. -ου, m. f.); τρέφ-ω, *to nourish,* τροφ-ός, *nurse;* ἀείδω, *to sing,* ἀοιδός, *minstrel.*

REMARK. Some verbals of Class 3 are applied to things; as, ῥαίω, *to beat,* ῥαιστήρ, *beater, hammer,* ζωστήρ, *girdle,* ἀήτης, *wind* (blower), ἐμβολεύς, *stopper.*

§ 307. 4.) The PLACE, INSTRUMENT, or other means of the action. These are formed by adding to the root of the verb,

a. -τήριον (G. -ου, n.), more frequently expressing *place;* as, ἀκροά-ομαι, *to hear,* ἀκροα-τήριον, *place of hearing, auditory;* δικαστήριον (δικάζω), *court of justice;* ποτήριον (πίνω), *drinking-cup.* Cf. §§ 314. b, 315. α.

b. -τρον (G. -ου, n.), or -τρᾱ (G. -ᾱς, f.), more frequently expressing *means;* as, ξύω, *to curry,* ξύστρον and ξύστρα, *currycomb,* λύτρον (λύω), *ransom* (means of releasing), ὀρχήστρα (ὀρχέομαι), *orchestra.*

REMARK. Terminations of verbals are affixed, in general, with the same euphonic changes as the similar affixes of inflection; i. e. those beginning with σ follow the analogy of -σω of the Fut. or -σαι of the Perf. pass.; those beginning with μ and τ, of -μαι and -ται of the Perf. pass.; and those beginning with a vowel, of the 2d Perf. It is convenient to remember, that verbal nouns following the 1st Pers. of the Perf. pass. more frequently denote the *thing done;* the 2d, the *doing;* and the 3d, the *doer.* Thus,

πε-ποίη-μαι,	πε-ποίη-σαι,	πε-ποίη-ται,
ποίη-μα, *poem,*	ποίη-σις, *poesy,*	ποιη-τής, *poet.*

§ 308. II. FROM ADJECTIVES. Nouns formed from adjectives (or from common radicals, § 303. α) usually express the ABSTRACT of the adjective, and are formed in,

a. -ίᾱ (G. -ίᾱς, f.), or, if the root ends in ε or ο, -ιᾰ forming, with the final vowel of the root, -ειᾰ or -οιᾰ; as, σοφ-ός, *wise,* σοφ-ίᾱ, *wisdom;* εὐδαίμων, -ον-ος, *happy,* εὐδαιμον-ίᾱ, *happiness;* ἀληθής, -έ-ος, *true,* ἀλήθειᾰ, *truth;* εὔνο-ος, contr. εὔνους, *kind,* εὔνοιᾰ, *kindness.* See §§ 92. β, γ, 315. a.

b. -της (G. -τητος, f.), from adjectives in -ος and -υς; as, ἴσος, *equal*, ἰσότης *equality*; ταχύς, *swift*, ταχυτής, *swiftness*.

c. -σύνη (G. -ης, f.), from adjectives in -ος and -ων; as, δίκαιος, *just*, δικαιοσύνη, *justice*; σώφρων, *discreet*, σωφροσύνη, *discretion*.

d. -ος (G. -εος, n.), chiefly from adjectives in -υς; as, βαθύς, *deep*, βάθος, *depth*; εὐρύς, *broad*, εὖρος, *breadth*.

e. -άς (G. -άδος, f.), from numerals; as, δύο, *two*, δυάς, *duad*. See ¶ 25. III.

§ **309.** III. From Other Nouns. Nouns derived from other nouns are,

1.) Patrials (patria, *native land*), and similar words denoting *persons related to some object*. These end in,

a. -της (G. -του) masc., and -τις (§ 134. α; G. -τιδος) fem. (with the preceding vowel long in patrials; thus, -ίτης, -ήτης, -άτης, -ιάτης, -ιώτης; and also in other nouns in -ιτης); as, Σύβαρις, *Sybaris*, Συβαρίτης, *a man of Sybaris, a Sybarite*, Συβαρῖτις, *a woman of Sybaris*; Αἰγινήτης, Πισάτης, Σπαρτιάτης, Σικελιώτης, *a man of Ægina*, &c.; πόλις, *city*, πολίτης, *citizen*, πολῖτις, *female citizen*; τόξον, *bow*, τοξότης, *archer*, τοξότις, *archeress*.

b. -εύς (G. -έως) masc., and -ις (G. -ιδος) fem. (§ 118. 3); as, Μέγαρα, *Megara*, Μεγαρεύς, *Megarian man*, Μεγαρίς, *M. woman*; φάρμακον, *drug*, φαρμακεύς, *dealer in drugs, sorcerer*, φαρμακίς, *sorceress*; ἵππος, *horse*, ἱππεύς, *horseman, knight*.

§ **310.** 2.) Patronymics (so called from containing the father's or ancestor's name, πατρὸς ὄνομα). These end in,

a. -ίδης (G. -ου) masc. (uniting with ε or ο preceding), and -ίς (G. -ίδος) fem.; -άδης (G. -ου) masc., and -άς (G. -άδος) fem., from names of Dec. I.; and -ιάδης (G. -ου) masc., and -ιάς (G. -ιάδος) fem., from names in -ιος, and (especially in hexameter verse for the sake of the measure) from many which have the last syllable of the root long; as, Πρίαμος, *Priam*, Πριαμίδης, *son of P.*, Πριαμίς, *daughter of P.*; Κέκροψ, Κεκροπίδης, Κεκροπίς· Πηλεύς, -έως, Πηλείδης· Ἡρακλῆς, -έους, Ἡρακλείδης· Λητώ, -όος, Λητοίδης· Βορέας, *Boreas*, Βορεάδης, *son of B.*, Βορεάς, -δος, *daughter of B.*; Θέστιος, Θεστιάδης, Θεστιάς· Φέρης, -ητ-ος, Φερητιάδης· Πηλεύς, Ep. G. -ῆος, Ep. Πηληιάδης, A. 1.

b. -ίων (G. -ίωνος, rarely -ίονος) masc., and -ιώνη or -ίνη (G. -ης) fem., only poetic; as, Κρόνος, *Saturn*, Κρονίων, -ίωνος or -ίονος, *son of S.*, A. 397; Πηλεύς, Πηλείων, A. 188; Ἀκρίσιος, Ἀκρισιώνη, *daughter of A.*, Ξ. 319; Ἄδρηστος, Ἀδρηστίνη E. 412.

Remark. Patronymics appear to have been, in their origin, *diminutives* thus, Πριαμίδης, *little Priam*. See § 312. Akin to the above are a few words in -ιδέος, contr. -ιδοῦς, — *son*, -ιδέα, contr. -ιδῆ, — *daughter*; as, θυγατριδοῦς, -ιδῆ, *daughter's son*, — *daughter*, ἀδελφιδοῦς, -ιδῆ, *nephew, niece*.

§ **311.** 3.) Female Appellatives. These end in,

a. -ις (G. -ιδος), chiefly from masculines of Dec. I., and from those in -εύς as, δεσπότης, *master*, δεσπότις, *mistress* (also δέσποινα, cf. b). See § 134. α.

b. -αινᾰ (G. -ης), chiefly from masculines in -ων; as, λέων, -οντος, *lion*, λέαινα, *lioness*; τέκτων, -ονος, *artisan*, τέκταινα· Λάκων, -ωνος, *Spartan*, Λάκαινα. Also from some in -ος; as, θεός, *god*, θέαινα, *goddess* (§ 74. ε), λύκος *wolf*, λύκαινα.

c. -εια (G. -είας), from βασιλεύς, *king*, and ἱερεύς, *priest*; thus, βασίλεια, *queen*, ἱέρεια, *priestess*.

d. -σσᾰ (-ττᾰ, § 70. 1; G. -ης), from several endings of Dec. III.; as, Κίλιξ, -ικος, *Cilician*, Κίλισσα (cf. § 273), ἄναξ, -κτος, *sovereign*, ἄνασσα, θής, -τός, *hireling*, θῆσσα, Λίβυς, -υος, *Lybian*, Λίβυσσα.

NOTE. See, also, §§ 306. N., 309, 310.

§ 312. 4.) DIMINUTIVES (sometimes expressing *affection*, often *contempt*). These end in,

a. -ιον (G. -ιου, n.), with a syllable often prefixed (-ίδιον, -άριον, -ύλλιον, -ύδριον, -ύφιον, &c.). — b. -ίσκος (G. -ου, m.), -ίσκη (G. -ης, f.). Thus, παῖς, *child*, Diminutives, παιδίον, *little child*, παιδίσκος, *young boy*, παιδίσκη, *young girl*, παιδάριον, παιδαρίδιον, παιδαρύλλιον, παιδαρίσκος, παιδισκάριον· μεῖραξ, *youth*, μειράκιον, μειρακίδιον, μειρακύλλιον, μειρακυλλίδιον, μειρακίσκος, μειρακίσκη· κόρη, *girl*, κόριον, κορίσκη, κορίσκιον, κορίδιον, κοράσιον (for -άριον, on account of the preceding ρ), κορασίδιον· νῆσος, *island*, νησύδριον· ζῷον, *animal*, (ζωΐδιον) ζῴδιον, ζωδάριον, ζωΰφιον. Ὦ Σώκρατες, ὦ Σωκρατίδιον, *O Socrates! dear Socky!* Ar. Nub. 222.

c. -ίς (G. -ίδος and -ῖδος, f.); as, κρήνη, *fountain*, κρηνίς, -ῖδος· πίναξ, *table*, πινακίς, -ίδος, *tablet*.

d. -ιδεύς (G. -έως, m., only of the young of animals); as, ἀετός, *eagle*, ἀετιδεύς, *eaglet*; λαγώς, *hare*, λαγιδεύς.

e. -ίχνη, -άκνη, -υλλίς, -ύλος (Dor.), &c.; as, πόλις, *city*, πολίχνη· πίθος, *wine-jar*, πιθάκνη· ἀκανθίς, *finch*, ἀκανθυλλίς· ἔρως, -ωτος, *love*, ἐρωτύλος, *darling*, Theoc. 3. 7.

NOTE. Some diminutives (especially in -ιον) have lost their peculiar force· thus, θήρ, commonly in prose θηρίον, *wild beast*. Some *proper names* have diminutive forms, sometimes made by abbreviation; as, Μέγιλλος (μέγας *great*), Ἀμαρυλλίς (ἀμάρα, *channel*), Διονῦς, Μηνᾶς (§ 126. 2).

§ 313. 5.) AUGMENTATIVES, words implying *increase* either of *number*, *size*, or *degree*. They end in,

a. -ων (G. -ωνος, m.). This ending may express either a *place*, an *animal*, or a *person*, in which any thing exists *in numbers*, or *in large size* or *degree*; as, ἄμπελος, *vine*, ἀμπελών, *vineyard*, ἱππών (ἵππος), *horse-stable*, ἀνδρών, γυναικών (ἀνήρ, γυνή), *apartments for men, women*, οἰνών (οἶνος), *wine-cellar*; χεῖλος, *lip*, χειλών, a fish with a long snout; γνάθος, *jaw*, γνάθων, *glutton*; πλάτος, *breadth*, Πλάτων. As a designation of place, -ωνία is also used; as, ῥοδωνία (ῥόδον), *rose-bed*.

b. -αξ (G. -ακος, m.), applied, like the preceding, to persons and animals, but harsher in its expression; as, πλοῦτος, *wealth*, πλούταξ, *a rich churl*. So λάβρος, *greedy*, λάβραξ, *sea-wolf*.

REMARK. Many derivative nouns are properly adjectives used substantively.

B. Adjectives.

§ **314.** I. From Verbs. These end in,

a. -ικός, -ή, -όν, *active;* as, ἄρχω, *to rule*, ἀρχικός, *able to rule;* γράφω, *to describe*, γραφικός, *descriptive, graphic.* This ending is more frequently preceded by τ (cf. § 306. a, b); as, ποιητικός (ποιέω), *poetic.* But see § 315. b.

b. -τήριος, -ᾱ, -ον, *active;* as, σώζω, *to save*, σωτήριος, *saving* (cf. § 306. b).

c. -ιμος, -ον (and -ος, -η, -ον), implying *fitness*, both *active* and *passive*, and annexed after the analogy of different verbal nouns; as, τρέφω, τροφή (§ 305. b), τρόφιμος, *fitted to impart* or *to receive nourishment, nutritious, vigorous*, χρήσιμος (χράομαι, χρῆσις), *fit for use.*

d. -μων, -μον (G. -μονος), *active;* as, ἐλεέω, *to pity*, ἐλεήμων, *compassionate*, μνήμων (μέμνημαι), *mindful.*

e. -τός, -ή, -όν, *passive*, signifying *that which is done*, either as a matter of *fact* (like the Lat. Part. pass. in *-tus*), or more commonly as a matter of *habit* or *possibility;* thus, ὁράω, *to see*, ὁρᾱτός, *seen, visible.*

f. -τέος, -ᾱ, -ον, *passive*, expressing *necessity* or *obligation* (like the Lat. Part. in *-ndus*); as, ποιέω, *to make*, ποιητέος, *that which is to be made.*

Note. Verbals in -τός and -τέος commonly follow, in respect to the form of the root, the analogy of the 1 Aor. pass.; as, αἱρέω, *to take*, Pf. P. ᾕρημαι, A. P. ᾑρέθην, αἱρετός, αἱρετέος · παύω, *to stop*, Pf. P. πέπαυμαι, A. P. ἐπαύσθην, παυστός, παυστέος.

g. -νός, -ή, -όν, *passive* (compare the Part. in -μενος); as, σέβω, *to revere*, (σεβ-νός) σεμνός, *revered*, ποθεινός (ποθέω), *longed for.*

h. -ἀρός (-ᾱ, -όν), -ᾰς (G. -ᾰδος), &c.; as, χαλάω, *to slacken*, χαλαρός, *slack;* φέρω, *to bear*, φοράς, *fruitful;* λέγω, *to choose*, λογάς, *chosen;* λοιπός (λείπω), *remaining.*

§ **315.** II. From Nouns. These have the following endings, with, in general, the significations that are annexed:

a. -ιος, *belonging to;* if a vowel precedes, commonly uniting with it in a diphthong (-αιος, -ειος, -οιος, -ῳος, -υιος), and often, without respect to this, assuming the form -ειος (Ion. -ήϊος, § 46. B.), especially from names of persons and animals. Many *patrials* (properly adjectives, but often used substantively) belong to this class. Thus, οὐρανός, *heaven*, οὐράνιος, *belonging to heaven, heavenly*, φόνιος (φόνος), *of murder, murderous;* ἀγοραῖος (ἀγορά), *pertaining to the forum*, Ἀθηναῖος (Ἀθῆναι), *Athenian*, θεῖος (θε-ός), *divine*, Ἀργεῖος (Ἄργος, -ε-ος), *Argive*, ἑῷος (ἕως), Ion. ἠοῖος (ἠώς, -ό-ος), *of the morning*, πήχυιος (πῆχυς), *of a cubit's length;* ἀνθρώπειος (ἄνθρωπος), *human*, Ὁμήρειος (Ὅμηρος), *Homeric*, θήρειος (θήρ), *of wild beasts.*

Notes. *α.* From the neuter of these adjectives has come a class of substantives denoting an appropriated *building* or other *place, instrument*, &c.; as, Ἀθήναιον (Ἀθηνᾶ), Θησεῖον, Μουσεῖον, *temple of Minerva, of Theseus, of the Muses*, κουρεῖον (κουρεύς), *barber's shop*, γραμματεῖον (γραμματεύς), *writing-tablet*, cf. § 307.

β. Before -ιος and -ιᾱ (§ 308. a), τ often passes into σ; as, ἐνιαυτός, *year*, ἐνιαύσιος, *of a year*, Μιλήσιος (Μίλητος), *Milesian*, ἀθανασία (ἀθάνατος), *immortality.*

b. -ικός, -ή, -όν (if υ precede, -κός: if simple ι or ει, -ακός; while -αιος commonly makes -αϊκός), *relating to.* These adjectives in -κός are often formed from words that are themselves derivative. They apply to *things* rather than to *persons*. When used of the latter, they commonly signify *related to in quality*, or *fit for*, and are mostly derived from personal appellations. Thus, τέχνη, *art*, τεχνικός, *relating to art, artistic;* δοῦλος, *slave*, δουλικός, *servile;* Λίβυς, *Libyan*, Λιβυκός, *pertaining to the Libyans* or *Libya;* Κορίνθιος, *Corinthian*, Κορινθιακός· σπονδεῖος, *spondee*, σπονδειακός, *spondaïc;* Ἀχαιός, *Achæan*, Ἀχαϊκός, and less Att. Ἀχαιϊκός· ποιητής, *poet*, ποιητικός, *poetic*, ῥητορικός, (ῥήτωρ), *rhetorical*, στρατηγικός (στρατηγός), *fit for a general.* See § 314. a.

c. -εος, -ᾶ, -ουν, and -ινος, -η, -ον (proparoxytone), denoting *material, -en;* as, χρυσός, *gold*, χρύσεος (¶ 18), *golden*, ξύλινος (ξύλον), *wooden*.

d. -ινός, seldom -ινός, expressing *time* or *prevalence;* as, ἡμερινός (ἡμέρα), *by day*, πεδινός (πέδον), *level*, ὀρεινός (ὄρος, -ε-ος), *mountainous*.

e. -ῖνος, -ηνός, -ᾱνός, *patrials*, from names of cities and countries out of Greece; as, Ταραντῖνος (Τάρας, -αντος), *Tarentine*, Κυζικηνός (Κύζικος), *Cyzicene*, Σαρδιανός (Σάρδεις), *Sardian*.

f. -ρός, -ερός, -ηρός, -αλέος, -ηλός, -ωλός, -εις (-εσσα, -εν, G. -εντος), -ώδης (-ες, G. -εος; contr. from -ο-ειδής, from εἶδος, *form*), expressing *fulness* or *quality;* as, αἰσχρός (αἶσχος), *shameful*, φοβερός (φόβος), *fearful*, πονηρός (πόνος), *painful*, θαρσαλέος (θάρσος), *courageous*, ἀπατηλός (ἀπάτη), *deceitful*, φειδωλός (φειδώ), *parsimonious*, ὑλήεις (ὕλη), *woody*, πυρόεις (πῦρ, -υρός), *fiery*, χαρίεις (χάρις), *graceful*, σφηκώδης (σφήξ), *wasp-like*, ψαμμώδης (ψάμμος), *sandy*.

§ 316. III. From Adjectives and Adverbs. 1. From some adjectives and adverbs, derivatives are formed in the same manner as from nouns; thus, καθαρός, *clean*, καθάριος, *cleanly*, ἐλευθέριος (ἐλεύθερος), *liberal*, θηλυκός (θῆλυς), *feminine*, χθεσινός (χθές), *of yesterday*.

2. The adjective has in Greek, as in other languages, two strengthened forms, of which the one may be termed *dual*, denoting choice between *two* objects, and the other *plural*, denoting choice among a *number* of objects.

The most obvious examples of these strengthened forms are the *comparative* and *superlative degrees*, commonly so called. Other examples of the *comparative* or *dual strengthened form* are, (*a*) the *correlatives* πότερος; *whether of the two?* ποτερός, ἕτερος (formed from the 3d Pers. pron. as the positive, ¶ 23, § 141, or, as some think, from the numeral εἷς), *one of the two*, οὐδέτερος, ὁπότερος, ἑκάτερος, ἀμφότερος (see ¶ 63, and compare the Lat. *uter*, *neuter*, *alter*, and the Eng. *whether*, *either*, *neither*, *other*); (*b*) the following implying a consideration of *two objects* or *properties;* δεξιτερός (poet.), Lat. dexter, *right* (rather than left), ἀριστερός, sinister, *left*, δεύτερος, *second*, ἡμέτερος, noster, *our* (rather than yours, or any one's else), ὑμέτερος, vester, *your*, σφέτερος, *their*, &c. (¶ 24). Other examples of the *superlative* or *plural strengthened form* are, (*c*) the *correlatives* πόστος; *which in order?* or, *one of how many?* ὁπόστος, ἕκαστος (¶ 63); (*d*) all *ordinals* except δεύτερος (see ¶ 25).

C. Pronouns.

§ 317. For the formation of the most common pronouns,

see §§ 141–154. The Greek abounds in correlative pronouns and adverbs (see ¶ 63), in respect to many of which it will be observed that, when they begin with π-, they are *indefinite*, or *interrogative* (with a change of accent); with τ-, *definite* or *demonstrative*; with the *rough breathing*, *relative definite*, and with ὁπ-, *relative indefinite*. Thus, πόσος; *how much?* ποσός, *of a certain quantity*, τόσος, τοσοῦτος and τοσόσδε (§ 150. α), *so much*, ὅσος, *as much*, ὁπόσος, *how much soever*; πότε; *when?* ποτέ, *at some time*, τότε, *then*, ὅτε, *when*, ὁπότε, *whensoever*.

D. Verbs.

§ **318.** I. From Nouns and Adjectives. Of these the chief endings and the prevailing significations are as follows.

a. -έω, -εύω, and (mostly from nouns of Dec. I.) -άω, *to be* or *do* that which is pointed out by the primitive; as, φίλος, *friend*, φιλέω, *to be a friend, to love*, εὐδαιμονέω (εὐδαίμων, -ονος), *to be prosperous*, ἀτυχέω (ἀτυχής), *to be unfortunate*, πολεμέω (πόλεμος), *to wage war*; δουλεύω (δοῦλος), *to be a slave, to serve*, βασιλεύω (βασιλεύς), *to reign*, χορεύω (χορός), *to dance*; τολμάω (τόλμα), *to be bold, to dare*, τιμάω (τιμή), *to honor*.

b. -όω (mostly from words of Dec. II.), -αίνω and -ύνω (mostly from adjectives), *to make* that which is pointed out by the primitive; as, δῆλος, *evident*, δηλόω, *to make evident*, δουλόω (δοῦλος), *to make one a slave, to enslave*, χρυσόω (χρυσός), *to make golden, to gild*, πτερόω (πτερόν), *to make winged, to furnish with wings*, στεφανόω (στέφανος), *to crown*; λευκαίνω (λευκός), *to whiten*, σημαίνω (σῆμα), *to signify*, ἡδύνω (ἡδύς), *to sweeten*.

c. -ίζω, and (chiefly when formed from words which have α or η in the last syllable, or when preceded by ι, cf. §§ 310. a, 315. b) -άζω; from names of persons or animals, *imitative* (denoting the adoption of the *manners, language, opinions, party*, &c.); from other words, used in various senses, but mostly active; as, Μηδίζω (Μῆδος), *to imitate or favor the Medes*, Ἑλληνίζω, *to speak Greek*, Δωρίζω and Δωριάζω, *to live, talk, sing*, or *dress like the Dorians*, Φιλιππίζω, *to be of Philip's party*, ἀλωπεκίζω (ἀλώπηξ), *to play the fox*; πλουτίζω (πλοῦτος), *to make rich*, εὐδαιμονίζω, *to esteem happy*, θερίζω (θέρος), *to harvest*, ἐρίζω (ἔρις), *to contend*, ἑορτάζω (ἑορτή), *to make a feast*, δικάζω (δίκη), *to judge*, θαυμάζω (θαῦμα), *to wonder*.

d. -ω with simply a strengthening of the penult, more frequently *active*; as, καθαρός, *pure*, καθαίρω, *to purify*, ποικίλλω (ποικῖλος), *to variegate*, μαλάσσω (μαλακός), *to soften*.

§ **319.** II. From Other Verbs. These are

1.) *Desideratives*, formed in -σείω, from the Fut.; as, γελάω, *to laugh*, γελασείω, *to wish to laugh*, Pl. Phædo, 64 b, πολεμησείω (πολεμέω), *to wish for war*, Th. i. 33. Desideratives are also formed in -ιάω (rarely -άω), chiefly from verbal nouns; as, μανθάνω, *to learn*, μαθητής, *disciple*, μαθητιάω, *to wish to become a disciple*, Ar. Nub. 183, στρατηγιάω (στρατηγός), *to desire military command*, vii. 1. 33, θανατάω (θάνατος), *to desire death*, Pl. Phædo, 64 b.

2.) Various prolonged forms in -ζω, -σκω, &c. (see §§ 265–300), sometimes *frequentative* or *intensive*, as, ῥίπτω, *to throw*, ῥιπτάζω, *to throw to and fro*, στένω, *to sigh*, στενάζω, *to sigh deeply*; sometimes *inceptive*, as, ἡβάω, *to be at the age of puberty*, ἡβάσκω, *to come to the age of puberty*; sometimes *causative*, as, μεθύω, *to be intoxicated*, μεθύσκω, *to intoxicate*; sometimes *diminutive*, as, ἐξαπατάω, *to cheat*, ἐξαπατύλλω (cf. § 312), *to cheat a little, to humbug*, Ar. Eq. 1144; but often scarce differing in force from the primitive form (§§ 254–258, 265).

E. Adverbs.

§ **320.** Most adverbs belong to the following classes.

I. Oblique Cases of Nouns and Adjectives, employed as circumstantial adjuncts (see Syntax). With an adjective thus employed, a noun is strictly to be supplied. Many of these *oblique cases* have antique forms, and many belong to themes that are not in use. Examples,

1. Genitives, (*a*) in -θεν, denoting the *place whence* (§ 91): (*b*) in -ου, denoting the *place where*; as, οὗ [sc. τόπου or χωρίου], *in which place, where*, αὐτοῦ, *there*, ὁμοῦ, *in the same place*, οὐδαμοῦ, *nowhere*: (*c*) in -ης; as, αἴφνης, *of a sudden*, ἑξῆς, *in order*: (*d*) προικός (προίξ), *of a gift, gratis*, &c.

2. Datives, (*a*) in -οι, -οθι of Dec. II. sing., and in -ησι(ν), -ᾶσι(ν) of Dec. I. pl., denoting the *place where* (in adverbs in -οι derived from pronouns, this commonly passes into the idea of *whither*, see ¶ 63, and compare the familiar use of *where, there*, &c., in English); as, Ἀθήνησι, *at Athens*; see §§ 90, 96. 5: (*b*) in -ῃ (-η), -ᾳ (-α), -αι of Dec. I., and in -ι of Dec. III., denoting *way, place where*, or *time when*; as, ταύτῃ, [sc. ὁδῷ] *in this way, thus*, [sc. χώρᾳ] *in this place, here*, πανταχῆ, *every way, everywhere*, πεζῇ, *on foot*, ἰδίᾳ, *privately*, χαμαί, *on the ground*, πάλαι, *in olden time*, ἕκητι, *by the will of*, ἶφι (§ 89. β. *d*), ἄγχι, *near*, ἦρι, *early*, I. 360.

Note. Adverbial Datives of Dec. I. are written by most editors with an ι subsc., except when they have no Nom. in use, and by some even then. See § 25. β.

3. Accusatives; as, ἀκμήν, *at the moment*, χάριν, *on account of*, δίκην, *like*, and the Neut. sing. and pl. of adjectives.

§ **321.** II. Derivatives signifying, (1.) Manner, in,

a. -ως, from adjectives. The adverb may be formed by changing ν of the Gen. pl. into ς; as, σοφός, G. pl. σοφῶν, *wise*, σοφῶς, *wisely*, ταχύς, ταχέων, *swift*, ταχέως, *swiftly*, σαφῶς (σαφής, -έων, -ῶν), Ion. σαφέως, *evidently*.

b. -ηδον or -δον (perhaps kindred with εἶδος, *form*), chiefly from nouns; -δην or -άδην, chiefly from verbs (those in -άδην commonly conforming to other verbals); and -δα; as, πλινθηδόν (πλίνθος), *in the form of bricks*, Hdt. ii. 96, βοτρυδόν (βότρυς), *in clusters*, B. 89, ἀναφανδόν, or -δά (ἀναφαίνω), *openly*, κρύβδην, or -δα (κρύπτω), *secretly*, σποράδην (σπείρω, σποράς), *scatteringly*. These appear to be Acc. forms (cf. § 320. 3); thus, Sing. fem. -δην, neut. -δον, Pl. neut. -δα.

c. -ί or -εί, especially from imitative verbs (§ 318. c, -ίζω becoming -ιστί), and in compounds of ἀ- *privative*, αὐτός, and πᾶς· as, Μηδιστί, *like the Medes*, Ἑλληνιστί, *in the Greek language*, ἀμισθί (μισθός), *without pay*, ἀμαχεί and *ἀμαχητεί*, or *-ί*, *without battle*, *αὐτοχειρί* (*χείρ*), *with one's own hand*, *πανδημεί* (*δῆμος*), *with the whole people*. These appear to be Dat. forms (cf. § 320. 2).

d. *-ξ* added to a palatal; as, *ἀνα-μίγνυμι* (r. *μιγ-*, § 294), *to mix up*, *ἀναμίξ*, *confusedly*, *pellmell*, *παραλλάξ* (*παρ-αλλάσσω*, § 274. γ), *alternately*.

(2.) Time when, in *-τε* (Dor. *-κα*), or, for more specific expression, in *-ίκα*; as, *ἄλλοτε* (*ἄλλος*), *at another time*, *αὐτίκα* (*αὐτός*), *at the very moment*. See ¶ 63.

(3.) Place whither, in *-σε* (which appears to be a softened form of *-δε*, § 322. III., or at least kindred with it); as, *οὐρανόσε*, *to heaven*, *ἐκεῖσε*, *thither*, *ἑτέρωσε*, *to the other side*. See ¶ 63.

(4.) Number, in *-άκις*. See ¶ 25. II.

§ **322.** III. Prepositions with their Cases; as, (πρὸ ἔργου) προὔργου, *before the work*, *to the purpose*, παραχρῆμα, *upon the affair*, *immediately*, (δι' ὅ) διό, *on account of which*, *wherefore*, (ἐν ποδῶν ὁδῷ) ἐμποδών, *in the way* of the feet, Ἀθήναζε (from Ἀθήνας, and -δε, an inseparable preposition denoting *direction towards*, §§ 51. N., 150. 4), *to Athens*.

IV. Derivatives from Prepositions, or Prepositions used without Cases; as, ἔξω (ἐξ), *without*, εἴσω (εἰς), *within* πρός, *besides*.

II. Formation of Compound Words.

§ **323.** In composition, the word which modifies or limits the other, usually precedes; as, νομο-θέτης (νόμος, τίθημι) *law-maker*.

The exceptions consist mainly of a verb or preposition followed by a noun, and are for the most part poetic. Among the verbs which are most frequently so placed in prose are *φιλέω*, *to love*, and *μισέω*, *to hate*; thus, *φιλ-άνθρωπος*, *man-loving*, *μισο-πέρσης*, *Persian-hater*.

§ **324.** A. The first word has commonly its radical form with simply euphonic changes. These changes, besides those which the general rules of orthoëpy require, consist chiefly,

1.) In the insertion of a *union-vowel*, which, after a *substantive* or *adjective*, is commonly *-ο-*, but sometimes *-η-*, *-α-*, or *-ι-*; and, after a *verb*, *-ε-*, *-ι-*, *-ο-*, *-οι-*, or *-αι-*; as, *παιδ-ο-τρίβης* (*παῖς*, *-δός*, *τρίβω*), *instructer*, *δικ-ο-λόγος* (*δίκη*, *λέγω*), *advocate*, *δημιουργός* (Ion. *δημι-ο-εργός*, from *δήμιος* and *ἔργον*), *artisan*, (*γα-ο-μετρία*, from *γάα*, contr. *γῆ*, and *μετρέω*, §§ 35, 98. α) *γεωμετρία*, *geometry*, (*να-ο-κόρος* · *ναός*, *νεώς*, and *κορέω*) *νεωκόρος*, *keeper of a temple*, *θανατ-ο-φόρος* and *-η-φόρος* (*θάνατος*, *φέρω*), *death-bringing*, Æsch. Ag. 1176, Cho. 369, *ξιφ-η-φόρος* and *-ο-φόρος* (*ξίφος*, *-εος*, *φέρω*), *sword-bearing*, *ἀγορ-α-νόμος* (*ἀγορά*, *νέμω*), *clerk of the market*, *ποδ-ά-νιπτήρ* (*πούς*, *νίζω*), *foot-bath*, Hdt. ii. 172, *πυρ-ι-γενής* (*πῦρ*, *γίγνομαι*), *fire-born*, *ὁδ-οι-πόρος* (*ὁδός*, *πόρος*), *wayfarer*, *μεσ-αι-πόλιος* (*μέσος*, *πολιός*), *half-gray*, N. 361; *ἀρχ-έ-χορος* (*ἄρχω*, χορός), *chorus-leading*, τερπ-ι-κέραυνος (τέρπω, κεραυνός), *delighting in thunder*, A. 419, λιπ-ο-ταξία (λείπω, τάξις), *leaving one's post.*

2.) In the insertion of σ, commonly connected by a union-vowel either to the succeeding or preceding word, and sometimes even to both; as, (ῥίπ-σ-ασπις) ῥίψασπις (ῥίπτω, ἀσπίς), *coward*, τελε-σ-φόρος (τέλος, -ε-ος, φέρω), *fulfilling*, κερασφόρος, *horned*, φωσφόρος, *light-bringing*; λυ-σι-τελής (λύω, τέλος), *income-paying, profitable*, ναυ-σί-πορος (ναῦς, πόρος) *navigable*, (μιγ-σο-β.) μιξο-βάρβαρος (μίγνυμι, βάρβαρος), *mixed with barbarians*; θε-οσ-εχθρία (θεός, ἐχθρός), *impiety*, φερ-έσ-βιος (φέρω, βίος), *life-giving*; ταμ-εσί-χρως (τέμνω, χρώς), *wounding*, Δ. 511. In some of these cases, the σ appears to have been borrowed from the theme or the Dat. pl. of nouns, and in others, perhaps, from the Aor. of verbs, or a verbal.

3.) In adopting a *shorter form* from the theme, or an early root; as, αἱμ-ο-βαφής (αἷμα, -ατος, βάπτω), *blood-bathed*, φιλ-ό-πονος (φιλέ-ω from φίλος, πόνος), *labor-loving.*

NOTES. α. The mode in which the constituent words are united often depends, especially in verse, upon the quantity of the syllables which compose them.

β. In some compounds, chiefly poetic, the first word has a form like that of the Dat. sing. or pl. without change; as, νυκτι-πόλος, *roaming by night*, Eur. Ion, 718, τειχεσι-πλήτης, *wall-approacher*, E. 31.

§ **325.** REMARKS. 1. If the first word is a *particle*, it is commonly unchanged except by the general laws of euphony. For elision in prepositions, see §§ 41, 42, 192. 1. Ἀμφί, like περί, often retains its vowel. In the other prepositions, the elision is rarely omitted, except in the Ion., particularly in the Ep. before some words which begin with the digamma. For elision before a consonant, see § 48. 2. Πρό sometimes unites with a vowel following by crasis; as, πρό-οπτος προὖπτος, προ-έχω προὔχω, κ. 90; see § 192. 1.

2. Some particles occur only in composition, and are hence called *inseparable*. Of these, the most important are,

a.) ἀ-, commonly denoting *privation* or *negation*, and then called *ἀ- privative*, as, ἄ-παις, *without children*, ἄ-σοφος, *unwise*; but sometimes denoting *union, collection*, or *intensity*, as, ἀ-δελφός (δελφύς), *brother*, ἀ-τενής (τείνω), *strained*. Ἀ- *privative* (commonly ἀν- before a vowel) is akin to ἄνευ, *without*, to the Lat. *in-*, and to the Eng. and Germ. *un-*; ἀ- *copulative* appears to be akin to ἅμα, *together*. Akin to ἀ *priv.* is νη- (Lat. *ne*); thus, νηλεής (ἔλεος), *merciless.*

b.) δυσ-, *ill, mis-, un-*; as, δύσ-φημος, *ill-omened*, δυσ-τυχία, *mis-fortune*, δυσ-δαίμων, *un-happy.*

c.) The *intensive* ἀρι- (kindred with Ἄρης, § 161. R.), ἐρι-, ζα-, and δα-; as, ἀρί-δακρυς, *very tearful*, ζά-πλουτος, *very rich.*

§ **326.** B. The form of the LAST WORD depends upon the part of speech to which the compound belongs.

1. If the compound is a NOUN or ADJECTIVE, it commonly takes the most obvious form which is appropriate to the class

of words to which it belongs. Often, the last word, if itself a *noun* or *adjective*, undergoes no change; as, ὁμό-δουλος, *fellow-slave*, ἄ-παις, *childless*. If the last element is a *verb*, the compound adjective or masculine substantive ends commonly in,

a. -ος. This ending (which is far the most common) has both an *active* and a *passive* sense, distinguished, for the most part, by the accent, which, if the penult is short, the *active* compound commonly takes upon the *penult*, but the *passive* upon the *antepenult*; as, λιθο-βόλος (λίθος, βάλλω), *throwing stones*, λιθό-βολος, *thrown at with stones*.

b. -ης (-ες, G. -εος); as, εὐ-πρεπής, *becoming*, αὐτάρκης, *self-sufficing*.

c. -ης or -ας (G. -ου), and -ηρ or -ωρ, denoting the *agent* (§ 306. a, b); as, νομο-θέτης, *legislator*, μυρο-πώλης (§ 92. 2), ὀρνιθο-θήρας, *bird-catcher*, μηλο-βότηρ, *shepherd*, Σ. 529, παιδ-ολέτωρ, *child-murderer*.

REMARK. In compounds of this class, if the last word begins with ἄ, ε, or ο, followed by a single consonant, this vowel is commonly lengthened to η or ω; as, στρατηγός (στρατός, ἄγω), *general*, δυσήλατος (δυσ-, ἐλαύνω), *hard to drive over*, ἀνώνυμος (ἀ-, ὄνομα, § 44. 5), *nameless*.

§ **327.** 2. If the compound is a VERB, it is important to observe that verbs are compounded directly and without change with prepositions only; and that, in other cases, compound verbs are derivatives from compound nouns or adjectives existing or assumed.

Thus, λαμβάνω, *to take*, unites directly with the prep. ἀνά, *up*, to form ἀναλαμβάνω, *to take up*; but it cannot so unite with the noun ἔργον, *work*, and hence the idea *to take work, to contract*, is expressed by ἐργο-λαβέω, derived from the compound verbal ἐργο-λάβος, *contractor*. So the verb compounded of ἵππος, *horse*, and τρέφω, *to feed*, is ἱπποτροφέω from ἱπποτρόφος, *horse-keeper*. Sometimes the form of the verb happens not to be changed in passing through the compound verbal; thus, from σῖτος and ποιέω, is formed σιτο-ποιός, *bread-maker*, and from this again σιτο-ποιέω, *to make bread*.

REMARKS. 1. The union of the preposition with the verb, as not affecting the form of the verb, and admitting of separation by *tmesis* (§ 328. N.), is termed *loose* or *improper composition*, in distinction from that *close* or *proper composition* which forms one inseparable word.

§ **328.** 2. In PRONOUNS and PARTICLES there is a still looser form of composition, consisting in the aggregation of words, sometimes really and sometimes only apparently combined in sense. In these aggregates, the orthography varies, the words being sometimes written together, chiefly when the last is an enclitic, and sometimes separately. Among the chief words that are thus affixed to others are,

a. The INDEFINITE PRONOUN τὶς· as, ὅστις, *whoever*, οὔτις, *no one*, εἴτις, *if any one*.

b. The PARTICLES,

ἄν (Ep. κέ or κέν, Dor. κᾶ), contingent or indefinite; as, ὅς ἄν, *whoever*, ὅταν or ὅτ' ἄν, *whenever*.

γέ (Dor. γᾶ), *at least*, emphatic as, ἔγωγε, *I at least*, σύγε, *you surely*, τοῦτό γε, *this certainly*, ἐπεί γε, *since at least*.

δή, *now* (shorter form of ἤδη); as, ὅστις δή, *whoever now*, νῦν δή, *just now*.

δήποτε (δή ποτε), *ever now*; as, ὁστισδήποτε, *whosoever now*, τί δήποτε; *what in the world?*

οὖν (contr. from ἐόν, *it being so*, ¶ 55), *then*, *therefore*, *yet*, often added to an indefinite pronoun or adverb to strengthen the expression of indefiniteness; as, ὁστισοῦν, *whoever then*, ὁπωσδηποτοῦν, *howsoever now then*.

πέρ (shorter form of περί), *very*, *particularly*, *just*; as, ὅσπερ, *who in particular*, ὥσπερ, *just as*.

ποτέ, *at any time*, *ever*, often added to interrogatives to strengthen the expression; as, τί ποτέ ἐστι τοῦτο; [what at any time is this?] *what in the world is this?* or, *what can this be?*

τέ, the simplest sign of connection, and hence often joined to other connective words, before their use was established, to mark them as such. In the Ep. and Ion. this is found to a great extent; but in the Att. scarce occurs, except in ἅτε, and ὥστε, *as*, οἷός τε, *able*, *possible*, and ἐφ' ᾧτε, *on condition that*.

NOTE. In cases of loose composition, other words, especially particles, are sometimes interposed. When a preposition is thus separated from a verb, the figure is called *Tmesis* (τμῆσις, *cutting*); as, ἐκ δὲ πηδήσας, *and leaping forth*, Eur. Hec. 1172.

BOOK III.

SYNTAX.

Μύθους ὑφαίνειν.
Homer.

§ 329. SYNTAX, as the DOCTRINE OF SENTENCES, treats either of the offices and relations of words as arranged in sentences, or of the offices and relations of these sentences themselves.

NOTE. For a general view of the OFFICES OF WORDS, as *subject, predicate, copula, attribute, compellative* (person addressed), *appositive* (substantive in apposition), *adjunct* (modifying or limiting substantive not in apposition), whether complement or circumstance (i. e. regarded as *completing* the idea of the modified word, especially as a direct or indirect object, or as denoting some *circumstance* respecting it, as time, place, means, &c.), whether exponential or nude (i. e. attached with or without a preposition), *exponent* (sign of office or relation, as preposition, conjunction, &c.), &c.: of their RELATIONS, as *agreement* or *concord, government* or *regimen,* &c.: of the DISTINCTIONS OF SENTENCES, as *simple* or *compound, distinct* (in which the predicate has a distinct form as a *finite verb*) or *incorporated* (in which the predicate is incorporated in another sentence as an *infinitive* or *participle*), *intellective* or *volitive* (expressing an act of the *understanding*, or of the *will*), *declarative* or *interrogative, actual* or *contingent* (having respect to *fact*, or founded upon *supposition*), *positive* or *negative, leading* or *dependent, substantive, adjective,* or *adverbial* (performing the office of a *substantive, adjective,* or *adverb* in another sentence), *protasis* (introduction, condition) or *apodosis* (conclusion), &c.: of their MODES OF CONNECTION, *incorporation, subordination, coördination,* and *simple succession:* of their EXPONENTS, as *connective* or *characteristic* (denoting the *connection* of sentences, or simply distinguishing their *character*); *conjunctions,* copulative, final (denoting purpose), conditional, complementary (introducing a sentence used *substantively*), &c.; *connective pronouns* and *adverbs,* whether relative or complementary (referring to an *antecedent*, or introducing a sentence used *substantively*); *characteristic particles, pronouns,* and *adverbs;* &c.: of the ARRANGEMENT OF WORDS AND SENTENCES, as *logical, rhetorical, rhythmical, periodic,* &c.: and of the FIGURES OF SYNTAX, as, ELLIPSIS (omission), *syllepsis* and *zeugma* (varieties of *compound construction*, according as the word referring to a compound subject has the form required by *all* the substantives in the subject taken *together*, or that which is required by *one* of them taken *singly*); PLEONASM (redundance), *periphrasis* or *circumlocution;* ENALLAGE (use of one word or form for another), *metaphor, metonymy, synecdoche, synesis* (when the construction follows the *sense*, in disregard of grammatical form), *attraction* (when a word is drawn from its appropriate form by the influence of another word), *anacolūthon* (a want of agreement between two parts of a sentence, arising from a change of construction), *vision*, *change of number*; HYPERBATON (disregard of the common laws of arrangement), *anastrophe* (inversion) *parenthesis*, &c., see General Grammar.

§ **330.** Among the especial causes of VARIETY in the syntax of the Greek are,

1.) Its freedom in the use of either *generic* or *specific* forms of expression. In the development of a language, new forms arise to express more specifically what has been generically expressed by some older form. This older form thus becomes narrowed in its appropriate sphere, and itself more specific in its expression. But habit, which is mighty everywhere, is peculiarly the arbiter of language;—

"Usus,
Quem penes arbitrium est et jus et norma loquendi";—

and, wherever the new distinction is unimportant, there is a tendency to employ the old and familiar form in its original extent of meaning. The result is, that an idea may be often expressed by two or more forms, which differ from each other in being more or less specific; and the same form may have different uses, according as it is employed more generically, or more specifically. These remarks apply both to the words of a language, to the forms of those words, and to the methods of construction. They apply with peculiar force to the Greek, from the freedom and originality of its development, the copiousness of its vocabulary, the fulness of its forms, and the variety of its constructions.

2.) The prevalence of different *dialects* in states intimately connected with each other by commerce, by alliances, and by national festivals; and also in different departments of literature, without respect to local distinctions (§ 6). It cannot be thought strange, that forms of expression appropriate to the different dialects should have been sometimes interchanged or commingled; or that the laws of syntax should have acquired less rigidity in the Greek, than in languages which have but a single cultivated dialect.

3.) The *vividness of conception and emotion*, the *spirit of freedom*, the *versatility*, the *love of variety*, and the *passion for beauty*, which so preëminently characterized the Greek mind, and left their impress upon all its productions. The Greek language was the development in speech of these characteristics, the vivacious, free, versatile, varied, and beautiful expression of Greek genius and taste.

CHAPTER I.

SYNTAX OF THE SUBSTANTIVE.

I. AGREEMENT OF THE SUBSTANTIVE.

§ **331.** RULE I. An APPOSITIVE agrees in *case* with its *subject*; as,

Παρύσατις . . ἡ μήτηρ, *Parysatis, the mother*, i. 1. 4. Ὁ Μαίανδρο ποταμός, *the river Mæander*, i. 2. 7. Τὰ δὲ ἆθλα ἦσαν στλεγγίδες Ib. 10 Ὁ ποταμὸς λέγεται Μαρσύας Ib. 8. Ὄνομα αὐτῷ εἶναι Ἀγάθωνα Pl. Prot 315 e. Ἧς αὐτὸν σατράπην ἐποίησε i. 1. 2. Λαβὼν Τισσαφέρνην ὡς φίλον Ib.

§ **332.** Remarks. 1. Appositives, more frequently, agree with their subjects in *gender* and *number*, as well as in case; as, Ἐπύαξα, ἡ Συεννέσιος γυνή, τοῦ Κιλίκων βασιλέως, *Epyaxa, the wife of Syennesis, the king of the Cilicians*, i. 2. 12. Σοφαίνετον δὲ τὸν Στυμφάλιον, καὶ Σωκράτην τὸν Ἀχαιόν, ξένους ὄντας καὶ τούτους i. 1. 11.

2. Ellipsis. The appositive or the subject may be omitted, when it can be supplied from the connection; as, Λύκιος ὁ Πολυστράτου [sc. υἱός], *Lycius, the son of Polystratus*, iii. 3. 20. Θεμιστοκλῆς ἥκω παρὰ σέ [sc. ἐγώ], *I, Themistocles, have come to thee*, Th. i. 137.

3. The sign of *special application* (ὡς, *as*) is often omitted; as, Διφθέρας, ἃς εἶχον σκεπάσματα, *the skins which they had* as *coverings*, i. 5. 10. Κλέαρχον δὲ καὶ εἴσω παρεκάλεσε σύμβουλον i. 6. 5.

4. Synesis. An appositive sometimes agrees with a subject which is implied in another word; as, Ἀθηναῖος ὢν πόλεως τῆς μεγίστης, *being an Athenian, a city the greatest*, Pl. Apol. 29 d (here πόλεως agrees with Ἀθηνῶν, *of Athens*, implied in Ἀθηναῖος). Ἀφίκοντο εἰς Κοτύωρα, πόλιν Ἑλληνίδα, Σινωπέων ἀποίκους, οἰκοῦντας v. 5. 3 (here ἀποίκους refers to πολίτας, implied in πόλιν); cf. iv. 8. 22, v. 3. 2. Σὸν τοῦ πρέσβεως Ar. Ach. 93.

§ **333.** 5. Attraction. A substantive intimately related to another is sometimes put in apposition with it by attraction. In this construction, the appositive usually denotes a *part*, or a *circumstance*, and is often joined with a *participle*, taking the place of the *Genitive absolute*. Thus, Εὔφλεκτα δὲ τὰ πρόθυρα αὐτῶν, φοίνικος μὲν αἱ θύραι πεποιημέναι, *their portals are easily set on fire, the doors being made of the palm-tree*, Cyr. vii. 5. 22. Ἄλλο τρίτον ἅρμα ἐξήγετο, φοινικίσι καταπεπταμένοι οἱ ἵπποι Ib. viii. 3. 12.

6. Some relations may be expressed either by an *appositive* or an *adjunct*; and one of these constructions is sometimes used where the other would seem more appropriate. Thus, Τούτου τὸ εὖρος δύο πλέθρα, *of this the breadth is two plethra*, i. 2. 5; but, Τοῦ δὲ Μαρσύου τὸ εὖρός ἐστιν εἴκοσι καὶ πέντε ποδῶν, *and the breadth of the Marsyas is twenty-five feet*, Ib. 8. Ποταμὸς . εὖρος δύο πλέθρων Ib. 23; but, Τάφρος . ., τὸ μὲν εὖρος ὀργυιαὶ πέντε i. 7. 14. Δέκα μναῖ εἰσφορά· but, Δυοῖν μναῖν πρόσοδον, Vect. iii. 9, 10. Ἔστι δὲ ἡ χώρα . . ὡς εἴκοσι στάδιοι v. 3. 11. Πασῶν Ἀθῆναι τιμιωτάτη πόλις Soph. Œd. C. 108; but, Ἔστ' ἄρ' Ἀθηνῶν ἔστ' ἀπόρθητος πόλις Æsch. Pers. 348.

7. Anacoluthon. An appositive sometimes differs in case from its subject, through a change of construction; as, Μητρί τ', Ἐρίβοιαν λέγω, *and to my mother, Eribœa I mean* (for Μητρί τ' Ἐριβοίᾳ, *and to my mother Eribœa*), Soph. Aj. 569. See also § 344.

§ **334.** 8. A word, in apposition with a *sentence not used substantively*, is commonly in the *Accusative*, as expressing the effect of the action; but is sometimes in the *Nominative*, as if an inscription marking the character of the sentence. Thus, Ἑλένην κτάνωμεν, Μενέλεῳ λύπην πικράν, *let us slay*

Helen, [which would be] *a bitter grief to Menelāus*, Eur. Or. 1105. Στέφη μιαίνεται πόλει τ' ὄνειδος καὶ θεῶν ἀτιμία, *our garlands are profaned, a dishonor to the city, and an insult to the gods*, Eur. Heracl. 72. Τὸ δὲ πάντων μέγιστον . ., τὴν μὲν σὴν χώραν αὐξανομένην ὁρᾷς, *but the greatest thing of all, you see your own territory increasing*, Cyr. v. 5. 24. Τὸ λοίσθιον δὲ, θριγκὸς ἀθλίων κακῶν, δούλη γυνὴ γραῦς Ἑλλάδ' εἰσαφίξομαι Eur. Tro. 489. Ἡμῶν δὲ γεννωμένων, τὸ τοῦ κωμῳδοποιοῦ, οὐδ' οἱ γείτονες σφόδρα τι αἰσθάνονται, 'as the comic poet says,' Pl. Alc. 121 d.

NOTE. This use of the Nom. and Acc. may be often explained by attraction (§ 333) to the subject or object of the verb.

9. The *whole* and its *parts*, or a *part*, are often found in the same case, either by regular apposition (as when the whole is simply *divided* into its parts, or the parts *united* to form the whole), or by attraction (§ 333), or from their sustaining similar relations to the same word. This construction has received the general name of σχῆμα καθ' ὅλον καὶ μέρος, *construction by the whole and the part.*

II. USE OF THE NUMBERS.

§ **335.** I. The SINGULAR is sometimes used for the Plural in the Greek, as in other languages, to give to the expression greater *individuality* or *unity*; as, Τὸν Ἕλληνα, *the Greek* (= *the Greeks*), Hdt. i. 69. Ἕρπει δάκρυον ὀμμάτων ἄπο, *the tear trickles from my eyes*, Soph. El. 1231. Πίμπλημ' εὐθὺς ὄμμα δακρύων Ib. 906.

REMARK. A *chorus*, from its strict unity, commonly speaks of itself as an *individual*, and is often so addressed or spoken of by others. Not unfrequently, the two numbers are mingled; as, ΧΟΡ. Ἐγὼ μὲν, ὦ παῖ, καὶ τὸ σὸν σπεύδουσ' ἅμα, καὶ τοὐμὸν αὐτῆς, ἦλθον· εἰ δὲ μὴ καλῶς λέγω, σὺ νίκα· σοὶ γὰρ ἑψόμεσθ' ἅμα Soph. El. 251. Ὦ ξεῖνοι, μὴ δῆτ' ἀδικηθῶ σοὶ πιστεύσας Id. Œd. C. 174. Ἡμῖν μὲν ἤδη πᾶν τετόξευται βέλος· μένω δέ Æsch. Eum. 676. Ὀργὰς ξυνοίσω σοι . . Ὑμεῖς δέ Ib. 848.

§ **336.** II. The use of the PLURAL for the Singular is particularly frequent in Greek, especially in *abstract nouns*, in *adjectives used substantively*, in the names of *things composed of distinct parts*, and in *vague expressions for persons or things*; as,

Καὶ ψύχη καὶ θάλπη καὶ πόνους φέρειν, *to endure both heat, and cold, and labor*, iii. 1. 23. Τὰ δεξιὰ τοῦ κέρατος, *the right of the wing*, i. 8. 4. Πάτροκλος, ὅς σοι πατρὸς ἦν τὰ φίλτατα, *Patroclus, who was thy father's best-beloved*, Soph. Ph. 434. Τὰ Συεννέσιος βασίλεια, *the palace of Syennesis*, i. 2. 23; cf. iii. 4. 24, iv. 4. 2, 7. Ξὺν τοῖσδε τόξοις, *with this bow*, Soph. Ph. 1335; cf. Τόξον τόδε 288. Τῶν Διός τ' ἐχθρῶν ὕπερ στένεις, 'for the foes' (Prometheus), Æsch. Pr. 67. Χάλα τοκεῦσιν εἰκότως θυμουμένοις, 'parents' (a mother), Eur. Hec. 403.

REMARKS. *a.* An *individual* often speaks of himself in the *Plur.*, as if others were associated with him; and a *woman* so speaking of herself, uses the *masculine*, as the generic gender (§ 330. 1); thus, Αἰδούμεθα γὰρ τὰ λελεγμένα μοι, *for I am ashamed of what I have said*, Eur. Hipp. 244. Σοῦ *γὰρ φθιμένης οὐκέτ' ἂν εἴην· ἐν σοὶ δ' ἐσμὲν καὶ ζῆν καὶ μή* Id. Alc. 277 'ΑΛΚ. *'Αρκοῦμεν ἡμεῖς οἱ προθνήσκοντες σέθεν* Ib. 383. ΜΗΔ. *'Ημεῖς κτενοῦμεν, οἵπερ ἐξεφύσαμεν* Id. Med. 1241. 'ΗΛ. *Πεσούμεθ', εἰ χρή, πατρὶ τιμωρούμενοι* Soph. El. 399. So a chorus of women (§ 335. R.) uses the masc. sing. (if the text is correct), *Κεύθων λείπομαι, . . λεύσσων* Eur. Hipp. 1105.

β. The *Plur.* may be used with a *singular compellative*, when the person addressed is *associated with others*; as, *"Ιτ', ἔφη, ὑμεῖς, ὦ 'Ηριππίδα, καὶ διδάσκετε αὐτὸν βουληθῆναι ἅπερ ἡμεῖς. Οἱ μὲν δὴ ἀναστάντες ἐδίδασκον* H. Gr. iv. 1. 11. *Ὦ τέκνον, ἦ πάρεστον;* Soph. Œd. C. 1102. *Προσέλθετ', ὦ παῖ, πατρί* Ib. 1104.

§ **337.** III. In speaking of *two*, both the PLURAL and the DUAL are used, the one as the *more generic*, and the other as the *more specific* form (§ 330. 1); thus, *Παῖδες δύο, two children;* but, *Τὼ παῖδε, the two children*, i. 1. 1. Compare *Τῶν ἀνδρῶν* vi. 6. 29, *τὼ ἄνδρε* 30, *τοὺς ἄνδρας· . . τούτων, . . τὼ ἄνδρε* 31, *τούτων* 32, *τώ τε ἄνδρε* 34.

> *Σφῷν δ' εὐοδοίη Ζεύς, τάδ' εἰ τελεῖτέ μοι*
> *Θανόντ', ἐπεὶ οὔ μοι ζῶντί γ' αὖθις ἕξετον.*
> *Μέθεσθε δ' ἤδη, χαίρετόν τ'· οὐ γάρ μ' ἔτι*
> *Βλέποντ' ἐσόψεσθ' αὖθις.* Soph. Œd. C. 1435.

REMARKS. α. Hence, the *union of the Plur. and Du.* is not regarded as a violation of the laws of agreement; e. g. *Προσέτρεχον δύο νεανίσκω, there ran up two young men*, iv. 3. 10. *Δυνάμεις δὲ ἀμφότεραι ἐστὸν, δόξα τε καὶ ἐπιστήμη* Pl. Rep. 478 b. *'Εγελασάτην οὖν ἄμφω βλέψαντες εἰς ἀλλήλω* Pl. Euthyd. 273 d.

β. In the old poetic language, a few examples occur in which the Dual is used of more than two (§§ 85, 172); as, *Ξάνθε τε καὶ σύ, Πόδαργε, καὶ Αἴθων Λάμπε τε δῖε, νῦν μοι τὴν κομιδὴν ἀποτίνετον . . · ἀλλ' ἐφομαρτεῖτον καὶ σπεύδετον* Θ. 185. *Πείθεσθε . . · κάθετον, λύσαντε βοείας* Hom. Ap. 486. Some think that the Dual is never thus used, except when *two pairs* or *sets* are spoken of.

III. USE OF THE CASES.

§ **338.** Cases serve to distinguish the relations of substantives. These relations are regarded, in Greek, I. as either DIRECT or INDIRECT, and, II. as either *subjective, objective*, or *residual.*

I. Of these distinctions, the first is chiefly founded upon the *directness* with which the substantive is related to the *verb* of the sentence. The principal DIRECT RELATIONS are those of the *subject* and *direct object* of the verb, and that of *direct address.* Other relations are, for the most part, regarded as INDIRECT.

II. The second distinction is founded upon the *kind* or *character* of the relation. The relation is,

1. SUBJECTIVE, when the substantive denotes the SOURCE, or SUBJECT, of *motion*, *action*, or *influence*; or, in other words THAT FROM WHICH ANY THING COMES.

2. OBJECTIVE, when the substantive denotes the END, or OBJECT, of *motion*, *action*, or *influence*; or, in other words, THAT TO WHICH ANY THING GOES.

3. RESIDUAL (residuus, *remaining*), when it is not referred to either of the two preceding classes.

§ **339.** The latter of the two distinctions appears to have had its origin in the *relations of place*, which relations are both the earliest understood, and, through life, the most familiar to the mind. These relations are of two kinds; those of MOTION, and those of REST. Motion may be considered with respect either to its SOURCE or its END; and both of these may be regarded either as *direct* or *indirect*. We may regard as the DIRECT SOURCE of motion, that which *produces* the motion, or, in other words, that which *moves*; as the INDIRECT SOURCE, that *from* which the motion *proceeds*; as the DIRECT END, that which *receives* the motion, or that *to* or *upon* which the motion *immediately goes*; and as the INDIRECT END, that *towards* which the motion *tends*. By a natural analogy, the relations of *action and influence in general*, whether subjective or objective, may be referred to the relations of motion; while the relations which remain without being thus referred may be classed together as *relations of rest*. These *residual* relations, or relations of rest, may likewise be divided, according to their office in the sentence (§ 338), into the *direct* and the *indirect*. We have, thus, six kinds of relation, which may be characterized in general as follows, and each of which, with a single exception, is represented in Greek by an appropriate case.

A. DIRECT RELATIONS.

1. Subjective.	*That which acts.*	THE NOMINATIVE
2. Objective.	*That which is acted upon.*	THE ACCUSATIVE.
3. Residual.	*That which is addressed.*	THE VOCATIVE.

B. INDIRECT RELATIONS.

1 Subjective.	*That from which any thing proceeds.*	THE GENITIVE.
2. Objective.	*That towards which any thing tends.*	THE DATIVE.
3. Residual.	*That with which any thing is associated.*	THE DATIVE.

§ **340.** REMARKS. *a.* For the historical development of the Greek cases, see §§ 83-88. From the *primitive indirect case* (which remained as the Dat.), a special form was separated to express the *subjective* relations, but none to express the *objective*. The primitive form, therefore, continued to express the *objective* relations, as well as all those relations which, from any cause, *were not referred* to either of these two classes; and hence the Dat. is both an *objective* and a *residual* case.

β. In the Latin case-system, which has a close correspondence with the Greek, there is a partial separation of the *indirect objective* and *residual*, or, as they are termed in Lat., DATIVE and ABLATIVE cases. This separation, however, does not appear at all in the Plural, or in Dec. II., and, wherever it occurs, may be explained by the mere precession or contraction of final vowels. A more important difference between the two languages appears in the extensive use of the Lat. ABLATIVE. The Romans were more controlled than the Greeks by the power of habit, while they were less observant of the minuter shades of thought, and niceties of relation. Hence, even after the full development of the Lat. case-system, the *primitive indirect case* continued to retain, as it were by the mere force of possession, many of the subjective relations. It is interesting to observe how the old Ablative, the once undisputed lord of the whole domain of indirect relations, appears to have contested every inch of ground with the new claimant that presented himself in the younger Genitive. But we must leave the particulars of the contest to the Latin grammarian, and content ourselves with merely referring to two or three familiar illustrations. Thus, in Lat., the Gen. (as well as the Dat.) was excluded from all *exponential adjuncts* (§ 329), because in these the relation was sufficiently defined by the preposition. The *Gen. of place* obtained admission into the Sing. of Dec. I. and II., but not into Dec. III. (the primitive declension, cf. § 86) or into the Plur. The *Gen. of price* secured four words (*tanti, quanti, pluris,* and *minoris*), but was obliged to leave all others to the Abl. After words of *plenty* and *want*, the use of the two cases was more nearly equal. In the construction of *one substantive as the complement of another*, the Gen. prevailed, yet even here the Abl. not unfrequently maintained its ground, if an adjective was joined with it as an ally. In some constructions, the use of the Gen. was only a poetic license, in imitation of the Greek.

γ. The NOMINATIVE, from its high office as denoting the subject of discourse, became the *leading case*, and was regarded as the representative of the word in all its forms (its *theme*). Hence it was employed when the word was spoken of *as a word*, or was used *without grammatical construction* (§ 343).

§ 341. There are no dividing lines either between DIRECT and INDIRECT, or between *subjective, objective,* and *residual* relations. Some relations seem to fall with equal propriety under two, or even three heads, according to the view which the mind takes of them. Hence the use of the cases not only varies in different languages, and in different dialects of the same language, but even in the same dialect, and in the compositions of the same author.

A. THE NOMINATIVE.

§ 342. RULE II. The SUBJECT OF A FINITE VERB is put in the Nominative; as,

Ἐπειδὴ δὲ ἐτελεύτησε Δαρεῖος, καὶ κατέστη εἰς τὴν βασιλείαν Ἀρταξέρξης, Τισσαφέρνης διαβάλλει τὸν Κῦρον, *and when now Darius was dead, and Artaxerxes was established in the royal authority, Tissaphernes accuses Cyrus*, i. 1. 3.

§ 343. RULE III. SUBSTANTIVES INDEPEND-

ENT OF GRAMMATICAL CONSTRUCTION are put in the Nominative.

NOTE. The Nominative thus employed is termed the *Nominative independent* or *absolute* (absolūtus, *released, free,* sc. from grammatical fetters). See § 340. γ.

To this rule may be referred the use of the Nom.,

1.) In the *inscription of names, titles*, and *divisions;* as, *Κύρου Ἀνάβασις, The* EXPEDITION *of Cyrus; Βιβλίον Πρῶτον, Book First.*

2) In *exclamations;* as, Ὦ δυστάλαιν' ἐγώ, *O wretched me!* Eur. Iph. A. 1315. *Θάλαττα, Θάλαττα, the Sea! the Sea!* iv. 7. 24.

3.) In *address.*

The appropriate case of address is the *Voc.* (§ 85). But there is often no distinct form for this case, and even when there is, the Nom. is sometimes employed in its stead (§ 81). (*a*) The Nom. is particularly used, when the address is *exclamatory* or *descriptive*, or when the *compellative* is the same with the *subject* of the sentence; as, Ὦ φίλος, ὦ φίλος, *my beloved! my beloved!* Ar. Nub. 1167. Ἱππίας ὁ καλός τε καὶ σοφὸς, *O Hippias, the noble and the wise!* Pl. Hipp. Maj. 281 a. (*b*) To the head of *descriptive address* belong those *authoritative, contemptuous,* and *familiar* forms, in which the person who is addressed is described or designated as if he were a *third person;* as, Οἱ δὲ οἰκέται, . . ἐπίθεσθε, *but the servants, . . do you put,* Pl. Conv. 218 b. Ὁ Φαληρεὺς . . οὗτος Ἀπολλόδωρος, οὐ περιμενεῖς; *The Phalerian there, Apollodorus, stop! wont you?* Ib. 172 a. (*c*) In forms of address which are both direct, and likewise exclamatory or descriptive, the Voc. and Nom. may be associated; as, Ὦ φίλος ὦ φίλε Βάκχιε Eur. Cycl. 73. Ὦ οὗτος, Αἶαν Soph. Aj. 89. Οὗτος ὦ, ποῖ σὸν πόδ' αἴρεις, δέσποτα Eur. Hel. 1627. Ἀριαῖε, καὶ οἱ ἄλλοι ii. 5. 39.

§ **344.** ANACOLUTHON, &c. From the office of the Nom. in denoting the subject of discourse, and from its independent use, it is sometimes employed where the construction would demand a different case: —

1.) In the *introduction* of a sentence; as, Ὑμεῖς δὲ, . . νῦν δὴ καιρὸς ὑμῖν δοκεῖ εἶναι; *You then, . . does it now seem to you to be just the time?* vii. 6, 37. Ἐπιθυμῶν ὁ Κῦρος . ., ἔδοξεν αὐτῷ, *Cyrus desiring . ., it seemed best to him,* Cyr. vii. 5. 37. Καὶ ἐνταῦθα μαχόμενοι καὶ βασιλεὺς καὶ Κῦρος, καὶ οἱ ἀμφ' αὐτοὺς ὑπὲρ ἑκατέρων, ὁπόσοι μὲν τῶν ἀμφὶ βασιλέα ἀπέθνησκον i. 8. 27. Ὄπισθεν δὲ ἡ φάλαγξ ἐφεπομένη, . . οἱ προστυγχάνοντες τῶν ἀρχόντων ἐπεμέλοντο Cyr. vi. 3. 2.

2.) In *specification, description,* or *repetition;* as, Ἄλλους δ' ὁ μέγας . . Νεῖλος ἔπεμψεν· Σουσισκάνης, Πηγασταγών, κ. τ. λ., *and others the vast Nile hath sent; Susiskānes, P., &c.,* Æsch. Pers. 33. Τὰ περὶ Πύλον ὑπ' ἀμφοτέρων κατὰ κράτος ἐπολεμεῖτο· Ἀθηναῖοι μὲν . . περιπλέοντες . ., Πελοποννήσιοι δὲ . . στρατοπεδευόμενοι Th. iv. 23. Λόγοι δ' ἐν ἀλλήλοισιν ἐρρόθουν κακοὶ, φύλαξ ἐλέγχων φύλακα Soph. Ant. 259. Θυγάτηρ μεγαλήτορος Ἠετίωνος, Ἠετίων, ὃς ἔναιεν Z. 395.

3.) In speaking of *names* or *words as such*; thus, Προσείληφε τὴν τῶν πονηρῶν κοινὴν ἐπωνυμίαν συκοφάντης, *he has obtained the common appellation of the vile*, SYCOPHANT, Æschin. 41. 15. Παρεγγύα ὁ Κῦρος σύνθημα, Ζεὺς ξύμμαχος καὶ ἡγεμών, *Cyrus gave out as the pass-word*, JOVE OUR ALLY AND LEADER, Cyr. iii. 3. 58.

B. THE GENITIVE.

§ **345.** THAT FROM WHICH ANY THING PROCEEDS (§ 339) may be resolved into, I. That from which any thing proceeds, as its POINT OF DEPARTURE; and, II. That from which any thing proceeds, as its CAUSE. Hence the Greek Genitive is either, (I.) the GENITIVE OF DEPARTURE, or, (II.) the GENITIVE OF CAUSE; and we have the following general rule for subjective adjuncts (§§ 329, 338): The POINT OF DEPARTURE AND THE CAUSE ARE PUT IN THE GENITIVE.

NOTE. The *Gen. of departure* is commonly expressed in English by the preposition *from*, and the *Gen. of cause*, by the preposition *of*.

(I.) GENITIVE OF DEPARTURE.

§ **346.** Departure may be either in *place* or in *character*. Hence,

RULE IV. Words of SEPARATION and DISTINCTION govern the Genitive.

NOTE. There is no line of division between the two classes of words which are mentioned in this rule. Many words which are commonly used to denote distinction of character referred originally to separation of place (cf. § 339). And, on the other hand, words which usually denote separation of place, are often employed, by a metaphorical or transitive use, to express departure or difference in other respects.

1. *Genitive of Separation.*

§ **347.** Words of SEPARATION include those of *removal* and *distance*, of *exclusion* and *restraint*, of *cessation* and *failure*, of *abstinence* and *release*, of *deliverance* and *escape*, of *protection* and *freedom*, &c.; as,

Χωρίζεσθαι ἀλλήλων, *to be separated from each other*, Pl. Conv. 192 c. Χωρὶς τῶν ἄλλων, *apart from the rest*, i. 4. 13. Σώματος δίχα Cyr. viii. 7. 20. Ὑποχωρῇ τοῦ πεδίου Ib. ii. 4. 24. Διέσχον ἀλλήλων, *were distant from each other*, i. 10. 4. Πόῤῥω . . αὐτοῦ, *far from him*, i. 3. 12. Κωλύσειε τοῦ καίειν, *he would prevent them from burning*, i. 6. 2. Εἰ θαλάττης εἴργοιντο H. Gr. vii. 1. 8. Τοῦ πρὸς ἐμὲ πολέμου παύσασθαι, *to cease from the war against me*, i. 6. 6. Τούτους . . οὐ παύσω τῆς ἀρχῆς Cyr. viii. 6. 3. Βίου τελευτήσω Ib. 7. 17. Οὗτος μὲν αὐτοῦ ἥμαρτεν, *this man missed him*, i. 5. 12. Ἐψεύσθη τῆς ἐλπίδος H. Gr. vii. 5. 24. Γυναικὸς ἐσθλῆς ἤμπλακες Eur. Alc. 418. Ἐπέσχομεν τοῦ δακρύειν, *we refrained from weeping*, Pl. Phædo, 117 e. Κακῶν . . λυτήριον Soph. El. 1489. Σῶσαι κακοῦ Id. Ph. 919. Νόσου πεφευγέναι, Ib. 1044. Ἀλύξετον μόρου Id. Ant. 488. Δύο ἄνδρας ἕξει τοῦ μὴ καταδῦναι, *will keep two men from sinking*, iii. 5. 11. Ἐλεύθεροι πόνων, ἐλεύθεροι . . Εὐρυσθέως Eur. Heracl. 873. Ἄνευ αἰσχύνης καὶ βλάβης ii. 6. 6. Γάμων τε ἁγνοὶ ζῶσιν Pl. Leg. 840 d. Καθαρὸς ἀδικίας, Pl. Rep. 496 d. Ἕως ἂν καθήρῃ σωφροσύνης Ib. 573 b. Νοσφιεῖς με τοῦδε δευτέρου νεκροῦ; Eur. Alc. 43.

§ **348.** REMARKS. α. Words of SPARING imply *refraining from*, and those of CONCEDING, RESIGNING, REMITTING, and SURRENDERING, imply *parting with*, or *retiring from*. Hence, τῶν μὲν ὑμετέρων ἡδύ μοι φείδεσθαι, *it is my pleasure to spare your property*, Cyr. iii. 2. 28. Κἀκεῖνος ὑπεχώρησεν αὐτῷ τοῦ θρόνου, *and he* [Sophocles] *conceded to him* [Æschylus] *the throne*, Ar. Ran. 790. Ἀλλὰ τῆς ὀργῆς ἀνέντες, *but resigning your anger*, Ib. 700. Τῆς τῶν Ἑλλήνων ἐλευθερίας . . παραχωρῆσαι Φιλίππῳ, *to surrender to Philip the freedom of the Greeks*, Dem. Cor. 247. 24. Τοῖς πρεσβυτέροις . . καὶ ὁδῶν καὶ θάκων καὶ λόγων ὑπείκειν Cyr. viii. 7. 10.

β. The Gen. denoting *that from which motion proceeds* is, in prose, commonly joined to *words not in themselves expressing separation* by a preposition; but in poetry, often without a preposition (cf. § 429. α); as, Δόμων . . φέρουσαν, *bringing from the house*, Soph. El. 324. Τούσδε παῖδας γῆς ἐλᾷν, *to drive these children from the land*, Eur. Med. 70. Ἀνακουφίσαι κάρα βυθῶν Soph. Œd. T. 23. Ὑμεῖς μὲν βάθρων ἵστασθε Ib. 142. Τό τ' οὐρανοῦ πέτημα Eur. Iph. T. 1384. For *adverbs* in -θεν, properly genitives, see §§ 91, 320.

γ. In a few rare phrases, the Gen. denotes the *time from which*, without a preposition; as, Μετ' ὀλίγον δὲ τούτων, *and* [after a little from these things] *a little after these things*, H. Gr. i. 1. 2. Τρίτῳ . . ἔτεϊ τουτέων, *in the third year* [from] *before these things*, Hdt. vi. 40. Δευτέρῳ δὲ ἔτεϊ τουτέων, '[from] after,' Ib. 46.

2. *Genitive of Distinction.*

§ **349.** Words of DISTINCTION include those of *difference* and *exception*, of *superiority* and *inferiority*, &c.; as,

Διώρισται τέχνης, *is distinct from the art*, Pl. Polit. 260 c. Ἠλέκτρου οὐδὲν διέφερεν, *differed in nothing from amber*, ii. 3. 15. Πᾶσαι πλὴν Μιλήτου, *all except Milētus*, i. 1. 6. Διάφορον τῶν ἄλλων πόλεων, *superior to the other states*, Mem. iv. 4. 15. Πλήθει . . ἡμῶν λειφθέντες, *inferior to us in number*, vii. 7. 31. Τὰ δίκαια . ., ἢ ἄλλα τῶν δικαίων; Mem. iv. 4. 25. Ἕτερον δὲ τὸ ἡδὺ τοῦ ἀγαθοῦ Pl. Gorg. 500 d. Πότερόν ἐστιν ἐπιστήμη ἡ ἀρετή, ἢ ἀλλοῖον ἐπιστήμης Pl. Meno, 87 c. Οὐδὲν ἀλλότριον ποιῶν οὔτε τῆς ἑαυτοῦ πατρίδος οὔτε τοῦ τρόπου (cf. § 405) Dem. Cor. 289. 14. Οὕτω πλούτου ἀρετὴ διέστηκεν Pl. Rep. 550 e. Τῶν ἀρκούντων περιττά Cyr. viii. 2. 21.

REMARK. The verb λείπομαι governs the Gen. in a variety of senses, which are naturally connected with each other, but which might be referred, in syntax, to different heads. Thus, Στρατὸν . . τὸν λελειμμένον δορός, 'left from [*or* by] the spear,' *i. e.* 'the relics of war' (§§ 347, 381), Æsch. Ag. 517. Κίρκοι πελειῶν οὐ μακρὰν λελειμμένοι, 'not left far behind,' *i. e.* 'closely pursuing,' Id. Pr. 857. Γνώμῃ δ' ἀδελφοῦ Μελεάγρου λελειμμένος, 'left behind by,' *i. e.* 'inferior to,' Eur. Suppl. 904. Καὶ τίς βίος μοι σοῦ λελειμμένῃ φίλος; 'bereft of' (§ 357), Soph. Ant. 548. Γνώμας λειπομένα, *devoid of understanding*, Soph. El. 474. Λέλειμμαι τῶν ἐν Ἕλλησιν νόμων, 'am ignorant of,' Eur. Hel. 1246.

§ **350.** Words of SUPERIORITY include, —

α.) Words of *authority*, *power*, *precedence*, and *preëminence*. Thus,

Τισσαφέρνην ἄρχειν αὐτῶν, *that Tissaphernes should govern them*, I. 1. 8. Ἐγκρατεῖς . . πάντων, *sovereign over all*, v. 4. 15. Ἡγεῖτο τοῦ στρατεύματος, *led the army*, iv. 1. 6. Πρεσβεύειν τῶν πολλῶν πόλεων, *to take rank of most cities*, Pl. Leg. 752 e. Ἐκράτησαν τῶν Ἑλλήνων iii. 4. 26. Ὃς κραίνει στρατοῦ Soph. Aj. 1050. Ὃς αἰσυμνᾷ χθονός Eur. Med. 19. Βασιλεύων αὐτῶν v. 6. 37. Δεσπόζειν δόμων Eur. Ion, 1036. See also § 389.

Οὐκ αὐτὸς ἐξέπλευσεν, ὡς αὑτοῦ κρατῶν;
Ποῦ σὺ στρατηγεῖς τοῦδε; ποῦ δὲ σοὶ λεῶν
Ἔξεστ' ἀνάσσειν ὧν ὅδ' ἡγεῖτ' οἴκοθεν;
Σπάρτης ἀνάσσων ἦλθες, οὐχ ἡμῶν κρατῶν. Soph. Aj. 1099

REMARK. The primitive sense of the verb ἄρχω appears to have been *to take the lead*. But, in early warfare, the same individual led the march, ruled the host, and began the onset. Hence this verb came to signify *to rule*, and *to begin*; and, in both these senses, it retained the Gen. which belonged to it as a verb of *precedence*. Thus, Ἀνθρώπων ἄρχειν, *to rule men*, Cyr. i. 1. 3. Φυγῆς ἄρχειν, *to begin flight*, iii. 2. 17. Τοῦ λόγου δὲ ἤρχετο ὧδε iii. 2. 7. Καινοῦ λόγου κατῆρχεν Symp. 8. 1.

§ **351.** *β.*) *Adjectives* and *adverbs* in the *comparative degree*, and words *derived from them.*

All comparatives may be ranked with words of *superiority*, as denoting the possession of a property in a *higher degree.*

RULE V. The COMPARATIVE DEGREE governs the Genitive; as,

Κρείττονι ἑαυτοῦ, *more powerful than himself*, i. 2. 26. Τῶν ἵππων ἔτρεχον θᾶττον, *they ran faster than the horses*, i. 5. 2. Τούτου δεύτερον Pl. Leg. 894 d. Ἀνωτέρω τῶν μασθῶν i. 4. 17. Ὑμᾶς οὐ πολὺ ἐμοῦ ὕστερον i. 5. 16. Ἀβροκόμας δὲ ὑστέρησε τῆς μάχης, *but Abrocomas came after the battle*, i. 7. 12. Τῇ ὑστεραίᾳ τῆς μάχης Pl. Menex. 240 c. Ἡττώμεθα αὐτοῦ Cyr. v. 3. 33. Τιμαῖς τούτων ἐπλεονεκτεῖτε iii. 1. 37.

§ **352.** *γ.*) *Multiple* and *proportional* words (§ 138). Thus,

Πολλαπλασίους ὑμῶν αὐτῶν, *many times your own number*, iii. 2. 14. Ἤρχετο δὲ διαιρεῖν ὧδε· μίαν ἀφεῖλε τοσοῦτον ἀπὸ παντὸς μοῖραν· μετὰ δὲ ταύτην, ἀφῄρει διπλασίαν ταύτης· τὴν δ' αὖ τρίτην, ἡμιολίαν μὲν τῆς δευτέρας, τριπλασίαν δὲ τῆς πρώτης· τετάρτην δὲ, τῆς δευτέρας διπλῆν· πέμπτην δὲ, τριπλῆν τῆς τρίτης· τὴν δ' ἕκτην, τῆς πρώτης ὀκταπλασίαν· ἑβδόμην δὲ, ἑπτακαιεικοσαπλασίαν τῆς πρώτης (a. $b = 2\,a$. $c = 1\frac{1}{2}\,b = 3\,a$. $d = 2\,b$. $e = 3\,c$. $f = 8\,a$. $g = 27\,a$) Pl. Tim. 35, b, c. Δὶς τόσω ἐμὲ κτείνας ἀδελφῆς ζῶσαν Eur. El. 1092.

(II.) Genitive of Cause.

§ **353.** To the head of CAUSE may be referred, I. That from which any thing is DERIVED, FORMED, SUPPLIED, OR TAKEN; II. That which exerts an influence, as an EXCITEMENT, OCCASION, OR CONDITION; III. That which produces any thing, as its ACTIVE OR EFFICIENT CAUSE; and IV. That which CONSTITUTES any thing WHAT IT IS.

In the first of these divisions, the prevailing idea is that of *source;* in the second, that of *influence;* in the third, that of *action;* and in the fourth, tnat of *property.* Or we may say, in general, that the first division presents the *material cause;* the second, the *motive cause;* the third, the *efficient cause;* and the fourth, the *constituent cause.* It scarcely needs to be remarked, that the four divisions are continually blending with each other in their branches and analogies.

§ **354.** I. That from which any thing is DERIVED, FORMED, SUPPLIED, OR TAKEN. To this division belong, 1. the *Genitive of Origin,* 2. the *Genitive of Material,* 3. the *Genitive of Supply,* and 4. the *Genitive of the Whole,* or the *Genitive Partitive.*

1 and 2. *Genitive of Origin and of Material.*

§ **355.** RULE VI. The ORIGIN, SOURCE, and MATERIAL are put in the Genitive; as,

Δαρείου καὶ Παρυσάτιδος γίγνονται παῖδες δύο, *of Darīus and Parysatis are born two children,* i. 1. 1. Φοίνῖκος μὲν αἱ θύραι πεποιημέναι, *the doors being made of the palm-tree,* Cyr. vii. 5. 22. Μιᾶς μητρὸς . . φύντες Pl. Menex. 239 a. Ὧν δ' ἔβλαστεν Soph. Tr. 401. Οὔτε τῆς νεοζύγου νύμφης τεκνώσει παῖδα Eur. Med. 804. Τί ἀπολαύσαις ἂν τῆς ἀρχῆς; *What advantage should you derive from your authority?* Cyr. vii. 5. 56. Διψήσας τῶν ἡδίστων ποτῶν ἀπολαύσεται Ib. 81. Χρημάτων ὀνήσομαι Eur. Hel. 935. Εὐωχοῦ τοῦ λόγου Pl. Rep. 352 b Τῆς κεφαλῆς ὄζω Ar.

Eccl. 524. Οἶνος φοινίκων πολύς ii. 3. 14 (cf. Οἶνον τε κ. τ. λ. i. 5. 10) Περιστεφῆ .. ἀνθέων Soph. El. 895. Λίμνην .. ζέουσαν ὕδατος καὶ πηλοῦ, 'boiling with water,' Pl. Phædo, 113 a. Μεθυσθεὶς τοῦ νέκταρος Pl Conv. 203 b. Τῶν λόγων ὑμᾶς Λυσίας εἱστία; Pl. Phædr. 227 b.

Note. The *Gen. of source* or *material* occurs, especially in the Epic poets, for other forms of construction, particularly the *instrumental Dat.*; as, Πρῆσαι δὲ πυρὸς δηΐοιο θύρετρα, *and burn the gates with raging fire* [from fire, as the source], B. 415. Πυρὸς μειλισσέμεν H. 410. Χεῖρας νιψάμενος πολιῆς ἁλός, *having washed his hands* [with water from] *in the foaming sea*, β. 261. Λούεσθαι ἐϋῤῥεῖος ποταμοῖο Z. 508.

§ **356.** That of which one discourses or thinks may be regarded as the *material* of his discourse or thoughts; thus we speak of the *matter of discourse*, a *matter of complaint*, the *subject-matter of a composition*, &c. Hence, not unfrequently both in immediate dependence upon another word, and even in the introduction of a sentence,

Rule VII. The theme of discourse or of thought is put in the Genitive. Thus,

Τοῦ τοξότου οὐ καλῶς ἔχει λέγειν, ὅτι, κ. τ. λ., *it is not well to say of the bowman, that, &c.*, Pl. Rep. 439 b. Διαθεώμενος αὐτῶν, ὅσην μὲν χώραν καὶ οἵαν ἔχοιεν, *observing in respect to them, how great and what a country they have*, iii. 1. 19. Τῆς δὲ γυναικός, εἰ .. κακοποιεῖ, *but in respect to the wife, if she manages ill*, Œc. 3. 11. Τοῦ κασιγνήτου τί φής; Soph. El. 317. Κλύουσα παιδός, *having heard respecting her son*, Id. Ant. 1182. Μαντεῖα, .. ἃ τοῦδ' ἐχρήσθη σώματος Id. Œd. C. 354. Καταμαθεῖν δὲ τοῦ Κύρου δοκοῦμεν, ὡς .. ἐνόμιζε Cyr. viii. 1. 40. Τοῦ δὲ οἴκαδε πλοῦ μᾶλλον διεσκόπουν, ὅπη κομισθήσονται Th. i. 52. Οἶσθα γάρ που τῶν γενναίων κυνῶν, ὅτι τοῦτο φύσει αὐτῶν τὸ ἦθος Pl. Rep. 375 e. Τὸ Μεγαρέων ψήφισμα καθαιρεῖν Id. i. 140 (cf. Τὸ περὶ Μεγαρέων ψήφισμα καθελοῦσι 139). Τί δὲ τῶν πολλῶν καλῶν, οἷον ἀνθρώπων, ἢ ἵππων, ἢ ἱματίων, .. ἆρα κατὰ τὰ αὐτὰ ἔχει; *But what of, &c.?* Pl. Phædo, 78 d. Τῆς δὲ σῆς φρενός, ἔν σου δέδοικα Eur Andr. 361. Cf. § 438. γ.

Note. For the *Gen. of the theme* may be often substituted another case, more frequently the Nom., in the succeeding clause; thus, Εἰ δὲ ἡ γυνὴ κακοποιεῖ, *but if the wife manages ill.*

3. *Genitive of Supply.*

§ **357.** Supply may be either *abundant* or *defective.* Hence,

Rule VIII. Words of plenty and want govern the Genitive; as,

α. Of Plenty. Ἀγρίων θηρίων πλήρης, *full of wild beasts*, i. 2. 7. Διφθέρας .. ἐπίμπλασαν χόρτου, *they filled the skins with hay*, i. 5. 10. Τούτων ἅλις, *enough of these things*, v. 7, 12. Κώμας πολλῶν καὶ ἀγαθῶν γεμούσας iv. 6, 27. Μεστὴ γὰρ πολλῆς ἀπορίας ἐστίν ii. 5. 9. Τῶν δὲ ἱππέων ὁ λόφος ἐνεπλήσθη i. 10. 12. Παραδείσου .. δασέος παντοίων δένδρων ii. 4. 14. Κορέσαι στόμα . . ἐμᾶς σαρκός Soph. Ph. 1156. Ὁ δαίμων δ' ἐς με πλούσιος κακῶν Eur. Or. 394. Πλουτεῖ . . φίλων vii. 7. 42. Τριήρης . . σεσαγμένη ἀνθρώπων Œc. 8. 8.

β. OF WANT. Τῶν ἐπιτηδείων σπανιεῖ, *he will want provisions*, ii. 2. 12. Σφενδονητῶν . . δεῖ, *there is need of slingers*, iii. 3. 16. Οἵων ἂν ἐλπίδων ἐμαυτὸν στερήσαιμι, *of what hopes I should deprive myself*, ii. 5. 10. Ἀνθρώπων ἀπορῶν i. 7. 3. Ἡ ψυχὴ γυμνὴ τοῦ σώματος Pl. Crat. 403 b. Γυμνωτέος δὴ πάντων Pl. Rep. 361 b. Ὀλίγου δεήσαντος καταλευσθῆναι i. 5. 14. Πολλῶν ἐνέδει αὐτῷ, ὥστε vii. 1. 41. Ὑμῶν δ' ἐρημωθεὶ' i. 3. 6. Ἅρματα . . κενὰ ἡνιόχων i. 8. 20. Οἴμοι, τί δράσω δῆτα σοῦ μονούμενος; Eur. Alc. 380. Ὀρφανὴν φίλου πατρός Eur. El. 914. Χρημάτων δὲ δὴ πένητες Ib. 37. Ἐψιλοῦτο δ' ὁ λόφος τῶν ἱππέων i. 10. 13.

NOTE. The Gen. which belongs to δέομαι and χρήζω as *verbs of want* may be retained by them in the derived senses, *to desire, to request, to entreat.* Thus, Ἄλλου οὔτινος ἂν δέησθε, *whatever else you may desire*, i. 4. 15. Ἐμοὶ χάρισαι ὧν ἂν σοῦ δεηθῶ, *grant me what I would entreat of you* (§ 380), Cyr. v. 5. 35. Αἰσχρὸν γὰρ ἄνδρα τοῦ μακροῦ χρήζειν βίου Soph. Aj. 473.

4. *Genitive Partitive.*

§ **358.** RULE IX. The WHOLE OF WHICH A PART IS TAKEN is put in the Genitive; as,

Ἥμισυ τοῦ ὅλου στρατεύματος, *half of the whole army*, vi. 2. 10.

NOTE. This Gen. has received the names of *the Gen. of the whole*, and the *Gen. partitive;* the former from its denoting *the whole*, and the latter from its denoting this whole in a state of *division* (partio or partior, *to divide*, from pars, *part*).

§ **359.** REMARKS. 1. The partitive construction may be employed,—

α.) To express *quantity*, *degree*, *condition*, *place*, *time*, &c. considered as a limitation of a general idea, or as a part of an extended whole. Thus,

Μικρὸν δ' ὕπνου λαχών, *obtaining a little sleep* [a small portion of sleep], iii. 1. 11. Ἐν τοιούτῳ . . τοῦ κινδύνου προσιόντος, *in such imminent danger* [in such a degree of], i. 7. 5. Ὁ δ' εἰς τοῦθ' ὕβρεως ἐλήλυθεν, 'to such a pitch of insolence,' Dem. 51. 1. Καὶ οἱ μὲν ἐν τούτῳ παρασκευῆς ἦσαν, 'in this state of preparation,' Th. ii. 17. Ξυνέπεσον ἐς τοῦτο ἀνάγκης Th. i. 49. Ἐπὶ μέγα ἐχώρησαν δυνάμεως Ib. 118. Ἐμβαλεῖν που τῆς ἐκείνων χώρας, *to make an incursion somewhere upon their territory*, or *upon some part of*, &c., Cyr. vi. 1. 42. Ἦν μέσον ἡμέρας, *it was mid-day*, i. 8. 8. Τῆς ἡμέρας ὀψὲ ἦν, *it was late in the day* [at a late hour of the day], H. Gr. ii. 1. 23. Εἰς τόδ' ἡμέρας, *to this day*, Eur. Alc. 9, Phœn. 425.

β.) To express the whole as the sum of all the parts. Thus,

Ἐν τοῖς ἀγαθοῖσι δὲ πάντ' ἔνεστιν σοφίας, *and in the good dwell all the qualities of wisdom*, Eur. Alc. 601. Οἱ μὲν Ἀθηναῖοι ἐν παντὶ δὴ ἀθυμίας ἦσαν Th. vii. 55. Ἐν παντὶ κακοῦ εἴη Pl. Rep. 579 b.

§ **360.** 2. The whole is sometimes put in the case which

belongs to the part, the part agreeing with the whole instead of governing it (§§ 333. 5, 334. 9); as,

Ἀκούομεν ὑμᾶς . . ἐνίους σκηνοῦν ἐν ταῖς οἰκίαις, *we hear that you, some of you, quarter in the houses;* for ὑμῶν ἐνίους, κ. τ. λ. v. 5. 11. Πελοποννήσιοι καὶ οἱ ξύμμαχοι τὰ δύο μέρη . . ἐσέβαλον, for Πελοποννησίων καὶ τῶν ξυμμάχων, κ. τ. λ. Th. ii. 47. Δίδυμα τέκεα πότερος ἄρα πότερον αἱμάξει Eur Ph. 1289.

Note. This form of construction chiefly occurs when several parts are successively mentioned; as, Οἰκίαι, αἱ μὲν πολλαὶ ἐπεπτώκεσαν, ὀλίγαι δὲ περιῆσαν, *the houses, the greater part had been demolished, and but few remained,* Th. i. 89. Οὐ γὰρ τάφου νῷν τὼ κασιγνήτω Κρέων, τὸν μὲν προτίσας, τὸν δ' ἀτιμάσας ἔχει; Soph. Ant. 21. In the following example, the second part has three subdivisions; Καὶ οἱ ξένοι, οἱ μὲν . . ἀποχωροῦσιν· οἱ δὲ, . . οἱ μὲν . . ἀπέρχονται, οἱ δὲ . ., εἰσὶ δ' οἵ Th. vii. 13.

3. It is often at the option of the writer whether he will employ the Gen. partitive or a simpler form of construction. The two forms are sometimes combined; as, Εἴτ' οὖν θεὸς, εἴτε βροτῶν ἦν ὁ ταῦτα πράσσων, 'a god, or one of mortals,' Soph. El. 199. Ποῦ τις θεῶν ἢ δαίμων ἐπαρωγός; Eur. Hec. 164. Οἶδε . . φαίνουσι τινὲς δαίμονες, ἢ θεῶν τῶν οὐρανίων Id. El. 1233.

§ 361. According to Rule IX., any word referring to a part, whether *substantive, adjective, adverb,* or *verb,* may take with it a Gen. denoting the whole. Thus,

A. Substantives.

Τὸ τρίτον μέρος τοῦ . . ἱππικοῦ, *the third part of the cavalry,* Cyr. ii. 1. 6. Τῶν πελταστῶν τις ἀνήρ, *a certain man of the targeteers,* iv. 8. 4. Τῶν Ἑλλήνων δὲ ἔχων ὁπλίτας ἀνέβη τριακοσίους i. 1. 2. Τριάκοντα μυριάδας στρατιᾶς i. 4. 5. Εἶτ' ἀνὴρ τῶν ῥητόρων Ar. Eq. 425.

Remarks. *α.* When place is designated by mentioning both the *country* and the *town,* the former, as the whole, may be put in the Gen., and may precede the latter; as, Οἱ δὲ Ἀθηναῖοι . . ὡρμίσαντο τῆς Χεῤῥονήσου ἐν Ἐλεοῦντι, *and the Athenians touched upon the Cherronese at Eleüs* [at Eleüs, a town of the Cherronese], H. Gr. ii. 1. 20. Οἱ Πελοποννήσιοι τῆς Ἀττικῆς ἐς Ἐλευσῖνα καὶ Θρίωζε ἐσβαλόντες, *the Peloponnesians invading Attica as far as Eleusis and Thria,* Th. i. 114. Ὁ δὲ στρατὸς τῶν Πελοποννησίων προϊὼν ἀφίκετο τῆς Ἀττικῆς ἐς Οἰνόην πρῶτον, 'came upon Attica first at Œnoë,' Id. ii. 18.

β. The Gen., in all cases in which it is strictly *partitive,* may be regarded as properly depending upon a substantive denoting the part; and therefore the use of this Gen. in connection with adjectives, verbs, and adverbs may be referred to ellipsis. Thus, Τῶν ἄλλων Ἑλλήνων τινὲς [sc. ἄνδρες]. Ἐξεκύμαινέ τι [sc. μέρος] τῆς φάλαγγος (§ 362. *β*). Εἰσὶ δ' αὐτῶν [sc. ποταμοί τινες], οὓς οὐδ' ἂν παντάπασι διαβαίητε. Πολέμου, καὶ μάχης οὐ μετῆν [sc. μέρος] αὐτῇ (§ 364). Γῆς γε οὐδαμοῦ, i. e. ἐν οὐδενὶ μέρει τῆς γῆς (§ 363).

γ. If the substantive denoting the part is expressed, and that denoting the whole is a form of the same word, the latter is commonly omitted; as, Τρεῖς ἄνδρες τῶν γεραιτέρων [sc. ἀνδρῶν], *three men of the more aged,* v. 7. 17. Δύο τῶν πρεσβυτάτων στρατηγοί, iii. 2. 37. Εἰσεφέρετο τῇ ὀρχηστρίδι τροχὸς τῶν κεραμεικῶν Symp. 7. 2.

§ 362. B. ADJECTIVES.

NOTE. The adjectives which are most frequently used to denote a part are termed *partitives.*

α. THE ARTICLE. Τοὺς μὲν αὐτῶν ἀπέκτεινε, τοὺς δ' ἐξέβαλεν, *slew some of them, and banished others*, i. 1. 7.

β. ADJECTIVE PRONOUNS. Τῶν ἄλλων Ἑλλήνων τινές, *some of the other Greeks*, i. 7. 8. Ὅστις . . τῶν παρὰ βασιλέως i. 1. 5. Οἳ ὕστερον ἐλήφθησαν τῶν πολεμίων i. 7. 13. Τῶν δὲ βαρβάρων . . ἄλλοις i. 2. 18. Τοῖς τοιούτοις τῶν ἔργων Mem. ii. 8. 3. Εἰ δέ τι καὶ ἄλλο ἐνῆν ὕλης ἢ καλάμου i. 5. 1. Ἐξεκύμαινέ τι τῆς φάλαγγος i. 8. 18. Ἐν τῷ ξυμφορᾶς διεφθάρης; Soph. Ant. 1229. See § 359. *α.*

γ. NUMERALS. Εἷς τῶν στρατηγῶν, *one of the generals*, vii. 2. 29. Τοὺς τρεῖς . . τῶν δακτύλων Ar. Vesp. 95. Εἰς ἓν μοίρας Eur. Andr. 1172. Ὁπόσοι μὲν τῶν ἀμφὶ βασιλέα ἀπέθνησκον i. 8. 27. Πολλὰ τῶν ὑποζυγίων i. 5. 5. Ὀλίγοι μὲν αὐτῶν iii. 1. 3.

δ. SUPERLATIVES, and words derived from them (by virtue of the included adjective, cf. § 351). Ἐν τοῖς ἀρίστοις Περσῶν, *among the best of the Persians*, i. 6. 1. Τοῦ πιστοτάτου τῶν Κύρου σκηπτούχων Ib. 11. Ἐπὶ πλεῖστον ἀνθρώπων Th. i. 1. Τῆς γῆς ἡ ἀρίστη Ib. 2. Τῶν καθ' ἑαυτοὺς ἀνθρώπων ἀριστεύσαντες [= ἄριστοι γενόμενοι], *being the best of the men of their age*, Mem. iii. 5. 10. Δῶρ', ἃ καλλιστεύεται τῶν νῦν ἐν ἀνθρώποισιν Eur. Med. 947. Οὐ δευτέρων πρωτεύουσιν Ages. i. 3.

ε. PARTICIPLES. Σὺν τοῖς παροῦσι τῶν πιστῶν, *with those present of his faithful attendants*, i. 5. 15. Καὶ τῶν ἄλλων τὸν βουλόμενον, *and of the rest any one that wished*, i. 3. 9. Ἥκει δέ τις ἢ τῶν προβάτων λελυκωμένα φέρων, ἢ τῶν βοῶν κατακεκρημνισμένα Cyr. viii. 3. 41.

ζ. OTHER ADJECTIVES. Ἔχων τῶν ὀπισθοφυλάκων τοὺς ἡμίσεις, *having half of the rear guard*, iv. 2. 9. Ὦ τάλαινα παρθένων, *O ill-fated of virgins*, Eur. Heracl. 567. Τοὺς ἀγαθοὺς τῶν ἀνθρώπων, *the good among men*, Ar. Plut. 495. Δειλαία δειλαίων κυρεῖς, *wretched of the wretched art thou!* Soph. El. 849. Τὸ λοιπὸν τῆς ἡμέρας iii. 4. 6. Ἔτεμον τῆς γῆς τὴν πολλήν Th. ii. 56. Ὦ φίλα γυναικῶν Eur. Alc. 460. Δῖε Πελασγῶν Æsch. Suppl. 967. Ἄνοια μεγάλη λείπειν ἐχθροὺς ἐχθρῶν Eur. Andr. 521. Τῶν ἄλλων σκευῶν τὰ περιττά iii. 2. 28.

§ 363. C. ADVERBS.

α. Of PLACE and TIME (§ 359. *α*). Οὐδ' ὅπου γῆς ἐσμὲν οἶδα, *I know not where on earth* [upon what part of the earth] *we are*, Ar. Av. 9. Γῆς γε οὐδαμοῦ Pl. Rep. 592 b. Πανταχοῦ τῆς γῆς Pl. Phædo, 111 a. Ποῦ ποτ' εἶ φρενῶν; Soph. El. 390. Τηλοῦ γὰρ οἰκῶ τῶν ἀγρῶν, 'in a remote part of the country,' *i. e.* 'far from town,' Ar. Nub. 138. Ἐνταῦθα τοῦ οὐρανοῦ ἀναστρέφεσθαι Mem. iv. 3. 8. Ἐνταῦθα ἤδη εἶ τῆς ἡλικίας, *you are now at that point of life*, Pl. Rep. 328 c. Δεῦρο τοῦ λόγου Pl. Conv. 217 e. Οὐχ ὁρᾷς ἵν' εἶ κακοῦ; Soph. Aj. 386. Οἷ προελήλυθεν ἀσελγείας ἄνθρωπος Dem. 42. 24. Ποῖ τις φροντίδος ἔλθῃ; Soph. Œd. C. 170. Ἐφύλαττον ἄλλος ἄλλοθεν τοῦ Ὀνείου H. Gr. vii. 1. 15. Μὴ πρόσω δὲ τοῦ ποταμοῦ προβαίνειν, *but not to advance far into the river*, iv. 3. 28. Ἐκάθευδον μέχρι πόῤῥω τῆς ἡμέρας H. Gr. vii. 2. 19. Ὁπηνίκα . . τῆς ὥρας, *at whatever point of time*, iii. 5. 18. Πηνίκ' ἐστὶν ἄρα τῆς ἡμέρας; Ar. Av. 1498. Πρωϊαίτατα . . τῆς ἡλικίας, *at the earliest age*, Pl. Prot. 326 c.

β. Of State or Condition (§ 359. α; especially with the verbs ἔχω and ἥκω). Τῆς τύχης γὰρ ὧδ' ἔχω, *for I am thus in* [have myself in this state of] *fortune*, Eur. Hel. 857. Ἀναμνήσας, ὡς εἶχε φιλίας πρός τε τὴν . . πόλιν, 'in what a state of friendship he was,' *i. e.* 'what friendship he bore, H. Gr. ii. 1. 14. Διώξαντες, ὡς τάχους ἕκαστος εἶχεν, *having pursued, as each one had himself in respect to speed*, i. e. *every man according to his speed*, Ib. iv. 5. 15. Ὡς ὀργῆς ἔχω Soph. Œd. T. 345. Πῶς ἀγῶνος ἥκομεν *how do we come on in the strife?* Eur. El. 751. Οὕτω τρόπου . . ἔχεις Cyr. vii. 5. 56. Γένους μὲν ἥκεις ὧδε τοῖσδε, *thus are you related to these*, Eur Heracl. 213. Ἔχοντας εὖ φρενῶν, *of good judgment*, Eur. Hipp. 462. Ἀνδράσι μέλλουσιν εὖ σώματος ἕξειν Pl. Rep. 404 d. Ὅταν . . ὑγιεινῶς τις ἔχῃ αὐτὸς αὑτοῦ Ib. 571 d.

γ. Of the Superlative Degree. Ἀφειδέστατα πάντων, *most unsparingly of all*, i. 9. 13. Προτιμηθῆναι μάλιστα τῶν Ἑλλήνων i. 6. 5. Οἱ μὲν ἐγγύτατα τῶν πολεμίων ii. 2. 17.

§ 364. D. Verbs.

The Genitive partitive, in connection with a verb, may perform the office either of a *subject*, an *appositive*, or a *complement;* taking the place of any case which the verb would require, if referring to the whole. See § 361. β.

α. The Genitive Partitive as a Subject.

(1.) *Of a Finite Verb.* Εἰσὶ δ' αὐτῶν, οὓς οὐδ' ἂν παντάπασι διαβαίητε, *and there are some of them, which you could not pass at all*, ii. 5. 18. Ἦν δὲ τούτων τῶν σταθμῶν, οὓς πάνυ μακροὺς ἤλαυνεν, i. 5. 7. Τῶν δὲ Σαμίων . . ξυνθέμενοι . . διέβησαν Th. i. 115. Πολέμου, καὶ μάχης οὐ μετῆν αὐτῇ, *of war and battle, there fell to her no share*, Cyr. vii. 2. 28. Οὐδ' ὡς ἡμῖν νῦν προσήκει οὔτε πλησμονῆς πω οὔτε μέθης Cyr. iv. 2. 20.

(2.) *Of an Infinitive.* Καὶ ἐπιμιγνύναι σφῶν τε πρὸς ἐκείνους, καὶ ἐκείνων πρὸς αὐτούς, *that there even mingled some of themselves with those, and some of those with them*, iii. 5. 16. Οὐκ ᾤετο προσήκειν οὐδενὶ ἀρχῆς, *he thought that no authority belonged to any one*, Cyr. viii. 1. 37. Δοκεῖ δίκαιον εἶναι, πᾶσι τῶν ἀρχῶν μετεῖναι Rep. Ath. 1. 2.

§ 365. β. The Genitive Partitive as an Appositive.

The Gen. partitive in the place of an appositive is most common with *substantive verbs*, but is likewise found with other verbs, particularly those of *reckoning, esteeming*, and *making*. Thus, Οὐκ ἐγὼ τούτων εἰμί, *I am not one of these*, Cyr. viii. 3. 45. Τῶν φιλτάτων ἔμοιγ' ἀριθμήσει τέκνων, *thou shalt be numbered as one of my dearest children*, Eur. Bacch. 1318. Ἐτύγχανε γὰρ καὶ βουλῆς ὢν Th. iii. 70. Καὶ ἐμὲ τοίνυν . . θὲς τῶν πεπεισμένων Pl. Rep. 424 c. Τοὺς δούλους . . τῶν περὶ ἑαυτὸν δορυφόρων ποιήσασθαι Ib. 567 e. Τῶν φευγόντων ὀνομάζεσθαι Isocr. 380 d.

§ 366. γ. The Genitive Partitive as a Complement.

The Genitive partitive is used as a complement,

I.) *Generally*, with any verb, when its action affects not the whole object, but a *part* only; as,

Λαβόντας τοῦ βαρβαρικοῦ στρατοῦ, *taking a part of the barbarian army*, i. 5. 7. Τῶν κηρίων . . ἔφαγον, *ate of the honeycombs*, iv. 8. 20. Ἀφιεὶς δὲ τῶν αἰχμαλώτων, *and sending some of the captives*, vii. 4. 5. Συγκαλέσαντες λοχαγοὺς καὶ πελταστὰς καὶ τῶν ὁπλιτῶν iv. 1. 26. Χειρίσοφος πέμπει τῶν ἐκ τῆς κώμης σκεψομένους iv. 5. 22. Καὶ τῆς τε γῆς ἔτεμον Th. ii. 56. Μαντικῆς ἔχον τέχνης Soph. Œd T. 709. Ξυνελέγοντο τῶν λίθων Ar. Ach. 184. Τῶν κρεῶν ἔκλεπτον Ar. Eq. 420. Παροίξας τῆς θύρας, *just opening the door*, Ar. Pax, 30.

§ **367.** II.) *Particularly*, with verbs which, in their ordinary use, imply *divided* or *partial action*.

NOTE. The Gen. partitive may be connected with other parts of speech upon the same principle. Hence the rule is expressed in a general form.

RULE X. Words of SHARING and TOUCH govern the Genitive.

1. Words of SHARING include those of *partaking* (part-taking), *imparting*, *obtaining by distribution*, &c. Thus,

Τῶν κινδύνων μετέχειν, *to share in the dangers*, ii. 4. 9. Τῆσδε κοινωνῶ τύχης, *I partake of this fortune*, Eur. Med. 303. Τῶν εὐφροσυνῶν μεταδιδόντες, *imparting our joys*, Œc. 9. 12. Κοινωνοὺς ἁπάντων, vii. 2. 38. Ἄνδρες οἱ ξυναράμενοι τοῦδε τοῦ κινδύνου Th. iv. 10. Ξυλλήψομαι δὲ τοῦδέ σοι κἀγὼ πόνου Eur. Med. 946. Μειονεκτεῖ τῶν εὐφροσυνῶν ὁ τύραννος, 'has less of,' Hier. 1. 29. Τοῦ ἡλίου πλεονεκτοῦντα, 'bearing more of,' Cyr. i. 6. 25. Πᾶσιν ἀφθόνως ἐπήρκει τῶν ἑαυτοῦ Mem. i. 2. 60. Τοῦ λόγου προσδοὺς Eur. Suppl. 350. Ξυμβάλλεται . . τοῦδε δείματος Eur. Med. 284. Ἀγαθὴ δὲ συλλήπτρια τῶν ἐν εἰρήνῃ πόνων, βεβαία δὲ τῶν ἐν πολέμῳ σύμμαχος ἔργων, ἀρίστη δὲ φιλίας κοινωνός Mem. ii. 1. 32.

§ **368.** 2. TOUCH may be regarded as a species of partial action, affecting only the point of contact. To this head belong, either by direct connection or by obvious analogy, verbs of *laying hold of*, *hitting*, *meeting with*, &c. Thus,

Ἅπτεσθαι τῆς κάρφης, *to touch the hay*, i. 5. 10. Ἐπιλαμβάνεται αὐτοῦ τῆς ἴτυος, *lays hold of his shield-rim*, iv. 7. 12. Φεραύλα τυγχάνει, *hits Pheraulas*, Cyr. viii. 3. 28. Ἐξικνεῖσθαι τῶν σφενδονητῶν, *to reach the slingers*, iii. 3. 7. Ἀνδρῶν ἀγαθῶν παιδὸς ὑπαντήσας, *having met with the son of brave heroes*, Soph. Ph. 719. Ὅταν δὲ τούτων τινὸς θίγῃς Cyr. i. 3. 5. Τούς τε τῆς τραγικῆς ποιήσεως ἁπτομένους Pl. Rep. 602 b. Δυσχερὲς ψαύειν νοσοῦντος ἀνδρός Eur. Or. 793. Αὐτὸς δὲ λαβόμενος τῆς δεξιᾶς τοῦ Κυαξάρους Cyr. v. 5. 7. Ἀντιλήψονται τῶν πραγμάτων Cyr. ii. 3. 6. Ἑξόμεθα αὐτοῦ, *we shall keep hold of him*, vii. 6. 41. Κοινῇ τῆς σωτηρίας ἔχεσθαι, *to strive in common for our safety*, vi. 3. 17. Ἐχόμενοι δὲ τούτων, *and following these*, i. 8. 9. Τῆς ἐλπίδος γὰρ ἔρχομαι δεδραγμένος Soph. Ant. 235. Λέγεται τῆς τελευτῆς τυχεῖν, 'to have come to his end,' ii. 6. 29. Ὁποίων τινῶν ἡμῶν ἔτυχον, *what kind of men they found us*, v. 5. 15.

§ **369.** REMARKS. *a.* Hence, the *part taken hold of* is put in the Gen., in connection with other forms of construction; as,

Ἔλαβον τῆς ζώνης τὸν Ὀρόντην, *they took Orontes by the girdle*, i. 6. 10. Τὰ παιδάρι' εὐθὺς ἀνέλκει . . τῆς χειρός Ar. Vesp. 568. Τὰς δὲ κεχειρωμένας ἄγεσθαι . . πλοκάμων Æsch. Theb. 326. Νὶν . . ψαύειν χερός Eur. Herc. 968. Τὴν μὲν κρεμαστὴν αὐχένος Soph. Ant. 1221.

β. To the analogy of verbs of touch may be referred expressions like the following: Τῆς κεφαλῆς κατέαγε, *he broke* [was fractured in] *his head*, Ar. Ach. 1180. Ξυνετρίβη τῆς κεφαλῆς Ar. Pax, 71. Ἠτιῶντο τὸν Κρατῖνον συντρῖψαι τῆς κεφαλῆς αὐτῆς, *they charged Cratinus with having broken her head*. Isocr. 381 a. Εἶτα κατάξειέ τις αὐτοῦ μεθύων τῆς κεφαλῆς Ar. Ach. 1166. Cf. § 437.

§ **370.** 3. Several words of *obtaining*, *attaining*, and *receiving*, govern the Genitive, from their referring primarily either to distribution or to touch. Thus,

Ἵνα τῆς προσηκούσης μοίρας λαγχάνῃ, *that it may receive its proper portion*, Pl. Leg. 903 e. Κληρονομεῖν οὐδενός, *to inherit nothing*, Dem. 1065. 25. Τῶν δικαίων τυγχάνειν, *to obtain your rights*, vii. 1. 30. ἘΠΕΙΔΗ ΘΝΗΤΟΥ ΜΕΝ ΣΩΜΑΤΟΣ ἘΤΥΧΕΣ, ἈΘΑΝΑΤΟΥ ΔΕ ΨΥΧΗΣ, ΠΕΙΡΩ ΤΗΣ ΨΥΧΗΣ ἈΘΑΝΑΤΟΝ ΤΗΝ ΜΝΗΜΗΝ ΚΑΤΑΛΙΠΕΙΝ Isocr. 22 b. Κἀκεῖθεν, οὔτε του τάφου ἀντιάσας, οὔτε γόων παρ' ἡμῶν Soph. El. 868. Οἵας ἀμοιβῆς ἐξ Ἰάσονος κυρεῖ Eur. Med. 23.

NOTE. The student can hardly fail to have remarked the great variety of metaphorical and transitive meanings in which words of sharing and of touch are employed, not only in Greek, but likewise in our own and in other languages.

§ **371.** II. That which exerts an influence as an EXCITEMENT, OCCASION, or CONDITION. To this division belong the following rules, respecting, 1. the *motive*, *reason*, and *end in view*; 2. *price*, *value*, *merit*, and *crime*; 3. the *sensible* and *mental object*; and 4. *time* and *place*.

1. *Genitive of Motive, &c.*

§ **372.** RULE XI. The MOTIVE, REASON, and END IN VIEW are put in the Genitive.

To this rule may be referred the use of the Gen., both in *regular construction* and in *exclamation*, to express the person or thing, *on account of* which, *in consequence of* which, *for the sake of* which, *in honor of* which, or *to affect* which, any thing is felt, said, or done. Thus,

α. WITH VERBS. Τούτου σε . . ζηλῶ, *on this account I envy you*, Cyr. viii. 4. 23. Μισθοῦ ὑπηρετοῦντες, *serving for hire*, Ib. vi. 2. 37. Μηδὲν αὐτῶν καταθείς, *paying nothing for them*, Ib. iii. 1. 37. Τοῦ μὲν πάθους ᾤκτειρεν αὐτόν Ib. v. 4. 32. Ζηλῶ σε τοῦ νοῦ, τῆς δὲ δειλίας στυγῶ Soph. El. 1027. Ἢ φίλου δείσας . . ἢ χαὐτοῦ Id. Œd. T. 234. Ταύτης ἱκνοῦμαί σε, *I beseech you for her sake*, Eur. Or. 671. Ἱκετεύω σε τῶνδε γουνάτων καὶ σοῦ γενείου δεξιᾶς τ' εὐδαίμονος, 'by these knees,' &c., Eur. Hec. 752. Σπεῖσον ἀγαθοῦ δαίμονος, 'in honor of,' Ar. Eq. 106. Τοῦ δώδεκα μνᾶς Πασίᾳ; *For what do I* [*owe*] *Pasias twelve minæ?* Ar. Nub. 23. Προπέποται τῆς παραυτίκα ἡδονῆς καὶ χάριτος τὰ τῆς πόλεως πράγματα, 'for the sake of present pleasure and favor,' Dem. 34. 23. Καταῤῥοφοῦσι, τοῦ . . μὴ λυσιτελεῖν αὐτοῖς, 'so that it may not profit,' Cyr. i. 3. 9.

β. WITH ADJECTIVES. Εὐδαίμων . . τοῦ τρόπου Pl. Phædo, 58 e. Ὦ μακάρις τῆς τέχνης, *Blessed in thy trade!* Ar. Av. 1423. Ὦ τάλαιν' ἐγὼ σέθεν Soph. El. 1209. Ὦ δυστάλαινα τῆς ἐμῆς αὐθαδίας Eur. Med. 1028.

γ. WITH ADVERBS. Ταύτης ἕνεκα τῆς παρόδου, *on account of this pass*, i. 4. 5. Τοῦ μὴ φεύγειν ἕνεκα, *lest they should escape*, iii. 4. 35. Πέμπει μ' ἐκείνη τοῦδε τοῦ φόβου χάριν Soph. El. 427. Πενθικῶς δὲ ἔχουσαν τοῦ ἀδελφοῦ τεθνηκότος Cyr. v. 2. 7. Χαλεπῶς φέρειν αὐτῶν Th. ii. 62.

δ. WITH NOUNS. Ἐμοὶ πικρὰς ὠδῖνας αὐτοῦ προσβαλών, 'pangs on his account,' Soph. Tr. 41. Πολλὰς γενείου τοῦδ' ἂν ἐκτεῖναι λιτάς, 'by this beard,' Eur. Or. 290. Οἴαξ, τὸ Τροίας μῖσος ἀναφέρων πατρί Ib. 432.

ε. WITH INTERJECTIONS. Φεῦ τοῦ ἀνδρός, *Alas for the noble man!* Cyr. iii. 1. 39. Αἰαῖ κακῶν Eur. Herc. 899. Οἴμοι δάμαρτος καὶ τέκνων, οἴμοι δ' ἐμοῦ Ib. 1374. Ὀὰ Περσικοῦ στρατεύματος τοῦδε Æsch. Pers 116. Ἰατταταιὰξ τῶν κακῶν Ar. Eq. 1.

ζ. IN SIMPLE EXCLAMATION. Τῆς τύχης, *My ill-luck!* Cyr. ii. 2. 3. Τῆς μωρίας, *What folly!* Ar. Nub. 818. Ὦ Ζεῦ βασιλεῦ, τῆς λεπτότητος τῶν φρενῶν Ib. 153. Ἄπολλον ἀποτρόπαιε, τοῦ χασμήματος Ar. Av. 61.

§ **373.** REMARKS. 1. The Genitive of the END IN VIEW is put with some words of *direction*, *claim*, and *dispute*. Words of *direction* include those of *aiming at*, *throwing at*, *going towards*, and *reaching after*. Thus,

Ἀνθρώπων στοχάζεσθαι, *to take aim at men*, Cyr. i. 6. 29. Αὐτοῦ χερμάδας . . ἔῤῥιπτον, *they threw stones at him*, Eur. Bacch. 1096. Εὐθὺ Πελλήνης πέτεσθαι, *to fly straight to Pellene*, Ar. Av. 1421. Τίς γὰρ αὐτῷ ἐστιν ὅστις τῆς ἀρχῆς ἀντιποιεῖται; *For who is there that disputes with him the sovereignty* [makes for the sovereignty in opposition to him]? ii. 1. 11. Ὥστε τοξόται σκοποῦ, τοξεύετ' ἀνδρὸς τοῦδε Soph. Ant. 1033. Ὤη, ῥίψω πέτρον τάχα σου Eur. Cycl. 51. Ἰέναι τοῦ πρόσω, *to go towards that which is farther on*, i. e. *to go farther*, *to proceed*, i. 3. 1. Λήγει δ' ἔρις δραμοῦσα τοῦ προσωτάτω Soph. Aj. 731. Οὗτοι ἀντεποιοῦντο ἀρετῆς, *these were rivals in valor*, iv. 7. 12. Βασιλικῆς μεταποιουμένους τέχνης, *laying claim to the kingly art*, Pl. Pol. 289 e. Τοῦ δὲ φρονεῖν εὖ . . ἀμφισβητῶ Isocr. 98 c.

2. The student cannot fail to remark the ease with which verbs of *motion* pass into those of simple *effort* and *desire*. Thus, ἵεμαι, and, more commonly, ἐφίεμαι, *to send one's self to*, *to rush to*, *to strive for*, *to seek*, *to desire*; ὀρέγομαι, *to reach after*, *to strive for*, *to seek*, *to court*, *to desire*; as, Ἱέμενοι λεχέων Soph. Tr. 514. Τοῖς δόξης ἐφιεμένοις Cyr. iii. 3. 10. Ὀρέξασθαι τῆς ὁμιλίας αὐτοῦ Mem. i. 2. 15. Σωκράτους ὠρεχθήτην Ib. 16. Τιμῆς ὀρέγεσθαι Hier. 7. 3.

2. *Genitive of Price, &c.*

§ **374.** RULE XII. PRICE, VALUE, MERIT, and CRIME are put in the Genitive.

α. PRICE. Ἵππον, ὃν . . ἀπέδοτο πεντήκοντα δαρεικῶν, *the horse, which he had sold for fifty darics*, vii. 8. 6. Ὠνεῖσθαι . . μικρὰ μέτρα πολλοῦ ἀργυρίου iii. 2. 21. Πολλοῦ τοῖς ἄλλοις ἐπώλουν Mem. i. 2. 60. Τῶν δ' ἐμῶν παίδων φυγὰς ψυχῆς ἂν ἀλλαξαίμεθ', οὐ χρυσοῦ μόνον Eur. Med. 967 Δόξα δὲ χρημάτων οὐκ ὠνητή Isocr. 21 b. Ἀμφίλοχον . . ἀπελύτρωσε ταλάντων ἐννέα Dem. 159. 13.

β. VALUE AND MERIT. Πολλοῦ ἄξιος τῇ στρατίᾳ, *worth much to the army*, iv. 1. 28. Ἄνδρες ἄξιοι τῆς ἐλευθερίας i. 7. 3. Τῶν καλλίστων ἑαυτὸν ἀξιώσαντα iii. 2. 7. Τὸ μνῆμα πολλοὶ χώσουσιν ἀξίως ὑμῶν Cyr. vii. 3. 11. Παῖδα . . ἀνάξιον μὲν σοῦ, κατάξιον δ' ἐμοῦ Soph. Ph. 1008. Ἕκαστον θέντος τῆς ἴσης ἀξίας Pl. Pol. 257 b. Μείζονος αὐτὰ τιμῶνται οἱ λαμβάνοντες Cyr. ii. 1. 13. Εἰ οὖν δεῖ με κατὰ τὸ δίκαιον τῆς ἀξίας τιμᾶσθαι, τούτου τιμῶμαι τῆς ἐν Πρυτανείῳ σιτήσεως Pl. Apol. 36 e. Πρέπον γέ τἂν ἦν δαίμονος τοὐμοῦ τάδε Soph. Aj. 534. Πρεπόντως τῶν πραξάντων Pl. Menex. 239 c (for the common construction of πρέπω, see § 403).

γ. CRIME. Ἀσεβείας φεύγοντα, *accused of impiety*, Pl. Apol. 35 d. Δικάζουσι δὲ καὶ ἐγκλήματος, . . ἀχαριστίας Cyr. i. 2. 7. Διώξομαί σε δειλίας Ar. Eq. 368. Καλοῦμαι Πεισθέταιρον ὕβρεως Ar. Av. 1046. Τῷ πατρὶ φόνου ἐπεξέρχομαι Pl. Euthyph. 4 d. Ἐπαιτιασάμενός με φόνου Dem. 552. 1. Οὐδεὶς ἔνοχός ἐστι λειποταξίου οὐδὲ δειλίας Lys. 140. 1. Τῆς αὐτῆς ἀγνοίας ὑπεύθυνος εἶ τοῖς ἄλλοις Dem. 293. 28.

NOTE. The Gen. is sometimes used to express the *punishment*; as, Θανάτου δὲ οὗτοι κρίνουσι, *and these pronounce sentence of death*, Cyr. i. 2. 14. Συλλαμβάνοντες ὑπῆγον θανάτου H. Gr. ii. 3. 12. Ἀνθρώπων καταψηφισθέντων θανάτου ἢ φυγῆς Pl. Rep. 558 a. Ὥστ' ἔνοχοι δεσμοῦ γεγόνασι Dem. 1229. 11. — In this construction (which is rare except with θανάτου), the *punishment* appears to be regarded either as the *desert* of the crime, or as the *end in view* (§ 372) in judicial procedings.

3. *Genitive of Sensible and Mental Object.*

§ **375.** The object of sensation, thought, or emotion may be regarded as its *exciting cause*, and, in this view, may be put in the Genitive. Hence,

RULE XIII. Words of SENSATION, and of MENTAL STATE or ACTION govern the Genitive; as,

α. OF SENSATION. Σίτου ἐγεύσαντο, *tasted of food*, iii. 1. 3. Γεῦσαι τῆς θύρας, 'have a smack of,' *i. e.* 'try,' *or* 'knock at,' Ar. Ran. 462. Τοὺς παῖδας . . γευστέον αἵματος, 'give a taste of,' Pl. Rep. 537 a. Οἴνου . . ὀσφραίνεσθαι, *to catch the scent of wine*, v. 8. 3. Θορύβου ἤκουσε διὰ τῶν τάξεων ἰόντος, 'heard,' i. 8. 16. Τοῦ δὲ πάντων ἡδίστου ἀκούσματος, ἐπαίνου σεαυτῆς, ἀνήκοος εἶ Mem. ii. 1. 31. Οὐκ ἀκροώμενοι δὲ τοῦ ᾄδοντος Cyr. i. 3. 10. Κλύων σάλπιγγος Soph. Aj. 290. Οὐδεὶς δὲ πώποτε Σωκράτους οὐδὲν ἀσεβὲς οὐδὲ ἀνόσιον οὔτε πράττοντος εἶδεν, οὔτε λέγοντος ἤκουσεν Mem. i. 1. 11.

β. Of Perception, Knowledge, Reflection, Experience, and Habit Τῆς . . ἐπιβουλῆς οὐκ ᾐσθάνετο, *he did not perceive the plot*, i. 1. 8. Ὅσοι ἀλλήλων ξυνίεσαν Th. i. 3. Ἐνθυμοῦ δὲ τῶν εἰδότων Mem. iii. 6. 17 Ἐπιστήμων εἶναι τῶν ἀμφὶ τάξεις ii. 1. 7. Θέλω δ' ἄϊδρις μᾶλλον ἢ σοφὸς κακῶν εἶναι Æsch. Sup. 453. Ἰδιώτης . . τούτου τοῦ ἔργου, 'unskilled in,' Œc. 3. 9. Τῆς ἀρετῆς . . οὐδένα δεῖ ἰδιωτεύειν Pl. Prot. 326 e. Κύρου . . ἐν πείρᾳ γενέσθαι, *to have been well acquainted with Cyrus* [in the knowledge of Cyrus by proof], i. 9. 1. Πειρώμενοι ταύτης τῆς τάξεως, 'making trial of,' iii. 2. 38. Τῶν τειχῶν ἡμῶν πειρᾶν, 'attempt,' Th. vii. 12. Ἔμπειροι γὰρ ἦσαν τῆς Παφλαγονίας v. 6. 1. Ἄπειροι ὄντες αὐτῶν iii. 2. 16. Τῶν ἐμπείρως αὐτοῦ ἐχόντων ii. 6. 1. Ξένως ἔχω τῆς ἐνθάδε λέξεως Pl. Apol. 17 d. Οὐ τρίβων ὢν ἱππικῆς Ar. Vesp. 1429. Ἠθάς εἰμί πως τῶν τῆσδε μύθων Soph. El. 372. Ἀήθεις τοῦ κατακούειν Dem. 15. 27.

§ 376. γ. Of Memory. Τούτων οὐδεὶς μέμνηται, *these things no one remembers*, v. 8. 25. Οὐδενὸς ἔτι τούτων ἐμέμνητο, 'made mention of,' vii. 5. 8. Τῆς ἀρχῆς μνημονεύομεν Isocr. 12 c. Τούτου δὲ αὐτοὺς ὑπομιμνήσκετε Cyr. iii. 3. 37. Μή μ' ἀναμνήσῃς κακῶν Eur. Alc. 1045. Βίου δὲ τοῦ παρόντος οὐ μνείαν ἔχεις; Soph. El. 392. Τῶν πάροιθε μὲν λόγων λαθώμεθ' ἄμφω, 'forget,' Eur. Hipp. 288. Ὕπνον τε, λήθην τῶν καθ' ἡμέραν κακῶν Eur. Bacch. 282.

δ. Of Care. Κήδεσθαι Σεύθου, *to care for Seuthes*, vii. 5. 5. Τούτου σοι δεῖ μέλειν, *of this there must be to you a care*, i. e. *you must take care of this*, Cyr. i. 6. 16. Τῶν παρ' ἑαυτῷ δὲ βαρβάρων ἐπεμελεῖτο i. 1. 5. Ἀμελεῖν ἡμῶν αὐτῶν, 'to be careless of,' 'to neglect,' i. 3. 11. Ἐπιμελὴς ἀγαθῶν, ἀμελὴς κακῶν Pl. Conv. 197 d. Ἡ τῆς ὑγιείας ἐπιμέλεια Cyr. i. 6. 16. Μὴ μεταμέλειν σοι τῆς ἐμῆς δωρεᾶς, 'repent of,' Cyr. viii. 3. 32. Εἰ νομίζοιμι θεοὺς ἀνθρώπων τι φροντίζειν, οὐκ ἂν ἀμελοίην αὐτῶν Mem. i. 4. 11. Φυλασσομένους τῶν νεῶν Th. iv. 11. Ὅπως αὐτῶν ἀνακῶς ἕξουσιν Id. viii. 102.

ε. Of Desire. Ἐρῶντες τούτου, *desiring this*, iii. 1. 29. Εἴ τις δὲ χρημάτων ἐπιθυμεῖ, 'desires' [sets his mind upon; cf. § 373. 2], iii. 2. 39. Γλιχόμενος τοῦ ζῆν, *eager for life*, or *clinging to life* (§ 370. N.), Pl. Phædo, 117 a. Πεινήσας χρημάτων, *having hungered for wealth*, Cyr. viii. 3. 39. Πόλις ἐλευθερίας διψήσασα Pl. Rep. 562 c. Κιττῶντες τῆς εἰρήνης Ar. Pax, 497.

ζ. Of Various Emotion. Ἄγαμαι λήματος, *I admire the spirit*, Eur. Rhes. 244. Οὓς οὐκ ἂν ἀνασχέσθαι αὐτοῦ βασιλεύοντος, *who would not endure him as their king*, ii. 2. 1. Ὧν ἐγώ σοι οὐ φθονήσω, *which I shall not grudge to you*, Cyr. viii. 4. 16. Αἰσχρὸν στέγης γε φθονῆσαι, *it is mean to grudge him our roof*, i. e. *to refuse him admission*, Symp. 1. 12. Μηδέ μοι φθονήσῃς εὐγμάτων, 'deny,' or 'reject,' Æsch. Pr. 583. Ἀλλ' οὐ μεγαίρω τοῦδέ σοι δωρήματος Ib. 626.

§ 377. Remarks. 1. The idea of *hearing* passes, by an easy transition, into that of *obedience* (obēdio, *to give ear to, to listen to, to obey*, from ob and audio, *to hear*). Hence, *words of obedience* govern the Gen. (cf. § 405. *n*); as, Τούτους . . βασιλέως οὐκ ἀκούειν, *that these did not obey* [or *were not subject to*] *the king*, iii. 5. 16. Οἱ δὲ Καρδοῦχοι οὔτε καλούντων ὑπήκουον, 'regarded their invitations [listened to them calling],' iv. 1. 9. Ὑπήκοοι τῶν Μοσσυνοίκων, *subject to the Mossynœci*. Κατήκοοί τε ἦσαν τῶν νόμων Pl. Criti. 120 e. Ἀνηκουστεῖν δὲ τῶν πατρὸς λόγων οἷόν τε πῶς; Æsch. Prom. 40. Σφῶν πείθεσθαι Th. vii. 73. Πῶς χρὴ καλοῦντος ἀπειθεῖν Cyr. iv. 5. 19.

2. Verbs of *sight* commonly govern the Acc.; and many verbs which are followed by the Gen. according to this rule sometimes or often take the Acc. (especially of a neuter adjective); as, Εἴδομεν τοὺς πολεμίους vi. 5. 10. Αἰσθάνονται ἕκαστα Mem. i. 4. 5. See §§ 424. 2, 432. 2.

4. *Genitive of Time and Place.*

§ **378.** The *time* and *place* in which any thing is done may be regarded as *essential conditions* of the action, or as *coöperating* to produce it. Hence,

RULE XIV. The TIME and PLACE *IN WHICH* are put in the Genitive (cf. §§ 420, 439); as,

1. TIME. Ὤιχετο τῆς νυκτός, *he went in the night*, vii. 2. 17. Ταῦτα μὲν τῆς ἡμέρας ἐγένετο, 'in the day,' vii. 4. 14. Τῆς δείλης δὲ ἥκειν, 'in the evening,' vii. 2. 16. Ὥστε τῆς ἡμέρας ὅλης διῆλθον .., ἀλλὰ δείλης ἀφίκοντο iii. 3. 11. Εἴτε νυκτὸς δέοι τι, εἴτε καὶ ἡμέρας, 'whether by night or by day,' iii. 1. 40. Βασιλεὺς οὐ μαχεῖται δέκα ἡμερῶν, 'within ten days,' i. 7. 18. Ὅτι οὔπω δὴ πολλοῦ χρόνου .. ἐπιτύχοι, 'now for a long time,' i. 9. 25. Ἐξιόντες δ' ἑκάστης ἡμέρας, 'every day,' vi. 6. 1. Πολλάκις τῆς ἡμέρας, *many times a day*, Ar. Eq. 250. Ποιεῖ δὲ τοῦτο πολλάκις τοῦ μηνός Cyr. i. 2. 9. Τρία ἡμιδαρεικὰ τοῦ μηνός, *three half-darics a month*, i. 3. 21. Τοῦ δ' αὐτοῦ θέρους Th. ii. 28, 79, 80. Τοῦ δ' ἐπιγιγνομένου χειμῶνος Ib. v. 13, 36, 51, 56, 116. Ἐξ ἐτῶν ἄλουτος Ar. Lys. 280. Οὔτε τις ξένος ἀφῖκται χρόνου συχνοῦ Pl. Phædo, 57 a. Μέτεισιν .. οὐ μακροῦ χρόνου Soph. El. 477. Οὐκέτι τοῦ λοιποῦ [sc. χρόνου] πάσχοιμεν ἂν κακῶς Dem. 44. 12.

§ **379.** 2. PLACE. Αὐτοῦ [sc. τόπου] μείναντες, *remaining in that place*, i. 10. 17. Τόνδ' εἰσεδέξω τειχέων, 'within the walls,' Eur. Ph. 451. Ἐρκέων .. ἐγκεκλῃμένους Soph. Aj. 1274. Κατέκλεισαν .. Μακεδονίας Ἀθηναῖοι Περδίκκαν Th. v. 83. Τῆς δὲ Ἰωνίας καὶ ἄλλοθι πολλαχοῦ αἰσχρὸν νενόμισται Pl. Conv. 182 b. Μήτ' ἐμβατεύειν πατρίδος Soph. Œd. T. 825. Γῆς δὲ μὴ 'μβαίνῃς ὅρων Id. Œd. C. 400. Πεδίων ἐπινίσσεται Ib. 689. Ἐσχάτης δ' ὁρῶ πυρᾶς νεωρῆ βόστρυχον Soph. El. 900. Ἑστίας μεσομφάλου ἕστηκεν ἤδη μῆλα Æsch. Ag. 1056. Λαιᾶς δὲ χειρὸς οἱ σιδηροτέκτονες οἰκοῦσι Χάλυβες Id. Pr. 714. ΚΥΚΛ. Ποτέρας τῆς χερός; ΧΟΡ. Ἐν δεξιᾷ σου Eur. Cycl. 681.

REMARKS. α. This use of the Gen., to denote the *place where*, occurs very rarely in prose, except in those adverbs of place which are properly genitives (§ 320. 1); as, οὗ [sc. τόπου], *in which place, where*, αὐτοῦ, *there*, ὁμοῦ, *in the same place*, οὐδαμοῦ, *nowhere*, &c. Cf. § 421. β.

β. In Epic poetry, this Gen. is sometimes employed to denote the *place upon or over which* any thing moves; as, Ἔρχονται πεδίοιο, *they advance upon the plain*, B. 801. Ἔκαμον πολέος πεδίοιο θέουσαι Δ. 244. Ἑλκέμεναι νειοῖο βαθείης πηκτὸν ἄροτρον K. 353.

γ. The ideas of *place* and *time* are combined in expressions like those which follow, relating to *journeying* (Fr. journée, *a day's-march*, from Lat. diurnus, from dies, *day*); Ἑπτακαίδεκα γὰρ σταθμῶν τῶν ἐγγυτάτω οὐδὲν εἴχομεν λαμβάνειν, 'during the last seventeen day's-marches,' ii. 2. 11. Ἡμερεύοντας .. μακρᾶς κελεύθου Æsch. Cho. 710.

δ. In the phrase μιᾶς χειρός, in the following passage, the idea of *time* is combined with that of *action*; Ἐξὸν μιᾶς μοι χειρὸς εὖ θέσθαι τάδε, 'at a single stroke,' 'once for all,' Eur. Herc. 938.

§ **380.** III. That which produces any thing, as its ACTIVE or EFFICIENT CAUSE; or, in other words, that *by* which, as its *author*, *agent*, or *giver*, any thing is *made*, *written*, *said*, *done*, *bestowed*, &c., or *from* which any thing is *obtained*, *heard learned*, *inquired*, *requested*, *demanded*, &c.

To this division, which must obviously refer chiefly to *persons*, belongs the following rule, which will of course be understood as applying only to *adjuncts*.

Genitive Active.

RULE XV. The AUTHOR, AGENT, and GIVER are put in the Genitive; as,

α. With Verbs of Obtaining, Hearing, Learning, Inquiring, Requesting, &c. Ταῦτα δέ σου τυχόντες, *and obtaining this of you*, vi. 6. 32. Ὧν δέ σου τυχεῖν ἐφίεμαι, ἄκουσον (§ 370) Soph. Phil. 1315. Ἀκούων Κύρου ἔξω ὄντα . . βασιλέα i. 8. 13. Τῶν καταλελειμμένων ἐπυνθάνοντο, ὅτι οἱ μὲν Θρᾷκες . . ᾤχοντο, 'learned by inquiry from,' vi. 3. 23. Καὶ ἐπυνθάνοντο οἱ Ἀρκάδες τῶν περὶ Ξενοφῶντα, τί τὰ πυρὰ κατασβέσειαν, 'inquired of,' Ib. 25. Μάθε δέ μου, ὦ παῖ, καὶ τάδε Cyr. i. 6. 44. Δέονται δέ σου καὶ τοῦτο vi. 6. 33. Ἐμοὶ χάρισαι ὧν ἂν σοῦ δεηθῶ (§ 357. N.) Cyr. v. 5. 35. Σοῦ γὰρ . . βραχύν τιν' αἰτεῖ μῦθον Soph. Œd. C. 1161.

§ **381.** β. With Passive Verbs and Verbals. Πληγεὶς θυγατρὸς τῆς ἐμῆς, *smitten by my daughter*, Eur. Or. 497. Φωτὸς ἠπατημένη Soph. Aj. 807. Τῶν φίλων νικώμενος Ib. 1353. Ποίας μερίμνης τοῦθ' ὑποστραφεὶς λέγεις; Soph. Œd. T. 728. Τοῦ κακοῦ πότμου φυτευθείς Id. Œd. C. 1323. Ἄθικτος ἡγητῆρος Ib. 1521. Γήρως ἄλυπα Ib. 1519. Κακῶν γὰρ δυσάλωτος οὐδείς Ib. 1722. Φίλων ἄκλαυτος Soph. Ant. 847. Κείνης διδακτά Id. El. 343. — This use of the Gen. is poetic, and is most frequent with the Participle.

γ. With Substantives. Ξενοφῶντος Κύρου Ἀνάβασις, *Xenophon's Expedition of Cyrus.* Οἱ μὲν νέοι τοῖς τῶν πρεσβυτέρων ἐπαίνοις χαίρουσιν, οἱ δὲ γεραίτεροι ταῖς τῶν νέων τιμαῖς ἀγάλλονται, *the young rejoice in the praises of their elders, and the old delight in the honors paid them by the young*, Mem. ii. 1. 33. Ἥρας ἀλατείαις, *wanderings caused by Juno*, Æsch. Pr. 900. Νότου ἢ Βορέα . . κύματα Soph. Tr. 113.

§ **382.** IV. That which CONSTITUTES any thing WHAT IT IS. To this head may be referred whatever serves to *complete the idea of a thing or prop-*

erty, by adding some *distinction* or *characteristic* Hence,

Genitive Constituent.

RULE XVI. AN ADJUNCT DEFINING A THING OR PROPERTY is put in the Genitive; as,

Τὸ Μένωνος στράτευμα, *the army of Meno*, i. 2. 21.

§ **383.** REMARKS. α. The THING OR PROPERTY DEFINED may be either *distinctly expressed by its appropriate word*, or may be *involved in another word;* as, βασιλεύς in βασιλεύω, σατράπης in σατραπεύω (§ 389). Cf. §§ 351, 362. δ, 391. δ, 394, 395. δ.

NOTE. In particular, adjectives in which a substantive is compounded with ἀ-*privative* (§ 325), have often a Gen. defining the substantive. See § 395.

§ **384.** β. A genitive *defining a substantive* is sometimes connected with it by an *intervening word*, which is usually a *substantive verb*. See, for examples, §§ 387, 390; cf. § 365. — This form of construction may be referred to *ellipsis;* thus, Ἦν [ἄνθρωπος] ἐτῶν ὡς τριάκοντα, *he was* [*a man*] *of about thirty years* (§ 387).

§ **385.** γ. A substantive governing the Gen. is often *understood*, particularly υἱός, *son*, οἶκος, *house*, and other words denoting *domestic relation* or *abode*. Thus, Γλοῦς ὁ Ταμώ, *Glus, the son of Tamos*, ii. 1. 3. Ὦ Διὸς [sc. θύγατερ] Ἄρτεμις Eur. Iph. A. 1570. Βυρσίνης τῆς Ἱππίου [sc. γυναικός] Ar. Eq. 449. Θύραζέ μ' ἐξενέγκατ' ἐς τοῦ Πιττάλου [sc. οἶκον], 'to Pittalus's [house],' Ar. Ach. 1222. Εἰς οὐδενὸς διδασκάλου πώποτε φοιτήσαντα Cyr. ii. 3. 9. Τῶν ἐν Ἀδμήτου κακῶν Eur. Alc. 761 (cf. Ἐν Ἀδμήτου δόμοις 68). Ἐν Ἅιδου Soph. Ant. 654 (cf. Εἰν Ἅιδου δόμοις 1241). Ἐν Ἀσκληπιοῦ [sc. ἱερῷ] Mem. iii. 13. 3. Εἰς Τροφωνίου [sc. ἄντρον] Ar. Nub. 508.

δ. The Gen. is often used in *periphrasis*, particularly with χρῆμα, *thing*, and, by the poets, with δέμας, *form*, *body*, κάρα, *head*, ὄνομα, *name*, and similar words. Thus, Δέμας Ἀγαμέμνονος = Ἀγαμέμνονα Eur. Hec. 723. Ὦ φίλτατον γυναικὸς Ἰοκάστης κάρα Soph. Œd. T. 950. Ὦ ποθεινὸν ὄνομ' ὁμιλίας ἐμῆς Eur. Or. 1082. See § 395. α.

ε. A substantive governing the Gen. is sometimes used by the poets instead of an *adjective;* as, Χρυσὸν . . ἐπῶν, *the gold of words*, for Ἔπη χρυσᾶ, *golden words*, Ar. Plut. 268. Ὦ μητρὸς ἐμῆς σέβας Æsch. Pr. 1091. Πολυνεικους βίαν Eur. Ph. 56.

§ **386.** An adjunct defining a THING either expresses a *property* of that thing, or points out *another thing related* to it. An adjunct defining a PROPERTY points out a *thing related* to that property. Hence the CONSTITUENT GENITIVE is either, 1. the *Genitive of Property*, or 2. the *Genitive of Relation.*

1. *Genitive of Property.*

§ **387.** The Genitive of property expresses *quality*, *dimension*, *age*, &c. Thus,

Ἦν ἐτῶν ὡς τριάκοντα, *he was about thirty years old* [of about thirty years], ii. 6. 20. Ποταμὸν ὄντα τὸ εὖρος πλέθρου i. 4. 9, *a river being* [*of*] *a plethrum in breadth* (cf. Ποταμὸν τὸ εὖρος πλεθριαῖον i. 5. 4, and see § 333. 6). [Τεῖχος] εὖρος εἴκοσι ποδῶν, ὕψος δὲ ἑκατόν· μῆκος δ' ἐλέγετο εἶναι εἴκοσι παρασαγγῶν ii. 4. 12. Ὁ δὲ τᾶς ἡσυχίας βίοτος, *but a life of quiet* [= βίοτος ἥσυχος, *a quiet life*], Eur. Bac. 388. Στολίδα . . τρυφᾶς [= τρυφεράν] Eur. Ph. 1491. Τοσόνδ' ἔχεις τόλμης πρόσωπον [= οὕτω τολμηρόν]; Soph. Œd. T. 533. Τὸ δὲ συμπνεῦσαι . . χρόνου πολλοῦ [ἐστι], καὶ παγχάλεπον Pl. Leg. 708 d. Ἔστιν ὁ πόλεμος οὐχ ὅπλων τοπλέον, ἀλλὰ δαπάνης Th. i. 83. Ὅσοι τῆς αὐτῆς γνώμης ἦσαν Ib. 113. Τοῦθ' ὁρῶ πολλοῦ πόνου Eur. Ph. 719.

NOTE. It is obvious from the examples above, that the *Gen. of property* performs the office of an *adjective*. Its use to express *quality*, in the strict sense of the term, is chiefly poetic.

2. *Genitive of Relation.*

§ **388.** The Genitive of relation, in its full extent, includes much which has been already adduced, under other and more specific heads. The relations which remain to be considered are, (a.) those of *domestic*, *social*, and *civil life*, (b.) those of *possession* and *ownership*; (c.) that of the *object of an action* to the *action* or *agent*; (d.) those of *time* and *place*; (e.) those of simple *reference*, of *explanation*, &c.

The Genitives expressing these relations may be termed, (a.) the *Gen. of social relation*, (b.) the *Gen. possessive*, (c.) the *Gen. objective*, (d.) the *Gen. of local* and *temporal relation*, (e.) the *Gen. of reference*, *of explanation*, *&c.*

§ **389.** a. GENITIVE OF SOCIAL RELATION.

Ὁ τῆς βασιλέως γυναικὸς ἀδελφός, *the brother of the king's wife*, ii. 3. 17. Τῶν Ὀδρυσῶν βασιλέα vii. 3. 16. Δούλους τούτων i. 9. 15. Ἧς αὐτὸν σατράπην ἐποίησε i. 1. 2. Βασιλεύων [= Βασιλεὺς ὢν § 383. α] αὐτῶν v. 6. 37. Τῷ σατραπεύοντι [= σατράπῃ ὄντι] τῆς χώρας iii. 4. 31. (See also § 350.) Γείτων . . τῆς Ἑλλάδος (cf. § 399) iii. 2. 4. Τῆς πόλεως ἐχθροῖς Ven. 13. 12. Τοὺς ἐκείνου ἐχθίστους, . . τοὺς Κύρου φίλους iii. 2. 5. Διὰ τῆς ἑαυτῶν πολεμίας χώρας, *through the country of their enemies*, iv. 7. 19.

REMARK. To this analogy may be referred the use of the Gen. for the Dat., with some *adjectives implying intimate connection*; as, Ὁ δὲ φήσας ποτὲ συγγενὴς τοῦ Κύρου εἶναι, *and he who once said that he was related to Cyrus*, or *a relative of Cyrus*, Cyr. v. 1. 24. Οὐδ' ἡ ξύνοικος τῶν κάτω θεῶν Δίκη Soph. Ant. 451. Λακεδαίμονος δὲ γαῖά τις ξυνώνυμος; Eur. Hel. 495. Βάκχον εὔιον, Μαινάδων ὁμόστολον Soph. Œd. T. 212. Τὸν Σωκράτους μὲν ὁμώνυμον Pl. Soph. 218 b. Γῆς ἰσόμοιρ' ἀήρ Soph. El. 87. Ἀκόλουθα ταῦτα πάντα ἀλλήλων Œc. 11. 12. Ὦ φέγγος ὕπνου διάδοχον Soph. Ph. 867. Ὁ κυβερνήτης τὸ τῆς νεὼς καὶ ναυτῶν ἀεὶ ξυμφέρον παραφυλάττων

Pl. Pol. 296 e. Τὰ πρόσφορα τῆς νῦν παρούσης συμφορᾶς Eur. Hel. 508 Cf. §§ 399, 400, 403. — It will be observed, that, in some of these examples the adjective may be regarded as used substantively, and that this construction is not confined to the names of persons.

b. GENITIVE POSSESSIVE.

§ 390. The Genitive possessive denotes that to which anything *belongs* as a *possession*, *power*, *right*, *duty*, *quality*, &c. Thus,

Τὰ Συεννέσιος βασίλεια, *the palace of Syennesis*, i. 2. 23. Ἦσαν αἱ Ἰωνικαὶ πόλεις Τισσαφέρνους, *the Ionian cities belonged to Tissaphernes*, i. 1. 6. Τῶν μὲν γὰρ νικώντων τὸ κατακαίνειν, τῶν δὲ ἡττωμένων τὸ ἀποθνήσκειν ἐστί, *for it is the part of victors to kill, but of the vanquished to die*, iii. 2. 39. Κρήνη ἡ Μίδου καλουμένη i. 2. 13. Αὐτοῦ γὰρ εἶναί φησιν, ἐπείπερ Κύρου ἦσαν ii. 5. 38. Τούτου τὸ εὖρος δύο πλέθρα i. 2. 5. Τῶν γὰρ νικώντων ἐστὶ καὶ τὰ ἑαυτῶν σώζειν, καὶ τὰ τῶν ἡττωμένων λαμβάνειν iii. 2. 39. Ἢν ὑμῶν αὐτῶν ἐθελήσητε γενέσθαι, 'your own men,' *i. e.* 'independent,' Dem. 42. 10. Τῆς πόλεως ὄντας, *true to the state*, Isocr. 185 b. Ὥστ' οὐ Κρέοντος προστάτου γεγράψομαι Soph. Œd. T. 411. Ἀλλ' ἐστὶ τοῦ λέγοντος, ἢν φόβους λέγῃ, 'at the mercy of the speaker,' Ib 917. Μηδ' ἃ μὴ ἔθιγες ποιοῦ σεαυτῆς, 'make yours,' Id. Ant. 546.

§ 391. REMARKS. *α.* The idea of possession is sometimes modified or strengthened by an adjective or adverb; as, Ἱερὸς ὁ χῶρος τῆς Ἀρτέμιδος, *the spot is sacred to Diana* [consecrated to be Diana's], v. 3. 13. Ἰδίων ἑαυτοῦ κτημάτων, *of his own acquisitions*, Pl. Menex. 247 b. Οἱ δὲ κίνδυνοι τῶν ἐφεστηκότων ἴδιοι Dem. 26. 11. Τὸ οἰκεῖον ἑκατέρου σημεῖον Pl. Theæt 193 c. Τὸν ἔρωτα τοῦτον πότερα κοινὸν οἴει εἶναι πάντων ἀνθρώπων; Pl. Conv. 205 a. Τῆς ἡμετέρας Μούσης ἐπιχώριον Ib. 189 b.

β. A *neuter adjective used substantively* takes the Gen. possessive, in connection with *verbs* of *praise*, *blame*, and *wonder*; as, Τοῦτο ἐπαινῶ Ἀγησιλάου, *I commend this in Agesilaus* [this characteristic of Agesilaus], Ages. 8. 4. Ὃ μέμφονται μάλιστα ἡμῶν Th. i. 84. Ἄλλα τέ σου πολλὰ ἄγαμαι Symp. 8. 12. Ἐθαύμασα αὐτοῦ πρῶτον μὲν τοῦτο Pl. Phædo, 89 a. Τοῦτο . . ἐν τοῖς κυσὶ κατόψει, ὃ καὶ ἄξιον θαυμάσαι τοῦ θηρίου Pl. Rep. 376 a.

γ. ELLIPSIS. The *possessor* is sometimes put in the case belonging to the *thing possessed*, with an ellipsis of the latter, particularly in *comparison*; as, Ἅρματα . . ὅμοια ἐκείνῳ [= τοῖς ἐκείνου ἅρμασι], *chariots similar to his* [*chariots*], Cyr. vi. 1. 50 (cf. [Ἅρματα] ὅμοια τοῖς Κύρου 2. 7). Ὁμοίαν ταῖς δούλαις εἶχε τὴν ἐσθῆτα Cyr. v. 1. 4. Ὡπλισμένοι . . τοῖς αὐτοῖς Κύρῳ ὅπλοις Cyr. vii. 1. 2. Ἔχομεν σώματα ἱκανώτερα τούτων, *we have bodies better able than theirs*, iii. 1. 23. Μηδ' ἐξισώσῃς τάσδε [= τὰ τῶνδε κακὰ] τοῖς ἐμοῖς κακοῖς Soph. Œd. T. 1507. Ἄρχοντες μέσον ἔχοντες τὸ αὐτῶν i. 8. 22 (cf. Βασιλεὺς δὴ τότε μέσον ἔχων τῆς αὐτοῦ στρατιᾶς 23).

δ. The verbs ὄζω, *to smell*, πνέω, *to breathe*, and προσβάλλω, *to emit*, may take a Gen. defining a noun implied in these verbs (§ 383. *α*) or understood with them; thus, Ὄζουσι πίττης, *they smell of pitch* [emit the smell of pitch], Ar. Ach. 190. Τῆς κεφαλῆς ὄζω μύρου (§ 355) Ar. Eccl. 524. Τῶν ἱματίων ὀζήσει δεξιότητος, 'there will be a smell of,' Ar. Vesp. 1058. Ὡς ἡδύ μοι προσέπνευσε χοιρείων κρεῶν Ar. Ran. 338. Πόθεν βροτοῦ με προσέβαλε; Ar. Pax, 180.

ε. It will be observed, that the *Genitive possessive* is the exact converse of the *Genitive of property* (§ 387), the one denoting *that which possesses,* and the other, *that which is possessed.*

c. GENITIVE OBJECTIVE.

§ **392.** The object of an action, *regarded as such*, is put in the *Accusative* or *Dative* (§ 339). But if the action, instead of being predicated by a verb, is merely *represented as a thing or property* (or *as implied in a thing or property*), by a *noun, adjective*, or *adverb*, then its object is usually regarded simply as something *defining that thing or property*, and is consequently put in the *Genitive*. Thus,

1. GENITIVE OF THE DIRECT OBJECT. Ὁ φρούραρχος τὰς φυλακὰς ἐξετάζει, *the commander of a garrison reviews his troops,* Œc. 9. 15; but, Κῦρος ἐξέτασιν ποιεῖται τῶν Ἑλλήνων, *Cyrus makes a review of the Greeks,* i. 7. 1; Τῶν τοιούτων ἔργων ἐξεταστικόν, *fitted to review such matters,* Mem. i. 1. 7. Τὸν ὄλεθρον τῶν συστρατιωτῶν i. 2. 26. Ἰὼ γάμοι .. ὀλέθριοι φίλων Æsch. Ag. 1156 (cf. Σπόγγος ὤλεσεν γραφήν 1329). Τῇ ὑπερβολῇ τοῦ ὄρους iv. 4. 18 (cf. Ὑπερέβαλλον τὰ ὄρη 20). Καρδίας δηκτήρια Eur. Hec. 235 (cf. Δάκνει φρένα Id. Heracl. 483). Διδασκαλικὸν .. σοφίας Pl. Euthyph. 3 c. Μαθητὰς ἰατρικῆς Pl. Rep. 599 c. Ἄλλους τοιούτων τινῶν μαθητικούς Ib. 475 e. Ἀρτιμαθὴς κακῶν Eur. Hec. 686. Ὀψιμαθῆ .. τῶν πλεονεξιῶν Cyr. i. 6. 35. Τοξικῆς τε καὶ ἀκοντίσεως φιλομαθέστατον i. 9. 5 (cf. Σωφροσύνην καταμάθοι 3). Λάθρα δὲ τῶν στρατιωτῶν, *but without the knowledge of the soldiers,* i. 3. 8 (cf. Λαθεῖν αὐτὸν ἀπελθών 17). Κρύφα τῶν Ἀθηναίων Th. i. 101. Ἀπαθῆ κακῶν vii. 7. 33. Ἀπαιδεύτους μουσικῆς Cyr. iii. 3. 55.

2. GENITIVE OF THE INDIRECT OBJECT. Εὔχεσθαι τοῖς .. θεοῖς, *to pray to the gods,* iv. 3. 13; but, Θεῶν εὐχάς, *prayers to the gods,* Pl. Phædr. 244 e. Τὰ τῆς θεοῦ θύματα Eur. Iph. T. 329 (cf. Θύειν θεᾷ 1035). Τὴν τῶν κρεισσόνων δουλείαν Th. i. 8 (cf. Ταῖς ἡδοναῖς δουλεύων Mem. i. 5. 5). Ἐπιβουλευτοῦ στρατοῦ, *of a plotter against the host,* Soph. Aj. 726 (cf. Ἐπιβουλεύοι αὐτῷ i. 1. 3). Συγγνώμων τῶν ἀνθρωπίνων ἁμαρτημάτων Cyr. vi. 1. 37 (cf. Ἐγώ σοι συνεγίγνωσκον Ib. vii. 5. 50).

§ **393.** REMARKS. α. In like manner, the *Gen.* is employed with *nouns*, to denote relations, which, with the corresponding *adjectives*, are denoted by the *Dat.*; as, Τῆς τῶν Ἑλλήνων εὐνοίας, *from good-will to the Greeks,* iv. 7. 20 (cf. Εὔνους δέ σοι ὤν vii. 3. 20). Τίς δῆτ' ἂν ἀνδρὸς εὐμένειαν ἐκβάλοι τοιοῦδε Soph. Œd. C. 631 (cf. Τὸν εὐμενῆ πόλει Id. Ant. 212).

β. The Gen. is sometimes employed, in like manner, for a preposition with its case; as, Ἐν ἀποβάσει τῆς γῆς, *in a descent upon the land,* Th. i. 108 (cf. Ἀπέβη ἐς τὴν γῆν H. Gr. i. 1. 18).

γ. To the *Gen. of the direct object* may be referred the Gen. with αἴτιος and its derivatives; as, Τὸ αἴτιον τῆς σπουδῆς, *the cause of the haste* [that which was causative of, &c.], iv. 1. 17. Τούτων οὐ σὺ αἰτία, *you are not responsible for* [the cause of] *these things,* Œc. 8. 2. Οἱ τοῦ πολέμου αἰτιώτατοι, *the principal authors of the war,* H. Gr. iv. 4. 2. Τούτου Σωκράτην ὁ κατήγορος αἰτιᾶται, *for this the accuser blames Socrates* [makes S. the author of this], Mem. i. 2. 26. See § 374.

δ. The Gen. in its more active uses (when employed to denote *agent*, *possessor*, &c.) has received the special designation of the *Gen. subjective*, in distinction from the Gen. objective. The following passages contain examples of both kinds: Τὴν Πέλοπος μὲν ἁπάσης Πελοποννήσου κατάληψιν, *Pelops's seizure of all Peloponnesus*, Isocr. 249 a. Τὰς τῶν οἰκείων προπηλακίσεις τοῦ γήρως Pl. Rep. 329 b. Τὴν ἐκείνων μέλλησιν τῶν ἐς ἡμᾶς δεινῶν Th. iii. 12. Adjectives taking the place of the Gen. are, in like manner, used both *subjectively* and *objectively*. See § 503.

d. GENITIVE OF LOCAL AND TEMPORAL RELATION.

§ **394.** The Genitive is extensively employed in defining local and temporal relation, particularly with *adverbs of place* and *time*, and with words *derived* from them. Thus,

Ἄγχι γῆς, *near the land*, Soph. Œd. C. 399. Ἀντίον τῆς Λαμψάκου H. Gr. ii. 1. 21. Τούτου ἐναντίον vii. 6. 23. Ἀντιπέρας τῶν πλαγίων Cyr. vii. 1. 7. Ἄνω τῶν ἱππέων iv. 3. 3. Ἄχρι τοῦ μὴ πεινῆν Symp. 1. 37. Ἐγγὺς παραδείσου ii. 4. 14. Ἐγγὺς μυρίων, *nearly ten thousand*, v. 7. 9. Εἴσω τῶν ὁρίων i. 2. 21. Ἐκτὸς τοῦ τείχους Mag. Eq. 7. 4. Ἐκτὸς ὀλίγων, *except a few* (§ 349), H. Gr. i. 6. 35. Σκηνῆς ἔνδον Soph. Aj. 218. Ἔνερθε γῆς Æsch. Pers. 229. Ἔνθεν καὶ ἔνθεν σφῶν iv. 3. 28. Ποταμῶν ἐντός ii. 1. 11. Τοῦ Πλούτωνος ἑξῆς Ar. Ran. 765. Ἔξω τῶν πυλῶν i. 4. 5. Κεῦθει κάτω δὴ γῆς Soph. Œd. T. 968. Κύκλῳ τοῦ στρατοπέδου Cyr. iv. 5. 5. Τὸ μέσον τῶν τειχῶν, *the distance between the walls*, i. 4. 4. Ἐν μέσῳ ἡμῶν καὶ βασιλέως ii. 2. 3. Μεσοῦσι . . τῆς πορείας Pl. Pol. 265 b. Μεταξὺ τοῦ ποταμοῦ καὶ τῆς τάφρου i. 7. 15. Μέχρι τοῦ Μηδίας τείχους Ib. Ὄπισθεν ἑαυτῶν i. 7. 9. Δούλης ποδῶν πάροιθεν Eur. Hec. 48. Βωμοῦ πέλας Æsch. Ag. 210. Πλησίον εἶναι τοῦ τείχους vii. 1. 39. Ἐπλησίαζον . . τῶν ἄκρων Cyr. iii. 2. 8. Πέραν τοῦ ποταμοῦ ii. 4. 28. Πρόσθεν τῶν ὅπλων iii. 1. 33. Ὕπερθε βωμοῦ Æsch. Ag. 232. — It will be observed, that, in some of these examples, the word governing the Gen. is used in a secondary sense. For the Dat. after some of these words, see §§ 399, 405.

e. GENITIVE OF REFERENCE, EXPLANATION, EMPHASIS, &c.

§ **395.** The CONSTITUENT GENITIVE has likewise other uses, of which the principal are those of *simple reference*, of *explanation*, and of *emphatic repetition*.

NOTE. In some of these uses, the Gen. rather denotes a relation between *two expressions for the same thing*, than between *two different things*. In such cases, an *appositive* might be substituted for it (§ 333. 6); and, indeed, in some of the examples which follow (particularly with the compounds of ἀ-*privative*, § 383. N.), we might regard the Gen. as in apposition with a substantive implied.

α. With SUBSTANTIVES. Πρόφασις . . τοῦ ἀθροίζειν, *pretext for assembling*, i. 1. 7. Τριῶν μηνῶν μισθόν, *three months' pay*, i. 1. 10. Θανάτου τέλος, *the end* [*sc.* of life], *which is found in death*, or simply, *death*, Æsch. Sept. 906. Θανάτου τελευτάν Eur. Med. 152 (cf. Βίου τελευτή Soph. Œd. C. 1473). Τέρμα τῆς σωτηρίας Soph. Œd. C. 725. Εἰ πέρας μηδὲν ἔσται σφίσι τοῦ ἀπαλλαγῆναι τοῦ κινδύνου Th. vii. 42. Μέγα . . χρῆμα . . τῆς ἐμπίδος, *a monster of a gnat* (§ 385. δ), Ar. Lys. 1031. Συὸς μέγιστον χρῆμα Soph. Fr. 357 (cf. Καταβάλλει τὴν ἔλαφον, καλόν τι χρῆμα καὶ μέγα Cyr. i. 4. 8). Τὸ χρῆμα τῶν νυκτῶν Ar. Nub. 2. Σφενδονητῶν πάμπολύ τι χρῆμα Cyr. ii. 1. 5. Διὰ τὴν τῆς ἀδελφῆς ἀτιμίαν τῆς κανηφορίας, *on account of his sister's being denied the honor of bearing the sacred basket*, Pl. Hipparch. 229 c. See also § 333. 6.

β. With ADJECTIVES. Ἄπαις δέ εἰμι ἀῤῥένων παίδων, *and I am childless as to male children*, Cyr. iv. 6. 2. Ὦ τέκεα πατρὸς ἀπάτορα Eur. Herc. 114. Ἄφιλος φίλων Id. Hel. 524. Ἄπεπλος φαρέων λευκῶν Id. Ph. 324. Πληγῶν ἄθῳον Ar. Nub. 1413. Χρημάτων . . ἀδωρότατος Th. ii. 65. Ἄσκευον . . ἀσπίδων Soph. El. 36. Ἀνάριθμος ὧδε θρήνων Ib. 232. Ἄφωνοι τῆσδε τῆς ἀρᾶς Id. Œd. C. 865. Ἐν ἀσφαλεῖ εἰσι τοῦ μηδὲν παθεῖν Cyr. iii. 3. 31. Θρασὺς εἶ πολλοῦ [sc. θράσους], *you are very audacious* [bold with much boldness], Ar. Nub. 915. Θυγάτηρ . . γάμου ἤδη ὡραία Cyr. iv. 6. 9. Τέλειον εἶναι τῆς . . ἀρετῆς Pl. Leg. 643 d. Τυφλὸς δὲ τῶν ἄλλων ἁπάντων Symp. 4. 12.

γ. With ADVERBS. Ἐξέσται ἡμῖν, ἐκείνου ἕνεκα, *it will be permitted us, as far as respects him*, Cyr. iii. 2. 30. Ὅμοιοι τοῖς τυφλοῖς ἂν ἦμεν, ἕνεκά γε τῶν ἡμετέρων ὀφθαλμῶν, 'for all the good our eyes would do us,' Mem. iv. 3. 3. Καλῶς παράπλου κεῖται, *it is well situated in regard to the voyage*, Th. i. 36. Τοῦ πρὸς Ἀθηναίους πολέμου καλῶς αὐτοῖς ἐδόκει ἡ πόλις καθίστασθαι Id. iii. 92. Τῆς τε ἐπὶ Θρᾴκης παρόδου χρησίμως ἕξειν Ib. (See also § 363. β.) Ὑμᾶς οἴονται ἐμποδὼν γενέσθαι τοῦ ἄρξαι αὐτοὺς τῶν Ἑλλήνων H. Gr. vi. 5. 38.

δ. With VERBS. Τῆς ἐπωβελίας . . κινδυνεύοντα [= ἐν κινδύνῳ ὄντα], *being in danger of the fine for false accusation*, Dem. 835. 14. Τάφου . . τὸν μὲν προτίσας, τὸν δ' ἀτιμάσας, *having bestowed upon the one, and denied to the other, the honor of sepulture* (τάφου defining τιμήν implied in προτίσας and ἀτιμάσας, § 383. α), Soph. Ant. 21.

§ 396. GENERAL REMARK. Great care is requisite in distinguishing the various uses of the Genitive, inasmuch as,

1.) The Gen. may have different uses in connection with the same word; as, with ἀκούω and κλύω (§§ 356, 375, 380), with δέομαι (§§ 357. N., 380), with πλεονεκτέω (§§ 351, 367), with περιττός (§§ 349, 362. ζ), with πόῤῥω and πρόσω (§§ 347, 363). — The use of the Gen. with substantives is especially various.

2.) A word may have two or more adjuncts in the Gen. expressing different relations; as, Ἀνάβασις (§ 381. γ), ὄζω (§ 391. δ), τυγχάνω and δέομαι (§ 380. α). See § 393. δ.

C. THE DATIVE OBJECTIVE.

§ 397. THAT TOWARDS WHICH ANY THING TENDS (§ 339) may be resolved into, I. That towards which any thing tends, as an OBJECT OF APPROACH; and II. That towards which any thing tends, as an OBJECT OF INFLUENCE. Hence the Dative objective is either, (I.) the DATIVE OF APPROACH, or (II.) the DATIVE OF INFLUENCE; and we have the following general rule: THE OBJECT OF APPROACH AND OF INFLUENCE IS PUT IN THE

DATIVE; Or, in other words, since neither approach nor influence are regarded as *direct action*, AN INDIRECT OBJECT IS PUT IN THE DATIVE.

NOTES. *α.* The *Dat. of approach* is commonly expressed in Eng. by the preposition *to*, and the *Dat. of influence*, by the prepositions *to* and *for*.

β. The DATIVE OBJECTIVE is the converse of the GENITIVE; the *Dat. of approach* contrasting with the *Gen. of departure*, and the *Dat. of influence* with the *Gen. of cause*. See §§ 338, 339, 345.

(I.) DATIVE OF APPROACH.

§ 398. Approach, like its opposite, *departure* (§ 346), may be either in *place* or in *character*. Hence,

RULE XVII. Words of NEARNESS and LIKENESS govern the Dative.

NOTES. *α.* Words of *likeness* are related to those of *nearness*, in the same manner as words of *distinction* are related to those of *separation* (§ 346. N.).

β. For the *Genitive* after some words of *nearness* and *likeness*, see §§ 389, 394.

1. *Dative of Nearness.*

§ 399. Words of nearness may imply either *being near*, *coming near*, or *bringing near*; and to this class may be referred words of *union* and *mixture*, of *companionship* and *intercourse*, of *meeting* and *following*, of *sending to* and *bringing to*, &c. Thus,

Πελάσαι .. τῇ εἰσόδῳ, *to approach the entrance*, iv. 2. 3. Οἴνῳ κεράσας αὐτήν, *having mixed it with wine*, i. 2. 13. Ἕψονται ὑμῖν, *they will follow you*, iii. 1. 36. Πέμπων αὐτῷ ἄγγελον, *sending a messenger to him*, i. 3. 8. Ἐν τῷ πλησιαιτάτῳ δίφρῳ Σεύθῃ καθήμενος vii. 3. 29. Σοὶ πέλας θρόνους ἔχειν Æsch. Sup. 208. Ἐγγὺς ἡμῖν γενέσθαι Cyr. iii. 2. 8. Σκόπει δή, ἔφη, τὰ ἑξῆς ἐκείνοις Pl. Phædo, 100 c. (Cf. § 394.) Γείτων οἰκῶ τῇ Ἑλλάδι ii. 3. 18 (cf. § 389). Ἐπορεύετο .. ἅμα Τισσαφέρνει ii. 4. 9. Ἅμα τῇ ἐπιούσῃ ἡμέρᾳ ἥκοντες, 'at daybreak,' i. 7. 2. Ὁμοῦ .. τοῖς Ἕλλησι στρατοπεδευσάμενοι H. Gr. iii. 2. 5. Ἀναμεμιγμένοι τοῖς Ἕλλησι iv. 8. 8. Εἰ ὁμιλησαίτην ἐκείνῳ Mem. i. 2. 15. Σωκράτει ὁμιλητὰ γενομένω Ib 12 (cf. Ib. 48, and § 389). Ἀριαίῳ .. οἰκειότατος ii. 6. 28. Κοινωνὸ ἡμῖν τοῦ πολιχνίου (§ 367) Pl. Rep. 370 d. Κοινωνεῖν ἀλλήλοις Pl. Leg. 844 c. Ἔχει κοινωνίαν ἀλλήλοις ἡ τῶν γενῶν φύσις Pl. Soph. 257 a. Ἀπαντᾷ τῷ Ξενοφῶντι Εὐκλείδης vii. 8. 1. Οὔτε τότε Κύρῳ ἰέναι ἤθελε i. 2. 26. Αὐτῷ ἀφίκοντο Ib. 4. Ἀμεινοκλῆς Σαμίοις ἦλθε Th. i. 13. Ἥκει ἡμῖν ἀνὴρ ἄριστος Cyr. vi. 3. 15. Ἧκέ μοι γένει, *it belonged* [came] *to me by birth*, Soph. Œd. C. 738. Τὰ ἐμοὶ προσήκοντα Cyr. v. 1. 15 (see § 364). Πίπτοντος πέδῳ Soph. El. 747. Τὰ τούτοις ἀκόλουθα πάσχοντος Pl. Tim. 88 d (cf. § 389. R.). Ἀκολουθῶν τῇ φύσει Pl. Leg. 836 c. Τῷ ἡμερινῷ ἀγγέλῳ τὸν νυκτερινὸν διαδέχεσθαι Cyr. viii. 6. 18. Διάδοχος

Κλεάνδρῳ vii. 2. 5 (cf. § 389. R.). Ἡ διαδοχὴ τῇ πρόσθεν φυλακῇ Cyr. i. 4. 17. Δῶρα ἄγοντες αὐτῷ vii. 3. 16. Αὐτῷ τὸ κέρας ὀρέξαι Ib. 29.

REMARKS. α. *Traffic* is a species of intercourse; hence, Πόσου πρίωμαί σοι τὰ χοιρίδια; *How can I trade with you for your pigs?* Ar. Ach. 812 (§ 374). Ὠνήσομαί σοι, *I will buy of you*, Ib. 815. Ἐγὼ πρίωμαι τῷδε; Ar. Ran. 1229.

β. A substantive is sometimes repeated in the Dat., with an ellipsis, to express *succession;* as, Ἀλλὰ φόνῳ φόνος Οἰδιπόδα δόμον ὤλεσεν, *but slaughter upon slaughter* [slaughter following slaughter] *has destroyed the house of Œdipus,* Eur. Ph. 1496. Μὴ τίκτειν σ' ἄταν ἄταις Soph. El. 235.

2. *Dative of Likeness.*

§ **400.** Words of likeness include those of *resemblance, assimilation, comparison, identity, equality,* &c. Thus,

Ὅμοιοι τοῖς ἄλλοις, *like the rest,* vi. 6. 16. Ἐμὲ δὲ θεῷ μὲν οὐκ εἴκασεν, *but me he did not liken to a god,* Apol. 15. Τὸ ἀληθὲς ἐνόμιζε τὸ αὐτὸ τῷ ἠλιθίῳ εἶναι, *he thought sincerity to be the same with folly,* ii. 6. 22. Ἴσους . . τούτοις ἀριθμόν, *equal to these in number,* Mag. Eq. ii. 3. Ὁμοίως τοῖς ἄλλοις Mem. iv. 7. 8. Ὁμοιοῦν ἑαυτὸν ἄλλῳ Pl. Rep. 393 c. Ὁμοίωσις θεῷ Pl. Theæt. 176 b. Τὸ τῷ καλῷ ἀνόμοιον Mem. iii. 8. 4. Ὁμογνωμονῶ σοι καὶ τοῦτο Mem. iv. 3. 10. Ὁμόδρομος ἡλίῳ Pl. Epin. 987 b. Σάκαι γε μὴν ὅμοροι ἡμῖν Cyr. v. 2. 25. Ἀλλήλοις ὁμοσκηνοῦντες Ib. ii. 1. 25. Κλεάρχῳ καὶ ὁμοτράπεζος γενόμενος iii. 2. 4. Ὁμώνυμος ἐμοί Pl. Rep. 330 b (cf. § 389. R.). Παραδείγματα ὁμοιοπαθῆ τοῖς πονηροῖς Ib. 409 b. Προσῳδὸς ἡ τύχη τῶμῷ πάθει Eur. Ion, 359. Σφηξὶν ἐμφερεστάτους Ar. Vesp. 1102. Τὰ δὲ κρέα . . ἦν παραπλήσια τοῖς ἐλαφείοις i. 5. 2. Ἀλλὰ φιλοσόφῳ μὲν ἔοικας ii. 1. 13. Ποταμοῦ ῥοῇ ἀπεικάζων τὰ ὄντα Pl. Crat. 402 a. Προσίεσθαι εἰς ταὐτὸ [= τὸ αὐτό, § 39] ἡμῖν αὐτοῖς iii. 1. 30. Ἐν τῷ αὐτῷ κινδύνῳ τοῖς φαυλοτάτοις αἰωροῦμαι Th. vii. 77. Ὅς ἐμοὶ μιᾶς ἐγένετ' ἐκ ματρὸς Eur. Ph. 151. Οὐ καὶ σὺ τύπτει τὰς ἴσας πληγὰς ἐμοί; Ar. Ran. 636. Τοῖς ἐκ τοῦ ἴσου ἡμῖν οὖσι, 'on an equality with us,' Hier. 8. 5. Ὁ σίδηρος ἀνισοῖ τοὺς ἀσθενεῖς τοῖς ἰσχυροῖς Cyr. vii. 5. 65. Διεῖλε ψυχὰς ἰσαρίθμους τοῖς ἄστροις Pl. Tim. 41 d. Ἰσῆλιξ τοῖς ἀειγενέσι θεοῖς Symp. 8. 1.

(II.) DATIVE OF INFLUENCE.

§ **401.** The Dative of influence expresses a person or thing which is *affected* by an action, property, &c., without being *directly acted upon.*

Influence has every variety and degree. On the one hand, it may be so *immediate,* that it can scarcely be distinguished from direct action, and the Dat. expressing it is used interchangeably with the Acc.; and, on the other hand, it may be so *remote,* that it can scarcely be appreciated, and the Dat. expressing it might have been omitted without impairing the sense.

RULE XVIII. The OBJECT OF INFLUENCE is put in the Dative.

§ **402.** The Dative is governed, according to this rule by,

α. Words of ADDRESS, including those of *call* and *command*, of *conversation* and *reply*, of *declaration* and *confession*, of *exhortation* and *message*, of *oath* and *promise*, of *reproach* and *threatening*, &c. Thus,

Οὗτος Κύρῳ εἶπεν, *this man said to Cyrus*, i. 6. 2. Τῷ Κλεάρχῳ ἐβόα, *called out to Clearchus*, i. 8. 12. Διαλεχθέντες ἀλλήλοις, *having conversed with each other*, ii. 5. 42. Τοῖς τε ναυκλήροις ἀπεῖπε μὴ διάγειν vii. 2. 12. Λέγει τὴν μαντείαν τῷ Σωκράτει iii. 1. 7. Τῷ Ἐνυαλίῳ ἐλελίζουσι i. 8. 18. Τοῖς νεανίσκοις ἐγχεῖν ἐκέλευε iv. 3. 13. Ἡ παρακέλευσις τῷ ἐρῶντι παρὰ πάντων θαυμαστή Pl. Conv. 182 d. Ἀλλήλοις διεκελεύοντο iv. 8. 3. Ἀφήγησαι τούτῳ, τί σοι ἀπεκρινάμην vii. 2. 26. Ἀγγέλλουσι τοῖς στρατιώταις i. 3. 21. Παρήγγειλε τοῖς φρουράρχοις i. 1. 6. Ὑπισχνοῦμαί σοι δέκα τάλαντα i. 7. 18. Οὐ μέμφομαι, ἔφη, τούτοις Mem. iii. 5. 20. Εἰ δέ τις αὐτῷ . . ὀνειδίζοι Ib. ii. 9. 8. Ἠπείλουν αὐτῷ v. 6. 34. Ἐκήρυξε τοῖς Ἕλλησι συσκευάσασθαι iii. 4. 36. Ὁπόταν πλάτανος πτελέᾳ ψιθυρίζῃ Ar. Nub. 1008. Ἀνεῖλεν αὐτῷ ὁ Ἀπόλλων iii. 1. 6. Ὥσπερ αὐτῷ μαντευτὸς ἦν vi. 1. 22. Ὁ Θρῃξὶ μάντις, *the prophet to the Thracians*, i. e. *the Thracian prophet*, Eur. Hec. 1267. Ἀλλ' ἤνεσ' ἀνδρὶ πάντα Eur. Med. 1157.

§ **403.** *β.* Words of ADVANTAGE and DISADVANTAGE, including those of *benefit* and *injury*, of *assistance* and *service*, of *favor* and *fidelity*, of *necessity* and *sufficiency*, of *fitness* and *unfitness*, of *convenience* and *trouble*, of *ease* and *difficulty*, of *safety* and *danger*, &c. Thus,

Παρύσατις . . ὑπῆρχε τῷ Κύρῳ, *Parysatis favored Cyrus*, i. 1. 4. Χρήσιμα . . τοῖς Κρησί, *useful to the Cretans*, iii. 4. 17. Ὅπῃ ἂν τῇ στρατιᾷ συμφέρῃ iii. 2. 27. Πρόσφορά θ' ὑμῖν Soph. Œd. C. 1774 (cf. § 389. R.). Ἀγαθὰ ἀμφοτέροις Cyr. viii. 5. 22. Κρείττω ἑαυτῷ iii. 1. 4. Χεῖρόν ἐστιν αὐτῷ vii. 6. 4. Λυμαινόμενον τοῖς μειρακίοις Ar. Nub. 928. Οὕτως ἐβοήθουν ἀλλήλοις iv. 2. 26. Τούτοις ἐπικουρεῖτε v. 8. 21. Οἵ σοι ὑπηρετοῖμεν ii. 5. 14. Τοῖς θανοῦσι πλοῦτος οὐδὲν ὠφελεῖ Æsch. Pers. 842. Ἀνθρώποισιν ὠφελήματα Id. Pr. 501. Τοῖς φίλοις ἀρήγειν Cyr. i. 5. 13. Ὃς ἠθέλησε τιμωρεῖν πατρί Eur. Or. 924. Ἐὰν αὐτῷ ταῦτα χαρίσωνται ii. 1. 10. Πιστοὶ ὄντες Κύρῳ ii. 4. 16. Δεῖ ἐπισάξαι τὸν ἵππον Πέρσῃ ἀνδρί iii. 4. 35. Πολλῶν μέν σοι δεήσει (§ 357) Cyr. i. 6. 9. Ἐμοὶ μὲν ἀρκεῖ περὶ τούτων τὰ εἰρημένα v. 7. 11. Χωρίον ἱκανὸν μυρίοις ἀνθρώποις οἰκῆσαι vi. 4. 3. Ἐνοχλοῦντα ἀεὶ τῇ ὑμετέρᾳ εὐδαιμονίᾳ ii. 5. 13. Ἐγώ τινι ἐμποδών εἰμι; v. 7. 10. Ἐμπόδιος γάρ σοι ὁ Ζεύς vii. 8. 4. Τῇ ἡλικίᾳ ἔπρεπε i. 9. 6. Εὖ ἁρμόττοντα αὐτῷ Cyr. i. 4. 18. Ἄλλῳ γὰρ ἢ 'μοὶ χρή γε τῆσδ' ἄρχειν χθονός; Soph. Ant. 736. Ἑτοίμους εἶναι αὐτῷ τοὺς ἱππέας i. 6. 3. Ὁδὸς . . ἀμήχανος εἰσελθεῖν στρατεύματι i. 2. 21. Ἡ τραχεῖα τοῖς ποσὶν ἀμαχεὶ ἰοῦσιν εὐμενέστερα iv. 6. 12. Ἀσφαλέστερόν γέ σοι οἶδα ὄν vii. 7. 51. Ἐπικίνδυνον μοί ἐστιν Ib. 54.

§ **404.** γ. Words of APPEARANCE, including those of *seeming*, *showing*, *clearness*, *obscurity*, &c. Thus,

Πᾶσι δῆλον ἐγένετο, *it was evident to all*, H. Gr. vi. 4. 20. Σοὶ αὖ δηλώσω ὅθεν ἐγὼ περὶ σοῦ ἀκούω ii. 5. 26. Ἄδηλον μὲν παντὶ ἀνθρώπῳ ὅπῃ τὸ μέλλον ἕξει vi. 1. 21. Αἰσχύνεσθαί μοι δοκῶ i. 7. 4. Μὴ ἀποδόξῃ ἡμῖν ii. 3. 9. Τοῖς δὲ παισὶν ἐδείκνυσαν iv. 5. 33. Πᾶσι σαφές Vect. 4. 2. Αὐτοῖς πάλιν φαίνεται ὁ Μιθριδάτης iii. 4. 2. Λαμβάνειν τοὺς πολεμίους . . φανερούς σοι ὄντας, ἀφανὴς ὢν αὐτὸς ἐκείνοις Cyr. i. 6. 35.

δ. Words of GIVING, including those of *offering*, *paying distributing*, *supplying*, &c. Thus,

Δίδωσι δὲ αὐτῷ Κῦρος μυρίους δαρεικούς, *and Cyrus gives him ten thousand darics*, ii. 6. 4. Τῇ δ' οὖν στρατιᾷ τότε ἀπέδωκε Κῦρος μισθόν i. 2. 12. Τὰ δὲ ἄλλα διανεῖμαι τοῖς στρατηγοῖς vii. 5. 2. Τοῖς στρατηγοῖς δωροῦ Ib. 3. Τοῖς λοχαγοῖς κατεμερίσθη Ib. 4. Εἴπερ ἐμοὶ ἐτέλει τι Σεύθης, οὐχ οὕτως ἐτέλει δήπου, ὡς ὧν τε ἐμοὶ δοίη στεροῖτο, καὶ ἄλλα ὑμῖν ἀποτίσειεν vii. 6. 16. Θώρακες αὐτοῖς ἐπορίσθησαν iii. 3. 20. Τὴν τοῦ θεοῦ δόσιν ὑμῖν Pl. Apol. 30 d. Σῶν Ἡρακλεῖ δωρημάτων Soph. Tr. 668. Βασιλεῖ δασμός iv. 5. 34. Οὔτε ἐκεῖνος ἔτι ἡμῖν μισθοδότης i. 3. 9.

ε. Words of OBLIGATION and VALUE. Thus,

Τοῖς στρατιώταις ὠφείλετο μισθός, *pay was due to the soldiers*, i. 2. 11. Βασιλεῖ ἂν πολλοῦ ἄξιοι γένοιντο (§ 374), 'worth much to the king,' ii. 1. 14. Ἄξιος . . θανάτου τῇ πόλει, *meriting death from* [to] *the city*, Mem. i. 1. 1. Ὡς οὐκ ἄξιον εἴη βασιλεῖ ἀφεῖναι, 'unworthy of the king,' *or* 'disgraceful to the king,' ii. 3. 25. Ὑμῖν εἴσεται χάριν i. 4. 15.

§ **405.** ζ. Words of OPPOSITION, including those of *contention*, *dispute*, *enmity*, *resistance*, *rivalry*, *warfare*, &c. Thus,

Λιμὸν ὑμῖν ἀντιτάξαι, *to oppose to you famine*, ii. 5. 19. Ἐρίζοντά οἱ περὶ σοφίας, *contending with him in skill*, i. 2. 8. Ἥρᾳ Παλλάδι τ' ἔριν Eur. Iph. A. 183. Ἀντίοι ἰέναι τοῖς πολεμίοις i. 8. 17. Στασιάζοντα αὐτῷ ii. 5. 28. Τύραννος ἅπας ἐχθρὸς ἐλευθερίᾳ καὶ νόμοις ἐναντίος Dem. 72. 2. Ἡμῖν ἐναντιώσεται vii. 6. 5. Ἀντίπορον λόφον τῷ μαστῷ iv. 2. 18. Οὔτε βασιλεῖ ἀντιποιούμεθα τῆς ἀρχῆς (§ 373) ii. 3. 23. Ἀλλοτριωτάτας ταύτῃ Dem. 72. 1 (cf. § 349). Ὑποστῆναι αὐτοῖς Ἀθηναῖοι τολμήσαντες iii. 2. 11. Τῷ ἐμῷ ἀδελφῷ πολέμιος i. 6. 8. Τισσαφέρνει . . πολεμοῦντα i. 1. 8. Οὐδεὶς αὐτῷ ἐμάχετο i. 8. 23. Φαμὲν γὰρ Μαραθῶνί τε μόνοι προκινδυνεῦσαι τῷ βαρβάρῳ Th. i. 73. Ὠστιοῦνται . . ἀλλήλοισι Ar. Ach. 24. Ὡς ἐπιβουλεύοι αὐτῷ i. 1. 3. Ἐπιβουλὴ ἐμοί v. 6 29. Δικαζόμενος τῷ πατρί Pl. Euthyph. 4 e.

η. Words of YIELDING, SUBJECTION, and WORSHIP, including those of *homage*, *obedience* (cf. § 377. 1), *prayer*, *sacrifice*, &c. Thus,

Πάντα τοῖς θεοῖς ὕποχα, *all things are subject to the gods*, ii. 5. 7. Ἐμοὶ οὐ θέλετε πείθεσθαι, *you are not willing to obey me*, i. 3. 6. Ἐάν μοι πεισθῆτε, *if you will listen to me*, i. 4. 14. Εὔχεσθαι τοῖς . . θεοῖς, *to pray to the gods*, iv. 3. 13. Ἡ στρατιά σοι ὑφεῖτο vi. 6. 31. Ὑποχωρῆσαι τὸν ποταμὸν Κύρῳ i. 4. 18. Εἰ ὑποχείριος ἔσται Λακεδαιμονίοις vii. 6. 43.

Οἱ νῦν σοι *ὑπήκοοι* vii. 7. 29 (cf. § 377. 1). Κύρῳ καλῶς *πειθαρχεῖν* i. 9. 17. *Ἀπιστεῖν* ἐκείνῳ ii. 6. 19. Ἔ*θυε* τῷ Διί vii. 6. 44. *Θυσίαν* ἐποίει τῇ θεῷ v. 3. 9. *Σφαγιάσασθαι* τῷ ἀνέμῳ iv. 5. 4. *Ὀρχησάμενοι* θεοῖσιν Ar. Lys. 1277.

§ **406.** ϑ. Words expressing a MENTAL ACT OF FEELING which is regarded as *going out towards an object*; as those of *friendship* and *hatred*, *pleasure* and *displeasure*, *joy* and *sorrow*, *contentment* and *envy*, *belief* and *unbelief*, *trust* and *distrust*, &c. Thus,

Κύρῳ *φιλαίτερον*, *more friendly to Cyrus*, i. 9. 29. *Ἐχαλέπαινον* τοῖς στρατηγοῖς, *were angry with the generals*, i. 4. 12. Ἐπίστευον γὰρ αὐτῷ, *for they trusted him*, i. 2. 2. *Εὐνοϊκῶς* ἔχοιεν αὐτῷ i. 1. 5. *Κακόνους* τοῖς Ἕλλησιν ii. 5. 27. Τούτοις ἥσθη Κῦρος i. 9. 26. Μένων *ἠγάλλετο* τῷ ἐξαπατᾷν ii. 6. 26. Οὐδενὶ οὕτω *χαίρεις* ὡς φίλοις ἀγαθοῖς Mem. ii. 6. 35. Εἴ τινα εὕροιτε καὶ ὑμῖν καὶ ἐμοὶ *ἀχθόμενον* vi. 1. 29. *Ὠργίζοντο* ἰσχυρῶς τῷ Κλεάρχῳ i. 5. 11. *Χαλεπῶς φέρω* τοῖς παροῦσι πράγμασιν i. 3. 3. *Στέργειν* τοῖς παροῦσιν, 'to be content with,' Isocr. 159 e. *Ἀγαπήσας* τοῖς πεπραγμένοις Dem. 13. 11. *Φθονῶν* τοῖς φανερῶς πλουτοῦσιν i. 9. 19. Ὧν ἐγώ σοι οὐ φθονήσω (§ 376. ζ) Cyr. viii. 4. 16. Ἡμῖν *ἀπιστεῖν* ii. 5. 15. Τῇ τύχῃ *ἐλπίσας* Th. iii. 97. Ἔστασαν *ἀποροῦντες* τῷ πράγματι i. 5. 13. *Ἀθυμῶν* τοῖς γεγενημένοις vi. 2. 14. *Θαυμάζω* δὲ τῇ τε ἀποκλείσει μου τῶν πυλῶν Th. iv. 85. *Ὑπέπτησσον* οἱ ἥλικες αὐτῷ Cyr. i. 5. 1.—Some of these constructions may perhaps be referred to the instrumental Dat. (§ 416).

§ **407.** ι. Words expressing the POWER OF EXCITING EMOTION; as, *pleasure*, *displeasure*, *care*, *fear*, &c. Thus,

Ἀπεχθάνεσθαι τοῖς στρατιώταις, *to displease the soldiers*, ii. 6. 19. Ἐμοὶ *μελήσει*, *it shall be my care*, i. 4. 16. Ὅτι αὐτῷ *μέλοι*, [that it should be a care to him] *that he would take care*, i. 8. 13. Διὰ τὸ μέλειν ἅπασιν, *through the interest which all felt*, vi. 4. 20. Ζηνὶ τῶν σῶν, οἶδ' ἐγώ, μέλει πόνων (§ 376. δ) Eur. Heracl. 717. Ὦ φίλτατον *μέλημα* δώμασιν πατρός Æsch. Cho. 235. *Μεταμέλει* μοι, *it is a regret to me, I repent*, Cyr. v. 3. 6. Μεταμέλειν τί σοι ἔφησθα i. 6. 7. (See § 376. δ.) Τοῖς μὲν πολλοῖς . . *ἤρεσκον* ii. 4. 2. Ἡ*δὺ* συμμαθόντι τὸ πόμα ἦν iv. 5. 27. Ὑμῖν Μυσοὺς *λυπηροὺς* ὄντας ii. 5. 13. *Φοβερώτατον* τοῖς πολεμίοις iii. 4. 5.

κ. VERBAL ADJECTIVES AND ADVERBS, having a *passive* signification. The property expressed by these verbals has relation to an agent; which, as if affected by the property, is put in the Dat. Adjectives of this kind usually end in -τός or -τέος (§ 314). Thus,

Θαυμαστὸν πᾶσι, *wonderful to all* [to be wondered at by all], iv. 2. 15. Ἡμῖν . . οἶμαι πάντα ποιητέα, *I think that every thing should be done by us*, iii. 1. 35. Τὸν μὲν οἴκαδε βουλόμενον ἀπιέναι, τοῖς οἴκοι *ζηλωτὸν* ποιήσω ἀπελθεῖν, 'an object of envy to his countrymen,' i. 7. 4. Ἵνα μοι *εὐπρακτότερον* ᾖ ii. 3. 20. Οἱ ποταμοὶ . . προϊοῦσι πρὸς τὰς πηγὰς *διαβατοὶ* γίγνονται, 'can be passed by those who ascend [become passable to those who ascend],' iii. 2. 22. *Εὐεπίθετον* ἦν ἐνταῦθα τοῖς πολεμίοις iii. 4. 20. Ποταμὸς . . ἡμῖν ἐστ. *διαβατέος*, 'for us to pass [to be passed by us],' ii. 4. 6

§ **408.** λ. Substantive Verbs, when employed to denote *possession*. These verbs and their compounds are used with the Dat., in a variety of expressions, which are variously translated into English. Thus,

Ἐνταῦθα Κύρῳ βασίλεια ἦν, *here Cyrus had a palace* [there was a palace to Cyrus], i. 2. 7. Τοῖς δὲ ὑποψία μὲν ἦν, *they had a suspicion*, or *they suspected*, i. 3. 21. Δρόμος ἐγένετο τοῖς στρατιώταις, [to the soldiers there came to be a running] *the soldiers began to run*, i. 2. 17. Ὥστε πᾶσιν αἰσχύνην εἶναι, *so that all were ashamed*, ii. 3. 11. Ὑπάρχει γὰρ νῦν ἡμῖν οὐδὲν ii. 2. 11. Ὡς νόμος αὐτοῖς εἰς μάχην [sc. ἐστί] i. 2. 15. Ἀνάγκη δή μοι [sc. ἐστί], *I am now compelled*, i. 3. 5. Ἦν αὐτῷ πόλεμος, *he made war*, i. 9. 14. Πόλις . . ᾗ ὄνομα Σιττάκη, *a city named Sittace*, ii. 4. 13. Ἐγένετο καὶ Ἕλληνι καὶ βαρβάρῳ . . πορεύεσθαι, *both Greek and barbarian could go*, i. 9. 13. Οὐ γὰρ ἦν ἀθρόοις περιστῆναι iv. 7. 2. Νῦν σοι ἔξεστιν . . ἀνδρὶ γενέσθαι vii. 1. 21. Οὐδενὸς ἡμῖν μετείη iii. 1. 20 (see § 364). Τί γάρ ἐστ' Ἐρεχθεῖ καὶ κολοιοῖς; *for what has Erechtheus to do with jackdaws* [what is there to Erechtheus, and also to jackdaws]? Ar. Eq. 1022. Μηδὲν εἶναι σοὶ καὶ Φιλίππῳ πρᾶγμα, *that you had no connection with Philip*, Dem. 320. 7. Τί τῷ νόμῳ καὶ τῇ βασάνῳ; Id. 855. 5. Ἐκείνῳ βουλομένῳ ταῦτ' ἐστί, *these things are* [to him willing] *according to his will*, or *agreeable to him*, H. Gr. iv. 1. 11. Εἰ αὐτῷ γε σοὶ βουλομένῳ ἐστὶν ἀποκρίνεσθαι Pl. Gorg. 448 d. Εἴ σοι ἡδομένῳ ἐστίν, *if it is your pleasure*, Pl. Phædo, 78 b. Θέλοντι κἀμοὶ τοῦτ' ἂν ἦν Soph. Œd. T. 1356. Ἦν δὲ οὐ τῷ Ἀγησιλάῳ ἀχθομένῳ ταῦτα, 'displeasing to Agesilaus,' H. Gr. v. 3. 13. Νικίᾳ προσδεχομένῳ ἦν τὰ περὶ τῶν Ἐγεσταίων, 'were as Nicias had expected,' Th. vi. 46.

§ **409.** μ. And, in general, words expressing *any action*, *property*, &c., which is represented as being *to* or *for* some person or thing. Thus,

Προπίνω σοι, *I drink to you*, vii. 3. 26. Κενοτάφιον αὐτοῖς ἐποίησαν, *they made for them a cenotaph*, vi. 4. 9. Μέγιστον κόσμον ἀνδρί, *the greatest ornament to a man*, i. 9. 23. Ὥρα ἦν ἀπιέναι τοῖς πολεμίοις, *it was time for the enemy to withdraw*, iii. 4. 34. Στράτευμα αὐτῷ συνελέγετο i. 1. 9. Ὃς Χειρισόφῳ ὑπεστρατήγει v. 6. 36. Βασίλειον εἶχε τῷ σατράπῃ iv. 4. 2. Ἔχω γὰρ καὶ αὐτὸς αὐτῷ μαρτυρῆσαι vii. 6. 39. Ἡμῖν τὸν μισθὸν ἀναπρᾶξαι Ib. 40. Ἐγὼ σιωπῶ τῷδε; Ar. Ran. 11. 34. Εἴργειν τεκούσῃ μητρὶ πολέμιον δόρυ Æsch. Sept. 416. Ἐμοὶ δὲ μίμνει σχισμὸς ἀμφήκει δορί, 'awaits me [is waiting for me],' Id. Ag. 1149. Νόμιμον ἄρα ὑμῖν ἐστιν iv. 6. 15. Πᾶσι κοινὸν εἶναι καὶ ἀναγκαῖον ἀνθρώποις iii. 1. 43. Λοιπόν μοι εἰπεῖν iii. 2. 29. Ἀγαθοῦ . . αἴτιος τῇ στρατιᾷ vi. 1. 20. Ἡ . . πατρῴα ὑμῖν οἰκία Pl. Charm. 157 e. Ξένος ὢν ἐτύγχανεν αὐτῷ i. 1. 10. Ὑμᾶς ἐμοὶ εἶναι καὶ πατρίδα καὶ φίλους i. 3. 6. Ἱμάτια τῇ γυναικί vii. 3. 27. Τριήρεσι . . πλοῦς vi. 4. 2. Αἱ δὲ εἴσοδοι τοῖς μὲν ὑποζυγίοις ὀρυκταί iv. 5. 25. Ἡ δὲ [sc. ὁδός τινι] διαβάντι τὸν ποταμὸν iii. 5. 15. Κακὰς ἐγὼ γυναῖκας υἱέσι στυγῶ Soph. Ant. 571. Λύπη τε φρενῶν χερσίν τε πόνος Eur. Hipp. 189.

§ **410.** Remarks. 1. The remoter relations expressed by the Dat. (§ 401) are various in their character, having respect to *place*, *time*, *sensation*, *thought*, *feeling*, *expression*, *action*, &c. They are expressed in two ways; (a.) by the

Dat. simply, and (b.) by an elliptical form of construction, in which the Dat. is preceded by ὡς. Thus,

Ἡ Θρᾴκη αὕτη ἐστὶν . . ἐπὶ δεξιὰ εἰς τὸν Πόντον εἰσπλέοντι [sc. τινί or σοί], *this Thrace is upon the right to one sailing into the Pontus*, or *as you sail into the Pontus*, vi. 4. 1 (cf. Th. i. 24). Ἦν δ' ἦμαρ ἤδη δεύτερον πλέοντί μοι, *and it was now the second day of my voyage* [to me sailing], Soph. Ph. 354. Θυομένῳ οἱ . . ὁ ἥλιος ἀμαυρώθη, *while he was sacrificing the sun was eclipsed*, Hdt. ix. 10 (this mode of defining time by a Dat. with a participle is especially Ion.). Καὶ τίς χρόνος τοῖσδ' ἐστὶν οὐξεληλυθώς; 'since this event,' Soph. Œd. T. 735. Τὸ μὲν ἔξωθεν ἁπτομένῳ σῶμα οὐκ ἄγαν θερμὸν ἦν, 'to the external touch,' Th. ii. 49. Εἶ γενναῖος, ὡς ἰδόντι [sc. φαίνει], 'as you appear to one beholding,' 'in appearance,' Soph. Œd. C. 75. Ἐμοὶ γὰρ, ὅστις ἄδικος ὢν σοφὸς λέγειν πέφυκε, πλείστην ζημίαν ὀφλισκάνει, 'according to my judgment,' Eur. Med. 580. Καίτοι σ' ἐγὼ 'τίμησα τοῖς φρονοῦσιν εὖ Soph. Ant. 904. Κρέων γὰρ ἦν ζηλωτὸς, ὡς ἐμοὶ [sc. ἐδόκει], ποτέ, 'as it seemed to me,' 'in my opinion,' Ib. 1161. Οὐ μὰ τὸν Δί', ἔφη, οὔκουν, ὥς γ' ἐμοὶ ἀκροατῇ. Ἀλλ' ὡς ἐμοὶ, ἦν δ' ἐγὼ, ῥήτορι Pl. Rep. 536 c. Τὸ μὲν οὖν νόσημα, πολλὰ καὶ ἄλλα παραλιπόντι . ., τοιοῦτον ἦν Th. ii. 51. Θεὸς γὰρ ἐκσώζει με, τῷδε δ' οἴχομαι, 'so far as lay in him,' Soph. Aj. 1128. Μακρὰν γὰρ, ὡς γέροντι, προὐστάλης ὁδόν, 'for an old man [as journeys are to an old man],' Id. Œd. C. 20. Τόδε δὲ μάλιστα πάντων μέμνησό μοι, μηδέποτε ἀναμένειν, *but this most of all remember* [for me], *I pray you, never to defer*, Cyr. i. 6. 10. Ἐς τί μοι βλέψασα θάλπει Soph. El. 887. Οἶμαί σοι ἐκείνους τοὺς ἀγαθοὺς τὰ πεζικὰ ῥᾳδίως νικήσειν Cyr. i. 3. 15. Οὕτως ἐγώ σοι . . τάγε δίκαια παντάπασιν ἤδη ἀκριβῶ Ib. 17.

NOTE. The use of the Dat. to express remote relation is particularly frequent in the *pronouns of the first and second person*. In the Greek, as in our own and in other languages, the Dat. of these pronouns is often inserted, simply to render the discourse more emphatic or subjective. Observe the examples just above.

§ 411. 2. Words governing the Gen. sometimes take a Dat. in its stead, to express the exertion of an influence; as,

Ἡγεῖτο δ' αὐτοῖς ὁ κωμάρχης, *and the bailiff led the way for them*, i. e. *guided them*, iv. 6. 2. Οἱ γὰρ βλέποντες τοῖς τυφλοῖς ἡγούμεθα Ar. Plut. 15. Ἡμῖν πᾶσιν ἐξηγούμενος Soph. Œd. C. 1589. Ἀνάσσει βαρβάροισι βάρβαρος Θόας Eur. Iph. T. 31. Ὦ Θήβαισιν εὐίπποις ἄναξ Id. Ph. 17. Δαρὸν γὰρ οὐκ ἄρξει θεοῖς Æsch. Prom. 940. Μάχας δέ σοι καὶ πολέμους ἀφαιρῶ Cyr. vii. 2. 26. Ἦ βέβηκεν ἡμῖν ὁ ξένος; Soph. Œd. C. 81. Πέφευγεν ἐλπὶς τῶνδέ μοι σωτηρίας Eur. Heracl. 452. Τὰ ἄκρα ἡμῖν . . προκαταλαμβάνειν i. 3. 16. Τυράννοις ἐκποδὼν μεθίστασο Eur. Ph. 40. Cf. §§ 347, 350, 421. 2.

§ 412. 3. A *Dat. depending upon a verb* is often used instead of a *Gen. depending upon a substantive*; as,

Οἱ . . ἵπποι αὐτοῖς δέδενται, *the horses are tied for them*, = οἱ ἵπποι αὐτῶν δέδενται, *their horses are tied*, iii. 4. 35. Ἡ . . τοῦ παντὸς ἀρχὴ Χειρισόφῳ ἐνταῦθα κατελύθη vi. 2. 12 (cf. Ἥ τε Χειρισόφου ἀρχὴ τοῦ παντὸς κατελύθη vi. 3. 1). Διὰ τὸ διεσπάρθαι αὐτῷ τὸ στράτευμα ii. 4. 3. Τοῖς βαρβάροις τῶν τε πεζῶν ἀπέθανον πολλοὶ, καὶ τῶν ἱππέων . . ἐλήφθησαν iii. 4. 5. Οἵους ἡμῖν γνώσεσθε τοὺς ἐν τῇ χώρᾳ ὄντας ἀνθρώπους [= ἐν τῇ ἡμῶν χώρᾳ]

i. 7. 4. *Ἀθηναίων . . , ἐπειδὴ αὐτοῖς οἱ βάρβαροι ἐκ τῆς χώρας ἀπῆλθον* Th. i. 89. *Οὐκέτι σοι τέκνα λεύσσει φάος* Eur. Ph. 1547.

NOTE. The Dat. (chiefly of the personal pronoun) is sometimes placed as a simple adjunct of the substantive; and in some instances, when so placed, appears to depend strictly upon a participle understood. Thus, *Ἀπόβλεπε . . πρὸς τὴν νέαν ἡμῖν πόλιν*, *look upon our new state* (i. e. the new state established for us in the dialogue), Pl. Rep. 431 b. *Οἱ δέ σφι βόες . . οὐ παρεγίνοντο* Hdt. i. 31.

§ **413.** 4. Sometimes two datives following the same word, especially in Epic poetry, appear to be most naturally, though not unavoidably, referred to the *Σχῆμα καθ' ὅλον καὶ μέρος* (§ 334. 9); as, *Σθένος ἔμβαλ' ἑκάστῳ καρδίῃ*, *imparted strength* [to each one, to the heart] *to the heart of each one*, *Λ*. 11. *Ἀγαμέμνονι ἥνδανε θυμῷ* *Α*. 24. Cf. § 438. *β*.

D. THE DATIVE RESIDUAL.

§ **414.** The Dative residual is used in expressing adjuncts, which are not viewed as either subjective or objective (§§ 338, 340. *α*). It simply denotes indirect relation, without specifying the character of that relation; or, in other words, it denotes mere *association* or *connection*. Hence we have the general rule: AN ATTENDANT THING OR CIRCUMSTANCE, SIMPLY VIEWED AS SUCH, IS PUT IN THE DATIVE.

NOTES. *α*. In accordance with this rule, the Dat. is sometimes used in expressing an adjunct, which, upon a more exact discrimination of its character, would be expressed by either the *Gen.* or *Acc.* See §§ 340. *α*, 341.

β. The DATIVE RESIDUAL is expressed in Eng. most frequently by the preposition *with*, but likewise by the prepositions *by*, *in*, *at*, &c. Cf. §§ 345. N., 397. *α*.

§ **415.** The Dative residual may be resolved into, (I.) the INSTRUMENTAL and MODAL DATIVE, and (II.) the TEMPORAL and LOCAL DATIVE.

(I.) INSTRUMENTAL AND MODAL DATIVE.

RULE XIX. The MEANS and MODE are put in the Dative.

§ **416.** INSTRUMENTALITY and MODE may be either *external* or *internal*, and MODE may apply either to *action* or *condition*. Hence, to these heads may be referred,

1.) The *instrument*, *force*, or *other means*, with which any thing is done, or through which any thing comes to pass Thus,

Αὐτὸν ἀκοντίζει τις παλτῷ, *one shoots him with a dart*, i. 8. 27. Ἐφείποντο . . ἱππικῷ, *pursued with cavalry*, vii. 6. 29. Θανάτῳ ζημιοῦν, *to punish with death*, Cyr. vi. 3. 27. Σχεδίαις διαβαίνοντες i. 5. 10. Ἴησι τῇ ἀξίνῃ Ib. 12. Λίθοις σφενδονᾶν iii. 3. 17. Δώροις ἐτίμα i. 9. 14. Λόγοις ἔπεισε ii. 6. 4. Τεκμαίρεσθαι δ' ἦν τῷ ψόφῳ iv. 2. 4. Γέφυρα δὲ ἐπῆν ἐζευγμένη πλοίοις ἑπτά i. 2. 5. Ὡπλισμένοι θώραξι i. 8. 6. Ὠικοδομημένον πλίνθοις ii. 4. 12. Κῦρος ἀνέβη ξενικῷ ii. 5. 22. Τοῖς δὲ λειπομένοις ἐς Πλάταιαν ἐλθόντες, τὴν γῆν ἐδῄουν Th. ii. 12. Εἶχον δεινῶς τῇ ἐνδείᾳ vi. 4. 23. Ἀποθνήσκει νόσῳ vii. 2. 32. Φιλίᾳ μὲν καὶ εὐνοίᾳ ἑπομένους ii. 6. 13. Οἳ δὲ μὴ παρεῖεν, τούτους ἡγεῖτο ἢ ἀκρατείᾳ τινὶ ἢ ἀδικίᾳ ἢ ἀμελείᾳ ἀπεῖναι Cyr. viii. 1. 16. Προνοεῖν μέν γε ἔξω πάντα τῇ ἀνθρωπίνῃ γνώμῃ, ταῖς δὲ χερσὶν ὁπλοφορήσω, διώξομαι δὲ τῷ ἵππῳ, τὸν δ' ἐναντίον ἀνατρέψω τῇ τοῦ ἵππου ῥώμῃ Cyr. iv. 3. 18. Πάσας κινήσεις τῷ σώματι Pl. Leg. 631 c. Ἡ τοῖς βέλεσιν ἔφεσις Ib. 717 a. Τὰ γὰρ δόλῳ τῷ μὴ δικαίῳ κτήματ' οὐχὶ σώζεται Soph. Œd. C. 1026. — The Dat. of the missile with verbs of throwing will be specially observed.

§ **417.** Remark. Dative of the Agent. The Dat. sometimes expresses *that through whose agency* any thing takes place; as,

Πάνθ' ἡμῖν πεποίηται, *all things have been done by us*, i. e. *our work is done*, i. 8. 12. Εἰ δέ τι καλὸν . . ἐπέπρακτο ὑμῖν vii. 6. 32. Τὰ πυρὰ κεκαυμένα εἴη τῷ Σεύθῃ vii. 2. 18. Τοῖς δὲ Κερκυραίοις . . οὐχ ἑωρῶντο Th. i. 51. Τοῖς Ἕλλησι μισοῖντο Id. iii. 64. Πορσπόλοις φυλάσσεται Soph. Aj. 539. Ὥς σοι δύσφορ' εἴργασται κακά Eur. Hec. 1085. Τίνι γάρ ποτ' ἂν . . πρόσφορον ἀκούσαιμ' ἔπος, 'through whom,' i. e. 'from whom,' Soph. El. 226. Δέξατό οἱ σκῆπτρον, *received from him the sceptre*, B. 186 (the Dat. following δέχομαι, instead of the Gen. with παρά, is especially Epic, and might perhaps be referred to § 409, thus, *took for him the sceptre*). Θέμιστι . . δέκτο δέπας O. 87.

Note. This use of the Dat. is most frequent with *verbs in the Perf. and Plup.* This dative of the agent with *passive verbs*, and that with *passive verbals* (§ 407. κ), might perhaps have been referred to the same analogy.

§ **418.** 2.) The *way* or *manner*, in which any thing is done or affected, together with *attendant circumstances*. Thus,

Οὐ γὰρ κραυγῇ, ἀλλὰ σιγῇ . . προσῄεσαν, *for they advanced not with clamor, but in silence*, i. 8. 11. Παρελθεῖν οὐκ ἦν βίᾳ i. 4. 4. Ὥσπερ ὀργῇ ἐκέλευσε i. 5. 8. Ἐλαύνων ἀνὰ κράτος ἱδροῦντι τῷ ἵππῳ i. 8. 1. Ψιλαῖς ταῖς κεφαλαῖς ἐν τῷ πολέμῳ διακινδυνεύειν Ib. 6. Δρόμῳ θεῖν Ib. 18. Τούτῳ τῷ τρόπῳ ἐπορεύθησαν σταθμοὺς τέτταρας iii. 4. 23. Πορευόμενοι . . τῇ ὁδῷ Ib. 30. Τὰς βίᾳ πράξεις Pl. Pol. 280 d.

Remark. The pronoun αὐτός is sometimes joined to the Dat. of an associated object to give emphasis; as, Μὴ ἡμᾶς αὐταῖς ταῖς τριήρεσι καταδύσῃ, *lest he should sink us, triremes and all* [with the triremes themselves], i. 3. 17. Πολλοὺς γὰρ ἤδη αὐτοῖς τοῖς ἵπποις κατακρημνισθῆναι Cyr. i. 4. 7. Τριήρεις αὐτοῖς πληρώμασι διεφθάρησαν Isocr. 176 b. — The preposition σύν, which is common in such adjuncts if the *αὐτός* be omitted, is sometimes expressed even with it; as, Ὅπως . . ξὺν αὐτοῖσι τοῖς κηρίοις ἐκτετμῆσθον Pl. Rep. 564 c. Cf. Ξ. 498 and Υ. 482.

3.) The *respect* in which any thing is taken or applied (cf § 437). Thus,

Πλήθει γε ἡμῶν λειφθέντες, *inferior to us in number* [in respect to number], vii. 7. 31 (§ 349). Πόλις . . Θάψακος ὀνόματι i. 4. 11. Τῇ ἐπιμελείᾳ περιεῖναι τῶν φίλων i. 9. 24. Τῇ φωνῇ τραχύς ii. 6. 9. Χρήμασι καὶ τιμαῖς τούτων ἐπλεονεκτεῖτε (§ 351) iii. 1. 37. Ταῖς ψυχαῖς ἐῤῥωμενέστεροι Ib. 42. Ἑνὶ δὲ μόνῳ προέχουσιν οἱ ἱππεῖς ἡμᾶς iii. 2. 19. Τῷ βελτίστῳ τοῦ ὁπλιτικοῦ βλαφθῆναι Th. iv. 73. Ῥίζῃ μὲν μέλαν ἔσκε κ. 304.

§ 419. 4.) The *measure of difference*, especially with the Comparative. Thus,

Χρόνῳ δὲ συχνῷ ὕστερον, *and sometime after* [later by a considerable time], i. 8. 8. Πολλῷ δὲ ὕστερον ii. 5. 32. Νομίζων, ὅσῳ μὲν θᾶττον ἔλθοι, τοσούτῳ ἀπαρασκευαστοτέρῳ βασιλεῖ μάχεσθαι, ὅσῳ δὲ σχολαιότερον, τοσούτῳ πλέον συναγείρεσθαι βασιλεῖ στράτευμα, *thinking that* [by how much] *the more rapidly he should advance,* [by so much] *the more unprepared he should find the king for battle, &c.*, i. 5. 9. Ἐνιαυτῷ πρεσβύτερος, *a year older*, Ar. Ran. 18. Προύλαβε πολλῷ Th. vii. 80. Χρόνῳ μετέπειτα πολλῷ Hdt. ii. 110.

5.) The Dative with *χράομαι*, *to use* [to supply one's need with, § 284. 3]. Thus,

Μαντικῇ χρώμενος, *using divination*, Mem. i. 1. 2. Ἐχρῆτο τοῖς ξένοις, 'employed,' i. 3. 18. Τοῖς ἵπποις ἄριστα χρῆσθαι, 'manage,' i. 9. 5. Χειμῶνι χρησάμενον, 'having met with,' Dem. 293. 3. Τοὺς χρωμένους ἑαυτῷ, 'associating with,' Mem. iv. 8. 11. Ἡ Κύρῳ πολεμίᾳ ἐχρῆτο, *which was hostile to Cyrus*, ii. 5. 11. Σφόδρα πειθομένοις ἐχρῆτο ii. 6. 13.

NOTE. Νομίζω has sometimes the Dat. after the analogy of χράομαι· as, Θυσίαις διετησίοις νομίζοντες, 'observing,' Th. ii. 38. Εὐσεβείᾳ μὲν οὐδέτεροι ἐνόμιζον Id. iii. 82.

(II.) TEMPORAL AND LOCAL DATIVE.

§ 420. RULE XX. The TIME and PLACE *AT WHICH* are put in the Dative (cf. §§ 378, 439); as,

1. TIME. Τῇ δ' ὑστεραίᾳ [sc. ἡμέρᾳ] ἧκεν ἄγγελος, *but the next day there came a messenger*, i. 2. 21. Ὤιετο γὰρ ταύτῃ τῇ ἡμέρᾳ μαχεῖσθαι βασιλέα i. 7. 14. Τῇ ὑστεραίᾳ οὐκ ἐφάνησαν οἱ πολέμιοι, οὐδὲ τῇ τρίτῃ· τῇ δὲ τετάρτῃ, νυκτὸς προσελθόντες, καταλαμβάνουσι χωρίον ὑπερδέξιον, 'but on the fourth, having passed them in the night (§ 378),' iii. 4. 37. Λύσανδρος δὲ τῇ ἐπιούσῃ νυκτί, ἐπεὶ ὄρθρος ἦν, ἐσήμηνεν H. Gr. ii. 1. 22. Τρίτῳ μηνὶ ἀνήχθη ἐπ' Ἄνδρου Ib. i. 4. 21. Τῷ δ' ἐπιόντι ἔτει, ᾧ ἦν Ὀλυμπιάς, ᾗ τὸ στάδιον ἐνίκα Κροκίνας Ib. ii. 3. 1. Τῷ δ' αὐτῷ χρόνῳ, *and at the same time*, Ib. i. 2. 18. Ὁ δὲ Ἀγησίλαος χρόνῳ ποτὲ εἶπεν, 'at length,' Ib. iv. 1. 34. Ὡς δεκασπόρῳ χρόνῳ ἀλόχους τε καὶ τέκν' εἰσίδωσιν Eur. Tro. 20. Cf. §§ 378, 439.

2. PLACE. Τὰ τρόπαια τά τε Μαραθῶνι καὶ Σαλαμῖνι καὶ Πλαται-

αῖς, *the victories at Marathon and Salamis and Platæa*, Pl. Menex. 245 a. Τῶν τε Μαραθῶνι μαχεσαμένων καὶ τῶν ἐν Σαλαμῖνι ναυμαχησάντων Ib. 241 b. Τὴν παλαιὰν φηγὸν αὐδῆσαί ποτε Δωδῶνι Soph. Tr. 171. Θύραισ κειμένου Id. Œd. C. 401. Σοῖς ὅταν στῶσιν τάφοις Ib. 411. Ὁδοῖς κυκλῶν ἐμαυτόν Id. Ant. 226. Κείμενον πέδῳ Αἴγισθον Eur. El. 763.

§ **421.** Remarks. α. To the local dative may be referred the use of the Dat. to denote *persons among whom*, or *in whom any thing occurs;* as, Δύναμιν ἀνθρώποις ἔχειν, 'among men,' Eur. Bac. 310. Εὐδοκιμήσεις τοῖς τότε ἀνθρώποις Pl. Prot. 343 c. Οὐκ ἂν ἐξεύροις ἐμοὶ ἁμαρτίας ὄνειδος οὐδέν, 'in me,' Soph. Œd. C. 966. Οἷα καὶ Ὁμήρῳ Διομήδης λέγει, 'in Homer,' Pl. Rep. 389 e. Ὀδυσσεὺς γὰρ αὐτῷ [Ὁμήρῳ] λοιδορεῖ τὸν Ἀγαμέμνονα Pl. Leg. 706 d. Ἀριπρεπέα Τρώεσσιν Z. 477. Οὗ κράτος ἐστὶ μέγιστον πᾶσιν Κυκλώπεσσι α. 71.

β. The use of the local dative in prose is chiefly confined to those *adverbs of place* which are properly datives; as, ταύτῃ [sc. χώρᾳ], *in this region, here* (iv. 5. 36), τῇδε, *here* (vii. 2. 13), ᾗ and ᾗπερ, *where* (ii. 2. 21), ἄλλῃ, *elsewhere* (ii. 6. 4), κύκλῳ, *in a circuit, around* (i. 5. 4; iii. 5. 14), οἴκοι (= οἴκῳ), *at home* (i. 1. 10), Ἀθήνησι (= Ἀθήναις), *at Athens* (vii. 7. 57). See §§ 320. 2, 379. α.

E. The Accusative.

§ **422.** The office of the Accusative is to express direct termination or limit (§ 339); and the general rule for its use is the following: An Adjunct expressing Direct Limit is put in the Accusative.

Remark. In a general sense, all the oblique cases may be said to express limit; but the *Gen.* and *Dat.* express it less simply and less directly than the *Acc.* In some connections, however, these *indirect cases* are used interchangeably with the Acc. See §§ 341, 401, 414. α, 424. 2.

The Accusative, as the case of *direct limit*, is employed, —

(i.) To limit an action, by expressing its *direct object* or its *effect*. — Acc. of Direct Object and Effect.

(ii.) To limit a word or expression, by applying it to a *particular part, property, thing*, or *person*. — Acc. of Specification.

(iii.) To express limits of *time, space*, and *quantity*. — Acc. of Extent.

(IV.) To limit a word or expression, by denoting *degree*, *manner*, &c. — ADVERBIAL ACC.

NOTES. (*a.*) These uses are not only intimately allied, but sometimes blend with each other. (*b.*) For the use of the Acc. to denote the *subject of the Infinitive*, see the syntax of that mode.

(I.) ACCUSATIVE OF THE DIRECT OBJECT AND EFFECT.

§ **423.** RULE XXI. The DIRECT OBJECT and the EFFECT of an action are put in the Accusative.

Λαβὼν Τισσαφέρνην, *taking Tissaphernes*, i. 1. 2. *Ἐποιεῖτο τὴν συλλογήν*, *he made the levy*, i. 1. 6. *Ὑπώπτευε τελευτήν* i. 1. 1. *Διαβάλλει τὸν Κῦρον* Ib. 3. *Φιλοῦσα αὐτόν* Ib. 4. *Ὁ δὲ Κῦρος ὑπολαβὼν τοὺς φεύγοντας, συλλέξας στράτευμα ἐπολιόρκει Μίλητον* Ib. 7.

NOTE. The distinction between the *direct object* and the *effect* of an action is not always obvious, and it sometimes appears doubtful to which head an adjunct is best referred.

§ **424.** REMARKS. 1. The term *action* is employed in this rule to denote *whatever is signified by a verb;* and the rule properly applies only to the adjuncts of *verbs* (§ 392). *Adjectives* and *nouns*, however, sometimes take the Acc. after the analogy of kindred verbs; thus, *Σὲ . . φύξιμος*, *able to escape you*, Soph. Ant. 788 (cf. *Ἦ μὴ φύγω σε;* Id. El. 1503). *Ἐπιστήμονες δὲ ἦσαν τὰ προσήκοντα* Cyr. iii. 3. 9. *Ἐξάρνῳ εἶναι τὰ ἐρωτώμενα* Pl. Charm. 158 c. *Τά τε μετέωρα φροντιστής* Pl. Apol. 18 b (cf. *Τῶν μετεώρων φροντιστής* Symp. 6. 6). *Χοὰς προπομπός* Æsch. Cho. 23. *Τῆς θυμοβόρου φρένα λύπης* Id. Ag. 103. *Συνίστορα . . κακά* Ib. 1090. See also § 431. 1.

2. Many verbs, which according to the preceding rules govern the *Gen.* or the *Dat.*, are likewise construed with the *Accusative* (see §§ 341, 401, 422. R.); as, *Ὠφελεῖν μὲν τοὺς φίλους, . . βλάπτειν δὲ τοὺς ἐχθρούς* Pl. Rep. 334 b (cf. § 403). *Προέχουσιν οἱ ἱππεῖς ἡμᾶς* iii. 2. 19 (cf. § 350). *Ἀνὴρ κατῆρχε λόγου* Pl. Euthyd. 283 b (cf. § 350. R.). *Δύναμαι οὔτε σε αἰσθέσθαι* ii. 5. 4 (cf. § 375. β). *Μεταδοῖεν αὐτοῖς πυρούς* iv. 5. 5 (cf. Ib. 6, and § 367). *Λέγειν τε ἐκέλευεν αὐτούς* vii. 5. 9 (cf. § 402).

§ **425.** 3. ATTRACTION. A word which is properly construed otherwise sometimes becomes the direct object of a verb by *attraction* (§ 329. N.), especially in the poets. This sometimes results in *hypallage*, or an interchange of construction (*ὑπαλλαγή*, *exchange*). Thus, *Εἰ δέ μ' ὧδ' ἀεὶ λόγους ἐξῆρχες* [= *μοι λόγους* or *λόγων*], *if you had always begun your addresses to me thus*, Soph. El. 556. *Δεσπόταν γόοις . . κατάρξω*, *I will begin lamentations for my master*, Eur. Andr. 1199. Cf. §§ 427. 9, 431, 433.

4. A verb, of which the proper object or effect is a distinct sentence, often takes the subject (or some other prominent word) of that sentence in the Acc., by attraction; as, *Ἤιδει αὐτὸν, ὅτι μέσον ἔχοι*, *he knew* [him] *that he occupied the centre*, i. 8. 21. *Τὴν γὰρ ὑπερβολὴν τῶν ὀρέων ἐδεδοίκεσαν, μὴ προκαταληφθείη* iii. 5. 18. *Ἤλεγχον τὴν κύκλῳ πᾶσαν χώραν, τίς ἑκάστη εἴη* Ib. 14. *Οἶνον ἔφρασεν, ἔνθα ἦν κατορωρυγμένος* iv. 5. 29. *Ὡς ὁρᾷ τὸν Καλλίμαχον, ἃ ἐποίει* iv. 7. 11.

5. PERIPHRASIS. The place of a verb is often supplied by an *Acc. of the kindred noun* joined with such verbs as ποιέω (or more frequently ποιέομαι), ἄγω, ἔχω, τίθημι, &c.; thus, Κῦρος ἐξέτασιν καὶ ἀριθμὸν τῶν Ἑλλήνων ἐποίησεν [= ἐξήτασε καὶ ἠρίθμησε τοὺς Ἕλληνας], *Cyrus made a review and numbering of* [= reviewed and numbered] *the Greeks*, i. 2. 9. Ἐξέτασιν ποιεῖται Ib. 14. Τὴν πορείαν ἐποιεῖτο i. 7. 20.

6. Such periphrases sometimes take an Acc. by virtue of the implied verb, as, Σκεύη μὲν καὶ ἀνδράποδα ἁρπαγὴν ποιησάμενος [= ἁρπάσας], Th. viii. 62. Τὴν χώραν καταδρομαῖς λείαν ἐποιεῖτο [= ἐλεηλάτει] Ib. 41. Ἃ χρῆν σε μετρίως . . σπουδὴν ἔχειν [= σπεύδειν] Eur. Herc. 709. Τὰ δ' ἐν μέσῳ ἢ λῆστιν ἴσχεις Soph. Œd. C. 583. Τίν' ἀεὶ τάκεις ὧδ' ἀκόρεστον οἰμωγὰν . . Ἀγαμέμνονα [= τί ὧδ' ἀκορέστως οἰμώζεις Ἀγαμέμνονα] Id. El. 122. In like manner, Τοῦτο κἄμ' ἔχει πόθος [= τοῦτο καὶ ἐγὼ ποθῶ] Eur. Ion, 572. Yet see §§ 333. 5, 434.

§ **426.** 7. ELLIPSIS. The *verb* which governs the Acc. is sometimes *omitted*; particularly,

α.) In EMPHATIC ADDRESS; as, Οὗτος, ὦ σέ τοι [sc. λέγω or καλῶ], *You there, ho! you I mean*, Ar. Av. 274 (§ 343. *b*). Σὲ δή, σὲ τὴν νεύουσαν ἐς πέδον κάρα, φῂς, ἢ καταρνεῖ μὴ δεδρακέναι τάδε; Soph. Ant. 441.

β.) In ENTREATY; as, Μή, πρός σε θεῶν [sc. ἱκετεύω], τλῇς με προδοῦναι, *I beseech you by the gods, do not forsake me*, Eur. Alc. 275. (Observe the arrangement, which is frequent in earnest entreaty; and compare, in Lat., *Per omnes te deos oro* Hor. Ode i. 8. 1. *Per te ego deos oro* Ter. Andr. iii. 3. 6.)

γ.) In PROHIBITION; as, Μὴ τριβὰς ἔτι [sc. ποιεῖτε], *No more delays!* Soph. Ant. 577. Μή μοι μυρίους, μηδὲ δισμυρίους ξένους [sc. λέγε], *Don't talk to me of your ten thousand or twenty thousand mercenaries*, Dem. 45. 11. Μή μοι πρόφασιν Ar. Ach. 345.

δ.) In SWEARING; as, Οὐ, τόνδ' Ὄλυμπον [sc. ὄμνυμι. Cf. § 428], *No, by this Olympus!* Soph. Ant. 758. Οὐ τὰν Διὸς ἀστραπάν Id. El. 1063. — By this ellipsis may be explained the use of the Acc. with the particles νή, ναί, and μά (of which the two first are *affirmative*, and the last, unless preceded by ναί, commonly *negative*), according to the following

SPECIAL RULE. ADVERBS OF SWEARING are followed by the Accusative; as, Νὴ Δία, *Yes, by Jupiter!* i. 7. 9. Ναὶ τὼ Σιώ vi. 6. 34. Ἀλλά, μὰ τοὺς θεούς, οὐκ ἔγωγε αὐτοὺς διώξω, *but, by the gods, I will not pursue them*, i. 4. 8. Ναὶ μὰ Δία, *Yes, indeed!* v. 8. 6.

§ **427.** 8. The *Acc.* required by a transitive verb is sometimes *omitted*; as, Ὁπότε ἢ πρὸς ὕδωρ βούλοιτο διατελέσαι [sc. τὴν ὁδόν] i. 5. 7. Cf. iv. 5. 11. Λύκιος ἤλασε [sc. τὸν ἵππον] i. 10. 15. Compare Παρελαύνοντος Cyr. viii. 3. 28, with Ἐλαύνοντος τὸν ἵππον Ib. 29; and Παρελαύνων τὸν ἵππον, with Προσελαύνων αὐτοῖς Cyr. v. 3. 55.

9. An elliptical or unusual construction of a verb and Acc. is sometimes employed, especially by the poets, for energy of expression; as, Ἔκειρε [= κείρων ἐποίει] πολύκερων φόνον Soph. Aj. 55. Αἷμ' ἔδευσα [= αἷμα τὴν γῆν δεῦον ἔχεα, or αἵματι τὴν γῆν ἔδευσα] Ib. 376. Τέγγει δακρύων ἄχναν Id. Tr. 849. Τρώσῃς φόνον Eur. Sup. 1205. Cf. §§ 425, 431, 433.

1. *Accusative of the Direct Object.*

§ **428.** I. This Acc. is often translated into English with a *preposition ;* thus,

Ὄμνυμι θεοὺς καὶ θεάς, *I swear* by *gods and goddesses,* vi. 6. 17. Οὗτοι μὲν γὰρ αὐτοὺς ἐπιωρκήκασιν, *for these have been guilty of perjury* against *them,* iii. 1. 22. Ἡμᾶς . . εὖ ποιῶν, *doing well* to *us,* i. e. *treating us well,* ii. 3. 23. Ὁ δὲ σίγλος δύναται ἑπτὰ ὀβολούς, *the siglus is equivalent* to *seven oboli,* i. 5. 6. Οὐδὲν ἄλλο δυναμένη ii. 2. 13. Μάχας θαρρεῖτε, *you have no fear* of *battles,* iii. 2. 20. Φυλαττόμενον . . ἡμᾶς, *guarding* against *us,* ii. 5. 3. Ἀποδεδρακότες πατέρας, *having run away* from *their fathers,* vi. 4. 8. Ὁ κολοιός μ' οἴχεται, *the jackdaw has departed* from *me,* i. e. *has left me,* Ar. Av. 86. Ἠισχύνθημεν καὶ θεοὺς καὶ ἀνθρώπους προδοῦναι αὐτόν, *we were ashamed* before *both gods and men to desert him,* ii. 3. 22. Αἰσχύνεται τὸ πρᾶγμα, *he is ashamed* of *the act,* Eur. Ion, 367. Τοὺς γὰρ εὐσεβεῖς θεοὶ θνήσκοντας οὐ χαίρουσι, *for the gods do not rejoice* in *the death of the pious,* Id. Hipp. 1340. Αἵ σε . χορεύουσι, τὸν ταμίαν Ἴακχον, 'dance in honor of,' Soph. Ant. 1153. Ἑλίσσετ' . . Ἄρτεμιν Eur. Iph. A. 1480.

§ **429.** II. To this head may be referred the use of the Acc. with VERBS OF MOTION, to denote the *place* or *person to which* (§§ 339, 422); as,

Ἀφίξεται τόπον ὑλώδη, *will come to a woody spot,* Ven. 10. 6. Ἄστυ Καδμεῖον μολών Soph. Œd. T. 35. Ἦλθον πατρὸς ἀρχαῖον τάφον Id. El. 893. Πύργους γῆς ἔπλευσ' Ἰωλκίας Eur. Med. 7. Ἀφίκετο χθόνα Ib. 12. Τήνδε ναυστολεῖς χθόνα Ib. 682. Ἥβης τέλος μολόντας Ib. 920. Χρεία τίς σε Θεσσαλῶν χθόνα πέμπει ; Id. Alc. 479. Κνίσση δ' οὐρανὸν ἷκεν A. 317. Ἔβαν νέας γ. 162.

NOTES. *α.* This use of the Acc. is chiefly poetic, and especially Epic, instead of the common construction with a preposition.

β. The poets sometimes even join an Acc. of the place with verbs of *standing, sitting,* or *lying* (as implying *occupation*) ; thus, Στῆθ' αἱ μὲν ὑμῶν τόνδ' ἁμαξήρη τρίβον, αἱ δ' ἐνθάδ' ἄλλον οἶμον Eur. Or. 1251. Θάσσοντ' ἄκραν Ib. 871. Τρίποδα καθίζων Φοῖβος Ib. 956. Τόπον . . ὅντινα κεῖται Soph. Ph. 144.

§ **430.** III. CAUSATIVES govern the Acc., together with the case of the included verb ; as,

Μή μ' ἀναμνήσῃς κακῶν, *do not remind me of* [cause me to remember] *my woes,* Eur. Alc. 1045 (§ 376. *γ*). Ἀναμνήσω γὰρ ὑμᾶς καὶ τοὺς . . κινδύνους iii. 2. 11 (§ 424. 2). Βούλει σε γεύσω πρῶτον ἄκρατον μέθυ ; Eur. Cycl. 149. Τοὺς παῖδας . . γευστέον αἵματος Pl. Rep. 537 a (§ 375. *α*). Πολλὰ καὶ ἡδέα καὶ παντοδαπὰ εὐώχουν ὑμᾶς Pl. Gorg. 522 a. See also § 357.

REMARK. The verbs δεῖ and χρή are sometimes construed by the poets as *causatives ;* thus, Σὲ δεῖ Προμηθέως, *you have need of* [it needs you of] *a Prometheus,* Æsch. Prom. 86 (§ 357). Πόνου πολλοῦ με δεῖ Eur. Hipp. 23. Τί γάρ μ' ἔδει παίδων ; Eur. Suppl. 789 (cf. Σοί τε γὰρ παίδων τί δεῖ Id. Med. 565, and § 403). Τί χρὴ φίλων ; Id. Or. 667 (but Porson reads Τί δεῖ φίλων, denying that this use of χρή is Attic). Σὲ χρὴ . . αἰδοῦς γ. 14.

2. *Accusative of the Effect.*

§ **431.** The EFFECT of a verb includes whatever the agent does or makes. Hence any verb may take an Acc. expressing or defining its action. The Acc. thus employed is either, α. a *noun kindred, in its origin or signification, to the verb*, or β. a *neuter adjective used substantively*, or γ. a *noun simply defining or characterizing the action.*

α. KINDRED NOUN.

Οἱ δὲ Θρᾷκες ἐπεὶ εὐτύχησαν τοῦτο τὸ εὐτύχημα, *and when the Thracians had gained this success*, vi. 3. 6. Ὡς ἀκίνδῡνον βίον ζῶμεν, *how secure a life we live*, Eur. Med. 248. Στρατηγήσοντα ἐμὲ ταύτην τὴν στρατηγίαν i. 3. 15. Γαμεῖν γάμον τόνδε Eur. Med. 587. Τί προσγελᾶτε τὸν πανύστατον γέλων; Ib. 1041. Ἐπιμελοῦνται πᾶσαν ἐπιμέλειαν Pl. Prot. 325 c. Βασιλείαν πασῶν δικαιοτάτην βασιλευόμενοι Pl. Leg. 680 e. Φευγέτω ἀειφυγίαν Ib. 877 c. Τὸν ἱερὸν καλούμενον πόλεμον ἐστράτευσαν Th. i. 112. Ἦιξαν δρόμημα δεινόν Eur. Ph. 1379. Πήδημα κοῦφον ἐκ νεὼς ἀφήλατο Æsch. Pers. 305. Λεύσσων φονίου δέργμα δράκοντος Ib. 79. Τήνδ' ὁ προσθᾱκῶν ἕδραν Soph. Œd. C. 1166. Ὠρχοῦντο τὴν καρπαίαν vi. 1. 7. Πορευτέον δ' ἡμῖν τοὺς πρώτους σταθμούς ii. 2. 12. Ἔλθοι τὴν ὁδόν iii. 1. 6. Ἔφη ἡγήσεσθαι . . ὁδόν iv. 1. 24. Τρέπεται τριφασίας ὁδούς Hdt. vi. 119.

REMARKS. 1. In like manner, an *adjective* sometimes takes an Acc. of the kindred noun (§ 424. 1); as, Μήτε τι σοφὸς ὢν τὴν ἐκείνων σοφίαν, μήτε ἀμαθὴς τὴν ἀμαθίαν, *being neither wise with their wisdom, nor foolish with their folly*, Pl. Apol. 22 e. Κακοὺς πᾶσαν κακίαν Pl. Rep. 490 d. Δοῦλος τὰς μεγίστας θωπείας καὶ δουλείας Ib. 579 d.

2. It will be observed, that usually an adjective is joined with the Acc. of the kindred noun, and the whole phrase is an emphatic substitution for an adverb. Thus, Ὡς ἀκίνδῡνον βίον ζῶμεν = Ὡς ἀκινδύνως ζῶμεν. This adjective not unfrequently occurs with an ellipsis of the noun; as, Τὸ Περσικὸν ὠρχεῖτο [sc. ὄρχημα] vi. 1. 10. Hence appears to have arisen the construction in § 432.

§ **432.** β. NEUTER ADJECTIVE.

Τοιαῦτα μὲν πεποίηκε, τοιαῦτα δὲ λέγει, [he has done such things, and says such things] *such has been his conduct, and such is his language*, i. 6. 9. Λέγεις οὐκ ἀχάριστα ii. 1. 13. Ταῦτα χαρίσωνται Ib. 10. Τὰ Λύκαια ἔθῡσε i. 2. 10. Μηδὲν ψεύδεσθαι i. 9. 7. Μέγα φρονήσας iii. 1. 27. Ἀνέκραγέ τε πολεμικόν vii. 3. 33. Χρήσασθαί τι τῇ στρατιᾷ, *to make some use of the army*, Cyr. viii. 1. 14. Τί αὐτῷ χρήσῃ; *what would you do with him?* Ib. i. 4. 13. Τί σεμνὸν καὶ πεφροντικὸς βλέπεις; *why do you look grave and thoughtful?* Eur. Alc. 773. Καλὸν βλέπω Id. Cycl. 553. Κλέπτον βλέπει Ar. Vesp. 900.

REMARKS. 1. This construction (upon which see § 431. 2) is closely allied with the *adverbial use* of the neuter adjective § 440), and is, perhaps, its origin.

2. The *Acc. of the neuter adjective* is very extensive in its use, and often occurs where a *substantive* would have been constructed differently; thus, Τάδε μέντοι πλεονεκτῶν οὐκ ᾐσχύνετο, ἐν μὲν τῷ θέρει τοῦ ἡλίου, ἐν δὲ τῷ

χειμῶνι τοῦ ψύχους Ages. 5. 3. ΧΡ. Ὀσφραίνει τι; ΔΙΚ. Τοῦ ψύχους Ar. Plut. 896.

3. The Acc. of the *neuter pronoun* is sometimes used to denote that *on account of which* any thing is done (viewed originally as the *effect* or *result* of the action); as, Ἃ δ' ἦλθον, *but what I came for*, Soph. Œd. C. 1291. Ταῦτ' ἐγὼ ἔσπευδον, *therefore* [on account of these things] *I made haste*, iv. 1. 21. Τί τὰ πυρὰ κατασβέσειαν, 'why,' vi. 3. 25. Τοῦτ' ἀφικόμην Id. Œd. T. 1005. Ἀλλ' αὐτὰ ταῦτα καὶ νῦν ἥκω Pl. Prot. 310 e. Νεώτατος δ' ἦν Πριαμιδῶν· ὃ καί με γῆς ὑπεξέπεμψεν Eur. Hec. 13. Ἐκεῖνο δὲ ἀθυμῶ, ὅτι μοι δοκεῖ Mem. iv. 3. 15.

NOTE. So with χρῆμα, *thing*, expressed, Τί χρῆμα κεῖσαι; *why do you lie there?* Eur. Heracl. 633. See Ib. 646, 709; Id. Alc. 512; &c.

§ **433.** γ. DEFINITIVE NOUN.

Φόβον βλέπων, *looking terror*, Æsch. Sept. 498. Ἡ βουλὴ .. ἔβλεψε νᾶπυ, *the senate looked mustard*, Ar. Eq. 629. Ἄρη δεδορκότων Æsch. Sept. 53. Ἀλφιτὸν πνέων Ar. Av. 1121. Ἄιδων τὸν Σιτάλκαν vi. 1. 6. Ἐλπίδας λέγων i. 2. 11. Ὀλύμπια νενικηκότι, *having conquered in the Olympic games*, Th. i. 126. Νενικήκατε ναυμαχίας Id. vii. 66. Νενικηκότα αὐτὸν παγκράτιον Symp. i. 2. Ἠγωνίζοντο δὲ παῖδες μὲν στάδιον, .. πάλην δὲ καὶ πυγμὴν καὶ παγκράτιον ἕτεροι iv. 8. 27. Πολλὰς μάχας ἥττηνται Isocr. 71 e. Χορηγοῦντα παισὶ Διονύσια Dem. 535. 13.

3. *Double Accusative.*

§ **434.** The same verb often governs TWO ACCUSATIVES, which may be,

I.) The DIRECT OBJECT and the EFFECT, *in apposition* with each other (§ **331**); as with verbs of *making*, *appointing*, *choosing*, *esteeming*, *naming*, &c. Thus,

Βασιλέα σε ἐποίησαν, *they made you king*, vii. 7. 22. Στρατηγὸν δὲ αὐτὸν ἀπέδειξε, *and he had appointed him general*, i. 1. 2. Πατέρα ἐμὲ ἐκαλεῖτε, *you called me father*, vii. 6. 38. Ὅστις δ' ἂν ἑαυτὸν ἕληται στρατηγόν v. 7. 28. Οὓς οἱ Σύροι θεοὺς ἐνόμιζον i. 4. 9. Ὃν ὠνόμαζε Διομήδην πατήρ Eur. Sup. 1218. Ὄνομα τί σε καλεῖν ἡμᾶς χρεών; Id. Ion, 259. Θεμιστοκλῆς Κλεόφαντον τὸν υἱὸν ἱππέα μὲν ἐδιδάξατο ἀγαθόν Pl. Meno, 93 d. Οὓς ἡγεμόνας πόλεων ἐπαιδεύσασθε Pl. Rep. 546 b. Κῦρος τὸ στράτευμα κατένειμε δώδεκα μέρη, *Cyrus divided the army into twelve parts*, Cyr. vii. 5. 13.

NOTE. The infinitive εἶναι is often used with these verbs; as, Νομίζω γὰρ ὑμᾶς ἐμοὶ εἶναι καὶ πατρίδα καὶ φίλους i. 3. 6. Σοφιστὴν δή τοι ὀνομάζουσι .. τὸν ἄνδρα εἶναι Pl. Prot. 311 e.

§ **435.** II.) The DIRECT OBJECT and the EFFECT, *not in apposition;* as with verbs of *doing*, *saying*, &c. Thus,

Εἴ τίς τι ἀγαθὸν ἢ κακὸν ποιήσειεν αὐτόν, *if any one had done him any good or evil*, i. 9. 11. Τὰ μέγιστα κακὰ ἐργαζόμενοι τὰς πόλεις Pl. Rep. 495 b. Ἠδικήσαμεν τοῦτον οὐδέν vii. 6. 22. Ἡλίκα ταῦτ' ὠφέλησεν ἅπαντας Dem. 255. 7. Ἀποτίσασθαι δίκην ἐχθρούς Eur. Heracl. 852.

Ταῦτα καὶ καθύβρισ' αὐτόν Id. Bac. 616. Ὅταν ἐν ταῖς τραγῳδίαις ἀλλήλους τὰ ἔσχατα λέγωσιν, 'say the worst things to each other,' Mem. ii. 2. 9. Πολλὰ πρὸς πολλούς με δὴ ἐξεῖπας Soph. El. 520. Τὰ σέμν' ἔπη κόλαζ' ἐκείνους Id. Aj. 1107. Ἔπη κλύων, ἃ νῦν σὺ τήνδ' ἀτιμάζεις πόλιν Id. Œd. T. 339. Ἐψευσάμην οὐδέν σε Id. Œd. C. 1145. Τί . . γράψειεν ἄν σε μουσοποιὸς ἐν τάφῳ; Eur. Tro. 1188. Τοσοῦτον ἔχθος ἐχθαίρω σ' ἐγώ Soph. El. 1034. Ὥρκωσαν πάντας τοὺς στρατιώτας τοὺς μεγίστους ὅρκους Th. viii. 75. Μέλιτός με ἐγράψατο τὴν γραφὴν ταύτην Pl. Apol. 19 a. Γαμεῖ με δυστυχέστερον γάμον Eur. Tro. 357. Κτύπησε κρᾶτα μέλεον πλαγάν Id. Or. 1467. Ἀλλ' ἁγνὸν ὅρκον σὸν κάρα κατώμοσα Id. Hel. 835. Ἀναδῆσαι βούλομαι εὐαγγέλιά σε Ar. Plut. 764. Μιλτιάδης ὁ τὴν ἐν Μαραθῶνι μάχην τοὺς βαρβάρους νικήσας Æschin. 79. 36.

§ **436.** III.) Two OBJECTS differently related, but which are both regarded as DIRECT; as with verbs of *asking* and *requiring*, of *clothing* and *unclothing*, of *concealing* and *depriving*, of *persuading* and *teaching*, &c. Thus,

Κῦρον αἰτεῖν πλοῖα, *to ask vessels of Cyrus*, or *to ask Cyrus for vessels*, i. 3. 14. Μήτοι με κρύψῃς τοῦτο, *do not hide this from me*, Æsch. Pr. 625. Ἡμᾶς δὲ ἀποστερεῖ τὸν μισθόν, *but us he robs of our pay*, vii. 6 9. Σὲ διδάσκειν τὴν στρατηγίαν, *to teach you the military art*, Mem. iii. 1. 5. Πρὸς τί με ταῦτα ἐρωτᾷς; Mem. iii. 7. 2. Ἀνήρεθ' ἡμᾶς τούς τ' ἐν Ἰλίῳ πόνους, . . ἀνηρώτα τ' ἐμὲ γυναῖκα, παῖδάς τε Eur. Iph. T. 661. Τοσαῦτά σ' ὦ Ζεῦ, προστρέπω Soph. Aj. 831. Ὑμᾶς δὲ ὁ βασιλεὺς τὰ ὅπλα ἀπαιτε ii. 5. 38. Ἐὰν πράττητε αὐτὸν τὰ χρήματα, 'demand,' 'exact,' vii. 6. 17 Οἱ Λοκροὶ . . τέλη τοὺς καταπλέοντας ἐξέλεγον Æschin. 69. 29. Ταῦτα προὐκαλεῖτο τοὺς συνόντας Cyr. i. 4. 4. Τοῦτο μὲν δὴ μὴ ἀνάγκαζέ μ Pl. Rep. 473 a. Τὸν μὲν ἑαυτοῦ [sc. χιτῶνα] ἐκεῖνον ἠμφίεσε Cyr. i. 3. 17. Τὸν δῆμον ὑμῶν χλαῖναν ἤμπισχον Ar. Lys. 1156. Ἐκδύων ἐμὲ χρηστηρίαν ἐσθῆτα Æsch. Ag. 1269. Ἀφαιρεῖσθαι τοὺς ἐνοικοῦντας Ἕλληνας τὴν γῆν i. 3. 4 (cf. § 411). Ὅς με . . ψιλὸν ὄμμ' ἀποσπάσας Soph. Œd. C. 866. Τὴν μὲν γὰρ θεὸν τοὺς στεφάνους σεσυλήκασι Dem. 616. 19. Σὲ ταῦτα μὴ πείθων Soph. Œd. C. 797. Σύ τε γάρ με εὐθὺς τοῦτο . . ἐπαίδευες Cyr. i. 6. 20. Οὐκ ἐάσει τοῦτό γ' ἡ δίκη σε Soph. Ant. 538. Ὅς σε κωλύσει τὸ δρᾶν Id. Phil. 1241. Γυναῖκ' ἀρίσταν λίμναν Ἀχεροντίαν πορεύσας Eur. Alc. 442. Ποῖ μ' ὑπεξάγεις πόδα; Eur. Hec. 812 (cf. Ὁ κολοιός μ' οἴχεται, § 428). Χρόα νίζετο . . ἅλμην ζ. 224. Διατρίβησιν Ἀχαιοὺς ὃν γάμον β. 204. See also § 430.

(II.) ACCUSATIVE OF SPECIFICATION.

§ **437.** RULE XXII. An adjunct applying a word or expression to a PARTICULAR PART, PROPERTY, THING, or PERSON, is put in the Accusative; as,

Τὼ χεῖρε δεδεμένον, [bound as to the hands] *with his hands bound*, vi. 1. 8. Ποταμὸς, Κύδνος ὄνομα, εὖρος δύο πλέθρων, *a river, Cydnus by name, two plethra in breadth*, i. 2. 23. Πάντα κράτιστος, *best in every thing*, i. 9. 2 (cf. § 359. β). Ἀποτμηθέντες τὰς κεφαλάς, *beheaded*, ii. 6. 1, 29. Τὰ ὦτα τετρυπημένον iii. 1. 31. Θαυμάσιαι τὸ κάλλος καὶ τὸ μέγεθος ii. 3. 15.

Πλῆθος ὡς δισχίλιοι iv. 2. 2. Παῖδας . . οὐ πολλοῦ δέοντας ἴσους τὸ μῆκος καὶ τὸ πλάτος εἶναι, ποικίλους δὲ τὰ νῶτα, καὶ τὰ ἔμπροσθεν πάντα ἐστιγμένους ἀνθέμιον v. 4. 32. Δεινός εἰμι ταύτην τὴν τέχνην Cyr. viii. 4. 18. Πόλιν τὴν οὐδὲν αἰτίαν vii. 1. 25 (cf. § 393. γ). Ὅσα δέ μοι χρήσιμοι ἐστε ii. 5. 23. Cf. §§ 369, 418. 3.

§ **438.** Remarks. α. This use of the Acc. is often termed *synecdoche*, from its analogy to the rhetorical figure bearing that name.

β. Where a verb is in this way followed by two accusatives, the construction (which is most frequent in Epic poetry) may be often referred to the Σχῆμα καθ' ὅλον καὶ μέρος (§ 334. 9); as, Ποῖόν σε ἔπος φύγεν ἕρκος ὀδόντων, *What language has escaped* [you, the hedge of the teeth] *the hedge of your teeth!* α. 64. Τόνγε . . λίπ' ὀστέα θυμός Υ. 406. Cf. § 413.

γ. An Acc. of specification sometimes introduces a sentence; as, Τοὺς μέντοι Ἕλληνας, τοὺς ἐν τῇ Ἀσίᾳ οἰκοῦντας, οὐδὲν πω σαφὲς λέγεται, εἰ ἕπονται, 'but as to the Greeks,' Cyr. ii. 1. 5. Τὸ μὲν οὖν σύνταγμα τῆς τότε πολιτείας καὶ τὸν χρόνον, ὅσον αὐτῇ χρώμενοι διετελέσαμεν, ἐξαρκούντως δεδήλωται Isocr. 264 c. Τὸν δὲ πόνον τὸν κατὰ τὸν πόλεμον, μὴ γίνηταί τε πολύς Th. ii. 62. Τοὺς ἀγρονόμους τούτους . . ἐπειδὴ φερέσθωσαν Pl. Leg. 761 e.—This construction may usually be referred to *anacolūthon* or *ellipsis*.

δ. The Acc. is sometimes used in *exclamations*, to specify the object of emotion (cf. §§ 343. 2, 372. ε, ζ); as, Ἰώ, ἰὼ λιγείας μόρον ἀηδόνος, *oh, oh for the fate of the melodious nightingale*, Æsch. Ag. 1146. Δεινόν γε τὸν κήρυκα τὸν παρὰ τοὺς βροτοὺς οἰχόμενον, εἰ μηδέποτε νοστήσει πάλιν Ar. Av. 1269.—This construction, which is unfrequent, should perhaps be referred to ellipsis.

(III.) Accusative of Extent.

§ **439.** Rule XXIII. Extent of time and space is put in the Accusative (cf. §§ 378, 420); as,

α. Time. Ἔμεινεν ἡμέρας ἑπτά, *he remained seven days*, i. 2. 6. Ἐδάκρυε πολὺν χρόνον i. 3. 2. Ζῶν αἰκισθεὶς ἐνιαυτόν ii. 6. 29. Ἔπλεον ἡμέραν καὶ νύκτα vi. 1. 14. Πορευόμενοι τὸ λοιπὸν τῆς ἡμέρας iii. 4. 6. Τοὺς μὲν γὰρ κύνας τοὺς χαλεποὺς τὰς μὲν ἡμέρας διδέασι, τὰς δὲ νύκτας ἀφιᾶσι· τοῦτον δέ, ἢν σωφρονῆτε, τὴν νύκτα μὲν δήσετε, τὴν δὲ ἡμέραν ἀφήσετε v. 8. 24. Οἱ τριάκοντα ἔτη γεγονότες, 'thirty years old,' ii. 3. 12. Τὴν θυγατέρα τοῦ κωμάρχου ἐνάτην ἡμέραν γεγαμημένην iv. 5. 24. Τρίτην ἡμέραν αὐτοῦ ἥκοντος Th. viii. 23. Δέκατον αἰχμάζεις ἔτος Eur. Rhes. 444. Ὃς τέθνηκε ταῦτα τρία ἔτη, 'these three years,' Lys. 109. 12.

β. Space. Ἐξελαύνει διὰ Φρυγίας σταθμὸν ἕνα, παρασάγγας ὀκτώ, *he advances through Phrygia one day's-march, eight parasangs*, i. 2. 6. Ἀπέχουσα τοῦ ποταμοῦ σταδίους πεντεκαίδεκα ii. 4. 13. Μυρίας ἐμέ γε κατὰ γῆς ὀργυιὰς γενέσθαι vii. 1. 30. Τὸ βέλος αὐτῶν καὶ διπλάσιον [sc. διάστημα] φέρεσθαι τῶν Περσικῶν σφενδονῶν iii. 3. 16. Ὁπόσον δὲ προδιώξειαν οἱ Ἕλληνες, τοσοῦτον πάλιν ἐπαναχωρεῖν μαχομένους ἔδει iii. 3. 10.

Note. In the simple designation of *time* and *place*, the genitive commonly expresses the time and place *in which* (§ 378); the dative, *at which* (§ 420); and the accusative, *through which*. To a certain extent, however, the offices of the several cases blend with each other.

(IV.) ADVERBIAL ACCUSATIVE.

§ **440.** RULE XXIV. The Accusative is often used ADVERBIALLY, to express *degree*, *manner*, *order*, &c.; as,

Τόνδε τὸν τρόπον, *in this way*, or *thus*, i. 1. 9. Τὸν αὐτὸν τρόπον vi. 5. 6 (cf. Τῷ αὐτῷ τρόπῳ iv. 2. 13, and § 418). Τέλος δὲ εἶπε, *and finally* [at the end] *he said*, ii. 3. 26. Ἀρχὴν μὴ πλουτῆσαι, 'in the first place,' 'at all,' vii. 7. 28. Ὁ ὄχλος ἀκμὴν διέβαινε iv. 3. 26. Τούτου χάριν, *on account of this*, Mem. i. 2. 54. Κυνὸς δίκην, *like a dog*, Æsch. Ag. 3. Καιρὸν δ' ἐφήκεις, 'opportunely,' Soph. Aj. 34. Ἀωρίαν ἥκοντες Ar. Ach. 23. Τὴν ὥρην ἐπαγινέειν Hdt. ii. 2. Συντάττεσθαι τὴν ταχίστην [sc. ὁδόν] i. 3. 14 (cf. i. 2. 20). Οὐκοῦν, ἔφη, καὶ περὶ πολέμου συμβουλεύειν τήν γε πρώτην ἐπισχήσομεν, 'for the present,' Mem. iii. 6. 10. See § 320. 3.

§ **441.** REMARKS. α. This rule applies especially to the Acc. *neut.* of *adjectives*, both sing. and plur.; as, Τὸ ἀρχαῖον, *formerly*, i. 1. 6. Τὰ μὲν . ., τὰ δέ, *partly* . ., *partly*, iv. 1. 14, v. 6. 24. Μικρὸν ἐξέφυγε τὸ μὴ καταπετρωθῆναι i. 3. 2. Τυχόν, *perhaps*, vi. 1. 20. Τὸ λοιπόν, *henceforth*, ii. 2. 5. Εἴ τινος μέγα ἦν τὸ σῶμα φύσει ἢ τροφῇ ἢ ἀμφότερα Pl. Gorg. 524 b. Τοσοῦτον γὰρ πλήθει περιῆν βασιλεύς i. 8. 13. Θυμοειδέστεροι δὲ πολύ iv. 5. 36 (cf. § 419). See especially § 162.

β. A strict analysis would refer the adverbial Acc. in part to the Acc. of *effect* (§ 432), in part to that of *specification* (§ 437), and in part to that of *extent* (§ 422. III.).

F. THE VOCATIVE.

§ **442.** RULE XXV. The COMPELLATIVE of a sentence is put in the Vocative (§§ 329. N., 340. α); as,

Κλέαρχε καὶ Πρόξενε, . . οὐκ ἴστε ὅ τι ποιεῖτε, *Clearchus and Proxenus, you know not what you do*, i. 5. 16. Ὦ θαυμασιώτατε ἄνθρωπε, *O most wonderful man*, iii. 1. 27.

§ **443.** REMARKS. α. The *sign of address*, in Greek, as in other languages, is commonly ὦ.

β. The term of respectful address to a company of men is ἄνδρες, with which may be likewise connected a more specific appellation; thus,

Ὁρᾶτε μέν, ὦ ἄνδρες, *you see, gentlemen*, iii. 2. 4. Ἄνδρες στρατιῶται, μὴ θαυμάζετε, *fellow-soldiers, do not wonder*, i. 3. 3. Ὦ ἄνδρες Ἕλληνες ii. 3. 15. Ὦ ἄνδρες στρατηγοὶ καὶ λοχαγοί iii. 1. 34.

CHAPTER II.

SYNTAX OF THE ADJECTIVE.

I AGREEMENT OF THE ADJECTIVE.

§ 444. RULE XXVI. An ADJECTIVE agrees with its *subject* in *gender*, *number*, and *case*.

The word *adjective* is here used in its largest sense (§ 73). Thus, Παράδεισος μέγας ἀγρίων θηρίων πλήρης, *a large park full of wild beasts*, i. 2. 7. Τὼ παῖδε ἀμφοτέρω, *both the children*, i. 1. 1. Αἱ Ἰωνικαὶ πόλεις . . δεδομέναι Ib. 6. Τόνδε τὸν τρόπον Ib. 9. Ἔχων ὁπλίτας χιλίους καὶ πελταστὰς Θρᾷκας ὀκτακοσίους i. 2. 9. Θεοὺς πάντας καὶ πάσας vi. 1. 31.

NOTES. *α*. An adjective either assists in describing the thing which is spoken of, or forms a part of that which is said of it. In the former case, the adjective is said to be used as an *epithet* (ἐπίθετον, from ἐπιτίθημι, *to add*); in the latter, as an *attribute* (attribūtus, *ascribed*). In the sentence, "A good man is merciful," "good" is an epithet, and "merciful" an attribute. The agreement of the *attribute* with its subject is far less strict than that of the *epithet*; while the agreement of the *pronoun* (§ 495) is still less strict than that of the *attribute*.

β. An exception to this rule, which is merely apparent, consists in the use of the *masculine* form for the *feminine* in adjectives of three terminations (§ 133. *γ*, *δ*).

§ 445. REMARKS. 1. Infinitives, clauses used substantively, and words or phrases spoken of as such, are regarded as *neuter*; thus,

Εὔηθες εἴη ἡγεμόνα αἰτεῖν, *it would be foolish to ask a guide*, i. 3. 16. Δῆλον ἦν ὅτι ἐγγύς που βασιλεὺς ἦν ii. 3. 6. Οὐ τὸ ζῆν περὶ πλείστου ποιητέον, ἀλλὰ τὸ εὖ ζῆν Pl. Crito, 48 b. Ὑμεῖς, ὦ ἄνδρες Ἀθηναῖοι· τὸ δ' ὙΜΕΙΣ ὅταν εἴπω, τὴν πόλιν λέγω, *You, men of Athens; and when I say* YOU, *I mean the state*, Dem. 255. 4. Τὸ ΜΗ καὶ τὸ ΟΥ προτιθέμενα, *the* NOT *and the* NO *prefixed*, Pl. Soph. 257 b. Χρῆσθαι . . τῷ καθ' αὑτό, *to use the phrase* καθ' αὑτό Ib. 252 c.

NOTE. Grammarians often speak of a word, with an ellipsis of the part of speech to which it belongs; as, Ἔστιν ὁ [sc. σύνδεσμος] ἀλλά ἀντὶ τοῦ δέ, *the* [*conjunction*] ἀλλά *is instead of* δέ Soph. Œd. C. 237, Schol. Λείπει ἡ [sc. πρόθεσις] διά, [*the preposition*] διά *is wanting*, Ib. 1291, Schol.

§ 446. 2. In COMPOUND CONSTRUCTION, both *syllepsis* and *zeugma* are frequent (§ 329. N.). (*α*.) In *syllepsis*, when *persons* of both sexes are spoken of, the adjective is *masculine*; when *things* are spoken of, it is commonly *neuter*; as,

Ὡς δὲ εἶδε πατέρα τε καὶ μητέρα καὶ ἀδελφοὺς καὶ τὴν ἑαυτοῦ γυναῖκα αἰχμαλώτους γεγενημένους Cyr. iii. 1. 6. *Λίθοι τε καὶ πλίνθοι καὶ ξύλα καὶ κέραμος ἀτάκτως μὲν ἐῤῥιμμένα οὐδὲν χρήσιμά ἐστιν* Mem. iii. 2. 7.

(*β*.) In *zeugma*, the adjective sometimes agrees with the *most prominent* substantive, sometimes with the *nearest;* as,

Ἑπτὰ ὀβολοὺς καὶ ἡμιωβόλιον Ἀττικούς, seven Attic oboli and a half, i. 5. 6. *Πυθόμενος . . τὸν Στρομβιχίδην καὶ τὰς ναῦς ἀπεληλυθότα* Th. viii. 63. *Παῖδας ἢ γυναῖκας συναρμοζούσας* Cyr. vii. 5. 60. *Μητρός τε καὶ τοῦ σοῦ πατρός* Soph. Œd. T. 417.

§ **447.** 3. Ellipsis. The subject of the adjective is often *omitted*, especially if it is a familiar word. The words most frequently omitted are,

α. Masculine, *ἀνήρ* or *ἄνθρωπος, man, χρόνος, time;* as, *Συντάξαι δὲ ἕκαστον τοὺς ἑαυτοῦ* [sc. *ἄνδρας*], *and that each one should arrange his own* [*men*], i. 2. 15. *Τῶν παρὰ βασιλέως* i. 1. 5. *Τοὺς φεύγοντας, the exiles,* Ib. 7. *Τοὺς κακούργους καὶ ἀδίκους* [sc. *ἀνθρώπους*] i. 9. 13. *Ἐνταῦθα ἔμειναν ἡμέρας τρεῖς· ἐν ᾧ* [sc. *χρόνῳ*] *Κῦρος ἀπέκτεινεν* i. 2. 20. *Ἐν τούτῳ καὶ βασιλεὺς δῆλος ἦν* i. 10. 6 (cf. *Ἐν τούτῳ τῷ χρόνῳ* iv. 2. 17).

β. Feminine, *γυνή, woman, γῆ* or *χώρα, land, ὁδός, way, ἡμέρα, day, χείρ, hand, γνώμη, opinion, μοῖρα, portion, ὥρα, season;* as, *Ἡ Κίλισσα* [sc. *γυνή*] i. 2. 12. *Πορεύεσθαι ὡς διὰ φιλίας* ii. 3. 27 (cf. *Ὅστις διὰ φιλίας τῆς χώρας ἀπάξει* i. 3. 14). *Εἰς τὴν φιλίαν ἐλθεῖν* vi. 6. 38 (cf. *Εἰς φιλίαν γῆν ἀφίκοιντο* v. 1. 1. See also § 421. *β*). *Τὴν λοιπὴν* [sc. *ὁδὸν*] *πορευσόμεθα* iii. 4. 46. *Καὶ αὐτοὶ μὲν ἂν ἐπορεύθησαν ᾗ οἱ ἄλλοι, τὰ δὲ ὑποζύγια οὐκ ἦν ἄλλῃ ἢ ταύτῃ ἐκβῆναι* iv. 2. 10. *Ἰέντες μακράν* iii. 4. 17. *Τῇ ὑστεραίᾳ* [sc. *ἡμέρᾳ*] *οὐκ ἐφάνησαν οἱ πολέμιοι, οὐδὲ τῇ τρίτῃ, τῇ δὲ τετάρτῃ* iii. 4. 37 (§ 420). *Ἐν δὲ τῇ δεξιᾷ* [sc. *χειρί*] v. 4. 12. *Ἐν δεξιᾷ, on the right,* i. 5. 1. *Ἐν ἀριστερᾷ* vi. 1. 14. *Ἐκ τῆς νικώσης* [sc. *γνώμης*] *ἔπραττον πάντα*, 'according to the vote of the majority,' vi. 1. 18. *Ἀπὸ τῆς ἴσης* [sc. *μοίρας*], *on equal terms,* Th. i. 15. *Ἐπὶ τῇ ἴσῃ καὶ ὁμοίᾳ* Id. i. 27. *Ἡ πεπρωμένη, destiny,* Eur. Hec. 43. *Ἀπὸ πρώτης* [sc. *ὥρας*], *from the first,* Th. i. 77.

γ. Neuter, *πρᾶγμα* or *χρῆμα, affair, thing, μέρος, part, πλῆθος, collection, body, στράτευμα, military force, κέρας, wing of an army, χωρίον, place, ground;* as, *Τὰ μὲν δὴ Κύρου* [sc. *πράγματα*] . ., *τὰ ἡμέτερα* i. 3. 9 (cf. *Τὰ Ὀδρυσῶν πράγματα* vii. 2. 32). *Εἰς τὸ ἴδιον* [sc. *χρῆμα*] i. 3. 3. *Τὰ ἐπιτήδεια, the necessaries of life,* i. 5. 10. *Τῷ ὄντι, really,* v. 4. 20. *Ξενοφῶντος Ἑλληνικά, Xenophon's Affairs of Greece,* or *Greek History.* *Ἐξεκύμαινέ τι* [sc. *μέρος*] *τῆς φάλαγγος* i. 8. 18. *Τὰ δεξιὰ τοῦ κέρατος* Ib. 4. *Τοῦ . . ξενικοῦ* [sc. *πλήθους* or *στρατεύματος*], *the mercenary force* [= *τῶν ξένων, the mercenaries*], i. 2. 1. *Τοῦ Ἑλληνικοῦ* [= *τῶν Ἑλλήνων*] i. 4. 13 (cf. i. 2. 1). *Τὸ ξυνεστηκός* (cf. *Τοῖς ξυνεστῶσι*) Th. viii. 66. *Τὸ θῆλυ γάρ πως μᾶλλον οἰκτρὸν ἀρσένων* Eur. Herc. 536. *Τὸ κοινὸν τὸ ἡμέτερον* v. 7. 17. *Τὸ δὲ εὐώνυμον* i. 2. 15 (cf. *Τὸ εὐώνυμον κέρας* i. 8. 4). *Ἐν τῷ ὁμαλῷ* [sc. *χωρίῳ*] iv. 2. 16. *Ἀπὸ τοῦ ὑψηλοῦ εἰς τὸ πρανὲς ἔβαλλον* iii. 4. 25. See also § 379. *α*.

Notes. (a.) In cases of familiar ellipsis, the adjective is commonly said to be used *substantively.* The substantive use becomes especially prominent in such expressions as, *Τοῖς μὲν ὑμετέροις δυσμενέσι*, 'your foes,' H. Gr. v. 2. 33; *Ὅ τ' ἐκείνου τεκών*, 'his father,' Eur. El. 335. (b.) The substantive omitted is sometimes contained or implied in another word; as, *Ἀμυγδάλινον ἐκ τῶν* πικρῶν [sc. ἀμυγδάλων] iv. 4. 13. Γεωργεῖν τὸν μὲν πολλήν [sc. γῆν] Ar. Eccl. 592. Καλοῦσι δ' Ἰοκάστην με· τοῦτο [sc. ὄνομα] γὰρ πατὴρ ἔθετο Eur. Ph. 12. (c.) In the phrase ἐν ἡμετέρου, *in our palace, at our court* (Hdt. i. 35, vii. 8. 4), there is either a double ellipsis for the sake of dignity (ἐν ἡμετέρου οἴκου δώμασιν); or a blending of the two forms of expression, ἐν ἡμῶν οἴκῳ, and ἐν ἡμετέρῳ οἴκῳ.

§ **448.** 4. Many words which are commonly employed as substantives are properly adjectives, or may be used as such. Thus,

Ὀρόντης δὲ Πέρσης ἀνήρ, *and Orontes, a Persian man*, i. 6. 1. Ὦ ἄνδρες στρατιῶται, . . ἀνδρῶν στρατηγῶν iii. 2. 2. Ἄνδρα νεανίαν Cyr. ii. 2. 6. Νεανίας λόγους Eur. Alc. 679. Ἕλλην τις ἀνήρ Cyr. vi. 3. 11. Ἕλλην' ἐς οἶκον Eur. Med. 1331. Στολήν γ' Ἑλληνα Id. Heracl. 130. Ἑλλάδος γῆς Soph. Phil. 256. Στρατιᾶς Ἑλλάδος Eur. Rhes. 233. Γυναῖκα Τρῳάδα Id. Andr. 867. Τρῳάδος χθονός Id. El. 1001. Σκύθην ἐς οἶμον Æsch. Prom. 2. Τύχη δὲ σωτήρ Id. Ag. 664. — These words, as substantives, are commonly appellations of persons or countries, ἀνήρ, γυνή, γῆ, &c., being understood.

§ **449.** 5. Use of the Neuter. The substantive use of the neuter adjective (§ 447. a) exhibits itself in a variety of forms. Thus,

α.) A neuter adjective with the article often supplies the place of an *abstract noun*; as, Τὸ δ' ἁπλοῦν καὶ τὸ ἀληθὲς ἐνόμιζε τὸ αὐτὸ τῷ ἠλιθίῳ εἶναι, *but sincerity and truth he thought to be the same with folly*, ii. 6. 22. Σὺν τῷ δικαίῳ (cf. Μετὰ ἀδικίας) Ib. 18. Τὸ χαλεπὸν [= ἡ χαλεπότης] τοῦ πνεύματος iv. 5. 4. Οὐ γὰρ ἀριθμός ἐστιν ὁ ὁρίζων τὸ πολὺ καὶ τὸ ὀλίγον, 'the much and the little,' vii. 7. 36. Τὸ πιστόν [= ἡ πίστις] Th. i. 68. Διὰ τὸ ἀναίσθητον ὑμῶν Ib. 69. Ὑπὸ γὰρ τοῦ περιχαροῦς τῆς νίκης Id. vii. 73. Τό γ' ἐμὸν πρόθυμον Eur. Med. 178. Τῷ διαλλάσσοντι τῆς γνώμης, *the* [differing] *difference of opinion*, Th. iii. 10 (Thuc. is especially fond of this use of the Partic.). Τὸ μὲν δεδιὸς αὐτοῦ . ., τὸ δὲ θαρσοῦν, *his* [being afraid] *fear* . ., *but his confidence*, Id. i. 36. Ἐν τῷ μὴ μελετῶντι Ib. 142.

β.) Neuter adjectives (both with and without the article) are used with prepositions to form many *adverbial phrases*; as, Ἀπὸ τοῦ αὐτομάτου, *of their own accord*, i. 2. 17. Ἔν γε τῷ φανερῷ, *openly*, i. 3. 21. Διὰ ταχέων, *rapidly*, i. 5. 9. Ἐξ ἴσου iii. 4. 47. Ἐκ τῶν δυνατῶν iv. 2. 23. Ἀπὸ τοῦ πρώτου iv. 3. 9. Κατὰ ταὐτά, *in the same way*, v. 4. 22. Ἐπὶ δεξιά vi. 4. 1. Διὰ παντός, *throughout*, vii. 8. 11.

§ **450.** γ.) Neuter adjectives are used in connection with words of different gender and number (commonly as appositives, § 331); as, Φοβερώτατον δ' ἐρημία, *and solitude is the most terrible thing of all*, ii. 5. 9 (cf. Ξυμβουλὴ ἱερὸν χρῆμα Pl. Theag. 122 b). Τί οὖν ταῦτα ἐστίν; ii. 1. 22. Τοὺς δὲ ποταμοὺς ἄπορον νομίζετε εἶναι iii. 2. 22. Μυκῆναι μικρὸν ἦν, *Mycenæ was a small affair*, Th. i. 10. Εὔβοια γὰρ αὐτοῖς . . πάντα ἦν, *for Eubœa was every thing to them*, Ib. viii. 95. Ἀσθενέστερον γυνὴ ἀνδρός Pl. Rep. 455 e. Ἄνδρες οἱ ἡμέτεροι πλούσιοι εἰσὶν οὐδέν Ib. 556 d. Ἕκτορα τὸ μηδὲν εἶναι Eur. Rhes. 818. Πρὸς τὸν οὐδὲν [sc. ὄντα] Ib. Ph. 598. Τὴν μηδὲν εἰς τὸ μηδέν Soph. El. 1166. Ταῦτα δὲ ἀδύνατον ἐφάνη, 'an impossibility,' Pl. Parm. 160 a.

Λύρα καλὴ οὐ καλόν; Id. Hipp. Maj. 288 c. Ἔμοιγε φίλτατον πόλις Eur Med. 329. Οἶμαι γὰρ ὑμᾶς τῆσδε γῆς Κορινθίας τὰ πρῶτ' ἔσεσθαι Ib. 916. Κρίνασα δ' ἀστῶν τῶν ἐμῶν τὰ βέλτατα Æsch. Eum. 487. — In these cases, an adjective agreeing in gender and number with the substantive would either express a different idea, or would express the same idea with less emphasis.

δ.) The neuters πλεῖον or πλέον, μεῖον or ἔλαττον, ὅσον, μηδέν, and τὶ are sometimes used as indeclinable adjectives or substantives; thus, Μυριάδας πλεῖον ἢ δώδεκα, *myriads more than twelve in number*, v. 6. 9 (cf. Κρῆτες πλείους ἢ ἑξήκοντα iv. 8. 27). Μισθὸς πλέον ἢ τριῶν μηνῶν i. 2. 11. Οὔσης αὐτῆς ἐτῶν πλέον ἢ τετταράκοντα H. Gr. iii. 1. 14. Ἅλυν, οὐ μεῖον δυοῖν σταδίοιν, *the Halys, not less than two stadia in breadth*, v. 6. 9. Φοίνιξι θεμελιώσας οὐ μεῖον ἢ πλεθριαίοις Cyr. vii. 5. 11. Ἀποκτείνουσι τῶν ἀνδρῶν οὐ μεῖον πεντακοσίους vi. 4. 24. Φρουροὺς παρ' αὐτῷ οὐκ ἔλαττον τετρακισχιλίων H. Gr. iv. 2. 5 (cf. Σφενδονῆται . . οὐκ ἐλάττους τετρακοσίων Ib. 16). Πελτασταὶ ὅσον [= τοσοῦτοι ὅσοι] διακόσιοι, *targeteers as many as two hundred*, vii. 2. 20 (cf. Ἡμεῖς τοσοῦτοι ὄντες ὅσους σὺ ὁρᾷς ii. 1. 16). Λίθων . . ὅσον μναιαίων Eq. 4. 4. Λίθους . . ὅσον μναιαίους καὶ πλεῖον καὶ μεῖον Mag. Eq. 1. 16 (cf. Ὀλοιτρόχους ἁμαξιαίους καὶ μείζους καὶ ἐλάττους iv. 2. 3). Ὅτ' οὐδὲν ὢν τοῦ μηδὲν ἀντέστης ὕπερ Soph. Aj. 1231. Γέροντος . . τὸ μηδὲν ὄντος Eur. Heracl. 166. Κρείσσω τῶν τὸ μηδὲν Id. Tro. 412. Δοκούντων εἶναί τι, *appearing to be something*, i. e. *of some consequence*, Pl. Gorg. 472 a. (If μηδέν and τὶ did not here remain without change, they would be confounded with the masc., and the expressions would lose their peculiar force.)

NOTES. (*a*) So, with the plur. form instead of the sing., Παραμένει ἡμέρας πλείω ἢ τρεῖς Pl. Menex. 335 b. (*b*) In some of these cases, the neut. adjective appears to be used like an adverb. See § 529. β.

§ 451. ε.) A neuter adjective used substantively, or as an attribute of an infinitive or clause of a sentence, is often *plur.* instead of *sing.* (§ 336); as, Εἰ τοῦτο τὸ ὀφειλόμενον ἀποδοθείη, ἢ εἰ ταῦτά τε ὀφείλοιντο, *if this which is due should be paid, or if both this should be due*, vii. 7. 34. Οὐ τοῦτο λέξων ἔρχομαι . . · εἰ γὰρ ταῦτα λέγοιμι Ages. 2. 7. Ὅταν μέν τι ἀγαθὸν ἔχωσι, παρακαλοῦσί με ἐπὶ ταῦτα Symp. 4. 50. Σὲ μὲν τοσαῦτα χρὴ ποιεῖν, κλάειν ἐλεινῶς Ar. Thesm. 1062. Ἆρ' οὐχ ὕβρις τάδε; Soph. Œd. C. 883. Ἀπόλλων τάδ' ἦν . . ὁ κακὰ κακὰ τελῶν, 'it was Apollo,' Id. Œd. T. 1329. Οὐκ Ἴωνές τάδε εἰσίν, *there are here no Ionians*, Th. vi. 77. Ἀδύνατα ἦν ἐπιχειρεῖν Id. i. 125. Δεδογμένʼ, ὡς ἔοικε, τήνδε κατθανεῖν Soph. Ant. 576. Οὓς οὐ παραδοτέα τοῖς Ἀθηναίοις ἐστίν Th. i. 86.

NOTE. This use of the Plur. for the Sing. appears to have arisen from the want of a noun, or definite object of sense, to give strict unity to the conception. It is very frequent in demonstrative pronouns, and in verbals in -τός and -τέος.

§ 452. 6. An adjective often takes a substantive in the *Genitive partitive*, instead of agreeing with it. In this construction, the adjective is either in the *same gender* with the substantive, or in the *neuter* (commonly the *neut. sing.*). Thus,

Μηδὲ τὰ σπουδαῖα τῶν πραγμάτων [for πράγματα], μηδὲ τοὺς εὖ φρονοῦντας τῶν ἀνθρώπων [for ἀνθρώπους], *neither virtuous actions* [the virtuous of actions], *nor wise men* [the wise of men] Isocr. 24 d. Λαμπρότητός τι [for λαμπρότης τις], *some distinction* [something of distinction], Th. vii. 69. 'Αβρὰ παρηΐδος [for ἁβρὰν παρηΐδα, *soft cheek* [softnesses of cheek], Eur. Ph. 1486. Ἄσημα . . βοῆς Soph. Ant. 1209.

NOTE. In this way, greater prominence and distinctness of expression, and sometimes a species of independence or abstractness (§ 449. α), are given to the adjective. Upon the whole subject, see §§ 358 – 362.

§ **453.** 7. SYNESIS. The adjective often agrees in *gender* and *number* with the *idea of the speaker*, instead of the subject expressed; particularly with,

α. COLLECTIVE NOUNS, and words used *collectively*; as, Ἡ δὲ βουλὴ . ., οὐκ ἀγνοοῦντες, *and the senate, not ignorant*, H. Gr. ii. 3. 55. Κραυγὴ ἦν τοῦ Ἑλληνικοῦ στρατεύματος [= στρατιωτῶν] διακελευομένων iii. 4. 45. Τὴν πόλιν [πολίτας] . . ὄντας Th. iii. 79. Λέσβος . . ἀπέστη ἀπ' Ἀθηναίων, βουληθέντες Ib. 2. Ναῦν ἐκ τῶν Ἀθηνῶν ἧκουσαν ἐπί τε Ἀλκιβιάδην, ὡς κελεύσοντας Id. vi. 53. Οὐδ' ὄρνις εὐσήμους ἀποῤῥοιβδεῖ βοὰς, ἀνδροφθόρου βεβρῶτες αἵματος λίπος Soph. Ant. 1021.

β. Words in the *plural* used for the *singular* (chiefly ἡμεῖς for ἐγώ); as, Ἱκετεύομεν . . προσπίτνων, *we* [= *I*] *beseech you, falling down*, Eur. Herc. 1206. Ἥλιον μαρτυρόμεσθα δρῶσ' ἃ δρᾶν οὐ βούλομαι Ib. 858. Διωκόμεσθα . . κρατηθεῖσα Id. Ion, 1250.

γ. Nouns of which the *gender* does not follow the *sex* (§ 75); as, Ὦ φίλτατ', ὦ περισσὰ τιμηθεὶς τέκνον, *O dearest, O most fondly cherished son*, Eur. Tro. 735. Τόδ' ἔρνος . . κατθανόντα Id. Bac. 1307. Τέκνα θαμίν' ἐπαναβοῶντες Ar. Plut. 292. Κολλικοφάγε Βοιωτίδιον Ar. Ach. 872. Τὰ τέλη καταβάντας Th. iv. 15.

δ. Words for which others might have been used; as, Ἡ νόσος [= νόσημα] πρῶτον ἤρξατο γενέσθαι τοῖς Ἀθηναίοις, λεγόμενον Th. ii. 47 (cf. Τὸ μὲν οὖν νόσημα Ib. 51; yet see § 450. γ). Πᾶσα δὲ γέννα [= λαός] Φρυγῶν . . δώσων Eur. Tro. 531.

ε. Words governing a *Genitive*, to which, as the *more important word*, the adjective conforms in gender and number; as, Φίλτατ' Αἰγίσθου βία, *dearest majesty of Ægisthus*, Æsch. Cho. 893. Τροίαν ἑλόντες δήποτ' Ἀργείων στόλος Id. Ag. 577 (cf. α). Τὸ δὲ τῶν πρεσβυτέρων . . θεωροῦντες Pl. Leg. 657 d. Τὰ τῶν διακόνων . . ποιούμενοι Soph. Phil. 497. Ἀκούω φθόγγον ὀρνίθων, κακῷ κλάζοντας οἴστρῳ Id. Ant. 1001. — In these expressions, the Gen. and the word which governs it usually form simply a *periphrasis*, and are treated accordingly.

§ **454.** 8. An adjective sometimes agrees with a Genitive *implied* in another adjective (commonly a *possessive*); as,

Τὸ σὸν [= σοῦ] μόνης δώρημα, *the gift of you alone*, Soph. Tr. 775. Τοῖς ἡμετέροις [= ἡμῶν] αὐτῶν φίλοις, *our own friends* (§ 505. 3), vii. 1. 29. Τὰ ὑμέτερ' αὐτῶν ἀνηλίσκετε Dem. 25. 5. Θρῆνον . . ἐμὸν τὸν αὐτῆς Æsch. Ag. 1322. Τὸν ἐμὸν μὲν αὐτοῦ τοῦ ταλαιπώρου . . βίον Ar. Plut. 33. Τἀμὰ δυστήνου κακά Soph. Œd. C. 344. Σὴν ἀνδρίαν καὶ μεγαλοφροσύνην ἀναβαίνοντος Pl. Conv. 194 a. Cf. §§ 332. 4, 383. α. — In like manner, as the Dat. may be used for the Gen. (§ 412), Ἐμοῖσιν [= ἐμοὶ] ὄσσοις ὁμίχλα προσῇξε . . εἰσιδούσᾳ Æsch. Pr. 144.

§ **455.** 9. ATTRACTION. An adjective is sometimes attracted by a substantive either, (α.) *governing*, or (β.) *in apposition with*, its real subject; as,

α. Τοὐμὸν αἷμα . . πατρός, *the blood of my father*, Soph. Œd. T. 1400 Θυμὸς . . παῖς παιδὸς Eur. Andr. 584. Ξένων πρὸς ἄλλην ἑστίαν πορεύσομαι Id. Alc. 538. Μέλανα στολμὸν πέπλων Ib. 215. Νεῖκος ἀνδρῶν ξύναιμον Soph. Ant. 793. Πολιᾶς πόντου θινὸς Id. Ph. 1123. Ἡ τέκνων δῆτ' ὄψις . . βλαστοῦσα Id. Œd. T. 1375. — In most of these cases, the Gen. with the word which governs it may be regarded as forming a *complex idea*, which the adjective modifies. This construction is chiefly poetic.

β. Οἱ γὰρ ὀφθαλμοί, κάλλιστον ὄν [for ὄντες], *for the eyes, being the most beautiful of objects* (§ 450), Pl. Rep. 420 c. Τοὺς γὰρ μέγιστα ἐξημαρτηκότας, ἀνιάτους δὲ ὄντας, μεγίστην δὲ οὖσαν [for ὄντας] βλάβην πόλεως, ἀπαλλάττειν εἰώθεν Pl. Leg. 735 e. Πάντα ἃ δὴ ὡς ἰδέας αὐτὰς οὔσας [for αὐτὰ ὄντα] ὑπολαμβάνομεν Pl. Parm. 153 a. Ἥλιος . . πάντων λαμπρότατος, *the sun, the most splendid* [sc. *thing*] *of all things*, Mem. iv. 7. 8 (this is the common construction when the *superlative* is followed by a *Gen. partitive* of different gender from the subject of the sentence).

NOTE. An adjective is sometimes, in the poets, attracted by a Voc.; as, Ὄλβιε κῶρε γένοιο [for ὄλβιος, κῶρε, γ.], *may you be happy, boy*, Theoc. 17. 66. Ἰὼ δύστηνε σύ, δύστηνε [for -ος] . . φανείς Soph. Ph. 759. Cf. *Sic venias hodierne* Tibull. i. 7. 58.

§ **456.** 10. An adjective sometimes *agrees* with a substantive instead of *governing* it in the *Gen. partitive* (§§ 358–360); as,

Περὶ μέσας νύκτας, *about midnight* [the middle of the night], i. 7. 1 (cf. Ἐν μέσῳ νυκτῶν Cyr. v. 3. 52). Διὰ μέσης δὲ τῆς πόλεως, *and through the midst of the city*, i. 2. 23. Τὸ ἄλλο στράτευμα, *the rest of the army*, Ib. 25. Ἐν δ' ἄκροισι βὰς ποσί, *and going on* [the extremities of the feet] *tiptoe*, Eur. Ion, 1166.

§ **457.** 11. Adjectives are often used for *adverbs* and *adjuncts*, and, by the poets, even for *appositives*, and *dependent clauses;* to express,

α. TIME; as, Ἀφικνοῦνται . . τριταῖοι [= τῇ τρίτῃ ἡμέρᾳ], *they arrive on the third day*, v. 3. 2 (cf. iii. 4. 37, and § 420). Σκοταῖοι προσιόντες ii. 2. 17. Προτέρα Κύρου . . ἀφίκετο i. 2. 25. Τελευτῶν ἐχαλέπαινεν, *at last he became angry*, iv. 5. 16.

β. PLACE; as, Σκηνοῦμεν ὑπαίθριοι, *we encamp in the open air*, v. 5. 21 (cf. Ὑπὸ τῆς αἰθρίας iv. 4. 14). Δεξιὸν φθεγγόμενον vi. 1. 23. Ἑζόμεσθ' ἐφέστιοι Soph. Œd. T. 32. Θαλάσσιον ἐκρίψατε Ib. 1411. Φοιτᾷς δ' ὑπερπόντιος Id. Ant. 785. Θυραῖον οἰχνεῖν Id. El. 313. Μετακύμιος ἄτας, *amid the waves of woe*, Eur. Alc. 91 (§ 383. α). Πολλὰ δ' ὁρῶ ταῦτα [= ταύτῃ or τῇδε, § 421. β] πρόβατα, *and I see here many sheep*, iii. 5. 9. Ἠρόμην ὅπου αὐτὸς εἴη. Οὗτος, ἔφη, ὄπισθεν προσέρχεται, 'here he comes,' Pl. Rep. 327 b. Ὡς ἀνὴρ ὅδε, *as the man is here*, Soph. Œd. C. 32. Πορεύονται γὰρ οἵδε δή τινες Ib. 111. Ἀλλ' ἥδ' ὀπαδῶν ἐκ δόμων τις ἔρχεται Eur. Alc. 137. Ὅδ' εἴμ' Ὀρέστης Id. Or. 380. Ἶρος ἐκεῖνος . . ἧσται, 'sits there,' σ. 239.

γ. MANNER; as, Συνεβάλλοντο . . αἱ Ἑλλησποντιακαὶ πόλεις ἑκοῦσαι, *the Hellespontic cities contributed willingly*, i. 1. 9. Ὁ μὲν ἑκὼν πεινῶν (cf. Ὁ μὲν ἑκουσίως ταλαιπωρῶν) Mem. ii. 1. 18. Οἱ δὲ στρατιῶται ἐδέξαντο ἡδέως καὶ εὐθὺς εἵποντο ἄσμενοι vii. 2. 9. Κατῄνεσεν τάδ' ὅρκιος δράσειν Soph. Œd. C. 1637. Ἀνύσας τρέχε, *run with all speed*, Ar. Plut. 229. Τοὺς νεκροὺς ὑποσπόνδους ἀπεδίδοσαν H. Gr. ii. 4. 19.

δ. EFFECT; as, Εὔφημον [= ὥστε εὔφημον εἶναι] . . κοίμησον στόμα, *hush your mouth to silence* [so that it should be silent], Æsch. Ag. 1247. Τῶν σῶν ἀδέρκτων ὀμμάτων τητώμενος, [deprived of your sightless eyes] *rendered sightless by the loss of your eyes*, Soph. Œd. C. 1200. Σὺ καὶ δικαίων ἀδίκους φρένας παρασπᾷς Id. Ant. 791. Μεῖζον' ἐκτενῶ λόγον Id. Tr. 679. Χέρα τοξήρη . . ὁπλίσας Eur. Alc. 35.

ε. VARIOUS RELATIONS AND CIRCUMSTANCES; as, Ἄλλοι δὲ ἦσαν ἑξακισχίλιοι ἱππεῖς, 'besides,' i. 7. 11. Οὐ γὰρ ἦν χόρτος οὐδὲ ἄλλο οὐδὲν δένδρον i. 5. 5. Ξύλιναι πεποιημέναι, *made of wood*, v. 2. 5. Ἀνδροφθόρου [= ἀνδρὸς φθαρέντος] . . αἵματος, *homicidal blood*, Soph. Ant. 1022. Ματροκτόνον αἷμα, *the blood of a mother slain*, Eur. Or. 833. Πολύδακρυν [= πολλῶν δακρύων] ἀδονάν Id. El. 126. Μελαμπέπλους στολμούς Id. Alc. 819. Ἀριστόχειρ . . ἀγών Soph. Aj. 935. Ὀξύχειρι [= ὀξεῖ χειρῶν] σὺν κτύπῳ Æsch. Cho. 23. Παμμῆτόρ [= πάντων μῆτερ] τε γῆ Id. Pr. 90. Τοῦδε παμμήτωρ [= πάντως or κατὰ πάντα μήτηρ] νεκροῦ Soph. Ant. 1282. Ἕλενος ἀριστόμαντις [= ἄριστος μάντις] Id. Ph. 1338.

§ **458.** NOTES. 1. In cases like the above, the adjective form appears to be assumed through the *attraction of the substantive*, or in other words, for the sake of binding together more closely the different parts of the sentence, and giving greater unity to the expression. It will be observed that, in some of the examples, the adjective simply forms an emphatic pleonasm.

2. In some instances, a *Genitive with its adjective* appear to have been changed into *two adjectives agreeing with the governing substantive*; as, Πόντιόν τ' Αἰγαίων' [for πόντου τ' Αἰγαίου] ἐπ' ἀκτὰν ἀλίμενον, *and upon the harbourless coast of the Ægēan Sea*, Eur. Alc. 595. Ποταμίᾳ νερτέρᾳ τε [for ποταμοῦ νερτέρου] κώπᾳ, *with the oar of the nether stream*, Ib. 459.

3. *Derivative* and *compound adjectives* are formed in Greek with great freedom, and the latter, especially among the *poets*, often appear to have taken the place of a *simple adjective* or *noun*, by a species of *emphatic* or *graphic pleonasm*; as, Μονάμπυκας [= μόνους] πώλους, *singly-bridled* [= single] *horses*, Eur. Alc. 428. Ἀγέλαις βουνόμοις [= βοῶν] Soph. Œd. T. 26. — The poets often repeat a noun in composition with ἀ- *privative* or a similar word, to express emphatically the idea of *negation* or of *evil*; as, Μήτηρ ἀμήτωρ, *our* [unmotherly mother] *mother, yet no mother*, Soph. El. 1154. Γάμον ἄγαμον Eur. Hel. 690 (cf. *Innuptis . . nuptiis* Cic. de Or. iii. 58). Ὦ πάτερ αἰνόπατερ Æsch. Cho. 315.

§ **459.** 12. ANACOLUTHON. An adjective sometimes differs in case from its subject, through a change of construction (cf. § 333. 7); as,

Ξενίᾳ . . ἥκειν παραγγέλλει λαβόντα τοὺς ἄνδρας, *he commands Xenias to come, taking his men* (cf. Παραγγέλλει τῷ τε Κλεάρχῳ λαβόντι ἥκειν), i. 2. 1. Διαβαινόντων μέντοι ὁ Γλοῦς αὐτοῖς ἐπιφάνη ii. 4. 24. Ἀποβλέψας . . ἔδοξέ μοι Pl. Leg. 686 e. See the syntax of the Infinitive and Participle.

NOTE. The use of other cases with the *Genitive partitive* (as in §§ 364 366) may be referred to simple ellipsis.

II. USE OF THE DEGREES.

[The following observations apply both to ADJECTIVES and ADVERBS.]

§ 460. I. Words are compared not only by *inflection* (§§ 155–163), but also by the use of *adverbs* denoting *more* and *most ;* as,

Μᾶλλον φίλον, *more agreeable*, Soph. Ph. 886. Τοὺς μάλιστα φίλους, *the most friendly*, vii. 8. 11. Ὦ πλεῖστα μῶροι Soph. El. 1326.

NOTES. (*a*) The two methods are sometimes united for emphasis or perspicuity (cf. §§ 161. 1, 462) ; as, Θανὼν δ' ἂν εἴη μᾶλλον εὐτυχέστερος ἢ ζῶν, *and dying he would be happier, far happier than living*, Eur. Hec. 377. Τίς ἄλλος μᾶλλον ἐνδικώτερος ; Æsch. Sept. 673. Πολὺ οὖν κρεῖττον . . μᾶλλον ἢ iv. 6. 11 (cf. Ib. 12). Μάλιστα δεινότατος Th. vii. 42. Τὴν πλεῖστον ἡδίστην θεῶν Κύπριν Eur. Alc. 790. Ὦ μέγιστον ἐχθίστη γύναι Id. Med. 1323. (*b*) So the Comp. and Sup. are united, Ὦ πασᾶν κείνα πλέον ἁμέρα ἐλθοῦσ' ἐχθίστα δή μοι Soph. El. 201.

§ 461. II. The COMPARATIVE is commonly construed with the particle ἤ, *than*, or with the *Genitive of distinction ;* and the SUPERLATIVE with the *Genitive partitive*. Thus,

Φιλοῦσα αὐτὸν μᾶλλον ἢ . . Ἀρταξέρξην, *loving him more than Artaxerxes*, i. 1. 4. See §§ 351, 362. δ, 363. γ.

REMARKS. 1. The Comp. is sometimes construed with other particles, which commonly strengthen the expression (cf. 460. *a*) ; as, Κάλλιον . . πρὸ τοῦ φεύγειν, *more honorable* [in preference to fleeing] *than to flee*, Pl. Phædo, 99 a. Ἀντὶ σοῦ πλέον, *more* [instead of you] *than you*, Soph. Tr. 577. Πυκνότεραι παρὰ τὰ . . μνημονευόμενα, *more frequent* [beyond] *than the recollections*, Th. i. 23. Πρὸς ἅπαντας . . πλείω, *more* [in comparison with all] *than all*, Id. vii. 58. Πέρα τοῦ δέοντος σοφώτεροι Pl. Gorg. 487 d. Ἔστιν ὁ πόλεμος οὐχ ὅπλων τὸ πλέον, ἀλλὰ δαπάνης, [war is not of arms the more, but of expenditure] *war does not require arms more than money*, Id. i. 83 (§ 387). Ταῦτ' ἐστὶ κρείσσω πλὴν ὑπ' Ἀργείοις πεσεῖν, 'better [but not to fall] than to fall,' Eur. Heracl. 231. Ἀποθνήσκουσι πρότερον πρὶν δῆλοι γίγνεσθαι οἷοι ἦσαν Cyr. v. 2. 9 (cf. Πρότερον ἢ οἱ φίλοι παρῆσαν Ib. vii. 5. 41). Οὐ πρότερον ἐπαύσαντο, ἕως . . κατέστησαν Lys. 174. 6. Ἐπὶ γαστέρι κύντερον η. 216. — In the most of these examples, two forms of construction appear to have been united.

2. The construction of the Gen. with the Comp. is often *elliptical;* as, Ἐπεὶ πλείων χρόνος, ὃν δεῖ μ' ἀρέσκειν τοῖς κάτω, τῶν ἐνθάδε, *since the time is greater, which I must please those below, than those here* [than that during which I must please those here], Soph. Ant. 74. See § 391. γ.

3. By a mixture of the two methods of construction which belong to the Comp., — (*a*) When a numeral, or other word of quantity, follows πλεῖον, πλείω, ἔλαττον, or μεῖον, ἤ is sometimes omitted, though the Gen. is not employed ; as, Ἀποκτείνουσι τῶν ἀνδρῶν οὐ μεῖον πεντακοσίους, 'not less than 500,' vi. 4. 24. See § 450. δ, and cf. *Non amplius erant quingenti*, Cæs. viii. 10.—

(*b*) To the Gen. governed by the Comp., a specification is sometimes annexed with ἤ; as, Τί τοῦδ' ἂν εὕρημ' εὗρον εὐτυχέστερον, ἢ παῖδα γῆμαι βασιλέως; Eur. Med. 553. Τὸν νοῦν τ' ἀμείνω τῶν φρενῶν, ἢ νῦν φέρει Soph. Ant. 1090. Οὔ τί ἂν μᾶλλον σπουδάσειέ τις . ., ἢ τοῦτο; Pl. Gorg. 500 c. See also § 464. N. — (*c*) The Gen. sometimes follows ἤ, instead of the appropriate case; as, Οὐ προῄει πλέον τῆς ἡμέρας, ἢ δέκα ἢ δώδεκα σταδίων H. Gr. iv. 6. 5 (see § 439).

§ 462. III. The *positive* is sometimes added to the *superlative* for the sake of *emphasis;* as,

Ὦ κακῶν κάκιστε, *O vilest of the vile,* Soph. Œd. T. 334. Ἀγαθῶν ἱππέων κράτιστος ὢν ἱππεύς Cyr. i. 3. 15.

ΕΡΜ. Ὦ βδελυρὲ καὶ τολμηρὲ κἀναίσχυντε σύ,
Καὶ μιαρὲ, καὶ παμμίαρε, καὶ μιαρώτατε,
Πῶς δεῦρ' ἀνῆλθες, ὦ μιαρῶν μιαρώτατε;
Τί σοί ποτ' ἔστ' ὄνομ'; οὐκ ἐρεῖς; ΤΡ. Μιαρώτατος. Ar. Pax, 182.

NOTES. α. By *doubling* the *Pos.* or the *Sup.*, we obtain similar forms of expression, the one less and the other even more emphatic than the above; as, Ἄρρητ' ἀρρήτων, *horrible of the horrible,* i. e. *most horrible,* Soph. Œd. T. 465. Δειλαία δειλαίων Id. El. 849 (§ 362. ζ). Ἔσχατ' ἐσχάτων κακά, *the most violent of the most violent reproaches,* Id. Ph. 65 (cf. §§ 161. 1, 460. α). Ὃ δὴ δοκεῖ ἐν τοῖς μεγίστοις μέγιστον εἶναι Pl. Crat. 427 e.

β. From the doubling of the Sup., as in the last example, appears to have arisen the phrase ἐν τοῖς, which is used with the Sup. to increase its force, and, as an adverbial expression, without change of gender; thus, Ἐν τοῖς [sc. πρώτοις] πρῶτοι, *first* [among the first] *of all,* Th. i. 6. Ἐν τοῖς πρώτη Id. iii. 81. Ἐν τοῖς πλεῖσται δὴ νῆες Ib. 17. Ἐν τοῖς χαλεπώτατα διῆγον Id. vii. 71. Ἐν τοῖς μάλιστα, *most of all,* Pl. Crito, 52 a.

γ. The *numeral* εἷς is sometimes used with the Sup., to render the idea of *individuality* prominent; as, Δῶρα δὲ πλεῖστα . ., εἷς γε ὢν ἀνὴρ, ἐλάμβανε, *he received the most presents,* [at least being one man] *for a single individual,* i. e. *more than any one man beside,* i. 9. 22. Πλεῖστα εἷς ἀνὴρ . . δυνάμενος ὠφελεῖν Th. viii. 68.

δ. The Greeks are fond of expressing the Sup. *negatively;* as, Οὐχ ἥκιστα [= μάλιστα], *not the least, especially,* Mem. i. 2. 23. Ἀνδρῶν οὐ τῶν ἀδυνατωτάτων Th. i. 5. Μέγιστον δὲ καὶ οὐχ ἥκιστα Id. vii. 44.

§ 463. IV. Certain special forms of comparison deserve notice; e. g.

1.) The Comp., with a Gen. expressing *hope, duty, power of description,* &c.; as, Μεῖζον ἐλπίδος, *greater than could have been hoped, above hope,* Æsch. Ag. 266. Μᾶλλον τοῦ δέοντος, *more than is proper, too much,* Mem. iv. 3. 8. Κρεῖσσον λόγου, *beyond description,* Th. ii. 50.

2.) The Comp. followed by ἢ κατά, or sometimes ἢ πρός· as, Μείζω, ἢ κατὰ δάκρυα [sc. ἐστιν], [greater than is in accordance with tears] *too great for tears,* Th. vii. 75. Βελτίονος ἢ κατ' ἄνθρωπον Mem. iv. 4. 24. Μείζω . . ἢ κατ' ἐμὲ καὶ σὲ ἐξευρεῖν, *too great for me and you to discover,* Pl. Crat. 392 b. Ἐνδεεστέρως . . ἢ πρὸς τὴν ἐξουσίαν Th. iv. 39. Cf. *Prœlium atrocius, quam pro numero pugnantium* Liv. 21. 29.

3.) The Comp. followed by ἢ ὥστε (or ὡς) and the Infinitive; as, Βραχύτερα ἠκόντιζον ἢ ὡς ἐξικνεῖσθαι, *they shot* [a shorter distance than they must in order to reach] *too short a distance to reach*, iii. 3. 7. Μεῖζον ἢ ὥστε φέρειν δύνασθαι κακόν Mem. iii. 5. 17.—We likewise find the Infin. without ὥστε or ὡς, and also the Pos. for the Comp.; as, Τὸ γὰρ νόσημα μεῖζον ἢ φέρειν, *for the malady is too great to bear*, Soph. Œd. T. 1293. Ταπεινὴ ὑμῶν ἡ διάνοια ἐγκαρτερεῖν, *your mind is too weak to persevere*, Th. ii. 61. Ψυχρὸν, ἔφη, ὥστε λούσασθαι ἐστίν Mem. iii. 13. 3.

§ **464.** 4.) The Comp. and Sup. (for the most part joined with αὐτός) followed by a *reflexive pronoun*, to denote the comparison of an object with itself; the Comp. representing it as above that which it has been or would be in other circumstances, and the Sup. representing it as at its highest point. Thus, Ἀνδρειότερος γίγνεται αὐτὸς αὑτοῦ, *he becomes more manly than he was before*, Pl. Rep. 411 c. Ὅσῳ δυνατώτεροι αὐτοὶ αὑτῶν ἐγίγνοντο Th. iii. 11. Ὅτε δεινότατος σαυτοῦ ταῦτα ἦσθα, *when you were the most skilled in these matters that you ever were*, i. e. *when your skill in these matters was at its highest point*, Mem. i. 2. 46. Ἵν' αὐτὸς αὑτοῦ τυγχάνει βέλτιστος ὤν Pl. Gorg. 484 e.

NOTE. To the Comp. thus construed, a specification is sometimes annexed with ἢ (§ 461. *b*); as, Αὐτοὶ ἑαυτῶν [θαῤῥαλεώτεροί εἰσιν], ἐπειδὰν μάθωσιν, ἢ πρὶν μαθεῖν, *they have themselves more confidence when they have learned, than they had before learning*, Pl. Prot. 350 a. Τό γ' ὑπόλοιπον αὐτῶν τῆς δόξης ἀσθενέστερον αὐτὸ ἑαυτοῦ ἐστιν, ἢ εἰ μηδ' ᾠήθησαν Th. vii. 56.

5.) *Two comparatives connected by* ἢ, to denote that the one property exists in a higher degree than the other; as, Στρατηγοὶ πλείονες ἢ βελτίονες, *generals more numerous than good*, Ar. Ach. 1078. Ὡς λογογράφοι ξυνέθεσαν ἐπὶ τὸ προσαγωγότερον τῇ ἀκροάσει, ἢ ἀληθέστερον Th. i. 21. Πρόθυμος μᾶλλον ἢ σοφωτέρα Eur. Med. 485.

§ **465.** V. The comparative and superlative are often used *without an express object of comparison*. In this case, the SUPERLATIVE *increases* the force of the positive, while the COMPARATIVE may either *increase* or *diminish* it, according to the object of comparison which is implied. Thus,

Ὦ θαυμασιώτατε ἄνθρωπε, *O most wonderful man*, iii. 1. 27. Ὦ θαυμαστότατοι vii. 7. 10. Τὴν ταχίστην, *immediately*, iii. 3. 16. Πλείω [sc. τοῦ δέοντος] λέλεκται, [more than is proper] *too much has been said*, Eur. Alc. 706 (cf. Μᾶλλον τοῦ δέοντος, § 463. 1). Νεώτερος ὢν ἐς τὸ ἄρχειν, *being too young for the command*, Th. vi. 12. Μακρότερον . . διηγήσασθαι, *it is rather long* [*than otherwise*] *to relate*, Pl. Conv. 203 a (cf. § 464. 5). Ὁ δὲ αὐθαδέστερόν τέ τι ἀπεκρίνατο, *but he answered them* [somewhat more insolently than he might have done] *with a degree of insolence*, Th. viii. 84. Μέλος εὔτονον, ἀγροικότερον, *an energetic strain, somewhat rough*, Ar. Ach. 673. Τοῖν δὲ ἑτέροιν καὶ ἀλογώτερα, 'quite confounding,' Th. vi. 46. Τὶς τῶν ἀπειροτέρων, *one of the more inexperienced*, v. i. 8.

NOTE. The Comp. and Sup., when used without direct comparison, are said to be used *absolutely*. When thus employed, the Comp. is often translated into Eng. by the simple Pos., or by the Pos. with *too* or *rather*; and the Sup. by the Pos. with *very*. In addition to the examples above, see § 466.

§ **466.** VI. The degrees are more freely *interchanged*

and *mixed*, than in English. It may be however remarked in general, that the use of a higher degree for a lower renders the discourse more emphatic, and the converse, less so. Thus,

Ταύτην μάλιστα [for πολὺ μᾶλλον] τῆς κόρης ἀσπάζεται, *this she chooses far rather than the virgin*, Eur. Iph. A. 1594. Σεῖο . . μακάρτατος, *more completely happy than you*, λ. 482. Ἀξιολογώτατον τῶν προγεγενημένων, [the most remarkable of those which had preceded it] *more remarkable than any which had preceded it*, Th. i. 1. Ὦ βέλτιστε τῶν σαυτοῦ φίλων Ar. Plut. 631. Τὸ κάλλιστον . . τῶν προτέρων φάος Soph. Ant. 100. Ἡμῶν ὁ γεραίτερος [for γεραίτατος], *the oldest of us* (though none of them were old), Cyr. v. 1. 6. Ἐμοὶ πικρὸς τέθνηκεν [sc. μᾶλλον, § 460], ἢ κείνοις γλυκύς, *his death has been more bitter to me than sweet to them*, Soph. Aj. 965 (cf. § 464. 5). Ἀνέκραγον πάντες ὡς ὀλίγας [sc. πληγὰς] παίσειεν, *they all cried out that he had given him too few blows*, v. 8. 12 (cf. § 465). Ὦ φίλα γυναικῶν, *O* [beloved of] *dearest of women*, Eur. Alc. 460 (§ 362. ζ). Οἱ πολλοί, *the greater number*, or *the most*, Mem. i. 1. 19 (cf. Οἱ πλεῖστοι Ib. 11 ; Τοῖς πλείοσι H. Gr. ii. 3. 34). Ὀλίγους . ., τὸ δὲ πολύ i. 7. 20. Οἱ δὲ γεραίτεροι, *but the* [older] *old men*, Cyr. i. 2. 4. Οἱ μὲν νέοι τοῖς τῶν πρεσβυτέρων ἐπαίνοις χαίρουσιν Mem. ii. 1. 33. Ἵππον . . παλαίτερον iv. 5. 35. Τί νεώτερον, ὦ Σώκρατες, γέγονεν, *what new thing has happened, Socrates*, Pl. Euthyphr. 2 a. Νεωτέρων τινὲς ἐπιθυμοῦντες πραγμάτων, 'a revolution,' H. Gr. v. 2. 9. Οὐδὲν καινότερον, *nothing* [more recent] *new*, Pl. Phædo, 115 b. Οὐ γὰρ χεῖρον πολλάκις ἀκούειν Ib. 105 a. Πολλὰ ἂν οὐ βέλτιον αὐτοῖς στέρεσθαι, 'not well for them,' Cyr. v. 1. 12. Τί μοι ζῆν δῆτα κύδιον; *what then does it profit me to live?* Eur. Alc. 961 (cf. Τί δῆτ' ἐμοὶ ζῆν κέρδος Æsch. Pr. 747). Φαιήκων ἀνδρῶν προγενέστερος, 'oldest,' η. 156.

CHAPTER III.

SYNTAX OF THE ARTICLE.

§ **467.** The article (ὁ, ἡ, τό) appears, in the Epic language, as a GENERAL DEFINITIVE, performing the office not only of an *article as usually understood*, but still more frequently of a *demonstrative*, *personal*, or *relative pronoun* (see §§ 147, 148) ; as,

Ὁ γέρων, *the old man*, A. 33. Τά τ' ἐόντα, τά τ' ἐσσόμενα A. 70. Τά τ' ἄποινα δέχεσθαι, *and accept this ransom*, A. 20. Ὁ γάρ, *for he*, A. 9. Ἕως ὁ ταῦθ' ὥρμαινε A. 193. Τόν, *whom*, A. 36. Τὰ μὲν πολίων ἐξ ἐπράθομεν, τὰ δέδασται, 'those things which,' A. 125.

REMARKS. 1. These uses are intimately allied, inasmuch as, — (*a*) The art., as usually understood, is simply a *less emphatic form* of the *demonstr. pron.* Compare, in Eng., "*That* man whom you see," and "*The* man whom you see." — (*b*) The personal pron. of the 3d Pers. is a *substantive demonstr. pron.* Compare, in Eng., "*Those* that love me," and "*Them* that love me"; "*Those* that seek me," and "*They* that hate me," Prov. viii. 17, 21, 36. (The personal pron., like the art., is commonly *less emphatic* than the demonstrative usually so named.) — (*c*) The demonstr. pron. used *connectively* becomes a *relative;* as, in Eng., "Blessed are they *that* mourn." — Observe the resemblance in form between the English article *the*, and the pronouns *that, this, he, they*, &c.; the derivation of the definite art. in the French, Italian, &c., from the Lat. demonstr. *ille;* and the extensive use of the German article *der die, das.*

§ **468.** 2. In Epic poetry, — (*a*) The article, in its proper use as such, is commonly not expressed. The same omission prevails to a great extent in other kinds of elevated poetry. — (*b*) When used as a personal pronoun, it is most frequently connected with the same particles as in Attic Greek (§§ 490, 491); and is not unfrequently followed in the same sentence by the substantive to which it refers; as, Ἡ δ' ἕσπετο Παλλὰς Ἀθήνη, *and she, Pallas Minerva, followed*, α. 125. Αἱ δ' ἐπέμυξαν Ἀθηναίη τε καὶ Ἥρη Δ. 20. Cf. § 499. — (*c*) As a demonstrative, it sometimes follows its substantive before a relative; as, Ἀποπέμπειν ἄνδρα τὸν, ὅς κε θεοῖσιν ἀπέχθηται κ. 73. Συνθεσιάων τάων, ἃς ἐπέτελλε Ε. 319. — (*d*) The article when used as a personal or demonstrative pronoun has sometimes, from its position (see § 491. R.), or for the sake of the metre, the same form in the Nom. with the common relative; as, Ὃς γὰρ δεύτατος ἦλθεν, *for he returned last*, α. 286. Μηδ' ὃς φύγοι Ζ. 59. Ὃ γὰρ γέρας ἐστὶ θανόντων, 'for this,' Ψ. 9.

3. In the later Ion. and in the Dor. writers, this extended use of the article was, in great measure, retained. E. g. in Hdt., the relative has in the Nom. sing. and pl. the forms ὅς, ἥ, τό, οἵ, αἵ, τά· and has elsewhere the τ- forms of the article, except after prepositions which suffer elision, and in the phrases, ἐξ οὗ, ἐν ᾧ, ἐς ὅ, μέχρι οὗ.

4. Traces of the earlier and freer use of the article likewise remained in the Attic and common Greek; so that we shall treat of the Att. use of the article under two heads, (I.) *its use as an article*, and, (II.) *its use as a pronoun*, combining with the latter the use of the *relative forms* (§ 148. 2) as *demonstrative* or *personal*. We ought, perhaps, to premise, what might be inferred from § 467. 1, that no precise line of division can be drawn between the use of the article as such, and its use as a pronoun.

I. The Article as an Article.

§ 469. Rule XXVII. The Article is prefixed to substantives, to mark them as *definite*.

Notes. 1. The Greek article is commonly translated into English by the *definite article* THE; but often when used substantively, and sometimes when used adjectively, by a *demonstrative pronoun* (§§ 476, 479, 486. 1). With a *participle* following, it is most frequently translated by a *relative and verb*, preceded, if no antecedent is expressed, by a personal or demonstrative pronoun (§ 476). It is often *omitted* in translation, especially with *proper names, abstract nouns, nouns used generically*, and *pronouns* (§§ 470, 471, 473); and must be often *supplied* in translation when not expressed (§§ 485, 486).

2. A substantive used *indefinitely* wants the article; as, Καλὸς γὰρ θησαυρὸς, παρ' ἀνδρὶ σπουδαίῳ χάρις ὀφειλομένη, a *favor due from* a *good man is* an *excellent treasure*, Isocr. 8 b. See § 518. α.

§ 470. A substantive used DEFINITELY is either *employed in its full extent, to denote that which is known*, or, if not employed in its full extent, *denotes a definite part.*

A.) A substantive *employed in its full extent, to denote that which is known*, may be,

1.) A substantive used *generically*, i. e. denoting a *whole class;* as, ὁ ἄνθρωπος, *man* (referring to the whole race), ἡ γυνή, *woman*, οἱ ἄνθρωποι, *men*, οἱ Ἀθηναῖοι, *the Athenians* (the whole nation). Thus, Ὁ ἄνθρωπος "ἄνθρωπος" ὠνομάσθη, *man was named* ἄνθρωπος, Pl. Crat. 399 c. Ὁ γὰρ σύμβουλος καὶ ὁ συκοφάντης . . ἐν τούτῳ πλεῖστον ἀλλήλων διαφέρουσιν Dem. 291. 15. Καὶ τῶν Ἑλλήνων δὲ ἔχων ὁπλίτας . . τριακοσίους, 'of Greeks,' i. 1. 2. Cf. § 485. β.

NOTE. To this head may be referred substantives used *distributively*, which consequently take the article; as, Κῦρος ὑπισχνεῖται . . τρία ἡμιδαρεικὰ τοῦ μηνὸς τῷ στρατιώτῃ, *Cyrus promises three half-darics* [the month to the soldier] *a month to each soldier*, i. 3. 21. — Even with ἕκαστος· as, Ἕκαστον τὸ ἔθνος, *each nation*, i. 8. 9. Κατὰ τὸν ὁπλίτην ἕκαστον δύο μναῖ Th. v. 49 (cf. Ἕκαστον ἀσκὸν iii. 5. 10. For the position of ἕκαστος, see § 472. α.

2.) A substantive expressing an *abstract* idea; as, Ἡ ἀρετή, *virtue*, ἡ κακία, *vice*, ἡ σοφία, *wisdom*, τὸ καλόν, *the beautiful* (§ 449. α). Ἡ σωφροσύνη, καὶ ἡ ἐγκράτεια, καὶ ἡ ἀλκή Cyr. vii. 5. 75. Cf. § 485. β.

3.) An *infinitive* or *clause used substantively*, or *a word spoken of as such;* as, Τὸ ζῆν, *to live, life* (§ 445). Διὰ τὸ φοβεῖσθαι, *through fear*, v. 1. 13. Εἰς τὸ μὴ διὰ τὸ ἐγγὺς εἶναι φοβεῖσθαι vii. 8. 20. Τὸ ὄνομα ὁ ἄνθρωπος, *the name* ἄνθρωπος Pl. Crat. 399 c. Τὸ ὄνομα ἡ μηχανή Ib. 415 d. Τοὔνομα τὴν ἀρετήν Ib. e. (In the three last examples, the article conforms by *attraction* to the noun following, instead of being *neuter* (§ 445), inasmuch as the word ὄνομα expressed sufficiently shows that ἄνθρωπος, &c., are spoken of merely as words.)

§ 471. 4.) The name of a *monadic object;* i. e. of an object which exists *singly* in nature, or which is so regarded (μοναδικός, *single*); as, ὁ ἥλιος, *the sun*, ἡ σελήνη, *the moon*, ἡ γῆ, *the earth*, ὁ οὐρανός, *the heavens*. Thus, Ἔχει τροφὴν ἡ γῆ ἀπὸ τοῦ οὐρανοῦ, *the earth receives nutriment from the heavens*, Œc. 17. 10. Cf. § 485. α.

5.) The name of an *art* or *science;* as, Ἡ ἰατρικὴ καὶ ἡ χαλκευτικὴ καὶ ἡ τεκτονική, *medicine and brasiery and carpentry*, Œc. i. 1. Cf. § 485. β.

6.) A *proper name*, which has been before *mentioned* or *implied*, or which is *well known;* as, Κῦρον δὲ μεταπέμπεται . .. Ἀναβαίνει οὖν ὁ Κῦρος, *But he sends for Cyrus. Cyrus therefore goes up*, i. 1. 2. Διὰ Φρυγίας . .. Τῆς Φρυγίας πόλιν i. 2. 6, 7. Κῦρος τὴν Κίλισσαν εἰς τὴν Κιλικίαν ἀποπέμπει, *Cyrus sends the Cilician qeeen to Cilicia*, i. 2. 20. Ὑπὲρ τῆς Ἑλλάδος, *in behalf of Greece* (their native land), i. 3. 4. Cf. § 485. α.

NOTES. (*a*) Proper names appear to take the article, from their being, in their origin, either *adjectives used substantively* (§ 448), or *common nouns used distinctively* (§ 479). Thus, Ἡ Ἑλλάς [sc. γῆ], [the Greek land] *Greece* (comp. *England*, the land of the Angles, in French L'Angleterre, *Scotland*,

Ireland); Ὁ Ἑλλήσποντος, [the sea of Helle] *the Hellespont;* Ὁ Περικλῆς [sc. ἀνήρ], [the Illustrious Man] *Pericles;* Ὁ Φίλιππος, [the Horse-lover] *Philip;* Ἀνὴρ Μυσὸς τὸ γένος καὶ τοὔνομα τοῦτο ἔχων v. 2. 29. (*b*) The adjective construction is especially retained in names of *rivers;* as, Ὁ Μαίανδρος ποταμός i. 2. 7. Τοῦ Μαρσύου ποταμοῦ Ib. 8. So, in Eng., *the Connecticut river.*

§ 472. B.) A substantive *not employed in its full extent* may be rendered *definite,*

I.) By a *limiting word* or *phrase.*

This word or phrase is usually placed, either *between the article and its substantive,* or *after the substantive;* and in the latter case, the article is often *repeated,* either for perspicuity or emphasis. Thus, Μέχρι τοῦ Μηδίας τείχους, *as far as the wall of Media,* i. 7. 15. Τὸ περὶ τὸν Πειραιᾶ τεῖχος H. Gr. iv. 8. 9. Τὰ μακρὰ τείχη τῶν Κορινθίων Ib. 4. 18. Τὸ τεῖχος τὸ Περινθίων vii. 2. 11 (cf. Καὶ Ταναγραίων τὸ τεῖχος περιεῖλον Th. i. 108). Τὸ μὲν ἔσωθεν [τεῖχος] πρὸ τῆς Κιλικίας . ., τὸ δὲ ἔξω τὸ πρὸ τῆς Συρίας i. 4. 4. Ὁ τῆς βασιλέως γυναικὸς ἀδελφός ii. 3. 28. Τὸ τῆς τοῦ ξαίνοντος τέχνης ἔργον Pl. Pol. 281 a. Ἐν ταῖς κώμαις ταῖς ὑπὲρ τοῦ πεδίου τοῦ παρὰ τὸν Κεντρίτην ποταμόν iv. 3. 1.

NOTES. *α.* On the other hand, words and phrases not belonging to the definition or description of the substantive, but to *that which is said about it in the sentence,* either *precede the article,* or *follow the substantive without the article;* as, Ὅτι κενὸς ὁ φόβος εἴη, καὶ οἱ ἄρχοντες σῶοι, *that the fear was groundless, and the generals safe,* ii. 2. 21. Ψιλὴν ἔχων τὴν κεφαλήν, *having the head bare,* i. 8. 6. Ἐλαύνων ἀνὰ κράτος ἱδροῦντι τῷ ἵππῳ Ib. 1. Κατέστησεν ἀντίαν τὴν φάλαγγα i. 10. 10. Ἕπεσθε ἡγεμόνι τῷ Ἡρακλεῖ, *follow Hercules as leader,* vi. 5. 24 (cf. Τῷ Ἡγεμόνι Ἡρακλεῖ vi. 2. 15). Διὰ μέσου δὲ τοῦ παραδείσου, *through the midst of the park,* i. 2. 7 (§ 456). Ἐν τῇ ἀγορᾷ μέσῃ Dem. 848. 13 (but, Τὸ μέσον στῖφος, *the centre division,* i. 8. 13). Πολλῶν τῶν ἐπιτηδείων μεστάς, *full of the necessaries of life in great abundance,* iv. 4. 7. Τὰ δὲ ἐπιτήδεια πολλὰ ἦν λαμβάνειν iv. 1. 8. Σὺν ὀλίγοις τοῖς περὶ αὐτόν, *with those about him few,* i. e. *with few attendants,* i. 5. 12 (but, Σὺν τοῖς ὀλίγοις περὶ αὐτόν, *with the few about him*). Ἐπιχωρῆσαι ὅλην τὴν φάλαγγα, i. 2. 17. Τῆς ἡμέρας ὅλης iii. 3. 11. Πᾶσι . . τοῖς κριταῖς καὶ τοῖς θεαταῖς πᾶσιν, *to all the judges and all the spectators,* Ar. Av. 445. Ψιλὴ ἦν ἅπασα ἡ χώρα, *the country was all bare,* i. 5. 5. Ἕκαστον τὸ ἔθνος i. 8. 9 (§ 470. N.). Τὸ κέρας ἑκάτερον vii. 1. 23. Ἀμφότερα τὰ ὦτα, *both his ears* iii. 1. 31. Αὐτὼ τὼ Λάκωνε, *the Spartans themselves,* vii. 7. 19 (but, Τὼ αὐτὼ Λάκωνε, *the same Spartans*). Τούς τε ἄνδρας αὐτοὺς ii. 5. 39.

β. When the substantive is preceded or followed by *successive modifications,* the article is sometimes *repeated* with each; as, Τὸ ἐν Ἀρκαδίᾳ τὸ τοῦ Διὸς Λυκαίου ἱερόν, *the temple of Lycæan Jove in Arcadia,* Pl. Rep. 565 d. Ἐν τῇ τοῦ Διὸς τῇ μεγίστῃ ἑορτῇ Th. i. 126. Τά τε τείχη τὰ ἑαυτῶν τὰ μακρὰ ἀπετέλεσαν Ib. 108.

§ 473. REMARKS. 1. It is common to employ the article even when the substantive is rendered definite by a *possessive* or *demonstrative pronoun;* as,

α. POSSESSIVE. Ὁ ἐμὸς πατήρ, *my father,* i. 6. 6. Ὄμμα τοὐμόν [= τὸ ἐμόν, § 39] Cyr. viii. 7. 26. Τὴν ἡμετέραν χώραν iv. 8. 6. Τῷ νόμῳ τῷ ὑμετέρῳ vii. 3. 39.

β. DEMONSTRATIVE. The pronouns οὗτος and ὅδε, as themselves beginning with the article (§ 150), do not take it before them, and ἐκεῖνος follows their analogy. The arrangement, therefore, with these pronouns is the same as in § 472. α. Thus, Ταύτας τὰς πόλεις, *these cities*, i. 1. 8. Τὸν ἄνδρα τοῦτον i. 6. 9. Τόνδε τὸν τρόπον, i. 1. 9. Ὁ μὲν ἀνὴρ ὅδε Apol. 29. Ἐκείνης τῆς ἡμέρας i. 7. 18.

NOTE. In prose, when the article is *omitted* with a demonstrative pronoun and a common noun, the *pronoun* is usually employed as a *subject*, and the *noun* as an *attribute*; thus, Ἔστι μὲν γὰρ πενία αὕτη σαφής, *for this is manifest poverty*, Œc. 8. 2 (cf. Αὕτη ἡ ἔνδεια Ib.). Κίνησις γὰρ αὕτη μεγίστη . . ἐγένετο Th. i. 1. Αὕτη αὖ ἄλλη πρόφασις ἦν i. 1. 7.

§ **474.** 2. Upon the same principle, the article is prefixed to words and phrases, which are joined with a *proper name* or a *personal pronoun* to give *definiteness* or *emphatic distinction*; as,

Τὸν βασιλεύοντα Ἀρταξέρξην, [the reigning Artaxerxes] *Artaxerxes the king*, i. 1. 4. Μένων ὁ Θετταλός, *Meno the Thessalian*, i. 2. 6. Ἐπύαξα, ἡ Συεννέσιος γυνή, τοῦ Κιλίκων βασιλέως Ib. 12. Ἀριστόδημον τὸν μικρὸν ἐπικαλούμενον Mem. i. 4. 2. Ἐγὼ . . ὁ ἐξηπατηκὼς . ., ὑμεῖς δὲ οἱ ἐξηπατημένοι v. 7. 9. Ἡ τάλαιν' ἐγώ, *I, the wretched one* (by eminence), i. e. *most miserable*, Soph. El. 1138. Ὁρῶν σε τὸν δύστηνον Id. Œd. C. 745. Ὁ παντλήμων ἐγώ, *I, the all-wretched*, Id. Œd. T. 1379. Τὸν πατροφόντην, τὸν ἀσεβῆ με Ib. 1441. So, when the pronoun is implied in a verb, Ὀλεκόμαν ὁ τάλας Soph. Tr. 1015. Ὁ τλήμων . . ἥκω Eur. Andr. 1070.

NOTE. If, on the other hand, *no distinction is designed*, the article is *omitted*; as, Ξενοφῶν Ἀθηναῖος, *Xenophon, an Athenian*, i. 8. 15. Παταγύας ἀνὴρ Πέρσης Ib. 1. Ἐγὼ τάλας, *I, unhappy man*, Soph. Œd. C. 747. Ἀφέλκομαι δύστηνος Ib. 844.

§ **475.** 3. An *adverb preceded by an article* has often the force of an *adjective*. This construction may be explained by supposing the ellipsis of a participle, commonly ὤν or γενόμενος. Thus,

Τὸν νῦν χρόνον, *the* [now time] *present time*, vi. 6. 13 (cf. Τὸν ὄντα νῦν χρόνον Eur. Ion, 1349). Ἐν τῷ πρόσθεν [sc. γενομένῳ] λόγῳ ii. 1. 1. Ὁ νῦν βασιλεὺς οὗτος, καλέσαντος τοῦ τότε βασιλέως, πατρὸς δὲ τοῦ νῦν Cyr. iv. 6. 3. Τὴν τήμερον ἡμέραν iv. 6. 9. Τῆς οἴκαδε ὁδοῦ iii. 1. 2. Τοῖς πάνυ τῶν στρατιωτῶν, *the best soldiers*, Th. viii. 1. Κάδμου τοῦ πάλαι Soph. Œd. T. 1.

NOTES. (*a*) This adjective may again, like any other adjective, be used either *substantively* or *adverbially* (§§ 476 – 478). (*b*) A *preposition with its case* may be used in the same way; as, Τοῦ ἐν Δελφοῖς χρηστηρίου, *the Delphic oracle*, Cyr. vii. 3. 15. Ἀρμενία . . ἡ πρὸς ἑσπέραν, *Western Armenia*, iv. 4. 4.

§ **476.** 4. The substantive which is modified is often omitted; in which case the article may commonly be regarded as *used substantively with the word or phrase following* (see §§ 447, 469. 1). Thus,

Τῶν παρὰ βασιλέως [sc. ἀνδρῶν], *of those from the king*, i. 1. 5. Τῶν περὶ τὴν θήραν, *those engaged in the hunt*, or *the hunters*, Pl. Soph. 220 d. Οἱ τοῦ δήμου Th. viii. 66. Οἵ τ' ἔνδον . . καὶ οἱ ἔξω, *both those within, and those without*, ii. 5. 32. Τὸ πέραν τοῦ ποταμοῦ, *the opposite side of the river*, iii. 5. 2. Τοῦ πρόσω, i. 3. 1. Εἰς τοὔμπαλιν [τὸ ἔμπαλιν], *back*, i. 4. 15. Οἱ ἐκ τοῦ ἐπέκεινα, *those of the country beyond*, v. 4. 3. Τοῖς παροῦσι τῶν πιστῶν i. 5. 15. Τί τὸ κωλῦον εἴη εἰσελθεῖν, *what it was which prevented their entering*, iv. 7. 4. Ὁ μηδὲν ὤν, *he that is nothing*, Soph. Aj. 767. Τοῦ μηδὲν [ὄντος] Ib. 1231. See § 450.

Note. The phrases οἱ ἀμφί and οἱ περί, followed by the name of a person, commonly include the *person himself*, with his attendants or associates; and sometimes, by a species of vague periphrasis, denote little more than the *person merely*. Thus, Οἱ ἀμφὶ Ἀριαῖον, [those about Ariæus] *Ariæus and those with him*, iii. 2. 2. Οἱ περὶ Ξενοφῶντα, *Xenophon with his men*, vii. 4. 16. Οἱ δὲ ἀμφὶ Τισσαφέρνην iii. 5. 1 (cf. Τισσαφέρνης καὶ οἱ σὺν αὐτῷ Ib. 3). Τοὺς ἀμφὶ Θράσυλλον καὶ Ἐρασινίδην, *Thrasyllus and Erasinides with their colleagues*, Mem. i. 1. 18. Οἱ μὲν περὶ τοὺς Κορινθίους ἐν τῇ Νεμέᾳ ἦσαν, οἱ δὲ Λακεδαιμόνιοι καὶ οἱ ξύμμαχοι ἐν τῷ Σικυῶνι, 'the Corinthians with their allies,' H. Gr. iv. 2. 14. Πιττακοῦ τε καὶ Βίαντος, καὶ τῶν ἀμφὶ τὸν Μιλήσιον Θαλῆν Pl. Hipp. Maj. 281 c.

§ 477. 5. When the *neuter article* is used *substantively* with a word or phrase following, (α.) the precise idea (as, in English, of '*thing*' or '*things*') must be determined from the connection, and (β.) not unfrequently the whole expression may be regarded as a *periphrasis for an included substantive*. Thus,

α. Τὰ τοῦ γήρως, *the evils of old age*, Apol. 6. Τὰ ἀμφὶ τὸν πόλεμον, *military exercises*, Cyr. ii. 1. 21. Τὰ περὶ Προξένου, *the fate of Proxenus*, ii. 5. 37. Ἐν τοῖς ἐπάνω, [in the above] *in the preceding narrative*, vi. 3. 1. Τὰ μὲν δὴ Κύρου δῆλον ὅτι οὕτως ἔχει πρὸς ἡμᾶς, ὥσπερ τὰ ἡμέτερα πρὸς ἐκεῖνον, 'the relation of Cyrus to us is the same as ours to him,' i. 3. 9. Τὰ παρ' ἐμοὶ ἑλέσθαι ἀντὶ τῶν οἴκοι, *to prefer remaining with me to returning home*, i. 7. 4. Ἐπεὶ δὲ τὰ τῶν θεῶν καλῶς εἶχεν, *and when the gods had been duly honored*, iii. 2. 9. Τὰ περὶ τῆς δίκης, *the circumstances of the trial*, Pl. Phædo, 57 b. Χειρίσοφος μὲν ἤδη τετελευτήκει, . . τὰ δ' ἐκείνου Νέων Ἀσιναῖος παρέλαβε, 'his place or office,' vi. 4. 11. Ἐπιστήμων εἶναι τῶν ἀμφὶ τάξεις, *to be skilled in tactics*, ii. 1. 7. Τοὺς τὰ Ἀθηναίων φρονοῦντας, *those that favor the cause of the Athenians*, Th. viii. 31. Φρονεῖν τὰ πρὸς σέ vii. 7. 30. Τὸ τῶν ἁλιέων, *the habit of fishermen*, Œc. 16. 7. Ὡς δὲ τὸ τοῦ ποταμοῦ οὕτως ἐπορσύνετο, 'the diversion of the river,' Cyr. vii. 5. 17. Τὸ τοῦ Ἰβυκείου ἵππου πεπονθέναι, *to be in the condition of the horse of Ibycus*, Pl. Parm. 136 e. Δεδιέναι τὸ τῶν παίδων, *to have the boyish fear*, Id. Phædo, 77 d (§ 432). Τὸ τοῦ Σοφοκλέους, *what is said by Sophocles*, Id. Rep. 329 c. Τὸ τῶν παρόντων, *the convenience of those who are present*, Id. Gorg. 458 b. See § 447. γ.

β. Τὸ τῆς τύχης, *the course of fortune*, = ἡ τύχη, *fortune*, Eur. Alc. 785. Τὸ τῶν πνευμάτων, *the state of the winds*, = τὰ πνεύματα, *the winds*, Dem. 49. 7. Τὸ δὲ τῶν χρημάτων, *but the matter of the money*, = τὰ χρήματα, Id. 47. 24. Τὰ τῆς ὀργῆς = ἡ ὀργή, Th. ii. 60. Ἐπῄνει τὰ βασιλέως, *extolled the king*, H. Gr. vii. 1. 38. Τὰ θεῶν οὕτω βουλόμεν' ἔσται Eur. Iph. A. 33. Τὰ βαρβάρων γὰρ δοῦλα πάντα πλὴν ἑνός Id. Hel. 276. Ὡς δὴ σὺ σώφρων, τἀμὰ [τὰ ἐμὰ = ἐγὼ] δ' οὐχὶ σώφρονα Id. Andr. 235. Εἰ τὸ τῶνδ' εὔνουν πάρα Soph. El. 1203. See §§ 447. γ, 453. ε.

§ 478. 6. The NEUTER ACCUSATIVE of the article is often used in forming *adverbial phrases* (§§ 440, 441), in connection with,

α. ADVERBS (§ 475. *a*); as, Τὸ πάλαι [sc. ὄν], *as to that which was of old*, i. e. *formerly*, *anciently*, Pl. Phædr. 251 b. Τὸ πρόσθεν, *before*, i. 10. 10. Τὸ πρίν Eur. Alc. 977. Τοὔμπαλιν [τὸ ἔμπαλιν], *back*, vi. 6. 38. Τό γε παραυτίκα Ar. Vesp. 833. Τὸ παράπαν Ag. 7. 7. Τὸ πάμπαν Pl. Tim. 41 b.

β. ADJECTIVES; as, Τὸ πρῶτον, *at first*, i. 10. 10. Τὰ πρῶτα, *first*, Soph. Tr. 757. Τὸ πρότερον, *before*, iv. 4. 14. Τὸ τρίτον i. 6. 8. Τὸ παλαιόν iii. 4. 7. Τοὐλάχιστον [τὸ ἐλάχιστον], *at least*, v. 7. 8. See § 441.

γ. PREPOSITIONS followed by their cases; as, Τὸ ἀπὸ τοῦδε, *as to that after this*, i. e. *henceforth*, Cyr. v. 1. 6. Τὸ ἐκ τοῦδε Ib. 5. 43. Τὸ πρὸς ἑσπέραν, *to the west*, vi. 4. 4. See § 475. *b*.

§ 479. II.) By *previous mention*, *mutual understanding*, *general notoriety*, or *emphatic distinction*; as,

Θορύβου ἤκουσε διὰ τῶν τάξεων ἰόντος, καὶ ἤρετο τίς ὁ θόρυβος εἴη, *he heard a noise passing through the ranks, and inquired what the noise was*, i. 8. 16. Οἱ δ' ἐπεδίωκον μέχρι κώμης τινός· ἐνταῦθα δ' ἔστησαν οἱ Ἕλληνες· ὑπὲρ γὰρ τῆς κώμης γήλοφος ἦν, .. τῶν δὲ ἱππέων ὁ λόφος ἐνεπλήσθη i. 10. 11. Τὰ πλοῖα αἰτεῖν i. 3. 16 (cf. Αἰτεῖν πλοῖα Ib. 14). Δουλεύομεν θεοῖς, ὅ τι ποτ' εἰσὶν οἱ θεοί Eur. Or. 418. Ὅτε Ξέρξης ὕστερον ἀγείρας τὴν ἀναρίθμητον στρατιὰν ἦλθεν, 'that innumerable army,' iii. 2. 13. Τίνος ποινῆς τὰ πολλὰ πνεύματ' ἔσχ' ἐν Αὐλίδι Soph. El. 563. Τὸν ἄνδρα ὁρῶ, *I see* THE MAN [i. e. Artaxerxes], i. 8. 26. Ἀνακαλοῦντες τὸν προδότην, *exclaiming*, 'the traitor!' vi. 6. 7. Ἀνακαλοῦντες τὸν εὐεργέτην, τὸν ἄνδρα τὸν ἀγαθόν Cyr. iii. 3. 4.

§ 480. REMARKS. 1. From a reference to something which precedes, or is mutually understood, the article may be even joined,

α.) With an INTERROGATIVE PRONOUN; as, Ἄλλα τοίνυν, ἔφη ὁ Ἰσχόμαχος, θέλω σοι .. διηγήσασθαι. .. Τὰ ποῖα; ἔφην ἐγώ, *I will then, said Ischomachus, relate to you other things.* [The what?] *What are they? said I*, Œc. 10. 1. ΚΡ. Ἃ δ' ἐμποδὼν μάλιστα, ταῦθ' ἥκω φράσων. ἘΤ. Τὰ ποῖα ταῦτα; Eur. Ph. 706. ΤΡ. Πάσχει δὲ θαυμαστόν. ἙΡ. Τὸ τί; Ar. Pax, 696. ἙΡ. Οἶά μ' ἐκέλευσεν ἀναπυθέσθαι σου. ΤΡ. Τὰ τί; Ib. 693 (Τὰ plur. with reference to οἷα, and τί sing. for plur.; cf. Τί οὖν ταῦτα ἐστίν; § 450. γ). Εἴφ' ὅ τι παθεῖν δεῖ· τί με τὸ δεινὸν ἐργάσει; Eur. Bac. 492. Ποτέρῳ οὖν ὁμοιότερον τῷ εἴδει Pl. Phædo, 79 b. See § 528. 1.

β. With a PERSONAL PRONOUN; as, Δεῦρο δή, ἦ δ' ὅς, εὐθὺς ἡμῶν οὐ παραβάλλεις; .. Ποῖ, ἔφην ἐγώ, λέγεις, καὶ παρὰ τίνας τοὺς ὑμᾶς; *Will you not, said he, come hither directly to us? Whither, said I, do you say, and to whom* [as the you?] *do I go, in going to you?* Pl. Lys. 203 b. Τὸν ἐμέ, *the me*, i. e. *me, of whom you speak*, Id. Phil. 20 a.

γ.) With a PRONOUN OF QUALITY OR QUANTITY; as, Τὸ τοιοῦτον ὄναρ, *such a dream as I have described*, or, *such a dream as this*, iii. 1. 3. Ἀγορα-στὴν τὸν τοιοῦτον Mem. i. 5. 2. Τὴν τηλικαύτην ἀρχὴν Pl. Leg. 755 b.

2. A *numeral* preceded by ἀμφί, *about*, has commonly the article, the round number being apparently regarded as an object familiar to the mind, or as a definite standard to which an approach is made; thus, Ἅρματα . . ἀμφὶ τὰ εἴκοσι, *chariots about the* [number of] *twenty*, i. e. *about twenty in number*, i. 7 10. Πελτασταὶ δὲ ἀμφὶ τοὺς δισχιλίους i. 2. 9. Ἀμφὶ τὰ πεντήκοντα ἔτη ii. 6. 15. So, Εἰς τὰ ἑκατὸν ἅρματα Cyr. vi. 1. 50.

§ 481. III.) By the *connection in which it is employed*; as,

Ἐπειδὴ δὲ ἐτελεύτησε Δαρεῖος, καὶ κατέστη εἰς τὴν βασιλείαν Ἀρταξέρξης, 'had succeeded to the throne [sc. of Persia],' i. 1. 3. Ἰόντες ἐπὶ τὰς θύρας, i. 2. 11. Αἱ λόγχαι καὶ αἱ τάξεις καταφανεῖς ἐγίγνοντο i. 8. 8. Οἱ δ' ἐπεὶ ἦλθον πρὸς τοὺς προφύλακας, ἐζήτουν τοὺς ἄρχοντας ii. 3. 2.

§ 482. REMARK. With substantives which are rendered definite by the connection, the article has often the force of a *possessive* (see § 503); as,

Ἐβούλετο τὼ παῖδε ἀμφοτέρω παρεῖναι, *he wished* [the] *his children to be both present*, i. 1. 1. Τισσαφέρνης διαβάλλει τὸν Κῦρον πρὸς τὸν ἀδελφόν Ib. 3. Κῦρός τε καταπηδήσας ἀπὸ τοῦ ἅρματος τὸν θώρακα ἐνέδυ, καὶ ἀναβὰς ἐπὶ τὸν ἵππον τὰ παλτὰ εἰς τὰς χεῖρας ἔλαβε i. 8. 3.

§ 483. IV.) By *contrast*.

This may give a degree of definiteness to expressions which are otherwise quite indefinite; and may even lead to the employment of the article with the *indefinite pronoun* τὶς. Thus,

Ἐν ἑκάστῳ τρεῖς ἄνδρας, ὧν οἱ μὲν δύο ἐκβάντες εἰς τάξιν ἔθεντο τὰ ὅπλα, ὁ δὲ εἷς ἔμενε, 'of whom two . ., but the third,' v. 4. 11. Τῶν δὲ πολεμίων οἱ μέν τινες αἰσθόμενοι πάλιν ἔδραμον . ., οἱ δὲ πολλοὶ . . φανεροὶ ἦσαν φεύγοντες, 'some . ., but the most,' iv. 3. 33. Ἵππους . ., τοὺς μέν τινας παρ' ἐμοί, τοὺς δὲ τῷ Κλεάρχῳ καταλελειμμένους iii. 3. 19. Cf. § 490. R.

§ 484. GENERAL REMARKS. 1. The article is sometimes found without a substantive, through *anacolūthon* (§ 329. N.) or *aposiopēsis* (ἀποσιώπησις, *the becoming silent*, i. e. the leaving a sentence unfinished, from design, strong emotion, or any other cause); as,

Ἡ τῶν ἄλλων Ἑλλήνων ——, εἴτε χρὴ κακίαν, εἴτ' ἄγνοιαν, εἴτε καὶ ἀμφότερα ταῦτ' εἰπεῖν, *the* ——, *whether I should say* cowardice, *or* folly *of the rest of the Greeks, or* both these together, Dem. 231. 21. Τῆς γὰρ ἐμῆς, εἰ δή τίς ἐστι σοφία καὶ οἵα, μάρτυρα ὑμῖν παρέξομαι Pl. Apol. 20 e. Μὰ τὸν ——, οὐ σύ γε. *Not you, by* —— (the name of the god omitted, as the old grammarians say, through reverence), Ib. Gorg. 466 e.

§ 485. 2. OMISSION OF THE ARTICLE. With substantives which will be at once recognized as definite without the article, it is often *omitted;* particularly with,

α. *Proper names,* and *other names resembling these* from their being *specially appropriated* or *familiar appellations of persons* (§ 471); thus, Διαβάλλει τὸν Κῦρον. . . Συλλαμβάνει Κῦρον i. 1. 3. Πρὸς Κῦρον Ib. 6, 7. Πρὸς τὸν Κῦρον Ib. 10. Ὁ δὲ Κῦρος Ib. 7, 10. Κῦρος δὲ i. 2. 5. See i. 5, 11, 12. Εἰς τὴν Κιλικίαν i. 2. 20, 21. Εἰς Κιλικίαν Ib. 21. Ἅμα ἡλίῳ δύνοντι ii. 2. 13. Ἅμα τῷ ἡλίῳ δυομένῳ Ib. 16. Τοῖς ἄρχουσι τῆς θαλάττης, . . τοῖς τῆς γῆς Rep. Ath. 2. 4. Τοῖς μὲν κατὰ θάλατταν ἄρχουσιν, . . τοῖς δὲ κατὰ γῆν Ib. 5. Πρὸς ἑσπέραν, . . πρὸς ἕω v. 7. 6. Ὅτι βορέας . . φέρει, νότος δὲ Ib. 7. Τὸ ἐκείνων πλοῖον. . . Ἔχω γε αὐτῶν καὶ τέκνα καὶ γυναῖκας i. 4. 8. Λαβεῖν ἂν καὶ αὐτὸν καὶ γυναῖκα καὶ παῖδας καὶ τὰ χρήματα vii. 8. 9. Σὺν τοῖς θεοῖς iii. 1. 23. Πρὸς τῶν θεῶν Ib. 24. Σὺν θεοῖς vii. 7. 7. Πρὸς θεῶν v. 7. 5. Δίκαιόν ἐστι καὶ πρὸς θεῶν καὶ πρὸς ἀνθρώπων i. 6. 6. Τὰ πρὸς τοὺς θεοὺς, . . τὰ πρὸς τοὺς ἀνθρώπους Lac. 13. 11.—Hence βασιλεύς, in its familiar application to the *King of Persia,* commonly wants the article; as, Πορεύεται ὡς βασιλέα, *goes to the king,* i. 2. 4. Cf. Τὸν βασιλέα ii. 4. 4.

β. *Abstract nouns, names of arts and sciences,* and *generic terms* (§ 470); thus, Εὖρος εἴκοσι ποδῶν, ὕψος δὲ ἑκατόν ii. 4. 12. Τὸ εὖρος πεντήκοντα ποδῶν, καὶ τὸ ὕψος πεντήκοντα iii. 4. 10. Ὑπὸ κάλλους καὶ μεγέθους ἀδιήγητον Cyr. viii. 7. 22. Θαυμάσιαι τὸ κάλλος καὶ τὸ μέγεθος ii. 3. 15. Καὶ ἀνδρεία, καὶ σωφροσύνη, καὶ δικαιοσύνη Pl. Phædo, 69 b. Γεωργίαν τε καὶ τὴν πολεμικὴν τέχνην Œc. 4. 4. Ὅτι ἐπὶ θάνατον ἄγοιτο i. 6. 10. Θεοσεβέστατον . . ζώων ἄνθρωπος Pl. Leg. 902 b.

§ 486. γ. Substantives *followed by the article with a defining word or phrase;* thus, Κύρου ἀποτέμνεται ἡ κεφαλὴ καὶ χεὶρ ἡ δεξιά i. 10. 1. Ἐπὶ σκηνὴν ἰόντες τὴν Ξενοφῶντος vi. 4. 19.

NOTES. 1. Proper names, followed by the article, are rarely preceded by it, except with special demonstrative force. Thus, Παρύσατις . . ἡ μήτηρ i. 1. 4. Σοφαίνετος δὲ ὁ Στυμφάλιος . ., Σωκράτης δὲ ὁ Ἀχαιός i. 2. 3. Ἐν Χεῤῥονήσῳ τῇ καταντιπέρας Ἀβύδου i. 1. 9 (cf. Ἐκ τῆς Χεῤῥονήσου i. 3. 4). But, Ὁ δὲ Σιλανὸς ὁ Ἀμβρακιώτης, *but that Silanus the Ambraciot* (who had been the chief soothsayer of the army), vi. 4. 13.

2. In this construction, the substantive is sometimes *first introduced as indefinite,* and *then defined;* and this subsequent definition sometimes respects simply the *kind* or *class.* Thus, Κρήνη ἡ Μίδου καλουμένη, *a fountain* [that called Midas's] *which was called the fountain of Midas,* i. 2. 13. Πολλοὶ δὲ στρουθοὶ οἱ μεγάλοι, *and many struthi, the large ones,* i. e. *ostriches,* i. 5. 2. Κάρυα . . πολλὰ τὰ πλατέα, 'of the broad kind,' v. 4. 29.

δ. *Two or more nouns coupled together;* as, Περὶ δὲ τῶν τοιῶνδε τί σε κωλύει διελθεῖν, οἷον Ἡλίου τε καὶ σελήνης καὶ ἄστρων καὶ γῆς καὶ αἰθέρος καὶ ἀέρος καὶ πυρὸς καὶ ὕδατος καὶ ὡρῶν καὶ ἐνιαυτοῦ; Pl. Crat. 408 d (cf. Τὸν ἥλιον, Ἡ σελήνη, Τὰ ἄστρα Ib. 408, 409). See other examples in § 485.

ε. *Ordinals* and *Superlatives;* as, Καὶ τρίτον ἔτος τῷ πολέμῳ ἐτελεύτα Th. ii. 103. Εἰς Ἰσσοὺς, τῆς Κιλικίας ἐσχάτην πόλιν i. 4. 1.

§ 487. 3. The PARTS OF A SENTENCE may be ranked as follows, with respect to the frequency of their taking the article: (*a*) An *appositive,* appended for *distinction.* See §§ 472, 474. (*b*) The *subject* of the sentence.

(*c*) An *adjunct not governed by a preposition.* (*d*) An *adjunct governed by a preposition.* (*e*) An *attribute.* This commonly wants the article, as simply denoting that the subject is one of a class. To this head belongs the *second Acc.* after verbs of *making, naming,* &c. (§ 434).

4. Hence the article is often used in *marking the subject of a sentence,* and sometimes appears to be used chiefly for this purpose. Thus, Μὴ φυγὴ εἴη ἡ ἄφοδος, *lest the departure should be a flight,* vii. 8. 16. Ἐμπόριον δ' ἦν τὸ χωρίον i. 4. 6. Ἦσαν δὲ ζειαὶ αἱ πλεῖσται, *and the greater part was spelt,* v. 4. 27 (§ 455). Καλοῦσί γε ἀκολασίαν τὸ ὑπὸ τῶν ἡδονῶν ἄρχεσθαι Pl. Phædo, 68 e. Ἆρ' οὖν παραπλησίως εἰσὶν ἀγαθοὶ καὶ κακοὶ οἱ ἀγαθοί τε καὶ οἱ κακοί; Id. Gorg. 498 c. Τὰ δὶς πέντε δέκα ἐστίν, *twice five is ten,* Mem. iv. 4. 7. Οἱ μύριοι ἱππεῖς οὐδὲν ἄλλο ἢ μύριοί εἰσιν ἄνθρωποι, *ten thousand horsemen are nothing else than ten thousand men,* iii. 2. 18. Καὶ ΘΕΟΣ ἦν Ὁ ΛΟΓΟΣ St. Jn. 1. 1.

> Τίς δ' οἶδεν, εἰ τὸ ζῆν μέν ἐστι κατθανεῖν,
> Τὸ κατθανεῖν δὲ ζῆν κάτω νομίζεται. Eur. Pol. Fr. 7.

§ **488.** 5. There are some words, with which it is especially important to observe the insertion or omission of the article; as, Ἄλλο δὲ στράτευμα, *and another army,* i. 1. 9. Τὸ ἄλλο στράτευμα, *the rest of the army,* i. 2. 25. Ἀμφικράτης καὶ ἄλλοι, 'and others,' iv. 2. 17. Ἐπορεύθησαν, ἢ οἱ ἄλλοι, 'the others,' 'the rest,' Ib. 10. Πολὺ τοῦ στρατεύματος, 'much of,' iv. 1. 11. Τὸ μὲν δὴ πολὺ τοῦ Ἑλληνικοῦ, 'the greater part,' i. 4. 13. Πολλοί, *many,* iv. 6. 26. Τοὺς πολλούς, *the most,* Ib. 24 (§ 466). Ὀλίγοι ἀπέθνησκον, *few died,* iv. 2. 7. Πλείω τούτων ἀπολαύει ὁ ὄχλος ἢ οἱ ὀλίγοι, 'the few,' 'the aristocracy,' Rep. Ath. 2. 10. See § 472. α.

6. When two words or phrases are connected by a conjunction, if they refer to *different objects,* the article is more frequently *repeated;* but otherwise, *not;* as, Τό τε βαρβαρικὸν καὶ τὸ Ἑλληνικὸν ἐνταῦθα στράτευμα i. 2. 1. Τῶν Ἑλλήνων καὶ τῶν βαρβάρων Ib. 14. Τοὺς πιστοὺς καὶ εὔνους καὶ βεβαίους i. 9. 30. Τῆς πρόσθεν φιλίας ὑπομνήματα καὶ πίστεως i. 6. 3. Ὁ δ' αὖ διὰ τέλους τὸν ἅπαντα χρόνον γεγονώς τε καὶ ὢν καὶ ἐσόμενός ἐστι μόνος Pl. Tim. 38 c.

7. When two nouns are related to each other in a clause, and have the same extent of meaning, the article is commonly joined with *both,* or with *neither;* as, Πλήθει μὲν χώρας καὶ ἀνθρώπων ἰσχυρὰ οὖσα, τοῖς δὲ μήκεσι τῶν ὁδῶν καὶ τῷ διεσπάσθαι τὰς δυνάμεις ἀσθενής i. 5. 9. Οὐδέποτ' ἄρα . . λυσιτελέστερον ἀδικία δικαιοσύνης Pl. Rep. 354 a. Λυσιτελέστερον ἡ ἀδικία τῆς δικαιοσύνης Ib. b. Ἡ σώμασι φάρμακα [ἀποδιδοῦσα τέχνη]. . . Ἡ τοῖς ὄψοις τὰ ἡδύσματα Ib. 332 c.

§ **489.** 8. The insertion or omission of the article often depends, both in poetry and prose, upon *euphony* and *rhythm,* and upon those *nice distinctions in the expression of our ideas,* which, though they may be readily felt, are often transferred with difficulty from one language to another. In general, the *insertion* of the article promotes the *perspicuity,* and its *omission,* the *vivacity* of discourse. It is, consequently, more employed in *philosophical* than in *rhetorical* composition, and far more in *prose* than in *poetry.* It should be remarked, however, that, even in prose, there is none of the minutiæ of language in which manuscripts differ more, than in respect to its insertion or omission, especially with proper names.

9. The article is sometimes so closely united with the word following, that

a *second article is prefixed*, as if to a single word; thus, Λόγος δὲ ὁ κατὰ ταὐτὸν [= τὸ αὐτὸ, § 97. N.] ἀληθὴς γιγνόμενος, περί τε θάτερον [= τὸ ἕτερον, § 39] ὤν, καὶ περὶ τὸ ταὐτὸν . ., καὶ ὁ τοῦ θατέρου κύκλος Pl. Tim. 37 b. Τό τε θάτερον καὶ τὸ ταὐτόν Ib. 44 b (see §§ 479, 480). Τῶν τὸ μηδέν [sc. ὄντων], *those who are that which is nothing*, Eur. Tro. 412 (see §§ 450. δ, 476).

II. The Article as a Pronoun.

§ **490.** A. The ARTICLE, if we include both its *aspirated* and its τ- *forms*, is used as a PRONOUN, by Attic writers, only *in connection with certain particles.*

NOTE. By the use of the article *as a pronoun*, is meant its *substantive use independent of a modifying word or phrase* (§ 476). This use is explained, as in the case of other adjectives (§ 447), by the ellipsis of a noun. As a pronoun, the article in Attic writers is either *demonstrative* or *personal*, the cases in § 493 excepted.

1. With μέν and δέ; as, Ὁ δὲ [sc. ἀδελφὸς] πείθεται, *and he* [the brother] *is persuaded*, i. 1. 3. Οἱ μὲν ᾤχοντο, Κλέαρχος δὲ περιέμενε, *they* (Chirisophus and Meno) *went, but Clearchus stayed*, ii. 1. 6. Πᾶς σε Καδμείων λεὼς καλεῖ δικαίως, ἐκ δὲ τῶν μάλιστ' ἐγώ Soph. Œd. C. 741.

REMARK. The article with μέν and δέ is commonly used for *contradistinction* (cf. § 483), and we may translate ὁ μὲν . ., ὁ δέ, *this . ., that, the one . ., the other, one . ., another*, &c., and οἱ μὲν . ., οἱ δέ, *these . ., those, some . ., others*, &c. Thus, Ὁ μὲν μαίνεται, ὁ δὲ σωφρονεῖ, *the one is mad, the other is rational*, Pl. Phædr. 244 a. Οἱ μὲν ἐπορεύοντο, οἱ δ' εἵποντο, *the one party* (the Greeks) *marched on, and the other* (the Persians) *followed*, iii. 4. 16. Βασιλεύς τε καὶ οἱ Ἕλληνες . ., οἱ μὲν διώκοντες . ., οἱ δ' ἁρπάζοντες, 'these . . those,' i. 10. 4. Τοὺς μὲν αὐτῶν ἀπέκτεινε, τοὺς δ' ἐξέβαλεν, 'some . . others,' i. 1. 7 (§ 362. α). Ἐν μὲν ἄρα τοῖς συμφωνοῦμεν, ἐν δὲ τοῖς οὔ Pl. Phædr. 263 b. Ἔπειτα φωνὴν πᾶσαν ἀκούοντες, ἐξελέξαντο τοῦτο μὲν ἐκ τῆς, τοῦτο δὲ ἐκ τῆς Rep. Ath. 2. 8. Τὰ μὲν ἔπαθεν, . . τέλος δὲ κατέκτανε, *he received some wounds, but finally slew*, i. 9. 6. Ὁ μὲν ἦρχεν, οἱ δὲ ἐπείθοντο, *he* (Clearchus) *commanded, and the rest obeyed*, ii. 2. 5. Τῇ μὲν γὰρ ἄνοδον, τῇ δὲ εὔοδον, εὑρήσομεν τὸ ὄρος, *for we shall find the mountain, here easy, and there difficult, of ascent*, iv. 8. 10 (§ 421. β). Τὰ μέν τι μαχόμενοι, τὰ δὲ καὶ ἀναπαυόμενοι, '[as to some things . . as to others] *partly . . partly*,' '*now . . now*,' iv. 1. 14 (§ 441).

§ **491.** 2.) In poetry, with γάρ; as, Παρ' ἀνδρὸς Φανοτέως ἥκων· ὁ γὰρ μέγιστος αὐτοῖς τυγχάνει δορυξένων, 'for he,' Soph. El. 45. Τῆς γὰρ πέφυκα μητρός Soph. Œd. T. 1082. Τὸ γὰρ . . σπάνιον μέρος, *for this is a rare lot*, Eur. Alc. 473.

3.) As the subject of a verb, after καί, *and*; as, Καὶ τὸν κελεῦσαι δοῦναι, *and that he bade him give it*, Cyr. i. 3. 9. Καὶ τὸν ἀποκρίνασθαι λέγεται Ib. iv. 2. 13.

REMARK. The *proclitics in the nominative* (ὁ, ἡ, οἱ, αἱ, § 148) require, from the very laws of accent, that the particle, in connection with which they are used, should follow them. If, therefore, it precedes, they become *orthotone*, or, in other words, take the forms which commonly belong to the *relative pronoun* (§ 148. 2). This change takes place with καί uniformly, and with δέ when it follows ἤ for ἔφη (§ 228); thus, Καὶ ὃς ἐθαύμασε, *and he wondered*, i. 8. 16. Καὶ ἥ, "Οὐκ εὐφημήσεις;" ἔφη Pl. Conv. 201 e. Καὶ οἳ εἶπον vii 6. 4. Ἦ δ' ὅς, *said he*, Pl. Rep. 327 c. Ἦ δ' ὅς, ὁ Γλαύκων, *said he*, i. e. *Glauco*, Ib. b. Ἦ δ' ἥ, *said she*, Id. Conv. 205 c.

§ 492. B. The article *in its* τ- *forms* likewise occurs,

I.) As a DEMONSTRATIVE or PERSONAL PRONOUN,

1.) Before the *relatives* ὅς, ὅσος, and οἷος; as, Τοῦ ὅ ἐστιν, *of that which is*, Pl. Phædo, 92 d. Περὶ τὸ ἐφ' ᾧ λυπεῖται Id. Phil. 37 e. Καὶ τὸν ὅς ἔφη, δεσπότης τούτου εἶναι Lys. 167. 15. Περὶ τεχνῶν τῶν ὅσαι περὶ ταῦτά εἰσι Pl. Soph. 241 e. Προσήκει καὶ μισεῖν τοὺς οἷόσπερ οὗτος Dem. 613. 9. — The sentence introduced by the relative may be regarded as a *defining clause*, to which the article is prefixed (see § 472).

2.) In *particular forms of expression*; viz.

α. Πρὸ τοῦ (also written προτοῦ), *before this*; thus, Τό γε πρὸ τοῦ παῖς ἦσθα Pl. Alc. 109 e. Οἱ δ' οἰκέται ῥέγκουσιν· ἀλλ' οὐκ ἂν πρὸ τοῦ Ar. Nub. 5. Οἱ πρὸ τοῦ φίλοι, 'former friends,' Eur. Med. 696. See § 475. *b*.

β. Τῷ, [through this as a cause, § 416] *for this reason, therefore*; thus, Τῷ τοι . . μᾶλλον σκεπτέον Pl. Theæt. 179 d.

γ. Τό γε, followed by ὅτι; as, Τό γε εὖ οἶδα, ὅτι . ., *this I well know, that* . ., Pl. Euthyd. 291 a. Τό γε δὴ κατανοητέον . ., ὅτι Id. Pol. 305 c.

δ. The article *doubled with* καί or ἤ; as, Εἰ τὸ καὶ τὸ ἐποίησεν ἄνθρωπος οὑτοσί, οὐκ ἂν ἀπέθανεν, *if this man had done this and that, he would not have died*, Dem. 308. 3. Τὰ καὶ τὰ πεπονθώς Id. 560. 17. Ἀφικνοῦμαι ὡς τὸν καὶ τόν, *I go to this one and that*, Lys. 94. 3. With the article again repeated; Ἔδει γὰρ τὸ καὶ τὸ ποιῆσαι, καὶ τὸ μὴ ποιῆσαι, *for this and that we ought to have done, and this not to have done*, Dem. 128. 16. Ὅς ἔφη δεῖν οὕτω προαιρεῖσθαι κινδυνεύειν τὸν στρατηγόν, ὅπως μὴ τὰ ἢ τὰ γενήσεται, ἀλλ' ὅπως τά, 'not these or those, but THESE,' Id. 1457. 16. The nominative ὃς καὶ ὅς (§ 491. R.) occurs, Hdt. iv. 68.

3.) Through *poetic license*, in imitation of the earlier Greek; as, Τὸν . . φθίσον, *him destroy*, Soph. Œd. T. 200. Ταῖν μοι μέλεσθαι, *take care of these for me*, Ib. 1466. Μία γὰρ ψυχή· τῆς ὑπεραλγεῖν μέτριον ἄχθος Eur. Alc. 883. Ἀστέρας, ὅταν φθίνωσιν, ἀντολάς τε τῶν Æsch. Ag. 7.

§ 493. II.) As a RELATIVE PRONOUN.

This substitution of the τ- for the *aspirated* forms (§ 147) occurs in no Attic writers except the *tragedians*, and scarcely in these, except to *avoid hiatus*, or *lengthen a short syllable*. Thus, Κτείνασα τοὺς οὐ χρῆν κτανεῖν, *having slain those whom she ought not to slay*, Eur. Andr. 810. Τὸν θεόν, τὸν νῦν ψέγεις, *the god, whom you now blame*, Ib. Bac. 712. Νοεῖς ἐκεῖνον, ὅντιν' ἀρτίως μολεῖν ἐφιέμεσθα, τὸν θ' οὗτος λέγει; Soph. Œd. T. 1054. Ἀγάλμαθ' ἱερά, τῶν . . ἀπεστέρησ' ἐμαυτόν Ib. 1379. Ἄγος . . δεικνύναι, τὸ μήτε γῆ . . προσδέξεται Ib. 1426.

REMARK. On the other hand, the *aspirated forms* are sometimes found with μέν and δέ for the τ- *forms* (§ 490. 1); thus, Πόλεις Ἑλληνίδας, ἃς μὲν ἀναιρῶν, εἰς ἃς δὲ τοὺς φυγάδας κατάγων, 'some destroying, and to others,

Dem. 248. 18. Ἃς μὲν κατείληφε πόλεις τῶν ἀστυγειτόνων, τινὰς δὲ πορθεῖ. Id. 282. 11. Γνώμα δ' οἷς μὲν ἄκαιρος ὄλβου, τοῖς δ' εἰς μέσον ἥκει Eur. Iph. T. 419. So, Ὁτὲ μὲν . ., ὁτὲ δέ, *sometimes . ., at other times*, Th. vii. 27 Ὁτὲ δέ Ven. 5. 8.

CHAPTER IV.

SYNTAX OF THE PRONOUN.

I. AGREEMENT OF THE PRONOUN.

§ 494. RULE XXVIII. A PRONOUN agrees with its *subject* in *gender*, *number*, and *person*.

By the *subject of a pronoun* is meant the *substantive which it represents*. The rule, therefore, has respect either to *substantive pronouns*, or to *adjective pronouns used substantively*. The construction of adjective pronouns *regarded as such* belongs to RULE XXVI., and even their substantive use is explained by ellipsis (§ 447. a). Thus,

Βασιλεὺς τῆς μὲν πρὸς ἑαυτὸν [i. e. βασιλέα] ἐπιβουλῆς οὐκ ᾐσθάνετο, *the king did not perceive the plot against himself*, i. 1. 8. Ἀπὸ τῆς ἀρχῆς, ἧς [sc. ἀρχῆς] αὐτὸν σατράπην ἐποίησε, *from the government, of which* [government] *he had made him satrap*, i. 1. 2. Πάντων ὅσοι . . ἀθροίζονται Ib. Πρὸς τὸν ἀδελφόν, ὡς ἐπιβουλεύοι αὐτῷ. Ὁ δὲ πείθεται (§ 490) Ib. 3. Ὑμᾶς . ., ὅσοι ἐστέ iv. 6. 14. Θαυμαστὸν ποιεῖς, ὃς . . δίδως Mem. ii. 7. 13.

§ 495. The remarks upon the agreement of the ADJECTIVE (§§ 444 - 459) likewise apply, so far as *gender* and *number* are concerned, to that of the PRONOUN, and some of them to even a greater extent (§ 444. α). Thus,

a. MASCULINE FORM FOR FEMININE.

Ὥσπερ εἰ τὼ χεῖρε, ἃς ὁ θεὸς ἐπὶ τὸ συλλαμβάνειν ἀλλήλοιν ἐποίησεν, ἀφεμένω τούτου τράποιντο πρὸς τὸ διακωλύειν ἀλλήλω Mem. ii. 3. 18. See § 444. β.

NOTE. In speaking of persons *vaguely*, or *generally*, or simply *as persons*, the *masculine* gender often takes the place of the *feminine*, both in pronouns and in other substantive words which admit it; thus, Ξὺν οἷς τ' οὐ χρῆν [= τῇ μητρὶ] μ' ὁμιλῶν Soph. Œd. T. 1184. Οὐδὲ γὰρ κακῶς πάσχοντι μῖσος ὧν τέκῃ προσγίγνεται Id. El. 770. Ἡ στεῖρος οὖσα μόσχος οὐκ ἀνέξεται τίκτοντας ἄλλους [= τίκτουσαν ἄλλην] Eur. Andr. 711. Συνεληλύθασιν ὡς ἐμὲ καταλελειμμέναι ἀδελφαί τε καὶ ἀδελφιδαῖ καὶ ἀνεψιαὶ τοσαῦται, ὥστ' εἶναι ἐν τῇ οἰκίᾳ τεσσαρεσκαίδεκα τοὺς ἐλευθέρους. . . Χαλεπὸν μὲν οὖν ἐστιν, ὦ Σώκρατες, τοὺς οἰκείους περιορᾶν ἀπολλυμένους, ἀδύνατον δὲ τοσούτους τρέφειν Mem. ii. 7. 2 (cf. Ib. 8). See § 336. α.

§ 496. b. Use of the Neuter.

Τί γὰρ τούτου μακαριώτερον, τοῦ γῇ μιχθῆναι; Cyr. viii. 7. 25 (§ 445). Ἐνεδρεύσαμεν, ὅπερ ἡμᾶς καὶ ἀναπνεῦσαι ἐποίησε iv. 1. 22. Τίς οὐκ ἂν ὁμολογήσειεν αὐτὸν βούλεσθαι μήτ' ἠλίθιον μήτ' ἀλαζόνα φαίνεσθαι τοῖς συνοῦσιν; Ἐδόκει δ' ἂν ἀμφότερα ταῦτα, εἰ . . Mem. i. 1. 5 (§ 450). — The *neuter referring to words of other genders*, and the *neuter plural for the singular* (§§ 450, 451), are particularly frequent in pronouns.

c. Compound Construction.

Ἀρτάοζος καὶ Μιθριδάτης, οἳ ἦσαν ii. 5. 35. Πολλοὺς δὲ ἄνδρας καὶ γυναῖκας καλὰς κτήσῃ, οὓς οὐ ληΐζεσθαι δεήσει, ἀλλ' αὐτοὶ . . παρέσονται vii. 3 31. Ἀσφάλειαν καὶ εὔκλειαν, ἃ οὔτε κατασήπεται Cyr. viii. 2. 22. Πολλὰ δ' ὁρῶ πρόβατα καὶ αἶγας καὶ βοῦς καὶ ὄνους, ἃ ἀποδαρέντα iii. 5. 9. Ἀπαλλαγέντες πολέμων καὶ κινδύνων καὶ ταραχῆς, εἰς ἣν . . καθέσταμεν Isocr. 165 b. See § 446. — Zeugma is far less frequent in the construction of the *pronoun* than in that of the *adjective.*

§ 497. d. Synesis.

Τὸ Ἀρκαδικὸν ὁπλιτικὸν, ὧν ἦρχε Κλεάνωρ iv. 8. 18. Τὰ δόξαντα ἂν πλήθει, οἵπερ δικάσουσιν Pl. Phædr. 260 a. Βασιλεύς . . · οἱ δ' ἁρπάζοντες i. 10. 4 (cf. Ib. 2 and 5). Οἰκτρὰ γὰρ πεπόνθαμεν, ἣ . . κενὴν κατέσχον ἐλπίδα Eur. Iph. A. 985. Ὦ μελέα ψυχὰ, ὃς . . ἤσθη Soph. Phil. 714. Ὦ ἀγαθὴ καὶ πιστὴ ψυχὴ, οἴχῃ δὴ ἀπολιπὼν ἡμᾶς; Cyr. vii. 3. 8. Τέκνων, . . οὓς Eur. Suppl. 12. See § 453.

Notes. 1. In the construction of the pronoun, the *number is often changed* for the sake of *individualizing* or *generalizing* the expression; as, Ὅστις δ' ἀφικνεῖτο . ., πάντας . . ἀπεπέμπετο, *and whoever came, he sent them all back*, i. 1. 5. Ἀσπάζεται πάντας, ᾧ ἂν περιτυγχάνῃ Pl. Rep. 566 d. Ὃς ἂν κάμνῃ τῶν οἰκετῶν, τούτων σοι ἐπιμελητέον πάντων, ὅπως θεραπεύηται Œc. 7. 37. Τούτους . ., ᾧ ἂν . . πολλοὶ ἕπονται Ib. 21. 8. Ἄλλους δ' ἐκέλευε λέγειν, διὰ τί ἕκαστος ἐπλήγη, *and he bade the rest say, on what account each one had been struck*, v. 8. 12. Προσιὼν ἑνὶ ἑκάστῳ, οὕστινας ᾤετο ἔχειν τι vii. 3. 16. Πεῖραν λαβεῖν . . οἷος ἕκαστός ἐστι, καὶ τὴν ἀξίαν ἑκάστοις διανεῖμαι vi. 6. 33. Ἦν ἀφθονία τῶν θελόντων κινδυνεύειν, ὅπου τις οἴοιτο Κῦρον αἰσθήσεσθαι i. 9. 15 (see Ib. 16). Ἢν δέ τις τούτων τι παραβαίνει, ζημίαν αὐτοῖς ἐπέθεσαν Cyr. i. 2. 2. Εἰ δέ τι κἀκεῖ πλέον ἔστ' ἀγαθοῖς, τούτων μετέχουσα Eur. Alc. 744. Ἀληθὴς ἦν φίλος · . . ὧν ἀριθμὸς οὐ πολύς, *he was a true friend; of whom the number is not great*, Id. Suppl. 867. Αὐτουργός, οἵπερ καὶ μόνοι σώζουσι γῆν Id. Or. 720. Θησαυροποιὸς ἀνὴρ · οὓς δὴ καὶ ἐπαινεῖ τὸ πλῆθος Pl. Rep. 554 a.

2. A pronoun often refers to a subject which is *implied in another word* (cf. § 454); as, Φεύγει . . ἐς Κέρκυραν, ὧν αὐτῶν [i. e. τῶν Κερκυραίων] εὐεργέτης, *he flies to Corcyra, being a benefactor of theirs*, Th. i. 136. Ἀπὸ Πελοποννήσου . ., οἳ τῶνδε κρείσσους εἰσί Id. vi. 80. Τῆς ἐμῆς ἐπεισόδου, ὃν [i. e. ἐμὲ] μήτ' ὀκνεῖτε Soph. Œd. C. 730. Πατρῴα θ' ἑστία κατεσκάφη, αὐτὸς δὲ . . πίτνει Eur. Hec. 22. Ἀνυμέναιος, ὧν [i. e. ὑμεναίων] μ' ἐχρῆν τυχεῖν Ib. 416.

§ 498. e. Attraction.

A pronoun is sometimes attracted by a word in its own clause, or a word in apposition with its real subject (cf. § 455); as, Βισάνθην οἴκησιν δώσω, ὅπερ [for ἥπερ] ἐμοὶ κάλλιστον χωρίον ἐστί, *I will give you, as a residence, Bisanthe, which is my finest town*, vii. 2. 38. Ἑστίας, οὗ οὔτε ὁσιώτερον χωρίον Cyr. vii. 5. 56. Οὐδὲν ἄδικον διαγεγένημαι ποιῶν· ἥνπερ [for ὅπερ, § 445] νομίζω μελέτην εἶναι καλλίστην ἀπολογίας Apol. 3. Θανεῖν· . . αὕτη γὰρ ἦν ἂν πημάτων ἀπαλλαγή Æsch. Pr. 754. Ἐπὶ πύλας τῆς Κιλικίας καὶ τῆς Συρίας. Ἦσαν δὲ ταῦτα [for αὗται] δύο τείχη i. 4. 4. Καὶ δίκη ἐν ἀνθρώποις πῶς οὐ καλὸν, ὃ πάντα ἡμέρωκε τὰ ἀνθρώπινα; Pl. Leg. 937 d. — This construction may be commonly explained by *ellipsis*; thus, Ἑστίας, οὗ [χωρίου] οὔτε ὁσιώτερον χωρίον, *the hearth, than which* [spot] *there is no holier spot.*

§ **499.** ADDITIONAL REMARKS. 1. A pronoun, for the sake of perspicuity or emphasis, is often used in *anticipation or repetition of its subject*, or is *itself repeated*; as, Τί γὰρ τούτου μακαριώτερον, τοῦ γῇ μιχθῆναι; *For what is happier than this, to mingle with the earth?* Cyr. viii. 7. 25. Τούτου τιμῶμαι, τῆς ἐν Πρυτανείῳ σιτήσεως Pl. Apol. 37 a. Κεῖνο κάλλιον, τέκνον, ἰσότητα τιμᾷν Eur. Ph. 535. Ἀγίας δὲ ὁ Ἀρκὰς καὶ Σωκράτης ὁ Ἀχαιὸς, καὶ τούτω ἀπεθανέτην, 'these also died,' ii. 6. 30. Βασιλέα . ., οὐκ οἶδα ὅ τι δεῖ αὐτὸν ὀμόσαι ii. 4. 7. Ἀλκιβιάδης . ., οὕτω κἀκεῖνος ἠμέλησεν αὑτοῦ Mem. i. 2. 24. Σκέψαι δὲ, οἵῳ ὄντι μοι περὶ σὲ, οἷος ὢν περὶ ἐμὲ, ἔπειτά μοι μέμφῃ Cyr. iv. 5. 29. Οἶμαι δέ σοι . . ἔχειν ἂν ἐπιδεῖξαί σοι Œc. 3. 16. Ἔστι γάρ τις οὐ πρόσω Σπάρτης πόλις τις Eur. Andr. 733.

NOTE. Homer often uses the personal pron. οὗ, with its noun following; as, Ἦν ἄρα οἱ θεράπων ἔχε ποιμένι λαῶν N. 600. Ἣ μιν ἔγειρεν Ναυσικάαν εὔπεπλον ζ. 48. Cf. § 468. *b*.

§ **500.** 2. A change of PERSON sometimes takes place; — (*a*) From the union of *direct* and *indirect* modes of speaking, especially in *quotation*; as, Ἄγοιτ' ἂν μάταιον ἄνδρ' ἐκποδὼν, ὃς . . κάκτανον, *take out of the way a senseless man, me, who have slain*, Soph. Ant. 1339. Καὶ οὗτος ἔφη "ἐθέλειν πορεύεσθαι, προσλαβὼν ἐθελοντὰς ἐκ παντὸς τοῦ στρατεύματος. Ἐγὼ γὰρ," ἔφη, "οἶδα" iv. 1. 27. See i. 3. 20; iii. 3. 12; iv. 1. 19; v. 6. 25, 26. — (*b*) From a speaker's addressing a company, now as *one with them*, and now as *distinct from them*; as, Λανθάνειν ὑμᾶς εἰς ὅσην ταραχὴν ἡ πόλις ἡμῶν καθέστηκεν· ἐοίκατε γὰρ . ., οἵτινες τεθύκαμεν Isocr. 141 d.

II. SPECIAL OBSERVATIONS ON THE PRONOUNS.

§ **501.** Of the observations which follow, many apply equally to PRONOUNS and ADVERBS of the *same classes*.

A. PERSONAL, POSSESSIVE, AND REFLEXIVE.

§ **502.** In the use of the pronouns, especially those of the classes named above, it is important to distinguish between the *stronger* and the *weaker* forms of expression; that is, between those forms which are *more distinctive*, *emphatic*, or *prominent*, and those which are *less* so.

I. In the *weaker* form, the FIRST and SECOND PERSONAL PRONOUNS are *omitted* in the *Nom.*, and are *enclitic* in the *oblique cases sing.*; but in the *stronger* form, they are *expressed* in the *Nom.*, and are *orthotone* throughout. In the *weaker* form, the THIRD PERSONAL PRONOUN is *omitted* in the *Nom.*, and is commonly *supplied by αὐτός* in the *oblique cases;* in the *stronger* form, it is *supplied by* ὁ and ὅς, which are simply *distinctive* and are limited in their use (§§ 490 – 492), and by οὗτος, ὅδε and ἐκεῖνος, which are both *distinctive* and *demonstrative.* Thus,

Ἅπαντα σῶα ἀπέδωκά σοι, ἐπεὶ καὶ σὺ ἐμοὶ ἀπέδειξας τὸν ἄνδρα, *I gave you back every thing safe, when* you *also had shown to* me *the man,* v. 8. 7. Ἐγὼ μὲν, ὦ ἄνδρες, ἤδη ὑμᾶς ἐπαινῶ· ὅπως δὲ καὶ ὑμεῖς ἐμὲ ἐπαινέσετε, ἐμοὶ μελήσει, ἢ μηκέτι με Κῦρον νομίζετε i. 4. 16. Οὔτε γὰρ ἡμεῖς ἐκείνου ἔτι στρατιῶται, ἐπεί γε οὐ συνεπόμεθα αὐτῷ, οὔτε ἐκεῖνος ἔτι ἡμῖν μισθοδότης i. 3. 9. Οὔτε σὺ ἐκείνας φιλεῖς, οὔτε ἐκεῖναι σέ Mem. ii. 7. 9. Εἶχε δὲ τὸ μὲν δεξιὸν Μένων καὶ οἱ σὺν αὐτῷ, τὸ δὲ εὐώνυμον Κλέαρχος, καὶ οἱ ἐκείνου i. 2. 15. Κῦρος δὲ καὶ ἱππεῖς τούτου i. 8. 6. Τούτῳ συγγενόμενος ὁ Κῦρος, ἠγάσθη τε αὐτὸν, καὶ δίδωσιν αὐτῷ i. 1. 9. Ἦδ' οὖν θανεῖται Soph. Ant. 751. Κεῖνος τὰ κείνου στεργέτω, κἀγὼ τάδε Id. Aj. 1039. See §§ 490 – 492.

§ **503.** II. In the *stronger* form, the *Gen. subjective* (§ 393. δ) *with a substantive* is commonly supplied in the FIRST and SECOND PERSONS, and sometimes in the THIRD, by the *possessive adjective* (cf. §§ 457, 458); in the *weaker* form, it is often *omitted*, especially with the article (§ 482). The *Gen. objective* (§ 392) sometimes follows the same analogy. Thus,

"Οἴει γάρ σοι μαχεῖσθαι, ὦ Κῦρε, τὸν ἀδελφόν;" "Νὴ Δί'," ἔφη ὁ Κῦρος, "εἴπερ γε Δαρείου καὶ Παρυσάτιδός ἐστι παῖς, ἐμὸς δὲ ἀδελφός;" i. 7. 9. Τῶν σωμάτων στερηθῆναι. . . Περὶ τῶν ὑμετέρων ἀγαθῶν ii. 1. 12. Κείνου τε καὶ σὴν ἐξ ἴσου κοινὴν χάριν Soph. Tr. 485. Τὸ σὸν λέχος, *the marriage you talk of,* Soph. Ant. 573. Τὸ σὸν γὰρ Ἄργος οὐ δέδοικ' ἐγώ Eur. Heracl. 284. Σὰν ἔριν, ὦ Ἑλένη, 'the dispute for you,' Eur. Hel. 1160. Εὐνοίᾳ καὶ φιλίᾳ τῇ ἐμῇ, *good-will and affection to me,* Cyr. iii. 1. 28. Φιλίᾳ τῇ σῇ, *love to you,* vii. 7. 29. Μὴ μεταμέλειν σοι τῆς ἐμῆς δωρεᾶς, *that you may not regret your present to me,* Cyr. viii. 3. 32. Θρῆνος οὑμός Æsch. Pr. 388. See §§ 454, 482.

NOTES. (*a*) The POSSESSIVE PRONOUN is *modified* like the *personal pronoun* of which it supplies the place; as, Τόν γε σὸν [ὀφθαλμὸν], τοῦ πρεσβέως, *at least yours* [your eye], *the ambassador,* Ar. Ach. 93 (§ 332. 4). See § 454. So, since πότμος may be followed by the *Dat.*, as well as the *Gen.* (§§ 403, 411), Ἁμετέρου [= ἡμῖν] πότμου, κλεινοῖς Λαβδακίδαισιν Soph. Ant. 860. (*b*) The only POSSESSIVE of the 3d Pers., which has a place in Attic prose, is σφέτερος, *their;* and even this is used *reflexively,* and with no great frequency. Thus, Ὡς ἑώρων πονοῦντας τοὺς σφετέρους, *when they saw their own men in distress,* Cyr. i. 4. 21. (*c*) The *Dat. for the Gen.* belongs particularly to the weaker form of expression. See § 412.

§ **504.** III. In REFLEX REFERENCE, the *weaker* form is the same with that of the *common personal pronoun;* the *stronger* form is the so-called *reflexive* (§ 144). The weaker form belongs chiefly to those cases in which the reflex reference is *indirect* and *unemphatic;* the stronger, to those in which this reference is either *direct*, or, if indirect, is specially *emphatic* or *distinctive.* Thus,

Πράττετε ὁποῖον ἄν τι ὑμῖν οἴησθε μάλιστα συμφέρειν, *do whatever you think will be most advantageous to yourselves*, ii. 2. 2. Κελεύουσι διασώσαντα αὐτοῖς τὰ πρόβατα, τὰ μὲν αὐτὸν λαβεῖν, τὰ δὲ σφίσιν ἀποδοῦναι vi. 6. 5. Καὶ οὗτος δή, ὃν ᾤετο πιστόν οἱ εἶναι, ταχὺ αὐτὸν εὗρε Κύρῳ φιλαίτερον, ἢ ἑαυτῷ i. 9. 29. Ὡς εἶδον ὁρμῶντας καθ' αὐτούς, σαφῶς νομίζοντες ἐπὶ σφᾶς ἴεσθαι v. 7. 25. Λέγειν τε ἐκέλευεν αὐτούς, ὅτι οὐδὲν ἂν ἧττον σφεῖς ἀγάγοιεν τὴν στρατιάν, ἢ Ξενοφῶν vii. 5. 9. Εἰς τὴν ἑαυτοῦ σκηνὴν . . τῶν περὶ αὐτόν· . . περὶ τὴν αὐτοῦ σκηνήν i. 6. 4. Ἐκέλευε τοὺς φίλους τοῖς τὰ ἑαυτῶν σώματα ἄγουσιν ἵπποις ἐμβάλλειν τοῦτον τὸν χιλόν, ὡς μὴ πεινῶντες τοὺς ἑαυτοῦ φίλους ἄγωσιν i. 9. 27. Ποίαν δ' ἡλικίαν ἐμαυτῷ ἐλθεῖν ἀναμένω; . . Ἐὰν τήμερον προδῶ ἐμαυτόν iii. 1. 14. Ἐμαυτῷ γε δοκῶ συνειδέναι vii. 6. 11. Πολλοῦ μοι δοκῶ δεῖν Ib. 18. Σὺ μὲν ἡγούμενος αὐτὰς ἐπιζημίους εἶναι σεαυτῷ, ἐκείνας δὲ σὲ ὁρῶσαι ἀχθόμενον ἐφ' ἑαυταῖς Mem. ii. 7. 9. Ἀμελεῖν ἡμῶν αὐτῶν i. 3. 11. Πολλαπλασίους ὑμῶν αὐτῶν ἐνικᾶτε iii. 2. 14 (§ 352).

§ **505.** REMARKS. 1. As pronouns are used mainly for *distinction*, the choice or rejection of a pronoun in a particular instance depends greatly upon the *use of other pronouns* in the connection. The use of the pronouns is likewise much influenced in *poetry* by the *metre*, and even in *prose*, to some extent, by *euphony* and *rhythm*.

2. With respect to POSITION, the *weaker form of the Genitive*, from its want of distinctive emphasis, commonly follows § 472. α, but the *stronger form*, and the *possessive adjective*, § 472. I. Thus, Ἐπιλαμβάνεται αὐτοῦ τῆς ἴτυος iv. 7. 12. Ἣν δέ τις αὐτῶν τρέψῃ τὰς γνώμας iii. 1. 41. Τῷ σώματι αὐτοῦ . ., τὸ μὲν ἑαυτοῦ σῶμα i. 9. 23. Ἡ ἐκείνων ὕβρις καὶ ἡ ἡμέτερα ὑποψία iii. 1. 21. Τὰ ὑποζύγια τὰ ἐκείνου i. 3. 1. Ἀπέπεμψέ μου τὸν δεσπότην Ar. Plut. 12. Τὸν βίον τὸν ἐμαυτοῦ Pl. Gorg. 488 a.

3. The place of the *Gen. possessive* of the reflexive pron. is commonly supplied in the plur. by the possessive pron. with αὐτῶν. In the sing. this form of expression is poetic. See § 454.

§ **506.** 4. The *third person* being expressed *demonstratively* in other ways, the pronoun οὗ became simply a *retrospective* pronoun, i. e. a pronoun referring to a person or thing previously mentioned. As such, it performed the office both of an *unemphatic reflexive* (§ 504), and of a *simple personal pronoun*, and was sometimes used as a *general reflexive*, without respect to person. In this last use, it was sometimes imitated by its derivatives (even in the Attic, by ἑαυτοῦ and σφέτερος). Thus, Βουλεύοιτε μετὰ σφίσιν [= ὑμῖν], 'among yourselves,' K. 398. Δώμασιν οἷσιν [= σοῖς] ἀνάσσοις α. 402. Φρεσὶν ᾗσιν [= ἐμαῖς] ἔχων δεδαϊγμένον ἦτορ ἠλώμην ν. 320. Δεῖ ἡμᾶς ἀνερέσθαι ἑαυτούς [= ἡμᾶς αὐτούς], *we ought to ask ourselves*, Pl. Phædo, 78 b. Εὐλαβούμενοι, ὅπως μὴ ἐγὼ ὑπὸ προθυμίας ἅμα ἑαυτόν [= ἐμαυτόν] τε καὶ ὑμᾶς ἐξαπατήσας Ib. 91 c. Κλαίω . . αὐτὴ πρὸς αὐτήν Soph. El. 283. Αἰσχύνεις πόλιν τὴν αὐτὸς αὑτοῦ, *you yourself disgrace your own city*, Id. Œd. C. 929. Οὐδὲ γὰρ τὴν ἑαυτοῦ [= σεαυτοῦ] σύ γε ψυχὴν ὁρᾷς Mem. i. 4. 9. Μόρον τὸν αὐτῆς οἶσθα Æsch. Ag. 1397. Εἴπερ ὑπὲρ σωτηρίας αὑτῶν [= ὑμῶν αὐτῶν] φροντίζετε Dem. 9. 13. Σφετέρῃ [= ὑμετέρῃ] ἀπὸ μητέρι τίνετ' ἀμοιβήν Ap. Rh. 4. 1327.

§ **507.** 5. Some of the forms of οὗ are used with great latitude of number and gender; thus, (*a*) μίν and νίν commonly sing., but also plur. (especially νίν); as, νίν, *him*, Æsch. Pr. 333, *her*, Eur. Hec. 515, *it*, Soph. Tr. 145, *them*, masc. Soph. Œd. T. 868, fem. Id. Œd. C. 43, neut. Æsch. Pr.

55; μίν, *them*, Ap. Rh. 2. 8: (*b*) σφέ properly plur., but also (especially in the tragic poets) sing.; as, σφέ, *them*, masc. A. 111, fem. Soph. Œd. T. 1505, *him*, Æsch. Pr. 9, *her*, Eur. Alc. 834: (*c*) σφίν rarely sing.; as, Hom. H. 19 19, Æsch. Pers. 759: (*d*) ἕ commonly sing. masc. and fem., but sing. neut. A. 236, plur. Hom. Ven. 268. (*e*) So the derived *possessives*; as, ἑός, *their* Hes. Op. 58; σφέτερος, *his*, Id. Sc. 90, Pind. O. 13. 86, *my*, Theoc. 25. 163 (§ 506), *thy*, Id. 22. 67; σφωΐτερος, *his*, Ap. Rh. 1. 643.

6. The place of οὗ as a reflexive is commonly supplied in Att. prose by ἑαυτοῦ, and as a simple personal pron., by αὐτός. The plural occurs far oftener than the singular, which, except the Dat., is in Att. prose very rare. The disuse of the Nom. sing. of this pron. (§ 143. 4) is explained by its reflexive character (cf. § 144).

7. A *common reflexive* is sometimes used for the *reciprocal pronoun*; as, Οἵ γε, ἀντὶ μὲν τοῦ συνεργεῖν ἑαυτοῖς τὰ συμφέροντα, ἐπηρεάζουσιν ἀλλήλοις, καὶ φθονοῦσιν ἑαυτοῖς μᾶλλον ἢ τοῖς ἄλλοις ἀνθρώποις Mem. iii. 5. 16. Ἀντὶ ὑφορωμένων ἑαυτάς, ἥδέως ἀλλήλας ἑώρων Ib. ii. 7. 12. Συννενικήκατε μετ' ἀλλήλων· τῶν δὲ πολεμίων οἱ πολλοὶ μὲν συνήττηνται μεθ' ἑαυτῶν Cyr. vi. 3. 14.

B. ΑΥΤΟΣ.

§ **508.** The pronoun αὐτός marks a return of the mind to the same person or thing (§ 149). This *return* takes place,

I.) In speaking of REFLEX ACTION OR RELATION. Hence αὐτός is used with the personal pronouns in forming the REFLEXIVES. See §§ 144, 504.

II.) In designating a person or thing as THE SAME which has been previously mentioned or observed. When thus employed, αὐτός (like the corresponding *same* in English), being used for *distinction*, is preceded by the article (§ 472). Thus,

Τῇ δὲ αὐτῇ ἡμέρᾳ, *and upon the same day*, i. 5. 12. Εἰς τὸ αὐτὸ σχῆμα i. 10. 10. Οὗτος δὲ ὁ αὐτός, *and this same person*, vii. 3. 3. Ἐκεῖνα τὰ αὐτά Mem. iv. 4. 6. Ταὐτὰ ἔπασχον iii. 4. 28 (§ 39). See § 400.

§ **509.** III.) For the sake of EMPHASIS, one of the most familiar modes of expressing which is *repetition*. When αὐτός is thus employed in connection with the article, its position conforms to § 472. *α*. Thus,

Αὐτὸς Μένων ἐβούλετο, *Meno himself wished it*, ii. 1. 5. Ὅστις . . αὐτὸς ὀμόσας ἡμῖν, αὐτὸς δεξιὰς δούς, αὐτὸς ἐξαπατήσας συνέλαβε τοὺς στρατηγούς iii. 2. 4. Κῦρος παρελαύνων αὐτὸς σὺν Πίγρητι i. 8. 12. Αὐτὰ τὰ ἀπὸ τῶν οἰκιῶν ξύλα, *the very wood from the houses*, ii. 2. 16. Καὶ θεοσεβέστατον αὐτό ἐστι πάντων ζώων ἄνθρωπος, 'the very most religious,' Pl. Leg. 902 b. Οὗτοι δ' αὖ πρὸ αὐτοῦ βασιλέως τεταγμένοι ἦσαν, 'before the person of the king,' i. 7. 11. Πρὸς αὐτῷ τῷ στρατεύματι, [by the army itself] *close to the army*, i. 8. 14. Ὑπὲρ αὐτοῦ τοῦ ἑαυτῶν στρατεύματος, 'directly above,' iii. 4. 41. Εἰ αὐτοὶ οἱ στρατιῶται . . οἴχοιντο, 'of their own accord,' vii. 7. 33. Εἰ αὐτοῖς τοῖς ἀνδράσι σπένδοιτο ἰοῦσι, 'with simply the men,' ii. 3. 7. Ἐάν τις ἄνευ τοῦ σίτου τὸ ὄψον αὐτὸ ἐσθίῃ, 'by itself,' *or* 'alone,' Mem. iii. 14. 3. Αὐτοὺς τοὺς στρατηγοὺς ἀποκαλέσας, *having called the generals apart*, vii. 3. 35. See §§ 418. R., 472. *α*.

§ **510.** Remarks. 1. The emphatic αὐτός is joined with pronouns in both their *stronger* and their *weaker forms.* Hence it is often used in the *Nominative* with a pronoun which is *understood* (§ 502). Thus, Οἱ δὲ στρατιῶται, οἵ τε αὐτοῦ ἐκείνου καὶ οἱ ἄλλοι, 'both his own,' i. 3. 7. Αὐτοῦ τούτου ἕνεκεν, *on this very account*, iv. 1. 22. Αὐτῷ ἐμοὶ . . δόξει Pl. Phædo, 91 a. Αὐτῷ μοι ἔοικεν Ib. 60 c. Ὡς αὐτὸς σὺ ὁμολογεῖς i. 6. 7. Ὡς ἔφη αὐτός Ib. 6. Αὐτὸς σὺ ἐπαίδευσας Œc. 7. 4. Αὐτὸς ἐπαίδευσας Ib. 7. Αὐτός εἰμι, ὃν ζητεῖς ii. 4. 16. Αὐτοὶ καίουσιν, *they themselves burn*, iii. 5. 5. Ἰᾶσθαι αὐτὸς τὸ τραῦμά φησι, 'that he himself healed,' i. 8. 26. Χωρεῖ αὐτός, *he goes alone*, iv. 7. 11. Αὐτοὶ γάρ ἐσμεν, *for we are by ourselves*, Pl. Leg. 836 b. ΣΤΡ. Τίς γὰρ οὗτος οὑπὶ τῆς κρεμάθρας ἀνήρ; ΜΑΘ. Αὐτός. ΣΤΡ. Τίς αὐτός; ΜΑΘ. Σωκράτης. '[Himself] The great man. What great man?' Ar. Nub. 218.

2. In like manner, αὐτός is used without another pronoun expressed, in the *oblique cases of the third person;* as, Δῶρα ἄγοντες αὐτῷ τε καὶ τῇ γυναικί, *bringing presents both for himself and for his wife*, vii. 3. 16. Ἔπεμψεν . . στρατιώτας οὓς Μένων εἶχε, καὶ αὐτόν i. 2. 20. Πολλοὺς μὲν τῶν ἁρπαζόντων ἀπέκτειναν, οἱ δὲ καὶ αὐτῶν ἀπέθανον i. 10. 3.

Notes. *α.* From the gradual extension of this use to cases in which there was no special emphasis, appears to have arisen the familiar employment of αὐτός in the *oblique cases*, as the *common pronoun of the third person.* See § 502. In this unemphatic use, αὐτός must not begin a clause.

β. Sometimes (chiefly in the Epic), αὐτός occurs in the oblique cases, with the ellipsis of a pron. of the 1st or 2d Pers.; as, Αὐτῶν γὰρ ἀπωλόμεθ' ἀφραδίῃσιν [sc. ἡμῶν] κ. 27. Αὐτήν [sc. σέ] ζ. 27.

§ **511.** 3. The emphatic αὐτός often precedes a *reflexive*, agreeing with the subject of the latter. *Hyperbaton* (§ 329. N.) is sometimes employed to bring the two pronouns into immediate connection. Thus, Ἀποκτεῖναι λέγεται αὐτὸς τῇ ἑαυτοῦ χειρὶ Ἀρταγέρσην, *and he is said* [himself] *with his own hand to have slain Artagerses*, i. 8. 24. Οἱ δὲ Ἕλληνες . . αὐτοὶ ἐφ' ἑαυτῶν ἐχώρουν, 'by themselves,' ii. 4. 10. Τὸ δὲ ὄψον αὐτὸ καθ' αὑτὸ ἐσθίοντα Mem. iii. 14. 2 (cf. Ib. 3, and § 509). Τοῖς τ' αὐτὸς αὑτοῦ πήμασιν βαρύνεται Æsch. Ag. 836. Τοῖον παλαιστὴν νῦν παρασκευάζεται ἐπ' αὐτὸς αὑτῷ Id. Pr. 920. See §§ 464, 506.

4. The emphasis of αὐτός sometimes lies in mere *contradistinction;* as, Ἀλλ' αὐτὰ σιγῶ· . . τἀν βροτοῖς δὲ πήματα ἀκούσατε, 'those things I omit; but hear,' Æsch. Pr. 442. Ὅτι καὶ ἐπὶ τὰ ἡδέα, ἐφ' ἅπερ μόνα δοκεῖ ἡ ἀκρασία τοὺς ἀνθρώπους ἄγειν, αὐτὴ μὲν οὐ δύναται ἄγειν, ἡ δ' ἐγκράτεια Mem. iv. 5. 9. Ὅς, ὦ παῖ, σέ τ' οὐχ ἑκὼν κάκτανον, σέ τ' αὐτάν, *who involuntarily have slain both you, my son, and you, too, my wife*, Soph. Ant. 1340.

5. The use of αὐτός with *ordinals* deserves remark; thus, Περικλῆς . . στρατηγὸς ὢν Ἀθηναίων δέκατος αὐτός, *Pericles being general of the Athenians* [himself the tenth] *with nine colleagues*, Th. ii. 13 (cf. Ἀρχεστράτου . . μετ' ἄλλων δέκα στρατηγοῦντος Id. i. 57). Ἐξέπεμψαν Λυσικλέα πέμπτον αὐτὸν στρατηγόν Id. iii. 19. Ἡρέθη πρεσβευτὴς δέκατος αὐτός H. Gr. ii. 2. 17. But, with the omission of αὐτός, Δαρεῖος . . λαβὼν αὐτήν [i. e. τὴν ἀρχήν] ἕβδομος, 'with six confederates,' Pl. Leg. 695 c.

C. Demonstrative.

§ **512.** I. Of the primary demonstratives, the more

distant and *emphatic* is ἐκεῖνος· the *nearer* and *more familiar* is οὗτος or ὅδε (§ 150). Thus,

Ἐὰν ἐκείνοις δοκῇ, καὶ τούτους κακῶς ποιήσουσι, *if* those *should wish it, they will even injure* these, Pl. Phædr. 231 c. Ἐκεῖνος μὲν σκληφρὸς, οὗτος δὲ προφερής Id. Euthyd. 271 b.

NOTES. α. The two may be combined to mark the connection of the MORE REMOTE with the NEARER; as of the *past* with the *present*, of a *saying* with its *illustration*, of that which *has been mentioned* with that which *is present before us*, &c. Thus, Τοῦτ' [sc. ἐστὶ] ἐκεῖν' οὐγὼ ἔλεγον, *this is that which I said*, Ar. Ach. 41. Τοῦτ' ἐκεῖνο· "Κτᾶσθ' ἑταίρους, μὴ τὸ συγγενὲς μόνον" Eur. Hec. 804. Τόδ' ἐκεῖνο, *this is what I spoke of*, Id. Med. 98. Ἥδ' ἔστ' ἐκείνη τοὔργον ἡ 'ξειργασμένη Soph. Ant. 384.

β. Οὗτος sometimes marks the *ordinary*, and ἐκεῖνος the *extraordinary*; as, Ἔχοντες τούτους τε τοὺς πολυτελεῖς χιτῶνας, *having on the rich tunics which they are in the habit of wearing*, i. 5. 8 (see Cyr. i. 3. 2). Γεγόνασι ῥήτορες ἔνδοξοι καὶ μεγάλοι πρὸ ἐμοῦ, Καλλίστρατος ἐκεῖνος, κ. τ. λ., 'that wonderful Callistratus,' Dem. 301. 17. Τὸν Ἀριστείδην ἐκεῖνον Id. 34. 20.

§ 513. II. The pronouns οὗτος and ὅδε have in general the same force, and the choice between them often depends upon euphony or rhythm; as, τούτῳ φιλεῖν χρή, τῷδε χρὴ πάντας σέβειν Soph. Ant. 981. Yet they are not without distinction. Οὗτος, as formed by composition with αὐτός, is properly a pronoun of *identification* or *emphatic designation* (it may be regarded as a *weaker form* of ὁ αὐτός, *the same*, § 502); while ὅδε, arising from composition with δε, is strictly a *deictic* pronoun (δεικτικός, from δείκνυμι, *to point out*), pointing to an object as before us (see § 150). Hence,

1.) If reference is made to that which *precedes*, or which is *contained in a subordinate clause*, οὗτος is commonly used; but if reference is made to that which *follows* and is *not* contained in a subordinate clause, ὅδε. Thus,

Τεκμήριον δὲ τούτου καὶ τόδε, *and of this* (which has been stated), *this* (which follows) *is also a proof*, i. 9. 29. Ἐπὶ τούτοις Ξενοφῶν τάδε εἶπε, *to this Xenophon replied as follows*, ii. 5. 41. Τοῦτο, ὅ τι ἂν δοκῇ τοῖς θεοῖς, πάσχειν iii. 2. 6. Τοῦτό γε ἐπίστασθε, ὅτι βορέας .. φέρει v. 7. 7. Τοῦτο πρῶτον ἠρώτα, πότερον λῷον εἴη iii. 1. 7.

NOTE. To the *retrospective character* of οὗτος may be referred, —(*a*) Its use, preceded by καί, in *making an addition to a sentence*, the pronoun either serving as a *repetition* of a *substantive* in the sentence, or, in the *neuter Acc.* or *Nom.* (commonly *plur.*), of the *sentence* itself (cf. §§ 334, 451). The construction may be explained by *ellipsis*. Thus, Ξένους προσήκει σοι πολλοὺς δέχεσθαι, καὶ τούτους [sc. δέχεσθαι] μεγαλοπρεπῶς, *it becomes you to entertain many guests, and these magnificently*, Œc. 2. 5. Συμμάχων δεήσεται, καὶ τούτων πλειόνων Mem. ii. 6. 27. Ἐβοήθησαν τῇ Λακεδαίμονι, καὶ ταῦτα [sc. ἐποίησαν] εἰδότες, *they assisted Lacedæmon, and* [they did] *that knowing*, Ag. 1. 38. Μένωνα δὲ οὐκ ἐζήτει, καὶ ταῦτα παρ' Ἀριαίου ὤν, *but Meno he did not ask for, and that although he was from Ariæus*, ii. 4. 15. Διεφύλαξε τὴν πόλιν, καὶ *ταῦτα ἀτείχιστον οὖσαν* Ag. 2. 24. — (*b*) The use of *τοῦτο* and *ταῦτα* in *assent*; as, "*Ἆρ' οὐ πλουσίοις ἀνδράσι μαχοῦνται αὐτοὶ ὄντες πολέμου ἀθληταί;*" "*Ναὶ τοῦτό γε* [sc. *ἔστι*]," *ἔφη*, 'Certainly it is so,' Pl. Rep. 422 b. Π. *Οὔκουν ἕτερόν γέ τιν' ἐκ Λακεδαίμονος μέτει ἀνύσας τι;* Κ. *Ταῦτ', ὦ δέσποτα* Ar. Pax, 274. ΒΔ. *Ἀλλ' εἰσίωμεν.* Φ. *Ταῦτά νυν, εἴπερ δοκεῖ* Id. Vesp. 1008.

§ 514. 2.) *Ὅδε* surpasses in *demonstrative vivacity*; but *οὗτος* in *emphatic force* and in the *extent of its substantive use*. Thus,

ΟΙΔ. *Ἦ τόνδε φράζεις;* ἈΓΓ. *Τοῦτον, ὅνπερ εἰσορᾷς*, Œd. *Is* THIS *the man you speak of?* Mess. *The* VERY MAN, *whom you behold*, Soph. Œd. T. 1120. ΘΕΡ. *Ποῖον ἄνδρα καὶ λέγεις;* ΟΙΔ. *Τόνδ', ὃς πάρεστιν* Ib. 1126. *Σὺν τοῖσδε τοῖς παροῦσι νῦν* ii. 3. 19. *Καταλιπόντες τόνδε τὸν ἄνδρα· . . ἐπεὶ οὗτος αὐτὸς ὁμολογεῖ* vi. 6. 26. *Ἡμᾶς τούσδε λαβόντες*, *taking us who are here*, Th. i. 53.

NOTE. To the *deictic* power of *ὅδε* (§ 513), may be referred the very frequent use of this pronoun by the Epic and Dramatic poets for an *adverb of place* (§ 457. β); and perhaps, in no small degree, the general fact, that it is far more extensively employed in *poetry* than in *prose*.

§ 515. 3.) In the emphatic designation of the *first* and *second persons* by a *demonstrative*, *ὅδε* commonly denotes the *first* person, as the nearer object; and *οὗτος*, the *second*. In denoting the *first* person, the demonstrative may be regarded as simply *deictic* (§ 513); in denoting the *second*, as expressive of *impatience*, *authority*, *contempt*, *familiarity*, &c. For the use of *οὗτος* in *address*, which is employed both with and without *σύ*, see § 343. 3. Thus,

Μὴ θνῆσχ' ὑπὲρ τοῦδ' ἀνδρὸς [= *ἐμοῦ*], *οὐδ' ἐγὼ πρὸ σοῦ*, *do not you die for this man* [for me], *nor yet I for you*, Eur. Alc. 690. *Φονεὺς ὢν τοῦδε τἀνδρὸς* [= *ἐμοῦ*] *ἐμφανῶς* Soph. Œd. T. 534 (but, *Ἀνὴρ ὅδ'* [= *σὺ*], *ὡς ἔοικεν, εἰς τριβὰς ἐλᾷ* Ib. 1160). *Τῆσδέ γε ζώσης ἔτι*, *at least, while I am yet alive*, Id. Tr. 305. *Τάδε* [= *ἡμεῖς*, § 450] . . *πιστὰ καλεῖται, καὶ φύλακες* Æsch. Pers. 1. *Οὑτοσὶ ἀνὴρ* [= *σὺ*] *οὐ παύσεται φλυαρῶν.* *Εἰπέ μοι, ὦ Σώκρατες, οὐκ αἰσχύνῃ* Pl. Gorg. 489 b. *Οὗτος σὺ, ὦ πρέσβυ*, [This you, *or* You there, § 457. β], *Ho there! old man*, Soph. Œd. T. 1121. *Οὗτος σὺ, πῶς δεῦρ' ἦλθες;* *Ho villain! how camest thou hither?* Ib. 532. *Αὕτη σὺ, ποῖ στρέφει;* Ar. Thesm. 610. *Οὗτος, τί σεμνὸν . . βλέπεις;* *Fellow! why that solemn look?* Eur. Alc. 773 (§ 432). See § 343. 3. — This use of *ὅδε* is very frequent in the tragedians.

§ 516. III. Other compounds of *αὐτός* and *δε* (§ 150. α) are distinguished in like manner with *οὗτος* and *ὅδε*· thus,

Ὁ Κῦρος ἀκούσας τοῦ Γωβρύου τοιαῦτα, τοιάδε *πρὸς αὐτὸν ἔλεξε* Cyr. v. 2. 31 (§ 513. 1). *Ὁ μὲν* οὕτως *εἶπεν* ii. 3. 23. *Κλέαρχος μὲν οὖν* τοσαῦτα *εἶπε· Τισσαφέρνης δὲ* ὧδε *ἀπημείφθη* ii. 5. 15. Οὕτως *ἐστὶ δεινὸς λέγειν, ὥστε σε πεῖσαι* Ib. *Ἐγένετο* οὕτως, *ὥσπερ σὺ ἔλεγες* vii. 2. 27. Τοσοῦτον *εἶπεν, ὅτι οὐ τῶν νικώντων εἴη* ii. 1. 9. *Ἡμεῖς* τοσοῦτοι *ὄντες, ὅσους σὺ ὁρᾷς* Ib. 16. *Ἡμεῖς* τοσοίδε *ὄντες ἐνικῶμεν τὸν βασιλέα* ii. 4. 4 (§ 514). ὈΡ. *Ὕποπτος οὖσα γιγνώσκει πόλει.* ΠΡ. Τοιαῦτα· *μισεῖται γὰρ ἀνόσιος γυνή*, 'Even so,' Eur. El. 644 (§ 513. *b*).

D. Indefinite.

§ 517. Of the indefinite pronouns, the most extensive in its use is τὶς, which is the *simplest expression of indefiniteness or general reference.* As such, it is not only joined directly with *substantives*, or used *by itself* substantively or adverbially, but it is also joined with *other pronouns*, with *numerals* and other *adjectives*, and with *adverbs*. It more frequently *follows* the word with which it is thus joined, and is never placed at the beginning of a sentence, unless perhaps when it is emphatic. It is variously translated into English, and is sometimes best omitted in translation. Thus,

Ἄνθρωπός τις ἠρώτησε, *a certain man asked*, ii. 4. 15. Παρὰ Χάρωνί τινι, *with a certain Charon*, H. Gr. v. 4. 3. Τρόπῳ τινί, *in some way*, ii. 2. 17. Εἴ τῳ ὑπόσχοιτό τι, *if he made any promise to any one*, i. 9. 7. Δειπνεῖν ὅ τι τις ἔχει, *to make a supper of what one has*, or *each one has*, ii. 2. 4. Εὖ μέν τις δόρυ θηξάσθω, 'each one,' B. 382. Μισεῖ τις ἐκεῖνον, *there are those who hate him*, or *many a one hates him*, Dem. 42. 17. Ἤ τινα ἢ οὐδένα οἶδα, *I know* [either some one or none] *scarcely an individual*, Cyr. vii. 5. 45. Ἡ μὲν γὰρ γραφὴ κατ' αὐτοῦ τοιάδε τις ἦν, *for the accusation against him was something like this*, or *to this effect*, Mem. i. 1. 1. Ὁποίων τινῶν ἡμῶν ἔτυχον, *what sort of persons they found us*, v. 5. 15. Πόση τις εἴη χώρα, *how extensive a country it was*, ii. 4. 21. Πᾶς δέ τις . . ἕν γέ τι, ὧν εἰλήφει, ἐδωρεῖτο, *and every one presented at least some one thing of what he had taken*, Cyr. v. 5. 39. Λέγει τις εἷς, *a certain one speaks*, Soph. Ant. 269. Ἡμέρας μὲν ἑβδομήκοντά τινας, *some* [i. e. *about*] *seventy days*, Th. vii. 87. Τέτταρ' ἄττα ῥεύματα Pl. Phædo, 112 e. Τὴν ἔλαφον, καλόν τι χρῆμα Cyr. i. 4. 8. Οὐ πολλῷ τινι ὑποδεέστερον, *not inferior in any great degree*, Th. vi. 1. Πολλοὺς δέ τινας ἑλιγμοὺς ἄνω καὶ κάτω, 'quite a number of turnings,' Cyr. i. 3. 4. Μικρόν τι μέρος, *quite a small part*, Ib. vi. 14. Μικροῦ τινος ἄξια, *worth but little*, Mem. ii. 1. 19. Ὀλίγοι τινὲς ὄντες, *being* [some few] *but few*, iv. 1. 10. Ὡς δεινήν τινα λέγεις δύναμιν τοῦ φιλήματος εἶναι, 'what a fearful one,' *or* 'how fearful,' Mem. i. 3. 12. Ἐγὼ τυγχάνω ἐπιλήσμων τις ὢν ἄνθρωπος Pl. Prot. 234 c. Εἰμί τις γελοῖος ἰατρός Ib. 340 d. Μᾶλλόν τι ἀνιάσεται, *will suffer somewhat more*, iv. 8. 26. Ἧττόν τι ἀπέθανεν; *Did he die at all the less?* v. 8. 11. Σχεδόν τι πᾶσα ἡ στρατιά vi. 4. 20. Οὐ πάνυ τι νομίζω ἀσφαλὲς εἶναι τοῦτο vi. 1. 26. Πώς τι ὑπακούειν Œc. 9. 1. Διαφερόντως τι Th. i. 138.

§ 518. Remarks. *α.* Τὶς may be regarded as the Greek *indefinite article*; but it is not commonly expressed with a substantive, unless some *prominence* is given to the idea of indefiniteness. See iv. 3. 11, and § 469. 2.

β. Τὶς is sometimes *emphatic* and consequently *orthotone* (yet editors differ); as, Σεμνύνεσθαι ὥς τὶ ὄντε, *to pride themselves as if they were something*, Pl. Phædr. 242 e. Εὔελπίς εἰμι εἶναί τὶ τοῖς τετελευτηκόσι, *I am confident that there is something for the dead*, Id. Phædo, 63 c. Ἔδοξε τὶ εἰπεῖν, *he seemed to* [say something] *have reason* or *to be in the right*, Id. Amat. 133 c.

γ. An *indefinite form of expression* is sometimes employed for a *definite*; thus, Εἰ οὖν τις τούτοις ὑφέξει ἑαυτόν, *if therefore one gives himself up to these* [= if I give myself up], Cyr. vii. 5. 44. Βουλεύεσθαι, πῶς τις τοὺς ἄνδρας ἀπελᾷ, *to counsel, how one* [= we] *shall drive off the men*, iii. 4. 40. Κακὸν ἥκει τινί [= σοι] Ar. Ran. 552. Εἰ μέν τις ἐᾷ ἡμᾶς ἀπιέναι, *if one permits* [= you permit] *us to depart*, iii. 3. 3.

E. Relative.

§ **519.** I. Relatives refer to an antecedent either as *definite* or as *indefinite*; and are, hence, divided into the DEFINITE and the INDEFINITE RELATIVES.

REMARKS. 1. In the *logical order* of discourse, the antecedent, according to its name, *precedes* the relative, but this order may be *inverted*, whenever the *perspicuity*, *energy*, or *beauty* of the sentence is promoted by the change.

2. INDEFINITE RELATIVES are formed, either from the *definite relatives* by adding *τὶς* or a particle (commonly *ἄν*), or from the *simple indefinites* by prefixing *ὅς* (in the shortened form *ὁ-*); thus, *ὅστις* or *ὅς ἄν*, *whoever*, *ὁποῖος*, *of what kind soever*, *ὁπόσος*, *how much soever*, *ὁπότε*, *whensoever*. See §§ 153, 317, 328.

§ **520.** II. The DEFINITE RELATIVE is often used for the *indefinite*, as a simpler and shorter form; and the INDEFINITE sometimes takes the place of the *definite*, giving, however, a somewhat different turn to the expression. Thus,

Οὓς ἑώρα ἐθέλοντας κινδυνεύειν, τούτους καὶ ἄρχοντας ἐποίει, *whomsoever he saw willing to incur danger, these he both made rulers*, i. 9. 14. *Ἔκαιον πάντα ὅσα καύσιμα ἑώρων* vi. 3. 19 (cf. *Καίειν ἅπαντα ὅτῳ ἐντυγχάνοιεν καυσίμῳ* Ib. 15; and, *Ἔθαπτον πάντας ὁπόσους ἐπελάμβανε τὸ κέρας* vi. 5. 5). *Ὁρᾶτε δὲ τὴν Τισσαφέρνους ἀπιστίαν, ὅστις λέγων* . ., *and see the perfidy of Tissaphernes*, [one] *a man who saying* . ., iii. 2. 4. *Οὐκ αἰσχύνεσθε οὔτε θεοὺς οὔτ' ἀνθρώπους, οἵτινες ὀμόσαντες . . ἀπολωλέκατε* ii. 5. 39. *Τάσδε τύχας λεύσσων βασιλέως, ὅστις . . βιοτεύσει*, 'one who will live,' Eur. Alc. 239 (see Ib. 659). *Νοεῖς ἐκεῖνον, ὅντιν' ἀρτίως μολεῖν ἐφιέμεσθα*; Soph. Œd. T. 1054. *Χαλεπὰ μὲν τὰ παρόντα, ὁπότε ἀνδρῶν στρατηγῶν τοιούτων στερόμεθα* iii. 2. 2 (§ 521. *β*). See § 525. *β*.

NOTES. (*a*) After the plural *πάντες*, *all*, *ὅστις* and *ὅς ἄν* are used in the *singular*, but *ὅσοι* and *ὁπόσοι* in the *plural*. See above and §§ 497. 1, 521. (*b*) The use of *an indefinite relative referring to a definite antecedent* belongs particularly to those cases in which the relative clause is added, not to *distinguish*, but to *characterize*, thus representing the antecedent as *one of a class*.

§ **521.** III. The relative should correspond with its antecedent in *specific meaning*, as well as in grammatical form. Thus, the definite relative with *οὗτος* should be *ὅς*· with *τοιοῦτος*, *οἷος*· with *τοσοῦτος*, *ὅσος*· &c. The exceptions to this rule arise mostly from the use of a *simpler*, *more familiar*, or *more emphatic pronoun*, in the place of that which is strictly appropriate. Some apparent exceptions arise from *ellipsis*. Thus,

Μηδ' ἐπιθυμεῖν τοιαύτης δόξης ἧς [= *οἵας*] *πολλοὶ . . τυγχάνουσιν, ἀλλὰ τῆς τηλικαύτης τὸ μέγεθος ἣν* [= *ἡλίκην*] *μόνος ἂν σὺ τῶν νῦν ὄντων κτήσασθαι δυνηθείης· μηδ' ἀγαπᾷν λίαν τὰς τοιαύτας ἀρετὰς ὧν* [= *οἵων*] *καὶ τοῖς φαύλοις μέτεστιν, ἀλλ' ἐκείνας ὧν οὐδεὶς ἂν πονηρὸς κοινωνήσειε*, 'such glory as many obtain, &c.,' Isocr. 408 d. *Πάντων, ὅσοι* [for *οἵ*, or sc. *τοσούτων*] *εἰς Καστωλοῦ πεδίον ἀθροίζονται*, 'of all who muster,' *or* 'of all, as many as muster,' i. 1. 2

(cf. Πᾶσιν, οἷς ἐτύγχανεν, ἔδοα i. 8. 1). Πᾶν, ὅσον ἐγὼ ἐδυνάμην vii. 6. 36. "Ταῦτ'," ἔφη, "χρὴ ποιεῖν, ὅσα ὁ θεὸς ἐκέλευσεν" iii. 1. 7. Ἑπτὰ γὰρ ἡμέρας, ὅσασπερ ἐπορεύθησαν διὰ τῶν Καρδούχων iv. 3. 2.

REMARKS. α. Ὅς is also used for οἷος with an ellipsis of the antecedent; as, Ἕωσπερ ἂν ᾖς ὅς [= τοιοῦτος οἷος] εἶ, *as long as you are what* [= such as] *you are*, Pl. Phædr. 243 e. Ὧν γε ὅς εἰμι Id. Theæt. 197 a.

β. The place of a relative pronoun is often supplied by a RELATIVE ADVERB, chiefly in designations of *place, time*, and *manner;* as, Εἰς χωρίον, ὅθεν ὄψονται θάλατταν, *to a place* [whence], *from which they would behold the sea*, iv. 7. 20. Ἐν τῷ ὄρει, ἔνθαπερ ἐσκήνουν iv. 8. 25. Τὸ αὐτὸ σχῆμα . . ὥσπερ τὸ πρῶτον μαχούμενος συνῄει, *the same order* [as] *with that in which he first advanced to the battle*, i. 10. 10. Ὁμοῖα γάρ μοι δοκοῦσι πάσχειν, ὥσπερ εἴ τις πολλὰ ἐσθίων μηδέποτε ἐμπίπλαιτο Symp. iv. 37. Καί σοι θεοὶ πόροιεν, ὡς ἐγὼ θέλω Soph. Œd. C. 1124.

§ **522.** IV. The relative pronouns belong to the class of *adjectives* (§ 73), and, as such, agree with a substantive expressed or understood. This substantive, or one corresponding to it, is also the *antecedent* of the relative. It is commonly *expressed in but one* of the two clauses, more frequently the *former*, but often the *latter;* and may be *omitted in both*, if it is a word which will be readily supplied (§ 447). Thus,

Συνέπεμψεν αὐτῇ στρατιώτας, οὓς [sc. στρατιώτας] Μένων εἶχε, *he sent with her the soldiers, which* [soldiers] *Meno had*, i. 2. 20. Ἀποπέμψαι πρὸς ἑαυτὸν [sc. τὸ στράτευμα,] ὃ εἶχεν στράτευμα, *to send back to him the force which he had* [what force he had], Ib. 1. Κῦρος δὲ ἔχων οὓς εἴρηκα, *and Cyrus having the men whom I have mentioned*, Ib. 5. Εἰς δὲ ἣν ἀφίκοντο κώμην, [sc. αὕτη ἡ κώμη] μεγάλη τε ἦν iv. 4. 2. Κατασκευάζοντά τε ἧς ἄρχοι χώρας i. 9. 19. Λαβόντες [sc. τοσούτους βοῦς,] ὅσοι ἦσαν βόες vii. 8. 16. Ἕτεροι γάρ εἰσιν, οἷσιν εὔχομαι θεοῖς Ar. Ran. 889. Οἶδ', ἣν ἔθρεψεν Ἑρμιόνην μήτηρ ἐμή Eur. Or. 1184.

REMARKS. 1. Other words, belonging alike to both clauses, are subject to a similar ellipsis; thus, Τισσαφέρνης ἐπεφάνη [sc. ἔχων], οὕς τε αὐτὸς ἱππέας ἦλθεν ἔχων, *Tissaphernes appeared, having both the cavalry which he had himself brought* [had come having], iii. 4. 13. Οἷς τοσούτων πέρι σκέψις, ὅσων ἡμῖν, πρόκειται [= Οἷς πρόκειται σκέψις περὶ τοσούτων, περὶ ὅσων ἡμῖν σκέψις πρόκειται] Pl. Rep. 533 e.

2. It will be observed, that when the antecedent is expressed in the same clause with the relative, it is commonly put at the *end*, as though the rest of the clause were regarded as modifying it like an *adjective*. See § 526.

§ **523.** 3. The ELLIPSIS of a *demonstrative pronoun* before the relative is very frequent; as, indeed, of the *whole antecedent*, when it can be supplied from the relative. When this ellipsis of the antecedent takes place, ἔστ often unites with the relative to form a species of *compound pronoun* or *adverb*, remaining itself *unchanged*, whatever may be the appropriate number, tense, or mode. Thus, Προυβάλλοντο πρέσβεις πρῶτον μὲν Χειρίσοφον, ὅτι ἄρχων ᾕρητο· ἔστι δ' οἳ [= ἦσαν δ' ἐκεῖνοι, οἳ] καὶ Ξενοφῶντα, *they proposed as ambassadors, first Chirisophus, because he had been chosen commander; and some also* [there were also those who proposed] *Xenophon*, vi. 2. 6. Πλὴν Ἰώνων, καὶ

'Ἀχαιῶν, καὶ ἔστιν ὧν ἄλλων ἐθνῶν Th. iii. 92. Καὶ ἔστι μὲν οὓς αὐτῶν κατέβαλον H. Gr. ii. 4. 6. Ἔστιν οὕστινας ἀνθρώπων τεθαύμακας ἐπὶ σοφίᾳ; Mem. i. 4. 2. (Cf. Εἰσὶ δ' αὐτῶν οὓς οὐδ' ἂν παντάπασι διαβαίητε ii. 5. 18; Ἦσαν δὲ οἳ καὶ πῦρ προσέφερον v. 2. 14; and, with the *singular* for the *plural* in the *Imperfect* also, Ἦν δὲ τούτων τῶν σταθμῶν οὓς πάνυ μακροὺς ἤλαυνεν i. 5. 7. See § 364.) Ὡς καὶ αὐτῷ μεταμέλειν ἔσθ' ὅτε, so *that* [there were times when] *sometimes he even regretted it,* ii. 6. 9. Ἔστι δὲ ἔνθα, *and there are places where,* or *in some places,* Cyr. viii. 2. 5. Ἔστιν ὅπως τις ἂν ὑμᾶς ἐξαπατήσαι; *Is there any way in which one could deceive you?* or, *Is it possible that one should deceive you?* v. 7. 6. Οὐ γάρ ἐσθ' ὅπου μ' ὀλεῖς Soph. Œd. T. 448.

NOTES. (*a*) From a similar union of ἔνι [= ἔνεστι] with the relative, have arisen the compounds ἔνιοι, *some,* and ἐνίοτε, *sometimes.* (*b*) The ellipsis sometimes extends even to the substantive verb itself; thus, Ὅπου [for Ἔστιν ὅπου], *in some places,* Lac. 10. 4.

§ **524.** V. The intimate relation of clauses connected by a *relative pronoun,* or a *kindred particle,* often produces an ATTRACTION, sometimes simply *affecting the position or form of particular words,* and sometimes even *uniting the two clauses in one.* Not unfrequently a combination results, which may be regarded as a species of *compound* or *complex pronoun.* Thus,

§ **525.** A.) A word or phrase is often made a part of the *relative,* instead of the *antecedent, clause;* and sometimes the two clauses are *blended in their arrangement.* Thus,

Λόγους ἀκούσον, οὓς σοι δυστυχεῖς ἥκω φέρων, *hear the sad tidings which I bring you,* Eur. Or. 853. Εἰς Ἀρμενίαν ἥξειν, ἧς Ὀρόντας ἦρχε πολλῆς καὶ εὐδαίμονος [for πολλὴν καὶ εὐδαίμονα] iii. 5. 17. Εἰπὲ παῖδ', ὃν ἐξ ἐμῆς χερὸς Πολύδωρον ἔκ τε πατρὸς ἐν δόμοις ἔχεις, εἰ ζῇ, 'tell me respecting my son Polydorus, whom you have,' Eur. Hec. 986. Ταύτην γ' ἰδὼν θάπτουσαν, ὃν σὺ τὸν νεκρὸν ἀπεῖπας Soph. Ant. 404. Ἕτερα τοιαῦτα, ἃ δή τινες τὰ φαντάσματα ὑπὸ ἀπειρίας ἀληθῆ καλοῦσιν Pl. Theæt. 167 b. Οὗτοι, ἐπεὶ εὐθέως ᾔσθοντο τὸ πρᾶγμα, ἀπεχώρησαν [for ἐπεὶ ᾔσθοντο τὸ πρᾶγμα, εὐθέως ἀπεχώρησαν], *these, when they understood the matter, immediately withdrew,* H. Gr. iii. 2. 4. See § 522.

REMARK. We observe this construction particularly,

α.) In expressions of *time* and *possibility* with the *superlative;* as, Πειρασόμεθα παρεῖναι, ὅταν τάχιστα διαπραξώμεθα [for παρεῖναι τάχιστα, ὅταν διαπραξώμεθα], *we shall endeavour to be present* [most quickly, when] *as soon as we have accomplished,* Cyr. iv. 5. 33. Ὡς τάχιστα ἕως ὑπέφαινεν, ἐθύοντο iv. 3. 9. Ἐπεὶ ἦλθε τάχιστα, . . ἀπέδοτο, *as soon as he had come, he sold,* vii. 2. 6. Ἤγαγον . . ὁπόσους ἐγὼ πλείστους ἐδυνάμην, *I have brought* [the most which] *as many as I could,* Cyr. iv. 5. 29. Ἔχων ἱππέας ὡς ἂν δύνηται πλείστους, *bringing as many horse as he should be able,* i. 6. 3 (§ 521. *β*). Ὡς μάλιστα ἐδύνατο ἐπικρυπτόμενος i. 1. 6. Ἀπήγοντο . . ὅποι ἐδύναντο προσωτάτω vi. 6. 1. Ἐλαύνων ὡς δυνατὸν ἦν τάχιστα, *riding as fast as was possible,* Cyr. v. 4. 3. Πείσομαι ᾗ δυνατὸν [sc. ἔσται] μάλιστα i. 3. 15. Διέβαινον . . ὡς οἷόν τε [sc. ἦν] μάλιστα πεφυλαγμένως ii. 4. 24. Ἕως ἂν ταῦτα ὡς ἔνι [= ἔνεστι] ἥδιστα γίνηται Mem. iv. 5. 9.

NOTE. The word denoting *possibility* is often understood; thus, Ὡς τάχιστα [sc. δυνατὸν ἦν] πορεύεσθαι, *to march as quickly as possible*, i. 3. 14 Πῶς ἂν πορευοίμεθά τε ὡς ἀσφαλέστατα, καὶ . . ὡς κράτιστα μαχοίμεθα iii 2. 27. Ἵνα ὡς πλεῖστοι μὲν ἡμῶν ἐν τοῖς ὅπλοις ὦσιν, ὡς ἐλάχιστοι δὲ σκευοφορῶσι Ib. 28. Διαβιβάζειν εἰς τὴν Ἀσίαν ὅτι τάχιστα [sc. ἂν δύνηται] vii. 2. 8 (ὅτι in this construction with the superlative is the *neuter of* ὅστις, used *adverbially*). Ὅπως ὅτι ἀπαρασκευαστότατον λάβοι βασιλέα, *that he might take the king as unprepared as possible*, i. 1. 6. Ὅτι πλείστους καὶ βελτίστους Ib Ὅπως δ' ἄριστα Æsch. Ag. 600. Ὅσον τάχιστα Soph. El. 1433.

β.) In the use of the *indefinites*, which, even in composition with ὅς (§ 519. 2), often seem to belong in force to the antecedent clause; thus, Ἡγεμόνα αἰτεῖν Κῦρον, ὅστις . . ἀπάξει [= ἡγεμόνα τινὰ, ὅς], *to ask Cyrus for some guide, who would conduct them*, i. 3. 14. Ἔστιν ὅ τι [= τί, ὅ] σε ἠδίκησα; *Is there aught in which I have wronged you?* i. 6. 7. Καὶ ἄλλον ὅντινα ἂν δυνώμεθα v. 5. 12. Οὐ διατρίβων, ὅπου μὴ ἐπισιτισμοῦ ἕνεκα . . ἐκαθίζετο, '[anywhere, where he did not] except where,' i. 5. 9. See §§ 520, 523.

§ **526.** B.) The RELATIVE takes the *case of the antecedent*. This is the common construction, when the ANTECEDENT is a *Genitive* or *Dative*, and the RELATIVE would properly be an *Accusative depending upon a verb*. Thus,

Ἐκ τῶν πόλεων, ὧν Τισσαφέρνης ἐτύγχανεν ἔχων, *from the cities, which Tissaphernes happened to have*, i. 1. 8. Τῷ ἀνδρὶ, ᾧ ἂν ἕλησθε, πείσομαι, *I will obey the man, whom you may choose*, i. 3. 15. Ἄξιοι τῆς ἐλευθερίας, ἧς κέκτησθε i. 7. 3. (Cf. Ἐν ταῖς σπονδαῖς, ἃς . . ἐποίησαν iv. 1. 1. Τοῖς κτήνεσιν, ἃ ἐκ τῶν Ταόχων ἔλαβον iv. 7. 17.) Τούτων, ὧν σὺ δεσποινῶν [= ἃ σὺ δεσποίνας, § 434] καλεῖς Œc. ii. 1. Ἄρχοντας ἐποίει ἧς κατεστρέφετο χώρας i. 9. 14 (§ 522. 2). Ξὺν ᾧπερ εἶχον οἰκετῶν πιστῷ μόνῳ Soph. Œd. C. 334. Μεταδίδως οὗπερ αὐτὸς ἔχεις σίτου Mem. ii. 7. 13. Χειμῶνός γε ὄντος οἵου λέγεις v. 8. 3.

REMARKS. α. If the ANTECEDENT is a *demonstrative*, it is commonly *omitted*; as, Σὺν [sc. ἐκείνοις] οἷς ἔχω, *with those whom I have*, vii. 3. 48. Ἀμφὶ ὧν εἶχον iv. 5. 17. Ἀνθ' ὧν εὖ ἔπαθον i. 3. 4. Ἡμιόλιον πᾶσι δώσειν οὗ πρότερον ἔφερον Ib. 21. Ἐδήλωσε δὲ τοῦτο οἷς τῇ ὑστεραίᾳ ἔπραττε ii. 2. 18.

β. Sometimes, though rarely, the *Dat.* and even the *Nom.* are attracted in like manner; as, Ὧν [= ἐκείνων, οἷς] ἠπίστει, πολλούς, *many of those whom he distrusted*, Cyr. v. 4. 39. Ἐξ ὧν [= ἐκείνων, ἃ] μεθ' ἑκατέρων γέγονεν, *from what he has been with either party*, Isocr. 69 c (§ 450). Βλάπτεσθαι ἀφ' ὧν [= ἐκείνων, ἃ] ἡμῖν παρεσκεύασται, *to be injured by those things which have been prepared by us* [in respect to which preparation has been made by us], Th. vii. 67. Οὐδὲν κω εἰδότες τῶν ἦν περὶ Σάρδις Hdt. i. 78.—When the *subject of a verb* is attracted, the verb, if retained, becomes impersonal. Cf. § 529.

γ. The *relative followed by* βούλει may, as if a *compound pronoun* (§ 524), agree with the antecedent in any case; thus, Περὶ Πολυγνώτου, ἢ ἄλλου ὅτου [= ὅντινα] βούλει, *respecting Polygnotus, or any other one whom you please*, Pl. Io, 533 a. Τὰ δέκα, ἢ ὅστις βούλει ἄλλος ἀριθμός Id. Crat. 432 a. Οἷα τούτων ὃς βούλει εἴργασται Id. Gorg. 517 b. Compare, in Lat., *quivis*.

δ. RELATIVE ADVERBS are likewise affected by attraction; thus, Διεκομίζοντο εὐθὺς ὅθεν [= ἐκεῖθεν ὅπου] ὑπεξέθεντο παῖδας, *they immediately brought over their children* [whence] *from the places where they had put them for safety*,

Th. i. 89. Ἐκ δὲ γῆς, ὅθεν [= οὗ] προὔκειτο Soph. Tr. 701. Χωρεῖν χρεὼν ὅποι [= ἐκεῖσε ὅπου] χθονὸς κρύψαντε λήσομεν δέμας Eur. Iph. T. 118. Cf. §§ 527. R., 531. β.

§ **527.** C.) The ANTECEDENT takes the *case of the relative.* This is termed INVERTED ATTRACTION. Thus,

Ἀνεῖλεν αὐτῷ ὁ Ἀπόλλων θεοῖς [= θεοὺς] οἷς ἔδει θύειν, *Apollo made known to him the gods to whom he must sacrifice*, iii. 1. 6 (cf. Θυσάμενος οἷς ἀνεῖλεν ὁ θεός Ib. 8). Ὅτι Λακεδαιμόνιοι πάντων [= πάντα], ὧν δέονται, πεπραγότες εἶεν H. Gr. i. 4. 2. Ἁνδάνουσα μὲν φυγῇ πολιτῶν [= πολίταις] ὧν ἀφίκετο χθόνα Id. Med. 11. Τάσδε [= Αἵδε] δ' ἅσπερ εἰσορᾷς, ἐξ ὀλβίων ἄζηλον εὑροῦσαι βίον, χωροῦσι πρὸς σὲ Soph. Tr. 283. Λόγος δ' ὃς ἐμπέπτωκεν ἀρτίως ἐμοὶ στείχοντι δεῦρο, συμβαλοῦ γνώμην Id. Œd. C. 1150. Τὸν ἄνδρα τοῦτον, ὃν πάλαι ζητεῖς, . . οὗτός ἐστιν ἐνθάδε Id. Œd. T. 449 (§ 499). Κοτυωρίτας δὲ, οὓς ὑμετέρους φατὲ εἶναι, εἴ τι αὐτῶν εἰλήφαμεν, αὐτοὶ αἴτιοί εἰσιν v. 5. 19.

REMARK. Inverted attraction appears also in ADVERBS; thus, Βῆναι κεῖθεν [= κεῖσε], ὅθεν περ ἥκει, *to return thither, whence he came*, Soph. Œd. C. 1227. Καὶ ἄλλοσε [= ἀλλαχοῦ], ὅποι ἂν ἀφίκῃ, ἀγαπήσουσί σε Pl. Crito, 45 b. Cf. §§ 526. δ, 531. β.

§ **528.** D.) The two clauses are *brought into one* by the *ellipsis of a substantive verb* (cf. § 538). This is termed CONDENSED CONSTRUCTION, or CONDENSATION. The verb is omitted either (a.) *with the antecedent*, or (b.) *with the relative.*

a.) WITH THE ANTECEDENT. We here distinguish the following cases: —

1.) After a *demonstrative pronoun* or *article*, the RELATIVE is also *omitted*, and the ANTECEDENT takes its place in the construction. This form of condensation is particularly frequent in *questions* and *exclamations*, especially with the poets. Thus, Τί τόδ' αὐδᾷς [= Τί ἐστι τόδε, ὃ αὐδᾷς]; *What is this, which you say?* Eur. Alc. 106. Τίν' ἄνδρα τόνδ' [= τίς ἀνήρ ἐστι ὅδε, ὃν] ἐπὶ σκηναῖς ὁρῶ; *What man is this, whom I see by the tents?* Id. Hec. 733. Τί τοῦτ' ἀρχαῖον ἐννέπεις κακόν; Soph. Œd. T. 1033. Οἵαν ἔχιδναν τήνδ' ἔφυσας! *What a viper is this, which thou hast produced!* Eur. Ion, 1262. Τοῦτο μὲν οὐδὲν θαυμαστὸν λέγεις Pl. Prot. 318 b. Τίς ὁ πόθος [= Τίς ἐστι ὁ πόθος, ὃς] αὐτοὺς ἵκετο; Soph. Ph. 601 (see § 480. α). Καλόν γέ μοι τοὔνειδος ἐξωνείδισας, *the reproach which you have cast upon me is an honor*, Eur. Iph. A. 305. In the following sentence, there appears to be a union between an *exclamation without a verb*, and a relative clause; Τοὺς ἐμὸς ἴδε πατὴρ θανάτους αἰκεῖς [= Ὦ θάνατοι αἰκεῖς, οὓς ἴδε πατὴρ ἐμός]! *The cruel death my father saw!* Soph. El. 205. — Expressions like the following are still more elliptical; Ἔνθα ἡ Τριπυργία [= ἐστὶ χωρίον, ὃ Τριπυργία] καλεῖται, *where there is a place, which is called Tripyrgia*, H. Gr. v. 1. 10. Ἐν ᾧ καλοῦμεν τὸ ζῆν, *in which is that which we call* LIFE, Pl. Phædo, 107 c.

2.) Οὐδείς with ὅστις οὐ (or sometimes ὅς οὐ) forms a species of *compound pronoun* (§ 524); as, Οὐδεὶς ὅστις οὐκ ἀφέξεται, *there is no one, who will not not refrain*, Ven. 12. 14 (cf. Οὐδεὶς ἦν, ὅστις οὐκ ᾤετο H. Gr. vii. 5. 26). Καταγελῷ ἂν ἡμῶν οὐδεὶς ὅστις οὐ, *every body would laugh at us*, Pl. Hipp. Maj. 299 a. Οὐδεὶς ὅς οὐχὶ τῶνδ' ὀνειδιεῖ Soph. Œd. T. 373. Οὐδενὸς [= οὐδείς ἐστι,] ὅτου οὐ πάντων ἂν ὑμῶν καθ' ἡλικίαν πατὴρ εἴην Pl. Prot. 317 c. Οὐδενὶ ὅτῳ οὐκ ἀποκρινόμενος Id. Meno, 70 c. Περὶ ὧν οὐδένα κίνδυνον [= οὐδεὶς κίνδυνος ἦν,] ὅντιν' οὐχ ὑπέμειναν οἱ πρόγονοι Dem. 295. 7. — So, with an interrogative for οὐδείς, Τίνα οἴεσθε ὅντινα οὐ βραχείᾳ προφάσει ἀποστήσεσθαι Th. iii. 39.

§ **529.** b.) With the Relative. This occurs with the *relatives of comparison*, οἷος, ὅσος, ἡλίκος, which then unite with the substantive or adjective following, to form a species of *compound adjective*. To this, as to other adjectives, the article may be prefixed (§ 472). Thus,

Χαριζόμενον οἵῳ σοὶ ἀνδρὶ [= ἀνδρὶ τοιούτῳ, οἷος σὺ εἶ], *obliging a man such as you are* [a SUCH AS YOU man], Mem. ii. 9. 3. Οἱ δὲ οἷοί περ ὑμεῖς ἄνδρες, *but* [the SUCH AS YOU men] *men of your rank*, or *men like you*, Cyr. vi. 2. 2. Πρὸς ἄνδρας τολμηροὺς οἵους καὶ 'Αθηναίους Th. vii. 21. Ὄντος τοῦ πάγου οἵου δεινοτάτου [= τοιούτου, οἷός ἐστι δεινότατος], *the cold being* [such as is most dreadful] *of the most intense kind* Pl. Conv. 220 b (see iv. 8. 2 ; vii. 1. 24). Μαχαίριον ὅσον ξυήλη Λακωνικὴν [= τοσοῦτον, ὅση ἐστὶ ξυήλη Λακωνική], *a knife about the size of the Spartan small-sword*, iv. 7. 16. Εἰκὸς ἄνδρα κυφὸν, ἡλίκον Θουκυδίδην [= τηλικοῦτον, ἡλίκος Θουκυδίδης ἐστί], ἐξολέσθαι Ar. Ach 703. Δεινὸν τοῖσιν ἡλίκοισι νῷν Id. Eccl. 465. — In like manner, Τοῦ περιττοῦ ὄντος οὐχ οὕπερ τῆς τριάδος Pl. Phædo, 104 a.

Remarks. α. A substantive *of a different number* following the relative remains in the *Nominative*; as, Νεανίας δ' οἵους [= τοιούτους, οἷος] σύ, *but young men such as you*. Τῶν οἵωνπερ αὐτὸς ὄντων, *of men like him*, H. Gr. i. 4. 16.

β. In this construction, ὅσος is commonly used in the *neuter form* ὅσον, as *indeclinable*, and may be often regarded as a mere *adverb* (§ 450. δ, *b*) ; thus, Οἱ ἱππεῖς τούτου ὅσον ἑξακόσιοι, 'as many as 600,' or, 'about 600,' i. 8. 6. Λαβὼν . . ὅσον τριχοίνικον ἄρτον vii. 3. 23. 'Απέχει ὅσον παρασάγγην, 'about a parasang,' iv. 5. 10. Καὶ πρόβατα ὅσον θύματα, *and sheep* [as many as the sacrifices would be] *enough for sacrifice*, vii. 8. 19. So, doubled, Ὅσον ὅσον στίλην Ar. Vesp. 213. See § 450. δ.

γ. In the Epic, the demonstrative is sometimes expressed instead of the relative; as, Τύμβον . . ἐπιεικέα τοῖον [= τοῖον, οἷός ἐστι ἐπιεικής] Ψ. 246.

§ **530.** E.) A relative pronoun takes the place of *a demonstrative pronoun and a connective particle.*

The term *demonstrative pronoun*, as here used, includes the *personal pronoun* and the *article*. See § 467. 1. Of this form of attraction there are two kinds, according as the demonstrative belongs to the *first* or the *second* of the two clauses which are united.

a.) When the demonstrative belongs to the *first clause*. In this kind of attraction the pronoun is commonly either *governed by a preposition or adverb*, or is itself *used adverbially*. Thus, 'Εφ' ᾧ [= ἐπὶ τούτῳ, ὥστε] μὴ καίειν τὰς κώμας, *upon this condition, that they should not burn the villages*, iv. 2. 19 (cf. 'Επὶ τοῖσδε, ὥστε Th. iii. 114). 'Εφ' ᾧ τε [= ἐπὶ τούτῳ, ὥστε] πλοῖα συλλέγειν, *for the purpose of collecting* [for this purpose, that we might collect] *vessels*, vi. 6. 22. Μέχρι οὗ [= τοῦ χρόνου, ὅτε] εἶδον, *until* [the time when] *they saw*, v. 4. 16 (cf. Μέχρι τοσούτου, ἕως Th. i. 90). Μέχρι οὗ [= τοῦ χωρίου, ἔνθα] διὰ καῦμα οὐ δύνανται οἰκεῖν ἄνθρωποι, 'to the region where,' i. 7. 6

Διώξας ἄχρι οὗ [= τοῦ τόπου, οἷ] ἀσφαλὲς ᾤετο εἶναι, 'as far as,' Cyr. v. 4. 16. Ἐπεὶ προπέμψειαν τοὺς Ἀμυκλαιεῖς μέχρι ὁπόσου αὐτοὶ κελεύοιεν H. Gr. iv. 5. 12. Ἐξ ὅτου ἀπεδήμησε, *since he had been abroad*, vii. 8. 4. Ἐν ᾧ δὲ ὡπλίζοντο, *and whilst they were arming*, ii. 2. 15. Οὗτος δέ μοι φίλος μέγιστος, οὕνεκ' [οὗ ἕνεκα = τούτου ἕνεκα, ὅτι] Ἀτρείδας στυγεῖ, 'because,' Soph. Ph. 585. Ἀνθ' ὧν [= Ἀντὶ τούτου, ὅτι], *because*, Id. Ant. 1068. Οὐ δοκεῖ σοι . . διαφέρειν τὰ ἑκούσια τῶν ἀκουσίων, ᾗ [= ταύτῃ, ὅτι] ὁ μὲν ἑκὼν πεινῶν φάγοι ἄν, ὁπότε βούλοιτο Mem. ii. 1. 18.

NOTE. Hdt. sometimes uses μέχρι οὗ or ὅτου as a compound adverb governing the Gen. (§ 394); as, Μέχρι οὗ ὀκτὼ πύργων i. 181. Μέχρι ὅτου πληθώρης ἀγορῆς ii. 173.

§ **531.** b.) When the demonstrative belongs to the *second clause*; as, Τίς οὕτω μαίνεται, ὅστις [= ὥστε ἐκεῖνος] οὐ βούλεταί σοι φίλος εἶναι; *Who is so mad, that he does not wish* [or *as not to wish*] *to be your friend?* ii. 5. 12 (see Ib. 6. 6; vii. 1. 28). Ἀπόρων ἐστὶ . ., οἵτινες ἐθέλουσι, *it is the part of those without resource, that they should wish*, or *to wish*, ii. 5. 21. Οὐκ ἔστιν οὕτω μῶρος, ὃς θανεῖν ἐρᾷ Soph. Ant. 220. Τοσοῦτον ἄλγος, οὗ [= ὥστε αὐτοῦ] ποτ' οὐ λελήσεται, *such grief, that he will never forget it*, Eur. Alc. 198. Κατοικτείρων τήν τε γυναῖκα, οἵου ἀνδρὸς [= ὅτι τοιούτου ἀνδρὸς] στέροιτο, καὶ τὸν ἄνδρα, οἵαν [= ὅτι τοιαύτην] γυναῖκα καταλιπὼν οὐκέτ' ὄψοιτο, *commiserating, both the wife, that she had lost such a husband, and the husband, that, leaving such a wife, he would never behold her more*, Cyr. vii. 3. 13. Οἱ δὲ δεσπότιν στένωσιν, οἵαν ἐκ δόμων ἀπώλεσαν Eur. Alc. 948 (§ 425. 4).

NOTES. *α*. Akin to this construction is the extensive use of the relative in *explanation*, or the *assignment of reason or purpose*; as, Θαυμαστὸν ποιεῖς, ὃς . . δίδως, *you conduct strangely*, [who give] *that you give*, or *in giving*, Mem. ii. 7. 13. Ὅπλα κτῶνται, οἷς ἀμυνοῦνται τοὺς ἀδικοῦντας, *they prepare arms, that with these they may repel assailants*, Ib. 1. 14. Καὶ πόλει πέμψον τιν', ὅστις σημανεῖ, *and send some one to the city, to give notice*, Eur. Iph. T. 1208.

β. RELATIVE ADVERBS likewise exhibit this form of attraction (cf. §§ 526. δ, 527. R.); as, Εὐδαίμων γάρ μοι ὁ ἀνὴρ ἐφαίνετο, . . ὡς [= ὅτι οὕτως] ἀδεῶς καὶ γενναίως ἐτελεύτα, *for the man appeared to me happy, that he died so fearlessly and nobly*, Pl. Phædo, 58 e. Σοφήν σ' ἔθρεψεν Ἑλλάς, ὡς ᾔσθου καλῶς Eur. Iph. T. 1180.

§ **532.** REMARK. FORMS OF COMPARISON are especially liable to attraction and ellipsis (cf. §§ 391. γ, 461); thus,

Μόνοι τε ὄντες ὅμοια ἔπραττον, ἅπερ [= ἐκείνοις, ἅπερ] ἂν μετ' ἄλλων ὄντες, [like things, which] *things like to those which*,' v. 4. 34. Ἐὰν μὲν ἡ πρᾶξις ᾖ παραπλησία, οἵαπερ καὶ πρόσθεν ἐχρῆτο τοῖς ξένοις i. 3. 18. Οὔτε γὰρ πυρὸς οὔτ' ἄστρων ὑπέρτερον βέλος, οἷον [= τοιούτου, οἷον] τὸ τᾶς Ἀφροδίτας ἵησιν ἐκ χερῶν Ἔρως Eur. Hipp. 530. Τοσοῦτον δὲ διαφέρειν ἡμᾶς δεῖ τῶν δούλων, ὅσον οἱ μὲν δοῦλοι ἄκοντες τοῖς δεσπόταις ὑπηρετοῦσιν, ἡμᾶς δὲ . . ἑκόντας δεῖ ποιεῖν, 'insomuch as this, that slaves,' Cyr. viii. 1. 4. Τοσοῦτον μόνον σε ἐγίγνωσκον, ὅσον [= ὅσον τοῦτο, ὅτι] ἤκουον Ἀθηναῖον εἶναι, 'so far as this, that I heard,' iii. 1. 45. Τὸν μὲν ἄνδρα τοσοῦτον ἐγίγνωσκον, ὅτι [= ὅσον τοῦτο, ὅτι] εἷς ἡμῶν εἴη v. 8. 8. Δεινότερος γεγονέναι τὴν τέχνην τοσούτῳ, ὅσῳ ὁ μὲν τὰ αὑτοῦ μόνον ἐποίει Pl. Euthyphr. 11 d. Ἐπεί νιν τῶνδε πλεῖστον ᾤκτισα βλέπουσ', ὅσῳπερ καὶ φρονεῖν οἶδεν μόνη, 'inasmuch as,' Soph. Tr. 312. Προελθόντες ὅσον ἂν δοκῇ καιρὸς εἶναι εἰς τὸ δειπνοποιεῖσθαι, 'until,' vi. 3. 14.

NOTE. Ὅσον οὐ, [just so much as not to be] *only not, all but*, is used as a simple adverb (also written ὁσονού); thus, Τὸν μέλλοντα καὶ ὅσον οὐ πάροντα πόλεμον Th. i. 36. Ὅσον οὐ παρείη ἤδη vii. 2. 5.

§ **533.** VI. A RELATIVE sometimes introduces a clause which (α.) has *another connective* or a *participle absolute*, or which (β.) is properly *coördinate;* and, on the other hand, a COÖRDINATE CLAUSE sometimes (γ.) takes the *place of a relative clause*, or (δ.) is used in *continuation of it*. Thus,

α. Πολλὰ ἂν εἰπεῖν ἔχοιεν Ὀλύνθιοι νῦν, ἃ τότ' εἰ προείδοντο, οὐκ ἂν ἀπώλοντο, *the Olynthians could now mention many things, which, had they then foreseen, they would not have perished*, Dem. 128. 17. Ὃς ἐπειδὴ κατέμαθεν . ., ἐκεῖνος . . ἠνάγκασε, [when who perceived . ., he compelled] *who, when he perceived . ., compelled*, Lac. 10. 4. Οἷς ἐξὸν [= οἷ, ἐξὸν αὐτοῖς] πάντα ἔχειν τὰ τῶν πολιτῶν, οὐδὲν ἔχοιεν Pl. Rep. 466 a. Cf. § 539. 2.

β. Τοιαῦτα φῆμαι μαντικαὶ διώρισαν· ὧν ἐντρέπου σὺ μηδέν, *such things were decreed by prophetic responses; to which do you pay no regard*, Soph. Œd. T. 723. ΟΡ. Ψῆφον ἀμφ' ἡμῶν πολίτας ἐπὶ φόνῳ θέσθαι χρεών. ΠΥΛ. Ἣ κρινεῖ τί χρῆμα; '[Which will decide what?] *And what will this decide?* Eur. Or. 756.

γ. Ἐξετάσαι . . Ὀδυσσέα, ἢ Σίσυφον, ἢ ἄλλους μυρίους ἄν τις εἴποι, *to examine Ulysses, or Sisyphus, or* [one might mention ten thousand others] *ten thousand others whom one might mention*, Pl. Apol. 41 b.

§ **534.** δ. Κῦρον δὲ μεταπέμπεται ἀπὸ τῆς ἀρχῆς, ἧς αὐτὸν σατράπην ἐποίησε, καὶ στρατηγὸν δὲ αὐτὸν ἀπέδειξε i. 1. 2. This construction is adopted chiefly to avoid the repetition of the relative, in accordance with the following

REMARK. The *repetition of the relative is commonly avoided*, either by *ellipsis*, or by the substitution of a *demonstrative* or of a *personal pronoun*, as,

Ἀριαῖος δέ, ὃν ἡμεῖς ἠθέλομεν βασιλέα καθιστάναι, καὶ [sc. ᾧ] ἐδώκαμεν καὶ [sc. παρ' οὗ] ἐλάβομεν πιστὰ μὴ προδώσειν ἀλλήλους, *and Ariæus whom we wished to make king, and to whom we gave and from whom we received pledges that we would not betray each other*; iii. 2. 5. Ἐκεῖνοι, οἷς τι μέλει τῆς αὐτῶν ψυχῆς, ἀλλὰ μὴ σώματα πλάττοντες ζῶσι Pl. Phædo, 82 d. Ἡμᾶς δέ, οἷς κηδεμὼν μὲν οὐδεὶς πάρεστιν, ἐστρατεύσαμεν δὲ ἐπ' αὐτόν iii. 1. 17. Ποῦ δὴ ἐκεῖνός ἐστιν ὁ ἀνήρ, ὃς συνεθήρα ἡμῖν, καὶ σύ μοι μάλα ἐδόκεις θαυμάζειν αὐτόν; *Where now is that man, who hunted with us, and whom you seemed to me greatly to admire?* Cyr. iii. 1. 38. Ἐκεῖνοι τοίνυν, οἷς οὐκ ἐχαρίζονθ' οἱ λέγοντες, οὐδ' ἐφίλουν αὐτοὺς Dem. 35. 3. Καὶ νῦν τί χρὴ δρᾶν; ὅστις ἐμφανῶς θεοῖς ἐχθαίρομαι, μισεῖ δέ μ' Ἑλλήνων στρατὸς Soph. Aj. 457. — So, when the pronoun is repeated in the same sentence (§ 499); as, Γυναῖκα βάρβαρον, ἥν χρῆν σ' ἐλαύνειν τήνδ' ὑπὲρ Νείλου ῥοάς, 'whom you ought to drive [her],' Eur Andr. 649.

F. COMPLEMENTARY.

§ **535.** From the *connective*, and, at the same time, *indefinite* character of the complementary pronouns and adverbs

(§ 329. N.), their proper forms are those of the *indefinite relatives* (§ 519. 2). But, when there will be no danger of mistake, there is often employed, for the greater brevity and vivacity, in place of the full compound form, one or the other element, either the *relative* or the *indefinite*. Of these, the latter is far the more frequently used, but with this distinction from the *indefinite in its proper sense*, that the *accentuation of the compound form* is retained, as far as possible. Thus,

Πρὶν δῆλον εἶναι, ὅ τι οἱ ἄλλοι Ἕλληνες ἀποκρινοῦνται, *before it is evident, what the other Greeks will answer*, i. 4. 14. Πρὶν δῆλον εἶναι, τί ποιήσουσιν οἱ ἄλλοι Ἕλληνες Ib. 13. Ὡς δηλοίη, οὕς τιμᾷ i. 9. 28. Ἤρετο, τίς ὁ θόρυβος εἴη. . . Καὶ ἤρετο, ὅ τι εἴη τὸ σύνθημα i. 8. 16. Διάγνωσιν φρενῶν, ὅστις τ' ἀληθής ἐστιν, ὅς τε μὴ φίλος Eur. Hipp. 924. Ὁποίοις μὲν λόγοις ἔπεισε Κῦρον, ἄλλῃ γέγραπται ii. 6. 4. Ὁρῶν, ἐν οἵοις ἐσμέν iii. 1. 15. Οὐκ οἶδα, οὔτ' ἀπὸ ποίου ἂν τάχους οὔτε ὅποι ἄν τις φεύγων ἀποφεύγοι, οὔτ' εἰς ποῖον ἂν σκότος ἀποδραίη, οὔθ' ὅπως ἂν εἰς ἐχυρὸν χωρίον ἀποσταίη ii. 5. 7. Τὸ τῆς τύχης γὰρ ἀφανὲς, οἷ προβήσεται Eur. Alc. 785. Συνεβουλεύετό τε πῶς ἂν τὴν μάχην ποιοῖτο i. 7. 2. Οἱ δ' ἠρώτων αὐτὸν τὸ στράτευμα, ὁπόσον τε εἴη καὶ ἐπὶ τίνι συνειλεγμένον iv. 4. 17. Ἠρώτα αὐτὸν, πόσον χρυσίον ἔχει vii. 8. 2.

§ **536.** REMARKS. 1. The indefinites thus employed and accented are termed in Etymology, from the most prominent of their offices, INTERROGATIVES (§§ 152. 2, 317). As complementary words, they were employed in indirect question; and hence appears to have arisen their use as *direct interrogatives*, through an ellipsis. Thus, from the indirect question, *Εἰπὲ, τίνα γνώμην ἔχεις περὶ τῆς πορείας*, *say, what opinion you have respecting the march* (ii. 2. 10), by the omission of *εἰπὲ*, comes the direct question, *Τίνα γνώμην ἔχεις περὶ τῆς πορείας;* *What opinion have you respecting the march?* So, from *Λέξατε οὖν πρός με, τί ἐν νῷ ἔχετε*, *tell me, therefore, what you have in mind* (iii. 3. 2), comes, *Τί ἐν νῷ ἔχετε;* *What have you in mind?*

NOTES. α. In other languages, as the Lat., with those derived from it, and the Eng., the complementary use of the *simple relatives* has prevailed; and hence, in these languages, the general identity of the *relatives* and the *interrogatives*. Thus, *who*, *which*, *when*, &c., are both relative and interrogative.

β. In direct question, the Greek employs only one of the two shorter forms above mentioned, but in *exclamation* it employs both; thus, Οἴμοι, πάτερ, τί εἶπας! οἷά μ' εἴργασαι! *O my father, what have you said! how you treat me!* Soph. Tr. 1203. Οἷ' ἔργ' ἀκούσεσθ', οἷα δ' εἰσόψεσθ', ὅσον δ' ἀρεῖσθε πένθος! Id. Œd. T. 1223.

§ **537.** 2. A COMPLEMENTARY PRONOUN OR ADVERB, used as *an echo to an interrogative*, has, for distinction's sake, its full form; thus,

ΛΑΜ. Τίς γὰρ εἶ; ΔΙΚ. [Sc. Ἐρωτᾷς] Ὅστις; Πολίτης χρηστός.

Lam. *For who are you?* Dic. [*Do you ask*] *Who? A good citizen*, Ar. Ach. 594. ΧΑΡ. Οὗτος, τί ποιεῖς; ΔΙΟΝ. Ὅ τι ποιῶ; Id. Ran. 198. ΕΥΘ. Τίνα γραφήν σε γέγραπται; ΣΩΚΡ. Ἥντινα; Οὐκ ἀγεννῆ, ἔμοιγε δοκεῖ Pl. Euthyphr. 2 b. ΚΛ. Πῶς ἂν ταῦτά γ᾽ ἔτι ξυγχωροῖμεν; ᾿ΑΘ. Ὅπως; Εἰ θεὸς ἡμῖν . . δοίη τις συμφωνίαν Id. Leg. 662 a.

3. A complementary clause often expresses merely a *condition* or a *circumstance;* and the *complementary* construction is sometimes used where the *relative* might have been. Thus,

Δόθ᾽, ἥτις ἐστί, *give it, whoever she may be*, Soph. El. 1123. Τὸν ἄνδρ᾽ ἀπαυδῶ τοῦτον, ὅστις ἐστὶ, γῆς Id. Œd. T. 236. Δουλεύομεν θεοῖς, ὅ τι ποτ᾽ εἰσὶν οἱ θεοί Eur. Or. 418. Καὶ ἱκανοὺς κρίνεις συνεργοὺς εἶναι, ὅ τι τυγχάνοι βουλόμενος κατεργάζεσθαι i. 9. 20 (cf. Συνεργὸς . . εἶναι τούτου, ὅτου Ib. 21). Ἥδιστ᾽ ἂν ἀκούσαιμι τὸ ὄνομα, τίς οὕτως ἐστὶ δεινὸς λέγειν [= ὄνομα τούτου, ὅστις], *most gladly should I hear the name, who there is of such power in speaking* [= the name of him who is], ii. 5. 15. Ἆθλα ὁπότεροι ἂν ἡμῶν ἄνδρες ἀμείνονες ὦσιν iii. 1. 21.

§ **538.** 4. Condensation. The antecedent and complementary clauses are sometimes *brought into one* by the *ellipsis of a substantive verb* (cf. § 528). The verb is omitted either (α.) in the *antecedent*, or (β.) in the *complementary* clause.

α. In the antecedent clause. This occurs with *adjectives of admiration*, which unite with the complementary word (commonly ὅσος or ὡς) to form a *complex adjective* or *adverb* (cf. §§ 528. 2, 529); thus, Θαυμαστὴν ὅσην [= Θαυμαστόν ἐστιν, ὅσην] περὶ σὲ προθυμίαν ἔχει, *it is wonderful how much regard he has for you*, Pl. Alc. 151 a. Μετὰ ἱδρῶτος θαυμαστοῦ ὅσου Id. Rep. 350 d. Θαυμαστόν τινα χρόνον ὅσον Id. Epin. 982 c. Θαυμαστῶς ὡς [= Θαυμαστόν ἐστιν, ὡς] ἐπείσθην Id. Phædo, 92 a. Θαυμαστῶς μοι εἶπες ὡς παρὰ δόξαν Ib. 95 a. Ἀμήχανον ὅσον χρόνον, *an inconceivably long time*, Ib. 80 c. Ἀνέβλεψέ τέ μοι τοῖς ὀφθαλμοῖς ἀμήχανόν τι οἷον Id. Charm. 155 c. Ὑπερφυῶς ὡς χαίρω Id. Conv. 173 c. Ἦν περὶ αὐτὸν ὄχλος ὑπερφυὴς ὅσος Ar. Plut. 750. Ἄφθονοι ὅσοι Hdt. iv. 194.

β. In the complementary clause. To this ellipsis may be referred the employment of a complementary word (commonly with οὖν or δή), as a *mere indefinite;* thus, Μηδ᾽ ὁντιναοῦν μισθὸν [= μισθόν τινα, ὅστις οὖν εἴη] προσαιτήσας, *not demanding any pay whatever* [it might be], vii. 6. 27. Ἢ ἄλλ᾽ ὁτιοῦν, *or any thing else whatever*, Cyr. i. 6. 22. Οὐδ᾽ ὁτιοῦν περὶ τούτου ἐπεμνήσθη, *he made not the least mention of this*, Ib. 12. Ὁπωσοῦν, *in any way whatever*, Ib. ii. 1. 27. Ὅτου δὴ παρηγγυήσαντος, *some one* [whosoever it might have been] *having suggested it*, iv. 7. 25. Ἔστι γὰρ ὁτιοῦν πρᾶγμα ὅτῳ δὴ ὁπωσοῦν ἔχοντι ἄμεινον ἀγνοεῖν ἢ γιγνώσκειν; Pl. Alc. 143 c. Μήτε διακονίαν μηδ᾽ ἥντινα κεκτημένος Pl. Leg. 919 d. Εἴ τις ἀδικοίη ὁποτέρους Cyr. iii. 2. 23.

Note. For an additional remark upon complementary words, see § 539. 2.

G. Interrogative.

§ **539.** The interrogatives are, in Greek, simply the *indefinites with a change of accent.* For their *origin*, their *complementary use*, and their *use in exclamation*, see §§ 535, 536

For the use of the *article* with interrogatives, see § 480. For examples of *condensed interrogative sentences*, see § 528. 1.

REMARKS. 1. The *neuter τί* unites with several *particles* to form *elliptical expressions;* which, with various specific offices, serve in general to promote the *vigor* and *vivacity* of the discourse; as, Τί γάρ [sc. ἐστιν, or λέγετε]; ἄρχοντας αἱρουμένων ὑμῶν, ἐγώ τινι ἐμποδὼν εἰμι; 'What then?' v. 7. 10. Τί οὖν; v. 8. 11. Τί δέ; Mem. ii. 1. 3. Τί δῆτα; Vect. 4. 28.

2. The Greek idiom (*a*) admits a *greater freedom* than the English, in the *construction* and *position* of both INTERROGATIVE and COMPLEMENTARY WORDS; and even (*b*) allows the use of *more than one* in the same clause. Thus, — (*a*) Τί . . ἰδὼν ποιοῦντα, ταῦτα κατέγνωκας αὐτοῦ; [Having seen him doing what] *What have you seen him do, that you thus judge of him?* Mem. i. 3. 10. Ὅταν τί ποιήσωσι, νομιεῖς αὐτοὺς σοῦ φροντίζειν; Ib. 4. 14. Ἐγὼ οὖν τὸν ἐκ ποίας πόλεως στρατηγὸν προσδοκῶ ταῦτα πράξειν; iii. 1. 14. Εἴ τις ἔροιτο ἡμᾶς, τῶν τί σοφῶν εἰσιν οἱ ζωγράφοι ἐπιστήμονες Pl. Prot. 312 c. Ἵνα τί [sc. γένηται] ταῦτα λέγεις; [That what may be] *With what intent*, or *Why, do you say this?* Id. Apol. 26 d. ΠΥΛ. Ὡς τί δὴ τόδε; ΟΡ. Ὥς νιν ἱκετεύσω με σῶσαι Eur. Or. 796. Ὅτι δὴ τί γε [sc. ἐστίν]; [Because there is what?] *Why so?* Pl. Charm. 161 c. Εἶτ' ἐλαυνομένων, καὶ ὑβριζομένων, καὶ τί κακὸν οὐχὶ πασχόντων, πᾶσα ἡ οἰκουμένη μεστὴ γέγονε προδοτῶν, 'what evil not suffering?' i. e. 'suffering every evil,' Dem. 241. 28. Cf. § 533. — (*b*) Τίς τίνος αἴτιός ἐστι, γενήσεται φανερόν, *it will become evident who is guilty* [and] *of what*, Dem. 249. 8. Τίνας οὖν, ἔφη, ὑπὸ τίνων εὕροιμεν ἂν μείζονα εὐεργετημένους, ἢ παῖδας ὑπὸ γονέων; Mem. ii. 2. 3. Πότερος ἄρα πότερον αἱμάξει; Eur. Phœn. 1288. Τίς ἂν πᾶ πόρος κακῶν γένοιτο; Id. Alc. 213. Λεύσσετε, . . οἷα πρὸς οἵων ἀνδρῶν πάσχω Soph. Ant. 940. Οὐδ' ἔχω, ὅπα πρὸς πότερον ἴδω Id. 1342.

H. ἌΛΛΟΣ.

§ 540. The pronoun ἄλλος is not only used *retrospectively*, but also *prospectively* and *distributively;* that is, it may denote, not only a different person or thing from one which *has been* mentioned, but also, from one which *is to be* mentioned; or it may, in general, denote a difference among the several individuals or parties which compose the whole number spoken of.

When ἄλλος is *prospective*, and is followed by another ἄλλος or an equivalent pronoun used *retrospectively*, it is commonly translated by *one*. When it is *distributive*, it is combined with another ἄλλος, or with one of its derivatives, and is commonly translated by two pronouns, as *one . . another*, *this . . that*, &c., the sentence being resolved into two. Examples are subjoined of ἄλλος and its derivatives, as used,

α.) RETROSPECTIVELY. Ὅπου δὲ ἱκανὸν ἔργον ἑνὶ ἕψειν κρέα, ἄλλῳ ὀπτᾶν, ἄλλῳ δὲ ἰχθὺν ἕψειν, ἄλλῳ ὀπτᾶν, ἄλλῳ ἄρτους ποιεῖν, 'for one man to boil meat, for another to roast it, &c.,' Cyr. viii. 2. 6. Μείναντες δὲ ταύτην τὴν ἡμέραν, τῇ ἄλλῃ ἐπορεύοντο, 'on the next,' iii. 4. 1. See § 457. ε.

§ 541. β.) PROSPECTIVELY. Τά τε ἄλλα ἐτίμησε, καὶ μυρίους ἔδωκε δαρεικούς, *both honored me in every other respect, and gave me ten thousand darics*, i. 3. 3 (§§ 432, 488. 5). Οὐδὲν ἄλλο πράξαντες ἢ δῃώσαντες, *having done nothing else than ravage*, H. Gr. vii. 4. 17.

NOTES. (a.) The neuter ἄλλο is often used with τί, τὶ, οὐδέν, and μηδέν, with the ellipsis of a verb, commonly ποιῶ, πράσσω, πάσχω, εἰμί, or γίγνομαι thus, Τί ἄλλο οὗτοι [sc. ἐποίησαν] ἢ ἐπεβούλευσαν; *What else have they done but plot against us?* Th. iii. 39. Ἄλλο τι ἂν ἢ . . ἀγωνιζοίμεθα; ii. 5. 10. Ἐκεῖνος οὐδὲν ἄλλο ἢ τοὺς πεπτωκότας περιελαύνων ἐθεᾶτο, 'did nothing but,' Cyr. i. 4. 24. Εἰ . . μηδὲν ἄλλο ἢ μετενέγκοις Ib. 6. 39. — (b.) Hence arises the use of ἄλλο τι ἤ, or, the ἤ omitted, ἄλλο τι (also written ἄλλοτι), as an *interrogative phrase;* thus, Ἄλλο τι ἢ περὶ πλείστου ποιῇ; *Do you* [do any thing else than regard] *not regard it of the highest consequence?* Pl. Apol. 24 c. Ἄλλο τι ἢ οὐδὲν κωλύει; *Does any thing whatever forbid?* iv. 7. 5. Ἄλλο τι οὖν οἵ γε φιλοκερδεῖς φιλοῦσι τὸ κέρδος; *Do not then the covetous love gain?* Pl. Hipparch. 226 e.

§ **542.** γ.) PROSPECTIVELY and RETROSPECTIVELY. Ἄλλος ἄλλον εἷλκε, *one drew up another,* v. 2. 15. Ἄλλος ἄλλον . . ἔθραυε, *they were dashing, one against another,* Soph. El. 728 (cf. § 145). Τότ' ἄλλος, ἄλλοθ' ἅτερος, *now one, and then the other,* Ib. 739. Ἄλλοτε καὶ ἄλλοτε, [at one time and at another] *now and then,* ii. 4. 26. So, when two are spoken of, Ὁ ἕτερος τὸν ἕτερον παίει, *the one strikes the other,* vi. 1. 5.

δ.) DISTRIBUTIVELY. Οὗτοι μέν, ὦ Κλέαρχε, ἄλλος ἄλλα λέγει, *these men, Clearchus, say, one one thing, and another another,* ii. 1. 15 (§§ 451, 497. 1). Οἱ δὲ πολέμιοι . . ἄλλος ἄλλῃ ἐτράπετο iv. 8. 19. Οὐ μὴν ἔτι ἀθρόοι, ἀλλ' ἄλλοι ἄλλοθεν, *no longer in a body, but some in this direction, and others in that,* i. 10. 13. Εἴκαζον δὲ ἄλλοι ἄλλως i. 6. 11. Ἄλλοτε ἄλλῃ ἀποβαίνων H. Gr. i. 5. 20.

CHAPTER V.

SYNTAX OF THE VERB.

I. AGREEMENT OF THE VERB.

§ **543.** RULE XXIX. A VERB agrees with its *subject* in *number* and *person;* as,

Ἐγὼ λήψομαι, *I shall take,* i. 7. 9. Σὺ ὁρᾷς ii. 1. 12. Ἠσθένει Δαρεῖος i. 1. 1. Ὑμεῖς δόξετε i. 4. 15. Διειχέτην τὼ φάλαγγε i. 8. 17.

NOTE. AGREEMENT, whether in the *appositive,* the *adjective,* the *pronoun,* or the *verb,* has the same general foundation, and, to a great extent, the same varieties and exceptions. The four rules of agreement may be thus presented in a tabular form: —

An APPOSITIVE	agrees with its subject in			CASE.	
An ADJECTIVE		GENDER,	NUMBER, and	CASE.	
A PRONOUN		GENDER,	NUMBER,		and PERSON.
A VERB			NUMBER,		and PERSON

§ **544.** REMARKS. 1. In COMPOUND CONSTRUCTION, both *syllepsis* and *zeugma* are common (§ 329. N.); thus,

Ἀπολελοίπασιν ἡμᾶς Ξενίας καὶ Πασίων i. 4. 8. Κύρου ἀποτέμνεται ἡ κεφαλὴ καὶ χεὶρ ἡ δεξιά. Βασιλεὺς δὲ καὶ οἱ σὺν αὐτῷ διώκων εἰσπίπτει i. 10. 1 Βασιλεὺς δὲ καὶ οἱ σὺν αὐτῷ τά τε ἄλλα πολλὰ διαρπάζουσι Ib. 2. Κῦρός τε καὶ ἡ στρατιὰ παρῆλθε, καὶ ἐγένοντο i. 7. 16. Ἐγὼ καὶ σφὼ βαρείᾳ συμφορᾷ πεπλήγμεθα Eur. Alc. 404. Σὺ δ' ἡ μακαρία μακάριός θ' ὁ σὸς πόσις ἥκετον Eur. Or. 86. Δοκεῖς σύ τε καὶ Σιμμίας Pl. Phædo, 77 d. Cf. §§ 446, 497

NOTES. α. When the subject is *divided* or *distributed*, the verb sometimes agrees with the *whole*, and sometimes with *one of the parts*; thus, Ὅπη ἐδύναντο ἕκαστος, *where they each could*, iv. 2. 12. Ἀνεπαύοντο δὲ, ὅπου ἐτύγχανεν ἕκαστος iii. 1. 3. Πάντες δὲ οὗτοι κατὰ ἔθνη, ἐν πλαισίῳ πλήρει ἀνθρώπων ἕκαστον τὸ ἔθνος ἐπορεύετο i. 8. 9. Ἄλλος πρὸς ἄλλον διέβαλλον H. Gr. ii. 3. 23. Οὗτοι . . ἄλλος ἄλλα λέγει ii. 1. 15. See §§ 360, 497. 1, 542. δ.

β. In syllepsis, the poets sometimes adopt the following arrangement (termed by grammarians Σχῆμα Ἀλκμανικόν); Πυριφλεγέθων τε ῥέουσιν Κώκυτός τε κ. 513. Εἰ δέ κ' Ἄρης ἄρχωσι μάχης ἢ Φοῖβος Υ. 138.

§ **545.** 2. ELLIPSIS. When the *subject* is sufficiently indicated by the *form of the verb* or the *context*, and no stress is laid upon it, it is commonly *omitted*. This remark applies,

a.) To the *first* and *second personal pronouns*, and likewise to the *third*, when its reference is sufficiently determined by the connection; thus, Ἐπεὶ δὲ ἠσθένει Δαρεῖος . ., ἐβούλετο, *and when Darius was sick, he wished*, i. 1. 1. See § 502.

NOTE. The personal pronouns are implied in the very affixes of the verb. See §§ 171, 172.

§ **546.** b.) To the *third personal pronoun*, when referring to a subject which is *indefinite*, or *general*, or *implied in the verb itself*; thus,

Ἐπεὶ συνεσκότασε, *when it grew dark*, Cyr. iv. 5. 5. Ἔσεισε, *there was an earthquake*, Th. iv. 52. Κατένιψε χιόνι τὴν Θρᾴκην ὅλην, καὶ τοὺς ποταμοὺς ἔπηξε Ar. Ach. 138. Ὀψὲ ἦν, *it was late*, ii. 2. 16. Ἦν ἀμφὶ ἀγορὰν πλήθουσαν i. 8. 1. Ὡς ἔοικεν, *as it seems*, vi. 1. 30. Οὕτω δὲ ἔχει, [and it has itself thus] *and thus the matter stands*, v. 6. 12. Ἐν τούτῳ ἴσχετο vi. 3. 9. Καλῶς ἔσται vii. 3. 43. Ἐδήλωσε δέ Mem. i. 2. 32. Ὡς δὲ αὐτῷ οὐ προυχώρει, *but when* [it did not succeed to him] *he met with no success*, Th. i. 109. Κάτω διεχώρει αὐτοῖς iv. 8. 20. Μάχης δεῖ, *there is need of a battle*, or *there must be fighting*, ii. 3. 5 (see §§ 357, 430. R.). Ἐμοὶ μελήσει περὶ τροφῆς αὐτῶν, [there shall be to me a care] *I will take care of their support*, Cyr. iv. 5. 17 (see § 376. δ.). Τοῖς μὲν πειθομένοις αὐτῷ συνέφερε, τοῖς δὲ μὴ πειθομένοις μετέμελε Mem. i. 1. 4. Λέγουσιν, ὅτι ἐπὶ τοῦτο ἔρχονται, 'they say,' Cyr. i. 2. 6. Καὶ οὐδὲν μέντοι οὐδὲ τοῦτον παθεῖν ἔφασαν (cf. Τοξευθῆναί τις ἐλέγετο) i. 8. 20. Ὅπερ πάσχουσιν ἐν τοῖς μεγάλοις ἀγῶσι Th. vii. 69. Οὔτε ἄρα ἀνταδικεῖν δεῖ, . . ὁτιοῦν πάσχῃ, *it is not right then to return an injury, whatever one may suffer*, Pl. Crito, 49 c. Ἡ τοῦ οἴεσθαι εἰδέναι [ἀμαθία], ἃ οὐκ οἶδεν, *the folly of one's supposing that he knows what he does not know*, Pl. Apol. 29 b. Ἐπεὶ ἐσάλπιγξε [sc. ὁ σαλπιγκτής], *when* [he blew the trumpet] *the trumpeter blew*, or *at the sound of the trumpet*, i. 2. 17. Ἐσήμηνε τοῖς Ἕλλησι τῇ σάλπιγγι iii. 4. 4 (cf. Ἐν τούτῳ σημαίνει ὁ σαλπιγκτής iv. 3. 32). Ἐκήρυξε τοῖς Ἕλλησι [sc. ὁ κήρυξ], *proclamation was made to the Greeks*, iii. 4. 36. Τὸν νόμον ὑμῖν αὐτὸν ἀναγνώσεται Dem. 465. 14. Οἰνοχοεύει [sc. ὁ οἰνοχόος] φ. 142.

Notes. α. When the pronoun is wholly indefinite in its reference, or, in other words, when the verb simply expresses an action or state without predicating it of any person or thing, the verb is termed *impersonal* (in, *not*, persōna, *person*). A verb thus employed is a compendious form of expression for the *kindred noun* with a *substantive* (or *other appropriate*) *verb*; thus, *It rains* = *There is rain*, or *Rain falls*. An impersonal verb, from its very nature, is in the 3*d pers. sing.*; and an *adjective* joined with it is in the *neut. sing.*, or in the *neut. plur. for the sing.* (§ 451).

β. A verb is often *introduced as impersonal*, of which the subject is afterwards expressed in an *Inf.* or *distinct clause*; as, Ἐπεὶ δ' ἐδόκει αὐτῷ ἤδη πορεύεσθαι, *and when now it seemed best to him to march*, i. 2. 1. Οἷς καθήκει εἰς Καστωλοῦ πεδίον ἀθροίζεσθαι i. 9. 7. Δῆλον ἦν, ὅτι ἐγγύς που βασιλεὺς ἦν ii. 3. 6. Οὐκ ἦν λαβεῖν, [it was not, to take them, *i. e.* there was no such thing as taking them] *it was not possible to take them*, i. 5. 2. Ἔστι λαμβάνειν Ib. 3. Ἔξεστιν ὑμῖν πιστὰ λαβεῖν, *it is permitted you to take pledges*, ii. 3. 26. Ἔξεστιν ὁρᾶν, *you can see*, iii. 4. 39. Ἐγένετο . . πορεύεσθαι i. 9. 13. See § 523.

γ. Personal and impersonal constructions are so blended and interchanged, that it is often difficult to determine, whether a verb is to be regarded in a particular instance as *personal* or *impersonal*, and whether a neuter pronoun or adjective connected with it is to be regarded as *Nom.* or *Acc.*; as, Τί δεῖ αὐτὸν αἰτεῖν; [What needs him, *or*, What does it need him, § 432] *What need is there that he should ask?* ii. 1. 10. For the change of impersonal to personal constructions by attraction, see § 551.

δ. For the construction of verbs with the Gen. partitive, see §§ 361. β, 364.

§ 547. 3. The substantive verb is very often *omitted*, especially if it is merely a *copula*. Its omission is particularly frequent with *verbals in* -τέος, in *general remarks* and *relative clauses*, and with such words as ἀνάγκη, χρεών, εἰκός, θέμις, καιρός, ὥρα, δῆλος, ἕτοιμος, φροῦδος, δυνατός, οἷός τε, ῥᾴδιος, χαλεπός. Thus,

Τοῦτο οὐ ποιητέον [sc. ἐστί], *this must not be done*, i. 3. 15. Ἐν τῷ ἄντρῳ ὅθεν αἱ πηγαί, *in the cave, whence the springs*, i. 2. 8. Ποταμόν, οὗ τὸ εὖρος στάδιον (cf. Οὗ ἦν τὸ εὖρος) i. 4. 1. Δυσχρήστους εἶναι ἀνάγκη ἀτάκτους ὄντας (cf. Ἀνάγκη γάρ ἐστιν) iii. 4. 19. Ὡς τὸ εἰκός iii. 1. 21. Ὥρα λέγειν i. 3. 12. Δῆλον γάρ ii. 4. 19. Cf. §§ 528, 538.

§ 548. 4. Synesis affects the number of the verb in two ways: —

I.) A *plural verb* may be joined with a *singular Nom.*, if *more than one* are referred to; as,

Τὸ πλῆθος ἐψηφίσαντο, *the majority voted*, Th. i. 125. Ὁ ἄλλος στρατὸς ἀπέβαινον Id. iv. 32. Δημοσθένης μετὰ τῶν ξυστρατηγῶν Ἀκαρνάνων σπένδονται Id. iii. 109. Τὸ δὲ τῶν πρεσβυτέρων ἡμῶν . . ἡγούμεθα Pl. Leg. 657 d. See §§ 453, 497, 544. α.

§ **549.** II.) A *singular verb* may be joined with a *plural Nom.* regarded as but a *single object of thought*. This occurs chiefly in two cases: — (*a*) When the nominative is neuter, according to the following

SPECIAL RULE. The NEUTER PLURAL has its VERB in the *singular*.

That the want of agreement has in this case become the rule, seems to have arisen from the fact, that the neuter plural commonly denotes a mass of lifeless things, and likewise to be connected with the usage in §§ 336, 451. Exceptions are, however, frequent; chiefly, when things that have life are denoted, or when the idea of plurality is prominent, or in the non-Attic poets for the sake of the metre. Thus, Τὰ ἐπιτήδεια ἐπέλιπε, *provisions failed*, iv. 7. 1. Πλοῖα δ' ὑμῖν πάρεστιν v. 6. 20. Ταῦτα ἐδόκει ὠφέλιμα εἶναι, *these things* [or *this*] *seemed to be useful*, i. 6. 2 (cf. § 451). Ἐνταῦθα Κύρῳ βασίλεια ἦν i. 2. 7 (cf. Ib. 8). Ἐνταῦθα ἦσαν τὰ Συεννέσιος βασίλεια Ib. 23 (§ 336). Τὰ τέλη τῶν Λακεδαιμονίων ὀμόσαντα αὐτὸν ἐξέπεμψαν, 'the rulers,' Th. iv. 88 (cf. § 453. γ). Ὑποζύγια νέμοιντο ii. 2. 15 (cf. iv. 5. 25). Τὰ ὑποζύγια ἐλαύνετο iv. 7. 24 (cf. i. 5. 5). Ἦσαν δὲ ταῦτα δύο τείχη i. 4. 4. Φανερὰ ἦσαν καὶ ἵππων καὶ ἀνθρώπων ἴχνη πολλά i. 7. 17. Τὰ δ' ἅρματα ἐφέροντο i. 8. 20. Ἄστρα ἐν τῇ νυκτὶ ἀνέφηναν, ἃ ἡμῖν τὰς ὥρας τῆς νυκτὸς ἐμφανίζει Mem. iv. 3. 4. Ἔργα γένοντο Λ. 310. For such examples as Ὅσσε δαίεται ζ. 131, see § 337.

NOTE. In the following example, apparently upon the same principle, a series of feminine plurals denoting natural. phenomena is followed after an interval by a substantive verb in the singular; Καὶ γὰρ πάχναι καὶ χάλαζαι καὶ ἐρυσίβαι ἐκ πλεονεξίας καὶ ἀκοσμίας περὶ ἄλληλα τῶν τοιούτων γίγνεται ἐρωτικῶν Pl. Conv. 188 b. Cf. *b*.

(*b*) When the *verb precedes*, and is hence introduced as though its subject were, as yet, *undetermined* (cf. § 546. β). This construction is almost confined in prose to ἔστι and ἦν (compare, in French, the use of *il est*, and *il y a*). Thus,

Ἔστι γὰρ ἔμοιγε καὶ βωμοὶ καὶ ἱερά, *for* [there is to me] *I have both altars and sacred rites*, Pl. Euthyd. 302 c. Ἦν δ' ἀμφίπλεκτοι κλίμακες Soph. Tr. 520. Ἔστι τούτω διττὼ τὼ βίω Pl. Gorg. 500 d. Γίγνηται . . ἀρχαί τε καὶ γάμοι Id. Rep. 363 a. See § 523.

REMARK. A few other examples of the Nom. pl. masc. or fem. with a verb in the sing. occur in the poets; as, Κόμαι κατενήνοθεν Hom. Cer. 280. Ὕμνοι . . τέλλεται Pind. Ol. 11. 4. This construction was termed by the old grammarians Σχῆμα Πινδαρικόν or Βοιώτιον.

§ **550.** 5. ATTRACTION. The verb is sometimes attracted by a *word in apposition with the subject;* usually an *attribute* coming *between* the subject and the verb; as,

Τὸ χωρίον τοῦτο, ὅπερ πρότερον Ἐννέα Ὁδοὶ ἐκαλοῦντο, *this place, which was before called The Nine Ways*, Th. iv. 102. Ἔστον δὲ δύο λόφω ἡ Ἰδομένη ὑψηλώ Id. iii. 112. Ἄπαν δὲ τὸ μέσον τῶν τειχῶν ἦσαν στάδιοι ρεῖς i. 4. 4.

§ **551.** 6. A verb, of which the proper subject is an *Inf.* or *distinct clause* (or which is *impersonal* with an Inf. or clause dependent), often takes for a Nom. the *subject* of tha Inf. or clause. In this case, the Inf. sometimes becomes a Part. Thus,

Λέγεται Ἀπόλλων ἐκδεῖραι Μαρσύαν, *Apollo is said to have flayed Marsyas*, = Λέγεται, Ἀπόλλωνα ἐκδεῖραι Μαρσύαν, *it is said, that Apollo flayed Marsyas*, i. 2. 8 (cf. Λέγεται δὲ καὶ τοὺς ἄλλους Πέρσας . . διακινδυνεύειν i. 8. 7). Ἐλέγοντό τινες, ὡς γιγνώσκουσι Vect. i. 1. Ὁ Ἀσσύριος εἰς τὴν χώραν αὐτοῦ ἐμβαλεῖν ἀγγέλλεται Cyr. v. 3. 30. Ὡς ἀγγέλλοιτο ὁ μὲν Πείσανδρος τετελευτηκώς, *that* [Pisander was announced as having died] *it was announced, that Pisander was dead*, H. Gr. iv. 3. 13. Ὁμολογεῖται πρὸς πάντων κράτιστος δὴ γενέσθαι i. 9. 20 (cf. Ὁμολογεῖται . ., τοὺς ζῶντας ἐκ τῶν τεθνεώτων γεγονέναι Pl. Phædo, 72 a). Ὁ μὲν οὖν πρεσβύτερος παρὼν ἐτύγχανε [= Τὸν πρεσβύτερον παρεῖναι ἐτύγχανε], *the elder, therefore, happened to be present*, i. e. *it happened, that the elder was present*, i. 1. 2. Ὅτι πονηρότατοί γέ εἰσιν, οὐδὲ σὲ λανθάνουσιν [= λανθάνει] Œc. i. 19. Ἀρκέσω θνήσκουσ' ἐγώ [= Ἀρκέσει ἐμὲ θνήσκειν], *it will be enough that I should die*, Soph. Ant. 547. Ἅλις [sc. εἰμὶ] νοσοῦσ' ἐγώ Id. Œd. T. 1061. Τοσοῦτον ἀρκῶ σοι σαφηνίσαι μόνον, 'it is enough that I communicate,' Æsch. Pr. 621. Οὐ προσήκομεν κολάζειν τοῖσδε, *it does not belong to these to punish us*, Eur. Or. 771. Κρείσσων γὰρ Ἅιδᾳ κεύθων, *for* [he were better lying] *it were better he were lying in the grave*, Soph. Aj. 635. Δῆλός τε ἦν πᾶσιν, ὅτι ὑπερεφοβεῖτο, *it was manifest to all, that he was exceedingly alarmed*, Cyr. i. 4. 2 (cf. Ὅτι μὲν σφόδρα ἠνιάθησαν, πᾶσι δῆλον ἐγένετο H. Gr. vi. 4. 20). Δῆλος ἦν ἀνιώμενος, *it was evident that he was sad*, or, *he was evidently sad*, i. 2. 11. Στέργων δὲ φανερὸς μὲν ἦν οὐδένα, ὅτῳ δὲ φαίη φίλος εἶναι, τούτῳ ἔνδηλος ἐγίγνετο ἐπιβουλεύων ii. 6. 23. Σὺ οὖν ἡμῖν δίκαιος εἶ ἀντιχαρίζεσθαι, *it is therefore just that you should requite us*, Cyr. iv. 1. 20. Τοὺς σοφοὺς . . πολλοῦ δέω [= πολλοῦ δεῖ ἐμὲ] βατράχους λέγειν, [much is wanting in order that I should call] *I am far from calling the wise frogs*, Pl. Theæt 167 b. Οἵ τοσούτου δέουσι μιμεῖσθαι τὴν πρᾳότητα τὴν ὑμετέραν Isocr. 300 a. In like manner, Αὐτοῦ ὀλίγου δεήσαντος καταλευσθῆναι, *when he had* [wanted little of] *narrowly escaped being stoned to death*, i. 5. 14. See § 546. γ.

NOTE. Sometimes the two modes of construction are united; as, Σοὶ γὰρ δὴ λέγεται πάνυ γε τεθεραπεῦσθαι ὁ Ἀπόλλων, καί σε πάντα ἐκείνῳ πειθόμενον πράττειν Cyr. vii. 2. 15. Ἤγγελται . . ἥ τε μάχη πάνυ ἰσχυρὰ γεγονέναι, καὶ ἐν αὐτῇ πολλοὺς . . τεθνάναι Pl. Charm. 153 b. Ἔδοξεν αὐτῷ, βροντῆς γενομένης, σκηπτὸς πεσεῖν εἰς τὴν πατρῴαν οἰκίαν, καὶ ἐκ τούτου λάμπεσθαι πᾶσαν iii. 1. 11.

§ **552.** 7. The verb ἔφη is often separated from its subject by some of the words quoted; and is often thrown in *pleonastically*; as, "Εὖ λέγεις," ἔφη, "ὦ Σιμμία," ὁ Κέβης, "*You speak well, Simmias,*" *said Cebes*, Pl. Phædo, 77 c. Ὁ Ἡρακλῆς ἀκούσας ταῦτα, "Ὦ γύναι," ἔφη, "ὄνομα δέ σοι τί ἐστιν;" Mem. ii. 1. 26. Ἀποκρίνεται ὁ Χειρίσοφος· "Βλέψον," ἔφη, "πρὸς τὰ ὄρη" iv. 1. 20. See v. 1. 2; vi. 1. 31.

II. USE OF THE VOICES.

§ **553.** For a general statement of the use of the voices, see §§ 165, 166. *Irregularity* and *variety* in their use arise chiefly from the following sources: — (*a*) From the use of the same verb as *transitive* and *intransitive*, or as *causative* and *immediate*. See § 555. — (*b*) From the formation of a *new theme*, with a *strengthened meaning*. See §§ 265, 319. 2. — (*c*) From the variety and extent of the *reflexive* uses of the verb, and their intimate connection, on the one hand, with the *intransitive*, and on the other, with the *passive* use. See §§ 165, 166, 557 - 561. — (*d*) From a *transition of meaning* in the verb. See §§ 556, 561. 2. — (*e*) From *ellipsis*. See § 555.

§ **554.** As in most of the tenses the same form is both *mid.* and *pass.*, it is but natural that the distinction should be sometimes neglected in the *Fut.* and *Aor.* (§ 166). This occurs chiefly,

α.) In the use of the *Fut. mid.* for the *Fut. pass.*, as a shorter and more euphonic form; thus, Ἐξ ἐμοῦ τιμήσεται, *he shall be honored by me*, Soph. Ant. 210. Ψῆφος καθ' ἡμῶν οἴσεται τῇδ' ἡμέρᾳ Eur. Or. 440. Μαστιγώσεται, στρεβλώσεται, δεδήσεται, ἐκκαυθήσεται τὤφθαλμώ Pl. Rep. 361 e.

β.) In the use of the *Aor. pass.* for the *Aor. mid.* This occurs chiefly in *deponents* (§ 166. 2), and in other verbs in which the proper passive is wanting or rare. Thus, Ἠγάσθη τε αὐτόν, *admired him*, i. 1. 9. Διαλεχθέντες ἀλλήλοις, *having conversed with each other*, ii. 5. 42. Συναλλαγέντι i. 2. 1. Δεηθῆναι Ib. 14. Ἥσθη Ib. 18. Ἐδυνήθησαν iii. 1. 35. Ἐπιμεληθείητε Ib. 38. Φοβηθέντες ἀλλήλους ii. 5. 5.

NOTES. (1.) Whether verbs of the classes just mentioned employ the *mid.* or the *pass.* form of the *Aor.* must be determined by observation. (2.) Sometimes, though rarely, the *Fut. pass.* occurs as *mid.*, and the *Aor. mid.* as *pass.*; thus, Ἐπιμεληθησόμεναι Mem. ii. 7. 8. Κατέσχετο ἔρωτι δεινῷ Eur. Hipp. 27.

A. ACTIVE.

§ **555.** I. In many verbs in which the active voice is commonly or often transitive, it is likewise used *intransitively* or *reflexively* (§ 553). This use may be often explained by the ellipsis of a noun or reflexive pronoun (§ 427). Thus,

Ὁ δὲ βασιλεὺς ταύτῃ μὲν οὐκ ἦγεν [sc. τὸ στράτευμα], *but the king did not* [lead on his army] *advance in this direction*, i. 10. 6. Ἄγε δή, *come now*, ii. 2. 10. Φέρε δὴ τοίνυν Rep. Ath. 3. 5. Βάλλ' [sc. σεαυτόν] ἐς κόρακας! [Throw yourself to the crows] *Go, feed the crows! Go to the dogs!* Ar. Plut. 782. Ἡδονῇ δούς [sc. ἑαυτόν], *giving* [*himself*] *up to pleasure*, Eur. Ph. 21. Ἀνακάλυπτ', ὦ κασίγνητον κάρα Id. Or. 294. Ἐντεῦθεν ἐξελαύνει i. 2. 7 (cf. § 427). Οὕτω δὲ ἔχει, *and thus* [it has itself] *the matter stands*, v. 6. 12. Εἶχον δεινῶς, *they were in a sad condition*, vi. 4. 23 (see § 363. *β*). Προσέχειν [sc. τὸν νοῦν], *to give attention*, Mem. iv. 5. 6. Ὑποδείκνυσιν [sc. ἑαυτό] v. 7. 12. Παῦε τοῦ λόγου Ar. Ran. 580 (cf. i. 6. 6, and see § 560. 1).

NOTES. (*a*) Ἔχω used reflexively with an *adverb* is commonly equivalent to εἰμί with an *adjective*; thus, Εὐνοϊκῶς ἔχοιεν = Εὐνοϊκοὶ εἴησαν i. 1. 5.

Ἀθύμως ἔχοντες = Ἄθυμοι ὄντες iii. 1. 3. The poets even join ἔχω with an adjective; as, Ἔχ' ἥσυχος, [hold still] *be quiet*, Eur. Med. 550. (*b*) For the *intransitive* use of the *second tenses*, see § 257. β.

§ **556.** II. The active voice, through a *transition of meaning*, sometimes supplies the place of the *passive;* as,

Εὖ ἀκούω, *to hear agreeably*, and hence, from the bewitching sweetness of praise, *to be commended* or *spoken well of;* as, Μέγα δὲ εὖ ἀκούειν ὑπὸ ἑξακισχιλίων ἀνθρώπων vii. 7. 23. Ἵνα μὴ αὐτοὶ ἀκούωσι κακῶς, *that they themselves may not be spoken ill of*, Rep. Ath. 2. 18. Κλύειν ἄναλκις, *to be called a coward*, Æsch. Pr. 868. (Cf., in Lat., *bene audire*, *male audire*.) Ἀπέθανεν ὑπὸ Νικάνδρου, *he* [died] *was killed by Nicander*, v. 1. 15 (see § 295, κτείνω). Ἐδύνατο . . ἑλεῖν. . . Οὕτως ἑάλω. *He was able to take it. . . It was thus taken*, iii. 4. 12 (see § 301. 1). Οἱ ἐκπεπτωκότες Ῥοδίων ὑπὸ τοῦ δήμου, *those of the Rhodians who had* [fallen out of the city] *been banished by the people*, H. Gr. iv. 8. 20. Ὅτι φεύγοιεν οἴκοθεν ὑπὸ τοῦ δήμου, *that they were* [fleeing] *banished from home by the people*, H. Gr. i. 1. 27. Ἀσεβείας φεύγοντα ὑπὸ Μελίτου, *accused of impiety by Melitus*, Pl. Apol. 35 d (§ 374). Καταστὰς ὑφ' ὑμῶν, *appointed by you*, Dem. 49. 11. Cf. § 561. 2. — For the Inf. *act.* instead of *pass.*, see § 621. β.

B. Middle.

§ **557.** The reflexive sense of the middle voice is far from being uniform either in kind or force. It not only varies in different verbs, but often in the same verb when used in different connections. It is,

a.) Direct; so that the middle is equivalent to the active with the *Acc.* of the *reflexive pronoun;* as, Λοῦται [= Λούει ἑαυτόν], *he is washing himself*, or *bathing*, Cyr. i. 3. 11. Πάντες μὲν ἠλείφοντο, *they all anointed themselves*, H. Gr. iv. 5. 4. Στεφανοῦσθαι πάντας Ag. 2. 15. Ὅταν δ' ἐγὼ ἐγκαλύψωμαι Cyr. viii. 7. 26. Ἐπιφερομένην, *bearing herself on*, i. e. *rushing on*, i. 9. 6. Τῶν ἀδίκων ἀπεχόμενος, *refraining* [holding himself] *from injustice*, Mem. iv. 8. 4. Ὁ δ' ἄλλος στρατὸς . . ἐξωπλίζετο πολλοῖς μὲν καὶ καλοῖς χιτῶσι· . . ὥπλιζον δὲ καὶ ἵππους προμετωπιδίοις Cyr. vi. 4. 1. Φυγῇ ἄλλος ἄλλῃ ἐτράπετο iv. 8. 19 (cf. Εἰς φυγὴν ἔτρεψε τοὺς ἑξακισχιλίους i. 8. 24).

§ **558.** b.) Indirect; so that the middle is equivalent to the active with the *Dat.* or *Gen.* of the *reflexive pronoun;* as, Στρατηγοὺς μὲν ἑλέσθαι [= ἑλεῖν ἑαυτοῖς] ἄλλους, τὰ δ' ἐπιτήδεια ἀγοράζεσθαι [= ἀγοράζειν ἑαυτοῖς], *to* [take for themselves] *choose other generals, and to supply themselves with necessaries*, i. 3. 14. Παῖδα . . σὲ ποιοῦμαι, *I make you a son to myself*, or *I make you my son*, Cyr. iv. 6. 2. Ἀπὸ γεωργίας τὸν βίον ποιεῖσθαι Œc. 6. 11. Ὅτι περὶ πλείστου ποιοῖτο, *that he* [made it to himself] *esteemed it of the utmost consequence*, i. 9. 7. Καταστρεψάμενος μὲν πάντας Σύρους, 'having subjected to himself,' Cyr. i. 5. 2. Κῦρον δὲ μεταπέμπεται, *but he sends for Cyrus* (to come to himself), i. 1. 2. Τοῦτον φυλάττεσθαι, *to watch him for your own safety, to be on your guard against him*, i. 6. 9. Φέρονται δὲ οἴκοθεν . . κώθωνα, ὡς ἀπὸ τοῦ ποταμοῦ ἀρύσασθαι Cyr. i. 2. 8. Σπασάμενον τὸν ἀκινάκην, *drawing his scymitar*, i. 8. 29. Θέσθαι τὰ ὅπλα i. 6. 4. Κρέα θέμενος ἐπὶ τὰ γόνατα, 'upon his own knees,' vii. 3. 23. Ἀπόφηναι γνώμην, *express your opinion*, i. 6. 9. Παῖδά μ' ὠνόμαζετο, *he called me his son*, Soph. Œd. T. 1021. — Ἀποδίδομαι, *to give up for one's own profit*, hence *to sell;* as, Ταῦτα ἀποδόμενος, οὔτε Σεύθῃ ἀπέδωκεν οὔτε ἡμῖν τὰ γιγνόμενα, *having sold these things, he has neither paid over the proceeds to Seuthes nor to us,* vii. 6. 41. Λύομαι, *to loose for one's self, to deliver, to ransom, to redeem;* as, Εἴ τινας ἐκ τῶν πολεμίων ἐλυσάμην Dem. 316. 3. Τίθημι or γράφω νόμον, *to make a law for another,* τίθεμαι or γράφομαι νόμον, *to make a law for one's self;* as, Θεοὺς οἶμαι τοὺς νόμους τούτους τοῖς ἀνθρώποις θεῖναι, *I think that the gods have instituted these laws for men.* Οἱ ἄνθρωποι αὐτοὺς ἔθεντο, *men have instituted them for themselves,* Mem. iv. 4. 19. Νόμον οὗτοι ἔγραψαν, *these men* (the Thirty) *enacted a law,* H. Gr. ii. 3. 52. Ἢν νόμους καλοὺς γράψωνται, *if they* (the citizens) *should enact good laws,* Œc. 9. 14. Βουλεύω, *to give counsel to another,* βουλεύομαι, *to give counsel to one's self, to deliberate, to resolve* (¶ 35). Τιμωρέω, *to take vengeance for another, to avenge,* τιμωρέομαι, *to take vengeance for one's self, to punish.*

§ **559.** c.) Reciprocal; so that the middle is equivalent to the active with the *reciprocal pronoun;* as, Μαχόμενοι καὶ βασιλεὺς καὶ Κῦρος καὶ οἱ ἀμφ' αὐτούς, 'fighting with each other,' i. 8. 27. Ἀμφὶ ὧν εἶχον διαφερόμενοι, 'quarrelling,' iv. 5. 17. Διηλλάξαντο [τοὺς ἵππους], 'exchanged,' Cyr. viii. 3. 32. — Hence the middle is extensively used in expressing actions which imply mutual relation; as those of *agreement* and *contention,* of *greeting* and *companionship,* of *intercourse* and *traffic,* of *question* and *answer,* &c. Thus, Συντίθεμαι, *to agree,* διαλύομαι, *to become reconciled,* σπένδομαι, [to pour out libations together] *to make a treaty,* ἀγωνίζομαι, *to contend,* ἁμιλλάομαι, *to vie,* μάχομαι, *to fight,* ἀσπάζομαι, *to embrace, to salute,* ἕπομαι, *to attend upon, to follow,* διαλέγομαι, *to converse,* ὠνέομαι, *to buy,* πυνθάνομαι, *to inquire,* ἀποκρίνομαι, *to answer,* &c.

d.) Causative; so that the middle denotes what a person *procures to be done* for himself; as, Θώρακα ἐποιήσατο, *she had a corselet made,* Cyr. vi. 1. 51. Ἃ ὁ πάππος . . ἐπεποίητο Ib. i. 4. 18. Ἀπόλλωνος ἀνάθημα ποιησάμενος v. 3. 5. Ἐγὼ γάρ σε ταῦτα ἐπίτηδες ἐδιδαξάμην, *for I had you taught these things on purpose,* Cyr. i. 6. 2. Τράπεζάν τε Περσικὴν παρετίθετο Th. i. 130. Ἐκέλευον ἀπογράφεσθαι πάντας, *they commanded all to* [have their names registered] *give in their names,* H. Gr. ii. 4. 8. — Γράφομαί τινα, *to have the name of any one taken down as a criminal,* hence *to accuse;* as, Οἱ γραψάμενοι Σωκράτην Mem. i. 1. 1. Πρεσβεύω, *to go as an ambassador,* πρεσβεύομαι, *to send an ambassador;* as, Ὅσπερ ἐπρέσβευεν αὐτῷ πάντοτε vii. 2. 23; Οἱ πολέμιοι ἐπρεσβεύοντο Ag. 2. 21. Μισθόω, *to let upon hire,* μισθόομαι, [to procure to be let to one's self upon hire] *to hire;* as, Πλοῖον μισθωσάμενος vi. 4. 13.

§ **560.** e.) Subjective; so that the middle represents the action as *more nearly concerning the subject,* than the active (see § 174). Thus, (1.) if the active is a *causative* verb, the middle may form the corresponding *immediate,* (2.) if the active expresses an *external* or *physical* action, the middle may express the analogous *internal* or *mental* action; (3.) if the active represents a person as *having* a particular office, condition, or character, the middle may represent him as making it more his own by *acting in accordance* with it. Thus, —(1.) Γεύω, *to make another taste,* γεύομαι, *to taste for one's self* (see §§ 375, 430). Παύω, *to make to cease,* παύομαι, *to cease;* as, Ἔπαυσε μὲν τούτων πολλούς Mem. i. 2. 2; Ταῦτα εἰπὼν ἐπαύσατο i. 3. 12. Φοβέω, *to cause to fear, to terrify,* φοβέομαι, *to fear;* as, Τοὺς ἑπομένους πολεμίους φοβῆσαι iv. 5. 17; Ἐφοβοῦντο αὐτόν i. 9. 9. Αἰσχύνω, *to put to shame,* αἰσχύνομαι, *to be ashamed.* Ἵστημι, *to make to stand, to station,* ἵσταμαι, *to stand* (¶ 48). Κοιμάω, *to put to sleep,* κοιμάομαι, *to sleep.* Ὀρέγω, *to stretch out,* ὀρέγομαι, *to reach after,* hence *to desire.* Πείθω, *to persuade,* πείθομαι, *to believe, to obey.* Περαιόω, *to carry across,* περαιόομαι, *to go across.* Στέλλω, *to fit out, to send,* στέλλομαι, *to set out, to go.* Φαίνω, *to show,* φαίνομαι, *to appear.* — (2.) Ὁρίζω, *to bound,* ὁρίζομαι, *to determine;* as, Ποταμὸν, . . ὃς ὁρίζει τὴν Ἀρμενίαν iv. 3. 1; Οἱ πλεῖστοι ὁρίζονται τοὺς εὐεργέτας ἑαυτῶν ἄνδρας ἀγαθοὺς εἶναι H. Gr. vii. 3. 12. Σκοπέω, *to view, to observe,* σκοπέομαι, *to consider;* as, Οἱ λοχᾶγοὶ ἐσκόπουν, εἰ οἷόν τε εἴη τὴν ἄκραν λαβεῖν· . . σκοπουμένοις δὲ αὐτοῖς ἔδοξε παντάπᾶσιν ἀνάλωτον εἶναι τὸ χωρίον v. 2. 20. Ἀγάλλω, *to adorn,* ἀγάλλομαι, *to pride one's self.* Φράζω, *to tell,* φράζομαι, *to tell one's self, to reflect.* — (3.) Πολιτεύω (from πολίτης, *citizen*), *to be a citizen,* πολιτεύομαι, *to conduct one's self as a citizen, to engage in politics, to manage state affairs;* as, Φυγάδα ἐξ Ἀθηνῶν, . . πολιτεύοντα παρ' αὐτοῖς [i. e. τοῖς Θυριεῦσι] H. Gr. i. 5. 19; Οἱ μὲν πολιτευόμενοι ἐν ταῖς πατρίσι καὶ νόμους τίθενται Mem. ii. 1. 14.

§ **561.** Remarks. 1. If the reflexive action is *direct* or *prominent,* the *reflexive pronoun* is commonly employed; more frequently with the active voice (if in use), but often with the middle; as, Ἐκεῖνος ἀπέσφαξεν ἑαυτόν, *he slew himself,* Dem. 127. 3. Οἱ μέν φασι βασιλέα κελεῦσαί τινα ἐπισφάξαι αὐτὸν Κύρῳ, οἱ δὲ ἑαυτὸν ἐπισφάξασθαι i. 8. 29. Ἐπισφαλεστέραν αὐτὴν . . κατεσκεύακεν ἑαυτῷ Dem. 22. 13. Ἑαυτῷ ὄνομα καὶ δύναμιν περιποιήσασθαι v. 6. 17. Διελέγοντό τε ἑαυτοῖς, *they talked with themselves,* v. 4. 34 (cf. § 559). Μετεπέμπετο τὸν Συέννεσιν πρὸς ἑαυτόν i. 2. 26 (cf. § 558). Συνεγένοντο ἀλλήλοις Ib. 27. See § 504.

2. The middle voice, by a transition of meaning, (*a*) often becomes in its force the active of a new verb; and (*b*) sometimes, like the active, supplies the place of the passive (§ 556). Thus, — (*a*) Κόπτω, *to smite,* κόπτομαι, *to smite one's self through grief,* hence *to bewail;* as, Κόπτεσθ' Ἄδωνιν Ar. Lys. 396. See §§ 558 – 560. — (*b*) Ἀπώλοντο ὑπό τε τῶν πολεμίων καὶ χιόνος, 'were destroyed by,' v. 3. 3. Ἀκούσομαι κακός, *I shall be called a villain,* Soph. Œd. C. 988 (cf. § 556). Οὐδὲ τούτων στερήσονται, *they shall not* [want] *be deprived of these,* i. 4. 8.

3. In many cases, the reflex reference is so *obvious,* or so *indistinct,* that it may be either expressed or omitted without affecting the sense; that is, the *active* or the *middle* may be employed at pleasure; thus, Αἰτεῖ αὐτόν i. 1. 10. Ἠιτούμην βασιλέα ii. 3. 19. Πολὺ φέροιεν. . . Μικρὸν φερομένων Mem. iii. 14. 1. Πολύν γε μισθὸν . . φέροιτο Œc. i. 4. Μισθὸν τούτου φέροι Ib. 6. Παφλαγόνας ξυμμάχους ποιήσεσθε· . . φίλον ποιήσομεν τὸν Παφλαγόνα v. 5. 22 (cf. Ib. 12, § 558). Οἱ στρατιῶται ἠγόραζον τὰ ἐπιτήδεια i. 5. 10 (cf. i. 3. 14, § 558). Εἶπεν ὅτι θῦσαί τι βούλοιτο. Καὶ ἀπελθὼν ἐθύετο vii. 2. 14. Ἐστράτευσαν ἐπὶ βασιλέα ii. 6. 29. Ἐπὶ τὸν ἀδελφὸν Ἀρταξέρξην ἐστρατεύετο ii. 1. 1. — In some verbs, the use of the mid. form is poetic, especially Epic.

4. It follows naturally from the distinction between the two voices, that the *middle* is more inclined to take its object in an *indirect* case than the *active;* thus, Οἱ δὲ φύλακες προσελάσαντες ἐλοιδόρουν αὐτόν Cyr. i. 4. 8. Ὁ θεῖος αὐτῷ ἐλοιδορεῖτο Ib. 9.

C. Passive.

§ **562.** The passive voice has for its subject an *object of the active,* commonly (α.) a *direct,* but sometimes (β.) an *indirect* object. Any *other word* governed by the active *remains unchanged* with the passive. The subject of the ac-

TIVE is expressed, with the passive, by the *Gen. with a preposition* (commonly ὑπό, but sometimes ἀπό, ἐξ, παρά, or πρός), or, less frequently, by the *simple Gen.* or *Dat.* (§§ 381, 417), or, yet more rarely (chiefly in poetry, especially Ep.), by the *Dat. with* ὑπό. Thus,

α. Περιεῤῥεῖτο δ' αὐτὴ ὑπὸ τοῦ Μάσκα, *and it was surrounded by the Mascas* [= Περιέῤῥει δ' αὐτὴν ὁ Μάσκας, *and the Mascas surrounded it*], i. 5. 4. Οὐδένα κρίνω ὑπὸ πλειόνων πεφιλῆσθαι, *I judge that no one has been loved by more* [= Κρίνω πλείους πεφιληκέναι οὐδένα, *I judge that more have loved no one*], i. 9. 28. Εἰ θαλάττης εἴργοιντο, *if they should be excluded from the sea*, H. Gr. vii. 1. 8 (§ 347). Τῶν δ' ἱππέων ὁ λόφος ἐνεπλήσθη i. 10. 12 (§ 357). Ἠξίου . . δοθῆναι οἱ ταύτας τὰς πόλεις i. 1. 8 (§ 404. δ). Μουσικὴν μὲν ὑπὸ Λάμπρου παιδευθείς, *having been taught music by Lamprus* Pl. Menex. 236 a (§ 436). Ἐγὼ ἐπείσθην τε ταῦτα ὑπὸ σοῦ Cyr. v. 5. 16. Συληθεὶς γὰρ Ἡρακλῆς τὰς βοῦς . . ὑπὸ Νηλέως, *for Hercules having been robbed of his kine by Neleus*, Isocr. 119 d. Τί δῆτα . . οὐ καὶ σὺ τύπτει τὰς ἴσας πληγὰς ἐμοί, *why then are not you beaten the same number of blows with me*, Ar. Ran. 635 (§ 435). Τοιοῦτον τμῆμα τέμνεται τὸ τετμημένον, οἷον τὸ τέμνον τέμνει, *the thing cut is cut such a cut as the cutter cuts*, Pl. Gorg. 476 d. Τὰ μεγάλα [sc. μυστήρια] μεμύησαι, πρὶν τὰ σμικρά, *you have been initiated into the greater mysteries before the less*, Ib. 497 c. Ἄλλαι τε γνῶμαι ἀφ' ἑκάστων ἐλέγοντο Th. iii. 36. Ἐκ βασιλέως δεδομέναι i. 1. 6. Παρὰ πάντων ὁμολογεῖται i. 9. 1. Ὁμολογεῖται πρὸς πάντων Ib. 20. Ὑπὸ πόλεως τεταγμένοι, ἢ ὑπὸ τοῦ δεῖσθαι ἢ ἄλλῃ τινὶ ἀνάγκῃ κατεχόμενοι ii. 6. 13. Υἱὸς ὑπὸ τῷ πατρὶ τεθραμμένος, 'brought up [under] by his father,' Pl. Rep. 558 d.

β. Κατεφρονήθην ὑπ' αὐτοῖν, *I was despised by them* [= Κατεφρονησάτην μου, *they despised me*], Pl. Euthyd. 273 c (§ 375). Τὸ κρατεῖν ἡδονῶν. . . Κρατοῖντ' ἂν ὑπὸ τοῦ Ἔρωτος Id. Conv. 196 c (§ 350). Ἀπιστοῦνται δ' ὑφ' ἁπάντων Πελοποννησίων, *and they are distrusted by all the Peloponnesians* [= Οἱ δὲ Πελοποννήσιοι ἅπαντες ἀπιστοῦσιν αὐτοῖς], Isocr. 92 a (§ 406). Οἱ τῶν Ἀθηναίων ἐπιτετραμμένοι τὴν φυλακήν, *those of the Athenians who had been intrusted with the guard* [= οἷς ἡ φυλακὴ ἐπετέτραπτο, *to whom the guard had been intrusted*], Th. i. 126. Οἱ Κορίνθιοι ταῦτα ἐπεσταλμένοι, *the Corinthians having received these directions*, Id. v. 37.

§ 563. REMARKS. 1. When the active has more than one object, it is commonly determined which shall be the subject of the passive by one or the other of the following preferences; — (*a*) *The passive prefers, as its subject, a direct to an indirect object of the active.* — (*b*) *The passive prefers, as its subject, the name of a person to that of a thing.* — If these preferences conflict, sometimes the one prevails, and sometimes the other. The latter preference often leads to construction by *synecdoche* (§ 438); thus, Ἀποτμηθέντες τὰς κεφαλάς, *cut off as to their heads* [= Ἀποτμηθεισῶν τῶν κεφαλῶν, *their heads being cut off*], ii. 6. 1 (cf. Κύρου ἀποτέμνεται ἡ κεφαλή i. 10. 1). Διεφθαρμένοι . . τοὺς ὀφθαλμούς [= Ἔχοντες τοὺς ὀφθαλμοὺς διεφθαρμένους] iv. 5. 12. Τὰ ὦτα τετρυπημένον, *having his ears bored*, iii. 1. 31.

§ 564. 2. The passive is sometimes the converse of the *middle* rather than of the active; and hence *deponents* may have a passive. Thus, Μισθωθῆναι δὲ οὐκ ἐπὶ τούτῳ ἔφασαν, 'that they had not been hired,' i. 3. 1 (§ 559. d). Θώρακας εὖ εἰργασμένας, *corselets well made*, Mem. iii. 10. 9 (cf. Ἀνδριάντας καλῶς εἰργασμένον, 'having made,' Ib. ii. 6. 6). Ἐργασθήσεται, *it shall be* *performed*, Soph. Tr. 1218. Ἐωνήθη δὲ ἔρια, *and wool was bought*, Mem. ii. 7 12 (§ 301. 8). Τὸ θεαθέν Th. iii. 38. Ὡς βιάζομαι τάδε Soph. Ant. 66. — This passive occurs chiefly in the *Perf.*, *Plup.*, and *Aor.*

3. If an active or middle which has *no object* is changed to a passive, it becomes, *of course*, IMPERSONAL (§ 546. α); and it *may* become so, with an *indirect object*. Thus, Ὑπῆρκτο, *a beginning had been made* [= Ὑπῆρξαν, *they had begun*], Th. i. 93. Ἐπειδὴ αὐτοῖς παρεσκεύαστο, *when preparation had been made by them* [= Ἐπειδὴ παρεσκευασμένοι ἦσαν, *when they had made preparation*], Ib. 46. Καλῶς ἄν σοι ἀπεκέκριτο [= ἄν ἀπεκέκρισο]; *Would* [it have been answered well by you] *your answer have been a good one?* Pl. Gorg. 453 d.

III. Use of the Tenses.

§ **565.** A general view of the distinctive offices of the Greek tenses, particularly as employed in the Indicative, has already been presented (§§ 167, 168). In explanation and completion of that view, it is essential to observe,

I. That, *out of the Ind.*, the tenses, except the *Fut.*, have no direct reference to a distinction of time, but simply to the RELATION OR STATE of the action as *indefinite*, *definite*, or *complete*, or, in other words, as *doing*, *done*, or *having been done* (§ 168).

Hence, if we omit the Fut., each of the three states or relations has but a *single tense-form* out of the Ind. This form, as it marks the distinction of time only occasionally and indirectly, may be termed *achronic* (ἀ-, *not*, χρονικός, *relating to time*); while the forms of the *Ind.*, as they properly and directly mark this distinction (though sometimes used *achronically*), may be termed *chronic*. The time of an action expressed by an achronic tense must be inferred from the connection. Thus (the star denoting that a form is wanting),

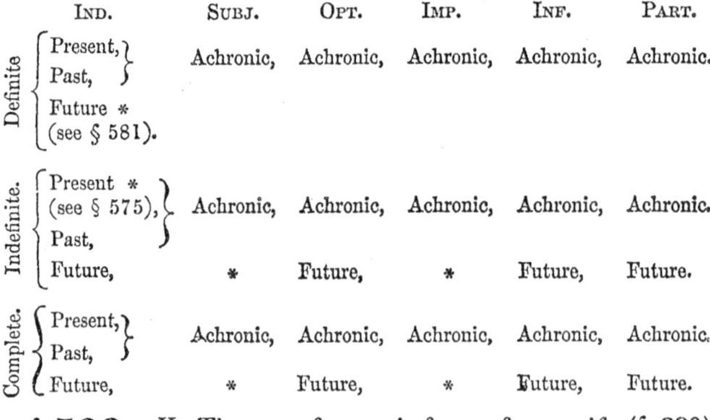

	Ind.	Subj.	Opt.	Imp.	Inf.	Part.
Definite	Present, Past,	Achronic,	Achronic,	Achronic,	Achronic,	Achronic.
	Future * (see § 581).					
Indefinite.	Present * (see § 575), Past,	Achronic,	Achronic,	Achronic,	Achronic,	Achronic.
	Future,	*	Future,	*	Future,	Future.
Complete.	Present, Past,	Achronic,	Achronic,	Achronic,	Achronic,	Achronic.
	Future,	*	Future,	*	Future,	Future.

§ **566.** II. The use of *generic* forms for *specific* (§ 330) has a peculiar prominence in the doctrine of the Greek tenses.

REMARKS. *α.* The PRES., in its widest generic sense, includes *all the other tenses* (see *β*); as a definite tense used *achronically* (§ 565), it includes the *Impf.* The IMPF., in its widest generic sense, includes *all the past tenses* (§ 173); and the AOR., *all the indefinite and complete tenses.* The PERF., as a generic tense, includes the *Plup.*

β. The distinction of *generic* and *specific* belongs not merely to grammatical forms, but also to the ideas which these forms represent. Thus the idea of PRESENT TIME, which applies specifically only to the passing moment, extends in its generic application to any period including this moment; and we speak of the *present month*, the *present century*, &c. In its widest extent, therefore, it includes all time. Hence *general truths, existing states and habits,* and *oft-recurring facts,* belong appropriately to the *present time.*

§ **567.** III. The relations of time have nothing sensible to fix the conceptions of the mind. It ranges therefore with freedom through all time, the past, the present, and the future; and, without difficulty, conceives of the *past* or *future* as present, and even of the *present* or *future* as already past. That the Greek language should have a peculiar freedom in the interchange of tenses, is but the natural consequence of the wonderful vivacity of the Greek mind. See §§ 330. 3, 576, 584, 585.

REMARKS. *α.* The Pres. tense, when employed by the figure of *vision*, in speaking of past events, is termed the HISTORIC PRESENT. See § 576.

β. Common facts, imagined scenes, and general assertions, not being confined to any particular time, may often be expressed in the present, past, or future, according to the view which the speaker chooses to take. E. g. we may say, "The wisest often err," or "The wisest have often erred," or "The wisest will often err." Thus, Ἡ *μὲν γὰρ εὐταξία σώζειν δοκεῖ, ἡ δὲ ἀταξία πολλοὺς ἤδη ἀπολώλεκεν, for good order seems to preserve, but disorder has already destroyed many,* iii. 1. 38. Οὐδέν *ἐστι κερδαλεώτερον τοῦ νικᾶν· ὁ γὰρ κρατῶν ἅμα πάντα συνήρπακε* Cyr. iv. 2. 26. Ἡ *δὲ ψυχὴ, . . ἀπαλλαττομένη τοῦ σώματος, εὐθὺς διαπεφύσηται καὶ ἀπόλωλεν* Pl. Phædo, 80 c. Κ*ρατεῖ δὲ μηχαναῖς ἀγραύλου θηρὸς ὀρεσσιβάτα, λασιαύχενά θ' ἵππον ὑπάξεται* Soph. Ant. 348. Ἄ*πορος ἐπ' οὐδὲν ἔρχεται τὸ μέλλον·* Ἅ*ιδα μόνον φεῦξιν οὐκ ἐπάξεται* Ib. 360. Ἐ*ν πολλοῖς μὲν, ὦ Δημόνικε, πολὺ διεστώσας εὑρήσομεν τάς τε τῶν σπουδαίων γνώμας καὶ τὰς τῶν φαύλων διανοίας· πολὺ δὲ μεγίστην διαφορὰν εἰλήφασιν ἐν ταῖς πρὸς ἀλλήλους συνηθείαις.* Οἱ *μὲν γὰρ φίλους παρόντας μόνον τιμῶσιν, οἱ δὲ καὶ μακρὰν ἀπόντας ἀγαπῶσι· καὶ τὰς μὲν τῶν φαύλων συνηθείας ὀλίγος χρόνος διέλυσε, τὰς δὲ τῶν σπουδαίων φιλίας οὐδ' ἂν ὁ πᾶς αἰὼν ἐξαλείψειεν* Isocr. 2 a. See §§ 575–578.

NOTE. The use of the Aor. by Homer in comparisons is particularly frequent; as, Ἤ*ριπε δ', ὡς ὅτε τις δρῦς ἤριπεν* Π. 482, cf. Γ. 33, &c. See also § 575. 2.

γ. A past tense may be used, in *speaking of that which is present, with reference to some past opinion, feeling, remark, action,* or *obligation;* thus, Κ*ύπρις οὐκ ἄρ' ἦν θεός, Venus was not then merely a goddess* (as we supposed her to be), Eur. Hipp. 359. Ἆ*ρ' οὐ τόδε ἦν τὸ δένδρον, ἐφ' ὅπερ ἦγες ἡμᾶς;* Pl. Phædr. 230 a. Δ*ιαφθεροῦμεν ἐκεῖνο καὶ λωβησόμεθα, ὃ τῷ μὲν δικαίῳ βέλτιον ἐγίγνετο, τῷ δὲ ἀδίκῳ ἀπώλλυτο, we shall corrupt and injure that, which* (as we said) *is* *improved by justice, and ruined by injustice*, Pl. Crito, 47 d. Ἱέναι σ' ἐκέλευον οἱ στρατηγοὶ τήμερον Ar. Ach. 1073. Ὤφελε μὲν Κῦρος ζῆν, [Cyrus ought to be living] *Would that Cyrus were living!* ii. 1. 4. Οὐκ ἐχρῆν μέντοι σκοπεῖν; *But ought you not to be considering?* Apol. 3. Cf., in English, the familiar use of *ought*, the Impf. of *owe*, as a Pres.

§ **568.** IV. The tense may vary according as an action is viewed in its relation to the *present time*, or to the *time of another action, either past or future.* The tense of an *Inf.* or *Part.* is commonly determined by its connection with another verb, without regard to the present time. In the *Ind.*, the tense is properly determined by the relation of the action to the present time; but in Greek, if the Ind. is dependent upon another verb, its tense is often determined by the time of that verb, particularly in *indirect quotation.* In the *Subj.* and *Opt.* modes, from their very nature, there is commonly a union of the two considerations. Thus,

Ὑπέσχετο ἀνδρὶ ἑκάστῳ δώσειν, *he promised to give each man* (the giving future at the time of the promise), i. 4. 13. Ἔχων ὁπλίτας ἀνέβη τριακοσίους, *he went up, having* (at the time of his going up) *three hundred hoplites,* i. 1. 2. Ἀνίσταντο . . λέξοντες ἃ ἐγίγνωσκον, *they rose to say* (future at the time of the rising) *what they thought* (past at the time of the narration), i. 3. 13. Πιστευθεὶς ἀληθεύσειν, ἃ ἔλεγες, ἐπῆρας vii. 7. 25. Εἶπε . ., στρατηγοὺς μὲν ἑλέσθαι ἄλλους ὡς τάχιστα, εἰ μὴ βούλεται Κλέαρχος ἀπάγειν · . . ἡγεμόνα αἰτεῖν Κῦρον, ὅστις . . ἀπάξει, *recommended, that they should immediately choose other generals, if Clearchus* [is] *was unwilling to lead them; that they should ask Cyrus for a guide, who* [will] *would conduct them back,* i. 3. 14. Τοῖς δὲ ὑποψία μὲν ἦν, ὅτι ἄγει πρὸς βασιλέα, *and they had indeed a suspicion, that he was leading them against the king,* i. 3. 21. Ἐθαύμασε, τίς παραγγέλλει i. 8. 16. Ἐπεμελεῖτο, ὅ τι ποιήσει βασιλεύς Ib. 21.

REMARK. An INFINITIVE, denoting an action which must be future, from the very nature of the governing word, often employs the *Fut.*, but far more frequently the appropriate *achronic* tense; thus, Συμπράξειν ὑπισχνεῖτο · ἐδεῖτο δὲ τὰς κώμας μὴ καίειν vii. 7. 19. Ὑπισχνῶνται προθυμότερον αὐτοῖς συστρατεύεσθαι Ib. 31. Μεμνῆσθαι ὑπισχνεῖσθε vii. 6. 38. Ὑπέσχετό μοι βουλεύσασθαι, ἐρέσθαι δέ με ὑμᾶς ἐκέλευσεν ii. 3. 20. See § 583.

A. DEFINITE AND INDEFINITE.

§ **569.** The INDEFINITE and the DEFINITE tenses are thus distinguished. The former represent an action *simply as performed;* the latter represent it *definitely as performing.* The former merely express that an action has been, is, or will be performed; the latter present a picture of the action in the course of its performance. The former take a single glance at it, as one complete act conceived of as momentary; the latter observe its progress, as begun and going forward by continued or repeated effort, but not yet complete.

If action is conceived of as *motion in a straight line,* the definite tenses may be said to present a *side view* of this line, so that it is seen *in its full length;* but the indefinite tenses to present only an *end view* of it, so that it appears as a *mere point.* Thus,

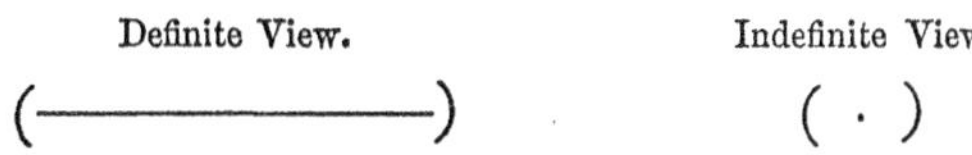

§ **570.** Hence an action is represented,

a.) By the definite tenses, as *continued* or *prolonged;* but by the Aor., as *momentary* or *transient.* Thus,

Τοὺς μὲν οὖν πελταστὰς ἐδέξαντο οἱ βάρβαροι καὶ ἐμάχοντο· ἐπειδὴ δὲ ἐγγὺς ἦσαν οἱ ὁπλῖται, ἐτράποντο. Καὶ οἱ μὲν πελτασταὶ εὐθὺς εἵποντο διώκοντες. *The barbarians then received the targeteers* (momentary) *and fought with them* (continued); *but when now the hoplites were near, they turned to flight* (momentary). *And the targeteers immediately followed pursuing them* (continued). v. 4. 24. Ἵνα ἢ . . ἡσυχίαν ἔχῃ, ἢ . . ἀφύλακτος ληφθῇ Dem. 45. 2. Διαλέγου, καὶ μάθε πρῶτον τίνες εἰσίν, *converse with them, and learn first who they are,* iv. 8. 5. Ἐπειδὰν ἅπαντα ἀκούσητε, κρίνατε, καὶ μὴ πρότερον προλαμβάνετε Dem. 44. 2. Δοθῆναί οἱ ταύτας τὰς πόλεις μᾶλλον, ἢ Τισσαφέρνην ἄρχειν αὐτῶν i. 1. 8. Λαβών, *having taken* (momentary). Ἔχων, *having* (continued), i. 1. 2.

NOTES. 1. Any dwelling of the mind upon the *agent*, *mode*, or *circumstances* of an action, and any attempt at *graphic description*, commonly lead to the use of the *definite tenses;* thus, Ἀπεκρίναντο (Κλέαρχος δ' ἔλεγεν), *they answered* (*and Clearchus was the speaker*), ii. 3. 21 (cf. ii. 5. 39; iii. 3. 3). Ἔλεγε Ξενοφῶν, ἡρμήνευε δὲ Τιμησίθεος v. 4. 4. See § 576.

2. In the IMPERATIVE, the momentary character of the AOR. is peculiarly favorable to *vivacity*, *energy*, and *earnestness* of expression; thus, Σὺ οὖν πρὸς θεῶν συμβούλευσον ἡμῖν ii. 1. 17. Ἀκούσατε οὖν μου πρὸς θεῶν v. 7. 5. "Βλέψον," ἔφη, "πρὸς τὰ ὄρη, καὶ ἴδε ὡς ἄβατα πάντα ἐστί" iv. 1. 20.

§ **571.** b.) By the definite tenses, as a *habit* or *continued course of conduct;* but by the Aor., as a *single act.* Thus,

Ἐπεὶ δὲ εἶδον αὐτὸν, οἵπερ πρόσθεν προσεκύνουν, καὶ τότε προσεκύνησαν, *and when those saw him who were before in the habit of prostrating themselves before him, they prostrated themselves even then,* i. 6. 10. Διέφθειρον γὰρ προσιόντες τοὺς στρατιώτας, καὶ ἕνα γε λοχαγὸν διέφθειραν iii. 3. 5. Ὅστις δ' ἀφικνεῖτο . . πρὸς αὐτὸν, πάντας οὕτω διατιθεὶς ἀπεπέμπετο i. 1. 5. Πολλάκις ἰόντες ἐπὶ τὰς θύρας ἀπῄτουν. Ὁ δὲ ἐλπίδας λέγων διῆγε i. 2. 11. Στρουθὸν δὲ οὐδεὶς ἔλαβεν· οἱ δὲ διώξαντες τῶν ἱππέων ταχὺ ἐπαύοντο i. 5. 3.—Hence the great use of the definite tenses in the description of character. See Anab. i. ch. 9; ii. ch. 6.

§ **572.** c.) By the definite tenses, as *doing at the time of*, or *until another action;* but by the Aor., simply as *done in its own time.* Thus,

Τούτῳ τῷ τρόπῳ ἐπορεύθησαν σταθμοὺς τέτταρας. Ἡνίκα δὲ τὸν πέμπτον ἐπορεύοντο, εἶδον βασίλειόν τι. *In this way, they made four day's-marches. And while they were making the fifth, they saw a palace.* iii. 4. 23. Ἀπέκτειναν συχνοὺς, . . καὶ ἐδίωκον μέχρι οὗ εἶδον, *they slew many, and continued the pursuit until they saw*, v. 4. 16. Τοῦτον ἐκέλευσε διαφυλάξαι αὐτῷ τήν τε γυναῖκα καὶ τὴν σκηνήν Cyr. v. 1. 2. Ταύτην οὖν ἐκέλευσεν ὁ Κῦρος διαφυλάττειν τὸν Ἀράσπην, ἕως ἂν αὐτὸς λάβῃ Ib. 3.

§ **573.** d.) By the definite tenses, as *begun*, *attempted*, or *designed* (doing, not done); but by the Aor., as *accomplished* (done). Thus,

Κλέαρχος τοὺς αὑτοῦ στρατιώτας ἐβιάζετο ἰέναι· οἱ δὲ αὐτόν τε ἔβαλλον. . . Τότε μὲν μικρὸν ἐξέφυγε τὸ μὴ καταπετρωθῆναι, ὕστερον δ' ἐπεὶ ἔγνω, ὅτι οὐ δυνήσεται βιάσασθαι. *Clearchus attempted to force his soldiers to proceed; but they began to stone him. He then narrowly escaped being stoned to death* (the completion of the act of stoning); *and afterwards, when he became convinced that he should not be able to prevail by force* (to accomplish his attempt). i. 3. 1. Ὅπως νῷν ἐγένεθ' υἱὸς οὑτοσὶ, . . περὶ τοὐνόματος δὴ 'ντεῦθεν ἐλοιδορούμεθα. Ἡ μὲν γὰρ ἵππον προσετίθει πρὸς τοὔνομα, . . ἐγὼ δὲ τοῦ πάππου 'τιθέμην Φειδωνίδην. . . Τῷ χρόνῳ κοινῇ ξυνέβημεν, κἀθέμεθα Φειδιππίδην. *When this son was born to us, thereupon we began to quarrel about the name. For she insisted on tacking* ἵππος *to his name, and I was for giving him his grandfather's name, Phidonides. At last we made a compromise, and named him Phidippides.* Ar. Nub. 60. Ὅτ' ἐξέβαλλον τοὺς θεοὺς, *when I was for expelling the gods*, Ib. 1477. Ἐκαινόμην ξίφει· ἀλλ' ἐξέκλεψεν . . Ἄρτεμις Eur. Iph. T. 26. Ὠνεομένοισι ἔδωκε δωτίνην Hdt. i. 69.

Notes. *α.* Hence the definite tenses are often used with a negative to *deny the attempt* as well as the *accomplishment* of an action; thus, Κλέαρχος οὐκ ἀνεβίβαζεν ἐπὶ τὸν λόφον, *Clearchus did not undertake to march upon the hill*, i. 10. 14. Ξενοφῶν τοὺς μὲν πελταστὰς οὐκ ἦγεν iii. 4. 39. Ἐπεὶ δὲ οὐδεὶς ἀντέλεγεν, εἶπεν iii. 2. 38. Ἐπεὶ δὲ οὐδὲν ὠφέλιμον ἔλεγεν, ὁρῶντος τοῦ ἑτέρου κατεσφάγη. Ὁ δὲ λοιπὸς ἔλεξεν. *And when he would say nothing useful, he was put to death in the sight of the other. But the second said.* iv. 1. 23.

β. A person is often spoken of as *having done* what he *has attempted to do*; thus, MEN. Δίκαια γὰρ τόνδ' εὐτυχεῖν κτείναντά με; TEYK. Κτείναντα; Δεινόν γ' εἶπας, εἰ καὶ ζῇς θανών. MEN. Θεὸς γὰρ ἐκσώζει με, τῷδε δ' οἴχομαι. Men. *For is it right that he should prosper, having slain me?* Teuc. *Having slain you? You tell a wonder, indeed, if, being dead, you are yet alive.* Men. *For heaven preserves me, but, so far as lay in him, I am no more.* Soph. Aj. 1126 (§ 410). Σὰν ψυχὰν ἀπέβαλον, τέκνον· ἔκτεινά σ' ἄκουσα Eur. Ion, 1498.

§ **574.** e.) By the definite tenses, as *introductory;* but by the Aor., as *conclusive*. Thus,

Οἳ ἠρώτων Κῦρον· . . ὁ δ' ἀπεκρίνατο, *who asked Cyrus; and he answered*, i. 3. 20 (cf. Ἀξιοῦν· . . ἀναγγεῖλαι Ib. 19). Ἀκούσαντες ταῦτα ἐπείθοντο καὶ διέβησαν i. 4. 16. Οἱ Ἕλληνες ἐβουλεύοντο· καὶ ἀπεκρίναντο ii. 3. 21.

Note. Verbs of *asking, inquiring, commanding, forbidding, deliberating, attempting, endeavouring, besieging, wounding*, and some others, are introductory in their very nature, and hence incline to the use of the definite tenses; thus, Τί δεῖ αὐτὸν αἰτεῖν, καὶ οὐ λαβεῖν ἐλθόντα; *Why must he ask for them* (which of itself accomplishes nothing), *and not come and take them* (which is final)? ii. 1. 10. Συλλέξας στράτευμα, ἐπολιόρκει Μίλητον καὶ κατὰ γῆν καὶ κατὰ θάλατταν, καὶ ἐπειρᾶτο κατάγειν τοὺς ἐκπεπτωκότας i. 1. 7. Καὶ πολλοὺς κατετίτρωσκον, καὶ ἐκράτησαν τῶν Ἑλλήνων iii. 4. 26.

§ **575.** REMARKS. 1. As the Aor. is an achronic tense, except in the Ind. (§ 565), it is in this mode only that the *Pres. indefinite* is wanting (§ 168. α). It is commonly supplied by the *Pres. definite*, but sometimes by the *Aor.* or *Perf.* See REM. 2, and §§ 233, 577, 578.

2. The AOR. in the *Ind.* is properly a *past tense;* but, from the want of the *Pres. indefinite*, it often supplies the place of this tense, or is used *achronically*. In these uses, it differs from the Pres. definite, in representing the action either *more simply* or *singly*, or with a certain expression of *instantaneousness*, *energy*, *decisiveness*, or *completeness*. Ἀνὴρ δ' ὅταν τοῖς ἔνδον ἄχθηται ξυνών, ἔξω μολὼν ἔπαυσε καρδίαν ἄσης, *and when a man becomes weary of the society of those at home, going abroad he relieves his heart at once of its disgust*, Eur. Med. 244. Καὶ ναῦς γὰρ ἐνταθεῖσα πρὸς βίαν ποδὶ ἔβαψεν, ἔστη δ' αὖθις, ἢν χαλᾷ πόδα Id. Or. 706. Ὅταν δ' ἐκ πλεονεξίας καὶ πονηρίας τις, ὥσπερ οὗτος, ἰσχύσῃ, ἡ πρώτη πρόφασις καὶ μικρὸν πταῖσμα ἅπαντα ἀνεχαίτισε καὶ διέλυσεν, 'instantly tosses off and dissipates,' Dem. 20. 25. Ταχὺ εἶπεν Pl. Rep. 406 d. Ἐπῄνεσ' ἔργον, *I fully approve the act*, Soph. Aj. 536. Σοὶ ταῦτα . . παρῄνεσα Id. Phil. 1433 Σὲ . . εἶπον τῆσδε γῆς ἔξω περᾶν, 'I bid you peremptorily,' Eur. Med. 271. Ὤιμωξα δ' οἷον ἔργον ἔστ' ἐργαστέον Ib. 791. Ἀπέπτυσα τοιάνδε συγγένειαν ἀλλήλων πικράν Id. Iph. A. 509. Ἥσθην ἀπειλαῖς, ἐγέλασα ψολοκομπίαις, ἀπεπυδάρισα μόθωνα, περιεκόκκυσα, *I enjoy your threats, I laugh at your boastings of smoke*, &c., Ar. Eq. 696. Ἐδεξάμην τὸ ῥηθέν, *I welcome the omen*, Soph. El. 668.

§ **576.** 3. The Greek has the power of giving to narration a wonderful variety, life, and energy, from the freedom with which it can employ and interchange the Aor., Impf., and Historical Pres. Without circumlocution, it can represent an action as continued or momentary; as attempted or accomplished; as introductory or conclusive. It can at pleasure retard or quicken the progress of the narrative. It can give to it dramatic life and reality by exhibiting an action as doing, or epic vivacity and energy by dismissing it as done. It can bring a scene forward into the strong light of the present, and instantly send it back again into the shade of the past. The variety, vivacity, and dramatic life of Greek narrative can be preserved but very imperfectly in translation, from the fact that the English has no definite tenses, except by circumlocution, and has far less freedom than the Greek in uniting the past and present tenses. Thus, Ἐπεὶ δὲ καὶ ἐνταῦθ' ἐχώρουν οἱ Ἕλληνες, λείπουσι δὴ καὶ τὸν λόφον οἱ ἱππεῖς· οὐ μὴν ἔτι ἀθρόοι, ἀλλ' ἄλλοι ἄλλοθεν· ἐψιλοῦτο δ' ὁ λόφος τῶν ἱππέων· τέλος δὲ καὶ πάντες ἀπεχώρησαν. Ὁ οὖν Κλέαρχος οὐκ ἀνεβίβαζεν ἐπὶ τὸν λόφον, ἀλλ' ὑπὸ αὐτὸν στήσας τὸ στράτευμα, πέμπει Λύκιον τὸν Συρακόσιον καὶ ἄλλον ἐπὶ τὸν λόφον, καὶ κελεύει, κατιδόντας τὰ ὑπὲρ τοῦ λόφου, τί ἐστιν, ἀπαγγεῖλαι. Καὶ ὁ Λύκιος ἤλασέ τε, καὶ ἰδὼν ἀπαγγέλλει, ὅτι φεύγουσιν ἀνὰ κράτος. Σχεδὸν δ' ὅτε ταῦτα ἦν, καὶ ἥλιος ἐδύετο. Ἐνταῦθα δ' ἔστησαν οἱ Ἕλληνες, καὶ θέμενοι τὰ ὅπλα ἀνεπαύοντο· καὶ ἅμα μὲν ἐθαύμαζον, ὅτι οὐδαμοῦ Κῦρος φαίνοιτο, οὐδ' ἄλλος ἀπ' αὐτοῦ οὐδεὶς παρείη i. 10. 13–16. See iii. 4. 25–27, 38, 39; i. 8. 23–27; iv. 7. 10–14; v. 4. 16, 17; vi. 1. 5–13.

4. There is no precise line of division between the offices of the definite and indefinite tenses. In some cases it seems to be indifferent which are employed. And the definite tenses, as the *generic forms* (§ 566. α), often occur, where the indefinite would seem to be more strictly appropriate. The use of the Impf. for the Aor. occurs especially in Hom. and Hdt.

5. In verbs in which the Aor. was not formed, or was formed with a different signification, the Impf. remained as both the definite and indefinite past tense; as ἦν and ἔφην (¶¶ 53, 55, § 301. 7), which are more frequently used as Aor.

B. Indefinite and Complete.

§ **577.** I. The indefinite and the complete tenses are thus distinguished. The former represent an action as *performed in the time contemplated;* the latter represent it as, *at the time contemplated, having already been performed.* In the former, the view is directed to the action simply; in the latter, it is specially directed to the completion of the action, and to the state consequent upon its performance. Hence arise two special uses of the complete tenses; the one to mark emphatically the *entire completion* or the *termination* of an action; and the other, to express the *continuance of the effects* of an action. Thus,

Τοιαῦτα μὲν πεποίηκε, *such things has he done* (and is now upon trial for), i. 6. 9. Ἔπειτ' ἀναγκάζω πάλιν ἐξεμεῖν ἅττ' ἂν κεκλόφωσί μου, 'whatever they may have stolen from me (and may have in their possession),' Ar. Eq. 1147. Ἦλθον οἱ Ἰνδοὶ ἐκ τῶν πολεμίων, οὓς ἐπεπόμφει Κῦρος ἐπὶ κατασκοπῇ, καὶ ἔλεγον, ὅτι Κροῖσος μὲν ἡγεμὼν . . ᾑρημένος εἴη τῶν πολεμίων· δεδογμένον δ' εἴη πᾶσι τοῖς συμμάχοις . . παρεῖναι· . . πεπομφέναι δὲ Κροῖσον καὶ εἰς Λακεδαίμονα περὶ ξυμμαχίας Cyr. vi. 2. 9. Περὶ μὲν οὖν τῶν ἰδίων ταῦτά μοι προειρήσθω· περὶ δὲ τῶν κοινῶν . ., 'let these things have been premised,' Isocr. 43 d. Ὡρίσθω ὑμῶν ἡ βραδύτης· νῦν δὲ . . βοηθήσατε, *let your sluggishness have reached its full limits; and do you now assist,* Th. i. 71. Ταῦτα μὲν οὖν, ὦ Εὐθύδημέ τε καὶ Διονυσόδωρε, πεπαίσθω τε ὑμῖν, καὶ ἴσως ἱκανῶς ἔχει· τὸ δὲ δὴ μετὰ ταῦτα ἐπιδείξατον Pl. Euthyd. 278 d. Ἀπειργάσθω δὴ ἡμῖν καὶ αὕτη . . ἡ πολιτεία Id. Rep. 552 e. Πεπειράσθω, [let it have been tried] *let a trial be made,* Ar. Vesp. 1129. Ἐξιόντες δὲ εἶπον τὴν θύραν κεκλεῖσθαι, *and going out they commanded the door* [to be closed and to remain so] *to be kept closed,* H. Gr. v. 4. 7.

§ **578.** Remarks. *α.* The consequences of an action are usually more obvious and more permanent in that which *is acted upon,* than in that which *acts.* The receiver feels the blow more deeply and longer than the giver. We find here a reason why the complete tenses are used so much more in the *passive* than in the *active,* and why, in the *active,* so many verbs want them altogether (§§ 256, 580).

β. As the object of the complete tenses is to ascribe the consequences of an action, rather than to narrate the action, they naturally occur more frequently in the *Part.* than in the other modes. Some modern languages, as the English, the French, the German, have no pass. form by inflection, except the Perf. Part.

γ. For the same reason, the transition in § 233 is natural and easy. We subjoin an example, which marks strikingly the distinction between the Perf. used as a Pres. and the Aor.; Τεθνᾶσιν οἱ θανόντες, *those who have died* (referring to the past event) *are dead* (referring to the present state consequent upon the event), Eur. Alc. 541 (but, Θνήσκω, *I am dying,* Ib. 284).

δ. In the Epic, the use of the Plup. as Impf. or Aor. is more extended than in the Attic, and has perhaps some connection with the usage in § 194. 3. Thus, Βεβήκει, *went*, A. 221. Βεβλήκει E. 66.

§ **579.** ε. The Perf. is sometimes called a *past*, and sometimes a *present* tense; and neither without reason, since it marks the relation of a *past action* to the *present time*. The *action* which it denotes is *past*; but the *state consequent*, to which it also refers, is *present*. The tense is therefore in its *time*, as in many languages in its *form*, COMPOUND, having both a *past* and a *present* element. The comparative prominence of these elements varies in different languages, in different words in the same language, and in different uses of the same word. We remark, in general, that the *present element* has a far greater prominence in the *Greek* than in the *English* Perf.

ζ. An action is sometimes so regarded as continued in its effect, that the *Pres.* supplies the place of the *Perf.* This is the common use of the Pres. in ἥκω, *to come*, and οἴχομαι, *to go* (cf., in Eng., *I am come*, and *I am gone*); and is not unfrequent in ἀκούω and κλύω, *to hear*, μανθάνω, *to learn*, νικάω, *to conquer*, and some other verbs. In these verbs, the *Impf.* may supply the place of the *Plup.* Thus, Εἰς καλὸν ἥκετε, *you* [come] *have come opportunely*, iv. 7. 3. Κῦρος δὲ οὔπω ἧκεν, *and Cyrus had not yet come*, i. 5. 12. Οὔτε ἀποδεδράκᾱσιν, οἶδα γὰρ ὅπῃ οἴχονται, 'whither they have gone,' i. 4. 8. Ὡς ἡμεῖς ἀκούομεν, *as we* [hear] *have heard*, v. 5. 8. Ἄρτι μανθάνω Eur. Bac. 1297. Νικῶμέν τε βασιλέα ii. 1. 4.

§ **580.** II. Unless the attention is specially directed to the *effect* of an action, the *generic Aor.* more frequently supplies the place of the *specific Perf. and Plup.* (§ 566. α), as a more familiar, more vivacious, and often a shorter or more euphonic form. This use prevails especially in the *active voice* (§ 578. α). The Aor. often occurs in immediate connection with the Perf. or Plup. Thus,

Ἐφ' ᾗ [κρήνῃ] λέγεται Μίδας τὸν Σάτυρον θηρεῦσαι, οἴνῳ κεράσας αὐτήν, *at which* [*fountain*] *Midas is said to have caught the Satyr, having mixed it with wine* i. 2. 13. Ταύτην τὴν πόλιν ἐξέλιπον οἱ ἐνοικοῦντες, *this city its inhabitants had left*, Ib. 24. Νυνὶ δὲ Θετταλοῖς . . ἐβοήθησε, *and now it has aided the Thessalians*, Dem. 22. 7. Τοιαῦτα παθὼν καὶ πάσχων, *having suffered and suffering such things*, Id. 576. 18. Ἀποδεδρακότες πατέρας καὶ μητέρας, οἱ δὲ καὶ τέκνα καταλιπόντες vi. 4. 8. Πενεστέρους πεποίηκε, καὶ πολλοὺς κινδύνους ὑπομένειν ἠνάγκασε, καὶ πρὸς τοὺς Ἕλληνας διαβέβληκε Isocr. 163 a. Οὐχ ὁ ἐσκεμμένος οὐδ' ὁ μεριμνήσας τὰ δίκαια λέγειν Dem. 576. 22. ΣΤΡ. Ἵνα με διδάξῃς, ὧνπερ οὕνεκ' ἐλήλυθα. ΣΩ. Ἦλθες δὲ κατὰ τί; Ar. Nub. 238.

NOTE. The use of the Aor. for the Perf. is especially common in the *Part.*

C. FUTURE.

§ **581.** I. The dim, shadowy future has little occasion for precise forms to mark the *state* of the action. It is commonly enough to mark the action *simply as future*. Hence the inflection of most verbs has but a single Fut., the *indefinite*; leaving the *definite* and *complete Futures*, if they require to be distinguished from this, to be expressed by a *Participle and substantive verb*; as,

Σκῦρος ἐξαρκοῦσά μοι ἔσται τὸ λοιπόν, *Scyros shall hereafter content me* (continued, § 570) Soph. Ph. 459. Τοῖσδ' ἔσται μέλον Id. Œd. C. 653. Ἄνδρα κατακανόντες ἔσεσθε, *you will have slain a man*, vii. 6. 36. Τὰ δέοντα ἐσόμεθα ἐγνωκότες, καὶ λόγων ματαίων ἀπηλλαγμένοι Dem. 54. 22.

§ **582.** II. The Future Perfect expresses the sense of the Perf. with a change of the time; that is, it represents the state consequent upon the completion of an action as future. As it carries the mind at once over the act itself to its completion and results, it is sometimes used to express a future action as *immediate*, *rapid*, or *decisive*, and hence received its old name of *paulo-post-future* (paulo post futurus, *about to be a little after*). In verbs in which the Perf. becomes a *new Pres.*, the Fut. Perf. becomes a *new Fut.* (§§ 233, 239). Thus,

Ἢν δὲ μὴ γένηται, μάτην ἐμοὶ κεκλαύσεται, *but if there should not be, I shall have wept in vain*, Ar. Nub. 1435 (§ 564. 3). Οὐδεὶς . . μετεγγραφήσεται, ἀλλ', ὥσπερ ἦν τὸ πρῶτον, ἐγγεγράψεται, *no one shall be enrolled* (the simple act) *elsewhere, but shall remain enrolled* (the state consequent upon the act of enrolment) *as he was at first*, Id. Eq. 1370. Φράζε καὶ πεπράξεται, *speak and it* [shall be done at once] *is done*, Id. Plut. 1027. Ὅταν δὴ μὴ σθένω, πεπαύσομαι, 'I shall desist at once,' Soph. Ant. 91. Νομίζετε ἐν τῇδε τῇ ἡμέρᾳ ἐμέ τε κατακεκόψεσθαι, καὶ ὑμᾶς οὐ πολὺ ἐμοῦ ὕστερον, 'shall be immediately cut down,' i. 5. 16. Ἐὰν γὰρ ἄρα ἐμοὶ δόξῃ τινὰ . . αὐτίκα μάλα δεῖν τεθνάναι, τεθνήξει οὗτος, 'he shall be dead,' i. e. 'he shall die instantly,' Pl. Gorg. 469 d (cf. Κατεαγὼς ἔσται, Διεσχισμένον ἔσται Ib.). Μεμνησόμεθα, *we shall remember*, Cyr. iii. 1. 27 (§ 233). Εὐθὺς Ἀριαῖος ἀφεστήξει· ὥστε φίλος ἡμῖν οὐδεὶς λελείψεται, *Ariæus will immediately withdraw; so that no friend will remain to us*, ii. 4. 5.

§ **583.** III. A future action may be represented more expressly as *on the point of accomplishment*, or as *connected with destiny, necessity, will, purpose*, &c., by the verbs μέλλω, ἐθέλω or θέλω, βούλομαι, δεῖ, χρή, &c., with the Inf. This Inf. may be *Pres.*, *Aor.*, or *Fut.*, according to the view taken of the action in respect to definiteness and nearness (§ 568. R.). Thus, Ἰδὼν παῖδα . . μέλλοντα ἀποθνήσκειν, *seeing a boy about to die*, vii. 4. 7. Ὁ σταθμὸς ἔνθα ἔμελλε καταλύειν i. 8. 1. Μελλήσαντά τι παθεῖν Cyr. vi. 1. 40. Εἰ μὲν πλοῖα ἔσεσθαι μέλλει ἱκανά, *if there are to be vessels enough*, v. 6. 12. Οὐκ ἐθέλω ἐλθεῖν, *I am not willing to go*, or *I will not go*, i. 3. 10. Ἐγὼ θέλω, ὦ ἄνδρες, διαβιβάσαι ὑμᾶς iii. 5. 8. Βουλεύεσθαι, ὅ τι χρὴ ποιεῖν i. 3. 11.

Remarks. (*a*) The ideas of *destiny*, *purpose*, &c., are often expressed by the simple Fut. Especially is the *Fut. Part.*, both with and without ὡς, used continually to express *purpose* (§ 635). Thus, Οἱ εἰς τὴν βασιλικὴν τέχνην παιδευόμενοι . . τί διαφέρουσι τῶν ἐξ ἀνάγκης κακοπαθούντων, εἴ γε πεινήσουσι καὶ διψήσουσι καὶ ῥιγώσουσι καὶ ἀγρυπνήσουσι, 'if they must hunger and thirst,' Mem. ii. 1. 17. Τὸν ὀρθῶς βιωσόμενον, *he that would live well*, Pl. Gorg. 491 e. Συλλαμβάνει Κῦρον ὡς ἀποκτενῶν, *he apprehends Cyrus* [as about to put him to death] *with the design of putting him to death*, i. 1. 3. Ἔπεμψέ τινα ἐροῦντα, *he sent one to say*, ii. 5. 2. Πεμφθεὶς παρὰ βασιλέως κελεύσων ii. 1. 17. Μαχούμενος συνήσει i. 10. 10. See § 531. α. — (*b*) Instead of the Fut. Part., the Pres. is sometimes employed to denote purpose, according to § 573, especially with verbs of motion; thus, Ταῦτ' ἐκδικάζων ἦλθον, *I went to avenge this wrong*, Eur. Suppl. 154.

§ 584. IV. A future action, in view of its *nearness*, its *certainty*, its *rapidity*, or its *connection with another action*, may be conceived of as *now doing*, or even as *already done* (§ 567); and may hence be expressed by the *Pres.*, *Aor.*, or *Perf.* Thus, Κακὸν ἥκει τινί, *evil is coming upon some one*, Ar. Ran. 552 (cf. Δώσει τις δίκην Ib. 554). Ἀπωλόμεσθ' ἄρ', εἰ κακὸν προσοίσομεν νέον παλαιῷ, πρὶν τόδ' ἐξηντληκέναι Eur. Med. 78. Εἴ με τόξων ἐγκρατὴς αἰσθήσεται, ὄλωλα, καὶ σὲ προσδιαφθερῶ, *if, while possessed of the bow, he shall discover me, I am undone, and I shall destroy you besides*, Soph. Ph. 75. Εἰ δὲ δὴ κατακτενεῖτέ με, ὁ νόμος ἀνεῖται Eur. Or. 940. Οὐκ εἶ ξυνέρξων, ἡνίκ' ἢ σεσώσμεθα κείνου βίον σώσαντος, ἢ οἰχόμεσθ' ἅμα; Soph. Tr. 83. Ἀπέσταλκά σοι τόνδε τὸν λόγον δῶρον Isocr. 2 b. — For *presents* which are commonly used as *futures*, see § 200. b.

§ 585. V. The FUTURE sometimes occurs for a *present* or *past* tense, as a less direct and positive form of expression, or as though the action were not yet finished; thus, Τοὐμὸν δ' ἐγὼ . . σπέρμ' ἰδεῖν βουλήσομαι, 'I shall wish,' i. e. 'am resolved,' Soph. Œd. T. 1076. ΧΟΡ. Παῖδες τεθνᾶσι χειρὶ μητρῴᾳ σέθεν. ἸΑΣ. Οἴμοι, τί λέξεις; Ὥς μ' ἀπώλεσας, γύναι Eur. Med. 1309. Πῶς φής; τί λέξεις; Ὥς μ' ἀπώλεσας, γύναι Id. Hel. 780. This exclamatory use of τί λέξεις for τί λέγεις or τί ἔλεξας, as though the communication were not yet finished, belongs particularly to Euripides.

IV. USE OF THE MODES.

§ 586. For a classification and designation of the modes according to the character of the sentences which they form (§ 329. N.), see ¶ 27.

A. INTELLECTIVE.

§ 587. Intellective sentences express the *actual* or the *contingent* (§ 329. N.). The idea of contingency is expressed in two ways; by the form of the verb, and by a particle, commonly ἄν (Ep. κέ or κέν, Dor. κά). The two ways are often united for the stronger expression; and they may be both neglected, if the idea is either not prominent, or is too obvious to require expression. The forms of the verb which in themselves express contingency are the *Subjunctive* and *Optative* modes (§ 169). Intellective sentences not employing these modes (either because they are actual, or because their contingency is simply expressed by a particle or is not expressed at all) employ the *Indicative*, which is the generic mode (§§ 177, 330. 1).

REMARKS. 1. It may be said in general, that *the Ind. expresses the actual; the Subj. and Opt., the contingent.* But it must be understood that this, like all similar statements in grammar, has primary reference to the conceptions of the mind, rather than to the reality of things; that is, to employ the technical language of philosophy, it must be taken *subjectively*, rather than *objectively*. The contingent is often, from strong assurance or vivid fancy, spoken of as actual; while, on the other hand, the actual, from diffidence or courtesy or some other cause, is not unfrequently spoken of as contingent. This statement is also limited by the generic use of the Ind., as mentioned above.

2. An action which is now future has, from the very nature of things, some degree of contingency; and therefore, in the Fut. tense, no distinction is made between the Ind. and the Subj., but any rule requiring in other tenses the Subj. in this requires the Ind. And even the use of the Fut. opt. appears to be limited to the *oratio obliqua*, in which it takes the place of the Fut. ind. in the *oratio recta* (§§ 607, 608).

§ **588.** 3. The particle of contingence, ἄν, may commonly be distinguished from the conjunction ἄν for ἐάν (§ 603) by its position, as it never stands first in its clause, which is the usual place of the conjunction. It chiefly occurs with the past tenses of the Ind. and with the Opt., to mark them as depending upon some condition expressed or implied; with the Subj. after various connectives; and with the Inf. and Part., when the distinct modes to which they are equivalent would have this particle. It is extensively used with the Subj., in cases where it would have been omitted with the Opt., for the reason, as it would seem, that the separation, in form, of the Subj. from the Ind. was later and less strongly marked than that of the Opt. (§ 177). The insertion or omission of ἄν for the most part follows general rules, but in some cases appears to depend upon nice distinctions of sense, which it is difficult to convey in translation, or upon mere euphony or rhythm. Upon its use in not a few cases, manuscripts differ, and critics contend. Verbs with which ἄν is connected are commonly translated into Eng. by the potential mode.

§ **589.** Contingency is viewed as either present or past; that is, a contingent event is regarded either as one of which there is some chance at the present time, or merely as one of which there was some chance at some past time. PRESENT CONTINGENCY is expressed either by *the Subj.*, or by *the primary tenses of the Ind.*; and PAST CONTINGENCY, either by *the Opt.*, or by *the secondary tenses of the Ind.*

The tenses of the Subj. and Opt. are therefore related to each other as *present* and *past* tenses, or, in sense as well as in form (§§ 168, 196), as *primary* and *secondary* tenses; and the rule above may be thus given in a more condensed form: —

PRESENT CONTINGENCY IS EXPRESSED BY THE PRIMARY TENSES; PAST CONTINGENCY, BY THE SECONDARY.

NOTE. Future contingency is contained in present; for that which *will be* contingent, is of course contingent *now*.

§ **590.** REMARKS. 1. It cannot be kept too carefully in mind, that the distinction above has no reference to the time of the *occurrence* of an event, but only to the time of its *contingency*. Thus, in the two sentences, "I can go if I wish," and "I could go, if I wished," the time of the *going* itself is in both the same, i. e. *future*. But in the former sentence, the *contingency* is *present*, because it is left undecided what the person's wish is, and therefore there is still some chance of his going; while in the latter, the *contingency* is *past*, because it is implied that the person does not wish to go, and therefore, although there was some chance of his going before his decision, there is now no chance. Hence, in the former sentence, present tenses are employed; and in the latter, past.

2. The limits of past are far wider than those of present contingency; for there is nothing which it is proper for us to suppose at all, of which we may not conceive that there was some chance at some distant period in past eternity. The dividing line between present and past contingency may perhaps be thus drawn; whatever is supposed *with some degree of present expectation*, or in *present view of a decision yet to be had*, belongs to the head of *present contingency*; but whatever is supposed *without this present expectation or view of a decision*, to the head of *past contingency*. Past contingency, therefore, includes, (1.) all *past* supposition, whether with or without expectation at that time; (2.) all supposition, whether present or past, which *does not imply expectation, or contemplate a decision*, that is, all *mere supposition*; (3.) all supposition, whether present or past, in despite of a prior decision. Thus:

A. PRESENT CONTINGENCY.

I will go, if I can have leave (and I intend to ask for it).
I think, that I may go, if I can have leave.
I wish, that you may go.

B. PAST CONTINGENCY.

(1.) Past supposition.

I thought, that I might go, if I could have leave.
I wished, that you might go.

(2.) Present supposition not implying expectation or contemplating a decision.

I would go, if I should have leave (but I have no thought of asking for it).
I could go with perfect ease.
I should like to go.

(3.) Present supposition in despite of a prior decision.

α. In regard to the present.

I would go, if I had leave (but I have none, and therefore I shall not go).

β. In regard to the past.

I would have gone, if I had had leave (but I had none, and therefore did not go).

§ 591. 3. As the difference between the Subj. and Opt. is one of time, rather than of essential office, some have chosen to consider them as only different tenses of a *general conjunctive* or *contingent mode*. With this change, the number and offices of the Greek modes are the same with those of the Latin, and the correspondence between the Greek conjunctive and the English potential modes becomes somewhat more obvious (see ¶ 33). According to this classification, which deserves the attention of the student, although it is questionable whether it is best to discard the old phraseology, the

Present Subjunctive	becomes the	Definite Present (or the Present) Conjunctive
Present Optative	" "	Definite Past (or the Imperfect) Conjunctive.
Aorist Subjunctive	" "	Aorist Present (or Primary) Conjunctive.
Aorist Optative	" "	Aorist Past (or Secondary) Conjunctive.
Perfect Subjunctive	" "	Perfect Present (or the Perfect) Conjunctive.
Perfect Optative	" "	Perfect Past (or the Pluperfect) Conjunctive.

4. Contingent sentences, like actual (§§ 566 – 568, 576, 584, 585), are liable to an interchange and blending of tenses. Past contingency is often conceived of as present; and present, as past. Hence, primary tenses take the place of secondary, and secondary of primary. This interchange may be observed particularly between the Subj. and Opt. modes.

§ **592.** The Subj. and Opt. occur, for the most part, in dependent clauses; and indeed some grammarians have refused to regard them as being ever strictly independent. It results from the principles already laid down, that, in their use as dependent modes, *the Subj., for the most part, follows the primary tenses; and the Opt., the secondary.* To this general rule, however, there are many exceptions.

Note. In the application of this rule, the tenses of the *Imperat.*, as from its very nature referring to present or future time, are to be regarded as *primary* tenses; those of the *Inf.* and *Part.*, as *primary* or *secondary*, according to the finite verbs, whose places they occupy, or, in general, according to those upon which they themselves depend.

§ **593.** In the expression of contingency, the Ind. is properly distinguished from the Subj. and Opt. by the greater positiveness with which it implies or excludes present anticipation. Thus supposition with present anticipation is expressed by the primary tenses; but there is here this general distinction, that the Fut. Ind. anticipates without expressing doubt, while the Subj. expresses doubt. On the other hand, supposition without present anticipation is expressed by the secondary tenses; but with this general distinction, that the Opt. supposes, either with some past anticipation, or without regard to any decision, while the secondary tenses of the Ind. suppose in despite of a prior decision.

Remarks. α. In the expression of contingency, the *Impf.* ind. has commonly the same difference from the *Aor.* and *Plup.*, as, in English, the Impf. ind. and potential from the Plup. In respect to the time of the action, therefore, the contingent Impf. ind. commonly refers to *present* time, and the Aor. and Plup. to *past*. See §§ 599, 601. δ, 603. δ.

β. We may, say in general, that *supposition as fact* is expressed by the appropriate tense of the Ind. (§§ 587, 603. α); *supposition that may become fact*, by the Subj.; *supposition without regard to fact*, by the Opt.; and *supposition contrary to fact*, by the past tenses of the Ind.; while in these tenses there is this distinction, that the Impf. expresses supposition *contrary to present fact*, but the Aor. and Plup. *contrary to past fact.*

γ. The Epic sometimes joins κέ with the Fut. ind., when it depends upon a condition expressed or understood; as, Εἰ δ' Ὀδυσεὺς ἔλθοι . ., αἶψά κε . . ἀποτίσεται ρ. 539. A similar use of ἄν in the Att. is rare and doubtful.

§ **594.** δ. Indefiniteness constitutes a species of contingency. Hence (1.) the construction with the relative indefinite (§ 606); and (2.) the use of ἄν with the past tenses of the Ind. to denote an action, not as occurring at a definite time, but from time to time, as the occasion might occur, or, in other words, to denote a *habitual action;* thus, Πολλάκις γὰρ ἔφη μὲν ἄν τινος ἐρᾶν, *for he would often say, that he was in love with some one,* Mem. iv. 1. 2. Εἰ δέ τινα ὁρῴη δεινὸν ὄντα οἰκονόμον . ., οὐδένα ἂν πώποτε ἀφείλετο, ἀλλ' ἀεὶ πλείω προσεδίδου i. 9. 19. Εἴ τις αὐτῷ δοκοίη . . βλακεύειν, . . ἔπαισεν ἄν, καὶ ἅμα αὐτὸς προσελάμβανεν ii. 3. 11.

§ **595.** The contingent modes are often used where the Ind. might have been employed. The Opt. with ἄν for the (α.) Pres. or (β.) Fut. ind. is particularly frequent; and often serves, by suggesting instead of asserting, to give to the discourse that tone of moderation and refined courtesy, which was so much studied by the Greeks, especially the Athenians. (See §§ 604. b, 605. 5.) The use of the Subj. for the Ind. is more limited, and occurs chiefly (for the Fut.) in (γ.) earnest inquiry respecting one's self, and in (δ.) strong denial. Thus,

α. Αὐτὸ ἂν . . τὸ δέον εἴη· θᾶττον γὰρ ἀναλώσουσι, *this* [would be] *is the very thing we want; for they will sooner expend,* iv. 7. 7. Καὶ θηρῶντες μὲν οὐκ ἂν ἀριστήσαιεν, ἢν δέ τι δεήσῃ . ., θηρῶσι μέχρι δείπνου Cyr. i. 2. 11 (cf. § 594). ΣΩΚ. Δημηγορία ἄρα τίς ἐστιν ἡ ποιητική. ΚΑΛ. Φημί. ΣΩΚ. Οὐκοῦν ῥητορικὴ δημηγορία ἂν εἴη Pl. Gorg. 502 d. This use of the Opt. is particularly frequent in argumentative conclusions.

β. Φημί, καὶ οὐκ ἂν ἀρνηθείην, *I confess, and* [would not] *will not deny it,* Dem. 576. 17. Ἀλλ' οὐκέτ' ἂν κρύψαιμι Ar. Plut. 284. ΜΕΝ. Οὐκ ἂν μεθείμην. ΠΡ. Οὐδ' ἔγωγ' ἀφήσομαι Eur. Iph. A. 310. — This use of the Opt. is particularly frequent in the first person.

γ. Ποῖ βῶ; πᾶ στῶ; τί λέγω; *Whither* [can] *shall I go? where stop? what say?* Eur. Alc. 864. Εἴπωμεν, ἢ σιγῶμεν, ἢ τί δράσομεν; Id. Ion, 758. Εἰπεῖν τι δώσεις, ἢ στραφεὶς οὕτως ἴω; Soph. Ant. 315. Κἀμπλάκω τοῦ σοῦ μόρου; Ib. 554. See § 611. 3.

NOTE. In the Epic language, the use of the Subj. for the Fut. ind. is more extended.

δ. Οὐ γάρ σε μὴ . . γνῶσ' οὐδ' ὑποπτεύσουσιν, *for they* [cannot] *will not know nor suspect you,* Soph. El. 42. Αἱρήσεις, καὶ ἀποχωρῶν οὐ μὴ δείσῃς vii. 3. 26. Ὁ πλησίον βοηθήσει· ἤν τε . ., οὐδεὶς μηκέτι μείνῃ iv. 8. 13.

NOTES. (1.) This use is most frequent in those forms of the Subj. which have no forms of the Ind. closely resembling them, viz., the Aor. pass. and the 2d Aor. It is, on the other hand, less frequent in the Pres., resembling the Pres. *ind.*, and in the 1st Aor. act. and mid., resembling the Fut. ind. (cf. 601. N.). In this emphatic negation, the Subj. is regularly preceded by a double negative, οὐ μή. The construction may be explained by supplying a word or phrase expressing fear (cf. § 602. 3); thus, Οὐ δέδοικα μὴ γνῶσι, *I have no fear that they would know.* Compare such passages as, Οὐ φόβος, μή σε ἀγάγω Mem. ii. 1. 25; Οὐχὶ δέος, μή σε φιλήσῃ Ar. Eccl. 650. (2.) The similar use of οὐ μή with the Fut. ind. is to be explained in the same manner; as, Οὔ σοι μὴ μεθέψομαί ποτε, *never will I follow you*, Soph. El. 1052.

§ **596.** We proceed to the application of the general principles which govern the use of the distinct modes, to particular kinds of sentences, which may be termed, from their offices or connectives, *desiderative* (expressing wish, from desidero, *to desire*), *final*, *conditional*, *relative*, and *complementary* (§ 329. N.).

(1.) *Desiderative.*

§ **597.** A wish is expressed either with or without a definite looking forward to its realization. In the former case, it is expressed by the *primary* tenses; in the latter case, by the *secondary*. In the former case, (α.) if the wish is expressed with an *assurance* that it will be realized, the *Ind. Fut.* is used; but, (β.) otherwise, the *Subj.* mode. In this use, both the Ind. Fut. and the Subj. may be regarded as less direct modes of expression instead of the *Imperat.* In the latter case, (γ.) if the time for realizing the wish is already *past*, the *secondary tenses of the Ind.* are used with εἰ γάρ and εἴθε· but, (δ.) otherwise, the *Opt.* mode. (See §§ 590, 593.) Hence the Opt. becomes the simplest and most general form of expressing a wish; and from the frequency of this use, it has derived its name (§ 169. 3). Thus,

(α.) Ὡς οὖν ποιήσετε, καὶ πείθεσθέ μοι, *thus then* [you will do] *do, and listen to me*, Pl. Prot. 338 a. Μηδὲν τῶνδ' ἐρεῖς Æsch. Sept. 250.

NOTES. (1.) A wish is often expressed in the form of a question. Hence in Greek, as in other languages, the interrogative Fut. often supplies the place of the Imperat.; as, Οὐκ ἄξεθ' ὡς τάχιστα; καὶ . . ἄφετε μόνην, [Will you not carry] *Carry her away instantly, and leave her alone*, Soph. Ant. 885. Ἄξει τις ἐλθὼν δεῦρο τὸν βοτῆρά μοι; Ταύτην δ' ἐᾶτε Id. Œd. T. 1069. Οὐ μὴ λαλήσεις, ἀλλ' ἀκολουθήσεις ἐμοί; [Won't you not talk] *Don't talk, but follow me*, Ar. Nub. 505. (2.) For the Fut. with ὅπως in the place of the Imperat., see § 602. 3. (3.) The Aor. and Pres. are also used with τί οὖν οὐ, or τί οὐ, in the earnest expression of a wish; as, Τί οὖν, ἔφη ὁ Κῦρος, οὐ . . ἔλεξάς μοι; *Why then, said Cyrus, have you not told me?* i. e. *tell me*, Cyr. ii. 1. 4. Τί οὖν, ἦ δ' ὅς, οὐκ ἐρωτᾷς; Pl. Lys. 211 d.

§ **598.** (β.) Μὴ ἀναμένωμεν, *let us not wait*, iii. 1. 24. Μὴ μέλλωμεν, ὦ ἄνδρες, ἀλλ' ἀπελθόντες ἤδη αἱρεῖσθε Ib. 46. Δύο τῶν πρεσβυτάτων στρατηγοὶ ἐπιμελείσθων· ὀπισθοφυλακῶμεν δ' ἡμεῖς iii. 2. 37. Ἀλλά μ' ἔκ γε τῆσδε γῆς πόρθμευσον ὡς τάχιστα, μηδ' αὐτοῦ θάνω Soph. Tr. 801. Φέρ', ἐκπύθωμαι Eur. Herc. 529. Μὴ ποιήσῃς ταῦτα, *do not do this*, vii. 1. 8. Μηδὲν ἀθυμήσητε ἕνεκα τῶν γεγενημένων· ἔστι γάρ v. 4. 19.

NOTES. (1.) The use of the Subj. as Imperat. occurs chiefly in the 1*st Pers.* (where the Imperat. is wanting, § 170. N.), and in the *Aor. with μή*. In the 2d Pers., the distinction is rarely neglected, that *in prohibitions with μή and its compounds, the Pres. is put in the Imperat., but the Aor. in the Subj.*; as, Μὴ ἐκδῶτέ με· . . μήτε πολεμεῖτε vi. 6. 18. Μήτ' ὀκνεῖτε, μήτ' ἀφῆτ' ἔπος Soph. Œd. C. 731. Μηδ' ἐπίκευθε π. 168. Μηδ' ἐπικεύσῃς ο. 263. In the 3d Pers., the distinction is less observed. The foundation of the distinction seems to have been this; that the Pres. forbids an action more definitely than the Aor. (§ 569), and hence naturally adopts a more direct form of expression. Thus, prohibition in the Pres. is often designed to arrest an action now doing, while prohibition in the Aor. merely forbids, in general, that it should be done; as, Μὴ θαυμάζετε, *be not wondering,* i. 3. 3 (see Οἱ δὲ ὁρῶντες ἐθαύμαζον Ib. 2); but Μηδὲ . . δόξητε, *nor should you think,* iii. 2. 17. (2.) The use of the Subj. as Imperat. may be explained by ellipsis; thus, Ὁρᾶτε μὴ ἀναμένωμεν, *see that we do not wait.* Σκόπει μὴ ποιήσῃς ταῦτα. See §§ 592, 601, 602. 3; and compare §§ 595. γ, δ, 611. 3.

§ **599.** (γ.) Εἴθε σοι . . τότε συνεγενόμην, *Would that I had then been with you!* Mem. i. 2. 46. Εἴθ' εἶχες . . βελτίους φρένας, *Would that you had a better spirit,* Eur. El. 1061. Εἰ γὰρ τοσαύτην δύναμιν εἶχον Id. Alc. 1072. — In these expressions of wish there is properly an ellipsis; thus, Εἴθ' εἶχες βελτίους φρένας, καλῶς ἂν εἶχε, or ἡδόμην ἄν, *if you had a better spirit, it would be well,* or *I should be glad.* See §§ 600. 2, 603. δ.

NOTE. A wish in opposition to fact may be also expressed by the Aor. ὤφελον (§ 268), *ought.* With this verb, the particles of wishing are sometimes combined for the sake of greater strength of expression. Thus, Ὤφελε μὲν Κῦρος ζῆν, [C. ought to be living] *Would that Cyrus were living!* ii. 1. 4. Ὀλέσθαι δ' ὤφελον, *Would that I had perished!* Soph. Œd. T. 1157. Εἴθ' ὤφελ' Ἀργοῦς μὴ διαπτάσθαι σκάφος Eur. Med. 1. Εἰ γὰρ ὤφελον Pl. Crito, 44 d. So the Impf. ὤφειλον, Eur. Iph. A. 1291. In later writers, ὤφελον and ὤφελε are sometimes used as particles.

§ **600.** (δ.) Οἱ θεοὶ ἀποτίσαιντο, *May the gods requite!* iii. 2. 6. Πολλά μοι κἀγαθὰ γένοιτο v. 6. 4. Μήτε πολεμεῖτε Λακεδαιμονίοις, σώζοισθέ τε vi. 6. 18. Πράξας δ' ὃ μὴ τύχοιμι, νοστήσαιμι γάρ Eur. Alc. 1023.

NOTES. 1. The Opt. of wish is sometimes used, especially in the 3d Pers., as a less direct form for the Imperat. Sometimes the two forms are united, and these again with the Subj. (§ 598); as, Ἄγεθ', ἡμεῖς πέρ μιν ἀποτρωπῶμεν . ., ἤ τις . . Ἀχιλῆϊ παρσταίη, δοίη δὲ κράτος μέγα, μηδέ τι θυμῷ δευέσθω Υ. 119. See Soph. Ant. 151.

2. The Opt. of wish may be introduced by the particles εἰ, εἴθε, εἰ γάρ (Ep. and Dor. αἴθε, αἰ γάρ), ὡς, and in interrogation by πῶς ἄν. Εἴ μοι γένοιτο φθόγγος, *O, that I had a voice!* Eur. Hec. 836. Εἴθε μήποτε γνοίης Soph. Œd. T. 1068. Εἰ γὰρ γένοιτο Cyr. vi. 1. 38. Ὡς ὄλοιτο παγκάκως Eur. Hipp. 407. Πῶς ἂν ὀλοίμην; [How might I die?] *Would that I might die!* Id. Alc. 865 — These expressions, except the last, are elliptical; thus, Εἴ μοι γένοιτο φθόγγος, ἡδοίμην ἄν, *If there were a voice to me, I should be glad;* Βουλοίμην ἂν ὡς ὄλοιτο παγκάκως. See §§ 599, 603. γ. — Very rarely, εἴθε is joined with the Subj. in the expression of wish; as, Εἴθ' . . ἕλωσι Soph. Ph. 1092.

3. Except in interrogation, ἄν is not used with the Opt. of wish, which is thus often distinguished from the Opt. in its other uses. Thus, Ὦ παῖ, γένοιο πατρὸς εὐτυχέστερος, τὰ δ' ἄλλ' ὅμοιος· καὶ γένοι' ἂν οὐ κακός, *My son,*

may you be more fortunate than your father, but in other respects like him; and then you would not be bad, Soph. Aj. 550.

(II.) *Final.*

§ **601.** After final conjunctions (ἵνα, ὅπως, ὡς, μή · ὄφρα poet.), a *present purpose* is expressed by (α.) the *Subj.*, or (β.) in the *Fut.*, by the *Ind.*; but a *past purpose* by (γ.) the *Opt.*, or sometimes (δ.), when the *realization is now impossible*, by the *past tenses of the Ind.* (See §§ 589, 593). In final sentences, introduced by a relative (§ 531. α), the modes are used in the same manner. Thus,

(α.) Ἵνα εἰδῆτε, *so that you may know*, i. 3. 15. Ἐμοὶ δὸς αὐτὰ, ὅπως .. διαδῶ Cyr. i. 4. 10. Συμβουλεύω ἐγὼ, τὸν ἄνδρα τοῦτον ἐκποδὼν ποιεῖσθαι ὡς τάχιστα · ὡς μηκέτι δέῃ i. 6. 9. — After ὅπως and ὡς, ἄν is sometimes inserted; as, Ἄξεις ἡμᾶς, ὅπως ἂν εἰδῶμεν Cyr. iii. 2. 21. Θυμῷ βάλ', ὡς ἂν τέρματ' ἐκμάθῃς Æsch. Pr. 706.

(β.) Ἀλλ' ὅπως τοι μὴ ἐπ' ἐκείνῳ γενησόμεθα, πάντα ποιητέον, *but surely we must do every thing, that we may never come into his power*, iii. 1. 18.

NOTE. After ὅπως, the 1st Aor. subj. is rarely used in the active and middle voices, but instead of it the Fut. ind. Cf. § 595. δ.

(γ.) Κῦρος τὰς ναῦς μετεπέμψατο, ὅπως ὁπλίτας ἀποβιβάσειεν, *Cyrus sent for the ships, in order that he might land hoplites*, i. 4. 5. Βαρβάρων ἐπεμελεῖτο, ὡς πολεμεῖν τε ἱκανοὶ εἴησαν i. 1. 5. Ἐδόκει αὐτοῖς ἀπιέναι .., μή τις ἐπίθεσις γένοιτο iv. 4. 22. Εἰσάγει (Hist. Pres., § 567. α) δόμους, ἵν' ἄλλος μή τις εἰδείη Eur. Hec. 1148.

(δ.) Τί μ' οὐ .. ἔκτεινας εὐθὺς, ὡς ἔδειξα μήποτε ἐμαυτόν; *Why did you not instantly slay me, so that I might never have shown myself?* Soph. Œd. T. 1391. Ἵν' ἦ τυφλός Ib. 1389. Οὐκοῦν ἔχρην σε Πηγάσου ζεῦξαι πτερὸν, ὅπως ἐφαίνου Ar. Pax, 135. Ἵνα μηδεὶς αὐτοὺς διέφθειρεν, ἀλλ' ἐπειδὴ ἀφίκοιντο εἰς τὴν ἡλικίαν, χρήσιμοι γίγνοιντο Pl. Meno, 89 b. Ἔδει τὰ ἐνέχυρα τότε λαβεῖν, ὡς μηδ', εἰ ἐβούλετο, ἐδύνατο ἂν ταῦτα ἐξαπατᾶν vii. 6. 23.

§ **602.** REMARKS. 1. A past purpose, still continued or conceived of as present (§ 591. 4), may be expressed by the Subj.; and on the other hand, a present purpose, viewed as doubtful or as connected with something past, distant, or contingent (§ 590), may be expressed by the Opt. The Subj. for the Opt. may be remarked particularly after the Aor. used for the Perf. (§ 580), and in indirect quotation (§ 610). The two modes are sometimes both used in the same connection. Thus, Ἐπίτηδές σε οὐκ ἔγειρον, ἵνα ὡς ἥδιστα διάγῃς Pl. Crito, 43 b. Ἐξῆλθον δόμων, μή μοί τι μέμψησθε Eur. Med. 214. Ὤιχετο πρέσβεις ἄγουσα, οἵπερ τὰ σφέτερα φράσωσιν Th. vii. 25. Προσελθεῖν ἐκέλευον, εἴ τις εἴη .., ἵνα ἀπαγγείλωσι ii. 5. 36. Compare ἐπιθοῖντο and ἐπιθῶνται iii. 4. 1, 34. Ἴσως δέ που ἢ ἀποσκάπτει τι ἢ ἀποτειχίζει, ὡς ἄπορος εἴη ἡ ὁδός ii. 4. 4. Στῆσόν με κἀξίδρυσον, ὡς πυθοίμεθα Soph. Œd. C. 11. Αἰτεῖν πλοῖα, ὡς ἀποπλέοιεν · .. πέμψαι δὲ καὶ προκαταληψομένους τὰ ἄκρα, ὅπως μὴ φθάσωσι i. 3. 14. Ὡς ὕβριν δείξωμεν Αἰγίσθου θεοῖς, γόους τ' ἀφείην Eur. El. 58.

2. After words of *fear*, the final conjunction μή, *lest*, is commonly used, but sometimes also the fuller ὅπως μή, or some other connective; thus, Ἐφοβοῦντ

μὴ ἐπιθοῖντο αὐτοῖς . . οἱ πολέμιοι, *they feared* [lest the enemy should attack] *that the enemy would attack them*, iii. 4. 1. Δεδιὼς, μὴ λαβών με δίκην ἐπιθῇ i. 3. 10. Φοβοῦμαι δὲ, μή τινας ἡδονὰς ἡδοναῖς εὑρήσομεν ἐναντίας Pl. Phil. 13 a. Ἐφοβεῖτο . . μὴ οὐ δύναιτο iii. 1. 12. Κίνδυνος μὴ λάβωσι vii. 7. 31. Δέδοιχ' ὅπως μὴ τεύξομαι, *I am afraid* [as to this, *viz.* how I shall not find] *that I shall find*, Ar. Eq. 112. Ὅπως λάθω, δέδοικα, *I fear* [as to this, *viz.* how I may escape] *that I cannot escape*, Eur. Iph. T. 995. Μὴ τρέσῃς, ὅπως σέ τις . . ἀποσπάσει, *fear not that any one will tear you*, Id. Heracl. 248. Μὴ δείσῃς ποθ', ὡς . . ὄψεται Soph. El. 1309. Ἐφοβεῖτο, ὅτι ὀφθήσεσθαι ἔμελλε Cyr. iii. 1. 1. Φοβούμενοι δὲ, πῶς χρὴ ἀπειλοῦντι ὑπακοῦσαι Ib. iv. 5. 19. Ἀτὰρ φόβος, εἰ πείσω δέσποιναν Eur. Med. 184.

3. A verb of *attention*, *care*, or *fear*, is sometimes to be supplied before ὅπως or μή· as, Ὅπως οὖν ἔσεσθε ἄνδρες [sc. ὁρᾶτε, σκοπεῖτε, or ἐπιμελεῖσθε], *see then that you be men*, i. 7. 3. Δεῖ [sc. σκοπεῖν] σ', ὅπως πατρὸς δείξεις ἐν ἐχθροῖς, οἷος ἐξ οἵου 'τράφης Soph. Aj. 556. Ἀλλ' ὅπως μὴ οὐχ οἷός τ' ἔσομαι [sc. δέδοικα] Pl. Meno, 77 a. Μὴ . . διαφθείρῃ Eur. Alc. 315. Cf. §§ 595. δ, 598. 2.

(III.) *Conditional.*

§ **603.** In sentences connected by conditional conjunctions, there is a great variety of conception, and consequently of expression. The CONDITION may be assumed, either (α.) as *a fact*, or (β.) as *that which may become a fact*, or (γ.) as a *mere supposition without regard to fact*, or (δ.) *as contrary to fact*. In the first case (α.), it is expressed by the *appropriate tense of the Ind.;* in the second (β.), by the *Subj.;* in the third (γ.), by the *Opt.;* and in the fourth (δ.), by a *past tense of the Ind.* (see §§ 590, 593). Of these modes, the Ind. and Opt. are usually connected by εἰ, and the Subj. by ἐάν (= εἰ and ἄν the contingent particle) or its shortened forms, ἤν and ἄν· exceptions (ε.), however, occur, though rare in the Att. writers, and some of them doubtful. — The form of the CONCLUSION is, for the most part, determined by that of the condition. In the first case (α.), the conclusion is regularly made by the *appropriate tense of the Ind.;* in the second (β.), by the *Fut. ind.;* in the third (γ.), by the *Opt. with ἄν·* and in the fourth (δ.), by a *past tense of the Ind. with ἄν*. The form of the conclusion (ζ.), however, often depends upon other causes, besides its relation to the condition, and cases of *anacoluthon* are very frequent. There is (η.) sometimes even a union of different forms in the same construction. If (ϑ.) the conclusion is itself a dependent clause, its form is commonly determined by this dependence, and the condition usually conforms. Thus,

(α.) Εἰ μὲν ὑμεῖς ἐθέλετε ἐξορμᾶν ἐπὶ ταῦτα, ἕπεσθαι ὑμῖν βούλομαι· εἰ δ' ὑμεῖς τάττετέ με ἡγεῖσθαι, οὐδὲν προφασίζομαι iii. 1. 25. Εἴπερ ἐμοὶ ἐτέλει τι Σεύθης, οὐκ οὕτως ἐτέλει vii. 6. 16.

REMARK. Supposition is sometimes made in the Greek, as in other languages, by the Ind. without a conjunction; as, Καὶ δὴ παρεῖκεν· εἶτα πῶς . . σωθησόμεσθα Eur. Hel. 1059.

(β.) Ἢν γὰρ τοῦτο λάβωμεν, οὐ δυνήσονται μένειν, *for if we take this, they will not be able to remain*, iii. 4. 41. Ἢν δὲ φεύγῃ, ἡμεῖς ἐκεῖ πρὸς ταῦτα βουλευσόμεθα i. 3. 20. Ἐάν μοι πεισθῆτε, . . προτιμήσεσθε i. 4. 14. See Ib. 15. — (α. and β.) Οὐκ ἄρα ἔτι μαχεῖται, εἰ ἐν ταύταις οὐ μαχεῖται ταῖς ἡμέραις· ἐὰν δ' ἀληθεύσῃς, ὑπισχνοῦμαι [= δώσω] i. 7. 18.

Note. The place of the Fut. in the conclusion may be supplied by the same forms of expression as are elsewhere substitutes for this tense; thus, Ἐὰν οὖν κατὰ μέρος φυλάττωμεν καὶ σκοπῶμεν, ἧττον ἂν δύναιντο ἡμᾶς θηρᾷν οἱ πολέμιοι v. 1. 9 (§ 595. β). Ἢν γὰρ εὑρεθῇ λέγων σοί ταὔτ', ἔγωγ' ἂν ἐκπεφευγοίην πάθος Soph. Œd. T. 839. Ἢν δ' ἡμεῖς νικήσωμεν, ἡμᾶς δεῖ . . ποιῆσαι i. 7. 7 (§ 583). Κἂν τοῦτ', ἔφη, νικῶμεν, πάνθ' ἡμῖν πεποίηται i. 8. 12 (§ 584).

(γ.) Οὐκ ἂν οὖν θαυμάζοιμι, εἰ οἱ πολέμιοι . . ἐπακολουθοῖεν, *I should not, then, wonder if the enemy should pursue*, iii. 2. 35. Εἰ οὖν ὁρῴην ὑμᾶς σωτήριόν τι βουλευομένους, ἔλθοιμι ἂν πρὸς ὑμᾶς iii. 3. 2.

(δ.) Εἰ μὲν ἑώρων ἀποροῦντας ὑμᾶς, τοῦτ' ἂν ἐσκόπουν . . Ἐπεὶ δὲ ὁρῶ, κ. τ. λ., *If I saw you in want, I should be considering this . . But since I see*, &c., v. 6. 30. Οὐκ ἂν ἐποίησεν Ἀγασίας ταῦτα, εἰ μὴ ἐγὼ αὐτὸν ἐκέλευσα, *Agasias would not have done this if I had not commanded him*, vi. 6. 15. Εἰ δὲ τοῦτο πάντες ἐποιοῦμεν, ἅπαντες ἂν ἀπωλόμεθα v. 8. 13. Εἰ μὴ ὑμεῖς ἤλθετε, ἐπορευόμεθα ἂν ii. 1. 4. — (γ. and δ.) Εἰ μὲν πρόσθεν ἠπιστάμην, οὐδ' ἂν συνηκολούθησά σοι· καὶ νῦν ἄπειμι. Οὐδὲ γὰρ ἂν Μήδοκός με ὁ βασιλεὺς ἐπαινοίη, εἰ ἐξελαύνοιμι τοὺς εὐεργέτας. *Had I known this before, I had never accompanied you; and now I shall depart. For King Medocus would by no means commend me, should I drive out our benefactors.* vii. 7. 11.

(ε.) Εἴ σου στερηθῶ Soph. Œd. C. 1443. — The use of εἰ with the Subj. is almost entirely confined to the Ion. and Dor.

(ζ.) Εἰ μὲν ἐπαινῶ αὐτὸν, δικαίως ἄν με καὶ αἰτιῷσθε καὶ μισοῖτε vii. 6. 15. Εἰ δὲ καὶ δυνηθεῖτε τά τε ὄρη κλέψαι . ., ἥξετε ἐπὶ τοὺς ποταμούς (cf. Ἐφ' ὃν ἔλθοιτε ἄν, εἰ τὸν Ἅλυν διαβαίνητε) v. 6. 9. Εἰ ἔχοιμι, ὡς τάχιστα ὅπλα ἐποιούμην Cyr. ii. 1. 9. Οὐκ ἂν προβαίην τὸν πόδα τὸν ἕτερον, εἰ μὴ ταῦτ' ἀκριβωθήσεται Ar. Eccl. 161. Εἰ γὰρ γυναῖκες ἐς τόδ' ἥξουσιν θράσους, . . παρ' οὐδὲν αὐταῖς ἦν ἂν ὀλλύναι πόσεις Eur. Or. 566.

(η.) Εἰ οὖν εἰδεῖεν τοῦτο . ., ἵεντο ἂν ἐπὶ τοὺς πόνους . ., καὶ κατεργάζοιντο ἂν αὐτήν Ven. 12. 22. Δεινὸν ἂν εἴη, εἰ νῦν μὲν . . συγγνώμην . . ἔχοιτε, ἐν δὲ τῷ τέως χρόνῳ . . θανάτῳ ἐκολάζετε Lys. 179. 32. Εἰ μὲν πλοῖα ἔσεσθαι μέλλει ἱκανὰ . ., ἡμεῖς ἂν πλέοιμεν· εἰ δὲ μέλλοιμεν v. 6. 12. Οὐκ ἂν . . ἀγόρευες, οὐδέ κε . . ἀνιείης β. 184.

(θ.) Ἐπορευόμην, ἵνα, εἴ τι δέοιτο, ὠφελοίην αὐτόν i. 3. 4 (§ 601). Ἐπιβουλεύουσιν, ὡς, ἢν δύνωνται, ἀπολέσωσιν iii. 1. 35. Εἶπεν, εἰ αὐτῷ δοίη ἱππέας χιλίους, ὅτι . . κατακάνοι ἂν i. 6. 2.

§ 604. Remarks. 1. The condition is often (α.) understood; or (β.) instead of being expressed in a distinct clause, is incorporated in the conclusion; or (γ.) is expressed by a relative clause, or by an independent instead of a dependent sentence. In all these cases, the form of the conclusion is properly the same as if the condition had been formally expressed. Thus,

(α.) Ἔτι οὖν ἂν γένοιο τῷ ἐμῷ ἀδελφῷ πολέμιος, ἐμοὶ δὲ φίλος; *Would you then* [if I should now forgive you] *be in future an enemy to my brother, and a friend to me?* i. 6. 8.

NOTES. a. Among the conditions most naturally supplied, and therefore most frequently omitted, are those of inclination with possibility and of possibility with inclination; since these are the two great conditions of human conduct. Hence the frequent use of the Opt. and past tenses of the Ind. with ἂν to denote one of these ideas, the other being implied as a condition; thus, Οὐκ ἂν δύναιτο, *he would not be able* (if he should wish), i. e. *he could not*, i. 9. 23. Οὐδὲ τοῦτ' ἄν τις εἴποι, *nor could any one say this*, i. 9. 13. Αὐτοὶ μὲν ἂν ἐπορεύθησαν, *they could themselves have marched* [might if they had chosen], iv. 2. 10. Ἡμᾶς δ' ἂν ἔφην ἔγωγε χρῆναι, *and I might have said that we ought*, iii. 2. 24 Οὐδ' αὐτὸν ἀποκτεῖναι ἂν ἐθέλοιμεν, *nor should we wish to slay him* (if we could), ii. 3. 23. Ἥδιστ' ἂν ἀκούσαιμι, *I should most gladly hear* (if I might hear), ii. 5. 15. Τὴν ἐλευθερίαν ἑλοίμην ἂν i. 7. 3. Ὀκνοίην μὲν ἂν i. 3. 17. Ἐβουλόμην γ' ἄν, *I should have wished*, Pl. Phædr. 228 a.

b. To the use of the Opt. with ἂν just noticed, may be referred its employment to express *permission*, or *command in the softened or indifferent language of permission*; as, Σὺ μὲν κομίζοις ἂν σεαυτόν, *you may now betake yourself* [might if you wished], Soph. Ant. 444. Ἄγοιτ' ἂν μάταιον ἄνδρ' ἐκποδών Ib. 1339. Χωροῖς ἂν εἴσω σὺν τάχει Id. El. 1491. — Its use for the Pres. and Fut. ind. (§ 595) may be referred in like manner to ellipsis.

c. From the different idiom of the two languages, the Opt. is often best translated, as in the examples just given, by our Pres. potential; thus, Ἀλλ' εἴποιτε ἄν, *but you may say* [might if you were disposed], vii. 6. 16. Φαίητε ἂν Ib. 23. See also § 600.

(β.) Βουλοίμην δ' ἄν, ἄκοντος ἀπιὼν [= εἰ ἀπίοιμι] Κύρου, λαθεῖν αὐτόν i. 3. 17. Οὔτε γάρ, βοὸς ἂν ἔχων σῶμα [= εἰ βοὸς εἶχε σῶμα], ἀνθρώπου δὲ γνώμην, ἠδύνατ' ἂν πράττειν ἃ ἐβούλετο Mem. i. 4. 14. Ἄνευ τοῦ τὰ τοιαῦτα ἔχειν [= εἰ μὴ τὰ τοιαῦτα εἶχεν], . . οὐκ ἂν οἷός τ' ἦν Pl. Phædo, 99 a. Νικῶντες μὲν οὐδένα ἂν κατακάνοιεν, ἡττηθέντων δὲ αὐτῶν οὐδεὶς ἂν λειφθείη iii. 1. 2. Ὥσπερ ἂν δράμοι τις περὶ νίκης i. 5. 8. Ἅπερ ἂν ἄνθρωποι ἐν ἐρημίᾳ ποιήσειαν, ἄλλως δὲ οὐκ ἂν τολμῷεν v. 4. 34.

(γ.) Ὅστις δὲ τούτων σύνοιδεν [= εἴ τις συνειδείη] αὑτῷ παρημεληκώς, τοῦτον ἐγὼ οὔποτ' ἂν εὐδαιμονίσαιμι ii. 5. 7.

§ **605.** 2. The place of the Opt. in the conclusion is sometimes supplied by the Ind. expressing such ideas as *possibility*, *propriety*, *necessity*, *habit*, or *unfinished action*, commonly without ἂν· as, Οὐκ ἦν λαβεῖν, εἰ μὴ . . θηρῷεν i. 5. 2. Οὐδὲ γάρ, εἰ πάνυ προθυμοῖτο, ῥᾴδιον ἦν iii. 4. 15. Εἴ τις αὐτῷ φανερὸς γίνοιτο ἐπιδείκνυσθαι βουλόμενος, περὶ πάντος ἐποιεῖτο i. 9. 16. See Ib. 18, 19, 28; ii. 3. 11; iv. 1. 14; and § 594. Ὤικτειρον, εἰ ἁλώσοιντο i. 4. 7. Αἰσχρὸν γὰρ ἦν τὰ μὲν ἐμὰ διαπεπρᾶχθαι, 'for it would have been base,' vii. 7. 40 (§ 604. β).

3. The conclusion has sometimes a second condition, to which its verb conforms; as, Ἐὰν δ' ἐμὲ ἔλησθε, οὐκ ἂν θαυμάσαιμι, εἴ τινα εὕροιτε vi. 1. 29. Ἤκουον . . ὅτι, εἰ διέλθοιεν . ., ἢν μὲν βούλωνται, διαβήσονται iv. 1. 3.

4. The particle ἂν is sometimes omitted where it would regularly be insert-

ed; as, Ἠισχυνόμην μέντοι, εἰ . . ἐξηπατήθην, *I certainly should be ashamed, if I had been deceived,* vii. 6. 21. Εἰ δ' ἀμείνον' οἱ θεοὶ γνώμην ἔχουσιν, εὐτυχὴς εἴην ἐγώ Eur. Ph. 1200. Εἰ δὲ μὴ . . ᾔσμεν . ., φόβον παρέσχεν Id. Hec. 1111. Δύνασιν τίς ἀνδρῶν ὑπερβασίᾳ κατάσχοι; Soph. Ant. 604. Οὔτε δρῶσ' ἐλάνθανεν, *nor could she have done it unobserved,* Id. El. 914.

5. Attic courtesy (§ 595) often gives the conditional form to complementary clauses after words of emotion; as, Τόδε ἐθαύμασα, εἰ [= ὅτι] . . τίθης, *this I wonder at, that you place,* Pl. Rep. 348 e.

(IV.) *Relative.*

§ **606.** A sentence, which is introduced by a relative (or by a similar particle of time or place) referring to that which is *indefinite* or *general* or *not yet determined,* has a species of contingency (§ 594), and may hence employ the *Subj.* or *Opt.;* the Subj., when a future determination is now contemplated, but otherwise, the Opt. (§ 590. 2). Which mode should be employed will commonly depend upon the preceding verb (§ 592). After these connectives ἄν is regularly used with the Subj. (sometimes compounded with the connective); but not with the Opt., unless for some additional reason. Thus,

Εὔηθες εἴη, ἡγεμόνα αἰτεῖν παρὰ τούτου, ᾧ [definite, viz. *Cyrus*] λυμαινόμεθα τὴν πρᾶξιν. Εἰ δὲ καὶ τῷ ἡγεμόνι πιστεύσομεν, ᾧ [indefinite] ἂν Κῦρος διδῷ, 'the guide whom Cyrus may give us,' i. 3. 16. Ἐγὼ γὰρ ὀκνοίην μὲν ἂν εἰς τὰ πλοῖα ἐμβαίνειν, ἃ ἡμῖν δοίη, . . φοβοίμην δ' ἂν τῷ ἡγεμόνι, ᾧ δοίη, ἕπεσθαι, 'the vessels which he might give us,' Ib. 17. Ὅ τι ἂν δέῃ, πείσομαι Ib. 5. Ὅτῳ δὲ φαίη φίλος εἶναι, τούτῳ ἔνδηλος ἐγίγνετο ἐπιβουλεύων ii. 6. 23. Σὺν ὑμῖν μὲν ἂν οἶμαι εἶναι τίμιος, ὅπου ἂν ὦ i. 3. 6. Ὅπου μὲν στρατηγὸς σῶος εἴη, τὸν στρατηγὸν παρεκάλουν· ὁπόθεν δὲ οἴχοιτο, τὸν ὑποστρατηγόν iii. 1. 32. Πορευτέον δ' ἡμῖν τοὺς πρώτους σταθμοὺς ὡς ἂν δυνώμεθα μακροτάτους ii. 2. 12. Σιτοῦνται . ., ὅταν [= ὅτε ἂν] οἱ ἄρχοντες σημήνωσι Cyr. i. 2. 8. Ὅτε δ' ἔξω τοῦ δεινοῦ γένοιντο, . . ἀπέλειπον ii. 6. 12. Ἐγὼ δὲ, ὁπόταν [= ὁπότε ἂν] καιρὸς ᾖ, ἥξω vii. 3. 36. Ἐθήρευεν ἀπὸ ἵππου, ὁπότε γυμνάσαι βούλοιτο i. 2. 7. Τί οὖν, ἔφη, ποιοῦσιν, ἐπὴν [= ἐπεὶ ἂν] αἴσθωνται; Cyr. iii. 2. 1. Ἐπὰν [= ἐπεὶ ἂν] δὲ πάλιν ἁλισθῇ ii. 4. 3. Ἐπεί τις διώκοι, προδραμόντες ἕστασαν i. 5. 2. Ἕως μὲν ἂν παρῇ τις, χρῶμαι· ἐπειδὰν [= ἐπειδὴ ἂν] δὲ ἀπιέναι βούληται, . κακῶς ποιῶ i. 4. 8. Ἕως Κύρῳ συμμίξειαν ii. 1. 2. Ἐπειδὴ δέ τι ἐμφάγοιεν, ἀνίσταντο iv. 5. 8. Δεῖται αὐτοῦ, μὴ πρόσθεν καταλῦσαι . ., πρὶν ἂν αὐτῷ συμβουλεύσηται i. 1. 10. Πρὶν αὐτοὺς καταγάγοι i. 2. 2. Μέχρι ἂν καταστήσῃ i. 4. 13.

NOTES. (*a*) The omission of ἄν with the Subj., in sentences like the preceding, is most frequent in the Ep. poets, and rarest in Att. prose. (*b*) In Epic similes, as presenting imagined scenes, the Subj. sometimes occurs in relative clauses; as, Ὥστε λῖς ἠϋγένειος, ὅν ῥα κύνες . . δίωνται P. 109. Ὡς δ' ὅτε πορφύρῃ πέλαγος Ξ. 16.

(V.) *Complementary.*

§ **607.** As the complementary sentences which it is most important here to notice occur in what is termed the *oratio oblīqua*, it will be necessary to remark upon the character of this form of discourse, and upon its distinction from the *oratio recta*.

There are two ways of quoting the words of a person. In the first, we simply repeat his words, without change or incorporation into our own discourse; as, *He said*, "*I will go.*" This is termed DIRECT QUOTATION, or in Lat., ORATIO RECTA. In the second, we make such changes and insert such connectives as will render the quotation an integral part of our own discourse; thus, *He said*, *that he would go.* This is termed INDIRECT QUOTATION, or in Lat., ORATIO OBLĪQUA. This distinction likewise applies to the thoughts and feelings of persons, and even to general truths and appearances.

NOTE. Of these two methods of quotation, the former is *dramatic* in its character, presenting before us the speaker in the utterance of his own words; but the latter is *narrative*, simply relating what the speaker has said. This relation is made in Greek, by the use either of the distinct modes with their connectives or of the incorporated modes. We have occasion at present to treat only of the use of the distinct modes. For the use of the incorporated modes, see § 619.

§ **608.** In the *oratio obliqua*, a thing is presented not as actual, but as dependent upon the statement, thoughts, or feelings of some person, and consequently as having some degree of contingency. Hence it is properly expressed by a contingent mode. This use, however, is confined to the Opt., which limitation may be explained as follows. The *oratio obliqua*, from the very nature of quotation, commonly respects the past, and the cases in which it respects the actual present are too few and unimportant to require special provision; while in those cases, so constantly recurring, in which the past is spoken of as present, the very vivacity and dramatic character of this form of narrative forbids the use of a contingent mode. Hence the Subj. is used in the *oratio obliqua* only in such cases as would admit it in the *oratio recta*, while, on the other hand, of the distinct modes,

The optative is the mode appropriate to the oratio obliqua in past time.

With this Opt. *ἄν* is not joined, unless for some additional reason. Thus,

Ἧκεν ἄγγελος λέγων, ὅτι λελοιπὼς εἴη Συέννεσις τὰ ἄκρα, *a messenger came saying, that Syennesis had left the heights*, i. 2. 21. *Αὗται ἠρώτων αὐτοὺς, τίνες εἶεν. Ὁ δὲ ἑρμηνεὺς εἶπε Περσιστὶ, ὅτι παρὰ βασιλέως πορεύοιντο πρὸς τὸν σατράπην. Αἱ δὲ ἀπεκρίναντο, ὅτι οὐκ ἐνταῦθα εἴη, ἀλλ' ἀπέχοι ὅσον παρασάγγην* iv. 5. 10. *Ὡς εἶπεν ὁ Σάτυρος ὅτι οἰμώξοιτο, εἰ μὴ σιωπήσειεν, ἐπήρετο· "Ἂν δὲ σιωπῶ, οὐκ ἄρ'," ἔφη, "οἰμώξομαι;"* H. Gr. ii. 3. 56. *Ὅ τι δὲ ποιήσοι, οὐ διεσήμηνε* ii. 1. 23. *Ἤισθοντο οἱ μὲν Ἕλληνες, ὅτι βασιλεὺς . . ἐν τοῖς σκευο φόροις εἴη, βασιλεὺς δ' αὖ ἤκουσε Τισσαφέρνους, ὅτι οἱ Ἕλληνες νικῷεν* i. 10. 5 *Ἐγιγνώσκετο, ὅτι ὑπόπεμπτος εἴη* iii. 3. 4. *Σαφὲς πᾶσιν ἤδη ἐδόκει εἶναι, ὅτι ὁ στόλος εἴη* iii. 1. 10. *Ἠγνόει, ὅ τι τὸ πάθος εἴη* iv. 5. 7. *Ἐρωτώμενος δὲ, ποδαπὸς εἴη* iv. 4. 17. *Ἐπυνθάνετο περὶ τοῦ Σεύθου, πότερα πολέμιος εἴη ἢ φίλος,* vii. 1. 14. *Ἐκάλει . ., μνήμην παλαιῶν σπερμάτων ἔχουσ', ὑφ' ὧν θάνοι μὲν αὐτός* Soph. Œd. T. 1245. *Σκοπῶν, εἰ διαβαίνοιεν* ii. 4. 24. *Ὁ δ' ἐχαλέπαινεν, ὅτι . . πρᾴως λέγοι* i. 5. 14. *Ἐθαύμαζον, ὅτι οὐδαμοῦ Κῦρος φαίνοιτο* i. 10. 16. *Τισσαφέρνης διαβάλλει* (Hist. Pres., § 567. *α*) *τὸν Κῦρον πρὸς τὸν ἀδελφὸν, ὡς ἐπιβουλεύοι αὐτῷ* i. 1. 3. See i. 6. 3.

§ **609.** Remarks. 1. The Greek, from its peculiar spirit of freedom, vivacity, variety, and dramatic life (§§ 330, 576), often interchanges and blends the forms of indirect and direct quotation, commonly passing from the former to the latter, but sometimes the reverse. Thus,

A.) A sudden change is often made from indirect to direct quotation. This change may be made either (*α.*) after the introductory particle; or (*β.*) in the body of the quotation, commonly after a relative, a parenthetic clause, or one of the larger pauses, and in the last case with the frequent insertion of *ἔφη*. Thus, — (*α.*) *Πρόξενος εἶπεν, ὅτι* "*Αὐτός εἰμι, ὃν ζητεῖς,*" *Proxenus said,* "*I am the very person you inquire for,*" ii. 4. 16. *Οἱ δὲ εἶπον, ὅτι* "*ἱκανοί ἐσμεν*" v. 4. 10. *Ἴσως ἂν εἴποιεν, ὅτι* "*ὦ Σώκρατες, μὴ θαύμαζε τὰ λεγόμενα*" Pl. Crito, 50 c. — (*β.*) *Ἐπιδεικνὺς δὲ,* "*ὡς εὔηθες εἴη, ἡγεμόνα αἰτεῖν παρὰ τούτου, ᾧ λυμαινόμεθα τὴν πρᾶξιν*" i. 3. 16. "*Λόγον*" *ἔφασαν* "*χρῆναι διδόναι, μεμνημένους ὅσας τε ναυμαχίας αὐτοὶ καθ' αὑτοὺς νενικήκατε καὶ ναῦς εἰλήφατε*" H. Gr. i. 1. 28. *Ἔλεγεν, ὅτι* "*ὀρθῶς ᾐτιῷντο . .. Ἀλλ' ἐγὼ,*" *ἔφη,* "*ἠναγκάσθην.*" *Ἀπεκρίνατο, ὅτι* "*οὐδὲν ἂν τούτων εἴποι εἰς τὴν στρατιάν· ὑμεῖς δὲ ξυλλέξαντες,*" *ἔφη,* "*εἰ βούλεσθε, λέγετε*" v. 6. 37.

§ **610.** B.) Indirect quotation, without losing entirely its character, often adopts, in whole or in part, the modes and tenses of direct quotation, as the Pres., Fut., and Perf. ind. for the Opt., the Subj. for the Opt., &c. Thus, *Ἐπεὶ εἶπον, ὅτι ἐπὶ τὸ στράτευμα ἥκουσιν, ἔλεγεν, ὅτι τὸ στράτευμα ἀποδίδωσι, When they said, that they* [are] *were come for the army, he replied, that he* [resigns] *resigned the army* (here the regular forms of indirect quotation would be *ἥκοιεν* and *ἀποδιδοίη*, while those of direct quotation would be *ἥκομεν* and *ἀποδίδωμι*, so that the person of the one form is united with the mode of the other), vii. 6. 3. *Ἔγνω, ὅτι οὐ δυνήσεται* i. 3. 2. *Ὑποψία μὲν ἦν, ὅτι ἄγει* (cf. *Ὅτι δὲ ἐπὶ βασιλέα ἄγοι*) Ib. 21. *Οὗτοι ἔλεγον, ὅτι Κῦρος μὲν τέθνηκεν, Ἀριαῖος δὲ πεφευγὼς ἐν τῷ σταθμῷ εἴη* ii. 1. 3. *Ἧκον λέγοντες . . ὅτι οὐχ ἱππεῖς εἰσιν, ἀλλὰ ὑποζύγια νέμοιντο* ii. 2. 15. See iii. 5. 13; vi. 3. 11; vii. 1. 34. *Ἐδόκει δῆλον εἶναι, ὅτι αἱρήσονται αὐτὸν, εἴ τις ἐπιψηφίζοι* vi. 1. 25. *Ἔλεγον, ὅτι περὶ σπονδῶν ἥκοιεν, ἄνδρες, οἵτινες ἱκανοὶ ἔσονται* ii. 3. 4. See Ib. 6.

§ **611.** 2. The use of the Opt. in the *oratio obliqua* may extend not merely to the leading verbs in the quotation, but also to verbs joined with these by relatives and other connectives (cf. § 619. *α*); as, *Ἔλεγον, ὅτι . . εἴη . ., δι' ἧσπερ ἥκοιεν,* 'through which they had come,' iii. 5. 15. *Ἔλεγον . ., ὅτι παντὸς ἄξια λέγοι Σεύθης· χειμὼν γὰρ εἴη,* 'for it was winter,' vii. 3. 13. Even though an infinitive precedes; as, *Ἐβόα, ἄγειν τὸ στράτευμα κατὰ μέσον τὸ τῶν πολεμίων, ὅτι ἐκεῖ βασιλεὺς εἴη,* 'because there was the king,' i. 8. 12.

3. In complementary sentences, where doubt is expressed, and a primary

tense precedes, the *Subj.* is sometimes used, especially in the 1*st Pers.* The connective is sometimes omitted, and even the leading verb itself. Thus, Οὐκ οἶδ', εἰ Χρυσάντᾳ τούτῳ δῶ Cyr. viii. 4. 16. Βούλει [sc. ὡς] λάβωμαι; *Wilt thou I take?* Soph. Ph. 761. Θέλεις μείνωμεν; Id. El. 80. Εἶτε τι βούλει προσθῇς ἢ ἀφέλῃς Pl. Phædo, 95 d. ΔΙ. Παραινῶ σοι σιωπᾶν. . . ΑΙΣΧ. [Sc. Παραινεῖς ὡς] Ἐγὼ σιωπῶ; Bacch. *I advise you to be silent.* Æsch. *I be silent?* Ar. Ran. 1132 (cf. § 537).—The use of the Subj. in § 595. γ may in like manner be explained by ellipsis.

B. Volitive.

§ **612.** The most direct expression of an act of the will (§ 329. N.) is by the *Imperative mode* (§ 169. 4). For other less direct methods, see §§ 597–600, 602. 3, 604. b.

Remarks. 1. From the fondness of the Greeks for passing from indirect to direct forms of expression (cf. §§ 576, 609, 670), the Imperat. is sometimes found in *dependent* sentences; thus, Θνητὸς δ' Ὀρέστης· ὥστε μὴ λίαν στένε, *and Orestes was mortal; so that* [do not grieve] *you should not grieve to excess,* Soph. El. 1172. Γράψω δέ, ὥστε, ἂν βούλησθε, χειροτονήσατε, *and I will propose it in writing, so that if you will,* [vote it] *you may vote it,* Dem. 129. 1. Δεῖξαι, ὅτι, ὧν μὲν ἐφίενται, . . κτάσθωσαν, *to show them, that, what they desire* [let them gain] *they must gain,* Th. iv. 92. Ἐπανερωτῶ πάλιν, τῶν ἐκμαγείων ταῖς ᾠδαῖς εἰ πρῶτον ἐν τοῦθ' ἡμῖν ἀρέσκον κείσθω Pl. Leg. 800 e. Οἶσθ' οὖν ὃ δρᾶσον; *Do you know then, what* [do] *you should do?* Eur. Hec. 225 (cf. Οἶσθ' οὖν ὃ δράσεις; Id. Cycl. 131). Οἶσθ' ὡς ποίησον; ἀντὶ τῶν εἰρημένων ἴσ' ἀντάκουσον, κᾆτα κρῖν' αὐτὸς μαθών Soph. Œd. T. 543. Ἀλλ' οἶσθ' ὅ μοι σύμπραξον; Eur. Heracl. 451. Οἶσθά νυν ἅ μοι γενέσθω; *Do you know then, what* [let be done] *must be done for me?* Id. Iph. T. 1203. Φυλάκους, οἳ λεγόντων Hdt. i. 89.

§ **613.** 2. In general but earnest address, the 2d Pers. of the Imperat. is sometimes used with πᾶς, or τὶς, or both, instead of the 3d Pers.; as, Χώρει δεῦρο πᾶς ὑπηρέτης· τόξευε, παῖε· σφενδόνην τίς μοι δότω, *Come hither every man* [alias, *bird*] *of you! Shoot, smite. Let some one give me a sling,* Ar. Av. 1186. Φύλαττε πᾶς τις Ib. 1191. Ἴτω τις, εἰσάγγελλε Eur. Bac. 173. See § 500. *a.*

3. Such familiar imperatives as ἄγε, εἰπέ, ἰδέ, and φέρε, may be used in the singular, as interjections, though more than one are addressed; thus, Ἄγε δή, ἀκούσατε Apol. 14. Εἰπέ μοι, τί πάσχετ', ὦνδρες; Ar. Pax, 383.

4. An act of the will may respect either the real or the ideal. Hence in Greek, as in other languages, the Imperat. may be used to express supposition or condition; thus, Ὅμως δὲ εἰρήσθω μοι, *but yet* [let it have been said by me] *suppose me to have said,* Mem. iv. 2. 19. Πλούτει τε γὰρ . ., καὶ ζῆ Soph. Ant. 1168.

C. Incorporated.

§ **614.** I. The Greek has great freedom in respect to the employment of distinct or incorporated sentences, and in respect to the mode of their incorporation. Thus (α.) a dependent clause may be *preserved entirely distinct*; or (β.) its *subject* or *most prominent substantive* may be *incorporated* in the leading clause, leaving it otherwise distinct; or (γ.) its *verb* may be also incorporated as an *Infinitive;* or (δ.) its *verb* may be incorporated yet more closely as a *Participle.* The union often becomes still closer by an attraction, which renders *the subject of the Inf. or Part.* the same with *the subject or an adjunct of the principal verb.* This attraction has three forms; in the first (ε.), the principal verb adopts the subject of the dependent clause; in the second (ζ.), the Inf. or Part., referring to the same person or thing with the principal verb, adopts the same grammatical subject; in the third (η.), the Inf. or Part. adopts for its grammatical subject, an adjunct of the principal verb. E. g.

α. Ἤισθετο, ὅτι τὸ Μένωνος στράτευμα ἤδη ἐν Κιλικίᾳ ἦν, *he perceived, that the army of Meno was now in Cilicia,* i. 2. 21. Λέγουσιν, ὅτι ἐπὶ τοῦτο ἔρχονται Cyr. i. 2. 6. Παρεσκευάζοντο, ὅπως κατὰ κορυφὴν ἐσβαλοῦσιν Th. ii. 99.

β. Ἤισθετο τό τε Μένωνος στράτευμα, ὅτι ἤδη ἐν Κιλικίᾳ ἦν, *he perceived the army of Meno, that it was now in Cilicia,* i. 2. 21 *v. l.* Ἐλέγοντό τινες, ὡς γιγνώσκουσι Vect. i. 1. See §§ 425. 4, 551. — α and β. For examples, see § 551. N.

γ. Αἰσθανόμενος αὐτοὺς μέγα παρὰ βασιλεῖ Δαρείῳ δύνασθαι, *perceiving them to have great influence with King Darius,* Th. vi. 59. Παρεσκευάζετο βοηθεῖν Th. iii. 110. Πιστοὺς πέμπει ἐπισκοπεῖν Œc. 4. 6. Ἦλθεν . . βοηθεῖν τῇ πατρίδι Ages. i. 36.

δ. Οὐ δύναμαι . . σὲ αἰσθέσθαι πειρώμενον, *I cannot perceive you attempting,* ii. 5. 4. Παρεσκευάζετο γὰρ πορευσόμενος H. Gr. iv. 2. 41 (§ 583. *a*). Ἔπεμψέ τινα ἐροῦντα ii. 5. 2. Ἐρχόμεθα . . βοηθήσοντες τούτοις vii. 7. 17. — γ and δ. Ἔδοξεν αὐτοῖς παριτητέα ἐς τοὺς Λακεδαιμονίους εἶναι, τῶν μὲν ἐγκλημάτων πέρι μηδὲν ἀπολογησομένους, . . δηλῶσαι δέ Th. i. 72.

ε. For examples, see § 551.

ζ. Ἐνομίζομεν ἄξιοι εἶναι [= ἡμᾶς ἀξίους εἶναι], *we thought that we were worthy,* Cyr. vii. 5. 72 (cf. Νομίζοιμι γὰρ ἐμαυτὸν ἐοικέναι Ib. v. 1. 21). Νόμιζε . . ἄνδρα ἀγαθὸν ἀποκτείνων [= σεαυτὸν ἀποκτείνοντα], *consider yourself putting to death a good man,* vi. 6. 24. Οἶμαι εἶναι τίμιος i. 3. 6 (cf. Οἶμαι μέν, ἦν δ' ἐγώ, ληρεῖν με Pl. Charm. 173 a). Ὁρῶ μὲν ἐξαμαρτάνων Eur. Med. 350 (cf. Ὁρῶ δέ μ' ἔργον δεινὸν ἐξειργασμένην Soph. Tr. 706). Οὐκ ἃ κρείττων ᾔδει ὤν, ταῦτα προὐκαλεῖτο τοὺς συνόντας, ἀλλ' ἅπερ εὖ ᾔδει ἑαυτὸν ἥττονα ὄντα, ταῦτα ἐξῆρχε Cyr. i. 4. 4. Δηλοῖ τιμῶν τὸν πλοῦτον Ar. Plut. 587 (cf. Ἀποφήνω μόνην ἀγαθῶν ἁπάντων οὖσαν αἰτίαν ἐμέ Ib. 468). Σαφῆ σημεῖα φαίνεις ἐσθλὸς εἰς ἡμᾶς γεγώς Soph. El. 23. See §§ 627, 633. — ζ and δ. Ἑώρων οὐ κατορθοῦντες, καὶ τοὺς στρατιώτας ἀχθομένους, *they saw that they were unsuccessful and the soldiers displeased,* Th. vii. 47.

η. Ἔδοξεν οὖν αὐτοῖς συσκευασαμένοις ἃ εἶχον καὶ ὁπλισαμένοις προϊέναι, *it therefore seemed best to them, that having packed up what they had, and equipped themselves in full armor, they should advance,* ii. 1. 2 (§ 627. α). Εὖ γὰρ φρονοῦντος ὄμμα σοῦ κατηγορεῖ, *for your eye proves that you feel kindly,* Æsch. Ag. 271 (§ 633).

§ 615. Remarks. 1. An especial variety of construction is observed with such words as σύνοιδα, συγγιγνώσκω, ἔοικα, ὅμοιός εἰμι. Ἐγώ σοι σύνοιδα [sc. σε] . . πρωῒ ἀνιστάμενον (*v. l.* ἀνισταμένῳ), *I* [know with you your rising] *remember your rising early*, Œc. 3. 7. Συνίσασι γὰρ τοῖς μὲν . . γεγενημένοις (*v. l.* τοὺς . . γεγενημένους), τοὺς δὲ . . εἰληφότας Isocr. 319 e. Ξύνοιδα ἐμαυτῷ σοφὸς ὤν Pl. Apol. 21 b. Ἐμαυτῷ γὰρ ξυνῄδειν οὐδὲν ἐπισταμένῳ Ib. 22 d. Ἐμαυτῷ ξύνοιδα, ὅτι . . λέγω Ib. Ion, 533 c. Ἔοικας βασιλεὺς εἶναι, *you seem to be king*, Cyr. i. 4. 9. Ἐοίκατε τυραννίσι μᾶλλον ἢ πολιτείαις ἡδόμενοι, 'you seem more pleased,' H. Gr. vi. 3. 8. Ἔοικας ἀληθῆ εἰρηκότι, *you seem like one who has spoken the truth*, i. e. *you seem to have spoken the truth*, Pl. Alc. 124 b. Ἔοικε γὰρ ὥσπερ αἴνιγμα ξυντιθέντι Pl. Apol. 26 e. Ὅμοιοί ἐσμεν οὐκ ὀρθῶς ὡμολογηκόσι Id. Meno, 97 a. Ὅμοιοι ἦσαν θαυμάζειν (*v. l.* θαυμάζοντες), *they seemed to be wondering*, iii. 5. 13.

2. The contingent particle ἄν may be joined with the Inf. and Part., wherever it would be joined with the distinct modes of which they supply the place. The Inf. and Part. are then commonly translated into Eng. by the potential mode (§ 588). Thus, Εἰ δέ τις ἐξαπατηθῆναι ἂν οἴεται, *if any one thinks that he could be deceived*, v. 7. 11 (§ 604. a). Ὥστε καὶ ἰδιώτην ἂν γνῶναι vi. 1. 31. Τί ἂν οἰόμεθα παθεῖν (cf. τί οἰόμεθα πείσεσθαι); iii. 1. 17. See vi. 1. 20, and § 595. β. Ὡς οὕτω περιγενόμενος ἂν τῶν ἀντιστασιωτῶν, *as though he would thus prevail over his opponents*, i. 1. 10. Ὡς ἁλόντος ἂν τοῦ χωρίου v. 2. 8.

§ 616. 3. From the intimate union prevailing between the Inf. or Part., and the principal verb of the sentence, a word properly modifying the one is sometimes placed in immediate connection with the other. We remark, in particular, — (*a*) Such adverbs as ἅμα, αὐτίκα, εὐθύς, ἐξαίφνης, and μεταξύ, joined with the Part. instead of the principal verb; as, Ἅμα ταῦτ' εἰπὼν ἀνέστη [saying this, he at the same time rose up], *as soon as he had said this, he rose up*, iii. 1. 47. Ὅπως μή, ἅμα ἀποθνήσκοντος τοῦ ἀνθρώπου, διασκεδάννυται ἡ ψυχή Pl. Phædo, 77 b. Εὐθὺς οὖν με ἰδὼν ὁ Κέφαλος ἠσπάζετο, *immediately, therefore, upon seeing me, Cephalus saluted me*, Pl. Rep. 328 c. Ἦν αὐτοῖς ἐπιχώριον, τὸ μεταξὺ πορευομένους μήτε ἐσθίειν μήτε πίνειν, *it was their custom, while marching* [in the mean time], *neither to eat nor drink*, Cyr. viii. 8. 11.— (*b*) A particle joined with the principal verb instead of the Inf. or Part., particularly ἄν, and οὐκ with φημί· as, Σὺν ὑμῖν μὲν ἂν οἶμαι εἶναι τίμιος, *with you, I think that I should be honored*, i. 3. 6. Χρήσιμοι ἂν ἐδόκουν εἶναι v. 6. 1. Οὐκ ἔφασαν ἰέναι, *they said they would not go*, i. 3. 1. Ἐπήρετο αὐτόν, εἰ ὁπλιτεύοι. Οὐκ ἔφη [sc. ὁπλιτεύειν], 'He said *No*,' v. 8. 5.

4. In the use of the incorporated modes with adjuncts, there is often a union of two constructions; as, Ἄγγελλε δ' ὅρκῳ προστιθείς [uniting ἄγγελλε δ' ὅρκῳ and ἄγγελλε δ', ὅρκον προστιθείς], *and announce* [with an oath, adding it], *adding an oath*, Soph. El. 47. Ὅτι βάλλειν δεήσοι ἀναιρουμένους ταῖς βώλοις Cyr. ii. 3. 17. Τί ἡμῶν δεήσεσθε χρήσασθαι [uniting τί ἡμῶν δεήσεσθε and τί δεήσεσθε ἡμῖν χρήσασθαι]; [What shall you want of us to do with us?] *In what shall you wish to employ us?* v. 4. 9. Ἐπιθυμίᾳ τῶν ἀνδρῶν τῶν ἐκ τῆς νήσου κομίσασθαι Th. v. 15.

§ 617. 5. The Inf. and Part. may be used *impersonally*, as well as the finite modes (§ 546); thus, Ὥστε καὶ αὐτῷ μεταμέλειν ii. 6. 9. Μεταμέλον αὐτοῖς Pl. Phædo, 113 e.

6. From the familiar association of the Acc. with the Inf. (§ 626), and the Gen. with the Part. (§ 638), words commonly governing other cases are often followed by these in connection with an Inf. or Part. Thus, Ὑμᾶς προσήκει

καὶ ἀμείνονας καὶ προθυμοτέρους εἶναι iii. 2. 15 (cf. Ἀγαθοῖς τε ὑμῖν προσήκει εἶναι iii. 2. 11). Παραγγείλας τὴν πρώτην χιλιοστὺν ἕπεσθαι Cyr. ii. 4. 3 (see §§ 402, 424. 2). Οὐδὲν ἤχθετο αὐτῶν πολεμούντων, *he was not at all displeased with their being at war*, i. 1. 8 (cf. Σεύθης δὲ ἤχθετο αὐτῷ vii. 5. 7. See §§ 372. α, 406). Ὡς ἕρποντος εἰσορᾷς ἐμοῦ Soph. Tr. 394 (§§ 375, 377. 2) Sometimes the Acc. occurs for another case with the Part., if its use is analogous to that of the Inf.; as, Σὲ μὲν εὖ πράσσοντ' ἐπιχαίρω Soph. Aj. 136. Ἥσθην . . εὐλογοῦντά σε Id. Phil. 1314. Cf. § 406.

§ **618.** II. The relations of dependent sentences are expressed with *greater explicitness* by the *distinct modes with their connectives;* but with *greater brevity*, and often *greater energy and vivacity*, by the *incorporated modes*. There are few of these relations which cannot be expressed by the latter. Hence, in the wide range of their use, these modes may express the *subject*, the *direct* or *indirect object*, the *time*, *cause*, *purpose*, *manner*, *means*, *condition*, *restriction*, *preliminaries*, *result*, &c., of the verbs with which they are connected.

Remarks. 1. The use of both the incorporated modes is far more extensive in Greek than in English. Hence we often translate the Greek Inf. and Part. by finite verbs with connectives (*that, when, while, as, and, if, although, because, since, in order that*, &c.). Sometimes, also, from a difference of idiom, the Inf. and Part. are interchanged in translation; as, Τὰ δὲ τῶν φίλων μόνος ᾤετο εἰδέναι ῥᾷστον ὂν ἀφύλακτα λαμβάνειν, *but he thought that he alone knew it to be most easy to seize the unguarded property of friends*, ii. 6. 24. Πρωτεύειν παρ' οἷς ἐβούλετο ἑαυτὸν φιλεῖσθαι, *to hold the first place with those by whom he wished himself beloved*, Cyr. viii. 2. 26.

§ **619.** 2. The use of the incorporated modes, particularly the Inf., is very great in the *oratio obliqua* (§ 607), sometimes (α.) extending even to subsidiary clauses (cf. § 611. 2); and being interchanged and blended not only (β.) with other forms of the *oratio obliqua*, but also (γ.) with those of the *oratio recta*. Thus,

α. Πολλοὺς φαίη Ἀριαῖος εἶναι Πέρσας ἑαυτοῦ βελτίονας, οὓς οὐκ ἀνασχέσθαι ii. 2. 1. Ἔφη δέ, ἐπειδὴ οὗ ἐκβῆναι τὴν ψυχήν, πορεύεσθαι . . εἰς τόπον . ., ἐν ᾧ . . δύ' εἶναι χάσματε Pl. Rep. 614 b.

β. Ἀγγέλλει Δερκυλλίδας, ὅτι νικῷέν τε αὖ Λακεδαιμόνιοι, καὶ αὐτῶν μὲν τεθνάναι οὐκ τῶ H. Gr. iv. 3. 1. Ὡς μὲν στρατηγήσοντα ἐμὲ . . μηδεὶς ὑμῶν λεγέτω . . · ὡς δὲ πείσομαι i. 3. 15 (§ 640). Ἀπήγγελλον τῷ Κύρῳ, ὅτι τοσαῦτα εἴη ἔνδον ἀγαθά, ὅσα . . μὴ ἂν ἐπιλείπειν Cyr. v. 2. 4. See § 628.

Note. Ὅτι and ὡς are sometimes even followed, after an intervening sentence, by an Inf. or Part., instead of a finite verb; as, Εἶπε δέ, ὅτι, "ἐπειδὰν τάχιστα ἡ στρατεία λήξῃ, εὐθὺς ἀποπέμψειν αὐτόν" iii. 1. 9. Ἐνόμισεν ὅτι, εἴ τι οὗτος πάθοι, αὐτὸς ἂν λαβεῖν Cyr. v. 4. 1. Ἐγὼ γάρ, εὖ ἴσθ' ὅτι, ὡς ἐμαυτὸν πείθω, . . ἐμὲ εἶναι τούτων ἕνα Pl. Gorg. 453 b. Αἰσθάνομαι οὖν σου . ., ὅτι, ὁπόσ' ἂν φῇ . ., οὐ δυναμένου Ib. 481 d. Γνοὺς δὲ ὁ Κλέων καὶ ὁ Δημοσθένης, ὅτι, εἰ καὶ ὁποσονοῦν μᾶλλον ἐνδώσουσι, διαφθαρησομένους αὐτούς Th. iv. 37.

γ. Ἔφη "ἐθέλειν πορεύεσθαι . .. Ἐγὼ γάρ," ἔφη, "οἶδα" iv. 1. 27. Κλέανδρος, "Μάλα μόλις," ἔφη, "διαπραξάμενος ἥκω · λέγειν γὰρ Ἀναξίβιον ὅτι οὐκ ἐπιτήδειον εἴη. . . Ὅμως δὲ εἰσιέναι," ἔφη, "ἐκέλευεν" vii. 1. 39.

β and *γ*. Ἀπεκρίνατο, ὅτι "ἀκούοι Ἀβροκόμαν, ἐχθρὸν ἄνδρα, ἐπὶ τῷ Εὐφράτῃ ποταμῷ εἶναι . . · κἂν μὲν ᾖ ἐκεῖ, τὴν δίκην" ἔφη "χρῄζειν ἐπιθεῖναι αὐτῷ· ἢν δὲ φεύγῃ, ἡμεῖς ἐκεῖ πρὸς ταῦτα βουλευσόμεθα" i. 3. 20.

(I.) *The Infinitive.*

§ **620.** I. The general rule for the construction of the Infinitive is the following: —

RULE XXX. The INFINITIVE is construed as a *neuter noun* (§ 445). Hence,

(*a*) The Inf. may be the SUBJECT of any word which would agree with a noun; whether *appositive*, *adjective*, *article*, *pronoun*, or *verb*. (*b*) The Inf. may DEPEND upon any word which would govern a noun; whether *substantive*, *adjective*, *verb*, *adverb*, or *preposition*. (*c*) The Inf. may be used, like a noun, to express a CIRCUMSTANCE; particularly such as are denoted by the *instrumental and modal Dat.* (§ 415), and by the *Acc. of specification* (§ 437). Thus,

Φεύγειν αὐτοῖς ἀσφαλέστερόν ἐστιν ἢ ἡμῖν, *to fly is safer for them than for us*, iii. 2. 19. Ὡς οὐκ ἀκόλουθα εἴη τό τε ἐπιθήσεσθαι καὶ λύσειν τὴν γέφυραν ii. 4. 19. Δεῦρ' ἐνίκησεν μολεῖν σοί Soph. Ant. 233. Οὐδὲν οἷόν ἐστ' [= τοιοῦτόν ἐστιν, οἷον] ἀκοῦσαι, *there is nothing* [such as] *like hearing*, or, *it is best to hear*, Ar. Av. 966. Οὐδὲν οἷον τὸ αὐτὸν ἐρωτᾶν Pl. Gorg. 447 c. Ἐν γὰρ τῷ κρατεῖν ἐστι καὶ τὸ λαμβάνειν v. 6. 32. Πρόφασις . . τοῦ ἀθροίζειν στράτευμα, *pretext for assembling an army*, i. 1. 7. Πρόφασιν στρατεύειν ἐπὶ τοὺς Θηβαίους H. Gr. iii. 5. 5. Ἀντιπάσχειν δὲ οὐδεὶς κίνδυνος ii. 5. 17. Ἄρξαντες τοῦ διαβαίνειν i. 4. 15. Τύχη τοιάδ' ἐπέστη, θαυμάσαι μὲν ἀξία, σπουδῆς γε μέντοι τῆς ἐμῆς οὐκ ἀξία Soph. Œd. T. 776. Κωλύσεις τοῦ καίειν ἐπιόντας i. 6. 2 (§ 347). Οὐκ ἐκώλυε βασιλεὺς τὸ Κύρου στράτευμα διαβαίνειν i. 7. 19. Ἀπεγνωκέναι τοῦ μάχεσθαι Ib. Διὰ τοῦ ἐπιορκεῖν ii. 6. 22. Ἠγάλλετο τῷ ἐξαπατᾶν δύνασθαι, τῷ πλάσασθαι ψευδῆ Ib. 26. Μανθάνειν γὰρ ἥκομεν Soph. Œd. C. 12. Φοβούμενοι οὐχ ἡμᾶς μόνον, ἀλλὰ καὶ τὸ καταπεσεῖν iii. 2. 19. Διὰ τὸ πολλοὺς ἔχειν ὑπηρέτας καὶ διὰ τὴν ἐπιμέλειαν i. 9. 27. Ὡς πολεμεῖν τε ἱκανοὶ εἴησαν i. 1. 5. Ἀμήχανος εἰσελθεῖν στρατεύματι i. 2. 21. Φαγεῖν δεινός, *a terrible fellow to eat*, vii. 3. 23. Δεινὸς λέγειν ii. 5. 15. Ὁρᾶν στυγνὸς ἦν, καὶ τῇ φωνῇ τραχύς ii. 6. 9. Πρέπει γὰρ ὡς τύραννος εἰσορᾶν Soph. El. 664. Ἐπὶ γὰρ ταῖς ναυσὶ ῥᾷστοί εἰσιν ἀμύνεσθαι Th. iv. 10. Ῥᾷσται δὲ ἐς τὸ βλάπτεσθαι Id. vii. 67. Πεύσει δὲ χάρμα μεῖζον ἐλπίδος κλύειν Æsch. Ag. 266. Πλέω λέγειν Ib. 868. Μῦθος κυριώτερος λέγειν Eur. Iph. A. 318. Ὦ, πλὴν γυναικὸς οὕνεκα στρατηλατεῖν, τἄλλ' οὐδέν, ὦ κάκιστε τιμωρεῖν φίλοις Eur. Or. 718. Οὔθ' ὅμοιον οὐδὲν οὔτ' ἴσον βροτοῖς, πλὴν ὀνομάσαι, 'in nothing except name,' Eur. Ph. 501.

§ **621.** NOTES. *α*. In some cases it seems indifferent whether the Inf. is regarded as the subject of a verb, or as depending upon the verb used impersonally. See § 546. *β*, *γ*.

β. In Greek, as in Eng., the Inf. *Act.* is often used, where the Inf. *Pass.* might have been used with reference to a nearer, more explicit, or more natural subject; as, Τύπτειν παρέχοντα, *giving himself up* [for beating] *to be beaten*,

Pl. Gorg. 480 d (cf. Παράσχῃ . . θεραπευθῆναι Id. Charm. 157 b). Παρέχοντες ἡμᾶς αὐτοὺς εὖ ποιεῖν ii. 3. 22. Δίδωσι βουκόλοισιν ἐκθεῖναι βρέφος Eur Ph. 25. Τοῖς ῥᾴστοις ἐντυγχάνειν, *the easiest things to meet with*, Mem. i. 6. 9. Ἀκοῦσαι μὲν ἴσως τισὶν ἀηδῆ, ῥηθῆναι δ' οὐκ ἀσύμφορον Isocr. 265 c.

§ **622.** REMARKS. 1. The article is often prefixed to the Inf. to give prominence to its substantive character, or to define the relation which it sustains as a substantive, by marking the case. If the Inf. is governed by a preposition, the insertion of the article is required. The article is often prefixed, especially in the tragedians, where it would not have been expected, and is often in the Acc. (of *direct object*, *effect*, or *specification*), where another case might have been expected. Thus,

Τὸ δρᾶν οὐκ ἠθέλησαν, [willed not the doing it] *were not willing to do it*, Soph. Œd. C. 442. Πείθομαι τὸ δρᾶν Id. Ph. 1252. Ὅς σε κωλύσει τὸ δρᾶν Ib. 1241. Ἐλπίδος . . τὸ μὴ παθεῖν Soph. Ant. 235. Τεύξεται τὸ μὴ θανεῖν Ib. 778 (cf. § 370). Καρδίας δ' ἐξίσταμαι τὸ δρᾶν Ib. 1105. Ἐγὼ αἴτιος . . τὸ σὲ ἀποκρίνασθαι Pl. Lach. 190 e. Τό τε μὴ βλέπειν ἑτοίμα, *and ready to leave the light*, Soph. El. 1079. Τὸ μὲν προσταλαιπωρεῖν . . πρόθυμος Th. ii. 53. Τὸ σιγᾶν οὐ σθένω Eur. Iph. A. 655. Ἐγὼ γὰρ ἐκβαλεῖν μὲν αἰδοῦμαι δάκρυ, τὸ μὴ δακρῦσαι δ' αὖθις αἰδοῦμαι τάλας Ib. 451. For other examples, see §§ 620, 623.

NOTE. The Inf. with τοῦ as the *Gen. of motive* (§ 372) is particularly frequent with a negative; as, Τοῦ μή τινας ζητῆσαι, *in order that none may inquire*, Th. i. 23.

§ **623.** 2. The Inf., both with and without the article, is used in a great variety of expressions which may be referred to the *Acc. of specification*, and the *adverbial Acc.* When thus employed, it may be termed the INFINITIVE OF SPECIFICATION, and the ADVERBIAL INFINITIVE. In these uses it is variously translated, and in some of them it is often said, though not in the strict sense of the term (§ 343. N.), to be *absolute.* Thus,

Ἐκ δείματός του νυκτέρου, δοκεῖν ἐμοί, *from some night vision*, [according to the seeming] *as it seems to me*, or *methinks*, Soph. El. 410. Ἀλλ' εἰκάσαι μὲν, ἡδύς, *but to guess, joyous*, Id. Œd. T. 82. Ἐν ᾧ γὰρ ἦν μοι πάντα, γιγνώσκειν καλῶς Eur. Med. 228. Ἐς τὸ ἀκριβὲς [= ἀκριβῶς, § 449. β] εἰπεῖν, *to speak correctly*, Th. vi. 82. Ὀλίγου δεῖν πλείους ἀπεκτόνασιν, *have slain* [to want little] *almost a greater number*, H. Gr. ii. 4. 21. Μικροῦ δεῖν Isocr. 70 e. Ὀλίγου [sc. δεῖν] πᾶσαι, *almost all*, Pl. Phædr. 258, e. Καὶ μικροῦ [sc. δεῖν] κἀκεῖνον ἐξετραχήλισεν Cyr. i. 4. 8. Ἐς δέον πάρεσθ' ὅδε Κρέων, τὸ πράσσειν καὶ τὸ βουλεύειν Soph. Œd. T. 1416. For other examples, see §§ 620, 622.

NOTE. The use of εἶναι as the *Inf. of specification*, or the *adverbial Inf.*, will be particularly remarked, (α.) with ἑκών, chiefly in negative sentences; (β.) with some *adverbs* and *prepositions, followed by their cases*, chiefly preceded by τό. Thus, Οὔτε συνθήκας ἂν ψευδοίμην ἑκὼν εἶναι, *nor would I prove false to my engagements*, [as to the being willing] *so far as depends upon my own will*

Cyr. v. 2. 10. Οὐδὲ ξένοις ἑκὼν εἶναι γέλωτα παρέχεις, 'willingly,' Ib. ii. 2. 15. Τὸ νῦν εἶναι, *as to the* [now being] *present state of affairs, for the present,* iii. 2. 37. Τὸ μὲν τήμερον εἶναι, *for to-day,* Pl. Crat. 396 d. Τὸ κατὰ τοῦτον εἶναι, *as to the situation of affairs with respect to him,* i. e. *so far as regards him,* i. 6. 9. Τὸ ἐπὶ τούτοις εἶναι, so *far as depends upon these,* Lys. 180. 41. Τὸ ἐπὶ σφᾶς εἶναι Th. iv. 28.

§ **624.** 3. Pleonasm and Ellipsis. The Inf. (α.) is sometimes *redundant,* and (β.) is sometimes *omitted.* It (γ.) not unfrequently depends upon a word omitted, or implied in another verb, especially in indirect quotation. Thus,

(α.) Χάριν ἀντιδίδωσιν ἔχειν, *in return gives* [to have] *pleasure,* Soph. Œd. C. 232. Αἰτήσομαι δέ σ' οὐ μακρὸν γέρας λαχεῖν Id. Aj. 825. The Inf. added for the sake of expressing an idea more fully or precisely is termed the *Inf. epexegetic* (ἐπεξηγητικός). — (β.) Εἰς τὸ βαλανεῖον βούλομαι [sc. ἰέναι] Ar. Ran. 1279. Ἐκέλευσε . . τοὺς ἕνδεκα ἐπὶ τὸν Θηραμένην H. Gr. ii. 3. 54. Ἔφη ὁ Ὀρόντης [sc. οὕτω ποιῆσαι], *Orontes* [said that he had so done] *assented,* i. 6. 7. — (γ.) Οἱ δὲ σφάττειν ἐκέλευον· οὐ γὰρ ἂν δύνασθαι πορευθῆναι [sc. ἔφασαν], *but they bade him kill them; for* [they said that] *they were unable to proceed,* iv. 5. 16. See vii. 7. 19.

§ **625.** 4. The Inf. often forms an elliptical *command, request, counsel, salutation, exclamation,* or *question;* as,

Σύ μοι φράζειν [sc. ἔθελε], *do you* [*please to*] *tell me,* Pl. Soph. 262 e. Μὴ ἐμὲ αἰτιᾶσθαι τούτων, *do not blame me for these,* Ib. 218 a. Οἷς μὴ πελάζειν Æsch. Pr. 712. Θεοὶ πολῖται, μή με δουλείας τυχεῖν [sc. δότε]! *Ye gods of the city, O* [*grant*] *that I may not fall into slavery!* Id. Sept. 253 (cf. Ὦ Ζεῦ, δός με τίσασθαι μόρον πατρός Id. Cho. 18). Νίκη, ξυγγενοῦ, . . θέσθαι τροπαῖον ἡμᾶς, *O Victory, befriend, grant that we may erect a trophy,* Ar. Lys. 317. Καὶ παραστῆναι παντί [sc. ἔατε, παραινῶ, or δεῖ], *and let it be impressed upon every one,* Th. vi. 34 (cf. Παραστήτω δέ τινι καὶ τόδε Ib. 68). ΚΗΡ. Ἀκούετε, λεῴ· τοὺς ὁπλίτας . . ἀπιέναι [sc. κελεύεται, δεῖ, or χρή], Herald. *Hear, ye people; it is ordered that the hoplites depart,* or *the hoplites must depart,* Ar. Av. 448. Τὸν δὲ ἔχοντα . . καταδύειν v. 3. 13. Τὸν Ἴωνα χαίρειν [sc. κελεύω], *I bid Ion hail,* Pl. Ion, 530 a. Ἐμὲ παθεῖν τάδε [sc. δεινόν ἐστι], φεῦ! *That I should suffer such things* [is horrible], *alas!* Æsch. Eum. 837. Ὦ βασιλεῦ, κότερον λέγειν . . ἢ σιγᾶν [sc. χρή, or κελεύεις]; Hdt. i. 88. Ἆ δειλοί, πόσ' ἴμεν; κ. 431.

Notes. α. In exclamation, the *article* is usually prefixed; as, Φεῦ, τὸ καὶ λαβεῖν πρόσφθεγμα τοιοῦδ' ἀνδρός! *Ah, the hearing the voice of such a man!* Soph. Ph. 234. Τῆς τύχης! Τὸ ἐμὲ νῦν κληθέντα δεῦρο τυχεῖν! *My ill-luck! That I should happen now to have been summoned hither!* Cyr. ii. 2. 3 (§ 372. ζ). ΠΕΙΣΘ. Τὸ δ' ἐμὲ κορώνῃ πειθόμενον, τὸν ἄθλιον! ὁδοῦ περιελθεῖν στάδια πλεῖν ἢ χίλια! ΕΥ. Τὸ δ' ἐμὲ κολοιῷ πειθόμενον, τὸν δύσμορον! ἀποσποδῆσαι τοὺς ὄνυχας τῶν δακτύλων! Ar. Av. 5.

β. In a few poetic passages, the Inf. follows αἲ γάρ or εἴθε, to express wish (cf. §§ 597, 600. 2); as, Αἲ γὰρ . . ἐχέμεν η. 311. See ω. 376.

§ **626.** II. The *subject of the Inf.* is very often, either properly or by attraction (§§ 425. 4, 614), the *direct object* of a preceding verb, and consequently in the *Acc.* Hence has arisen an association between this case and the Inf., which has led to the following rule.

NOTE. The Inf., on the other hand, extensively constitutes an *indirect object* of the verb or other word on which it depends. From the prevalence of this use appears to have arisen the resemblance in form of the Greek and Lat. Inf. to the Dat., and the use of the prepositions *to* and *zu* before the Inf. in Eng. and German. Thus, Πέπεικε τὸν μάντιν λέγειν, *had persuaded the prophet* [to the saying] *to say*, vi. 4. 14. Τοὺς φυγάδας ἐκέλευσε σὺν αὐτῷ στρατεύεσθαι, *he invited the exiles* [to the serving] *to serve with him*, i. 2. 2.

RULE XXXI. The SUBJECT OF THE INFINITIVE is put in the *Accusative* ; as,

Ἠξίου . . δοθῆναί οἱ ταύτας τὰς πόλεις μᾶλλον, ἢ Τισσαφέρνην ἄρχειν αὐτῶν, *he requested that these cities should be given to him, rather than that Tissaphernes should rule them*, i. 1. 8. Κινδυνεύειν οὐκ ἐβούλοντο, ὑπὸ λιμοῦ τι παθεῖν αὐτούς, *did not wish to incur the risk* [that they should suffer any thing] *of their suffering from hunger*, Th. iv. 15. Νεῶν ποίησιν ἐπέμενον τελεσθῆναι Id. iii. 2. Φασὶ δ' οἱ σοφοὶ, . . θεοὺς καὶ ἀνθρώπους τὴν κοινωνίαν συνέχειν Pl. Gorg. 507 e.

§ **627.** REMARKS. 1. This rule applies to the subject of the Inf. *considered simply as such.* If, on the other hand, (α.) the subject of an Inf. has a *prior grammatical relation*, it may be in any case which this prior relation requires. If it is the same with the subject of the principal verb, it is seldom repeated, except for special emphasis or distinction (§ 614. ζ) ; and is then commonly repeated (as in other emphatic repetitions) in the same case (cf. § 499). Not unfrequently (β.) there is a mixture of constructions which may be referred to *ellipsis* or *anacoluthon.* Thus,

α. Ἦλθον ἐπί τινα τῶν δοκούντων σοφῶν εἶναι, *I came to one of those who were thought to be wise*, Pl. Apol. 21 b. Τοὺς οὐδενὶ ἐπιτρέψοντας κακῷ εἶναι, *who will permit no one to be bad*, iii. 2. 31. Νῦν σοὶ ἔξεστιν, ὦ Ξενοφῶν, ἀνδρὶ γενέσθαι vii. 1. 21. Ὁμολογεῖς οὖν περὶ ἐμὲ ἄδικος [= ἄδικόν σε] γεγενῆσθαι ; *Do you confess then* [to have been unjust] *that you have been unjust to me?* i. 6. 8. Τοῦτο δ' ἐποίει ἐκ τοῦ χαλεπὸς εἶναι, *and this he effected by being severe*, ii. 6. 9. Ἰᾶσθαι αὐτὸς τὸ τραῦμά φησι, *he says that he himself healed the wound*, i. 8. 26. Ὁ δὲ εἶπεν, ὅτι σπείσασθαι βούλοιτο, ἐφ' ᾧ μήτε αὐτὸς τοὺς Ἕλληνας ἀδικεῖν, μήτε ἐκείνους καίειν τὰς οἰκίας iv. 4. 6. Νομίζεις ἡμᾶς μὲν ἀνέξεσθαί σου, αὐτὸς δὲ τυπτήσειν ; καὶ ἡμᾶς μὲν ἀποψηφιεῖσθαί σου, σὺ δὲ οὐδὲ οὕτω παύσεσθαι ; Dem. 580. 9. See § 614. ζ.

β. Δέομαι ὑμῶν, ὦ ἄνδρες δικασταὶ, τὰ δίκαια [sc. ὑμᾶς] ψηφίσασθαι, ἐνθυμουμένους, *I entreat you, Judges,* [that you would vote] *to vote what is right, reflecting*, Lys. 118. 2. Κακούργου μὲν γάρ ἐστι, κριθέντ' ἀποθανεῖν· στρατηγοῦ δὲ, μαχόμενον τοῖς πολεμίοις Dem. 54. 1. Οὐ γὰρ ἦν πρὸς τοῦ Κύρου τρόπου, ἔχοντα μὴ διδόναι i. 2. 11. Συμβουλεύει τῷ Ξενοφῶντι, ἐλθόντα εἰς Δελφοὺς [sc. ἐκεῖνον] ἀνακοινῶσαι τῷ θεῷ, *he advises Xenophon* [that going to D. he should consult] *to go to Delphi and consult the god*, iii. 1. 5. Ἔδοξεν αὐτοῖς, προφύλακας καταστήσαντας συγκαλεῖν iii. 2. 1. Τοῖς πελτασταῖς πᾶσι παρήγγελλε διηγκυλωμένους ἰέναι, . . καὶ τοὺς τοξότας ἐπιβεβλῆσθαι v. 2. 12. Οἷς ἐξ ἀρχῆς ὑπῆρξεν, ἢ βασιλέων υἱέσιν εἶναι, ἢ αὐτοὺς τῇ φύσει ἱκανούς Pl. Gorg. 492 b. Ἧι πάρεστι μὲν στένειν πλούτου πατρῴου κτῆσιν ἐστερημένη, πάρεστι δ' ἀλγεῖν ἐς τοσόνδε τοῦ χρόνου ἄλεκτρα γηράσκουσαν Soph. El. 959. 'Εννέπω σὲ [for which σοὶ might have been used, if allowed by the metre] τῷ κηρύγματι, ᾧπερ προεῖπας, ἐμμένειν, . . ὡς ὄντι γῆς τῆσδ' ἀνοσίῳ μιάστορι Id. Œd. T. 350. See § 459.

2. Cases of special attraction and anacoluthon likewise occur in connection with the Inf.; as, 'Ελπίζων . . οὐδ' ὢν αὐτὸς, οὐδὲ οἱ [for τοὺς] ἐξ αὐτοῦ, παύσεσθαι Hdt. i. 56. Τοὺς δὲ ἀποκρίνασθαι, . . αὐτοὶ δώσειν Ib. 2.

3. The subject of the Inf. is very often indefinite, and is then commonly omitted. It follows from the rule, that words agreeing with this omitted subject are in the Acc. Thus, ΣΩΚ. Οὐδαμῶς ἄρα δεῖ ἀδικεῖν. ΚΡ. Οὐ δῆτα. ΣΩΚ. Οὐδὲ ἀδικούμενον ἄρα ἀνταδικεῖν. Soc. *One ought then by no means to injure.* Cr. *Surely not.* Soc. *Not then, when injured, to injure in turn.* Pl. Crito, 49 b.

§ **628.** III. By a mixture of constructions, the Inf. is often used after a connective (commonly ὡς, ὥστε, οἷος, or ὅσος), instead of a finite verb, or of the Inf. without a connective; as,

Καὶ κατέβαινον ὡς ἐπὶ τὸν ἕτερον ἀναβαίνειν, *and were descending, so as to ascend the second* [= ὡς ἀναβαῖεν, *that they might ascend*, which is the reading of Dindorf and Krüger], iii. 4. 25. 'Υπελάσας ὡς συναντῆσαι, *riding up to meet him*, i. 8. 15. Ποταμὸς τοσοῦτος τὸ βάθος, ὡς μηδὲ τὰ δόρατα ὑπερέχειν iii. 5. 7. 'Ως μὲν συνελόντι [sc. λόγῳ] εἰπεῖν, [so as to speak with a discourse bringing all together] *to speak comprehensively, to say all in a word*, iii. 1. 38. 'Ως δ' ἐν βραχεῖ εἰπεῖν, *but to speak in brief*, Ag. 7. 1. 'Ως ἔπος εἰπεῖν, *so to speak*, Pl. Gorg. 450 d. "Ως γε οὑτωσὶ δόξαι Id. Rep. 432 b. 'Ως μικρὸν μεγάλῳ εἰκάσαι Th. iv. 36. "Ως γ' ἐμοὶ χρῆσθαι κριτῇ Eur. Alc. 801. 'Ιόλην ἔλεξας, ὥς γ' ἐπεικάζειν ἐμέ, *you speak of Iole*, [at least for me to conjecture] *methinks*, Soph. Tr. 1220. 'Ως παλαιὰ εἶναι, *considering* [that they are ancient] *their antiquity*, Th. i. 21. Βούλεται πονεῖν, ὥστε πολεμεῖν, *chooses toil, so as to be* [or *that he may be*] *at war*, ii. 6. 6. "Εχω γὰρ τριήρεις, ὥστε ἑλεῖν τὸ ἐκείνων πλοῖον, 'so as to take,' *i. e.* 'so that I can take,' i. 4. 8. 'Εποίησα, ὥστε δόξαι αὐτῷ i. 6. 6. Κραυγὴν πολλὴν ἐποίουν καλοῦντες ἀλλήλους, ὥστε καὶ τοὺς πολεμίους ἀκούειν· ὥστε οἱ μὲν ἐγγύτατα τῶν πολεμίων καὶ ἔφυγον ii. 2. 17. 'Εφ' ᾧ μὴ καίειν iv. 2. 19 (see § 530). 'Εφ' ᾧ τε πλοῖα συλλέγειν vi. 6. 22. "Οπως τὴν ἀρχὴν μὴ τοιοῦτοι ἔσονται οἱ πολῖται, οἷοι πονηροῦ τινος ἢ αἰσχροῦ ἔργου ἐφίεσθαι, 'such as to desire' [= τοιοῦτοι οἷοι ἂν ἐφίοιντο, such as would desire], Cyr. i. 2. 3. Τοιούτους ἀνθρώπους, οἵους μεθυσθέντας ὀρχεῖσθαι Dem. 23. 16. "Οσον μόνον γεύσασθαι ἑαυτῷ καταλιπών [= τοσοῦτον μόνον ὅσον ἂν γεύσαιτο], *leaving for himself so much only as* [he could taste] *to taste*, i. e. *merely enough for a taste*, vii. 3. 22. Νεμόμενοί τε τὰ αὐτῶν ἕκαστοι ὅσον ἀποζῆν, 'merely enough for subsistence,' Th. i. 2. 'Ελείπετο τῆς νυκτὸς ὅσον σκοταίους διελθεῖν τὸ πεδίον iv. 1. 5. "Οσα μέντοι ἤδη δοκεῖν αὐτῷ, *but so far as* [seemed to him] *he could judge at present*, Th. vi. 25. "Οσον γέ μ' εἰδέναι Ar. Nub. 1252. "Ο τι κἄμ' εἰδέναι Id. Eccl. 350.

§ **629.** REMARKS. 1. It will be observed, that, in some of the examples above, there is an ellipsis before the connective, and that in some the connective itself suffers attraction. From the frequent use of οἷος as above, with an ellipsis of its corresponding demonstrative (§ 523), it seems to have been at length regarded, especially in connection with τε, as a simple adjective of quality, and to have been construed accordingly; thus, "Οἷοί τε ἔσεσθε ἡμῖν συμπρᾶξαι περὶ τῆς διόδου;" Οἱ δὲ εἶπον, ὅτι "ἱκανοί ἐσμεν εἰς τὴν χώραν εἰσβάλλειν." "*Shall you be* [such as to] *able to coöperate with us respecting the passage?*" *And they replied,* "*We are able to make an irruption into the country.*" v. 4. 9. Ὁ γὰρ οἷός τε ὢν γιγνώσκειν τε τοὺς ὠφελίμους αὐτοῖς, καὶ τούτους δυνάμενος ποιεῖν ἐπιθυμεῖν ἀλλήλων Symp. 4. 64 (§ 507. 7). Οὐχ οἷόν τε ἦν . . διώκειν, [there was not such a state of things that one could pursue] *it was not possible to pursue,* iii. 3. 9. Οὐχ οἷόν τέ σοι λανθάνειν, *it is not possible for you to conceal it,* vii. 7. 22 (§ 403). Οὐ γὰρ ἦν ὥρα οἵα τὸ πεδίον ἄρδειν, *for it was not a time* [such as to irrigate] *suitable for irrigating the plain,* ii. 3. 13. Τὸ πρᾶγμα μέγα εἶναι, καὶ μὴ οἷον νεωτέρῳ βουλεύσασθαι, 'not suitable for a young man to direct,' Th. vi. 12. Ξυγγράφεσθαι λόγους οἵους εἰς τὰ δικαστήρια, *to compose discourses adapted to courts of justice,* Pl. Euthyd. 272 a.

2. By a similar mixture of constructions, πρὶν ἤ, πρότερον ἤ, ὕστερον ἤ, are sometimes followed by the Inf. instead of another mode; as, Ὕστερον . . ἢ αὐτοὺς οἰκίσαι [for ὕστερον ἢ ᾤκισαν or ὕστερον τοῦ οἰκίσαι] Th. vi. 4.

(II.) *The Participle.*

§ **630.** I. The Participle, in its common uses, is either *preliminary*, *circumstantial*, *complementary*, *prospective*, or *definitive;* that is, it either (1.) denotes something preceding the main action of the sentence; or (2.) it expresses some circumstance of that action; or (3.) it serves as a complement of the action (§ 329); or (4.) it denotes a purpose or consequence of the action; or (5.) it defines some person or thing connected with the action. See § 618.

§ **631.** 1. As a *Preliminary Part.*, the *Aor.* is especially common. It is often best translated into Eng. by a finite verb with a connective, or by the Pres. Part.; as,

Κῦρος ὑπολαβὼν τοὺς φεύγοντας, συλλέξας στράτευμα, ἐπολιόρκει Μίλητον, *Cyrus received the exiles, and raising an army besieged Miletus,* i. 1. 7. Μάνθαν' ἐλθών, *Go and learn,* Ar. Nub. 89.

NOTE. To the *preliminary Part.* may be referred the use of μαθών and παθών with τί or ὅ τι, to form an intensive (and often severe or sarcastic) '*why*' or '*because*'; thus, Τί γὰρ μαθόντ' ἐς τοὺς θεοὺς ὑβρίζετην; *For having learned what new wisdom did you insult the gods?* i. e. *Why did you insult them?* or, *What possessed you to insult them?* Ar. Nub. 1506. Τί παθοῦσαι . . εἴξασι γυναιξίν; *Having experienced what change do they resemble women?* i. e. *How is it that they resemble?* Ib. 340. Δικαιότερον τὸν ὑμέτερον πατέρα τύπτοιμι, ὅ τι μαθὼν σοφοὺς υἱεῖς οὕτως ἔφυσεν, 'because he begat,' Pl. Euthyd. 299 a.

§ **632.** 2. The *Circumstantial Part.* is very common in Greek, especially in the Pres. It may sometimes be translated by an adverb or a circumstantial adjunct; as,

Δύναμιν ἤθροιζεν ὡς μάλιστα ἐδύνατο ἐπικρυπτόμενος, 'as secretly as possible,' i. 1. 6. Ἅπερ καὶ ἀρχόμενος εἶπον, 'in the beginning,' Th. iv. 64. Τοὺς πολλοὺς . . ἀπὸ Θρασυμάχου ἀρξαμένους, *the most* [beginning with] *and particularly Thrasymachus,* Pl. Rep. 498 c. Τελευτῶν ἐχαλέπαινεν iv. 5. 16 (§ 457. *a*).

Ἀνύσας τρέχε Ar. Plut. 229 (§ 457. γ). Ἧκε Μένων ὁ Θετταλὸς, ὁπλίτας ἔχων χιλίους, 'with 1000 hoplites,' i. 2. 6. Οἳ ληϊζόμενοι ζῶσι, *who live by plundering*, Cyr. iii. 2. 25.

NOTE. The participle ἔχων, both with and without an Accusative, is joined with some verbs, chiefly of *trifling* and *delay*, to give the idea of *continuance* or *persistency* (cf. § 637. a); as, Ποῖα ὑποδήματα φλυαρεῖς ἔχων; [Holding on upon what shoes are you trifling?] *What shoes are you trifling so pertinaciously about?* Pl. Gorg. 490 e. Ἔχων φλυαρεῖς, [you trifle, holding on upon it] *you persist in trifling*, Id. Euthyd. 295 c. Ληρεῖς ἔχων Id. Gorg. 497 a; Ar. Ran. 512. Τί κυπτάζεις ἔχων περὶ τὴν θύραν; Ar. Nub. 509. Τί δῆτα ἔχων στρέφῃ; Pl. Phædr. 236 e.

§ **633.** 3. The *Complementary Part.* is particularly frequent with verbs of *sensation*, of *mental state and action*, of *showing* and *informing*, of *appearance* and *discovery*, of *concealment* and *chance*, of *conduct* and *success*, of *permission* and *endurance*, of *commencement* and *continuance*, of *weariness* and *cessation*, of *anticipation* and *omission*. Thus,

Ἤκουσε Κῦρον ἐν Κιλικίᾳ ὄντα, *he heard* [of Cyrus being in C.] *that Cyrus was in Cilicia*, i. 4. 5. Ἑώρα πλείονος ἐνδέον, *he saw that there was need of more*, vi. 1. 31. Ἴσθι μέντοι ἀνόητος ὤν, *but know that you are senseless*, ii. 1. 13 (§ 614. ζ. Cf. "And knew not eating death," *Par. Lost*, ix. 792). Κατέμαθον ἀναστὰς μόλις v. 8. 14. Εἰδέναι συνοῖσον, *to know that it would be advantageous*, Dem. 55. 2. Πρὸς ἀνδρὸς ᾔσθετ' ἠδικημένη Eur. Med. 26. Σύνοιδα ἐμαυτῷ πάντα ἐψευσμένος i. 3. 10 (§ 615. 1). Φρόνει βεβὼς Soph. Ant. 996. Ἐμέμνητο γὰρ εἰπὼν Cyr. iii. 1. 31. Τιμώμενοι χαίρουσιν, *they delight in being honored*, Eur. Hipp. 8. Ἀπολείποντες αὐτὸν ἄχθονται. . . Ἥδονται πράττοντες Mem. ii. 1. 33. Μετεμέλοντο ἀποδεδωκότες Th. v. 35. Δεδρακυῖαν γελᾷν Soph. Ant. 483. Ἐπαισχύνεσθε . . κινοῦντες Id. Œd. T. 635. Δείξω πρῶτα μὲν σοφὸς γεγὼς, ἔπειτα σώφρων Eur. Med. 548. Κῦρόν τε ἐπιστρατεύοντα πρῶτος ἤγγειλα ii. 3. 19. Ἐμμένομεν οἷς ὡμολογήσαμεν δικαίοις οὖσιν; Pl. Crito, 50 a. Οὐ γὰρ φθονῶν τοῖς φανερῶς πλουτοῦσιν ἐφαίνετο i. 9. 19. Εὕρισκον οὐδαμῶς ἂν ἄλλως τοῦτο διαπραξάμενος Isocr. 311 c. Οἳ ἂν ἐξελεγχθῶσι διαβάλλοντες ii. 5. 27. Τρεφόμενον ἐλάνθανεν, [was secret being maintained] *was secretly maintained*, i. 1. 9. Λαθεῖν αὐτὸν ἀπελθών, *to conceal from him our departure*, or, *to depart without his knowledge*, i. 3. 17. Ὅπως μὴ λάθῃς σεαυτὸν ἀγνοῶν, *that you may not be unconsciously ignorant*, Mem. iii. 5. 23. Ἔστ' ἂν λάθωμεν [sc. ἡμᾶς αὐτοὺς] ὑδροπόται γενόμενοι, *till insensibly we become water-drinkers*, Cyr. vi. 2. 29. Παρὼν ἐτύγχανε, *happened* [being] *to be present*, i. 1. 2. Ὅστις ἐχθρὸς ὢν κυρεῖ Eur. Alc. 954. Ἀδικεῖτε . . πολέμου ἄρχοντες, *you do wrong in beginning war*, Th. i. 53. Ἐλλείπεσθαι εὖ ποιῶν Mem. ii. 6. 5. Εἴπερ εὐτυχήσομεν . . ἑλόντες Eur. Or. 1212. Ἡ πόλις αὐτοῖς οὐκ ἐπιτρέψει παραβαίνουσι τὸν νόμον Isocr. 268 e. Νικωμένη γὰρ Παλλὰς οὐκ ἀνέξεται Eur. Heracl. 352. Ὑπήρξαμεν κακῶς ποιοῦντες v. 5. 9. Διάγουσι μανθάνοντες δικαιοσύνην, *they spend their time in learning justice*, Cyr. i. 2. 6. Διατρίβουσι μελετῶσαι Ib. 12. Διαγωνιζόμενοι . . διατελοῦσιν Ib. Μὴ κάμῃς φίλον ἄνδρα εὐεργετῶν Pl. Gorg. 470 c. Ἐπαύσαντο πολεμοῦντες vi. 1. 28. Ἃ οἶμαι ἂν παῦσαι ἐνοχλοῦντα ii. 5. 13. Ὅπως μὴ φθάσωσι μήτε ὁ Κῦρος μήτε οἱ Κίλικες καταλαβόντες, *that neither Cyrus nor the Cilicians might anticipate them in taking possession*, or *take possession before them*, i. 3. 14. Φθάνουσιν ἐπὶ τῷ ἄκρῳ γενόμενοι τοὺς πολεμίους iii. 4. 49. Οὐκ ἔφθησαν πυθόμενοι τὸν περὶ τὴν Ἀττικὴν πόλεμον, καὶ . . ἧκον, *they no sooner heard of the war around At-*

tica than they came, Isocr. 58 b. Φυτεύων παῖδας οὐκέτ' ἂν φθάνοις, *you cannot now be too soon in begetting children*, Eur. Alc. 662. Οὐκ ἂν φθάνοις . . λέγων *you cannot tell me too soon*, i. e. *tell me at once*, Mem. ii. 3. 11. Ἄλλα γε δὴ μυρία ἐπιλείπω λέγων Pl. Phil. 26 b.

§ **634.** Notes. *α*. With these verbs, the Part. ὤν is sometimes omitted (cf. § 547); as, Σῶς ἴσθι [sc. ὤν], *know that you are safe*, Soph. Œd. C. 1210. Εἰ γέρων κυρῶ Ib. 726. Σὲ δηλώσω κακόν [sc. ὄντα] Ib. 783. Δηλοῖ τὸ γέννημ' ὠμόν Id. Ant. 471. Νῦν δ' ἀγροῖσι τυγχάνει Id. El. 313.

β. Many of these verbs likewise take the Inf.; but often with this distinction from the Part.; viz. that the Inf. denotes something dependent upon the action of the verb, but the Part. something which exists independent of it. Thus, Ἂν ἅπαξ μάθωμεν ἀργοὶ ζῆν, *if we should once have learned to live in idleness*, iii. 2. 25. Ἵνα μάθῃ σοφιστὴς ὤν, *that he may learn that he is a schemer*, Æsch. Pr. 61. Γνῷ τρέφειν τὴν γλῶσσαν ἡσυχωτέραν, 'learn to keep,' Soph. Ant. 1089. Ἐπειδὰν γνῶσιν ἀπιστούμενοι, *when they perceive that they are distrusted*, Cyr. vii. 3. 17. Μεμνήσθω ἀνὴρ ἀγαθὸς εἶναι, *let him remember to be a brave man*, iii. 2. 39. Μέμνημαι . . ἀκούσας ποτέ, *I remember to have once heard*, Cyr. i. 6. 3. Τοῦτο μὲν οὐκ αἰσχύνομαι λέγων· τὸ δὲ . . αἰσχυνοίμην ἂν λέγειν, *I am not ashamed to say this* (which is said); *but I should be ashamed to say that* (which from the shame is not said), Cyr. v. 1. 21.

γ. The complementary Part. sometimes occurs with an impersonal expression, or with an adjective and verb supplying the place of a simple verb. When thus connected, the real subject of the sentence is sometimes implied in the Part. Thus, Ἐμοὶ πρέποι ἂν μάλιστα ἐπιμελομένῳ, *it would become me most of all to attend*, Œc. 4. 1. Οἷς οὐδὲ ἅπαξ ἐλυσιτέλησε πειθομένοις Isocr. 174. 14. Εἰ πολεμοῦσιν ἄμεινον ἔσται, *whether it would be better for them to go to war*, Th. i. 118. Μεστὸς ἦν θυμούμενος, *I was sated with passion*, Soph. Œd. C. 768. Δῆλος ἦν ἀνιώμενος i. 2. 11. Κατάδηλοι γίγνονται προσποιούμενοι μὲν εἰδέναι, εἰδότες δὲ οὐδέν Pl. Apol. 23 d. See §§ 551, 614. *ε*.

§ **635.** 4. *Prospective Part.* This appears chiefly in the *Fut. Part. denoting purpose*, commonly translated by the Inf. (§§ 583. *a*, 618. 1).

§ **636.** 5. The *Definitive Part.* is equivalent to a relative pronoun and finite verb, and is most frequently translated by these. It is often used substantively, and may not unfrequently be translated by a noun. It occurs chiefly with the article, but sometimes without it, if the class only is defined. Thus,

Αὖθις δὲ ὁ ἡγησόμενος οὐδεὶς ἔσται, *and again there will be no one who will guide us*, ii. 4. 5. Οἱ αὐτομολήσαντες (cf. Οἳ ὕστερον ἐλήφθησαν) i. 7. 13. Τοὺς ἐκπεπτωκότας, *those who had been banished*, or *the exiles*, i. 1. 7 (§ 556). Τοῖς γειναμένοις (cf. Τοῖς γονεῦσι) Apol. 20. Συναγαγὼν . . τοὺς προσελθόντας αὐτῷ καὶ τῶν ἄλλων τὸν βουλόμενον, '*and of the rest* [him that wished] *any one that wished*,' i. 3. 9. Ἡ Διομήδεια λεγομένη ἀνάγκη, *the so-called necessity of Diomed*, Pl. Rep. 493 d. Ἵν', ὥσπερ ἐκεῖνος ἔχει δύναμιν τὴν ἀδικήσουσαν καὶ καταδουλωσομένην ἅπαντας τοὺς Ἕλληνας, οὕτω τὴν σώσουσαν ὑμεῖς καὶ βοηθήσουσαν ἅπασιν ἑτοίμην ἔχητε Dem. 101. 10. Ἅπαντα γὰρ τολμῶσι δεινὰ φαίνεται, *for every thing appears fearful to those who are venturing*, Eur. Ph. 270. Πεπονθέναι . . εἰς βλάβην φέρον, *to have suffered* [what tends to harm] *any injury*, Soph. Œd. T. 516. Διαφέρει δὲ πάμπολυ μαθὼν μὴ μαθόντος, καὶ ὁ γυμνασάμενος τοῦ μὴ γεγυμνασμένου Pl. Leg. 795 b. See §§ 447. a, 449, 469, 476.

§ **637.** II. The Part. with such verbs as εἰμί, γίγνομαι, ἔχω, ἔρχομαι, οἴχομαι, &c., often takes the place of a finite verb, either to supply some deficiency in inflection, or for the sake of more definite or emphatic expression. Thus,

Πεποιηκὼς εἴη iv. 8. 26. Τεταγμένοι ἦσαν i. 7. 11. Ἦσαν ἐκπεπτωκότες ii. 3. 10. Ἦν δὲ οὐδὲν πεπονθώς vi. 1. 6. Εἴη ἔχων iv. 4. 18. Ταῦτα οὕτως ἔχοντά ἐστιν Pl. Leg. 860 e. Πῶς . . ἦτε πάσχοντες τάδε; Eur. Cycl. 381. Εἴη συγγνωσθείς Id. Alc. 464. Ἀντιδοὺς ἔσει Soph. Ant. 1067. Μισοῦντές τε γίγνονται, Pl. Leg. 908 b. Μὴ προδοὺς ἡμᾶς γένῃ Soph. Aj. 588. Πέλει δικαιωθείς Æsch. Ag. 392. Πολλὰ χρήματα ἔχομεν ἀνηρπακότες, [having plundered many things we have them] *we have plundered many things*, i. 3. 14. Ἃ νῦν καταστρεψάμενος ἔχεις vii. 7. 27. Τὰ ἐπιτήδεια πάντα εἶχον ἀνακεκομισμένοι iv. 7. 1. Τὰ ἐπιτήδεια ἐν τούτοις ἀνακεκομισμένοι ἦσαν Ib. 17. Τὸν λόγον δὲ σοῦ πάλαι θαυμάσας ἔχω Pl. Phædr. 257 c. Τὸν μὲν προτίσας, τὸν δ' ἀτιμάσας ἔχει Soph. Ant. 22. Κηρύξαντ' ἔχειν Ib. 32. Ἀτιμάσασ' ἔχε Ib. 77. Βεβουλευκὼς ἔχει Id. Œd. T. 701. Οὐ τοῦτο λέξων ἔρχομαι, *I am not going* [or *come*] *to say this*, Ages. 2. 7. Ἔρχομαι ἀποθανούμενος νυνί Pl. Theag. 129 a. Ὤιχετο ἀπιὼν νυκτός, *he* [departed going off] *went off in the night*, iii. 3. 5. Ὤιχετο ἀπελαύνων, *rode off*, ii. 4. 24. Οἴχεται θανὼν Soph. Ph. 414.

NOTES. (*a*) The *Perf. Part.* with εἰμί is especially common, particularly in the passive, either to supply the deficiencies in the inflection of the complete tenses (§§ 168. α, 169. β, 213. 2, 234), or to direct the attention more expressly to the state consequent upon an action. Ἔχω occurs most frequently with the *Aor. act. part.* and in the dramatists, commonly conveying the accessory idea of *possession*, *continuance*, or *persistency* (holding on upon an action. Cf. § 632. N.). Ἔρχομαι with the *Fut. Part.* forms a more immediate Fut. The Part. of a *verb of motion* with οἴχομαι is a stronger form of expression for the simple verb. (*b*) The substantive verb is sometimes omitted (§ 547); as, Δεδογμέν' [sc. ἐστὶν], ὡς ἔοικε, τήνδε κατθανεῖν Soph. Ant. 576.

§ **638.** III. A Part. with its subject, or an impersonal Part. (§ 617), often forms so distinct a clause, that it is said (though not in the strictest sense of the term, § 343. N.) to be put *absolute*. This occurs most frequently in the *Gen.*, and, after this, in the *Acc.* The far less frequent instances in which the *Nom.* and *Dat.* are used in the same way, may be commonly referred at once to anacoluthon, or other constructions already mentioned (§§ 344, 401, 410, 420). The Gen. and Acc. absolute may also be referred, though often less directly, to the *Gen.* and *Acc. of time* (§§ 378, 439); and as, in this use, a Part. and substantive commonly denote an *event*, but an impersonal Part. a *continued state*, the following general rule has arisen, which is not, however, without exception.

RULE XXXII. A PARTICIPLE AND SUBSTAN-

TIVE are put absolute in the *Genitive*; an IMPERSONAL PARTICIPLE, in the *Accusative*; as,

[NOTE. Among the following examples of the rule have been inserted some exceptions, for the sake of comparison.]

Τοῦτο δὲ λέγοντος αὐτοῦ, πτάρνυταί τις, *and* [he saying this] *upon his saying this, some one sneezes,* iii. 2. 9. Ὅστις, ἐξὸν μὲν εἰρήνην ἔχειν . ., αἱρεῖται πολεμεῖν, *who,* [it being permitted him to have] *while he might have peace, prefers war,* ii. 6. 6. Μετὰ δὲ ταῦτα, ἤδη ἡλίου δύνοντος ii. 2. 3. Ἀνέβη ἐπὶ τὰ ὄρη, οὐδενὸς κωλύοντος, 'without opposition,' i. 2. 22. Οὐδὲ μὴν βοηθῆσαι, πολλῶν ὄντων πέραν, οὐδεὶς αὐτοῖς δυνήσεται, λελυμένης τῆς γεφύρας, *nor, although there were many upon the other side, could any one come to their assistance, if the bridge were destroyed,* ii. 4. 20. Σίτου δὲ ἐπιλελοιπότος, οἴνου δὲ μηδ' ὀσφραίνεσθαι παρόν, ὑπὸ δὲ πόνων πολλῶν ἀπαγορευόντων v. 8. 3. Ἐν καλῷ παρατυχὸν σφίσι ξυμβαλεῖν, καὶ πανταχόθεν αὐτῶν ἀποκεκλεισμένων Th. v. 60. Εὖ δὲ παρασχόν, *but when a favorable opportunity offers,* Id. i. 120. Οὐ προσῆκον, *when it is no interest of ours,* Id. iv. 95. Ἀμφοτέροις μὲν δοκοῦν ἀναχωρεῖν, . . κυρωθὲν δὲ οὐδὲν . . ὁπηνίκα χρὴ ὁρμᾶσθαι, νυκτός τε ἐπιγενομένης Ib. 125. Δεδογμένον δὲ αὐτοῖς Id. i. 125. Δόξαν αὐτοῖς ἀπὸ ξυνόδου, ὥστε διαναυμαχεῖν Id. viii. 79. Δόξαντος δὲ τούτου H. Gr. i. 1. 36. Δοξάντων δὲ καὶ τούτων Ib. v. 2. 24. Δόξαντα δὲ ταῦτα καὶ περανθέντα Ib. iii. 2. 19. Δόξαν δὲ ταῦτα [sc. ποιεῖν, or the sing. and plur. joined, see §§ 450. 451, 549], *and this seeming best,* iv. 1. 13. Δόξαν ἡμῖν ταῦτα, ἐπορευόμεθα Pl. Prot. 314 c. Ἄδηλον ὄν, ὁπότε τις . . ἀφαιρήσεται Th. i. 2. Αἰσχρὸν ὂν τὸ ἀντιλέγειν Cyr. ii. 2. 20. Προσταχθὲν γὰρ αὐτῷ . . ἀναγράψαι Lys. 183. 12. Δηλωθέντος, ὅτι ἐν ταῖς ναυσὶ τῶν Ἑλλήνων τὰ πράγματα ἐγένετο Th. i. 74. Ἐσαγγελθέντων, ὅτι Φοίνισσαι νῆες ἐπ' αὐτοὺς πλέουσιν Ib. 116 (§ 451). Περὶ σωτηρίας [sc. βουλεύεσθαι] προκειμένου Ar. Eccl. 401.

§ **639.** REMARKS. 1. Absolute and connected constructions of the Part. are, in various ways, interchanged and mixed; the former giving more prominence to the Part., and sometimes arising from a change of subject; the latter showing more clearly the relation of the Part. to the rest of the sentence. Thus, Διαβαινόντων [sc. αὐτῶν] μέντοι, ὁ Γλοῦς αὐτοῖς ἐπεφάνη [= διαβαίνουσιν αὐτοῖς], *as they were crossing, however, Glus appeared to them,* ii. 4. 24. Τοῖς προτέροις μετὰ Κύρου ἀναβᾶσι . . · καὶ ταῦτα, οὐκ ἐπὶ μάχην ἰόντων [= ἰοῦσι], ἀλλὰ καλοῦντος τοῦ πατρὸς Κῦρον i. 4. 12. Δι' ἡμᾶς, ἐν τάξει τε ἰόντων καὶ μαχομένων v. 8. 13. Οὐκέτι ὧν οὗτοι κλέπτουσιν ὀργίζεσθε, ἀλλ' ὧν αὐτοὶ λαμβάνετε χάριν ἴστε, ὥσπερ ὑμεῖς τὰ τούτων μισθοφοροῦντες, ἀλλ' οὐ τούτων τὰ ὑμέτερα κλεπτόντων Lys. 178. 38.

2. The substantive is sometimes *omitted,* and sometimes, though less frequently, the Part. of the substantive verb (cf. § 547); as, Ἐντεῦθεν προϊόντων [sc. αὐτῶν], ἐφαίνετο ἴχνια, 'as they were advancing,' i. 6. 1. Οἱ δ' εἶπον, ἐρωτήσαντος [sc. αὐτοῦ], ὅτι Μάκρωνες iv. 8. 5. Πόσις μὲν ἄν μοι, κατθανόντος [sc. πόσεως], ἄλλος ἦν Soph. Ant. 909. Οὕτω δ' ἐχόντων [sc. ἑαυτὰ πραγμάτων], *and affairs* [having themselves, § 555] *standing thus,* iii. 2. 10. Οὕτω μὲν γιγνομένων, σαφῶς οἶδα Cyr. v. 3. 13. Ἄκοντος βασιλέως [sc. ὄντος] ii. 1. 19. Ἔξεστι φωνεῖν, ὡς ἐμοῦ μόνης πέλας Soph. Œd. C. 83. Ὡς ὑφηγητοῦ τινός Id. Œd. T. 1260.

3. The use of the Acc. for the Gen. absolute chiefly occurs after ὡς (§ 640), or when the subject is a neuter adjective (cf. § 432. 2).

§ 640. IV. A Part., whether absolute or dependent, is often preceded by ὡς (or a similar *particle of special application*), chiefly to mark it as *subjective*, i. e. as *expressing the view*, *opinion*, *feeling*, *intention*, *or statement of some one*, whether in accordance with or contrary to fact. The Part. thus construed often supplies the place of a finite verb or Inf. Thus,

Παρήγγειλε . ., ὡς ἐπιβουλεύοντος Τισσαφέρνους, *he gave command* [as he would give command, T. plotting] *as if Tissaphernes were plotting*, or *under pretence that T. was plotting*, i. 1. 6. Ὤιοντο ἀπολωλέναι, ὡς ἑαλωκυίας τῆς πόλεως, *they thought they were lost, inasmuch as the city was taken*, vii. 1. 19. Ἐκέλευσε . ., ὡς εἰς Πεισίδας βουλόμενος στρατεύεσθαι, ὡς πραγμάτων παρεχόντων Πεισιδῶν i. 1. 11. Ὡς ἐμοῦ οὖν ἰόντος, . . οὕτω τὴν γνώμην ἔχετε, [as if then I should go, so have your opinion] *be assured, then, that I shall go*, i. 3. 6. Ἔλεγε θαῤῥεῖν, ὡς καταστησομένων τούτων εἰς τὸ δέον Ib. 8. Τὰ πλοῖα αἰτεῖν κελεύοντος, ὥσπερ πάλιν τὸν στόλον Κύρου μὴ ποιουμένου Ib. 16. Ὡς οὐκέτ' ὄντων σῶν τέκνων, φρόντιζε δή Eur. Med. 1311. Στρατιὰν πολλὴν ἄγων, ὡς βοηθήσων βασιλεῖ, *bringing a large force to aid the king*, ii. 4. 25 (§ 583. *a*) Κατασκευάζεσθαι ὡς αὐτοῦ που οἰκήσοντας (cf. Μένειν παρασκευαζομένους) iii. 2. 24. Κατακείμεθα, ὥσπερ ἐξὸν ἡσυχίαν ἄγειν, *we lie down, as if it were permitted us to enjoy our ease*, iii. 1. 14. Διηγκυλωμένους ἰέναι, ὡς, ὁπόταν σημήνῃ, ἀκοντίζειν δεῆσον, v. 2. 12. Λέγουσιν ἡμᾶς ὡς ὀλωλότας Æsch. Ag. 672. Δηλοῖς δ' ὥς τι σημανῶν Soph. Ant. 242. Ὡς πολέμου ὄντος παρ' ὑμῶν ἀπαγγελῶ; ii. 1. 21. Ὡς μὲν στρατηγήσοντα ἐμὲ ταύτην τὴν στρατηγίαν, μηδεὶς ὑμῶν λεγέτω, *let no one of you speak, as though I were to take this command*, i. 3. 15. Ἀνέκραγον, ὡς οὐδὲν δέον vi. 4. 22. Ἀπὸ τῶν πονηρῶν ἀνθρώπων εἴργουσιν, ὡς τὴν μὲν τῶν χρηστῶν ὁμιλίαν ἄσκησιν τῆς ἀρετῆς, τὴν δὲ τῶν πονηρῶν, κατάλυσιν Mem. i. 2. 20. Εὔχετο δὲ πρὸς τοὺς θεοὺς ἁπλῶς τἀγαθὰ διδόναι, ὡς τοὺς θεοὺς κάλλιστα εἰδότας Ib. iii. 2. Ἡ δὲ γνώμη ἦν, ὡς εἰς τὰς τάξεις τῶν Ἑλλήνων ἐλῶντα [sc. τὰ ἅρματα], *and the plan was, that they should drive against the ranks of the Greeks*, i. 8. 10. See § 662.

§ 641. V. Anacoluthon. From the variety of the offices and relations of the Part., and its frequent separation from its subject, its syntax is peculiarly affected by anacoluthon; consisting either (α.) in the transition from one case to another, or (β.) in the transition from the Part. to another form of the verb, or the converse. Thus,

α. Ἦν δὲ ἡ γνώμη τοῦ Ἀριστέως [= ἔδοξε τῷ Ἀριστεῖ], τὸ μὲν μεθ' ἑαυτοῦ στρατόπεδον ἔχοντι ἐν τῷ ἰσθμῷ ἐπιτηρεῖν Th. i. 62. Ἔδοξεν αὐτοῖς [= ἐψηφίσαντο] . ., ἐπικαλοῦντες Id. iii. 36. Καὶ δημοσίᾳ κράτιστα διαθέντα τὰ τοῦ πολέμου, ἰδίᾳ ἕκαστοι τοῖς ἐπιτηδεύμασιν αὐτοῦ ἀχθεσθέντες Id. vi. 15. Αἰδώς μ' ἔχει [= αἰδοῦμαι] ἐν τῷδε πότμῳ τυγχάνουσα Eur. Hec. 970. Πέπαλται δ' αὖτέ μοι φίλον κέαρ [= τρόμος ἔχει με], τόνδε κλύουσαν οἶκτον Æsch. Cho. 410. Ὕπεστί μοι θράσος, . . κλύουσαν Soph. El. 479. Ἡμῖν [= ἡμῶν, § 412] δ' αὖτε κατεκλάσθη φίλον ἦτορ, δεισάντων φθόγγον ι. 256. For other examples see §§ 344, 459, 627, 639.

β. Ἄλλῳ τε τρόπῳ πειράσαντες, καὶ μηχανὴν προσήγαγον Th. iv. 100. Οἱ στρατηγοὶ ἐστασίαζον, Κλεάνωρ μὲν καὶ Φρυνίσκος πρὸς Σεύθην βουλόμενοι ἄγειν . . . Τιμασίων δὲ προὐθυμεῖτο vii. 2. 2. Ὡς τύχοι ναῦς καὶ προσπε σοῦσα, ἢ διὰ τὸ φεύγειν, ἢ ἄλλῃ ἐπιπλέουσα Th. vii. 70. In the following example, there is a remarkable transition from the infinitive construction to the participial; Διείργεται, τὸ μὴ ἤπειρος οὖσα [for εἶναι], *is separated, so as not to be main land* (see § 622), Th. vi. 1.

(III.) *Verbal in -τέος.*

§ **642.** From the verb is formed a passive adjective in -τέος, expressing *obligation* or *necessity* (§ 314. f). This verbal is often used *impersonally*, in the neut. sing. or plur., with ἐστί (§ 546. α). In this use, it is equivalent to the *Inf. act.* or *mid.* with δεῖ or χρή· thus, Σκεπτέον μοι δοκεῖ εἶναι [= σκέπτεσθαι δεῖν], *it seems to me that it is to be considered* [= *that we ought to consider*], i. 3. 11. Ἐδόκει διωκτέον εἶναι, *it seemed that they must pursue*, iii. 3. 8. Hence it imitates in two ways, as follows, the construction of this Inf., and is therefore treated of in this connection.

§ **643.** Impersonal verbals in -τέον, or -τέα, (α.) govern the same cases as the verbs from which they are derived; and (β.) have sometimes their agent in the *Acc.* instead of the *Dat.* (§ 407. κ). Thus,

(α.) Ὡς πειστέον εἴη Κλεάρχῳ, *that they must obey Clearchus*, ii. 6. 8 (§ 405. η). Πορευτέον δ' ἡμῖν τοὺς πρώτους σταθμούς ii. 2. 12 (§ 431). Πάντα ποιητέον iii. 1. 18 (cf. the personal form, Πάντα ποιητέα Ib. 35). Οὓς οὐ παραδοτέα τοῖς Ἀθηναίοις ἐστίν Th. i. 86. Γυναικὸς οὐδαμῶς ἡσσητέα Soph. Ant. 678 (§ 349). — (β.) Καταβατέον οὖν ἐν μέρει ἕκαστον, *each one therefore must descend in turn*, Pl. Rep. 520 d. Ὡς οὔτε μισθοφορητέον εἴη ἄλλους ἢ τοὺς στρατευομένους, οὔτε μεθεκτέον τῶν πραγμάτων πλείοσιν ἢ πεντακισχιλίοις Th. viii. 65.

§ **644.** REMARK. Constructions are sometimes blended; thus, — (*a.*) The *impersonal* with the *personal* construction of the verbal; as, Τὰς ὑποθέσεις τὰς πρώτας, καὶ εἰ πισταὶ ὑμῖν εἰσιν, ὅμως ἐπισκεπτέαι σαφέστερον [for τὰς ὑποθέσεις ἐπισκεπτέον, or αἱ ὑποθέσεις ἐπισκεπτέαι] Pl. Phædo, 107 b. — (*b.*) The *Dat.* of the agent with the *Acc.*; as, Ἡμῖν νευστέον . . ἐλπίζοντας Pl. Rep. 453 d. — (*c.*) The *verbal* with the *Inf.*; as, Ἐπιθυμίας φὴς οὐ κολαστέον, . . ἐῶντα δὲ αὐτὰς . . ἑτοιμάζειν Pl. Gorg. 492 d.

CHAPTER VI.

SYNTAX OF THE PARTICLE.

§ **645.** The particle, in its full extent, includes the ADVERB, the PREPOSITION, the CONJUNC-

TION, and the INTERJECTION. Of these, however, *the interjection is independent of grammatical construction.* The other particles are construed as follows.

A. The Adverb.

§ **646.** Rule XXXIII. Adverbs modify *sentences*, *phrases*, and *words*; particularly *verbs*, *adjectives*, and *other adverbs*. Thus,

Πάλιν ἠρώτησεν ὁ Κῦρος, *again Cyrus asked*, i. 6. 8. Ἡδέως ἐπείθοντο i. 2. 2. Ὀρθία ἰσχυρῶς Ib. 21. Ἠμελημένως μᾶλλον i. 7. 19. Τὴν οὐ περιτείχισιν, *the not blockading*, Th. iii. 95. Ἡ μὴ 'μπειρία Ar. Eccl. 115. Τῆς ἀπὸ τῶν Ἐπιπολῶν πάλιν καταβάσεως, 'the descent back,' Th. vii. 44.

Remarks. 1. An adverb modifying a sentence or phrase is usually parsed as modifying the verb or leading word of the sentence or phrase. Such particles may also give a special emphasis, or bear a special relation to other words in the sentence or phrase; thus, Ἡμεῖς γε νικῶμεν, we *at least are victorious* (here γε, in modifying the sentence ἡμεῖς νικῶμεν, exerts a special emphasis upon ἡμεῖς) ii. 1. 4. Ἤκουσεν οὐδεὶς ἔν γε τῷ φανερῷ i. 3. 21. Ἀριαῖος δὲ, .. καὶ οὗτος .. πειρᾶται, *and Ariæus, even* he *attempts*, iii. 2. 5. Καὶ μεταπεμπομένου αὐτοῦ, οὐκ ἐθέλω ἐλθεῖν, *even though he sends for me, I am not willing to go*, i. 3. 10. Προσεκύνησαν, καίπερ εἰδότες i. 6. 10. Εἰδότι τοί μοι τάσδ' ἀγγελίας ὅδ' ἐθώϋξεν Æsch. Pr. 1040.

§ **647.** 2. Of the negative particles οὐ and μή, the former is used in *simple, absolute negation*, and the latter in *dependent or qualified negation*, hence in *supposition*, *prohibition*, &c.; or, in the language of metaphysicians, οὐ is the *objective*, and μή the *subjective* negative (cf. § 587. 1). It follows that οὐ is most used with the Ind., and μή with the other modes; and that, with the same mode, οὐ is more decided and emphatic than μή. Thus, Οὐκ οἶδα, *I do not know*, i. 3. 5. Οὔποτε ἐρεῖ οὐδεὶς Ib. Ἐὰν δὲ μὴ διδῷ, *and if he would not give*, i. 3. 14. Ὅπως μὴ φθάσωσι Ib. Μηκέτι με Κῦρον νομίζετε i. 4. 16. Οὐκ ἀκούειν ἔστι, καὶ μὴ δρᾶν ἃ μὴ χρῄζεις; Soph. Œd. C. 1175. Ἐμοὶ τῶν σῶν λόγων ἀρεστὸν οὐδὲν, μηδ' ἀρεσθείη ποτέ Id. Ant. 499. Τὰ μὴ ὄντα ὡς οὐκ ὄντα iv. 4. 15.

Note. Interrogation is sometimes expressed by negative assertion, and assertion by negative interrogation. Hence negative particles sometimes appear to pass into interrogative or affirmative ones; as, Μή σοι δοκοῦμεν; [We do not seem to you, do we?] *Do we seem to you?* Æsch. Pers. 344. Ἦ μήτις .. ἐλαύνει; ἦ μήτις σ' αὐτὸν κτείνῃ; ι. 405. Οὐκοῦν .. πεπαύσομαι; [Shall I not then cease?] *I shall cease then*, Soph. Ant. 91. Οὐκοῦν .. ἱκανῶς ἐχέτω Pl. Phædr. 274 b.

B. The Preposition.

§ **648.** Rule XXXIV. Prepositions govern substantives in the oblique cases, and mark their relations; as,

Ὡρμᾶτο ἀπὸ Σάρδεων, καὶ ἐξελαύνει διὰ τῆς Λυδίας . . ἐπὶ τὸν Μαίανδρον ποταμόν, *he set out from Sardis, and marches through Lydia to the river Mæander*, i. 2. 5.

Or, more particularly,

Ἀντί, ἀπό, ἐξ, and πρό	govern the	Genitive.
Ἐν and σύν	" "	Dative.
Ἀνά and εἰς	" "	Accusative.
Ἀμφί, διά, κατά, μετά, and ὑπέρ	" "	Gen. and Acc.
Ἐπί, παρά, περί, πρός, and ὑπό	" "	Gen., Dat., and Acc.

NOTES. *α.* The Dative sometimes follows ἀμφί, ἀνά, and μετά in the poets; and ἀμφί even in prose, chiefly Ionic. Thus, Ἀμφὶ πλευραῖς Æsch. Pr. 71. Ἀνά τε νανσί Eur. Iph. A. 754. Μετὰ χερσίν Soph. Ph. 1110.

β. The words above mentioned (with their euphonic, poetic, and dialectic forms, as ἐκ for ἐξ, § 68, ξύν for σύν, ἐς for εἰς, ἐνί for ἐν, προτί and ποτί for πρός, ὑπαί for ὑπό) are all which are commonly termed prepositions in Greek, though other words may have a prepositional force (§ 657. *α*). These prepositions have primary reference to the relations of *place*, and are used to express other relations by reason of some *analogy*, either real or fancied (cf. § 339).

γ. Ἐν and πρό, by the addition of ς (expressing *motion* or *action*, cf. § 84), become (ἐνς, § 58) εἰς or ἐς (cf. § 57. 4), and πρός· thus, ἐν, *in*, εἰς, *into*.

δ. To the prepositions governing the Acc., must be added the Ep. suffix -δε, *to* (cf. §§ 150, 322); as, Οὔλυμπόνδε A. 425 (cf. Πρὸς Ὄλυμπον 420). Ἅλαδε A. 308 (cf. Εἰς ἅλα 314). Ἄϊδόσδε [= εἰς Ἄϊδος δόμον, § 385. *γ*] H. 330. It is sometimes used pleonastically; as, Ὅνδε δόμονδε β. 83. Εἰς ἅλαδε κ. 351.

§ **649.** REMARKS. 1. The use of the different cases with prepositions may be commonly referred with ease to familiar principles in the doctrine of the cases; thus,

GENITIVE, — (*α.*) Of DEPARTURE or MOTION FROM (§ 347). Ἀπὸ τῆς ἀρχῆς, *from the province*, i. 1. 2. Ἐκ Χεῤῥονήσου ὁρμώμενος Ib. 9. Παρὰ δὲ βασιλέως πολλοὶ πρὸς Κῦρον ἀπῆλθον i. 9. 29. Ἀλλόμενοι κατὰ τῆς πέτρας, *leaping down from the rock*, iv. ii. 17. — (*β.*) Of ORIGIN and MATERIAL (§ 355). Γεγονὼς ἀπὸ Δαμαράτου ii. i. 3. Οἶνόν τε ἐκ τῆς βαλάνου πεποιημένον τῆς ἀπὸ τοῦ φοίνικος i. 5. 10. — (*γ.*) Of THEME (§ 356). Περὶ ὑμῶν ἐνίων ἤκουον, *I heard respecting some of you*, vi. 6. 34. Τῆς δίκης . . τῆς ἀμφὶ τοῦ πατρός Cyr. iii. 1. 8. — (*δ.*) PARTITIVE (§ 358). Οἱ αὐτομολήσαντες ἐκ τῶν πολεμίων i. 7. 13. — (*ε.*) ACTIVE (§ 380). For examples, see § 562.

DATIVE, — (*ζ.*) Of NEARNESS (§ 399). Σὺν τοῖς φυγάσι, *with the exiles* i. 1. 11. Τῶν παρ᾽ ἑαυτῷ Ib. 5. — (*η.*) Of PLACE (§ 420). Βασίλεια ἐν Κελαιναῖς ἐρυμνά, ἐπὶ ταῖς πηγαῖς τοῦ Μαρσύου ποταμοῦ, ὑπὸ τῇ ἀκροπόλει i. 2. 8.

ACCUSATIVE, — (*ϑ.*) Of MOTION TO (§ 429). Ἀφικνεῖτο . . πρὸς αὐτόν, *came to him*, i. i. 5. Κατέβαινεν εἰς πεδίον i. 2. 22. Πέμψας . . παρὰ τοὺς στρατηγούς Ib. 17. Ἀνέβη ἐπὶ τὰ ὄρη Ib. 22. Κατὰ Σηλυβρίαν ἀφίκου vii.

2. 28 Ὑπ' αὐτὰ τὰ τείχη ἄγειν Cyr. v. 4. 43. — (ι.) Of SPECIFICATION (§ 437). Λαμπρὰ καὶ κατ' ὄμμα καὶ φύσιν Soph. Tr. 379. Κατὰ γνώμην ἴδρις Id. Œd. T. 1087.

§ **650.** NOTES. α. It is common to explain many of the uses of the cases mentioned in Ch. I. by supplying prepositions; when, in reality, the connection of the cases with the prepositions is rather to be explained, as above, by reference to these uses, and to the principles on which they are founded In many connections the preposition may be either employed or omitted, at pleasure; as, Ὥσπερ δέ τις ἀγάλλεται ἐπὶ θεοσεβείᾳ . ., οὕτω Μένων ἠγάλλετο τῷ ἐξαπατᾷν δύνασθαι ii. 6. 26. Καὶ κραυγῇ πολλῇ ἐπίασιν i. 7. 4. Σὺν πολλῇ κραυγῇ καὶ ἡδονῇ ᾖσαν iv. 4. 14.

β. The poets sometimes omit the preposition with the first, and insert it with the second, of two nouns similarly related; as, Ὁδὸς . . Δελφῶν κἀπὸ Δαυλίας Soph. Œd. T. 734. Ἀγρούς σφε πέμψαι κἀπὶ ποιμνίων νομάς Ib. 761.

§ **651.** γ. In the connection of the preposition with its case, we are to consider not only the force of the preposition in itself, but also that of the case with which it is joined. Thus παρά denotes the relation of *side* or *nearness*; and with the Gen., it signifies *from the side of*, or *from*; with the Dat., *at the side of*, or *beside, near, with*; with the Acc., *to the side of*, or *to*. E. g. Ταῦτα ἀκούσαντες, ὅτι οὐ φαίη παρὰ βασιλέα πορεύεσθαι, ἐπῄνεσαν· παρὰ δὲ Ξενίου καὶ Πασίωνος πλείους ἢ δισχίλιοι, λαβόντες τὰ ὅπλα καὶ τὰ σκευοφόρα, ἐστρατοπεδεύσαντο παρὰ Κλεάρχῳ i. 3. 7.

δ. An elliptic use of the adjective after a preposition deserves notice; thus, Ἱλαραὶ δὲ ἀντὶ σκυθρωπῶν [sc. γυναικῶν, or = ἀντὶ τοῦ αὐτὰς εἶναι σκυθρωπούς] ἦσαν, καὶ ἀντὶ ὑφορωμένων ἑαυτὰς ἡδέως ἀλλήλας ἑώρων, *they were cheerful instead of* [being] *downcast, &c.*, Mem. ii. 7. 12. Ἐξ ὀλβίων ἄζηλον εὑροῦσαι βίον Soph. Tr. 284.

ε. The omission of the preposition with the second of *two substantives having a similar construction* will be observed, not only *after a conjunction*, but also in the case of the *relative*, in the *questions and answers of a dialogue*, &c.; as, Ἀπό τε τῶν νεῶν καὶ τῆς γῆς H. Gr. i. 1. 2. Ἐν τῷ χρόνῳ, ᾧ ὑμῶν ἀκούω Symp. 4. 1 (cf. Ἀπ' ἐκείνου γὰρ τοῦ χρόνου, ἀφ' οὗ τούτου ἠράσθην Pl. Conv. 213 c). "Τοῦ τοιοῦδε πέρι." "Τίνος δή;" "Τοῦ ὑπολαμβάνειν" Pl. Rep. 456 d. Ὡς παρὰ φίλους καὶ εὐεργέτας, [sc. παρὰ] Ἀθηναίους ἀδεῶς ἀπιέναι Th. vi. 50.

ζ. The complement of a preposition is often omitted when a relative follows. See § 526. α. So Εἰς [sc. τὸν χρόνον] ὅτε β. 99. Ἐς οὗ, *until*, Hdt. i. 67.

§ **652.** 2. A preposition in composition (α.) often retains its distinct force and government as such. But (β.) it commonly seems to be regarded as a mere adverb (cf. § 657. β), and the compound to be construed just as a simple word would be of the same signification. Hence (γ.) the preposition is often repeated, or a similar preposition introduced. The adverbial force of the preposition in composition is particularly obvious (δ.) in *tmesis* (§ 328. N.), and (ε.) when the preposition is used with an ellipsis of its verb (chiefly ἐστί). Thus, α. Συνέπεμψεν αὐτῇ στρατιώτας, *he sent with her soldiers*, i. 2. 20.

β. Προσέπεμψε δὲ αὐτῷ τὴν θυγατέρα Cyr. viii. 5. 18 (cf. Πέμπει Ἀβροζέλμην . . πρὸς Ξενοφῶντα vii. 6. 43). Ἐπιπλεύσας αὐτῷ H Gr. i. 6. 23 (cf. Πλεῖν ἐπ' αὐτούς Ib. 1. 11).

NOTES. (1.) Hence verbs compounded with ἐπί, παρά, and πρός are commonly followed by the *Dat. of approach* (§ 398). (2.) The preposition, as such, and the general sense of the compound, often require the same case, as, particularly, in compounds of ἀπό, ἐξ, and σύν. See §§ 347, 399.

γ. Ἐπειρῶντο εἰσβάλλειν εἰς τὴν Κιλικίαν i. 2. 21. Παρὰ δὲ βασιλέως ἀπῆλθον i. 9. 29.

§ **653.** δ. Tmesis occurs chiefly in the earlier (especially the Ep.) Greek, when as yet the union of the preposition and verb had not become firmly cemented. In Att. prose it is very rare, and even in Att. poetry (where it occurs most frequently in the lyric portions), it seldom inserts any thing more than a mere particle between the preposition and the verb. Thus, Ἀπὸ λοιγὸν ἀμῦναι [= λοιγὸν ἀπαμῦναι], *to ward off destruction*, A. 67. Παρὰ δ' ἔγχεα μακρὰ πέπηγεν Γ. 135. Ἀπὸ μὲν σεωυτὸν ὤλεσας Hdt. iii. 36. Ἐκ δὲ πηδήσας, *and leaping forth*, Eur. Hec. 1172. Διά μ' ἔφθειρας, κατὰ δ' ἔκτεινας Id. Hipp. 1357. Ἀντ' εὖ πείσεται Pl. Gorg. 520 e.

NOTES. (1.) The preposition sometimes follows the verb; and is sometimes repeated without the verb; as, Πέμψαντος, ὦ γύναι, μετά Eur. Hec. 504. Ἀπολεῖ πόλιν, ἀπὸ δὲ πατέρα Id. Herc. 1055. Κατὰ μὲν ἔκαυσαν Δρύμον πόλιν, κατὰ δὲ Χαράδρην Hdt. viii. 33. So, Ὤρνυτο . . Ἀγαμέμνων, ἂν [sc. ὤρνυτο] δ' Ὀδυσεύς Γ. 267. Ἔλιπον . ., κὰδ δέ E. 480. (2.) In the earlier Greek, what is called *tmesis* is rather to be regarded as the adverbial use of the preposition (§ 657. β), than as the division of a word already compounded.

ε. Ἀλλ' ἄνα [for ἀνάστηθι] ἐξ ἑδράνων, *but* [rise] *up from the seats*, Soph. Aj. 194. Εἰσελθεῖν πάρα [for πάρεστι] Eur. Alc. 1114. Ἔνι [for ἔνεστι] δ' ἐν τῷ ἱερῷ χώρῳ καὶ λειμὼν καὶ ἄλση v. 3. 11.

C. The Conjunction.

§ **654.** RULE XXXV. CONJUNCTIONS connect sentences, and like parts of a sentence; as,

Ἠσθένει Δαρεῖος καὶ ὑπώπτευε, *Darius was sick and apprehended*, i. 1. 1. Τισσαφέρνης διαβάλλει τὸν Κῦρον πρὸς τὸν ἀδελφόν, ὡς ἐπιβουλεύοι αὐτῷ. Ὁ δὲ πείθεταί τε καὶ συλλαμβάνει Κῦρον i. 1. 3. Ὥστε αὐτῷ μᾶλλον φίλους εἶναι ἢ βασιλεῖ Ib. 5. Πλείους ἢ δισχίλιοι i. 3. 7. Ἐβόα καὶ βαρβαρικῶς κα Ἑλληνικῶς i. 8. 1.

REMARKS. 1. By *like parts of a sentence* are meant words and phrases of like construction, or performing like offices in the sentence, and which united by conjunctions form *compound subjects, predicates, adjuncts*, &c. Some connective adverbs also may sometimes be regarded as uniting like parts of a sentence.

2. Like parts of a sentence are commonly, but not necessarily, of the same part of speech and of similar form. In many cases, it seems to be indifferent whether we regard a conjunction as connecting like parts of a sentence, or (supplying an ellipsis) as connecting whole sentences.

3. A conjunction often connects the sentence which it introduces, not so much to the preceding sentence as a whole, as to some particular word or phrase in it; thus, Προσέβαλλουσι . . καταλιπόντες ἄφοδον τοῖς πολεμίοις, εἰ βούλοιντο φεύγειν iv. 2. 11.

§ **655.** 4. A twofold construction is sometimes admissible, according as a word is regarded as belonging to a compound part of a sentence, or to a new sentence; thus, Πλουσιωτέρῳ μὲν ἄν, εἰ ἐσωφρόνεις, ἢ ἐμοὶ ἐδίδους Cyr. viii. 3. 32. Ἐκ δεινοτέρων ἢ τοιῶνδε ἐσώθησαν Th. vii. 77. Τοῖς δὲ νεωτέροις καὶ μᾶλλον ἀκμάζουσιν, ἢ ἐγὼ [sc. ἀκμάζω], παραινῶ Isocr. 188 a. Ἡμῶν δὲ ἄμεινον, ἢ ἐκεῖνοι, τὸ μέλλον προορωμένων Dem. 287. 27. Οὐδαμοῦ γάρ ἐστιν Ἀγόρατον Ἀθηναῖον εἶναι, ὥσπερ Θρασύβουλον Lys. 136. 27. Ἔξεστί θ', ὥσπερ Ἡγέλοχος, ἡμῖν λέγειν Ar. Ran. 303.

5. In many connections, two forms of construction are equally admissible, the one with, and the other without, a connective. The two forms are sometimes blended. See §§ 461. 3, 609, 619. N., 628.

6. A conjunction is sometimes used in Greek, where none would be employed in English; e. g., when πολύς is followed by another adjective; as, Πολλά τε καὶ ἐπιτήδεια διελέγοντο v. 5. 25.

§ **656.** 7. The Greeks, especially the earlier writers, often employ the more generic for the more specific connectives (§ 330. 1), or instead of other forms of expression; as, Ἐκμάνθανε· σχολὴ δὲ πλείων ἢ θέλω πάρεστί μοι, '[and] for I have more leisure,' Æsch. Pr. 817. Τυγχάνω τε κλῇθρ' ἀνασπαστοῦ πύλης χαλῶσα, καί με φθόγγος οἰκείου κακοῦ βάλλει δι' ὤτων, 'just as I am drawing the bars, there strikes,' Soph. Ant. 1186. Καὶ ἤδη τ' ἦν ἐν τῷ τρίτῳ σταθμῷ, καὶ Χειρίσοφος αὐτῷ ἐχαλεπάνθη iv. 6. 2. Οὐχ ὁμοίως πεποιήκασι, καὶ Ὅμηρος (cf. § 400), *they have not composed in the same manner* [and] *as Homer*, or *with Homer*, Pl. Ion, 531 d (cf., in Lat., *similis atque*, &c.).

NOTE. The student will not fail to remark, — (*a*) The frequent use, in the Epic, of δέ for γάρ, and in general of *coördination* in the connection of sentences, for *subordination*. — (*b*) The frequent use of γάρ in specification, where we should use *that, namely, now*, &c.; as, Τῷδε δῆλον ἦν· τῇ μὲν γὰρ πρόσθεν ἡμέρᾳ . . ἐκέλευε ii. 3. 1.

D. CONCLUDING REMARKS.

§ **657.** I. In Greek, as in other languages, the different classes of particles often blend with each other in their use. Thus, (α.) adverbs sometimes take a case, as prepositions; (β.) prepositions are sometimes used without a case, as adverbs; (γ.) the same particle is used both as an adverb and as a conjunction, or as a connective and a non-connective adverb. E. g.

α. For examples, see §§ 347, 349, 372. γ, 394, 399. — Hom. uses εἴσω and ἔσω as protracted forms for εἰς· thus, Ἄγγελον . . Ἴλιον εἴσω Ω. 145 (cf. Εἰς Ἴλιον 143). Ἀγάγησιν ἔσω κλισίην Ω. 155.

β. Ἦ μὴν κελεύσω, κἀπιθωΰξω τε πρός [sc. τούτῳ], 'in addition to this,' 'besides,' Æsch. Pr. 73. Πρὸς δ' ἔτι iii. 2. 2. Ἐν δέ [sc. τούτοις], *and meanwhile*, Soph. Œd. T. 27.

γ. Κῦρον δὲ (conjunction) μεταπέμπεται . . · καὶ στρατηγὸν δὲ (adverb) αὐτὸν ἀπέδειξε i. 1. 2. Ὡς δὲ νῦν ἔχει, χαλεπόν, εἰ, οἰόμενοι ἐν τῇ Ἑλλάδι καὶ ἐπαίνου καὶ τιμῆς τεύξεσθαι, ἀντὶ δὲ τούτων οὐδ᾽ ὅμοιοι τοῖς ἄλλοις ἐσόμεθα vi. 6. 16. Σοφαίνετον δὲ τὸν Στυμφάλιον, καὶ (conjunction) Σωκράτην τὸν Ἀχαιόν, ξένους ὄντας καὶ (adverb) τούτους, ἐκέλευσεν i. 1. 11. Πρῶτον μὲν ἐδάκρυε . . εἶτα δὲ ἔλεξε i. 3. 2. Ἄλλος δὲ λίθῳ, καὶ ἄλλος, εἶτα πολλοί i. 5. 12 Ταῦτα ἐποίουν, μέχρι σκότος ἐγένετο iv. 2. 4 (cf. § 394). Πλὴν οἱ τὰ καπηλεῖα ἔχοντες i. 2. 24 (cf. § 349).

NOTE. The adverb πρίν is construed in four ways; (1.) as a connective, with the appropriate mode; thus, Μὴ πρόσθεν καταλῦσαι . ., πρὶν ἂν αὐτῷ συμβουλεύσηται, 'before he should consult,' i. 1. 10 (πρίν is followed by the Subj. or Opt., only when a negative or interrogative sentence precedes); (2.) as having a prepositional force, with the Inf.; thus, Πρὶν τέτταρα στάδια διελθεῖν, *before* [completing] *they had completed four stadia*, iv. 5. 19; (3.) as a simple adverb, with ἤ and the appropriate mode; thus, Πρὶν ἤ . . ἐγένοντο, *before that they had come*, Cyr. i. 4. 23; (4.) with ἤ and the Inf. instead of another mode (§ 629. 2). This construction is less Attic.

§ **658.** II. Both adverbs, and prepositions with their cases, are often used substantively. An adverb and a preposition governing it are often written together as a compound word. Thus,

Ὅταν δὲ τούτων ἅλις ἔχητε, *but when you have had enough of this*, v. 7. 12. Εἰς μὲν ἅπαξ καὶ βραχὺν χρόνον, *for once and a short time*, Dem. 21. 1. Εἰς νῦν Pl. Tim. 20 b. Μέχρι ἐνταῦθα v. 5. 4. Πρόπαλαι Ar. Eq. 1155. Ἔμπροσθεν iii. 4. 2. Παραυτίκα Cyr. ii. 2. 24. Ἦν . . ὑπὲρ ἥμισυ τοῦ ὅλου στρατεύματος Ἀρκάδες, *above half of the whole army were Arcadians*, vi. 2. 10. Αἰτεῖ αὐτὸν εἰς δισχιλίους ξένους i. 1. 10. Ἐκ τῶν ἀμφὶ τοὺς μυρίους v. 3. 3. Ξυνέδραμον ὡς εἰς ἑπτακοσίους H. Gr. iv. 1. 18. Συνειλεγμένων εἰς τὴν Φυλὴν περὶ ἑπτακοσίους Ib. ii. 4. 5.

§ **659.** III. One preposition or adverb is often used for another (or a preposition is used with one case for another), by reason of something associated or implied. This construction is termed, from its elliptic expressiveness, *constructio prægnans*. Thus,

α.) A PREPOSITION of *motion* for one of *rest*. Οἱ ἐκ τῆς ἀγορᾶς . . ἔφυγον [ἐκ for ἐν, by reason of ἔφυγον following], *those in the market fled* [from it], i. 2. 18. Αἱ δὲ πηγαὶ αὐτοῦ εἰσιν ἐκ τῶν βασιλείων Ib. 7. Ἀφικνοῦνται τῶν ἐκ τοῦ χωρίου τρεῖς ἄνδρες v. 7. 17. Τοῖς ἐκ Πύλου ληφθεῖσι, *those taken at Pylus and brought thence*, Ar. Nub. 186. Οἱ ἀπὸ τῶν καταστρωμάτων τοῖς ἀκοντίοις . . ἐχρῶντο Th. vii. 70. Εἰς ἀνάγκην κείμεθα, *we have come into necessity, and lie there*, Eur. Iph. T. 620. Ἐν δὲ τῇ ὑπερβολῇ τῶν ὀρῶν τῶν εἰς τὸ πεδίον, i. 2. 25.

β). A PREPOSITION of *rest* for one of *motion*. Ἐν Λευκαδίᾳ ἀπῆσαν [ἐν for εἰς, to imply that they were still there], *had gone to Leucadia*, or *were absent in L.*, Th. iv. 42. Οἱ δ᾽ ἐν τῷ Ἡραίῳ καταπεφευγότες (cf. Εἰς δὲ τὸ Ἡραῖον κατέφυγον) H. Gr. iv. 5. 5. Ἐν τῷ ποταμῷ ἔπεσον Ag. 1. 32.

γ.) An ADVERB of *motion* for one of *rest*. Τῶν ἔνδοθεν [for ἔνδον] τις εἰσενηνοχότω Ar. Plut. 228. Μετοίκησις τοῦ τόπου τοῦ ἐνθένδε εἰς ἄλλον τόπον Pl.

Apol. 40 c. Ποῖ κακῶν ἐρημίαν εὕρω; 'Whither can I go to find?' Eur. Herc. 1157.

δ.) An ADVERB of *rest* for one of *motion*. Ὅπου [for ὅποι] βέβηκεν, οὐδεὶς οἶδε, *no one knows where* [for *whither*] *he has gone*, Soph. Tr. 40. Πανταχοῦ πρεσβεύσομεν Ar. Lys. 1230.

§ **660.** IV. In the doctrine of particles, especially connectives, the figures of syntax hold an important place; thus,

A. ELLIPSIS.

Ellipsis here consists either (α.) in the omission of the particles themselves, or (β.), far more frequently, in that of words, and even whole sentences, connected or modified by them.

α. Among the particles most frequently omitted are copulative and complementary conjunctions (§ 329. N.); as,

Πόθου πατρίδων, γονέων, γυναικῶν, παίδων iii. 1. 3. Ἔχεις πόλιν, ἔχεις τριήρεις, ἔχεις χρήματα, ἔχεις ἄνδρας τοσούτους vii. 1. 21. Οὔτε πλινθυφεῖς δόμους προσείλους ᾖσαν, οὐ [for οὔτε] ξυλουργίαν Æsch. Pr. 450. Ὀμνύω ὑμῖν θεοὺς πάντας καὶ πάσας, [sc. ὅτι] ἦ μὴν . . ἐθυόμην vi. 1. 31. Ἀφειλόμην, ὁμολογῶ v. 6. 17. Ἀπάγγειλον πόσει, ἥκειν ὅπως τάχιστ' ἐράσμιον πόλει· γυναῖκα πιστὴν δ' ἐν δόμοις εὕροι Æsch. Ag. 604. See § 611. 3.

NOTE. Hdt. sometimes uses οὔκων with the ellipsis of a conditional or other conjunction; as, Οὔκων ποιήσετε ταῦτα, ἡμεῖς . . ἐκλείψομεν, *if then you will not do this, we shall desert*, iv. 118.

§ **661.** β. Connected sentences especially abound in ellipsis, from the ease with which the omission can be supplied from the connection. We notice, among the great variety of cases that might be mentioned, the frequent ellipses,

1.) In replies; as, "Ἔστιν ὅ τι σε ἠδίκησα;" Ὁ δ' ἀπεκρίνατο, ὅτι οὔ [= οὐκ ἔστιν] i. 6. 7. Εἰπόντος δὲ τοῦ Ὀρόντου, ὅτι οὐδὲν ἀδικηθεὶς Ib. 8.

NOTE. (*a*.) In a dialogue or address, a speaker often commences with a connective (most frequently an adversative or causal conjunction), from reference to something which has been expressed or which is mutually understood; as, Ἀλλ' ὁρᾶτε, *but you see*, iii. 2. 4. Ἐμοὶ δ' οὐ φαῦλον δοκεῖ εἶναι vi. 6. 12. Οἴει γάρ σοι μαχεῖσθαι, ὦ Κῦρε, τὸν ἀδελφόν; i. 7. 9. (*b*.) In like manner the Voc. is often followed by a connective; as, Ὦ γύναι, ἔφη, ὄνομα δέ σοι τί ἐστιν; Mem. ii. 1. 26. Ὦ Κίρκη, τίς γὰρ . . ἡγεμονεύσει; κ. 501.

2.) Between two connectives; as, Ἀλλὰ [sc. παύομαι] γὰρ καὶ περαίνειν ἤδη ὥρα iii. 2. 32. Cf. v. 7. 11. Ἀλλὰ γὰρ δέδοικα iii. 2. 25. Παρὰ τὴν θάλατταν ἥει· καὶ [sc. ταύτῃ ᾔει] γὰρ ἤδη ἠσθένει vi. 2. 18. Καὶ γὰρ καὶ καπνὸς ἐφαίνετο ii. 2. 15.— And yet, perhaps, in such examples as these, ἀλλὰ γάρ or καὶ γάρ may be regarded as forming but a single compound connective, or one of the particles may be regarded as a mere adverb (§ 657. γ).

§ **662.** 3.) With ὡς, especially in expressing *comparison*, *design*, *pretence*, *possibility*, &c.; as, Θᾶττον ἢ [sc. οὕτω ταχὺ] ὡς τις ἂν ᾤετο, *quicker than* [so quick as] *one would have thought*, i. 5. 8. Μείζονα ἡγησάμενος εἶναι ἢ ὡς ἐπὶ Πεισίδας τὴν παρασκευήν, *thinking that the preparation was greater than* [so great as] *it would be against the Pisidians*, i. 2. 4. Βραχύτερα ἠκόντιζον, ἢ ὡς ἐξικνεῖσθαι, *hurled* [a shorter distance than so as to reach] *too short a distance to reach*, iii. 3. 7. Ἐφάνη κονιορτὸς, ὥσπερ νεφέλη λευκή i. 8. 8. Ὡς εἰς μάχην παρεσκευασμένος, *arrayed as* [he would array] *for battle*, Ib. 1. Ἐπέκαμπτεν, ὡς εἰς κύκλωσιν Ib. 23. Φεύγουσιν ἀνὰ κράτος ὡς πρὸς τὴν ἀπὸ τοῦ ποταμοῦ ἔκβασιν iv. 3. 21. Ἀθροίζει, ὡς ἐπὶ τούτους i. 2. 1. Ὥσπερ ὀργῇ, ἐκέλευσε i. 5. 8. Ὡς ἐκ τῶν παρόντων [sc. ἐδύναντο], ξυνταξάμενοι Th. vi. 70. Κερασούντιοι, ὡς ἂν καὶ ἑωρακότες τὸ παρ' ἑαυτοῖς πρᾶγμα, δείσαντες, *the Cerasuntians alarmed, as they would naturally be having seen what had happened among themselves*, v. 7. 22. Ὡς ἐπὶ τὸ πολύ, *as things are for the most part, commonly*, iii. 1. 42. See §§ 410, 525. α, 640.

Notes. (*a.*) From the frequent use of ὡς with the accusative after verbs of motion to express the purposed end of the motion (§ 429), it came at last to be regarded as a mere preposition, supplying the place of πρός or εἰς, but chiefly before names of persons; as, Πορεύεται ὡς βασιλέα, *goes to the king*, i. 2. 4. (*b.*) Ὡς is often used to render expressions of quantity less positive; as, Ἔχων [sc. οὕτω πολλοὺς] ὡς πεντακοσίους, *having such a number as* 500, i. e. *about* 500, i. 2. 3.

§ **663.** 4.) With adversative conjunctions, with which we must sometimes supply the opposite of that which has preceded; as, Καὶ μή μ' ἄτιμον τῆσδ' ἀποστείλητε γῆς, ἀλλ' ἀρχέπλουτον καὶ καταστάτην δόμων [sc. δέξασθε] Soph. El. 71. Εἰ μὲν βούλεται, ἑψέτω· εἰ δ' [sc. μὴ βούλεται], ὅ τι βούλεται, τοῦτο ποιείτω Pl. Euthyd. 285 c.

5.) With ἤ, before which there is sometimes an ellipsis of μᾶλλον· as, Ζητοῦσι κερδαίνειν [sc. μᾶλλον], ἢ ὑμᾶς πείθειν Lys. 171. 8. Τὴν τῆς ὑμετέρας πόλεως τύχην ἂν ἑλοίμην, . . ἢ τὴν ἐκείνου Dem. 24. 16. See § 466.

6.) With conditional conjunctions; as, Εἰ μὲν σύ τι ἔχεις, ὦ Μηδόσαδες, πρὸς ἡμᾶς λέγειν [sc. λέγε δή]· εἰ δὲ μὴ [sc. ἔχεις], ἡμεῖς πρὸς σὲ ἔχομεν vii. 7. 15. Εἴτε ἄλλο τι θέλοι χρῆσθαι, εἴτ' ἐπ' Αἴγυπτον στρατεύειν, συγκαταστρέψαιντ' ἂν αὐτῷ ii. 1. 14. Καὶ νῦν, ἂν μὲν ὁ Κῦρος βούληται [καλῶς ἔχει]· εἰ δὲ μή, ὑμεῖς γε τὴν ταχίστην πάρεστε Cyr. iv. 5. 10. Ἔκαιον καὶ χιλὸν καὶ εἴ τι ἄλλο χρήσιμον ἦν [sc. ἔκαιον τοῦτο] i. 6. 1 (εἴ τις so used is equivalent to ὅστις). Οἱ δὲ ἄλλοι ἀπώλοντο ὑπό τε τῶν πολεμίων καὶ χιόνος, καὶ εἴ τις νόσῳ v. 3. 3. Ἐπείθοντο, πλὴν εἴ τίς τι ἔκλεψεν iv. 1. 14. Εὖνοι ἦσαν, πλὴν καθόσον εἰ τὴν Σικελίαν ᾤοντο αὐτοὺς δουλώσεσθαι Th. vi. 88. Ἄλλοι μενέουσι . . · εἰ δὲ καὶ αὐτοὶ [sc. οὐ μενέουσι], φευγόντων I. 45. Εἰ δ' ἄγε [= εἰ δὲ βούλει, ἄγε, *but if you will, come*] A. 302, and often in Hom.

Note. When two similar clauses are connected, a pronoun, preposition, or other word is sometimes (chiefly by the poets) omitted in the first clause, and, for the sake of emphasis or the metre, or by reason of other ellipses, inserted in the second; as, Ζώγρει, Ἀτρέος υἱέ, σὺ δ' ἄξια δέξαι ἄποινα Z. 46. Ἐκ Πύλου ἄξει ἀμύντορας . ., ἢ ὅ γε καὶ Σπάρτηθεν β. 326. See § 650. β.

B. Pleonasm.

§ **664.** Under this head we remark,

1.) The redundant use of negatives. This appears chiefly,

α.) In connection with indefinites, which in a negative sentence are all regularly combined with a negative; as, Οὔποτε ἐρεῖ οὐδείς i. 3. 5. Οὐδενὶ οὐδαμῇ οὐδαμῶς οὐδεμίαν κοινωνίαν ἔχει Pl. Parm. 166 a.

β.) In divided construction; as, Οὐκ αἰσχύνεσθε οὔτε θεοὺς οὔτ' ἀνθρώπους ii. 5. 39. Μηδὲν τελείτω μήτε ἐμοὶ μήτε ἄλλῳ vii. 1. 6. Οὐ γάρ ἐστιν ὅστις ἀνθρώπων σωθήσεται, οὔτε ὑμῖν οὔτε ἄλλῳ οὐδενὶ πλήθει γνησίως ἐναντιούμενος Pl. Apol. 31 e.

γ.) In the emphatic use of οὐδέ and μηδέ· as, Οὐ μὲν δὴ οὐδὲ τοῦτ' ἄν τις εἴποι i. 9. 13. Μὴ τοίνυν μηδέ vii. 6. 19. Οὔκουν βούλεται . ., οὐδὲ πολλοῦ δεῖ, *he does not therefore wish, no, far from it*, Dem. 100. 9.

§ 665. δ.) In the use of μή with the Infinitive, after words implying some negation; as, Ναυκλήροις ἀπεῖπε μὴ διάγειν, *he forbade the shipmasters to cross* [saying that they should not cross], vii. 2. 12. Ἐξέφυγε τὸ μὴ καταπετρωθῆναι i. 3. 2. Ἔξει τοῦ μὴ καταδῦναι iii. 5. 11 (cf. Σχήσω σε πηδᾷν Eur. Or. 263). Κωλύοντες μηδαμῇ . . πορίζεσθαι vii. 6. 29 (cf. Κωλύσεις τοῦ καίειν i. 6. 2). Κωλύματα μὴ αὐξηθῆναι Th. i. 16. Ἐμποδὼν τοῦ μὴ ἤδη εἶναι iv. 8. 14.

NOTE. Οὐ is sometimes used in like manner, with a finite verb supplying (with ὅτι or ὡς) the place of an Inf.; as, Ἀρνεῖσθαι . ., ὅτι οὐ παρῆν, *to deny that he was present*, Rep. Ath. 2. 17. Ὡς δ' οὐκ ἐκεῖνος ἐγεώργει τὴν γῆν, οὐκ ἠδύνατ' ἀρνηθῆναι Dem. 871. 14.

§ 666. ε.) In the use of μὴ οὐ with the Infinitive and Participle, as a *simple negative*. This chiefly occurs (1.) after *negative* and *interrogative* sentences, and (2.) after some expressions of *shame* and *fear*. Here μὴ οὐ takes the place of simple μή, and (3.) may even be wholly redundant after words where μή would be so (§ 665). Thus, (1.) Οὐδείς γέ μ' ἂν πείσειεν ἀνθρώπων τὸ μὴ οὐκ ἐλθεῖν, *none of men can persuade me not to go*, Ar. Ran. 65. Οὐ γὰρ ἂν μακρὰν ἴχνευον αὐτὸς, μὴ οὐκ ἔχων τι σύμβολον Soph. Œd. T. 220. Τίς μηχανὴ μὴ οὐχὶ πάντα καταναλωθῆναι; Pl. Phædo, 74 d. (2.) Ὥστε πᾶσιν αἰσχύνην εἶναι, μὴ οὐ συσπουδάζειν ii. 3. 11. (3.) Οὐκ ἐναντιώσομαι τὸ μὴ οὐ γεγωνεῖν Æsch. Pr. 787. Τί δῆτα μέλλεις μὴ οὐ γεγωνίσκειν; Ib. 627. Τί ἐμποδὼν μὴ οὐχὶ . . ἀποθανεῖν; iii. 1. 13.

ζ.) In the occasional use of οὐ to strengthen the negative idea implied in ἤ, *than*; as, Τί οὖν δεῖ ἐκεῖνον τὸν χρόνον ἀναμένειν, . . μᾶλλον ἢ οὐχ ὡς τάχιστα . . τὴν εἰρήνην ποιεῖσθαι, 'rather than make peace,' = 'and not rather make peace,' H. Gr. vi. 3. 15. Εἰ τοίνυν τις ὑμῶν . . ἄλλως πως ἔχει τὴν ὀργὴν ἐπὶ Μειδίαν, ἢ ὡς οὐ δέον αὐτὸν τεθνάναι Dem. 537. 3. Ἥκει γὰρ ὁ Πέρσης οὐδέν τι μᾶλλον ἐπ' ἡμέας, ἢ οὐ καὶ ἐπὶ ὑμέας Hdt. iv. 118. (Compare, in French and Ital., *Vous écrivez mieux que vous* ne *parlez*, *Egli era più ricco che voi* non *siete*.)

NOTES. (1.) Two negatives in the same sentence have commonly their distinct force, (α.) when one applies to the whole sentence, and the other to a part only; and (β.) when two sentences have been condensed into one. Thus, (α.) Οὐ περὶ μὲν σοῦ λέγω . ., περὶ ἐμοῦ δὲ οὔ, *I do not say it of you, and not of myself*, Pl. Alc. 124 c. Οὐ νῦν ἐκεῖνοι παιόμενοι, . . οὐδὲ ἀποθανεῖν οἱ τλήμονες δύνανται; iii. 1. 29. (β.) See the examples in § 528. 2; to which may be added, with an ellipsis of the relative, Οὐδεὶς οὐκ ἔπασχε Symp. i. 9. (2.) For οὐ μή, see §§ 595. 1, 2, 597. 1.

§ 667. 2.) The repetition of various particles for greater clearness or strength of expression, particularly after intervening clauses, in divided construction, and with important or emphatic words ; as,

Ἔλεγεν, ὅτι, εἰ μὴ καταβήσονται οἰκήσοντες καὶ πείσονται, ὅτι κατακαύσει vii. 4. 5. Δέδοικα, μὴ, ἂν ἅπαξ μάθωμεν ἀργοὶ ζῆν . ., μὴ, ὥσπερ οἱ λωτοφάγοι, ἐπιλαθώμεθα iii. 2. 25. Οὐκ ἂν ἱκανὸς εἶναι οἶμαι, οὔτ' ἂν φίλον ὠφελῆσαι, οὔτ' ἂν ἐχθρὸν ἀλέξασθαι i. 3. 6. Κοὐκ ἂν γυναικῶν ἥσσονες καλοίμεθ' ἂν Soph. Ant. 680. Τάχ' ἂν κἄμ' ἂν τοιαύτῃ χειρὶ τιμωρεῖν θέλοι Id. Œd. T. 139. Ὦ τέκνον ὦ γενναῖον Id. Phil. 799. Εἰ μὴ εἴ τις ὑπολάβοι Pl. Gorg. 480 b.

3.) The multiplication of particles of similar force, and the employment of needless connectives ; as,

Μὴ πρόσθεν καταλῦσαι πρὸς τοὺς ἀντιστασιώτας, πρὶν ἂν αὐτῷ συμβουλεύσηται i. 1. 10 (cf. i. 2. 2). Οὐ πρόσθεν πρὶν ἢ . . ἐγένοντο Ag. 2. 4. Ὅσον ἀπὸ βοῆς ἕνεκα Th. viii. 92. Τίνος δὴ χάριν ἕνεκα Pl. Leg. 701 d. See §§ 461. 3, 609 α, 619. N., 628, 655. 5.

C. Attraction.

§ **668.** The influence of attraction sometimes passes even beyond a connective ; as,

Οὐδέν γε ἄλλο ἐστὶν, οὗ ἐρῶσιν οἱ ἄνθρωποι, ἢ τοῦ ἀγαθοῦ [for τὸ ἀγαθὸν through the attraction of οὗ] Pl. Conv. 205 e. Ἠξίουν, Λέπρεον μὲν μὴ ἀποδοῦναι (τοὺς Λακεδαιμονίους), εἰ μὴ βούλονται · ἀναβάντες [for ἀναβάντας, by attraction to the subject of βούλονται] δὲ . ., ἀπομόσαι Th. v. 50. Ἑρμοκράτους καὶ εἴ του ἄλλου πειθόντων (see § 663. 6) Th. vii. 21. See § 627. 2.

D. Anacoluthon.

§ **669.** Anacoluthon is frequent in the connection of sentences. The clause completing the construction is often either omitted or changed in its form. Hence, also, the regular correspondence of particles is sometimes neglected. Thus,

Ὡς γὰρ ἐγὼ . . ἤκουσά τινος, ὅτι Κλέανδρος ὁ ἐκ Βυζαντίου ἁρμοστὴς μέλλει ἥξειν [for ὡς ἤκουσα, Κλέανδρος μέλλει, or ἤκουσα, ὅτι Κλέανδρος μέλλει] vi. 4. 18. Ἀνὴρ ὅδ' ὡς ἔοικεν οὐ νεμεῖν [for ὡς ἔοικεν, οὐ νεμεῖ, or ἔοικεν οὐ νεμεῖν] Soph. Tr. 1238. Ἀλλὰ μὴν, — ἐρῶ γὰρ καὶ ταῦτα, ἐξ ὧν ἔχω ἐλπίδας, καὶ σὲ βουλήσεσθαι φίλον ἡμῖν εἶναι · — οἶδα μὲν γάρ [for ἀλλὰ μὴν, ἐρῶ γὰρ, οἶδα, or ἀλλὰ μὴν ἐρῶ · οἶδα γάρ] ii. 5. 12. See iii. 2. 11. Τῶν δὲ Ἀθηναίων ἔτυχε γὰρ πρεσβεία πρότερον ἐν τῇ Λακεδαίμονι περὶ ἄλλων παροῦσα, καὶ . . ἔδοξεν αὐτοῖς Th. i. 72. Οὐκ ἔσθ' ὅ τι μᾶλλον, ὦ ἄνδρες Ἀθηναῖοι, πρέπει οὕτως, ὡς τὸν τοιοῦτον ἄνδρα ἐν Πρυτανείῳ σιτεῖσθαι [for ὅ τι μᾶλλον πρέπει, ἤ, or ὅ τι πρέπει οὕτως, ὡς] Pl. Apol. 36 d. Εἰδότες οὐκ ἂν ὁμοίως δυνηθέντες, καὶ εἰ ἐκ τῶν νεῶν πρὸς παρεσκευασμένους ἐκβιβάζοιεν, ἢ [for καὶ εἰ] κατὰ γῆν ἰόντες γνωσθείησαν Th. vi. 64.

§ **670.** Note. After a connective, a distinct sentence often takes the place of a part of a sentence, and sometimes the reverse ; as, Ἔρχονται . . κήρυκες · οἱ μὲν ἄλλοι βάρβαροι, ἦν δ' αὐτῶν Φαλῖνος εἷς Ἕλλην [for εἷς δ' αὐτῶν Φ. Ἑ.], *there come heralds ; the rest barbarians, but* [there was] *one of them Phalinus, a Greek*, ii. 1. 7. See i. 10. 12. Παρημέλουν ὄντες ἄποικοι ·

οὔτε γὰρ . . διδόντες [for οὔτε διδόντες, or οὔτε γὰρ ἐδίδοσαν. The construction might be made regular by repeating παρημέλουν] Th. i. 25. See § 641. *β*.

§ **671.** V. The Greek especially abounds in combinations of particles, and in elliptical phrases having the power of particles. The use of these sometimes extends farther than their origin and structure would strictly warrant. A few examples of these combinations and phrases are given below, but the subject in its details belongs to the lexicographer rather than the grammarian.

1. ἀλλὰ γάρ, καὶ γάρ, see § 661. 2.

2. ἀλλ' ἤ [from ἄλλο ἤ or ἄλλα ἤ], *other than, except;* as, Ἀργύριον μὲν οὐκ ἔχω, ἀλλ' ἤ μικρόν τι vii. 7. 53. Οὐδαμοῦ . ., ἀλλ' ἢ κατ' αὐτὴν τὴν ὁδόν iv. 6. 11.

3. ἄλλως τε καί, *both otherwise and in particular, especially;* as, Οὐδὲν νομίζω ἀνδρί, ἄλλως τε καὶ ἄρχοντι, κάλλιον εἶναι κτῆμα vii. 7. 41.

4. δῆλον ὅτι, *it is evident that, evidently,* εὖ οἶδ' ὅτι, οἶδ' ὅτι, σάφ' ἴσθ' ὅτι, and similar phrases, which are often inserted in sentences (quite like adverbs), or annexed to them; as, Τὰ μὲν δὴ Κύρου δῆλον ὅτι οὕτως ἔχει i. 3. 9. Οὔτ' ἂν ὑμεῖς, εὖ οἶδ' ὅτι, ἐπαύσασθε Dem. 72. 24. Μονώτατος γὰρ εἶ σὺ . ., εὖ ἴσθ' ὅτι Ar. Plut. 182.

5. εἰ γάρ, εἴθ' ὤφελον, see §§ 599, 600. 2.

6. εἰ δὲ μή, *but if not, otherwise,* used even after negative sentences; as, Μὴ ποιήσῃς ταῦτα· εἰ δὲ μή, ἔφη, αἰτίαν ἕξεις, *do not do this; otherwise, said he, you will have blame,* vii. 1. 8. Οὔτ' ἐν τῷ ὕδατι τὰ ὅπλα ἦν ἔχειν· εἰ δὲ μή, ἥρπαζεν ὁ ποταμός iv. 3. 6.

7. ἵνα τί, ὡς τί, and ὅτι τί, see § 539. *a*.

8. μή τί γε, *not to say aught surely,* i. e. *much less,* or *much more;* as, Οὐκ ἔνι δ' αὐτὸν ἀργοῦντα οὐδὲ τοῖς φίλοις ἐπιτάττειν ὑπὲρ αὑτοῦ τι ποιεῖν, μή τί γε δὴ τοῖς θεοῖς Dem. 24. 21.

9. Ὅτι μή after negatives, *except* [= ὅ τι μή ἐστι, *what is not*]; as, Οὐ γὰρ ἦν κρήνη, ὅτι μὴ μία Th. iv. 26.

10. οὐ γὰρ ἀλλά, *for it is not otherwise, but,* i. e. *for indeed;* as, Οὐ γὰρ ἀλλ' ἡ γῆ βίᾳ ἕλκει Ar. Nub. 232.

11. οὐ μέντοι ἀλλά, οὐ μὴν ἀλλά, *yet no, but,* i. e. *nevertheless,* or *nay rather;* as, Ὁ ἵππος πίπτει εἰς γόνατα, καὶ μικροῦ κἀκεῖνον ἐξετραχήλισεν· οὐ μὴν ἀλλ' ἐπέμεινεν ὁ Κῦρος Cyr. i. 4. 8.

12. οὐχ ὅτι, μὴ ὅτι, οὐχ ὅσον, οὐχ ὅπως, μὴ ὅπως, οὐχ οἷον, *I do not say that, not to say that,* &c., i. e. *not only,* or *not only not* (the three first phrases usually mean *not only,* and the three last *not only not*); as, Οὐχ ὅτι μόνος ὁ Κρίτων ἐν ἡσυχίᾳ ἦν, ἀλλὰ καὶ οἱ φίλοι αὐτοῦ, *not only was Crito himself unmolested, but also his friends,* Mem. ii. 9. 8. Μὴ γὰρ ὅτι ἄρχοντα, ἀλλὰ καὶ οὓς οὐ φοβοῦνται, . . αἰδοῦνται Cyr. viii. 1. 28. Ἄχρηστοι γὰρ καὶ γυναιξὶν . ., μὴ ὅτι ἀνδράσι, 'not to say men,' Pl. Rep. 398 e. Οὐχ ὅσον οὐκ ἠμύναντο, ἀλλ' οὐδ' ἐσώθησαν Th. iv. 62. Ὡς οἱ Λακεδαιμόνιοι οὐχ ὅπως τιμωρήσαιντο, ἀλλὰ καὶ ἐπαινέσαιεν, *that the Lacedæmonians had not only not punished, but*

had even commended, H. Gr. v. 4. 34. Οὐχ ὅπως δῶρα δούς vii. 7. 8. Μὴ ὅπως ὀρχεῖσθαι ἐν ῥυθμῷ, ἀλλ' οὐδ' ὀρθοῦσθαι ἐδύνασθε Cyr. i. 3. 10. Πεπαύμεθ' ἡμεῖς, οὐχ ὅπως σὲ παύσομεν Soph. El. 796.

NOTE. Οὐχ ὅτι is sometimes *although* [*not because*, denying an inference which might be drawn]; as, Ἐγγυῶμαι μὴ ἐπιλήσεσθαι, οὐχ ὅτι παίζει καὶ φησιν ἐπιλήσμων εἶναι Pl. Prot. 336 d.

13. οὕνεκα and ὁθούνεκα [= τούτου ἕνεκα, ὅτι, §§ 530, 40. δ, 372. γ], poet., *on account of this, that* —, *because*, and, with certain verbs, *that*; as, Ζηλῶ σ' ὁθούνεκ' ἐκτὸς αἰτίας κυρεῖς, *I envy you* [because] *that you are free from blame*, Æsch. Pr. 330. Ἴσθι τοῦτο πρῶτον, οὕνεκα Ἕλληνές ἐσμεν Soph. Ph. 232. Οὕνεκα is sometimes used by the Att. poets, like a simple adverb, with the Gen.; as, Γυναικὸς οὕνεκα, [because of] *for the sake of a woman*, Æsch. Ag. 823.

14. When two prepositions are combined, which occurs most frequently in the Epic, either one or both the prepositions are used adverbially (§ 657. β), or one of the prepositions with its substantive forms the complement of the other; as, Ἀμφὶ περὶ κρήνην, *round about the fountain*, B. 305. Δι' ἐκ μεγάροιο κ. 388. Περὶ πρὸ γὰρ ἔγχεϊ θῦεν Λ. 180. Διαπρό Ρ. 393. Πάρεξ τοῦ . . ἀργυρίου Hdt. iii. 91. Ὑπ' ἐκ βελέων, *from beneath the weapons*, Δ. 465.

§ **672.** VI. POSITION OF PARTICLES. 1. Prepositions regularly *precede* the words which they govern. For the accentuation when they follow (which is chiefly poet., and in Att. prose occurs only with περί governing the Gen.), see §§ 730, 731. N.

NOTE. The great fondness of the Greeks for connecting kindred or contrasting words as closely as possible often produces *hyperbaton* in the construction of the preposition with its case, as well as in other constructions; thus, Πρὸς ἄλλοτ' ἄλλον, for ἄλλοτε πρὸς ἄλλον, Æsch. Pr. 276. Παρὰ φίλης φίλῳ φέρειν γυναικὸς ἀνδρί Id. Cho. 89. See § 511. 3. For hyperbaton in earnest entreaty, see § 426. β.

§ **673.** 2. Connective and interrogative particles, with the exceptions mentioned below (NOTE α), commonly stand first in their clauses.

NOTES. α. The following particles cannot stand first in a clause; ἄν (not for ἐάν, § 588), ἄρα (paroxytone), αὖ (poet. αὖτε), αὖθις (Ion. αὖτις), γάρ, γέ, δαί, δέ, δή (except in Hom. and Pind.), δῆθεν, δῆτα, θήν (poet.), κέ (Ep.), μέν, μέντοι, μήν, νύν (enclitic; Ep. also νύ, § 66. α), οὖν, πέρ, τέ, τοί, τοίνυν, and the indefinite adverbs beginning with π (ποτέ, πού, &c., ¶ 63). Thus, Ὁ δὲ πείθεταί τε καὶ συλλαμβάνει, *and he is both persuaded and apprehends*, i. 1. 3.

β. Ὅτι is sometimes placed after a subordinate clause; as, Κύρῳ εἶπεν, εἰ αὐτῷ δοίη ἱππέας χιλίους, ὅτι . . κατακάνοι [for ὅτι, εἰ . ., κατακάνοι] i. 6. 2. Ἔφη αὐτῷ ταῦτα συμπροθυμηθέντι, ὅτι οὐ μεταμελήσει vii. 1. 5.

γ. A sentence introduced by a connective often follows the Vocative, instead of including it. By this arrangement, immediate attention is better secured. Thus, Ἥφαιστε, σοὶ δὲ χρὴ μέλειν ἐπιστολάς [for σοὶ δέ, Ἥφαιστε], *and you, Vulcan, must heed the commands*, Æsch. Pr. 3.

§ 674. 3. The adverbs ἕνεκα and χάριν commonly follow, but sometimes precede, the genitives which they govern (§ 372. γ). Observe the arrangement, Τῆς πρόσθεν ἕνεκα περὶ ἐμὲ ἀρετῆς i. 4. 8; and, Οὗπερ αὐτὸς ἕνεκα i. 9. 21.

4. A particle is sometimes placed in one clause which belongs more strictly to another (cf. § 616); as, Οὐκ' οἶδ' ἂν εἰ πείσαιμι [for οἶδ', εἰ πείσαιμ' ἂν] Eur. Med. 941.

5. In emphatic address, the sign ὦ is sometimes placed as follows; Ἔρεβος ὦ φαεννότατον Soph. Aj. 395. Θαυμάσι' ὦ Κρίτων Pl. Euthyd. 271 c. Ἡμῖν εἰπὲ ὦ πρὸς Διὸς Μέλιτε Id. Apol. 25 c.

BOOK IV.

PROSODY.

Γλώσσης μείλιγμα.
Æschylus, Eumen.

§ **675.** Prosody treats of QUANTITY, of VERSIFICATION, and of ACCENT.

CHAPTER I.

QUANTITY.

§ **676.** In Greek, all vowels and syllables are divided, in respect to QUANTITY (i. e. the *time of their utterance* according to the ancient pronunciation), into the *long* and the *short;* and the long are regarded as having *double* the time of the short.

NOTE. Hence the unit in measuring metrical quantity is the short syllable, or the *breve* (brevis, *short*), and a long vowel or syllable is equal to *two breves.* For the marks of quantity (— ⏑), see § 16. 4.

§ **677.** Quantity is of two kinds, *natural* and *local.* Natural quantity has respect to the length of the vowel in its own nature; but local quantity, to the effect which is produced by the position of the vowel in connection with other letters or syllables. With reference to the first distinction, vowels and syllables are said to be long or short *by nature;* with reference to the second, *by position.* Thus, in ὄμφαξ, both syllables are short by nature, i. e. in the natural quantity of the vowels; but both become long by the position of these short vowels before two consonants (§§ 51, 688).

NOTE. The quantity of a syllable is always the natural quantity of the vowel which it contains, unless some change is produced by position.

Hence it is usual, in prosody, to regard the vowel as the representative of the syllable; and language is often applied to the vowel which in strict propriety belongs only to the syllable. Thus, in ὄμφαξ, it is common to say that the vowels are long by position; while, in strict accuracy, the quantity of the vowels themselves is not changed, but the *syllables* become long from the time occupied in the utterance of the successive consonants.

I. NATURAL QUANTITY.

§ **678.** RULE I. The vowels η and ω, all diphthongs, all vowels resulting from contraction or crasis, and all circumflexed vowels, are long; as the vowels in ἡμῶν, πλείους, γλώσσᾱς (§ 34), δῡς (§ 58), κᾱν (§ 40), λᾶς, ἡμῖν, πῦρ.

REMARK. All vowels which result from the union of two vowels have, from their very nature, a double time. See §§ 25, 29 – 31, 723.

§ **679.** RULE II. The vowels ε and ο are short; as in φέρομεν.

§ **680.** RULE III. The doubtful vowels (§ 24. β) are commonly short; as in χλᾰμῠ́δῐ.

To this *general rule for the doubtful vowels* there are many exceptions; which renders it necessary to observe the ACCENT, the SPECIAL LAWS OF INFLECTION AND DERIVATION, the DIALECT, and the USAGE OF THE POETS.

A. ACCENT.

§ **681.** From the general rules of accent (§ 726), we learn, that in natural quantity,

α.) Every *circumflexed* vowel is long (§ 678).

β.) In *paroxytones*, if the vowel of the *ultima* is *short*, the vowel of the *penult* is also short; and, on the other hand, if the vowel of the *penult* is *long*, the vowel of the *ultima* is also long. Hence, in μαινάδος, καρκίνος, and χλαμύδος, the vowel of the penult is short; and, in Λήδα, φοίνιξ, and κώμυς, the vowel of the ultima is long.

γ.) In *proparoxytones* and *properispomes*, the vowel of the ultima is short; as in ἄρουρα, δύναμις, πέλεκυς· βῶλαξ, πρᾶξις, διῶρυξ.

B. INFLECTION.

§ **682.** In the common affixes of declension and conjugation, the doubtful vowels are short, except cases of contraction, -α in the Sing. of Dec. I., and -ᾱσῐ for νσῐ in the nude Present.

Thus, Dec. I., Pl. Acc. -ᾱς (§ 34), Du. Nom. -ᾱ (§ 86), Aor. Pt. -σᾱς, -σᾱσᾰ (§§ 58, 132), Pf. Pl. 3 -κᾱσι (§ 181. 2); see ¶¶ 5, 29, 30. — For special rules in regard to the Sing. of Dec. I., see §§ 92, 93; for -έᾱ, -έᾱς in Dec. III., see § 116. For the dialectic affixes, see ¶¶ 8, 10, 15, 32. For -ᾱος, becoming -εως in Dec. II., see § 98. β. For the doubtful vowels in the augment, see § 188.

§ **683.** Special Rules of the Third Declension. 1. The doubtful vowels are *long* in the *last syllable* of the *root*,

α.) If the characteristic is ν; as, παιάν, παιᾶνος· δελφίς, δελφῖνος· Φόρκυς, Φόρκῡνος. Except in the adjectives μέλᾱς, μέλᾰνος, τάλᾱς, τάλᾰνος, and in the pronoun τῐς, τῐνος.

β.) In most *palatals*, if a long syllable precede; as, θώραξ, θώρᾱκος· μάστιξ, μάστῑγος· πέρδιξ, πέρδῑκος· κῆρυξ, κήρῡκος.

γ.) In words in -ις, -ιθος, and in some *oxytones* in -ις, -ιδος; as, ὄρνις, ὄρνῑθος· κνημίς, κνημῖδος· σφραγίς, σφραγῖδος.

δ.) In a few other words; as, κέρας, κέρᾱτος· ψάρ, ψᾱρός· γρύψ, γρῡπός. — None of these words are *pures*, except γραῦς, γρᾱός, and ναῦς, νᾱός. None of them are *labials*, except a few monosyllables, in which π is the characteristic; as, ῥίψ, ῥῑπός· γύψ, γῡπός. None of them are neuters in -α, -ατος.

2. Monosyllabic themes are long; as, κίς, κῑός· μῦς, μῡός· πῦρ, πῡρός. Except the pronoun τῐς.

Note. In accordance with this analogy, the neuter πᾶν (¶ 19) is lengthened.

3. Nouns in -αων, and in -ιων, G. -ιονος, have commonly the α and ι long; as, ὀπάων, κίων (G. κίονος); but Δευκαλῐων (G. -ῐωνος). For comparatives in -ίων, see § 159. α.

§ **684.** Special Rules of Conjugation. 1. Before the open terminations,

a.) α is *short*, except in ἰᾱομαι, *to heal*, κᾱω, and κλᾱω (§ 267. 3). — In Epic and lyric poets, the α is sometimes long for the sake of the metre.

b.) ι is commonly *long*; thus, κονῑω, *to cover with dust*, πρῑω (§ 282) But ἀῑω (ῐ; § 189. 4), ἐσθῑω (§ 298); δέδῐα (¶ 58); πῐομαι, ἔπῐον (§ 278).

c.) υ is *variable*; thus, ἀνῡω (§ 272. β), δακρῡω, *to weep*, θῡω (§ 219), κωλῡω, *to hinder*; ἐῤῥῠην (§ 264).

2. Before the regular close terminations,

α.) In *lingual* and *liquid* verbs, the doubtful vowels are *short*; thus, ὀνομᾰσω, ὠνόμᾰκα, ἔπᾰσα, ἔβλῐσα (§ 275); κομῐσω, κεκόμῐκα (¶ 40); κλύζω, *to rinse*, F. κλῠσω, A. ἔκλῠσα· τέτᾰκα, ἐτᾰθην (§ 268); κέκρῐκα, κέκρῐμαι (§ 217. α); πέπλῠμαι (§ 270). Except βρίθω, *to weigh down*, F. βρῑσω, A. ἔβρῑσα.

β.) In *pure verbs*, — (*a*) α is *short*, except when the theme ends in -ιάω pure, or -ράω; thus, σπᾰσω, ἔσπᾰκα (§ 219); ἐσκέδᾰσα, γελᾰσομαι (§§ 219. α, 293);

but, εἴᾶσα, θηρᾱ́σω (§ 218). — (*b*) ι is commonly *long;* thus, κονῑ́ω (1. b), F. κονῑ́σω, Pf. P. κεκόνῑμαι. But ἔφθῐμαι, ἐφθῐ́μην, and, in the Att. poets, φθῑ́σω, ἔφθῑσα (§ 278). — (*c*) υ is *variable;* thus, F. ἀνῠ́σω, δακρῡ́σω (1. c). See, also, θύω (§ 219) and χέω (§ 264).

3. Before the TERMINATIONS OF VERBS IN -μι, the doubtful vowels are *short*, except in the *Ind. sing.* of the *Pres.* and *Impf. act.*, and in the *2d Aor. act.* See § 224.

4. Before a CHARACTERISTIC CONSONANT,

i.) In the *theme*, α is commonly *short*, but ι and υ *long;* thus, λαμβᾰ́νω, μανθᾰ́νω (§ 290); κλῑ́νω (§ 269); ἀλγῡ́νω, ὀδῡ́ρομαι (§ 270). But ἱκᾱ́νω (§ 292), τῑ́νω, φθῐ́νω Ep., φθῑ́νω Att. (§ 278).

ii.) In the *liquid Fut.*, and in the *2d Aor.* (§ 255. δ), the doubtful vowels are *short*, but in the *liquid Aor.*, and in the *2d Perf.*, they are *long;* thus, κρῐνῶ, πλῠνῶ, ἔκρῑνα, ἔπλῡνα (§ 56); ἔλᾰβον, ἔθῐγον, ἐπῠθόμην (§ 290); ἐπᾰ́γην, ἐμῐ́γην, ἐζῠ́γην (§ 294); λέλᾱκα, κέκρῑγα, μέμῡκα (§ 236. 2). — Except 2 A. ἐάγην (§ 294; Att. ᾱ, Ep. commonly ᾰ). See, also, § 236. E.

C. DERIVATION.

§ 685. RULE IV. DERIVATIVES follow the quantity of their *primitives*.

This rule applies to compounds, as well as to simple derivatives. In applying the rule, observe § 307. R. Thus, θηρᾱ́ω, F. θηρᾱ́σω, Pf. P. τεθήρᾱμαι· θηρᾱ́σιμος, θήρᾱμα, θηρᾱτής, θηρᾱτός· πρόθῡμος (πρό, θῡμός), ἔντῑμος (ἐν, τῑμή).

NOTES. (*a*) For the quantity of the different terminations of derivation, see ¶ 62, §§ 305 – 321. For ῑ *paragogic*, see § 150. γ. The final ι in compound adverbs (§ 321. c) is likewise sometimes long. (*b*) For the lengthening of an initial vowel in the second part of a compound, see § 326. R. In some compounds, α is lengthened without passing into η; as, λοχᾱγός (λόχος, ἄγω).

D. DIALECT.

§ 686. The Doric α for η is long; and α, where the Ionic uses η, is commonly long (§ 44. 1). See also § 47.

E. AUTHORITY.

§ 687. For doubtful vowels which are long, and which are not determined by the rules already given, observe the usage of the poets, and the marks of quantity in the lexicons.

Among the most familiar examples are ἄτη, *destruction*, ὀπᾱδός, *follower*, σφρᾱγίς, *seal*, τρᾱχύς, *rough*, φλῡᾱρός, *talkative*, αἰκῑ́α, *outrage*, ἀνία (ῑ), *grief*, ἀκρῑβής, *exact*, ἀξῑ́νη, *axe*, δῑ́νη, *whirlpool*, κάμῑνος, *oven*, κῑνέω, *to move*, κλῑ́νη, *bed*, λῑμός, *hunger*, μῑκρός, *small*, νῑ́κη, *victory*, ὅμῑλος, *crowd*, σῑγή, *silence*, χαλῑνός, *bridle*, ἄγκῡρα, *anchor*, γέφῡρα, *bridge*, εὐθῡ́νη, *account*, ἰσχῡρός, *strong*, κίνδῡνος, *danger*, λῡ́πη, *grief*, πῡρός, *wheat*, σῡλᾱ́ω, *to plunder*, ὕλη, *forest*, φῡλή, *tribe*, χρῡσός, *gold*, ψῡχή, *soul*.

NOTE. Vowels, whose quantity is not determined by general or special rules, are said to be long or short by *authority*, i. e. the authority of the poets.

II. LOCAL QUANTITY.

§ 688. RULE V. A vowel before two consonants or a double consonant is long (§§ 51, 677. N.); as in ὄμφαξ, ἐλπίζοντες μάψ.

NOTE. This rule of position holds, when either one or both of the consonants are in the same word with the vowel; and commonly, also, when both consonants or the double consonant begin the next word.

§ 689. EXCEPTION. When the two consonants are *a mute followed by a liquid in the same simple word*, the quantity of the vowel is often not affected, especially in Attic poetry.

NOTES. 1. This exception results from the easy flowing together of the mute and liquid, so that they produce the effect of only a single consonant.

2. In the Att., the quantity of the vowel is commonly not affected, if the mute is *smooth* or *rough*, or, if *middle*, is *followed by* ρ. A middle mute followed by any liquid except ρ commonly renders the vowel long. Thus, the penult is regularly short in πέπλος, τέκνον, πότμος, δίδραχμος, γενέθλη, Μελέαγρος, χαράδρα· and long in στρεβλός, ἁγνός.

3. According to Porson, the tragic poets sometimes leave a vowel short before the two liquids μν.

§ 690. REMARK. A short vowel is sometimes *lengthened before a single consonant or another vowel*, especially in Epic poetry. This occurs chiefly in the following cases:

1.) When the consonant may be regarded as *doubled in pronunciation*. This applies especially to the liquids, and in the case of these (chiefly initial ῥ, cf. § 64. 1) sometimes extends even to Attic poetry; as, Αἰόλου [as if -ολλ-] κ. 36, δὲ νέφος Δ. 274, πολλὰ λισσομένη E. 358, ἐμὲ ῥέπον Soph. Œd. T. 847, μέγα ῥάκος Æsch. Pr. 1023.

2.) When the *digamma* (§ 22. δ) has been dropped; as, γὰρ ἕθεν [Fέθεν, §§ 142. 4, 143. β] I. 419, κὲν ἑ κύνες X. 42, πρὸς οἶκον [Fοῖκον] I. 147.— Epic usage appears to have been variable in respect to the digamma. It sometimes appears to have had the force of a consonant, and sometimes only that of a breathing.

3.) Before a *masculine cæsura* (§ 699. 4), and sometimes, without a cæsura, by the mere force of the *arsis* (§ 695); as, ὄνομα· Οὖτιν ι. 366, ἀπὸ ἕθεν Z. 62, ἀπὸ ἔρσῃ Φ. 283, ἀθάνατος ὡς ζ. 309, θυγατέρα ἥν E. 371, ὅγ' ὀλοῇσι A. 342.

NOTE. In Hexameter verse, one of three successive short syllables, a short between two long syllables, and a short syllable at the beginning of a line, must of necessity be made long. The second case sometimes occurs in the *thesis* (§ 695). Thus, ἀπονέεσθαι Ξ. 46; Ἀσκληπιοῦ δύο B. 731 (cf. Ἀσκληπῐοῦ υἱόν Δ. 194), βλοσυρῶπῐς ἐστεφάνωτο Λ. 36, Ἕως ὅ ταῦθ' Α. 193 ; Ἐπειδή (ῐ) Χ. 379, Φῐ́λε κασίγνητε Δ. 145, Δῐὰ μέν Γ. 357 (cf. Καὶ δῐά 358), Ἆρες, Ἄρες Ε. 31. See other examples above.

§ 691. Rule VI. A long vowel or diphthong at the end of a word may be shortened, if the next word begins with a vowel.

Remarks. 1. In the thesis of Hexameter and Pentameter verse (§§ 704, 705), this shortening is the general rule; as, Ἡμετέρῳ ἐνὶ οἴκῳ ἐν Ἄργεϊ τηλόθι πάτρης. Α. 30. Υἷες, ὁ μὲν Κτεάτου, ὁ δ' ἄρ' Εὐρύτου Ἀκτορίωνος. Β. 621.

2. This rule does not apply to the Iambic and Trochaic metres of the drama, as there the hiatus is not allowed.

3. A long vowel or diphthong is sometimes shortened before another vowel, in the middle of a word; as, ἔμπαῐον υ. 379, οῖος (οῐ) Ν. 275, τοῐοῦτος Soph. Ph. 1049, δείλαῐος Ar. Plut. 850. See also § 150. γ.

4. Some explain this shortening by supposing the long vowel (η, ω, = εε, οο, § 29. α) or diphthong to be half elided before the following vowel (οἴκο' ἐν); or the subjunctive of the diphthong to be used with a consonant power (ἔμπαyον).

§ 692. Rule VII. The last syllable of every verse is common.

That is, the metrical pause at the end of the verse renders the quantity of the last syllable indifferent; and it may be regarded as either long or short according to the metre.

Note. In some kinds of verse, the scansion is continuous; i. e. the verses are formed into systems (§ 700), at the end of which only a common final syllable is allowed, the preceding syllables being all subject to the rules of prosody, as though in the middle of a verse.

§ 693. Remarks. 1. In respect to quantity, both natural and local, the different dialects and kinds of poetry vary greatly. The greatest license appears in Epic poetry, which arose before the laws and usage of the language became fixed; and the least in the dialogue of comedy, which conformed the most closely to the language of common life. Of elegiac, lyric, and tragic poetry, the two former approached more nearly to the Epic, and the latter to the comic.

2. In giving the rules of quantity, never adduce position, unless some change has been made from the natural length of the vowel. For convenient distinction in metrical analysis, a vowel whose quantity is to be referred to Rules I. and II. may be said to be long or short *by nature;* to Rule III., *by the general rule for the doubtful vowels*; to Rule IV., *by derivation*; to Rule V., *by position before two consonants*, or *a double consonant*; to Rule VI., *by position before a word beginning with a vowel;* to Rule VII., *by position at the end of the verse.* When the quantity is not determined by general rules, cite special rules; or if these do not apply, adduce *authority* (§ 687), *cæsura*, *arsis*, the *necessity of the verse* (§ 690), &c.

CHAPTER II.

VERSIFICATION.

§ **694.** Greek verse is founded upon RHYTHM, i. e. *the regular succession of long and short quantities.* The simplest and most familiar rhythms are those in which a long syllable alternates with *one*, or with *two* short syllables (_ ⏑ _ ⏑ _ ⏑ _, or _ ⏑ ⏑ _ ⏑ ⏑ _ ⏑ ⏑ _).

NOTE. In versification, the elementary combinations of syllables are termed FEET; regular combinations of feet, VERSES (versus, *a turn*); and regular combinations of verses, STANZAS, STROPHES (στροφή, *a turning round*), or SYSTEMS (§ 700).

§ **695.** The long syllables are naturally pronounced with a greater stress of the voice than the short. This stress is termed ARSIS (ἄρσις, *elevation*), while the alternate weaker tone is termed THESIS (θέσις, *depression*). These terms are also applied to the parts of the rhythm which are thus pronounced. In the exhibition of metres, the arsis (also termed *metrical ictus*) is marked thus (ʹ).

NOTES. *a.* As one long syllable is equal to two short, the partial substitution of ⏑́ ⏑ for _́ in the arsis, and of _ for ⏑ ⏑ in the thesis, may be made without affecting the rhythm. In this way, as the short syllables have more vivacity, ease, and lightness, and the long syllables, more gravity, dignity, and strength, the poet has the power of greatly varying the expression of the verse; while, at the same time, the facility of versification is very much increased.

b. In the common kinds of verse, the metrical ictus is determined by the prevailing foot. Hence in Trochaic and Dactylic verse, every foot receives the ictus upon the *first* syllable; while, in Iambic and Anapæstic verse, every foot receives it upon the *second,* except the anapæst and proceleusmatic, which receive it upon the *third.*

§ **696.** In the series _́ ⏑ ⏑ _́ ⏑ ⏑ _́ ⏑ ⏑, the thesis is equal in time to the arsis (§ 676), and the rhythm is termed *equal* or *quadruple* (_ ⏑ ⏑ = 4 breves); but in the series _́ ⏑ _́ ⏑ _́ ⏑, the thesis is half the arsis, and the rhythm is termed *triple* (_ ⏑ = 3 breves).

REMARKS. 1. Of these, the former is the more stately in its movement, and the more appropriate to those kinds of verse which are farthest removed from common discourse; while the latter has more nearly the movement of common conversation, and is hence better adapted to the more familiar kinds of verse, and to dialogue.

2. Not only do the equal and triple rhythms differ from each other in ex-

pression; but the same rhythm has a different expression, according as it commences with the arsis or the thesis. In the former case (*Dactylic* –́ ⏑ ⏑ | –́ ⏑ ⏑ | –́ ⏑ ⏑, and *Trochaic* –́ ⏑ | –́ ⏑ | –́ ⏑), the movement, passing from the heavier to the lighter, has more ease, grace, and vivacity; in the latter (*Anapæstic* ⏑ ⏑ –́ | ⏑ ⏑ –́ | ⏑ ⏑ –́, and *Iambic* ⏑ –́ | ⏑ –́ | ⏑ –́), the movement, passing from the lighter to the heavier, has more decision, emphasis, and strength.

3. Other rhythms are formed by doubling the arsis, or by prolonging the thesis, or by variously compounding simple rhythms. Thus, by doubling the arsis, we obtain the rhythms, ⏑ –́ –́ ⏑ –́ –́ ⏑ –́ –́ ⏑, and ⏑ ⏑ –́ –́ ⏑ ⏑ –́ –́ ⏑ ⏑ –́ –́ ⏑. Of these, the first, according to its division into feet (§ 697), is Cretic –́ ⏑ –́ | –́ ⏑ –́ | –́ ⏑ –́, Bacchic ⏑ –́ –́ | ⏑ –́ –́ | ⏑ –́ –́, or Antibacchic –́ –́ ⏑ | –́ –́ ⏑ | –́ –́ ⏑; and the second, Choriambic –́ ⏑ ⏑ –́ | –́ ⏑ ⏑ –́ | –́ ⏑ ⏑ –́, Antispastic ⏑ –́ –́ ⏑ | ⏑ –́ –́ ⏑ | ⏑ –́ –́ ⏑, Rising Ionic ⏑ ⏑ –́ –́ | ⏑ ⏑ –́ –́ | ⏑ ⏑ –́ –́, or Falling Ionic – –́ ⏑ ⏑ | –́ –́ ⏑ ⏑ | –́ –́ ⏑ ⏑. Verses, in which the equal and triple rhythms are united, are termed *logaœdic* (λογαοιδικός, from λόγος, *discourse*, and ἀοιδή, *song*; see REM. 1 above). The most irregular kinds of verse are termed *polyschematist* (πολυσχημάτιστος, *multiform*) and *asynartete* (ἀσυνάρτητος, *disjointed*).

§ 697. FEET of the same metrical length are termed *isochronous* (ἰσόχρονος, *of equal time*). In the table of feet below, the measure of Class I. is two breves; of Class II., three; of Class III., four, &c.

I.	Πυῤῥίχιος,	Pyrrhic,	⏑ ⏑	μένε.
II.	Ἴαμβος,	Iambus, Iamb,	⏑ –	μένω.
	Τροχαῖος, Χορεῖος,	Trochee, Choree,	– ⏑	μῆκος.
	Τρίβραχυς,	Tribrach,	⏑ ⏑ ⏑	μένομεν.
III.	Δάκτυλος,	Dactyl,	– ⏑ ⏑	δώσετε.
	Ἀνάπαιστος,	Anapæst,	⏑ ⏑ –	ἐθέλω.
	Σπονδεῖος,	Spondee,	– –	σώζω.
	Ἀμφίβραχυς,	Amphibrach,	⏑ – ⏑	ἔδωκεν.
	Προκελευσματικός,	Proceleusmatic,	⏑ ⏑ ⏑ ⏑	λεγόμενος.
IV.	Ἀμφίμακρος, Κρητικός,	Amphimacer, Cretic,	– ⏑ –	δώσομαι.
	Βακχεῖος,	Bacchīus,	⏑ – –	λέγωνται.
	Ἀντιβάκχειος	Antibacchīus,	– – ⏑	σώζωμεν.
	Παίων α',	Pæon I.,	– ⏑ ⏑ ⏑	δωσόμενος.
	Παίων β',	Pæon II.,	⏑ – ⏑ ⏑	ἐγείρομεν.
	Παίων γ',	Pæon III.,	⏑ ⏑ – ⏑	ἐθέλητε.
	Παίων δ',	Pæon IV.,	⏑ ⏑ ⏑ –	θεοσεβής.
V.	Χορίαμβος,	Choriamb,	– ⏑ ⏑ –	σωζομένων.
	Ἀντίσπαστος,	Antispast,	⏑ – – ⏑	ἐγείρωμεν.
	Διΐαμβος,	Diiamb,	⏑ – ⏑ –	σοφωτέρων.
	Διτρόχαιος,	Ditrochee,	– ⏑ – ⏑	αἰνέσαιτε.
	Ἰωνικὸς ἀπὸ μείζονος,	Falling Ionic,	– – ⏑ ⏑	βουλεύετε.
	Ἰωνικὸς ἀπ' ἐλάσσονος,	Rising Ionic,	⏑ ⏑ – –	ἐθελήσει.
	Μολοσσός,	Molossus,	– – –	μνηστήρων.

VI.	Ἐπίτριτος α′,	Epitrite I.,	⏑ — — —	ἐγείρωνται.
	Ἐπίτριτος β′,	Epitrite II.,	— ⏑ — —	εὐπροσώπων.
	Ἐπίτριτος γ′,	Epitrite III.,	— — ⏑ —	ἡγουμένων.
	Ἐπίτριτος δ′,	Epitrite IV.,	— — — ⏑	βουλεύσεις.
VII.	Δόχμιος,	Dochmius,	⏑ — — ⏑ —	ἐβουλευόμην.
	Δισπόνδειος,	Dispondee,	— — — —	βουλεύσωνται.

NOTES. *α.* The Pyrrhic appears to have been so named from its use in the *war-dance* (πυῤῥίχη); the Iamb, from its early use in invective (ἰάπτω, *to assail*); the Trochee from its rapid movement (τρέχω, *to run*); the Dactyl, from its resemblance to the *finger* (δάκτυλος) in containing one long part and two short ones, or from the use of the finger in measuring, or in keeping time; the Anapæst, as the Dactyl reversed (ἀνάπαιστος, *struck back*); the Spondee, from its use in solemn rites (σπονδή, *libation*); the Bacchīus and Pæon, from their use in songs to Bacchus and in pæans; the Tribrach as consisting of three short syllables; the Amphibrach, of a short on each side of a long; the Amphimacer, of a long on each side of a short; the Antibacchīus, of a Bacchīus reversed; the Choriamb, of a Choree and Iamb; the Diiamb, Ditrochee, and Dispondee, of two Iambs, &c. I shall be pardoned, I trust, for adding a few lines from Coleridge's Metrical Lesson to his Son.

> "Trōchĕe | trīps frŏm | lōng tŏ | shōrt.
> From long to long, in solemn sort,
> Slōw Spōn|dēe stālks; | strōng fōot! | yet ill able
> Ēvĕr tŏ | cōme ŭp wĭth | Dāctȳl trĭ|sȳllăblĕ.
> Ĭām|bĭcs mārch | frŏm shōrt | tŏ lōng.
> Wĭth ă lēap | ănd ă bōund | thĕ swĭft Ān|ăpæ̆sts thrōng.
> One syllable long, with one short at each side,
> Ămphībră|chȳs hāstes wĭth | ă stātelȳ | stride."

β. Iambic, Trochaic, and Anapæstic verses are commonly measured, not by single feet, but by *dipodies* or pairs of feet (διποδία, *double foot*, from δίς and πούς). When they are measured by single feet, a verse of one foot is termed a *monopody*; of two, a *dipody*; of three, a *tripody*; of four, a *tetrapody*, or *quaternarius*; of six, a *hexapody*, or *senarius*, &c.

§ 698. VERSES are named, — (1.) From the prevailing foot; as, *Iambic*, *Trochaic*, *Dactylic*, *Anapæstic*. — (2.) From some poet who invented or used them, or from the species of composition in which they were employed; as, *Alcaic*, from Alcæus; *Sapphic*, from Sappho; *Heroic*, from its use in celebrating the deeds of heroes. — (3.) From the number of measures (i. e. of feet, or dipodies, § 697. *β*) which they contain; as, *monometer* (μονόμετρος, *of one measure*), *dimeter* (δίμετρος, *of two measures*), *trimeter*, *tetrameter*. — (4.) From their degree of completeness; thus a verse is termed *acatalectic* (ἀκατάληκτος, *not leaving off*, sc. before its time, from ἀ- priv. and καταλήγω), when its measure is complete; *catalectic* (καταληκτικός), when its last foot is incomplete; *brachycatalectic* (βραχύς, *short*), when it wants a whole foot at the end; *hypercatalectic* (ὑπέρ, *over*), when it has one or two syllables over; and *ace-*

phalous (ἀκέφαλος, *headless*) when it wants a syllable at the beginning.

REMARKS. α. A catalectic verse is said to be *catalectic on one syllable* (in syllabam), *on two syllables* (in dissyllabum), &c., according as the imperfect foot has one, two, or more syllables. Dactylic verses ending with a spondee or trochee (§ 692) are by some regarded as acatalectic, and by others as catalectic on two syllables; e. g. the common Hexameter (§ 704).

β. A lyric verse sometimes begins with an introductory syllable, termed an *anacrusis* (ἀνάκρουσις, *striking up*); or with two such syllables, forming what is termed a *base* (βάσις, *foundation*). In these introductory syllables, the quantity is commonly indifferent. A base sometimes consists of more than two syllables, and the term is sometimes applied to a monometer in any species of verse.

γ. In the dramatic poets, exclamations often occur *extra metrum* (i. e. not included in the metre); as, Φεῦ! Eur. Alc. 536, 719, 1102. Τί φῶ; Soph. Œd. C. 315. Τάλαινα! Ib. 318.

§ **699.** CÆSURA. Composition in verse consists of two series; the *metrical series*, divided into feet and verses; and the *significant series*, divided into words and sentences. These two series must, of course, correspond in their great divisions; but if this correspondence is carried too far, it gives to the composition an unconnected, mechanical, and spiritless character. The life and beauty of poetry depend essentially upon the skilful and varied interweaving of the two series. The *cutting of the metrical series by the divisions of the significant series* is termed *cæsura* (Lat. from cædo, *to cut*). It is of two principal kinds; the *cæsura of the foot*, and the *cæsura of the verse*. The former is the cutting of a foot by the ending of a word; the latter is the cutting of a verse by a pause permitted by the sense (termed the *cæsural pause*).

REMARKS. 1. (*a*) The cæsura of the verse is more frequently, but not necessarily, a cæsura of the foot. (*b*) When a foot-cæsura separates the arsis from the thesis, it is likewise termed a *cæsura of the rhythm*. (*c*) A cæsura is sometimes allowed between the parts of a compound word; as, Καὶ μ' οὔ|τι μελι†||γλώσσοις | πειθοῦς. Æsch. Pr. 172. (*d*) A syllable immediately preceding a cæsura is termed a *cæsural syllable*.

2. The coincidence of the divisions of the metrical series with those of the significant series is termed *diæresis* (διαίρεσις, *division*). The most important diæreses are those at the end of verses, systems, or stanzas. A foot-diæresis occurs whenever the division of words corresponds with the division of feet. Hence a verse-cæsura may be a foot-diæresis; e. g. the pastoral (REM. 5).

3. The verse-cæsura (often called simply the cæsura) not only contributes to the proper interweaving of the metrical and significant series, but affords a grateful relief to both the voice and the ear. See REM. 6.

4. When the cæsura follows a syllable pronounced with the arsis, it is termed *masculine*; with the thesis, *feminine*. A cæsura in the second foot is

named *triemim* (τριημιμερής, from τρεῖς, *three*, ἡμι-, half, and μέρος, *part*, occurring after three half-feet); in the third, *penthemim* (πέντε, *five*); in the fourth, *hephthemim* (ἑπτά, *seven*); in the fifth, *enneëmim* (ἐννέα, *nine*), &c. These names are also given to verses, or parts of verses, consisting of 1½, 2½, &c., feet.

5. The cæsura often occurring in Hexameter verse after the fourth foot (which is then commonly a dactyl) is termed the ***bucolic*** or ***pastoral cæsura*** from its prevalence in pastoral poetry.

6. The expression of the verse is affected by the place of the cæsura. In general, the earlier cæsuras give to the verse more vivacity; the later, more gravity. The most frequent cæsura is the penthemim. The effect of the cæsura in producing metrical variety will be seen by observing that the two most common metres, the Hexameter and Iambic Trimeter, are divided by the two most common cæsuras, the penthemim and hephthemim, into two parts, having the ratio of 5 and 7, of which (with the partial exception produced by the feminine cæsura in the Hexameter), the *one* always *begins* and *ends* with the *arsis*, and the *other* with the *thesis*.

§ 700. Metrical composition is either in MONOSTICHS, SYSTEMS, or STANZAS. (*a*) MONOSTICHS (*μονόστιχος, of a single line*) are formed by the repetition of the same metrical line, as in Hexameter verse (§ 704), Iambic Trimeter (§ 712), &c. (*b*) SYSTEMS are formed by the repetition of similar rhythms, with continuous scansion (§ 692. N.) and an appropriate close. See §§ 708, 714, 718. (*c*) STANZAS (also called *strophes*) are formed by the union of different kinds of verse. A stanza consisting of two lines is called a *distich* (*δίστιχος, of two lines*); of three, a *tristich;* and of four, a *tetrastich.*

NOTES. 1. The most common systems are easily arranged in dimeters, with here and there a monometer; and close with a dimeter catalectic. See §§ 708. 2, 714, 718.

2. The Greek choral odes were written in stanzas of very varied structure, but commonly arranged in *duads* or *triads* (sometimes in *tetrads* or *pentads*). A duad consists of two stanzas, corresponding in metre throughout. Of these the first is termed the *strophe* (στροφή, *turning round, stanza*), and the second the *antistrophe* (ἀντιστροφή, *counter-turn*, or *-stanza*). A triad consists of a strophe and antistrophe, preceded, divided, or followed by a third stanza of different metre, which according to its place is termed *proöde* (προῳδός, from πρό, *before*, and ᾠδή, *ode*), *mesode* (μέσος, *middle*), or *epode* (ἐπί, *after*). Of these, the epode is far the most common. The odes of Pindar are written each in a peculiar metre, but nearly all in strophes, antistrophes, and epodes. In the same ode, the strophes and antistrophes are all written in one metre, and the epodes all in a second, different from the first. In the drama, on the contrary, the metre of one duad or triad is not repeated in a second.

§ 701. REMARKS. 1. In SCANNING, observe not only the division into dipodies and feet, but also the arsis or metrical ictus (§ 695), and the verse-cæsura (§ 699). Unless these are carefully marked, the metrical character and expression of the verse are lost.

2. SYNIZESIS (§ 30). (a.) In Epic poetry synizesis is very frequent,

especially when the first vowel is ε; thus, ε͡α, ε͡ᾳ, ε͡αι; ε͡ο, ε͡οι, ε͡ου; ε͡ω, ε͡ῳ; as, Πηληϊάδε͡ω A. 1; χρυσέ͡ῳ ἀ|νά 15; see § 121. 2, ¶ 23. We find more rarely α͡ε; ι͡α, ι͡αι, ι͡η, ι͡ῃ, ι͡ο; η͡ι; ο͡ο; υ͡οι; &c. Synizesis sometimes occurs between two words, when the first is ἤ, ἦ, δή, μή, ἐπεί, or a word ending in the affix -η or -ῳ; as, ἢ͡ οὐχ E. 349, δὴ͡ ὄγδο͡ον η. 261, Πηλείδη͡ ἔθελ' A. 277, ἀσβέστῳ͡ οὐδ' P. 87.

(b.) In Attic poetry, synizesis occurs chiefly, — (*a*) In the endings -εως, -εων, -εα of Dec. III. (§ 116. α). — (*b*) In a few single words and forms; as, θε͡ός Eur. Or. 399. — (*c*) In the combinations ἢ οὐ and μὴ οὐ, which are always pronounced as one syllable. — (*d*) In some other combinations in which the first word is ἤ, ἦ, μή, ἐπεί, or ἐγώ· as, μὴ͡ εἰδέναι Eur. Hipp. 1335, ἐγὼ͡ εἰμ' Soph. Ph. 585.

3. Hiatus. Hiatus between words was admitted the most freely in Epic poetry, where however it may be often removed by the insertion of the digamma (§ 22. δ). It was the most studiously avoided in Attic poetry, especially in the Tragic Trimeter (§ 712), where it was scarce allowed, except after the interrogative τί, and some interjections, or words used in exclamation; as, οἴ ἐγώ! ἐγώ! Æsch. Ag. 1257.

§ 702. 4. In the following exhibition of metres, the division of feet will be marked by a single bar (|); the division of dipodies by a double bar (‖); and the verse-cæsura by an obelisk (†), sometimes doubled (‡). A base is denoted by B. In the examples which are given, the accents and breathings are mostly omitted, that they may not interfere with the marks of quantity; and these marks are employed alike to denote the metrical quantity, whether natural or local. Hence the common syllable at the end of a line (§ 692) is marked according to the rhythm in which it occurs. Some examples are added of analogous metres in our own language.

A. Dactylic Verse.

§ 703. The place of the fundamental dactyl is often supplied by a spondee ($— \smile \smile = — —$).

§ 704. I. The common Hexameter or Heroic Verse consists of six feet, of which the first four are either dactyls or spondees, the fifth commonly a dactyl, and the sixth always a spondee.

Remarks. 1. When the fifth is a spondee, the verse is termed *spondaic*, and has commonly an expression of greater weight or dignity. This occurs most frequently when the verse ends with a word of four syllables.

2. The favorite cæsura of the verse is the penthemim, which is almost equally masculine and feminine (§ 699. 4). After this, the most frequent cæsuras are the masculine hephthemim, and the pastoral (§ 699. 5). — Even when the penthemim is not the principal verse-cæsura, it is yet seldom wanting as a foot-cæsura. It is stated, that in the first book of the Iliad, 290 lines have the masc. penthemim, 315 have the fem., and only 6 have neither.

36

SCHEME AND EXAMPLES.

1.	2.	3.	4.	5.	6.
⏗ ⏑ ⏑	⏗ ⏑ ⏑	⏗ † ⏑ † ⏑	⏗ † ⏑ ⏑ †	⏗ ⏑ ⏑	⏗ —
⏗ —	⏗ —	⏗ † —	⏗ † — †		

Ᾱλλᾰ κᾰ|κῶς ʼᾰφῐ|ει,† κρᾰτε̆|ρῡν δ᾽ ʼε̆πῐ | μῡθŏν ʺε̆|τε̄λλε̄ν. A. 25.
Στε̄μμᾰτ᾽ ʼε̆|χῶν ʼε̄ν | χε̄ρσῐν † ʽε̆|κη̄βŏλοῡ | ʼᾹπŏλ|λῶνŏς. A. 14.
Αῐ κε̄ν | πῶς ʼᾱρ|νῶν κνῑσ|σῆς † αῐ|γῶν τε̆ τε̄|λειῶν. A. 66.
ʼΗ-τοῐ ʽŏγ᾽ | ʽῶς εῐ|πῶν κᾰτ᾽ ʼᾰρ | ʽε̆ζε̆τŏ · †| τοῖσῐ δ᾽ ʼᾰ|νε̄στη̄. A. 68.
Βη̄ δε̆ κᾰτ᾽ | Οῡλῡμ|ποῖŏ κᾰ|ρη̄νῶν, †| χῶŏμε̆|νŏς κῆρ. A. 44.

Coleridge's "Homeric Hexameter Described and Exemplified."

Stróngly it | beárs us a|lóng † in | swélling and | límitless | bíllows,
Nóthing be|fóre and | nóthing be|hínd, † but the | ský and the | ócean.

§ **705.** II. The ELEGIAC PENTAMETER consists of two dactylic penthemims (§ 699. 4), the first containing two dactyls or spondees with a cæsural syllable, and the second two dactyls with a final syllable. It commonly alternates with the Hexameter, forming what is termed, from its early use in plaintive song, the Elegiac Metre.

SCHEME AND EXAMPLES.

⏗ ⏑ ⏑	⏗ ⏑ ⏑	⏗ †	⏗ ⏑ ⏑	⏗ ⏑ ⏑	⏗
⏗ —	⏗ —				

ʼᾹρτε̆μῐ | θη̄ρŏφŏ|νη̄, † θῠγᾰ|τε̄ρ Δῐŏς, †| ʽη̄ν ʼᾸγᾰ|με̄μνῶν
Εῐσᾰθ᾽, ʺŏτ᾽ | ʼε̄ς Τροῐ|η̄ν †| ʺε̄πλε̆ε̆ | νηῡσῐ θŏ|ῆς,
Εῡχŏμε̆|νῳ μοῐ | κλῡθῐ, † κᾰ|κᾱς δ᾽ ʼᾰπŏ | κη̄ρᾰς ʺᾰ|λᾱλκε̆.
Σοῐ με̄ν | τοῡτŏ, θε̆|ᾱ, †| σμῑκρŏν, ε̆|μοῐ δε̆ με̆|γᾱ. Theog. 11

Described and Exemplified by Coleridge.

'In the Hex|ámeter | rīses † the | foúntain's | sílvery | cólumn;
'In the Pen|támeter | áye †| fálling in | mélody | báck.

§ **706.** III. Other Dactylic Metres are, (a.) *Pure*, consisting of dactyls only; (b.) *Impure*, consisting of dactyls and spondees; (c.) *Æolic*, containing, in place of the first foot, a mere base (§ 698. β); (d.) *Logaœdic* (§ 696. 3), in which dactyls are united with trochees. Thus,

1. DIMETER.

(a.) Μῡστŏδŏ|κŏς δŏμŏς. Ar. Nub. 303.
(b.) ADONIC (⏗ ⏑ ⏑ | ⏗ —). Πŏτνῐᾰ, | θῡμōν. Sapph. 1. 4.
(b.) Hypercat., *Dactylic Penthemim.* ʽᾹλμη̄|ε̄ντᾰ πŏ|ρον. Æsch. Sup. 844.

2. TRIMETER.

(b.) Πŏλλᾰ γᾰρ | ʺῶστ᾽ ʼᾰκᾰ|μᾱντῐς. Soph. Tr. 112.
(c). PHERECRATIC (B. | ⏗ ⏑ ⏑ | ⏗ —). ʺ-Ελδε̆|αι φῐλŏν | ʼη̄τŏρ. Pind. O. 1. 6.
GLYCONIC. Τŏ σōν | τοῐ πᾰρᾰ|δειγμ᾽ ʼε̆χῶν,
(B. | ⏗ ⏑ ⏑ | ⏗ ⏑ ⏑) Τōν σōν | δαῐμŏνᾰ, | τōν σŏν, ʼῶ
Τλᾱμŏν | Οῐδῐπŏ|δᾱ, βρŏτῶν. Soph. Œd. T. 1193.

(d.) Μῆτῐν 'ŏ|πᾱ φῠ|γοῖμ' "ᾰν. Æsch. Pr. 907.
(a.) Hypercat. Πŏλλᾰ βρŏ|τῶν δῐᾰ|μειβŏμĕ|νᾱ. Æsch. Sup. 543.

3. Tetrameter.

(a.) Alcmanian. Μῶσ', 'ᾰγĕ, | Κᾰλλῐŏ|πᾱ θῠγᾰ|τĕρ Δῐŏς. Alcm.
(b.) Spondaic. Ζεῦς πŏλῠ|ᾱνŏρŏς | 'ᾱμφῐ γῠ|ναῖκŏς. Æsch. Ag. 62.
(c.) Γλῠκῠ|πῖκρŏν 'ᾰ|μᾱχᾰνŏν | "ŏρπĕτŏν. Sapph. 20 (37).
(d.) Lesser Alcaic (⏑́ ⏑ ⏑ | ⏑́ ⏑ ⏑ | ⏑́ ⏑ | ⏑́ ⏑).
Χρῡσŏκῠ|μᾱͅ Ζĕφῠ|ρῳ̄ μῐ|γεῖσᾰ. Alc. 5 (24).
(a.) Hypercat. Τῶν μĕγᾰ|λῶν Δᾰνᾰ|ῶν 'ῠπŏ|κλῇζŏμĕν|ᾱν. Soph. Aj. 225.

4. Pentameter.

(b.) 'Ᾱτρεῖ|δᾱς μᾰχῐ|μοῦς, † 'ĕδᾰ|ῆ Λᾰγŏ|δαῖτᾱς. Æsch. Ag. 123.
(c.) Οἰνŏς, | 'ῶ φῐλĕ | παῖ, † λĕγĕ|ταῖ, καῖ 'ᾰ|λᾱθĕᾰ. Theoc. 29. 1.
(d.) 'Ω‾ πŏλῐς, | 'ῶ γĕνĕ|ᾱ τᾰ|λαῖνᾰ, | νῦν σĕ. Soph. El. 1314.
Πῡρφŏρŏς | 'ŏς τŏτĕ | μαῖνŏμĕ|νᾱͅ ξῠν | 'ŏρμᾱͅ. Soph. Ant. 135.
Sapphic (⏑́ ⏑ | ⏑́ ⏓ | ⏑́ ⏑ ⏑ | ⏑́ ⏑ | ⏑́ ⏑).
Καῖ γᾰρ | αῖ φεῦ|γεῖ, τᾰχĕ|ως δῐ|ωξεῖ,
Αῖ δĕ | δῶρᾰ | μῆ δĕκĕτ', | 'ᾱλλᾰ | δῶσεῖ. Sapph. 1. 21.
Phalœcian (B. | ⏑́ ⏑ ⏑ | ⏑́ ⏑ | ⏑́ ⏑ | ⏑́ ⏑).
Τŏν λεῖ|ŏντŏμᾰ|χᾱν, τŏν | 'ŏξῠ|χεῖρᾰ. Theoc. Ep. 20.

5. Hexameter.

(a.) Πρŏς σĕ γĕ|νεῖᾰδŏς, | 'ῶ φῐλŏς, | 'ῶ δŏκῐ|μῶτᾰτŏς | '‾Ελλᾰδῐ. Eur. Sup. 277.
(b.) 'Ᾱλλ' 'ῶ | πᾱντοῖ|ᾱς φῐλŏ|τῆτŏς 'ᾰ|μειβŏμĕ|ναῖ χᾰρῐν. Soph. El. 134.
(c.) Κĕλŏ|μαῖ τῐνᾰ | τŏν χᾰρῐ|ĕντᾰ Μĕ|νῶνᾰ κᾰ|λĕσσαῖ. Alc. 49.
(d.) "Η‾ πᾰλᾰ|μᾱͅ τῐνῐ | τᾱν δῠσᾰ|λωτŏν 'ĕ|λῆ τῐς | 'ᾱρχᾱν. Æsch. Pr. 165.

B. Anapæstic Verse.

§ 707. The place of the fundamental anapæst is often supplied by a spondee or dactyl, and sometimes, though very rarely, by a proceleusmatic (⏑ ⏑ ‒ = ‒ ‒ = ‒ ⏑ ⏑ = ⏑ ⏑ ⏑ ⏑).

§ 708. I. The Anapæstic, from its strong, even movement, was a favorite metre for marching songs; and it was greatly employed in SYSTEMS, by the dramatic poets, as intermediate between the Iambic of the common dialogue, and the lyric metres of the choral odes.

Remarks. 1. The general distinction (to omit modifications and exceptions) was this. The Iambic portions of the drama were spoken while the performers were stationary; the lyric, while they were dancing; and the Anapæstic, while they were coming in, or going out, or marching to and fro.

2. These systems are scanned continuously (§ 692. N.), but are usually arranged, so far as convenient, in dimeters (whence the common name of this species of verse, the Anapæstic Dimeter). They uniformly close with the dimeter catalectic, called, from its use in proverbs (παροιμίαι), the *parœmiac* verse (see § 700. 1). The use of the parœmiac, however, is not confined to the close of regular systems.

3. This verse requires a *cæsura* after each dipody, except in the parœmiac. This cæsura is sometimes deferred, so as to follow a short syllable at the beginning of the next dipody.

4. In respect to the *feet*, the following should be observed. (*a*) An anapæst must not follow a dactyl in the same dipody, and rarely follows it in successive dipodies. (*b*) A dactyl rarely follows an anapæst or spondee in the same dipody. (*c*) The third foot of the parœmiac is regularly an anapæst; so that the system may close with the cadence of the common Hexameter. A spondee, however, is occasionally admitted (cf. § 704. 1).

SCHEME AND EXAMPLES.

Dimeter Acatalectic.				Parœmiac.			
1.	2.	3.	4.	1.	2.	3.	4.
⏑ ⏑ –́	⏑ ⏑ –́ † ‖	⏑ ⏑ –́	⏑ ⏑ –́	⏑ ⏑ –́	⏑ ⏑ –́ ‖	⏑ ⏑ –́	–
– –́	– –́ † ‖	– –́	– –́	– –́	– –́ ‖	(– –́)	
–́ ⏑ ⏑	– –́ ⏑ ⏑ † ‖	– –́ ⏑ ⏑	– –́ ⏑ ⏑	– –́ ⏑ ⏑	‖		

Ἀλλὰ σ᾽ ὁ | Μαίας †‖ πομπαῖ|ος ἄναξ
Πελάσει|ε δόμοις, †‖ ὧν τ᾽ ἐπί|νοιαν
Σπεύδεις | κατέχων †‖ πράξει|ας, ἐπεὶ
Γενναῖ|ος ἀνήρ,
Αἰγεῦ, | παρ᾽ ἐμοὶ ‖ δεδόκη|σαι. Eur. Med. 759.

Δέρχθηθ᾽ | οἵαις †‖ αἰκί|αισιν. Æsch. Pr. 93.
Ἧπερ | δὸρίληπ‖τος †ἔτ᾽ ἦν | λοιπή. Soph. Aj. 146.

Though her éye | shone oút, † ‖ yet the líds | were fíx'd,
And the glánce | that it gáve † ‖ was wíld | and unmíx'd
With áught | of chánge, † ‖ as the éyes | may seém
Of the rést|less who wálk † ‖ in a troúb|led dréam.
Byron's Siege of Corinth.

§ **709.** II. The combination of the regular dimeter with the parœmiac (cf. §§ 713, 717) forms the ANAPÆSTIC TETRAMETER CATALECTIC of comedy, also called, from its use by the great master of comic verse, the *Aristophanic.*

SCHEME AND EXAMPLES.

1.	2.	3.	4.	5.	6.	7.	8.
⏑ ⏑ –́	⏑ ⏑ –́ † ‖	⏑ ⏑ –́	⏑ ⏑ –́ ‡ ‖	⏑ ⏑ –́	⏑ ⏑ –́ ‖	⏑ ⏑ –́	–
– –́	– –́ † ‖	– –́	– –́ ‡ ‖	– –́	– –́ ‖		
– –́ ⏑ ⏑	– –́ ⏑ ⏑ † ‖	– –́ ⏑ ⏑	‖	– –́ ⏑ ⏑	‖		

Καὶ μὴν | εὐθύς γ᾽ † ‖ ἀπὸ βαλ|βίδων ‡ ‖ περὶ τῆς | ἀρχῆς ‖ ἀποδεί|ξω
Τῆς ἡ|μετέρας † ‖ ὡς οὐ|δεμιᾶς ‡ ‖ ἥττων | ἐστὶν ‖ βασιλεί|ας.
Τί γὰρ εὐ|δαιμῶν † ‖ καὶ μακα|ριστὸν ‡ ‖ μᾶλλον | νῦν ἐσ‖τὶ δικασ|τοῦ,
Ἢ τρυφε|ρώτερον, ‡ ‖ ἢ δει|νότερον ‡ ‖ ζῷον, | καὶ ταῦ‖τα γέρον|τος.
Ar. Vesp. 548.

At your wórd | off I gó, † ‖ and at stárt|ing will shów, ‡ ‖ convínc|ing the stíff‖est opín|ion,
That regá|lia and thróne, † ‖ sceptre, kíng|dom and crówn, ‡ ‖ are but dírt | to judí‖cial domín|ion.

First in pléas|ure and glée, † || who abóund | more than wé; ‡ || who with lúx|ury néar||er are wéd|ded?
Then for pán|ic and fríghts, † || the world throúgh | none excítes, ‡ || what your dí|cast does, é'en || tho' gray-héad|ed.

Mitchell's Translation.

§ **710.** III. Examples are added, from lyric poetry, of other kinds of Anapæstic verse, both common and *logaœdic* (§ 696. 3);

Monom. Hyperc. Τρῐσŏλῡμ|πῐŏνῑ||κᾱν. Pind. O. 13. 1.
Dim. Hyperc. Τŏτε̆ με̄ν | πε̆ρῐσσᾱ||μŏτᾰτōς | καὶ ᾰρῐσ||τōς. Eur. Herc. 1018
Trim. Brachyc. Σε̆ μὲν οὖν | κᾰτᾰλευ||σŏμε̄ν, ὦ|μῐᾰρη̄ || κε̆φᾰλή. Ar. Ach 285.

Logaœdic. 1 An., 1 Iam. Νε̆με̆ᾱͅ | δὲ τρεῖς. Pind. N. 6. 34.
1 An., 3 Iam. Δε̆χŏμε̄σ|θᾰ καὶ | θε̆ῶν | γε̆νōς. Ar. Thesm. 312.
1 An., 4 Iam. Cat. Χᾰρῐτων | ἕκᾱ|τι τōν|δε̆ κω̄|μōν. Pind. O. 4. 14.
2 An., 1 Iam. Τὸ μὲν Ἀρ|χῐλŏχου | με̆λōς. Pind. O. 9. 1.
2 An., 2 Iam. Cat. Ὀλῐγŏ|δρᾰνῐᾱν | ἄκῐ|κυν. Æsch. Pr. 547.
2 An., 3 Iam. Σῠνε̆κῦρ|σ' ᾰδŏκη|τōς ἡ|δōνᾱ; | πŏθε̆ν. Eur. Ion, 1447.
3 An., 2 Iam. Δῠλε̆ρōν | μὲν ἀεὶ | κᾰτᾰ πᾶν|τᾰ δη̄ | τρŏπōν. Ar. Av. 451.
4 An., 1 Iam. Ἰŏτᾱ|τι γᾰμω̄ν, | ὅτε̆ τᾱν | ὁμŏπᾱ|τρῐōν. Æsch. Pr. 558.

C. Iambic Verse.

§ **711.** The place of the fundamental iambus may be supplied by a tribrach (⏑ — = ⏑ ⏑ ⏑), except at the end of a line. To add dignity and variety to the verse, the first foot of a dipody is very often lengthened to a spondee, and not unfrequently to a dactyl or an anapæst.

Note. The comic poets admit the anapæst in every place except the last of a verse or system. The same license exists in tragedy in proper names containing two short between two long syllables.

§ **712.** I. The Iambic Trimeter Acatalectic (often called the *Senarius*, § 697. *β*) is the principal metre of dramatic dialogue (§ 708. 1).

Remarks. 1. This verse has for its cæsura the penthemim or the hephthemim, the former much the most frequently. The latter is sometimes *anticipated* by the elision of the syllable after which it would properly fall, forming what has been termed by Porson the *quasi-cæsura*. Lines occur, though rarely, which have neither of these cæsuras.

2. The Tragic Trimeter admits the tribrach in every place but the last; the spondee in the 1st, 3d, and 5th places; the dactyl in the 1st and 3d; and the anapæst in the 1st. The feet which are admitted only in comedy or in proper names (§ 711. N.) are placed within parentheses, in the following scheme.

SCHEME AND EXAMPLES.

1.	2.	3.	4.	5.	6.
⏑ –́	⏑ –́	⏑ † –́	⏑ † –́	⏑ –́	⏑ –́
⏑ ⏑́ ⏑	⏑ ⏑́ ⏑	⏑ † ⏑́ ⏑	⏑ † ⏑́ ⏑	⏑ ⏑́ ⏑	
– –́		– † –́		– –́	
– ⏑́ ⏑		– † ⏑́ ⏑		(– ⏑́ ⏑)	
⏑ ⏑ –́	(⏑ ⏑ –́	⏑ † ⏑ –́	⏑ † ⏑ –́	⏑ ⏑ –́)	

Ἐγὼ | δ' ἀτολ||μός εἰ|μὶ † συγ||γένη | θεόν. Æsch. Pr. 14.
Σκύθην | ἐς οἶ||μον, † ἄβα|τον εἰς || ἐρη|μίαν. Ib. 2.
Πάντως | δ' ἀνάγ||κη † τῶν|δέ μοι || τόλμαν | σχέθειν. Ib. 16.
Τῆς ὀρ|θοβού||λου Θέμι|δος † αἰ||πυμῆ|τα παῖ. Ib. 18.
Ἑκατογ|κάρη||νον † πρὸς | βίαν || χειρου|μένον. Ib. 353.
Τέταρ|τον Ἱπ||πομέδοντ' † | ἀπέ||στειλεν | πατήρ. Soph. Œd. C. 1317
Κέντει|τε μὴ || φείδεσθ' · † | ἐγὼ || ἔτεκον | Πάριν. Eur. Hec. 387.
Μενέλα|ε μὴ || γνώμας | ὑπο||στήσας | σοφάς. Soph. Aj. 1091.

Love wátch|ing Mád||ness † wíth | unál||terá|ble míen.
Byron's Childe Harold.

§ **713.** II. The IAMBIC TETRAMETER CATALECTIC is peculiar to comedy. It consists of two dimeters, the second catalectic (cf. §§ 709, 717); and has commonly a cæsura after the first dimeter.

NOTE. The same metre (following of course accent and not quantity) is a favorite verse of modern Greek poetry. In our own language, it is chiefly used in comic songs and ballads.

SCHEME AND EXAMPLES.

1.	2.	3.	4.	5.	6.	7.	8.
⏑ –́	⏑ –́	⏑ –́	⏑ –́ †	⏑ –́	⏑ –́	⏑ –́	⏑
⏑ ⏑́ ⏑	⏑ ⏑́ ⏑	⏑ ⏑́ ⏑	⏑ ⏑́ ⏑ †	⏑ ⏑́ ⏑	⏑ ⏑́ ⏑		
– –́		– –́		– –́			
– ⏑́ ⏑		– ⏑́ ⏑		– ⏑́ ⏑			
⏑ ⏑ –́	⏑ ⏑ –́	⏑ ⏑ –́	⏑ ⏑ –́ †	⏑ ⏑ –́	⏑ ⏑ –́	(⏑ ⏑ –́	in prop. names.)

Ὅτου | χάριν || μ' ὁ δέσ|ποτης † || ὁ σὸς | κέκλη||κε δεῦ|ρο.
Οὔκουν | πάλαι || δήπου | λέγω; † || σὺ δ' αὐ|τὸς οὐκ || ἀκού|εις.
Ὁ δέσ|ποτης || γάρ φη|σιν ὑ||μᾶς ἡ|δέως || ἅπαν|τας. Ar. Plut. 260.

Auró|ra rís||es ó'er | the hílls, † || by gráce|ful Hoúrs || atténd|ed,
And ín | her tráin, || a mér|ry troóp † || of bríght-|eyed Lóves || are blénd|ed
Percival's Classic Melodies.

§ **714.** III. The Iambic verse sometimes occurs in SYSTEMS of the common form (§ 700. 1); as,

Παῖ' αὐ|τὸν ἀν||δρικώ|τατα, καὶ
Γάστρι|ζε καὶ || τοῖς ἐν|τέροις
Καὶ τοῖς | κόλοις,
Χὤπως | κόλᾳ || τὸν ἄν|δρα. Ar. Eq. 453.

§ 715. IV. Examples are added, from lyric poetry, of other kinds of Iambic verse (for the iambus in logaœdic verse, see § 710).

Monom. Hyperc. 'Ἔ̄τοῐ|μό̄ς 'ῡμ||νῶν. Pind. P. 6. 7.
Dim. Brachyc. 'Ὕ̄πε̆σ|τῐ μοῐ || θρᾰσό̄ς. Soph. El. 479.
Dim. Hyperc. Σῠ τοῐ | σῡ τοῐ || κᾰτη̄|ξῐω̄||σᾰς. Soph. Ph. 1095.
Trim. Cat. 'Ὃ̆ς αῐ|ε̄ν 'ῠπε̆ρ||ὄχό̄ν | σθε̆νό̄ς || κρᾰταῐ|ό̄ν. Æsch. Pr. 429.
Tetram. Τᾱν δεῐ|νᾰ τλᾱ||σᾱν, δεῐ|νᾰ δ' εῡ||ρουσᾱν | πρὸ̄ς αῡ||θαῐμῶν | πᾰθῆ. Soph. Œd. C. 1077.

SCAZON (σκάζων, *limping*) or CHOLIAMBUS (χωλίαμβος, *lame Iambus*), a form of the Trimeter, introduced by Hipponax, and having, for satiric or comic effect, a spondee in the last place.

Ἔ̄ῐ δ' 'ε̆σ|σῐ κρη̄||γῠό̄ς | τε̆ † καῑ || πᾰρᾱ | χρη̄στῶν. Theoc. Ep. 21.

D. TROCHAIC VERSE.

§ 716. The place of the fundamental trochee may be supplied in any part of the verse by a tribrach (– ⏑ = ⏑ ⏑ ⏑). The last foot of a dipody is often lengthened to a spondee or anapæst. The dactyl is admitted in proper names, except in the 4th and 7th places.

§ 717. I. The TROCHAIC TETRAMETER CATALECTIC occurs in both tragedy and comedy. It consists of two dimeters, the second catalectic (cf. §§ 709, 713); and has commonly a cæsura after the first dimeter.

SCHEME AND EXAMPLES.

1.	2.	3.	4.	5.	6.	7.	8.
∠ ⏑	∠ ⏑	∠ ⏑	∠ ⏑ †	∠ ⏑	∠ ⏑	∠ ⏑	∠
⏑́ ⏑ ⏑	⏑́ ⏑ ⏑	⏑́ ⏑ ⏑	⏑́ ⏑ ⏑ †	⏑́ ⏑ ⏑	⏑́ ⏑ ⏑	⏑́ ⏑ ⏑	
	∠ –		∠ – †		∠ –		
	⏑́ ⏑ –		⏑́ ⏑ – †		⏑́ ⏑ –		
(∠ ⏑ ⏑	∠ ⏑ ⏑	∠ ⏑ ⏑		∠ ⏑ ⏑	∠ ⏑ ⏑ in prop. names.)		

Πō̆λλᾰ|χοῡ σκό̆||ποῡντε̆ς | 'ἡμᾱς † || εῐς 'ᾰ|πᾱνθ' εῡ||ρη̄σε̆|τε̄
Τοῡς τρό̆|ποῡς καῐ || τη̄ν δῐ|αιτᾱν † || σφη̄ξῐν | 'ε̄μφε̆||ρε̄στᾰ|τοῡς.
Ar. Vesp. 1101.

Smáll re|fléction || ánd in|spéction, † || néeds it, | friénds of || míne, to | sée,
I'n the | wásps and || ús your | chórus, † || wóndrous | sími||lári|ty.
Mitchell's Translation.

§ 718. II. The Trochaic verse sometimes occurs in SYSTEMS of the common form (§ 700. 1); as,

Τῶ φρε̆|νᾱτῐ, || τῶν τ' 'ε̆|λαῐῶν,
'Ὧ̄ν πό̆|θοῡμε̆ν, || 'ᾱντῐ | τοῡτῶν
Τη̄νδε̆ | νῡνῐ
Τη̄ν θε̆|ό̄ν πρό̄σ||εῐπᾰ|τε̄. Ar. Pax, 578.

§ **719.** III. Examples are added, from lyric poetry, of other kinds of Trochaic verse (for the trochee in logaœdic verse, see § 706).

Trim. Δωρί|ῳ φω||νὰν ἐν|αρμόξ||αι πέ|διλῳ. Pind. O. 3. 9.
Trim. Cat. Τὶν γὰρ | ἐν πόν||τῳ κυ|βερνῶν||ται θο|αί. Ib. 12. 4.
Tetram. Ἔστι | μοι θε||ῶν ἕ|κατι || μυρί|α πάν||τᾳ κέ|λευθος. Pind. I. 4. 1.

E. Other Metres.

§ **720.** The metres which remain are Lyric, and for the most part admit with great freedom isochronous feet, or the substitution of two short syllables for one long, or of one long for two short. Examples are given of some of the most important.

1. Cretic System. Φρόντισον | καὶ γένου
(–́ ⏑ –́) Πανδίκως | εὐσεβὴς | πρόξενος,
Τὰν φυγάδα | μὴ προδῷς,
Τὰν ἕκαθεν | ἐκβολαῖς
Δυσθέοις | ὀρμέναν. Æsch. Sup. 418.

2. Bacchic Tetram. Τίς ἀχώ, | τίς ὀδμὰ | προσέπτα | μ' ἀφεγγής.
(⏑ –́ –́) Æsch. Pr. 115.

3. Choriambic System, closing, as is usual, with a bacchius.
(–́ ⏑ ⏑ –́) Νῦν δὲ τὸν ἐκ | θημετέρου
Γυμνασίου | λέγειν τι δεῖ
Καινὸν ὅπως | φανήσει. Ar. Vesp. 526.

4. Rising Ionic System. Πεπέρακεν | μὲν ὁ περσέ|πτολις ἤδη
(⏑ ⏑ –́ –́) Βασίλειος | στρατὸς εἰς ἀν|τίπορον γεί|τονα χώραν,
Λινοδέσμῳ | σχεδίᾳ πορθ|μὸν ἀμείψας. Æsch. Pers. 65.

5. Pæonic Tetram. Cat. Ὦ μακάρι' | Αὐτόμενες, † | ὥς σε μακα|ρίζομεν,
(–́ ⏑ ⏑ ⏑) Παῖδας ἐφύ|τευσας ὅτι † | χειροτεχνι|κωτάτους.
Ar. Vesp. 1275.

6. Dochmiac System. Μέθειται στρατὸς | στρατόπεδον λιπών,
(⏑ –́ –́ ⏑ –́) Ῥεῖ πολὺς ὅδε λεὼς | πρόδρομος ἱππότας.
Αἰθερία κόνις | με πείθει φανεῖσ',
Ἄναυδος, σαφής, | ἔτυμος ἄγγελος. Æsch. Sept. 79.

§ **721.** Note. An *antispast* (ἀντίσπαστος, *drawn in contrary directions*) is a combination of an iambic with a trochaic rhythm, and admits in the first part any foot which is admitted into Iambic verse, with the appropriate ictus; and in the second part, any foot which is admitted into Trochaic verse, with the appropriate ictus. The addition to this combination of a long syllable (which, in connection with other rhythms, may be resolved into two short) forms a *dochmius* (δόχμιος, *oblique, crooked*), which has consequently a triple ictus, with great variety of structure. Thus (1.) ⏑ –́ –́ ⏑ –́; (2.) ⏑ ⏑́ ⏑ –́ ⏑ –́; (3.) ⏑ ⏑́ ⏑́ ⏑ ⏑ –́; (4.) ⏑ ⏑́ ⏑ ⏑́ ⏑ ⏑ –́; (5.) – –́ –́ ⏑ –́; (6.) – ⏑́ ⏑ ⏑́ ⏑ – –́; &c.

CHAPTER III.

ACCENT.

§ **722.** In every Greek word, one of the *three last* syllables was distinguished by a *special tone* of the voice.

REMARKS. 1. This tone is commonly spoken of simply as *the tone*, or *the accent*. Its precise nature we cannot now determine. It seems to have resembled, in some degree, but with important differences, that which we call *accent* in English orthoëpy. That it never fell upon any syllable before the antepenult, shows that the Greeks felt the same difficulty in the utterance of a long train of syllables after their accent which we feel after ours. See also § 733. 2.

2. The versification of the ancient Greeks was founded upon quantity without regard to accent; that of the modern Greeks is founded upon accent without regard to quantity. We cannot resist the conclusion from this, that in the ancient language the distinction of quantity was the more prominent to the ear; while in the modern language the reverse is strikingly true (§ 19). At the same time, the distinction of accent was evidently the more intellectual in its character (§ 734); and, if less marked by the ear, was far more so by the understanding.

3. To those who pronounce the Greek in the usual method, according to quantity, the study of the accent is still highly useful, as serving, — (*a*) To distinguish *different words*, or *different senses* of the same word; as εἰμί (enclitic, § 732), *to be*, εἶμι, *to go*; ὁ, *the* (§ 731), ὅ, *which*; πότε; *when?* ποτέ (encl.), *once*; ἄλλα, *other things*, ἀλλά, *but*; λιθοβόλος, *throwing stones*, λιθόβολος, *thrown at with stones* (§ 739. *b*). — (*b*) To distinguish *different forms* of the same word; as the Opt. βουλεύσαι, the Inf. βουλεῦσαι, and the Imp. βούλευσαι (¶¶ 34, 35). — (*c*) To ascertain the *quantity* of the doubtful vowels (§§ 681, 726). — (*d*) To show the *original form* of words. Thus the circumflex over τιμῶ, φιλῶ, δηλῶ, marks them as contract forms of the pure verbs τιμάω, φιλέω, δηλόω. — (*e*) To show how words are employed in the sentence; as in cases of anastrophe, and where the accent is retained by proclitics and enclitics (§§ 730 – 732).

4. Upon some of the minute points of accentuation, authorities and critics differ. But this only furnishes another point of analogy between the Greek accent and our own. Indeed, there is no subject, either in grammar or in any other science, upon all the minutiæ of which there is a perfect oneness of opinion.

§ **723.** In accentuation, a *long vowel or diphthong* in the *ultima*, and often in the *penult*, is regarded as forming *two* syllables (§§ 29. *a*, 676). — We may say, in such cases, that the vowel or syllable forms two *accentual places*.

REMARK. In accentuation, the *inflection-endings* αι and οι are not treated as long vowels, except in the *Optative* (cf. § 41).

NOTE. This treatment of final *αι* and *οι* as short vowels appears not to have prevailed in the earliest form of the language, nor in the Doric dialect, which was characterized by its closer adherence to old usage (§ 735. *a*). In the Opt., it seems not to have prevailed from the natural dwelling of the voice upon the termination (§ 177). Traces of the old usage appear in the accentuation of so many Inf. forms upon the penult (§ 746); although the circumflex accent is not here excluded (cf. 726. R.).

§ **724.** 1. Accentual places are counted according to the following method. The *ultima* is counted as the 1st place, if its *vowel* is *short*, but as the 1st and 2d places, if its *vowel* is *long*. If the ultima forms two places, the *penult* forms, of course, the 3d place, and completes the number which is allowed. If, on the other hand, the ultima forms only a single place, then the penult forms the 2d place; and, besides this, if its *vowel* is *long*, it *always* forms in *dissyllables*, and *sometimes* forms in *polysyllables*, the 3d place also. If the ultima and the penult form but two places, then the *antepenult* is the 3d place. In the following words, the numbers denote the accentual places;

1 | 21 | 3 21 | 2 1 | 3 21 | 32 1 | 32 1 | 3 21
θες, παις, λογου, λογος, πλουτου, πλουτος, πλουτοι, προσωποις,
3 2 1 | 3 21 | 32 1 | 32 1 | 3 21 | 3 2 1 | 3 2 1
προσωπον, ἑκουσαις, ἑκουσᾰ, ἑκουσαι, πολεμους, πολεμος, πολεμοι.

2. An ascending line (ʹ) was adopted by the Greek grammarians as the mark of an accented place, and a descending line (ˋ) as the mark of an unaccented place. A syllable in which an accented was followed by an unaccented place received, of course, a double mark (ʹˋ). The words above, in which the accentual places are numbered, are all accented as far from the end as possible. If, therefore, all their accentual places were distinctly marked, they would be written thus;

θές, πά̀ις, λόγὸὺ, λόγὸς, πλού̀τὸὺ, πλόὺτὸς, πλόὺτοὶ, προσώπὸὶς,
πρόσὼπὸν, ἑκού̀σὰὶς, ἑκόὺσὰ, ἑκόὺσαὶ, πολέμὸὺς, πόλὲμὸς, πόλὲμοὶ.

3. But it is evidently needless, except for grammatical illustration, to mark unaccented syllables, and when the two marks (ʹˋ) fall upon the same syllable, it is more convenient in writing to unite them into one (^, or, as rounded for greater ease in writing, ⁀ or ~). Dropping, therefore, the marks over the unaccented syllables, and uniting the double marks, we write thus;

θές, παῖς, λόγου, λόγος, πλούτου, πλοῦτος, πλοῦτοι, προσώποις,
πρόσωπον, ἑκούσαις, ἑκοῦσα, ἑκοῦσαι, πολέμους, πόλεμος, πόλεμοι.

4. The following words are accented upon the first place; δός, θήρ, θηρί, χείρ, παιδός, γυναιξί, βασιλεύς. The following, upon the second; βοῦς, φῶς, πῦρ, σοφοῦ, τιμῆς, νέος, νέοι, λόγε, φίλοι, ζῶναι, τέμνε, ὀστέον, βασιλέες, τιθέντι. The following, upon the third; λόγων, παῖδες, γυναῖκα, σῶμα, σώματος, σωμάτων, λείπω, λείπομεν, λείπουσι, ἔλειπον, λέλοιπα, ἐλελοίπειν, λεῖπε.

§ **725.** A syllable is termed *acute*, if it simply forms an accented place; *circumflexed*, if it forms an accented followed by an unaccented place; *grave*, if it receives no accent; as the final syllables in θηρί, βασιλεύς· σοφοῦ, τιμῆς· λόγε, σῶμα.

A word is termed an	OXYTONE, PERISPOME, BARYTONE,	if its Ultima is	Acute. Circumflexed. Grave.

A word is termed a { PAROXYTONE, PROPERISPOME, } if its Penult is { Acute. Circumflexed. PROPAROXYTONE, if its Antepenult is Acute.

NOTES. (*a*) The terms above are formed from the words τόνος (Lat. accentus), *tone*, ὀξύς (Lat. acūtus), *sharp*, περισπώμενος (Lat. circumflexus), *bent round*, *circumflexed*, βαρύς (Lat. gravis), *heavy*, *grave*, παρά, *near*, and πρό, *before*. (*b*) The *paroxytones*, *properispomes*, and *proparoxytones* are all included in the general class of *barytones*.

§ **726.** To the principles of Greek accentuation which have now been given, may be referred, almost throughout, the following general laws of accent and accentual changes.

I. GENERAL LAWS OF ACCENT.

1. One accent, and *only one*, belongs to each word.

Hence σύν and ὁδός, compounded, become σύνοδος· σύν and φέρω, συμφέρω.— For apparent exceptions, see §§ 731, 732.

2. The accent *never* falls upon any syllable before the antepenult.

Hence ὄνομα, μέγεθος become, in the Gen., ὀνόματος, μεγέθεος.

3. The *antepenult* can receive only the *acute* accent, and can receive this only when the *ultima* is *short*.

Hence θάλασσᾰ, ἄνθρωπος, πρόσωπον, become, in the Gen., θαλάσσης, ἀνθρώπου, προσώπου. — For θάλασσαι, ἄνθρωποι, see § 723. R.

NOTES. α. If the ultima is long merely by *position*, still the antepenult receives no accent; hence ἱεριβῶλαξ (ᾰ), though ἱερίβωλος.

β. In accentuation, ε before ω in the terminations of the Gen. and of the Attic Dec. II. is not regarded as forming a distinct syllable (§§ 35, 95. 3. α, 98, 116. α, δ); hence, Ἀτρείδεω, πόλεως, πόλεων· ἀνώγεων. So, also, with an intervening liquid, in adjectives compounded of γέλως and κέρας (§ 136. 1); as, φιλόγελως, ἄκερως· and, according to the same analogy, the compound adverbs ἔκπαλαι, πρόπαλαι.

4. The *circumflex* never falls upon any syllable that is not *long by nature*.

Hence βοῦς, μῦς, πᾶς, become, in the Nom. pl., βόες, μύες (ῠ), πάντες (ᾰ).

5. The *penult* can receive the *circumflex* only when the *ultima* is *short by nature*.

Hence μοῦσα, νῆσος, σῦκον, become, in the Gen., μούσης, νήσου, σύκου. — For μοῦσαι, νῆσοι, see § 723. R.

REMARK. In the old language and in the Dor. (cf. § 723. N.), a final syllable long merely by position appears to have forbidden both the acute upon the antepenult, and the circumflex upon the penult. From the common accentuation (which forbade ἱερίβωλαξ, but permitted ἱεριβῶλαξ, see N. α above), the circumflex upon the penult appears not to have been deemed quite so great a remove from the end of the word as the acute upon the antepenult (cf. 723. N.). Even after the dropping of τ in the 3d Pers. pl. of verbs (§ 181. 2), some forms of the Doric retained the old accentuation; as, ἐγράφοντ ἐγράφον.

6. If the *ultima* is *short by nature*, and the *penult* is *long by nature* and *accented*, it must be *circumflexed*.

Hence θήρ, αἰών, γνώμη, Ἀτρείδης, become, in the Nom. pl., θῆρες, αἶωνες, γνῶμαι (§ 723. R.), Ἀτρεῖδαι. — For εἶθε, ναίχι, ὥστε, &c., see § 732. d.

II. Accentual Changes.

§ **727.** The accent is subject to the following changes: — (*a*) The *acute* may be changed to the *circumflex;* as, θήρ, θῆρες. — (*b*) The *circumflex* may be changed to the *acute;* as, μοῦσα, μούσης. — (*c*) The *acute* may be *softened* upon the *ultima* (§ 729). — (*d*) The accent may be *thrown back*, that is, transferred to a preceding syllable; as, γράφω, ἔγραφον. — (*e*) The accent may be *brought forward*, that is, transferred to a succeeding syllable; as, θήρ, θηρός. — (*f*) The accent may be thrown upon the *preceding word;* as, σῶμά μου (§ 732). — (*g*) The accent may be *omitted;* as, ταὐτό· παρ' ἐμοί· ὁ νοῦς· φιλῶ σε (§§ 728. b, c, 731, 732).

§ **728.** Changes in the accent arise, principally, from,

I.) The addition or loss of syllables; as, ὄνομα, ὀνόματος (§ 726. 2); ῥίπτω, πτέω (§ 288); κοῦφος, κουφότερος (§ 156); πατέρος, πατρός (§ 741). See III. c.

II.) Change in the quantity of vowels. See § 726. 3 - 6.

III.) Contraction, crasis, or apostrophe, as follows.

a. Contraction. An *acute* syllable, *followed* by a grave, is contracted with it into a *circumflexed* (§§ 724. 3, 725); otherwise the accent is not affected by contraction, except as the general laws may require; as, νόος νοῦς, τιμάω τιμῶ· τίμαε τίμα, τιμαοίμην τιμῴμην· ἑσταότος ἑστῶτος (§ 726. 6).

Remark. Some contract forms are accented as though made by inflection without contraction; or fall into the analogy of other words. Thus,

1.) In contracts of Dec. II., — (*a*) The accent remains throughout upon the same syllable as in the theme; as, περίπλοος, περιπλόου, contr. περίπλους, περίπλου· Gen. ἀγήρω (¶ 17). — (*b*) The Nom. dual, if accented upon the ultima, is always oxytone; as, νώ, ὀστώ (¶ 9). — (*c*) Except in the Nom. dual, all simple contracts in -ους or -ουν are perispome; as, χρύσεος χρυσοῦς (¶ 18), κάνεον κανοῦν, *basket*. — (*d*) In oxytones of the Attic Dec., the Gen. sing. has the acute; which may be explained by supposing one ο to have been dropped from the original form (cf. § 243. 2); thus, νᾱός (¶ 9), G. ναόο (§ 86), ναό, by contraction νώ, νεώ (§ 98. β).

2.) The contract Acc. of nouns in -ώ is oxytone; as, ἠχόα ἠχώ (¶ 14). So Dat. (χρωτί) χρῷ perispome (§ 104). These cases follow the analogy of § 744.

3.) The contract Gen. pl. of τριήρης (¶ 14), αὐτάρκης, and compounds in ήθης is paroxytone; as, τριηρέων τριήρων.

4.) The *Subj. pass.* of verbs in -μι, and of Perfects used in the sense of the Pres., is often accented as though *uncontracted;* thus, τίθωμαι, τίθῃ, τίθηται· δίδωμαι· κέκτωμαι, μέμνωμαι (§ 234). And, on the other hand, the *Opt. pass.* of these verbs is accented by many as though *contracted;* thus, τιθεῖο, τιθεῖτο· διδοῖο· κεκτῇο, κεκτῇτο.

NOTE. In *diæresis*, or the resolution of a diphthong, a circumflexed syllable is resolved into an acute and a grave; as παῖς πάϊς.

b. CRASIS. In crasis, the accent of the first word is omitted. The accent of the second remains without change, except as required by § 726. 6; as, ταὐτό, for τὸ αὐτό· τἆλλα, for τὰ ἄλλα (yet some write τἄλλα).

c. APOSTROPHE. When an accented syllable is *elided*, the accent is thrown back upon the penult, as acute; thus, δεῖν' ἔπη, for δεινὰ ἔπη· πόλλ' ἔπαθον (πολλά). — Except in prepositions, and the particles ἀλλά, μηδέ, οὐδέ, and the poetic ἠδέ and ἰδέ· as, παρ' ἐμοί, ἀλλ' ἐγώ.

§ **729.** IV.) The CONNECTION OF WORDS in discourse, as follows.

A. GRAVE ACCENT. Oxytones, followed by other words in closely connected discourse, *soften* their tone, and are then marked with the *grave accent* (§ 14); as, ἐπὶ τὰ καλὰ καὶ ἀγαθά.

EXCEPTION. The interrogative τίς, and words followed by enclitics (§ 732), never take the grave; as, Τίς εἶ; *Who art thou?*

NOTES. α. In the application of this rule editors vary. The best usage, however, retains the acute accent only in the case of unconnected words or phrases, and before the period, colon, and such other pauses as require to be distinctly marked in reading.

β. The syllable over which the grave accent is written is still regarded as *acute*, although its tone is softened, and the word to which it belongs is still termed an *oxytone*. Syllables *strictly grave* are never marked, except for grammatical illustration, as in § 724.

§ **730.** B. ANASTROPHE. In *prepositions of two short syllables*, the accent is usually *thrown back* upon the penult, when they *follow* the words which they would regularly precede, or take the place of *compound verbs*, or are used *adverbially;* as, δόμων ὕπερ, for ὑπὲρ δόμων· ὀλέσας ἄπο ι. 534, for ἀπολέσας (§ 653); πάρα, for πάρεστι· ἄνα, for ἀνάστηθι (§ 653. ε); πέρι, in the sense of *exceedingly* (§ 657. β). This change of the accent is termed *anastrophe* (ἀναστροφή, *turning back*).

NOTES. (*a*) Grammarians except διά and ἀνά (except for ἀνάστηθι), to distinguish them from the Acc. Δία, and the Voc. ἄνα (¶¶ 11, 16). (*b*) Both in anastrophe and in the common accentuation of prepositions (§ 750. 2), the attraction of the accent towards the word upon which the preposition expresses its force will be observed.

§ **731.** C. PROCLITICS. A few *monosyllables*, beginning with a vowel, are commonly *connected* in accentuation with the *following* word, and *lose*, in consequence, their proper accent. They are hence called *atonics* (ἄτονα, *toneless*), or, with more precision, *proclitics* (προκλίνω, *to lean forward*). They are, (1.) the *aspirated* forms of the article, ὁ, ἡ, οἱ, αἱ· (2.) the adverb οὐ, *not*; (3.) the prepositions εἰς, *into*, ἐν, *in*, ἐξ, *out of*; (4.) the conjunctions εἰ, *if*, ὡς, *as*.

NOTE. The proclitics retain their accent when they close a sentence, or follow the word which they would regularly precede. Hence, οὐ δῆτα· but, πῶς γὰρ οὔ· ὡς θεός, but, θεὸς ὥς· ἐκ κακῶν, but, κακῶν ἔξ.

§ **732.** D. ENCLITICS. Some words are *attached*, in accentuation, to the *preceding* word, and are hence called *enclitics* (ἐγκλιτικός, from ἐγκλίνω, *to lean upon*). They are,— (I.) The following *oblique cases of the personal pronouns*; 1st Pers. μοῦ, μοί, μέ· 2d P. σοῦ, σοί, σέ· 3d P. οὗ, οἷ, ἕ· νίν, σφίσι, σφέ. For other enclitic forms of the personal pronouns, see ¶ 23. (II.) The *indefinite pronoun* τὶς, in all its cases, and the *indefinite adverbs* πώς, πώ, πή, ποί, πού, ποθί, ποθέν, ποτέ (¶ 63). (III.) The Pres. ind. of εἰμί, *to be*, and φημί, *to say*, except the 2d Pers. sing. — (IV.) The *particles* γέ, νύν, πέρ, τέ, τοί· the poetic θήν, κέ(ν), νύ, ῥά· and the inseparable -δέ. — See § 152. 2.

REMARKS. a. (*a*) An enclitic throws back its tone, in the form of the *acute* accent, upon the *ultima* of the preceding word; as, ἄνθρωπός ἐστι· δεῖξόν μοι· εἴ τίς τινά φησί μοι παρεῖναι. (*b*) If the ultima of the preceding word has already an accent, the accent of the enclitic unites with it, and disappears; as, ἀνήρ τις· φιλῶ σε. (*c*) The accent of the enclitic, if a monosyllable, is also lost after a paroxytone; as, φίλος μου.

b. An enclitic *retains* its accent,— (1.) At the *beginning* of a clause; as, Σοῦ γὰρ κράτος ἐστὶ μέγιστον. — (2.) After the *apostrophe*; as, πολλοὶ δ' εἰσίν. — (3.) If it is *emphatic*; as, οὐ Κῦρον, ἀλλὰ σέ, *not Cyrus, but you*. — (4.) If it is a *personal pronoun*, preceded by an *orthotone preposition* which governs it; as, παρὰ σοί, περὶ σοῦ, πρὸς σέ. But πρός με, and sometimes περί μου and πρός σε, occur. — (5.) If it is a *dissyllable*, preceded by a *paroxytone*; as, ἦν λόγος ποτὲ ἐναντίος σφίσιν.

c. When ἐστί is prominent in a sentence, it becomes a paroxytone; as, τοῦτ' ἔστιν, *it is so*.

d. (α.) An enclitic is often joined in writing to the preceding word, as if forming with it but one compound word; thus, μήτις, οὐδέποτε, ὥστε. (β.) This is always the case with the preposition -δέ, *to*; as, Ὄλυμπόνδε, *to Olympus*, Ἐλευσῖνάδε. (γ.) In pronouns and adverbs compounded with -δέ (§ 150, ¶ 63. IX.), the syllable preceding -δέ always takes the accent, which is acute or circumflex according to the rule in § 744. (δ.) In ἐγώ, ἐμοί, and ἐμέ, the accent is thrown back when γέ is affixed (§ 328. b); thus, ἔγωγε, ἔμοιγε, ἔμεγε. (ε.) Εἴθε and ναίχι are accented as if formed by the attachment of enclitics.

§ **733.** Notes. 1. A word, which neither *leans* upon the following nor upon the preceding word, but stands, as it were, *erect*, is called, in distinction from the proclitics and enclitics, an *orthotone* (ὀρθότονος, *erect in tone*).

2. Both proclitics and enclitics are more abundant in English than in Greek, and these classes of words furnish another strong analogy between the Greek and the English accent (§ 722. 1). The words in English which are used in translating the Greek proclitics and enclitics are themselves, for the most part, either proclitic or enclitic. Thus, in the sentence, *Give me the book* (pronounced *Gívme thebóok*), the pronoun *me* is enclitic, and the article *the*, proclitic. In the sentence, *If John's in the house, don't tell him a word of this*, the words *If*, *in*, *the*, *a*, and *of*, are proclitics, and the words *is*, *not*, and *him*, enclitics.

III. Determination of Accented Syllable.

§ **734.** General Principle. In each word, the accent belongs to that syllable *upon which the attention is most strongly fixed.*

Note. If, from the general laws of accentuation, this syll. cannot receive the accent, it draws it as near to itself as possible.

Remarks. 1. In the origin of language, the attention is absorbed by the greater distinctions of thought; but, as these become familiar to the mind, it passes to the less, and then to those that are still subordinate. Hence, in the progress of a language, its accent is subject to change, as well as the forms of its words, its vocabulary, and its constructions. In the Greek, as in other languages, the accent was originally confined to the syllables containing the essential ideas of words, i. e. to their radical syllables (see §§ 83, 171). But, in proportion as these became familiar, there was a tendency to throw the accent upon those syllables by which these ideas were modified, either through inflection, derivation, or composition. This tendency would of course vary greatly in different classes and forms of words. It would naturally be the strongest where the root was the most familiar; or where the formative part was the most significant or characteristic. On the other hand, any strengthening of the radical, or weakening of the formative part, would have a tendency to produce a contrary effect. In illustration of these tendencies (which of course are subject to the general laws of accent), it will be observed, that, —(*a*) In neuter nouns, the affix, from its inferior importance, almost never attracts the accent (§§ 737. *i*, 738. *d*). —(*b*) In demonstrative pronouns, the deictic -δε always draws the accent to the preceding syllable (§ 732. γ), and the still stronger -ι always takes it upon itself (§ 150. γ). —(*c*) In verbs, the accent is always attracted by the augment, while it can never pass beyond it (§ 748. 4). —(*d*) The old weak root of the 2d Aor. (§ 257. 1) yields the accent to the affix in several cases where the strengthened root of the Pres. retains it (§ 746 – 748). — (*e*) In derivative adjectives, those endings which express most strongly character or relation attract the accent (§§ 737 – 739). — (*f*) In composition, the accent is usually attracted by that word which defines the other, and thus gives its special character to the compound (§§ 323, 739). In the *active* compound verbals, the idea of the action is more prominent than in the *passive;* and hence appears to have arisen the distinction in § 739. *b.*

§ **735.** 2. That the different dialects should have often varied in accent will occasion no surprise in those who have compared the pronunciation of our own language in different parts of its native isle. That these differences are often neglected in our copies of the classics has arisen from the late period at which the marks of accent were introduced (§ 22. *a*), and the tendency at that time to conform every thing to the Attic standard (§ 4). From the testimony of the old grammarians we learn, that, — (*a*) The Doric was characterized by its adherence to general rules and old usage (§§ 723. N., 726. R.). — (*b*) The Lesbian Æolic was characterized by its tendency to throw the accent as far back as possible. In words of more than one syllable, it is said to have admitted the accent upon the ultima in prepositions and conjunctions only. — (*c*) The Attic (to which the Ionic appears to have more nearly approached) was characterized by an expressive variety of accent, and a greater inclination to mark the minuter shades of thought and species of relation.

A. Accent in Declension.

§ **736.** I. The accent of the THEME must be learned from special rules and from observation.

a. Rules for Simple Words.

Special Rules of Dec. I. All contracts are perispome; as, Ἑρμῆς, μνᾶ. Of other words, — (*a*) All in -ας are paroxytone; as, ταμίας. — (*b*) Most in -ης are paroxytone, except *verbals in* -της *from mute and pure roots of verbs in* -ω, which are commonly oxytone; as, Ἀτρείδης, ναύτης, ψάλτης, προφήτης, προστάτης· δικαστής, ποιητής. — (*c*) Nouns in -α short (§ 92) throw the accent as far back as possible; as, γλῶσσᾰ, λέαινᾰ, ἀλήθειᾰ, μυῖᾰ. — (*d*) Most abstracts in -ιᾱ, those in -συνη, and those in -ειᾱ from verbs in -εύω (§§ 305. b, 308. a, c), are paroxytone; as, σοφίᾱ, σωφροσύνη, παιδείᾱ. — (*e*) Most other verbals in -α long or -η, especially those formed after the analogy of the 2d Perf. (§ 307. R.), are oxytone; as, φυγή, φθορᾱ́.

§ **737.** Special Rules of Dec. II. (*a*) *Adjectives in* -ος *preceded by a mute* are commonly oxytone, especially those in -κος, verbals in -τος, and ordinals in -στος; as, κακός, ἀρχικός, ὁρᾱτός, εἰκοστός, χαλεπός, σοφός, δολιχός, ἀγαθός. — (*b*) On the contrary, *primitive nouns with a mute root* are more frequently accented as far back as possible; as, λόγος, κρόκος, πλοῦτος, ψάμαθος. — (*c*) All ordinals not ending in -στος are accented as far back as possible; as, δέκατος. — (*d*) Adjectives in -λος, -ρος, and -νος (except those in -ινος denoting *material* or *country*, § 315. c, e) are commonly oxytone; as, ἀπατηλός, φειδωλός, ψιλός, αἰσχρός, φοβερός, πονηρός, λιγυρός, χλωρός, σεμνός, πεδινός, Κυζικηνός, Σαρδιᾱνός· ξύλινος, Ταραντῖνος. — (*e*) Nouns in -μος with a long penult are commonly oxytone; while adjectives in -μος are commonly accented as far back as possible; as, ὀδυρμός, βωμός· χρήσιμος. — (*f*) Nouns in -ος *pure* are more frequently oxytone; as, ναός, θεός, υἱός, νυός. — (*g*) Verbals in -τεος (§ 314. f), multiples in -πλοος (§ 138. 4), and most adjectives in -αιος from nouns of Dec. I., in -οιος, and in -ῳος, are accented upon the penult; as, ποιητέος, διπλόος, ἀγοραῖος, ὁποῖος, ἑῷος. — (*h*) Adjectives in -ειος, in -ιος *preceded by a consonant*, and in -εος joined immediately to the root, are commonly accented as far back as possible, as, θήρειος, οὐράνιος, χρύσεος. — (*i*) Very few neuters are oxytone; and most neuters are accented as far back as possible (§ 734. *a*); as, μόριον, ποτήριον, κορίδιον, ὄρνεον, ἔλαιον.

§ **738.** Special Rules of Dec. III. (*a*) All nouns in -αν, -ευς, -ω, -ως (G. -οος), -ας (-αδος), -ῑς (-ῑδος), all masculines in -ηρ, nouns of more than one syllable in -ῡς, and almost all nouns in which the characteristic is ν preceded by ᾱ, ε, η, or ῑ, are oxytone; as, παιάν, ἱππεύς, ἠχώ, αἰδώς, λαμπάς, -άδος, σφραγίς, -ῖδος, ὁ πατήρ, λιμήν, -ένος, λειχήν, -ῆνος, δελφίς, -ῖνος. — (*b*) All nouns in -εων, names of months in -ων, and most feminines and augmentatives in -ων, are oxytone; other words in -ων are more frequently paroxytone; as, κυκεών, Ἀνθεστηριών, χελῑδών, ἀμπελών· Κρονίων, τρίβων, κλύδων. — (*c*) Monosyllabic nouns which have the Acc. in -α are commonly oxytone; those which are neuter (see *d* below), and most which have the Acc. in -ν, are perispome; as, αἴξ, πούς, θήρ, θώς· τὸ φῶς, τὸ πῦρ (so likewise the neut. adjective πᾶν, ¶ 19); βοῦς, ναῦς. — (*d*) In neuter nouns (§ 734. *a*), in words in -ξ and -ψ, in verbals in -τωρ, and in nouns in -ις or -υς with the Gen. in -εως, the accent is thrown as far back as possible; as, κέρας, τεῖχος, βούλευμα· κόραξ, καλαῦροψ (§ 726. R.); δύναμις, πέλεκυς. — (*e*) Female appellatives in -ις (§§ 306. N., 309 - 311) have the accent upon the same syllable as the masculine, except when this is a proparoxytone or dissyllabic barytone (in which case the feminine commonly becomes oxytone); as, αὐλητής, αὐλητρίς· πολίτης, πολῖτις· Πριαμίδης, Πριαμίς· αἰχμάλωτος, αἰχμαλωτίς· Πέρσης, Περσίς. — (*f*) Simple adjectives are commonly oxytone, if the characteristic is a vowel; paroxytone, if it is a consonant; as, σαφής, ἡδύς· μέλας, χαρίεις (¶¶ 17, 19).

b. Rules for Compound Words.

§ **739.** In composition, there is a general tendency to throw the accent as far back as possible. But, — (*a*) Compound adjectives in -ης are more frequently oxytone; as, εὐπρεπής (those in -ωδης are always paroxytone; so compounds of ἦθος, ἀρκέω, and some other words). — (*b*) Compounds in which -ος is affixed to the root of a verb united with a noun are commonly oxytone, if the *penult is long*; but if the *penult is short*, they are commonly paroxytone when *active* in sense, and proparoxytone when *passive*; as, σιτοποιός (§ 327); λιθοβόλος and λιθόβολος (§ 326. a). — (*c*) Compound adjectives of Dec. III., with a palatal or lingual characteristic, in which the latter part is a monosyllable derived from a verb, are commonly oxytone; e. g. all in -σφαξ, -πληξ, -ρωξ, -τρωξ, -βλης, -θνης, -κμης; as, ἀποῤῥώξ. — (*d*) Words derived from compound words are commonly not accented as though themselves compounded; but their compounds again follow the general rule; thus, κατασκευάζω, κατασκευαστός (§ 737. *a*), ἀ-κατασκεύαστος. — See § 734. *f*.

§ **740.** II. In declension, the accent commonly remains, so far as the general laws permit, upon the same syllable as in the theme.

Remarks. 1. In Dec. I., the affix -ων of the Gen. pl., as contracted from -άων (§ 95. 3), is always circumflexed. — Grammarians except, chiefly for the sake of distinction from other words, ἡ ἀφύη, *anchovy*, οἱ ἐτησίαι, *trade-*

winds, ὁ χλούνης, *wild-boar*, and ὁ χρήστης, *usurer*; Gen. pl. ἀφύων, &c. For an apparent exception in adjectives in -ος, see 2 below.

2. In adjectives in -ος, the feminine is accented throughout, so far as the general laws permit, upon the same syllable as the masculine; thus, φίλιος (¶ 18), φιλία, Pl. φίλιοι, φίλιαι, M. and F. φιλίων (as if a common form for the two genders, cf. § 133. α, γ, δ; the Dor. Gen. pl. in -αν, § 95. β, where the feminine has a special form, follows the rule in 1 above, as φιλιᾶν); while, from the noun ἡ φιλία, *friendship*, φιλίαι, φιλιῶν· so καρβάτιναι iv. 5. 14, as properly an adjective. — In other adjectives, the feminine retains the accent of the theme, but subject to the same changes as in nouns of Dec. I.; as, μέλας, μέλαινα, μελαίνης, μελαινῶν (¶ 19). Except poetic feminines in -εια, belonging to adjectives in -ής (§ 134. γ); as, ἠριγενής, ἠριγένεια. Observe the accentuation of μία, μιᾶς, &c. (¶ 21).

§ 741. 3. In Dec. III., *dissyllabic Genitives and Datives* throw the accent upon the *affix*; as, γυπός, αἰγί, τριχῶν, ποσί, κλεισοῖν (¶ 11); πατρός, ἀνδρῶν, κυσί, ἀρνί (¶ 12).

Notes. (*a*) Except those which have become dissyllabic by *contraction*, *participles*, and the *Gen. pl.* and *dual* of these ten nouns, δάς, δμώς, θώς, κάρα, οὖς, παῖς, σής, Τρώς, φῴς, φῶς (*light*), and of the adjective πᾶς· thus, πόλεϊ πόλει (¶ 14), ἔαρος ἦρος (§ 108. N.); δόντος, δόντι, δόντων (¶ 22); παίδων, φώτων, ὤτοιν (¶ 11). — (*b*) The contraction is not regarded in accenting the Gen. and Dat. of οἶς (¶ 14, § 121. *f*), οὖς, στέαρ, φρέαρ (§ 104. N.; yet see οὖς above), and Θρᾷξ (G. -κός). — (*c*) Observe the accentuation of οὐδείς (¶ 21), τίς, τὶς (¶ 24), γυνή (§ 101. γ), θυγάτηρ (§ 106. 2). — (*d*) The Attics are said to have made the Gen. pl. of numeral substantives in -άς perispome; thus, μυριαδῶν, as if contracted from the Ion. μυριαδέων (§ 120. 2).

§ 742. 4. From the natural tone of frequent address, the accent of the Voc. in a few familiar words is thrown back as far as the general laws permit; viz. Dec. I. δεσπότης, *master*; Dec. III. γυνή (§ 101. γ), Ἀπόλλων, Ποσειδῶν, σωτήρ (§ 105. R.), ἀνήρ, πατήρ, θυγάτηρ, Δημήτηρ (§ 106), δαήρ, *brother-in-law*; thus, δέσποτα, θύγατερ, Δήμητερ.

Note. In the Voc. sing., ευ and οι final are always circumflexed; as, ἱππεῦ, ἠχοῖ, αἰδοῖ (¶ 14).

§ 743. 5. The tendency in compounds and comparatives to throw the accent as far back as possible (§§ 739, 745) leads to the accentuation of the antepenult in the Voc. and Neut. sing. of some nouns and adjectives of Dec. III. whose theme is accented upon the penult. These are, — (*a*) Comparatives in -ων; as, ἡδίων, ἥδιον. — (*b*) Most compound paroxytones in -ων and -ης, except those in -φρων, -ήρης, -ώδης, -ώλης, and -ώρης; as, εὐδαίμων, Neut. and Voc. εὔδαιμον· αὐθάδης, N. and V. αὔθαδες· Ἀγαμέμνων, V. Ἀγάμεμνον· V. Σώκρατες, Ἡράκλεες (¶ 14).

6. (α.) Observe the accentuation of μήτηρ, θυγάτηρ, Δημήτηρ (¶ 12, § 106. 2), and of δέλεαρ (§§ 104. N., 728. R.). — (β.) The forms in -θε(ν), -φι, -θι (§§ 89 – 91, 320), follow the general rule, unless a short vowel precede, in which case they are commonly paroxytone. — (γ.) For the irregularities and peculiarities in the accentuation of the numerals and pronouns, see ¶¶ 21, 23, 24.

§ 744. III. A *long vowel in the ultima*, belonging to an *affix of declension*, can receive only the *acute* accent in the *direct*, and the *circumflex* in the *indirect* cases; as, τιμή, -ῆς, -ῇ, -ήν, -αί, -ῶν, -αῖς, -άς, -ά, -αῖν (¶ 7); ὁδοῦ, -ῷ, -οί, -ῶν, -οῖς, -ούς, -ώ, -οῖν (¶ 9); γυπῶν, -οῖν (¶ 11).

Except in the peculiar datives ἐμοί, μοί, σοί (¶ 23, § 141).

B. Accent in Comparison.

§ **745.** Comparatives and superlatives, whether adjectives or adverbs, are accented as far back as the general rules of accent permit; thus, ἡδύς, ἡδίων, ἥδῖον (§ 743. 5), ἥδιστος.

C. Accent in Conjugation.

§ **746.** Verbs are accented as far back as the general laws permit, with the following exceptions (see §§ 723. N., 734. *c*, *d*).

1. These forms are accented upon the PENULT; — (*a*) All *Infinitives in* -ναι; as, βεβουλευκέναι, βουλευθῆναι, ἱστάναι, ἑστάναι (¶ 48). Except dialectic forms in -μεναι (§ 250). — (*b*) The *Inf.* of the 1*st Aor. act.* and 2*d Aor. mid.*; as, βουλεῦσαι, λιπέσθαι (¶ 37). — (*c*) The *Perf. pass. Inf. and Part.*; as, βεβουλεῦσθαι, βεβουλευμένος. — Except a few *preteritive participles*; as, ἥμενος (¶ 59). So κείμενος, from κεῖμαι (§ 232), which otherwise is accented as an uncontracted Perf.; thus, κατάκειμαι, κατακεῖσθαι. In a few Epic forms, the retraction of the accent extends even to the Inf.; as, ἀκάχησθαι T. 335, ἀκαχήμενος E. 24 (§ 286). — (*d*) All dialectic infinitives in -μεν (§ 250).

§ **747.** 2. These forms are OXYTONE; — (*a*) *Participles in* -ς, *G.* -τος, except in the 1*st Aor. act.*; as, βεβουλευκώς, βουλευθείς, ἱστάς, στάς · but, βουλεύσας. — (*b*) The 2*d Aor. act. part.*; as, λιπών, στάς. — (*c*) The 2*d Aor. imperat. forms*, εἰπέ, *say*, ἐλθέ, *come*, εὑρέ, *find*, and, in strict Attic, ἰδέ, *see*, and λαβέ, *take*. Except in composition; thus, ἔξελθε, εἴσιδε.

§ **748.** 3. These forms are PERISPOME; — (*a*) The 2*d Aor. inf. in* -ειν; as, λιπεῖν. — (*b*) The 2*d Pers. sing.* of the 2*d Aor. mid. imp.*; as, λιποῦ, δοῦ (¶ 51). Except in *compounds* of more than two syllables from verbs in -μι; as, ἀπόδου · but προδοῦ. Some exceptions also occur in compound and even in simple verbs in -ω.

4. The accent of a verb in COMPOSITION can never be thrown farther back than the augment (§ 734. *c*), or farther than the tone syllable of the word prefixed; thus, παρέχω (παρά, ἔχω, § 300), παρεῖχον, παρέσχον, παράσχες.

§ **749.** REMARKS. *α*. In those forms in which the accent of the Perf. and 2 Aor. differs from that of the Pres., a want of uniformity has sometimes arisen from different views in regard to their etymology. Thus, 2 Aor. forms are sometimes accented as Pres.; as, *Inf.* ἀμυνάθειν, σχέθειν, *Pt.* σχέθων (§ 299); πρίασο, πρίω, πρίασθαι (¶ 49).

β. *Monosyllables long by nature*, except *Participles*, are generally *circumflexed*; thus, εἶ, ἦν, ἦ, ὦν (¶ 55); σχῶ, σχεῖν, σχών (§ 300).

γ. For the accentuation of φημί (¶ 53) and εἰμί (¶ 55), see § 732.

δ. The Ionics, in dropping one ε from -έεαι, -έεο, do not change the accent, thus, φοβέο (§ 243. 2). So ἔσται (¶ 55), as if syncopated from ἔσεται, remains paroxytone in composition; thus, παρέσται.

ε. Examples of *irregular* or *various accentuation* are φής, φάθι or φαθί, *Imp.* εἶπον or εἰπόν (§ 53); ἰών (§ 56); κίω, *to go*, poet., *Pt.* κιών · Ion. ἐών (¶ 55); χρή, ἐχρῆν, χρεών (§ 284. 4).

D. Accent in Particles.

§ **750.** 1. Adverbs. (*a*) Adverbs in -ως derived from adjectives are, with very few exceptions, accented like the Gen. pl. of their primitives (§ 321. a); as, σοφῶς, ταχέως. — (*b*) Derivative adverbs in -δον, -δα, -ι, -ει, and -ξ (§ 321. b, c, d) are commonly oxytone; those in -δην, -ακις (§ 321. b, 4), and -ω, paroxytone; as, πλινθηδόν, ἀναφανδά, Μηδιστί, ἀμαχεί, παραλλάξ · σποράδην, πολλάκις, ἔξω.

2. Prepositions. The primitive prepositions (§ 648. β) are all oxytone; as, ἀπό, κατά. For the removal or loss of the accent, see §§ 730, 731.

3. For proclitic and enclitic particles, see §§ 731, 732. The accentuation of those particles which remain is best learned by observation.

GREEK INDEX.

[In this and the following Index, figures immediately preceded by the mark ¶ refer to paragraphs in the Tables; other figures refer to sections in the body of the Grammar, with their subdivisions. The references to the Tables are usually followed by other references in illustration. The letter f immediately attached to a figure (thus, 32 f) signifies *and the following*. The signs > and < denote the change, by contraction or otherwise, of the words or letters at the opening into those at the angle. The sign ✕ denotes opposition or distinction. The abbreviation cj. stands for conjugation, contr. for contraction, const. for construction, cp. for comparison, dec. for declension, der. for derivation, encl. for enclitic, ins. for inserted, num. for numeral, pos. for position, r. for root, w. for with, &c.]

38

ENGLISH INDEX.

LIST OF AUTHORS AND WORKS CITED, AND OF ABBREVIATIONS.

[The works of Xenophon are commonly cited without naming the author, and the Anabasis without even naming the work (by simply giving the book, chapter, and section; thus, iv. 3. 17). The Iliad and Odyssey are commonly cited by giving simply the letter denoting the book, with the verse, using a capital letter if the citation is made from the Iliad, and a small letter if it is made from the Odyssey (thus, A. 232, for Il. i. 232; β. 305, for Od. ii. 305). In Homer, the references are made to the verses of Wolf; in Hesiod, to those of Gaisford; in Pindar, to those of Heyne; in the Dramatic Poets, to those of Dindorf; and in the Pastoral Poets, to those of Kiessling. In Herodotus, Thucydides, Xenophon, Diodorus Siculus, Dio Cassius, and Pausanias, they are made to books and chapters; and also, in Xenophon, to the sections of the usual more minute division as given by Schneider, Dindorf, &c. In Demosthenes, they are made to the pages and lines of Reiske; in the other Orators and in Plato (including Timæus Locrus) to the pages and lines or division-letters of Stephens; in Strabo to the pages, and in Athenæus to the pages and division-letters, of Casaubon. The fragments of Alcæus, Sappho, Corinna, Epicharmus, and Sophron are numbered according to Ahrens, with the numbers of other well known editions (as those of Alcæus by Matthiæ, and of Sappho by Neue) usually following in parentheses; those of Anacreon, according to Bergk; those of Callimachus, according to Blomfield; those of Hesiod, Simonides, and Tyrtæus, according to Gaisford; those of Hipponax, according to Welcker; those of Pindar, according to Böckh; those of the Dramatic Poets, according to Dindorf; &c. Cases of abbreviation not given below, and those in which the same abbreviation or initial stands for different words, are either explained by the immediate connection, or (as indeed many of those below) can scarce fail of being obvious in themselves.]

Accusative (Acc., A.).
Active (Act.).
Adjective (Adj.).
Æliānus.
Æolic (Æol., Æ.).
Æschines (Æschin.).
Æschylus (Æsch.): Agamemnon (Ag.), Choëphori (Cho.), Eumenides (Eum.), Persæ (Pers.), Promētheus (Prom., Pr.), Septem contra Thebas (Sept., Theb., Th.), Supplices (Suppl., Sup.).
Alcæus (Alc.).
Alcman (Alcm.).
Alexandrine (Alex.).
Anacreon (Anacr.).
Andocides (Andoc.).
Anthologia (Anth.).
Antimachus (Antim.).
Antipater Thessalonicensis (Antip. Th.).
Antiphilus (Antiphil.).
Aorist (Aor., A.).
Apollonius Dyscolus de Pronomine. [Rh.).
Apollonius Rhodius (Ap.
Apud (ap.) = *quoted in.*
Arātus (Arat.).
Archilochus (Archil.).
Aretæus.
Aristophanes (Ar.): Acharnenses (Ach.), Aves (Av.), Ecclesiazūsæ (Eccl.), Equites (Eq.), Lysistrata (Lys.), Nubes (Nub.), Pax, Plutus (Plut., Pl.), Ranæ (Ran.), Thesmophoriazūsæ (Thesm.), Vespæ (Vesp.).
Aristoteles (Aristl.).
Article (Art.).
Athenæus (Ath.).
Attic (Att., A.).
Augment (Augm.).
Bion.
Bœotic (Bœot., B.).
Cæsar (Cæs.).
Callimachus (Call.): Epigrammata (Ep.), Hymni in Delum (Del.), Diānam (Di.), Jovem (Jov.), Lavācrum Palladis (Lav.).
Cicero de Oratōre (Cic. de Or.).
Collateral (Collat.).
Common (Comm.), commonly (comm.).
Comparative (Compt., Comp.).
Confer (Cf.) = *compare, consult.*
Contracted, -ion (Contr.).
Dative (Dat., D.).
Declension (Declens., Dec.).
Demosthenes (Dem.).
Derivative, -ion (Deriv., Der.).
Dialects (Dial.).
Dinarchus (Dinarch.).
Dindorf's Edition (Dind.).
Dio Cassius (Dio Cass.).
Diodōrus Siculus (Diod.).
Diogenes Laërtius (Diog. Laërt.).
Doric (Dor., D.).
Dual (Du., D.).
Enclitic (Enclit., Encl.).
English (Eng.).
Epic (Ep., E.).
Epicharmus (Epicharm., Epich.).
Euripides (Eur.): Alcestis (Alc.), Andromache (Andr.), Bacchæ (Bacch., Bac.), Cyclops (Cycl.), Electra (El.), Hecuba (Hec.), Helena (Hel.), Heraclīdæ (Heracl.), Hercules Furens (Herc.), Hippolytus (Hipp.), Ion, Iphigenīa in Aulide (Iph. A.), Iphigenīa in Tauris (Iph. T.), Medēa (Med.), Orestes (Or.), Phœnissæ (Phœn., Ph.), Rhesus (Rhes., Rh.), Supplices (Suppl., Sup.), Troades (Tro.). — Fragmenta (Fr.), Archelāi (Arch.), Peleos (Pel.), Polyïdi (Pol.), Incerta (Inc.).
Exempli gratia (E. g.) = *for example.*
Feminine (Fem., F.).
Fragment (Fr.).
Future (Fut., F.).
Gaisford's Edition (Gaisf.).
Genitive (Gen., G.).
Göttling's Edition (Göttl.).
Hellenistic (Hellenist., Hel.).
Herōdes Atticus (Herod. Att.).
Herodotus (Hdt., Herod.).
Hesiodus (Hes.): Opera et Dies (Op.), Scutum Herculis (Sc.), Theogonia (Theog., Th.).
Hesychius (Hesych.).
Hippocrates (Hipp.).
Hipponax (Hippon.).
Homērus (Hom.): Batrachomyomachia (Batr.), Hymni (Hym., H.), in Apollinem (Ap.), Bacchum (Bac.), Cererem (Cer.), Mercurium (Merc.), Venerem (Ven.), Ilias (Il.), Odyssēa (Od.).
Horatius (Hor.).
Ibīdem (Ib.) = *in the same work or part of a work.*
Id est (i. e.) = *that is.*
Idem (Id.) = *the same author.*
Imperative (Imperat., Imp.).
Imperfect (Impf.).
Indicative (Ind.).
Infinitive (Infin., Inf.).
Inscriptiones (Inscr., Insc.), Bœotica (Bœot.), Cretica (Cret.), Cumæa (Cum.), Heracleënsis (Heracl.), Potidaïca (Potid.).

Intransitive (Intrans.).
Ionic (Ion., I.).
Isocrates (Isocr.).
Iterative (Iter., It.).
Καὶ τὰ λοιπά (κ. τ. λ.) = *&c.*
Laconic (Lacon., Lac.).
Latin (Lat.).
Livius (Liv.).
Lobeck on Phrynichus (Lob. ad Phryn.).
Luciānus (Luc.): de Historia Scribenda (de Hist. Scrib.), Parasītus (Paras.).
Lycophron (Lyc.).
Lycurgus (Lycurg.).
Lysias (Lys.).
Masculine (Masc., M.).
Megarian (Meg.).
Middle (Mid., M.).
Mimnermus (Mimn.).
Neuter (Neut., N.).
Nominative (Nom., N.).
Optative (Opt.).
Orpheus (Orph.): Argonautica (Arg.), Hymni (Hym.), Lithica (Lith.).
Participle (Partic., Part., Pt.).
Passive (Pass., P.).
Pausanias (Pausan.).
Perfect (Perf., Pf.).
Person (Pers., P.).
Philētas (Philet.).
Pindarus (Pind.): Isthmia (I.), Nemea (Nem., N.), Olympia (O.), Pythia (P.).
Plato (Pl.): Alcibiades (Alc.), Amatōres (Amat.), Apologia (Apol.), Axiochus (Ax.), Charmides (Charm.) Convivium (Conv.), Cratylus (Crat.), Critias (Criti.), Crito, Definitiones (Def.), Epinomis (Epin.), Euthydēmus (Euthyd.), Euthyphron (Euthyphr.), Gorgias (Gorg.), Hippias Major (Hipp. Maj.), Hipparchus (Hipparch.), Ion, Laches (Lach.), Leges (Leg.), Lysis (Lys.), Menexenus (Menex.), Meno, Parmenides (Parm.), Phædo, Phædrus (Phædr.), Philēbus (Phil.), Politicus (Polit., Pol.), Protagoras (Prot.), de Republica (Rep.), Sophista (Soph.), Theætētus (Theæt.), Theages (Theag.), Timæus (Tim.).
Plato Comicus: Metœci.
Plautus (Plaut.): Trinummus (Trinumm.).
Pluperfect (Plup.).
Plural (Plur., Pl., P.).
Plutarchus (Plut.).
Poetic (Poet., P.).
Pollux (Poll.).
Positive (Pos.).
Pratinas (Pratin.).
Present (Pres., Pr.).
Primitive (Prim.).
Pronoun (Pron.).
Quintus Smyrnæus (Quint.).
Reduplication (Redupl., Redpl.).
Root (r.).
Sappho (Sapph.).
Scholia (Schol.)
Scilicet (sc.) = *understand, namely.*
Scripta Sacra (S. S.): Septuagint (LXX.), Deuteronomy (Deut.), Psalms (Ps.), Matthew (St. Matth., Mt.), Mark (Mk.), Luke (Lk.), John (St. Jn.), Acts, Romans (Rom.), Ephesians (Ep. Ephes.), Revelations (Rev.).
Simonides (Simon.).
Singular (Sing., S.).
Sophocles (Soph.): Ajax (Aj.), Antigone (Ant.), Electra (El.), Œdipus Coloněus (Œd. C.), Œdipus Tyrannus (Œd. T.), Philoctētes (Phil., Ph.), Trachiniæ (Tr.).
Sophron (Sophr.).
Strabo (Strab.).
Subjunctive (Subj.).
Superlative (Superl., Sup.).
Syncope, -ated (Sync.).
Terentius (Ter.): Andria (Andr.).
Theocritus (Theoc.): Bucolica, Epigrammata (Ep.).
Theognis (Theog.).
Thucydides (Thuc., Th.).
Tibullus (Tibull.).
Timæus Locrus (Tim. Locr., Tim.).
Transitive (Trans.).
Tyrtæus (Tyrt.).
Varia lectio (*v. l.*) = *various reading.*
Vocative (Voc., V.).
Xenophanes (Xenophan.).
Xenophon (Xen.): Agesilāus (Ages., Ag.), Anabasis (Anab.), Cyropædīa (Cyr.), de Re Equestri (Eq.), Hiero (Hier.), Historia Græca (H. Gr.), Lacedæmoniorum Respublica (Lac.), Magister Equitum (Mag. Eq.), Memorabilia Socratis (Mem.), Œconomicus (Œc.), de Republica Atheniensium (Rep. Ath., Ath.), Symposium (Symp.), Vectigalia (Vect.), Venatio (Ven.).

THE END.

INDEX

OF

CITATIONS FROM XENOPHON'S ANABASIS

IN "A

GRAMMAR OF THE GREEK LANGUAGE, BY A. CROSBY, &c."

"Accomplished XENOPHON! thy truth hath shown
A brother's glory sacred as thy own.
O rich in all the blended gifts that grace
Minerva's darling sons of Attic race!
The Sage's olive, the Historian's palm,
The Victor's laurel, all thy name embalm!
Thy simple diction, free from glaring art,
With sweet allurement steals upon the heart;
Pure as the rill, that Nature's hand refines,
A cloudless mirror of thy soul it shines.
Thine was the praise, bright models to afford
To CÆSAR's rival pen, and rival sword:
Blest, had Ambition not destroyed his claim
To the mild lustre of thy purer fame!"

CITATIONS FROM THE ANABASIS.

[The following Index conforms to the Second (Stereotype) Edition of the Grammar The numbers inclosed in parentheses denote the sections of the Anabasis which are cited; those following them, the sections or the Grammar in which the citations are made.]

BOOK I.

654; (8) 392. 1, 399, 640; (9) 362. ε, 404. δ, 447. γ, 477. α, 502, 636, 671. 4; (10) 583, 602. 2, 633, 646. 1; (11) 376. δ, 504, 583, 642; (12) 347, 547, 560. 1; (13) 568; (14) 436, 440, 447. β, 479, 525. N., 525. β, 558, 561. 3, 568, 602. 1, 633, 637, 647; (15) 431, 525. α, 526, 547, 601. α, 619. β, 640; (16) 411, 445, 479, 606, 609, 640; (17) 194. N., 392. 1, 418. R., 604. a, 604. β, 606, 633; (18) 419. 5, 532; (19) 574; (20) 500, 574, 603. β, 619. β, γ; (21) 140. γ, 378, 382, 402, 408, 449. β, 470. N., 526. α, 568, 610, 646. 1.

Chap. IV. (1) 486. ε, 547; (2) 140; (3) 561. 2; (4) 394, 418. 2, 472, 498, 549. a, 550; (5) 361, 372. γ, 394, 601. γ, 633; (6) 487. 4; (7) 605. 2; (8) 426. δ, 485. α, 544, 579. ζ, 606, 628, 674. 3; (9) 387, 434; (11) 418. 3; (12) 406, 639. 1; (13) 347, 447. γ, 488. 5, 535, 568, 606; (14) 405. η, 535, 603. β; (15) 357. N., 404. ε, 476, 543, 603. β, 620; (16) 407. ι, 502, 574, 647; (17) 351; (18) 405. η.

Chap. V. (1) 362. β, 447. β; (2) 351, 400, 486. 2, 546. β, 605. 2, 606; (3) 546. β, 571; (4) 387, 421. β, 562. α; (5) 362. γ, 457. ε, 472. α, 549. a; (6) 428, 446. β; (7) 364. 1, 366, 427. 8, 523; (8) 418. 2, 512. β, 604. β, 662; (9) 275. ζ, 419. 4, 449. β, 488. 7, 525. β; (10) 332. 3, 355, 357. α, 368, 416, 447. γ, 561. 3, 649. β; (11) 406, 485. α; (12) 347, 416, 472. α, 485. α, 508, 579. ζ, 657. γ; (13) 237, 406; (14) 357. β, 551, 608; (15) 362. ε, 476; (16) 351, 442, 582.

Chap. VI. (1) 362. δ, 448, 639. 2, 663. 6; (2) 347, 402, 549. a, 603. ϑ, 620, 665, 673. β; (3) 403, 488. 6, 525. α, 608; (4) 504; (5) 332. 3, 363. γ; (6) 347, 473. α, 485. α, 510. 1, 555, 628; (7) 407. ι, 510. 1, 525. β, 624. β, 661. 1; (8) 405. ζ, 478. β, 831. α, 627. α, 646, 661. 1; (9) 432, 473. β, 558, 577, 601. α, 623. N.; (10) 369. α, 485. β, 571, 646. 1; (11) 362. δ, 542. δ.

Chap. VII. (1) 392. 1, 456; (2) 399, 535; (3) 191. 3, 357. β, 374. β, 526, 602. 3, 604. a; (4) 404. γ, 407. κ, 412, 477. α, 650. α; (5) 234. β 359. α; (6) 530; (7) 603. N.; (8) 362. β; (9) 394, 426. δ, 503, 543, 661. a; (10) 137. α, 480. 2; (11) 457. ε, 509, 637; (12) 351; (13) 362. β, 636, 649. δ; (14) 333. 6, 420. 1; (15) 394, 472; (16) 544; (17) 549. a; (18) 378, 402, 473. β, 603. β; (19) 620, 646; (20) 425. 5, 466.

Chap. VIII. (1) 418. 2, 472. α, 521, 546, 583, 654, 662; (3) 482. (4) 336, 447. γ; (6) 416, 418. 2, 472. α, 502, 529. β; (7) 551; (8) 359. α, 419. 4, 481, 662; (9) 368, 470. N., 472. α, 544. α; (10) 640; (11) 418. 2; (12) 402, 417, 509, 611. 2; (13) 380, 407. ι, 441, 472. α; (14) 509; (15) 474. N., 628; (16) 375. α, 479, 491. R., 535, 568; (17) 405. ζ, 543; (18) 263. 6, 362. β, 402, 418. 2, 447. γ; (20) 357. β, 546, 549. a; (21) 425. 4, 568; (22) 391. γ; (23) 391. γ, 405. ζ, 662; (23–27) 576; (24) 511. 3, 557; (26) 479, 510. 1, 627. α; (27) 344. 1, 362. γ, 416, 559. c; (29) 558, 561. 1.

Chap. IX. (1) 375. β, 562. α; (1 31) 571; (2) 437; (3) 392. 1; (5) 392. 1, 419. 5; (6) 403, 490. R., 557; (7) 153. γ, 226. 3, 432, 517, 546. β, 558; (9) 560. 1; (10) 226. 3; (11) 435; (13) 363. γ, 408, 447. α, 546. β, 604. a, 664. γ; (14) 408, 416, 520, 526; (15) 389, 497. 1; (16) 497. 1, 605. 2, (17) 405. η; (18) 605. 2; (19) 406, 522, 594, 605. 2, 633; (20) 537. 3, 551, 562. α; (21) 153. γ, 537. 3. 674. 3; (22) 462. γ; (23) 409, 505. 2,

BOOK II.

BOOK III.

BOOK IV.

BOOK V.

BOOK VI.

615. 2; (21) 404. γ; (22) 402, 640; (23) 457. β; (25) 610; (26) 517; (28) 633; (29) 406, 605. 3; (30) 546; (31) 444, 552, 615. 2, 633, 660.

CHAP. II. (1) 119. 2; (6) 523; (10) 358, 658; (12) 412; (14) 406; (15) 472. α; (18) 661. 2.

CHAP. III. (1) 412, 477. α; (2) 137. ε; (6) 431; (9) 546; (11) 610; (14) 532; (15) 520; (17) 368; (19) 520; (23) 380; (25) 380, 432. 3.

CHAP. IV. (1) 410, 449. β; (2) 409; (3) 403; (4) 478. γ; (8) 428, 580; (9) 409; (11) 194. 1, 477. α; (13) 194. 1, 486. 1, 559. d; (14) 626. N.; (18) 669; (19) 486. γ; (20) 407. ι, 517; (23) 416, 555; (24) 450. δ.

CHAP. V. (5) 520; (6) 440; (10) 234. α, 377. 2; (24) 472. α.

CHAP. VI. (1) 378, 525. α; (5) 504; (7) 479; (12) 661. α; (13) 475; (15) 603. δ; (16) 400, 657. γ; (17) 428; (18) 598. 1, 600; (22) 530, 628; (24) 614. ζ; (26) 514; (29) 337; (30) 337; (31) 337, 405. ζ; (32) 337, 380; (33) 380, 497. 1; (34) 337, 426. δ, 649. γ; (38) 447. β 457. α, 478. α.

BOOK VII.

CHAP. I. (5) 673. β; (6) 664. β; (8) 598, 671. 6; (14) 608; (19) 640; (21) 408, 627. α, 660; (23) 472. α; (24) 529; (25) 437; (28) 531; (29) 454; (30) 370, 439. β; (34) 610; (39) 394, 619. γ; (41) 357. β.

CHAP. II. (2) 641. β; (5) 399, 532. N.; (6) 525. α; (8) 525. N.; (9) 457. γ; (11) 472; (12) 402, 665; (13) 421. β; (14) 561. 3; (16) 378; (17) 378; (18) 417; (20) 450. δ; (23) 559. d; (26) 402; (27) 516; (28) 649. ϑ; (29) 362. γ; (32) 416, 447. γ; (38) 367, 498.

CHAP. III. (3) 508; (13) 611. 2; (16) 389, 399, 497. 1, 510. 2; (20) 194. 1, 393. α; (22) 628; (23) 529. β, 558, 620; (26) 409, 595. δ; (27) 409; (29) 399; (31) 496. c; (32) 119. 2; (33) 432; (35) 509; (36) 606; (39) 161. 2, 473. α; (43) 546; (46) 301. 5; (48) 526. α.

CHAP. IV. (5) 366, 667. 2; (7) 583; (14) 378; (16) 476. N; (19) 237.

CHAP. V. (2) 404. δ; (3) 404. δ; (4) 404. δ; (5) 376. δ; (7) 617. 6; (8) 376. γ; (9) 424. 2, 504.

CHAP. VI. (1) 137. γ; (3) 610; (4) 403, 491. R.; (5) 405. ζ; (9) 436; (11) 504; (15) 603. ζ; (16) 404. δ, 603. α, 604. c; (17) 436; (18) 504; (19) 664. γ; (21) 605. 4; (22) 435; (23) 394, 601. δ; (24) 153. γ; (27) 538. β; (29) 416, 665; (32) 417; (36) 521, 581; (37) 344 1; (38) 434, 568. R.; (39) 409; (40) 409; (41) 368, 558; (43) 405. η, 652 β; (44) 405. η.

CHAP. VII. (6) 237; (7) 485. α (8) 671. 12; (10) 465; (11) 603. δ; (15) 663. 6; (17) 614. δ; (19) 472 α, 568. R., 624. γ; (22) 434, 629. 1; (23) 556; (25) 568; (27) 637; (28 440; (29) 405. η, 503; (30) 477. α (31) 349, 418. 3, 568. R., 602. 2 (33) 509; (34) 451; (36) 449. α (40) 605. 2; (41) 671. 3; (42) 357 α; (51) 403; (53) 671. 2; (54) 403 (55) 200. N.; (57) 124. β. N., 421. β.

CHAP. VIII. (1) 399; (2) 535, (4) 403, 530; (6) 374. α; (9) 485. α; (11) 449. β, 460; (12) 119. 2; (16) 487. 4, 522; (19) 529. β; (20) 470. 3; (26) 140.

www.ingramcontent.com/pod-product-compliance
Lightning Source LLC
LaVergne TN
LVHW021128110826
845150LV00005B/960

* 9 7 8 1 4 2 5 5 5 1 0 9 4 *